The Routledge Drama

The Routledge Drama Anthology is an original compilation of works from key movements in the history of the modern theatre, from the late nineteenth to the early twenty-first century. This expanded new edition now features twenty new plays and critical essays spanning Naturalism and Symbolism, the Historical Avant-Garde, Political Theatres, Late Modernism, and Contemporary Performance, including:

- *The Exception and the Rule* – Bertolt Brecht
- *Endgame* – Samuel Beckett
- *The Dumb Waiter* – Harold Pinter
- *R.U.R.* – Karel Čapek
- *Six Characters in Search of an Author* – Luigi Pirandello
- *Dr Faustus Lights the Lights* – Gertrude Stein
- *The Balcony* – Jean Genet
- *Product* – Mark Ravenhill
- *The Bald Soprano* – Eugène Ionesco
- *Quartet* – Heiner Müller
- *Belle Reprieve* – Split Britches
- *Meerut* – The Workers' Theatre Movement

Each of the book's five sections comprises a selection of plays and performance texts that define the period, reproduced in full and accompanied by key theoretical writings from performers, playwrights and critics that inform and contextualize their reading. Substantial introductions from experts in the field also provide these sections with an overview of the works and their significance.

This textbook provides an unprecedented collection of comprehensive resource materials that will facilitate in-depth critical analysis. It enables a dialogue between playwrights and performance practitioners on one hand, and on the other, critics and theorists such as Roland Barthes, Jean Baudrillard, Walter Benjamin, André Breton, Martin Esslin, Michael Kirby, Hans-Thies Lehmann, Jacques Rancière and Theodor Adorno.

Maggie B. Gale is Chair of Drama at the University of Manchester, UK. She is the co-editor of *The Cambridge Companion to the Actress*; author of *West End Women: Women on the London Stage 1918–1962*, and *J. B. Priestley* from the series *Routledge Modern and Contemporary Dramatists*; and co-editor of *Fifty Modern and Contemporary Dramatists* (Routledge Key Guides) 2014.

John F. Deeney is Principal Lecturer in Contemporary Arts at Manchester Metropolitan University, UK, editor of *Writing Live*, author of the book *Mark Ravenhill* from the series *Routledge Modern and Contemporary Dramatists*, and co-editor of *Fifty Modern and Contemporary Dramatists* (Routledge Key Guides) 2014.

The Routledge Drama Anthology

From Modernism to Contemporary Performance

Second edition

Edited by Maggie B. Gale and John F. Deeney
(with Dan Rebellato and Carl Lavery)

Routledge
Taylor & Francis Group

LONDON AND NEW YORK

First published 2016
by Routledge
2 Park Square, Milton Park, Abingdon, Oxon OX14 4RN

and by Routledge
711 Third Avenue, New York, NY 10017

Routledge is an imprint of the Taylor & Francis Group, an informa business

British Library Cataloguing-in-Publication Data
A catalogue record for this book is available from the British Library

Library of Congress Cataloguing-in-Publication Data
The Routledge drama anthology : from modernism to contemporary performance / edited by Maggie B. Gale and John F. Deeney ; with Dan Rebellato and Carl Lavery. -- Second edition.
pages cm
Includes index.
1. Drama--19th century. 2. Drama--20th century. 3. Drama--19th century--History and criticism. 4. Drama--20th century--History and criticism. I. Gale, Maggie B. (Maggie Barbara), 1963- editor. II. Deeney, John F., editor. III. Rebellato, Dan, 1968- editor. IV. Lavery, Carl, 1969- editor.
PN6112.R68 2016
808.82--dc23
2015031675

ISBN: 978-0-415-72416-6 (hbk)
ISBN: 978-0-415-72417-3 (pbk)

Typeset in Bembo MT Pro
by Fakenham Prepress Solutions, Fakenham, Norfolk NR21 8NN

Printed and Bound in the United States of America by

Edwards Brothers Malloy on sustainably sourced paper.

Contents

Plays and Performance Texts

Critical Texts

Illustrations

Notes on Editors and Contributors

Maggie B. Gale is Professor and Chair of Drama at the University of Manchester, England. Her publications include, *West End Women: Women on the London Stage 1918–1962*, London: Routledge, 1996; *British Theatre Between the Wars 1918–1939*, Cambridge: Cambridge University Press, 2000, with Clive Barker; *The Cambridge Companion to the Actress*, Cambridge: Cambridge University Press, 2007, with John Stokes, *and J. B. Priestley: Routledge Modern and Contemporary Dramatists*, London: Routledge, 2008. She is editor of *Plays and Performance Texts by Women 1880–1930: An Anthology of Texts by British and American Women from the Modernist Period*, Manchester University Press, 2012, with Gilli Bush-Bailey and is co-editor of *Fifty Modern and Contemporary Dramatists: Routledge Keyguides*, London: Routledge, 2014.

John F. Deeney is Principal Lecturer in Contemporary Arts at Manchester Metropolitan University, UK. He is the author of many essays and articles on contemporary playwrights and performance, editor of *Writing Live: An Investigation of the Relationship between Writing and Live Art*, London: New Playwrights Trust/London Arts Board, 1998; co-editor of *Fifty Modern and Contemporary Dramatists: Routledge Keyguides*, London: Routledge, 2014, and author of *Mark Ravenhill: Routledge Modern and Contemporary Dramatists,* London: Routledge, 2016.

Dan Rebellato is Professor of Contemporary Theatre at Royal Holloway, University of London. He is also an award-winning playwright and the author of *1956 and All That: The Making of Modern British Drama*, London: Routledge, 1999, and *Theatre & Globalization*, Basingstoke: Palgrave Macmillan, 2009, co-editor with Maria M. Delgado of *Contemporary European Theatre Directors,* London: Routledge, 2010, and author of *The Suspect Culture Book,* London: Oberon, 2011, as well as many essays and articles on post-war and contemporary British theatre and drama.

Carl Lavery is Professor of Theatre and Performance at the University of Glasgow. He is author of many articles and essays on contemporary performance, ecology and performance and of *The Politics of Jean Genet's Late Theatre: Spaces of Revolution*, Manchester: Manchester University Press, 2010, and with Dee Heddon and Paul Smith, *Walking, Writing and Performance: Autobiographical Texts*, Bristol: Intellect, 2009. He has edited with Claire Finburgh and Maria Shevtsova *Jean Genet: Performance and Politics*, Basingstoke: Palgrave, 2006, and with Claire Finburgh, *Contemporary French Theatre and Performance*, Basingstoke: Palgrave, 2011.

Acknowledgements

We would like to thank the numerous people involved in the making of this second edition of the anthology. First, many thanks to all the artists and scholars who gave permission to reproduce their texts and photographs. Second, to all those at Routledge who have continued to be excited and engaged by the project and who have encouraged us, especially when the task seemed too vast, thanks to Ben Piggott in particular. We are grateful to the numerous readers for the proposal for the second edition, many of whose comments directly influenced our decisions as to what to include in this volume. We would also like to thank all our students at the University of Manchester, and Manchester Metropolitan University, UK, who have worked with many of the materials included in this anthology since the mid-2000s and whose thoughtful responses to them have impacted on the ways they are presented and discussed here. This project would not have been possible without the advice and encouragement of our friends and colleagues: Maria Delgado, Dan Rebellato, Carl Lavery, Rachel Clements, Simon Parry, Alison Jeffers, Hayley Jayne Bradley, Kate Dorney, Robin Nelson and Stephen Berwind. Editorial advice and detailed responses to the anthology in its early stages and to the essays from readers, teachers and practitioners were vital. Thanks also to friends and family, Eamon McKay, Jenny Hughes and to Oscar Partridge and Sol Partridge.

This book is again dedicated to the theatre and performance artists who have made our lives richer through their work.

Maggie B. Gale and John F. Deeney
Manchester 2016

The publishers wish to thank the following for their permission to publish work in full or extracts.

Émile Zola, *Thérèse Raquin*, translated and © Pip Broughton, Oberon Books/Absolute Classics, 2003.

August Strindberg, *Miss Julie, August Strindberg's Miss Julie*, new version translated by Frank McGuinness. Copyright © 2000 Frank McGuinness. Kind permission of Casarotto Ramsay & Associates Limited, London.

Anton Chekhov, *The Three Sisters* (Penguin) © 1954 Elisaveta Fen, pp. 247–330. Reproduced by kind permission of the Estate of Elisaveta Fen.

Henrik Ibsen, *When We Dead Awaken*, translation by William Archer, 1903. Public domain.

Maurice Maeterlinck, *Interior*, translation by Dan Rebellato. Reproduced by permission of Orlamonde Inc, on behalf of the Maeterlinck Estate.

Emile Zola, *Naturalism in the Theatre* (trans. A. Bermel), in Eric Bentley, *The Theory of the Modern*

Stage, pp. 351–72, 1968. Reprinted by permission of Helen Merrill, LLC. Copyright © Albert Bermel.

August Strindberg, *Preface* to *Miss Julie*, pp. 56–68. Copyright © 1998 Michael Robinson. Reprinted by permission of Oxford University Press.

Arthur Symons, 'A New Art of The Stage', in Eric Bentley, *The Theory of the Modern Stage*, pp.138–47, 1968. Reproduced by kind permission of the Estate of Arthur Symons.

Maurice Maeterlinck, *The Modern Drama* (1904), in Bernard Dukore, *Dramatic Theory and Criticism*, pp. 731–6. Copyright © Dukore. Translated by Alfred Sutro, Reprinted from Maeterlinck, *The Double Garden*, NY Dodd Mead and Co. 1904. Reproduced by permission of Orlamonde Inc, on behalf of the Maeterlinck Estate.

Excerpt from 'Tragedy in Everyday Life', pp. 32–42 (translation by Dan Rebellato). Reproduced by permission of Orlamonde Inc, on behalf of the Maeterlinck Estate.

Pierre Quillard, *On the Complete Pointlessness of Accurate Staging*, pp. 180–3 (1891), newspaper article translated by Dan Rebellato. Copyright © Dan Rebellato 2009.

King Ubu: Copyright in this translation © The Estate of Kenneth McLeish 1997. Reprinted by permission of the publishers Nick Hern Books: www.nickhernbooks.co.uk. Enquiries concerning any kind of performance of *King Ubu* should be directed to Nick Hern Books Ltd, 14 Larden Road, London W3 7ST, *fax* +44 (0) 20 8735 2500, *email* info@nickhernbooks.demon.co.uk. No performance may be given unless a licence has been obtained. The right of Kenneth McLeish to be identified as translator of this work has been asserted in accordance with the Copyright, Designs and Patents Act 1988.

The Breasts of Tiresias by Guillaume Apollinaire. English translation copyright © 1961 by Louis Simpson. Originally published as *Les mamelles de tirésias* by Éditions Sic copyright 1918. Reprinted by permission of Georges Borchardt, Inc., for Éditions Gallimard.

Antonin Artaud, *The Spurt of Blood*, from Antonin Artaud, *Collected Works*, vol. 1, pp. 62–5. Reproduced by kind permission of Calder Publications Ltd. Copyright © John Calder (Publishers) Ltd 1970.

Oskar Kokoschka, *Murderer the Women's Hope*, in *An Anthology of German Expressionist Drama*, ed. Walter Sokel, Cornell, 1984, pp. 17–22. Copyright © trans. Michael Hamburger. Translation reproduced by kind permission of the estate of Michael Hamburger. Original © Fondation Oskar Kokoshka/DACS 2013.

Umberto Boccioni, *Bachelor Apartment*, *Genius and Culture* and *Feet* (Marinetti), from *Futurist Performance*. Copyright © 1971, 1986 Michael Kirby. English translation of manifestos and playscripts. Copyright © 1971 Victoria Nes Kirby. Reprinted by permission of PAJ Publications.

Raoul Hausmann (1920), *Genius in a Jiffy or a Dadalogy*, in L. Senelick, ed. *Cabaret Performance: Europe 1890–1920*, New York: PAJ Publications, pp. 212–15, trans. Laurence Senelick 1989. Reproduced by kind permission of Laurence Senelick.

R.U.R. (Rossum's Universal Robots) © Karel Čapek, translated 1923 by P. Selver and Nigel Playfair, Methuen Drama, an imprint of Bloomsbury Publishing Plc.

English translation of *Six Characters in Search of an Author* (*Sei personaggi in cerca d'autore*) copyright © 1970 by Eric Bentley. Plays published 1998 by Northwestern University Press. All rights strictly reserved.

Gertrude Stein, *Dr Faustus Lights the Lights*, from *Last Operas and Plays*, published by Rinehart and Co. reproduced by kind permission of the estate of Gertrude Stein and David Higham Associates.

Filippo Marinetti, 'The Meaning of the Music Hall', in *Theatre Quarterly* Vol 1: 3 (1971) (originally from the *Daily Express*). Reprinted by permission of the heirs of Filippo Marinetti. Courtesy of Fausto Piermaria Salvati, Vicedirettore Sezione OLAF – SIAE v. le della Letteratura 30, 00144 Roma, Italia.

Antonin Artaud, 'Theatre of Cruelty: First Manifesto', from Antonin Artaud, *The Theatre and Its Double*, pp. 68–78. Reproduced by kind permission of Calder Publications Ltd. Copyright © John Calder (Publishers) Ltd 1970.

Andre Breton, 'The First Surrealist Manifesto', pp. 66–71, and 'The Second Surrealist Manifesto', pp. 76–80, from *Surrealism* by Patrick Waldberg. Copyright © Dumont Schauberg, Cologne 1965. This edition © 1965 and 1997 Thames & Hudson Ltd, London. Reprinted by kind permission of Thames & Hudson and the estate of Andre Breton.

E. Prampolini, *Futurist Scenography* (*Manifesto*), in E. T. Kirby, *Total Theatre: A Critical Anthology*, trans. Diana Clemmons from *Futurist Performance*. Copyright © Michael Kirby 1971, 1986. Reprinted by permission of PAJ Publications.

'Theater, Circus, Variety' by L. Moholy-Nagy from *The Theater of Bauhaus*, ed. Walter Gropius and Arthur Wensinger (Wesleyan University Press, 1971). Copyright © 1971 Walter Gropius and Arthur Wensinger. Reprinted by permission of Wesleyan University Press.

Cicely Hamilton and Christopher St John, *How the Vote Was Won*, in *How the Vote Was Won*, ed. Carol Hayman and Dale Spender, Methuen Publishing Ltd, 1985, pp. 23–33. Copyright © 1985, Sir Leslie Bower. Reproduced by kind permission of Lady Patricia Bower.

Ernst Toller, *Hoppla, We're Alive!* Reprinted with the translator's corrections from *Ernst Toller Plays One: Transformation, Masses Man, Hoppla, We're Alive!: A Prologue and Five Acts*. Translated and edited by Alan Raphael Pearlman. London: Oberon Books Ltd, 2000. Original works © Katharine Weber. Sixteen photographs from the original production have not been included in this anthology but are available along with other important pictorial material in the Oberon edition.

The Exception and the Rule © Bertolt Brecht, 1991, Methuen Drama, an imprint of Bloomsbury Publishing Plc.

Workers' Theatre Movement, *Meerut* and *How to Produce Meerut*, versions used from *Theatres of the Left 1880–1935* (Routledge, 1985) by Raphael Samuel, Ewan MacColl and Stuart Cosgrove.

Ronald Gow and Walter Greenwood, *Love on the Dole* in *Plays of the Thirties*, Pan Books Ltd, 1966, pp. 119–94. Copyright © 1938 Gow and Greenwood/Samuel French Acting Editions. Reprinted courtesy of Laurence Fitch Ltd.

Blues for Mister Charlie. Copyright © 1964 James Baldwin. Copyright renewed. Reprinted by arrangement with the James Baldwin Estate.

Susan Carlson, 'Suffrage Theatre: Community Activism and Political Commitment', in *A Companion to Modern British and Irish Drama*, ed. Mary Luckhurst, Oxford: Blackwell Publishing, 2006, pp. 99–109. Reproduced by permission of Blackwell Publishing Ltd.

Sheila Stowell, 'Rehabilitating Realism', in *Journal of Dramatic Theory and Criticism*, 6(2), 1992, pp. 81–8. Reprinted by kind permission of Sheila Stowell.

'The Work of Art in the Age of Mechanical Reproduction', from *Illuminations* by Walter Benjamin, translated by Harry Zohn © 1955 by Suhrkamp Verlag, Frankfurt A.M. English translation © 1968 and renewed 1996 by Houghton Mifflin Harcourt Publishing Company. Reproduced by permission of Houghton Mifflin Harcourt Publishing Company and Suhrkamp Verlag via Writers House LLC. All rights reserved.

Bertolt Brecht, 'Theatre for Pleasure or Theatre for Instruction' and 'The Street Scene', in *Brecht on Theatre*, ed. John Willett, London: Methuen, 1978, pp. 69–76 and pp. 120–9, translated by John Willett. Reproduced by kind permission of Suhrkamp Verlag. All rights reserved. And, Methuen Drama, an imprint of Bloomsbury Publishing Plc.

Michael Kirby, 'On Political Theatre', TDR/The Drama Review, 19:2 (June, 1975), pp. 129-35. © 1975 by New York University and the Massachusetts Institute of Technology.

Howard Barker, 'The Politics Beyond Politics', in H. Barker, *Arguments for a Theatre*, Manchester University Press, 1997, pp. 48–50. Reproduced by kind permission of the publisher.

The Bald Soprano by Eugene Ionesco. © 1958 by Grove Press, Inc. Used by Permission of Grove/Atlantic, Inc. Any third party use of this material, outside of this publication, is prohibited. Original version: *La Cantatrice chauve* © Editions Gallimard, Paris, 1964.

Samuel Beckett, *Endgame* © 1957 by The Estate of Samuel Beckett. Used by Permission of Grove/Atlantic, Inc and Faber and Faber Publishers. Any third party use of this material, outside of this publication, is prohibited.

The Balcony by Jean Genet © 1958, 1960 by Bernard Frechtman, © 1966 by Jean Genet and Bernard Frechtman. Used by Permission of Grove/Atlantic, Inc and Faber and Faber Ltd. Any third party use of this material, outside of this publication, is prohibited.

The Dumb Waiter © 1960 by Harold Pinter. Used by Permission of Grove/Atlantic, Inc and Faber and Faber Ltd. Any third party use of this material, outside of this publication, is prohibited.

Martin Esslin, 'The Absurdity of the Absurd', from *The Theatre of the Absurd* © 1961 Martin Esslin, Bloomsbury Methuen Drama.

Eugène Ionesco, *The London Controversy* from *Notes and Counter Notes*, translated by Donald Watson, London John Calder, pp. 90–100 © Calder Publications 1964.

Theodore Adorno, 'Trying to Understand *Endgame*', *The New German Critique* 26: Spring, pp. 119–150, 1982 © Suhrkamp Verlage. Used with permission.

Lucien Goldmann, translated by Pat Dreyfus, edited by Richard Schechner, 'The Theatre of Genet: A Sociological Study', TDR/The Drama Review, 12:2 (Winter 1968), pp. 51–61. © 1968 by New York University and the Massachusetts Institute of Technology.

Müller, H. *Quartet*, in *Hamletmachine and Other Texts for the Stage*, trans. Carl Weber. Copyright © Performing Arts Journal 1984, 1986. Reprinted by permission of PAJ Publications.

'Forced Entertainment', a new version of text from *Speak Bitterness*, in Tim Etchells, *Certain Fragments*, 2005 [1999], with an introduction by Tim Etchells in 2010. Printed here by courtesy of Tim Etchells and Forced Entertainment.

Split Britches, *Belle Reprieve*, in Sue-Ellen Case (ed.) (1996) *Split Britches: Lesbian Practice/Feminist Performance*, London: Routledge, pp. 149–184. Used with permission of the publishers.

SuAndi, *The Story of M*, reproduced by kind permission of the author.

Guillermo Gómez-Peña, 'Supernintendo Ranchero', from *BORDERScape 2000*, pp. 24–33, in Guillermo Gómez-Peña, *Dangerous Border Crossings*, London: Routledge, 2000. Reproduced by permission of Taylor & Francis Books UK.

Far Away. Copyright © 2000 Caryl Churchill Ltd. Reprinted by permission of the publishers Nick Hern Books: www.nickhernbooks.co.uk. The right of Caryl Churchill to be identified as author of this work has been asserted in accordance with the Copyright, Designs and Patents Act 1988.

Mark Ravenhill, *Product* from *Plays 2* © 2008 Mark Ravenhill author, Methuen Drama, an imprint of Bloomsbury Publishing Plc.

'The Death of the Author', from *Image, Music, Text* by Roland Barthes, translated by Stephen Heath. English translation © 1977 by Stephen Heath. Reprinted by permission of Hill and Wang, a division of Farrar, Strauss and Giroux, LLC, and of HarperCollins Publishers Ltd.

Eugenio Barba, 'Dramaturgy', pp. 66–71, and 'Montage', pp. 178–84, from *A Dictionary of Theatre Anthropology*. Copyright © 2006 (1991) Routledge. Reproduced by permission of Taylor & Francis Books UK and the author.

Jean Baudrillard, 'The Divine Irreference of Images', pp. 3–7, and 'The Strategy of the Real', pp. 19–27, in *Simulacra and Simulation*, Ann Arbor: University of Michigan Press, 1994. Originally published in French by Editions Galilee, 1981.

Jacques Rancière, 'The Emancipated Spectator', in *The Emancipated Spectator*, Verso, 2009, pp. 1–24. Used with permission of the publishers.

Hans-Thies Lehmann, 'Epilogue', from *Postdramatic Theatre*, London: Routledge, pp. 145–74.

German edition copyright © Verlag der Autoren, D-Frankfurt am Main, 1999; English edition copyright © Routledge 2006. Reproduced by permission of Taylor & Francis Books UK and Verlag der Autoren.

Guillermo Gómez-Peña, 'Away from the Surveillance Cameras of the Art World: Strategies for Collaboration and Community Activism', from Guillermo Gómez-Peña, *Dangerous Border Crossers*, pp. 167–87, London: Routledge, 2000. Reproduced by permission of Taylor & Francis Books UK.

Mark Ravenhill, 'Me, My iBook, and Writing in America', in *Contemporary Theatre Review*, 16(1), 2006, pp. 131–8, reprinted by permission of the publisher (Taylor & Francis Ltd, www.tandfonline.com).

Introduction

MAGGIE B. GALE

From modernism to contemporary practice: crisis and change

If I had to sum up the twentieth century, I would say it had raised the greatest hopes ever conceived by humanity, and destroyed all illusions and ideals. (Yehudi Menuhin qtd in Hobsbawm 2009: 2)

It works small the history thing. Small things make big changes. (Etchells 1999: 19)

THIS ANTHOLOGY INCLUDES MATERIALS – plays, performance texts, critical essays, commentaries, theories and manifestos – by innovatory practitioners and cultural critics, from the end of the nineteenth century to the early years of the twenty-first. So it has an ambitious and challenging remit in terms of representation. The bulk of the materials come from the twentieth century, which historian Eric Hobsbawm labelled an 'age of extremes' characterized by catastrophe, economic growth and decline, and culminating with the prediction of an 'apocalyptic future' (Hobsbawm 2009: 6). The texts included here encompass theatre and performance's reaction to, and interface with, such a history, but as Etchells suggests, they also reflect on history as a series of 'small things' – individual plays, performances, practitioners and critical works that have transformed the ways in which we conceptualize and practise theatre.

The volume is divided into five parts: Naturalism and Symbolism: Early Modernist Practice; The Historical Avant-Garde: Performance and Innovation; Political Theatres; Late Modernism; and Contemporary Theatre and Performance. The introductory chapters to each of the five parts – which cross over each other in terms of chronologies – provide more detailed overviews of the historical and social contexts for the materials included in the volume. This overview introduction draws out some of the themes which reverberate over the period covered as a whole.

Virtually all of the plays and texts in this volume reflect upon, are reflective of and sometimes collide with a context of social, political and aesthetic transition with which theatre and performance in Europe and America have been engaged, from the late nineteenth century onwards. All areas of human experience have been radically changed by the impact of war, technological advances, economic crises and shifting relationships between the social classes, the individual and the state, during the period the volume covers. The terrible impact of two World Wars was felt by Europe and America across the classes in the first half of the twentieth century, but the ripple effects were global with the redrawing of international boundaries in colonized territories and transformations in the power relations between colonizer and colonized, as well as an emergence of the United States as the dominant economic power. Some might suggest that the twentieth and twenty-first centuries thus far have been characterized by war itself, with very few countries ever existing in a state of peace. As performance theorist Richard Schechner (1934–) writes in

2008 – post the 9/11 attack on the World Trade Center in New York – for all but very few years of his own lifetime, the United States has been at war. He points out that the economic cost of this has been significant, but more importantly he notes the high cost of war in terms of 'the cultural, the personal and the spiritual' (Schechner 2008: 7).

In the opening decade of the twenty-first century, the supposed divide between West and East and actual disparities between the rich and the poor appeared to be ever stronger. As an economic system, capitalism was challenged by the rise of communism in the earlier part of the twentieth century, only to re-emerge as an all-powerful neo-liberal, globalized economic structure in the twenty-first century. Combined with this, the technological developments over the period covered in this volume, which transformed our production processes and transportation and communication systems, have completely altered the ways in which we live our lives – from increasing levels of geographical and social mobility to changing relationships between work and leisure time. They also threaten to potentially destroy the fine ecological balance of the physical world we inhabit. The period covered in this volume has therefore been one of unprecedented change, much of which has created a consistent and vibrant revaluation of the ways in which art overall, and theatre and performance in particular, can be used to question, express, experience and impact upon our world. In the final part of the volume we see artists embracing what Tim Etchells views as the 'small things [which] make big changes' (see above), whereby performance practice returns or perhaps re-embraces the complexities of individual experience and the expression of individuality, in a world where generality, uncertainty and the non-specificity of a 'global culture' appear to dominate.

The desire to use theatre as a means of thinking through the causal relationships between man/woman and their social environment embedded in the innovations brought about by the Naturalists in the late nineteenth century (see Part 1) was followed by the refusal of many in the historical avant-garde to see art as representational: art is not about meaning but should question and embrace the illogical, the anarchic, the subconscious and so on (see Part 2). The belief in theatre and performance as a form of social, political agency and critique which drives much of the work of the practitioners whose work is placed in Part 3 is complicated by the shift in beliefs brought about by the social upheavals and globalized contexts of the work in Part 5. Here and in Part 4, a crisis of subjectivity prevails; artists question the terms by which we might define 'truth' and 'self', and what kinds of art we might usefully or meaningfully make in a culture in crisis. Running through each of the Parts are questions about the reliance of theatre on text for the making of meaning – this is as much to do with a predicament about and distrust of text (the written word and the power of language) as it is about the dominance of the play text as a form through which theatre and performance are generated. Many of the practitioners we include in the volume, especially those in Parts 2 and 5, have been involved in undermining the dominance of text and the belief that text alone can represent experience or express meaning. Others have made formal textual innovations, breaking away from the traditional format of the well-made play prevalent in the late nineteenth century. All have been heavily influenced by innovations in art practices and theories of art and culture generally: some of the texts in this volume are hybrid forms which barely indicate what might be happening on stage or in front of our eyes (see 2.4 and 2.6) or which might more recognizably be viewed as performance poetry or prose (see 5.2 and 5.4).

The division of 'high' and 'low' culture dominant in the early years covered by this volume is problematized as early as 1896 in Alfred Jarry's *King Ubu* (2.1). Many of the practitioners whose work or ideas are included in the volume strongly argued against the idea of theatre as 'literary' and refuted its 'ownership' by the bourgeoisie or the ruling classes, instead celebrating popular cultural forms that they attempted to embrace in their work. The interrelationships between drama, text, performance, 'high' and 'low' art and theatricality are sometimes joyously and mischievously played with by, for example, the Surrealists at one end of the century (see 2.2) but also by artists like Forced Entertainment (5.2) and Split Britches (5.3) at the closing end of the same century. During the twentieth century, theatre has had to reposition itself alongside and in tandem with the development of other populist representational media such as film. The potential ways in which this repositioning might transform what we understand the role or function of art or theatre to be were critiqued early on by cultural philosophers such as Walter Benjamin (see 3.9), who questioned terms such as 'aura', 'replica' and 'authenticity' in his discussion about art practices in an age where 'art' objects could now be easily 'reproduced'.

The spaces in which theatre and performance events take place have been transformed, from the large-scale proscenium-arch stages of the nineteenth century, to the intimate chamber theatres craved by practitioners such as Strindberg in the early part of the twentieth century, to the cabaret venues of the avant-garde and the 'non-theatre', site-specific venues of the twenty-first century. There is a sense in which theorizing about how theatre and performance operate as cultural products has removed the traditional boundaries we might use to define what is and what is not theatre: this in turn has influenced the kinds of spaces in which theatre might take place. Yet, some of the practitioners included here from the earlier part of the twentieth century, such as Antonin Artaud, had ideas about the kinds of spaces and places in which theatre and performance might take place, which were decades ahead of their era.

One of the recurrent arguments about the unique quality of theatre and performance has focused on its reliance on interaction, on community and on its 'liveness' as an event, its non-reproducibility and inability to 'produce a tangible object which may enter into circulation as a marketable commodity' (Lehmann 2006: 16). This creates a problem in terms of what we use as a means of studying theatre and performance, especially historically. Ultimately 'you had to be there' to experience the event, but there are ephemera, an archive of possible materials which we might use to begin our explorations and conversations about how that event might have been experienced, how it functioned or what it might have signified. This anthology attempts therefore to provide a series of evidential 'objects' – texts – which it is hoped will provide a starting point for discussions about theatre and performance as a significant cultural product over a period of more than 100 years. Some of the texts are more indicative than they are representational, but we have included photographic materials which can also be used as routes into discussing the 'texts' as theatre and performance rather than as literature. So, for example, the photographs of two productions of *Three Sisters* (see Figures 5 and 6) come from two different historical moments, but offer interesting scenographic commonalities in terms of the ways in which the text has been framed visually in performance. Each creates demarcated 'spaces' where action might happen simultaneously. Thus the early twentieth-century Russian staging might be part of a 'Naturalist' tradition, but is clearly linked or referred to by the recent German production, where the architectural lines imply a similar division of a domestic space, predicated on providing the possibility of simultaneous stage action.

Divisions of culture: modernism and postmodernism

Numerous 'texts' in this volume challenge us to break away from 'traditional' theatre, with its presumed passive audiences and silent auditoria. We might reinvent what it is that theatre and performance offers as cultural products created within a 'politics of culture'; for they are part of, and impact upon, a wider social and cultural milieu. Here, politics – in the broadest sense of the word – 'are the condition of which culture is the product' (Eagleton 2000: 122). For it is clear that political thinking and political change – who has access to power and how that access might affect our everyday lives – have impacted on theatre as much as any other cultural product during the period covered in this volume.

Many of the materials in this volume, especially those in the earlier parts, respond to the cultural conditions from which they originate by means of manifestos for change and the demand for a transformation of theatre and, in turn, society. They represent 'emergent' cultures that challenged the 'residual' and 'dominant' cultures that surrounded them. Raymond Williams (1921–88), whose ideas greatly influenced the development of cultural theory in the late decades of the twentieth century, uses the terms 'residual' (the extant sense of community, for example, or established social practices which may seem out of kilter with the contemporary moment), 'dominant' (those cultural practices which appear to be the 'norm', the predominant at any one time) and the 'emergent' (innovatory, 'alternative' or oppositional practices). He uses these to illustrate the ways in which no cultural product is isolated, but rather reacts against, is dispensed with or is appropriated by the present historical moment (see Williams 2005: 31–49).

Most of the texts in this volume, at the point of creation, fall into the category of emergent culture. However, as the introductions to each of the Parts in the volume explore, the texts from the first half of the volume all came in fast succession. No sooner had Naturalism paved the way for a sociological perspective and a 'laboratory' of humanity through theatre (see Part 1), for example, than Symbolism interrupted by proposing that theatre was at its height of efficacy when working through the implied and the imagistic, through its poetic qualities as opposed to the constraints of the realist text. Similarly, no sooner had Symbolism drawn us back into the poetic of language, than Dada and Futurism turned text on its head, deconstructing language and its relation to performance altogether (see Part 2). By the early 1920s, even though some Naturalist plays were still banned for public performance in the UK – viewed as socially risqué and unsuitable for public consumption – Naturalism was part of the dominant culture and to some extent was fast becoming a residual culture from the late nineteenth century. For Williams, what came about during the twentieth century was in fact 'an increasingly close interweaving of all three categories', the residual, the dominant and the emergent (qtd in Eagleton 2000: 123). Certainly what we see in many of the aesthetic propositions of the Modernist and Postmodernist movements which dominate innovatory practice during the period covered in this volume, is the deliberate interplay, manipulation, refusal and hybridizing of all of Williams' categories of cultural product, to different degrees depending on which texts we focus on.

Modernism is notoriously difficult to define. Before the First World War, modernist cultural practice was driven by experiment and was more positive in its outlook despite its agenda of social critique and the disruption of cultural tradition. A belief in progress underpinned the work of many of the early modernists such as the Naturalists. After the First World War (1914–18), however, modernism was more characterized by fragmentation and a questioning of what might previously have been viewed as accepted knowledge – the chronology of time and the limitations of consciousness, for example. Immediately after the First World War, 'modernisms' traditionally grouped as the historical avant-garde, such as Futurism and Surrealism, often created a more violent and radical challenge to 'existing modes of representation' (Childs 2000: 4). Many of the practices they formulated have fed into developments typified in some later modernist and postmodern theatre and performance practices at the opposite end of the century (see Parts 4 and 5). Here we see a move from an interrogation of the ways in which we look at and reflect reality, to a questioning of any possibility of a consensual, united version or expression of reality as articulated in Baudrillard's work (5.10). Similarly, much modernist practice beyond the avant-garde as explored in Parts 3 and 4 questioned whose 'reality' we might represent and in some cases, how we represent it.

As practices which came under the umbrella of modernism melded and bled into each other, so too many of the theories produced in one historical moment find realization in another. We should also note that the postmodern – explored in more detail in Part 5 – cannot be totally distinguished from its antecedents. Although many argue that the postmodern marks a break from the modernist as a post-Second World War shift in cultural practices, general definitions allow for strong connections to be made between them. Thus the postmodern 'deliberately and playfully employs paradox to display its own artificiality and contradictions … alludes to both high and popular culture,' and is characterized by 'an incredulity to the grand narratives of progress', questioning 'the stability of traditional notions of reason and rationality' (Macey 2000: 306–7). Such a description of a general movement influencing theatre and performance from the late 1950s onwards, however, could just as easily be applied to the historical avant-garde which flourished during the modernist period in the earlier part of the same century. The point here is not to confuse or to oversimplify, but to note the crossovers, cross-currents and meeting points between the different cultural products included in this volume.

The spectrum of materials included in this new edition of the volume all represent some form of innovation driven by questions such as 'who is theatre for?', 'what can it represent and how?', 'how does it function and how might we transform its functionality?' As editors we have worked from the premise that the materials included are cultural products not literary works. They derive from a philosophical and pragmatic questioning of what theatre and performance are, and how they function within a politics of culture – from the alienating urban chaos of the late industrial revolution of the nineteenth century, through the social, political and domestic upheavals of the early and mid-twentieth century, to the globalized and seemingly anonymized culture of the first decades of the twenty-first.

How to use this volume

The plays, performance texts and critical texts included in this volume can and should be read both *with* and *against* each other. The contents to some extent are inevitably a compromise: pedagogically, we hope that there is a useful combination of the canonical and the marginal, the pan-European and American, the critical and the practical. Often copyright and financial constraints have been more influential over what has been excluded than any kind of intellectual or pedagogical rationale. We have reorganized some of the materials in this new edition of the *Routledge Drama Anthology*, and have included numerous new texts: plays by Pirandello, Čapek,

Gertrude Stein, Brecht, Beckett, Pinter, Ionesco, Jean Genet, Heiner Müller, and Split Britches, and critical texts by Theodor Adorno, Roland Barthes, and Jacques Rancière. We have included texts which we hope will usefully open out discussion: thus in Part 1, rather than have an early play by Ibsen we have included his last, in part to evidence the fluid nature of the infamous 'isms' of modernism: Ibsen is both a purveyor of Naturalism in the introduction to Part 1 and a Symbolist in terms of the play we include, *When We Dead Awaken* (1.4). In Part 5, the texts cannot possibly represent the 'contemporary' *per se*. It is hoped, however, that they provide points of focus and a 'way in' to exploring a range of contemporary practices, the evidence for which is perhaps more readily accessible than the practice represented by the materials in the opening parts of the anthology: many contemporary performance companies have sophisticated web pages and archive holdings accessible to the public, with clips of their work accessible on YouTube, Vimeo or on sites such as the Routledge Performance Archive. We advise that readers make use of these alongside readings of the texts reprinted in this volume.

Theatre and Performance Studies have undergone a significant transformation over the past few decades, but the materials with which students still need to engage in order to understand the relationships between theatre and performance practices of the past and those of the present remain relatively constant as reference points. Whilst 'information' about historical theatre and performance practices has become more easily and speedily accessible through the internet, many of the texts and performance documents which one might wish to refer students to remain either inaccessible or too costly.

Although the volume is divided into five parts, we refer the reader from one part to another wherever possible. So, for example, where Walter Benjamin's seminal essay, 'The Work of Art in the Age of Mechanical Reproduction' (3.9), is placed in Part 3, it might also be used to analyse materials and ideas explored in both Part 2 and Part 5. Similarly, a play like Caryl Churchill's *Far Away* (5.6), for example, can be read alongside or against any of the plays in Part 4, but it could also be fruitfully placed against many of the plays/performance texts in Part 3. The vision in operation when the volume was put together was that it could be multi-purpose in its potential usability, and that whilst the introduction and divisions of materials embrace an internal logic, the logic is not hermetically sealed to disallow any other grouping or connectivities being made between and amongst the texts included.

We hope the *Routledge Drama Anthology: From Modernism to Contemporary Performance* is a volume that students and teachers will buy and want to keep. It includes numerous plays and critical/performance texts seminal to an understanding of various developments in theatre and performance across Western Europe and America during the late nineteenth century and into the twenty-first. Despite its obvious limitations in terms of global coverage, we hope that this anthology allows for close, interconnected and fluid readings of the texts produced by some of the great European and American innovative theatre and performance artists and cultural theorists of the past 100-plus years.

Bibliography

Childs, Peter (2000) *Modernism*, London: Routledge.
Eagleton, Terry (2000) *The Idea of Culture*, Oxford: Blackwell.
Etchells, Tim (1999) *Certain Fragments*, London: Routledge.

Hobsbawm, Eric (2009 [1994]) *The Age of Extremes: 1914–1991*, London: Abacus.

Lehmann, Hans-Thies (2006) *Postdramatic Theatre*, London: Routledge.

Macey, David (2000) *The Penguin Dictionary of Critical Theory*, London: Penguin.

Schechner, Richard (2008) 'We Are, After All, at War', *The Drama Review*, 52(1) (T197), 7–10.

Williams, Raymond (2005 [1980]) *Culture and Materialism*, London: Verso.

Further reading

Bennett, Susan (1997) *Theatre Audiences: A Theory of Production and Reception*, London: Routledge.

Carey, John (1992) *The Intellectuals and the Masses: Pride and Prejudice among the Literary Intelligentsia 1880–1939*, London: Faber and Faber.

Eyre, Richard and Nicholas Wright (2001) *Changing Stages: A View of British and American Theatre in the Twentieth Century*, London and New York: Random House.

Hughes, Robert (1991 [1980]) *The Shock of the New: Art and a Century of Change*, London: Thames and Hudson.

Jürs-Munby, Karen, Jerome Caroll and Steve Giles (2013) *Postdramatic Theatre and the Political*, London: Bloomsbury.

Kershaw, Baz (1992) *The Politics of Performance: Radical Theatre as Cultural Intervention*, London: Routledge.

Knowles, Ric (2014) *How Theatre Means*, Basingstoke: Palgrave Macmillan.

McFarlane, James and Malcolm Bradbury (eds.) (1991 [1976]) *Modernism: A Guide to European Literature 1880–1930*, London: Penguin.

Radosavljvić, Duška (2013) *Theatre-Making: Interplay between Text and Performance in the 21st Century*, Basingstoke: Palgrave Macmillan.

Wiles, David (2003) *A Short History of Western Performance Space*, Cambridge: Cambridge University Press.

Williams, Raymond (1973) *Drama from Ibsen to Brecht*, London: Pelican.

Part 1
Naturalism and Symbolism: Early Modernist Practice

Timeline

	Social, cultural and political context	Theatre
1848	*The Communist Manifesto*: Karl Marx and Friedrich Engels	
1859	*The Origin of Species*: Charles Darwin	
1861–2	Manifesto on the emancipation of serfs and social unrest in Russia	
1864		Imperial decree liberates Paris theatres and leads to an upsurge of new theatres being constructed
		Émile Zola's letter to Antony Valabrègue sets out his theory of the 'realist screen'
1866		In 'Books of Today and Tomorrow' (essay) Émile Zola coins the word 'Naturalism' to describe his scientific approach to literature (*L'Événement*)
1870	Education Act in Britain, which provides equal access to elementary education for girls and boys	
1873		*Thérèse Raquin* (play): Émile Zola
		Saxe-Meiningen Theatre's first tour to Berlin
1874	First Impressionist Art Salon, Paris	
1876	Alexander Graham Bell invents the telephone	Wagner's *Ring* cycle premieres in Bayreuth
1877	Thomas Edison invents the phonograph	
1879		*A Doll's House*: Henrik Ibsen (Royal Theatre, Copenhagen)
1881		Electric lighting introduced into a number of British theatres
		Naturalist Novelists, *Naturalism in the Theatre* and *Our Dramatic Authors*: Émile Zola
1882		'On Realism: Some Viewpoints' (essay): August Strindberg
1883	The death of Karl Marx	
1885	Karl Benz patents the first gasoline-powered automobile (1885–6)	
1886		*Ghosts*: Henrik Ibsen (Meiningen Theatre)
		'Symbolist' (essay/manifesto): Jean Moréas (*Le Figaro*)
1887		Théâtre Libre founded by André Antoine in Paris
1888		Théâtre du Chat Noir opens its shadow puppet theatre
		Miss Julie: August Strindberg
1889		'On Modern Drama and Modern Theatre' (essay): August Strindberg
1890		Théâtre d'Art founded by Paul Fort

	Social, cultural and political context	Theatre
1891		*The Girl with the Severed Hands*: Pierre Quillard (Théâtre d'Art)
		'On the Complete Pointlessness of Accurate Staging' (essay): Pierre Quillard (*Revue d'Art Dramatique*)
		Intruder: Maurice Maeterlinck (Théâtre d'Art)
		The Blind: Maurice Maeterlinck (Théâtre d'Art)
1893		Théâtre de l'Oeuvre founded by Aurélien Lugné-Poë
		Miss Julie: August Strindberg (Théâtre Libre)
		The Weavers: Gerhart Hauptmann (Théâtre Libre)
1894	Thomas Edison opens his Kinetoscope Parlor in New York (early motion-picture device)	
1895	Auguste and Louis Lumière credited with the first public film screening in Paris	*Interior*: Maurice Maeterlinck (Théâtre de l'Oeuvre)
1896		Independent Theatre founded in Barcelona
		Ubu Roi: Alfred Jarry (Théâtre de l'Oeuvre)
		The Seagull: Anton Chekhov (Alexandrinsky Theatre, St Petersburg)
1897		Moscow Art Theatre founded by Konstantin Stanislavski and Vladimir Nemirovich-Danchenko
		Théâtre Antoine, successor to Théâtre Libre, founded, Paris
1898		*The Seagull*: Anton Chekhov (Moscow Art Theatre)
1899		*When We Dead Awaken*: Henrik Ibsen
1900	*The Interpretation of Dreams*: Sigmund Freud	
1901	Nobel Prize founded	*Three Sisters*: Anton Chekhov (Moscow Art Theatre)
1902		Death of Émile Zola
1903	The Wright brothers successfully fly an engine-powered aeroplane	
1904		*The Cherry Orchard*: Anton Chekhov (Moscow Art Theatre)
		Death of Chekhov
		Abbey Theatre, Dublin, founded
1905	Albert Einstein formulates his 'special theory of relativity'	Vsevolod Meyerhold opens the Moscow Art Studio Theatre
1906		Max Reinhardt founds the Kammerspielhaus in Berlin
		Death of Henrik Ibsen
1907	First Symbolist exhibition in Moscow (called *Blue Rose*)	Intimate Theatre, Stockholm, founded by August Strindberg and others
1908		*The Ghost Sonata*: August Strindberg (Intimate Theatre, Stockholm)
1911	Maurice Maeterlinck awarded the Nobel Prize for Literature	

Introduction

DAN REBELLATO

NATURALISM AND SYMBOLISM MARK the beginnings of modernist theatre and in many ways provided the template for much that followed. André Antoine's Théâtre Libre (1887–94) was perhaps the first independent experimental theatre company in the modern world and the Symbolist theatres that followed, while fiercely opposed to the Naturalism with which the Théâtre Libre was associated, followed Antoine's lead in choosing intimate small theatre spaces, producing short plays performed by amateur casts, and publishing journals to explain their work and ideas. Most modernist theatres which followed were a response to, and rejection of, Naturalism. For that reason, it is sometimes supposed that Naturalism was not a modernist theatre and that modernism emerged precisely in reaction to a perceived conservatism on the Naturalist stage.

In fact, Naturalism was foundational to modernist theatre practice and caused as much scandal, controversy and outrage as any of the radical, experimental theatres that came after it. The term 'naturalism', in particular, has become flattened out to refer to any theatrical production where the set and the acting attempt vaguely to resemble real life. Similarly, the term 'symbolism' can refer to any attempt to represent things and ideas through symbols. Naturalist and Symbolist theatre in their particular historical moments had a much more specific character and remit. The naturalism of Robert De Niro's acting or the symbolism in a play like Samuel Beckett's *Waiting for Godot* are very different from the Naturalism of *Thérèse Raquin* or the Symbolism of Maurice Maeterlinck's work.

The nineteenth century

Modernism was so called because it sought to capture the distinctive spirit of the modern age. The nineteenth century had wrought enormous changes across European society and culture. Industrialization, which had begun in Britain in the eighteenth century, had spread across Europe through the nineteenth century. This altered the economic organization of society which meant the emergence of unprecedentedly large industrial processes, including the building of huge factories, large-scale industrial machinery, whole towns of housing for the workers who operated it and, as a result, a transformation in the geography of Europe. Revolutionary developments in technology saw the invention, for example, of the typewriter, the battery, the light bulb, photography and cinema, the steam train and the bicycle, the elevator and escalator, phonograph, gramophone, telephone, and numerous industrial processes that would feed the development and spread of industrial capitalism across Europe.

By the beginning of the twentieth century, Europe's capital cities had expanded: thus London had gone from a population of under one million in 1800 to around six and a half million by 1900, and Paris from just over half a million to nearly three million. The emergence of cities as the centres of industry and the relative decline of agriculture meant a great migration from the countryside to the city. Cities were transformed to accommodate their new residents. This rapid expansion, with new classes being thrown together in the new city spaces, created new forms of cultural and social anxiety. There were new opportunities for vice and criminality and, not unconnected, new relationships between those with wealth and those with power.

The Eiffel Tower, and the 'Universal Exposition' of 1888 which it was built to mark, were examples of Paris's heightened awareness of itself as a powerful global city, a centre for international industry, culture and finance. Modernist theatre was also marked by these cosmopolitan flows of people and ideas. The repertoires of the Théâtre Libre and the Théâtre de l'Oeuvre – the two main Naturalist and Symbolist theatres in Paris – were pan-European, showing work from, among others, Sweden (Strindberg), Norway (Ibsen), Germany (Hauptmann), Belgium (Maeterlinck), Britain (Shelley) and Italy (Verga). Otherwise, Naturalism and Symbolism had very different relations to these dramatic changes. Symbolism, as the cultural theorist Walter Benjamin remarked (Benjamin 1999: 41), was an attempt to shield art from the onslaught of the modern world to appeal beyond it to something timeless, mysterious, profoundly unscientific. Naturalism, on the other hand, was to embrace the modern world with campaigning enthusiasm, bringing the scientific age's distinctive forms of analysis to bear on itself.

It was the emergence of a substantial middle class in Paris that gave Naturalism its main audience, while the city provided Naturalism with its subject matter. Thus much of Émile Zola's work focused on the particular conditions of Parisian life, showing particular delight in addressing the social problems and contradictions arising from rapid urban change – alcoholism, prostitution, consumerism, class conflict, decline of religion and so on. The critics who so vehemently railed against Naturalism did so in urban-industrial metaphors; when Strindberg's *Miss Julie* (1.2) was published in 1888, they called it 'water from … [a] dirty sewer' (Meyer 1985: 198). Ibsen distances himself from Zola in the same terms: 'Zola descends into the sewer to bathe in it; I to cleanse it' (qtd in Meyer 1974, 514–15).

As the income of the rising industrial class outstripped that of the declining aristocracy (whose income derived from land, which was suffering from economic competition with the Americas), the middle class bought up the gentry's town houses. These houses, with their steps up to the front door, literally elevated their residents above the mess and chaos of the city. Curtains and shutters prevented the public from seeing in. Naturalism, with its preference for making invisible the fourth wall, was a way of seeing into these homes, of showing the middle class to itself, stripped of its carefully presented respectability, laid bare in its greed, lust and hypocrisy. Pastor Manders, hearing of Mr Alving's affair with a maid, voices this architectural clash between outward respectability and domestic vice: 'all that in this very house! In this house!' (Ibsen 1994: 118).

Naturalism and the nineteenth-century stage

An immediate literary precedent for Naturalism lay in the rise of the 'realist' novel of the 1830s in the work of Balzac, Flaubert and Stendhal. A little later, in the 1850s, 'realism' emerged as a force in the visual arts, gaining particular notoriety when Gustave Courbet's paintings were rejected by the Paris International Exposition of 1855. It was in this atmosphere of controversy that Émile Zola began writing, first as a critic, then as a novelist. He was a great supporter of Courbet and his approach to the novel was entirely in the spirit of Flaubert's famous remark that 'great art is scientific and impersonal' (qtd in Cruickshank 1969: 3). However, Zola thought the term 'realism' too narrow and exclusive and instead, in an article for *L'Événement* published on

15 July 1866, coined the term 'Naturalism' to describe his new approach and for the next fifteen years campaigned for it indefatigably in the novel and, from the mid-1870s, on the stage. Zola collected many of his essays and articles in a series of books, including *The Experimental Novel* (1880) and *Naturalist Novelists, Naturalism in the Theatre* and *Our Dramatic Authors* in (1881). Zola had considerable success as a novelist and adapted some of his own novels for the stage, including *L'Assommoir* (1879), *Nana* (1881), *Pot-Bouille* (1883), *Le Ventre de Paris* (1887), and *Germinal* (1888). Only *Thérèse Raquin* (1873), however, adapted from his novel of 1867, has had any substantial theatrical afterlife.

If Zola thought that by using the word 'Naturalism' rather than 'Realism' he would avoid controversy, he was mistaken. The French stage in the 1870s was dominated by three playwrights – that 'illustrious trinity' wrote Antoine half in mockery, half in awe (Antoine 1964: 2) – Émile Augier, Victorien Sardou and Alexandre Dumas *fils*, the masters of the 'well-made play'. This form, developed and perfected through the century, was loosely based on Aristotle's rules for dramatic construction and took its hero through an increasingly complicated plot, characterized by secrets and misunderstandings, before being completely resolved in the 'scène à faire' (or 'obligatory scene') in which all secrets are revealed, all misunderstandings resolved. The moral world-view of the well-made play – usually articulated by a 'raisonneur', a character who voices the author's own moral judgment – was generally conservative. Further, the neatness of the narrative prevented it from connecting with the messy realities of nineteenth-century Europe, which had seen the unification of Germany and Italy, the spread of colonial empires, and multiple wars and revolutions. Yet, as the Naturalist playwright Henry Becque noted in 1888, 'from all these events we have not taken the action of a single drama, not one' (Schumacher 1996: 53).

Shortly after the publication of *Thérèse Raquin*, Zola's novel was condemned in the French newspaper *Le Figaro*. The article was entitled 'La Littérature Putride' (Putrid Literature) and its author, 'Ferragus', denounced *Thérèse Raquin* as 'a puddle of dirt and blood' and Naturalism as 'a monstrous school of novelists that tries to replace the eloquence of the body with the eloquence of the charnel house, that specializes in clinical abnormalities, that gathers the diseased together and invites us to admire their blemishes, that takes its inspiration from that great teacher, cholera, and make spurt forth the pus of conscience'. 'Ferragus' was a pseudonym for Louis Ulbach, a satirical writer and friend of Zola, so it is quite possible that Zola put him up to writing the article to gain publicity for his book. Nonetheless, his arguments shed light on the curious place of the theatre within French culture in his belief that *Thérèse Raquin's* (1.1) characters could not possibly be put on stage: they are 'impossible phantoms, who reek of death, who have never breathed life, who are but nightmares of reality' (Ferragus 1868: 1).[1] Zola invites us to treat his characters with contempt and disgust and, suggests Ferragus, this is not acceptable in the theatre.

What Ferragus means by this is that actors should be met with admiration, complicit laughter or tragic empathy, and nothing else. It would be unseemly to play a role that repelled the audience's sympathy. Indeed, Naturalist plays, if they weren't banned outright, were sometimes modified to conform to prevailing theatrical taste: when Ibsen's *A Doll's House* was first produced in Germany, for example, Hedwig Niemann-Raabe, the actress playing Nora, refused to play the ending in which Nora leaves her husband and children, declaring '*I* would never leave *my* children' (Meyer 1974: 480). To prevent the production from falling through, Ibsen had to write a new closing sequence in which Nora sees her children, imagines them motherless, and declares 'Oh, this is a sin against myself, but I cannot leave them' (Ibsen 1994: 87–8).

Thus Naturalism was a long time coming to the French stage. Zola's campaign was conducted as much in hope as conviction. In 'Naturalism in the Theatre' (1.6), perhaps as tacit acknowledgement of his own shortcomings as a dramatist, he confesses to not knowing what form Naturalist theatre will take, only the ideas it must embody, and he fervently bids a 'genius to come … with the expected word, the solution to the problem, the formula for real life on stage, combining it with the illusions necessary in the theatre' (1.6: 132). Zola presumed this genius would be a writer; though, as we will see, it was a director who would first make Naturalism a theatrical reality.

But what is 'Naturalism'? Even in its era, the term meant different things to different people. For Zola, it is very much the application of scientific method to the production of literature and theatre. For Strindberg, it was 'the poetic portrayal of nature' (Strindberg 1992: 512–13). Ibsen was uninterested in aligning himself with any movement.[2] However, one can see in Naturalism two main strands, which I will call 'the sociological imagination' and a 'visual culture'. Broadly, the first conveys something of Naturalism's attitude to the world, the second conveys its style of representing the world. Neither entails the other and much Naturalist theatre leans in one of the two directions.

The sociological imagination

'We are an age of method, of experimental science,' wrote Zola (1.6: 129), aligning the Naturalist movement with the nineteenth century's revolution in scientific ideas, in particular its impact on the study of society. Particularly important were Ernest Renan, Auguste Comte and Hippolyte Taine with their shared belief in bringing the principles of scientific investigation to bear on literature, religion and history, respectively. Comte, in particular, is one of the founders of modern sociology, which has its origins in the application of scientific method to the study of society (Comte's preferred term for such study was 'social physics' [Comte 1983: 77]). While their names have somewhat receded in importance, they were part of the climate of thought in the 1900s that produced the twentieth century, for good and bad. They certainly had a defining influence on Zola's conception of Naturalism.

For Renan, science had shown religion to be redundant; as he wrote in his posthumously published *The Future of Science*, 'It is not one single argument, but all the modern sciences together that produce this great conclusion: there is no such thing as the supernatural' (Renan 1890: 47). Such sceptical attitudes towards religion that he represents can be found in the generally unsympathetic representation of religious beliefs in Naturalist plays, including Kristin in *Miss Julie*, whose banal pieties are pointedly inadequate to the more complex dilemmas unfolding before us.

In his *Course in Positive Philosophy* (1830–42), Comte suggests that the history of humanity has fallen into three intellectual stages: 'the theological, or fictitious; the metaphysical, or abstract; and the scientific, or positive' (Comte 1983: 71). In the first, the world is explained through false religious ideas; in the second, the religious ideas have been abandoned in favour of abstract concepts; in the third, the positive stage, 'the mind has given over the vain search after absolute notions, the origin and destination of the universe, and the causes of phenomena, and applies itself to the study of their laws' (ibid: 72). These kinds of 'teleological' arguments were more popular in the nineteenth century than in ours and can be found in the work of thinkers as diverse as G.W.F. Hegel and Karl Marx (whose youngest daughter, Eleanor, was an early translator of Ibsen's work into English).

Comte's view of history confirmed Zola's view that Naturalism was progressive and modern, *the* literary and theatrical form of the positivist age. Indeed, Comte's three-stage history of human ideas finds its way, somewhat reinterpreted, into Zola's 'Naturalism in the Theatre'. Thus in his declaration that 'an irresistible current carries our society towards the study of reality ... the great naturalistic school, which has spread secretly, irrevocably, often making its way in darkness but always advancing, can finally come out triumphantly into the light of day' (1.6: 127), one can see traces of Comte's teleology. In describing previous forms of theatre as a 'necessary link' (ibid: 128) or a 'necessary revolution', the article shows a Comtean confidence in Naturalism as the inevitable outcome of theatre history.

For Zola, Comte's three phases of thought – theological, metaphysical and scientific – map onto three phases of French theatre: Classical, Romantic and Naturalist. The Classical theatre that dominated the seventeenth and eighteenth centuries arose from the rediscovery of ancient Greek theatre and, in particular, Aristotle's *Poetics*, which attempts to codify its rules. Associated with dramatists like Jean Racine and Pierre Corneille, neoclassicism was characterized by a certain grand austerity, heightened poetic language, stories drawn from classical mythology, great psychological complexity and with reason favoured over passion. Romanticism emerged in the theatre in the 1830s and now Shakespeare, rather than ancient Greece, provided the model. All the formal purity of neoclassicism was abandoned; action was vivid and intense, emotions ran high, the stories mixed comedy and tragedy, and often had medieval and Renaissance settings. Zola suggests that classicism, with its ancient cosmology, corresponds to the theological phase, while Romanticism, with its grand passions, its evocation of higher causes for which to fight, its speculation about the nature of the universe, corresponds to the metaphysical. With the advent of Naturalism, says Zola in clearly Comtean terms, we are seeing 'the gradual substitution of physiological man for metaphysical man' (ibid: 133).

A still greater influence on Zola's thinking comes from critic and historian Hippolyte Taine for whom the best way to understand a society is to read its literature. 'If the work is rich and one knows how to interpret it', Taine wrote, 'one can find in there the psychology of a soul, often of a century, and sometimes of an entire race. In this respect a great poem, a beautiful novel, the memoirs of a great man are more instructive than a mountain of historians and their history books' (Taine 1863: xlv). Taine believed that a work of literature bore the traces of three forces acting on it from the society in which it emerged: *race*, *milieu* and *moment*. Taine did not merely believe these were influences amongst others: these were the only possible causes of all events (xxxiii). Together, '*race*, *environment*, *moment*, in other words the internal dynamic, the external pressure and the momentum already acquired ... will impose a shape and direction on anything new' (xxxiii, xxx). Taine's *moment*, *milieu* and *race* find themselves paraphrased loosely in Strindberg's preface to *Miss Julie* (1.7), in which he describes his main character as a victim of 'the errors of an age, of circumstances, and of her own deficient constitution' (1.7: 139). If Comte left Zola with the belief that Naturalism was the modern theatre form *par excellence*, Taine persuaded him that literature and drama were unparalleled means of capturing the spirit of the age.

The word 'naturalism', before Zola picked it up, was a philosophical term denoting a belief that all things are part of the natural world, that nothing – not free will, ethics, passions, religion or art – escaped the laws of cause and effect and the natural forces at work in the physical universe. The publication of Charles Darwin's *The Origin of Species* (1859) was a naturalistic landmark in this sense: it erased much of the distinction between human beings and animals. It encouraged many thinkers – sociologists, economists and artists – to see animal behaviour in the patterns of human society. Although Darwin's evolutionary processes are only visible over hundreds of years, at the end of the century 'Social Darwinism' had appeared: this was a – probably illegitimate – application of Darwin's principle of 'natural selection' to human cultures, suggesting that ordinary human interactions were 'really' competitions for status and power. Naturalism in the theatre was, to some extent, part of this overexuberant adoption of Darwinian themes. Zola carries some of this meaning over into his view of the world and of art; of the novel *Thérèse Raquin* he writes:

In *Thérèse Raquin* I set out to study, not characters, but temperaments. Therein lies the whole essence of the book. I chose to portray individuals existing under the sovereign dominion of their nerves and their blood, devoid of free will and drawn into every act of their lives by the inescapable promptings of their flesh. (Zola 1992: 1–2)

Taine's philosophically naturalist remark that 'vice and virtue are products just like vitriol and sugar' (1863: xv) was Zola's epigraph to the first edition of *Thérèse Raquin*.

Influenced by French physiologist Claude Bernard, who sought to apply the principles of scientific enquiry to the practice of medicine and surgery, Zola compared the Naturalist author to a surgeon: 'I like to think of him as an anatomist of the soul and the flesh,' he wrote in 1866. 'He dissects man, studies the play of the passions, explores each fibre, analyses the whole organism. Like a surgeon, he has neither shame nor revulsion when he explores human wounds. He cares only for truth and lays before us the corpse of our heart. Modern science has provided him with the tools of analysis and the experimental method' (qtd in Becker 2002: 256). Defending his characterization of Thérèse and Laurent in his preface to *Thérèse Raquin* he insists: 'I simply carried out on two living bodies the same analytical examination that surgeons perform on corpses' (Zola 1992: 2).

Many Naturalist playwrights had connections with the world of medical science: Chekhov was a practising doctor; Ibsen was a pharmacist's apprentice for six years; Strindberg studied medicine for two years and in 1887 published a collection of stories and essays entitled *Vivisections: A Retired Doctor's Observations*. This is not to say that they were all reliable supporters of the latest scientific ideas: Zola's *Thérèse Raquin* uncomfortably marries a contemporary scientific viewpoint with the ancient theory of the 'humours' (1992: xvi–xxii). Ibsen's *Ghosts* (1881) relies on the belief that syphilis is hereditary. Strindberg's openness to the new science was, to put it mildly, undiscrimi-nating, and *Miss Julie* makes reference to telepathy in the battle between its antagonists. Chekhov, despite or perhaps because of his medical training, depicts most of his doctors as depressed, weary, cynical, even accidentally murderous.

Nonetheless, there is, widespread in Naturalist theatre, a determination to observe the world with all its flaws and disorders with the unsentimental clarity of a scientist, refusing any mystical, spiritual or otherwise non-physical explanations, crowned by a belief that the theatre has the vital social purpose of recording the observable truth of the world that is too important to be restrained by theatrical convention or moral squeamishness.

Visual culture

A determination to depict the truth of the world, understood in materialist terms, does not necessarily entail visual realism. It is therefore important to understand that Naturalism's visual style, its preference for a relation of resemblance between the stage and the world, is a particular – and contestable – decision. 'Realism' has never been a theatre movement as such; in the arts, realism doesn't mean much more than a determination to represent reality, however that reality is understood. The Naturalist version of realism understands reality in the sociological terms that I have described and chooses to represent that world through copying its surfaces – the details of human behaviour and its environment.

Changes in theatre technology made new kinds of realism possible through the nineteenth century. The move from oil to gas lighting at the beginning of the century, then to limelight in the mid-century, and finally to electric lighting towards the century's end, meant that the stage could be lit more brightly, with a whiter light, the intensity, level and direction of which could increasingly be controlled. This demanded increasingly sophisticated scene painting, as the backcloths were more exposed by the light; it also made obsolete some conventions of the early nineteenth century, including footlights, heavy stylized make-up and the necessity for the actor to stand downstage facing the audience if they were to be seen.

Particularly influential in making use of these innovations to create new realistic stage effects was the Meiningen Court Theatre, established in 1866 by George II, Duke of Saxe-Meiningen, a small independent state in the heart of what is now Germany. The Meiningen company became famous for the detailed, historically accurate composition of their stage pictures, in particular their crowd scenes, which were arranged with particular eye to realistic effect. André Antoine saw them in Brussels in 1888 and admired the 'extraordinarily convincing crowd scenes' and the sight of an actor with his back to the audience who thereby 'gives the impression that he is oblivious to the presence of the public and thus creates the perfect illusion' (Schumacher 1996: 80). Stanislavski saw them when they toured to Russia and the meticulously realized sound effects at the Moscow Art Theatre owed much to the similarly innovative sound design at the Meiningen.

If human beings are the products of their environment, then the environment must be represented with particular care. Zola's remark that 'the environment must determine the character' (1.6: 134) is directly echoed by Antoine's insistence that 'it is the environment that determines the movements of the character, not the movements of the characters that determine the environment' (qtd in Whitton 1987: 21). In both instances the French word for environment, 'milieu', both stands for 'set design' and reminds us of the second of Taine's forces. As such, Naturalism demanded a new detail and precision in stage design, the better to demonstrate the social and environmental forces acting on the characters. The actors, meanwhile, were required to subsume themselves within the ensemble and the stage picture so as to represent the place of the human within the natural world. The dramatist's medium being language, he or she has limited power to determine through words the stage environment. Naturalism gave new independent responsibility to the stage designer.

Jean Jullien's book *Le Théâtre Vivant* (1892) provides us with two widely used phrases to describe Naturalist theatre. One is that a Naturalist play is 'a slice of life'; the other is that the play is seen through 'a *fourth wall*, transparent for the audience, opaque for the actor' (1892: 11; my emphasis). The 'fourth wall' requires not only the actor to not acknowledge the audience, but the audience to join in the make-believe. To encourage this, the auditorium lights were dimmed; this is now so common in European and North American theatre as to seem unremarkable but at the Théâtre Libre, where they started dimming the house lights a year into their operation, it occasioned giggles and facetious kissing sounds (Chothia 1991: 64).

All of these techniques came together in perhaps the most important European theatre company of the nineteenth century, the Théâtre Libre, founded by André Antoine in March 1887. The Théâtre Libre was quickly associated with Naturalism, though in fact its repertoire was an eclectic mixture of Naturalist plays, farces, tragedies, poetic dramas, Symbolist plays, historical epics and documentary performances. Antoine was a member of the new middle class, initially supporting his company from his job as clerk at the Gas Company and the Palais de Justice; it was an amateur operation, a beneficiary of an Imperial decree deregulating the theatre industry in 1864, and it struggled on for barely seven years under Antoine's leadership. Yet it directly inspired the foundation of a dozen other experimental theatres across Europe, including Berlin's Freie Bühne (1889), London's Independent Theatre (1891), the Moscow Art Theatre (1897), as well as many theatres in Paris (see Henderson 1971).

August Strindberg: *Miss Julie* (1.2)

One theatre artist directly inspired by the example of the Théâtre Libre was August Strindberg, who formed the Scandinavian Experimental Theatre in 1888 to perform two one-act plays he had written that summer: *Miss Julie* and *Creditors*. *Miss Julie* and its preface reflect both Strindberg's brief but fervent advocacy of Zolaesque Naturalism and his own equally fervent misogyny. His philosophical naturalism was greatly influenced by his recent reading of the German philosopher Friedrich Nietzsche, from whom he appears to have taken the idea that the world is divided into the naturally weak and naturally strong, both groups engaged in perpetual, but unequal, battle for supremacy. For Strindberg, the weak included the lower classes, socialists and women. In the preface, he declares that a woman is a 'stunted form of human being' compared to 'man, the lord of creation, the creator of culture' (1.7: 139). Any talk of equality between men and women is absurd, he decides, because men and women are entirely different species; it would be as meaningless as demanding equality between ants and elephants. Feminism, an emergent political movement across Europe in the late nineteenth century, was therefore an attempt to deny nature or – and this is Strindberg at his most Nietzschean – for the weak to defeat the strong by stealth. In this he undoubtedly has his eye on Ibsen, whose *A Doll's House* (1879) was considered a form of feminist challenge to patriarchal convention.[3]

The play exploits some of this spurious logic. Julie is a woman whose upbringing and aristocratic privilege has encouraged her to try to dominate the men around her; challenging the traditional passive female position, she leads when dancing and was seen training her fiancé like a dog. She invades the scullery and flirts with the servants. However, when circumstances conspire to place her and Jean together in the latter's bedroom, her 'true' weakness as a woman is revealed, and she submits sexually to her servant. The possibility of equality between them is articulated in the play by Jean – 'Maybe deep down there is not such a difference between us all as people think' (1.2: 56) – but later it becomes clear that this was simply part of his seduction. Jean's male 'superiority' is revealed and, Strindberg suggests, there is no possible outcome for her than her own death. It is the tragedy of a woman trying to defy her nature.

Although it is unlikely that many modern theatregoers would be convinced by Strindberg's views about men and women, it is worth considering the view of feminist critic and thinker Germaine Greer, who has argued that Strindberg's genius lay in his unflinching honesty: in his torrid misogyny he 'glimpsed the archetypal conflict in all its terrible grandeur' and laid it bare (Greer 1986: 207). Perhaps one might defend this play as more honest about patriarchal attitudes and the 'battle of the sexes' than the more reasoned and liberal debates of Ibsen or Shaw. Let's also not overlook that Strindberg gives Julie a speech of violent female sexual revenge that has rarely been equalled for force and power:

JULIE: … I'm weak – am I – I'd like to see your blood, your brains smashed on the chopping block. I want to see every one of your sex swimming in a lake of blood like this one. I think I could drink out of your skull – I could wash my feet in your ripped stomach – I could roast your heart and eat. So you think I am weak … (1.2: 64).

On the other hand, one can consider the play as being complicated by Strindberg's own adherence to the principles of Naturalism. The preface shows just how closely Strindberg has followed the debates around Zola's work and the emergence of the Théâtre Libre. He calls for the lowering of the house lights and the actors to turn their backs on the audience, and describes the scenography in terms of a fourth wall, all of which recalls the Théâtre Libre's principles of staging, while his description of his characters as animals and his insistence that characters 'merge with their milieu' (1.7: 142) recall Zola. Some of his ideas go further; for example, in his suggestion that actors might improvise some of their dialogue (ibid), there is a moment where this is suggested in the play, and in his desire to create spaces for 'monologue, mime, and ballet' (1.7: 141 and 1.2: 53 for wordless and dance sequences).

But where the play is most modern is in its conception of character; unlike Zola's simplistic notion of individuals being ruled by a single temperament which Strindberg criticizes, or Taine's neat tripartite account of the forces acting on human action, Strindberg's characters are multiple: 'conglomerates of past and present stages of culture, bits out of books and newspapers, scraps of humanity, torn shreds of once fine clothing now turned to rags, exactly as the human soul is patched together' (ibid: 138). Strindberg lists at least thirteen different reasons to explain Julie's action, from the 'festive atmosphere of Midsummer Night' to the fact that she is menstruating during the action of the play (ibid: 137). This has an effect on the tumbling dialogue that frequently darts from thought to thought, giving a potent sense of a mind's wandering journey through a subject. The multiplicity of motives creates rich ambiguities in the play that perhaps undermine Strindberg's misogynistic intentions. Similarly, the psychological density of the play raises questions it cannot fully answer: what did happen in Jean's bedroom? Is Julie's fate truly inevitable? So many different thoughts crowd together in the play to explain the action that it becomes difficult to limit it to a woman's battle against her femininity.

In addition, the battle of the sexes threads through the play's battles between Naturalism and theatricality. Strindberg seems to conceive Naturalism as a 'masculine' form of theatre: in his preface, he explicitly addresses his thoughts on Naturalism only to men, since he believes women 'would rather be beautiful than truthful' (1.7: 143). Jean's talent for deception and seduction is repeatedly described in terms of theatre, and the preface to the play sees non-Naturalistic conventions as false. But the play is itself not always rigorously Naturalistic: several images – Julie and Jean's dreams of falling and climbing, the peasants' dance and the rather Ibsenite image of the greenfinch (or 'siskin') being beheaded – all take on meanings in the play beyond the strictly material and logical. The sexual politics of the play are worked out at the level of theatrical form as well as content.

Thérèse Raquin (1.1) and the contradictions of Naturalism

'Zola's *Thérèse Raquin*', wrote August Strindberg, 'will be accounted the first milestone of naturalist drama, thus ascribing the origin of the latter to 1873' (Strindberg 1996: 76). That was the year Zola's adaptation of his own novel opened at the Théâtre de la Renaissance. The play closed after seventeen performances which, for the time, was moderately successful, and was performed by a number of the Naturalist theatres across Europe. It is Zola's only play to be regularly revived and adapted.

The play, in some respects, programmatically represents Zola's naturalistic ideas. In the first few minutes we are given various aspects of *race*, *milieu* and *moment*, from Camille's sickly physiology to the Raquin family background, from the geography of their youth to the urban environment of Paris. Unlike the book, which is able to roam freely between different locations, the entire play is set in one room. This has the benefit of creating an even more cramped setting to suggest the pressing in of the bourgeois *milieu* on the lives of the characters. Animal imagery supports the Naturalistic representation of these characters as natural beings. The first act establishes, like an equation, a series of conditions – (a) Camille is weak, (b) Laurent is strong, (c) Thérèse is strong also, (d) They are having an affair, (e) Laurent may soon not be able to take time off work to see Thérèse, (f) Camille has agreed to go boating – such as to make the outcome seem like an inevitable consequence.

Within the play, Zola places a few images to steer the audience to an appreciation of his Naturalist intentions. Laurent is an artist and his work is admired as being lifelike – even to the point where it does not flatter its subject. Meanwhile much fun is had with the character of Michaud, who enjoys gruesome stories of what we would now call 'true crime': he horrifies Thérèse with his tales of the murderers who walk the streets unidentified, their victims undiscovered. His salacious voyeurism is presumably to be distinguished from the clinical objectivity of the Naturalist.

Later in the play, however, Laurent fails to recognize the portrait he's painted, believing it is actually Camille come back to accuse him, a moment that might stand as a metaphor for the way works of art can elude the grasp of their makers. Indeed, *Thérèse Raquin* does not consistently fulfil Zola's dream of a Naturalist theatre: the play is heavily indebted to the conventions of the well-made play and of the melodramatic stage. Zola artfully misdirects the audience, inviting us to think Thérèse dislikes Laurent before pulling off a major reversal in the fifth scene of Act 1. While this is ingenious, it works more as a technical plot twist than a Naturalist exposition of a human case study. The same is true of some of the play's elegant literary touches, such as the symmetry of Thérèse adding extra sugar to the syllabub in Act 1, and adding too much salt to the soup in Act 4. These seem out of place in a 'slice of life'. The play tips into melodrama from the end of Act 3 when Mme Raquin overhears Laurent's confession: 'She suddenly has an attack of spasms, staggers as far as the bed, tries to balance, but seizing onto one of the white bed curtains, leans against the wall a moment, panting and fearful' (1.1: 44). Such moments seem uncritically copied from the conventions of the mid-century Paris Boulevard theatre. When Thérèse asks, 'What is the good of acting out this comedy of the past?' (1.1: 43), she might have been referring to the play itself.

In a very early attempt to explain Naturalism in a letter to his friend, the poet and critic Antony Valabrègue, Zola suggested that art was like a window onto the world, and the type of art was the type of glass, or 'screen', in that window. Unlike the 'classical' or 'romantic' screen, what characterizes the 'realist'[4] screen is that it is

> a simple pane of glass, very thin and clear, which aims to be so perfectly transparent that images pass straight through it and are therefore reproduced in all their reality. Thus a precise, accurate, and simple reproduction that does not alter line or colour. The realist screen denies its own existence … However clear, thin, and transparent it may be, it has its own tint and a certain thickness; it colours objects, it refracts everything as something else. Nonetheless, I gladly consider the images it offers the most real; it achieves a high degree of exact reproduction.
>
> (Becker 2002: 238)

Zola claims that the realist screen is entirely transparent; then he accepts that such a transparency is impossible; and then he seems to put that consideration to one side. The image of the transparent screen suggests that the stage need only represent the *appearance* of the world. However, Naturalist theatre represents more of an experimental project than this suggests. It broke theatrical form, it introduced new subject matter, it expressed new attitudes towards the world and expressed those attitudes in new ways. As such, it cannot but have drawn attention to itself as theatre, in the choices it made, and in the artistic and political decisions underlying the performances. In such circumstances, it will have been difficult, perhaps impossible, to look transparently through the theatrical screen to the world it is depicting. All of these contradictions are part of what continues to fascinate theatre makers and audiences about Naturalism. It perhaps explains why, well over a century later, it is not uncommon to find writers, actors, directors and theatre companies wishing to challenge Naturalism, to seek out alternative forms. It is also why those same people return to those early Naturalist plays to subvert them and explore and exploit their contradictions.

The Symbolist movement

Barely three years after the Théâtre Libre had opened its doors, Naturalism was challenged by a rival avant-garde theatre movement. Symbolist theatre – declared Paul Fort, director of Théâtre d'Art – would not concern itself, like Naturalism, with the 'trivial and accidental details of actuality' (qtd in Whitton 1987: 28). In the manifesto that announced the Symbolist movement, Jean Moréas neatly belittled Naturalism as 'a legitimate but ill-advised protest against the blandishments of a few then-fashionable novelists' (1886: 2). Symbolism had a much grander aim: nothing less than to represent the mystical harmony of the universe.

Just as Naturalist theatre was rehearsed in the novel, Symbolist theatre was prefigured in poetry. Charles Baudelaire's *Les Fleurs du Mal* (The Flowers of Evil) (1857) and Arthur Rimbaud's 'Le Bateau Ivre' (The Drunken Boat) (1871), and *Une Saison en Enfer* (A Season in Hell) (1873) were particular inspirations in their elusive attempts to capture mysterious patterns beyond what was known. Baudelaire's poem 'Correspondances' (1857) is an important example as it presents an experience of the world thick with mysterious symbols between which there are curious harmonies, where a perfume can resemble a child's body, the sound of an oboe or a verdant meadow.

The Symbolists were interested in everything the Naturalists usually tried to repress in their work: ambiguity, metaphor, mysticism. The 'symbols' of Symbolism were those images that seemed to have more significance than is explained by their mere existence. As the critic John Cruickshank put it, writing of the great poet and theorist of Symbolism Stéphane Mallarmé, his poems 'aspire towards mystical presences hinted at by such things as blue sky, open windows, the sound of bells, a woman's hair, ships leaving port' (Cruickshank 1969: 142). In the specifi-cally literary figures of symbol, metaphor, allegory, echo, parallel, repetition and rhyme, usually non-literal connections are drawn between two quite different experiences or objects. This affinity is a third quality that gives us a glimpse, so the Symbolists felt, of a broader cosmic harmony far deeper and more fundamental than the banal and accidental happenstance of material life.

Where the Naturalists pronounced the end of the supernatural and the ubiquity of material reality, the Symbolists denounced material reality as an illusion and sought experiences of the supernatural. Put another way, Naturalism was materialist and Symbolism was idealist. Where the Naturalists saw clarity and transparency as virtues, the Symbolists preferred to be ambiguous, cryptic, difficult. Where the Naturalists sought a wide public for their work, the Symbolists were avowedly elitist, preferring to speak to a small coterie of close initiates. Where the Naturalists embraced the modern world and believed themselves to be its direct expression, the Symbolists turned away from it and sought the ancient and the timeless. Where the preferred environment of the Naturalists was a scientific laboratory, the Symbolists would probably have been more at home in a cathedral.

Like the Naturalists, the Symbolists faced enormous difficulties in realizing their ideas on the stage but if anything their problem was more fundamental. One of their most devoted admirers, Camille Mauclair, admitted that 'if ever a literary movement has been incapable by its very essence of adapting itself to the stage, it was Symbolism' (qtd in Whitton 1987: 32). The problem was the materiality of the stage itself; how was it possible to attain a glimpse of the 'Eternal' on a solid stage made of wood, with painted backdrops, fleshly actors? Many Symbolists considered great plays to be better read than performed; Maurice Maeterlinck, perhaps Symbolism's most accomplished playwright, believed that 'most of the great poems of humanity are not fit for the stage. Lear, Hamlet, Othello, Macbeth, Anthony and Cleopatra cannot be represented, and it is dangerous to see them on the stage. Something of Hamlet died for us the day we saw him die onstage' (qtd in Dorra 1995: 145). Mallarmé bemoaned 'the solid set and the real actor' of the conventional theatre (1885: 195). In 1902, the Russian Symbolist writer Bryusov wrote in reference to the avalanche at the end of Ibsen's *When We Dead Awaken* (1.4) performed by the Moscow Art Theatre, 'When an avalanche of cotton batting comes crashing down on stage, the spectators ask each other: how did they do that? If Rubek and Irene simply went backstage, the spectator would more readily believe in their destruction' (Schumacher 1996: 220). The Symbolists were entranced by the mystical power of words and saw the clumsy materialism of the stage as a barrier to the 'Infinite'.

An early clue to a possible Symbolist staging practice came from the work of the composer Richard Wagner, in particular his vision of the *Gesamtkunstwerk* (total work of art). There was a view, associated with Walter Pater but very widespread, that all art aspired towards the condition of music. Music's communicative form being abstract and (usually) non-literal suggested itself as a direct example of art that was not mimetic of anything in the world and which might, therefore, represent some higher reality than mere appearance. The example of music encouraged writers to think more abstractly about words not just as bearers of meaning but also as bearers of rhythms, textures, their own kind of music. And if music and poetry could represent complementary arts that led towards the higher Idea, perhaps other art forms could too. Ultimately, the most perfect expression of the Idea might be a 'total work of art' that combined all others in a single experience. And what art form seems to combine all others? 'There is only one medium,' wrote Richard Wagner, 'in which all these united artforms can transform their intentions into glorious reality, and that is the drama' (qtd in Schumacher 1996: 162).

Symbolist staging

Paul Fort was only 18 years old and still a student when he formed the Théâtre d'Art as an avowedly Symbolist theatre. It was a short-lived enterprise, existing for less than sixteen months and producing only eight productions. Their second performance in January 1891 was given over to a raw but potent staging of Shelley's *The Cenci*, uncut and lasting until 2.00 a.m. However, it was unusual for Théâtre d'Art to give an evening over to one play; more often, bills would contain several items – plays, staged poems and readings. Also, it was not uncommon for evenings to be interrupted by arguments and fights in the auditorium, ending late in the night.

The Théâtre d'Art produced some of the most radically experimental theatre of the nineteenth century, setting a template for later experiments in Expressionism, Dada and Surrealism (see Part 2). In particular, there was a consistent attempt to find a way of bypassing the materiality of the theatre and restore the poetic in language to the stage. In March 1891 the Théâtre d'Art staged Pierre Quillard's *The Girl with the Severed Hands*. The play is a medieval verse fantasy about a girl mutilated by her abusive father, who escapes to a mystical land where her hands are restored and a choir of angels bid her to accept the love of a Poet-King. At the Théâtre d'Art, a thin gauze separated the audience from the stage; upstage was a gold backcloth adorned with paintings of angels kneeling in prayer. In front of the gauze to the left stood a narrator, Susan Gay, wearing a long blue robe and standing at a lectern. She intoned the stage directions while the poetic dialogue was recited without expression by the actors behind the gauze.

Several features of this staging are worth pointing out. The lack of movement and of any distracting 'realistic' detail allows the audience to concentrate on the words. As Pierre Quillard wrote, in a newspaper article responding to criticisms of that evening, '*The word creates the set and everything else as well*' (1.11: 161). The gold backcloth was a '*pure ornamental fiction which completes the illusion with colour and lines analogous to the drama*' (ibid: 162); in other words, rather than creating a realistic setting for the action, the backcloth is a symbolic analogy for the play, corresponding to an aspect of its atmosphere or ideas. The gauze served two purposes: first, it distanced the actors, made them harder to see, simplified their physical outline, making them seem less individual. Second, it served as a kind of analogy for the relation of the Symbolist to everyday life: by looking through the gauze's surface to discern its mystical depths, the audience was rehearsing their penetration of the surface of ordinary life to the deeper realities beyond. The narrator at the front of the gauze is like the Symbolist, a guide leading us through to the Ideal. The theatre, as Quillard puts it, is '*a chance to dream*' (ibid).

The lack of intonation in the verse-speaking was one attempt to solve the problem of the actor's presence. Camille Mauclair insisted that actors 'have no value except as incarnations of the Idea they symbolise' (qtd in Carlson 1993: 290). Aurélien Lugné-Poë, introducing his own Symbolist company, the Théâtre de l'Oeuvre, declared: 'the greatest virtue of the actor will be to efface himself' (qtd in Braun 1982: 46). There was considerable interest in finding alternatives to human performers; many theatre makers associated with Symbolism, including Alfred Jarry, Edward Gordon Craig, Paul Margueritte and Fyodor Sologub, were interested in using puppets, Margueritte admiring the way they seem to 'possess a quaint and mysterious life' (qtd in Henderson 1971: 134). Maeterlinck wrote some of his plays for puppets, and mused, 'one should perhaps eliminate the living being from the stage', considering a bewildering range of alternatives, from masks, sculptures, wax figures, shadows, reflections to even 'a projection of symbolic forms, or a being who would appear to be alive without being alive? I do not know; but the absence of man seems essential to me' (qtd in Dorra 1995: 145–6). In 1888, the Petit Théâtre de la Galerie Vivienne and Théâtre du Chat Noir opened puppet and shadow-puppet theatres, respectively.

If puppets were not feasible the next best thing was to turn human beings into puppets. This was initially achieved by minimizing the distinctive and individual human qualities of the actor by stripping the voice of any kind of conversational intonation, and the body of its ordinary movements and gestures. This was not always very effective; as one contemporary reviewer noted, the actors 'assume a perpetually ecstatic and visionary air. As if hallucinating, they stare before them, gazing afar, very far, vaguely, very vaguely. Their voices are cavernous, their diction chopped. They endeavour to give the impression that they are deranged. This is in order to awaken us to a sense of the Beyond' (qtd in Whitton 1987: 34). Correspondingly, Strindberg, in his Symbolist phase, described ideal acting as being somewhat like sleepwalking (1967: 23).

Maurice Maeterlinck and Symbolist playwriting

Where the Naturalists favoured precise, contemporary locations, the Symbolists preferred mystical, other-worldly locations, not anchored in time or space. Maeterlinck's *The Blind* (1891), for example, is set in 'an ancient forest in the North, with an aura of timelessness, beneath a sky deep in stars'. Maeterlinck, who moved to Paris in 1886, was quickly welcomed by the Symbolists. Strindberg initially dismissed his work – but after a stormy period in his life when he began to abandon Naturalism in favour of new, more fragmented and personal theatre forms, he revised his opinion: 'The theatre I seek is Maeterlinck's and not that of the past' (qtd in Mayer 1985), later recalling that on this rereading 'he struck me like a new country and a new age' (521).

Maeterlinck's plays are distinguished by stillness and inactivity, though this is not to say that they are not dramatic. In his famous essay 'Tragedy in Everyday Life' (1.10), Maeterlinck suggests that 'an old man sitting in his armchair, just waiting beneath his lamp ... lives, in reality, a profound, more human and more universal life than the lover who strangles his mistress, the captain who carries off the battle, or "the husband who avenges his honour"' (1.10: 158). Both poles of Symbolism saw the complex twisting narratives of Naturalism to be burdened with the bustle of everyday life and favoured stillness, contemplation and image. Maeterlinck's particular achievement was to recognize that this stillness and silence – and what might be going on within it – were worth dramatic attention, and in his best plays he strips away the grand rhetoric, the knights and castles, keeping the language very simple and the characters ordinary. The result is a series of one-act plays that find mystery and horror within everyday experience. In *Intruder* (1891), a family sit waiting for a nurse to attend their mother who has just given birth. The daughters somehow sense a figure, unseen by anyone else, enter the garden, then the house, climb the stairs and pass into the mother's antechamber, at which point the Nurse appears, announcing her death. In *The Blind* (1891), six blind men and six blind women are lost in a forest, because, unbeknown to them, their guide has died and his body sits lifeless among them.

In *Interior* (1894, 1.5), we are looking at the rear of a house. Through the windows, a family is sitting quietly together of an evening, unaware that one of the daughters has drowned. There is a telling homology between the stage picture in this play and the staging innovations of the Théâtre d'Art. The two men function like the narrator in Pierre Quillard's play, standing before the house, which has affinities with the gauze screen of that production. But the relations of the image are reversed; what we look at through the gauze is precisely a Naturalist setting, a domestic interior. Outside the house, we know the horrible truth about the death, news of which is imminently going to strike them and destroy their calm. Visually it is reframing a Naturalist play within a set of Symbolist concerns, reminding us that there is more to life than our particular existence. In the theatre there is a further visual rhyme: the windows of the house form a kind of proscenium arch; because it is dark outside and light indoors, the family cannot see the strangers in their garden. This reproduces the relationship we have, as a theatre audience, with the two strangers; we sit in the dark, watching them while they are unaware of our presence. In turn, this prompts the question, is someone watching *us*, aware of some cosmic injustice about to befall us? Symbolism gloried in drawing attention to the processes of theatre itself, creating theatre about theatre – or 'metatheatre' – which used the artifice and artistry of the theatre to talk about the world, contrasting with the Naturalists who wanted as far as possible for that artistry to be transparent.

Ibsen and Chekhov: between Symbolism and Naturalism

As we have seen, the Symbolists and Naturalists were opposed in many things. However, they also had much in common and their aggressively contrary viewpoints should not hide their shared roots in late nineteenth-century philosophy, science and ideas. Both Naturalism and Symbolism began as writers' theatres but their respective theatrical visions demanded the creation of the director to organize the visual field. They each demanded the effacement of the actor and endeavoured to contain some aspect of theatricality, whether that be its fictionalizing, metaphorical productivity or its dully material, physical existence. Symbolism's gauze is, in some ways, a version of the Naturalist 'fourth wall', both of them allowing access to some secret truth of the world; both conceived human beings as determined by forces outside of their control and of which they are usually unaware, whether they be natural laws or cosmic correspondences. Mallarmé, for example, declared that the poet's 'role is to understand and apply the universal laws of Analogy', which sounds Naturalistic, until the final word (qtd in Cruickshank 1969: 138). Naturalism being deterministic and Symbolism being fatalistic, they shared a belief that the future was fixed, even if we cannot know how.

Naturalism and Symbolism were, in many ways, contemporaries, in dialogue with each other, sharing theatre spaces, audiences and writers. Many of the major playwrights of the era were championed by both the Symbolists and the Naturalists. Some, like Strindberg and Hauptmann, moved very decisively from one to the other. Others, like Ibsen and Chekhov, maintained an ambiguous relationship with both. Henrik Ibsen is now so frequently considered to be a stern Naturalist that it can be surprising to read in a Symbolist journal of the time someone declaring, 'don't let [the Naturalists] get their hands on Ibsen' (qtd in Henderson 1971: 113). Ibsen had two successful productions at the Théâtre Libre but a commercial production of *Hedda Gabler* in 1891 was a failure. It fell to the Symbolists, and especially Lugné-Poë at the Théâtre de l'Oeuvre, to premiere most of his plays in Paris, including *Rosmersholm*, *An Enemy of the People* (1893), *The Master Builder* (1894), *Little Eyolf*, *Brand* (1895), *The Pillars of Society*, *Peer Gynt* (1896), *Love's Comedy* and *John Gabriel Borkman* (1897).

Why were the Symbolists so enamoured of Ibsen? Despite Ibsen's reputation as a Naturalist, his work shows signs of the sociological imagination only in four plays: *The Pillars of Society*, *A Doll's House*, *Ghosts* and *An Enemy of the People*. In each of these plays, a vision of society is plainly set out and truth is held out as an absolute virtue that must be defended regardless of the consequences. Over time, Ibsen's work increasingly exploited metaphor and symbolism. Although his characters and settings remained contemporary, the psychological worlds they inhabited became abstracted and elevated – literally so; *The Master Builder*, *John Gabriel Borkman* and *When We Dead Awaken* (1.4) all feature various kinds of journeys upwards.

By the time we reach his last play, *When We Dead Awaken*, Ibsen's stagecraft has begun to closely resemble some aspects of Symbolist theatre. The play is structured around two encounters in the first act that lead to two journeys up a mountain. Despite the grand sweep of the play's movement, it is a play of stillness and memory. Maia begins the play by expressing the idea that beneath the bustle of activity she seems to detect silence and death, which, as with the images of dead women walking through the gardens at night, sounds like something that might be expressed in a Maeterlinck play. The movement of the play lifts the action away from the sociality of the town to the sublime isolation of the mountain, an environment – like the medieval forests of the Symbolists – good for growing metaphors.

Rubek is an artist and in what we hear of his history we see a battle between Naturalism and Symbolism. The busts he sculpts of people secretly show them, he suggests, as animals underneath, which, taken together with the play's frequent animal images, points towards a certain Naturalistic view of the world. But Rubek's greatest work, *The Resurrection Day*, embodied quite different ideas. He wanted to 'embody the pure woman as I saw her awakening on the Resurrection Day … filled with a sacred joy at finding herself unchanged' (1.4: 105). (Some Symbolists, too, demanded that the stage treat woman as 'the eternal Object' [Henderson 1971: 113].) Rubek is confronted with Irene, the model who sat for him, and protests – like Zola – that as an artist he had to shut off any erotic feelings towards his subject. However, like Laurent in *Thérèse Raquin*, the artwork seemed to change beyond his control. He began to add other images and moved the Woman away from the centre, Meiningen-like, to create an overall image; in doing so he lost the sense of transcendence and the image fell back down to earth. The working title of *When We Dead Awaken* was *The Resurrection Day* and it is not hard to see the play as working through Ibsen's own disengagement from realism. *When We Dead Awaken* was first published in mid-December 1899 and first performed in Stuttgart on 26 January 1900, and as such marks a transition between the nineteenth- and twentieth-century theatre.

A year later, Chekhov's *Three Sisters* (1.3) premiered at the Moscow Art Theatre. By all accounts, the final curtain came down in silence, the audience too moved even to applaud.

Chekhov is an exquisite realist: his characters have the complexity Strindberg was aiming for in *Miss Julie* and his plotting escapes the conventions of the well-made play in a way that even Ibsen never managed. Chekhov once claimed that 'a writer must be as objective as a chemist; he must renounce subjectivity in life and know that dunghills play an important part in the landscape and evil passions are as much part of life as good ones' (qtd in Rayfield 1997: 149). This highly Zolaesque sentiment is reflected in his plays' unheroic characters. Key to understanding Chekhov is that we may be moved by the characters' plight, but we are not obliged to *like* any of them. The Prozorov sisters are self-obsessed, spoiled and consumed with their social superiority; and Colonel Vershinin is a philosophizing bore who embarks on an affair with Masha, leaving his suicidal wife at home. Chebutykin is a drunken surgeon who self-pityingly treats a botched operation as his own tragedy rather than the patient's.

Chekhov was a meticulous observer of human behaviour but, like Maeterlinck, found drama in silence and stillness and points a way towards the later twentieth-century dramaturgy of Samuel Beckett and Harold Pinter. Where Chekhov seems to be moving in a Symbolist direction in *Three Sisters* is in his deployment of stillness and subtext. The play has a vigorous plot that keeps one's interest and moves the action and characters forward, but this is disguised in various ways – first, several important actions take place offstage (like the departure of the soldiers) or only half visibly (like Irina's birthday party); second, when decisive actions do take place the audience's attention is elsewhere (when Soliony and Toozenbach fight their duel, it is offstage and Masha is now crying about being parted from Vershinin); third, each act begins with the promise of great activity and ends in stasis. Act 3, for example, begins with a bustle of activity, the sisters joining the relief effort to support those made homeless by the fire; by the end of the play they have forgotten about the fire and are left 'huddled together' on the stage (1.3: 96). As a result, the play, without being lethargic or boring, stages lethargy and boredom. It is a play in which silence speaks.

Conclusion

Modern theatre begins on the Théâtre Libre's tiny stage in Montmartre, Paris, in March 1887. From there comes an almost inexhaustible procession of experimental companies, most of them both promoting and challenging Naturalism, adopting and rejecting many of its characteristics. Integrally linked to Naturalism, Symbolism pushed the stage to unprecedented levels of formal innovation, challenging the theatre's relation with its audience and the world. As John Henderson suggests, both Naturalism and Symbolism were present at the birth of the avant-garde: Naturalism worked to strip the theatre of its decorative self-indulgence; Symbolism restored poetry to the stage and made the theatre into what Maurice Maeterlinck called 'the temple of dreams' (qtd in Dorra 1995: 144). The plays in this part show the journey from one genre to another and, read alongside and against each other, give an insight into the interrelation between two movements situated at the start of the modernist period in theatre.

Notes

1. All translations from original sources, unless otherwise indicated, are by the author.
2. In fact, most of the Naturalist writers seemed rather to dislike each other. Strindberg, while sometimes admitting to admiration of his Scandinavian colleague, more often thought of Ibsen as 'my enemy' (Strindberg 1992: 522), while Ibsen agreed, famously hanging a portrait of Strindberg ('my mortal enemy') above his desk claiming that

he liked to see those 'demonic eyes' staring down at him while he worked (Meyer 1974: 770). Ibsen also thought Tolstoy mad (823), while Tolstoy, in *What is Art?* (1897), mocked Ibsen and Zola, and pronounced Chekhov's *The Seagull* 'utterly worthless' (624). Chekhov in his turn partly wrote *The Seagull* in mockery of Ibsen's *The Wild Duck* and smirked his way through a performance of *When We Dead Awaken* (Rayfield 1997: 519). This should be borne in mind as a corrective to the impression that theatrical Naturalism was any kind of disciplined international dramatic movement.

3. Strindberg's disdain for Ibsen makes its way into the preface to *Miss Julie*; in its reference to 'pretentious talk of the joy of life', he is making a dig at Ibsen's *Ghosts* (Ibsen 1994: 145).

4. This is two years before he adopted the word 'Naturalism' to describe the new movement.

Bibliography

Antoine, A. (1964) *Memories of the Théâtre Libre*, Miami: University of Miami Press.

Becker, C. (2002) *Zola: Le Saut dans les Étoiles*, Paris: Presses de la Sorbonne Nouvelle.

Benjamin, W. (1999) *The Arcades Project*, Cambridge, MA: Harvard University Press.

Braun, E. (1982) *The Director and the Stage: From Naturalism to Grotowski*, London: Methuen.

Carlson, M. (1993) *Theories of the Theatre: A Historical and Critical Survey from the Greeks to the Present*, Ithaca and London: Cornell University Press.

Chothia, J. (1991) *André Antoine*, Cambridge: Cambridge University Press.

Comte, A. (1983) *Auguste Comte and Positivism: The Essential Writings*, Chicago and London: University of Chicago Press.

Cruickshank, J. (1969) *French Literature and its Background 5: The Late Nineteenth Century*, Oxford: Oxford University Press.

Deak, F. (1993) *Symbolist Theater: The Formation of an Avant-Garde*, Baltimore and London: Johns Hopkins University Press.

Dorra, H. (1995) *Symbolist Art Theories: A Critical Anthology*, Berkeley and Los Angeles: University of California Press.

Ferragus (1868) 'Lettres de Ferragus III: La Littérature Putride', *Le Figaro*, 23 January: 1.

Greer, G. (1986) *The Madwoman's Underclothes: Essays and Occasional Writings 1968–85*, London: Picador.

Henderson, J. A. (1971) *The First Avant-Garde 1887–1894: Sources of the Modern French Theatre*, London: Harrap.

Ibsen, H. (1980) *Plays: Two*, London: Methuen.

Ibsen, H. (1994) *Four Major Plays*, Oxford: Oxford University Press.

Jullien, J. (1892) *Le Théâtre Vivant*, Paris: Charpentier & Fasquelle.

Maeterlinck, M. (1979) *Théâtre*, Geneva: Slatkine Reprints.

Mallarmé, S. (1885) 'Richard Wagner: Rêverie d'un Poète Français', *La Revue Wagnérienne*, 8 August: 195.

Meyer, M. (1974) *Ibsen*, Harmondsworth: Penguin.

Meyer, M. (1985) *Strindberg: A Biography*, London: Secker and Warburg.

Moréas, J. (1886) 'Le Symbolisme', *Le Figaro*, Supplément Littéraire, 18 September: 2–3.

Quillard, P. (1976) *The Girl with Cut-Off Hands*, The Drama Review, 20(3), 123–8.

Rayfield, D. (1997) *Anton Chekhov: A Life*, London: HarperCollins.

Renan, E. (1890) *L'Avenir de la Science: Pensées de 1848*, Paris: Calmann Lévy.

Schumacher, C. (ed.) (1996) *Naturalism and Symbolism in European Theatre*, Theatre in Europe: A Documentary History, Cambridge: Cambridge University Press.

Strindberg, A. (1967) *Open Letters to the Intimate Theater*, Seattle and London: University of Washington Press.

Strindberg, A. (1992) *Letters*, vol. II: 1892–1912, Chicago: University of Chicago Press.

Strindberg, A. (1996) *Selected Essays*, Oxford: Oxford University Press.

Taine, H. (1863) *Histoire de la Littérature Anglaise*: vol. 1, Paris: Hachette.

Whitton, D. (1987) *Stage Directors in Modern France*, Manchester: Manchester University Press.

Zola, É. (1992) *Thérèse Raquin*, Oxford: Oxford University Press.

Further reading

Bentley, E. (ed.) (1976) *The Theory of the Modern Stage: An Introduction to Modern Theatre and Drama*, Harmondsworth: Penguin.

Bradbury, M. and J. McFarlane (eds) (1976) *Modernism 1890–1930*, Pelican Guides to European Literature, Harmondsworth: Penguin.

Cardullo, B. and R. Knopf (eds) (2001) *Theater of the Avant-Garde: A Critical Anthology*, New Haven and London: Yale University Press.

Chadwick, C. (1971) *Symbolism*, London: Methuen.

Deak, F. (1976) 'Symbolist Staging at the Théâtre d'Art', *The Drama Review*, 20(3) (T71), 117–22.

Emeljanow, V. (ed.) (1981) *Chekhov: The Critical Heritage*, London: Routledge.

Garner Jr, S. B. (2000) 'Physiologies of the Modern: Zola, Experimental Medicine, and the Naturalist Stage', *Modern Drama*, 43(4), 67–79.

Gerould, D. (1985) *Doubles, Demons, and Dreamers: An International Collection of Symbolist Drama*, New York: PAJ.

Gottlieb, V. (ed.) (2005) *Anton Chekhov at the Moscow Art Theatre: Archive Illustrations of the Original Productions*, Abingdon: Routledge.

Harrison, C., P. Wood and with J. Gaiger (eds) (1998) *Art in Theory 1815–1900: An Anthology of Changing Ideas*, Oxford: Blackwell.

McFarlane, J. (ed.) (1994) *The Cambridge Companion to Ibsen*, Cambridge Companions to Literature, Cambridge: Cambridge University Press.

Moi, T. (2006) *Henrik Ibsen and the Birth of Modernism*, Oxford: Oxford University Press.

Shattuck, R. (1969) *The Banquet Years: The Origins of the Avant-Garde in France from 1885 to World War I*, London: Jonathan Cape.

Stanislavski, K. (2008) *An Actor's Work: A Student's Diary*, Abingdon: Routledge.

Stanislavski, K. (2008) *My Life in Art*, Abingdon: Routledge.

Szondi, P. (1987) *Theory of the Modern Drama*, Cambridge and Oxford: Polity and Blackwell.

West, T. G. (1980) *Symbolism: An Anthology*, London: Methuen.

Worth, K. (1985) *Maeterlinck's Plays in Performance*, Cambridge: Chadwyck-Healey.

Zola, É. (1964) *The Experimental Novel and Other Essays*, New York: Haskell House.

1.1 THÉRÈSE RAQUIN (1873)

ÉMILE ZOLA

Translated by Pip Broughton

Émile Zola (1840–1902) was a French novelist and public intellectual who coined the term Naturalism in 1866 to refer to his new scientific model of fiction writing. Over the next fifteen years, he mounted a ceaseless press campaign for Naturalism in the novel and the theatre and gathered these articles in a series of books: The Experimental Novel *(1880),* Naturalist Novelists *(1881),* Naturalism in the Theatre *(1881) and* Our Dramatic Authors *(1881). Critical of the worn-out conventions of Romanticism and the artificiality of the well-made play, his ideas were widely admired by Antoine, Strindberg and Chekhov, and prepared the way for the emergence of stage Naturalism in the 1880s.* Thérèse Raquin *was originally published in serial form for the journal* L'Artiste, *then published as a novel in 1867. Zola adapted the novel for the stage in 1873. The play has often been revived – sometimes readapted from the original novel and often in radically non-Naturalist styles – and has also been made into three films, seven TV series, two operas and a Broadway musical. This translation was written by Pip Broughton for the Warehouse Theatre, Croydon, London, in 1984.*

———————————————

Characters

LAURENT
CAMILLE
THÉRÈSE RAQUIN
MADAME RAQUIN
GRIVET
MICHAUD
SUZANNE

The set

A large bedroom which also serves as dining room and parlour. The room is in the Pont-Neuf Passage. It is high, dark, in a state of decay, hung with faded grey wallpaper, furnished with threadbare poor furniture, littered with haberdashery cardboard boxes.

At the back: a door; to the right of the door, a wardrobe; to the left, a writing-desk. On the left: upstage, on a slant, a bed in an alcove with a window looking out onto a bare wall; midstage, a little door; downstage, a work-table. On the right: upstage, the top of the spiral staircase leading down to the shop; downstage, a fireplace; on the mantelpiece a columned clock and two bunches of artificial flowers under glass; photographs hang either side of the mirror. In the middle of the room: a round table with waxed tablecloth; two armchairs, one blue, the other green; other various chairs.

The set remains the same throughout the four acts.

Act 1

Eight o'clock one Thursday summer evening, after dinner. The table has not yet been cleared; the window is half open. There is a feeling of peace, of a sense of middle-class calm.

Scene 1
LAURENT, THÉRÈSE, MME RAQUIN, CAMILLE

CAMILLE is sitting in an armchair stage right, stiffly posing for his portrait, wearing his Sunday best. LAURENT is painting, standing at his easel in front of the window. Next to LAURENT sits THÉRÈSE, in a daydream, her chin in her hand. MME RAQUIN is finishing clearing the table.

CAMILLE: (*After a long pause.*) All right if I talk? Won't disturb you, will it?

LAURENT: Not in the least, so long as you don't move.

CAMILLE: I fall asleep after dinner if I don't talk … You're lucky, you're healthy. You can eat anything … I shouldn't have had that second helping of syllabub, it always makes me ill. My stomach is so delicate … You like syllabub, don't you?

LAURENT: Oh yes. It's delicious – so sweet.

CAMILLE: We know what you like here. Mother spoils you – she makes syllabub specially for you, even though she knows what it does to me … That's true, isn't it, Thérèse, that Mother spoils Laurent?

THÉRÈSE: (*Without raising her head.*) Yes.

MME RAQUIN: (*Carrying a pile of plates.*) Don't listen to them, Laurent. It was Camille who told me how much you love it, and Thérèse who wanted to put the extra sugar in it.

CAMILLE: Mother, you're such an egoist.

MME RAQUIN: Me, an egoist?!

CAMILLE: Yes, you … (*To LAURENT.*) Mother likes you because you're from Vernon, like her. Remember, when we were little, she used to give us money …

LAURENT: And you bought loads of apples.

CAMILLE: And you, you bought little penknives … What a stroke of luck it was bumping into each other here in Paris, I still can't believe it – after all that time! Oh, I was getting so bored, I was dying of boredom! Every evening, when I got home from the office, it was so miserable here … Can you still see properly?

LAURENT: Not really, but I want to get this finished.

CAMILLE: It's nearly eight o'clock. These Summer evenings are so long … I wanted to be painted in sunlight – that would have been more attractive. Instead of this dingy background, you could have done a landscape. But in the mornings I barely even have time to swallow my coffee before I have to set off for the office … I say, this can't be particularly good for the old digestive system, sitting still like this after a meal.

LAURENT: Don't worry, this is the last session.

MME RAQUIN comes back in and finishes clearing the table, then wipes it with a cloth.

CAMILLE: You would have got a better light in the mornings, though. We don't get the sun in here, but it shines onto the wall opposite; that lights the room … I really don't know why Mother got it into her head to rent this place. It's so damp. When it rains, it's like being in a cellar.

LAURENT: Bah! One place is as good as another for work purposes.

CAMILLE: I daresay you're right. They've got the haberdashery shop downstairs. It keeps them busy. I never go down there.

LAURENT: But the flat itself is comfortable though, isn't it?

CAMILLE: Not really! Apart from this room where we eat and sleep, we've only got the one room for Mother. You can't count the kitchen, which is a black hole no bigger than a cupboard. Nothing closes properly, so it's freezing cold. At night-time we get an abominable draught under that little door to the staircase. (*He indicates the little door, stage left.*)

MME RAQUIN: (*Who has finished her clearing up.*) My poor Camille, you're never satisfied. I did it all for the best. You're the one who wanted to come and work in Paris. I'd have been happy to open up another haberdashery shop in Vernon. But when you married your cousin Thérèse, I had to work again, in case you had children.

CAMILLE: Yes, well, I thought we'd be living in a busy street with lots of people passing. I could've sat at the window and watched the cars – that would've been fun … But here all I can see when I open the shutter is that big wall opposite and the glass roof of the passage below. The wall is black, the glass roof is all dirty from dust and cobwebs … I still prefer the windows at Vernon. You could watch the Seine from there, though that wasn't much fun either.

MME RAQUIN: I offered you the chance of going back there.

CAMILLE: Good God, no! Not now that I've found Laurent at the office … After all I'm out all day, I don't care if the street is damp, just so long as you're happy.

MME RAQUIN: Then don't tease me any more about the flat.

Bell from shop.

Thérèse, the shop.

THÉRÈSE seems not to have heard and stays still.

All right, I'll go. (*She goes down the spiral staircase.*)

Scene 2
LAURENT, THÉRÈSE, CAMILLE

CAMILLE: I don't like to contradict her, but the street is very unhealthy. I'm afraid of another collapsed lung. I'm not strong like you two … (*Silence.*) I say, can I have a rest? I can't feel my left arm any more.

LAURENT: Just a few more brush strokes and I'm finished.

CAMILLE: No good. I can't hold it any longer. I've got to walk about a bit. (*He gets up, paces, then goes over to THÉRÈSE.*) I've never been able to understand how my wife manages to stay perfectly still for hours at a time, without even moving a finger. It gets on my nerves, she's always miles away. Doesn't it bother you, Laurent, to feel her like that next to you? Come on, Thérèse, bustle up. Having fun are you?

THÉRÈSE: (*Without moving.*) Yes.

CAMILLE: I hope you're having a good time. Only animals amuse themselves like that ... When her father, Captain Degans, left her with Mother, those huge black eyes of hers used to frighten me ... And the Captain! – now *he* was a terrifying man. He died in Africa; never set foot in Vernon again ... That's right, isn't it, Thérèse? (*No reply.*) She'll talk herself to death! (*He kisses her.*) You're a good girl, though. We haven't quarrelled once since Mother married us ... You're not cross with me, are you?

THÉRÈSE: No.

LAURENT: (*Slapping* CAMILLE *on the shoulder.*) Come on, Camille, only ten minutes more.

CAMILLE sits.

Turn your head to the left ... That's it, now don't move!

CAMILLE: (*After a silence.*) Any news of your father?

LAURENT: No, the old man's forgotten me. Anyway I never write to him.

CAMILLE: Strange, though – between father and son. I couldn't do it.

LAURENT: Nah! My father always had his own ideas. He wanted me to be a lawyer, so I could handle his endless lawsuits with his neighbours. When he found out that I was blowing his money on visiting painters' workshops instead of law lessons, he stopped my allowance ... Who wants to be a lawyer!

CAMILLE: It's a good job. You've got to be brainy and the money's not bad.

LAURENT: I bumped into an old college friend of mine who paints. So I started to study painting, too.

CAMILLE: You should have kept it up. You might have won awards by now.

LAURENT: I couldn't. I was dying of hunger. So I chucked in the painting, and looked for a proper job.

CAMILLE: But you still know how to draw.

LAURENT: I'm not very good ... What I liked about painting was that it was fun and not too tiring ... God, how I missed that bloody studio when I started working at the office! I had this couch, where I slept in the afternoons. That couch could tell a story or two – what a life!

CAMILLE: You mean, you had affairs with the models?

LAURENT: Of course. There was one superb blonde ...

THÉRÈSE rises slowly and goes down to the shop.

Oh look! We've chased away your wife.

CAMILLE: You don't imagine she was listening, do you! She's not very clever. But she's a perfect nurse when I'm ill. Mother has taught her how to make the infusions.

LAURENT: I don't think she likes me very much.

CAMILLE: Oh you know, women! Haven't you finished yet?

LAURENT: Yes, you can get up now.

CAMILLE: (*Getting up and coming to look at the portrait.*) Finished? Have you really finished?

LAURENT: Just the frame to go on now.

CAMILLE: It's a huge success, isn't it. (*He leans over the spiral staircase.*) Mother! Thérèse! Come and look, Laurent's finished!

Scene 3

LAURENT, CAMILLE, MME RAQUIN, THÉRÈSE

MME RAQUIN: What? Finished already?

CAMILLE: (*Holding the portrait in front of himself.*) Yes ... Come and look.

MME RAQUIN: (*Looking at the portrait.*) Oh! ... Look at that! Particularly the mouth, the mouth is very striking ... Don't you think so, Thérèse?

THÉRÈSE: (*Without approaching.*) Yes.

She goes to the window where she day-dreams, her forehead against the glass.

CAMILLE: And the dress-suit, my wedding suit. I've only ever worn it four times! ... And the collar looks like real material!

MME RAQUIN: And the arm of the chair!

CAMILLE: Amazing! Real wood! ... My armchair, we bought it at Vernon; no-one but me may sit in it. Mother's is blue. (*Indicating other chair.*)

MME RAQUIN: (*To* LAURENT *who has put away the easel and paints.*) Why have you put a dark patch under the left eye?

LAURENT: That's the shadow.

CAMILLE: (*Putting the portrait on the easel, between the alcove and the window.*) It might have been more attractive without the shadow ... but never mind, I think I look very distinguished, as if I were out visiting.

MME RAQUIN: My dear Laurent, how can we thank you? Are you sure you won't let Camille pay for the materials?

LAURENT: He's the one to thank for having sat for me!

CAMILLE: No, no, that won't do. I'll go and buy a bottle of something. Damn it, we'll drink to your work of art!

LAURENT: Oh, well, if you insist, I'll just go and get the frame. Remember it's Thursday. Monsieur Grivet and the Michauds must find the portrait in its place.

He goes out. CAMILLE *takes off his jacket, changes tie, puts on an overcoat which his mother gives him and goes to follow* LAURENT.

Scene 4

THÉRÈSE, MME RAQUIN, CAMILLE

CAMILLE: (*Hesitating and coming back.*) What shall I buy?

MME RAQUIN: It must be something that Laurent likes. He's such a good, dear child! He's practically one of the family.

CAMILLE: Yes, he's a real brother ... What about a bottle of anisette?

MME RAQUIN: Are you sure he'd like that? A light wine would be better, perhaps, with some cakes?

CAMILLE: (*To* THÉRÈSE.) You're not saying much. Do you remember if he likes Malaga?

THÉRÈSE: (*Leaving the window and moving downstage.*) I'm sure he does. He likes everything. He eats and drinks like a pig.

MME RAQUIN: My child …!

CAMILLE: Do tell her off. She can't stand him. He's already noticed, he told me so. It's not very nice … (*To* THÉRÈSE.) I can't allow you to be against my friends. What have you got against him?

THÉRÈSE: Nothing … He's always here. Lunch, dinner, he eats here all the time. You always put the best food on his plate. Laurent this, Laurent that. It gets on my nerves, that's all … He's not particularly amusing, either. He's a greedy, lazy pig.

MME RAQUIN: Be charitable, Thérèse. Laurent is not happy. He lives in an attic and eats very badly at that place of his. It gives me pleasure to see him eat a good meal and feel warm and cosy here with us. He makes himself at home, has a smoke, that's nice to see … He's all alone in the world, the poor boy.

THÉRÈSE: Do what you like. Pamper him, coddle him, it's all the same to me.

CAMILLE: I know! I'll get a bottle of champagne, that'll be perfect.

MME RAQUIN: Yes, that'll pay him back for the portrait nicely … Don't forget the cakes.

CAMILLE: It's only half-past eight. Our friends won't arrive until nine. They'll get such a surprise! Champagne! (*He goes.*)

MME RAQUIN: (*To* THÉRÈSE.) You'll light the lamp, won't you, Thérèse. I'm going down to the shop.

Scene 5

THÉRÈSE, *later joined by* LAURENT

THÉRÈSE, *left alone, stays still a moment, looking around, then at last she lets out a sigh. Silently she moves downstage and stretches with lassitude and boredom. Then she hears* LAURENT *enter by the small side door and she smiles, shaking with joy. During this scene it gets darker and darker as night falls.*

LAURENT: Thérèse …

THÉRÈSE: Laurent, my darling … I felt you would come back, my love. (*She takes his hands and leads him downstage.*) I haven't seen you for a whole week. Every afternoon I waited for you, hoping you'd be able to escape from the office … If you hadn't come, I'd have done something stupid … *Why* have you stayed away for a whole week? I can't stand it any longer. Shaking hands every evening in front of the others you seem so cold.

LAURENT: I'll explain.

THÉRÈSE: You're afraid, aren't you? You big baby! Where could we be safer? (*She raises her voice and moves a few paces.*)

Who could guess we loved each other? Who would ever come and look for us in this room?

LAURENT: (*Pulling her back and taking her in his arms.*) Be sensible … No, I'm not afraid to come here.

THÉRÈSE: Then you're afraid of me, admit it … You're afraid that I love you too much, that I'll upset your life.

LAURENT: Why do you doubt me? Don't you know I can't sleep because of you. I'm going mad. ME! Who never took women seriously … Thérèse, I'm afraid because you have awoken something in the depths of my being – a man I never knew existed. Sometimes, it's true, I am not calm. It can't be natural to love anyone as I love you; and I'm afraid it will get out of control.

THÉRÈSE: (*Her head resting on his shoulder.*) That would be a pleasure without end, a long walk in the sun. (*They kiss.*)

LAURENT: (*Extricating himself rapidly.*) Did you hear someone on the stairs? (*They both listen.*)

THÉRÈSE: It's only the damp making the stairs creak. (*They come together again.*) Come here, let's love each other without fear, without regret. If only you knew … Oh, what a childhood I had! I have been brought up in the damp atmosphere of a sick man's room.

LAURENT: My poor Thérèse.

THÉRÈSE: Oh yes! I was so miserable. For hours on end I would squat in front of the fire stupidly watching over his infusions. If I moved, my aunt scolded me – mustn't wake Camille up, must we? I used to stammer; my hands shook like an old woman's. I was so clumsy that even Camille made fun of me. And yet I felt strong. I could feel my child's fists clench, I wanted to smash everything … They told me my mother was the daughter of a nomadic African chief. It must be true; so often I dreamt of escaping; roaming the roads and running barefoot in the dust, begging like a gypsy … you see, I preferred starving in the wild to their hospitality.

She has raised her voice: LAURENT, *distressed, crosses the room and listens at the staircase.*

LAURENT: Keep your voice down, your aunt will come up.

THÉRÈSE: Let her come up! It's their fault if I'm a liar. (*She leans on the table, arms crossed.*) I don't know why I ever agreed to marry Camille. It was a prearranged marriage. My aunt simply waited until we were of age. I was only twelve years old when she said, 'You will love your cousin, you will look after him.' She wanted him to have a nurse, an infusion-maker. She adored this puny child that she had wrestled from death twenty times, and she trained me to be his servant … And I never protested. They had made me cowardly. I felt pity for the child. When I played with him I could feel my fingers sink into his limbs like putty. On the evening of the wedding, instead of going to my room at the left on the top of the stairs, I went in Camille's, which was on the right. That was all … But you … you, my Laurent …

LAURENT: You love me? (*He takes her in his arms and slowly sits her down in the chair to the right of the table.*)

THÉRÈSE: I love you. I loved you the day Camille pushed you into the shop, remember? – when you'd bumped into each other at the office ... I really don't know how I loved you. It was more like hate. The very sight of you drove me mad, I couldn't bear it. The moment you were there, my nerves were strained to breaking point, yet I waited achingly for you to come, for the pain. When you were painting just now, I was nailed to the stool, at your feet, no matter how hard I secretly tried to fight it.

LAURENT: (*Kneeling at her feet.*) I adore you.

THÉRÈSE: And our only time of pleasure, Thursday evenings, when Grivet and old Michaud would arrive regular as clockwork, those Thursday evenings used to drive me mad – the eternal games of dominoes, eternal Thursdays, the same imbecilic boredom ... But now I feel proud and revenged. When we sit round the table exchanging polite remarks I can bask in such wicked pleasure; I sit there sewing and put on my half-baked expression while you all play dominoes; and in the midst of this bourgeois peace I'm reliving our moments of ecstasy.

LAURENT: (*Thinking he has heard a noise, getting up, terrified.*) I'm sure you're talking too loud. We'll be caught. I tell you your aunt will come up. (*He listens at the door to the spiral staircase.*) Where is my hat?

THÉRÈSE: (*Quietly getting up.*) Do you really think she will come up? (*She goes to the staircase and returns with lowered voice.*) Yes, you're right, you'd better go. You will come tomorrow, at two o'clock?

LAURENT: No, it's not possible.

THÉRÈSE: Why not?

LAURENT: The head-clerk has threatened to sack me if I'm absent again.

THÉRÈSE: You mean we won't see each other any more? You're leaving me? This is where all this caution has been leading? Oh, you coward!

LAURENT: No, we can have a peaceful existence, the two of us. It's only a matter of looking, of waiting for circumstances to change. How often I've dreamt of having you all to myself for a whole day; then my desire would grow and I wanted you for a month of happiness, then a year, then all my life ... All our lives to be together ... all our life to love each other. I would leave my job and would start painting again. You would do whatever you wished. We would adore each other for ever, for ever ... You'd be happy, wouldn't you?

THÉRÈSE: (*Smiling, swooning on his chest.*) Oh yes, very, very happy.

LAURENT: (*Breaking away from her, in a low voice.*) If only you were free ...

THÉRÈSE: (*Dreamily.*) We would marry, we would no longer be afraid of anything. Oh, Laurent, what a sweet life it would be.

LAURENT: All I can see are your eyes shining in the dim light, those eyes that would drive me mad. We must now say farewell, Thérèse.

THÉRÈSE: You're not coming tomorrow?

LAURENT: No. Trust me. If we have to spend some time apart without seeing each other, you must tell yourself that we are working towards our future happiness. (*He kisses her and then exits hastily through the secret door.*)

THÉRÈSE: (*Alone. A moment's silence as she dreams.*) If only I were free.

Scene 6

THÉRÈSE, MME RAQUIN, CAMILLE

MME RAQUIN: What, you still haven't lit the lamp! Oh, you daydreamer. Never mind, it's ready. I'll get it. (*She goes out to her bedroom.*)

CAMILLE: (*Arrives with a bottle of champagne and a box of cakes.*) Where is everyone? Why is it so dark in here?

THÉRÈSE: My aunt has gone for the lamp.

CAMILLE: Ah. (*Shaking.*) Oh it's you! You gave me a fright ... You could at least talk in a more natural tone of voice ... You know I hate it when people play jokes in the dark.

THÉRÈSE: I'm not playing jokes.

CAMILLE: I caught sight of you just then, all white like a ghost ... It's ridiculous, pranks like that ... Now if I wake up during the night, I'm going to think that a woman in white is pacing round my bed waiting to strangle me ... It's all very well for you to laugh.

THÉRÈSE: I'm not laughing.

MME RAQUIN: (*Enters with lamp.*) What's wrong?

The scene brightens.

CAMILLE: It's Thérèse, she's scaring me, she thinks it's funny. I nearly dropped the bottle of champagne ... That would have been three francs wasted.

MME RAQUIN: What? You only paid three francs? (*She takes bottle.*)

CAMILLE: Yes, I went as far as the boulevard St Michel, where I'd seen some advertised for three francs in a grocer's. It's just as good as the eight franc bottle. Everyone knows that the shopkeepers are a load of frauds. Here are the cakes.

MME RAQUIN: Give them to me. I'll put everything on the table so as to surprise Grivet and Michaud when they arrive. Could you get me two plates, Thérèse?

They set everything on the table, the champagne between two plates of cakes. Then THÉRÈSE goes and sits at her work table and begins to sew.

CAMILLE: Ah, quarter to nine. On the stroke of nine Monsieur Grivet will arrive. He's exactitude itself ... You will be nice to him, won't you? I know he's only the deputy chief clerk but he could be useful as regards my promotion. He's a very powerful man, so don't underestimate him. The old boys at the office swear that in twenty years he's never once been a minute late … Laurent is wrong to say he won't make his mark.

MME RAQUIN: Our friend Michaud is just as precise. When he was Police Superintendent at Vernon he arrived home precisely at eight o'clock exactly, do you remember? We always complimented him on it.

CAMILLE: Yes, but since he's retired and moved to Paris with his niece, he's become somewhat more erratic. That little Suzanne is always leading him up the garden path … But all the same I find it most agreeable to have good friends and to entertain them once a week. Anything more regular would cost too much … Oh, I've just remembered, before they arrive, I wanted to tell you, I hatched a plan when I was walking back.

MME RAQUIN: What plan?

CAMILLE: Mother, you know I promised to take Thérèse to Saint-Ouen one Sunday before the weather turns. She hates walking out round town with me, even though it is much more fun than the countryside. She says I wear her out, that I don't walk properly … So, I thought it'd be an idea to go for a walk in Saint-Ouen this coming Sunday, and to take Laurent with us.

MME RAQUIN: Yes, my children, you do that. My legs aren't good enough to come with you, but I think that's an excellent idea … That will make you square with Laurent for the portrait.

CAMILLE: Laurent is so funny in the countryside … Remember, Thérèse, the time we took him to Suresnes? He's so strong, like a horse! He can jump over streams of water and can throw stones to amazing heights. What a joker! On the wooden horse at Suresnes he did this impersonation of a hunt, cracking the whip, kicking the spurs. You know, he did it so well that a wedding party nearby almost wept with laughter. The bride almost had a seizure! Really! … Remember, Thérèse?

THÉRÈSE: He'd certainly had enough to drink at dinner to stimulate his wit.

CAMILLE: Oh you! You don't understand people having fun. If I had to rely on you for entertainment I would have a truly tedious time at Saint-Ouen … All she does – she just sits on the ground staring into the water … Now, if I bring Laurent, it's to keep me amused … Where the devil has he gone to get that frame? (*Bell rings in shop.*) Ah, that'll be him. Monsieur Grivet still has seven minutes left.

Scene 7

Same and LAURENT

LAURENT: (*Holding the frame.*) They always take so long in that shop. (*Looking at* MME RAQUIN *and* CAMILLE *who are talking in hushed voices.*) I bet you're plotting some treat.

CAMILLE: Guess.

LAURENT: You're going to invite me to dinner tomorrow night and there'll be chicken and rice.

MME RAQUIN: You greedy pig!

CAMILLE: Better than that … On Sunday I'm taking Thérèse to Saint-Ouen and you're coming with us … Would you like that?

LAURENT: Would I like to! (*He takes the portrait and a small hammer from* MME RAQUIN.)

MME RAQUIN: You will be careful, won't you, Laurent. I leave Camille in your hands. You are strong. I am happier when I know he is with you.

CAMILLE: Mother, you're such a worrier, it's boring. Just think, I can't even go to the end of the road without her imagining some catastrophe has happened … It's awful always being treated like a little boy … What we'll do, we'll take a cab as far as the ramparts, that way we'll only have to pay for the one journey. Then we'll walk back along the tow-path, spend the afternoon on the island, and in the evening we'll have a fish stew by the riverside. Is that settled, then?

LAURENT: (*Fixing the painting into the frame.*) Yes … but we could add the finishing touch to the programme.

CAMILLE: How?

LAURENT: (*Glancing at* THÉRÈSE.) With a trip on a rowing boat.

MME RAQUIN: No, no, no boating. I wouldn't feel happy.

THÉRÈSE: You don't think Camille would risk going on the water, do you? He's much too scared.

CAMILLE: Me scared?!

LAURENT: That's true, I forgot you were frightened of the water. When we used to go paddling in the Seine at Vernon, you'd just stay on the bank, shivering … All right, we'll give the boat a miss.

CAMILLE: But that's not true! *I'm* not scared! … We *shall* take a boat. What the devil are you doing, making me out to be an idiot? We'll see which of the three of us is the least brave. It's Thérèse who's frightened.

THÉRÈSE: My poor child, you look pale with fear already.

CAMILLE: Tease me if you like … We'll see! We'll see!

MME RAQUIN: Camille, my good Camille, give up this idea; do it for me.

CAMILLE: Please, Mother, don't torment me. You know it only makes me ill.

LAURENT: Very well, your wife will decide.

THÉRÈSE: Accidents can happen anywhere.

LAURENT: That's very true … in the street – your foot could slip, a tile could fall on your head.

THÉRÈSE: Besides, you know how much I adore the Seine.

LAURENT: (*To* CAMILLE.) All right then, that's settled. You win! We will take a boat.

MME RAQUIN: (*Aside to* LAURENT, *who's hanging up portrait.*) I can't tell you how worried this outing makes me. Camille is so insistent. You see how carried away he gets.

LAURENT: Don't be afraid. I'll be there … I must just quickly hang up the portrait. (*He hangs portrait over mantelpiece.*)

CAMILLE: It will catch the light there, won't it? (*Shop bell rings and the clock strikes nine.*) Nine o'clock. Here's Monsieur Grivet.

Scene 8

The same plus GRIVET

GRIVET: I'm first to arrive ... Good evening Ladies and Gentlemen.

MME RAQUIN: Good evening, Monsieur Grivet ... shall I take your umbrella? (*She takes it.*) Is it raining?

GRIVET: It's threatening to. (*She goes to put it to the left of fireplace.*) Not in that corner, not in that corner; you know my little habits ... In the other corner. There, thank you.

MME RAQUIN: Give me your galoshes.

GRIVET: No, no, I'll put them away myself. (*He sits on the chair she offers him.*) I have my own little system. Yes, yes, I like everything to be in its place, you understand. (*He places galoshes next to umbrella.*) That way I don't worry.

CAMILLE: Do you not bring any news, Monsieur Grivet?

GRIVET: (*Getting up and coming centre stage.*) I left the office at half-past four, dined at six at the Little Orléans restaurant, read my paper at seven at the Café Saturnin; and it being Thursday today, instead of going to bed at nine as is my habit, I came here. (*Reflecting.*) Yes, that's all, I think.

LAURENT: You didn't see anything on your way here?

GRIVET: Oh yes, of course, forgive me ... There was a crowd of people in the rue Saint-André-des-Arts. I had to cross to the other pavement ... That did put me out ... You understand, in the mornings I walk to the office along the left-hand pavement, and, in the evenings, I return along the other ...

MME RAQUIN: The right-hand pavement.

GRIVET: No, no, no, no. Allow me. (*Miming the action.*) In the mornings, I go like this, and in the evenings, I come back ...

LAURENT: Oh, very good. (*Clapping.*)

GRIVET: Always by way of the left-hand pavement, you see. I always keep to the left, like the railways. It's the best way of not getting lost *en route*.

LAURENT: But what was the crowd doing on the pavement?

GRIVET: I don't know. How should I know?

MME RAQUIN: No doubt, some accident.

GRIVET: Why, of course, that's true, it must have been an accident ... I hadn't thought of that ... My word, you put my mind at rest by saying it was an accident. (*He sits down at the table, on the left.*)

MME RAQUIN: Ah! Here's Monsieur Michaud.

Scene 9

The same plus MICHAUD *and* SUZANNE

SUZANNE *takes off her shawl and hat and goes to chat quietly to* THÉRÈSE, *who is still sitting at her work desk.* MICHAUD *shakes hands with everyone.*

MICHAUD: I believe I am late.

GRIVET, *who has taken out his watch and shows it with an air of triumph.*

I know, six minutes past nine. It was this little one's fault. (*Indicating* SUZANNE.) We had to stop at every shop. (*He goes to place his cane next to* GRIVET's *umbrella.*)

GRIVET: No, forgive me, but that's my umbrella's place ... You know full well that I don't like that. I have left you the other corner of the fireplace for your cane.

MICHAUD: Very well, very well, don't let's get angry.

CAMILLE: (*Aside to* LAURENT.) I say, I do believe Monsieur Grivet is annoyed because there's champagne. He's looked at the bottle three times without saying a thing. It's amazing that he's not more surprised than that!

MICHAUD: (*Turning and catching sight of the champagne.*) Well, blow me! You're going to send us home in a proper state. Cakes and champagne!

GRIVET: Gosh, champagne. I've drunk champagne only four times in my whole life.

MICHAUD: Whose saint's day are you celebrating?

MME RAQUIN: We are celebrating the portrait of Camille that Laurent finished this evening. (*She takes the lamp and goes over to the portrait to illuminate it.*) Look! (*They all follow her, except* THÉRÈSE, *who stays at her work table, and* LAURENT, *who leans on the fireplace.*)

CAMILLE: It's very striking, isn't it? I look as though I'm out visiting.

MICHAUD: Yes, yes.

MME RAQUIN: It's still quite fresh. You can still smell the paint.

GRIVET: That's what it is. I thought I could smell something ... That's the advantage of photographs – they don't smell.

CAMILLE: Yes, but when the paint dries ...

GRIVET: Oh, certainly, when the paint dries ... And it dries quite quickly ... But they painted a shop in the Rue de la Harpe and that took five days to dry!

MME RAQUIN: Well, Monsieur Michaud, do you think it's good?

MICHAUD: It's very good; very, very good. (*They all return and* MME RAQUIN *puts the lamp on the table.*)

CAMILLE: If you could serve tea now, Mother. We shall drink the champagne after the game of dominoes.

GRIVET: (*Sitting down again.*) Quarter past nine. We'll hardly have time to get a good game in.

MME RAQUIN: It'll only take five minutes ... You stay there, Thérèse, since you are not feeling well.

SUZANNE: (*Cheerfully.*) I am feeling very well. I will help you, Madame Raquin. I like playing the housewife. (*They go out to the kitchen.*)

Scene 10

THÉRÈSE, GRIVET, CAMILLE, MICHAUD, LAURENT

CAMILLE: Nothing new to report, Monsieur Michaud?

MICHAUD: No, nothing ... I took my niece to the Luxembourg to do her sewing. Oh, yes, of course, yes, there *is* news! There's the tragedy at the rue St-André-des-Arts.

CAMILLE: What tragedy? Monsieur Grivet saw a big crowd there on his way here.

MICHAUD: The crowd hasn't dispersed since this morning. (*To GRIVET.*) They were all looking up into the air, weren't they?

GRIVET: I couldn't say. I changed pavements ... So it *was* an accident? (*He puts on his skull-cap and cuffs, which were in his pocket.*)

MICHAUD: Yes, at the Hotel de Bourgogne they found a woman's body cut into four pieces, in the trunk belonging to a traveller who has since disappeared.

GRIVET: Is it possible?! Cut into four pieces! How can you cut a woman into four pieces?

CAMILLE: It's disgusting!

GRIVET: And I walked right past the place! ... I remember now, everyone was looking up into the air ... Did they see anything up there? – Was there anything to see?

MICHAUD: You could see the window of the bedroom where the crowd claim the trunk was found ... but they were, in fact, wrong. The window of the bedroom in question looked out onto the courtyard.

LAURENT: Has the murderer been arrested?

MICHAUD: No, one of my ex-colleagues who is conducting the inquiry told me this morning he is working in the dark and the murderer is still at large.

GRIVET chuckles, nodding his head.

The law is going to have some difficulty finding him!

LAURENT: But has the identity of the victim been established?

MICHAUD: No. The body was naked, and the head was not in the trunk.

GRIVET: It must have got mislaid.

CAMILLE: Please, dear sir! Your woman cut into four pieces is making my flesh creep.

GRIVET: Why, no! It's fun to be frightened, when one is absolutely sure that one is in no danger oneself. Monsieur Michaud's stories of his time as Police Superintendent are so amusing ... Remember the one about the policeman's body that had been buried in a carrot-patch and his fingers were pulled up with the carrots? He told us that story last autumn ... I found that one very interesting. What the devil, we know there aren't any murderers lurking behind our backs here. This is a house of God ... Now in a wood, that's different. If I were crossing a dark wood with Monsieur Michaud, I would ask him to keep quiet.

LAURENT: (*To MICHAUD.*) Do you think many crimes go unpunished?

MICHAUD: Yes, unfortunately. Disappearances, slow deaths, suffocations, sinister crushings, without a trace of blood, without a single cry. The law arrives and can't find any clues. There's more than one murderer freely walking the streets in broad daylight right now, you know.

GRIVET: (*Chuckling louder.*) Don't make me laugh. And no-one arrests them?

MICHAUD: If they are not arrested, my dear Monsieur Grivet, it is because nobody suspects they are murderers.

CAMILLE: So what's wrong with the police?

MICHAUD: Nothing's wrong with the force. But they can't do the impossible. I say again, there are criminals who right now are living, loved and respected ... You are wrong to scoff, Monsieur Grivet.

GRIVET: Let me scoff, let me scoff, leave me in peace.

MICHAUD: Maybe one of these men is an acquaintance of yours, and you shake hands with him every day.

GRIVET: Oh no, don't say things like that. That's not true, you know full well that's not true. I could tell you a story or two.

MICHAUD: Tell us your story, then.

GRIVET: Certainly ... It's the story of the thieving magpie. (*MICHAUD shrugs his shoulders.*) You may know it. You know everything. Once there was a servant-girl who was imprisoned for having stolen some table silver. Two months later some men were cutting down a poplar tree and they found the silver in a magpie's nest. The thief was the magpie! The girl was released ... so you see, the guilty are always punished.

MICHAUD: (*Sneering.*) So, did they put the magpie into prison?

GRIVET: (*Annoyed.*) A magpie in prison! A magpie in prison? Michaud is so stupid!

CAMILLE: Come, that's not what Monsieur Grivet meant. You are confusing things.

GRIVET: The police are inefficient, that's all ... It's immoral.

CAMILLE: Laurent, do you think that people can kill like that without anyone knowing about it?

LAURENT: What *I* think? (*He crosses the room, slowly getting nearer to THÉRÈSE.*) I think that Monsieur Michaud is making fun of you. He's trying to frighten you with his stories. How can he know what he claims nobody knows ... And if there are people out there who are that clever, good luck to them, that's what I say! (*Close to THÉRÈSE.*) Look, your wife is less gullible than you.

THÉRÈSE: Of course, what you don't know, doesn't exist.

CAMILLE: All the same, I'd prefer it if we talked about something else. Would you mind, let's talk about something else ...

GRIVET: With pleasure, let's talk about something else.

CAMILLE: Why, we haven't brought up the chairs from the shop ... Come and give me a hand, would you. (*He goes down.*)

GRIVET: (*Getting up, moaning.*) Is that what he calls talking about something else, going to fetch chairs?

MICHAUD: Are you coming, Monsieur Grivet?

GRIVET: After you ... The magpie in prison! Magpie in prison! Has anyone seen such a thing? ... For an ex-Police Superintendent, you have just told us a load of poppycock, Monsieur Michaud.

They go down the stairs.

LAURENT: (*Seizing THÉRÈSE's hands, lowering voice.*) Do you swear to obey me?

THÉRÈSE: (*Same.*) Yes, I belong to you. Do what you want with me.

CAMILLE: (*From below.*) Laurent, you lazy-bones ... You could at least have come and helped with the chairs, instead of leaving it to your elders and betters.

LAURENT: (*Raising voice.*) I stayed to flirt with your wife. (*To THÉRÈSE, gently.*) Have hope. We shall live together happily for ever.

CAMILLE: (*From below, laughing.*) Oh, that! I give my consent. Try to please her.

LAURENT: (*To THÉRÈSE.*) And remember what you said: what you don't know, doesn't exist. (*They hear steps on the stairs.*) Careful.

They separate hastily. THÉRÈSE resumes her bored attitude by her work desk. LAURENT breaks stage right. The others come back up, each with a chair, laughing heartily.

CAMILLE: (*To LAURENT.*) Oh, Laurent, you're such a card. Your jokes will be the death of me. All that palaver just to get out of carrying up a chair.

MME RAQUIN and SUZANNE enter with tea.

GRIVET: Ah! At last, here's the tea.

Scene 11

The same plus MME RAQUIN and SUZANNE

MME RAQUIN: (*To GRIVET, who's taken out his watch.*) Yes, it took me a quarter of an hour. Now, sit down and we will catch up on lost time.

GRIVET sits downstage left, behind him LAURENT. MME RAQUIN's armchair to the right: MICHAUD sits behind her. Finally, at the back in the centre, CAMILLE in his armchair. THÉRÈSE stays at her work table. SUZANNE joins her when she has finished serving the tea.

CAMILLE: (*Sitting.*) There, I'm in my chair. Pass the box of dominoes, Mother.

GRIVET: (*Beatifically.*) This is such a pleasure. Every Thursday, I wake up and say to myself, 'Why, this evening I shall go to the Raquins and play dominoes.' You won't believe how much ...

SUZANNE: (*Interrupting.*) Shall I sweeten yours, Monsieur Grivet?

GRIVET: With pleasure, Miss, how charming you are. Two lumps, remember? (*Resuming.*) Indeed, you won't believe how much ...

CAMILLE: (*Interrupting.*) Aren't you coming, Thérèse?

MME RAQUIN: (*Passing him the box of dominoes.*) Leave her. You know she is not feeling well. She doesn't like playing dominoes ... If we get a customer, why she can go down to the shop.

CAMILLE: It's upsetting, when everyone else is enjoying themselves, to have someone there who isn't. (*To MME RAQUIN.*) Come along, Mother, will you not sit down?

MME RAQUIN: (*Sitting.*) Yes, yes, here I am.

CAMILLE: Is everyone sitting comfortably?

MICHAUD: Certainly, and this evening I am going to thrash you, Monsieur Grivet ... Mme Raquin, your tea is a touch stronger than last Thursday ... But Monsieur Grivet was saying something.

GRIVET: Me? I was saying something?

MICHAUD: Yes, you had started a sentence.

GRIVET: A sentence? You think so? That surprises me.

MICHAUD: No, I assure you. Isn't that right, Mme Raquin? Monsieur Grivet said, 'Indeed, you won't believe how much ... '

GRIVET: 'Indeed, you won't believe how much.' No, I don't remember, nothing of the sort ... If you are making fun of me, Monsieur Michaud, you know full well that I find that mediocre.

CAMILLE: Is everyone sitting comfortably? Then I shall begin.

He noisily empties the box. Silence, while the players shuffle the dominoes and deal.

GRIVET: Monsieur Laurent is not playing and is forbidden to give advice. There, everyone take seven. No cheating, do you hear Monsieur Michaud? No cheating. (*Silence.*) Ah, me to start. I've got the double six!

End of Act 1.

Act 2

Ten p.m. The lamp is on. One year has passed without change to the room. Same peace. Same intimacy. MME RAQUIN and THÉRÈSE are in mourning.

Scene 1

THÉRÈSE, GRIVET, LAURENT, MICHAUD, MME RAQUIN, SUZANNE

All are seated exactly as at the end of Act 1. THÉRÈSE at her work table looking dreamy and unwell, her embroidery work on her knee. GRIVET, MICHAUD and MME RAQUIN at the round table. But CAMILLE's chair is empty. A silence during which MME RAQUIN and SUZANNE serve tea, exactly repeating their motions of Act 1.

LAURENT: You should relax, Mme Raquin. Give me the box of dominoes.

SUZANNE: Shall I sweeten yours, Monsieur Grivet?

GRIVET: With pleasure, Mademoiselle. You're so charming. Two lumps, remember? You're the only one to sweeten me.

LAURENT: (*Holding the domino box.*) Here are the dominoes. Do sit down, Mme Raquin. (*She sits.*) Is everyone sitting comfortably?

MICHAUD: Certainly, and tonight I am going to thrash you, Monsieur Grivet. Just let me put a little rum in my tea. (*He pours the rum.*)

LAURENT: Is everyone sitting comfortably? ... Then I shall begin. (*He noisily empties the box. The players shuffle and share out dominoes.*)

GRIVET: This is such a pleasure ... There, everybody take seven. No cheating. Do you hear, Monsieur Michaud, no cheating ...? (*Silence.*) No, it's not me to start today.

MME RAQUIN: (*Bursting suddenly into tears.*) I can't. I can't.

LAURENT and MICHAUD get up and SUZANNE comes over to stand behind MME RAQUIN's armchair.

When I see you all sitting round the table like in the old days, I remember, it breaks my heart ... My poor Camille used to be here.

MICHAUD: For heaven's sake, Mme Raquin, do try to be sensible.

MME RAQUIN: Forgive me, my old friend. I can't go on ... You remember how he loved playing dominoes. He was the one who always emptied the box, exactly as Laurent did just now. And if I didn't sit down straight away, he would scold me. I was always afraid of contradicting him – it always made me ill. Oh, those were such happy evenings. And now his chair is empty, you see!

MICHAUD: Come on, old girl, you mustn't upset yourself. You'll make yourself ill.

SUZANNE: (*Hugging MME RAQUIN.*) Don't cry, please. It hurts us all so much.

MME RAQUIN: You are right. I must be brave. (*She cries.*)

GRIVET: (*Pushing away his dominoes.*) I suppose it'd be better if we didn't play. It's a shame that it affects you in this way. Your tears won't bring him back.

MICHAUD: We are all mortal.

MME RAQUIN: Alas.

GRIVET: Our only intention in coming round here is to offer you some diversion.

MICHAUD: You must forget, my poor friend.

GRIVET: Certainly. Hang it all ... Let us not get downcast. We'll play for two sous a game, all right? Yes?

LAURENT: In a minute. Give Mme Raquin time to compose herself ... We all weep for our dear Camille.

SUZANNE: Listen to them, dear lady. We all weep for him, we weep for him with you. (*She sits at her feet.*)

MME RAQUIN: Yes, you are all so good ... Don't be angry with me for upsetting the game.

MICHAUD: We're not angry with you. It's just that it's a year now since the terrible incident happened and you should learn to think about it more calmly.

MME RAQUIN: I hadn't counted the days. I am crying because the tears come to my eyes. Forgive me. I can still see my dear boy beaten by the murky Seine water, and then I see him as a tiny boy falling asleep between two blankets as I sing to him. What a terrible way to die! How he must have suffered! I knew something terrible would happen. I begged him to abandon the idea of that boat trip. He wanted to be so brave ... If only you knew how I tended him in his cradle. Once when he had typhoid I held him for three weeks on end without a wink of sleep.

MICHAUD: (*Getting up.*) You've still got your niece. You mustn't distress her. You mustn't distress the kind friend who saved her, and whose eternal regret it will be that he was unable to rescue Camille as well. Your sorrow is selfish. You're bringing tears to Laurent's eyes.

LAURENT: These memories are so painful.

MICHAUD: Come now, you did all you could. When the boat capsized, by colliding with a stake, I believe – one of those stakes used to support the eel-nets, if I remember correctly ...

LAURENT: I believe so. The jolt sent all three of us flying into the water.

MICHAUD: Then, when you had fallen in, you were able to grab hold of Thérèse?

LAURENT: I was rowing, she was sitting next to me. All I had to do was to grab her clothes. When I dived back in, Camille had disappeared ... He had been sitting at the front of the boat, dipping his hands in the water ... he even made jokes, he said, 'Golly, it isn't half cold. It wouldn't be very nice to take a header in that brew.'

MICHAUD: You mustn't reawaken these painful memories. You acted like a hero – you dived in again three times.

GRIVET: (*Getting up.*) So I believe ... There was a superb article about it in my paper the next day. It said that Monsieur Laurent deserved a medal. I got goose pimples just reading how three people had fallen into the river while their dinner stood waiting for them at the bankside restaurant. And then a week later when they found poor Monsieur Camille, there was another article. (*To MICHAUD.*) Do you remember, it was Monsieur Laurent who came to fetch you to identify the body with him.

MME RAQUIN is seized by another weeping fit.

MICHAUD: (*Angrily, in lowered voice.*) Really, Monsieur Grivet, couldn't you have kept quiet? Mme Raquin was just beginning to calm down. Did you *have* to refer to such details?

GRIVET: (*Piqued, in lowered voice.*) A thousand pardons, it was you who started the story of the accident ... Seeing as we can't play, we have to say something.

MICHAUD: (*Raising his voice gradually.*) What! If you haven't quoted that article in your paper a hundred times! It's most disagreeable, understand? Now, Mme Raquin won't stop crying for *another* quarter of an hour.

GRIVET: (*Shouting.*) Well you started it.

MICHAUD: What! No. Damn it! You did.

GRIVET: You'll be calling me a fool in a minute.

MME RAQUIN: My dear friends, please don't argue.

They move upstage, muttering their discontent.

I will be good. I won't cry any more. These conversations are a great comfort. It helps to talk of my loss, it reminds me how much I owe you all ... My dear Laurent, give me your hand. Are you angry?

LAURENT: Yes, with myself, for not being able to give *both* of them back to you.

MME RAQUIN: (*Holding his hand.*) You are my child, and I love you. Every night I pray for you. You tried to save my son. Every night I beseech the Heavens to watch over your precious life ... You see, my son is up there and he will hear my prayers. You will owe your happiness to him. Each time you find joy, say to yourself that it was I who prayed and Camille who granted it.

LAURENT: Dear Madame Raquin!

MICHAUD: That's good, very good.

MME RAQUIN: (*To SUZANNE.*) And now my little one, back to your place. Look, I'm smiling – for you.

SUZANNE: Thank you. (*She gets up and kisses her.*)

MME RAQUIN: (*Slowly taking up the dominoes game.*) Who's to start?

GRIVET: Oh! Are you sure? ... Oh, how kind!

GRIVET, MICHAUD and LAURENT sit in their places.

Who's to start?

MICHAUD: Me. There! (*He starts the game.*)

SUZANNE: (*Who has moved over to THÉRÈSE.*) My dear friend, shall I tell you about the blue prince?

THÉRÈSE: The blue prince?

SUZANNE: (*Takes a stool and sits next to THÉRÈSE.*) There's so much to tell. I'll whisper it to you, I don't want my uncle to know. Imagine, this young man ... It's a young man, he's got a blue suit and a very fine chestnut moustache that really suits him.

THÉRÈSE: Be careful, your uncle is listening.

SUZANNE half rises and watches the players.

MICHAUD: (*Furiously to GRIVET.*) But you passed on five a minute ago, and now you're playing fives all over the place.

GRIVET: I passed on five? You are mistaken. Apologise!

MICHAUD protests, the game continues.

SUZANNE: (*Sitting again, in lowered voice.*) No need to worry about uncle when he plays dominoes ...! This young man used to come to the Luxembourg Gardens every day. You know my uncle usually sits on the terrace, by the third tree from the left, just by the newspaper kiosk? Well, the blue prince would sit by the fourth tree. He would put a book on his knee. Every time he turned the page he would look across at me. (*She stops from time to time to glance furtively at the players.*)

THÉRÈSE: Is that all?

SUZANNE: Yes, that's all that happened in the Luxembourg Gardens ... oh no, I forget ... one day he saved me from a hoop that a little girl threw at me at top speed. He gave the hoop a hard hit and it span off in the other direction – that made me smile. It made me think of lovers who throw themselves at wild horses. The blue prince must

have had the same idea: he started smiling too as he bowed to me.

THÉRÈSE: Is that the end of the story?

SUZANNE: No! That's just the beginning. The day before yesterday, my uncle had gone out. I was feeling very bored, because our maid is very stupid. So, to keep myself amused, I got out the big telescope – you know, the one that my uncle had in Vernon? Do you know that from our terrace you can see right to the edge of Paris? I was looking in the direction of Saint Sulpice ...

MICHAUD: (*Angrily, to GRIVET.*) What! No! A six! Go on, play it!

GRIVET: It's a six, it's a six, I can see very well. Heavens, I'll have to do my sums. (*The game continues.*)

SUZANNE: Wait! ... I saw chimneys, oh! so many chimneys, fields of them, oceans of them! When I moved the telescope slightly the chimneys started to march, faster and faster until they fell onto each other, marching at the double. The whole telescope was full of them ... Suddenly, who do I see between two chimneys ...? Guess! ... The blue prince.

THÉRÈSE: So he's a chimney sweep, your blue prince?

SUZANNE: No, silly. He was on a terrace like me, and what's even funnier, he was looking through a telescope, like me. I recognised him, of course, with his blue suit and moustache.

THÉRÈSE: So where does he live?

SUZANNE: But I don't know. You see I only saw him in the telescope. It was without doubt a long way away in the direction of Saint Sulpice. When I looked with my bare eyes, all I could see was grey, with blue patches of the slate roofs. Then I almost lost the spot. The telescope moved and I had to retrace an enormous journey across the sea of chimneys. Now I've got a landmark, the weathercock of the house next door.

THÉRÈSE: Have you seen him again?

SUZANNE: Yes, yesterday, today, every day ... Am I doing anything wrong? If only you knew how little and sweet he looks in the telescope. He's hardly any bigger than that; just like a little figure; I'm not frightened of him at all ... But I don't know where he is; I don't even know if what you see in the telescope is real. It's all so far away ... When he goes like this (*She blows a kiss.*) I draw back and all I can see is the grey again. I can believe that the blue prince didn't do that (*She repeats gesture of blowing a kiss.*) can't I, since he's not there any more, no matter how hard I stare out ...

THÉRÈSE: (*Smiling.*) You do me good ... love your blue prince forever – in your dreams.

SUZANNE: Oh no! Sh, the game's over.

MICHAUD: So, it's us two, the final set, Monsieur Grivet.

GRIVET: Are you ready, Monsieur Michaud? (*They mix up the pieces.*)

MME RAQUIN: (*Pushing her armchair stage right.*) Laurent, as you're on your feet, would you do me the favour of fetching my wool basket. I must have left it on the chest of drawers in my bedroom. Take the lamp.

LAURENT: There's no need. (*He goes out of the upstage door.*)

MICHAUD: You've got a true son, there. He's so obliging.

MME RAQUIN: Yes, he's very good to us. I entrust him with our little errands; and in the evenings, he helps us to shut up shop.

GRIVET: The other day I saw him selling some needles like a real shop girl. Ha! Ha! A shop girl with a beard!

He laughs. LAURENT *comes back suddenly, with a wild look in his eyes, as if he were being followed. For a moment he leans against the wardrobe.*

MME RAQUIN: Whatever's the matter?

MICHAUD: (*Rising.*) Are you not well?

GRIVET: Did you bump into something?

LAURENT: No, it's nothing, thank you. A fit of dizziness. (*He moves unsurely downstage.*)

MME RAQUIN: And the wool basket?

LAURENT: The basket ... I don't know ... I haven't got it.

SUZANNE: What! You were frightened. A man frightened!

LAURENT: (*Attempting to laugh.*) Frightened? Frightened of what? ... I didn't find the basket.

SUZANNE: Wait, I'll find it. And if I find your ghost, I'll bring him back with me. (*She goes.*)

LAURENT: (*Recovering gradually.*) You see, it's soon gone.

GRIVET: You are living too well. It's bad blood, that's your trouble.

LAURENT: (*Shaking.*) Yes, bad blood.

MICHAUD: (*Resitting.*) You need a refreshing infusion.

MME RAQUIN: As a matter of fact I've noticed you've been distracted for quite some time now. I'll prepare you some red vine-leaf. (*To* SUZANNE *returning with basket.*) Ah, you've found it!

SUZANNE: It was on the chest of drawers. (*To* LAURENT.) Monsieur Laurent, I didn't see your ghost. I must have scared him.

GRIVET: What a lot of spirit that girl has.

Bell from shop.

SUZANNE: Don't disturb yourselves. I'll go. (*She goes down.*)

GRIVET: A treasure, a real treasure. (*To* MICHAUD.) Let's say I've got thirty-two points to your twenty-eight.

MME RAQUIN: (*Having searched in the basket that she's placed on the fireplace.*) No, I can't find the wool I need. I'll have to go down for it (*She goes down.*)

Scene 2

THÉRÈSE, LAURENT, GRIVET, MICHAUD

GRIVET: (*In a lowered voice.*) It's not as jolly here as it used to be. The game was almost jeopardised just now.

MICHAUD: (*Ditto.*) What do you expect? When there's been a death in the house? ... But rest assured, I've found a way of bringing back our good old Thursdays. (*They play.*)

THÉRÈSE: (*Quietly to* LAURENT.) You're frightened, aren't you?

LAURENT: (*Quietly.*) Yes. Shall I come to you tonight?

THÉRÈSE: No, we must wait. Let's wait a bit longer. We must be careful.

LAURENT: We've been careful for a year. It's been a year since I last touched you. It would be so easy. I could come back through the little door. We are free now. Alone together in your room we wouldn't be afraid.

THÉRÈSE: No, let's not spoil the future. We need so much happiness, Laurent. Will we ever find enough?

LAURENT: Have confidence. We will find peace and happiness in each other's arms. We will fight the fear together. When shall I come?

THÉRÈSE: On our wedding night. It won't be long now ... Careful, my aunt.

MME RAQUIN: (*From off.*) Thérèse, will you come down. You're needed in the shop.

THÉRÈSE *goes out, wearily. They all watch her go.*

Scene 3

LAURENT, GRIVET, MICHAUD, MME RAQUIN

MICHAUD: Did you notice Thérèse just then? She can't hold her head up and is looking extremely pale.

MME RAQUIN: I watch her every day, the rings under her eyes, her hands that suddenly start shaking feverishly.

LAURENT: Yes, and her cheeks have the pink flame of consumption.

MME RAQUIN: Yes, you were the first to point it out to me, my darling Laurent, and now I see things getting worse. Will no pain be spared me!

MICHAUD: Rubbish, you're worrying about nothing. It's only her nerves. She'll recover.

LAURENT: No, she is heart-broken. There seems to be a feeling of farewell in her long silence, in her pale smiles ... It will be a long, slow death.

GRIVET: My dear man, you are being of small consolation. You ought to be cheering her up, not filling her head with macabre thoughts.

MME RAQUIN: Alas, my friend, Laurent is right. The sickness is in her heart. She has no wish to be consoled. Each time I try to make her see reason, she gets impatient, even angry. She is hiding in her pain like a wounded animal.

LAURENT: We must resign ourselves to it.

MME RAQUIN: That would be the final blow ... She's all I have. I was hoping she would be there to close my eyes. If she goes, I'll be all alone here in this shop ... left to die in a corner ... Oh, see how unhappy I am. What ill wind is shaking our house? (*She weeps.*)

GRIVET: (*Timidly.*) Well, are we playing or not?

MICHAUD: Wait, can't you. Damn you. (*He gets up.*) Look, I'm determined to find a cure. What the devil, at her age she can't be inconsolable ... Did she weep a lot after the terrible catastrophe at Saint-Ouen?

MME RAQUIN: No, she was never one for crying. She simply suffered a silent grief. She seemed overwhelmed by a weariness of mind and body; she seemed dazed, like after a long walk, but recently she's become extremely fearful.

LAURENT: (*Shaking.*) Extremely fearful?

MME RAQUIN: Yes ... One night I heard her shouting out in her sleep. I ran to her ... She didn't recognise me, she was babbling deliriously.

LAURENT: A nightmare ... And she was talking? What did she say?

MME RAQUIN: I couldn't make out the words. She was crying out for Camille ... Now in the evenings she doesn't dare go up to bed without the lamp. In the mornings she is exhausted, she drags herself around listlessly and looks at me blankly, it upsets me so ... I know only too well that she will leave us, that she wishes to join my other poor child.

MICHAUD: Very well, old girl, my enquiry is complete. I shall tell you exactly what I think. But first may we be left alone?

LAURENT: You wish to be left alone with Mme Raquin?

MICHAUD: Yes.

GRIVET: (*Getting up.*) Very well, we're going. You know you owe me two games, Monsieur Michaud. Remind me. I'll be waiting for you.

GRIVET and LAURENT go out.

Scene 4

MICHAUD and MME RAQUIN

MICHAUD: Now then, my old girl, I'll be blunt ...

MME RAQUIN: What is your advice? If only we could save her!

MICHAUD: (*Lowering his voice.*) You must marry her off.

MME RAQUIN: Marry her off! Oh, how cruel! It would be like losing my dear Camille all over again.

MICHAUD: Come, come, let's face the facts. I'm acting as your doctor and as your doctor I prescribe marriage.

MME RAQUIN: No, it's not possible ... You've seen her fears. She'd never accept. She hasn't forgotten my son. I begin to doubt your sense of delicacy, Michaud. Thérèse can't possibly remarry with Camille still in her heart. That would be a profanation.

MICHAUD: Don't start using big words with me! A woman who is afraid to go to her room alone at night is in need of a husband, damn it!

MME RAQUIN: What? And introduce a stranger to our midst! It would cloud the rest of my old age. We might make the wrong choice, disturb the little peace we have left ... No, no. Let me die in my mourning clothes. (*She sits.*)

MICHAUD: Obviously we have to find a good soul who would be both a good husband for Thérèse and a good son for you, who would replace Camille perfectly. In a word ... well, how about ... Laurent!

MME RAQUIN: Laurent!

MICHAUD: Why yes! They'd make such a lovely couple. That is my advice, old friend, they must be married.

MME RAQUIN: Those two, Michaud!

MICHAUD: I was sure you would be amused. I've been toying with the idea for some time now. Think it over and have faith in my professional experience. If, in order to add a final joy to your old age, you decide to marry Thérèse off and save her from this slow, consuming grief, then where would you find a better husband than Laurent?

MME RAQUIN: But they've always been like brother and sister.

MICHAUD: Come now, just think of yourself! I only want to see you all happy. It will be like the good old days again. You will have two children to comfort you in your old age.

MME RAQUIN: Do not tempt me ... You're right, I am in such need of consolation. But I fear we might be doing wrong ... My poor Camille would punish us for forgetting him so quickly.

MICHAUD: Who's talking about forgetting him? Laurent is forever mentioning his name. He'll still be part of the family, damn it.

MME RAQUIN: I am old. My legs are bad. All I ask is to die happy.

MICHAUD: You see, I've managed to convince you. It's the only way of avoiding a stranger in your midst. You would be simply strengthening your bond of friendship. And I want to see you a grandmother with little ones climbing on your knee ... You are smiling, you see, I knew I'd make you smile.

MME RAQUIN: Oh, it's wrong, it's wrong to smile. I feel so confused, my friend. They will never consent. They never think of such things.

MICHAUD: Bah, we will hustle things on. They are far too reasonable not to realise that their marriage is necessary to the happiness of this household. That's the logic we must use to them. I'll speak to Laurent. I'll talk him into it while I help him close up the shop. Meanwhile, you speak to Thérèse. And we'll have them engaged this very evening.

MME RAQUIN: (*Rising.*) I'm all of a tremble. (*THÉRÈSE enters.*)

MICHAUD: Look, here she is. I'll leave you. (*He goes.*)

Scene 5

MME RAQUIN and THÉRÈSE

MME RAQUIN: (*To THÉRÈSE, who enters, dejected.*) What's wrong with you, my child? You haven't said a word all evening. I beg you, try to be less sad. For the gentlemen's sake. (*THÉRÈSE makes a vague gesture.*) I know, I know you can't control sadness ... Are you in pain?

THÉRÈSE: No, I'm just very tired.

MME RAQUIN: If you are in pain, you must say so. It's not right to suffer without allowing us to look after you. Perhaps you're getting palpitations? Pains in your chest?

THÉRÈSE: No ... I don't know ... It's nothing ... It's as if everything in me has gone to sleep.

MME RAQUIN: Dear child ... you cause me so much anxiety, with your long silences. You are all I have.

THÉRÈSE: Are you asking me to forget?

MME RAQUIN: I didn't say that. I can't say that ... But it is my duty to see if there can be any consolation for you. I mustn't impose my mourning on you ... Tell me, frankly.

THÉRÈSE: I am so tired.

MME RAQUIN: You must tell me. You spend too much time alone and you are bored, is that it? At your age to be constantly weeping!

THÉRÈSE: I don't understand what you're trying to say.

MME RAQUIN: Nothing. I was just asking. I want to know what's wrong. I know it can't be much fun living alone with a sad old woman. I do understand. And your room is so big, so dark and perhaps you want ...

THÉRÈSE: I don't *want* anything.

MME RAQUIN: Listen. Don't be angry. I know it's a wicked idea we've had but ... We've thought you should remarry.

THÉRÈSE: Me! Never! Never! Why do you doubt me?

MME RAQUIN: (*Very emotional.*) I said to them, she can't have forgotten him, he's still in her heart ... It was they who forced me ... And they are right, you see, my child. This house is too sad. Soon everyone will desert us. Oh, you must listen to them.

THÉRÈSE: Never!

MME RAQUIN: Yes. Remarry. I can't remember how they put it ... they were so convincing ... I did agree with them. I took it upon myself to persuade you ... If you like, I'll call Michaud. He'll explain much better than I can.

THÉRÈSE: My heart is closed, it won't listen. Please can't you all leave me in peace? Remarry, good God, to whom!

Figure 1 The Italian actress Giacinta Pezzana as the mother in *Thérèse Raquin* at the Teatro dei Fiorentini in 1879.

Figure 2 Charlotte Emmerson as Thérèse and Ben Daniels as Laurent in *Thérèse Raquin* from a new version by Nicholas Wright, directed by Marianne Elliot at the Royal National Theatre, London, in 2006. (Photographer: Simon Annand and by permission of the Royal National Theatre archive.)

MME RAQUIN: They have had a good idea. They have found you someone. Michaud is below right now talking to Laurent.

THÉRÈSE: Laurent! The person you've chosen is Laurent! But I don't love him, don't want to love him.

MME RAQUIN: They are right, I promise you. Laurent is practically one of the family. You know how kind he is, how helpful he is to us. At first, like you, I felt hurt; it seemed wrong. Then, when I thought more about it, I realised that it would be more faithful to Camille's memory for you to marry his friend, your rescuer.

THÉRÈSE: But I still weep, still want to weep!

MME RAQUIN: And I am pleading against these tears of yours and against my own … You see, they only want us to be happy. They said I'd have two children, they said it'd surround me with something sweet and joyful to ease the wait for death … I am selfish, I need to see you smile … Do it for me.

THÉRÈSE: My sweet suffering. You know I have always resigned myself, that my only wish was to please you.

MME RAQUIN: Yes, you are a good girl. (*Trying to smile.*) Next spring will be my last. We will work out a cosy life together, we three. Laurent will love us both … You know, I'm marrying him too, a little … You will lend him to me for my little errands, for my old woman's whims.

THÉRÈSE: Dear aunt … I was so sure you would let me weep in peace.

MME RAQUIN: You give your consent, yes?

THÉRÈSE: Yes.

MME RAQUIN: (*Very moved.*) Thank you, my daughter. You make me so happy. (*Falls into armchair.*) Oh, my dear son, my poor dead child, I was the first to betray you.

Scene 6

THÉRÈSE, MME RAQUIN, MICHAUD, then: SUZANNE, GRIVET and LAURENT

MICHAUD: (*Quietly to MME RAQUIN.*) I've persuaded him. But my God, it wasn't without the greatest difficulty. He will do it for your sake, you understand; I pleaded your case … He'll be up in a minute, he's just locking up the front … and Thérèse?

MME RAQUIN: She consents.

MICHAUD crosses to THÉRÈSE, upstage left, and whispers to her.

SUZANNE: (*Arrives, followed by GRIVET, in mid-conversation.*) No, Monsieur Grivet, no! You are such an egoist, I *won't* dance with you at the wedding. So you never got married so as not to disturb your little habits?

GRIVET: Certainly, Miss.

SUZANNE: Huh, the objectionable man! … Not a single step of the quadrille, do you hear? (*She goes over to join THÉRÈSE and MICHAUD.*)

GRIVET: All little girls think it's fun to get married. I've tried it five times. (*To MME RAQUIN.*) You remember the

last time, that large unfeeling lady teacher. The banns were published, everything was going perfectly, until she confessed to drinking milky coffee in the mornings. I loathe milky coffee, *I* drink hot chocolate and have done for thirty years now. That would have upset my entire existence, so I broke it off. I did the right thing, didn't I?

MME RAQUIN: (*Smiling.*) Without doubt.

GRIVET: Ah! It's such a pleasure when people get on with each other. That's how Michaud saw straight away that Thérèse and Laurent were made for each other.

MME RAQUIN: (*Gravely.*) You are right, my friend. (*She gets up.*)

GRIVET: That's what the song says. (*He sings.*) Oh dear mother, shall I say, what torments me, night and day. (*Looks at watch.*) Gracious! Five to eleven! (*He sits down and puts on his galoshes, picks up his umbrella.*)

LAURENT: (*Who has come up, goes over to MME RAQUIN.*) I have just been discussing your happiness with Monsieur Michaud. Your children wish to make you happy … dear Mother.

MME RAQUIN: (*Very moved.*) Yes, call me your mother, my good Laurent.

LAURENT: Thérèse. Do you wish to give our mother a sweet and peaceful life?

THÉRÈSE: I do. We have a duty to fulfil.

MME RAQUIN: Oh, my children! (*Taking the hands of THÉRÈSE and LAURENT and holding them in her own hands.*) Marry her, Laurent: make her happy and my son will thank you. You make me so happy. I pray to the Heavens that we shall not be punished.

End of Act 2.

Act 3

Three a.m. The room is decorated, all white. Big open fire. One lamp burning. White curtains round the bed: bedspread edged with lace, squares of lace on the chairs. Large bouquets of roses everywhere, on the sideboard, mantelpiece, table.

Scene 1

THÉRÈSE, MME RAQUIN, SUZANNE, MICHAUD, GRIVET

THÉRÈSE, MME RAQUIN and SUZANNE in wedding outfits enter. MME RAQUIN and SUZANNE have already taken off their hats and shawls. THÉRÈSE is in grey silk: she goes to sit: she seems tired. SUZANNE stands at the door and argues a moment with GRIVET and MICHAUD (wearing black), who want to follow the women.

SUZANNE: No, uncle. No, Monsieur Grivet. You can't come into the bride's bedroom. What you're doing is very improper.

GRIVET and MICHAUD enter all the same.

MICHAUD: (*Quietly to SUZANNE.*) Sh, sh, it's a joke. (*To GRIVET.*) Have you got the packet of nettles, Monsieur Grivet?

GRIVET: Certainly, they've been in my pocket since this morning. They caused me a lot of bother both at the church and at the restaurant. (*He approaches the bed slyly.*)

MME RAQUIN: (*With a smile.*) Come on now, gentlemen, you can't be present for the undressing of the bride.

MICHAUD: The undressing of the bride! Oh, my dear lady, what a charming thought! If you need any help with the pins, here we are at your service. (*He joins* GRIVET.)

SUZANNE: (*To* MME RAQUIN.) I've never seen my uncle look so jolly. He was so red, very red during the dessert.

MME RAQUIN: Let them laugh. You're allowed to have fun on a wedding night. At Vernon we used to get up to all sorts of tricks. The wedding couple weren't allowed to get a wink of sleep all night.

GRIVET: (*In front of the bed.*) My word, this bed is so soft. Have a feel, Monsieur Michaud.

MICHAUD: By jove, three mattresses at least. (*Whispers.*) Have you hidden the stinging nettles in the bed?

GRIVET: (*Whispers.*) Right in the middle.

MICHAUD: (*Bursting out laughing.*) Ha! Ha! You are such a joker, honestly!

GRIVET: (*Also giggling.*) Ha, ha! This one will work all right.

MME RAQUIN: (*Smiling.*) Gentlemen, the bride is waiting.

SUZANNE: Look, will you leave? You're getting annoying now.

MICHAUD: Right, very well, we're going.

GRIVET: (*To* THÉRÈSE.) Our compliments, Madame, and good night.

THÉRÈSE: (*Getting up and sitting down again.*) Thank you, gentlemen.

GRIVET: You're not angry are you, my dear lady?

MME RAQUIN: What, my old friend, on a wedding night?! Goodnight.

MICHAUD and GRIVET leave slowly, spluttering with laughter.

SUZANNE: (*Shutting the door behind them.*) And don't come back. Uncle, wait for me downstairs. Only the groom will be allowed in and then only when we allow it.

Scene 2
THÉRÈSE, MME RAQUIN, SUZANNE

MME RAQUIN: You should get undressed, Thérèse. It's nearly three o'clock.

THÉRÈSE: I am exhausted. What with the ceremony, the coach-ride, that interminable meal … Leave that for a moment, please.

SUZANNE: (*To* MME RAQUIN.) Yes, it was so hot in that restaurant. It gave me a headache, but it went away in the cab. You are the one who must be tired, with your bad legs! Remember what the doctor said.

MME RAQUIN: He said a severe shock might be fatal, but today I just felt so happy. Everything went very smoothly, didn't you think? It was all very proper.

SUZANNE: The Mayor looked perfect, didn't he? When he began to read from his little red book, the groom bowed

his head … Monsieur Grivet's signature in the register looked superb.

MME RAQUIN: At the church, the priest was very touching.

SUZANNE: Ooh, and everyone was crying. I was watching Thérèse; she looked so serious … And then this afternoon, there were so many people on the streets. We must have travelled twice round Paris. People gave us funny looks … Half of the wedding party was asleep by the time we got to the restaurant. (*She laughs.*)

MME RAQUIN: Thérèse, you ought to get undressed, my child.

THÉRÈSE: Just a bit longer please. Keep talking, just a bit longer.

SUZANNE: Can I be your chamber-maid? Wait. Now, let me do it all. In that way, you won't get more tired.

MME RAQUIN: Give me her hat.

SUZANNE: (*Gives the hat to* MME RAQUIN.) There, you see, you don't even have to move. Oh, but I'm afraid you'll have to stand up if you want me to take off your dress.

THÉRÈSE: (*Standing up.*) How you torment me!

MME RAQUIN: It's late, my daughter.

SUZANNE: (*Unhooking the dress.*) A husband, that must be awful. One of my friends who got married cried and cried. Your waist is so small and you aren't holding yourself in. You're right to wear long bodices. Ah, this hook is really sticking. I've got a good mind to go and fetch Monsieur Grivet. (*She laughs.*)

THÉRÈSE: Hurry up, I've got the shivers.

SUZANNE: We'll go in front of the fire.

They both cross to the fire.

Oh! You've got a rip in your flounce. Oh, this silk is magnificent, so strong … Why you are so nervous, my darling friend. I can feel you shaking when I touch you, just like Thisbe. She's the cat my uncle gave me. I'm trying so hard not to tickle you.

THÉRÈSE: I'm a bit feverish.

SUZANNE: Nearly finished. There! (*She makes* THÉRÈSE *step out of the dress and hands it to* MME RAQUIN.) Finished! And now I will brush your hair for the night, would you like that?

MME RAQUIN: That's it. (*She takes the dress out of the upstage door.*)

SUZANNE: (*Having sat* THÉRÈSE *down in front of the fire.*) Now you're all nice and pink. You looked as pale as death just now.

THÉRÈSE: It's the fire.

SUZANNE: (*Standing behind her, brushing her hair.*) Lower your head a touch. You have such superb hair. Tell me, my dear friend, I'd like to ask a few questions. I'm so curious, you know … Your heart is beating so very fast, and that's why you are shaking, is that right?

THÉRÈSE: My heart isn't seventeen years old like yours, my dear.

SUZANNE: I hope I'm not annoying you! It's just I've been thinking all day long that if I were in your place I'd be so foolish; so I promised myself to watch how you prepared yourself for the night so that I wouldn't seem too awkward when it was my turn … You seem a bit sad, but you have courage; I'd be afraid of sobbing like an idiot.

THÉRÈSE: Is the blue prince such an awful prince, then?

SUZANNE: Don't tease me. You look good with your hair down. You look like a queen in those pictures … No plaits, just a simple bun, yes?

THÉRÈSE: Yes, just a simple knot, please. (*MME RAQUIN returns and takes a white nightdress from the wardrobe.*)

SUZANNE: (*Brushing THÉRÈSE'S hair.*) If you promise not to laugh, I'll tell you what I would be feeling in your place. I would be happy, oh, but happy like I'd never been before. And then, I'd be terribly scared. I'd think I was floating on a cloud, approaching something unknown, sweet and terrifying, with very gentle music, and very delicate perfumes. And I'd step into a white light, pushed forward in spite of myself by a joy that was so thrilling I would think I was dying … That's how you feel, isn't it?

THÉRÈSE: Yes … (*Softly.*) Music, perfumes, a great light, all the springtime of youth and love.

SUZANNE: You're still trembling.

THÉRÈSE: I can't get warm.

MME RAQUIN: (*Coming to sit by the fireplace.*) I'll warm your nightdress for you. (*She holds it against the fire.*)

SUZANNE: And when the blue prince was waiting, like Monsieur Laurent is doing, I would maliciously make him wait. Then, when he'd come to the door, oh! Then I would come over all silly, I'd make myself very small, very, very small, so that he couldn't find me. I don't know after that. I can't think about it, without feeling funny.

MME RAQUIN: (*Turning the nightdress, smiling.*) You ought not to think about it, little one. Children think of nothing but dolls, flowers and husbands.

SUZANNE: (*To THÉRÈSE.*) Is that not what you're feeling?

THÉRÈSE: Yes, it is. I'd have preferred not to have been married in winter, or in this room. At Vernon, in May, the acacia are in flower, the nights are warm.

SUZANNE: There! That's your hair done. Now you can put on your nice warm nightdress.

MME RAQUIN: (*Helping THÉRÈSE on with her nightdress.*) It's burning my hands.

SUZANNE: I hope you're not cold now.

THÉRÈSE: Thank you.

SUZANNE: (*Looking at THÉRÈSE.*) Ah, you are lovely. You look like a true bride in the lace.

MME RAQUIN: Now we will leave you alone, my child.

THÉRÈSE: Alone, no! Wait, I'm sure I've still something to tell you.

MME RAQUIN: No, don't talk; I'm avoiding talking, you note. I don't want to start us crying. If you knew what an effort it's been ever since this morning. My heart is breaking, and yet I must be, I *am* happy … It's all over. You saw how jolly our old friend Michaud was, you must be jolly, too.

THÉRÈSE: Yes, you are right. I've got a headache. Goodbye.

MME RAQUIN: Goodbye … Tell me, my daughter, you're not feeling sorrowful, you're not hiding anything from me …? What makes me strong is the thought of having made you happy … You will love your husband; he deserves both of our affection. You will love him like you loved … No, I've got nothing to say to you, I don't want to say anything. We have done the best we can and I wish you much happiness, my daughter, for all the comfort you are giving me.

SUZANNE: Anyone would think you were leaving Thérèse to a pack of wolves in a dark den. The den smells good. There are roses everywhere. Like a cosy nest.

THÉRÈSE: These flowers must have been expensive. You are mad.

MME RAQUIN: I know you love the springtime; I wanted to give you a corner of spring in your room for your wedding night. You could live out Suzanne's dream, and believe that you are visiting the garden of paradise. You see, you are smiling. Be happy amidst your roses. Good night my daughter (*She kisses her.*) Good night, little one.

SUZANNE: And me, aren't you going to give me a kiss, dear friend?

THÉRÈSE kisses her.

Now you've gone all pale again. The blue prince is here. Oh! It's wonderful, a room like this full of roses.

Scene 3

LAURENT *and* THÉRÈSE

THÉRÈSE, now alone. She slowly moves back to sit by the fire. Silence. LAURENT enters slowly, still in his wedding outfit. He closes the door and advances with embarrassment. Takes off his jacket and waistcoat.

LAURENT: Thérèse, my dear love …

THÉRÈSE: (*Pushing him away.*) No, wait, I'm cold.

LAURENT: (*After a silence.*) At last, we are alone, my Thérèse, far from the others, free to love each other … Life ahead is ours, this room is ours, you are mine, dear wife, because I won you, and you gave yourself willingly. (*He goes to kiss her.*)

THÉRÈSE: (*Pushing him away.*) No, in a minute, I am freezing.

LAURENT: My poor angel! Give me your feet so I can warm them with my hands. (*He kneels in front of her and tries to take her foot, which she withdraws.*) The time has come, you see. Remember, we've been waiting for a year, been working for a year towards this night of love. We need it, don't we, as payment for all our caution, our suffering, our pain?

THÉRÈSE: I remember … Don't stay there. Sit down a minute. Let's talk.

LAURENT: (*Getting up.*) Why are you shaking? I've closed the door, and I am your husband … Before, when I came to you, you never trembled, you laughed, you spoke out loud despite the risk of being found out. Now, you are talking in a whisper as if someone were listening through the walls ... Come, we can raise our voices, and laugh, and love each other. It is our wedding night. No one will come.

THÉRÈSE: (*Terrified.*) Don't say that. Don't say that ...! You are even paler than I am, Laurent, and you are stammering to get your words out. Don't pretend to be brave. Let's wait until we dare before we kiss. You are afraid of looking ridiculous by not taking me and kissing me. You are a child. We are not a normal newly wedded couple. Sit down. Let's talk.

He sits. She changes her tone of voice to a familiar and casual one.

It was very windy today.

LAURENT: Yes, it was a very cold wind. But it died down a little this afternoon.

THÉRÈSE: Yes. The apricot trees will do well not to flower too early.

LAURENT: In March, bouts of frost are very bad for fruit trees. You must remember, at Vernon ...

He stops. Both dream an instant.

THÉRÈSE: (*Quietly.*) At Vernon, that was our childhood. (*Assuming her familiar and indifferent tone of voice.*) Put a log on the fire, will you? It's beginning to be quite pleasant in here. Is it four o'clock yet?

LAURENT: (*Looking at the clock.*) No, not yet. (*He moves left and sits at the other end of the room.*)

THÉRÈSE: It's surprising, how long the night is ... Do you dislike cab rides as I do? There is nothing more stupid than riding for hours. It puts me to sleep ... And I detest eating in restaurants.

LAURENT: One is always more comfortable at home.

THÉRÈSE: That's not so in the country.

LAURENT: One can eat some excellent things in the country. Do you remember, the pleasure gardens by the water ... (*He gets up.*)

THÉRÈSE: Shut up! (*Suddenly getting up, rough voice.*) Why do you bring back those memories! I can hear them, pounding in your head and in mine, and the whole cruel story unfolds in front of my eyes ... No, let's not say anything, let us not think any more. Underneath your words, I hear others; I hear what you are thinking but don't say. Am I right? Just then you were thinking of the accident? Shut up! (*A silence.*)

LAURENT: Thérèse, say something, I implore you. This silence is too heavy to bear. Speak to me.

THÉRÈSE: (*Going to sit stage right, her hands clutching her forehead.*) Close your eyes. Try to disappear.

LAURENT: No. I need to hear your voice. Say something, anything you like, like you did just now, that the weather is bad, that the night is long ...

THÉRÈSE: All the same I think, I can't not think. You are right, silence is bad, it is better to talk ... (*Trying to smile, in a jolly tone.*) The town hall was so cold this morning. My feet were frozen. But I managed to warm them on a little stove in the church. Did you notice the little stove? It was just by the place where we knelt down.

LAURENT: Of course. Grivet stood over it throughout the whole ceremony. That devil Grivet had a triumphant smile on his face. He was so funny, wasn't he? (*They both force themselves to laugh.*)

THÉRÈSE: The church was a bit dark, due to the weather. Did you notice the lace of the altar cloth? That lace costs ten francs a metre at least, better than any we've got in the shop. The smell of the incense hung around; it smelt so sweet, it made me feel sick ... At first I thought we were alone inside that huge church; that pleased me. (*Her voice getting muffled.*) Then, I heard singing. You must have noticed it in a chapel on the other side of the nave.

LAURENT: (*Hesitating.*) I think I saw some people with candles.

THÉRÈSE: (*Suddenly seized by terror.*) It was a funeral. When I looked up I was confronted by the black cloth and the white cross ... The coffin passed close to us. I watched it. A poor, short, narrow, shabby coffin. Some poor creature, sordid and destitute.

She has gradually moved towards LAURENT and brushes his shoulder. They both shake. Pause. Then she resumes in a low voice.

Laurent, did you see him at the morgue?

LAURENT: Yes.

THÉRÈSE: Did he look as though he had suffered a lot?

LAURENT: Horribly.

THÉRÈSE: His eyes were wide open, and he looked straight at you?

LAURENT: Yes. He looked revolting, blue and swollen with the water. And he was smiling; the corner of his mouth was twisted.

THÉRÈSE: You say you think he was smiling ... Tell me, tell me everything, tell me how he looked. In my long sleepless nights, I've never seen him clearly, and I have a passion, a passion to see him.

LAURENT: (*In a terrible voice, shaking THÉRÈSE.*) Shut up! Wake up! We are both half asleep. What are you talking about? If I answered you, I was lying. I saw nothing. Nothing. Nothing. What is this ridiculous game we are playing?

THÉRÈSE: Ah! Feel how the words rise to our lips in spite of ourselves. Everything leads us back to him ... the apricot trees in flower, the pleasure gardens by the river, the coffin ... There can no longer be any indifferent conversation between us. He is at the bottom of all our thoughts.

LAURENT: Kiss me.

THÉRÈSE: I understand full well that you were talking about nothing but him, and that I replied about nothing but him. The awful story has formed inside us and we must complete it aloud.

LAURENT: (*Trying to take her in his arms.*) Kiss me Thérèse. Our kisses will cure us. We married so that we could find peace in each other's arms. Kiss me, and let us forget, dear wife.

THÉRÈSE: (*Pushing him away.*) No! I beg you, do not torment me. Just one more minute ... Reassure me, be good and light-hearted like before. (*A silence.* LAURENT *walks away, then he suddenly goes out of the main door, as if he's had a sudden idea.*)

Scene 4

THÉRÈSE alone

THÉRÈSE: He's left me alone ... Don't leave me, Laurent, I am yours. He's gone, and I am alone, now ... I think the lamp is going out. If it goes out ... If I am left in the dark ... I don't want to be alone. I don't want it to be night ... Oh, why did I not let him kiss me? I don't know what was wrong with me, my lips were icy cold; I thought his kiss would have killed me ... Where can he have gone? (*A knock at the little side door.*) Oh my God, now the other one has come back! He's come back for my wedding night. Can you hear him? He's knocking on the wood of the bed, he's calling me to my pillow ... Go away. I'm frightened ... (*She stays still, trembling, hands over her eyes. Another knock, she gradually calms herself and smiles.*) No, it's not the other one, it's my dear lover, it's my dear ... Thank you for that good thought, Laurent. I recognise your signal.

She goes and opens. LAURENT *enters.*

Scene 5

LAURENT and THÉRÈSE

They repeat exactly the same gestures as in Act 1 Scene Five.

THÉRÈSE: It's you, my Laurent! (*She flings her arms round his neck.*) I knew you would come, my dear love. I was thinking about you. It is so long since I've been able to hold you like this, all to myself.

LAURENT: Remember how you held me till I fell asleep. And I would dream of a way to stop us having to separate for ever ... Tonight, that beautiful dream is fulfilled. Thérèse ... you are there leaning against my chest for ever.

THÉRÈSE: An endless pleasure, a long walk in the sun.

LAURENT: Kiss me, then, dear wife.

THÉRÈSE: (*Suddenly breaking away, with a shout.*) No, then no! What is the good of acting out this comedy of the past? We don't love each other any more. We have murdered our love. Do you think I can't feel how cold you are in my arms? Let us stay calm and not move.

LAURENT: You are mine. I will have you. I will cure you of this nervous fear. What would be cruel, would be not to love each other any more, to find only a nightmare instead of the happiness we dreamt of. Come, put your arms round my neck again.

THÉRÈSE: No, we must not tempt suffering.

LAURENT: You must understand how ridiculous it is to spend the night like this; when we have loved each other so fearlessly. No one will come.

THÉRÈSE: (*Terrified.*) You've just said that. Don't repeat yourself, I implore you ... He might come.

LAURENT: Do you want to drive me mad? (*He goes towards her.*) I have given up too much, for you to refuse me now.

THÉRÈSE: (*Breaking away from him.*) Mercy! The sound of our kisses will call him I'm afraid, look, I'm afraid.

LAURENT goes to seize her in his arms, when he catches sight of CAMILLE's portrait, hanging above the sideboard.

LAURENT: (*Terrified, staggering backwards, pointing with his finger.*) There! There! Camille.

THÉRÈSE: I told you so. I felt a cold breeze behind my back. Where is he?

LAURENT: There, in the shadow.

THÉRÈSE: Behind the bed?

LAURENT: No, on the right. He's quite still, staring. He's watching us, staring ... He looks just as I saw him, pale and smudgy, with that twisted smile at the corner of his mouth.

THÉRÈSE: (*Looking.*) But, it's his portrait that you can see!

LAURENT: His portrait?

THÉRÈSE: Yes, the painting you did, you know?

LAURENT: No, I don't know. You think it's his portrait? I saw his eyes move ... Look. They're moving now. His portrait. Then go and take it down.

THÉRÈSE: No, I don't dare.

LAURENT: I beg you, do it.

THÉRÈSE: No.

LAURENT: Then let us turn it to face the wall, then we won't be afraid any more; perhaps we'll be able to kiss.

THÉRÈSE: No, why don't you do it yourself?

LAURENT: His eyes are still looking at me. I tell you his eyes are moving! They are following me, they are crushing me ... (*He slowly approaches.*) I will look down, and then I won't see him any more. (*He takes down the portrait in a single furious movement.*)

Scene 6

LAURENT, MME RAQUIN, THÉRÈSE

MME RAQUIN: (*In the doorway.*) What's wrong? I heard someone shouting.

LAURENT: (*Still holding the portrait and looking at it in spite of himself.*) He looks terrible. He looks just like he did when we threw him into the water.

MME RAQUIN: (*Advancing, staggering.*) Oh, just God! They killed my child!

THÉRÈSE, desperate, cries out in terror; LAURENT, bewildered, throws the portrait onto the bed, and falls back in front of MME RAQUIN, who stammers.

Murderers, murderers!

She suddenly has an attack of spasms, staggers as far as the bed, tries to balance, but seizing onto one of the white bed curtains, leans against the wall a moment, panting and fearful. LAURENT, hounded by her looks, hides behind THÉRÈSE.

LAURENT: It's the attack they warned her of. The paralysis is rising to her throat.

MME RAQUIN: (*Making a final supreme effort.*) My poor child. The wretches, the …

THÉRÈSE: It's horrible. She's all twisted, like in a vice. I don't dare help her. (*MME RAQUIN, thrown backwards, overwhelmed, collapses onto a chair.*)

MME RAQUIN: Misery! … I can't … I can't … (*She freezes stiff in her chair, her eyes fixed on THÉRÈSE and LAURENT.*)

THÉRÈSE: She's dying.

LAURENT: No, her eyes are living, her eyes are threatening us. Oh, that those lips and limbs were of stone!

End of Act 3.

Act 4

Five p.m. Five months later. The room is dark and humid once more. Dirty curtains. Neglected housework; dust, rags and clothes lying around on the furniture, dirty crockery left on the chairs. A rolled-up mattress thrown behind the bed curtain.

Scene 1

THÉRÈSE, SUZANNE

They are sitting at the work table, sewing.

THÉRÈSE: (*Gaily.*) So, at long last you found out where the blue prince lives? Love can't make you as stupid as they say, then.

SUZANNE: I wouldn't know. Myself, I'm pretty smart. In the end, you understand, it wasn't the least bit amusing to see my prince half a league away, always well-behaved like a picture. Between you and me, he was *too* well-behaved, much too much so.

THÉRÈSE: (*Laughing.*) So you like your lovers to be wicked, do you?

SUZANNE: Well, a lover you're not afraid of can't be a serious lover, can he? When I caught sight of my prince far away against the sky surrounded by chimney-pots, I thought I was looking at one of those angels in my Mass book who stand with their feet in the clouds. Very nice, but in the end extremely boring, you see! So, when it was my birthday, I told Uncle to give me a map of Paris.

THÉRÈSE: A map of Paris?

SUZANNE: Yes … Uncle was rather surprised, too … When I got the map … I set to work. I worked so hard! I drew lines with a ruler, measured distances with a pair of compasses, added, multiplied. And, when I thought I'd found the prince's terrace, I stuck a pin in the map on the

spot. Then, the next day, I forced Uncle to take a walk along the road where the house was.

THÉRÈSE: (*Cheerfully.*) My dear, it's such an amusing story. (*Looking at the clock and suddenly becoming very withdrawn.*) Five o'clock already. Laurent will be home.

SUZANNE: What's wrong? Just now you were so cheerful.

THÉRÈSE: (*Recovering.*) So the map helped you to discover the blue prince's address?

SUZANNE: Mm? No, my map was no help at all. Oh, if you only knew where it led me! One day it led me to a huge ugly house, where they make shoe polish; another day to a photographer's shop; another time to a seminary, then a prison, I don't know where else … You're not laughing. Come on, it *is* funny. … Are you feeling unwell?

THÉRÈSE: No, I thought my husband would be home. When you get married, you must frame that lucky map of yours!

SUZANNE: (*Getting up and moving stage right, passing behind THÉRÈSE.*) I've just told you it was useless. Haven't you been listening? Anyway, one afternoon, I went to the flower market at Saint Sulpice; I wanted to get some nasturtiums for our terrace. Who do I see in the middle of the market …? The blue prince, loaded down with flowers, pots in his pockets, pots under his arms, pots in his hands. He looked quite embarrassed with all his pots when he caught sight of me … Then he followed me; he didn't know how to get rid of the pots, poor dear! He said they were all for his terrace! Then, he made friends with Uncle, asked for my hand, and now I am marrying him – so there you are! I made a paper bird with the map and all I ever look at through the telescope is the moon … My dear friend, have you been listening?

THÉRÈSE: Yes, and your story is beautiful. And you still have your blue sky, and your flowers and your laughter. Oh, my dear, with your blue bird, if only you knew. (*Looks at the clock.*) Five o'clock. It is five o'clock isn't it? I must lay the table.

SUZANNE: I'll help you.

THÉRÈSE gets up. SUZANNE helps her to lay the table, three places.

Oh, how heartless of me to be so cheerful here, when I know that your happiness has been saddened by the cruel affliction of poor Mme Raquin … How is she today?

THÉRÈSE: She still can't move or talk but she doesn't seem to be in pain.

SUZANNE: The doctor did warn it could happen; she was always overdoing it … The paralysis has been merciless. As if she'd been struck by lightning and turned to stone, the poor, dear lady … When she's here with us, all stiff in her chair, her face all taut and white, her pale hands on her lap, she reminds me of one of those awful statues of mourning you see in churches, sitting at the feet of the tombs. I don't know why, but she makes me feel terrified. Can she still not move her hands?

THÉRÈSE: Her hands are dead like her legs.

SUZANNE: Oh Lord, it's such a shame! Uncle says she can't even hear or understand any more. He says it would be a Godsend for her mind to go completely.

THÉRÈSE: He's wrong. She can hear and understand everything. Her intelligence is still lucid and her eyes are alive.

SUZANNE: Yes, they seem to have got bigger; they are quite enormous now. They look so black and terrible in her dead face. I'm not easily scared as a rule, but during the night when I think of the poor lady I start to shake all over. You know those stories of people being buried alive? I imagine that she has been buried alive and that she is lying there at the bottom of a ditch with a ton of soil weighing on her chest preventing her from shouting out … What can she think about all day long? It's awful to be like that and yet to think all the time, *all* the time … But you are both so good to her!

THÉRÈSE: We are only doing our duty.

SUZANNE: And you are the only one who can understand what she's saying with her eyes, aren't you? I can't understand her at all. Monsieur Grivet prides himself on being able to interpret her slightest wish, yet he always replies at cross-purposes. She's so lucky that she's got you by her; she doesn't want for anything. Uncle's forever saying, 'The Raquins, that's a house of God.' Your happiness will come back, you'll see. Has the doctor given her any hope?

THÉRÈSE: Very little.

SUZANNE: I was here last time he came and he said the poor lady might possibly recover her voice and the use of her limbs.

THÉRÈSE: We mustn't count on it. We daren't count on it.

SUZANNE: Oh, but you must, you must have hope. (*They have finished laying the table and move downstage.*) And where's Monsieur Laurent? We hardly see him nowadays.

THÉRÈSE: Since he stopped working at the office and took up painting again, he leaves first thing in the morning and doesn't get home until the evening. He's working very hard – on a large painting that he wants to send to the next Salon.

SUZANNE: Monsieur Laurent has changed into a real gentleman. He no longer laughs too loud, he looks so distinguished. I never used to think I would like him as a husband, whereas now he would be just right … If you promise not to tell anyone, I'll tell you a secret …

THÉRÈSE: I'm hardly a gossip, you know.

SUZANNE: That's true, you keep everything to yourself. Then let me tell you that yesterday we were passing your husband's studio in the rue Mazarin, when Uncle suddenly had the idea of paying him a visit. Monsieur Laurent hates being disturbed, as you know, but he made us quite welcome … you'll never guess what he's working on.

THÉRÈSE: He's working on a big painting.

SUZANNE: No, the canvas for the big painting is still all white. We found him surrounded by lots of little canvases on which he had done rough sketches, children's heads, women's faces, old men … Uncle was most impressed; he claims that all of a sudden your husband has become a great painter; and he can't just be flattering him, because he always used to be so critical of his work. What I noticed was that all the faces seemed to resemble each other. They looked like …

THÉRÈSE: Who did they look like?

SUZANNE: I don't want to upset you … They all looked like poor Monsieur Camille.

THÉRÈSE: (*Shaking.*) Oh no … You must have imagined it.

SUZANNE: No, I assure you. All the children, women, old men, they have all got something that reminded me of the person I've just mentioned. My uncle thought they needed more colour, they are so pale. And they've all got a smile in the corner of their mouth.

We hear LAURENT *at the door.*

Ah! Here's your husband. Don't say anything. I think he wants to give you a surprise with all those faces.

Scene 2

LAURENT, SUZANNE, THÉRÈSE

LAURENT: Good evening, Suzanne. Have you both been working hard?

THÉRÈSE: Yes.

LAURENT: I am exhausted. (*He sinks wearily into a chair.*)

SUZANNE: It must be tiring having to stand up to paint, all day long.

LAURENT: I didn't do any work today. I walked as far as Saint-Cloud and then back again. Walking does me so much good … Thérèse, is the supper ready?

THÉRÈSE: Yes.

SUZANNE: I must go.

THÉRÈSE: Your uncle promised to fetch you; you must wait. You are not disturbing us.

SUZANNE: Well, then, I'll go down to the shop; I want to steal some tapestry needles.

As she is about to go down, the bell rings.

Why, a customer! Well, then, she will be served. (*She goes down.*)

Scene 3

LAURENT, THÉRÈSE

LAURENT: (*Pointing to the mattress left at the foot of the bed.*) Why didn't you hide the mattress? The idiots don't need to know that we sleep in separate beds. (*He gets up.*)

THÉRÈSE: You hide it. I do what I like.

LAURENT: (*Roughly.*) Woman, let's not start quarrelling. It's not night-time yet.

THÉRÈSE: Huh! So much the better for you if you can amuse yourself out of doors, if you can wear yourself out walking all day long. I'm fine when you are not there. As soon as you come back, all hell opens up … At least let me rest during the daytime since we don't sleep at night.

LAURENT: (*In a more gentle tone.*) Your voice is even more harsh than mine, Thérèse.

THÉRÈSE: (*After a silence.*) Are you going to bring in my aunt for supper? No, you'd better wait until the Michauds have gone; I'm always afraid when she is here when they are. For a while now I've seen an unrelenting thought in her eyes. She will find some way of talking, you'll see.

LAURENT: Bah! I get more afraid when he goes to her room. Michaud is bound to want to see his old friend. What on earth could she tell him? She can't even lift a finger. (*He goes out of door to* MME RAQUIN's *bedroom.*)

Scene 4

THÉRÈSE, MICHAUD, SUZANNE, *then* LAURENT *and* MME RAQUIN *in a chair, rigid and silent, white hair, dressed in black*

MICHAUD: Oh! The table is laid.

THÉRÈSE: Why, of course, Monsieur Michaud.

MICHAUD: So you are still living well, I see. These lovers have got a devilish appetite … On with your hat, Suzanne … (*Looking sad.*) And where is our good Mme Raquin?

LAURENT comes in, pushing MME RAQUIN. *He sits her at the table to her laid place.*

Ah, here she is, the old girl. Her eyes are shining – she is happy to see us. (*To* MME RAQUIN.) We two are old friends, aren't we …? Do you remember when I was Police Superintendent? I believe we first met at the time of the Wolf's Throat murder. You must remember, this woman and this man who had murdered a haulier, and I myself had to go and arrest them in their hovel. Damn it, they were guillotined at Rouen.

Scene 5

THÉRÈSE, LAURENT, MICHAUD, SUZANNE, MME RAQUIN, GRIVET

GRIVET: (*Who has heard* MICHAUD's *last few words.*) Ah! You're telling the story of the haulier; yes, I know that one. You told me that one, and I found it greatly interesting … Monsieur Michaud has a nose for sniffing out criminals. Good evening to you, one and all.

MICHAUD: And what are you doing here at this time, Monsieur Grivet?

GRIVET: Well, I was passing, and I thought I'd treat myself to a little debauchery; I've come for a chat with dear Mme Raquin. Oh! Were you about to sit down to eat, I hope I'm not disturbing you?

LAURENT: Not in the least.

GRIVET: It's just that we understand each other so well. A single glance and I know exactly what she means.

MICHAUD: Then, you'd better tell me what she means by staring at me all the time.

GRIVET: Wait, I can read her eyes like a book. (*He sits in front of* MME RAQUIN.) Now, let's chat like old friends … Have you got something you want to ask Monsieur Michaud? No? Nothing at all, just as I thought. (*To* MICHAUD.) You are making yourself out to be so important. She doesn't need you, you understand, it's me she wants to talk to. (*Turning back to* MME RAQUIN.) Now, what did you say? Yes, yes, I understand; you are hungry.

SUZANNE: (*Leaning against the back of the chair.*) Would you prefer if we left, dear Madame?

GRIVET: Gracious me! She *is* hungry … And she is inviting me to stay for a game this evening … A thousand pardons, Mme Raquin, but I can't accept, you know my little habits. But on Thursday, yes, I promise.

MICHAUD: Tut. She didn't say anything at all, Monsieur Grivet. Where do you get that idea from? Let me question her.

LAURENT: (*To* THÉRÈSE, *who has got up.*) Keep an eye on your aunt. You were right, she's got a terrible glint in her eye.

MICHAUD: Let's see, old girl, you know I am at your command. Why are you looking at me in this way? If only you could find a way of telling me what you want.

SUZANNE: You see what Uncle is saying, your every wish is sacred to us.

GRIVET: Hah. I've already explained what she wants – it's obvious.

MICHAUD: (*Insisting.*) You can't make yourself understood, can you, old girl. (*To* LAURENT, *who has come to the table.*) Laurent, look, how strangely she is continually staring at me.

LAURENT: No, I can't see anything special in her eyes.

SUZANNE: What about you, Thérèse, you can understand her slightest whim?

MICHAUD: Yes, please help us. Ask her for us.

THÉRÈSE: You are mistaken. She doesn't want anything, she always looks like that. (*She comes over and leans on the table opposite* MME RAQUIN, *but cannot stand to look her in the eyes.*) That's right, isn't it? You don't want anything …? No, nothing, I assure you. (*She moves away.*)

MICHAUD: Well, then, perhaps Monsieur Grivet was right.

GRIVET: Please yourselves, damn you. But I know what she says; she is hungry and she invites me to stay for a game.

LAURENT: Why don't you accept, Monsieur Michaud, you are more than welcome.

MICHAUD: Thank you, but I am busy this evening.

THÉRÈSE: (*Quietly, to* LAURENT.) For pity's sake, don't keep them here a moment longer.

MICHAUD: Goodbye, my friends. (*He is about to go.*)

GRIVET: Oh yes, goodnight, goodnight. (*He gets up and follows* MICHAUD.)

SUZANNE: (*Goes to kiss* MME RAQUIN.) Ah! Look! Her fingers are moving!

MICHAUD and GRIVET let out a shout of surprise and cross over to MME RAQUIN.

THÉRÈSE: (*Quietly to* LAURENT.) Oh God! She has made a superhuman effort. This is the punishment! (*They huddle together.*)

MICHAUD: (*To* MME RAQUIN.) Why, you are like a little girl again. Look at your fingers dancing the gavotte now.

A silence, during which MME RAQUIN *continues to move her fingers, with her eyes rooted on* THÉRÈSE *and* LAURENT.

GRIVET: Oho! We've become a proper little wanderer, haven't we, with our hands roving all over the place!

THÉRÈSE: (*Quietly.*) Great God, she is reviving – the stone statue is coming back to life.

LAURENT: (*Quietly.*) Be strong. Hands can't talk.

SUZANNE: It's as if she's making shapes on the tablecloth.

GRIVET: Yes, what is she doing?

MICHAUD: Can't you see? She is writing. That's a capital T.

THÉRÈSE: (*Quietly.*) Hands do talk, Laurent!

GRIVET: By God, it's true, she is writing. (*To* MME RAQUIN.) Take it gently and I will try to follow you. (*After a silence.*) No, start again, I lost you there. (*After another silence.*) It's incredible, I read: T.H.R.E.E.S. Threes! She undoubtedly wants me to stay for a game!

SUZANNE: No, Monsieur Grivet she has written the name of my dear friend, Thérèse.

MICHAUD: Really, Monsieur Grivet, can't you even read? (*Reading.*) 'Thérèse and.' Continue, Mme Raquin.

LAURENT: (*To* THÉRÈSE.) Revenging hand, hand once dead coming out of the coffin, each finger becoming a mouth. She shall not finish! (*He goes to take a knife from his pocket.*)

THÉRÈSE: (*Holding him back.*) For pity's sake, you will betray us!

MICHAUD: It's perfect, I understand, 'Thérèse and Laurent.' She is writing your names, my friends.

GRIVET: Both your names, upon my honour. It's incredible.

MICHAUD: (*Reading.*) 'Thérèse and Laurent have.' Have what? What do they have, these two dear children?

GRIVET: Oh! She's stopped … keep going, keep going.

MICHAUD: Finish the sentence, just a little effort …

MME RAQUIN looks at THÉRÈSE *and* LAURENT *for a long-held stare.*

Yes, we all want to know the end of the sentence.

She remains a moment motionless, enjoying the terror of the two murderers, then her hand falls.

Oh! She's let her hand drop, damn it.

SUZANNE: (*Touching the hand.*) It is stuck to her knee again like a hand of stone.

THÉRÈSE: I thought I saw our punishment. The hand is silent now. We are saved.

LAURENT: Don't fall. Lean on me. I thought I was choking.

The three gather round MME RAQUIN's *chair.*

GRIVET: It's too annoying that she didn't finish the sentence.

MICHAUD: Yes, I was following perfectly. What can she have wanted to say?

SUZANNE: That she is grateful for the care that Thérèse and Laurent heap upon her.

MICHAUD: This little one is brighter than we are. 'Thérèse and Laurent have all my blessings.' Of course, damn it, there's the finished sentence. That's right, isn't it, Mme Raquin, you are doing them justice. (*To* THÉRÈSE *and* LAURENT.) You are two courageous souls, you deserve a good reward, in this world or the next.

LAURENT: You would do as we do.

GRIVET: They are already rewarded. Do you know that in this district they are known as the turtle doves?

MICHAUD: Ah, and it was *we* who married them … Are you coming Monsieur Grivet? We must let them get on with their supper, after all. (*Coming back to* MME RAQUIN.) Have patience, old girl. Your little hands will come back to life, and your legs too. It's a good sign to have been able to move your fingers just a little; your recovery is near at hand. Goodbye. (*He leaves.*)

SUZANNE: (*To* THÉRÈSE.) Till tomorrow, good friend. (*She leaves.*)

GRIVET: (*To* MME RAQUIN.) There, I said we understood each other perfectly. Take courage, we will start up our Thursday dominoes again, and we will beat Monsieur Michaud between the two of us; yes, we will thrash him. (*On his way out, to* THÉRÈSE *and* LAURENT.) Goodbye, turtle doves, you are two turtle doves.

As MICHAUD, SUZANNE *and* GRIVET *leave by the spiral staircase,* THÉRÈSE *goes out of the upstage door and returns with the soup.*

Scene 6

THÉRÈSE, LAURENT, MME RAQUIN

During this scene, MME RAQUIN's *face reflects the emotions that she is feeling: anger, horror, and joy, total revenge. Her burning eyes hound the murderers, sharing their outbursts and sobs.*

LAURENT: She would have given us up.

THÉRÈSE: Shut up, leave her alone. (*She serves the soup.*)

LAURENT: (*Sitting at the table upstage.*) Do you think she would spare us if she could speak? Michaud and Grivet had a peculiar smile on their faces when they were talking about our happiness. They'll end up knowing everything, you'll see. Grivet put his hat on to one side, didn't he?

THÉRÈSE: (*Putting down the soup tureen.*) Yes, I believe so.

LAURENT: He buttoned his frock-coat and he put a hand into his pocket on his way out. At the office he always used to button his frock-coat like that when he wanted to look important. And the way he said, 'Goodbye, turtle doves.' The imbecile.

THÉRÈSE: (*Coming back.*) Be quiet; don't make it worse than it already is.

LAURENT: When he twists his mouth in that stupid manner, you know, it must be to laugh at us. I don't trust these people who play the fool … They know everything, I assure you.

THÉRÈSE: They are too innocent … It would be one end, if they gave us up; but they see nothing, they will continue to traipse through our pitiful lives with their oblivious bourgeois tread. (*She sits at the table.*) Let us talk about something else. You must be mad to raise the subject when she is still here.

LAURENT: I haven't got a spoon.

THÉRÈSE goes and fetches a spoon from the sideboard, gives it to LAURENT and sits.

Are you not going to feed her?

THÉRÈSE: Yes, when I've finished my soup.

LAURENT: (*Tasting the soup.*) Your soup is dreadful, it's too salty. (*He pushes it away.*) It's one of your wicked tricks. You know I hate salt.

THÉRÈSE: Laurent, please don't pick an argument with me. I am very tired. The tension just now has left me shattered.

LAURENT: Yes, make yourself listless … you torture me with your petty annoyances.

THÉRÈSE: You want us to have a quarrel, don't you?

LAURENT: I 'want' you to stop talking to me in that tone of voice.

THÉRÈSE: Oh really! (*In a rough voice, pushing away her plate.*) Very well, just as you please, we will not eat any more this evening, we will tear each other apart, and my aunt can listen. It's a treat we give her every day now.

LAURENT: Do you calculate the blows you give me? Why, you spy on me, you try to touch my open wounds and then you are happy when the pain drives me mad.

THÉRÈSE: It wasn't me who found the soup too salty! Here we go! The most ridiculous pretext is enough, isn't it! You just want to argue all evening, to dull your nerves so that you can sleep a little during the night.

LAURENT: You don't sleep any more than I do.

THÉRÈSE: Oh, you have made my whole existence appalling. As soon as night falls, we begin to shake. You know who is there, between us. Oh, what torture it is in this room!

LAURENT: It's your fault.

THÉRÈSE: My fault! Is it my fault if, instead of the rich life you dreamt of, all you have created is fear and disgust?

LAURENT: Yes, it's your fault.

THÉRÈSE: Stop it! I am not an idiot! Don't think I don't know you. You've always been a calculating thing. When you took me as your mistress, it was because I didn't cost anything … You don't even dare deny it … Oh, don't you see, I hate you!

LAURENT: Who's looking for a quarrel now, me or you?

THÉRÈSE: I hate you. You killed Camille!

LAURENT: (*Gets up and sits down again.*) Be quiet! (*Pointing to MME RAQUIN.*) A moment ago, you told me to be silent in front of her. Do not force me to recall the facts, to tell the truth all over again in her presence.

THÉRÈSE: Oh, let her hear, let her suffer! Haven't I suffered? The *truth* is that you killed Camille.

LAURENT: You're lying, admit that you are lying … If I threw him into the river, it was because you pushed me into the murder.

THÉRÈSE: Me? Me?

LAURENT: Yes, you. Don't play the innocent, don't make me drag it from you by force … I need you to confess to your crime, I need you to accept your share of the guilt. That gives me relief and calms me.

THÉRÈSE: But it wasn't I who killed Camille.

LAURENT: Yes it was, a thousand times yes! You were on the bank, and I said to you quietly, 'I am going to throw him into the river.' You consented, you got into the boat … You see very well that you killed him with me.

THÉRÈSE: That's not true … I was mad, I don't know what I did any more. I never wanted to kill him.

LAURENT: And, in the middle of the Seine, when I capsized the boat, didn't I warn you? You grabbed onto my neck. You left him to drown *like a dog*.

THÉRÈSE: It is not true, you killed him!

LAURENT: And, in the cab on the way back, didn't you put your hand into mine? Your hand fired my heart.

THÉRÈSE: *You* killed him.

LAURENT: (*To MME RAQUIN.*) She doesn't remember. She's deliberately not remembering. (*To THÉRÈSE.*) You intoxicated me with your caresses, here, in this room. You pushed me against your husband, you wanted to get rid of him. He didn't please you, he used to shiver with fever, you said. Three years ago was I like this? Was I a wretch then? I used to be an upright gentleman, I didn't do any harm to anyone … I wouldn't have even crushed a fly.

THÉRÈSE: *You* killed him!

LAURENT: Twice you turned me into a cruel brute … I used to be prudent and peaceful. And look at me now, I tremble at the least shadow like an easily frightened child. My nerves are just as wretched as yours. You have led me to adultery, to murder, without my even noticing. Now when I look back, I remain stupefied by what I have done. In my dreams I see policemen, the court, the guillotine, pass before my eyes. (*He rises.*) You play the innocent in vain – at night your teeth chatter with terror. You know very well that if the ghost were to come, he would strangle you first.

THÉRÈSE: (*Getting up.*) Don't say that. You killed him. (*Both standing at the table.*)

LAURENT: Listen, it is cowardly to refuse your share of the crime. You want to make my guilt the heavier, don't you? Since you push me to the edge, I prefer to make an end of it. You see, I am quite calm. (*He takes his hat.*) I am going to tell the whole story to the Police Superintendent for the area.

THÉRÈSE: (*Jeering.*) What a good idea!

LAURENT: We will *both* be arrested, we will soon see what the judge thinks of your innocence.

THÉRÈSE: Do you think you can scare me? I am more weary than you. I am the one who will go to the magistrate, if you don't.

LAURENT: I don't need you to accompany me – I will be able to tell them everything myself.

THÉRÈSE: Oh no, every time we quarrel, when you run out of reasons, you always bring up this threat. Well, today I want it to be serious. I am not a coward, like you. I am ready to follow you to the scaffold. Come on, let's go, I'll come with you. (*She goes with him as far as the spiral staircase.*)

LAURENT: (*Stammering.*) As you wish, we'll go together to the police.

He goes down – THÉRÈSE remains immobile, listening; she is gradually seized by a fit of shaking and terror – MME RAQUIN turns her head, her face lit up by a fierce smile.

THÉRÈSE: He's gone down. He's still down there. Will he have the courage to give us up? ... I don't want that, I will run after him, grab his arm and bring him back ... And what if he shouts out the whole story in the street. Oh, my God, I was wrong to push him to the limit. I should have been more reasonable ... (*Listening.*) He's stopped in the shop, the bell hasn't rung. What can he be doing? He's coming back up, oh I can hear him coming back up the stairs. I knew he was too much of a coward. (*Suddenly.*) The coward! Coward!

LAURENT: (*Coming in, sits down. He is broken, head in his hands.*) I can't, I can't.

THÉRÈSE: (*In a mocking tone.*) Oh! Back already, are you? What did they say? Oh, how I pity you, you have no blood in your veins.

LAURENT: (*In a lower voice.*) I can't.

THÉRÈSE: You ought to be helping me to carry the terrible memory, but you are feebler than I am ... How can you ask us to forget?

LAURENT: So you accept your part of the crime now, do you?

THÉRÈSE: Yes. I am guilty. If you like, I am more guilty than you. I should have saved my husband from your clutches. Camille was so good.

LAURENT: Let's not start again, I beg you. How you revel when you have driven me frantic. Don't look at me. Stop smiling. I will escape from you when I wish to. (*He takes out a little bottle from his pocket.*) Here is the remission, here is the peaceful sleep. Two drops of prussic acid will be enough.

THÉRÈSE: Poison! Oh no, you are too cowardly. I dare you to drink it. Drink, go on, Laurent, drink just a little, to see ...

LAURENT: Be quiet. Don't push me any further.

THÉRÈSE: I am calm, you won't drink it ... Camille was good, do you hear, and I wish you were in his place in the ground.

LAURENT: Be quiet!

THÉRÈSE: Why, you don't know a woman's heart. How can you expect me not to hate you, drenched as you are in Camille's blood?

LAURENT: (*Pacing back and forth, as if hallucinating.*) Will you be quiet! I can hear something hammering in my head. It will shatter my skull ... What is this infernal game of yours, to have regrets now, to weep louder and louder? I am living with him all the time now. He did this, he did that, he was good, he was generous. Oh, misery! I am going mad ... He is living with us. He sits on my chair, he sits at the table next to me, uses our furniture. He used to eat off my plate, he's still eating off it. I don't know any more, I am him, I am Camille ... I've got his wife, I've got his place at table, I've got his sheets. I am Camille, Camille, Camille!

THÉRÈSE: It's a cruel game *you're* playing putting his face in all your paintings.

LAURENT: Oh, so you know that, do you? (*Lowering his voice.*) Talk softer, it's terrible, my hands are no longer my own. I can't even paint any more, it's always his face that takes shape under my hand. No, these hands are no longer mine. They will kill me in the end, if I don't cut them off. They are his hands, he has taken them from me.

THÉRÈSE: It's the punishment.

LAURENT: Tell me I haven't got Camille's mouth. (*He kisses her.*) Look, did you hear that? I pronounced that phrase just as Camille would have done. Listen, 'I've got his mouth. I've got his mouth.' That's it, isn't it? I talk like him, I laugh like him. He is always there, in my head, punching with his clenched fists.

THÉRÈSE: It is the punishment.

LAURENT: (*Violently.*) Go away woman, you are driving me mad. Go away, or I'll ... (*He throws her to the ground in front of the table and raises his foot.*)

THÉRÈSE: (*On the ground.*) Kill me, like the other, make an end of it all ... Camille never laid a hand on me. You, you are a monster ... But kill me, like the other!

LAURENT, demented, backs away and breaks upstage. He sits down, his head in his hands. Meanwhile, MME RAQUIN manages to push a knife off the table, which lands in front of THÉRÈSE. THÉRÈSE slowly turns her head at this noise: she looks in turn at MME RAQUIN and at the knife.

You pushed it and made it fall. Your eyes are burning like two hell-holes. I know what you are saying. You are right, this man is making my existence intolerable. If he wasn't always there, reminding me of what I long to forget, I would be peaceful, I would work out a gentle life for myself. (*To MME RAQUIN, as she picks up the knife.*) You're looking at the knife, aren't you? Yes. I am holding the knife and I don't want this man to torture me any longer

... He killed Camille, who was in his way ... He is in my
way! (*She gets up, with the knife in her fist.*)

LAURENT: (*Who gets up, hiding the bottle of poison in his hand.*)
Let us make peace, let us finish our meal, shall we?

THÉRÈSE: If you like. (*To herself.*) I will never be patient
enough to wait till night. The knife is burning my hand.

LAURENT: What are you thinking about? Sit down at the table
... Wait, I will serve you with something to drink. (*He
pours some water into a glass.*)

THÉRÈSE: Better to end it all now. (*She approaches with the knife
raised. But she sees* LAURENT *pour the poison into the glass.*)
What are you pouring into it, Laurent?

LAURENT: (*Likewise sees the knife.*) Why are you raising your
arm?

A silence.

Drop the knife!

THÉRÈSE: Drop the poison.

*They look at each other with a terrible stare: then they let the
bottle and knife drop.*

LAURENT: At the same moment, in each mind, the same
thought, the horrible thought.

THÉRÈSE: Remember how we adored each other with such
passionate kisses, Laurent? And here we are, face to face,
with poison and a knife. (*She glances towards* MME RAQUIN
and shrieks with shock.) Laurent, look!

LAURENT: (*Getting up and turning towards* MME RAQUIN *with
terror.*) She was there, waiting to watch us die!

THÉRÈSE: But can't you see her lips are moving? She is smiling
... Oh, what a terrible smile!

LAURENT: She's coming back to life.

THÉRÈSE: She's going to speak, I tell you, she's going to speak!

LAURENT: I know how to stop her. (*He goes to leap on* MME
RAQUIN *when she slowly rises to her feet. He staggers back,
reeling.*)

MME RAQUIN: (*Standing up, in a low, deep voice.*) Murderer of
the child, dare to strike the mother!

THÉRÈSE: Oh mercy! Don't hand us over to the police.

MME RAQUIN: Hand you over! No, no ... I thought of it, just
now when I regained my strength. I began to write your
act of indictment on the table. But I stopped myself; I
thought that human justice would be too quick. And I
want to watch your slow death, here in this room, where
you stole from me all my happiness.

THÉRÈSE: (*Sobbing, throwing herself at* MME RAQUIN'S *feet.*) Forgive
me ... My fears are suffocating me ... I am a miserable
wretch ... If you wish to raise your foot, I will deliver up
my head, on the floor – here, so that you can crush it ...
Pity ... have pity!

MME RAQUIN: (*Leaning on the table.*) Pity? Did you have any for
the poor child I adored? Don't ask for pity. I have no more
pity. You have torn out my heart.

LAURENT falls to his knees.

I will not save you from each other. May your remorse
make you lash out at each other like enraged beasts. I shall
not give you up to justice. You are mine, only mine, and
I am watching over you.

THÉRÈSE: It is too much not to be punished ... We will judge
each other, and we will condemn each other.

*She picks up the bottle of prussic acid, drinks greedily and falls
to the ground at* MME RAQUIN'S *feet.* LAURENT, *who has seized
the bottle, also drinks and falls.*

MME RAQUIN stands over them, watching.

MME RAQUIN: Dead. They're dead.

1.2 MISS JULIE (1888)

AUGUST STRINDBERG

In a new version by Frank McGuinness (from a literal translation by Charlotte Barslund)

August Strindberg (1849–1912) wrote Miss Julie *in 1888. It was quickly identified as one of the first plays which embraced the principles of Naturalism and showed how they could be manifested in theatre.* Miss Julie *has since become part of the canon of modernist plays, though it was originally banned or refused performances in a number of countries, including Strindberg's homeland of Sweden, where it had to wait eighteen years for its first professional production. André Antoine mounted a celebrated production of the play at the Théâtre Libre in 1893 and it was often performed and adapted for the stage in Europe and America during the twentieth century. The play raises issues of gender, sexual politics and class relevant to the emancipatory era for which it was originally written, but which have a resonance still. The version printed here is by Frank McGuinness and was commissioned for a production at Theatre Royal, Haymarket, in London in 2000, directed by Michael Boyd.*

Characters

MISS JULIE
JEAN
KRISTIN

The stage

A large kitchen whose ceilings and side walls are hidden by drapes and borders. The back wall stretches in up from stage left. On the same wall there are shelves with copper, cast-iron and pewter pots. The shelves are decorated with embossed paper. Stage right three-quarters of a large arched exit is visible with two glass doors. Through them there is a fountain with a cupid, and flowering lilac bushes and tall upright poplars can be seen. The corner and some of the hood of a large tiled stove can be seen stage left. At stage right one end of the servants' white-painted pine dinner table stands surrounded by some chairs. The stove is decorated with leafy birch twigs. The floor is strewn with juniper twigs. On the end of the table there is a large Japanese spice jar with lilacs in bloom. There is an ice-box, a draining board and a sink. Above the door there is a large, old-fashioned bell, and on its left side there is a fixed speaking tube. Frying something in a pan, Kristin stands by the stove. She wears a light-coloured cotton dress and an apron. Jean enters, dressed in livery. He carries a large pair of riding boots with spurs. He places them somewhere visible on the floor.

JEAN: Off her head. The mistress. Julie. She's off her head, tonight.

KRISTIN: So – he's here now?

JEAN: The Count – I took his Lordship to the station. I come back, I'm going past the barn, I walk into the dance. What do I see? Miss Julie, dancing with the gamekeeper. She's leading. Then she catches sight of me. She runs full into my arms. She asks me to dance. She starts to waltz – never seen the like of it. She's off her head.

KRISTIN: She always was, but she's been worse the past two weeks since her engagement's been called off.

JEAN: What was the story there? Tell me that. He might not have had money but he had standing. People like that – if it's not one thing, it's something else. (*He sits down at the end of the table.*) I for one find it strange that a lady would rather stay at home with their servants than go off with her father to see her relatives. It's Midsummer Eve.

Figure 3 The first production in Stockholm of *Miss Julie* in November 1906, at The People's Theatre.

KRISTIN: Maybe she can't face people after the bother with her fiancé.

JEAN: Maybe. But at least he was his own man. Do you know what happened, Kristin? Do you know that I saw it all – though I pretended I saw nothing.

KRISTIN: You saw it?

JEAN: I did – I certainly did. The stable yard one evening, the two of them, Miss Julie putting him through his paces, that's what she called it. Do you know what happened? She had her riding whip and she made him leap over it. Like a dog. He leapt twice, and he felt the touch of the whip from her hand. Then he let her have it across the left cheek, he smashed the whip into a thousand pieces, and departed from the scene.

KRISTIN: That's what happened, is it? No. Just as you say?

JEAN: That's it exactly. Now come on, Kristin, have you anything nice for me?

She takes something from the frying pan and sets the table for JEAN.

KRISTIN: A bit of kidney, that's all. I cut it off the roast veal.

JEAN smells the food.

JEAN: Excellent. Delicious – a great *délice.* (*He touches the plate.*) You could have warmed the plate.

KRISTIN: Listen to him – more fussy than the Count himself when he sits down to eat.

She runs her hands affectionately through his hair. He responds crossly.

JEAN: Don't touch me. I'm a sensitive man, you know that.

KRISTIN: It's only because I'm mad about you and you know that.

JEAN eats and KRISTIN opens a bottle of beer.

JEAN: Beer? On Midsummer Eve? I think not, thank you. I can do something better for myself. (*He opens a drawer and takes out a bottle of red wine with yellow sealing wax on the cork.*) Look – yellow sealing wax. A glass if you please. One with a stem – this you drink *pur.*

KRISTIN returns to the stove and puts a small pot on it.

KRISTIN: God help the one who gets him for a husband. Such a fuss he makes.

JEAN: Is that so? I'd put money on you being delighted to land a strapping man like myself. I imagine you don't lose much face when people call me your intended. (*He tastes the wine.*) Good. Very good. Temperature not quite perfect though. (*He heats the glass in his hand.*) Dijon – that's where we bought this. Without the bottle it set us back four francs a litre. There's duty on top of that. What are you cooking now? It stinks like hell.

KRISTIN: Some dirty feed Miss Julie wants for her bitch, Diana.

JEAN: Kristin, would you please express yourself in a more ladylike manner? And why are you standing here sweating for that dog on Midsummer Eve? Is she not well?

KRISTIN: She's not well. She smelt out the gamekeeper's dog. Now she has a pack of pups inside her. Miss Julie wants rid of them.

JEAN: Miss Julie gets on her high horse about one thing and doesn't give a tinker's curse about another. Just like her dead mother, the Countess. She was in her element in the kitchen and the barn, but she'd go nowhere with just the one horse. Her cuffs might need washing, but every button had to bear the coat of arms. As for Miss Julie, she does not give a damn about herself and her reputation. She was leaping about the barn at the dance and she tore the gamekeeper from Anna's arms, she wanted to dance with him. We'd never do a thing like that. That's what happens when the gentry demean themselves. That's when they fall. Still, she is a grand looking woman. Magnificent. The shoulder on her! And everything else.

KRISTIN: Take it easy, will you? I know what Klara says, and she dresses her.

JEAN: Klara be damned. You women would eat each other out of jealousy. I've been out riding with her – and the way she dances.

KRISTIN: Jean – will you dance with me when I'm finished?

JEAN: I will, of course, yes.

KRISTIN: Is that a promise?

JEAN: Promise? When I say I will, then I will. The dinner was lovely, thank you.

He puts the cork in the bottle. MISS JULIE, in the doorway, speaks offstage.

JULIE: I will soon return. Carry on – carry on.

JEAN hides the bottle in the drawer. He gets up respectfully. MISS JULIE enters and goes to KRISTIN at the stove.

JULIE: Have you finished it?

KRISTIN indicates JEAN's presence. JEAN asks gallantly:

JEAN: Are the ladies conversing in secrets?

MISS JULIE hits him in the face with her handkerchief.

JULIE: Nosy-nosy.

JEAN: The beautiful smell of violets.

MISS JULIE flirts back.

JULIE: Impudent. He knows all about perfumes too. He certainly knows how to dance. Do not peep – just go away.

JEAN replies with a mixture of cheek and respect:

JEAN: Are the ladies brewing some witch's spell especially for Midsummer Eve? Will someone be telling fortunes? Will the stars show the man you'll marry?

MISS JULIE concludes sharply:

JULIE: If you can see that, then you must have extraordinary eyesight. (*She turns to Kristin.*) Throw that in a bottle, cork it tightly. Now, Jean, come and dance with me.

JEAN is reluctant.

JEAN: I don't wish to be disrespectful, but I promised this dance to Kristin.

JULIE: She can have another, can't she? What do you say, Kristin? May I borrow Jean? Will you let me?

KRISTIN: Not for me to say. If Miss Julie lowers herself to him, he could hardly say no. Let him go. He should thank her for the honour.

JEAN: I honestly want to cause no offence, but I doubt if it's wise that Miss Julie should have the same partner twice in a row. People soon get the wrong notion in these cases –

MISS JULIE flares up:

JULIE: Cases – what is he talking about? What are these notions – explain.

JEAN is evasive.

JEAN: If Miss Julie doesn't care to follow me, then I will have to explain. It does not look well if you favour one servant above others – they might come to expect the same –

JULIE: Favour! The idea of it! I am shocked! I am mistress of this house. I honour the servants' dance with my presence. When I actually want to dance, I wish to do so with a partner who can lead. That way I do not look ridiculous.

JEAN: Miss Julie's word is my command.

MISS JULIE grows gentler.

JULIE: Not command – don't say that. We're happy tonight – celebrating – we've stripped away all the titles. Give me your arm, go on. Kristin, don't worry. I won't run away with your fiancé.

JEAN offers her his arm and escorts MISS JULIE off the stage.

PANTOMIME

This is acted as if the actress really is alone in the room. She turns her back to the audience. She doesn't look into the auditorium. There is the faint violin music of a Scottish reel. KRISTIN hums to the music as she clears up after JEAN. She washes the plate, dries it and puts it away in a cupboard. She takes off her cook's apron. She takes out a small mirror from a drawer in the table. She tilts it against the jar of lilacs. She lights a candle, heats a hairpin and curls her fringe. She goes to the door and listens. She returns again to the table. She finds MISS JULIE's handkerchief. She picks it up and smells it, spreads it out pensively, smoothes it, stretches it and folds it into four parts.

Jean enters on his own.

JEAN: Off her head – she really is. Dancing in that manner. People standing mocking her behind the doors. Well, Kristin, what do you say to that?

KRISTIN: She's not herself, it's her time of the month and then she's always strange. But what about yourself – will you dance with me now?

JEAN: I hope you're not cross because I left.

KRISTIN: I'm not. Very little to make me cross there. I do know my place.

JEAN puts his arms around her waist.

JEAN: Kristin, you're a sound girl and you'll make a sound wife.

MISS JULIE enters, is unpleasantly surprised and remarks with forced jollity:

JULIE: So you have abandoned your partner – how charming.

JEAN: Not so, Miss Julie. I've run back to the one I left behind.

MISS JULIE paces the floor.

JULIE: No one dances as well as you do, do you know that? Why are you wearing your uniform on Midsummer Eve? Take if off immediately.

JEAN: Then I must ask you, Mam, to excuse yourself – my black coat is hanging over there.

JULIE: Is he shy in front of me? Too shy to change a jacket? Run into your room and then toddle back. No, maybe you should stay and I won't peep.

JEAN: Whatever you wish, my lady.

He exits the stage right.

His arm is visible as he changes his jacket.

JULIE: Jean is so casual with you – is he really your fiancé?

KRISTIN: Fiancé? He is my intended, if you like. That's what we call it.

JULIE: Call it?

KRISTIN: Well, Miss Julie, yourself, had a fiancé and –

JULIE: That's true, but we were properly engaged –

KRISTIN: So properly the engagement ended.

JEAN enters wearing a black coat and black hat.

JULIE: *Très gentil, monsieur Jean, très gentil – très gentil.*

JEAN: *Vous voulez plaisanter, Madame.*

JULIE: *Et vous voulez parler français.* Where did you learn it?

JEAN: Switzerland. I was *sommelier* in one of the biggest hotels at Lucerne.

JULIE: In those clothes you look so like a gentleman. *Charmant.* (*She sits down at the table.*)

JEAN: You're flattering me.

MISS JULIE is hurt.

JULIE: I'm flattering you?

JEAN: I'm modest by nature. That modesty prevents me from imagining that you would utter truthful compliments to one in my position, so I must take the liberty of assuming that you have exaggerated – you have indulged in flattery.

JULIE: Where did you learn such phraseology? You must have gone to the theatre often.

JEAN: I have indeed. I have been in many theatres – I have.

JULIE: Weren't you born here on the estate?

JEAN: My father worked as a labourer on the next-door estate – the Attorney's. I used to see Miss Julie when she was a child, but Miss Julie did not notice me.

JULIE: No – is that so?

JEAN: Yes, that's so, I remember very clearly once – no, I can't speak about that.

JULIE: You can, you can, just for me. Make one exception.

JEAN: I can't really. Perhaps another time.

JULIE: Another time may never arrive. What's the danger in telling me now?

JEAN: No danger – I just don't want to. Look at that one.

He points to KRISTIN who has fallen asleep in a chair by the stove.

JULIE: That one will make the most divine wife – she will. Does she snore as well, perhaps?

JEAN: She doesn't – she does talk in her sleep though.

MISS JULIE asks cynically:

JULIE: She talks in her sleep – how do you know?

He replies cheekily:

JEAN: I've heard her.

There is a pause and they watch each other.

JULIE: Sit down – won't you?

JEAN: In your presence I am now allowed to sit?

JULIE: If I command you?

JEAN: I'll obey.

JULIE: Sit down – no, wait. Fetch me something to drink first.

JEAN: I don't know if we have anything cold. Beer – that's all – I think.

JULIE: That's all right. I have simple tastes. Beer suits me more than wine.

He takes a bottle of beer from the ice-box. He looks in the cupboard for a glass and plate. He serves her.

Thank you. Have one yourself – go on.

JEAN: I'm not a beer man. But if Miss Julie commands –

JULIE: Commands? My good sir, I believe it is manners to keep your lady company.

JEAN: That is absolutely true. (*He opens another bottle and takes a glass.*)

JULIE: Now – drink a toast to me.

He hesitates.

I do believe the poor boy is shy.

On his knees, parodying, he raises his glass.

JEAN: Oh mistress mine!

JULIE: Bravo! Kiss my shoe – now – you have to – then it is finished.

He hesitates, but then grasps her foot gamely and kisses it lightly.

Excellent. You should have been an actor.

He gets up.

JEAN: This is not right, Miss Julie. What if someone came in and saw us –

JULIE: What if?

JEAN: People gossip. That's what if. If Miss Julie knew how their tongues were wagging up there just now –

JULIE: What were they saying? Talking about me? Sit down.

He sits down.

JEAN: I don't want to insult you – there were statements made that cast aspersions of the kind that – you know yourself. You're not a child. They see a lady on her own drinking at night with a man, even a servant, then –

JULIE: What then? Anyway, we're not on our own. Kristin, she's here.

JEAN: She's dead to the world.

She rises.

JULIE: Kristin? Are you sleeping?

KRISTIN mumbles in her sleep.

Kristin? She has a gift for this. Sleeping.

KRISTIN mutters in her sleep.

KRISTIN: Boots – polish the Count's – coffee – hurry – make coffee – hurry.

MISS JULIE grabs KRISTIN's nose.

JULIE: Wake up.

JEAN answers her sternly:

JEAN: Don't disturb her sleep.

MISS JULIE reacts sharply:

JULIE: What?

JEAN: A woman slaving over a stove all day has the right to be tired at night-time. You should respect the sleep –

MISS JULIE is pacing the floor.

JULIE: A beautiful thought – it does him great credit. Thank you. (*She offers him her hand.*) Now gather some lilacs with me.

JEAN: With Miss Julie?

JULIE: Me!

JEAN: That is not right. Absolutely not.

JULIE: I don't follow your way of thinking. Have you imagined something and you believe it?

JEAN: I don't, but the servants will –

JULIE: Believe I'm in love with a servant?

JEAN: I'm not an arrogant man, but there have been cases, and the servants will say anything. Nothing is sacred.

JULIE: I do believe the man's an aristocrat.

JEAN: I am. Yes.

JULIE: I demean myself –

JEAN: Miss Julie, don't demean yourself. Listen to me. Not a living soul will believe you did it by choice. People will swear that you fell.

JULIE: I think more of people than you do. Go on – come on. (*She looks at him pleadingly.*)

JEAN: You're a strange being – do you know that?

JULIE: Am I? Are you? Yes. Everything is strange. Life itself. All of us. Everything. A mess, tossing and turning across the water and then it sinks – it sinks. I'm suddenly thinking of a dream I always have. I'm on top of a pillar. I've climbed up here, and I see no way of getting down, but I do not have the courage to throw myself. I want so much to fall, but I don't fall, and I'll have no peace until I come down, no rest until down I come, down to the field. And when I reach the field, I want to walk into the earth. Have you ever felt anything like that?

JEAN: No. When I dream, I'm lying beneath a big tree in a deep forest. I want to get up, right up to the top, I want to be able to see where the sun shines bright over the whole countryside. I want to rob the bird's nest and steal the golden eggs. I climb and I climb, but the tree trunk is thick, it's slippery, and the first branch is so far away. I do know that if I could only reach that first branch, then I could climb to the top – like stepping up a ladder. I've not reached it yet, I can't, but I will, even if I'm only dreaming.

JULIE: I'm standing talking to you about dreams – come on. To the fields.

She offers him her arm and they move to go.

JEAN: If we step on top of nine flowers tonight, Miss Julie, then our dreams will come true this Midsummer Night.

They go to the doorway. JEAN puts one hand up to his eye.

JULIE: What have you got in your eye? Let me see.

JEAN: Nothing. Just dirt. It'll pass.

JULIE: My dress – the sleeve has scratched you. Sit down, I'll help you.

She takes his arm and sits him down. She clasps his head and pulls it backwards. With the corner of her handkerchief she tries to clean his eye.

Sit still. Absolutely still. (*She slaps his hand.*) Do as I tell you. Now – now – a big strong boy – (*She feels his upper arm.*) Such strength.

JEAN warns her:

JEAN: Miss Julie –

KRISTIN wakes up and walks sleepily offstage right to lie down.

JULIE: Yes, monsieur Jean.

JEAN: *Attention. Je ne suis qu'un homme.*

JULIE: Sit still. Listen to me. Say thank you, kiss my hand.

JEAN: Miss Julie, listen to me. Kristin has gone to lie down. Listen to me – will you?

JULIE: First kiss my hand.

JEAN: Listen to me.

JULIE: First kiss my hand.

JEAN: Yes, but on your own head be it.

JULIE: Be what?

JEAN: You're twenty-five – are you still a child? Do you not know you can be burnt playing with fire?

JULIE: Not me – I'm insured.

JEAN: You are not – no. Even if you are, there is still dangerous fire around here.

JULIE: Are you referring to yourself?

JEAN: I am. I am a young man –

JULIE: Of beautiful appearance. What arrogance. Beyond belief. You are Don Juan, perhaps. Or Joseph. My God, I believe he is a Joseph.

JEAN: You believe that.

JULIE: I'm half frightened.

JEAN tries to put his arms around her and kiss her. She slaps him across the face.

JULIE: No.

JEAN: Are you playing or are you serious?

JULIE: Serious.

JEAN: You always are – even when you're playing. That's what's dangerous. Now I'm tired of playing. Give me permission to return to my work. The Count will need his boots on time, and it's well after midnight.

JULIE: Put the boots away.

JEAN: No. That's my job – I do it well, that's my duty. I've never imagined myself as your playmate, I never will be, I think too much of myself to be that.

JULIE: Proud, aren't you?

JEAN: Sometimes I am, other times I'm not.

JULIE: Have you ever known love?

JEAN: We don't say that word. There's been girls I like. One time I couldn't get the girl I wanted, and I was sick. I couldn't eat, I couldn't drink for love, just like the princes in the Arabian Nights.

JULIE: Who was she?

JEAN is silent.

Who was she?

JEAN: You can't make me tell you that.

JULIE: If I ask you as a friend – an equal – who was she?

JEAN: You.

MISS JULIE sits down.

JULIE: How entertaining.

JEAN: If you like, yes. Ridiculous. That was the story I couldn't tell you before. I will now. Do you know what the world looks like from down here – no, you don't. You're like the hawk and the falcon. They fly so high above you rarely see their backs. I lived in a hovel on the estate. Seven brothers and sisters – a pig as well – in a dirty field where there wasn't a tree growing. From the window though, I could see the wall around the Count's park, and the orchard of apples rising above it. It was the Garden of Eden. And standing guard there were multitudes of evil angels with their swords on fire. But still I was like the other lads – I discovered the way to the tree of life – you despise me now –

JULIE: Do I? All boys thieve apples.

JEAN: You say that now, but you still despise me. It doesn't matter. I went with my mother one day into the vegetable garden to weed the onion beds. There was a Turkish pavilion beside the garden. Jasmine trees shaded it, the honeysuckle drowned it. I didn't know what it was for but I'd never set eyes before on such a beautiful building. People went in and out again, and one day the door was left open. I sneaked in, I saw the wall covered with pictures, kings and emperors. Red curtains with tassels covered the windows. Do you know where I was now – you do – I – (*He picks a lilac flower and holds it under MISS JULIE's nose.*) I'd never been inside a big house – never seen anything but the church, but this was more lovely. No matter where my thoughts wandered, they always came back to – that. Bit by bit the desire was eating me that one day I would enjoy the pleasure of –. *Enfin*, I did sneak in, I saw and wondered. Then somebody came in, into the beautiful pavilion. There was one exit for the gentry out of there. For my kind there was another. I had to climb through that stinking pit – no choice in it.

MISS JULIE has taken the lilac and let it drop on to the table.

I leapt out and I ran through the raspberries, all across the strawberries and I finished up on the rose terrace. I could see a pink dress there – a pair of white stockings.

It was you. I crawled under a pile of weeds. Imagine me hiding under thistles prickling me, all damp and soiled and stinking. I watched you walk among the roses. I thought that if it's true a thief can get into Heaven and live among the angels, then it's strange that the child of a man who labours on God's earth can't enter the park and play with the Count's daughter.

MISS JULIE asks painfully:

JULIE: Wouldn't all poor children think the same thing as you did if they were where you were?

JEAN hesitates at first, then is convinced.

JEAN: All poor – they would – yes – of course.

JULIE: Poverty must be awful.

In deep pain, JEAN is very moved.

JEAN: Miss Julie – Miss Julie. A dog might lie on the Countess's sofa, a lady's hand might caress a horse's nose, but a poor child – (*He walks.*) A man might pull himself up by his own boot laces, if he has it in him. So they say, but how often does that happen? So, do you know what I did? I waded into the stream with my clothes on. Hauled out and beaten blue. The next Sunday, my father and the rest of the house had gone off to my grandmother's, I arranged that I could stay at home. I washed myself with warm water and soap. I donned my Sunday best and went to church where I would see you. I did see you and I went home wanting to die – going to die. I wanted to do it beautifully – in complete comfort, with no pain. I remembered then it was dangerous to sleep under an elder bush. We had one which was just bursting into bloom. I ripped all its flowers from it and I made a bed in the oat bin. Oats are so smooth – have you noticed? They touch like skin, human soft – anyway, I slammed the lid shut and nodded off. I fell asleep and woke up a very sick boy. But as you can see, I did not die. What was I doing? Don't ask me. I had no hope of winning. You were a sign that I should abandon hope of ever rising from the class I was born into.

JULIE: You know, you have a charming way with words. Did you go to school?

JEAN: A short while. I have read a lot of novels and I've gone to the theatre. I've heard the gentry talking as well – that's where I learned the most.

JULIE: You stand there listening to us speak, do you?

JEAN: I do. And I've heard plenty, let me tell you, when I'm sitting on the coachman's seat or rowing the boat. I once heard Miss Julie and a lady friend –

JULIE: Did you – what did you hear?

JEAN: That would be telling, wouldn't it? I did raise my eyebrows a little – where did you learn those words? That I couldn't understand. Maybe deep down there is not such a difference between us all as people think.

JULIE: How dare you. We don't behave the way you do when we're engaged.

JEAN fixes her with his eyes.

JEAN: You're sure? Miss Julie, please don't act the innocent –

JULIE: I gave my love to a good-for-nothing.

JEAN: Women always say that – afterwards.

JULIE: Always?

JEAN: I'd say always. I've heard it said so many times in so many different cases.

JULIE: What cases?

JEAN: This one for instance. The last time –

JULIE: Stop. I don't want to hear any more.

JEAN: She didn't either. Very strange. So I ask your permission to go to bed.

She answers softly:

JULIE: Go to bed? On Midsummer Eve?

JEAN: Yes. I'm not in the mood for leaping about with the herd up there.

JULIE: Get the key to the boat and row me out on the lake. I want to see the sun rise.

JEAN: Is that wise?

JULIE: Are you worried about my reputation?

JEAN: Why shouldn't I be? I'd prefer not to be taken for a fool. I'd prefer not to be sacked without a reference now that I'm starting to stand on my own two feet. And I think I have a certain obligation to Kristin.

JULIE: I understand – it's Kristin now –

JEAN: It's you as well. Take my advice, go upstairs and go to bed.

JULIE: Am I to do as you command?

JEAN: Yes, for once – for your own sake. I'm begging you. Night's falling. Tiredness is like drink, it makes your head light. Go to bed. If I'm not mistaken, I can hear people coming to look for me. If they find the two of us, you have had it.

The crowd's voices are heard singing.

VOICES:
A lady she walked by the shore
She was wanting to wash her feet
She was looking for sailors and more
And a handsome young man she did meet

Will you lie down with me on the sand
And I'll take you from here to Peru
I'll kiss more than your lily white hand
I'll leave your dainty cheek black and blue

The lady she laid on her back
Her petticoats sheets in the wind
The bucko he emptied his sack
And they called it original sin

Will you lie down with me on the sand

And I'll take you from here to Peru
I'll kiss more than your lily white hand
I'll leave your dainty cheek black and blue

A lady she walked by the shore
She was wanting to wash her feet
She was looking for sailors and more
And a handsome young man she did meet

JULIE: I know my servants. I love them the way they love me. You'll see. Let them come.

JEAN: They do not love you, Miss Julie. They eat your food, and afterwards they spit at you. Believe me. Listen to them. Listen to the words they are singing. No, don't listen.

She listens.

JULIE: What are they singing?

JEAN: A dirty song. About you and me.

JULIE: Damn them – they're filth –

JEAN: A pack of cowards. When you're in that kind of fight, you can only run –

JULIE: Run where? We can't get out. We can't go in to Kristin.

JEAN: We can't. My room? We have to. And you can trust me. I am your friend – a genuine friend.

JULIE: What if – what if they look in there?

JEAN: I'll bolt the door. If they break it down, I'll shoot. Come on. (*He gets on his knees.*) Come on.

MISS JULIE asks urgently:

JULIE: Promise me –

JEAN: I swear.

DANCE

Peasants enter in their best clothes, with flowers in their hats, led by a fiddler. A keg of beer and a bottle of schnapps, decorated with leaves, are placed on the table. Glasses are found. They drink. They form a circle and dance, singing 'A Lady She Walked by the Shore'. When this is over, they exit, singing. MISS JULIE enters on her own. She sees the mess in the kitchen and clasps her hands. She takes a powder puff and powders her face. JEAN enters, excited.

JEAN: You saw that – you heard it. Do you think we can stay here?

JULIE: We can't, no. What are we going to do?

JEAN: Leave, go abroad, far away.

JULIE: Go abroad? All right – where?

JEAN: Switzerland, or the Italian Lakes – you've never been there?

JULIE: No. Is it beautiful there?

JEAN: The summer lasts for ever. Orange trees and laurels.

JULIE: How will we live there?

JEAN: I'll open a hotel – first-class service, first-class guests.

JULIE: A hotel?

JEAN: Believe me, that's the way to live. New people all the time, new language. There's no such thing as an idle minute to complain or to worry. Always something to do – endless work. The bell rings night and day. The train whistles. The carriage coming and going. And the gold piles in. That's the life.

JULIE: Yes, that's living. And me –

JEAN: The mistress of the house. The hotel's pride and joy. You have looks, you have style – it has to be a success, it's bound to. Mighty. You'll rule like a queen behind the counter – you'll press an electric bell and the slaves will come running. The guests file past your throne and lay their gifts upon your table – you'll terrify them. You won't believe how it puts the wind up people to be presented with a bill. I'll salt the bills and you'll sugar them with your sweetest smile. We'll get away from this place. (*He takes a timetable from his pocket.*) The next train, now. We'll hit Malmö by six-thirty, Hamburg tomorrow morning, eight-forty. Frankfurt – Basle – a day later through the St Gothard Pass into Como, let me see, in three days. Three days.

JULIE: This is all grand, but Jean, give me courage – you must. Tell me you love me. Put your arms about me.

He hesitates.

JEAN: I want to – but I daren't. Not in this house again. I have no doubt – I love you – can you doubt that, Miss Julie?

She answers shyly, very womanly:

JULIE: Julie. Call me Julie. We're equals now. Julie.

He is tormented.

JEAN: I can't. We are not equals as long as we're standing in this house. The past is between us, there's the Count. I respect him more than any other I've ever met. If I see his gloves lying on a chair it's enough to make me a small child. If I hear the bell ringing I leap like a frightened horse. I can see him, boots standing there, so straight and proud, and I can feel my back bending. (*He kicks the boots.*) Old woman's talk – bigotry – we drank it in our mother's milk and it's as easy to spew out. We'll go to another country – a republic – they will grovel before me in my servant's uniform. They can grovel, I won't. I wasn't born to do that. I have something in me. I have a man's nature. If I can only grab that first branch, then watch me climb. I might be a servant today, but next year I'll own a hotel. In ten years' time I'll be living off my money. I'll travel then to Romania and get myself a decoration. I may – note that I say may – just end up a Count.

JULIE: Good, excellent.

JEAN: In Romania you can buy a Count's title and then I'll make you a Countess after all. My Countess.

JULIE: I'm leaving all that behind me. I care nothing about that. Say you love me. If you don't – yes, if you don't – what am I?

JEAN: I'll say it till it's coming out your ears – just wait – but not here, not here. Above all else show no feelings in this place, or we'll be lost. We have to look at things with a cold eye. Behave like logical people.

He takes out a cigar, cuts it and lights it.

You sit there – I'll sit here – we'll talk as if nothing happened.

JULIE: God almighty, have you no feelings?

JEAN: Feelings? I am the most passionate man, but I can control myself.

JULIE: You kissed my shoe a minute ago – and now –

JEAN: That was then – now we've other things to talk about.

JULIE: Don't speak so roughly to me.

JEAN: I'm speaking wisely. We've made one foolish mistake, we're not making another. The Count could walk in at any minute and before that happens we have to decide what's to be our destiny. What do you make of my plans for our future – do you approve?

JULIE: They seem sensible enough, but I do have one question. Such a big undertaking is going to need a lot of capital. Do you have any?

He chews on his cigar.

JEAN: Me? I certainly do. I'm an expert in my field, I have enormous experience. I'm fluent in many languages. That's what I call capital.

JULIE: But it won't buy you a railway ticket.

JEAN: Very true – that's why I'm looking for a partner who can provide the funds.

JULIE: Where are you going to find one at such short notice?

JEAN: That's your job if you want to come with me.

JULIE: I can't do that, I own nothing myself.

There is a pause.

JEAN: Then that's that –

JULIE: So.

JEAN: Things stay as they are.

JULIE: Do you think I'll live in this house as your whore? Do you think I'll let people point the finger at me? Do you think I can look my father in the face after this? No. Get me away from this place. I am humiliated – I am disgraced. Christ, what have I done – Christ – (*She sobs.*)

JEAN: Please don't start on that same old song. What have you done? The same as many have done before you.

She screams convulsively.

JULIE: You take me now. I've fallen – I'm falling –

JEAN: Fall down to my level and I'll lift you up again.

JULIE: What power drove me to you? The terror of the weak before the strong? As I fall, you rise – is that it? Or was it love? Is this love? Do you know what love is?

JEAN: I'd say I do, yes. Do you think I've not done it before?

JULIE: The way you speak and the way you think –

JEAN: It's what I learned, it's what I'm like. Don't act the lady – we're two peas in the pod now. That's right, girl, come on and I'll feed you a drink. (*He opens the drawer in the table and takes out the wine bottle. He fills up two used wine glasses.*)

JULIE: That wine – where did you get it?

JEAN: The cellar.

JULIE: My father's burgundy.

JEAN: Isn't it good enough for his son-in-law?

JULIE: And I was drinking beer – me –

JEAN: Just goes to show you have poorer taste than myself.

JULIE: Thief.

JEAN: Are you going to tell Daddy?

JULIE: Jesus, have I been aiding and abetting a thief? Have I been drunk or dreaming this Midsummer Night? A night of innocent games –

JEAN: Innocent my arse.

She paces up and down the room.

JULIE: Am I the most unfortunate alive on this earth?

JEAN: Why are you unfortunate? Look what you've won. Think of Kristin in there. Maybe you don't believe she has feelings as well.

JULIE: I did think so once. Not now. A servant is a servant –

JEAN: And a whore is a whore.

She is on her knees with her hands clasped.

JULIE: God above, end my life. Save me from the filth I've fallen into. Save me – please.

JEAN: I must admit I am sorry for you. When I was hiding in the onion beds watching you in the rose garden you must know I was entertaining the same dirty thoughts every other boy thinks.

JULIE: You said you would die for me.

JEAN: In the oat bin? Talking rubbish.

JULIE: You were lying?

Jean begins to grow sleepy.

JEAN: I suppose I was. I think I read the story in some newspaper – a chimney sweep lay down in a box of lilacs – he'd been ordered to pay child maintenance –

JULIE: And that's your like, is it?

JEAN: I had to think of something. Women fall for fancy stories.

JULIE: Pig.

JEAN: *Merde.*

JULIE: Now you've seen the hawk on its back –

JEAN: Not quite on its back –

JULIE: And I was to be the first branch –

JEAN: But the branch was rotten –

JULIE: I was to be the sign above the hotel –

JEAN: And I was to be the hotel –

JULIE: Trapped behind your counter, tempting the guests, cheating on the bills –

JEAN: I would do that myself –

JULIE: Could a human being sink so low in the dirt?

JEAN: Then clean it.

JULIE: Servant – lackey – get to your feet when I speak.

JEAN: Servant's whore – lackey's lick – shut up and get out. You stand here telling me that I'm filth? None of my kind has acted the filthy way you did tonight. Do you think any serving girl would throw herself at a man the way you did? Have you ever seen a girl from my class hand herself over like that? I've seen it with animals, I've seen it with whores. Oh, I know your class lets it happen. What do they call it? Being liberated. Emancipated – something fancy like that. Yes, I've seen great ladies wag their arses at soldiers and waiters.

She is crushed.

JULIE: That's right. Hit me. Walk on me. I deserve no better. I'm an unfortunate woman – so help me. Show me how to get out of this if you know a way.

He speaks more gently.

JEAN: I won't deny my share in the honour of seducing you – that would be shaming myself. But do you really believe a man in my position would have dared to look at you unless you offered the invitation yourself? I am still amazed –

JULIE: And are you proud of it –

JEAN: Why should I not be? I do admit though that I won too easily to give me complete pleasure.

JULIE: Go on – hit me again.

He gets up.

JEAN: No – forgive what I have just said. I wouldn't hit a defenceless man, let alone a woman. Yes, it's good to learn that you blinded us beneath you with fool's gold – the hawk's back was not too fine, the porcelain cheeks were powdered and the elegant nails had black beneath them. The handkerchief may smell of perfume but it's soiled. Still, it hurts me to know that what I wanted amounted to so little, so very, very little. It hurts me to see you fall so low that you're far beneath your cook. It hurts me the way flowers in the harvest are washed away by the rain and churned into dirt.

JULIE: You're talking as if you're already looking down on me.

JEAN: I do – I do. You see, I could make you a Countess, but you can never turn me into a Count.

JULIE: But I'm still the child of a Count, and you can never be that.

JEAN: True, but I could father Counts if –

JULIE: You thieve – I don't.

JEAN: Thieving's not that bad. There's worse you could learn to do. By the way, as a servant of this establishment I count myself to some extent a part of the family. A child of the house, you might say. It's not really thieving when the child grabs a berry from the branches that are full.

(*His passion is aroused once more.*) Miss Julie, you are an extraordinary woman. Far too good for my like. You were drunk, you made a mistake, and you want to cover that up by believing that you're in love with me. You are not – maybe you fancy my fine features – and so your love's no better than mine. Me though, I'd hate to be your animal, and I can never win your heart.

JULIE: Are you sure about that?

JEAN: You're going to say that I can. I should be able to love you absolutely. You are beautiful, and wealthy – (*He moves closer to her and takes her hand.*) Clever, kind when you choose to be, and when you have a man on fire, those flames will never die.

He puts his arms around her waist.

You're a strong wine – warm – the smell is powerful – and to kiss you –

He attempts to lead her offstage, but she quickly frees herself.

JULIE: Get your hands off me. You won't win me like that – no.

JEAN: How then? No sweet nothings – not like that – no caresses? Not by planning the future, saving you from disgrace – how do I win you?

JULIE: How? I don't know how. I do not know. I hate you the way I hate a rat, but I can't get away from you.

JEAN: Escape with me.

She straightens up.

JULIE: Escape – we'll escape, yes. I am tired out. Get me a glass of wine.

JEAN pours the wine.
MISS JULIE looks at her watch.

JULIE: We have to talk first – we have a bit of time – (*She empties her glass and holds it out for more.*)

JEAN: Stop drinking so much – you'll get drunk.

JULIE: Who cares?

JEAN: Who cares? It's bad manners to get drunk. What were you going to say to me?

JULIE: We must escape. But first of all we need to talk – I mean I need to talk. So far you've done all the talking. You've told me about your life. I want to tell you now about mine. Before we begin our journey, we have to know each other completely.

JEAN: Hold on. Make sure you won't regret spilling out your life's secrets.

JULIE: Are you not my friend?

JEAN: Sometimes I am, but don't count on me.

JULIE: You don't mean that. Anyway, my secrets are everybody's business. My mother had no noble blood. She came from very ordinary stock. She was reared in the ideas of her time – woman's emancipation, equality, all that sort of thing. And she loathed marriage. When my

father proposed, she said she could never be his wife, but he could be her lover. He told her he didn't wish the woman he loved to receive less respect than he himself would. She told him that such things meant nothing to her, and being madly in love he agreed to her terms. From that day on his own kind didn't recognise him. This imprisoned him in family life, and that did not satisfy him. I was born and, as far as I can understand it, my mother did not want that. My mother wanted to rear me as a child of nature. I also had to learn everything a boy is taught. I was to become an example of how a woman could be just as good as a man. I wore boy's clothes. I was taught to tame horses, but never to milk in the barn. I had to groom and harness. I had to learn about farming – hunting – even slaughtering. It was frightening. Throughout the estate men were ordered to do women's work, and the women to do men's. So, the estate fell to ruin. We were the laughing stock of the whole neighbourhood. My father must have finally come out from under his spell. He turned against it all and everything was changed to the way he wanted it. My parents were soon married quietly. My mother took ill – I don't know from what – she hid in the garden – some nights she stayed outside. You've heard about the big fire – that came next. The house, the stable, the barn – all burned down in mysterious circumstances. It was probably an act of arson, because the catastrophe happened the day after the quarterly insurance had run out. My father had sent the renewal premium, but it was delayed – the servant carrying it was careless – and it didn't arrive on time. (*She fills the glass and drinks wine.*)

JEAN: Don't drink any more.

JULIE: Who cares? We were left with the clothes we stood in. We had to sleep in the carriages. My father had neglected most of his old friends. They had forgotten him completely. He didn't know where to get money to build the house up again. My mother remembered a friend from her youth. A brickmaker – he lived near here. My mother urged my father to borrow from this man. He did borrow and he was not allowed to pay a penny interest. That astonished him. So the house rose again from the ashes. (*She drinks again.*) Do you know who burned down the house?

JEAN: Your most exalted mother?

JULIE: Do you know who the brickmaker was?

JEAN: Your mother's lover.

JULIE: Do you know whose money it was?

JEAN: Hold on – I don't know – whose?

JULIE: My mother's.

JEAN: Then it was the Count's as well, unless they made a marriage settlement.

JULIE: There was no settlement. My mother had a small fortune. She didn't want my father to manage it. She gave it into the safe keeping of her – friend.

JEAN: And he did keep it.

JULIE: He did. My father finds this all out, but he can't take him to court, he can't pay his wife's lover back, and he can't prove that it is his wife's money. He wanted to shoot himself – they say he tried and failed. He recovered. He made my mother pay for what she had done. I loved my father, but I sided with my mother. I didn't know the ins and outs of it all. I've learned from her to hate men – she hated all men, you've heard that – I swore to her I would not be a slave to any man.

JEAN: Then you got yourself engaged to the County Attorney.

JULIE: So that he would become my slave.

JEAN: Did he not want to?

JULIE: He wanted to, but I wouldn't let him. I grew bored of him.

JEAN: I saw it – in the stableyard.

JULIE: What did you see?

JEAN: What I saw. He broke off the engagement.

JULIE: Lie. I did that. Has he claimed he did, the good-for-nothing?

JEAN: He's not that, I think. Miss Julie, you hate men.

JULIE: Yes. Always – almost. I get weak – then – Christ –

JEAN: You hate me as well?

JULIE: I hate you. I would like to put you down like an animal –

JEAN: Have the animal put down, and those who abused it get two years' hard labour, isn't that the law?

JULIE: It is.

JEAN: That law doesn't apply. No animals here. What are we going to do?

JULIE: Get away from here.

JEAN: And torment each other to death?

JULIE: No. Two days to love – eight days – as long as you can love – and then – die.

JEAN: Die? Ridiculous. It's better to open a hotel.

She is not listening to him.

JULIE: By Lake Como. The sun shines there all the time. The laurels are green at Christmas, and the oranges burn red –

JEAN: It pisses rain on Lake Como. The only oranges I saw were on fruit stalls. But it's a nice trap for tourists. There's loads of villas there for happy couples to rent. There's big profit in that. Do you know why? They lease for six months – and they leave after three weeks.

She asks naively:

JULIE: Three weeks? Why?

JEAN: They fight. But the rent still has to be paid. Then they lease it out again. That's the way it happens. There's plenty of love – even if it doesn't last too long.

JULIE: You don't want to die with me?

JEAN: I don't want to die at all. I enjoy my life, and I think suicide is sinful, it's against God who gave us life.

JULIE: You believe in God?

JEAN: Naturally I do, yes. I go to church every second Sunday. Look, I'm really tired of this – I'm off to bed.

JULIE: I see – you believe I can be tossed aside like that? Do you know when a man shames a woman he owes her a debt?

JEAN takes out his wallet and throws a silver coin on the table.

JEAN: There you go. I wouldn't be in debt to anyone.

MISS JULIE pretends not to have noticed the insult.

JULIE: Do you know what the law says –

JEAN: It's sad the law doesn't say when a woman's seduced a man, how she should be punished.

JULIE: Do you see any other escape – we go away, get married and then separate.

JEAN: And if I do not want to be part of this damaging marriage?

JULIE: Damaging?

JEAN: Most definitely. You see I come from a much better background than you do. None of my ancestors indulged in arson.

JULIE: You're sure of that?

JEAN: You can't contradict it – nobody recorded my family's history, apart from the parish. I've looked up your breeding in a book on the drawing-room table. Do you know who started your noble line? He was a miller. During the war with Denmark he let the king screw his wife. I can't boast such ancestors. I don't have a single ancestor, but I can become one myself.

JULIE: This is what I get for giving my heart to a dog – for dishonouring my family –

JEAN: Dishonour – yes, well, I told you so. You shouldn't drink because then you start talking. And really one should not talk.

JULIE: I do regret it – I really do. If you loved me at least –

JEAN: For the last time – what are you talking about? Do you want me to weep? Will I leap over your riding whip? Will I kiss you? Trick you into running away to Lake Como, stay with you for three weeks and then – what will I do then? What will you do? This is beginning to pain me. That's what happens when a man interferes in women's business. Miss Julie, I see the misery you're in. I know you're suffering, but I do not understand you. We're not like you. We don't have your sort of hatred. Love's like a game to us. When we've time off work, we play, but we don't have all night and day like you do! I think you're a sick woman, and your mother was seriously mad. Whole parishes about here have been affected by her kind of madness.

JULIE: Be gentle with me – you're talking to me now like a human being.

JEAN: You act like a human being as well. You spit on me, yet you won't let me wipe the spit dry – on you.

JULIE: Just help me, will you? What way should I go?

JEAN: In Christ's name, I wish I knew myself.

JULIE: Crazy – I've been insane – but there must surely be some way of saving myself.

JEAN: Calm – just be calm. Nobody knows a thing.

JULIE: That's not possible. Those people know – Kristin knows.

JEAN: They don't imagine anything like this happening – they couldn't.

She hesitates.

JULIE: But it could happen again.

JEAN: True.

JULIE: And what will they do?

JEAN: What will they do – I didn't think of that, have I taken leave of my senses? There's only one thing to do – get away. Now. You have to go on your own – everything's lost if I'm seen to follow you. Just get away – anywhere –

JULIE: Anywhere – on my own – I can't –

JEAN: You must. Before the Count comes back. We know what's going to happen if you stay. The harm's done. If you fall once, you fall again – you get to care less and less. That way you're found out. Just leave. Write to the Count later on. Tell him everything. But don't mention my name. He'll never ever guess that. And I don't imagine he would be too keen to know.

JULIE: Come with me and I'll go.

JEAN: Woman, are you a lunatic? Miss Julie runs off with her servant. It would be read in every newspaper the day after tomorrow. The Count could not survive that.

JULIE: How do I leave? How do I stay? Help me. I am worn out – my very bones are aching. Order me what to do. Force me to do something – I can't think anything, I can't do anything.

JEAN: Do you see now what you're cut from? Why do you give yourself such airs and walk the earth as if you owned it? All right, I'll order you. Get upstairs – get dressed. Get money together for the journey – then get downstairs.

She asks half-audibly:

JULIE: Come upstairs with me.

JEAN: To your bedroom? You're off your head again – (*He hesitates a moment.*) No – get out – now.

He takes her hand and leads her offstage. She asks as she exits:

JULIE: Jean, speak kindly to me.

JEAN: You don't give orders of kindness, you bark them. Now you know what it feels like.

On his own, JEAN heaves a sigh of relief. He sits down by the table and takes out a notebook and pencil. He calculates something out loud. This continues in dumb mime until KRISTIN enters dressed for church. She holds a shirtfront and a white tie in her hand.

KRISTIN: I've slept like a log.

JEAN: Dressed for church already, are you?

KRISTIN: I am. What about yourself? You promised to come to communion with me today.

JEAN: I did, true enough. I see you've got my Sunday best. Come on then.

He sits down. KRISTIN *starts to dress him in the shirtfront and white tie. There is a pause. He asks sleepily:*

JEAN: What's the reading for today?

KRISTIN: John the Baptist getting his head chopped off.

JEAN: That one goes on and on. Watch, you're hanging me. I could sleep for a month, I really could.

KRISTIN: Well, what has the big man been doing up all night? Look at the green face on him.

JEAN: I've been stuck here talking to Miss Julie.

KRISTIN: That lady does not know the meaning of modesty.

There is a pause.

JEAN: Kristin?

KRISTIN: What?

JEAN: Isn't it peculiar when you think of it – her –

KRISTIN: What's peculiar?

JEAN: Everything.

There is a pause. KRISTIN *looks at the half-empty glasses standing on the table.*

KRISTIN: Have you been boozing together as well?

JEAN: We have.

KRISTIN: To hell with you – it's not possible – is it?

He considers this briefly.

JEAN: Yes – it is.

KRISTIN: I don't believe it – I can't, no – oh God –

JEAN: You're not jealous of her, are you?

KRISTIN: Not of her – no. Klara or Sofi – either of them – I would have had your eyes. That's the way it is. Why – I don't know. But it's a dirty act.

JEAN: Are you in a rage against her?

KRISTIN: A rage against you. That was a rotten thing to do – really rotten. Foolish girl. I'll tell you one thing. I won't stay any longer in this house when I can no longer look up to my betters.

JEAN: Why do you have to look up to them?

KRISTIN: The smart boy here can explain that to me. Do you want to dance attendance on people who have no decency? Do you? We'll all be tarred with the same brush, I say.

JEAN: Yes, but it's comforting for us to know they're not a bit better.

KRISTIN: I take no comfort from it. If they are the dregs, there's not much point in us trying to improve ourselves. Think of the Count. Think of the suffering that man's endured in his day. Good Jesus. I will stay no longer in this house. And she did it with the likes of this boy. If it had been the County Attorney – if it had been someone from her own class –

JEAN: What then?

KRISTIN: Well, you're no better nor worse than you should be, but there are distinctions between people. No, I cannot get over this. Miss Julie so haughty, so hard on all men – who would believe she'd throw herself at any man – especially a man like this. She's the one who insisted the bitch should be put down because she ran after the gamekeeper's dog. I'm saying it out straight. I'll stay here no longer. Come the twenty-fourth of October, I'll be gone.

JEAN: What then?

KRISTIN: Then you might start looking for work seeing that we're supposed to get married. That's what then.

JEAN: So what should I look for? When I'm a married man I can't get a position like this.

KRISTIN: No, you can't. You'll have to look for a job as a caretaker or a porter in a government office. The money at the Civil Service is bad, but it's a safe job with a pension for the wife and children –

He grimaces.

JEAN: Is that so? I don't intend to die just yet for my wife and children. I must admit my ambitions were slightly higher.

KRISTIN: Oh, you have ambitions, do you? You have obligations as well. You might think of them.

JEAN: Don't preach to me about obligations. I know what I've got to do. (*He listens to what's happening offstage.*) We'll have time enough to think about that. Get yourself ready, we'll head off to church.

KRISTIN: Who's that wandering about upstairs?

JEAN: Maybe it's Klara.

KRISTIN: It wouldn't be the Count – he wouldn't have come home and no one's heard him?

JEAN is frightened.

Figure 4 Sandra Prinsoo and John Kani as Miss Julie and Jean in The Baxter Theatre Centre's 1985 production of *Miss Julie*. (Photographer: Bee Berman. Reprinted by permission of The Baxter Theatre Centre, Cape Town, South Africa.)

JEAN: The Count? No – that's not true – he would have rang for me – I know that.

KRISTIN exits.

KRISTIN: God, look down on us. I've never found myself in the likes of this before.

The sun rises. It lights the tops of the trees in the park. The light moves slowly until it falls in a slant through the windows. JEAN goes over to the door and gives MISS JULIE a sign. MISS JULIE enters dressed in travelling clothes. She carries a small bird-cage, covered with a towel. She places it on a chair.

JULIE: I'm ready now.

JEAN: Hold your tongue. Kristin is awake.

MISS JULIE is growing increasingly nervous.

JULIE: Does she suspect anything?

JEAN: Nothing – she knows nothing. Christ, the look of you.

JULIE: What? How do I look?

JEAN: You're as pale as a ghost. I'm sorry to say this – your face is filthy.

JULIE: Let me clean it then. (*She goes to the washing bowl and cleans her face and hands.*) Give me a towel. Look – the sun's rising.

JEAN: Then the demons' work is done.

JULIE: They were busy last night. Jean, listen to me. Come with me. I have the money now.

He hesitates.

JEAN: Enough money?

JULIE: Enough to make a start. Come with me – I can't travel alone today. It's Midsummer. Imagine being stuck on that train, surrounded by people. Every eye would be fixed on me. I wouldn't be able to breathe. We would have to stop at every train station when what we want to do is fly, fly. No. I can't, I can't. The memories would start. I'd remember when I was a child – the church on Midsummer Day was thick with leaves and branches. Birch twigs and lilacs. We'd feast at the happy table, friends, relations – and the afternoon in the garden, dancing, music, flowers, playing games. You can run away for the rest of your life, but the memories, they weigh you down like your luggage. They bring you remorse, they hurt your conscience.

JEAN: I will go with you. It has to be now before it's too late. I mean now, this minute.

JULIE: Get dressed then. (*She takes the bird-cage.*)

JEAN: Take no luggage. That will give the game away.

JULIE: Nothing, no. Only what we can carry and ourselves.

JEAN has taken his hat.

JEAN: What's that – what have you there?

JULIE: My greenfinch – that's all. I can't leave it behind.

JEAN: Is that so – we're bringing a bird-cage, are we? You are off your head. Let it go.

JULIE: This is all I'm taking from my own home. The one living creature that cares for me since Diana betrayed me. Don't be cruel. Let me keep it.

JEAN: I'm saying, let it go. Keep your voice down. Kristin will hear us.

JULIE: I'm not handing it to strangers – I'd rather kill it.

JEAN: Give me the bastard and I'll wring its neck.

JULIE: All right, but don't let it suffer, don't – I can't, no –

JEAN: Give me it – I can do it.

She takes the bird from the cage and kisses it.

JULIE: My tiny Serine, are you going to die and leave Mama?

JEAN: Please, no scenes. We're talking about your life, your survival. Come on, quickly.

He takes the bird from her, goes to the chopping board and takes the kitchen axe. MISS JULIE turns away.

JEAN: You wasted your time learning to shoot with a gun. Better for you to behead a few chickens. (*He chops.*) You might not faint then at the sight of a drop of blood.

She screams.

JULIE: Take my life as well – take it. That creature is innocent. You can kill it and your hands don't shake. I despise – I hate you. There is blood between us. I curse the day I set eyes on you, I curse the day I was conceived in my mother's womb.

JEAN: Your curses won't help you. Get a move on.

She approaches the chopping board as if drawn against her will.

JULIE: No – not yet – I don't want to – I can't – I need to see – ssh, there's a carriage coming up the road – (*She listens, her eyes firmly fixed all the while on the chopping board and axe.*) I can't stomach the sight of blood – that's what you think – I'm weak – am I – I'd like to see your blood, your brains smashed on the chopping block. I want to see every one of your sex swimming in a lake of blood like this one. I think I could drink out of your skull – I could wash my feet in your ripped stomach – I could roast your heart and eat. So you think I am weak. You think I love you – and blessed be your seed in my womb. You think I'll carry your child beneath my heart and my blood will nourish it – I'll give you a child and I'll take your name. Tell me, what is your name? I've never heard your surname. Have you got one? I don't suppose you do. So I'll become Mrs Doorman – or maybe Mrs Shitspreader – you are a dog who wears my collar – you are the son of a labourer – you wear my coat of arms on your buttons. I have to share you with my cook. I am my servant's rival. Dear sweet God! You think I'm a coward who wants to run away. No, I'll stay now. What will be, will be. My father will return home. He'll find his desk broke open. His money vanished. He'll ring then – on that bell there. Ring twice for his lackey. He'll send for the police. And I will tell him everything. Everything. It will be wonderful to put an end to this – if only that could be the end. His heart will break. He will die. That will be the end for each and every one of us. Quiet – we will all be at peace – eternal rest – they break the coat of arms over the coffin – the Count's line has ended. The lackey's child survives in an orphanage – he will win the praise of the gutter and end up behind bars.

JEAN: Listen to the spouting of the royal blood. Well done, Miss Julie. Bury the miller in his sack.

KRISTIN enters, dressed for church, with a hymn-book in her hand. MISS JULIE rushes towards her. She falls into her arms, as if seeking protection.

JULIE: Kristin, help me. Save me from this man.

KRISTIN is unmoved and cold.

KRISTIN: What sort of racket are you making on a Sunday morning? (*She notices the chopping board.*) Look at the state of that. What are you doing? Why are you roaring and screaming like this?

JULIE: You're a woman, Kristin, and you're my friend. Take care against that good-for-nothing.

JEAN is disconcerted.

JEAN: The ladies are engaged in conversation, so I'll go and shave.

He slips out stage right.

JULIE: You have to understand me – you have to listen –

KRISTIN: I do not understand this carry on. Where is my lady going dressed in travelling clothes? Why is Jean wearing a hat? Why is that?

JULIE: Kristin, listen to me, I'll tell you everything, listen –

KRISTIN: I want to know nothing –

JULIE: Listen – you have to listen –

KRISTIN: About what? This silly nonsense with Jean, is that it? I do not care in the slightest. But if you think you'll trick him into eloping with you, I can put a sure stop to your gallop.

MISS JULIE is even more nervous.

JULIE: Please be calm, Kristin, and listen to me. I can't stay here – Jean can't stay here – we have to get away.

KRISTIN eyes her and MISS JULIE brightens up.

JULIE: So I've had this idea, you see. The three of us go together – go abroad – Switzerland. We start a hotel together – I've money, you see – Jean and I, we'd take care of everything. And I thought that you would take charge of the kitchen. Wouldn't that be lovely? Say yes, please. Come away with us – then everything will be settled. Say yes, do, please.

She embraces KRISTIN and pats her back. KRISTIN eyes her coldly and thoughtfully. MISS JULIE speaks at great speed.

JULIE: Kristin, you've never travelled. Get out and see the world – do. Such fun to travel by train. New people constantly – new places – we'll visit the zoo in Hamburg – you'll like that – the theatre and the opera – in Munich we'll get to the museum – Rubens, Raphael, great painters you know – you have heard about Munich – where King Ludwig lived – the king who went mad, you know – we'll see his castle – exactly like in fairy tales and it's not far from there to Switzerland – the Alps, you know – the Alps – imagine – snow on top in the middle of the summer – oranges grow there and laurels green all year round.

JEAN can be seen in the wings sharpening his razor on a strap which he holds with his teeth and left hand. He listens to the conversation with a pleased expression, nodding approval in places. MISS JULIE speaks with even greater speed than before.

JULIE: We'll open a hotel – I'll keep guard behind the counter and Jean will greet the guests – does the shopping – writes a letter – believe me, it's a fine life – the train whistles, the carriage arrives, the bell rings upstairs, it rings in the restaurant – I'll write the bills – I'll salt them, I will – you would not believe how paying bills scares the wits out of the guests – you – you will be in charge of the kitchen. You won't be standing over a stove – no – no – you'll be well-dressed because you'll be introduced to people – and I'm not flattering you – you'll land yourself a husband one fine day with your looks. You'll see – a grand English gentleman – these people are very easy to – (*She slows down.*) Land. We'll grow rich. Build ourselves a villa at Lake Como. It does rain there – sometimes it does rain – but – (*Her voice falters.*) The sun has to shine there once in a while – just when it's at its darkest – and – then – if it doesn't – we can go back home, can't we – and just go back – (*She pauses.*) Here – or some place else –

KRISTIN: Stop this. Do you yourself believe any of it, Miss Julie?

MISS JULIE is crushed.

JULIE: Do I believe it?

KRISTIN: Yes.

MISS JULIE is exhausted.

JULIE: I don't know. I don't believe in anything any more. (*She collapses on the bench and drops her head between her arms on the table.*) Nothing at all. Nothing.

KRISTIN turns to where JEAN is standing.

KRISTIN: So he was thinking of doing a runner.

Disconcerted, JEAN puts the razor down on the table.

JEAN: A runner? That's putting it too harshly. You've heard

what Miss Julie is proposing. She may be exhausted without her night's sleep but we can still carry out her proposal.

KRISTIN: Listen to that. Was the intention that I would cook for that –

JEAN *interrupts sharply:*

JEAN: Keep a decent tongue in your head when you're addressing your mistress. Do you hear?

KRISTIN: Mistress?

JEAN: Yes.

KRISTIN: Listen to that. Listen to him.

JEAN: Listen to you – listen more and talk less. Miss Julie is your mistress. You spit on her now but you might spit on yourself for the same reason.

KRISTIN: I've always had enough respect for myself –

JEAN: Enough to spit on others –

KRISTIN: Enough to never lower myself beneath my station. No man can say that the Count's cook threw herself at the stableboy or the pig-keeper. No man can say that.

JEAN: Yes, you've been enjoying yourself with the right gentleman – that's been your good luck.

KRISTIN: A right gentleman, yes – he steals oats from the Count's stables –

JEAN: You're a fine one to talk. You take your cut from the grocery money – you take bribes from the butcher.

KRISTIN: What are you saying?

JEAN: And you, yes you, you can no longer respect your betters.

KRISTIN: Are you coming to church? After your big talk you could do with a good sermon.

JEAN: I'm not going to church today, no. Go by yourself, fall on your knees and confess your sins.

KRISTIN: I'll do that, yes. And I'll come home and forgive you as well. The Saviour suffered on the cross. He died for all our sins. If we come to him with faith, if we repent, he will take all our guilt on himself.

JEAN: Will he forgive those who stole food?

JULIE: Do you believe that, Kristin?

KRISTIN: As sure as I'm alive, as I'm standing here, that is my faith. The faith of my childhood. I've stayed firm in it, Miss Julie. Where there is a multitude of sin, there is a multitude of grace.

JULIE: If I had your faith – if I –

KRISTIN: You can't have it. It comes only through the grace of God and he does not grant it to everyone –

JULIE: So who does he grant it to?

KRISTIN: The last shall be the first – that's the great mystery of grace, Miss Julie. God doesn't have favourites. The last –

JULIE: So he favours the last –

KRISTIN *continues:*

KRISTIN: Shall be first, and it is easier for a camel to pass through the eye of a needle than for a rich man to enter

the Kingdom of God. That's the way God planned it, Miss Julie. Well I'm going now – going on my own. I'll tell the stableboy when I'm leaving not to lend anybody any horses – someone might want to do a runner before the Count gets home. Farewell. (*She exits.*)

JEAN: There goes the devil. And all this because of a greenfinch.

MISS JULIE *is numb.*

JULIE: Leave the greenfinch out of it. Do you see any ending – any way out of this?

JEAN: No.

JULIE: If you were in my place, what would you do?

JEAN: Me – in your place – wait a minute. If I were of noble blood – If I were a woman who – fell – I don't know. I do – I do know.

She has taken the razor and makes a gesture.

JULIE: This?

JEAN: Yes. But I wouldn't do it. Make a note of that. That's the difference between us.

JULIE: You're a man, and I am a woman – what difference is that?

JEAN: The same difference between a man and a woman.

MISS JULIE *has the razor in her hand.*

JULIE: I want to. I can't. My father couldn't either, the time he should have.

JEAN: No, he shouldn't have. He needed his revenge first.

JULIE: And now through me, my mother gets her revenge.

JEAN: Have you never loved your father, Miss Julie?

JULIE: I love him with all my heart and soul, but I loathe him too. I did that without knowing it. He brought me up to hate my own sex. I am woman, and I am man. Who's to blame for what happened? My father? My mother? Myself? Is it myself? Have I nothing that is mine? Every thought I've had, I took from my father. Every passion I've felt came from my mother. And the last hope – everybody is equal – that I got from the man I was to marry, and for that reason I call him good-for-nothing. How can it be my own fault? Should I blame Jesus, like Kristin did – no, I won't do that. I think too much of myself, I know myself too well – thank you, Father, for teaching me that. A rich man can't enter the Kingdom of God – what a lie. Kristin has money saved in the bank – so she's barred for sure. Who's to blame? Who gives a curse who's to blame? In the end I will take the blame on my own two shoulders, and I will face the music.

JEAN: Yes, but –

The bell rings sharply twice. MISS JULIE *leaps to her feet.* JEAN *changes his coat.*

JEAN: The Count – he's home. What if Kristin – (*He goes to the speaking tube, taps it and listens.*)

JULIE: Has he been to his desk yet?

JEAN listens. The audience does not hear what the Count says.

JEAN: Yes, my Lord. (*He listens.*) At once, my Lord. (*He listens.*) In half an hour – yes.

She is even more distressed.

JULIE: What did he say? In the name of Jesus, what did he say?

JEAN: His boots – his coffee – he wants them in half an hour.

JULIE: Half an hour, I am worn out. I can do nothing. I can't say I'm sorry, can't run away, can't stay, I cannot live, I cannot die. Help me. Bark me an order and I'll obey like a dog. Save my honour, save my name – do me that one last favour. You know what I want to do. I can't. Force me to do it. Command me to do it.

JEAN: I can't – I don't know why either – I don't understand – I put on this coat and it makes me – I can't order you about – now since the Count spoke to me – I can't say what I mean – but – I will live and die a servant – if that man the master were to walk in and order me to cut my throat, I believe I would do it here and now.

JULIE: Pretend you're him, and I'm you. You acted so well when you were on your knees – then you had blue blood – or have you ever been to the theatre and seen a hypnotist –

JEAN indicates he has.

JULIE: He says, take the broom, and you take it. He says, sweep, and you sweep.

JEAN: You have to be asleep first though –

MISS JULIE is in ecstasy.

JULIE: I think I'm sleeping already. I think the whole room is filled with smoke. You look like an iron stove, and it looks like a man dressed in black, wearing a top hat, and your eyes, they're like coal glowing when the fire's dying, and your face is the colour of ashes.

The sun's rays stretch across the floor and lighten JEAN.

JULIE: It's so warm – so very warm – (*She rubs her hands as if warming them before a fire.*) Full of light – peace –

JEAN takes the razor and puts it in her hand.

JEAN: Here – go into the daylight – into the barn – and –

He whispers in her ear. She is awake now.

JULIE: Thank you. I can go to my rest now. Tell me this – the first and the last – can the first receive the gift of grace? Tell me, even if you don't believe it.

JEAN: The first? I can't, no. Miss Julie – wait. You're no longer among the first. You're standing among the last.

JULIE: I am among the last. I am the last. Still – I can't go now. Tell me again to go.

JEAN: I can't – I can't.

JULIE: And the last shall be the first.

JEAN: Stop thinking about it – stop. You're draining my strength, you're turning me into a coward. Look, I think I heard the bell – no. Will we put some paper round it? Frightened of a bell, so frightened. It's not just a bell – there is someone behind it – a hand makes it move – and something else makes the hand move – put your hands over your ears – put your hands over your ears – just do that. I will, and he'll ring louder. He'll keep ringing until you answer. It will be too late then. The police will be here – then –

The bell rings twice, forcefully. JEAN startles, then straightens up.

Savage – there is no other way out – go.

MISS JULIE exits through the door with complete determination.

1.3 THREE SISTERS (1900)

ANTON CHEKHOV

Translated by Elisaveta Fen

Anton Chekhov (1860–1904) wrote Three Sisters *fitfully through the spring, summer and winter of 1900, suffering greatly from tuberculosis. In October, he read a first draft of the play to the Moscow Art Theatre, who were to produce the play, and received a muted reaction from the company, some of whom were expecting a comedy, but the play became one of the Art Theatre's greatest successes. Along with* The Seagull, Uncle Vanya *and* The Cherry Orchard, Three Sisters *has become one of the most widely performed plays of the twentieth century. The puzzles of the play – why don't the sisters just go to Moscow? What happened to Vershinin's wife? – have fostered their own minor industry of radical reworkings, sequels and homages, including The Wooster Group's* Brace Up!, *Brian Friel's* Afterplay, *Dijana Milošević's* The Story of Tea, *Janusz Glowacki's* The Fourth Sister, *Beth Henley's* Crimes of the Heart *and Diane Samuels'* Three Sisters on Hope Street, *several movies, a ballet,* Winter Dreams, *choreographed by Kenneth MacMillan, and a rock musical,* Three Sistahs. *The translation from Russian republished here is by Elisaveta Fen and was originally published in 1959 by Penguin Classics.*

Characters

PROZOROV ANDREY SERGHYEEVICH
NATASHA (Natalia Ivanovna), his fiancée, afterwards his wife
OLGA (Olga Serghyeevna, Olia) ⎫
MASHA (Maria Serghyeevna)   ⎬ his sisters
IRENA (Irena Serghyeevna)   ⎭
KOOLYGHIN, Fiodor Ilyich, master at the High School for boys, husband of Masha
VERSHININ, Alexandr Ignatyevich, Lieutenant-Colonel, Battery Commander
TOOZENBACH, Nikolai Lvovich, Baron, Lieutenant in the Army
SOLIONY, Vassily Vassilich, Captain
CHEBUTYKIN, Ivan Romanych, Army Doctor
FEDOTIK, Aleksey Petrovich, Second Lieutenant
RODÉ, Vladimir Karlovich, Second Lieutenant
FERAPONT (Ferapont Spiridonych), an old porter from the County Office
ANFISA, the Prozorovs' former nurse, an old woman of 80

The action takes place in a county town.

Act 1

A drawing-room in the Prozorovs' house; it is separated from a large ballroom[1] at the back by a row of columns. It is midday; there is cheerful sunshine outside. In the ballroom the table is being laid for lunch. OLGA, *wearing the regulation dark-blue dress of a secondary school mistress, is correcting her pupils' work, standing or walking about as she does so.* MASHA, *in a black dress, is sitting reading a book, her hat on her lap.* IRENA, *in white, stands lost in thought.*

OLGA: It's exactly a year ago that Father died, isn't it? This very day, the fifth of May – your Saint's day, Irena. I remember it was very cold and it was snowing. I felt then as if I should never survive his death; and you had fainted and were lying quite still, as if you were dead. And now – a year's gone by, and we talk about it so easily. You're wearing white, and your face is positively radiant …

A clock strikes twelve.

The clock struck twelve then, too. (*A pause.*) I remember when Father was being taken to the cemetery there was a military band, and a salute with rifle fire. That was because he was a general, in command of a brigade. And yet there weren't many people at the funeral. Of course, it was raining hard, raining and snowing.

IRENA: Need we bring up all these memories?

Baron TOOZENBACH, CHEBUTYKIN *and* SOLIONY *appear behind the columns by the table in the ballroom.*

OLGA: It's so warm today that we can keep the windows wide open, and yet there aren't any leaves showing on the birch trees. Father was made a brigadier eleven years ago, and then he left Moscow and took us with him. I remember so well how everything in Moscow was in blossom by now, everything was soaked in sunlight and warmth. Eleven years have gone by, yet I remember everything about it, as if we'd only left yesterday. Oh, Heavens! When I woke up this morning and saw this flood of sunshine, all this spring sunshine, I felt so moved and so happy! I felt such a longing to get back home to Moscow!

CHEBUTYKIN: (*to* TOOZENBACH.) The devil you have!

TOOZENBACH: It's nonsense, I agree.

MASHA: (*Absorbed in her book, whistles a tune under her breath.*)

OLGA: Masha, do stop whistling! How can you? (*A pause.*) I suppose I must get this continual headache because I have to go to school every day and go on teaching right into the evening. I seem to have the thoughts of someone quite old. Honestly, I've been feeling as if my strength and youth were running out of me drop by drop, day after day. Day after day, all these four years that I've been working at the school.… I just have one longing and it seems to grow stronger and stronger.…

IRENA: If only we could go back to Moscow! Sell the house, finish with our life here, and go back to Moscow.

OLGA: Yes, Moscow! As soon as we possibly can.

(CHEBUTYKIN *and* TOOZENBACH *laugh.*)

IRENA: I suppose Andrey will soon get a professorship. He isn't likely to go on living here. The only problem is our poor Masha.

OLGA: Masha can come and stay the whole summer with us every year in Moscow.

MASHA: (*Whistles a tune under her breath.*)

IRENA: Everything will settle itself, with God's help. (*Looks through the window.*) What lovely weather it is today! Really, I don't know why there's such joy in my heart. I remembered this morning that it was my Saint's day, and suddenly I felt so happy, and I thought of the time when we were children, and Mother was still alive. And then such wonderful thoughts came to me, such wonderful stirring thoughts!

OLGA: You're so lovely today, you really do look most attractive. Masha looks pretty today, too. Andrey could be good-looking, but he's grown so stout. It doesn't suit him. As for me, I've just aged and grown a lot thinner. I suppose it's through getting so irritated with the girls at school. But today I'm at home, I'm free, and my headache's gone, and I feel much younger than I did yesterday. I'm only twenty-eight, after all.… I suppose everything that God wills must be right and good, but I can't help thinking sometimes that if I'd got married and stayed at home, it would have been a better thing for me: (*A pause.*) I would have been very fond of my husband.

TOOZENBACH: (*To* SOLIONY.) Really, you talk such a lot of nonsense, I'm tired of listening to you. (*Comes into the drawing-room.*) I forgot to tell you: Vershinin, our new battery commander, is going to call on you today. (*Sits down by the piano.*)

OLGA: I'm very glad to hear it.

IRENA: Is he old?

TOOZENBACH: No, not particularly. Forty, forty-five at the most. (*Plays quietly.*) He seems a nice fellow. Certainly not a fool. His only weakness is that he talks too much.

IRENA: Is he interesting?

TOOZENBACH: He's all right, only he's got a wife, a mother-in-law and two little girls. What's more, she's his second wife. He calls on everybody and tells them that he's got a wife and two little girls. He'll tell you about it, too, I'm sure of that. His wife seems to be a bit soft in the head. She wears a long plait like a girl, she is always philosophizing and talking in high-flown language, and then she often tries to commit suicide, apparently just to annoy her husband. I would have run away from a wife like that years ago, but he puts up with it, and just grumbles about it.

SOLIONY: (*Enters the drawing-room with* CHEBUTYKIN.) Now I can only lift sixty pounds with one hand, but with two I can lift two hundred pounds, or even two hundred and forty. So I conclude from that that two men are not just twice as strong as one, but three times as strong, if not more.

CHEBUTYKIN: (*Reads the paper as he comes in.*) Here's a recipe for falling hair … two ounces of naphthaline, half-a-bottle of methylated spirit … dissolve and apply once a day.… (*Writes it down in a notebook.*) Must make a note of it. (*To* SOLIONY.) Well, as I was trying to explain to you, you cork the bottle and pass a glass tube through the cork. Then you take a pinch of ordinary powdered alum, and ….

IRENA: Ivan Romanych, dear Ivan Romanych!

CHEBUTYKIN: What is it, my child, what is it?

IRENA: Tell me, why is it I'm so happy today? Just as if I were sailing along in a boat with big white sails, and above me the wide, blue sky, and in the sky great white birds floating around?

CHEBUTYKIN: (*Kisses both her hands, tenderly.*) My little white bird!

IRENA: You know, when I woke up this morning, and after I'd got up and washed, I suddenly felt as if everything in the world had become clear to me, and I knew the way I ought to live. I know it all now, my dear Ivan Romanych. Man must work by the sweat of his brow whatever his class, and that should make up the whole meaning and purpose of his life and happiness and contentment. Oh, how good it must be to be a workman, getting up with the sun and breaking stones by the roadside – or a shepherd – or a schoolmaster teaching the children – or an engine-driver on the railway. Good Heavens! it's better to be a mere ox or horse, and work, than the sort of young woman who wakes up at twelve, and drinks her coffee in bed, and then takes two hours dressing.... How dreadful! You know how you long for a cool drink in hot weather? Well, that's the way I long for work. And if I don't get up early from now on and really work, you can refuse to be friends with me any more, Ivan Romanych.

CHEBUTYKIN: (*Tenderly.*) So I will, so I will....

OLGA: Father taught us to get up at seven o'clock and so Irena always wakes up at seven – but then she stays in bed till at least nine, thinking about something or other. And with such a serious expression on her face, too! (*Laughs.*)

IRENA: You think it's strange when I look serious because you always think of me as a little girl. I'm twenty, you know!

TOOZENBACH: All this longing for work.... Heavens! how well I can understand it! I've never done a stroke of work in my life. I was born in Petersburg, an unfriendly, idle city – born into a family where work and worries were simply unknown. I remember a valet pulling off my boots for me when I came home from the cadet school.... I grumbled at the way he did it, and my mother looked on in admiration. She was quite surprised when other people looked at me in any other way. I was so carefully protected from work! But I doubt whether they succeeded in protecting me for good and all – yes, I doubt it very much! The time's come: there's a terrific thunder-cloud advancing upon us, a mighty storm is coming to freshen us up! Yes, it's coming all right, it's quite near already, and it's going to blow away all this idleness and indifference, and prejudice against work, this rot of boredom that our society is suffering from. I'm going to work, and in twenty-five or thirty years' time every man and woman will be working. Every one of us!

CHEBUTYKIN: I'm not going to work.

TOOZENBACH: You don't count.

SOLIONY: In twenty-five years' time you won't be alive, thank goodness. In a couple of years you'll die from a stroke – or I'll lose my temper with you and put a bullet in your head, my good fellow. (*Takes a scent bottle from his pocket and sprinkles the scent over his chest and hands.*)

CHEBUTYKIN: (*Laughs.*) It's quite true that I never have done any work. Not a stroke since I left the university. I haven't even read a book, only newspapers. (*Takes another newspaper out of his pocket.*) For instance, here.... I know from the paper that there was a person called Dobroliubov, but what he wrote about I've not the faintest idea.... God alone knows....

Someone knocks on the floor from downstairs.

There! They're calling me to come down: there's someone come to see me. I'll be back in a moment.... (*Goes out hurriedly, stroking his beard.*)

IRENA: He's up to one of his little games.

TOOZENBACH: Yes. He looked very solemn as he left. He's obviously going to give you a present.

IRENA: I do dislike that sort of thing ....

OLGA: Yes, isn't it dreadful? He's always doing something silly.

MASHA: 'A green oak grows by a curving shore, And round that oak hangs a golden chain' .... (*Gets up as she sings under her breath.*)

OLGA: You're sad today, Masha.

MASHA: (*Puts on her hat, singing.*)

OLGA: Where are you going?

MASHA: Home.

IRENA: What a strange thing to do.

TOOZENBACH: What! Going away from your sister's party?

MASHA: What does it matter? I'll be back this evening. Goodbye, my darling. (*Kisses* IRENA.) And once again – I wish you all the happiness in the world. In the old days when Father was alive we used to have thirty or forty officers at our parties. What gay parties we had! And today – what have we got today? A man and a half, and the place is as quiet as a tomb. I'm going home. I'm depressed today, I'm sad, so don't listen to me. (*Laughs through her tears.*) We'll have a talk later, but goodbye for now, my dear. I'll go somewhere or other....

IRENA: (*Displeased.*) Really, you are a....

OLGA: (*Tearfully.*) I understand you, Masha.

SOLIONY: If a man starts philosophizing, you call that philosophy, or possibly just sophistry, but if a woman or a couple of women start philosophizing you call that ... what would you call it, now? Ask me another!

MASHA: What are you talking about? You are a disconcerting person!

SOLIONY: Nothing.
  'He had no time to say "Oh, oh!"'
  Before that bear had struck him low'....

A pause.

MASHA: (*To* OLGA, *crossly.*) Do stop snivelling!

Enter ANFISA *and* FERAPONT, *the latter carrying a large cake.*

ANFISA: Come along, my dear, this way. Come in, your boots are quite clean. (*To* IRENA.) A cake from Protopopov, at the Council Office.

IRENA: Thank you. Tell him I'm very grateful to him. (*Takes the cake.*)

FERAPONT: What's that?

IRENA: (*Louder.*) Tell him I sent my thanks.

OLGA: Nanny, will you give him a piece of cake? Go along, Ferapont, they'll give you some cake.

FERAPONT: What's that?

ANFISA: Come along with me, Ferapont Spiridonych, my dear. Come along. (*Goes out with* FERAPONT.)

MASHA: I don't like that Protopopov fellow, Mihail Potapych, or Ivanych, or whatever it is. It's best not to invite him here.

IRENA: I haven't invited him.

MASHA: Thank goodness.

Enter CHEBUTYKIN, *followed by a soldier carrying a silver samovar. Murmurs of astonishment and displeasure.*

OLGA: (*Covering her face with her hands.*) A samovar! But this is dreadful! (*Goes through to the ballroom and stands by the table.*)

IRENA: My dear Ivan Romanych, what are you thinking about?

TOOZENBACH: (*Laughs.*) Didn't I tell you?

MASHA: Ivan Romanych, you really ought to be ashamed of yourself!

CHEBUTYKIN: My dear, sweet girls, I've no one in the world but you. You're dearer to me than anything in the world! I'm nearly sixty, I'm an old man, a lonely, utterly unimportant old man. The only thing that's worth anything in me is my love for you, and if it weren't for you, really I would have been dead long ago. (*To* IRENA.) My dear, my sweet little girl, haven't I known you since the very day you were born? Didn't I carry you about in my arms?... didn't I love your dear mother?

IRENA: But why do you get such expensive presents?

CHEBUTYKIN: (*Tearfully and crossly.*) Expensive presents!... Get along with you! (*To the orderly.*) Put the samovar over there. (*Mimics* IRENA.) Expensive presents!

The orderly takes the samovar to the ballroom.

ANFISA: (*Crosses the drawing-room.*) My dears, there's a strange colonel just arrived. He's taken off his coat and he's coming up now. Irenushka, do be nice and polite to him, won't you? (*In the doorway.*) And it's high time we had lunch, too.... Oh, dear! (*Goes out.*)

TOOZENBACH: It's Vershinin, I suppose.

Enter VERSHININ.

TOOZENBACH: Lieutenant-Colonel Vershinin!

VERSHININ: (*To* MASHA *and* IRENA.) Allow me to introduce myself – Lieutenant-Colonel Vershinin. I'm so glad, so very glad to be here at last. How you've changed! Dear, dear, how you've changed!

IRENA: Please, do sit down. We're very pleased to see you, I'm sure.

VERSHININ: (*Gayly.*) I'm so glad to see you, so glad! But there were three of you, weren't there? – three sisters. I remember there were three little girls. I don't remember their faces, but I knew your father, Colonel Prozorov, and I remember he had three little girls. Oh, yes, I saw them myself. I remember them quite well. How time flies! Dear, dear, how it flies!

TOOZENBACH: Alexandr Ignatyevich comes from Moscow.

IRENA: From Moscow? You come from Moscow?

VERSHININ: Yes, from Moscow. Your father was a battery commander there, and I was an officer in the same brigade. (*To* MASHA.) I seem to remember your face a little.

MASHA: I don't remember you at all.

IRENA: Olia, Olia! (*Calls towards the ballroom.*) Olia, do come!

OLGA enters from the ballroom.

IRENA: It seems that Lieutenant-Colonel Vershinin comes from Moscow.

VERSHININ: You must be Olga Serghyeevna, the eldest. And you are Maria.... And you are Irena, the youngest ....

OLGA: You come from Moscow?

VERSHININ: Yes. I studied in Moscow and entered the service there. I stayed there quite a long time, but then I was put in charge of a battery here – so I moved out here, you see. I don't really remember you, you know, I only remember that there were three sisters. I remember your father, though, I remember him very well. All I need to do is to close my eyes and I can see him standing there as if he were alive. I used to visit you in Moscow.

OLGA: I thought I remembered everybody, and yet ....

VERSHININ: My Christian names are Alexandr Ignatyevich.

IRENA: Alexandr Ignatyevich, and you come from Moscow! Well, what a surprise!

OLGA: We're going to live there, you know.

IRENA: We hope to be there by the autumn. It's our home town, we were born there.... In Staraya Basmannaya Street.

Both laugh happily.

MASHA: Fancy meeting a fellow townsman so unexpectedly! (*Eagerly.*) I remember now. Do you remember, Olga, there was someone they used to call 'the lovesick Major'? You were a Lieutenant then, weren't you, and you were in love with someone or other, and everyone used to tease you about it. They called you 'Major' for some reason or other.

VERSHININ: (*Laughs.*) That's it, that's it.... 'The lovesick Major', that's what they called me.

MASHA: In those days you only had a moustache.... Oh, dear, how much older you look! (*Tearfully.*) How much older!

VERSHININ: Yes, I was still a young man in the days when they called me 'the lovesick Major'. I was in love then. It's different now.

OLGA: But you haven't got a single grey hair! You've aged, yes, but you're certainly not an old man.

VERSHININ: Nevertheless, I'm turned forty-two. Is it long since you left Moscow?

IRENA: Eleven years. Now what are you crying for, Masha, you funny girl? ... (*Tearfully.*) You'll make me cry, too.

MASHA: I'm not crying. What was the street you lived in?

VERSHININ: In the Staraya Basmannaya.

OLGA: We did, too.

VERSHININ: At one time I lived in the Niemietzkaya Street. I used to walk from there to the Krasny Barracks, and I remember there was such a gloomy bridge I had to cross. I used to hear the noise of the water rushing under it. I remember how lonely and sad I felt there. (*A pause.*) But what a magnificently wide river you have here! It's a marvellous river!

OLGA: Yes, but this is a cold place. It's cold here, and there are too many mosquitoes.

VERSHININ: Really? I should have said you had a really good healthy climate here, a real Russian climate. Forest, river ... birch trees, too. The dear, unpretentious birch trees – I love them more than any of the other trees. It's nice living here. But there's one rather strange thing, the station is fifteen miles from the town. And no one knows why.

SOLIONY: I know why it is. (*Everyone looks at him.*) Because if the station were nearer, it wouldn't be so far away, and as it is so far away, it can't be nearer.

An awkward silence.

TOOZENBACH: You like your little joke, Vassily Vassilich.

OLGA: I'm sure I remember you now. I know I do.

VERSHININ: I knew your mother.

CHEBUTYKIN: She was a good woman, God bless her memory!

IRENA: Mamma was buried in Moscow.

OLGA: At the convent of Novo-Dievichye.

MASHA: You know, I'm even beginning to forget what she looked like. I suppose people will lose all memory of us in just the same way. We'll be forgotten.

VERSHININ: Yes, we shall all be forgotten. Such is our fate, and we can't do anything about it. And all the things that seem serious, important and full of meaning to us now will be forgotten one day – or anyway they won't seem important any more. (*A pause.*) It's strange to think that we're utterly unable to tell what will be regarded as great and important in the future and what will be thought of as just paltry and ridiculous. Didn't the great discoveries of Copernicus – or of Columbus, if you like – appear useless and unimportant to begin with? – whereas some rubbish, written up by an eccentric fool, was regarded as a revelation of great truth?

It may well be that in time to come the life we live today will seem strange and uncomfortable and stupid and not too clean, either, and perhaps even wicked ...

TOOZENBACH: Who can tell? It's just as possible that future generations will think that we lived our lives on a very high plane and remember us with respect. After all, we no longer have tortures and public executions and invasions, though there's still a great deal of suffering!

SOLIONY: (*In a high-pitched voice as if calling to chickens.*) Cluck, cluck, cluck! There's nothing our good Baron loves as much as a nice bit of philosophizing.

TOOZENBACH: Vassily Vassilich, will you kindly leave me alone? (*Moves to another chair.*) It's becoming tiresome.

SOLIONY: (*As before.*) Cluck, cluck, cluck!...

TOOZENBACH: (*To* VERSHININ.) The suffering that we see around us – and there's so much of it – itself proves that our society has at least achieved a level of morality which is higher....

VERSHININ: Yes, yes, of course.

CHEBUTYKIN: You said just now, Baron, that our age will be called great; but people are small all the same.... (*Gets up.*) Look how small I am.

A violin is played offstage.

MASHA: That's Andrey playing the violin; he's our brother, you know.

IRENA: We've got quite a clever brother.... We're expecting him to be a professor. Papa was a military man, but Andrey chose an academic career.

OLGA: We've been teasing him today. We think he's in love, just a little.

IRENA: With a girl who lives down here. She'll be calling in today most likely.

MASHA: The way she dresses herself is awful! It's not that her clothes are just ugly and old-fashioned, they're simply pathetic. She'll put on some weird-looking, bright yellow skirt with a crude sort of fringe affair, and then a red blouse to go with it. And her cheeks look as though they've been scrubbed, they're so shiny! Andrey's not in love with her – I can't believe it; after all, he has got some taste. I think he's just playing the fool, just to annoy us. I heard yesterday that she's going to get married to Protopopov, the chairman of the local council. I thought it was an excellent idea. (*Calls through the side door.*) Andrey, come here, will you? Just for a moment, dear.

Enter ANDREY.

OLGA: This is my brother, Andrey Serghyeevich.

VERSHININ: Vershinin.

ANDREY: Prozorov. (*Wipes the perspiration from his face.*) I believe you've been appointed battery commander here?

OLGA: What do you think, dear? Alexandr Ignatyevich comes from Moscow.

ANDREY: Do you, really? Congratulations! You'll get no peace from my sisters now.

VERSHININ: I'm afraid your sisters must be getting tired of me already.

IRENA: Just look, Andrey gave me this little picture frame today. (*Shows him the frame.*) He made it himself.

VERSHININ: (*Looks at the frame, not knowing what to say.*) Yes, it's ... it's very nice indeed.... .

IRENA: Do you see that little frame over the piano? He made that one, too.

ANDREY waves his hand impatiently and walks off.

OLGA: He's awfully clever, and he plays the violin, and he makes all sorts of things, too. In fact, he's very gifted all round. Andrey, please, don't go. He's got such a bad habit – always going off like this. Come here!

MASHA and IRENA take him by the arms and lead him back, laughing.

MASHA: Now just you come here!

ANDREY: Do leave me alone, please do!

MASHA: You are a silly! They used to call Alexandr Ignatyevich 'the lovesick Major', and he didn't get annoyed.

VERSHININ: Not in the least.

MASHA: I feel like calling you a 'lovesick fiddler'.

IRENA: Or a 'lovesick professor'.

OLGA: He's fallen in love! Our Andriusha's in love!

IRENA: (*Clapping her hands.*) Three cheers for Andriusha! Andriusha's in love!

CHEBUTYKIN: (*Comes up behind ANDREY and puts his arms round his waist.*) 'Nature created us for love alone.' ... (*Laughs loudly, still holding his paper in his hand.*)

ANDREY: That's enough of it, that's enough.... (*Wipes his face.*) I couldn't get to sleep all night, and I'm not feeling too grand just now. I read till four o'clock, and then I went to bed, but nothing happened. I kept thinking about one thing and another ... and it gets light so early; the sun just pours into my room. I'd like to translate a book from the English while I'm here during the summer.

VERSHININ: You read English, then?

ANDREY: Yes. My father – God bless his memory – used to simply wear us out with learning. It sounds silly, I know, but I must confess that since he died I've begun to grow stout, as if I'd been physically relieved of the strain. I've grown quite stout in a year. Yes, thanks to Father, my sisters and I know French and German and English, and Irena here knows Italian, too. But what an effort it all cost us!

MASHA: Knowing three languages in a town like this is an unnecessary luxury. In fact, not even a luxury, but just a sort of useless encumbrance ... it's rather like having a sixth finger on your hand. We know a lot of stuff that's just useless.

VERSHININ: Really! (*Laughs.*) You know a lot of stuff that's

useless! It seems to me that there's no place on earth, however dull and depressing it may be, where intelligence and education can be useless. Let us suppose that among the hundred thousand people in this town, all of them, no doubt, very backward and uncultured, there are just three people like yourselves. Obviously, you can't hope to triumph over all the mass of ignorance around you; as your life goes by, you'll have to keep giving in little by little until you get lost in the crowd, in the hundred thousand. Life will swallow you up, but you'll not quite disappear, you'll make some impression on it. After you've gone, perhaps six more people like you will turn up, then twelve, and so on, until in the end most people will have become like you. So in two or three hundred years life on this old earth of ours will have become marvellously beautiful. Man longs for a life like that, and if it isn't here yet, he must imagine it, wait for it, dream about it, prepare for it, he must know and see more than his father and his grandfather did. (*Laughs.*) And you're complaining because you know a lot of stuff that's useless.

MASHA: (*Takes off her hat.*) I'll be staying to lunch.

IRENA: (*With a sigh.*) Really, someone should have written all that down.

ANDREY has left the room, unnoticed.

TOOZENBACH: You say that in time to come life will be marvellously beautiful. That's probably true. But in order to share in it now, at a distance so to speak, we must prepare for it and work for it.

VERSHININ: (*Gets up.*) Yes.... What a lot of flowers you've got here! (*Looks round.*) And what a marvellous house! I do envy you! All my life I seem to have been pigging it in small flats, with two chairs and a sofa and a stove which always smokes. It's the flowers that I've missed in my life, flowers like these!... (*Rubs his hands.*) Oh, well, never mind!

TOOZENBACH: Yes, we must work. I suppose you're thinking I'm a sentimental German. But I assure you I'm not – I'm Russian. I don't speak a word of German. My father was brought up in the Greek Orthodox faith. (*A pause.*)

VERSHININ: (*Walks up and down the room.*) You know, I often wonder what it would be like if you could start your life over again – deliberately, I mean, consciously.... Suppose you could put aside the life you'd lived already, as though it was just a sort of rough draft, and then start another one like a fair copy. If that happened, I think the thing you'd want most of all would be not to repeat yourself. You'd try at least to create a new environment for yourself, a flat like this one, for instance, with some flowers and plenty of light.... I have a wife, you know, and two little girls; and my wife's not very well, and all that.... Well, if I had to start my life all over again, I wouldn't marry.... No, no!

Enter KOOLYGHIN, in the uniform of a teacher.

KOOLYGHIN: (*Approaches* IRENA.) Congratulations, dear sister – from the bottom of my heart, congratulations on your Saint's day. I wish you good health and everything a girl of your age ought to have! And allow me to present you with this little book.... (*Hands her a book.*) It's the history of our school covering the whole fifty years of its existence. I wrote it myself. Quite a trifle, of course – I wrote it in my spare time when I had nothing better to do – but I hope you'll read it nevertheless. Good morning to you all! (*To* VERSHININ.) Allow me to introduce myself. Koolyghin's the name; I'm a master at the secondary school here. And a town councillor. (*To* IRENA.) You'll find a list in the book of all the pupils who have completed their studies at our school during the last fifty years. *Feci quod potui, faciant melior a potentes.* (*Kisses* MASHA.)

IRENA: But you gave me this book last Easter!

KOOLYGHIN: (*Laughs.*) Did I really? In that case, give it me back – or no, better give it to the Colonel. Please do take it, Colonel. Maybe you'll read it some time when you've nothing better to do.

VERSHININ: Thank you very much. (*Prepares to leave.*) I'm so very glad to have made your acquaintance....

OLGA: You aren't going, are you?... Really, you mustn't.

IRENA: But you'll stay and have lunch with us! Please do.

OLGA: Please do.

VERSHININ: (*Bows.*) I see I've intruded on your Saint's day party. I didn't know. Forgive me for not offering you my congratulations. (*Goes into the ballroom with* OLGA.)

KOOLYGHIN: Today is Sunday, my friends, a day of rest; let us rest and enjoy it, each according to his age and position in life! We shall have to roll up the carpets and put them away till the winter.... We must remember to put some naphthaline on them, or Persian powder.... The Romans enjoyed good health because they knew how to work *and* how to rest. They had *mens sana in corpore sano.* Their life had a definite shape, a form.... The director of the school says that the most important thing about life is form.... A thing that loses its form is finished – that's just as true of our ordinary, everyday lives. (*Takes* MASHA *by the waist and laughs.*) Masha loves me. My wife loves me. Yes, and the curtains will have to be put away with the carpets, too.... I'm cheerful today, I'm in quite excellent spirits.... Masha, we're invited to the director's at four o'clock today. A country walk has been arranged for the teachers and their families.

MASHA: I'm not going.

KOOLYGHIN: (*Distressed.*) Masha, darling, why not?

MASHA: I'll tell you later.... (*Crossly.*) All right, I'll come, only leave me alone now.... (*Walks off.*)

KOOLYGHIN: And after the walk we shall all spend the evening at the director's house. In spite of weak health, that man is certainly sparing no pains to be sociable. A first-rate, thoroughly enlightened man! A most excellent person! After the conference yesterday he said to me: 'I'm tired, Fiodor Ilyich. I'm tired!' (*Looks at the clock, then at his watch.*) Your clock is seven minutes fast. Yes, 'I'm tired,' he said.

The sound of the violin is heard offstage.

OLGA: Will you all come and sit down, please! Lunch is ready. There's a pie.

KOOLYGHIN: Ah, Olga, my dear girl! Last night I worked up to eleven o'clock, and I felt tired, but today I'm quite happy. (*Goes to the table in the ballroom.*) My dear Olga!

CHEBUTYKIN: (*Puts the newspaper in his pocket and combs his beard.*) A pie? Excellent!

MASHA: (*Sternly to* CHEBUTYKIN.) Remember, you mustn't take anything to drink today. Do you hear? It's bad for you.

CHEBUTYKIN: Never mind. I've got over that weakness long ago! I haven't done any heavy drinking for two years. (*Impatiently.*) Anyway, my dear, what does it matter?

MASHA: All the same, don't you dare to drink anything. Mind you don't now! (*Crossly, but taking care that her husband does not hear.*) So now I've got to spend another of these damnably boring evenings at the director's!

TOOZENBACH: I wouldn't go if I were you, and that's that.

CHEBUTYKIN: Don't you go, my dear.

MASHA: Don't go, indeed! Oh, what a damnable life! It's intolerable.... (*Goes into the ballroom.*)

CHEBUTYKIN: (*Follows her.*) Well, well!...

SOLIONY: (*As he passes* TOOZENBACH *on the way to the ballroom.*) Cluck, cluck, cluck!

TOOZENBACH: Do stop it, Vassily Vassilich. I've really had enough of it....

SOLIONY: Cluck, cluck, cluck!...

KOOLYGHIN: (*Gaily.*) Your health, Colonel! I'm a schoolmaster ... and I'm quite one of the family here, as it were. I'm Masha's husband. She's got a sweet nature, such a very sweet nature!

VERSHININ: I think I'll have a little of this dark vodka. (*Drinks.*) Your health! (*To* OLGA.) I do feel so happy with you people!

Only IRENA *and* TOOZENBACH *remain in the drawing-room.*

IRENA: Masha's a bit out of humour today. You know, she got married when she was eighteen, and then her husband seemed the cleverest man in the world to her. It's different now. He's the kindest of men, but not the cleverest.

OLGA: (*Impatiently.*) Andrey, will you please come?

ANDREY: (*Offstage.*) Just coming. (*Enters and goes to the table.*)

TOOZENBACH: What are you thinking about?

IRENA: Oh, nothing special. You know, I don't like this man Soliony, I'm quite afraid of him. Whenever he opens his mouth he says something silly.

TOOZENBACH: He's a strange fellow. I'm sorry for him, even though he irritates me. In fact, I feel more sorry for him than irritated. I think he's shy. When he's alone with me, he can be quite sensible and friendly, but in company he's offensive and bullying. Don't go over there just yet, let them get settled down at the table. Let me stay beside you for a bit. Tell me what you're thinking about. (*A pause.*) You're twenty ... and I'm not thirty yet myself. What years and years we still have ahead of us, a whole long succession of years, all full of my love for you!...

IRENA: Don't talk to me about love, Nikolai Lvovich.

TOOZENBACH: (*Not listening.*) Oh, I long so passionately for life, I long to work and strive so much, and all this longing is somehow mingled with my love for you, Irena. And just because you happen to be beautiful, life appears beautiful to me! What are you thinking about?

IRENA: You say that life is beautiful. Maybe it is – but what if it only seems to be beautiful? Our lives, I mean the lives of us three sisters, haven't been beautiful up to now. The truth is that life has been stifling us, like weeds in a garden. I'm afraid I'm crying.... So unnecessary.... (*Quickly dries her eyes and smiles.*) We must work, work! The reason we feel depressed and take such a gloomy view of life is that we've never known what it is to make a real effort. We're the children of parents who despised work....

Enter NATALIA IVANOVNA. She is wearing a pink dress with a green belt.

NATASHA: They've gone in to lunch already.... I'm late.... (*Glances at herself in a mirror, adjusts her dress.*) My hair seems to be all right.... (*Catches sight of IRENA.*) My dear Irena Serghyeevna, congratulations! (*Gives her a vigorous and prolonged kiss.*) You've got such a lot of visitors.... I feel quite shy.... How do you do, Baron?

OLGA: (*Enters the drawing-room.*) Oh, there you are, Natalia Ivanovna! How are you, my dear?

They kiss each other.

NATASHA: Congratulations! You're such a lot of people here, I feel dreadfully shy....

OLGA: It's all right, they're all old friends. (*Alarmed, dropping her voice.*) You've got a green belt on! My dear, that's surely a mistake!

NATASHA: Why, is it a bad omen, or what?

OLGA: No, but it just doesn't go with your dress ... it looks so strange....

NATASHA: (*Tearfully.*) Really? But it isn't really green, you know, it's a sort of dull colour.... (*Follows OLGA to the ballroom.*)

All are now seated at the table; the drawing-room is empty.

KOOLYGHIN: Irena, you know, I do wish you'd find yourself a good husband. In my view it's high time you got married.

CHEBUTYKIN: You ought to get yourself a nice little husband, too, Natalia Ivanovna.

KOOLYGHIN: Natalia Ivanovna already has a husband in view.

MASHA: (*Strikes her plate with her fork.*) A glass of wine for me, please! Three cheers for our jolly old life! We keep our end up, we do!

KOOLYGHIN: Masha, you won't get more than five out of ten for good conduct!

VERSHININ: I say, this liqueur's very nice. What is it made of?

SOLIONY: Black beetles!

IRENA: Ugh! ugh! How disgusting!

OLGA: We're having roast turkey for dinner tonight, and then apple tart. Thank goodness, I'll be here all day today ... this evening, too. You must all come this evening.

VERSHININ: May I come in the evening, too?

IRENA: Yes, please do.

NATASHA: They don't stand on ceremony here.

CHEBUTYKIN: 'Nature created us for love alone.' ... (*Laughs.*)

ANDREY: (*Crossly.*) Will you stop it, please? Aren't you tired of it yet?

FEDOTIK and RODÉ come in with a large basket of flowers.

FEDOTIK: Just look here, they're having lunch already!

RODÉ: (*In a loud voice.*) Having their lunch? So they are, they're having lunch already.

FEDOTIK: Wait half a minute. (*Takes a snapshot.*) One! Just one minute more!... (*Takes another snapshot.*) Two! All over now.

They pick up the basket and go into the ballroom where they are greeted uproariously.

RODÉ: (*Loudly.*) Congratulations, Irena Serghyeevna! I wish you all the best, everything you'd wish for yourself! Gorgeous weather today, absolutely marvellous. I've been out walking the whole morning with the boys. You do know that I teach gym at the high school, don't you?...

FEDOTIK: You may move now, Irena Serghyeevna, that is, if you want to. (*Takes a snapshot.*) You do look attractive today. (*Takes a top out of his pocket.*) By the way, look at this top. It's got a wonderful hum.

IRENA: What a sweet little thing!

MASHA: 'A green oak grows by a curving shore, And round that oak hangs a golden chain.' ... A green chain around that oak.... (*Peevishly.*) Why do I keep on saying that? Those lines have been worrying me all day long!

KOOLYGHIN: Do you know, we're thirteen at table?

RODÉ: (*Loudly.*) You don't really believe in these old superstitions, do you? (*Laughter.*)

KOOLYGHIN: When thirteen people sit down to table, it means that some of them are in love. Is it you, by any chance, Ivan Romanych?

CHEBUTYKIN: Oh, I'm just an old sinner.... But what I can't make out is why Natalia Ivanovna looks so embarrassed.

Loud laughter. NATASHA runs out into the drawing-room, ANDREY follows her.

ANDREY: Please, Natasha, don't take any notice of them! Stop ... wait a moment.... Please!

Figure 5 From the Moscow Art Theatre 1901 production of *Three Sisters*.

NATASHA: I feel so ashamed.... I don't know what's the matter with me, and they're all laughing at me. It's awful of me to leave the table like that, but I couldn't help it.... I just couldn't.... (*Covers her face with her hands.*)

ANDREY: My dear girl, please, please don't get upset. Honestly, they don't mean any harm, they're just teasing. My dear, sweet girl, they're really good-natured folks, they all are, and they're fond of us both. Come over to the window, they can't see us there.... (*Looks round.*)

NATASHA: You see, I'm not used to being with a lot of people.

ANDREY: Oh, how young you are, Natasha, how wonderfully, beautifully young! My dear, sweet girl, don't get so upset! Do believe me, believe me.... I'm so happy, so full of love, of joy.... No, they can't see us here! They can't see us! How did I come to love you, when was it? ... I don't understand anything. My precious, my sweet, my innocent girl, please – I want you to marry me! I love you, I love you as I've never loved anybody.... (*Kisses her.*)

Enter two officers and, seeing NATASHA *and* ANDREY *kissing, stand and stare in amazement.*

Act 2

The scene is the same as in Act 1.

It is eight o'clock in the evening. The faint sound of an accordion is heard coming from the street.

The stage is unlit. Enter NATALIA IVANOVNA *in a dressing-gown, carrying a candle. She crosses the stage and stops by the door leading to* ANDREY's *room.*

NATASHA: What are you doing, Andriusha? Reading? It's all right, I only wanted to know.... (*Goes to another door,*

opens it, looks inside and shuts it again.) No one's left a light anywhere....

ANDREY: (*Enters with a book in his hand.*) What is it, Natasha?

NATASHA: I was just going round to see if anyone had left a light anywhere. It's carnival week, and the servants are so excited about it ... anything might happen! You've got to watch them. Last night about twelve o'clock I happened to go into the dining-room, and – would you believe it? – there was a candle alight on the table. I've not found out who lit it. (*Puts the candle down.*) What time is it?

ANDREY: (*Glances at his watch.*) Quarter past eight.

NATASHA: And Olga and Irena still out. They aren't back from work yet, poor things! Olga's still at some teachers' conference, and Irena's at the post office. (*Sighs.*) This morning I said to Irena: 'Do take care of yourself, my dear.' But she won't listen. Did you say it was a quarter past eight? I'm afraid Bobik is not at all well. Why does he get so cold? Yesterday he had a temperature, but today he feels quite cold when you touch him.... I'm so afraid!

ANDREY: It's all right, Natasha. The boy's well enough.

NATASHA: Still, I think he ought to have a special diet. I'm so anxious about him. By the way, they tell me that some carnival party's supposed to be coming here soon after nine. I'd rather they didn't come, Andriusha.

ANDREY: Well, I really don't know what I can do. They've been asked to come.

NATASHA: This morning the dear little fellow woke up and looked at me, and then suddenly he smiled. He recognized me, you see. 'Good morning, Bobik,' I said, 'good morning, darling precious!' And then he laughed. Babies understand everything, you know, they understand us perfectly well. Anyway, Andriusha, I'll tell the servants not to let that carnival party in.

ANDREY: (*Irresolutely.*) Well ... it's really for my sisters to decide, isn't it? It's their house, after all.

NATASHA: Yes, it's their house as well. I'll tell them, too.... They're so kind.... (*Walks off.*) I've ordered sour milk for supper. The doctor says you ought to eat nothing but sour milk, or you'll never get any thinner. (*Stops.*) Bobik feels so cold. I'm afraid his room is too cold for him. He ought to move into a warmer room, at least until the warm weather comes. Irena's room, for instance – that's just a perfect room for a baby: it's dry, and it gets the sun all day long. We must tell her: perhaps she'd share Olga's room for a bit.... In any case, she's never at home during the day, she only sleeps there.... (*A pause.*) Andriusha, why don't you say anything?

ANDREY: I was just day-dreaming. ... There's nothing to say, anyway....

NATASHA: Well.... What was it I was going to tell you? Oh, yes! Ferapont from the Council Office wants to see you about something.

ANDREY: (*yawns*). Tell him to come up.

NATASHA goes out. ANDREY, bending over the candle which she has left behind, begins to read his book. Enter FERAPONT in an old shabby overcoat, his collar turned up, his ears muffled in a scarf.

ANDREY: Hullo, old chap! What did you want to see me about?

FERAPONT: The chairman's sent you the register and a letter or something. Here they are. (*Hands him the book and the letter.*)

ANDREY: Thanks. That's all right. Incidentally, why have you come so late? It's gone eight already.

FERAPONT: What's that?

ANDREY: (*Raising his voice.*) I said, why have you come so late? It's gone eight already.

FERAPONT: That's right. It was still daylight when I came first, but they wouldn't let me see you. The master's engaged, they said. Well, if you're engaged, you're engaged. I'm not in a hurry. (*Thinking that ANDREY has said something.*) What's that?

ANDREY: Nothing. (*Turns over the pages of the register.*) Tomorrow's Friday, there's no meeting, but I'll go to the office just the same ... do some work. I'm so bored at home! ... (*A pause.*) Yes, my dear old fellow, how things do change, what a fraud life is! So strange! Today I picked up this book, just out of boredom, because I hadn't anything to do. It's a copy of some lectures I attended at the University.... Good Heavens! Just think – I'm secretary of the local council now, and Protopopov's chairman, and the most I can ever hope for is to become a member of the council myself! I – a member of the local council! I, who dream every night that I'm a professor in Moscow University, a famous academician, the pride of all Russia!

FERAPONT: I'm sorry, I can't tell you. I don't hear very well.

ANDREY: If you could hear properly I don't think I'd be talking to you like this. I must talk to someone, but my wife doesn't seem to understand me, and as for my sisters ... I'm afraid of them for some reason or other, I'm afraid of them laughing at me and pulling my leg.... I don't drink and I don't like going to pubs, but my word! how I'd enjoy an hour or so at Tyestov's, or the Great Moscow Restaurant! Yes, my dear fellow, I would indeed!

FERAPONT: The other day at the office a contractor was telling me about some business men who were eating pancakes in Moscow. One of them ate forty pancakes and died. It was either forty or fifty, I can't remember exactly.

ANDREY: You can sit in some huge restaurant in Moscow without knowing anyone, and no one knowing you; yet somehow you don't feel that you don't belong there.... Whereas here you know everybody, and everybody knows you, and yet you don't feel you belong here, you feel you don't belong at all.... You're lonely and you feel a stranger.

FERAPONT: What's that? (*A pause.*) It was the same man that told me – of course, he may have been lying – he said that there's an enormous rope stretched right across Moscow.

ANDREY: Whatever for?

FERAPONT: I'm sorry, I can't tell you. That's what he said.

ANDREY: What nonsense! (*Reads the book.*) Have you ever been to Moscow?

FERAPONT: (*After a pause.*) No. It wasn't God's wish. (*A pause.*) Shall I go now?

ANDREY: Yes, you may go. Goodbye.

FERAPONT goes out.

Goodbye. (*Reading.*) Come in the morning to take some letters.... You can go now. (*A pause.*) He's gone.(*A bell rings.*) Yes, that's how it is.... (*Stretches and slowly goes to his room.*)

Singing is heard offstage; a nurse is putting a baby to sleep. Enter MASHA and VERSHININ. While they talk together, a maid lights a lamp and candles in the ballroom.

MASHA: I don't know. (*A pause.*) I don't know. Habit's very important, of course. For instance, after Father died, for a long time we couldn't get accustomed to the idea that we hadn't any orderlies to wait on us. But, habit apart, I think it's quite right what I was saying. Perhaps it's different in other places, but in this town the military certainly do seem to be the nicest and most generous and best-mannered people.

VERSHININ: I'm thirsty. I could do with a nice glass of tea.

MASHA: (*Glances at her watch.*) They'll bring it in presently. You see, they married me off when I was eighteen. I was afraid of my husband because he was a school-master, and I had only just left school myself. He seemed terribly learned

Figure 6 *Drei Schwestern* (Three Sisters) at the Schaubühne am Lehniner Platz in Berlin, 2009. (Photograph Arno Declair.)

then, very clever and important. Now it's quite different, unfortunately.

VERSHININ: Yes.... I see....

MASHA: I don't say anything against my husband – I'm used to him now – but there are such a lot of vulgar and unpleasant and offensive people among the other civilians. Vulgarity upsets me, it makes me feel insulted, I actually suffer when I meet someone who lacks refinement and gentle manners, and courtesy. When I'm with the other teachers, my husband's friends, I just suffer.

VERSHININ: Yes, of course. But I should have thought that in a town like this the civilians and the army people were equally uninteresting. There's nothing to choose between them. If you talk to any educated person here, civilian or military, he'll generally tell you that he's just worn out. It's either his wife, or his house, or his estate, or his horse, or something.... We Russians are capable of such elevated thoughts – then why do we have such low ideals in practical life? Why is it, why?

MASHA: Why?

VERSHININ: Yes, why does his wife wear him out, why do his children wear him out? And what about *him* wearing out his wife and children?

MASHA: You're a bit low-spirited today, aren't you?

VERSHININ: Perhaps. I haven't had any dinner today. I've had nothing to eat since morning. One of my daughters is a bit off colour, and when the children are ill, I get so worried. I feel utterly conscience-stricken at having given them a mother like theirs. Oh, if only you could have seen her this morning! What a despicable woman! We started quarrelling at seven o'clock, and at nine I just walked out and slammed the door. (*A pause.*) I never talk about these things in the ordinary way. It's a strange thing, but you're the only person I feel I dare complain to. (*Kisses her hand.*) Don't be angry with me. I've nobody, nobody but you.... (*A pause.*)

MASHA: What a noise the wind's making in the stove! Just before Father died the wind howled in the chimney just like that.

VERSHININ: Are you superstitious?

MASHA: Yes.

VERSHININ: How strange. (*Kisses her hand.*) You really are a wonderful creature, a marvellous creature! Wonderful, marvellous! It's quite dark here, but I can see your eyes shining.

MASHA: (*Moves to another chair.*) There's more light over here.

VERSHININ: I love you, I love you, I love you. ... I love your eyes, I love your movements.... I dream about them. A wonderful, marvellous being!

MASHA: (*Laughing softly.*) When you talk to me like that, somehow I can't help laughing, although I'm afraid at the same time. Don't say it again, please. (*Half-audibly.*) Well, no ... go on. I don't mind.... (*Covers her face with her hands.*) I don't mind.... Someone's coming.... Let's talk about something else....

Enter IRENA *and* TOOZENBACH *through the ballroom.*

TOOZENBACH: I have a triple-barrelled name – Baron Toozenbach-Krone-Alschauer – but actually I'm a Russian. I was baptized in the Greek-Orthodox faith, just like yourself. I haven't really got any German characteristics, except maybe the obstinate patient way I keep on pestering you. Look how I bring you home every evening.

IRENA: How tired I am!

TOOZENBACH: And I'll go on fetching you from the post office and bringing you home every evening for the next twenty years – unless you send me away.... (*Noticing* MASHA *and* VERSHININ, *with pleasure.*) Oh, it's you! How are you?

IRENA: Well, here I am, home at last! (*To* MASHA.) A woman came into the post office just before I left. She wanted to send a wire to her brother in Saratov to tell him her son had just died, but she couldn't remember the address. So we had to send the wire without an address, just to Saratov. She was crying and I was rude to her, for no reason at all. 'I've no time to waste,' I told her. So stupid of me. We're having the carnival crowd today, aren't we?

MASHA: Yes.

IRENA: (*Sits down.*) How nice it is to rest! I am tired!

TOOZENBACH: (*Smiling.*) When you come back from work, you look so young, so pathetic, somehow.... (*A pause.*)

IRENA: I'm tired. No, I don't like working at the post office, I don't like it at all.

MASHA: You've got thinner.... (*Whistles.*) You look younger, too, and your face looks quite boyish.

TOOZENBACH: It's the way she does her hair.

IRENA: I must look for another job. This one doesn't suit me. It hasn't got what I always longed for and dreamed about. It's the sort of work you do without inspiration, without even thinking.

Someone knocks at the floor from below.

That's the Doctor knocking. (*To* TOOZENBACH.) Will you answer him, dear? ... I can't.... I'm so tired.

TOOZENBACH: (*knocks on the floor.*)

IRENA: He'll be up in a moment. We must do something about all this. Andrey and the Doctor went to the club last night and lost at cards again. They say Andrey lost two hundred roubles.

MASHA: (*With indifference.*) Well, what are we to do about it?

IRENA: He lost a fortnight ago, and he lost in December, too. I wish to goodness he'd lose everything we've got, and soon, too, and then perhaps we'd move out of this place. Good Heavens, I dream of Moscow every night. Sometimes I feel as if I were going mad. (*Laughs.*) We're going to Moscow in June. How many months are there till June? ... February, March, April, May ... nearly half-a-year!

MASHA: We must take care that Natasha doesn't get to know about him losing at cards.

IRENA: I don't think she cares.

Enter CHEBUTYKIN. *He has been resting on his bed since dinner and has only just got up. He combs his beard, then sits down at the table and takes out a newspaper.*

MASHA: There he is. Has he paid his rent yet?

IRENA: (*Laughs.*) No. Not a penny for the last eight months. I suppose he's forgotten.

MASHA: (*Laughs.*) How solemn he looks sitting there!

They all laugh. A pause.

IRENA: Why don't you say something, Alexandr Ignatyevich?

VERSHININ: I don't know. I'm just longing for some tea. I'd give my life for a glass of tea! I've had nothing to eat since morning....

CHEBUTYKIN: Irena Serghyeevna!

IRENA: What is it?

CHEBUTYKIN: Please come here. *Venez ici!*

IRENA goes over to him and sits down at the table.

I can't do without you.

IRENA lays out the cards for a game of patience.

VERSHININ: Well, if we can't have any tea, let's do a bit of philosophizing, anyway.

TOOZENBACH: Yes, let's. What about?

VERSHININ: What about? Well ... let's try to imagine what life will be like after we're dead, say in two or three hundred years.

TOOZENBACH: All right, then.... After we're dead, people will fly about in balloons, the cut of their coats will be different, the sixth sense will be discovered, and possibly even developed and used, for all I know.... But I believe life itself will remain the same; it will still be difficult and full of mystery and full of happiness. And in a thousand years' time people will still be sighing and complaining: 'How hard this business of living is!' – and yet they'll still be scared of death and unwilling to die, just as they are now.

VERSHININ: (*After a moment's thought.*) Well, you know ... how shall I put it? I think everything in the world is bound to change gradually – in fact, it's changing before our very eyes. In two or three hundred years, or maybe in a thousand years – it doesn't matter how long exactly – life will be different. It will be happy. Of course, we shan't be able to enjoy that future life, but all the same, what we're living for now is to create it, we work and … yes, we suffer in order to create it. That's the goal of our life, and you might say that's the only happiness we shall ever achieve.

MASHA: (*Laughs quietly.*)

TOOZENBACH: Why are you laughing?

MASHA: I don't know. I've been laughing all day today.

VERSHININ (*To* TOOZENBACH.) I went to the same cadet school as you did but I never went on to the Military Academy. I read a great deal, of course, but I never know what books I ought to choose, and probably I read a lot of stuff that's not worth anything. But the longer I live the more I seem to long for knowledge. My hair's going grey and I'm getting on in years, and yet how little I know, how little! All the same, I think I do know one thing which is not only true but also most important. I'm sure of it. Oh, if only I could convince you that there's not going to be any happiness for our own generation, that there mustn't be and won't be…. We've just got to work and work. All the happiness is reserved for our descendants, our remote descendants. (*A pause.*) Anyway, if I'm not to be happy, then at least my children's children will be.

FEDOTIK and RODÉ enter the ballroom; they sit down and sing quietly, one of them playing on a guitar.

TOOZENBACH: So you won't even allow us to dream of happiness! But what if I *am* happy?

VERSHININ: You're not.

TOOZENBACH: (*Flinging up his hands and laughing.*) We don't understand one another, that's obvious. How can I convince you?

MASHA: (*Laughs quietly.*)

TOOZENBACH: (*Holds up a finger to her.*) Show a finger to her and she'll laugh! (*To* VERSHININ.) And life will be just the same as ever not merely in a couple of hundred years' time, but in a million years. Life doesn't change, it always goes on the same; it follows its own laws, which don't concern us, which we can't discover anyway. Think of the birds that migrate in the autumn, the cranes, for instance: they just fly on and on. It doesn't matter what sort of thoughts they've got in their heads, great thoughts or little thoughts, they just fly on and on, not knowing where or why. And they'll go on flying no matter how many philosophers they happen to have flying with them. Let them philosophize as much as they like, as long as they go on flying.

MASHA: Isn't there some meaning?

TOOZENBACH: Meaning? … Look out there, it's snowing. What's the meaning of that? (*A pause.*)

MASHA: I think a human being has got to have some faith, or at least he's got to seek faith. Otherwise his life will be empty, empty…. How can you live and not know why

the cranes fly, why children are born, why the stars shine in the sky! … You must either know why you live, or else … nothing matters … everything's just wild grass…. (*A pause.*)

VERSHININ: All the same, I'm sorry my youth's over.

MASHA: 'It's a bore to be alive in this world, friends,' that's what Gogol says.

TOOZENBACH: And I feel like saying: it's hopeless arguing with you, friends! I give you up.

CHEBUTYKIN: (*Reads out of the paper.*) Balsac's marriage took place at Berdichev.[2]

IRENA: (*Sings softly to herself.*)

CHEBUTYKIN: Must write this down in my notebook. (*Writes.*) Balsac's marriage took place at Berdichev. (*Reads on.*)

IRENA: (*Playing patience, pensively.*) Balsac's marriage took place at Berdichev.

TOOZENBACH: Well, I've thrown in my hand. Did you know that I'd sent in my resignation, Maria Serghyeevna?

MASHA: Yes, I heard about it. I don't see anything good in it, either. I don't like civilians.

TOOZENBACH: Never mind. (*Gets up.*) What sort of a soldier do I make, anyway? I'm not even good-looking. Well, what does it matter? I'll work. I'd like to do such a hard day's work that when I came home in the evening I'd fall on my bed exhausted and go to sleep at once. (*Goes to the ballroom.*) I should think working men sleep well at nights!

FEDOTIK: (*To* IRENA.) I've got you some coloured crayons at Pyzhikov's, in Moscow Street. And this little penknife, too….

IRENA: You still treat me as if I were a little girl. I wish you'd remember I'm grown up now. (*Takes the crayons and the penknife, joyfully.*) They're awfully nice!

FEDOTIK: Look, I bought a knife for myself, too. You see, it's got another blade here, and then another … this thing's for cleaning your ears, and these are nail-scissors, and this is for cleaning your nails….

RODÉ: (*In a loud voice.*) Doctor, how old are you?

CHEBUTYKIN: I? Thirty-two.

Laughter.

FEDOTIK: I'll show you another kind of patience. (*Sets out the cards.*)

The samovar is brought in, and ANFISA *attends to it. Shortly afterwards* NATASHA *comes in and begins to fuss around the table.*

SOLIONY: (*Enters, bows to the company and sits down at the table.*)

VERSHININ: What a wind, though!

MASHA: Yes. I'm tired of winter. I've almost forgotten what summer is like.

IRENA: (*Playing patience.*) I'm going to go out. We'll get to Moscow!

FEDOTIK: No, it's not going out. You see, the eight has to go on the two of spades. (*Laughs.*) That means you won't go to Moscow.

CHEBUTYKIN: (*Reads the paper.*) Tzitzikar. Smallpox is raging....

ANFISA: (*Goes up to* MASHA.) Masha, the tea's ready, dear. (*To* VERSHININ.) Will you please come to the table, your Excellency? Forgive me, your name's slipped my memory....

MASHA: Bring it here, Nanny. I'm not coming over there.

IRENA: Nanny!

ANFISA: Comi-ing!

NATASHA: (*To* SOLIONY.) You know, even tiny babies understand what we say perfectly well! 'Good morning, Bobik,' I said to him only today, 'Good morning, my precious!' – and then he looked at me in such a special sort of way. You may say it's only a mother's imagination, but it isn't, I do assure you. No, no! He really is an extraordinary child!

SOLIONY: If that child were mine, I'd cook him up in a frying pan and eat him. (*Picks up his glass, goes into the drawing-room and sits down in a corner.*)

NATASHA: (*Covers her face with her hands.*) What a rude, ill-mannered person!

MASHA: People who don't even notice whether it's summer or winter are lucky! I think I'd be indifferent to the weather if I were living in Moscow.

VERSHININ: I've just been reading the diary of some French cabinet minister – he wrote it in prison. He got sent to prison in connection with the Panama affair. He writes with such a passionate delight about the birds he can see through the prison window – the birds he never even noticed when he was a cabinet minister. Of course, now he's released he won't notice them any more.... And in the same way, you won't notice Moscow once you live there again. We're not happy and we can't be happy: we only want happiness.

TOOZENBACH: (*Picks up a box from the table.*) I say, where are all the chocolates?

IRENA: Soliony's eaten them.

TOOZENBACH: All of them?

ANFISA: (*Serving* VERSHININ *with tea.*) Here's a letter for you, Sir.

VERSHININ: For me? (*Takes the letter.*) From my daughter. (*Reads it.*) Yes, of course.... Forgive me, Maria Serghyeevna, I'll just leave quietly. I won't have any tea. (*Gets up, agitated.*) Always the same thing....

MASHA: What is it? Secret?

VERSHININ: (*In a low voice.*) My wife's taken poison again. I must go. I'll get away without them seeing me. All this is so dreadfully unpleasant. (*Kisses* MASHA's *hand.*) My dear, good, sweet girl.... I'll go out this way, quietly.... (*Goes out.*)

ANFISA: Where's he off to? And I've just brought him some tea! What a queer fellow!

MASHA: (*Flaring up.*) Leave me alone! Why do you keep worrying me? Why don't you leave me in peace? (*Goes to the table, cup in hand.*) I'm sick and tired of you, silly old woman!

ANFISA: Why.... I didn't mean to offend you, dear.

ANDREY's voice: (*Offstage*). Anfisa!

ANFISA: (*Mimics him.*) Anfisa! Sitting there in his den! ... (*Goes out.*)

MASHA: (*By the table in the ballroom, crossly.*) Do let me sit down somewhere! (*Fumbles up the cards laid out on the table.*) You take up the whole table with your cards! Why don't you get on with your tea?

IRENA: How bad-tempered you are, Mashka!

MASHA: Well, if I'm bad-tempered, don't talk to me, then. Don't touch me!

CHEBUTYKIN: (*Laughs.*) Don't touch her! ... Take care you don't touch her!

MASHA: You may be sixty, but you're always gabbling some damn nonsense or other, just like a child....

NATASHA: (*Sighs.*) My dear Masha, need you use such expressions? You know, with your good looks you'd be thought so charming, even by the best people – yes, I honestly mean it – if only you wouldn't use these expressions of yours! *Je vous prie, pardonnez moi, Marie, mais vous avez des manières un peu grossières.*

TOOZENBACH: (*With suppressed laughter.*) Pass me.... I say, will you please pass me.... Is that cognac over there, or what? ...

NATASHA: *Il parait que mon Bobik déjà ne dort pas....* I think he's awake. He's not been too well today. I must go and see him ... excuse me. (*Goes out.*)

IRENA: I say, where has Alexandr Ignatyevich gone to?

MASHA: He's gone home. His wife's done something queer again.

TOOZENBACH: (*Goes over to* SOLIONY *with a decanter of cognac.*) You always sit alone brooding over something or other – though what it's all about nobody knows. Well, let's make it up. Let's have a cognac together. (*They drink.*) I suppose I'll have to play the piano all night tonight – a lot of rubbishy tunes, of course.... Never mind!

SOLIONY: Why did you say 'let's make it up'? We haven't quarrelled.

TOOZENBACH: You always give me the feeling that there's something wrong between us. You're a strange character, no doubt about it.

SOLIONY: (*Recites.*) 'I am strange, but who's not so? Don't be angry, Aleko!'

TOOZENBACH: What's Aleko got to do with it? ... (*A pause.*)

SOLIONY: When I'm alone with somebody I'm all right, I'm just like other people. But in company, I get depressed and shy, and ... I talk all sorts of nonsense. All the same, I'm a good deal more honest and well-intentioned than plenty of others. I can prove I am.

TOOZENBACH: You often make me angry because you keep on pestering me when we're in company – but all the same, I do like you for some reason.... I'm going to get drunk tonight, whatever happens! Let's have another drink!

SOLIONY: Yes, let's. (*A pause.*) I've never had anything against you personally, Baron. But my temperament's rather like Lermontov's. (*In a low voice.*) I even look a little like Lermontov, I've been told.... (*Takes a scent bottle from his pocket and sprinkles some scent on his hands.*)

TOOZENBACH: I have sent in my resignation! Finished! I've been considering it for five years, and now I've made up my mind at last. I'm going to work.

SOLIONY: (*Recites.*) 'Don't be angry, Aleko.... Away, away with all your dreams!'

During the conversation ANDREY *enters quietly with a book in his hand and sits down by the candle.*

TOOZENBACH: I'm going to work!

CHEBUTYKIN: (*Comes into the drawing-room with* IRENA.) And the food they treated me to was the genuine Caucasian stuff: onion soup, followed by chehartma – that's a meat dish, you know.

SOLIONY: Chereshma isn't meat at all; it's a plant, something like an onion.

CHEBUTYKIN: No-o, my dear friend. Chehartma isn't an onion, it's roast mutton.

SOLIONY: I tell you chereshma is a kind of onion.

CHEBUTYKIN: Well, why should I argue about it with you? You've never been to the Caucasus and you've never tasted chehartma.

SOLIONY: I haven't tasted it because I can't stand the smell of it. Chereshma stinks just like garlic.

ANDREY: (*Imploringly.*) Do stop it, friends! Please stop it!

TOOZENBACH: When's the carnival crowd coming along?

IRENA: They promised to be here by nine – that means any moment now.

TOOZENBACH: (*Embraces* ANDREY *and sings.*) 'Ah, my beautiful porch, my lovely new porch, my ...'[3]

ANDREY: (*Dances and sings.*) 'My new porch all made of maple-wood....'

CHEBUTYKIN: (*Dances.*) 'With fancy carving over the door....'

Laughter.

TOOZENBACH: (*Kisses* ANDREY.) Let's have a drink, the devil take it! Andriusha, let's drink to eternal friendship. I'll come with you when you go back to Moscow University.

SOLIONY: Which university? There are two universities in Moscow.

ANDREY: There's only one.

SOLIONY: I tell you there are two.

ANDREY: Never mind, make it three. The more the merrier.

SOLIONY: There are two universities in Moscow.

Murmurs of protest and cries of 'Hush!'

There are two universities in Moscow, an old one and a new one. But if you don't want to listen to what I'm saying, if my conversation irritates you, I can keep silent. In fact I can go to another room.... (*Goes out through one of the doors.*)

TOOZENBACH: Bravo, bravo! (*Laughs.*) Let's get started, my

friends, I'll play for you. What a funny creature that Soliony is! ... (*Sits down at the piano and plays a waltz.*)

MASHA: (*Dances alone.*) The Baron is drunk, the Baron is drunk, the Baron is drunk....

Enter NATASHA.

NATASHA: (*To* CHEBUTYKIN.) Ivan Romanych! (*Speaks to him, then goes out quietly.* CHEBUTYKIN *touches* TOOZENBACH *on the shoulder and whispers to him.*)

IRENA: What is it?

CHEBUTYKIN: It's time we were going. Goodnight.

IRENA: But really.... What about the carnival party?

ANDREY: (*Embarrassed.*) The carnival party's not coming. You see, my dear, Natasha says that Bobik isn't very well, and so. ... Anyway, I don't know ... and I certainly don't care....

IRENA: (*Shrugs her shoulders.*) Bobik's not very well! ...

MASHA: Never mind, we'll keep our end up! If they turn us out, out we must go! (*To* IRENA.) It isn't Bobik who's not well, it's her.... There! ... (*Taps her forehead with her finger.*) Petty little bourgeois housewife!

ANDREY *goes to his room on the right.* CHEBUTYKIN *follows him. The guests say goodbye in the ballroom.*

FEDOTIK: What a pity! I'd been hoping to spend the evening here, but of course, if the baby's ill.... I'll bring him some toys tomorrow.

RODÉ: (*In a loud voice.*) I had a good long sleep after lunch today on purpose, I thought I'd be dancing all night. I mean to say, it's only just nine o'clock.

MASHA: Let's go outside and talk it over. We can decide what to do then.

Voices are heard saying 'Goodbye! God bless you!' and TOOZENBACH *is heard laughing gaily. Everyone goes out.* ANFISA *and a maid clear the table and put out the lights. The nurse sings to the baby offstage. Enter* ANDREY, *wearing an overcoat and hat, followed by* CHEBUTYKIN. *They move quietly.*

CHEBUTYKIN: I've never found time to get married, somehow ... partly because my life's just flashed past me like lightning, and partly because I was always madly in love with your mother and she was married....

ANDREY: One shouldn't marry. One shouldn't marry because it's so boring.

CHEBUTYKIN: That may be so, but what about loneliness? You can philosophize as much as you like, dear boy, but loneliness is a dreadful thing. Although, really ... well, it doesn't matter a damn, of course! ...

ANDREY: Let's get along quickly.

CHEBUTYKIN: What's the hurry? There's plenty of time.

ANDREY: I'm afraid my wife may try to stop me.

CHEBUTYKIN: Ah!

ANDREY: I won't play cards tonight, I'll just sit and watch. I'm not feeling too well.... What ought I to do for this breathlessness, Ivan Romanych?

CHEBUTYKIN: Why ask me, dear boy? I can't remember – I simply don't know.

ANDREY: Let's go through the kitchen.

They go out. A bell rings. The ring is repeated, then voices and laughter are heard.

IRENA: (*Coming in.*) What's that?

ANFISA: (*In a whisper.*) The carnival party.

The bell rings again.

IRENA: Tell them there's no one at home, Nanny. Apologize to them.

ANFISA goes out. IRENA walks up and down the room, lost in thought. She seems agitated. Enter SOLIONY.

SOLIONY: (*Puzzled.*) There's no one here.... Where is everybody?

IRENA: They've gone home.

SOLIONY: How strange! Then you're alone here?

IRENA: Yes, alone. (*A pause.*) Well ... Goodnight.

SOLIONY: I know I behaved tactlessly just now, I lost control of myself. But you're different from the others, you stand out high above them – you're pure, you can see where the truth lies.... You're the only person in the world who can possibly understand me. I love you.... I love you with a deep, infinite ...

IRENA: Do please go away. Goodnight!

SOLIONY: I can't live without you. (*Follows her.*) Oh, it's such a delight just to look at you! (*With tears.*) Oh, my happiness! Your glorious, marvellous, entrancing eyes – eyes like no other woman's I've ever seen....

IRENA: (*Coldly.*) Please stop it, Vassily Vassilich!

SOLIONY: I've never spoken to you of my love before ... it makes me feel as if I were living on a different planet.... (*Rubs his forehead.*) Never mind! I can't force you to love me, obviously. But I don't intend to have any rivals – successful rivals, I mean.... No, no! I swear to you by everything I hold sacred that if there's anyone else, I'll kill him. Oh, how wonderful you are!

Enter NATASHA carrying a candle.

NATASHA: (*Pokes her head into one room, then into another, but passes the door leading to her husband's room.*) Andrey's reading in there. Better let him read. Forgive me, Vassily Vassilich, I didn't know you were here. I'm afraid I'm not properly dressed.

SOLIONY: I don't care. Goodbye. (*Goes out.*)

NATASHA: You must be tired, my poor dear girl. (*Kisses IRENA.*) You ought to go to bed earlier.

IRENA: Is Bobik asleep?

NATASHA: Yes, he's asleep. But he's not sleeping peacefully. By the way, my dear, I've been meaning to speak to you for some time but there's always been something ... either you're not here, or I'm too busy.... You see, I think that Bobik's nursery is so cold and damp.... And your room

is just ideal for a baby. Darling, do you think you could move into Olga's room?

IRENA: (*Not understanding her.*) Where to?

The sound of bells is heard outside, as a 'troika' is driven up to the house.

NATASHA: You can share a room with Olia for the time being, and Bobik can have your room. He is such a darling! This morning I said to him: 'Bobik, you're my very own! My very own!' And he just gazed at me with his dear little eyes.

The door bell rings.

That must be Olga. How late she is!

A maid comes up to NATASHA and whispers in her ear.

NATASHA: Protopopov! What a funny fellow! Protopopov's come to ask me to go for a drive with him. In a troika! (*Laughs.*) Aren't these men strange creatures! ...

The door bell rings again.

Someone's ringing. Shall I go for a short drive? Just for a quarter of an hour? (*To the maid.*) Tell him I'll be down in a minute.

The door bell rings.

That's the bell again. I suppose it's Olga. (*Goes out.*)

The maid runs out; IRENA sits lost in thought. Enter KOOLYGHIN and OLGA, followed by VERSHININ.

KOOLYGHIN: Well! What's the meaning of this? You said you were going to have a party.

VERSHININ: It's a strange thing. I left here about half an hour ago, and they were expecting a carnival party then.

IRENA: They've all gone.

KOOLYGHIN: Masha's gone, too? Where has she gone to? And why is Protopopov waiting outside in a troika? Who's he waiting for?

IRENA: Please don't ask me questions. I'm tired.

KOOLYGHIN: You ... spoilt child!

OLGA: The conference has only just ended. I'm quite worn out. The headmistress is ill and I'm deputizing for her. My head's aching, oh, my head, my head.... (*Sits down.*) Andrey lost two hundred roubles at cards last night. The whole town's talking about it....

KOOLYGHIN: Yes, the conference exhausted me, too. (*Sits down.*)

VERSHININ: So now my wife's taken it into her head to try to frighten me. She tried to poison herself. However, everything's all right now, so I can relax, thank goodness. ... So we've got to go away? Well, Goodnight to you, all the best. Fiodor Illych, would you care to come along with me somewhere or other? I can't stay at home tonight, I really can't.... Do come!

KOOLYGHIN: I'm tired. I don't think I'll come. (*Gets up.*) I'm tired. Has my wife gone home?

IRENA: I think so.

KOOLYGHIN: (*Kisses* IRENA's *hand.*) Goodnight. We can rest tomorrow and the day after tomorrow, two whole days! Well, I wish you all the best. (*Going out.*) How I long for some tea! I reckoned on spending the evening in congenial company, but – o, *fallacem hominum spem!* Always use the accusative case in exclamations.

VERSHININ: Well, it looks as if I'll have to go somewhere by myself. (*Goes out with* KOOLYGHIN, *whistling.*)

OLGA: My head aches, oh, my head.... Andrey lost at cards ... the whole town's talking.... I'll go and lie down. (*Going out.*) Tomorrow I'm free. Heavens, what a joy! Tomorrow I'm free, and the day after tomorrow I'm free.... My head's aching, oh, my poor head....

IRENA: (*Alone.*) They've all gone. No one's left.

Someone is playing an accordion in the street. The nurse sings in the next room.

NATASHA: (*Crosses the ballroom, wearing a fur coat and cap. She is followed by the maid.*) I'll be back in half an hour. I'm just going for a little drive. (*Goes out.*)

IRENA: (*Alone, with intense longing.*) Moscow! Moscow! Moscow!

Act 3

A bedroom now shared by OLGA *and* IRENA. *There are two beds, one on the right, the other on the left, each screened off from the centre of the room. It is past two o'clock in the morning. Offstage the alarm is being sounded on account of a fire which has been raging for some time. The inmates of the house have not yet been to bed.* MASHA *is lying on a couch, dressed, as usual, in black.* OLGA *and* ANFISA *come in.*

ANFISA: Now they're sitting down there, under the stairs.... I keep telling them to come upstairs, that they shouldn't sit down there, but they just cry. 'We don't know where our Papa is,' they say, 'perhaps he's got burned in the fire.' What an idea! And there are people in the yard, too ... half-dressed....

OLGA: (*Takes a dress out of a wardrobe.*) Take this grey frock, Nanny.... And this one.... This blouse, too.... And this skirt. Oh, Heavens! what is happening! Apparently the whole of the Kirsanovsky Street's been burnt down.... Take this ... and this, too.... (*Throws the clothes into* ANFISA's *arms.*) The poor Vershinins had a fright. Their house only just escaped being burnt down. They'll have to spend the night here ... we mustn't let them go home. Poor Fedotik's lost everything, he's got nothing left....

ANFISA: I'd better call Ferapont, Oliushka, I can't carry all this.

OLGA: (*Rings.*) No one takes any notice when I ring. (*Calls through the door.*) Is anyone there? Will someone come up, please!

A window, red with the glow of the fire, can be seen through the open door. The sound of a passing fire engine is heard.

How dreadful it all is! And how tired of it I am!

Enter FERAPONT.

Take this downstairs please.... The Kolotilin girls are sitting under the stairs ... give it to them. And this, too....

FERAPONT: Very good, Madam. Moscow was burned down in 1812 just the same. Mercy on us! ... Yes, the French were surprised all right.

OLGA: Go along now, take this down.

FERAPONT: Very good. (*Goes out.*)

OLGA: Give it all away, Nanny dear. We won't keep anything, give it all away.... I'm so tired, I can hardly keep on my feet. We mustn't let the Vershinins go home. The little girls can sleep in the drawing-room, and Alexandr Ignatyevich can share the downstairs room with the Baron. Fedotik can go in with the Baron, too, or maybe he'd better sleep in the ballroom. The doctor's gone and got drunk – you'd think he'd done it on purpose; he's so hopelessly drunk that we can't let anyone go into his room. Vershinin's wife will have to go into the drawing-room, too.

ANFISA: (*Wearily.*) Don't send me away, Oliushka, darling! Don't send me away!

OLGA: What nonsense you're talking, Nanny! No one's sending you away.

ANFISA: (*Leans her head against* OLGA's *breast.*) My dearest girl! I do work, you know, I work as hard as I can.... I suppose now I'm getting weaker, I'll be told to go. But where can I go? Where? I'm eighty years old. I'm over eighty-one!

OLGA: You sit down for a while, Nanny.... You're tired, you poor dear.... (*Makes her sit down.*) Just rest a bit. You've turned quite pale.

Enter NATASHA.

NATASHA: They're saying we ought to start a subscription in aid of the victims of the fire. You know – form a society or something for the purpose. Well, why not? It's an excellent idea! In any case it's up to us to help the poor as best we can. Bobik and Sofochka are fast asleep as if nothing had happened. We've got such a crowd of people in the house; the place seems full of people whichever way you turn. There's flu about in the town.... I'm so afraid the children might catch it.

OLGA: (*Without listening to her.*) You can't see the fire from this room; it's quiet in here.

NATASHA: Yes.... I suppose my hair is all over the place. (*Stands in front of the mirror.*) They say I've got stouter, but it's not true! I'm not a bit stouter. Masha's asleep ... she's tired, poor girl.... (*To* ANFISA, *coldly.*) How dare you sit down in my presence? Get up! Get out of here!

ANFISA goes out. A pause.

I can't understand why you keep that old woman in the house.

OLGA: (*Taken aback.*) Forgive me for saying it, but I can't understand how you. . . .

NATASHA: She's quite useless here. She's just a peasant woman, her right place is in the country. You're spoiling her. I do like order in the home, I don't like having useless people about. (*Strokes* OLGA'S *cheek.*) You're tired, my poor dear! Our headmistress is tired! You know, when my Sofochka grows up and goes to school, I'll be frightened of you.

OLGA: I'm not going to be a headmistress.

NATASHA: You'll be asked to, Olechka. It's settled.

OLGA: I'll refuse. I couldn't do it.... I wouldn't be strong enough. (*Drinks water.*) You spoke so harshly to Nanny just now.... You must forgive me for saying so, but I just can't stand that sort of thing ... it made me feel quite faint....

NATASHA: (*Agitated.*) Forgive me, Olia, forgive me. I didn't mean to upset you.

MASHA gets up, picks up a pillow and goes out in a huff.

OLGA: Please try to understand me, dear.... It may be that we've been brought up in a peculiar way, but anyway I just can't bear it. When people are treated like that, it gets me down, I feel quite ill.... I simply get unnerved....

NATASHA: Forgive me, dear, forgive me! ... (*Kisses her.*)

OLGA: Any cruel or tactless remark, even the slightest discourtesy, upsets me....

NATASHA: It's quite true, I know I often say things which would be better left unsaid – but you must agree with me, dear, that she'd be better in the country somewhere.

OLGA: She's been with us for thirty years.

NATASHA: But she can't do any work now, can she? Either I don't understand you, or you don't want to understand me. She can't work, she just sleeps or sits about.

OLGA: Well, let her sit about.

NATASHA: (*In surprise.*) What do you mean, let her sit about? Surely she is a servant! (*Tearfully.*) No, I don't understand you, Olia! I have a nurse for the children and a wet nurse and we share a maid and a cook. Whatever do we want this old woman for? What for?

The alarm is sounded again.

OLGA: I've aged ten years tonight.

NATASHA: We must sort things out, Olia. You're working at your school, and I'm working at home. You're teaching and I'm running the house. And when I say anything about the servants, I know what I'm talking about.... That old thief, that old witch must get out of this house tomorrow! ... (*Stamps her feet.*) How dare you vex me so? How dare you? (*Recovering her self-control.*) Really, if you don't move downstairs, we'll always be quarrelling. This is quite dreadful!

Enter KOOLYGHIN.

KOOLYGHIN: Where's Masha? It's time we went home. They say the fire's getting less fierce. (*Stretches.*) Only one block got burnt down, but to begin with it looked as if the whole town was going to be set on fire by that wind. (*Sits down.*) I'm so tired, Olechka, my dear. You know, I've often thought that if I hadn't married Masha, I'd have married you, Olechka. You're so kind. I'm worn out. (*Listens.*)

OLGA: What is it?

KOOLYGHIN: The doctor's got drunk just as if he'd done it on purpose. Hopelessly drunk.... As if he'd done it on purpose. (*Gets up.*) I think he's coming up here.... Can you hear him? Yes, he's coming up. (*Laughs.*) What a fellow, really! ... I'm going to hide myself. (*Goes to the wardrobe and stands between it and the wall.*) What a scoundrel!

OLGA: He's been off drinking for two years, and now suddenly he goes and gets drunk.... (*Walks with* NATASHA *towards the back of the room.*)

CHEBUTYKIN enters; walking firmly and soberly he crosses the room, stops, looks round, then goes to the wash-stand and begins to wash his hands.

CHEBUTYKIN: (*Glumly.*) The devil take them all ... all the lot of them! They think I can treat anything just because I'm a doctor, but I know positively nothing at all. I've forgotten everything I used to know. I remember nothing, positively nothing....

OLGA and NATASHA leave the room without his noticing.

The devil take them! Last Wednesday I attended a woman at Zasyp. She died, and it's all my fault that she did die. Yes.... I used to know a thing or two twenty-five years ago, but now I don't remember anything. Not a thing! Perhaps I'm not a man at all, but I just imagine that I've got hands and feet and a head. Perhaps I don't exist at all, and I only imagine that I'm walking about and eating and sleeping. (*Weeps.*) Oh, if only I could simply stop existing! (*Stops crying, glumly.*) God knows.... The other day they were talking about Shakespeare and Voltaire at the club.... I haven't read either, never read a single line of either, but I tried to make out by my expression that I had. The others did the same. How petty it all is! How despicable! And then suddenly I thought of the woman I killed on Wednesday. It all came back to me, and I felt such a swine, so sick of myself that I went and got drunk....

Enter IRENA, VERSHININ and TOOZENBACH. TOOZENBACH is wearing a fashionable new civilian suit.

IRENA: Let's sit down here for a while. No one will come in here.

VERSHININ: The whole town would have been burnt down but for the soldiers. They're a fine lot of fellows! (*Rubs his hands with pleasure.*) Excellent fellows! Yes, they're a fine lot!

KOOLYGHIN: (*Approaches them.*) What's the time?

TOOZENBACH: It's gone three. It's beginning to get light.

IRENA: Everyone's sitting in the ballroom and nobody thinks of leaving. That man Soliony there, too.... (*To* CHEBUTYKIN.) You ought to go to bed, Doctor.

CHEBUTYKIN: I'm all right.... Thanks.... (*Combs his beard.*)

KOOLYGHIN: (*Laughs.*) Half seas over, Ivan Romanych! (*Slaps him on the shoulder.*) You're a fine one! *In vino veritas*, as they used to say in Rome.

TOOZENBACH: Everyone keeps asking me to arrange a concert in aid of the victims of the fire.

IRENA: Well, who'd you get to perform in it?

TOOZENBACH: It could be done if we wanted to. Maria Serghyeevna plays the piano wonderfully well, in my opinion.

KOOLYGHIN: Yes, wonderfully well!

IRENA: She's forgotten how to. She hasn't played for three years ... or maybe it's four.

TOOZENBACH: Nobody understands music in this town, not a single person. But I do – I really do – and I assure you quite definitely that Maria Serghyeevna plays magnificently. She's almost a genius for it.

KOOLYGHIN: You're right, Baron. I'm very fond of Masha. She's such a nice girl.

TOOZENBACH: Fancy being able to play so exquisitely, and yet having nobody, nobody at all, to appreciate it!

KOOLYGHIN: (*Sighs.*) Yes.... But would it be quite proper for her to play in a concert? (*A pause.*) I don't know anything about these matters, my friends. Perhaps it'll be perfectly all right. But you know, although our director is a good man, a very good man indeed, and most intelligent, I know that he does hold certain views.... Of course, this doesn't really concern him, but I'll have a word with him about it, all the same, if you like.

CHEBUTYKIN: (*Picks up a china clock and examines it.*)

VERSHININ: I've got my clothes in such a mess helping to put out the fire, I must look like nothing on earth. (*A pause.*) I believe they were saying yesterday that our brigade might be transferred to somewhere a long way away. Some said it was to be Poland, and some said it was Cheeta, in Siberia.

TOOZENBACH: I heard that, too. Well, the town will seem quite deserted.

IRENA: We'll go away, too!

CHEBUTYKIN: (*Drops the clock and breaks it.*) Smashed to smithereens!

A pause. Everyone looks upset and embarrassed.

KOOLYGHIN: (*Picks up the pieces.*) Fancy breaking such a valuable thing! Ah, Ivan Romanych, Ivan Romanych! You'll get a bad mark for that!

IRENA: It was my mother's clock.

CHEBUTYKIN: Well, supposing it was. If it was your mother's, then it was your mother's. Perhaps I didn't smash it. Perhaps it only appears that I did. Perhaps it only appears to us that we exist, whereas in reality we don't exist at all. I don't know anything, no one knows anything. (*Stops at the door.*) Why are you staring at me? Natasha's having a nice little affair with Protopopov, and you don't see it. You sit here seeing nothing, and meanwhile Natasha's having a nice little affair with Protopopov.... (*Sings.*) Would you like a date?... (*Goes out.*)

VERSHININ: So.... (*Laughs.*) How odd it all is, really! (*A pause.*) When the fire started, I ran home as fast as I could. When I got near, I could see that our house was all right and out of danger, but the two little girls were standing there, in the doorway in their night clothes. Their mother wasn't there. People were rushing about, horses, dogs ... and in the kiddies' faces I saw a frightened, anxious, appealing look, I don't know what!... My heart sank when I saw their faces. My God, I thought, what will these children have to go through in the course of their poor lives? And they may live a long time, too! I picked them up and ran back here with them, and all the time I was running, I was thinking the same thing: what will they have to go through?

The alarm is sounded. A pause.

When I got here, my wife was here already ... angry, shouting!

Enter MASHA *carrying a pillow; she sits down on the couch.*

VERSHININ: And when my little girls were standing in the doorway with nothing on but their night clothes, and the street was red with the glow of the fire and full of terrifying noises, it struck me that the same sort of thing used to happen years ago, when armies used to make sudden raids on towns, and plunder them and set them on fire.... Anyway, is there any essential difference between things as they were and as they are now? And before very long, say, in another two or three hundred years, people may be looking at our present life just as we look at the past now, with horror and scorn. Our own times may seem uncouth to them, boring and frightfully uncomfortable and strange.... Oh, what a great life it'll be then, what a life! (*Laughs.*) Forgive me, I'm philosophizing my head off again ... but may I go on, please? I'm bursting to philosophize just at the moment. I'm in the mood for it. (*A pause.*) You seem as if you've all gone to sleep. As I was saying: what a great life it will be in the future! Just try to imagine it.... At the present time there are only three people of your intellectual calibre in the whole of this town, but future generations will be more productive of people like you. They'll go on producing more and more of the same sort until at last the time will come when everything will be just as you'd wish it yourselves. People will live their lives in your way, and then even you may be outmoded, and a new lot will come along who will be even better than you are.... (*Laughs.*) I'm in quite a special mood today. I feel full of a tremendous urge to live.... (*Sings.*)

'To Love all ages are in fee,
The passion's good for you and me.' ... (*Laughs.*)

MASHA: (*Sings.*) Tara-tara-tara....
VERSHININ: Tum-tum....
MASHA: Tara-tara. ...
VERSHININ: Tum-tum, tum-tum.... (*Laughs.*)

Enter FEDOTIK.

FEDOTIK: (*Dancing about.*) Burnt, burnt! Everything I've got burnt!

All laugh.

IRENA: It's hardly a joking matter. Has everything really been burnt?
FEDOTIK: (*Laughs.*) Everything, completely. I've got nothing left. My guitar's burnt, my photographs are burnt, all my letters are burnt. Even the little note-book I was going to give you has been burnt.

Enter SOLIONY.

IRENA: No, please go away, Vassily Vassilich. You can't come in here.
SOLIONY: Can't I? Why can the Baron come in here if I can't?
VERSHININ: We really must go, all of us. What's the fire doing?
SOLIONY: It's dying down, they say. Well, I must say it's a peculiar thing that the Baron can come in here, and I can't. (*Takes a scent bottle from his pocket and sprinkles himself with scent.*)
VERSHININ: Tara-tara.
MASHA: Tum-tum, tum-tum.
VERSHININ: (*Laughs, to* SOLIONY.) Let's go to the ballroom.
SOLIONY: Very well, we'll make a note of this. 'I hardly need to make my moral yet more clear: That might be teasing geese, I fear!' (*Looks at* TOOZENBACH.) Cluck, cluck, cluck! (*Goes out with* VERSHININ *and* FEDOTIK.)
IRENA: That Soliony has smoked the room out.... (*Puzzled.*) The Baron's asleep. Baron! Baron!
TOOZENBACH: (*Waking out of his doze.*) I must be tired. The brick-works.... No, I'm not talking in my sleep. I really do intend to go to the brick-works and start working there quite soon. I've had a talk with the manager. (*To* IRENA, *tenderly.*) You are so pale, so beautiful, so fascinating.... Your pallor seems to light up the darkness around you, as if it were luminous, somehow.... You're sad, you're dissatisfied with the life, you have to live.... Oh, come away with me, let's go away and work together!
MASHA: Nikolai Lvovich, I wish you'd go away.
TOOZENBACH: (*Laughs.*) Oh, you're here, are you? I didn't see you. (*Kisses* IRENA's *hand.*) Goodbye, I'm going. You know, as I look at you now, I keep thinking of the day – it was a long time ago, your Saint's day – when you talked to us about the joy of work.... You were so gay and high-spirited then.... And what a happy life I saw ahead of me! Where is it all now? (*Kisses her hand.*) There are tears in your eyes. You should go to bed, it's beginning to get light ... it's almost morning.... Oh, if only I could give my life for you!

MASHA: Nikolai Lvovich, please go away! Really now....
TOOZENBACH: I'm going. (*Goes out.*)
MASHA: (*Lies down.*) Are you asleep, Fiodor?
KOOLYGHIN: Eh?
MASHA: Why don't you go home?
KOOLYGHIN: My darling Masha, my sweet, my precious Masha....
IRENA: She's tired. Let her rest a while, Fyedia.
KOOLYGHIN: I'll go in a moment. My wife, my dear, good wife! ... How I love you! ... only you!
MASHA: (*Crossly.*) Amo, amas, amat, amamus, amatis, amant!
KOOLYGHIN: (*Laughs.*) Really, she's an amazing woman! – I've been married to you for seven years, but I feel as if we were only married yesterday. Yes, on my word of honour, I do! You really are amazing! Oh, I'm so happy, happy, happy!
MASHA: And I'm so bored, bored, bored! (*Sits up.*) I can't get it out of my head.... It's simply disgusting. It's like having a nail driven into my head. No, I can't keep silent about it any more. It's about Andrey.... He's actually mortgaged this house to a bank, and his wife's got hold of all the money – and yet the house doesn't belong to him, it belongs to all four of us! Surely, he must realize that, if he's got any honesty.
KOOLYGHIN: Why bring all this up, Masha? Why bother about it now? Andriusha owes money all round.... Leave him alone.
MASHA: Anyway, it's disgusting. (*Lies down.*)
KOOLYGHIN: Well, we aren't poor, Masha. I've got work, I teach at the county school, I give private lessons in my spare time.... I'm just a plain, honest man.... *Omnia mea mecum porto*, as they say.
MASHA: I don't ask for anything, but I'm just disgusted by injustice. (*A pause.*) Why don't you go home, Fiodor?
KOOLYGHIN: (*Kisses her.*) You're tired. Just rest here for a while.... I'll go home and wait for you.... Go to sleep. (*Goes to the door.*) I'm happy, happy, happy! (*Goes out.*)
IRENA: The truth is that Andrey is getting to be shallow-minded. He's ageing and since he's been living with that woman he's lost all the inspiration he used to have! Not long ago he was working for a professorship, and yet yesterday he boasted of having at last been elected a member of the County Council. Fancy him a member, with Protopopov as chairman! They say the whole town's laughing at him, he's the only one who doesn't know anything or see anything. And now, you see, everyone's at the fire, while he's just sitting in his room, not taking the slightest notice of it. Just playing his violin. (*Agitated.*) Oh, how dreadful it is, how dreadful, how dreadful! I can't bear it any longer, I can't, I really can't! ...

Enter OLGA. *She starts arranging things on her bedside table.*

Figure 7 From the Moscow Art Theatre 1901 production of *Three Sisters.*

IRENA: (*Sobs loudly.*) You must turn me out of here! Turn me out; I can't stand it any more!

OLGA: (*Alarmed.*) What is it? What is it, darling?

IRENA: (*Sobbing.*) Where.... Where has it all gone to? Where is it? Oh, God! I've forgotten.... I've forgotten everything ... there's nothing but a muddle in my head.... I don't remember what the Italian for 'window' is, or for 'ceiling'.... Every day I'm forgetting more and more, and life's slipping by, and it will never, never come back.... We shall never go to Moscow.... I can see that we shall never go....

OLGA: Don't, my dear, don't....

IRENA: (*Trying to control herself.*) Oh, I'm so miserable! ... I can't work, I won't work! I've had enough of it, enough! ... First I worked on the telegraph, now I'm in the County Council office, and I hate and despise everything they give me to do there.... I'm twenty-three years old, I've been working all this time, and I feel as if my brain's dried up. I know I've got thinner and uglier and older, and I find no kind of satisfaction in anything, none at all. And the time's passing ... and I feel as if I'm moving away from any hope of a genuine, fine life, I'm moving further and further away and sinking into a kind of abyss. I feel in despair, and I don't know why I'm still alive, why I haven't killed myself....

OLGA: Don't cry, my dear child, don't cry.... It hurts me.

IRENA: I'm not crying any more. That's enough of it. Look, I'm not crying now. Enough of it, enough! ...

OLGA: Darling, let me tell you something.... I just want to speak as your sister, as your friend.... That is, if you want my advice.... Why don't you marry the Baron?

IRENA: (*Weeps quietly.*)

OLGA: After all, you do respect him, you think a lot of him.... It's true, he's not good-looking, but he's such a decent, clean-minded sort of man.... After all, one doesn't marry for love, but to fulfil a duty. At least, I think so, and I'd marry even if I weren't in love. I'd marry anyone that proposed to me, as long as he was a decent man. I'd even marry an old man.

IRENA: I've been waiting all this time, imagining that we'd be moving to Moscow, and I'd meet the man I'm meant for there. I've dreamt about him and I've loved him in my dreams.... But it's all turned out to be nonsense ... nonsense....

OLGA: (*Embracing her.*) My darling sweetheart, I understand everything perfectly. When the Baron resigned his commission and came to see us in his civilian clothes, I thought he looked so plain that I actually started to cry.... He asked me why I was crying.... How could I tell him? But, of course, if it were God's will that he should marry you, I'd feel perfectly happy about it. That's quite a different matter, quite different!

NATASHA, *carrying a candle, comes out of the door on the right, crosses the stage and goes out through the door on the left without saying anything.*

MASHA: (*Sits up.*) She goes about looking as if she'd started the fire.

OLGA: You're silly, Masha. You're the stupidest person in our family. Forgive me for saying so.

A pause.

MASHA: My dear sisters, I've got something to confess to you. I must get some relief, I feel the need of it in my heart. I'll confess it to you two alone, and then never again, never to anybody! I'll tell you in a minute. (*In a low voice.*) It's a secret, but you'll have to know everything. I can't keep silent any more. (*A pause.*) I'm in love, in love.... I love that man.... You saw him here just now.... Well, what's the good? ... I love Vershinin....

OLGA: (*Goes behind her screen.*) Don't say it. I don't want to hear it.

MASHA: Well, what's to be done? (*Holding her head.*) I thought he was queer at first, then I started to pity him ... then I began to love him ... love everything about him – his voice, his talk, his misfortunes, his two little girls....

OLGA: Nevertheless, I don't want to hear it. You can say any nonsense you like, I'm not listening.

MASHA: Oh, you're stupid, Olia! If I love him, well – that's my fate! That's my destiny.... He loves me, too. It's all rather frightening, isn't it? Not a good thing, is it? (*Takes* IRENA *by the hand and draws her to her.*) Oh, my dear! ... How are we going to live through the rest of our lives? What's going to become of us? When you read a novel, everything in it seems so old and obvious, but when you fall in love yourself, you suddenly discover that you don't really know anything, and you've got to make your own decisions.... My dear sisters, my dear sisters! ... I've confessed it all to you, and now I'll keep quiet.... I'll be like that madman in the story by Gogol – silence ... silence! ...

Enter ANDREY *followed by* FERAPONT.

ANDREY: (*Crossly.*) What do you want? I don't understand you.

FERAPONT: (*Stopping in the doorway, impatiently.*) I've asked you about ten times already, Andrey Serghyeevich.

ANDREY: In the first place, you're not to call me Andrey Serghyeevich – call me 'Your Honour'.

FERAPONT: The firemen are asking Your Honour if they may drive through your garden to get to the river. They've been going a long way round all this time – it's a terrible business!

ANDREY: All right. Tell them it's all right.

FERAPONT *goes out.*

They keep on plaguing me. Where's Olga?

OLGA *comes from behind the screen.*

I wanted to see you. Will you give me the key to the cupboard? I've lost mine. You know the key I mean, the small one you've got ...

OLGA *silently hands him the key.* IRENA *goes behind the screen on her side of the room.*

ANDREY: What a terrific fire! It's going down though. That Ferapont annoyed me, the devil take him! Silly thing he made me say.... Telling him to call me 'Your Honour'! ... (*A pause.*) Why don't you say anything, Olia? (*A pause.*) It's about time you stopped this nonsense ... sulking like this for no reason whatever.... You here, Masha? And Irena's here, too. That's excellent! We can talk it over then, frankly and once for all. What have you got against me? What is it?

OLGA: Drop it now, Andriusha. Let's talk it over tomorrow. (*Agitated.*) What a dreadful night!

ANDREY: (*In great embarrassment.*) Don't get upset. I'm asking you quite calmly, what have you got against me? Tell me frankly.

VERSHININ'S VOICE: (*Offstage.*) Tum-tum-tum!

MASHA: (*In a loud voice, getting up.*) Tara-tara-tara! (*To* OLGA.) Goodbye, Olia, God bless you! (*Goes behind the screen and kisses* IRENA.) Sleep well.... Goodbye, Andrey. I should leave them now, they're tired ... talk it over tomorrow.... (*Goes out.*)

OLGA: Really, Andriusha, let's leave it till tomorrow.... (*Goes behind the screen on her side of the room.*) It's time to go to bed.

ANDREY: I only want to say one thing, then I'll go. In a moment.... First of all, you've got something against my wife, against Natasha. I've always been conscious of it from the day we got married. Natasha is a fine woman, she's honest and straightforward and high-principled.... That's my opinion. I love and respect my wife. You understand that I respect her, and I expect others to respect her, too. I repeat: she's an honest, high-principled woman, and all your grievances against her – if you don't mind my saying so – are just imagination, and nothing more.... (*A pause.*) Secondly, you seem to be annoyed with me for not making myself a professor, and not doing any academic work. But I'm working in the Council Office, I'm a member of the County Council, and I feel my service there is just as fine and valuable as any academic work I might do. I'm a member of the County Council, and if you want to know, I'm proud of it! (*A pause.*) Thirdly ... there's something else I must tell you.... I know I mortgaged the house without asking your permission.... That was wrong, I admit it, and I ask you to forgive me.... I was driven to it by my debts.... I'm in debt for about thirty-five thousand roubles. I don't play cards any more, I've given it up long ago. ... The only thing I can say to justify myself is that you girls get an annuity, while I don't get anything ... no income, I mean.... (*A pause.*)

KOOLYGHIN: (*Calling through the door.*) Is Masha there? She's not there? (*Alarmed.*) Where can she be then? It's very strange.... (*Goes away.*)

ANDREY: So you won't listen? Natasha is a good, honest woman, I tell you. (*Walks up and down the stage, then stops.*) When I married her, I thought we were going to be happy, I thought we should all be happy.... But ... oh, my God! ... (*Weeps.*) My dear sisters, my dear, good sisters, don't believe what I've been saying, don't believe it.... (*Goes out.*)

KOOLYGHIN: (*Through the door, agitated.*) Where's Masha? Isn't Masha here? Extraordinary! (*Goes away.*)

The alarm is heard again. The stage is empty.

IRENA: (*Speaking from behind the screen.*) Olia! Who's that knocking on the floor?

OLGA: It's the doctor, Ivan Romanych. He's drunk.

IRENA: It's been one thing after another all night. (*A pause.*) Olia! (*Peeps out from behind the screen.*) Have you heard? The troops are being moved from the district ... they're being sent somewhere a long way off.

OLGA: That's only a rumour.

IRENA: We'll be left quite alone then.... Olia!

OLGA: Well?

IRENA: Olia, darling, I do respect the Baron.... I think a lot of him, he's a very good man.... I'll marry him, Olia, I'll agree to marry him, if only we can go to Moscow! Let's go, please do let's go! There's nowhere in all the world like Moscow. Let's go, Olia! Let's go!

Act 4

The old garden belonging to the Prozorovs' house. A river is seen at the end of a long avenue of fir-trees, and on the far bank of the river a forest. On the right of the stage there is a verandah with a table on which champagne bottles and glasses have been left. It is midday. From time to time people from the street pass through the garden to get to the river. Five or six soldiers march through quickly.

CHEBUTYKIN, radiating a mood of benevolence which does not leave him throughout the act, is sitting in a chair in the garden. He is wearing his army cap and is holding a walking stick, as if ready to be called away at any moment. KOOLYGHIN, with a decoration round his neck and with his moustache shaved off, TOOZENBACH and IRENA are standing on the verandah saying Goodbye to FEDOTIK and RODÉ, who are coming down the steps. Both officers are in marching uniform.

TOOZENBACH: (*Embracing* FEDOTIK.) You're a good fellow, Fedotik; we've been good friends! (*Embraces* RODÉ.) Once more, then.... Goodbye, my dear friends!

IRENA: Au revoir!

FEDOTIK: It's not 'au revoir'. It's Goodbye. We shall never meet again!

KOOLYGHIN: Who knows? (*Wipes his eyes, smiling.*) There! you've made me cry.

IRENA: We'll meet some time.

FEDOTIK: Perhaps in ten or fifteen years' time. But then we'll hardly know one another.... We shall just meet and say: 'How are you?' coldly.... (*Takes a snapshot.*) Wait a moment.... Just one more, for the last time.

RODÉ: (*Embraces* TOOZENBACH.) We're not likely to meet again.... (*Kisses* IRENA's *hand.*) Thank you for everything ... everything!

FEDOTIK: (*Annoyed.*) Do just wait a second!

TOOZENBACH: We'll meet again if we're fated to meet. Do write to us. Be sure to write.

RODÉ: (*Glancing round the garden.*) Goodbye, trees! (*Shouts.*) Heigh-ho! (*A pause.*) Goodbye, echo!

KOOLYGHIN: I wouldn't be surprised if you got married out there, in Poland.... You'll get a Polish wife, and she'll put her arms round you and say: Kohane![4] (*Laughs.*)

FEDOTIK: (*Glances at his watch.*) There's less than an hour to go. Soliony is the only one from our battery who's going down the river on the barge. All the others are marching with the division. Three batteries are leaving today by road and three more tomorrow – then the town will be quite peaceful.

TOOZENBACH: Yes, and dreadfully dull, too.

RODÉ: By the way, where's Maria Serghyeevna?

KOOLYGHIN: She's somewhere in the garden.

FEDOTIK: We must say Goodbye to her.

RODÉ: Goodbye. I really must go, or I'll burst into tears. (*Quickly embraces* TOOZENBACH *and* KOOLYGHIN, *kisses* IRENA's *hand.*) Life's been very pleasant here....

FEDOTIK: (*To* KOOLYGHIN.) Here's something for a souvenir for you – a note-book with a pencil.... We'll go down to the river through here. (*They go off, glancing back.*)

RODÉ: (*Shouts.*) Heigh-ho!

KOOLYGHIN: (*Shouts.*) Goodbye!

At the back of the stage FEDOTIK *and* RODÉ *meet* MASHA, *and say Goodbye to her; she goes off with them.*

IRENA: They've gone.... (*Sits down on the bottom step of the verandah.*)

CHEBUTYKIN: They forgot to say Goodbye to me.

IRENA: Well, what about you?

CHEBUTYKIN: That's true, I forgot, too. Never mind, I'll be seeing them again quite soon. I'll be leaving tomorrow. Yes ... only one more day. And then, in a year's time I'll be retiring. I'll come back here and finish the rest of my life near you. There's just one more year to go and then I get my pension.... (*Puts a newspaper in his pocket and takes out another.*) I'll come back here and lead a reformed life. I'll be a nice, quiet, well-behaved little man.

IRENA: Yes, it's really time you reformed, my dear friend. You ought to live a different sort of life, somehow.

CHEBUTYKIN: Yes. ... I think so, too. (*Sings quietly.*) Tarara-boom-di-ay.... I'm sitting on a tomb-di-ay....

KOOLYGHIN: Ivan Romanych is incorrigible! Incorrigible!

CHEBUTYKIN: Yes, you ought to have taken me in hand. You'd have reformed me!

IRENA: Fiodor's shaved his moustache off. I can't bear to look at him.

KOOLYGHIN: Why not?

CHEBUTYKIN: If I could just tell you what your face looks like now – but I daren't.

KOOLYGHIN: Well! Such are the conventions of life! *Modus vivendi*, you know. The director shaved his moustache off, so I shaved mine off when they gave me an inspectorship. No one likes it, but personally I'm quite indifferent. I'm content. Whether I've got a moustache or not, it's all the same to me. (*Sits down.*)

ANDREY passes across the back of the stage pushing a pram with a child asleep in it.

IRENA: Ivan Romanych, my dear friend, I'm awfully worried about something. You were out in the town garden last night – tell me what happened there?

CHEBUTYKIN: What happened? Nothing. Just a trifling thing. (*Reads his paper.*) It doesn't matter anyway.

KOOLYGHIN: They say that Soliony and the Baron met in the town garden outside the theatre last night and ....

TOOZENBACH: Don't, please! What's the good? ... (*Waves his hand at him deprecatingly and goes into the house.*)

KOOLYGHIN: It was outside the theatre.... Soliony started badgering the Baron, and he lost patience and said something that offended him.

CHEBUTYKIN: I don't know anything about it. It's all nonsense.

KOOLYGHIN: A school-master once wrote 'nonsense' in

Russian over a pupil's essay, and the pupil puzzled over it, thinking it was a Latin word. (*Laughs.*) Frightfully funny, you know! They say that Soliony's in love with Irena and that he got to hate the Baron more and more.... Well, that's understandable. Irena's a very nice girl. She's a bit like Masha, she tends to get wrapped up in her own thoughts. (*To* IRENA.) But your disposition is more easy-going than Masha's. And yet Masha has a very nice disposition, too. I love her, I love my Masha.

From the back of the stage comes a shout: 'Heigh-ho!'

IRENA: (*Starts.*) Anything seems to startle me today. (*A pause.*) I've got everything ready, too. I'm sending my luggage off after lunch. The Baron and I are going to get married tomorrow, and directly afterwards we're moving to the brick-works, and the day after tomorrow I'm starting work at the school. So our new life will begin, God willing! When I was sitting for my teacher's diploma, I suddenly started crying for sheer joy, with a sort of feeling of blessedness.... (*A pause.*) The carrier will be coming for my luggage in a minute....

KOOLYGHIN: That's all very well, but somehow I can't feel that it's meant to be serious. All ideas and theories, but nothing really serious. Anyway, I wish you luck from the bottom of my heart.

CHEBUTYKIN: (*Moved.*) My dearest girl, my precious child! You've gone on so far ahead of me, I'll never catch you up now. I've got left behind like a bird which has grown too old and can't keep up with the rest of the flock. Fly away, my dears, fly away, and God be with you! (*A pause.*) It's a pity you've shaved your moustache off, Fiodor Illyich.

KOOLYGHIN: Don't keep on about it, please! (*Sighs.*) Well, the soldiers will be leaving today, and everything will go back to what it was before. Anyway, whatever they say, Masha is a good, loyal wife. Yes, I love her dearly and I'm thankful for what God has given me. Fate treats people so differently. For instance, there's an excise clerk here called Kozyrev. He was at school with me and he was expelled in his fifth year because he just couldn't grasp the *ut consecutivum*. He's dreadfully hard up now, and in bad health, too, and whenever I meet him, I just say to him: 'Hullo, *ut consecutivum!*' 'Yes', he replies, 'that's just the trouble – *consecutivum*' ... and he starts coughing. Whereas I – I've been lucky all my life. I'm happy, I've actually been awarded the order of Saint Stanislav, second class – and now I'm teaching the children the same old *ut consecutivum*. Of course, I'm clever, cleverer than plenty of other people, but happiness does not consist of merely being clever....

In the house someone plays 'The Maiden's Prayer'.

IRENA: Tomorrow night I shan't have to listen to the 'Maiden's Prayer'. I shan't have to meet Protopopov.... (*A pause.*) By the way, he's in the sitting-room. He's come again.

KOOLYGHIN: Hasn't our headmistress arrived yet?

IRENA: No, we've sent for her. If you only knew how difficult it is for me to live here by myself, without Olia! She lives at the school now; she's the headmistress and she's busy the whole day. And I'm here alone, bored, with nothing to do, and I hate the very room I live in. So I've just made up my mind – if I'm really not going to be able to live in Moscow, that's that. It's my fate, that's all. Nothing can be done about it. It's God's will, everything that happens, and that's the truth. Nikolai Lvovich proposed to me.... Well, I thought it over, and I made up my mind. He's such a nice man, it's really extraordinary how nice he is.... And then suddenly I felt as though my soul had grown wings, I felt more cheerful and so relieved somehow that I wanted to work again. Just to start work! ... Only something happened yesterday, and now I feel as though something mysterious is hanging over me....

CHEBUTYKIN: Nonsense!

NATASHA: (*Speaking through the window.*) Our headmistress!

KOOLYGHIN: Our headmistress has arrived! Let's go indoors.

Goes indoors with IRENA.

CHEBUTYKIN: (*Reads his paper and sings quietly to himself.*) Tarara-boom-di-ay.... I'm sitting on a tomb-di-ay....

MASHA *walks up to him;* ANDREY *passes across the back of the stage pushing the pram.*

MASHA: You look very comfortable sitting here....

CHEBUTYKIN: Well, why not? Anything happening?

MASHA: (*Sits down.*) No, nothing. (*A pause.*) Tell me something. Were you in love with my mother?

CHEBUTYKIN: Yes, very much in love.

MASHA: Did she love you?

CHEBUTYKIN: (*After a pause.*) I can't remember now.

MASHA: Is my man here? Our cook Marfa always used to call her policeman 'my man'. Is he here?

CHEBUTYKIN: Not yet.

MASHA: When you have to take your happiness in snatches, in little bits, as I do, and then lose it, as I've lost it, you gradually get hardened and bad-tempered. (*Points at her breast.*) Something's boiling over inside me, here. (*Looking at* ANDREY, *who again crosses the stage with the pram.*) There's Andrey, our dear brother.... All our hopes are gone. It's the same as when thousands of people haul a huge bell up into a tower. Untold labour and money is spent on it, and then suddenly it falls and gets smashed. Suddenly, without rhyme or reason. It was the same with Andrey....

ANDREY: When are they going to settle down in the house? They're making such a row.

CHEBUTYKIN: They will soon. (*Looks at his watch.*) This is an old-fashioned watch: it strikes.... (*Winds his watch which then strikes.*) The first, second and fifth batteries will be leaving punctually at one o'clock. (*A pause.*) And I shall leave tomorrow.

ANDREY: For good?

CHEBUTYKIN: I don't know. I may return in about a year. Although, God knows ... it's all the same....

The sounds of a harp and a violin are heard.

ANDREY: The town will seem quite empty. Life will be snuffed out like a candle. (*A pause.*) Something happened yesterday outside the theatre; everybody's talking about it. I'm the only one that doesn't seem to know about it.

CHEBUTYKIN: It was nothing. A lot of nonsense. Soliony started badgering the Baron, or something. The Baron lost his temper and insulted him, and in the end Soliony had to challenge him to a duel. (*Looks at his watch.*) I think it's time to go. ... At half-past twelve, in the forest over there, on the other side of the river.... Bang-bang! (*Laughs.*) Soliony imagines he's like Lermontov. He actually writes poems. But, joking apart, this is his third duel.

MASHA: Whose third duel?

CHEBUTYKIN: Soliony's.

MASHA: What about the Baron?

CHEBUTYKIN: Well, what about him? (*A pause.*)

MASHA: My thoughts are all in a muddle.... But what I mean to say is that they shouldn't be allowed to fight. He might wound the Baron or even kill him.

CHEBUTYKIN: The Baron's a good enough fellow, but what does it really matter if there's one Baron more or less in the world? Well, let it be! It's all the same.

The shouts of 'Ah-oo!' and 'Heigh-ho!' are heard from beyond the garden.

That's Skvortsov, the second, shouting from the boat. He can wait.

ANDREY: I think it's simply immoral to fight a duel, or even to be present at one as a doctor.

CHEBUTYKIN: That's only how it seems.... We don't exist, nothing exists, it only seems to us that we do.... And what difference does it make?

MASHA: Talk, talk, nothing but talk all day long! ... (*Starts to go.*) Having to live in this awful climate with the snow threatening to fall at any moment, and then on the top of it having to listen to all this sort of talk.... (*Stops.*) I won't go into the house, I can't bear going in there.... Will you let me know when Vershinin comes? ... (*Walks off along the avenue.*) Look, the birds are beginning to fly away already! (*Looks up.*) Swans or geese.... Dear birds, happy birds.... (*Goes off.*)

ANDREY: Our house will seem quite deserted. The officers will go, you'll go, my sister will get married, and I'll be left alone in the house.

CHEBUTYKIN: What about your wife?

Enter FERAPONT with some papers.

ANDREY: My wife is my wife. She's a good, decent sort of woman ... she's really very kind, too, but there's something about her which pulls her down to the level of an animal ... a sort of mean, blind, thick-skinned animal – anyway, not a human being. I'm telling you this as a friend, the only person I can talk openly to. I love Natasha, it's true. But at times she appears to me so utterly vulgar, that I feel quite bewildered by it, and then I can't understand why, for what reasons I love her – or, anyway, did love her....

CHEBUTYKIN: (*Gets up.*) Well, dear boy, I'm going away tomorrow and it may be we shall never see each other again. So I'll give you a bit of advice. Put on your hat, take a walking stick, and go away.... Go away, and don't ever look back. And the further you go, the better.

SOLIONY passes across the back of the stage accompanied by two officers. Seeing CHEBUTYKIN, he turns towards him, while the officers walk on.

SOLIONY: It's time, Doctor. Half past twelve already. (*Shakes hands with ANDREY.*)

CHEBUTYKIN: In a moment. Oh, I'm tired of you all. (*To ANDREY.*) Andriusha, if anyone asks for me, tell them I'll be back presently. (*Sighs.*) Oh-ho-ho!

SOLIONY: 'He had no time to say "Oh, oh!"
Before that bear had struck him low.' ...
(*Walks off with him.*) What are you groaning about, old man?

CHEBUTYKIN: Oh, well!

SOLIONY: How do you feel?

CHEBUTYKIN: (*Crossly.*) Like a last year's bird's-nest.

SOLIONY: You needn't be so agitated about it, old boy. I shan't indulge in anything much, I'll just scorch his wings a little, like a woodcock's. (*Takes out a scent bottle and sprinkles scent over his hands.*) I've used up a whole bottle today, but my hands still smell. They smell like a corpse. (*A pause.*) Yes.... Do you remember that poem of Lermontov's?

'And he, rebellious, seeks a storm,
As if in storms there were tranquillity.' ...

CHEBUTYKIN: Yes.

'He had no time to say "Oh, oh!"
Before that bear had struck him low.'

Goes out with SOLIONY.

Shouts of 'Heigh-ho!' 'Ah-oo!' are heard. Enter ANDREY and FERAPONT.

FERAPONT: Will you sign these papers, please?

ANDREY: (*With irritation.*) Leave me alone! Leave me alone, for Heaven's sake. (*Goes off with the pram.*)

FERAPONT: Well, what am I supposed to do with the papers then? They are meant to be signed, aren't they? (*Goes to back of stage.*)

Enter IRENA *and* TOOZENBACH, *the latter wearing a straw hat.* KOOLYGHIN *crosses the stage, calling: 'Ah-oo! Masha! Ah-oo!'*

TOOZENBACH: I think he's the only person in the whole town who's glad that the army is leaving.

IRENA: That's quite understandable, really. (*A pause.*) The town will look quite empty.

TOOZENBACH: My dear, I'll be back in a moment.

IRENA: Where are you going?

TOOZENBACH: I must slip back to the town, and then ... I want to see some of my colleagues off.

IRENA: It's not true.... Nikolai, why are you so absent-minded today? (*A pause.*) What happened outside the theatre last night?

TOOZENBACH: (*With a movement of impatience.*) I'll be back in an hour.... I'll be back with you again. (*Kisses her hands.*) My treasure! ... (*Gazes into her eyes.*) It's five years since I first began to love you, and still I can't get used to it, and you seem more beautiful every day. What wonderful, lovely hair! What marvellous eyes! I'll take you away tomorrow. We'll work, we'll be rich, my dreams will come to life again. And you'll be happy! But – there's only one 'but', only one – you don't love me!

IRENA: I can't help that! I'll be your wife, I'll be loyal and obedient to you, but I can't love you.... What's to be done? (*Weeps.*) I've never loved anyone in my life. Oh, I've had such dreams about being in love! I've been dreaming about it for ever so long, day and night ... but somehow my soul seems like an expensive piano which someone has locked up and the key's got lost. (*A pause.*) Your eyes are so restless.

TOOZENBACH: I was awake all night. Not that there's anything to be afraid of in my life, nothing threatening.... Only the thought of that lost key torments me and keeps me awake. Say something to me.... (*A pause.*) Say something!

IRENA: What? What am I to say? What?

TOOZENBACH: Anything.

IRENA: Don't, my dear, don't.... (*A pause.*)

TOOZENBACH: Such trifles, such silly little things sometimes become so important suddenly, for no apparent reason! You laugh at them, just as you always have done, you still regard them as trifles, and yet you suddenly find they're in control, and you haven't the power to stop them. But don't let us talk about all that! Really, I feel quite elated. I feel as if I was seeing those fir-trees and maples and birches for the first time in my life. They all seem to be looking at me with a sort of inquisitive look and waiting for something. What beautiful trees – and how beautiful, when you think of it, life ought to be with trees like these!

Shouts of 'Ah-oo! Heigh-ho!' are heard.

I must go, it's time.... Look at that dead tree, it's all dried-up, but it's still swaying in the wind along with the others. And in the same way, it seems to me that, if I die, I shall still have a share in life somehow or other. Goodbye, my dear.... (*Kisses her hands.*) Your papers, the ones you gave me, are on my desk, under the calendar.

IRENA: I'm coming with you.

TOOZENBACH: (*Alarmed.*) No, no! (*Goes off quickly, then stops in the avenue.*) Irena!

IRENA: What?

TOOZENBACH: (*Not knowing what to say.*) I didn't have any coffee this morning. Will you tell them to get some ready for me? (*Goes off quickly.*)

IRENA *stands, lost in thought, then goes to the back of the stage and sits down on a swing. Enter* ANDREY *with the pram;* FERAPONT *appears.*

FERAPONT: Andrey Serghyeech, the papers aren't mine, you know, they're the office papers. I didn't make them up.

ANDREY: Oh, where has all my past life gone to? – the time when I was young and gay and clever, when I used to have fine dreams and great thoughts, and the present and the future were bright with hope? Why do we become so dull and commonplace and uninteresting almost before we've begun to live? Why do we get lazy, indifferent, useless, unhappy? ... This town's been in existence for two hundred years; a hundred thousand people live in it, but there's not one who's any different from all the others! There's never been a scholar or an artist or a saint in this place, never a single man sufficiently outstanding to make you feel passionately that you wanted to emulate him. People here do nothing but eat, drink and sleep.... Then they die and some more take their places, and they eat, drink and sleep, too, – and just to introduce a bit of variety into their lives, so as to avoid getting completely stupid with boredom, they indulge in their disgusting gossip and vodka and gambling and law-suits. The wives deceive their husbands, and the husbands lie to their wives, and pretend they don't see anything and don't hear anything.... And all this overwhelming vulgarity and pettiness crushes the children and puts out any spark they might have in them, so that they, too, become miserable, half-dead creatures, just like one another and just like their parents! ... (*To* FERAPONT, *crossly.*) What do you want?

FERAPONT: What? Here are the papers to sign.

ANDREY: What a nuisance you are!

FERAPONT: (*Hands him the papers.*) The porter at the finance department told me just now ... he said last winter they had two hundred degrees of frost in Petersburg.

ANDREY: I hate the life I live at present, but oh! the sense of elation when I think of the future! Then I feel so light-hearted, such a sense of release! I seem to see light ahead, light and freedom. I see myself free, and my children, too, – free from idleness, free from *kvass*, free from eternal meals of goose and cabbage, free from after-dinner naps, free from all this degrading parasitism! ...

FERAPONT: They say two thousand people were frozen to death. They say everyone was scared stiff. It was either in Petersburg or in Moscow, I can't remember exactly.

ANDREY: (*With sudden emotion, tenderly.*) My dear sisters, my dear good sisters! (*Tearfully.*) Masha, my dear sister! ...

NATASHA: (*Through the window.*) Who's that talking so loudly there? Is that you, Andriusha? You'll wake Sofochka. *Il ne faut pas faire du bruit, la Sophie est dormie déjà. Vous êtes un ours.* (*Getting angry.*) If you want to talk, give the pram to someone else. Ferapont, take the pram from the master.

FERAPONT: Yes, Madam. (*Takes the pram.*)

ANDREY: (*Shamefacedly.*) I was talking quietly.

NATASHA: (*In the window, caressing her small son.*) Bobik! Naughty Bobik! Aren't you a naughty boy!

ANDREY: (*Glancing through the papers.*) All right, I'll go through them and sign them if they need it. You can take them back to the office later. (*Goes into the house, reading the papers.*)

FERAPONT wheels the pram into the garden.

NATASHA: (*In the window.*) What's Mummy's name, Bobik? You darling! And who's that lady? Auntie Olia. Say: 'Hullo, Auntie Olia.'

Two street musicians, a man and a girl, enter and begin to play on a violin and a harp; VERSHININ, OLGA and ANFISA come out of the house and listen in silence for a few moments; then IRENA approaches them.

OLGA: Our garden's like a public road; everybody goes through it. Nanny, give something to the musicians.

ANFISA: (*Giving them money.*) Go along now, God bless you, good people!

The musicians bow and go away.

Poor, homeless folk! Whoever would go dragging round the streets playing tunes if he had enough to eat? (*To IRENA.*) How are you, Irenushka? (*Kisses her.*) Ah, my child, what a life I'm having! Such comfort! In a large flat at the school with Oliushka – and no rent to pay, either! The Lord's been kind to me in my old age. I've never had such a comfortable time in my life, old sinner that I am! A big flat, and no rent to pay, and a whole room to myself, with my own bed. All free. Sometimes when I wake up in the night I begin to think, and then – Oh, Lord! Oh, Holy Mother of God! – there's no one happier in the world than me!

VERSHININ: (*Glances at his watch.*) We shall be starting in a moment, Olga Serghyeevna. It's time I went. (*A pause.*) I wish you all the happiness in the world ... everything.... Where's Maria Serghyeevna?

IRENA: She's somewhere in the garden. I'll go and look for her.

VERSHININ: That's kind of you. I really must hurry.

ANFISA: I'll come and help to look for her. (*Calls out.*) Mashenka, ah-oo!

Goes with IRENA towards the far end of the garden.

Ah-oo! Ah-oo!

VERSHININ: Everything comes to an end. Well, here we are – and now it's going to be 'Goodbye'. (*Looks at his watch.*) The city gave us a sort of farewell lunch. There was champagne, and the mayor made a speech, and I ate and listened, but in spirit I was with you here.... (*Glances round the garden.*) I've grown so ... so accustomed to you.

OLGA: Shall we meet again some day, I wonder?

VERSHININ: Most likely not! (*A pause.*) My wife and the two little girls will be staying on here for a month or two. Please, if anything happens, if they need anything....

OLGA: Yes, yes, of course. You needn't worry about that. (*A pause.*) Tomorrow there won't be a single officer or soldier in the town.... All that will be just a memory, and, of course, a new life will begin for us here.... (*A pause.*) Nothing ever happens as we'd like it to. I didn't want to be a headmistress, and yet now I am one. It means we shan't be going to live in Moscow....

VERSHININ: Well.... Thank you for everything. Forgive me if ever I've done anything.... I've talked a lot too much, far too much.... Forgive me for that, don't think too unkindly of me.

OLGA (*Wipes her eyes.*) Now ... why is Masha so long coming?

VERSHININ: What else can I tell you now it's time to say 'Goodbye'? What shall I philosophize about now? ... (*Laughs.*) Yes, life is difficult. It seems quite hopeless for a lot of us, just a kind of impasse.... And yet you must admit that it is gradually getting easier and brighter, and it's clear that the time isn't far off when the light will spread everywhere. (*Looks at his watch.*) Time, it's time for me to go.... In the old days the human race was always making war, its entire existence was taken up with campaigns, advances, retreats, victories.... But now all that's out of date, and in its place there's a huge vacuum, clamouring to be filled. Humanity is passionately seeking something to fill it with and, of course, it will find something some day. Oh! If only it would happen soon! (*A pause.*) If only we could educate the industrious people and make the educated people industrious.... (*Looks at his watch.*) I really must go....

OLGA: Here she comes!

Enter MASHA.

VERSHININ: I've come to say Goodbye....

OLGA walks off and stands a little to one side so as not to interfere with their leave-taking.

MASHA: (*Looking into his face.*) Goodbye! ... (*A long kiss.*)

OLGA: That'll do, that'll do.

MASHA: (*Sobs loudly.*)

VERSHININ: Write to me.... Don't forget me! Let me go ... it's time. Olga Serghyeevna, please take her away ... I must go ... I'm late already.... (*Deeply moved, kisses* OLGA'*s hands, then embraces* MASHA *once again and goes out quickly.*)

OLGA: That'll do, Masha! Don't, my dear, don't....

Enter KOOLYGHIN.

KOOLYGHIN: (*Embarrassed.*) Never mind, let her cry, let her. ... My dear Masha, my dear, sweet Masha.... You're my wife, and I'm happy in spite of everything.... I'm not complaining, I've no reproach to make – not a single one.... Olga here is my witness.... We'll start our life over again in the same old way, and you won't hear a word from me ... not a hint....

MASHA: (*Suppressing her sobs.*) 'A green oak grows by a curving shore, And round that oak hangs a golden chain.' ... 'A golden chain round that oak.' ... Oh, I'm going mad.... By a curving shore ... a green oak....

OLGA: Calm yourself, Masha, calm yourself. ... Give her some water.

MASHA: I'm not crying any more....

KOOLYGHIN: She's not crying any more ... she's a good girl.

The hollow sound of a gun-shot is heard in the distance.

MASHA: 'A green oak grows by a curving shore, And round that oak hangs a golden chain.' ... A green cat ... a green oak ... I've got it all mixed up.... (*Drinks water.*) My life's messed up.... I don't want anything now.... I'll calm down in a moment.... It doesn't matter.... What *is* 'the curving shore'? Why does it keep coming into my head all the time? My thoughts are all mixed up.

Enter IRENA.

OLGA: Calm down, Masha. That's right ... good girl! ... Let's go indoors.

MASHA: (*Irritably.*) I'm not going in there! (*Sobs, but immediately checks herself.*) I don't go into that house now, and I'm not going to....

IRENA: Let's sit down together for a moment, and not talk about anything. I'm going away tomorrow, you know.... (*A pause.*)

KOOLYGHIN: Yesterday I took away a false beard and a moustache from a boy in the third form. I've got them here. (*Puts them on.*) Do I look like our German teacher? ... (*Laughs.*) I do, don't I? The boys are funny.

MASHA: It's true, you do look like that German of yours.

OLGA: (*Laughs*). Yes, he does.

MASHA *cries.*

IRENA: That's enough, Masha!

KOOLYGHIN: Very much like him, I think!

Enter NATASHA.

NATASHA: (*To the maid.*) What? Oh, yes. Mr Protopopov is going to keep an eye on Sofochka, and Andrey Serghyeevich is going to take Bobik out in the pram. What a lot of work these children make! ... (*To* IRENA.) Irena, you're really leaving tomorrow? What a pity! Do stay just another week, won't you? (*Catching sight of* KOOLYGHIN, *shrieks; he laughs and takes off the false beard and moustache.*) Get away with you! How you scared me! (*To* IRENA.) I've grown so accustomed to you being here.... You mustn't think it's going to be easy for me to be without you. I'll get Andrey and his old violin to move into your room: he can saw away at it as much as he likes there. And then we'll move Sofochka into his room. She's such wonderful child, really! Such a lovely little girl! This morning she looked at me with such a sweet expression, and then she said: 'Ma-mma!'

KOOLYGHIN: It's quite true, she is a beautiful child.

NATASHA: So tomorrow I'll be alone here. (*Sighs.*) I'll have this fir-tree avenue cut down first, then that maple tree over there. It looks so awful in the evenings.... (*To* IRENA.) My dear, that belt you're wearing doesn't suit you at all. Not at all good taste. You want something brighter to go with that dress.... I'll tell them to put flowers all round here, lots of flowers, so that we get plenty of scent from them.... (*Sternly.*) Why is there a fork lying on this seat? (*Going into the house, to the maid.*) Why is that fork left on the seat there? (*Shouts.*) Don't answer me back!

KOOLYGHIN: There she goes again!

A band plays a military march offstage; all listen.

OLGA: They're going.

Enter CHEBUTYKIN.

MASHA: The soldiers are going. Well. ... Happy journey to them! (*To her husband.*) We must go home.... Where's my hat and cape? ...

KOOLYGHIN: I took them indoors. I'll bring them at once.

OLGA: Yes, we can go home now. It's time.

CHEBUTYKIN: Olga Serghyeevna!

OLGA: What is it? (*A pause.*) What?

CHEBUTYKIN. Nothing.... I don't know quite how to tell you.... (*Whispers into her ear.*)

OLGA: (*Frightened.*) It can't be true!

CHEBUTYKIN: Yes ... a bad business.... I'm so tired ... quite worn out.... I don't want to say another word.... (*With annoyance.*) Anyway, nothing matters! ...

MASHA: What's happened?

OLGA: (*Puts her arms round* IRENA.) What a dreadful day! ... I don't know how to tell you, dear....

IRENA: What is it? Tell me quickly, what is it? For Heaven's sake! ... (*Cries.*)

CHEBUTYKIN: The Baron's just been killed in a duel.

IRENA: (*Cries quietly.*) I knew it, I knew it....

CHEBUTYKIN: (*Goes to the back of the stage and sits down.*) I'm tired.... (*Takes a newspaper out of his pocket.*) Let them cry for a bit.... (*Sings quietly to himself.*) Tarara-boom-di-ay, I'm sitting on a tomb-di-ay.... What difference does it make? ...

The three sisters stand huddled together.

MASHA: Oh, listen to that band! They're leaving us ... one of them's gone for good ... for ever! We're left alone ... to start our lives all over again. We must go on living ... we must go on living....

IRENA: (*Puts her head on* OLGA's *breast.*) Some day people will know why such things happen, and what the purpose of all this suffering is.... Then there won't be any more riddles.... Meanwhile we must go on living ... and working. Yes, we must just go on working! Tomorrow I'll go away alone and teach in a school somewhere; I'll give my life to people who need it.... It's autumn now, winter will soon be here, and the snow will cover everything ... but I'll go on working and working! ...

OLGA: (*Puts her arms round both her sisters.*) How cheerfully and jauntily that band's playing – really I feel as if I wanted to live! Merciful God! The years will pass, and we shall all be gone for good and quite forgotten.... Our faces and our voices will be forgotten and people won't even know that there were once three of us here.... But our sufferings may mean happiness for the people who come after us.... There'll be a time when peace and happiness reign in the world, and then we shall be remembered kindly and blessed. No, my dear sisters, life isn't finished for us yet! We're going to live! The band is playing so cheerfully and joyfully – maybe, if we wait a little longer, we shall find out why we live, why we suffer. ... Oh, if we only knew, if only we knew!

The music grows fainter and fainter. KOOLYGHIN, *smiling happily, brings out the hat and the cape.* ANDREY *enters; he is pushing the pram with* BORIK *sitting in it.*

CHEBUTYKIN: (*Sings quietly to himself.*) Tarara-boom-diay.... I'm sitting on a tomb-di-ay.... (*Reads the paper.*) What does it matter? Nothing matters!

OLGA: If only we knew, if only we knew! ...

Notes

1   A large room, sparsely furnished, used for receptions and dances in Russian houses.
2   A town in western Russia well known for its almost exclusively Jewish population.
3   A traditional Russian dance-song.
4   A Polish word meaning 'beloved'.

1.4 WHEN WE DEAD AWAKEN (1899)

HENRIK IBSEN

Translated by William Archer

Henrik Ibsen (1828–1906). When We Dead Awaken *was the last play written by Ibsen. He was concerned that his health would fail him, believing that the play would be 'the best and the biggest I have ever written'. It is subtitled 'A Dramatic Epilogue' because he intended it to bring to an end the great sequence of twelve prose plays he had been writing since 1877 and which included all of his Naturalist plays. He had been drifting away from strict Naturalism since* The Wild Duck *but this play treads on Symbolist territory more decisively than ever: it is a play of stillness, memory, atmosphere, of persuasion and obsession, metaphor and symbol. The play was poorly received at the time, though a young James Joyce thought it one of Ibsen's finest achievements. The play is less often performed than the other prose plays, not least because of the technical challenge of producing the closing avalanche. The translation from Norwegian printed here was written by William Archer in 1903.*

Characters

PROFESSOR ARNOLD RUBEK, a sculptor
MRS MAIA RUBEK, his wife
THE INSPECTOR at the Baths
ULFHEIM, a landed proprietor
A STRANGER LADY
A SISTER OF MERCY
Servants, Visitors to the Baths and Children

The First Act passes at a bathing establishment on the coast; the Second and Third Acts in the neighbourhood of a health resort, high in the mountains.

Act 1

Outside the Bath Hotel. A portion of the main building can be seen to the right. An open, park-like place with a fountain, groups of fine old trees, and shrubbery. To the left, a little pavilion almost covered with ivy and Virginia creeper. A table and chair outside it. At the back a view over the fjord, right out to sea, with headlands and small islands in the distance. It is a calm, warm and sunny summer morning.

PROFESSOR RUBEK *and* MRS MAIA RUBEK *are sitting in basket chairs beside a covered table on the lawn outside the hotel, having just breakfasted. They have champagne and seltzer water on the table, and each has a newspaper.* PROFESSOR RUBEK *is an elderly man of distinguished appearance, wearing a black velvet jacket, and otherwise in light summer attire.* MAIA *is quite young, with a vivacious expression and lively, mocking eyes, yet with a suggestion of fatigue. She wears an elegant travelling dress.*

MAIA: (*Sits for some time as though waiting for the* PROFESSOR *to say something, then lets her paper drop with a deep sigh.*) Oh dear, dear, dear – !

RUBEK: (*Looks up from his paper.*) Well, Maia? What is the matter with you?

MAIA: Just listen how silent it is here.

RUBEK: (*Smiles indulgently.*) And you can hear that?

MAIA: What?

RUBEK: The silence?

MAIA: Yes, indeed I can.

RUBEK: Well, perhaps you are right, *mein Kind*. One can really hear the silence.

MAIA: Heaven knows you can – when it's so absolutely overpowering as it is here –

RUBEK: Here at the Baths, you mean?

MAIA: Wherever you go at home here, it seems to me. Of course there was noise and bustle enough in the town. But I don't know how it is – even the noise and bustle seemed to have something dead about it.

RUBEK: (*With a searching glance.*) You don't seem particularly glad to be at home again, Maia?

MAIA: (*Looks at him.*) Are you glad?

RUBEK: (*Evasively.*) I – ?

MAIA: Yes, you, who have been so much, much further away than I. Are you entirely happy, now that you are at home again?

RUBEK: No – to be quite candid – perhaps not entirely happy –

MAIA: (*With animation.*) There, you see! Didn't I know it!

RUBEK: I have been too long abroad. I have drifted quite away from all this – this home life.

MAIA: (*Eagerly, drawing her chair nearer him.*) There, you see, Rubek! We had much better get away again! As quickly as ever we can.

RUBEK: (*Somewhat impatiently.*) Well, well, that is what we intend to do, my dear Maia. You know that.

MAIA: But why not now – at once? Only think how cosy and comfortable we could be down there, in our lovely new house –

RUBEK: (*Smiles indulgently.*) We ought by rights to say: our lovely new home.

MAIA: (*Shortly.*) I prefer to say house – let us keep to that.

RUBEK: (*His eyes dwelling on her.*) You are really a strange little person.

MAIA: Am I so strange?

RUBEK: Yes, I think so.

MAIA: But why, pray? Perhaps because I'm not desperately in love with mooning about up here – ?

RUBEK: Which of us was it that was absolutely bent on our coming north this summer?

MAIA: I admit, it was I.

RUBEK: It was certainly not I, at any rate.

MAIA: But good heavens, who could have dreamt that everything would have altered so terribly at home here? And in

so short a time, too! Why, it is only just four years since I went away –

RUBEK: Since you were married, yes –

MAIA: Married? What has that to do with the matter?

RUBEK: (*Continuing.*) – since you became the Frau Professor, and found yourself mistress of a charming home – I beg your pardon – a very handsome house, I ought to say. And a villa on the Lake of Taunitz, just at the point that has become most fashionable, too –. In fact it is all very handsome and distinguished, Maia, there's no denying that. And spacious too. We need not always be getting in each other's way –

MAIA: (*Lightly.*) No, no, no – there's certainly no lack of house-room, and that sort of thing –

RUBEK: Remember, too, that you have been living in altogether more spacious and distinguished surroundings – in more polished society than you were accustomed to at home.

MAIA: (*Looking at him.*) Ah, so you think it is *I* that have changed?

RUBEK: Indeed I do, Maia.

MAIA: I alone? Not the people here?

RUBEK: Oh yes, they too – a little, perhaps. And not at all in the direction of amiability. That I readily admit.

MAIA: I should think you must admit it, indeed.

RUBEK: (*Changing the subject.*) Do you know how it affects me when I look at the life of the people around us here?

MAIA: No. Tell me.

RUBEK: It makes me think of that night we spent in the train, when we were coming up here –

MAIA: Why, you were sound asleep all the time.

RUBEK: Not quite. I noticed how silent it became at all the little roadside stations. I heard the silence – like you, Maia –

MAIA: H'm, – like me, yes.

RUBEK: – and that assured me that we had crossed the frontier – that we were really at home. For the train stopped at all the little stations – although there was nothing doing at all.

MAIA: Then why did it stop – though there was nothing to be done?

RUBEK: Can't say. No one got out or in; but all the same the train stopped a long, endless time. And at every station I could make out that there were two railway men walking up and down the platform – one with a lantern in his hand – and they said things to each other in the night, low, and toneless, and meaningless.

MAIA: Yes, that is quite true. There are always two men walking up and down and talking –

RUBEK: – of nothing. (*Changing to a livelier tone.*) But just wait till tomorrow. Then we shall have the great luxurious steamer lying in the harbour. We'll go on board her, and sail all round the coast – northward ho! – right to the polar sea.

MAIA: Yes, but then you will see nothing of the country – and of the people. And that was what you particularly wanted.

RUBEK: (*Shortly and snappishly.*) I have seen more than enough.

MAIA: Do you think a sea voyage will be better for you?

RUBEK: It is always a change.

MAIA: Well, well, if only it is the right thing for you –

RUBEK: For me? The right thing? There is nothing in the world the matter with me.

MAIA: (*Rises and goes to him.*) Yes, there is, Rubek. I am sure you must feel it yourself.

RUBEK: Why my dearest Maia – what should be amiss with me?

MAIA: (*Behind him, bending over the back of his chair.*) That you must tell me. You have begun to wander about without a moment's peace. You cannot rest anywhere – neither at home nor abroad. You have become quite misanthropic of late.

RUBEK: (*With a touch of sarcasm.*) Dear me – have you noticed that?

MAIA: No one that knows you can help noticing it. And then it seems to me so sad that you have lost all pleasure in your work.

RUBEK: That too, eh?

MAIA: You that used to be so indefatigable – working from morning to night!

RUBEK: (*Gloomily.*) Used to be, yes –

MAIA: But ever since you got your great masterpiece out of hand –

RUBEK: (*Nods thoughtfully.*) 'The Resurrection Day' –

MAIA: – The masterpiece that has gone round the whole world, and made you so famous –

RUBEK: Perhaps that is just the misfortune, Maia.

MAIA: How so?

RUBEK: When I had finished this masterpiece of mine – (*Makes a passionate movement with his hand.*) – for 'The Resurrection Day' is a masterpiece! Or was one in the beginning. No, it is one still. It must, must, must be a masterpiece!

MAIA: (*Looks at him in astonishment.*) Why, Rubek – all the world knows that.

RUBEK: (*Short, repellently.*) All the world knows nothing! Understands nothing!

MAIA: Well, at any rate it can divine something –

RUBEK: Something that isn't there at all, yes. Something that never was in my mind. Ah yes, that they can all go into ecstasies over! (*Growling to himself.*) What is the good of working oneself to death for the mob and the masses – for 'all the world'!

MAIA: Do you think it is better, then – do you think it is worthy of you, to do nothing at all but portrait-bust now and then?

RUBEK: (*With a sly smile.*) They are not exactly portrait-busts that I turn out, Maia.

MAIA: Yes, indeed they are – for the last two or three years – ever since you finished your great group and got it out of the house –

RUBEK: All the same, they are no mere portrait-busts, I assure you.

MAIA: What are they, then?

RUBEK: There is something equivocal, something cryptic, lurking in and behind these busts – a secret something, that the people themselves cannot see –

MAIA: Indeed?

RUBEK: (*Decisively.*) I alone can see it. And it amuses me unspeakably. – On the surface I give them the 'striking likeness', as they call it, that they all stand and gape at in astonishment – (*Lowers his voice.*) – but at bottom they are all respectable, pompous horse-faces, and self-opinioned donkey-muzzles, and lop-eared, low-browed dog-skulls, and fatted swine-snouts – and sometimes dull, brutal bull-fronts as well –

MAIA: (*Indifferently.*) All the dear domestic animals, in fact.

RUBEK: Simply the dear domestic animals, Maia. All the animals which men have bedevilled in their own image – and which have bedevilled men in return. (*Empties his champagne-glass and laughs.*) And it is these double-faced works of art that our excellent plutocrats come and order of me. And pay for in all good faith – and in good round figures too – almost their weight in gold, as the saying goes.

MAIA: (*Fills his glass.*) Come, Rubek! Drink and be happy.

RUBEK: (*Passes his hand several times across his forehead and leans back in his chair.*) I am happy, Maia. Really happy – in a way. (*Short silence.*) For after all there is a certain happiness in feeling oneself free and independent on every hand – in having at one's command everything one can possibly wish for – all outward things, that is to say. Do you not agree with me, Maia?

MAIA: Oh yes, I agree. All that is well enough in its way. (*Looking at him.*) But do you remember what you promised me the day we came to an understanding on – on that troublesome point –

RUBEK: (*Nods.*) – on the subject of our marriage, yes. It was no easy matter for you, Maia.

MAIA: (*Continuing unruffled.*) – and agreed that I was to go abroad with you, and live there for good and all – and enjoy myself. – Do you remember what you promised me that day?

RUBEK: (*Shaking his head.*) No, I can't say that I do. Well, what did I promise?

MAIA: You said you would take me up to a high mountain and show me all the glory of the world.

RUBEK: (*With a slight start.*) Did I promise you that, too?

MAIA: Me too? Who else, pray?

RUBEK: (*Indifferently.*) No, no, I only meant did I promise to show you – ?

MAIA: – all the glory of the world? Yes, you did. And all that glory should be mine, you said.

RUBEK: That is a sort of figure of speech that I was in the habit of using once upon a time.

MAIA: Only a figure of speech?

RUBEK: Yes, a schoolboy phrase – the sort of thing I used to say when I wanted to lure the neighbours' children out to play with me, in the woods and on the mountains.

MAIA: (*Looking hard at him.*) Perhaps you only wanted to lure me out to play, as well?

RUBEK: (*Passing it off as a jest.*) Well, has it not been a tolerable amusing game, Maia?

MAIA: (*Coldly.*) I did not go with you only to play.

RUBEK: No, no, I daresay not.

MAIA: And you never took me up with you to any high mountain, or showed me –

RUBEK: (*With irritation.*) – all the glory of the world? No, I did not. For, let me tell you something: you are not really born to be a mountain-climber, little Maia.

MAIA: (*Trying to control herself.*) Yet at one time you seemed to think I was.

RUBEK: Four or five years ago, yes. (*Stretching himself in his chair.*) Four or five years – it's a long, long time, Maia.

MAIA: (*Looking at him with a bitter expression.*) Has the time seemed so very long to you, Rubek?

RUBEK: I am beginning now to find it a trifle long. (*Yawning.*) Now and then, you know.

MAIA: (*Returning to her place.*) I shall not bore you any longer.

She resumes her seat, takes up the newspaper and begins turning over the leaves. Silence on both sides.

RUBEK: (*Leaning on his elbows across the table, and looking at her teasingly.*) Is the Frau Professor offended?

MAIA: (*Coldly, without looking up.*) No, not at all.

Visitors to the baths, most of them ladies, begin to pass, singly and in groups, through the park from the right, and out to the left.

Waiters bring refreshments from the hotel, and go off behind the pavilion.

THE INSPECTOR, *wearing gloves and carrying a stick, comes from his rounds in the park, meets visitors, bows politely and exchanges a few words with some of them.*

THE INSPECTOR: (*Advancing to* PROFESSOR RUBEK'S *table and politely taking off his hat.*) I have the honour to wish you good morning, Mrs Rubek. – Good morning, Professor Rubek.

RUBEK: Good morning, good morning, Inspector.

THE INSPECTOR: (*Addressing himself to* MRS RUBEK.) May I venture to ask if you have slept well?

MAIA: Yes, thank you; excellently – for my part. I always sleep like a stone.

THE INSPECTOR: I am delighted to hear it. The first night in a strange place is often rather trying. – And the Professor – ?

RUBEK: Oh, my night's rest is never much to boast of – especially of late.

THE INSPECTOR: (*With a show of sympathy.*) Oh – that is a pity. But after a few weeks' stay at the Baths – you will quite get over that.

RUBEK: (*Looking up at him.*) Tell me, Inspector – are any of your patients in the habit of taking baths during the night?

THE INSPECTOR: (*Astonished.*) During the night? No, I have never heard of such a thing.

RUBEK: Have you not?

THE INSPECTOR: No, I don't know of anyone so ill as to require such treatment.

RUBEK: Well, at any rate there is someone who is in the habit of walking about the park by night?

THE INSPECTOR: (*Smiling and shaking his head.*) No, Professor – that would be against the rules.

MAIA: (*Impatiently.*) Good Heavens, Rubek, I told you so this morning – you must have dreamt it.

RUBEK: (*Drily.*) Indeed? Must I? Thank you! (*Turning to* THE INSPECTOR.) The fact is, I got up last night – I couldn't sleep – and I wanted to see what sort of night it was –

THE INSPECTOR: (*Attentively.*) To be sure – and then – ?

RUBEK: I looked out at the window – and caught sight of a white figure in there among the trees.

MAIA: (*Smiling to* THE INSPECTOR.) And the Professor declares that the figure was dressed in a bathing costume –

RUBEK: – or something like it, I said. Couldn't distinguish very clearly. But I am sure it was something white.

THE INSPECTOR: Most remarkable. Was it a gentleman or a lady?

RUBEK: I could almost have sworn it was a lady. But then after it came another figure. And that one was quite dark – like a shadow – .

THE INSPECTOR: (*Starting.*) A dark one? Quite black, perhaps?

RUBEK: Yes, I should almost have said so.

THE INSPECTOR: (*A light breaking in upon him.*) And behind the white figure? Following close upon her – ?

RUBEK: Yes – at a little distance –

THE INSPECTOR: Aha! Then I think I can explain the mystery, Professor.

RUBEK: Well, what was it then?

MAIA: (*Simultaneously.*) Was the Professor really not dreaming?

THE INSPECTOR: (*Suddenly whispering, as he directs their attention towards the background on the right.*) Hush, if you please! Look there – don't speak loud for a moment.

A slender lady, dressed in fine, cream-white cashmere and followed by a SISTER OF MERCY *in black, with a silver cross hanging by a chain on her breast, comes forward from behind the hotel and crosses the park towards the pavilion in front on the left. Her face is pale, and its lines seem to have stiffened; the eyelids are drooped and the eyes appear as though they saw nothing. Her dress comes down to her feet and clings to the body in perpendicular folds. Over her head, neck, breast, shoulders and arms she wears a large shawl of white crêpe. She keeps her arms crossed upon her breast. She carries her body immovably, and her steps are stiff and measured. The* SISTER's *bearing is also measured, and she has the air of a servant. She keeps her brown piercing eyes incessantly fixed upon the lady. Waiters, with napkins on their arms, come forward in the hotel doorway, and cast curious glances at the strangers, who take no notice of anything, and, without looking round, enter the pavilion.*

RUBEK: (*Has risen slowly and involuntarily, and stands staring at the closed door of the pavilion.*) Who was that lady?

THE INSPECTOR: She is a stranger who has rented the little pavilion there.

RUBEK: A foreigner?

THE INSPECTOR: Presumably. At any rate they both came from abroad – about a week ago. They have never been here before.

RUBEK: (*Decidedly; looking at him.*) It was she I saw in the park last night.

THE INSPECTOR: No doubt it must have been. I thought so from the first.

RUBEK: What is this lady's name, Inspector?

THE INSPECTOR: She has registered herself as 'Madame de Satow, with companion'. We know nothing more.

RUBEK: (*Reflecting.*) Satow? Satow – ?

MAIA: (*Laughing mockingly.*) Do you know anyone of that name, Rubek? Eh?

RUBEK: (*Shaking his head.*) No, no one. – Satow? It sounds Russian – or in all events Slavonic. (*To* THE INSPECTOR.) What language does she speak?

THE INSPECTOR: When the two ladies talk to each other, it is in a language I cannot make out at all. But at other times she speaks Norwegian like a native.

RUBEK: (*Exclaims with a start.*) Norwegian? You are sure you are not mistaken?

THE INSPECTOR: No, how could I be mistaken in that?

RUBEK: (*Looks at him with eager interest.*) You have heard her yourself?

THE INSPECTOR: Yes. I myself have spoken to her – several times. – Only a few words, however, she is far from communicative. But –

RUBEK: But Norwegian it was?

THE INSPECTOR: Thoroughly good Norwegian – perhaps with a little north-country accent.

RUBEK: (*Gazing straight before him in amazement, whispers.*) That too?

MAIA: (*A little hurt and jarred.*) Perhaps this lady has been one of your models, Rubek? Search your memory.

RUBEK: (*Looks cuttingly at her.*) My models?

MAIA: (*With a provoking smile.*) In your younger days, I mean. You are said to have had innumerable models – long ago, of course.

RUBEK: (*In the same tone.*) Oh no, little Frau Maia. I have in reality had only one single model. One and only one – for everything I have done.

THE INSPECTOR: (*Who has turned away and stands looking out to the left.*) If you'll excuse me, I think I will take my leave. I see someone coming whom it is not particularly agreeable to meet. Especially in the presence of ladies.

RUBEK: (*Looking in the same direction.*) That sportsman there? Who is it?

THE INSPECTOR: It is a certain Mr Ulfheim, from –

RUBEK: Oh, Mr Ulfheim –

THE INSPECTOR: – the bear-killer, as they call him –

RUBEK: I know him.

THE INSPECTOR: Who does not know him?

RUBEK: Very slightly, however. Is he on your list of patients – at last?

THE INSPECTOR: No, strangely enough – not as yet. He comes here only once a year – on his way up to his hunting-grounds. – Excuse me for the moment –

Makes a movement to go into the hotel.

ULFHEIM'S VOICE: (*Heard outside.*) Stop a moment, man! Devil take it all, can't you stop? Why do you always scuttle away from me?

THE INSPECTOR: (*Stops.*) I am not scuttling at all, Mr Ulfheim.

ULFHEIM *enters from the left followed by a servant with a couple of sporting dogs in leash.* ULFHEIM *is in shooting costume, with high boots and a felt hat with a feather in it. He is a long, lank, sinewy personage, with matted hair and beard and a loud voice. His appearance gives no precise clue to his age, but he is no longer young.*

ULFHEIM: (*Pounces upon* THE INSPECTOR.) Is this a way to receive strangers, hey? You scamper away with your tail between your legs – as if you had the devil at your heels.

THE INSPECTOR: (*Calmly, without answering him.*) Has Mr Ulfheim arrived by the steamer?

ULFHEIM: (*Growls.*) Haven't had the honour of seeing any steamer. (*With his arms akimbo.*) Don't you know that I sail my own cutter? (*To the servant.*) Look well after your fellow-creatures, Lars. But take care you keep them ravenous, all the same. Fresh meat-bones – but not too much meat on them, do you hear? And be sure it's reeking raw and bloody. And get something in your own belly while you're about it. (*Aiming a kick at him.*) Now then, go to hell with you.

The servant goes out with the dogs, behind the corner of the hotel.

THE INSPECTOR: Would not Mr Ulfheim like to go into the dining-room in the meantime?

ULFHEIM: In among all the half-dead flies and people? No, thank you a thousand times, Mr Inspector.

THE INSPECTOR: Well, well, as you please.

ULFHEIM: But get the housekeeper to prepare a hamper for me as usual. There must be plenty of provender in it – and lots of brandy −! You can tell her that I or Lars will come and play Old Harry with her if she doesn't −

THE INSPECTOR: (*Interrupting.*) We know your ways of old. (*Turning.*) Can I give the waiter any orders, Professor? Can I send Mrs Rubek anything?

RUBEK: No thank you; nothing for me.

MAIA: Nor for me.

THE INSPECTOR goes into the hotel.

ULFHEIM: (*Stares at them for a moment; then lifts his hat.*) Why, blast me if here isn't a country tyke that has strayed into regular tip-top society.

RUBEK: (*Looking up.*) What do you mean by that, Mr Ulfheim?

ULFHEIM: (*More quietly and politely.*) I believe I have the honour of addressing no less a person than the great Sculptor Rubek.

RUBEK: (*Nods.*) I remember meeting you once or twice − the autumn when I was last at home.

ULFHEIM: That's many years ago, now. And then you weren't so illustrious as I hear you've since become. At that time even a dirty bear-hunter might venture to come near you.

RUBEK: (*Smiling.*) I don't bite even now.

MAIA: (*Looks with interest at ULFHEIM.*) Are you really and truly a bear-hunter?

ULFHEIM: (*Seating himself at the next table, nearer the hotel.*) A bear-hunter when I have the chance, madam. But I make the best of any sort of game that comes in my way − eagles, and wolves, and women, and elks and reindeer − if only it's fresh and juicy and has plenty of blood in it.

Drinks from his pocket-flask.

MAIA: (*Regarding him fixedly.*) But you like bear-hunting best?

ULFHEIM: I like it best, yes. For then one can have the knife handy at a pinch. (*With a slight smile.*) We both work in a hard material, madam − both your husband and I. He struggles with his marble blocks, I daresay; and I struggle with tense and quivering bear-sinews. And we both of us win the fight in the end − subdue and master our material. We never rest till we've got the upper hand of it, though it fight never so hard.

RUBEK: (*Deep in thought.*) There's a great deal of truth in what you say.

ULFHEIM: Yes, for I take it the stone has something to fight for too. It is dead, and determined by no manner of means to let itself be hammered into life. Just like the bear when you come and prod him up in his lair.

MAIA: Are you going up into the forests now to hunt?

ULFHEIM: I am going right up into the high mountain. − I suppose you have never been in the high mountain, madam?

MAIA: No, never.

ULFHEIM: Confound it all then, you must be sure and come up there this very summer! I'll take you with me − both you and the Professor, with pleasure.

MAIA: Thanks. But Rubek is thinking of taking a sea trip this summer.

RUBEK: Round the coast − through the island channels.

ULFHEIM: Ugh − what the devil would you do in those damnable sickly gutters − floundering about in the brackish ditchwater? Dishwater I should rather call it.

MAIA: There, you hear, Rubek!

ULFHEIM: No, much better come up with me to the mountain − away, clean away, from the trail and taint of men. You can't think what that means for me. But such a little lady −

He stops.

The SISTER OF MERCY *comes out of the pavilion and goes into the hotel.*

ULFHEIM: (*Following her with his eyes.*) Just look at her, do! That night-crow there! − Who is it that's to be buried?

RUBEK: I have not heard of anyone −

ULFHEIM: Well, there's someone on the point of giving up the ghost, then − in one corner. or another. − People that are sickly and rickety should have the goodness to see about getting themselves buried − the sooner the better.

MAIA: Have you ever been ill yourself, Mr Ulfheim?

ULFHEIM: Never. If I had, I shouldn't be here. − But my nearest friends − they have been ill, poor things.

MAIA: And what did you do for your nearest friends?

ULFHEIM: Shot them, of course.

RUBEK: (*Looking at him.*) Shot them?

MAIA: (*Moving her chair back.*) Shot them dead?

ULFHEIM: (*Nods.*) I never miss, madam.

MAIA: But how can you possibly shoot people!

ULFHEIM: I am not speaking of people −

MAIA: You said your nearest friends

ULFHEIM: Well, who should they be but my dogs?

MAIA: Are your dogs your nearest friends?

ULFHEIM: I have none nearer. My honest, trusty, absolutely loyal comrades − When one of them turns sick and miserable − bang! − and there's my friend sent packing − to the other world.

The SISTER OF MERCY *comes out of the hotel with a tray on which is bread and milk. She places it on the table outside the pavillion, which she enters.*

ULFHEIM: (*Laughs scornfully.*) That stuff there − is that what you call food for human beings! Milk and water and soft, clammy bread. Ah, you should see my comrades feeding. Should you like to see it?

MAIA: (*Smiling across to the* PROFESSOR *and rising.*) Yes, very much.

ULFHEIM: (*Also rising.*) Spoken like a woman of spirit, madam! Come with me, then! They swallow whole great thumping meat-bones − gulp them up and then gulp them down again. Oh, it's a regular treat to see them. Come along and

I'll show you – and while we're about it, we can talk over this trip to the mountains –

He goes out by the corner of the hotel, MAIA *following him.*

Almost at the same moment the STRANGE LADY *comes out of the pavillion and seats herself at the table.*

THE LADY *raises her glass of milk and is about to drink, but stops and looks across at* RUBEK *with vacant, expressionless eyes.*

RUBEK: (*Remains sitting at his table and gazes fixedly and earnestly at her. At last he rises, goes some steps towards her, stops, and says in a low voice.*) I know you quite well, Irene.

THE LADY: (*In a toneless voice, setting down her glass.*) You can guess who I am, Arnold?

RUBEK: (*Without answering.*) And you recognise me, too, I see.

THE LADY: With you it is quite another matter.

RUBEK: With me? – How so?

THE LADY: Oh, you are still alive.

RUBEK: (*Not understanding.*) Alive – ?

THE LADY: (*After a short pause.*) Who was the other? The woman you had with you – there at the table?

RUBEK: (*A little reluctantly.*) She? That was my – my wife.

THE LADY: (*Nods slowly.*) Indeed. That is well, Arnold. Someone, then, who does not concern me –

RUBEK: (*Nods.*) No, of course not –

THE LADY: – one whom you have taken to you after my lifetime.

RUBEK: (*Suddenly looking hard at her.*) After your – ? What do you mean by that, Irene?

IRENE: (*Without answering.*) And the child? I hear the child is prospering too. Our child survives me – and has come to honour and glory.

RUBEK: (*Smiles as at a far-off recollection.*) Our child? Yes, we called it so – then.

IRENE: In my lifetime, yes.

RUBEK: (*Trying to take a lighter tone.*) Yes, Irene. – I can assure you 'our child' has become famous all the wide world over. I suppose you have read about it.

IRENE: (*Nods.*) And has made its father famous too. – That was your dream.

RUBEK: (*More softly, with emotion.*) It is to you I owe everything, everything, Irene – and I thank you.

IRENE: (*Lost in thought for a moment.*) If I had then done what I had a right to do, Arnold –

RUBEK: Well? What then?

IRENE: I should have killed that child.

RUBEK: Killed it, you say?

IRENE: (*Whispering.*) Killed it – before I went away from you. Crushed it – crushed it to dust.

RUBEK: (*Shakes his head reproachfully.*) You would never have been able to, Irene. You had not the heart to do it.

IRENE: No, in those days I had not that sort of heart.

RUBEK: But since then? Afterwards?

IRENE: Since then I have killed it innumerable times. By daylight and in the dark. Killed it in hatred – and in revenge – and in anguish.

RUBEK: (*Goes close up to the table and asks softly.*) Irene – tell me now at last – after all these years – why did you go away from me? You disappeared so utterly – left not a trace behind –

IRENE: (*Shaking her head slowly.*) Oh Arnold – why should I tell you that now – from the world beyond the grave.

RUBEK: Was there someone else whom you had come to love?

IRENE: There was one who had no longer any use for my love – any use for my life.

RUBEK: (*Changing the subject.*) H'm – don't let us talk any more of the past –

IRENE: No, no – by all means let us not talk of what is beyond the grave – what is now beyond the grave for me.

RUBEK: Where have you been, Irene? All my inquiries were fruitless – you seemed to have vanished away.

IRENE: I went into the darkness – when the child stood transfigured in the light.

RUBEK: Have you travelled much about the world?

IRENE: Yes. Travelled in many lands.

RUBEK: (*Looks compassionately at her.*) And what have you found to do, Irene?

IRENE: (*Turning her eyes upon him.*) Wait a moment; let me see – Yes, now I have it. I have posed on the turntable in variety-shows. Posed as a naked statue in living pictures. Raked in heaps of money. That was more than I could do with you; for you had none. – And then I turned the heads of all sorts of men. That, too, was more than I could do with you, Arnold. You kept yourself better in hand.

RUBEK: (*Hastening to pass the subject by.*) And then you have married, too?

IRENE: Yes; I married one of them.

RUBEK: Who is your husband?

IRENE: He was a South American. A distinguished diplomatist. (*Looks straight in front of her with a stony smile.*) Him I managed to drive quite out of his mind; mad – incurably mad; inexorably mad. – It was great sport, I can tell you – while it was in the doing. I could have laughed within me all the time – if I had anything within me.

RUBEK: And where is he now?

IRENE: Oh, in a churchyard somewhere or other. With a fine handsome monument over him. And with a bullet rattling in his skull.

RUBEK: Did he kill himself?

IRENE: Yes, he was good enough to take that off my hands.

RUBEK: Do you not lament his loss, Irene?

IRENE: (*Not understanding.*) Lament? What loss?

RUBEK: Why the loss of Herr von Satow, of course.

IRENE: His name was not Satow.

RUBEK: Was it not?

IRENE: My second husband is called Satow. He is a Russian –

RUBEK: And where is he?

IRENE: Far away in the Ural Mountains. Among all his gold-mines.

RUBEK: So he lives there?

IRENE: (*Shrugs her shoulders.*) Lives? Lives? In reality I have killed him –

RUBEK: (*Start.*) Killed – !

IRENE: Killed him with a fine sharp dagger which I always have with me in bed –

RUBEK: (*Vehemently.*) I don't believe you, Irene!

IRENE: (*With a gentle smile.*) Indeed you may believe it, Arnold.

RUBEK: (*Looks compassionately at her.*) Have you never had a child?

IRENE: Yes, I have had many children.

RUBEK: And where are your children now?

IRENE: I killed them.

RUBEK: (*Severely.*) Now you are telling me lies again!

IRENE: I have killed them, I tell you – murdered them pitilessly. As soon as ever they came into the world. Oh, long, long before. One after the other.

RUBEK: (*Sadly and earnestly.*) There is something hidden behind everything you say.

IRENE: How can I help that? Every word I say is whispered into my ear.

RUBEK: I believe I am the only one that can divine your meaning.

IRENE: Surely you ought to be the only one.

RUBEK: (*Rests his hands on the table and looks intently at her.*) Some of the strings of your nature have broken.

IRENE: (*Gently.*) Does not that always happen when a young warm-blooded woman dies?

RUBEK: Oh Irene, have done with these wild imaginings –! You are living! Living – living!

IRENE: (*Rises slowly from her chair and says, quivering.*) I was dead for many years. They came and bound me – laced my arms together behind my back –. Then they lowered me into a grave-vault, with iron bars before the loop-hole. And with padded walls – so that no one on the earth above could hear the grave-shrieks –. But now I am beginning, in a way, to rise from the dead. (*She seats herself again.*)

RUBEK: (*After a pause.*) In all this, do you hold me guilty?

IRENE: Yes.

RUBEK: Guilty of that – your death, as you call it.

IRENE: Guilty of the fact that I had to die. (*Changing her tone to one of indifference.*) Why don't you sit down, Arnold?

RUBEK: May I?

IRENE: Yes. – You need not be afraid of being frozen. I don't think I am quite turned to ice yet.

RUBEK: (*Moves a chair and seats himself at her table.*) There, Irene. Now we two are sitting together as in the old days.

IRENE: A little way apart from each other – also as in the old days.

RUBEK: (*Moving nearer.*) It had to be so, then.

IRENE: Had it?

RUBEK: (*Decisively.*) There had to be a distance between us –

IRENE: Was it absolutely necessary, Arnold?

RUBEK: (*Continuing.*) Do you remember what you answered when I asked if you would go with me out into the wide world?

IRENE: I held up three fingers in the air and swore that I would go with you to the world's end and to the end of life. And that I would serve you in all things –

RUBEK: As the model for my art –

IRENE: – in frank, utter nakedness –

RUBEK: (*With emotion.*) And you did serve me, Irene – so bravely – so gladly and ungrudgingly.

IRENE: Yes with all the pulsing blood of my youth, I served you!

RUBEK: (*Nodding, with a look of gratitude.*) That you have every right to say.

IRENE: I fell down at your feet and served you, Arnold! (*Holding her clenched hand towards him.*) But you, you, – you – !

RUBEK: (*Defensively.*) I never did you any wrong! Never, Irene!

IRENE: Yes, you did! You did wrong to my innermost, inborn nature –

RUBEK: (*Starting back.*) I –!

IRENE: Yes, you! I exposed myself wholly and unreservedly to your gaze – (*More softly.*) And never once did you touch me.

RUBEK: Irene, did you not understand that many a time I was almost beside myself under the spell of all your loveliness?

IRENE: (*Continuing undisturbed.*) And yet – if you had touched me, I think I should have killed you on the spot. For I had a sharp needle always upon me – hidden in my hair – (*Strokes her forehead meditatively.*) But after all – after all – that you could –

RUBEK: (*Looks impressively at her.*) I was an artist, Irene.

IRENE: (*Darkly.*) That is just it. That is just it.

RUBEK: An artist first of all. And I was sick with the desire to achieve the great work of my life. (*Losing himself in recollection.*) It was to be called 'The Resurrection Day' – figured in the likeness of a young woman, awakening from the sleep of death –

IRENE: Our child, yes –

RUBEK: (*Continuing.*) It was to be the awakening of the noblest, purest, most ideal woman the world ever saw. Then I found you. You were what I required in every respect. And you consented so willingly – so gladly. You renounced home and kindred – and went with me.

IRENE: To go with you meant for me the resurrection of my childhood.

RUBEK: That was just why I found in you all that I required – in you and in no one else. I came to look on you as a thing hallowed, not to be touched save in adoring thoughts. In those days I was still young, Irene. And the superstition took hold of me that if I touched you, if I desired you with my senses, my soul would be profaned, so that I should be unable to accomplish what I was striving for. – And I still think there was some truth in that.

IRENE: (*Nods with a touch of scorn.*) The work of art first – then the human being.

RUBEK: You must judge me as you will; but at that time I was utterly dominated by my great task – and exultantly happy in it.

IRENE: And you achieved your great task, Arnold.

RUBEK: Thanks and praise be to you, I achieved my great task. I wanted to embody the pure woman as I saw her awakening on the Resurrection Day. Not marvelling at anything new and unknown and undivined; but filled with a sacred joy at finding herself unchanged – she, the woman of earth – in the higher, freer, happier region – after the long, dreamless sleep of death. (*More softly.*) Thus did I fashion her. – I fashioned her in your image, Irene.

IRENE: (*Laying her hands flat upon the table and leaning against the back of her chair.*) And then you were done with me –

RUBEK: (*Reproachfully.*) Irene!

IRENE: You had no longer any use for me –

RUBEK: How can you say that!

IRENE: – and began to look about you for other ideals –

RUBEK: I found none, none after you.

IRENE: And no other models, Arnold?

RUBEK: You were no model to me. You were the fountainhead of my achievement.

IRENE: (*Is silent for a short time.*) What poems have you made since? In marble I mean. Since the day I left you.

RUBEK: I have made no poems since that day – only frittered away my life in modelling.

IRENE: And that woman, whom you are now living with – ?

RUBEK: (*Interrupting vehemently.*) Do not speak of her now! It makes me tingle with shame.

IRENE: Where are you thinking of going with her?

RUBEK: (*Slack and weary.*) Oh, on a tedious coasting-voyage to the North, I suppose.

IRENE: (*Looks at him, smiles almost imperceptibly, and whispers.*) You should rather go high up into the mountains. As high as ever you can. Higher, higher, – always higher, Arnold.

RUBEK: (*With eager expectation.*) Are you going up there?

IRENE: Have you the courage to meet me once again?

RUBEK: (*Struggling with himself, uncertainly.*) If we could – oh, if only we could – !

IRENE: Why can we not do what we will? (*Looks at him and whispers beseechingly with folded hands.*) Come, come, Arnold! Oh, come up to me – !

MAIA enters, glowing with pleasure, from behind the hotel, and goes quickly up to the table where they were previously sitting.

MAIA: (*Still at the corner of the hotel, without looking around.*) Oh, you may say what you please, Rubek, but – (*Stops, as she catches sight of* IRENE.) – Oh, I beg your pardon – I see you have made an acquaintance.

RUBEK: (*Curtly.*) Renewed an acquaintance. (*Rises.*) What was it you wanted with me?

MAIA: I only wanted to say this: you may do whatever you please, but *I* am not going with you on that disgusting steamboat.

RUBEK: Why not?

MAIA: Because I want to go up on the mountains and into the forests – that's what I want. (*Coaxingly.*) Oh, you must let me do it, Rubek. – I shall be so good, so good afterwards!

RUBEK: Who is it that has put these ideas into your head?

MAIA: Why he – that horrid bear-killer. Oh you cannot conceive all the marvellous things he has to tell about the mountains. And about life up there! They're ugly, horrid, repulsive, most of the yarns he spins – for I almost believe he's lying – but wonderfully alluring all the same. Oh, won't you let me go with him? Only to see if what he says is true, you understand. May I, Rubek?

RUBEK: Yes, I have not the slightest objection. Off you go to the mountains – as far and as long as you please. I shall perhaps be going the same way myself.

MAIA: (*Quickly.*) No, no, no, you needn't do that! Not on my account!

RUBEK: I want to go to the mountains. I have made up my mind to go.

MAIA: Oh thanks, thanks! May I tell the bear-killer at once?

RUBEK: Tell the bear-killer whatever you please.

MAIA: Oh thanks, thanks, thanks! (*Is about to take his hand; he repels the movement.*) Oh, how dear and good you are today, Rubek!

She runs into the hotel.

At the same time the door of the pavilion is softly and noiselessly set ajar. The SISTER OF MERCY *stands in the opening, intently on the watch. No one sees her.*

RUBEK: (*Decidedly, turning to* IRENE.) Shall we meet up there then?

IRENE: (*Rising slowly.*) Yes, we shall certainly meet. – I have sought for you so long.

RUBEK: When did you begin to seek for me, Irene?

IRENE: (*With a touch of jesting bitterness.*) From the moment I realised that I had given away to you something rather indispensable, Arnold. Something one ought never to part with.

RUBEK: (*Bowing his head.*) Yes, that is bitterly true. You gave me three or four years of your youth.

IRENE: More, more than that I gave you – spend-thrift as I then was.

RUBEK: Yes, you were prodigal, Irene. You gave me all your naked loveliness –

IRENE: – to gaze upon –

RUBEK: – and to glorify –

IRENE: Yes, for your own glorification. – And the child's.

RUBEK: And yours too, Irene.

IRENE: But you have forgotten the most precious gift.

RUBEK: The most precious −? What gift was that?

IRENE: I gave you my young, living soul. And that gift left me empty within − soulless. (*Looking at him with a fixed stare.*) It was that I died of, Arnold.

The SISTER OF MERCY *opens the door wide and makes room for her. She goes into the pavilion.*

RUBEK: (*Stands and looks after her; then whispers.*) Irene!

Act 2

Near a mountain resort. The landscape stretches, in the form of an immense treeless upland, towards a long mountain lake. Beyond the lake rises a range of peaks with blue-white snow in the clefts. In the foreground on the left a purling brook falls in severed streamlets down a steep wall of rock, and thence flows smoothly over the upland until it disappears to the right. Dwarf trees, plants and stones along the course of the brook. In the foreground on the right a hillock, with a stone bench on the top of it. It is a summer afternoon, towards sunset.

At some distance over the upland, on the other side of the brook, a troop of children is singing, dancing and playing. Some are dressed in peasant costume, others in town-made clothes. Their happy laughter is heard, softened by distance, during the following.

PROFESSOR RUBEK is sitting on the bench, with a plaid over his shoulders, and looking down at the children's play.

Presently, MAIA *comes forward from among some bushes on the upland to the left, well back, and scans the prospect with her hand shading her eyes. She wears a flat tourist cap, a short skirt, kilted up, reaching only midway between ankle and knee, and high, stout lace-boots. She has in her hand a long alpenstock.*

MAIA: (*At last catches sight of* RUBEK *and calls.*) Hallo!

She advances over the upland, jumps over the brook, with the aid of her alpenstock, and climbs up the hillock.

MAIA: (*Panting.*) Oh, how I have been rushing around looking for you, Rubek.

RUBEK: (*Nods indifferently and asks.*) Have you just come from the hotel?

MAIA: Yes, that was the last place I tried − that fly-trap.

RUBEK: (*Looking at her for moment.*) I noticed that you were not at the dinner-table.

MAIA: No we had our dinner in the open air, we two.

RUBEK: 'We two'? What two?

MAIA: Why, I and that horrid bear-killer, of course.

RUBEK: Oh he.

MAIA: Yes. And first thing tomorrow morning we are going off again.

RUBEK: After bears?

MAIA: Yes. Off to kill a brown-boy.

RUBEK: Have you found the tracks of any?

MAIA: (*With superiority.*) You don't suppose that bears are to be found in the naked mountains, do you?

RUBEK: Where, then?

MAIA: Far beneath. On the lower slopes; in the thickest parts of the forest. Places your ordinary town-folk could never get through −

RUBEK: And you two are going down there tomorrow?

MAIA: (*Throwing herself down among the heather.*) Yes, so we have arranged. − Or perhaps we may start this evening. − If you have no objection, that's to say?

RUBEK: I? Far be it from me to −

MAIA: (*Quickly.*) Of course Lars goes with us − with the dogs.

RUBEK: I feel no curiosity as to the movements of Mr Lars and his dogs. (*Changing the subject.*) Would you not rather sit properly on the seat?

MAIA: (*Drowsily.*) No, thank you. I'm lying so delightfully in the soft heather.

RUBEK: I can see that you are tired.

MAIA: (*Yawning.*) I almost think I'm beginning to feel tired.

RUBEK: You don't notice it till afterwards − when the excitement is over −

MAIA: (*In a drowsy tone.*) Just so. I will lie and close my eyes. (*A short pause. With sudden impatience.*) Ugh, Rubek − how can you endure to sit there listening to these children's screams! And to watch all the capers they are cutting, too!

RUBEK: There is something harmonious − almost like music − in their movements, now and then; amid all the clumsiness. And it amuses me to sit and watch for these isolated moments − when they come.

MAIA: (*With a somewhat scornful laugh.*) Yes, you are always, always an artist.

RUBEK: And I propose to remain one.

MAIA: (*Lying on her side, so that her back is turned to him.*) There's not a bit of the artist about him.

RUBEK: (*With attention.*) Who is it that's not an artist?

MAIA: (*Again in a sleepy tone.*) Why, he − the other one, of course.

RUBEK: The bear-hunter, you mean?

MAIA: Yes. There's not a bit of the artist about him − not the least little bit.

RUBEK: (*Smiling.*) No, I believe there's no doubt about that.

MAIA: (*Vehemently, without moving.*) And so ugly as he is! (*Plucks up a tuft of heather and throws it away.*) So ugly, so ugly! Isch!

RUBEK: Is that why you are so ready to set off with him − out into the wilds?

MAIA: (*Curtly.*) I don't know. (*Turning towards him.*) You are ugly, too, Rubek.

RUBEK: Have you only just discovered it?

MAIA: No, I have seen it for long.

RUBEK: (*Shrugging his shoulders.*) One doesn't grow younger. One doesn't grow younger, Frau Maia.

MAIA: It's not that sort of ugliness that I mean at all. But there has come to be such an expression of fatigue, of utter weariness, in your eyes – when you deign, once in a while, to cast a glance at me.

RUBEK: Have you noticed that?

MAIA: (*Nods.*) Little by little this evil look has come into your eyes. It seems almost as though you were nursing some dark plot against me.

RUBEK: Indeed? (*In a friendly but earnest tone.*) Come here and sit beside me, Maia; and let us talk a little.

MAIA: (*Half rising.*) Then will you let me sit upon your knee? As I used to in the early days?

RUBEK: No, you mustn't – people can see us from the hotel. (*Moves a little.*) But you can sit here on the bench – at my side.

MAIA: No, thank you; in that case I'd rather lie here, where I am. I can hear you quite well here. (*Looks inquiringly at him.*) Well, what is it you want to say to me?

RUBEK: (*Begins slowly.*) What do you think was my real reason for agreeing to make this tour?

MAIA: Well – I remember you declared, among other things, that it was going to do me such a tremendous lot of good. But – but –

RUBEK: But – ?

MAIA: But now I don't believe the least little bit that that was the reason –

RUBEK: Then what is your theory about it now?

MAIA: I think now that it was on account of that pale lady.

RUBEK: Madame von Satow – !

MAIA: Yes, she who is always hanging at our heels. Yesterday evening she made her appearance up here too.

RUBEK: But what in all the world – !

MAIA: Oh, I know you knew her very well indeed – long before you knew me.

RUBEK: And had forgotten her, too – long before I knew you.

MAIA: (*Sitting upright.*) Can you forget so easily, Rubek?

RUBEK: (*Curtly.*) Yes, very easily indeed. (*Adds harshly.*) When I want to forget.

MAIA: Even a woman who has been a model to you?

RUBEK: When I have no more use for her –

MAIA: One who has stood to you undressed?

RUBEK: That means nothing – nothing for us artists. (*With a change of tone.*) And then – may I venture to ask – how was I to guess that she was in this country?

MAIA: Oh, you might have seen her name in a Visitor's List – in one of the newspapers.

RUBEK: But I had no idea of the name she now goes by. I had never heard of any Herr von Satow.

MAIA: (*Affecting weariness.*) Oh well then, I suppose it must have been for some other reason that you were so set upon this journey.

RUBEK: (*Seriously.*) Yes, Maia – it was for another reason. A quite different reason. And that is what we must sooner or later have a clear explanation about.

MAIA: (*In a fit of suppressed laughter.*) Heavens, how solemn you look!

RUBEK: (*Suspiciously scrutinising her.*) Yes, perhaps a little more solemn than necessary.

MAIA: How so – ?

RUBEK: And that is a very good thing for us both.

MAIA: You begin to make me feel curious, Rubek.

RUBEK: Only curious? Not a little bit uneasy.

MAIA: (*Shaking her head.*) Not in the least.

RUBEK: Good. Then listen. – You said that day down at the Baths that it seemed to you I had become very nervous of late –

MAIA: Yes, and you really have.

RUBEK: And what do you think can be the reason of that?

MAIA: How can I tell – ? (*Quickly.*) Perhaps you have grown weary of this constant companionship with me.

RUBEK: Constant – ? Why not say 'everlasting'?

MAIA: Daily companionship, then. Here have we two solitary people lived down there for four or five mortal years, and scarcely have an hour away from each other. – We two all by ourselves.

RUBEK: (*With interest.*) Well? And then – ?

MAIA: (*A little oppressed.*) You are not a particularly sociable man, Rubek. You like to keep to yourself and think your own thoughts. And of course I can't talk properly to you about your affairs. I know nothing about art and that sort of thing – (*With an impatient gesture.*) And care very little either, for that matter!

RUBEK: Well, well; and that's why we generally sit by the fireside, and chat about your affairs.

MAIA: Oh, good gracious – I have no affairs to chat about.

RUBEK: Well, they are trifles, perhaps; but at any rate the time passes for us in that way as well as another, Maia.

MAIA: Yes, you are right. Time passes. It is passing away from you, Rubek. – And I suppose it is really that that makes you so uneasy –

RUBEK: (*Nods vehemently.*) And so restless! (*Writhing in his seat.*) No, I shall soon not be able to endure this pitiful life any longer.

MAIA: (*Rises and stands for a moment looking at him.*) If you want to get rid of me, you have only to say so.

RUBEK: Why will you use such phrases? Get rid of you?

MAIA: Yes, if you want to have done with me, please say so right out. And I will go that instant.

RUBEK: (*With an almost imperceptible smile.*) Do you intend that as a threat, Maia?

MAIA: There can be no threat for you in what I said.

RUBEK: (*Rising.*) No, I confess you are right there. (*Adds after a pause.*) You and I cannot possibly go on living together like this –

MAIA: Well? And then – ?

RUBEK: There is no 'then' about it. (*With emphasis on his words.*) Because we two cannot go on living together alone – it does not necessarily follow that we must part.

MAIA: (*Smiles scornfully.*) Only draw away from each other a little, you mean?

RUBEK: (*Shakes his head.*) Even that is not necessary.

MAIA: Well then? Come out with what you want to do with me.

RUBEK: (*With some hesitation.*) What I now feel so keenly – and so painfully – that I require, is to have someone about me who really and truly stands close to me –

MAIA: (*Interrupts him anxiously.*) Don't I do that, Rubek?

RUBEK: (*Waving her aside.*) Not in that sense. What I need is the companionship of another person who can, as it were, complete me – supply what is wanting in me – be one with me in all my striving.

MAIA: (*Slowly.*) It's true that things like that are a great deal too hard for me.

RUBEK: Oh no, they are not at all in your line, Maia.

MAIA: (*With an outburst.*) And heaven knows I don't want them to be, either!

RUBEK: I know that very well. – And it was with no idea of finding any such help in my life-work that I married you.

MAIA: (*Observing him closely.*) I can see in your face that you are thinking of someone else.

RUBEK: Indeed? I have never noticed before that you were a thought-reader. But you can see that, can you?

MAIA: Yes, I can. Oh, I know you so well, so well, Rubek.

RUBEK: Then perhaps you can also see who it is I am thinking of?

MAIA: Yes, indeed I can.

RUBEK: Well? Have the goodness to – ?

MAIA: You are thinking of that – that model you once used for – (*Suddenly letting slip the train of thought.*) Do you know, the people down at the hotel think she's mad.

RUBEK: Indeed? And pray what do the people down at the hotel think of you and the bear-killer?

MAIA: That has nothing to do with the matter. (*Continuing the former train of thought.*) But it was this pale lady you were thinking of.

RUBEK: (*Calmly.*) Precisely, of her. – When I had no more use for her – and when, besides, she went away from me – vanished without a word –

MAIA: Then you accepted me as a sort of makeshift, I suppose?

RUBEK: (*More unfeelingly.*) Something of the sort, to tell the truth, little Maia. For a year or a year and a half I had lived there lonely and brooding, and had put the last touch – the very last touch, to my work. 'The Resurrection Day' went out over the world and brought me fame – and everything else that heart could desire. (*With greater warmth.*) But I no longer loved my own work. Men's laurels and incense nauseated me, till I could have rushed away in despair and hidden myself in the depths of the woods. (*Looking at her.*) You, who are a thought-reader – can you guess what then occurred to me?

MAIA: (*Lightly.*) Yes, it occurred to you to make portrait-busts of gentlemen and ladies.

RUBEK: (*Nods.*) To order, yes. With animals' faces behind the masks. Those I threw in gratis – into the bargain, you

understand. (*Smiling.*) But that was not precisely what I had in my mind.

MAIA: What, then?

RUBEK: (*Again serious.*) It was this, that all the talk about the artist's vocation and the artist's mission, and so forth, began to strike me as being very empty, and hollow, and meaningless at bottom.

MAIA: Then what would you put in its place?

RUBEK: Life, Maia.

MAIA: Life?

RUBEK: Yes, is not life in sunshine and in beauty a hundred times better worth while than to hang about to the end of your days in a raw, damp hole, and wear yourself out in a perpetual struggle with lumps of clay and blocks of stone?

MAIA: (*With a little sigh.*) Yes, I have always thought so, certainly.

RUBEK: And then I had become rich enough to live in luxury and in indolent, quivering sunshine. I was able to build myself the villa on the Lake of Taunitz, and the palazzo in the capital, – and all the rest of it.

MAIA: (*Taking up his tone.*) And last but not least, you could afford to treat yourself to me, too. And you gave me leave to share in all your treasures.

RUBEK: (*Jesting, so as to turn the conversation.*) Did I not promise to take you up to a high enough mountain and show you all the glory of the world?

MAIA: (*With a gentle expression.*) You have perhaps taken me up with you to a high enough mountain, Rubek – but you have not shown me all the glory of the world.

RUBEK: (*With a laugh of irritation.*) How insatiable you are, Maia.! Absolutely insatiable! (*With a vehement outburst.*) But do you know what is the most hopeless thing of all, Maia? Can you guess that?

MAIA: (*With quiet defiance.*) Yes, I suppose it is that you have gone and tied yourself to me – for life.

RUBEK: I would not have expressed myself so heartlessly.

MAIA: But you would have meant it just as heartlessly.

RUBEK: You have no clear idea of the inner workings of an artist's nature.

MAIA: (*Smiling and shaking her head.*) Good heavens, I haven't even a clear idea of the inner workings of my own nature.

RUBEK: (*Continuing undisturbed.*) I live at such high speed, Maia. We live so, we artists. I, for my part, have lived through a whole lifetime in the few years we two have known each other. I have come to realise that I am not at all adapted for seeking happiness in indolent enjoyment. Life does not shape itself that way for me and those like me. I must go on working – producing one work after another – right up to my dying day. (*Forcing himself to continue.*) That is why I cannot get on with you any longer, Maia – not with you alone.

MAIA: (*Quietly.*) Does that mean, in plain language, that you have grown tired of me?

RUBEK: (*Bursts forth.*) Yes, that is what it means! I have grown tired – intolerably tired and fretted and unstrung – in this life with you! Now you know it. (*Controlling himself.*) These are hard, ugly words I am using. I know that very well. And you are not at all to blame in this matter; – that I willingly admit. It is simply and solely I myself, who have once more undergone a revolution – (*Half to himself.*) – and awakening to my real life.

MAIA: (*Involuntarily folding her hands.*) Why in all the world should we not part then?

RUBEK: (*Looks at her in astonishment.*) Should you be willing to?

MAIA: (*Shrugging her shoulders.*) Oh yes – if there's nothing else for it, then –

RUBEK: (*Eagerly.*) But there is something else for it. There is an alternative –

MAIA: (*Holding up her forefinger.*) Now you are thinking of the pale lady again!

RUBEK: Yes, to tell the truth, I cannot help constantly thinking of her. Ever since I met her again. (*A step nearer her.*) For now I will tell you a secret, Maia.

MAIA: Well?

RUBEK: (*Touching his own breast.*) In here, you see – in here I have a little bramah-locked casket. And in that casket all my sculptor's visions are stored up. But when she disappeared and left no trace, the lock of the casket snapped to. And she had the key – and she took it away with her. – You, little Maia, you had no key; so all that the casket contains must lie unused. And the years pass! And I have no means of getting at the treasure.

MAIA: (*Trying to repress a subtle smile.*) Then get her to open the casket for you again –

RUBEK: (*Not understanding.*) Maia – ?

MAIA: – for here she is, you see. And no doubt it's on account of this casket that she has come.

RUBEK: I have not said a single word to her on this subject!

MAIA: (*Looks innocently at him.*) My dear Rubek – is it worth while to make all this fuss and commotion about so simple a matter?

RUBEK: Do YOU think this matter is so absolutely simple?

MAIA: Yes, certainly I think so. Do you attach yourself to whoever you most require. (*Nods to him.*) I shall always manage to find a place for myself.

RUBEK: Where do you mean?

MAIA: (*Unconcerned, evasively.*) Well – I need only take myself off to the villa, if it should be necessary. But it won't be; for in town – in all that great house of ours – there must surely, with a little good will, be room enough for three.

RUBEK: (*Uncertainly.*) And do you think that would work in the long run?

MAIA: (*In a light tone.*) Very well, then – if it won't work, it won't. It is no good talking about it.

RUBEK: And what shall we do then, Maia – if it does not work?

MAIA: (*Untroubled.*) Then we two will simply get out of each other's way – part entirely. I shall always find something new for myself, somewhere in the world. Something free! Free! Free! – No need to be anxious about that, Professor Rubek! (*Suddenly points off to the right.*) Look there! There we have her.

RUBEK: (*Turning.*) Where?

MAIA: Out on the plain. Striding – like a marble statue. She is coming this way.

RUBEK: (*Stands gazing with his hand over his eyes.*) Does not she look like the Resurrection incarnate? (*To himself.*) And her I could displace – and move into the shade! Remodel her –. Fool that I was!

MAIA: What do you mean by that?

RUBEK: (*Putting the question aside.*) Nothing. Nothing that you would understand.

IRENE advances from the right over the upland. The children at their play have already caught sight of her and run to meet her. She is now surrounded by them; some appear confident and at ease, others uneasy and timid. She talks low to them and indicates that they are to go down to the hotel; she herself will rest a little beside the brook. The children run down over the slope to the left, half way to the back. IRENE goes up to the wall of rock, and lets the rillets of the cascade flow over her hands, cooling them.

MAIA: (*In a low voice.*) Go down and speak to her alone, Rubek.

RUBEK: And where will you go in the meantime?

MAIA: (*Looking significantly at him.*) Henceforth I shall go my own ways.

She descends from the hillock and leaps over the brook, by aid of her alpenstock. She stops beside IRENE.

MAIA: Professor Rubek is up there, waiting for you, madam.

IRENE: What does he want?

MAIA: He wants you to help him to open a casket that has snapped to.

IRENE: Can I help him in that?

MAIA: He says you are the only person that can.

IRENE: Then I must try.

MAIA: Yes, you really must, madam.

She goes down by the path to the hotel. In a little while PROFESSOR RUBEK comes down to IRENE, but stops with the brook between them.

IRENE: (*After a short pause.*) She – the other one – said that you had been waiting for me.

RUBEK: I have waited for you year after year – without myself knowing it.

IRENE: I could not come to you, Arnold. I was lying down there, sleeping the long, deep, dreamful sleep.

RUBEK: But now you have awakened, Irene!

IRENE: (*Shakes her head.*) I have the heavy, deep sleep still in my eyes.

RUBEK: You shall see that day will dawn and lighten for us both.

IRENE: Do not believe that.

RUBEK: (*Urgently.*) I do believe it! And I know it! Now that I have found you again –

IRENE: Risen from the grave.

RUBEK: Transfigured!

IRENE: Only risen, Arnold. Not transfigured.

He crosses over to her by means of stepping-stones below the cascade.

RUBEK: Where have you been all day, Irene?

IRENE: (*Pointing.*) Far, far over there, on the great dead waste –

RUBEK: (*Turning the conversation.*) You have not your – your friend with you today, I see.

IRENE: (*Smiling.*) My friend is keeping a close watch on me, none the less.

RUBEK: Can she?

IRENE: (*Glancing furtively around.*) You may be sure she can – wherever I may go. She never loses sight of me – (*Whispering.*) Until, one fine sunny morning, I shall kill her.

RUBEK: Would you do that?

IRENE: With the utmost delight – if only I could manage it.

RUBEK: Why do you want to?

IRENE: Because she deals in witchcraft. (*Mysteriously.*) Only think, Arnold – she has changed herself into my shadow.

RUBEK: (*Trying to calm her.*) Well, well, well – a shadow we must all have.

IRENE: I am my own shadow. (*With an outburst.*) Do you not understand that!

RUBEK: (*Sadly.*) Yes, yes, Irene, I understand.

He seats himself on a stone beside the brook. She stands behind him, leaning against the wall of rock.

IRENE: (*After a pause.*) Why do you sit there turning your eyes away from me?

RUBEK: (*Softly, shaking his head.*) I dare not – I dare not look at you.

IRENE: Why dare you not look at me any more?

RUBEK: You have a shadow that tortures me. And I have the crushing weight of my conscience.

IRENE: (*With a glad cry of deliverance.*) At last!

RUBEK: (*Springs up.*) Irene – what is it!

IRENE: (*Motioning him off.*) Keep still, still, still! (*Draws a deep breath and says, as though relieved of a burden.*) There! Now they let me go. For this time. – Now we can sit down and talk as we used to – when I was alive.

RUBEK: Oh, if only we could talk as we used to.

IRENE: Sit there where you were sitting. I will sit here beside you.

He sits down again. She seats herself on another stone, close to him.

IRENE: (*After a short interval of silence.*) Now I have come back to you from the uttermost regions, Arnold.

RUBEK: Aye, truly, from an endless journey.

IRENE: Come home to my lord and master –

RUBEK: To our home; – to our own home, Irene.

IRENE: Have you looked for my coming every single day?

RUBEK: How dared I look for you?

IRENE: (*With a sidelong glance.*) No, I suppose you dared not. For you understood nothing.

RUBEK: Was it really not for the sake of someone else that you all of a sudden disappeared from me in that way?

IRENE: Might it not quite well be for your sake, Arnold?

RUBEK: (*Looks doubtfully at her.*) I don't understand you – ?

IRENE: When I had served you with my soul and with my body – when the statue stood there finished – our child as you called it – then I laid at your feet the most precious sacrifice of all – by effacing myself for all time.

RUBEK: (*Bows his head.*) And laying my life waste.

IRENE: (*Suddenly firing up.*) It was just that I wanted! Never, never should you create anything again – after you had created that only child of ours.

RUBEK: Was it jealousy that moved you, then?

IRENE: (*Coldly.*) I think it was rather hatred.

RUBEK: Hatred? Hatred for me?

IRENE: (*Again vehemently.*) Yes, for you – for the artist who had so lightly and carelessly taken a warm-blooded body, a young human life, and worn the soul out of it – because you needed it for a work of art.

RUBEK: And you can say that – you who threw yourself into my work with such saint-like passion and such ardent joy? – that work for which we two met together every morning, as for an act of worship.

IRENE: (*Coldly, as before.*) I will tell you one thing, Arnold.

RUBEK: Well?

IRENE: I never loved your art, before I met you. – Nor after either.

RUBEK: But the artist, Irene?

IRENE: The artist I hate.

RUBEK: The artist in me too?

IRENE: In you most of all. When I unclothed myself and stood for you, then I hated you, Arnold –

RUBEK: (*Warmly.*) That you did not, Irene! That is not true!

IRENE: I hated you, because you could stand there so unmoved –

RUBEK: (*Laughs.*) Unmoved? Do you think so?

IRENE: – at any rate so intolerably self-controlled. And because you were an artist and an artist only – not a man! (*Changing to a tone full of warmth and feeling.*) But that statue in the wet, living clay, that I loved – as it rose up, a vital human creature, out of those raw, shapeless masses – for that was our creation, our child. Mine and yours.

RUBEK: (*Sadly.*) It was so in spirit and in truth.

IRENE: Let me tell you, Arnold – it is for the sake of this child of ours that I have undertaken this long pilgrimage.

RUBEK: (*Suddenly alert.*) For the statue's – ?

IRENE: Call it what you will. I call it our child.

RUBEK: And now you want to see it? Finished? In marble, which you always thought so cold? (*Eagerly.*) You do not know, perhaps, that it is installed in a great museum somewhere – far out in the world?

IRENE: I have heard a sort of legend about it.

RUBEK: And museums were always a horror to you. You called them grave-vaults –

IRENE: I will make a pilgrimage to the place where my soul and my child's soul lie buried.

RUBEK: (*Uneasy and alarmed.*) You must never see that statue again! Do you hear, Irene! I implore you –! Never, never see it again!

IRENE: Perhaps you think it would mean death to me a second time?

RUBEK: (*Clenching his hands together.*) Oh, I don't know what I think. – But how could I ever imagine that you would fix your mind so immovably on that statue? You, who went away from me – before it was completed.

IRENE: It was completed. That was why I could go away from you – and leave you alone.

RUBEK: (*Sits with his elbows upon his knees, rocking his head from side to side, with his hands before his eyes.*) It was not what it afterwards became.

IRENE: (*Quietly but quick as lightning, half-unsheathes a narrow-bladed sharp knife which she carried in her breast, and asks in a hoarse whisper.*) Arnold – have you done any evil to our child?

RUBEK: (*Evasively.*) Any evil? – How can I be sure what you would call it?

IRENE: (*Breathless.*) Tell me at once: what have you done to the child?

RUBEK: I will tell you, if you will sit and listen quietly to what I say.

IRENE: (*Hides the knife.*) I will listen as quietly as a mother can when she –

RUBEK: (*Interrupting.*) And you must not look at me while I am telling you.

IRENE: (*Moves to a stone behind his back.*) I will sit here, behind you. – Now tell me.

RUBEK: (*Takes his hands from before his eyes and gazes straight in front of him.*) When I had found you, I knew at once how I should make use of you for my life-work.

IRENE: 'The Resurrection Day' you called your life-work. – I call it 'our child'.

RUBEK: I was young then – with no knowledge of life. The Resurrection, I thought, would be most beautifully and exquisitely figured as a young unsullied woman – with none of our earth-life's experiences – awakening to light and glory without having to put away from her anything ugly and impure.

IRENE: (*Quickly.*) Yes – and so I stand there now, in our work?

RUBEK: (*Hesitating.*) Not absolutely and entirely so, Irene.

IRENE: (*In rising excitement.*) Not absolutely –? Do I not stand as I always stood for you?

RUBEK: (*Without answering.*) I learned worldly wisdom in the years that followed, Irene. 'The Resurrection Day' became in my mind's eye something more and something – something more complex. The little round plinth on which your figure stood erect and solitary – it no longer afforded room for all the imagery I now wanted to add –

IRENE: (*Gropes for her knife, but desists.*) What imagery did you add then? Tell me!

RUBEK: I imagined that which I saw with my eyes around me in the world. I had to include it – I could not help it, Irene. I expanded the plinth – made it wide and spacious. And on it I placed a segment of the curving, bursting earth. And up from the fissures of the soil there now swarm men and women with dimly suggested animal-faces. Women and men – as I knew them in real life.

IRENE: (*In breathless suspense.*) But in the middle of the rout there stands the young woman radiant with the joy of light? – Do I not stand so, Arnold?

RUBEK: (*Evasively.*) Not quite in the middle. I had unfortunately to move that figure a little back. For the sake of the general effect, you understand. Otherwise it would have dominated the whole too much.

IRENE: But the joy in the light still transfigures my face?

RUBEK: Yes, it does, Irene – in a way. A little subdued perhaps – as my altered idea required.

IRENE: (*Rising noiselessly.*) That design expresses the life you now see, Arnold.

RUBEK: Yes, I suppose it does.

IRENE: And in that design you have shifted me back, a little toned down – to serve as a background-figure – in a group.

She draws the knife.

RUBEK: Not a background-figure. Let us say, at most, a figure not quite in the foreground – or something of that sort.

IRENE: (*Whispers hoarsely.*) There you uttered your own doom.

On the point of striking.

RUBEK: (*Turns and looks up at her.*) Doom?

IRENE: (*Hastily hides the knife, and says as though choked with agony.*) My whole soul – you and I – we, we, we and our child were in that solitary figure.

RUBEK: (*Eagerly, taking off his hat and drying the drops of sweat upon his brow.*) Yes, but let me tell you, too, how I have placed myself in the group. In front, beside a fountain – as it were here – sits a man weighed down with guilt, who cannot quite free himself from the earth-crust. I call him remorse for a forfeited life. He sits there and dips his fingers in the purling stream – to wash them clean – and he is gnawed and tortured by the thought that never, never will he succeed. Never in all eternity will he attain to freedom and the new life. He will remain for ever prisoned in his hell.

IRENE: (*Hardly and coldly.*) Poet!

RUBEK: Why poet?

IRENE: Because you are nerveless and sluggish and full of forgiveness for all the sins of your life, in thought and in act. You have killed my soul – so you model yourself in remorse, and self-accusation, and penance – (*Smiling.*) – and with that you think your account is cleared.

RUBEK: (*Defiantly.*) I am an artist, Irene. And I take no shame to myself for the frailties that perhaps cling to me. For I was born to be an artist, you see. And, do what I may, I shall never be anything else.

IRENE: (*Looks at him with a lurking evil smile, and says gently and softly.*) You are a poet, Arnold. (*Softly strokes his hair.*) You dear, great, middle-aged child, – is it possible that you cannot see that!

RUBEK: (*Annoyed.*) Why do you keep on calling me a poet?

IRENE: (*With malign eyes.*) Because there is something apologetic in the word, my friend. Something that suggests forgiveness of sins – and spreads a cloak over all frailty. (*With a sudden change of tone.*) But I was a human being – then! And I, too, had a life to live, – and a human destiny to fulfil. And all that, look you, I let slip – gave it all up in order to make myself your bondwoman. – Oh, it was self-murder – a deadly sin against myself! (*Half whispering.*) And that sin I can never expiate!

She seats herself near him beside the brook, keeps close, though unnoticed, watch upon him, and, as though in absence of mind, plucks some flowers from the shrubs around them.

IRENE: (*With apparent self-control.*) I should have borne children in the world – many children – real children – not such children as are hidden away in grave-vaults. That was my vocation. I ought never to have served you – poet.

RUBEK: (*Lost in recollection.*) Yet those were beautiful days, Irene. Marvellously beautiful days – as I now look back upon them –

IRENE: (*Looking at him with a soft expression.*) Can you remember a little word that you said – when you had finished – finished with me and with our child? (*Nods to him.*) Can you remember that little word, Arnold?

RUBEK: (*Looks inquiringly at her.*) Did I say a little word then, which you still remember?

IRENE: Yes, you did. Can you not recall it?

RUBEK: (*Shaking his head.*) No, I can't say that I do. Not at the present moment, at any rate.

IRENE: You took both my hands and pressed them warmly. And I stood there in breathless expectation. And then you said: 'So now, Irene, I thank you from my heart. This,' you said, 'has been a priceless episode for me.'

RUBEK: (*Looks doubtfully at her.*) Did I say 'episode'? It is not a word I am in the habit of using.

IRENE: You said 'episode'.

RUBEK: (*With assumed cheerfulness.*) Well, well – after all, it was in reality an episode.

IRENE: (*Curtly.*) At that word I left you.

RUBEK: You take everything so painfully to heart, Irene.

IRENE: (*Drawing her hand over her forehead.*) Perhaps you are right. Let us shake off all the hard things that go to the heart. (*Plucks off the leaves of a mountain rose and strews them on the brook.*) Look there, Arnold. There are our birds swimming.

RUBEK: What birds are they?

IRENE: Can you not see? Of course they are flamingoes. Are they not rose-red?

RUBEK: Flamingoes do not swim. They only wade.

IRENE: Then they are not flamingoes. They are sea-gulls.

RUBEK: They may be sea-gulls with red bills, yes. (*Plucks broad green leaves and throws them into the brook.*) Now I send out my ships after them.

IRENE: But there must be no harpoon-men on board.

RUBEK: No, there shall be no harpoon-men. (*Smiles to her.*) Can you remember the summer when we used to sit like this outside the little peasant hut on the Lake of Taunitz?

IRENE: (*Nods.*) On Saturday evenings, yes, – when we had finished our week's work –

RUBEK: – And taken the train out to the lake – to stay there over Sunday –

IRENE: (*With an evil gleam of hatred in her eyes.*) It was an episode, Arnold.

RUBEK: (*As if not hearing.*) Then, too, you used to set birds swimming in the brook. They were water-lilies which you –

IRENE: They were white swans.

RUBEK: I meant swans, yes. And I remember that I fastened a great furry leaf to one of the swans. It looked like a burdock-leaf –

IRENE: And then it turned into Lohengrin's boat – with the swan yoked to it.

RUBEK: How fond you were of that game, Irene.

IRENE: We played it over and over again.

RUBEK: Every single Saturday, I believe, – all the summer through.

IRENE: You said I was the swan that drew your boat.

RUBEK: Did I say so? Yes, I daresay I did. (*Absorbed in the game.*) Just see how the sea-gulls are swimming down the stream!

IRENE: (*Laughing.*) And all your ships have run ashore.

RUBEK: (*Throwing more leaves into the brook.*) I have ships enough in reserve. (*Follows the leaves with his eyes, throws more into the brook, and says after a pause.*) Irene, – I have bought the little peasant hut beside the Lake of Taunitz.

IRENE: Have you bought it? You often said you would, if you could afford it.

RUBEK: The day came when I could afford it easily enough; and so I bought it.

IRENE: (*With a sidelong look at him.*) Then do you live out there now – in our old house?

RUBEK: No, I have had it pulled down long ago. And I have

built myself a great, handsome, comfortable villa on the site – with a park around it. It is there that we – (*Stops and corrects himself.*) – there that I usually live during the summer.

IRENE: (*Mastering herself.*) So you and – and the other one live out there now?

RUBEK: (*With a touch of defiance.*) Yes. When my wife and I are not travelling – as we are this year.

IRENE: (*Looking far before her.*) Life was beautiful, beautiful by the Lake of Taunitz.

RUBEK: (*As though looking back into himself.*) And yet, Irene –

IRENE: (*Completing his thought.*) – yet we two let slip all that life and its beauty.

RUBEK: (*Softly, urgently.*) Does repentance come too late, now?

IRENE: (*Does not answer, but sits silent for a moment; then she points over the upland.*) Look there, Arnold, – now the sun is going down behind the peaks. See what a red glow the level rays cast over all the heathery knolls out yonder.

RUBEK: (*Looks where she is pointing.*) It is long since I have seen a sunset in the mountains.

IRENE: Or a sunrise?

RUBEK: A sunrise I don't think I have ever seen.

IRENE: (*Smiles as though lost in recollection.*) I once saw a marvel-lously lovely sunrise.

RUBEK: Did you? Where was that?

IRENE: High, high up on a dizzy mountain-top. – You beguiled me up there by promising that I should see all the glory of the world if only I –

She stops suddenly.

RUBEK: If only you – ? Well?

IRENE: I did as you told me – went with you up to the heights. And there I fell upon my knees and worshipped you, and served you. (*Is silent for a moment; then says softly.*) Then I saw the sunrise. (*Turning at him with a scornful smile.*) With you – and the other woman?

RUBEK: (*Urgently.*) With me – as in our days of creation. You could open all that is locked up in me. Can you not find it in your heart, Irene?

IRENE: (*Shaking her head.*) I have no longer the key to you, Arnold.

RUBEK: You have the key! You and you alone possess it! (*Beseechingly.*) Help me – that I may be able to live my life over again!

IRENE: (*Immovable as before.*) Empty dreams! Idle – dead dreams. For the life you and I led there is no resurrection.

RUBEK: (*Curtly, breaking off.*) Then let us go on playing.

IRENE: Yes, playing, playing – only playing!

They sit and strew leaves and petals over the brook, where they float and sail away.

Up the slope to the left at the back come ULFHEIM *and* MAIA *in hunting costume. After them comes the servant with the leash of dogs, with which he goes out to the right.*

RUBEK: (*Catching sight of them.*) Ah! There is little Maia, going out with the bear-hunter.

IRENE: Your lady, yes.

RUBEK: Or the other's.

MAIA: (*Looks around as she is crossing the upland, sees the two sitting by the brook, and calls out.*) Goodnight, Professor! Dream of me. Now I am going off on my adventures!

RUBEK: (*Calls back to her.*) What sort of an adventure is this to be?

MAIA: (*Approaching.*) I am going to let life take the place of all the rest.

RUBEK: (*Mockingly.*) Aha! So you too are going to do that, little Maia?

MAIA: Yes. And I've made a verse about it, and this is how it goes: (*Sings triumphantly.*) I am free! I am free! I am free! No more life in the prison for me! I am free as a bird! I am free! For I believe I have awakened now – at last.

RUBEK: It almost seems so.

MAIA: (*Drawing a deep breath.*) Oh – how divinely light one feels on waking.

RUBEK: Goodnight, Frau Maia – and good luck to –

ULFHEIM: (*Calls out, interposing.*) Hush, hush! – for the devil's sake let's have none of your wizard wishes. Don't you see that we are going out to shoot –

RUBEK: What will you bring me home from the hunting, Maia?

MAIA: You shall have a bird of prey to model. I shall wing one for you.

RUBEK: (*Laughs mockingly and bitterly.*) Yes, to wing things – without knowing what you are doing – that has long been quite in your way.

MAIA: (*Tossing her head.*) Oh, just let me take care of myself for the future, and I wish you then –! (*Nods and laughs roguishly.*) Goodbye – and a good, peaceful summer night on the upland!

RUBEK: (*Jestingly.*) Thanks! And all the ill-luck in the world over you and your hunting!

ULFHEIM: (*Roaring with laughter.*) There now, that is a wish worth having!

MAIA: (*Laughing.*) Thanks, thanks, thanks, Professor!

They have both crossed the visible portion of the upland, and go out through the bushes to the right.

RUBEK: (*After a short pause.*) A summer night on the upland! Yes, that would have been life!

IRENE: (*Suddenly, with a wild expression in her eyes.*) Will you spend a summer night on the upland – with me?

RUBEK: (*Stretching his arms wide.*) Yes, yes, – come!

IRENE: My adored lord and master!

RUBEK: Oh Irene!

IRENE: (*Hoarsely, smiling and groping in her breast.*) It will be only an episode – (*Quickly, whispering.*) Hush! – do not look round, Arnold!

RUBEK: (*Also in a low voice.*) What is it?

IRENE: A face that is staring at me.

RUBEK: (*Turns involuntarily.*) Where! (*With a start.*) Ah – !

The SISTER OF MERCY'S *head is partly visible among the bushes beside the descent to the left. Her eyes are immovably fixed on* IRENE.

IRENE: (*Rises and says softly.*) We must part then. No, you must remain sitting. Do you hear? You must not go with me. (*Bends over him and whispers.*) Till we meet again – tonight – on the upland.

RUBEK: And you will come, Irene?

IRENE: Yes, surely I will come. Wait for me here.

RUBEK: (*Repeats dreamily.*) Summer night on the upland. With you. With you. (*His eyes meet hers.*) Oh, Irene – that might have been our life. – And that we have forfeited – we two.

IRENE: We see the irretrievable only when –

Breaks off.

RUBEK: (*Looks inquiringly at her.*) When – ?

IRENE: When we dead awaken.

RUBEK: (*Shakes his head mournfully.*) What do we really see then?

IRENE: We see that we have never lived. (*She goes towards the slope and descends.*)

The SISTER OF MERCY *makes way for her and follows her.* PROFESSOR RUBEK *remains sitting motionless beside the brook.*

MAIA: (*Is heard singing triumphantly among the hills.*) I am free! I am free! I am free! No more life in the prison for me! I am free as a bird! I am free!

Act 3

A wild riven mountain-side, with sheer precipices at the back. Snow-clad peaks rise to the right, and lose themselves in drifting mists. To the left, on a stone-scree, stands an old, half-ruined hut. It is early morning. Dawn is breaking. The sun has not yet risen.

MAIA *comes, flushed and irritated, down over the stone-scree on the left.* ULFHEIM *follows, half angry, half laughing, holding her fast by the sleeve.*

MAIA: (*Trying to tear herself loose.*) Let me go! Let me go, I say!

ULFHEIM: Come, come! Are you going to bite now? You're as snappish as a wolf.

MAIA: (*Striking him over the hand.*) Let me, I tell you? And be quiet!

ULFHEIM: No, confound me if I will!

MAIA: Then I will not go another step with you. Do you hear? – not a single step!

ULFHEIM: Ho, ho! How can you get away from me, here, on the wild mountain-side?

MAIA: I will jump over the precipice yonder, if need be –

ULFHEIM: And mangle and mash yourself up into dogs'-meat! A juicy morsel! (*Lets go his hold.*) As you please. Jump over the precipice if you want to. It's a dizzy drop. There's only one narrow footpath down it, and that's almost impassable.

MAIA: (*Dusts her skirt with her hand, and looks at him with angry eyes.*) Well, you are a nice one to go hunting with!

ULFHEIM: Say rather, sporting.

MAIA: Oh! So you call this sport, do you?

ULFHEIM: Yes, I venture to take that liberty. It is the sort of sport I like best of all.

MAIA: (*Tossing her head.*) Well – I must say! (*After a pause; looks searchingly at him.*) Why did you let the dogs loose up there?

ULFHEIM: (*Blinking his eyes and smiling.*) So that they too might do a little hunting on their own account, don't you see?

MAIA: There's not a word of truth in that! It wasn't for the dogs' sake that you let them go.

ULFHEIM: (*Still smiling.*) Well, why did I let them go then? Let us hear.

MAIA: You let them go because you wanted to get rid of Lars. He was to run after them and bring them in again, you said. And in the meantime –. Oh, it was a pretty way to behave!

ULFHEIM: In the meantime?

MAIA: (*Curtly breaking off.*) No matter!

ULFHEIM: (*In a confidential tone.*) Lars won't find them. You may safely swear to that. He won't come with them before the time's up.

MAIA: (*Looking angrily at him.*) No, I daresay not.

ULFHEIM: (*Catching at her arm.*) For Lars – he knows my – my methods of sport, you see.

MAIA: (*Eludes him, and measures him with a glance.*) Do you know what you look like, Mr Ulfheim?

ULFHEIM: I should think I'm probably most like myself.

MAIA: Yes, there you're exactly right. For you're the living image of a faun.

ULFHEIM: A faun?

MAIA: Yes, precisely; a faun.

ULFHEIM: A faun! Isn't that a sort of monster? Or a kind of a wood demon, as you might call it?

MAIA: Yes, just the sort of creature you are. A thing with a goat's beard and goat-legs. Yes, and the faun has horns too!

ULFHEIM: So, so! – Has he horns too?

MAIA: A pair of ugly horns, just like yours, yes.

ULFHEIM: Can you see the poor little horns *I* have?

MAIA: Yes. I seem to see them quite plainly.

ULFHEIM: (*Taking the dogs' leash out of his pocket.*) Then I had better see about tying you.

MAIA: Have you gone quite mad? Would you tie me?

ULFHEIM: If I am a demon, let me be a demon! So that's the way of it! You can see the horns, can you?

MAIA: (*Soothingly.*) There, there, there! Now try to behave nicely, Mr Ulfheim. (*Breaking off.*) But what has become of that hunting-castle of yours, that you boasted so much of? You said it lay somewhere hereabouts.

ULFHEIM: (*Points with a flourish to the hut.*) There you have it, before your very eyes.

MAIA: (*Looks at him.*) That old pigsty!

ULFHEIM: (*Laughing in his beard.*) It has harboured more than one king's daughter, I can tell you.

MAIA: Was it there that that horrid man you told me about came to the king's daughter in the form of a bear?

ULFHEIM: Yes, my fair companion of the chase – this is the scene. (*With a gesture of invitation.*) If you would deign to enter.

MAIA: Isch! If ever I set foot in it –! Isch!

ULFHEIM: Oh, two people can doze away a summer night in there comfortably enough. Or a whole summer, if it comes to that!

MAIA: Thanks! One would need to have a pretty strong taste for that kind of thing. (*Impatiently.*) But now I am tired both of you and the hunting expedition. Now I am going down to the hotel – before people awaken down there.

ULFHEIM: How do you propose to get down from here?

MAIA: That's your affair. There must be a way down somewhere or other, I suppose.

ULFHEIM: (*Pointing towards the back.*) Oh, certainly! There is a sort of way – right down the face of the precipice yonder –

MAIA: There, you see. With a little goodwill –

ULFHEIM: – but just you try if you dare go that way.

MAIA: (*Doubtfully.*) Do you think I can't?

ULFHEIM: Never in this world – if you don't let me help you.

MAIA: (*Uneasily.*) Why, then come and help me! What else are you here for?

ULFHEIM: Would you rather I should take you on my back – ?

MAIA: Nonsense!

ULFHEIM: – or carry you in my arms?

MAIA: Now do stop talking that rubbish!

ULFHEIM: (*With suppressed exasperation.*) I once took a young girl – lifted her up from the mire of the streets and carried her in my arms. Next my heart I carried her. So I would have borne her all through life – lest haply she should dash her foot against a stone. For her shoes were worn very thin when I found her –

MAIA: And yet you took her up and carried her next your heart?

ULFHEIM: Took her up out of the gutter and carried her as high and as carefully as I could. (*With a growling laugh.*) And do you know what I got for my reward?

MAIA: No. What did you get?

ULFHEIM: (*Looks at her, smiles and nods.*) I got the horns! The horns that you can see so plainly. Is not that a comical story, madam bear-murderess?

MAIA: Oh yes, comical enough! But I know another story that is still more comical.

ULFHEIM: How does that story go?

MAIA: This is how it goes. There was once a stupid girl, who had both a father and a mother – but a rather poverty-stricken home. Then there came a high and mighty seigneur into the midst of all this poverty. And he took the girl in his arms – as you did – and travelled far, far away with her –

ULFHEIM: Was she so anxious to be with him?

MAIA: Yes, for she was stupid, you see.

ULFHEIM: And he, no doubt, was a brilliant and beautiful personage?

MAIA: Oh, no, he wasn't so superlatively beautiful either. But he pretended that he would take her with him to the top of the highest of mountains, where there were light and sunshine without end.

ULFHEIM: So he was a mountaineer, was he, that man?

MAIA: Yes, he was – in his way.

ULFHEIM: And then he took the girl up with him – ?

MAIA: (*With a toss of the head.*) Took her up with him finely, you may be sure! Oh no! he beguiled her into a cold, clammy cage, where – as it seemed to her – there was neither sunlight nor fresh air, but only gilding and great petrified ghosts of people all around the walls.

ULFHEIM: Devil take me, but it served her right!

MAIA: Yes, but don't you think it's quite a comical story, all the same?

ULFHEIM: (*Looks at her moment.*) Now listen to me, my good companion of the chase –

MAIA: Well, what is it now?

ULFHEIM: Should not we two tack our poor shreds of life together?

MAIA: Is his worship inclined to set up as a patching-tailor?

ULFHEIM: Yes, indeed he is. Might not we two try to draw the rags together here and there – so as to make some sort of a human life out of them?

MAIA: And when the poor tatters were quite worn out – what then?

ULFHEIM: (*With a large gesture.*) Then there we shall stand, free and serene – as the man and woman we really are!

MAIA: (*Laughing.*) You with your goat-legs yes!

ULFHEIM: And you with your –. Well, let that pass.

MAIA: Yes, come – let us pass – on.

ULFHEIM: Stop! Whither away, comrade?

MAIA: Down to the hotel, of course.

ULFHEIM: And afterward?

MAIA: Then we'll take a polite leave of each other, with thanks for pleasant company.

ULFHEIM: Can we part, we two? Do you think we can?

MAIA: Yes, you didn't manage to tie me up, you know.

ULFHEIM: I have a castle to offer you –

MAIA: (*Pointing to the hut.*) A fellow to that one?

ULFHEIM: It has not fallen to ruin yet.

MAIA: And all the glory of the world, perhaps?

ULFHEIM: A castle, I tell you –

MAIA: Thanks! I have had enough of castles.

ULFHEIM: – with splendid hunting-grounds stretching for miles around it.

MAIA: Are there works of art too in this castle?

ULFHEIM: (*Slowly.*) Well, no – it's true there are no works of art; but –

MAIA: (*Relieved.*) Ah! that's one good thing, at any rate!

ULFHEIM: Will you go with me, then – as far and as long as I want you?

MAIA: There is a tame bird of prey keeping watch upon me.

ULFHEIM: (*Wildly.*) We'll put a bullet in his wing, Maia!

MAIA: (*Looks at him a moment, and says resolutely.*) Come then, and carry me down into the depths.

ULFHEIM: (*Puts his arm round her waist.*) It is high time! The mist is upon us!

MAIA: Is the way down terribly dangerous?

ULFHEIM: The mountain is more dangerous still.

She shakes him off, goes to the edge of the precipice and looks over, but starts quickly back.

ULFHEIM: (*Goes towards her, laughing.*) What? Does it make you a little giddy?

MAIA: (*Faintly.*) Yes, that too. But go and look over. Those two, coming up –

ULFHEIM: (*Goes and bends over the edge of the precipice.*) It's only your bird of prey – and his strange lady.

MAIA: Can't we get past them – without their seeing us?

ULFHEIM: Impossible! The path is far too narrow. And there's no other way down.

MAIA: (*Nerving herself.*) Well, well – let us face them here, then!

ULFHEIM: Spoken like a true bear-killer, comrade!

PROFESSOR RUBEK and IRENE appear over the edge of the precipice at the back. He has his plaid over his shoulders; she has a fur cloak thrown loosely over her white dress, and a swansdown hood over her head.

RUBEK: (*Still only half visible above the edge.*) What, Maia! So we two meet once again?

MAIA: (*With assumed coolness.*) At your service. Won't you come up?

PROFESSOR RUBEK climbs right up and holds out his hand to IRENE, who also comes right to the top.

RUBEK: (*Coldly to MAIA.*) So you, too, have been all night on the mountain, – as we have?

MAIA: I have been hunting – yes. You gave me permission, you know.

ULFHEIM: (*Pointing downward.*) Have you come up that path there?

RUBEK: As you saw.

ULFHEIM: And the strange lady too?

RUBEK: Yes, of course. (*With a glance at MAIA.*) Henceforth the strange lady and I do not intend our ways to part.

ULFHEIM: Don't you know, then, that it is a deadly dangerous way you have come?

RUBEK: We thought we would try it, nevertheless. For it did not seem particularly hard at first.

ULFHEIM: No, at first nothing seems hard. But presently you may come to a tight place where you can neither get forward nor back. And then you stick fast, Professor! Mountain-fast, as we hunters call it.

RUBEK: (*Smiles and looks at him.*) Am I to take these as oracular utterances, Mr Ulfheim?

ULFHEIM: Lord preserve me from playing the oracle! (*Urgently, pointing up towards the heights.*) But don't you see that the storm is upon us? Don't you hear the blasts of wind?

RUBEK: (*Listening.*) They sound like the prelude to the Resurrection Day.

ULFHEIM: They are storm-blasts from the peaks, man! Just look how the clouds are rolling and sinking – soon they'll be all around us like a winding-sheet!

IRENE: (*With a start and shiver.*) I know that sheet!

MAIA: (*Drawing ULFHEIM away.*) Let us make haste and get down.

ULFHEIM: (*To PROFESSOR RUBEK.*) I cannot help more than one. Take refuge in the hut in the meantime – while the storm lasts. Then I shall send people up to fetch the two of you away.

IRENE: (*In terror.*) To fetch us away! No, no!

ULFHEIM: (*Harshly.*) To take you by force if necessary – for it's a matter of life and death here. Now, you know it. (*To MAIA.*) Come, then – and don't fear to trust yourself in your comrade's hands.

MAIA: (*Clinging to him.*) Oh, how I shall rejoice and sing, if I get down with a whole skin!

ULFHEIM: (*Begins the descent and calls to the others.*) You'll wait, then, in the hut, till the men come with ropes, and fetch you away.

ULFHEIM, with MAIA in his arms, clambers rapidly but warily down the precipice.

IRENE: (*Looks for some time at PROFESSOR RUBEK with terror-stricken eyes.*) Did you hear that, Arnold? – Men are coming up to fetch me away! Many men will come up here –

RUBEK: Do not be alarmed, Irene!

IRENE: (*In growing terror.*) And she, the woman in black – she will come too. For she must have missed me long ago. And then she will seize me, Arnold! And put me in the strait-waistcoat. Oh, she has it with her, in her box. I have seen it with my own eyes –

RUBEK: Not a soul shall be suffered to touch you.

IRENE: (*With a wild smile.*) Oh no – I myself have a resource against that.

RUBEK: What resource do you mean?

IRENE: (*Drawing out the knife.*) This!

RUBEK: (*Tries to seize it.*) Have you a knife?

IRENE: Always, always – both day and night – in bed as well!

RUBEK: Give me that knife, Irene!

IRENE: (*Concealing it.*) You shall not have it. I may very likely find a use for it myself.

RUBEK: What use can you have for it, here?

IRENE: (*Looks fixedly at him.*) It was intended for you, Arnold.

RUBEK: For me!

IRENE: As we were sitting by the Lake of Taunitz last evening –

RUBEK: By the Lake of –

IRENE: – outside the peasant's hut – and playing with swans and water-lilies –

RUBEK: What then – what then?

IRENE: – and when I heard you say with such deathly, icy coldness – that I was nothing but an episode in your life –

RUBEK: It was you that said that, Irene, not I.

IRENE: (*Continuing.*) – then I had my knife out. I wanted to stab you in the back with it.

RUBEK: (*Darkly.*) And why did you hold your hand?

IRENE: Because it flashed upon me with a sudden horror that you were dead already – long ago.

RUBEK: Dead?

IRENE: Dead. Dead, you as well as I. We sat there by the Lake of Taunitz, we two clay-cold bodies – and played with each other.

RUBEK: I do not call that being dead. But you do not understand me.

IRENE: Then where is the burning desire for me that you fought and battled against when I stood freely forth before you as the woman arisen from the dead?

RUBEK: Our love is assuredly not dead, Irene.

IRENE: The love that belongs to the life of earth – the beautiful, miraculous earth-life – the inscrutable earth-life – that is dead in both of us.

RUBEK: (*Passionately.*) And do you know that just that love – it is burning and seething in me as hotly as ever before?

IRENE: And I? Have you forgotten who I now am?

RUBEK: Be who or what you please, for aught I care! For me, you are the woman I see in my dreams of you.

IRENE: I have stood on the turn-table naked – and made a show of myself to many hundreds of men – after you.

RUBEK: It was I that drove you to the turn-table – blind as I then was – I, who placed the dead clay-image above the happiness of life – of love.

IRENE: (*Looking down.*) Too late – too late!

RUBEK: Not by a hairsbreadth has all that has passed in the interval lowered you in my eyes.

IRENE: (*With head erect.*) Nor in my own!

RUBEK: Well, what then! Then we are free – and there is still time for us to live our life, Irene.

IRENE: (*Looks sadly at him.*) The desire for life is dead in me, Arnold. Now I have arisen. And I look for you. And I find you. – And then I see that you and life lie dead – as I have lain.

RUBEK: Oh, how utterly you are astray! Both in us and around us life is fermenting and throbbing as fiercely as ever!

IRENE: (*Smiling and shaking her head.*) The young woman of your Resurrection Day can see all life lying on its bier.

RUBEK: (*Throwing his arms violently around her.*) Then let two of the dead – us two – for once live life to its uttermost – before we go down to our graves again!

IRENE: (*With a shriek.*) Arnold!

RUBEK: But not here in the half darkness! Not here with this hideous dank shroud flapping around us –

IRENE: (*Carried away by passion.*) No, no – up in the light, and in all the glittering glory! Up to the Peak of Promise!

RUBEK: There we will hold our marriage-feast, Irene – oh, my beloved!

IRENE: (*Proudly.*) The sun may freely look on us, Arnold.

RUBEK: All the powers of light may freely look on us – and all the powers of darkness too. (*Seizes her hand.*) Will you then follow me, oh my grace-given bride?

IRENE: (*As though transfigured.*) I follow you, freely and gladly, my lord and master!

RUBEK: (*Drawing her along with him.*) We must first pass through the mists, Irene, and then –

IRENE: Yes, through all the mists, and then right up to the summit of the tower that shines in the sunrise.

The mist-clouds close in over the scene – PROFESSOR RUBEK and IRENE, hand in hand, climb up over the snow-field to the right and soon disappear among the lower clouds. Keen storm-gusts hurtle and whistle through the air. The SISTER OF MERCY appears upon the stone-scree to the left. She stops and looks around silently and searchingly.

MAIA: I am free! I am free! I am free! No more life in the prison for me! I am free as a bird! I am free!

Suddenly a sound like thunder is heard from high up on the snow-field, which glides and whirls downwards with headlong speed. PROFESSOR RUBEK and IRENE can be dimly discerned as they are whirled along with the masses of snow and buried in them.

SISTER OF MERCY: (*Gives a shriek, stretches out her arms towards them and cries.*) Irene!

Stands silent a moment, then makes the sign of the cross before her in the air, and says.

Pax vobiscum!

MAIA's triumphant song sounds from still farther down below.

1.5 **INTERIOR** (1894)

MAURICE MAETERLINCK

Translated by Dan Rebellato

Maurice Maeterlinck (1862–1949) was a well-known and controversial fin-de-siècle *Belgian playwright and essayist. His most popular collection,* The Treasure of the Humble *(1896), included the essay* Tragedy in Everyday Life *(see 1.10), which offers a new approach to the writing of Symbolist drama. He shared the Symbolist aversion to the theatre, claiming, 'I always enjoy reading a play far more than I do seeing it acted', finding the fleshly presence of the actor damaging to the delicate ideas embodied in fine poetic language. For this reason he may have conceived* Interior *and some other plays (*The Blind *and* Intruder*) as puppet plays, although when it was first performed at the Théâtre de l'Oeuvre in March 1895* Interior *was performed by actors. In* Interior, *he uses the device of two men watching a family at peace, unaware of the terrible news that they are about to receive, to reflect on our – and, by implication, Naturalism's – tendency to ignore the ubiquity of death and the cruel ironies of fate. In its use of silence, hesitation and rich haunting atmosphere it looks forward to some aspects of 'absurd drama' in the 1950s and 1960s. It is translated from French for the present volume by Dan Rebellato.*

Characters

In the garden
THE OLD MAN
THE STRANGER
MARY
MARTHA
A FARMHAND
THE CROWD

In the house
THE FATHER
THE MOTHER
THE TWO GIRLS
THE CHILD

An old garden planted with willows. A house at the back, with three of its ground-floor windows lit up. We can clearly make out a family spending an evening together by the light of the lamp. THE FATHER *is sitting next to the fire.* THE MOTHER, *one elbow on the table, stares into space. Two young girls, dressed in white, are embroidering, dreaming and smiling in the calm of the room. A child sleeps, its head on the mother's left shoulder. When one of them gets up, walks or makes a movement, their movements appear serious, slow, sparse and as if hypnotized by the distance, the light and the slight veil of the windows.*

THE OLD MAN *and* THE STRANGER *cautiously make their way into the garden.*

OLD MAN: We're in the part of the garden that goes up round the back of the house. They never come here. The doors are on the other side. – They're locked and the shutters are closed. But there are no shutters this side and I saw the light … Yes; they're spending an evening by the light of the lamp. It's good that they didn't hear us; the mother or the young girls might have come out and then what would we have done? …

STRANGER: What are we going to do?

OLD MAN: First, I want to check they're all in the room. Yes, I can see the father sitting by the fire. He's waiting, his hands on his knees … the mother's leaning on the table.

STRANGER: She's looking at us …

OLD MAN: No; she is looking at nothing in particular. Her eyes aren't blinking. She can't see us; we're in the shade of the great trees. But don't get any nearer … the dead girl's two sisters are also in the room. They are working slowly at their embroidery; and the little child's asleep. The clock in the corner says nine … they suspect nothing and they say nothing.

STRANGER: Could we attract the father's attention, signal to him in some way? He's turned his head towards us. Would you like me to tap on one of the windows? One of them will have to find out before the others …

OLD MAN: I don't know what to do … we must be very careful … the father is old and frail … the mother too; and the sisters are too young … they never will love anyone the way they loved her … I've never seen a happier household … No, no, don't go near the window; that's the worst thing we could do … better to say it as simply as possible, like it's something ordinary, and not to seem too sad; otherwise, their grief has to compete with yours and they won't know what to do … let's go round to the other part of the garden. We'll knock on the door and go in like nothing's happened. I'll go in first; they won't be surprised to see me; I sometimes drop in of an evening, to bring them flowers or fruit, spend a couple of hours with them.

STRANGER: Why do I need to go with you? You go on your own; I'll wait till I'm called … they've never seen me … I'm just a passer-by; I'm a stranger …

OLD MAN: Better if I'm not alone. Bad news brought by two people is less blunt, less heavy … I was thinking about this on the way here … if I go in alone, I'll have to speak immediately; they'd know everything in a few words and I'd have nothing more to say; and the silence after bad news is terrifying … that's when the heart breaks. If we go in together, I can, for example, work my way round to telling them: she was found like this … floating on the river, her hands clasped together …

STRANGER: Her hands were not clasped; her arms were limp by her sides …

OLD MAN: You see how you let your tongue run away with itself … and the misfortune gets lost in the details … but if I go in alone, I know them: from the first words it'll all be so dreadful, God knows what will happen … but if we take turns to speak, they'll be listening to us and not to the terrible news … don't forget that the mother will be there and her life is so fragile … it's as well that the first wave founders on a handful of silly words … you have to be a bit roundabout with wretched people like this and make sure they are cushioned. Even the most careless visitors, without knowing it, take some of the sadness away with them … it just disperses soundlessly or effortlessly, like the air or the light …

STRANGER: Your clothes are wet and dripping on the flagstones.

OLD MAN: Just the bottom of my coat, I got it wet in the water. You look cold. You've got mud all down your front … I didn't notice it on the way, it was so dark …

STRANGER: I went into the water up to my waist.

OLD MAN: Did you find her long before I arrived?

STRANGER: Barely minutes before. I was on my way to the village; it was already late and getting dark on the river bank. I was walking, following the river because it was lighter than the path, and I see something strange by a clump of reeds … I get closer and see her hair rising almost in a circle round her head, swirling with the current …

In the room, the two young girls turn their heads towards the window.

OLD MAN: Did you see the two sisters' hair flutter on their shoulders?

STRANGER: They turned their heads this way … turned their heads that's all. Was I talking too loudly? (*The two young girls resume their original position.*) They've turned back now … I went into the water up to my waist and managed to grab her hand and drag her onto the bank easily enough … She was as beautiful as her sisters …

OLD MAN: Maybe more beautiful … I don't know why, I've lost my nerve …

STRANGER: What are you talking about, nerve? We did all anyone could … She'd been dead over an hour.

OLD MAN: She was alive this morning! … I met her coming out of church … She said she was going away, going to see her grandmother on the other side of that river where you found her … She didn't know when she'd be back … she seemed to be about to ask me something; but her courage failed her and she hurried off. I saw nothing but now I start to wonder … She smiled like one of those who smile instead of speaking for fear of being misunderstood … It always seemed like her hope was tinged with sorrow … her eyes were dim and she barely looked at me …

STRANGER: Some of the farmhands told me that they saw her wandering on the bank until the evening … They thought she was looking for flowers … it might be that her death …

OLD MAN: Who can say … what can we ever know? …

Maybe she was the type of person who doesn't like to talk but inside is carrying any number of reasons to end their life ... you can't see into the soul like you can into that room. Everyone's like this ... They come out with trivialities; and no one suspects anything's wrong ... you can spend months with someone who is no longer of this world, whose soul can't hold itself down any more; you talk to them without a second thought: and you see what happens ... they look like lifeless dolls but so many things are going on in their souls ... They don't know what they are themselves ... She would have lived like the others do ... She would have said up to her death: 'Sir, Madam, it looks like rain this morning' or even: 'Let's have dinner, we'll be thirteen at table': or even: 'The fruit hasn't ripened yet.' They smile, talking of falling blossom, and they cry in the dark ... Not even an angel could see what has to be seen; and we humans can only understand with hindsight ... Yesterday evening, there she was, by the lamp like her sisters, and if this hadn't happened you wouldn't be looking at them like this, but now we can't help look at them this way ... I feel like I'm looking at them for the first time ... Something new must enter our ordinary lives before we can understand them ... They're by your side, you look at them and look at them, but only really see them at the moment when they go for good ... And meanwhile, the strange little soul that she must have had; the poor, simple, unfathomable little soul that she must have had, dear child, to say what she must have said, to do what she must have done! ...

STRANGER: At this moment, they are smiling silently in their room ...

OLD MAN: They're relaxed ... they're not expecting her this evening ...

STRANGER: They smile without moving ... but now the father is placing a finger to his lips ...

OLD MAN: He's indicating the child asleep at its mother's breast ...

STRANGER: She doesn't dare lift her eyes, for fear of disturbing its sleep ...

OLD MAN: They are not working any more ... there is a heavy silence.

STRANGER: They have let the ball of white wool fall to the floor ...

OLD MAN: They are looking at the child ...

STRANGER: They don't know that they are being looked at ...

OLD MAN: We, too, are being looked at ...

STRANGER: They've raised their eyes ...

OLD MAN: But they can't see anything ...

STRANGER: They seem happy, but, I don't know, there's still something ...

OLD MAN: They think they're safe in there ... they have locked the doors; and the windows have iron bars on them ... they have reinforced the walls of their old house; they have bolted the three oak doors ... they have foreseen everything they could foresee ...

STRANGER: We're going to have to tell them eventually ... someone might turn up and tell them straight out ... there was a crowd of farmhands in the meadow where the dead girl was found ... if one of them knocks on the door ...

OLD MAN: Martha and Mary are with the little dead girl. The farmhands were going to make a stretcher out of leaves and branches; and I told the oldest to come and warn us immediately, as soon as they set off. Let's wait till she arrives; she'll go in with me ... we shouldn't have seen them like this ... I thought all we had to do was knock on the door, just go in, find the words to say and say them ... But I have spent too long watching them under their lamp.

MARY enters.

MARY: They're coming, grandfather.

OLD MAN: Is that you? – Where are they?

MARY: They are at the foot of the last hills.

OLD MAN: Are they coming in silence?

MARY: I told them to pray quietly. Martha is with them ...

OLD MAN: Are there many of them?

MARY: The whole village is walking alongside the pallbearers. They brought lanterns but I told them to put them out ...

OLD MAN: Which way are they coming?

MARY: They are coming along the footpaths. They are walking slowly ...

OLD MAN: It's time ...

MARY: Have you told them, grandfather?

OLD MAN: You can see perfectly well that we haven't ... they are still waiting by the lamp ... Look, my child, look: you'll see something of life ...

MARY: Oh! How calm they seem! ... it's almost like a dream ...

STRANGER: Be careful, I saw the two sisters give a start ...

OLD MAN: They are getting up ...

STRANGER: I think they're coming towards the windows ...

At this point, one of the two sisters comes up to the first window, the other, to the third; and, pressing their hands on the panes stare for a long time into the darkness.

OLD MAN: No one comes to the window in the middle ...

MARY: They are looking ... listening ...

OLD MAN: The older one smiles but doesn't see ...

MARY: And the second has eyes full of fear ...

OLD MAN: Be careful; we don't know how far beyond the body the soul can reach ...

A long silence. MARY nestles up to THE OLD MAN's chest and hugs him.

MARY: Grandfather! ...

OLD MAN: Don't cry, my child ... our turn will come ...

Silence.

STRANGER: They've been looking for a long time …

OLD MAN: They could look for a hundred thousand years and not see anything, the poor girls … the night is too dark … they're looking over here but the bad news is coming from over there …

STRANGER: Lucky they are looking this way … I don't know what that is coming from the direction of the meadows.

MARY: I think it's the crowd … they are so far away you can barely make them out …

STRANGER: They are following the path as it rises and falls … see, they appear again on that slope lit by the moon …

MARY: Oh! Looks like there's a lot of them … they were already coming in from the outskirts of the town when I arrived … They are taking the long route …

OLD MAN: They'll get here nonetheless, yes I can see them too. They're crossing the meadows … they look so small you can scarcely pick them out from the grasses … you might think they were children playing in the moonlight; and if the girls see them they wouldn't understand … they may well have their backs to it, but each step brings misery closer and it's been getting nearer for over two hours. They can't stop it, any more than the ones bringing it … it's their master too and they must serve it … it has its aim and follows its path … it's unstoppable and has only one thought … they have to submit to its power. They are sad but they come … they have pity but they must draw nearer.

MARY: The older one's not smiling any more, grandfather.

STRANGER: They're moving away from the windows.

MARY: They're kissing their mother.

STRANGER: The older one is stroking the sleeping child's curls …

MARY: Oh, look! The father wants a kiss too …

STRANGER: Now silence …

MARY: They're returning to their mother's side …

STRANGER: And the father's eyes are fixed on the great pendulum on the clock.

MARY: It's like they're praying without knowing it …

STRANGER: It's like they're listening to their souls …

Silence.

MARY: Grandfather, don't tell them, not this evening.

OLD MAN: You see how you also lose your nerve. I knew we shouldn't watch them. I'm nearly eighty-three and it's the first time I've seen life like this. Why does everything they do seem so strange and so serious to me? … they're waiting for night to fall, that's all, by the lamp, just like we would by ours. But I feel like I'm looking at them from high up, from another world, because I know a little truth that they don't … is that it, my children? But tell me why you're so pale too? Is there something else, perhaps, which cannot be said, but makes us weep? I didn't know life had anything this sad in it, anything which could terrify those who saw it … even if nothing had happened it would have terrified me to see them so still … they have too much faith in this world … there they are separated from the enemy by thin window panes … they think they're safe because they've locked the door and they don't realize that what happens happens in the soul and that the world doesn't stop at their front door … they are so certain of their little life, they have no idea how much more others know about it; and I, just a poor old man, I hold here, a couple of steps from their door, all their little happiness between my two old hands, and dare not open them …

MARY: Have pity, grandfather …

OLD MAN: We can pity them, my child, but no one pities us …

MARY: Tell them tomorrow, grandfather, tell them when it gets light … they won't be so sad …

OLD MAN: You may be right … it would be better to leave all this tonight. And light is gentle on sadness … But what would they say to us tomorrow? Misfortune makes us resentful; and those it hits want to be told before everyone else knows. They don't like it handled by strangers … it would be like we'd stolen something from them.

STRANGER: Besides, there's no more time; I can already hear the murmur of prayers …

MARY: They're here … they're passing behind the hedges …

MARTHA enters.

MARTHA: Here I am. I led them here. I told them to wait on the road.

The cries of children can be heard.

Ah, the children are still crying … I told them not to come … but they also wanted to see and their mother wouldn't listen to me … I'm going to tell them … No, they've gone quiet – Is everything ready? – I've brought the little ring we found on her. I laid her out on the stretcher myself. She looked like she was asleep. It was very difficult; her hair wouldn't do what I wanted … I got them to pick daisies … it's sad, there were no other flowers … what are you doing here? Why aren't you with them?

She looks through the windows.

They're not crying? … They … haven't you told them?

OLD MAN: Martha, Martha, there is too much life in your soul, you wouldn't understand.

MARTHA: Why wouldn't I?

After a silence, and in a very serious, reproachful tone –

You should have told them, grandfather.

OLD MAN: Martha, you don't understand …

MARTHA: I'll have to tell them.

OLD MAN: Stay here, my child, and watch for a moment.

MARTHA: Oh, they are so sad! … They mustn't be kept waiting any longer.

OLD MAN: Why not?

MARTHA: I don't know ... but it's not possible, not any more!

OLD MAN: Come here, my child.

MARTHA: They're so patient!

OLD MAN: Come here, my child.

MARTHA: (*Turning around.*) Where are you, grandfather? I'm so sad I can't make you out ... I, I don't know what to do now.

OLD MAN: Don't look at them any more; not until they know the full story.

MARTHA: I want to go in with you.

OLD MAN: No, Martha, wait here ... sit with your sister on the old stone bench by the wall of the house, and turn away ... you are too young, the memory would stay with you forever ... you shouldn't see what a face looks like when its eyes are filled with death ... there may be tears ... Don't turn round ... There may be nothing ... Above all, don't turn round if you hear nothing ... you never know in advance what path despair will take ... a few tiny sobs from the very depths and that's usually all ... I don't know what I'll do when I hear them ... it's not part of this life ... kiss me, my child, before I go.

The murmur of prayers gets gradually nearer. A part of the crowd enters the garden. We can hear the patter of soft footsteps and the murmur of low voices.

STRANGER: (*To the crowd.*) Stay here ... don't go near the window ... where is she?

FARMHAND: Who?

STRANGER: The others ... the pallbearers? ...

FARMHAND: They're taking the path that leads to the door.

THE OLD MAN leaves. MARTHA and MARY are seated on the bench, backs to the windows. Low muttering in the crowd.

STRANGER: Be quiet! ... Not a sound.

The older sister gets up and goes to the bolts on the door.

MARTHA: Is she opening it?

STRANGER: Far from it, she's locking it.

Silence.

MARTHA: Hasn't grandfather gone in?

STRANGER: No ... she's going back to sit next to her mother ... the others aren't stirring and the child's slept through the whole thing.

Silence.

MARTHA: My little sister, give me your hands.

MARY: Martha.

They hug and embrace.

STRANGER: He must have knocked ... they all raised their heads at the same time ... they're looking at each other ...

MARTHA: Oh! Oh! My poor sister ... I'm going to start crying too ...

She stifles her sobs on her sister's shoulder.

STRANGER: He must be knocking again ... the father's looking up this time. He's getting up.

MARTHA: My sister, my sister, I want to go in too ... they mustn't be alone any longer.

MARY: Martha, Martha.

She holds her back.

STRANGER: The father is at the door ... he's drawing back the bolts ... cautiously, he opens it ...

MARTHA: Oh! ... you can't see ...

STRANGER: What?

MARTHA: The pallbearers ...

STRANGER: He's not opened it very much ... I can only see the edge of the front garden and the fountain ... he's not letting go of the door ... he draws back ... He's saying something like 'Ah, it's you! ...' He raises his arms ... He's closing the door carefully ... Your grandfather's inside ...

The crowd has got up close to the windows. MARTHA and MARY rise hesitantly, before approaching as well, arms tight around each other. The dead girl's sisters get up; THE MOTHER gets up too, after having carefully sat the child in her armchair, in such a way that from outside the child can be seen sleeping, the head a little to one side, in the centre of the room. THE MOTHER goes up to meet THE OLD MAN and holds out her hand, but withdraws it before he has time to take it. One of the young girls goes to take the visitor's coat and the other offers him an armchair. But THE OLD MAN declines with a small gesture. THE FATHER smiles, bemused. THE OLD MAN looks towards the windows.

STRANGER: He can't bring himself to tell them ... He's looking at us.

Muttering in the crowd.

STRANGER: Be quiet! ...

THE OLD MAN, seeing the faces at the windows, quickly averts his gaze. One of the young girls is still offering the same armchair, and he finally sits down and rubs his forehead repeatedly.

STRANGER: He's sitting down ...

The other people in the room sit down as well, while THE FATHER speaks at length. Eventually THE OLD MAN opens his mouth and the sound of his voice appears to draw their attention. THE FATHER interrupts. THE OLD MAN carries on and, little by little, the others become still. Suddenly THE MOTHER gives a start, and stands up.

MARTHA: Oh! The mother begins to understand! ...

She turns around and buries her face in her hands. Further murmuring from the crowd. Some jockey for position. Children cry to be lifted up so that they can see too. Most of the mothers comply.

STRANGER: Silence! … He hasn't told them yet …

THE MOTHER can be seen, anxiously questioning THE OLD MAN. He says a few words more, then abruptly all the others get up too and seem to be asking him questions. He gives a slow nod of affirmation.

STRANGER: He's said it … He's come right out with it! …
VOICES IN THE CROWD: He's said it! … He's said it! …
STRANGER: There's not a sound to be heard.

THE OLD MAN gets up as well; and without turning round he indicates the door behind him. THE MOTHER, THE FATHER and the two young girls hurry to the door, which THE FATHER can't immediately get open. THE OLD MAN makes to stop THE MOTHER going out.

VOICES IN THE CROWD: They're coming out! They're coming out!

Pandemonium in the garden. Everyone hurls themselves towards the other side of the house and disappears, apart from THE STRANGER who stays at the windows. In the room, the double doors finally open; they all run out at once. The starry sky can be seen, the lawn and the fountain in the moonlight, while in the middle of the abandoned room, the child continues to sleep peacefully in the armchair. Silence.

STRANGER: The child has not awoken …

He leaves.

Notes

This is a new translation of Maeterlinck's play. The play was originally published in French in 1894 and collected in *Théâtre* (3 vols), ed. Martine de Rougemont, Paris and Brussels, 1901–2.

1.6 Naturalism in the Theatre (1881)

ÉMILE ZOLA

Translated by Albert Bermel

Naturalism

I

EACH WINTER AT THE beginning of the theatre season I fall prey to the same thoughts. A hope springs up in me, and I tell myself that before the first warmth of summer empties the playhouses, a dramatist of genius will be discovered. Our theatre desperately needs a new man who will scour the debased boards and bring about a rebirth in an art degraded by its practitioners to the simple-minded requirements of the crowd. Yes, it would take a powerful personality, an innovator's mind, to overthrow the accepted conventions and finally install the real human drama in place of the ridiculous untruths that are on display today. I picture this creator scorning the tricks of the clever hack, smashing the imposed patterns, remaking the stage until it is continuous with the auditorium, giving a shiver of life to the painted trees, letting in through the backcloth the great, free air of reality.

Unfortunately, this dream I have every October has not yet been fulfilled, and is not likely to be for some time. I wait in vain, I go from failure to failure. Is this, then, merely the naïve wish of a poet? Are we trapped in today's dramatic art, which is so confining, like a cave that lacks air and light? Certainly, if dramatic art by its nature forbids this escape into less restricted forms, it would indeed be vain to delude ourselves and to expect a renaissance at any moment. But despite the stubborn assertions of certain critics who do not like to have their standards threatened, it is obvious that dramatic art, like all the arts, has before it an unlimited domain, without barriers of any kind to left or right. Inability, human incapacity, is the only boundary to an art.

To understand the need for a revolution in the theatre, we must establish clearly where we stand today. During our entire classical period tragedy ruled as an absolute monarch. It was rigid and intolerant, never granting its subjects a touch of freedom, bending the greatest minds to its inexorable laws. If a playwright tried to break away from them he was condemned as witless, incoherent and bizarre; he was almost considered a dangerous man. Yet even within the narrow formula genius did build its monument of marble and bronze. The formula was born during the Greek and Latin revival; the artists who took it over found in it a pattern that would serve for great works. Only later, when the imitators – that line of increasingly weaker and punier disciples – came along, did the faults in the formula show up: outlandish situations, improbabilities, dishonest uniformity, and uninterrupted, unbearable declaiming. Tragedy maintained such a sway that two hundred years had to pass before it went out of date. It tried slowly to become more flexible, but without success, for the authoritarian principles in which it was grounded formally forbade any concession to new ideas, under pain of death. Just when it was trying to broaden its scope, it was overturned, after a long and glorious reign.

In the eighteenth century romantic drama was already stirring inside tragedy. On occasion the three unities were violated, more importance was given to scenery and extras, violent climaxes were now staged, where formerly they had been described in speeches so that the majestic tranquillity of psychological analysis might not be disturbed by physical action. In addition, the passion of the *grande époque* was replaced by commonplace acting; a grey rain of mediocrity and staleness soaked the stage. One can visualize tragedy, by the beginning of this century, as a long, pale, emaciated figure without a drop of blood under its white skin, trailing its tattered robes across a gloomy stage on which the footlights had gone dark of their own accord. A rebirth of dramatic art out of a new formula was inevitable. It was then that romantic drama noisily planted its standard in front of the prompter's box. The hour had come; a slow ferment had been at work; the insurrection advanced on to terrain already softened-up for the victory. And never has the word insurrection seemed more apt, for romantic drama bodily seized the monarch tragedy and, out of hatred for its impotence, sought to destroy every memory of its reign. Tragedy did not react; it sat still on its throne, guarding its cold majesty, persisting with its speeches and descriptions. Whereas romantic drama made action its rule, excesses of action that leapt to the four corners of the stage, hitting out to right and left, no longer reasoning or analysing, giving the public a full view of the blood-drenched horror of its climaxes. Tragedy had chosen antiquity for its setting, the eternal Greeks and Romans, immobilizing the action in a room or in front of the columns of a temple; romantic drama chose the Middle Ages, paraded knights and ladies, manufactured strange sets with castles pinnacled over sheer gorges, armories crowded with weapons, dungeons dripping with moisture, ancient forests pocked with moonlight. The war was joined on all fronts; romantic drama ruthlessly made itself the armed adversary of tragedy and assaulted it with every method that defied the old formula.

This raging hostility, which characterized the romantic drama at its high tide, needs to be stressed, for it offers a precious insight. The poets who led the movement undoubtedly talked about putting real passion on stage and laying claim to a vast new realm that would encompass the whole of human life with its contradictions and inconsistencies; it is worth remembering, for example, that romantic drama fought above all for a mixture of laughter and tears in the same play, arguing that joy and pain walk side by side on earth. Yet truth, reality, in fact counted for little – even displeased the innovators. They had only one passion, to overthrow the tragic formula that inhibited them, to crush it once and for all under a stampede of every kind of audacity. They did not want their heroes of the Middle Ages to be more real than the heroes of tragic antiquity; they wanted them to appear as passionate and splendid as their predecessors had appeared cold and correct. A mere skirmish over dress and modes of speech, nothing more: one set of puppets at odds with another. Togas were torn up in favour of doublets; a lady, instead of addressing her lover as 'My lord', called him 'My lion'. After the transition fiction still prevailed; only the setting was different.

I do not want to be unfair to the romantic movement. Its effect has been outstanding and unquestionable; it has made us what we are: free artists. It was, I repeat, a necessary revolution, a violent struggle that arose just in time to sweep away a tragic convention that had become childish. Still, it would be ridiculous to arrest the evolution of dramatic art at romanticism. These days, especially, it is astounding to read certain prefaces in which the 1830 movement is announced as the triumphal entry into human truth. Our forty-year distance is enough to let us see clearly that the alleged truth of the romanticists is a persistent and monstrous exaggeration of reality, a fantasy that has declined into excesses. Tragedy, to be sure, is another type of falseness, but it is not *more* false. Between the characters who pace about in togas, endlessly discussing their passions with confidants, and the characters in doublets who perform great feats and flit about like insects drunk with the sun, there is nothing to choose; both are equally and totally unacceptable. Such people have never existed. Romantic heroes are only tragic heroes bitten by the *mardi gras* bug, hiding behind false noses, and dancing the dramatic cancan after drinking. For the old sluggish rhetoric the 1830 movement substituted an excited, full-blooded rhetoric, and that is all.

Without believing that art progresses, we can still say that it is continuously in motion, among all civilizations, and that this motion reflects different phases of the human mind. Genius is made manifest in every formula, even in the most primitive and innocent ones, though the formulas become transmuted according to the intellectual breadth of each civilization; that is incontestable. If Aeschylus was great, Shakespeare and Molière showed themselves to be equally great, each within his differing civilization and formula. By this I mean that I set apart the creative genius who knows how to make the most of the formula of his time. There is no progress in human creation but there is a logical succession to the formulas, to methods of thought and expression. Thus, art takes the same strides as humanity, is its very language, goes where it goes, moves with it towards light and truth; but for that, we could never judge whether a creator's efforts were more or less great, depending on whether he comes at the beginning or end of a literature.

In these terms, it is certain that when we left tragedy behind, the romantic drama was a first step in the direction of the naturalistic drama, towards which we are now advancing. The romantic drama cleared the ground, proclaimed the freedom of art. Its love of action, its mixture of laughter and tears, its research into accuracy of costume and setting show the movement's impulse towards real life. Is this not how things happen during every revolution against a secular regime? One begins by breaking windows, chanting and shouting, wrecking relics of the last regime with hammer blows. There is a first exuberance, an intoxication with the new horizons faintly glimpsed, excesses of all kinds that go beyond the original aims and degenerate into the despotism of the old, hated system, those very abuses the revolution has just fought against. In the heat of the battle tomorrow's truths evaporate. And not until all is calm and the fever has abated is there any regret for the broken windows, any understanding of how the effort has gone awry, how the new laws have been prematurely thrown together so that they are hardly any improvement over the laws that were destroyed. Well, the whole history of romantic drama is there. It may have been the formula necessary for its time, it may have had truthful intuitions, it may have been the form that will always be celebrated because a great poet used it to compose his masterpieces. At the present time it is, none the less, a ridiculous, outdated formula, with a rhetoric that offends us. We now wonder why it was necessary to push in windows, wave swords, bellow without a break, to go a scale too shrill in sentiment and language. All that leaves us cold, it bores and annoys us. Our condemnation of the romantic formula is summed up in one severe remark: To destroy one rhetoric it was not necessary to invent another.

Today, then, tragedy and romantic drama are equally old and worn out. And that is hardly to the credit of the latter, it should be said, for in less than half a century it has fallen into the same state of decay as tragedy, which took two centuries to die. There it lies, flattened in its turn, overwhelmed by the same passion it showed in its own battle. Nothing is left. We can only guess at what is to come. Logically all that can grow up on that free ground conquered in 1830 is the formula of naturalism.

II

It seems impossible that the movement of inquiry and analysis, which is precisely the movement of the nineteenth century, can have revolutionized all the sciences and arts and left dramatic art to one side, as if isolated. The natural sciences date from the end of the last century; chemistry and physics are less than a hundred years old; history and criticism have been renovated, virtually re-created since the Revolution; an entire world has arisen; it has sent us back to the study of documents, to experience, made us realize that to start afresh we must first take things back to the beginning, become familiar with man and nature, verify what is. Thenceforward, the great naturalistic school, which has spread secretly, irrevocably, often making its way in darkness but always advancing, can finally come out triumphantly into the light of day. To trace the history of this movement, with the misunderstandings that might have impeded it and the multiple causes that have thrust it forward or slowed it down, would be to trace the history of the century itself. An irresistible current carries our society towards the study of reality. In the novel Balzac has been the bold and mighty innovator who has replaced the observation of the scholar with the imagination of the poet. But in the theatre the evolution seems slower. No eminent writer has yet formulated the new idea with any clarity.

I certainly do not say that some excellent works have not been produced, with characters in them who are ingeniously examined and bold truths taken right on to the stage. Let me, for instance, cite certain plays by M. Dumas *fils*, whose talent I scarcely admire, and M. Émile Augier, the most humane and powerful of all. Still, they are midgets beside Balzac; they lack the genius to lay down the formula. It must be said that one can never tell quite when a movement is getting under way; generally its source is remote and lost in the earlier movement from which it emerged. In a manner of speaking, the naturalistic current has always existed. It brings with it nothing absolutely novel. But it has finally flowed into a period favourable to it; it is succeeding and expanding because the human mind has attained the necessary maturity. I do not, therefore, deny the past; I affirm the present. The strength of naturalism is precisely that it has deep roots in our national literature which contains plenty of wisdom. It comes from the very entrails of humanity; it is that much the stronger because it has taken longer to grow and is found in a greater number of our masterpieces.

Certain things have come to pass and I point them out. Can we believe that *L'Ami Fritz* would have been applauded at the Comédie-Française twenty years ago? Definitely not! This play, in which people eat all the time and the lover talks in such homely language, would have disgusted both the classicists and the romantics. To explain its success we must concede that as the years have gone by a secret fermentation has been at work. Lifelike paintings, which used to repel the public, today attract them. The majority has been won over and the stage is open to every experiment. This is the only conclusion to draw.

So that is where we stand. To explain my point better – I am not afraid of repeating myself – I will sum up what I have said. Looking closely at the history of our dramatic literature, one can detect several clearly separated periods. First, there was the infancy of the art, farces and the mystery plays of the Middle Ages, the reciting of simple dialogues which developed as part of a naïve convention, with primitive staging and sets. Gradually, the plays became more complex but in a crude fashion. When Corneille appeared he was acclaimed most of all for his status as an innovator, for refining the dramatic formula of the time, and for hallowing it by means of his genius. It would be very interesting to study the pertinent documents and discover how our classical formula came to be created. It corresponded to the social spirit of the period. Nothing is solid that is not built on necessity. Tragedy reigned for two centuries because it satisfied the exact requirements of those centuries. Geniuses of differing temperaments had buttressed it with their masterpieces. And it continued to impose itself long afterwards, even when second-rate talents were producing inferior work. It acquired a momentum. It persisted also as the literary expression of that society, and nothing would have overthrown it if the society had not itself disappeared. After the Revolution, after that profound disturbance that was meant to transform everything and give birth to a new world, tragedy struggled to stay alive for a few more years. Then the formula cracked and romanticism broke through. A new formula asserted itself. We must look back at the first half of the century to understand the meaning of this cry for liberty. The young society was in the tremor of its infancy. The excited, bewildered, violently unleashed people were still racked by a dangerous fever; and in the first flush of their new liberty they yearned for prodigious adventures and superhuman love affairs. They gaped at the stars; some committed suicide, a very curious reaction to the social enfranchisement which had just been declared at the cost of so much blood. Turning specifically to dramatic literature, I maintain that romanticism in the theatre was an uncomplicated revolt, the invasion by a victorious group who took over the stage violently with drums beating and flags flying. In these early moments the combatants dreamed of making their imprint with a new form; to one rhetoric they opposed another: the Middle Ages to Antiquity, the exalting of passion to the exalting of duty. And that was all, for only the scenic conventions were altered. The characters remained marionettes in new clothing. Only the exterior aspect and the language were modified. But for the period that was enough. Romanticism had taken possession of the theatre in the name of literary freedom and it carried out its revolutionary task with incomparable bravura. But who does not see today that its role could extend no farther than that? Does romanticism have anything whatever to say about our present society? Does it meet one of our requirements? Obviously not. It is as outmoded as a jargon we no longer follow. It confidently expected to replace classical literature which had lasted for two centuries because it was based on social conditions. But romanticism was based on nothing but the fantasy of a few poets or, if you will, on the passing malady of minds overwhelmed by historical events; it was bound to disappear with the malady. It provided the occasion for a magnificent flowering of lyricism; that will be its eternal glory. Today, however, with the evolution accomplished, it is plain that romanticism was no more than the necessary link between classicism and naturalism. The struggle is over; now we must found a secure state. Naturalism flows out of classical art, just as our present society has arisen from the wreckage of the old society. Naturalism alone corresponds to our social needs; it alone has deep roots in the spirit of our times; and it alone can provide a living, durable formula for our art, because this formula will express the nature of our contemporary intelligence. There may be fashions and passing fantasies that exist outside naturalism but they will not survive for long. I say again, naturalism is the expression of our century and it will not die until a new upheaval transforms our democratic world.

Only one thing is needed now: men of genius who can fix the naturalistic formula. Balzac has done it for the novel and the novel is established. When will our Corneilles, Molières and Racines appear to establish our new theatre? We must hope and wait.   ·

III

The period when romantic drama ruled now seems distant. In Paris five or six of its playhouses prospered. The demolition of the old theatres along the Boulevard du Temple was a catastrophe of the first order. The theatres became separated from one another, the public changed, different fashions arose. But the discredit into which the drama has fallen proceeds mostly from the exhaustion of the genre – ridiculous, boring plays have gradually taken over from the potent works of 1830.

To this enfeeblement we must add the absolute lack of new actors who understand and can interpret these kinds of plays, for every dramatic formula that vanishes carries away its interpreters with it. Today the drama, hunted from stage to stage, has only two houses that really belong to it, the Ambigu and the Théâtre-Historique. Even at the Saint-Martin the drama is lucky to win a brief showing for itself, between one great spectacle and the next.

An occasional success may renew its courage. But its decline is inevitable; romantic drama is sliding into oblivion, and if it seems sometimes to check its descent, it does so only to roll even lower afterwards. Naturally, there are loud complaints. The tail-end romanticists are desperately unhappy. They swear that except in the drama – meaning their kind of drama – there is no salvation for dramatic literature. I believe, on the contrary, that we must find a new formula that will transform the drama, just as the writers in the first half of the century transformed tragedy. That is the essence of the matter. Today the battle is between romantic drama and naturalistic drama. By romantic drama I mean every play that mocks truthfulness in its incidents and characterization, that struts about in its puppet-box, stuffed to the belly with noises that flounder, for some idealistic reason or other, in pastiches of Shakespeare and Hugo. Every period has its formula; ours is certainly not that of 1830. We are an age of method, of experimental science; our primary need is for precise analysis. We hardly understand the liberty we have won if we use it only to imprison ourselves in a new tradition. The way is open: we can now return to man and nature.

Finally, there have been great efforts to revive the historical drama. Nothing could be better. A critic cannot roundly condemn the choice of historical subjects, even if his own preferences are entirely for subjects that are modern. It is simply that I am full of distrust. The manager one gives this sort of play to frightens me in advance. It is a question of how history is treated, what unusual characters are presented bearing the names of kings, great captains or great artists, and what awful sauce they are served up in to make the history palatable. As soon as the authors of these concoctions move into the past they think everything is permitted: improbabilities, cardboard dolls, monumental idiocies, the hysterical scribblings that falsely represent local colour. And what strange dialogue – François I talking like a haberdasher straight out of the Rue Saint-Denis, Richelieu using the words of a criminal from the Boulevard du Crime, Charlotte Corday with the weeping sentimentalities of a factory girl.

What astounds me is that our playwrights do not seem to suspect for a moment that the historical genre is unavoidably the least rewarding, the one that calls most strongly for research, integrity, a consummate gift of intuition, a talent for reconstruction. I am all for historical drama when it is in the hands of poets of genius or men of exceptional knowledge who are capable of making the public see an epoch come alive with its special quality, its manners, its civilization. In that case we have a work of prophecy or of profoundly interesting criticism.

But unfortunately I know what it is these partisans of historical drama want to revive: the swaggering and sword-play, the big spectacle with big words, the play of lies that shows off in front of the crowd, the gross exhibition that saddens honest minds. Hence my distrust. I think that all this antiquated business is better left in our museum of dramatic history under a pious layer of dust.

There are, undeniably, great obstacles to original experiments: we run up against the hypocrisies of criticism and the long education in idiocies that has been foisted on the public. This public, which titters at every childishness in melodramas, nevertheless lets itself be carried away by outbursts of fine sentiment. But the public is changing. Shakespeare's public and Molière's are no longer ours. We must reckon with shifts in outlook, with the need for reality which is everywhere getting more insistent. The last few romantics vainly repeat that the public wants this and the public wants that; the day is coming when the public will want the truth.

IV

The old formulas, classical and romantic, were based on the rearrangement and systematic amputation of the truth. They determined on principle that the truth is not good enough; they tried to draw out of it an essence, a 'poetry', on the pretext that nature must be expurgated and magnified. Up to the present the different literary schools disputed only over the question of the best way to disguise the truth so that it might not look too brazen to the public. The classicists adopted the toga; the romantics fought a revolution to impose the coat of mail and the doublet. Essentially the change of dress made little difference; the counterfeiting of nature went on. But today the naturalistic thinkers are telling us that the truth does not need clothing; it can walk naked. That, I repeat, is the quarrel.

Writers with any sense understand perfectly that tragedy and romantic drama are dead. The majority, though, are badly troubled when they turn their minds to the as-yet-unclear formula of tomorrow. Does the truth seriously ask them to give up the grandeur, the poetry, the traditional epic effects that their ambition tells them to put into their plays? Does naturalism demand that they shrink their horizons and risk not one flight into fantasy?

I will try to reply. But first we must determine the methods used by the idealists to lift their works into poetry. They begin by placing their chosen subject in a distant time. That provides them with costumes and makes the framework of the story vague enough to give them full scope for lying. Next, they generalize instead of particularizing; their characters are no longer living people but sentiments, arguments, passions that have been induced by reasoning. This false framework calls for heroes of marble or cardboard. A man of flesh and bone with his own originality would jar in such a legendary setting. Moreover, when we see the characters in romantic drama or tragedy walking about they are stiffened into an attitude, one representing duty, another patriotism, a third superstition, a fourth maternal love; thus, all the abstract ideas file by. Never the thorough analysis of an organism, never a character whose muscles and brain function as in nature.

These, then, are the mannerisms that writers with epic inclinations do not want to give up. For them poetry resides in the past and in abstraction, in the idealizing of facts and characters. As soon as one confronts them with daily life, with the people who fill our streets, they blink, they stammer, they are afraid; they no longer see clearly; they find everything ugly and not good enough for art. According to them, a subject must enter the lies of legend, men must harden and turn to stone like statues before the artist can accept them and make them fit the disguises he has prepared.

Now, it is at this point that the naturalistic movement comes along and says squarely that poetry is everywhere, in everything, even more in the present and the real than in the past and the abstract. Each event at each moment has its poetic, superb aspect. We brush up against heroes who are great and powerful in different respects from the puppets of the epic-makers. Not one playwright in this century has brought to life figures as lofty as Baron Hulot, Old Grandet, César Birotteau, and all the other characters of Balzac, who are so individual and so alive. Beside these real, giant creations Greek and Roman heroes quake; the heroes of the Middle Ages fall flat on their faces like lead soldiers.

With the superior works being produced in these times by the naturalistic school – works of high endeavour, pulsing with life – it is ridiculous and false to park our poetry in some antiquated temple and bury it in cobwebs. Poetry flows at its full force through everything that exists; the truer to life, the greater it becomes. And I mean to give the word poetry its widest definition, not to pin it down exclusively to the cadence of two rhymes, nor to bury it in a narrow coterie of dreamers, but to restore its real human significance which concerns the expansion and encouragement of every kind of truth.

Take our present environment, then, and try to make men live in it: you will write great works. It will undoubtedly call for some effort; it means sifting out of the confusion of life the simple formula of naturalism. Therein lies the difficulty: to do great things with the subjects and characters that our eyes, accustomed to the spectacle of the daily round, have come to see as small. I am aware that it is more convenient to present a marionette to the public and name it Charlemagne and puff it up with such tirades that the public believes it is watching a colossus; it is more convenient than taking a bourgeois of our time, a grotesque, unsightly man, and drawing sublime poetry out of him, making him, for example, Père Goriot, the father who gives his guts for his daughters, a figure so gigantic with truth and love that no other literature can offer his equal.

Nothing is as easy as persuading the managers with known formulas; and heroes in the classical or romantic taste cost so little labour that they are manufactured by the dozen, and have become standardized articles that clutter up our literature. But it takes hard work to create a real hero, intelligently analysed, alive and performing. That is probably why naturalism terrifies those authors who are used to fishing up great men from the troubled waters of history. They would have to burrow too deeply into humanity, learn about life, go straight for the greatness of reality and make it function with all their power. And let nobody gainsay this true poetry of humanity; it has been sifted out in the novel and can be in the theatre; only the method of adaptation remains to be found.

I am troubled by a comparison; it has been haunting me and I will now free myself of it. For two long months a play called *Les Danicheff* has been running at the Odéon. It takes place in Russia. It has been very successful here, but is apparently so dishonest, so packed with gross improbabilities, that the author, a Russian, has not even dared to show it in his country. What can you think of this work which is applauded in Paris and would be booed in St Petersburg? Well, imagine for a moment that the Romans could come back to life and see a performance of *Rome vaincue*. Can you hear their roars of laughter? Do you think the play would complete one performance? It would strike them as a parody; it would sink under the weight of mockery. And is there one historical play that could be performed before the society it claims to portray? A strange theatre, this, which is plausible only among foreigners, is based on the disappearance of the generations it deals with, and is made up of so much misinformation that it is good only for the ignorant!

The future is with naturalism. The formula will be found; it will be proved that there is more poetry in the little apartment of a bourgeois than in all the empty, worm-eaten palaces of history; in the end we will see that everything meets in the real: lovely fantasies that are free of capriciousness and whimsy, and idylls, and comedies, and dramas. Once the soil has been turned over, the task that seems alarming and unfeasible today will become easy.

I am not qualified to pronounce on the form that tomorrow's drama will take; that must be left to the voice of some genius to come. But I will allow myself to indicate the path I consider our theatre will follow.

First, the romantic drama must be abandoned. It would be disastrous for us to take over its outrageous acting, its rhetoric, its inherent thesis of action at the expense of character analysis. The finest models of the genre are, as has been said, mere operas with big effects. I believe, then, that we must go back to tragedy – not, heaven forbid, to borrow more of its rhetoric, its system of confidants, its declaiming, its endless speeches, but to return to its simplicity of action and its unique psychological and physiological study of the characters. Thus understood, the tragic framework is excellent; one deed unwinds in all its reality, and moves the characters to passions and feelings, the exact analysis of which constitutes the sole interest of the play – and in a contemporary environment, with the people who surround us.

My constant concern, my anxious vigil, has made me wonder which of us will have the strength to raise himself to the pitch of genius. If the naturalistic drama must come into being, only a genius can give birth to it. Corneille and Racine made tragedy. Victor Hugo made romantic drama. Where is the as-yet-unknown author who must make the naturalistic drama? In recent years experiments have not been wanting. But either because the public was not ready or because none of the beginners had the necessary staying-power, not one of these attempts has had decisive results.

In battles of this kind, small victories mean nothing; we need triumphs that overwhelm the adversary and win the public to the cause. Audiences would give way before the onslaught of a really strong man. This man would come with the expected word, the solution to the problem, the formula for a real life on stage, combining it with the illusions necessary in the theatre. He would have what the newcomers have as yet lacked: the cleverness or the might to impose himself and to remain so close to truth that his cleverness could not lead him into lies.

And what an immense place this innovator would occupy in our dramatic literature! He would be at the peak. He would build his monument in the middle of the desert of mediocrity that we are crossing, among the jerry-built houses strewn about our most illustrious stages. He would put everything in question and remake everything, scour the boards, create a world whose elements he would lift from life, from outside our traditions. Surely there is no more ambitious dream that a writer of our time could fulfil. The domain of the novel is crowded; the domain of the theatre is free. At this time in France an imperishable glory awaits the man of genius who takes up the work of Molière and finds in the reality of living comedy the full, true drama of modern society ...

Physiological man

... In effect, the great naturalistic evolution which comes down directly from the fifteenth century to ours has everything to do with the gradual substitution of physiological man for metaphysical man. In tragedy metaphysical man, man according to dogma and logic, reigned absolutely. The body did not count; the soul was regarded as the only interesting piece of human machinery; drama took place in the air, in pure mind. Consequently, what use was the tangible world? Why worry about the place where the action was located? Why be surprised at a baroque costume or false declaiming? Why notice that Queen Dido was a boy whose budding beard forced him to wear a mask? None of that mattered; these trifles were not worth stooping to; the play was heard out as if it were a school essay or a law case; it was on a higher plane than man, in the world of ideas, so far away from real man that any intrusion of reality would have spoiled the show.

Such is the point of departure – in Mystery plays, the religious point; the philosophical point in tragedy. And from that beginning natural man, stifling under the rhetoric and dogma, struggled secretly, tried to break free, made lengthy, futile efforts, and in the end asserted himself, limb by limb. The whole history of our theatre is in this conquest by the physiological man, who emerged more clearly in each period from behind the dummy of religious and philosophical idealism. Corneille, Molière, Racine, Voltaire, Beaumarchais and, in our day, Victor Hugo, Émile Augier, Alexandre Dumas *fils*, even Sardou, have had only one task, even when they were not completely aware of it: to increase the reality of our corpus of drama, to progress towards truth, to sift out more and more of the natural man and impose him on the public. And inevitably, the evolution will not end with them. It continues; it will continue forever. Mankind is very young ...

Costume, stage design, speech

Modern clothes make a poor spectacle. If we depart from bourgeois tragedy, shut in between its four walls, and wish to use the breadth of larger stages for crowd scenes we are embarrassed and constrained by the monotony and the uniformly funereal look of the extras. In this case, I think, we should take advantage of the variety of garb offered by the different classes and occupations. To elaborate: I can imagine an author setting one act in the main marketplace of Les Halles in Paris. The setting would be superb, with its bustling life and bold possibilities. In this immense setting we could have a very picturesque ensemble by displaying the porters wearing their large hats, the saleswomen with their white aprons and vividly coloured scarves, the customers dressed in silk or wool or cotton prints, from the ladies accompanied by their maids to the female beggars on the prowl for anything they can pick up off the street. For inspiration it would be enough to go to Les Halles and look about. Nothing is gaudier or more interesting. All of Paris would enjoy seeing this set if it were realized with the necessary accuracy and amplitude.

And how many other settings for popular drama there are for the taking! Inside a factory, the interior of a mine, the gingerbread market, a railway station, flower stalls, a racetrack, and so on. All the activities of modern life can take place in them. It will be said that such sets have already been tried. Unquestionably we have seen factories and railway stations in fantasy plays; but these were fantasy stations and factories. I mean, these sets were thrown together to create an illusion that was at best incomplete. What we need is detailed reproduction: costumes supplied by tradespeople, not sumptuous but adequate for the purposes of truth and for the interest of the scenes. Since everybody mourns the death of the drama our playwrights certainly ought to make a try at this type of popular, contemporary drama. At one stroke they could satisfy the public hunger for spectacle and the need for exact studies which grows more pressing every day. Let us hope, though, that the playwrights will show us real people and not those whining members of the working class who play such strange roles in boulevard melodrama.

As M. Adolphe Jullien has said – and I will never be tired of repeating it – everything is interdependent in the theatre. Lifelike costumes look wrong if the sets, the diction, the plays themselves are not lifelike. They must all march in step along the naturalistic road. When costume becomes more accurate, so do sets; actors free themselves from bombastic declaiming; plays study reality more closely and their characters are more true to life. I could make the same observations about sets I have just made about costume. With them, too, we may seem to have reached the highest possible degree of truth, but we still have long strides to take. Most of all we would need to intensify the illusion in reconstructing the environments, less for their picturesque quality than for dramatic utility. The environment must determine the character. When a set is planned so as to give the lively impression of a description by Balzac; when, as the curtain rises, one catches the first glimpse of the characters, their personalities and behaviour, if only to see the actual locale in which they move, the importance of exact reproduction in the decor will be appreciated. Obviously, that is the way we are going. Environment, the study of which has transformed science and literature, will have to take a large role in the theatre. And here I may mention again the question of metaphysical man, the abstraction who had to be satisfied with his three walls in tragedy – whereas the physiological man in our modern works is asking more and more compellingly to be determined by his setting, by the environment that produced him. We see then that the road to progress is still long, for sets as well as costume. We are coming upon the truth but we can hardly stammer it out.

Another very serious matter is diction. True, we have got away from the chanting, the plainsong, of the seventeenth century. But we now have a 'theatre voice', a false recitation that is very obtrusive and very annoying. Everything that is wrong with it comes from the fixed traditional code set up by the majority of critics. They found the theatre in a certain state and, instead of looking to the future, and judging the progress we are making and the progress we shall make by the progress we have already made, they stubbornly defend the relics of the old conventions, swearing that these relics must be preserved. Ask them why, make them see how far we have travelled; they will give you no logical reason. They will reply with assertions based on a set of conditions that are disappearing.

In diction the errors come from what the critics call 'theatre language'. Their theory is that on stage you must not speak as you do in everyday life. To support this viewpoint they pick examples from traditional practices, from what was happening yesterday – and is happening still – without taking account of the naturalistic movement, the phases of which have been established for us by M. Jullien's book [*Histoire du Costume au Théâtre*, 1880]. Let us realize that there is no such thing as 'theatre language'. There has been a rhetoric which grew more and more feeble and is now dying out. Those are the facts. If you compare the declaiming of actors under Louis XIV with that of Lekain, and if you compare Lekain's with that of our own artists today, you will clearly distinguish the phases, from tragic chanting down to our search for the natural, precise tone, the cry of truth. It follows that 'theatre language', that language of booming sonority, is vanishing. We are moving towards simplicity, the exact word spoken without emphasis, quite naturally. How many examples I could give if I had unlimited space! Consider the powerful effect that Geoffroy has on the public; all his talent comes from his natural personality. He holds the public because he speaks on stage as he does at home. When a sentence sounds outlandish he cannot pronounce it; the author has to find another one. That is the fundamental criticism of so-called 'theatre language'. Again, follow the diction of a talented actor and at the same time watch the public; the cheers go up, the house is in raptures when a truthful accent gives the words the exact value they must have. All the great successes of the stage are triumphs over convention.

Alas, yes, there is a 'theatre language'. It is the clichés, the resounding platitudes, the hollow words that roll about like empty barrels, all that intolerable rhetoric of our vaudevilles and dramas, which is beginning to make us smile. It would be very interesting to study the style of such talented authors as MM. Augier, Dumas and Sardou. I could find much to criticize, especially in the last two with their conventional language, a language of their own that they put into the mouths of all their characters, men, women, children, old folk; both sexes and all ages. This irritates me, for each character has his own language, and to create living people you must give them to the public not merely in accurate dress and in the environments that have made them what they are, but with their individual ways of thinking and expressing themselves. I repeat that that is the obvious aim of our theatre. There is no theatre language regulated by such a code as 'cadenced sentences' or sonority. There is simply a kind of dialogue that is growing more precise and is following – or rather, leading – sets and costumes towards naturalistic progress. When plays are more truthful, the actors' diction will gain enormously in simplicity and naturalness.

To conclude, I will repeat that the battle of the conventions is far from being finished, and that it will no doubt last forever. Today we are beginning to see clearly where we are going, but steps are still impeded by the melting slush of rhetoric and metaphysics.

Note

Translated by Albert Bermel, 1968. Selected extracts from *Naturalism in the Theatre*, from Eric Bentley, *The Theory of the Modern Stage*, London: Penguin, 1968, pp. 351–72.

1.7 **Preface to _Miss Julie_** (1888)

AUGUST STRINDBERG

Translated by Michael Robinson

LIKE ART IN GENERAL, the theatre has long seemed to me a _Biblia pauperum_,[1] a Bible in pictures for those who cannot read what is written or printed, and the dramatist a lay preacher who peddles the ideas of the day in a popular form, so popular that the middle classes which form the bulk of the audience can, without too much mental effort, understand what is going on. That is why the theatre has always been an elementary school for the young, the semi-educated, and women, who still retain the primitive capacity for deceiving themselves or for letting themselves be deceived, that is, for succumbing to illusions and to the hypnotic suggestions of the author. Nowadays, therefore, when the rudimentary and undeveloped kind of thinking that takes the form of fantasy appears to be evolving into reflection, investigation, and analysis, it seems to me that the theatre, like religion, is about to be discarded as a dying form of art, which we lack the necessary preconditions to enjoy. This supposition is supported by the serious theatrical crisis now prevailing throughout Europe, and especially by the fact that in England and Germany, those cultural heartlands which have nurtured the greatest thinkers of our age, the drama is dead, along with most of the other fine arts.

Again, in other countries people have believed in the possibility of creating a new drama by filling the old forms with new contents; but this approach has failed, partly because there has not yet been time to popularize the new ideas, so the public has not been able to understand what was involved; partly because party differences have so inflamed emotions that pure, dispassionate enjoyment has become impossible in a situation where people's innermost thoughts have been challenged and an applauding or whistling majority has brought pressure to bear on them as openly as it can do in a theatre; and partly because we have not yet found the new form for the new content, and the new wine has burst the old bottles.

In the following play I have not tried to accomplish anything new, for that is impossible, but merely to modernize the form according to what I believe are the demands a contemporary audience would make of this art. To that end I have chosen, or let myself be moved by, a theme that may be said to lie outside current party strife, for the problem of rising or falling on the social ladder, of higher or lower, better or worse, man or woman is, has been, and always will be of lasting interest. When I took this theme from a real incident that I heard about some years ago, it seemed to me a suitable subject for a tragedy, not least because of the deep impression it made on me; for it still strikes us as tragic to see someone favoured by fortune go under, and even more to see a whole family die out. But the time may come when we shall have become so highly developed, so enlightened, that we shall be able to look with indifference at the brutal, cynical, heartless drama that life presents, when we shall have laid aside those inferior, unreliable instruments of thought called feelings, which will become superfluous and harmful once our organs of judgement have matured. The fact that the heroine arouses our pity merely depends on our weakness in not being able to resist the fear that the same fate might overtake us. A highly sensitive spectator may still not feel that such pity is enough, while the man with faith in the future will probably insist on some positive proposals to remedy the evil, some kind of programme, in other words. But in the first place there is no such thing as absolute evil, for after all, if one family falls another now has the good fortune to rise, and this alternate rising and falling is one of life's greatest pleasures, since happiness is only relative. And of the man with a programme who wants to remedy the unpleasant fact that the bird of prey eats the dove and lice eat the bird of prey, I would ask: why should it be remedied? Life is not so idiotically mathematical that only the big eat the small; it is just as common for a bee to kill a lion or at least to drive it mad.

If my tragedy makes a tragic impression on many people, that is their fault. When we become as strong as the first French revolutionaries, we shall feel as much unqualified pleasure and relief at seeing the thinning out in our royal parks of rotten, superannuated trees, which have stood too long in the way of others with just as much right to their time in the sun, as it does to see an incurably ill man finally die. Recently, my tragedy *The Father* was criticized for being so tragic, as though tragedies were supposed to be merry. One also hears pretentious talk about the joy of life, and theatre managers commission farces as though this joy of life lay in behaving stupidly and depicting people as if they were all afflicted with St Vitus' dance or congenital idiocy. I find the joy of life in its cruel and powerful struggles, and my enjoyment comes from getting to know something, from learning something. That is why I have chosen an unusual case, but an instructive one, an exception, in other words, but an important exception that proves the rule, even though it may offend those who love the commonplace. What will also bother simple minds is that my motivation of the action is not simple, and that there is not a single point of view. Every event in life – and this is a fairly new discovery! – is usually the result of a whole series of more or less deep-seated motives, but the spectator usually selects the one that he most easily understands or that best flatters his powers of judgement. Someone commits suicide. 'Business worries', says the business man. 'Unrequited love', say the ladies. 'Physical illness', says the sick man, 'Shattered hopes', says the failure. But it may well be that the motive lay in all of these things, or in none of them, and that the dead man concealed his real motive by emphasizing quite a different one that shed the best possible light on his memory.

I have motivated Miss Julie's tragic fate with an abundance of circumstances: her mother's 'bad' basic instincts; her father's improper bringing-up of the girl; her own nature and the influence her fiancé's suggestions had on her weak, degenerate brain; also, and more immediately: the festive atmosphere of Midsummer Night; her father's absence; her period; her preoccupation with animals; the intoxicating effect of the dance; the light summer night; the powerful aphrodisiac influence of the flowers; and finally chance that drives these two people together in a room apart, plus the boldness of the aroused man.

So my treatment has not been one-sidedly physiological nor obsessively psychological. I have not attributed everything to what she inherited from her mother nor put the whole blame on her period, nor just settled for 'immorality', nor merely preached morality – lacking a priest, I've left that to the cook!

I flatter myself that this multiplicity of motives is in tune with the times. And if others have anticipated me in this, then I flatter myself that I am not alone in my paradoxes, as all discoveries are called.

As regards characterization, I have made my figures fairly 'characterless' for the following reasons:

Over the years the word 'character' has taken on many meanings. Originally it no doubt meant the dominant trait in a person's soul-complex, and was confused with temperament. Later it became the middle-class expression for an automaton, so that an individual whose nature had once and for all set firm or adapted to a certain role in life, who had stopped growing, in short, was called a character, whereas someone who goes on developing, the skilful navigator on the river of life who does not sail with cleated sheets but tacks with every change in the wind in order to luff again, was called characterless. In a derogatory sense, of course, because he was so hard to catch, classify, and keep track of. This bourgeois concept of the immobility of the soul was transferred to the stage, which has always been dominated by the bourgeoisie. There a character became a man who was fixed and set, who invariably appeared drunk or comical or sad; and all that was needed to characterize him was to give him a physical defect, a club-foot, a wooden leg, a red nose, or some continually repeated phrase such as 'That's capital' or 'Barkis is willin', etc.[2] This elementary way of viewing people is still to be found in the great Molière. Harpagon is merely a miser, although he could have been both a miser and an excellent financier, a splendid father, and a good citizen; and even worse, his 'defect' is extremely advantageous to his daughter and his son-in-law, who are his heirs and therefore ought not to criticize him even if they do have to wait a while before jumping into bed together. So I do not believe in simple stage characters, and the summary judgements that authors pass on people – this one is stupid, that one brutal, this one jealous, that one mean – ought to be challenged by naturalists, who know how richly complicated the soul is, and who are aware that 'vice' has a reverse side, which is very much like virtue.

As modern characters, living in an age of transition more urgently hysterical at any rate than the one that preceded it, I have depicted the figures in my play as more split and vacillating, a mixture of the old and the new, and it seems to me not improbable that modern ideas may also have permeated down by way of newspapers and kitchen talk to the level of the servants. That is why the valet belches forth certain modern ideas from within his inherited slave's soul. And I would remind those who take exception to the characters in our modern plays talking Darwinism,[3] while holding up Shakespeare to our attention as a model, that the gravedigger in *Hamlet* talks the then-fashionable philosophy of Giordano Bruno (Bacon),[4] which is even more improbable since the means of disseminating ideas were fewer then than now. Besides, the fact of the matter is, 'Darwinism' has existed in every age, ever since Moses' successive history of creation from the lower animals up to man; it is just that we have discovered and formulated it now!

My souls (characters) are conglomerates of past and present stages of culture, bits out of books and newspapers, scraps of humanity, torn shreds of once fine clothing now turned to rags, exactly as the human soul is patched together, and I have also provided a little evolutionary history by letting the weaker repeat words stolen from the stronger, and allowed these souls to get 'ideas', or suggestions as they are called, from one another, from the milieu (the death of the siskin),[5] and from objects (the razor). I have also facilitated *Gedankenübertragung* via an inanimate medium (the Count's boots, the bell). Finally, I have made use of 'waking suggestion', a variation of hypnotic suggestion, which is now so well known and popularized that it cannot arouse the ridicule or scepticism it would have done in Mesmer's time.[6]

Miss Julie is a modern character, which does not mean that the man-hating half-woman has not existed in every age, just that she has now been discovered, has come out into the open and made herself heard. Victim of a superstition (one that has seized even stronger minds) that woman, this stunted form of human being who stands between man, the lord of creation, the creator of culture, [and the child],[7] is meant to be the equal of man or could ever be, she involves herself in an absurd struggle in which she falls. Absurd because a stunted form, governed by the laws of propagation, will always be born stunted and can never catch up with the one in the lead, according to the formula: A (the man) and B (the woman) start from the same point C; A (the man) with a speed of, let us say, 100 and B (the woman) with a speed of 60. Now, the question is, when will B catch up with A? – Answer: *Never!* Neither with the help of equal education, equal voting rights, disarmament, or temperance – no more than two parallel lines can ever meet and cross.

The half-woman is a type who thrusts herself forward and sells herself nowadays for power, decorations, honours, or diplomas as formerly she used to do for money. She is synonymous with degeneration. It is not a sound species for it does not last, but unfortunately it can propagate itself and its misery in the following generation; and degenerate men seem unconsciously to select their mates among them so that they increase in number and produce creatures of uncertain sex for whom life is a torment. Fortunately, however, they succumb, either because they are out of harmony with reality or because their repressed instincts erupt uncontrollably or because their hopes of attaining equality with men are crushed. The type is tragic, offering the spectacle of a desperate struggle against nature, a tragic legacy of Romanticism which is now being dissipated by Naturalism, the only aim of which is happiness. And happiness means strong and sound species. But Miss Julie is also a relic of the old warrior nobility that is now giving way to the new aristocracy of nerve and brain; a victim of the discord which a mother's 'crime' has implanted in a family; a victim of the errors of an age, of circumstances, and of her own deficient constitution, which together form the equivalent of the old-fashioned concept of Fate or Universal Law. The naturalist has erased guilt along with God, but he cannot erase the consequences of an action – punishment, prison, or the fear of it – for the simple reason that these consequences remain, whether or not he acquits the individual. For an injured party is less forbearing than those who have not been harmed may be, and even if her father found compelling reasons not to seek his revenge, his daughter would wreak vengeance on herself, as she does here, because of her innate or acquired sense of honour which the upper classes inherit – from where? From barbarism, from their original Aryan home, from the chivalry of the Middle Ages, all of which is very beautiful, but a real disadvantage nowadays where the preservation of the species is concerned. It is the nobleman's *harakiri*, the inner law of conscience which makes a Japanese slit open his own stomach when someone insults him, and which survives in modified form in that privilege of the nobility, the duel. That is why Jean, the servant, lives, but Miss Julie, who cannot live without honour, does not. The slave has this advantage over the earl, he lacks this fatal preoccupation with honour, and there is in all of us Aryans a little of the nobleman or Don Quixote, which means that we sympathize with the suicide who has committed a dishonourable act and thereby lost his honour, and we are noblemen enough to suffer when we see the mighty fallen and reduced to a useless corpse, yes, even if the fallen should rise again and make amends through an honourable act. The servant Jean is the type who founds a species, someone in whom the process of differentiation may be observed. He was a poor tied-worker's son and has now brought himself up to be a future nobleman. He has been quick to learn, has finely developed senses (smell, taste, sight) and an eye for beauty. He has already come up in the world, and is strong enough not to be concerned about exploiting other people. He is already a stranger in his environment, which he despises as stages in a past he has put behind him, and which he fears and flees, because people there know his secrets, spy out his intentions, regard his rise with envy, and look forward to his fall with pleasure. Hence his divided, indecisive character, wavering between sympathy for those in high positions and hatred for those who occupy them. He calls himself an aristocrat and has learnt the secrets of good society, is polished on the surface but coarse underneath, and already wears a frock-coat with style, although there is no guarantee that the body beneath it is clean.

He respects Miss Julie but is afraid of Kristin because she knows his dangerous secrets, and he is sufficiently callous not to allow the events of the night to interfere with his future plans. With the brutality of a slave and the indifference of a master he can look at blood without fainting, and shake off misfortune without further ado. That is why he escapes from the struggle unscathed and will probably end up the proprietor of a hotel; and even if *he* does not become a Romanian count, his son will probably go to university and possibly become a government official.

Moreover, the information he gives about life as the lower classes see it from below is quite important – when he speaks the truth, that is, which he does not often do, for he tends to say what is to his own advantage rather than what is true. When Miss Julie supposes that everyone in the lower classes finds the pressure from above oppressive, Jean naturally agrees since his intention is to gain sympathy, but he immediately corrects himself when he sees the advantage of distinguishing himself from the common herd.

Apart from the fact that Jean is rising in the world, he is also superior to Miss Julie in that he is a man. Sexually he is the aristocrat because of his masculine strength, his more finely developed senses, and his ability to take the initiative. His inferiority arises mainly from the social milieu in which he temporarily finds himself and which he will probably discard along with his livery.

His slave mentality expresses itself in his respect for the Count (the boots) and his religious superstition; but he respects the Count mainly as the occupant of the high position that he covets; and this respect remains even when he has conquered the daughter of the house and seen how empty that pretty shell is.

I do not believe there can be any love in a 'higher' sense between two such different natures, so I let Miss Julie imagine she loves him as a means of protecting or excusing herself; and I let Jean suppose he could fall in love with her if his social circumstances were different. I suspect that love is rather like the hyacinth, which has to put its roots down into the darkness *before* it can produce a strong flower. Here it shoots up, blooms, and goes to seed all in a moment, and that is why it dies so quickly.

Kristin, finally, is a female slave. Standing over the stove all day has made her subservient and dull; like an animal her hypocrisy is unconscious and she overflows with morality and religion, which serve as cloaks and scapegoats for her sins whereas a stronger character would have no need of them because he could bear his guilt himself or explain it away. She goes to church to unload her household thefts onto Jesus casually and deftly, and to recharge herself with a new dose of innocence.

Moreover, she is a minor character, and therefore my intention was only to sketch her in as

I did the Pastor and the Doctor in *The Father*, where I just wanted to depict ordinary people as country parsons and provincial doctors usually are. And if some people have found my minor characters abstract, that is because ordinary people are to some extent abstract when working; which is to say, they lack individuality and show only one side of themselves while performing their tasks, and as long as the spectator feels no need to see them from several sides, my abstract depiction will probably suffice.

Finally, where the dialogue is concerned I have somewhat broken with tradition by not making my characters catechists who sit around asking stupid questions in order to elicit a witty reply. I have avoided the symmetrical, mathematical artificiality of French dialogue and allowed my characters' brains to work irregularly as they do in real life, where no subject is ever entirely exhausted before one mind discovers by chance in another mind a cog in which to engage. For that reason the dialogue also wanders, providing itself in the opening scenes with material that is later reworked, taken up, repeated, expanded, and developed, like the theme in a musical composition.

The action is sufficiently fecund, and since it really concerns only two people I have restricted myself to them, introducing only one minor character, the cook, and letting the father's unhappy spirit hover above and behind it all. I have done this because it seems to me that what most interests people today is the psychological process; our inquiring minds are no longer satisfied with simply seeing something happen, we want to know how it happened. We want to see the strings, look at the machinery, examine the double-bottomed box, try the magic ring to find the seam, and examine the cards to discover how they are marked.

In this regard I have had in mind the monographic novels of the Goncourt brothers,[8] which have attracted me more than anything else in contemporary literature.

As for the technical aspects of the composition, I have, by way of experiment, eliminated all act divisions. I have done this because it seems to me that our declining susceptibility to illusion would possibly be disturbed by intervals, during which the spectator has time to reflect and thereby escape from the suggestive influence of the dramatist-hypnotist. My play probably runs for about an hour and a half, and since people can listen to a lecture, a sermon, or a conference session for that length of time or even longer, I imagine that a ninety-minute play should not exhaust them. I attempted this concentrated form as long ago as 1872, in one of my first attempts at drama, *The Outlaw*, but with scant success. I had written the piece in five acts, but when it was finished I noticed what a disjointed and disturbing effect it had. I burned it and from the ashes arose a single, long, carefully worked-out act of fifty printed pages, which played for a full hour. Consequently the form is not new, though it seems to be my speciality, and current changes in taste may well have made it timely. In due course I would hope to have an audience so educated that it could sit through a single act lasting an entire evening, but this will require some preliminary experimentation. Meanwhile, in order to provide resting places for the audience and the actors without breaking the illusion for the audience I have used three art forms that belong to the drama, namely the monologue, mime, and ballet, all of which were part of classical tragedy, monody having become monologue and the chorus, ballet.

Nowadays our realists have banished the monologue as implausible, but given appropriate motivation it becomes plausible, and I can therefore use it to advantage. It is perfectly plausible for a speaker to walk up and down alone in his room reading his speech aloud, that an actor should run through his role aloud, a servant girl talk to her cat, a mother prattle to her child, an old maid chatter to her parrot, or a sleeper talk in his sleep. And in order to give the actor a chance, for once, to work on his own and to escape for a moment from the hectoring of an author, I have not written out the monologues in detail but simply suggested them. For, in so far as it does not influence the action, it is quite immaterial what is said while asleep or to the cat, and a talented actor who is absorbed in the situation and mood of the play can probably improvise better than the author, who cannot calculate in advance just how much needs to be said, or for how long, before the theatrical illusion is broken.

As we know, some Italian theatres have returned to improvisation, producing actors who are creative in their own right, although in accordance with the author's intentions. This could really be a step forward or a fertile, new form of art that may well deserve the name *creative*.

Where a monologue would be implausible, I have resorted to mime, and here I leave the actor even greater freedom to create – and so win independent acclaim. But in order not to try the audience beyond its limits, I have let the music – well-motivated by the Midsummer dance, of course – exert its beguiling power during the silent action, and I would ask the musical director to select this music with great care so that the wrong associations are not aroused by recollections of the latest operettas or dance tunes or by the use of ultra-ethnographic folk music.

I could not have substituted a so-called crowd scene for the ballet I have introduced because crowd scenes are always badly acted, with a pack of simpering idiots seeking to use the occasion to show off and so destroy the illusion. Since ordinary people do not improvise their malicious remarks but use ready-made material that can be given a double meaning, I have not composed a malicious song but taken a little-known singing game which I noted down myself in the neighbourhood of Stockholm. The words do not hit home precisely, but that is the intention, for the cunning (weakness) of the slave does not permit him to attack directly. So: no speaking buffoons in a serious play, no coarse smirking over a situation that puts the lid on a family's coffin.

As for the scenery, I have borrowed the asymmetry and cropped framing of impressionist painting, and believe I have thereby succeeded in strengthening the illusion; for not being able to see the whole room or all the furniture leaves us free to conjecture, that is, our imagination is set in motion and we complete the picture ourselves. This also means that I have avoided those tiresome exits through doors, particularly stage doors that are made of canvas and sway at the slightest touch; they do not even permit an angry father to express his anger after a bad dinner by going out and slamming the door behind him 'so the whole house shakes'. (In the theatre it sways!) I have likewise restricted myself to a single set, both to allow the characters time to merge with their milieu and to break with the custom of expensive scenery. But when there is only a single set, one is entitled to demand that it be realistic. Yet nothing is more difficult than to get a room on stage to resemble a real room, no matter how easy the scene-painter finds erupting volcanoes and waterfalls. Even if the walls do have to be of canvas, it is surely time to stop painting shelves and kitchen utensils on them. There are so many other stage conventions in which we are asked to believe that we might be spared the effort of believing in painted saucepans.[9]

I have placed the rear wall and the table at an angle so that the actors have to play face on or in half profile when they are seated opposite each other at the table. In a production of *Aida* I have seen an angled backdrop which led the eye out into an unknown perspective, nor did it give the impression of having been put there simply to protest the boredom of straight lines.

Another perhaps desirable innovation would be the removal of the footlights. I understand that the purpose of lighting from below is to make the actors' faces fatter, but I would like to ask: why all actors have to have fat faces? Does not this underlighting obliterate a great many features in the lower parts of the face, especially around the jaws, distort the shape of the nose, and cast shadows over the eyes? Even if this is not the case, one thing is certain: it hurts the actors' eyes, so that their full expressiveness is lost, for footlights strike the retina in places that are normally protected (except in sailors, who cannot avoid seeing the sun reflected in water), and therefore we seldom see any other play of the eyes except crude glances either to the side or up to the balcony, when the white of the eye is visible. This probably also accounts for the tiresome way that actresses in particular have of fluttering their eyelashes. And when anyone on stage wants to speak with the eyes, the actor has sadly no alternative but to look straight at the audience, with which he or she then enters into direct contact outside the frame of the set – a bad habit rightly or wrongly called 'counting the house'.

Would not sufficiently strong side lighting (using parabolic reflectors or something similar) give the actor this new resource, of strengthening his facial expression by means of the face's greatest asset: the play of the eyes?

I have hardly any illusions about getting the actor to play for the audience and not with it, although this would be desirable. Nor do I dream of seeing the full back of an actor[10] throughout an important scene, but I do fervently wish that vital scenes should not be performed next to the prompter's box, as duets designed to elicit applause, but rather located to that part of the stage the action dictates. So, no revolutions, simply some small modifications, for to turn the stage into a room with the fourth wall removed and some of the furniture consequently facing away from the audience, would probably have a distracting effect, at least for the present.

When it comes to a word about make-up I dare not hope to be heard by the ladies, who would rather be beautiful than truthful. But the actor really might consider whether it is to his advantage to paint his face with an abstract character that will sit there like a mask. Picture an actor who gives himself a pronounced choleric expression by drawing a line with soot between his eyes, and suppose that, in spite of being in so permanently enraged a state, he needs to smile on a certain line. What a horrible grimace that would be! And how can the old man get the false forehead of his wig to wrinkle with anger when it is as smooth as a billiard ball?

In a modern psychological drama, where the subtlest movements of the soul should be mirrored more in the face than in gestures and sounds, it would probably be best to experiment with strong side lighting on a small stage and with actors wearing no make-up, or at least a bare minimum.

If we could then dispense with the visible orchestra with its distracting lights and faces turned towards the audience; if we could have the stalls raised so that the spectator's eyes were on a line higher than the actor's knees; if we could get rid of the private proscenium boxes with their giggling drinkers and diners; if we could have complete darkness in the auditorium; and finally, and most importantly, if we had a *small* stage and a *small* auditorium, then perhaps a new drama might arise, and the theatre would at least be a place where educated people might once again enjoy themselves. While waiting for such a theatre, we shall just have to go on writing for our desk drawers, preparing the repertoire whose time will come.

I have made an attempt! If it fails, there will surely be time to try again!

Notes

1. A 'poor man's Bible', a medieval work of edification richly illustrated with pictures from the Bible, aimed at those with little or no education.
2. The Yarmouth carrier Barkis' recurring phrase in *David Copperfield* (1850) by Charles Dickens (1812–70). Strindberg was otherwise an enthusiastic admirer of Dickens' novels.
3. Darwin's *Origin of Species* appeared in 1859 and had been translated into Swedish in 1871.
4. Italian philosopher Giordano Bruno (1548–1600) was burnt at the stake by the Inquisition. Bacon is the English statesman and philosopher Francis Bacon (1561–1626). The theory that Bacon wrote Shakespeare's plays was one to which Strindberg sometimes subscribed.
5. Siskin is translated as greenfinch by McGuinness.
6. The German doctor and practitioner of hypnotism Anton Mesmer (1734–1815) was mainly active in Vienna and Paris.
7. 'and the child' was inserted by the translator to make sense of a passage that closely echoes similar arguments in Strindberg's essays and letters on women. This paragraph has not been included in previous translations of the *Preface*.
8. Edmond (1822–96) and Jules (1830–70) de Goncourt together wrote several novels of psychological realism focusing closely on a central female character (e.g. *Soeur Philomène* (1861) and *Germaine Lacerteux* (1864)).
9. The use of real props was already standard practice at the court theatre of the Duke of Saxe-Meiningen (1826–1914), as was the kind of asymmetrical set design which Strindberg is advocating here.
10 The acting style associated with the newly opened Théâtre Libre in Paris; Strindberg was hoping this *Preface* would help sell the play to its director, André Antoine (1858–1943).

From *Miss Julie and Other Plays*, translated with an introduction and notes (edited) by Michael Robinson, Oxford and New York: Oxford University Press, 1998, pp. 56–68. Notes: pp. 291–3.

1.8 A New Art of the Stage (1907)

ARTHUR SYMONS

1

IN THE REMARKABLE EXPERIMENTS of Mr Gordon Craig, I seem to see the suggestion of a new art of the stage, an art no longer realistic, but conventional, no longer imitative, but symbolical. In Mr Craig's staging there is the incalculable element; the element that comes of itself, and cannot be coaxed into coming. But in what is incalculable there may be equal parts of inspiration and of accident. How much, in Mr Craig's staging, is inspiration, how much is accident? That is, after all, the important question.

Mr Craig, it is certain, has a genius for line, for novel effects of line. His line is entirely his own; he works in squares and straight lines, hardly ever in curves. He drapes the stage into a square with cloths; he divides these cloths by vertical lines, carrying the eye straight up to an immense height, fixing it into a rigid attention. He sets squares of pattern and structure on the stage; he forms his groups into irregular squares, and sets them moving in straight lines, which double on themselves like the two arms of a compass; he puts square patterns on the dresses, and drapes the arms with ribbons that hang to the ground, and make almost a square of the body when the arms are held out at right angles. He prefers gestures that have no curves in them; the arms held straight up, or straight forward, or straight out sideways. He likes the act of kneeling, in which the body is bent into a sharp angle; he likes a sudden spring to the feet, with the arms held straight up. He links his groups by an arrangement of poles and ribbons, something in the manner of a maypole; each figure is held to the centre by a tightly stretched line like the spoke of a wheel. Even when, as in this case, the pattern forms into a circle, the circle is segmented by straight lines.

This severe treatment of line gives breadth and dignity to what might otherwise be merely fantastic. Mr Craig is happiest when he can play at children's games with his figures, as in almost the whole of *The Masque of Love*.[1] When he is entirely his own master, not dependent on any kind of reality, he invents really like a child, and his fairy-tale comes right, because it is not tied by any grown-up logic. Then his living design is like an arabesque within strict limits, held in from wandering and losing itself by those square lines which rim it implacably round.

Then, again, his effects are produced simply. Most of the costumes in *The Masque of Love* were made of sacking, stitched roughly together. Under the cunning handling of the light, they gave you any illusion you pleased, and the beggars of the masque were not more appropriately clothed than the kings and queens. All had dignity, all reposed the eye.

The aim of modern staging is to intensify the reality of things, to give you the illusion of an actual room, or meadow, or mountain. We have arrived at a great skill in giving this crude illusion of reality. Our stage painters can imitate anything, but what they cannot give us is the emotion which the playwright, if he is an artist, wishes to indicate by means of his scene. It is the very closeness of the imitation which makes our minds unable to accept it. The eye rebounds, so to speak, from this canvas as real as wood, this wood as real as water, this water which is actual water. Mr Craig aims at taking us beyond reality; he replaces the pattern of the thing itself by the pattern which that thing evokes in his mind, the symbol of the thing. As, in conventional art, the artist unpicks the structure of the rose to build up a mental image of the rose, in some formal pattern which his brain makes over again, like a new creation from the beginning, a new organism, so, in this new convention of the stage, a plain cloth, modulated by light, can stand for space or for limit, may be the tight walls of a tent or the sky and the clouds. The eye loses itself among these severe, precise, and yet mysterious lines and surfaces; the mind is easily at home in them; it accepts them as readily as it accepts the convention by which, in a poetical play, men speak in verse rather than in prose.

Success, of course, in this form of art lies in the perfecting of its emotional expressiveness. Even yet Mr Craig has not done much more, perhaps, than indicate what may be done with the material which he finds in his hands. For instance, the obvious criticism upon his mounting of *Acis and Galatea*[2] is, that he has mounted a pastoral, and put nothing pastoral into his mounting. And this criticism is partly just. Yet there are parts, especially the end of Act I, where he has perfectly achieved the rendering of pastoral feeling according to his own convention. The tent is there with its square walls, not a glimpse of meadow or sky comes into the severe design, and yet, as the nymphs in their straight dresses and straight ribbons lie back laughing on the ground, and the children, with their little modern brown straw hats, toss paper roses among them, and the coloured balloons (which you may buy in the street for a penny) are tossed into the air, carrying the eye upward, as if it saw the wind chasing the clouds, you feel the actual sensation of a pastoral scene, of country joy, of the spring and the open air, as no trickle of real water in a trough, no sheaves of real corn among painted trees, no imitation of a flushed sky on canvas, could trick you into feeling it. The imagination has been caught; a suggestion has been given which strikes straight to the 'nerves of delight'; and be sure those nerves, that imagination, will do the rest, better, more effectually, than the deliberate assent of the eyes to an imitation of natural appearances.

Take again some of those drawings of stage scenery which we have not yet been able to see realized, the decoration for Hofmannsthal's *Elektra* and *Venice Preserved*, and for *Hamlet* and for *The Masque of London*. Everywhere a wild and exquisite scenic imagination builds up shadowy structures which seem to have arisen by some strange hazard, and to the sound of an unfamiliar music, and which are often literally like music in the cadences of their design. All have dignity, remoteness, vastness; a sense of mystery, an actual emotion in their lines and faint colours. There is poetry in this bare prose framework of stage properties, a quality of grace which is almost evasive, and seems to point out new possibilities of drama, as it provides new, scarcely hoped for, possibilities to the dramatist.

Take, for instance, *The Masque of London*. It is Piranesi, and it is London of today, seen in lineal vision, and it is a design, not merely on paper, but built up definitely between the wings of the stage. It is a vast scaffolding, rising out of ruins, and ascending to toppling heights; all its crazy shapes seem to lean over in the air, and at intervals a little weary being climbs with obscure patience. In one of the *Hamlet* drawings we see the room in the castle at Elsinore into which Ophelia is to come with her bewildered singing; and the room waits, tall, vague, exquisitely still and strange, a ghostly room, prepared for beauty and madness. There is another room, with tall doors and windows and abrupt pools of light on the floor; and another, with its significant shadows, its two enigmatic figures, in which a drama of Maeterlinck might find its own atmosphere awaiting it. And in yet another all is gesture; walls, half-opened doors, half-seen windows, the huddled people at a doorway, and a tall figure of a woman raised up in the foreground, who seems to motion to them vehemently. Colour cooperates with line in effects of rich and yet delicate vagueness; there are always the long, straight lines, the sense of height and space, the bare surfaces, the subtle, significant shadows, out of which Mr Craig has long since learned to evoke stage pictures more beautiful and more suggestive than any that have been seen on the stage in our time.

The whole stage art of Mr Craig is a protest against realism, and it is to realism that we owe whatever is most conspicuously bad in the mounting of plays at the present day. Wagner did some of the harm; for he refused to realize some of the necessary limitations of stage illusion, and persisted in believing that the stage artist could compete successfully with nature in the production of landscape, light, and shadow. Yet Wagner himself protested against the heaps of unrealizing detail under which Shakespeare was buried, in his own time, on the German stage, as he is buried on the English stage in our own. No scene-painter, no scene-shifter, no limelight man, will ever delude us by his moon or meadow or moving clouds or water. His business is to aid the poet's illusion, that illusion of beauty which is the chief excuse for stage plays at all, when once we have passed beyond the 'rose-pink and dirty drab', in Meredith's sufficing phrase, of stage romance and stage reality. The distinction, the incomparable merit, of Mr Craig is that he conceives his setting as the poet conceives his drama. The verse in most Shakespearean revivals rebounds from a backcloth of metallic solidity; the scenery shuts in the players, not upon Shakespeare's dream, but upon as nearly as possible 'real' historical *bric-à-brac*. What Mr Craig does, or would do if he were allowed to do it, is to open all sorts of 'magic casements', and to thrust back all kinds of real and probable limits, and to give at last a little scope for the imagination of the playwright who is also a poet.

I do not yet know of what Mr Craig is capable, how far he can carry his happy natural gifts towards mastery. But he has done so much already that I want to see him doing more; I want to see him accepting all the difficulties of his new art frankly, and grappling with them. For the staging of Maeterlinck, especially for such a play as *La Mort de Tintagiles* [Maeterlinck's *The Death of Tintagiles*, 1894], his art, just as it is, would suffice. Here are plays which exist anywhere in space, which evade reality, which do all they can to become disembodied in the very moment in which they become visible. They have atmosphere without locality, and that is what Mr Craig can give us so easily. But I would like to see him stage an opera of Wagner, *Tristan*, or the *Meistersinger* even. Wagner has perfected at Bayreuth his own conception of what scenery should be; he has done better than any one else what most other stage-craftsmen have been trying to do. He allows more than they do to convention, but even his convention aims at convincing the eye; the dragon of the *Ring* is as real a beast as Wagner could invent in his competition with nature's invention of the snake and the crocodile. But there are those who prefer Wagner's music in the concert-room to Wagner's music even at Bayreuth. Unless the whole aim and theory of Wagner was wrong, this preference is wrong. I should like, at least as an experiment, to see what Mr Craig would make of one of the operas. I am not sure that he would not reconcile those who prefer Wagner in the concert-room to this new kind of performance on the stage. He would give us the mind's attractive symbols of all these crude German pictures; he would strike away the footlights from before these vast German singers, and bring a ghostly light to creep down about their hoods and untightened drapings; he would bring, I think, the atmosphere of the music for the first time upon the stage.

Then I would like to see Mr Craig go further still; I would like to see him deal with a purely modern play, a play which takes place indoors, in the house of middle-class people. He should mount the typical modern play, Ibsen's *Ghosts*. Think of that room 'in Mrs Alving's country-house, beside one of the large fjords in Western Norway'. Do you remember the stage directions? In the first act the glimpse, through the glass windows of the conservatory, of 'a gloomy fjord landscape, veiled by steady rain'; in the second 'the mist still lies heavy over the landscape'; in the third the lamp burning on the table, the darkness outside, the 'faint glow from the conflagration'. And always 'the room as before'. What might not Mr Craig do with that room! What, precisely, I do not know; but I am sure that his method is capable of an extension which will take in that room, and, if it can take in that room, it can take in all of modern life which is of importance to the playwright.

2

Most people begin with theory, and go on, if they go on, to carry their theory into practice. Mr Gordon Craig has done a better thing, and, having begun by creating a new art of the stage on the actual boards of the theatre, has followed up his practical demonstration by a book of theory, in which he explains what he has done, telling us also what he hopes to do. *The Art of the Theatre* is a little book, hardly more than a pamphlet, but every page is full of original thought. Until I read it, I was not sure how much in Mr Craig's work was intention and how much happy accident. Whether or not we agree with every part of his theory, he has left no part unthought out. His theory, then, in brief, is this: he defines the theatre as 'a place in which the entire beauty of life can be unfolded, and not only the external beauty of the world, but the inner beauty and meaning of life'. He would make the theatre a temple in which a continual ceremony unfolds and proclaims the beauty of life, and, like the churches of other religions, it is to be, not for the few, but for the people. The art of the theatre is to be 'neither acting nor the play, it is not scene nor dance, but it consists of all the elements of which these things are composed: action, which is the very spirit of acting; words, which are the body of the play; line and colour, which are the very heart of the scene; rhythm, which is the very essence of dance'. The art of the theatre is addressed in the first place to the eyes, and the first dramatist spoke through 'poetic action, which is dance, or prose action, which is gesture'. In the modern theatre a play is no longer 'a balance of actions, words, dance and scene, but it is either all words or all scene'. The business of the stage director, who is to be the artist of the theatre, is to bring back the theatre to its true purpose. He begins by taking the dramatist's play, and sets himself to interpret it visibly on the boards. He reads it and gets his general impression:

> he first of all chooses certain colours, which seem to him to be in harmony with the spirit of the play, rejecting other colours as out of tune. He then weaves into a pattern certain objects – an arch, a fountain, a balcony, a bed – using the chosen object as the centre of his design. Then he adds to this all the objects which are mentioned in the play, and which are

necessary to be seen. To these he adds, one by one, each character which appears in the play, and gradually each movement of each character, and each costume. . . . While this pattern for the eye is being devised, the designer is being guided as much by the sound of the verse or prose as by the sense or spirit.

At the first rehearsal the actors are all in their stage dresses, and have all learned their words. The picture is there; the stage director then lights his picture. He then sets it in motion, teaching each actor to 'move across our sight in a certain way, passing to a certain point, in a certain light, his head at a certain angle, his eyes, his feet, his whole body in tune with the play'. The play is then ready to begin, we may suppose? By no means. 'There will not be any play,' says the stage director to the sheep-like playgoer who has been meekly drifting with the current of dialogue, 'there will not be any play in the sense in which you use the word. When,' he is told, 'the theatre has become a masterpiece of mechanism, when it has invented a technique, it will without any effort develop a *creative art* of its own.' And that art is to be created out of three things, the three bare necessities of the stage: action, scene and voice. By action is meant 'both gestures and dancing, the prose and poetry of action'; by scene, 'all which comes before the eye, such as the lighting, costume, as well as the scenery'; by voice,

the spoken word or the word which is sung, in contradiction to the word which is read; for the word written to be spoken and the word written to be read are two entirely different things.

Up to this last surprising point, which, however, has been stealthily led up to by a very persuasive semblance of logic, how admirable is every definition and every suggestion! Everything that is said is as self-evidently true as it is commonly and consistently neglected. Who will deny that the theatre is a visible creation of life, and that life is, first of all, action; to the spectator, in the stalls or in the street, a thing first of all seen, and afterwards, to the measure of one's care or capability, heard and understood? That life should be created over again in the theatre, not in a crude material copy, but in the spirit of all art, 'by means of things that do not possess life until the artist has touched them': this also will hardly be denied. This visible creation of life is (until the words come into it) like a picture, and it is made in the spirit of the painter, who fails equally if in his picture he departs from life, or if he but imitates without interpreting it. But is it not, after all, through its power of adding the life of speech to the life of motion that the theatre attains its full perfection? Can that perfection be attained by limiting its scope to what must remain its only materials to work with: action, scene and voice?

The question is this: whether the theatre is the invention of the dramatist, and of use only in so far as it interprets his creative work; or whether the dramatist is the invention of the theatre, which has made him for its own ends, and will be able, when it has wholly achieved its mechanism, to dispense with him altogether, except perhaps as a kind of prompter. And the crux of the question is this: that to the supreme critic of literature, to Charles Lamb, a play of Shakespeare, *Lear* or *Hamlet*, seems too great for the stage, so that when acted it loses the rarest part of its magic; while to the ideal stage director, to Mr Gordon Craig, *Hamlet* should not be acted because it is not so calculated for the theatre that it depends for its ultimate achievement on gesture, scene, costume, and all that the theatre has to offer; not, that is, that it is greater or less in its art, but that it is different. If we are content to believe both, each from his own point of view, is it not Craig who will seem the more logical? For why, it will be asked, should the greatest dramatist of the world have produced his greatest work under an illusion, that is for acting? Why should all the vital drama of the world, the only drama that is vital as literature, have been thus produced? If all this has indeed been produced under an illusion, and in the face of nature, how invaluable must such an illusion be, and how careful should we be to refrain from destroying any of its power over the mind!

An illusion is one thing, a compromise is another, and every art is made up in part of more and more ingenious compromises. The sculptor, who works in the round, and in visible competition with the forms of life, has to allow for the tricks of the eye. He tricks the eye that he may suggest, beyond the literal contour, the movement of muscle and the actual passage of blood under the skin, the momentary creasing of flesh; and he balances his hollows and bosses that he may suggest the play of air about living flesh: all his compromises are with fact, to attain life. May not the art of the dramatist be in like manner a compromise with the logic of his mechanism, a deliberate and praiseworthy twisting of ends into means? The end of technique is not in itself, but in its service to the artist; and the technique, which Mr Craig would end with, might, if it were carried out, be utilized by the dramatist to his own incalculable advantage.

Notes

1. A reference to the production of the masque from Purcell's *Dioclesian* in 1901.
2. A reference to the production of Handel's *Acis and Galatea* in 1902.

Originally published in *Studies in Seven Arts*, New York: Dutton, 1907.

1.9 **The Modern Drama** (1904)

MAURICE MAETERLINCK

Translated by Alfred Sutro

· · · T HE FIRST THING THAT strikes us in the drama of the day is the decay, one might almost say the creeping paralysis, of external action. Next we note a very pronounced desire to penetrate deeper and deeper into human consciousness, and place moral problems upon a high pedestal; and finally the search, still very timid and halting, for a kind of new beauty, that shall be less abstract than was the old.

It is certain that, on the actual stage, we have far fewer extraordinary and violent adventures. Bloodshed has grown less frequent, passions less turbulent; heroism has become less unbending, courage less material and less ferocious. People still die on the stage, it is true, as in reality they still must die, but death has ceased – or will cease, let us hope, very soon – to be regarded as the indispensable setting, the *ultima ratio*, the inevitable end, of every dramatic poem. In the most formidable crises of our life – which, cruel though it may be, is cruel in silent and hidden ways – we rarely look to death for a solution; and for all that the theatre is slower than the other arts to follow the evolution of human consciousness, it will still be at last compelled, in some measure, to take this into account.

When we consider the ancient and tragical anecdotes that constitute the entire basis of the classical drama; the Italian, Scandinavian, Spanish or mythical stories that provided the plots, not only for all the plays of the Shakespearian period, but also – not altogether to pass over an art that was infinitely less spontaneous – for those of French and German romanticism, we discover at once that these anecdotes are no longer able to offer us the direct interest they presented at a time when they appeared highly natural and possible, at a time, when at any rate, the circumstances, manners, and sentiments they recalled were not yet extinct in the minds of those who witnessed their reproduction.

To us, however, these adventures no longer correspond with a living and actual reality. Should a youth of our time love, and meet obstacles not unlike those which, in another order of ideas and events, beset Romeo's passion, we need no telling that his adventure will be embellished by none of the features that gave poetry and grandeur to the episode of Verona. Gone beyond recall is the entrancing atmosphere of a lordly, passionate life; gone the brawls in picturesque streets, the interludes of bloodshed and splendor, the mysterious poisons, the majestic, complaisant tombs! And where shall we look for that exquisite summer's night, which owes its vastness, its savor, the very appeal that it makes to us, to the shadow of an heroic, inevitable death that already lay heavy upon it? Divest the story of Romeo and Juliet of these beautiful trappings, and we have only the very simple and ordinary desire of a noble-hearted, unfortunate youth for a maiden whose obdurate parents deny him her hand. All the poetry, the splendor, the passionate life of this desire, result from the glamour, the nobility, tragedy, that are proper to the environment wherein it has come to flower; nor is there a kiss, a murmur of love, a cry of anger, grief or despair, but borrows its majesty, grace, its heroism, tenderness – in a word, every image that has helped it to visible form – from the beings and objects around it; for it is not in the kiss itself that the sweetness and beauty are found, but in the circumstance, hour, and place wherein it was given. Again, the same objections would hold if we chose to imagine a man of our time who should be jealous as Othello was jealous, possessed of Macbeth's ambition, unhappy as Lear; or, like Hamlet, restless and wavering, bowed down beneath the weight of a frightful and unrealizable duty.

These conditions no longer exist. The adventure of the modern Romeo – to consider only the external events which it might provoke – would not provide material for a couple of acts. Against this it may be urged that a modern poet, who desires to put on the stage an analogous poem of youthful love, is perfectly justified in borrowing from days gone by a more decorative setting, one that shall be more fertile in heroic and tragical incident. Granted; but what can the result be of such an expedient? Would not the feelings and passions that demand for their fullest, most perfect expression and development the atmosphere of today (for the passions and feelings of a modern poet must, in despite of himself, be entirely and exclusively modern) would not these suddenly find themselves transplanted to a soil where all things prevented their living? ...

But we need dwell no further on the necessarily artificial poems that arise from the impossible marriage of past and present. Let us rather consider the drama that actually stands for the reality of our time, as Greek drama stood for Greek reality, and the drama of the Renaissance for the reality of the Renaissance. Its scene is a modern house, it passes between men and women of today. The names of the invisible protagonists – the passions and ideas – are the same, more or less, as of old. We see love, hatred, ambition, jealousy, envy, greed; the sense of justice and idea of duty; pity, goodness, devotion, piety, selfishness, vanity, pride, etc. But although the names have remained more or less the same, how great is the difference we find in the aspect and quality, the extent and influence, of these ideal actors! Of all their ancient weapons not one is left them, not one of the marvelous moments of olden days. It is seldom that cries are heard now; bloodshed is rare, and tears not often seen. It is in a small room, round a table, close to the fire, that the joys and sorrows of mankind are decided. We suffer, or make others suffer, we love, we die, there in our corner; and it were the strangest chance should a door or a window suddenly, for an instant, fly open, beneath the pressure of extraordinary despair or rejoicing. Accidental, adventitious beauty exists no longer; there remains only an external poetry that has not yet become poetic. And what poetry, if we probe to the root of things – what poetry is there that does not borrow nearly all of its charm, nearly all of its ecstasy, from elements that are wholly external? Last of all, there is no longer a God to widen, or master, the action; nor is there an inexorable fate to form a mysterious, solemn, and tragical background for the slightest gesture of man; nor the somber and abundant atmosphere that was able to ennoble even his most contemptible weaknesses, his least pardonable crimes.

There still abides with us, it is true, a terrible unknown; but it is so diverse and elusive, it becomes so arbitrary, so vague and contradictory, the moment we try to locate it, that we cannot evoke it without great danger; cannot even, without the mightiest difficulty avail ourselves of it, though in all loyalty, to raise to the point of mystery the gestures, actions, and words of the men we pass every day. The endeavor has been made; the formidable, problematic enigma of heredity, the grandiose but improbable enigma of inherent justice, and many others beside, have each in their turn been put forward as a substitute for the vast enigma of the Providence or Fatality of old.

And it is curious to note how these youthful enigmas, born but of yesterday, already seem older, more arbitrary, more unlikely, than those whose places they took in an access of pride ...

... Incapable of outside movement, deprived of external ornament, daring no longer to make serious appeal to a determined divinity or fatality, [the modern drama] has fallen back on itself, and seeks to discover, in the regions of psychology and of moral problems, the equivalent of what once was offered by exterior life. It has penetrated deeper into human consciousness; but has encountered difficulties there no less strange than unexpected.

To penetrate deeply into human consciousness is the privilege, even the duty, of the thinker, the moralist, the historian, novelist, and, to a degree, of the lyrical poet; but not of the dramatist. Whatever the temptation, he dare not sink into inactivity, become mere philosopher or observer. Do what one will, discover what marvels one may, the sovereign law of the stage, its essential demand, will always be *action*. With the rise of the curtain, the high intellectual desire within us undergoes transformation; and in place of the thinker, psychologists, mystic or moralist there stands the mere instinctive spectator, the man electrified negatively by the crowd, the man whose one desire it is to see something happen ... And there are no words so profound, so noble and admirable, but they will soon weary us if they leave the situation unchanged, if they lead to no action, bring about no decisive conflict, or hasten no definite solution.

But whence is it that action arises in the consciousness of man? In its first stage it springs from the struggle between diverse conflicting passions. But no sooner has it raised itself somewhat – and this is true, if we examine it closely, of the first stage also – than it would seem to be solely due to the conflict between a passion and a moral law, between a duty and a desire. Hence the eagerness with which modern dramatists have plunged into all the problems of contemporary morality; and it may safely be said that at this moment they confine themselves almost exclusively to the discussion of these different problems.

This movement was initiated by the dramas of Alexandre Dumas *fils*, dramas which brought the most elementary of moral conflicts on to the stage; dramas, indeed, whose entire existence was based on problems such as the spectator, who must always be regarded as the ideal moralist, would never put to himself in the course of his whole spiritual existence, so evident is their solution. Should the faithless husband or wife be forgiven? Is it well to avenge infidelity by infidelity? Has the illegitimate child any rights? Is the marriage of inclination – such is the name it bears in those regions – preferable to the marriage for money? Have parents the right to oppose a marriage for love? Is divorce to be deprecated when a child has been born of the union? Is the sin of the adulterous wife greater than that of the adulterous husband? etc., etc.

Indeed, it may be said here that the entire French theatre of today, and a considerable proportion of the foreign theatre, which is only its echo, exist solely on questions of this kind, and on the entirely superfluous answers to which they give rise.

On the other hand, however, the highest point of human consciousness is attained by the dramas of Björnson, of Hauptmann, and, above all, of Ibsen. Here we touch the limit of the resources of modern dramaturgy. For, in truth, the further we penetrate into the consciousness of man, the less struggle do we discover. It is impossible to penetrate far into any consciousness unless that consciousness be very enlightened; for, whether we advance ten steps, or a thousand, in the depths of a soul that is plunged in darkness, we shall find nothing there that can be unexpected, or new; for darkness everywhere will only resemble itself. But a consciousness that is truly enlightened will possess passions and desires infinitely less exacting, infinitely more peaceful and patient, more salutary, abstract, and general, than are those that reside in the ordinary consciousness. Thence, far less struggle – or at least a struggle of far less violence – between these nobler and wiser passions; and this for the very reason that they have become vaster and loftier; for if there be nothing more restless, destructive and savage than a dammed-up stream, there is nothing more tranquil, beneficent and silent than the beautiful river whose banks ever widen.

Again, this enlightened consciousness will yield to infinitely fewer laws, admit infinitely fewer doubtful or harmful duties. There is, one may say, scarcely a falsehood or error, a prejudice, half-truth or convention, that is not capable of assuming, that does not actually assume, when the occasion presents itself, the form of a duty in an uncertain consciousness. It is thus that honor, in the chivalrous, conjugal sense of the word (I refer to the honor of the husband, which is supposed to suffer by the infidelity of the wife), that revenge, a kind of morbid prudishness, pride, vanity, piety to certain gods, and a thousand other illusions, have been, and still remain, the unquenchable source of a multitude of duties that are still regarded as absolutely sacred, absolutely incontrovertible, by a vast number of inferior consciousnesses. And these so-called duties are the pivot of almost all the dramas of the Romantic period, as of most of those of today. But not one of these somber, pitiless duties, that so fatally impel mankind to death and disaster, can readily take root in the consciousness that a healthy, living light has adequately penetrated; in such there will be no room for honor or vengeance, for conventions that clamor for blood. It will hold no prejudices that exact tears, no injustice eager for sorrow. It will have cast from their throne the gods who insist on sacrifice, and the love that craves for death. For when the sun has entered into the consciousness of him who is wise, as we may hope that it will some day enter into that of all men, it will reveal one duty, and one alone, which is that we should do the least possible harm and love others as we love ourselves; and from this duty no drama can spring.

Let us consider what happens in Ibsen's plays. He often leads us far down into human consciousness, but the drama remains possible only because there goes with us a singular flame, a sort of red light, which, somber, capricious – unhallowed, one almost might say – falls only on singular phantoms. And indeed nearly all the duties which from the active principle of Ibsen's tragedies are duties situated no longer within, but without, the healthy, illumined consciousness; and the duties we believe we discover outside this consciousness often come perilously near an unjust pride, or a kind of soured and morbid madness.

Let it not be imagined, however – for indeed this would be wholly to misunderstand me – that these remarks of mine in any way detract from my admiration for the great Scandinavian poet. For, if it be true that Ibsen has contributed few salutary elements to the morality of our time, he is perhaps the only writer for the stage who has caught sight of, and set in motion, a new, though still disagreeable poetry, which he has succeeded in investing with a kind of savage, gloomy beauty and grandeur (surely too savage and gloomy for it to become general or definitive); as he is the only one who owes nothing to the poetry of the violently illumined dramas of antiquity or of the Renaissance.

But, while we wait for the time when human consciousness shall recognize more useful passions and less nefarious duties, for the time when the world's stage shall consequently present more happiness and fewer tragedies, there still remains in the depths of every heart of loyal intention a great duty of charity and justice that eclipses all others. And it is perhaps from the struggle of this duty against our egoism and ignorance that the veritable drama of our century shall spring. When this goal has been attained – in real life as on the stage – it will be permissible perhaps to speak of a new theatre, a theatre of peace, and of beauty without tears.

Note

This excerpt from Maurice Maeterlinck's *The Double Garden* (New York: Dodd, Mead & Co., 1904) was translated by Alfred Sutro.

1.10 Tragedy in Everyday Life (1896)

MAURICE MAETERLINCK

Translated by Dan Rebellato

THERE IS A TRAGIC aspect to everyday life which is much more real, much more profound and much more akin to our real self than the tragedy of grand adventures. We can all sense it but it's not easy to demonstrate, because the essence of this tragedy is neither merely psychological nor material. It's not in a determined struggle of one person against another, one desire against another, or the eternal battle between passion and duty. Rather it means making visible what is overwhelming in the simple fact of being alive. Rather it means making visible the existence of a soul in itself, in the midst of an unsleeping vastness. Instead, it would mean making heard, beneath the commonplace exchanges of reason and sentiment, the more sombre, uninterrupted dialogue between the individual and his destiny. Instead, it would mean making us follow the hesitant and painful footsteps of someone approaching or retreating from truth, from beauty, or from God. Again, it means showing us and making us listen to a thousand things that the tragic poets let us glimpse only in passing. But this is the essential point: should we not try to show those things first of all? What we hear within King Lear, within Macbeth, within Hamlet, for example, the mysterious song of the infinite, the portentous silence of souls or the gods, the eternity which rumbles towards the horizon, the destiny or fate that one perceives inwardly without being able to say how – is there any way of bringing those to the fore and, by some unprecedented reversal of roles, distancing us from the actors? And is it rash to claim that the real tragedy of life, the ordinary, deep and universal tragedy, only begins at the moment when what we call adventures, misfortunes and perils have passed? Does joy not have a longer reach than woe, and do some of its powers not touch the human soul? Is it absolutely necessary to wail like the Atrides for an eternal God to manifest himself in our life and does he never come to us when we are seated motionless beneath a lamp? When you think about it, isn't stillness, watched over by the stars, a terrible thing; and does a sense of life unfold in tumult or in silence? Shouldn't a great unease come over us when we are told at the end of those stories, 'They lived happily ever after'? What happens while they live happily? Isn't there more that is serious and substantial to be found in happiness, in a simple moment of peace, than in the excitation of the passions? Isn't it then that the march of time and many other hidden currents become finally visible as the hours rush headlong into nothing? Doesn't this all cut deeper than the dagger blows of conventional drama? Isn't it when a man believes himself to be protected against the approach of death that the strange and silent tragedy of being and infinity opens the doors to its own theatre? Is it when I flee from a drawn sword that my existence touches on its most interesting feature? Is it always in a kiss that it is most sublime? Are there not other moments in which one hears more constant and purer voices? Does your soul only flourish at night in the heart of a thunderstorm? You might well think that's what we've always believed. Most of our tragic authors find dramatic life only in violence and history; and one might well say that all of our theatre is anachronistic and that the dramatic art is as behind the times as sculpture. It's not the same for the fine arts or serious music, for example, which recognized the need to bring out those hidden qualities, grave and astonishing of life today. They realized that a life that discards surface decoration only grows in depth, meaning and spiritual weight. A good painter won't paint Marius, conqueror of the Cimbri, or the assassination of the Duke of Guise any more because the psychology of victory or murder is primitive and abnormal, and the empty clamour of a violent act drowns out more profound but hesitant and discreet voices. He or she will depict a house lost in the countryside, an open door at the end of a corridor, a face or hands at rest; these simple images could add something to our awareness of life; and once we have it, we can never lose it.

But like those mediocre painters who waste their time in painting historical scenes, our tragic authors devote their works to the violence of their stories. And they claim it's entertainment to show us the same kinds of thing that used to delight barbarians accustomed to the conspiracies, murders and treacheries they show us. But most of our lives are spent far away from blood, cries and swords, and the tears of men have become silent, invisible and almost spiritual ...

When I go to the theatre, I feel like I am spending a few hours among my ancestors, who had a simple, harsh and brutal understanding of life, which I no longer recognize and in which I can no longer take part. I watch a deceived husband kill his wife, a woman poisoning her lover, a son avenge his father, a father who slays his children, children who bring about their father's death, assassinated kings, virgins deflowered, merchants imprisoned, and that whole sublime tradition – alas! So superficial, and so materialistic: blood, fake tears and death. Who can show me someone who doesn't just have one *idée fixe* and can take the time to live without having to put a rival or a mistress to death?

I had come in hope of seeing something of how life is tied to its source and its mystery by links which I have neither the opportunity nor strength to perceive every day. I had come in hope of glimpsing a moment of the beauty, grandeur and gravity of my humble everyday existence. I had hoped I might be shown some kind of presence, some power or some god who lived alongside me in my own room. I longed for unfamiliar heightened moments among my most mundane hours; and mostly I just got a man telling me at great length of his jealousy, or why he is going to poison someone or why he has to kill himself.

I admire Othello, but he seems to me not to live the noble daily life of a Hamlet, who, because he does not act, has time to live. Othello is admirably jealous. But isn't it perhaps an old error to think that it is at the moments where we are possessed by this kind of passion (or others of similar intensity) that we truly live? I have come to believe that an old man sitting in his armchair, just waiting beneath his lamp, hearing without knowing it all the eternal laws which range around his house, interpreting without understanding the silence of doors and windows and, in the frail voice of the light, giving himself up to the presence of his soul and his destiny, his head slightly inclined to one side, not realizing that the powers of the world all throng around him, watching over him in the room like attentive servants, unaware that the sun itself is keeping the little table on which he leans from tipping into the void, and that there is no star in the heavens nor an impulse in the soul which is indifferent to the movement of a closing eyelid or a rising thought – I have come to believe that this motionless old man lives, in reality, a profound, more human and more universal life than the lover who strangles his mistress, the captain who carries off the battle, or 'the husband who avenges his honour'.

It will perhaps be said that a motionless life would be barely visible, that one really needs to animate it with varied movement and that these varied movements must necessarily resolve themselves only into the small number of passions employed hitherto. I'm not so sure a static theatre is impossible. As far as I can see, it already exists. The majority of Aeschylus' tragedies are static tragedies. I'm not talking about *Prometheus* and *The Suppliants* where nothing happens; but the great tragedy of *The Libation Bearers*, certainly the most terrible drama of antiquity, which lurks like a bad dream around the tomb of Agamemnon, until murder erupts, like a bolt of lightning, from out of the accumulated layering of prayers. From this point of view, look at several other of the best ancient tragedies: *Eumenides*, *Antigone*, *Electra*, *Oedipus at Colonnus*. 'They admired,' says Racine in his preface to *Berenice*, 'they admired Sophocles' *Ajax*, which consists only in Ajax killing himself from sorrow after his rage at being refused the armour of Achilles. They admired *Philoctetes*, the whole of which concerns Ulysses coming to seize Hercules' arrows. *Oedipus* itself, although full of recognition scenes, is less substantial than the simplest contemporary tragedy.'

What is this but motionless life? Usually, there isn't even psychological action, which is a thousand times better than material action and which it seems impossible to do without, but which it manages nonetheless to do away with or to reduce remarkably, so as not to let anything get in the way of the place of man in the universe. In these plays, we are no longer among barbarians, and man no longer acts in the heat of primitive passions which are not the only things of interest about him. We have time to watch him in repose. It's no longer a matter of a singular violent moment in existence, but of existence itself. There are thousands of laws, more powerful and revered than the laws of passion; but these gentle laws, discreet and silent, like everything endowed with irresistible force, are only sensed in the twilight and contemplation in the still hours of one's life.

When Ulysses and Neoptolemus come to demand Hercules' armour from Philoctetes, their action is in itself as simple and unremarkable as that of a man today going into a house to visit a sick person, a traveller who knocks on the door of an inn, or a mother who waits by the fire for her child to return. Sophocles cursorily stamps the character of his heroes. But perhaps the main interest of tragedy is found not in the struggle between cunning and loyalty, between patriotism, resentment and stubborn pride? There is something else; and that is the higher existence of man which must be made visible. The poet adds to ordinary life that unknown element which is the secret of poets, and all at once it appears in its extraordinary grandeur, in its submission to mysterious powers, in its infinite connections and its solemn woe. A chemist releases some mysterious droplets into a test tube which only seems to contain clear water: and at once a world of crystals springs up at its rim and reveals to us everything that has been in suspension, where our partial vision saw nothing. Thus in *Philoctetes*, the slender psychology of its three principal characters is just the glass of the test tube containing the clear water of ordinary life into which the poet releases the revelatory droplets of his genius ...

Also, is it not in the words, rather than the actions, that we find the beauty and grandeur of the most beautiful and grandest tragedies? Do we find these qualities only in words that accompany and explain action? No; there must be something more than the superficially necessary dialogue.

It is almost only those words which at first appear unnecessary which give the work its value. It is in them that the soul may recognize itself. Alongside the necessary dialogue, there is almost always another dialogue which seems superfluous. Look carefully and you will see that it's the only thing that the soul hears deeply, because this is the only place where the soul is addressed. You will also recognize that it's the quality and expanse of this empty dialogue which determines the quality and the inexpressible reach of the work. For certain in ordinary dramas the necessary dialogue in no way responds to reality; and what makes for the mysterious beauty of the most beautiful tragedies is found precisely in the words which are spoken alongside the apparently rigid truth. What sustains the poem are those words that are true to the deeper and incomparably more immediate truth of the invisible soul. One might even say that the poem gets closer to beauty and to a higher truth to the extent that it eliminates words which explain action and replaces them with words which explain not what is sometimes called 'the state of the soul' but those unknown elusive and ceaseless struggles of the soul towards its beauty and its truth. This is also the measure of how far it approaches true life. It happens to everyone in their everyday life that they have to negotiate very serious situations through words. Imagine it for a second. At such moments, is it always (or ever?) what you say or how you respond that matters the most? Are other forces, other words which we do not hear, at work determining what happens? What I say often counts for little; but my presence, the attitude of my soul, my future and past, what will be born in me, what has died in me, a secret thought, the stars supporting me, my destiny, thousands of mysteries encircling me, surrounding you – that is what speaks to you at that moment of tragedy and that is what answers. Beneath each of my words and beneath each of yours, all of that exists, and it is principally this that we see and principally this that we hear, despite ourselves. If you appeared, you 'the scorned husband', 'the deceived lover', 'the abandoned wife', with the intention of killing me, it is not my most eloquent pleas that would stay your hand. But it may be that you will come up against one of these unforeseen forces and that my soul, which knows that they throng around me, utters a secret word which disarms you. Those are the realms in which these episodes are decided, this is the dialogue for whose echo one should listen. And it's that echo – extremely weak and intermittent, it's true – which one really hears in a few of those works which I have spoken a little about. But couldn't one try to get a little nearer to those realms in which everything takes place 'really'?

I think the effort is being made. Recently, working on *The Master Builder*, the play of Ibsen's in which this 'second level' dialogue resonates most tragically, I tried once again to clumsily penetrate its secrets. And yet, these are the analogous traces of the hand of the same blind man on the same wall and which direct themselves also towards the same glimmers. In *The Master Builder*, I would ask what has the poet added to life to make it appear so strange, so profound and so disturbing beneath its apparent simplicity? It's not easy to discern and the old master keeps more than one secret. It is even as though what he wanted to say is nothing against what he was *compelled* to say. He has released certain powers of the soul which had never been given their freedom, and perhaps he was taken over by them. 'See, Hilde,' exclaims Solness, 'See! There is sorcery in you just as there is in me. It is that sorcery which stirs up the powers out there. And we *have* to accept them. Whether you want to or not, you *have to*.'[1]

There is sorcery in them just as in all of us. Hilde and Solness are, I think, the first heroes who felt themselves to be living in the environment of their soul and the essential life that they have discovered in themselves, beyond everyday life, terrifies them. Hilde and Solness are two souls that have glimpsed their position in the true life. There is more than one way to know someone. There are, for example, two or three people that I see more or less every day. It is probable for a long time that I will only identify them by their gestures, their outward and inward habits, their ways of feeling, acting and thinking. But, in a really long friendship, there comes a curious moment when we perceive, as it were, the exact place of our friend in relation to the unknown which surrounds us, and the attitude of destiny towards him. It's from that moment on that he really belongs to us. We have seen once and for all the way things are through his eyes. We know that however much he withdraws to the privacy of his home, and stays as still as he can for fear of disturbing something in the great chasms of the future, his caution will do no good, and those numberless things destined for him will knock at each of his doors in turn, and find him wherever he hides himself. And yet, we also know that he will go out, seeking pointlessly for any adventure. He will always come back empty-handed. The day our eyes are opened like this, it is as though a perfect science beyond the scope of mere reason were born in our soul, and we know that events which may seem to be within his grasp, within such a man's reach, will never come to pass.

From that moment, a special part of the soul presides over the friendship even of the dullest and the most humble. There is a kind of transposition of life. And when we bump into one of those who knows us like this, while all the time talking to us about the snow falling or the women passing by, there is in each of us a little something that acknowledges, examines, questions without knowing it; takes an interest in circumstances and speaks of events impossible for us to understand ...

I believe that Hilde and Solness find themselves in that state and understand each other like this. Their conversations do not resemble anything that we have heard before now, because the poet has tried to contain that internal and external dialogue in the same language. Who knows what new forces govern this sleepwalking drama? Everything said in it both conceals and reveals the sources of an unknown life. And if at times we are overwhelmed, we must not lose sight of the fact that, to our dim eyes, our soul often seems a wholly deranged force, and that there are many aspects to mankind more fertile, more profound and more interesting than those of reason and intelligence ...

Notes

1. The quotation comes from near the end of Act 2. See Henrik Ibsen, *Four Major Plays*, trans. James MacFarlane and Jens Arup, ed. James MacFarlane. World's Classics. 2nd edn. Oxford: Oxford University Press, 1994, p. 323.

The extract is from *Le Trésor des Humbles* (The Treasure of the Humble), Préface de Marc Rombaut, Lecture d'Albert Spinette. Espace Nord. Bruxelles: Éditions Labor, 1986, pp. 101–10. Translated by Dan Rebellato. This is a chapter from Maeterlinck's book of poetic-philosophical meditations, *The Treasure of the Humble*. Here he defends the stillness, silence and mystery of his plays, which stand in sharp contrast to the clamorous action of Romantic drama, the intricate plotting of the well-made play and the mundane detail of naturalism. Instead he argues for a kind of anti-dramatic drama of stillness and contemplation, the better to reveal our place in the mysterious universe.

1.11 On the Complete Pointlessness of Accurate Staging (1891)

PIERRE QUILLARD

Translated by Dan Rebellato

Sir,

IN THE 15TH APRIL issue of *Revue d'Art Dramatique*, your contributor M. Pierre Véber reported, with politely ironic neutrality, on the performance at the Théâtre d'Art, on Friday 27 March.[1] He briefly refers to one of the aspects of what we attempted that evening, in *The Girl with the Severed Hands*: a complete simplification of the dramatic means. Please permit me a little space to set out in a little more detail and without obscurity the innovation in staging I attempted. Also, the *mise en scène* necessarily depends on the dramatic system adopted, and since there are symbols, the *mise en scène* is a sign and a symbol in itself.

Nowhere is the inanity of Naturalism more clearly apparent than in the theatre. Think of the splendours of the Théâtre Libre. Time and time again, we've watched Monsieur Antoine die there with accomplished art (for want of a better word); men and women, whores and pimps have had the most banal conversations there and made the crudest remarks, *just like in real life*; each statement, on its own, was truthful and the author might have heard them from his caretaker, his lawyer, or from people passing on the street or any dull ordinary person you like. But this dialogue showed nothing whatever of how one character differed from his neighbour or what constitutes in him the *quid proprium* that distinguishes one monad from another. To create the complete illusion of life, it was thought clever to build scrupulously accurate sets, real fountains murmuring centre stage and meat dripping blood on the butcher's stall.[2] And yet, despite the meticulous care with which the whole exterior of things is represented, the drama was misplaced and unfathomable and the illusion entirely lacking. The truth is that Naturalism, by which I mean making use of specific facts, of trifling and arbitrary documents, is the very opposite of theatre.

The whole of drama is above all a synthesis: Prometheus, Orestes, Oedipus, Hamlet, Don Juan are creatures of a general humanity, in whom a single-minded and commanding passion is embodied with extraordinary intensity. The poet has breathed supernatural life into them; he created them by force of language, and set them off across the world, pilgrims in eternity. Dress them in tattered smocks and if Aeschylus or Shakespeare has crowned them, they will be kings, and their absent ermine robes will shine forth joyously, if they gleam in the verse. A universe unfolds around them, sadder or more magnificent than our own, and the grotesque backcloths of the travelling circus are the dream architecture that the poet places in the mind of the willing spectator. *The word creates the set and everything else as well.*

So what's left of the stagehand's job? All that's required is that the staging does not disturb the illusion in any way and to do that it should be as simple as possible. I write 'a marvellous palace'; even if a scene-painter were somehow to represent it using the most ingenious artistry they can devise, the effect produced by all that trickery will never equal 'a marvellous palace' for anyone; in each person's soul these words evoke a particular, personal image, which will be in conflict with any crude scenic representation; far from aiding the free play of the imagination, painted canvas impairs it. *The set must be a pure ornamental fiction which completes the illusion with colour and lines analogous to the drama.* Generally, a backdrop and some moveable drapes are all you need to suggest the infinite multiplicity of time and place. The spectator will not be distracted from the action any more by noises in the wings, or an incongruous prop; he will give himself up completely to the will of the poet and see, depending on his soul, terrible and enchanting figures and imaginary worlds that none but he will enter; the theatre will be what it has to be: *a chance to dream.*

This aesthetic is by no means new, indeed it is as old as history. In the first act of *The Recognition of Śakuntalā*, on a motionless chariot, the driver mimes the passion of a race; the horses, he says, 'thrust the air apart, their wake / Is thunder; in our tracks they leave for dust / The very dust they raised ...';[3] for those willing souls who were present at the traditional recital of this ancient masterpiece, this is undoubtedly a more perfect illusion of a wild-horse ride than that given to those sophisticated Parisians, sitting in the *Variétés* watching the horses of *Paris Pont de Mer*;[4] the latter know perfectly well that it's nothing more than ingenious stage machinery, but the former wouldn't even have contemplated such childish artifice. We need only recall Greek theatre and its masks, or the featureless stages of classical tragedy. These are similar means by which an informed spectator would collaborate in the drama: why would he not give himself, now as then, to this sacred art when he happily puts up with vaudeville's most wretched contrivances?

At least for one evening the audience didn't have to ignore the inadequacy of the set: listening to and deservedly applauding Mme Rachilde's *Lady Death*;[5] however, the characters were *contemporary* and perhaps one might have expected some confusion or surprise; but they existed, *in themselves*, over and above their time and its happenstance, with such independence that no one noticed how unusual the middle-class dining room was in which they moved; for everyone, the stage perfectly represented the sombre, black-draped smoking room where Paul Dartigny dies, since the dialogue hung funeral veils over your face and deepened the mysterious and sacred shadow around you.

It would be childish arrogance to say that all drama should be like this in the future. But we might say that an art form of this kind in which the poet, putting aside all other means and using only the word and the human voice, has no room for trickery – the work stands quite naked, stripped of make-up, reveals right away its native beauty or its original stain. Perhaps this kind of honesty is arrogant, but nothing is without risk.

Notes

1. Pierre Véber, 'Au Théâtre d'Art', *Revue d'Art Dramatique*, 22 (1891): 115–17. The passage to which Quillard seems particularly to be responding is: 'finally, Mr Quillard's experiment may be summarized as follows: a complete simplification of the dramatic means; a narrator, placed at the corner of the proscenium, describes the stage, the setting and the action. The main focus is on poetic language. Theatre as such disappears entirely, to make way for a series of declamations in dialogue form, a kind of decorative poetry. Maeterlinck never went so far' (p. 117). – *Translator.*

2. On 20 October 1888, Antoine staged Giovanni Verga's *Cavelleria Rusticana* and Fernand Icres' *The Butchers* and his decisions to create a working fountain for the Verga and to hang real meat in the butcher's shop set attracted both admiration and ridicule. – *Translator.*

3. I have quoted these lines from a modern translation of this first-millennium Sanskrit play: Kālidāsa, *The Recognition of Śakuntalā*, trans. W. J. Johnson, World's Classics, Oxford: Oxford University Press, 2001, pp. 7–8. The play was eventually performed at the Théâtre de l'Oeuvre in December 1895. – *Translator.*

4. *Paris Port de Mer* was a spectacular theatrical revue by Henri Blondeau and Hector Monréal which opened at the Théâtre des Variétés in March 1891 and included a celebrated staging of a horse race. – *Translator.*

5. Mme Rachilde's *Lady Death* (*Madame La Mort*) was performed on the same evening as Quillard's *The Girl with the Severed Hands*. Its central character is Paul Dartigny. – *Translator.*

Pierre Quillard (1864–1912) was a poet, playwright and journalist who published his first play, *The Girl with the Severed Hands*, in *La Pléiade* (1886), a journal he had co-founded two years earlier. This mystical work was performed at the Théâtre d'Art in March 1891, in a visionary and experimental production. When a reviewer in *Revue d'Art Dramatique* lightly mocked the evening, Quillard wrote a celebrated defence of Symbolist theatre practices (and attacked Naturalism as he did so), which we publish here. His 'On the Complete Pointlessness of Accurate Staging' is translated for the present volume by Dan Rebellato from Pierre Quillard, 'De l'inutilité absolue de la mise on scène exacte', *Revue d'Art Dramatique*, 22 (1 May 1891): 180–3.

Part 2
The Historical Avant-Garde: Performance and Innovation

Timeline

	Social, cultural and political context	Theatre
1893	*On the Psychical Mechanism of Hysterical Phenomena*: Sigmund Freud and Josef Breuer	
1895	First films made	
1896		*King Ubu* (*Ubu Roi*): Alfred Jarry, Paris
1900	*The Interpretation of Dreams*: Sigmund Freud	
1901	*A Dream Play*: August Strindberg	
1902	First transatlantic radiotelegraph message (Guglielmo Marconi)	
1907		Alfred Jarry dies
1909		*Foundation and Manifesto of Futurism* published on the front page of Parisian newspaper *Le Figaro*
		Murderer the Women's Hope: Oskar Kokoschka
1910		First Futurist *serate*, Italy
1911		*On the Art of the Theatre*: Edward Gordon Craig
		Manifesto of Futurist Playwrights (*The Pleasure of Being Booed*)
1912	The sinking of the *Titanic*	
1913	Post-Impressionism and Cubism introduced in New York	Marinetti's *Variety Theatre Manifesto*
1914	Start of the First World War (1914–1918)	
1916		Dada exhibitions and Cabaret Voltaire, Zurich
1917	America enters the First World War	*The Breasts of Tiresias*: Guillaume Apollinaire
	Russian Revolution	First Dada Exhibition, Paris
	Carl Jung's *The Psychology of the Unconscious* translated into English	Tristan Tzara launches the movement Dada and publishes *Dada 1*
	Marcel Duchamp, famous for his Dada 'ready-mades', submits his sculpture *Fountain* (a porcelain urinal, signed by R. Mutt) to an exhibition of the Society for Independent Artists in New York	Pablo Picasso creates the designs for Jean Cocteau's *Parade*, Paris
1918	End of the First World War	*Baal*: Bertolt Brecht (first produced in 1923)
		Gas: Georg Kaiser, Berlin
1919	*The Cabinet of Dr Caligari* (Expressionist film)	
1920	The League of Nations formed	First Paris Dada event

	Social, cultural and political context	Theatre
1921		*The Wedding on the Eiffel Tower*: Jean Cocteau
		Dada Festival at the Salle Gaveau, with performance of work by Tristan Tzara and André Breton
		First production of *Six Characters in Search of an Author*: Luigi Pirandello
1922	Mussolini elected to power in Italy	American premiere of *R.U.R (Rossum's Universal Robots)*: Karel Čapek
1923		London premiere of *R.U.R (Rossum's Universal Robots)*: Karel Čapek
1924		*First Surrealist Manifesto*: André Breton
1925		*The Spurt of Blood*: Antonin Artaud (unperformed until the late 1960s)
1926	British General Strike	Théâtre Alfred Jarry founded in Paris by Antonin Artaud and Roger Vitrac
1927	*Metropolis* (Expressionist film by Fritz Lang, Germany)	
1929	Surrealist artist Salvador Dalí collaborates with the Surrealist film director Luis Buñuel on the film *Un Chien Andalou (An Andalusian Dog)*	*The Second Surrealist Manifesto*: André Breton
	Wall Street Financial Crash	
1932		*First Manifesto of the Theatre of Cruelty*: Antonin Artaud
1933		*Second Manifesto of The Theatre of Cruelty*: Antonin Artaud
1936	Start of the Spanish Civil War (1936–9)	
	First public television broadcast	
1938		Gertrude Stein's *Dr Faustus Lights the Lights* written
		Artaud's seminal book *The Theatre and Its Double* published in French

Introduction

MAGGIE B. GALE

What has our culture lost in 1980 that the *avant-garde* had in 1890? ... above all the sense that art, in the most disinterested and noble way, could find the necessary metaphors by which a radically changing culture could be explained to its inhabitants. (Hughes 1991: 9)

The Modernists struggled against entrenched rules and conventions, yet never challenged the guardians of established cultural institutions ... avant-garde art was not only characterized by opposition, protest, negativity; it also experimented with new forms of expression and anticipated in its creations a liberated arts practice. (Berghaus 2005: 39)

THE HISTORICAL AVANT-GARDE, WHICH provides the overarching framework for the materials included in Part 2, is named as such here and elsewhere in order to distinguish between it and 'new' avant-garde art and performance which emerged towards the end of the twentieth century. It is firmly located within the turbulence of Europe at the end of the nineteenth century and the years immediately preceding and following the First World War (1914–18). The original contexts for productions of the materials included in Part 2 vary, from cabaret venues to mainstream theatres. With a focus on four prominent and inter-connecting modernist movements within the historical avant-garde – Dada, Surrealism, Expressionism and Futurism – often characterized by their anti-establishment, anti-traditionalist, politically and socially inflammatory and intertextual or hybrid nature, Part 2 also includes plays which are clearly influenced by avant-garde practices, but which do not adhere to any one 'ism' (see 2.8; 2.9; 2.10).

The historical avant-garde: a context

The experimental practices from the early decades of the twentieth century have continued to influence the development of performance as a social practice, aesthetic proposition and cultural product in the twenty-first century. Many of these demanded a radical transformation in the meaning and function of theatre, and challenged existing forms and practices. They also linked theatre to developments in innovative art practices and mark a definite turning point in the move away from the dominance of the literary text.

For a number of historians and critics, 'the avant-garde typically expresses itself through obscure and innovative techniques deliberately resisting easy assimilation into popular or mass culture' (Edgar and Sedgwick 2008: 33). The paradox is that much avant-garde theorizing about the role and function of theatre and performance sought to respond to and engage the 'masses' and counter the lack of representation or connection they found in the bourgeois theatres of the day. However, John Carey suggests that the modernists stigmatized what they saw as 'the masses', the crowd, the common man, playing into cultural anxieties about the new levels of relatively increased social agency which the proletariat began to experience during the early twentieth century (see Carey 1992). Numerous theoretical and performance texts produced by the historical avant-garde made reference to the validity of popular cultural and performance forms which they perceived as the art of the masses. For example, they embraced popular non-literary performance – circus, variety or, as in the case of Antonin Artaud, traditional non-Western performance styles (Balinese dance) – as a means of extricating theatre and performance from the stranglehold of the bourgeois and the literary, the text, the word.

The end of the nineteenth and beginning of the twentieth centuries were times of great social and cultural upheaval, and the devastation caused by the First World War had a profound impact both globally and locally. The historical avant-garde both developed before and cut across the war and operated, in a constant state of flux, until well into the middle of the twentieth century. Whilst it often removed itself from a direct engagement with the 'class' war (see Part 3), many practitioners whose work is aligned with the historical avant-garde were driven by political concerns from one end of the political spectrum to another – from the political left to fascism – but with a shared agenda for subversion and a countercultural stance. As had the Naturalists and the Symbolists before them, avant-garde artists asked questions about the function, purpose and cultural value of the artwork, through poetry, film, photography, painting, performance or hybrid performance events.

The historical avant-garde: definitions

> The historical roots of the term 'avant-garde' lie in French military terminology. The term was apparently first tied to art by Henri de Saint Simon (1760–1825) … In his last major work *Opinions littéraires, philosophiques et industrielles* (1925) [he] … proposed a utopian society to be led by a triumvirate of scientists, industrialist-artisans, and artists, with the last constituting an elite force within this group of leaders. (Aronson 2000: 6)

The historical avant-garde set out to restructure 'the way in which an audience views and experiences the very act of theatre, which in turn must transform the way in which the spectators view themselves and their world' (ibid: 7), and to 'transform society while standing apart from it' (ibid: 6). There is no other movement which so radically transformed what we understand as theatre or performance. Günter Berghaus notes that the historical avant-garde 'modified the categories of representation and enriched them with new techniques that went beyond the traditional "art holding a mirror to nature" concepts connected with Realism and to some extent Naturalism' (Berghaus 2005: 33; see also Part 1). It is certainly the case that a performance text such as Alfred Jarry's *King Ubu*, for example (see 2.1), or Gertrude Stein's *Dr Faustus Lights the Lights* (2.10), could not be further removed in terms of an artistic agenda from a play such as Strindberg's *Miss Julie* (1.2). But go further forward in the career of a playwright such as Strindberg and a play like his *Ghost Sonata* (1907) might have much more in common with avant-garde concerns. Similarly, despite its lack of logic or sense of cause and effect, Apollinaire's Surrealist *The Breasts of Tiresias* (2.2) has very little immediately in common with Kokoschka's Expressionist *Murderer the Women's Hope* (2.4). At times there are only broad similarities and shared discourses between the work and theory of those who we would consider to belong to the historical avant-garde. Certainly many of its practitioners critiqued what they saw as the 'destructive forces of industrialisation' and the ways in which the rapid development of the 'urban wastelands' of the mid- to late nineteenth century had created a society in which humankind experienced alienation and estrangement (Berghaus 2005: 32). But others, such as the Futurists, famously celebrated the possibilities of destruction brought about by war, the alienating characteristics of urban and industrial modernization and so on.

The historical avant-garde: the philosophical, the populist and the primitive

Christopher Innes's framework of the philosophical, the populist and the primitive is useful as a means of understanding the diversity of the historical avant-garde. He has suggested that although the 'signature' of the historical avant-garde was an 'unremitting hostility to contemporary civilisation', there was always an underlying agenda to find a 'utopian alternative to the *status quo*' (Innes 1993: 6). Innes identifies three strands to this project: the philosophical, the populist and the primitive. In line with the ideas promoted by the Russian anarchist philosopher Mikhail Bakunin (1814–76), the politics of the historical avant-garde in general terms leaned towards the anarchistic, founded as they were upon a belief in individualism and a 'fluid sense of individual fulfillment' (ibid). But there are still inherent contradictions: for example, many of their political ideas implied collective action, as in fact did Bakunin's and those of his followers. What many of the historical avant-garde did share in common, however, was a determined anti-establishment position manifest in their continual barrage against the cultural dominance of the bourgeoisie. They saw the bourgeoisie as watering down or flattening out the revolutionary potential of the arts, promoting and consuming a level of mediocrity, which in turn reflected nothing but the staid quality of their own lives.

Innes also sees the historical avant-garde as connecting to 'populist' culture in its alignment with Mikhail Bakhtin's (1895–1975) identification of the 'counter-cultural' potential of the carnivalesque (ibid: 7). Writing in the 1930s, philosopher and cultural theorist Bakhtin described the performance of carnival – with its reversals of hierarchy, sensual materiality, and displays of both the grotesque and the beautiful, its mixture of the bodily and the communal – as revolutionary. He saw folk traditions as 'multi-tonal or dialogic' – a model that allows for fluid interchange of ideas and experience rather than the solidification of culture as represented by the bourgeois hegemony. Reflecting on what he viewed to be the contemporary crisis in Russian culture, Bakhtin saw carnival as belonging to 'the borderline between art and life' (Bakhtin 1984: 7). This deconstruction and reformulation of the relationship between art and life are also central to a great deal of practice within the historical avant-garde. Similarly for Bakhtin, physical, embodied, communal and festive cultures should be valued against the literary, hierarchical, non-collective world of bourgeois art. Others have pointed to the way in which Bakhtin's 'carnivalesque' validates the collective experience and the democratic and utopian vision of the 'texture of public life' which carnival offers (Hirschkop and Shepherd 1989: 35). We can see echoes of these ideas in Jarry's *King Ubu* (2.1) and Apollinaire's *The Breasts of Tiresias* (2.2).

The last aspect of Innes's framework for analysis here is the primitive. Whilst some of the historical avant-garde, such as the Futurists, celebrated the excitement and promise of catastrophe provided by the speed and impact of technological development on our experience of the world, others showed a generic 'hostility to modern society and all the artistic forms that reflect its assumptions' (Innes 1993: 9). There was a significant element of the historical avant-garde that turned to the non-European – to African art or Balinese dance, for example. Here the attraction was related to a desire to move away from what was seen as the rational, the intellectual, the logical – towards art which reflected the primal, the ritualistic, the shamanistic, the earthy, the spiritual and the subliminal. This turn to the primitive might be viewed in retrospect as a form of colonialism – an imbuing of non-Western art with an essentialist character of the exotic 'other'. As contemporary performance artist Coco Fusco, writing from the perspective of the end of the twentieth century, notes, the historical avant-garde fetishized the 'primitive' – aligning it with a binary of civilized versus savage (see Fusco 2002: 270 and *The Breasts of Tiresias*, 2.2). It is certainly the case that the historical avant-garde adopted particular aspects of non-Western cultures and often decontextualized them as a means of finding an alternative to the staid bourgeois culture with which they saw themselves as being surrounded. Here Elin Diamond's observation is pertinent: 'primitivism sits on a pile of simple ahistorical essentialisms … To the "civilized" eye, the primitive signifies an enticing and inferior otherness, a projection of white culture's repressed libidinal forces' (Diamond 2006: 113). Whilst she notes that primitivism was a 'pervasive aesthetic' adopted by numerous and differing modernist playwrights, she sees it as one of modernism's many 'transatlantic curiosities' (ibid: 114). There was indeed a colonial context for what was thought at the time to be a radical and revolutionary cultural positioning. Whilst Innes notes the colonialist roots of an idea such as 'primitivism', he suggests, 'the attempt to reproduce the effects of the "primitive" … helps to explain avant-garde elements that might otherwise seem puzzling, such as the apparent incompatibility of stressing emotional authenticity and using stylized movement or unnatural gesture to express it' (Innes 1993: 18). This is particularly apparent in works such as Artaud's *The Spurt of Blood* (2.3) and Kokoschka's *Murderer the Women's Hope* (2.4), to which we return later.

Taking into account Innes's three tropes as frameworks for exploring the historical avant-garde – the philosophical, the populist and the primitive – it is useful to turn to an exploration of the play that signalled the beginnings of the historical avant-garde, Jarry's seminal *King Ubu* (2.1), which although written and first performed at the end of the nineteenth century, heavily influenced and is integral to an understanding of the development of the historical avant-garde in Europe.

Alfred Jarry (1873–1907): *King Ubu* (2.1)

Alfred Jarry's *King Ubu* opens with a play on the French word for shit, 'Merde' or as it is translated in the version included in this anthology, 'Shikt'. The uproar and outrage after this utterance in the original production notoriously halted the stage action (Melzer 1994: 110–11). First produced in the respected and largely middle-class Parisian theatre of 1896, the play caused a public outcry. Jarry himself was no stranger to controversy and even courted it; 'eccentric to the point of mania and lucid to the point of hallucination', Jarry's public persona reflected his alcoholism and his disrespect for the social habits of the bourgeoisie (Shattuck and Taylor 1980: 9). Known for his social pranks, such as painting himself entirely green with the intention of eliciting shock from his friends when he entered a café, Jarry became obsessed with the character he created in *King Ubu*. He wrote many plays and sketches centred on Ubu, as well as numerous articles on philosophy, art, politics and theatre (see Schumacher 1985). Jarry's collection of articles, which he titled *The Green Candle*, was not published until over sixty years after his death, in 1969 (ibid: 33), but his novel, *Exploits and Opinions of Dr Faustroll, Pataphysician*, published in 1898, was later recognized by the Surrealists as 'one of the most influential books written in the nineteenth century' (ibid: 34).

King Ubu bears little relation to any dramatic text that came before it in terms of character, action or plot, but it adapts the deceptively conventional structuring device of a Shakespearian play – five acts divided into short scenes.

The play opens with Ma Ubu persuading Ubu to take up arms:

MA UBU: … Thane of Four-door, you used to be. Now who follows you? Fifty sausage-knotters in procession. Forget Four-door. Get your loaf measured for the crown of Baloney. (2.1: 190)

Her ambitious suggestions for Ubu's career development and the reference to the Thane of Four-door (an indirect reference to the place Cawdor in *Macbeth*) immediately reminds us of Lady Macbeth. Indeed, Jarry deliberately plays with the classic, subverting and borrowing at will from Shakespeare's play. With his army officer Dogpile and the Barmpots, Ubu sets out to conquer through violence, dishonesty and sheer dogged determination. Jarry speeds the audience through the five short acts, which move from private rooms to palace courtyards, to the parade ground, to a cave in the mountains, to a dungeon, to a camp outside the city, to 'the middle of nowhere' and finally ends 'on board a ship skimming the ocean'. An unspeakable monster who is content to destroy everyone in his path, Ubu is pompous and violent but also witty. He is 'amoral, anti-social … self serving' and greedy, and, as Innes notes, 'a figure symbolizing all that bourgeois morality condemns is claimed to be representative of the real basis of bourgeois society' (Innes 1993: 23). Claude Schumacher suggests that the 'basic material' of the play is 'that of all revenge tragedies – or Shakespeare's histories', pointing out, however, that just as Jarry had no intention of writing a 'history play so too none of the characters in the play relate to any "real" people', just as the country in which the play is set – 'Poland' – is 'devoid of any geographical reality' (Schumacher 1985: 45). Jarry subverted an existing cultural referent to create something new and this he had in common with many of the historical avant-garde whom he later inspired. For Jarry, 'a play ought to be a kind of public holiday' (Shattuck and Watson Taylor 1965: 87) – an idea which links directly to the carnivalesque – and this is borne out in the playfulness of *King Ubu*. Just as the text is removed from the traditional dramatic literature of its day – it has more in common with the Surrealist and later Absurdist texts (see Esslin 2001 and Part 4) – so too the staging requirements of the play went beyond anything available in the theatre of the time – such quick location changes were not possible in a box set or proscenium-arch theatre with minimally flexible stage machinery. Jarry disliked the staging conventions of the '1890s as an unacceptable compromise between artefact and nature', and wanted for his play 'an abstract set, an artificial environment' (Schumacher 1985: 48). He made the set with innovative artists of the day including Pierre Bonnard (1867–1947) and Henri Toulouse-Lautrec (1864–1901), and in his famous letter to director Lugné-Poë (1869–1840) (see Part 1: Introduction) Jarry insisted on the use of masks, cardboard horses' heads referring to the fact that he had originally wanted to write *King Ubu* as a puppet play – plain backdrop, crowds being played by single performers, special vocal intonation and non-referential costumes, 'divorced as far as possible from local colour or chronology' (Melzer 1994: 110–11). The testimony from W. B. Yeats is perhaps most useful in its ability to give a sense of the way in which the play created the potential for a seismic cultural shift:

I go to the first performance of Jarry's *Ubu Roi* ... with Rhymer ... [who] explains to me what is happening on the stage. The players are supposed to be dolls, toys, marionettes, and now they are all hopping like wooden frogs, and I can see for myself that the chief personage, who is some kind of king, carries for a sceptre a brush of the kind we use to clean a closet [toilet]. Feeling bound to support the most spirited party, we have shouted for the play ... I am very sad ... after our own verse ... what more is possible? After us the Savage God. (qtd in Melzer 1994: 118)

Yeats astutely observed, in retrospect, that for all the innovations and advances made by the new wave of artists at the end of the nineteenth century – and this would include those whose work was discussed in Part 1 of this anthology – what Jarry's play indicated – anarchic, fast-paced and irreverent as it is – was a completely new direction, the response to which combined 'disgust and wonder, fear and awe, distance and familiarity', a form of what would later be termed as 'estrangement' (Taxidou 2007: 1; and see Part 3).

Jarry died in abject poverty at a young age, but not before he had befriended the influential art critic – amongst his many other occupations – Guillaume Apollinaire (1880–1918). Apollinaire, who also died very young, was one of a coterie of artists which included Pablo Picasso (1881–1973) and Max Jacob (1876–1944), and was central to the artistic and philosophical developments brought about by the historical avant-garde, especially those of the Surrealists. Before moving on to explore Surrealism and its impact on theatre and performance practice, however, it is useful to briefly explore Dada, the movement which preceded it and which, in part, Surrealism was a reaction to.

Dada

Much Dada performance – improvisational and characterized by the rough and ready – happened in a cabaret setting. During the First World War, many artists fled to Zurich, which was not operating under the same censorious atmosphere created in many European cities by the war. Here there were no ration stamps and 'newspapers printed what they pleased' (Melzer 1994: 11). It was in this atmosphere of relative freedom that Dada and Dadaism developed at the Cabaret Voltaire where, from 1916, cabaret evenings with an audience capacity of around fifty and organized by a group of artists including Hugo Ball (1886–1927), Emmy Hennings (1885–1948), Hans Arp (1886–1966) and Tristan Tzara (1896–1963) – who heavily influenced the Surrealists – took place. The evenings consisted of performances centred on poetry, music and language play, where the semantic meaning of words gave way to their tonal and rhythmic qualities, just as the word Dada has no meaning but is, rather, a play on sounds. As the cabaret developed, so the performances became more experimental in nature with consistent use of masks and sound poems. For Hugo Ball, 'The Dadaist loves the extraordinary and the absurd ... He therefore welcomes any kind of mask. Any game of hide and seek, with its inherent power to deceive' (Melzer 1994: 33), and his reading of what happens to the performer when they wear a mask takes us back to Innes's recognition of the historical avant-garde's obsession with the primitive to some extent. 'Man suddenly finds himself placed before an image of himself which he didn't suspect existed and which plunges him into terror ... at the limits of his reason' (ibid: 33). Melzer notes that the conceptualization and practice of Dada happened incrementally with theory and practice developing alongside one another. She identifies key characteristics of this development, with simultaneity and montage as central: so one poem might be read/performed by any number of performers in different rhythms at the same time as each other, for example. There was within Dada, which is perhaps why Tristan Tzara formed an early association with the Surrealists, a refusal to adhere to logic or to pander to the desire to 'make meaning' in art. Heavily influenced by painters such as Wassily Kandinsky (1886–1944), there are relatively few extant performance texts compared to the artworks and poetry produced from within Dada. As a movement, Dada's boundaries are blurred and its definitions flexible, as Melzer notes: 'Dada's raging manifestos do not help to clarify the movement; rather, they reinforce its many ambiguities' (ibid: 57). This was deliberate for a movement which critiqued the commodification of art objects and focused more on experimenting with art as *process* and as *action*. Such a critique of the commodification of art is no more evident than in the famous *Fountain* by Marcel Duchamp, a porcelain urinal signed by the imaginary artist R. Mutt and submitted to an exhibition of contemporary art in New York (Part 2: Timeline). *Fountain* is a ready-made, everyday object transformed into 'art' through its cultural/commodity framing – it has a title, is signed by an 'artist' and is submitted to a gallery as an exhibit.

In the Dada performance text included in this volume, *Genius in a Jiffy or a Dadalogy* by Raoul Hausmann (2.7), there is a critical exploration of the relationship between the artist and the artwork. The text was written in 1920 by Hausmann (1886–1971), who had been part of the Expressionist movement in Germany, working on the art/philosophy magazine *Der Sturm*. A painter and photographer by trade, he developed a photomontage technique the use of which became common practice amongst the avant-garde. Hausmann's play opens on a darkened stage where 'breakfast rolls rain down in the moonlight' (2.7: 228). The Engineer Dada enters the stage, 'Out of the past', and states that he is expecting something to happen in the 'present revolutionary atmosphere' (ibid). He curses those who know nothing about art, one of whom, the Dadasophist, enters the stage and complains that he has sprained his hand and can't produce, calling the Engineer a 'wage-slave'. The Engineer tells him to get on with his work and that he should be paid for his own ideas. They then discuss the meaning of Dada, get 'eaten up by two Berlin Daily editors' and someone in the audience shouts that 'Dada's a hoax'. The text is playful but almost entirely self-referential, reflecting the infighting and disagreement which was characteristic of many of the movements within the historical avant-garde, but in particular amongst the conflictual Dadaists, whose desire to constantly reinvent themselves and the philosophy of Dada is one reason why the movement in its purest form was short-lived. Although only a brief text, Hausmann's play typifies the Dadaist 'adversarial position towards accepted moral attitudes and assailed them by means of satire' (Senelick 1989: 9). Such hostility to traditional art forms and the deliberate embracing of the illogical and the satirical characterize a great deal of Surrealist practice, and is epitomized in the earliest 'surrealist' drama, *The Breasts of Tiresias*.

Guillaume Apollinaire: *The Breasts of Tiresias* (2.2)

Named by Apollinaire as a 'surrealist drama', his 1917 play *The Breasts of Tiresias* caused as much outrage as Jarry's had done more than twenty years earlier. The play has all the aesthetic and philosophical earmarks of the Surrealist movement, which, led by André Breton (1896–1966), was to follow in Paris in the mid-1920s. Apollinaire had a coterie of followers, and it was they who flocked to see the production of the play along with the critics of many of the leading Parisian newspapers and journals. As with Jarry's earlier play, the structure of *The Breasts of Tiresias* adheres to a traditional act and scene format; even so the production caused great scandal because of its subject matter, modes and registers of performance, and the synthetic décor such as masks, a patchwork of houses on the backdrop, unconventional musical instruments and the giant child's wooden horse ridden by the Policeman. Set largely in the public space of 'The market place at Zanzibar', the play exposes an anxiety about the 'battle of the sexes' as much as it suggests a bizarre world in which one of the Husband's young children is an entrepreneurial businessman making his father a great deal of money in 'the curdled milk trade', and another is a best-selling novelist. Thérèse (Tiresias) opens the play by declaring that:

> I am a feminist and I do not recognize the authority of men … Men have been doing what they like long enough … I want to make war and not make children. No Mister Husband you won't give me orders. (2.2: 207)

After this her breasts, 'one red, the other blue', fly off 'like toy balloons', but 'remain attached by strings' and she sprouts a beard and moustache. Whilst the theme of the play is clearly underpinned by cultural anxiety around women's increased levels of social agency, it is neither a feminist nor an anti-feminist text. Athough Apollinaire states his disquiet, in the preface to the play, about the falling French birth rate, 'we don't make children in France anymore because we don't make love enough. That is all there is to it!' (Apollinaire 1964: 59), this is not a polemical play despite its astute social and cultural critique. The text vacillates between declaration and dialogue, between fast-paced banter and ranting provocation. Music and dialogue intersect and interplay with one another as the action is punctuated by a cacophony of sounds. This is a play which makes unashamed reference to the 'primitive' in its setting and its appropriation of a 'savage' protocol of human relations. More than anything, however, the comic and grotesque are embedded within the anti-logic of the text: the play 'tells a story' but not in any strictly chronological sense nor in any way which allows us to identify with any of the characters, some of whom represent social types – Policeman, Reporter – or simply an embodied object – Kiosk.

Apollinaire, as is the case for many of the historical avant-garde artists who followed him, theorized about the need to transform the theatre, to make it more reflective of the disorientating chaos of a world – that is, Europe – in flux. He also wanted it to embrace more popular performance forms, and move away from concrete representation towards abstraction. As he states in the preface to the play:

> After all, the stage is no more the life it represents than the wheel is a leg. Consequently it is legitimate … to bring to the theatre new and striking aesthetic principles which accentuate the roles of the actors and increase the effect of the production … to protest against that 'realistic' theatre which is predominating theatrical art today. This 'realism', which is no doubt suited to the cinema, is, I believe, as far removed as possible from the art of drama. (Apollinaire 1964: 59–60)

For Apollinaire, theatre has the potential to raise 'humanity above the mere appearance of things' (ibid) and he saw the refusal to pander to tradition as a means of achieving this. Similar to the Symbolists who came before him (see Part 1), Apollinaire believed theatre and performance could thrive on the exploration of what lies under the surface of the 'real' with which the Naturalists were concerned; that theatre could explore the repressed, the unstated and so on. We can see this belief reflected in the 'Surrealist Manifestos' which are examined later (2.13), but a further investigation of both Apollinaire's suggestions for the production and the original critical reception of the play gives us a better sense of how his ideas were borne out in practice.

In the prologue he suggests that 'We're trying to bring a new spirit into the theatre' and that a new theatre would be a 'circular theatre with two stages':

> One in the middle and the other like a ring
> Around the spectators permitting
> The full unfolding of our modern art
> Often connecting in unseen ways as in life
> Sounds gestures colors cries tumults
> Music dancing acrobatics poetry painting
> Choruses actions and multiple sets
>
> …
>
> For the theatre must not be 'realistic' (Apollinaire 1964: 66)

This call for a new spirit for theatre, with the integration and hybridization of different art forms on a stage, resonates with many of the ideas developed by others who were part of the historical avant-garde.

The production was full of noise and action, with the stage wings covered in long strips of coloured paper, and the actors dressed in extraordinary costumes which made them appear as puppets or dolls – note the similarity with the original production of *King Ubu*. One actor played the newspaper kiosk and was covered in newspapers, another played 'the people of Zanzibar' and used 'all manner of musical sound effects' – a toy flute, cymbals, 'wood blocks and broken dishes', the noise of which was interspersed with the action on the rest of the stage (Melzer 1994: 129–30). The reaction to the production was equally full of commotion, and some reports suggest the crowd went crazy. One critic likened the play to Jarry's but like 'Jarry to the twentieth power' (ibid). Melzer notes that in the days following the event, critics were at a loss as to how to define the performance. We have to remember that France was still at war during 1917 and a play such as *The Breasts of Tiresias* did not fit into any ready-made framework; although similar in impact to Jarry's play some twenty years earlier, nothing like it had been witnessed in the theatres of Paris. Whilst other experiments had been taking place in the arts in Europe, many of which – including those of the Dada artists in Zurich in 1916 – Apollinaire would have been aware of, his play signalled a new direction in performance, as Breton later testified:

> Never again, as at that evening, did I plumb the depths of the gap which would separate the new generation from that preceding it. (qtd in Melzer 1994: 133)

André Breton: the First and Second Surrealist Manifestos (2.13)

Influenced by the Dadaist Tristan Tzara (1896–1963), with whom he later argued, André Breton wrote the 'First Surrealist Manifesto' in 1924. Whilst the word 'surreal' carries the connotations of 'bizarre', 'outlandish' or simply 'weird' in contemporary parlance, surrealism as defined by Breton was rooted in a connection with the irrational, the subconscious and the world of the dream. As Breton states:

> SURREALISM, noun, masc., Pure psychic automatism by which it is intended to express, either verbally or in writing, the true function of thought. Thought dictated in the absence of all control exerted by reason, and outside all aesthetic or moral preoccupations.
>
> ENCYCL. *Philos.* Surrealism is based on the belief in the superior reality of certain forms of association heretofore neglected, in the omnipotence of the dream, and in the disinterested play of thought. It leads to the permanent destruction of all other psychic mechanisms and to its substitution for them in the solution of the principal problems of life. (2.13: 306)

Breton's project involved a validation of the irrational and an attack on the fragmentation of consciousness – the 'dream' should be integrated into our view of 'reality' – it was also a call for man to 'escape from the control of reason as well as from the imperatives of a moral order' (Waldberg 1978: 17). The automatic writing practised by some of the Surrealists was not some form of message received from a 'spiritual' world, rather it was a technique which aimed at releasing thoughts and images from the unconscious, through disengaging the rational and intellectual conventionally considered to be at the root of the creative process of writing. Similarly, Surrealist art explores the workings of the mind beyond its ability to rationally formulate 'reality'. As Breton states in the 'First Surrealist Manifesto', 'Could not the dreams as well be applied to the solution of life's fundamental problems?' (2.13: 303). For Breton, because the rational mind functioned in a prohibitive environment and in the dream world, 'The agonizing question of possibility does not arise' (ibid: 304), creativity is stilted without recourse to the irrational world of dreams. Breton was familiar with Freud's ideas and psychoanalytic technique (see Freud 2006 and 1937), in part through his work as a medic helping the shell-shocked soldiers of the First World War. Here he observed that when the 'critical faculty of the subject' is removed from the process of the production of text, something new, vital, 'unencumbered by any reticence', emerges (2.13: 305). The Surrealists philosophized about areas related to performance but did not engage with performance at the same level as they did with art and writing. Their influence is more discernible from a historical perspective. By the time of the 'Second Surrealist Manifesto' in 1929 (2.13) Breton was more assertively linking a re-evaluation of the dream state with the call to political and ideological arms, seeing the 'raising of problems of love, dream, madness, art and religion' as paramount to any revolutionary impulse.

Surrealism offers a conceptualization of the possibilities of art, theatre and performance, which implicate the individual, the unconscious and the irrational. This connects to Jarry and Apollinaire's ideas and practice of theatre, and further, links to the innovative theatre theories of Artaud. The Surrealists were largely located in Paris during the 1920s but their ideas reverberated well into the 1930s and 1940s and well beyond Paris. Similarly, Antonin Artaud, originally affiliated with the Surrealist movement for a short time, created theories of theatre and performance which have been seminal to the development of innovative practice through the mid- and late twentieth-century European and American experimental theatre. That his ideas and his practice had less impact in his own lifetime is a reflection of the 'conservative' state of much theatre during that historical moment. It is also a reflection of the fact that, for numerous reasons – economic, technical and practical – many of his ideas were simply unrealizable. This volume includes one of Artaud's writings on theatre, 'Theatre of Cruelty – First Manifesto' (2.12) – which later became part of the seminal collection of his theatre theories, *The Theatre and Its Double* (Artaud 1981 [1968]) as well as the extraordinary, filmic performance text *The Spurt of Blood* (2.3); both pieces help to map out Artaud's ideas and their connection to the historical avant-garde and beyond.

Antonin Artaud

Artaud (1896–1948) worked as an actor (noted in particular for his role as Massieu the monk in Dreyer's 1928 film *Le Passion de Jeanne d'Arc*), director and writer during the 1920s and 1930s, but he is less remembered for his actual professional theatre work than for his ideas about theatre. Little is written, for example, about his running of the Alfred Jarry Theatre in Paris during the mid-1920s, where, along with Roger Vitrac, he introduced Paris to numerous experimental European plays: although one critic of the time noted his 'strikingly sensitive, intelligent, careful illustration of the subtlest meanings in the text' in relation to his production of Strindberg's *A Dream Play* (1901) in the mid-1920s (qtd in Leach 2004: 159). Plagued by mental illness and poverty, he was one of the most prolific theatre theorists of the early part of the twentieth century – he also wrote extensively about the occult, philosophy and culture – and his ideas have influenced numerous theatre groups and directors throughout the twentieth century. After his death his ideas have achieved an almost cult status (see Hayman 1977 and Esslin 1976).

For Artaud, as for many of the artists of the historical avant-garde, life and art were almost indistinguishable. He wanted to make theatre significant outside the framework of dominant bourgeois culture. As with the Surrealists, his was a project of disruption to create theatre which moved its audiences physically, emotionally and intellectually. Artaud used a host of metaphors and analogies to present his ideas about theatre, one of the most infamous being his comparison of theatre with the plague. Here he proposed that theatre must create societal upheaval, a psycho-physical reaction similar to that created by the plague: he wanted audiences to be shifted from a position of passive consumption to one of active involvement, bringing about physiological as much as social upheaval:

> If fundamental theatre is like the plague, this is not because it is contagious, but because like the plague it is a revelation, urging forward the exteriorisation of a latent undercurrent of cruelty through which all the perversity of which the mind is capable, whether in a person or a nation, becomes localised. (Artaud 1968: 19)

Just as the Surrealists wanted art to 'infect' us, to reach into our subconscious, to stay with us after the event, so too Artaud believed that theatre had the potential to alter not only the way we perceive our world but the world itself in which we live.

Artaud also turned to the gestural and hieroglyphic nature of non-Western art forms in traditions such as Balinese dance which he witnessed for the first time at the Paris Colonial Exposition of 1931. Here, he perceived a performance form which was predicated on a non-textual language as more capable, he thought, of expressing the human experience. He believed that 'theatre language captivates and bewitches our senses' (2.12: 297), and in 'Theatre of Cruelty: First Manifesto' (2.12) Artaud suggests that theatre must 'rediscover the idea of a kind of unique language somewhere in between gesture and thought', and that we must 'create word, gesture and expressive metaphysics, in order to rescue theatre from its human, psychological prostration' (ibid: 296). The 'Manifesto' includes notes on 'Technique' suggesting that theatre should be able to enslave 'our attention', and affect us on an 'inner level' (ibid: 297). He wanted staging to be not simply the realization of a text but more the 'starting point for theatrical creation', with 'Shouts, groans … surprise … brilliant lighting … incantation … puppets many feet high … a special use of inflexions' (ibid: 298). He gives notes on musical instruments, on lighting and costume, on objects and masks and on the possibility of a coded theatrical language of movement and gesture. For Artaud theatre needed to create a total experience, one which worked organically on the audience, to 'transgress the ordinary limits of art … to produce a kind of total creation *in real terms*, where man must reassume his position between dreams and events' (ibid: 298).

Like Apollinaire, Artaud suggested that the audience should literally be at the centre of the performance with the action happening around them; this way theatre might affect them in the same way vibration affects the movement of a snake. For Artaud the theatre could be a place where 'violent physical images pulverise, mesmerise the audience's sensibilities, caught in the drama as if in a vortex of higher forces' (Artaud 1993: 63). As Esslin notes, Artaud expressed a desire to create a theatre capable of communicating the 'fullness of human experience and emotion through bypassing the discursive use of language and by establishing contact between the artist and his audience at a level above – or perhaps below – the merely cerebral appeal of the verbal plane' (Esslin 1976: 70). To some extent we are limited in our ability to map Artaud's ideas against his actual practice as very few of his performance texts have survived. Where they have, it is sometimes difficult to imagine them working in practice, certainly on the stages of his day.

The Spurt of Blood (2.3)

Unproduced professionally until 1964, by Peter Brook and Charles Marowitz in London (see Hayman 1977), *The Spurt of Blood* (1925) is a short text that reads as a blueprint for performance, a *performance score* rather than a play. For Christopher Innes the text is rife with the 'hallucinatory shock effects of surrealistic film' (Innes 1984: 92). Peopled by characters with names which reflect their social or public roles – Knight, Wetnurse, Priest, Whore and so on – the performance text has a filmic quality, evidenced for Innes in the extensive stage directions, '*At that moment two stars collide, and a succession of limbs of flesh fall. Then feet, hands, scalps, masks … falling slower and slower as if through space … and a scarab which lands with heart-breaking, nauseating slowness*' (2.3: 217). Similarly the performance 'score' ends with an extraordinary and grotesque image: '*A host of scorpions crawl out from under the wetnurse's dress and start swarming in her vagina which swells and splits, becomes transparent and shimmers like the sun.*' The text, which could last half an hour or two hours depending on the production choices made, begins with romantic clichés – 'I love you and everything is fine', 'I love you, I am great' – but disintegrates into the ridiculous:

… the knight enters and throws himself on the wetnurse, shaking her violently.
KNIGHT: (*In a terrible voice.*) Where did you put it? Give me my Gruyère.

The Spurt of Blood is full of violent and sexual imagery, and unlike Eve who bit the apple in the Garden of Eden, the whore bites God's wrist, eliciting a 'spurt of blood' which flies across the stage, at which point the stage is strewn with dead bodies. This is not a performance text aimed at exploring or expressing some kind of 'meaning' in a social sense; rather we are bombarded with the chaotic imagery of culture in a state of disintegration and a world in disarray. Far more potent and virulent than anything by Apollinaire, the text expresses a strange apocalyptic vision. The imagery is, however, almost ritualistic and this it shares with an earlier performance text by the Expressionist painter Oskar Kokoschka (1886–1980), although Innes suggests that Artaud knew nothing of Kokoschka's *Murderer the Women's Hope* (1909, 2.4).

Expressionism and *Murderer the Women's Hope* (2.4)

Expressionism begins to emerge in art at the end of the nineteenth century. It signified the move away from literal representation towards a style which embraced the externalizing of internal psychology and social angst and as a means of exploring feeling, thought and spirit: as such it had some common features with other 'isms' of the historical avant-garde. In art, Expressionism was often characterized by intense colour, by the manipulation of spatial construction, by canvases filled with the irregular rhythms of frenetic brushstrokes – a famous early example of this being Edvard Munch's (1863–1944) 1893 painting, *The Scream*. What is manifest here is a representation of an internal state of mind rather than an attempt to replicate an external 'reality'. Thus the artist's subjective vision of the world is imposed onto the representation of it. Just as the Surrealists and the Symbolists before them (see Part 1) had no interest in representing surface reality, so, too, the Expressionists made use of emblematic modes. Later forms of Expressionist playwriting in America, typified by works such as Elmer Rice's *The Adding Machine* (1923) or Sophie Treadwell's *Machinal* (1928) – retitled *The Life Machine* in the first English production – made use of the abstraction present in earlier Expressionism. Here stark sets and telegraph-type speech – short, rhythmic, repetitive language – convey the internal states of characters who embodied social angst, or the alienation created by technological development whereby man/woman was often pitted against machine, as is literally the case with Karel Čapek's *R.U.R* reprinted in this volume (2.8) Here the Expressionist style links more to early German film, such as *The Cabinet of Dr Caligari* (1919) or Fritz Lang's *Metropolis* (1927), than a text like Kokoschka's, but the sense of alienation, of ritualized existence, of extremes of human emotion resonate (see Styan 1981: 3). J. L. Styan notes that early Expressionist drama in Germany was a reaction against the 'pre-war authority of the family and community … and … the mechanization of life' (ibid). He sees it as a 'violent drama of youth', and Kokoschka is not untypical in spirit. Styan gives a useful breakdown of the key characteristics of early Expressionist drama which it is worth noting in shorthand here. First, the atmosphere was often 'vividly dreamlike and nightmarish'; plot and structure were 'disjointed, broken into episodes' without the conflict or sense of cause and effect of a well-made play; characters were often social types rather than individuals; dialogue switched between the 'poetical' and 'telegraphese' – short words or speeches delivered in a rhythmical or repetitive manner; and lastly the acting or performance style was puppet-like and gestural (ibid: 4–5). Many of these characteristics can be found in Kokoschka's performance text.

Murderer the Women's Hope (1909, 2.4) opens under a night sky with torches offering the only light. Figures appear in relief before a tower with a large red grille as its door. The characters have clothes covered in symbols and are 'savage in appearance'. The text has the feeling of a medieval procession as a chorus walks around the stage. The ritualistic quality of the language builds as the piece progresses – Woman is spellbound by the mystical qualities of the man who strode 'through the fire, his feet unharmed' (2.4: 221). The girls warn Woman that they must escape and the movement and fearful expressions of the crowd climax in a moment of threat in which the men are sadistically ordered to brand Woman with a hot iron, to mark her: 'MAN: (*Enraged.*) My men, now brand her with my sign, hot iron into her red flesh' (ibid). In her struggle Woman manages to wound Man. Her need for revenge is heightened to the point where she states that she will not let him live: 'you feed on me, weaken me, woe to you … Your love imprisons me …', at which point she writhes on the steps to the tower in convulsions. Man then kills the frenzied crowd as they attempt to escape, their torches showering them with sparks, and the stage is left piled with dead bodies as, '*From very far away*' we hear the crowing of cocks (ibid: 222).

A man who courted public controversy, Kokoschka wrote the play, 'as an antedote to the torpor that, for the most part, one experiences in the theatre today' (Berghaus 2005: 65). The text has a prehistoric feel – located as it is in some ancient place – and focuses on a primal version of the battle of the sexes. The females are constructed in animalistic terms: woman '*creeps round the cage like a panther*' (ibid: 221), and the violence in the play is almost sadomasochistic in tone. Again, parallels might be drawn with Artaud's *The Spurt of Blood*, similarly violent in terms of the imagery and the relationship between male and female that it depicts. There is also a strong reference in both to the 'primitive' framed by a Western notion of the uncivilized rather than, as in Apollinaire's 'Zanzibar', as a reference to a particular non-Western geography. For Styan the play is 'unique in its violent eroticism' with scenes which 'correspond to the seven stations of the cross' (Styan 1981: 45). He also notes that the actors in the first production were not given the script, and the improvisational and free expressive form of the text alongside its musical and gestural properties present the possibility that in fact the extant text came out of its performance as much as the other way round (ibid).

Expressionist theatre, perhaps more than any other of the 'isms' of the historical avant-garde, developed a number of styles which altered the formal qualities of the text in a sustained manner. For example, although a later play such as *Hoppla, We're Alive!* (3.2), explored in Part 3, could not be more different from Kokoschka's text, we can identify a resonance with earlier Expressionist plays. The Expressionists were less concerned with the politics of the aesthetics of performance than were the Dadaists, and did not engage in the same level of self-reflection and critique of the artwork as other modernists. Such conscious critique was, however, absolutely embedded within Futurist performance practice, evidenced here in Umberto Boccioni's *Genius and Culture* and *Bachelor Apartment* (2.5), and in Filippo Tommaso Marinetti's *Feet* (2.6).

Futurism: Filippo Tommaso Marinetti (1876–1944) and Umberto Boccioni (1882–1916)

The Futurists shared much with the other historical avant-garde movements that developed during the first three decades of the twentieth century – an abhorrence of tradition, a desire to disrupt, a belief in art as action and process, and so on. Marinetti is viewed as the founding father of Futurism, which declared itself – through the publication on the front page of Parisian daily newspaper *Le Figaro* of 'The Foundation and Manifesto of Futurism' in 1909 – by launching a 'violently upsetting incendiary manifesto'. The manifesto lays out the tenets of Italian Futurism as Marinetti states that the Futurists intended to:

> sing of the love of danger ... courage, audacity, and revolt will be the essential elements of our poetry ... the world's magnificence has been enriched by ... the beauty of speed ... no work without an aggressive character can be a masterpiece ... we will glorify war – the world's only hygiene – militarism, patriotism, the destructive gesture of freedom-bringers, beautiful ideas worth dying for and scorn for woman ... we will sing of the polyphonic tides of revolution.

Whilst historians have noted Marinetti's fascism – he became a great friend of the Fascist Italian dictator Benito Mussolini – others point to his earlier associations with the 'amorphous pool of radicals and subversives of the extreme Left in Italy' (Berghaus 2005: 95). Futurism's intention to 'effect a total overhaul of society' was not, however, based on socialist ideological affiliations, and politically, Marinetti had far more in common with anarchist beliefs and those which later developed into the foundations of fascism. Fascism works through autocratic systems of representation rather than dialectical ones, and gained power as a political movement in Europe – specifically Germany, Spain and Italy – during the 1920s and 1930s. Walter Benjamin (see Part 3: Introduction and 3.9) argued vociferously against both Marinetti's glorification of war, and Futurism's aestheticization of politics, and from a contemporary standpoint it is difficult to disassociate an appreciation of Futurism from its ultimate foundations in an exclusionary politics. Keeping this in mind, the task here is to look at the ways in which the Futurists influenced developments in theatre and performance, and Marinetti's 'The Meaning of the Music Hall' (2.11) along with Enrico Prampolini's 'Futurist Scenography' (2.14) go some way towards opening this discussion. Originally published in an English newspaper, the *Daily Mail*, in 1913, Marinetti's analysis of the British popular music hall, which flourished as a mode of performance practice from the last decades of the nineteenth century into the first few of the twentieth, is an interesting one. For Marinetti the music hall thrived on having 'no masters, no dogmas' and on subsisting 'on the moment', it set out to entertain the audience with the comic or the 'startling to the imagination'. Here the audience 'does not remain static and stupidly passive, but participates noisily in the action'. Based on the expression and display of physical skill, risk and daring, many music hall acts appealed to the Futurists for whom text-based theatres were the epitome of bourgeois indulgence. Marinetti makes direct reference to the primitive in relation to this performance form and states that Futurism could perfect 'variety theatre by transforming it into the theatre of wonders' (2.11: 294). Enrico Prampolini's (1894–1956) suggestions for theatre are more concerned with the specifics of production, and reveal a desire to develop a 'dynamic synthesis' in production, to move away from classicism towards intuitive staging that makes use of the poetic and vibrant qualities of colour; the non-representational where the scenography, and specifically the lighting, will come across as a character in and of itself (see 2.14). Between the two we can see an embracing of both so-called 'low' and 'high art'. Whilst Marinetti perhaps misunderstood and underestimated the 'traditions' which operated within the music hall, he focused on its populist appeal. Prampolini, on the other hand, wanted to create 'luminous dynamic architectures' in staging, which, like many of Artaud's ideas, would have been technically unrealizable in his historical moment.

The Futurist performances of which Marinetti's *Feet* (2.6) and the Boccioni texts would have been a component were called *serate*, evenings of performances, readings of manifestos and exhibitions of Futurist artworks, in large theatres. Most *serate* turned into a battleground where the audience noisily and sometimes violently disrupted the performances, which, much to the joy of the Futurists, brought their ideas more noticeably into the public realm. By around 1914 the disruptive potential of these evenings had reached its limit, as the element of surprise was harder to manufacture and Marinetti turned to other performance escapades to develop Futurism's performance practices (see Berghaus 2005).

The scripts or *sintesi* which we have reprinted here do not really give a full sense of the vibrant, violent and disruptive essence of Futurism; what they do give us, however, is a sense – especially in the case of *Feet* (2.6) – of what the Futurists might have been aiming to achieve in performance. *Genius and Culture* and *Bachelor Apartment* (2.5) subvert bourgeois domestic settings, and link with Dada's critique of the commodification of both artist and artwork as the Critic in the former states:

> I am not a man, I am a critic. I am a man of culture. The artist is a man, a slave, a baby … In him nature is chaos. The critic and history are between nature and the artist. History is history, in other words subjective fact. (2.5: 224)

Thus, whilst the artist is human, the critic can remove himself from humanity and be 'a man of culture', which he can critique subjectively, and present his critique as fact or truth. Similarly the relationship between the sexes in both texts is presented in what might now be seen as rather traditionalist terms, with the Woman in *Genius and Culture* (2.5) as the supportive nurturer of the Artist and as the manipulative seductress in *Bachelor Apartment* (2.5). Marinetti's *Feet* (2.6), however, does more in terms of performative innovation. Broken into seven sections, scenes or simply moments, the audience sit in front of a stage curtain which is only a third raised above the stage and therefore sees only 'legs in action'. The actors are required to give 'greatest expression to the attitudes and movements of their lower extremities' (2.6: 226). Attention is drawn to the seven 'episodes', none of which lasts longer than a few lines of text, via our hearing of snippets of conversation, just as a camera might focus on small elements of a larger scene. So, we see the bottom of two armchairs whilst we witness a failed seduction scene as a bachelor says, 'All, all for one of your kisses' and a married woman replies, 'No! … Don't talk to me like that! …' (ibid: 226). Later our attention is drawn to three women sitting on a couch having a conversation about which of three men sitting on another couch they prefer. The last episode is simply a man running away – presumably offstage – whilst another kicks at him shouting 'Imbecile!' (ibid: 227). What the performance text achieves is a retuning of our attention: we are asked, as it were, to fill in the missing pieces, there is no exposition – we don't know where we are, who is there or why – there is minimal reference to the usual signifiers which operate in theatre and they are manipulated so as to remove the possibility of presenting a picture or a scene. Just as a camera pans in on specific aspects of a filmic composition, so Marinetti plays with our desire to know where we are and what the characters on stage are doing there; we cannot see their faces, their expressions, nor can we identify or empathize with them in any real way. Something else apart from our intellect comes into play. Marinetti's text genuinely opens up questions about how performance works as practice, linking him with others from the avant-garde such as Artaud and Moholy-Nagy (1895–1946), who, like Marinetti, turned to an analysis of variety and circus performance as a way of breaking theatre and performance away from the dominance of text.

László Moholy-Nagy's 'Theater, Circus, Variety' (2.15) is self-explanatory and has been included in this volume because of the way it discusses the relationship between popular performance forms and innovative theories of staging. Like others from the historical avant-garde, Moholy-Nagy believed that the actor has to work in synchronicity with the other elements of staging (sound, motion, space, form) in a 'theatre of totality' which he saw as an 'organism' – something removed from the traditional storytelling qualities of bourgeois theatre which did not facilitate the 'creative relationships and reciprocal tensions' which he believed a theatre of totality could achieve.

The historical avant-garde and the mainstream experimental

As we have seen, much of the historical avant-garde can be identified with a desire to genuinely investigate the potential of theatre and performance beyond its subservience to text, to literature and the written word. Some played with language and sound, removing meaning through the repetition or deconstruction of the tonal and rhythmic qualities of language, and through creating a different hierarchy between language and the other elements of theatre, the visual, the physical and so on. This introduction draws to its close with an exploration of three texts which were generated through engagement with the cultural questions raised by the historical avant-garde, but which have found either popularity or longevity outside of the experimental perimeters of the original historical avant-garde performance contexts in which they were created.

Karel Čapek (1890–1938): *R.U.R. (Rossum's Universal Robots)* (2.8)

Čapek's play (1920) is well known for its insertion of the word 'robot' into the English language: indeed motifs and even character names from the play have reverberated in popular culture from *Star Trek* to *Doctor Who*. A kind of dystopic science fiction, *R.U.R.* has tones of a melodramatic romance as well as borrowing from the rhythms and psychic anxieties of Expressionism. Located on a remote island at some point in the future, Robots are being manufactured in order to replace human labour at a lower cost and to ostensibly create more leisure time for humans, so they can 'only do what they enjoy'. As the play progresses, some of the Robots who have been given larger brains and therefore emotions initiate a revolution, realizing that they are being exploited. As Kara Reilly notes, '*R.U.R.* examines the workers' ongoing struggle against the machine' (Reilly 2011: 161). It also shares with Expressionist art an anxiety about the role of technology in the formation of human experience. With humans almost extinct, the scientist Alquist cannot compensate for the fact that the formula for making Robots has been destroyed and so the Robots cannot reproduce nor can they be altered. The play ends with the revelation that whilst humanity has been wiped out, two of the Robots have fallen in love – a human emotion not associated with mechanical beings.

Critics were at pains to point out the play's anti-war and anti-technological stances but Harold Segel has suggested that, 'The dehumanization threatened by the machine culture was paralleled … by the demoralization attributable to false values and artificiality for which capitalism and commercialization were responsible' (qtd in Reilly 2011: 169 from Segel 1995: 303).

Luigi Pirandello (1867–1936): *Six Characters in Search of an Author* (2.9)

The first night of the original production of *Six Characters in Search of an Author* in Rome (1921) ended in riots, but the play was revived in Milan a few months later to an ecstatic reception (see Bassnett 1989). Banned by the Lord Chamberlain's office because of the perceived obscenities within the play, it was first produced in the UK in 1922 by the Stage Society, an independent non-commercial organization that could avoid the censorship licensing laws in operation in the UK until 1968 (Bassnett 1983: 8). It was produced in the US in the same year. The play has been produced regularly since then, and remains one of the best known of Pirandello's theatrical works. Some critics suggest that it is foolish to try to summarize Pirandello's plays through a delineation of their plot lines: his plays are often much more to do with the exposition of philosophical discussions about the possibility of truth, and about the human condition, and are driven largely by 'the process that develops inside the souls of his characters', (qtd in Bassnett 1989: 41). At the opening of *Six Characters in Search of an Author*, however, we assume we are in a rehearsal for the production of a play, another by Pirandello. The rehearsal is interrupted by six characters, who are looking for the theatre and its players to help them tell their own story. As the plot unfolds we see the disruption of the orderly rehearsal, with actors going in and out of character and the visiting 'family' shifting from a standard nuclear family unit – father, mother, children – to one which disintegrates before our eyes, as their tale of marriage breakdown and abuse is revealed. It is not always clear who is acting, telling their story or instructing others as to how it should be told. Thus the boundaries between the 'real' of the rehearsal, the telling or acting out of a past and what is happening in the present is never precisely clear – the truth is illusive as the 'boundary between reality and fiction has broken down' (ibid). The play is divided into three 'acts' with language that is naturalistic, but it is centred around 'two fundamental issues: the problem of defining the limitations of theatre and the distinction between rehearsing and living a scene' (ibid: 38), in other words, the fluid relation between *performing* and *being* aligns it with the central concerns of much historical avant-garde performance and the concerns of performance at the other end of the century, in the work, for example, of Forced Entertainment (see Part 5 and 5.2). Pirandello's experimentation with the limitations of the form and language of theatre, exemplified in this play, situate his work amongst the most deceptively experimental of the twentieth century.

Gertrude Stein, the last of the practitioners examined here, could not be more different in her approach to theatre: in most of her works for the theatre, she refused traditional structure or form and was not interested in linearity, narrative or the comfort of plot lines reliant on a symbiotic relationship of cause and effect.

Gertrude Stein (1874–1946): *Dr Faustus Lights the Lights* (2.10)

Gertrude Stein was, like Čapek, heavily influenced by Cubism, in part inspired by her friendships with Pablo Picasso (1881–1973) and Juan Gris (1887–1927), and was concerned with literary composition, with form, rhythm and the shape of language, more than its semantic content or meaning. Stein's work, especially the plays *Four Saints in Three Acts* (performed 1934) and *The Mother of Us All* (1946) have been celebrated and produced by a number of generations of experimental theatre and opera makers in the latter decades of the twentieth century and beyond. She wrote over 100 plays and performance texts (Shaughnessy 2007: 94).

Like many artists from the historical avant-garde, Stein also had a level of economic independence and so could afford not to earn a living from her writing until quite late into her career: this meant that much of her writing is playful, artful and sometimes impenetrable. Whilst Stein's use of the Faust story in *Dr Faustus Lights the Lights* (1938, 2.10) 'situates her play within the mainstream theatrical tradition' (ibid: 96), the text bears little relation to anything that would have been considered to be mainstream in its day. Not produced in her lifetime, there have been a number of landmark productions of the play in the US, with Robert Wilson's 1992 production set on a 'bare stage sparely furnished with suspended lightbulbs', where 'words, music and setting … become independent of one another' (qtd in Shaughnessy 2007: 102–3). The play itself is the first of Stein's to use 'identifiable characters and attribute[s] specific dialogue to them' (Bay-Cheng 2004: 71). Full of 'punning non-sequiturs and repetition', the play explores themes of 'isolation and chaos' (ibid: 72), and for some 'represents the culmination of Stein's thinking about the modern world: its wars: its technology and its humanity' (ibid: 73). Critics have read the play in a number of different ways, as feminist, as a Jungian analysis of the self, and as a play that cements Stein's relationship to the Surrealists and Dadaists (see Bay-Cheng 2004 and Shaughnessy 2007). In her bid to 'express things seen not as one knows them but as they are when one sees them without remembering having looked at them' (qtd in Souhami 1993: 145), the sparse abstract landscape of the play, its repetitions and uncertainties and its 'representation of a technologically tormented modern world without end' (Bay-Cheng 2004: 92) connect Stein's work to that of the late modernists explored in Part 4 of this volume.

Conclusion

With no formal beginning or end, the historical avant-garde was a movement made up of different and interconnected elements. Its inventions and practices, however, reverberate through to the early twenty-first century, as James M. Harding notes, there has been 'an "avant-garde urge" that has continued to thrive in contemporary theater, our understanding of that urge … is largely contingent upon a sense of the dynamics that characterized the historical avant-garde' (Harding 2000: 6).

Many of the dynamic theories about art, and more specifically theatre and performance, which the varying movements within the historical avant-garde developed, could not be realized in practice within the technological limitations of their time. But many of these ideas have become embedded in the approach to theatre of practitioners working at the other end of the century (see Part 5). As the timeline at the beginning of Part 2 illustrates, Dada, Surrealism, Expressionism and Futurism were all practices which interrelated and circulated during the same decades. The reach of Part 2 has been largely France, Germany and Italy, but the avant-garde in Russia and the US equally influenced far less esoteric and far more politically directed performance. Where the historical avant-garde refused to adhere specifically or permanently to a particular ideological position, some of their ideas were often adopted by those who wanted to transform theatre as part of a 'class' war and a battle with political systems subservient to the economic inequities of capitalism.

Bibliography

Apollinaire, Guillaume (1964) *The Breasts of Tiresias*, trans. Louis Simpson, in Michael Benedikt and George Welwarth (eds) *Modern French Theatre: An Anthology of Plays from Jarry to Ioneso*, London: Faber and Faber, pp. 55–92.

Aronson, Arnold (2000) *American Avant-Garde Theatre: A History*, London: Routledge.

Artaud, Antonin (1981 [1968 and 1993]) *The Theatre and Its Double*, London: John Calder.

Bakhtin, Mikhail (1984 [1965]) *Rabelais and His World*, Bloomington: Indiana University Press.

Bay-Cheng, Sarah (2004) *MAMA DADA: Gertrude Stein's Avant-Garde Theater*, New York and London: Routledge.

Bassnett, Susan (1983) *Luigi Pirandello*, New York: Grove Press.

Bassnett, Susan (1989) *File on Pirandello*, London: Methuen.

Berghaus, Günter (2005) *Theatre, Performance and the Historical Avant-Garde*, Basingstoke: Palgrave Macmillan.

Carey, John (1992) *The Intellectuals and the Masses*, London: Faber and Faber.

John F. Deeney and Maggie B. Gale (2014) *Fifty Key Dramatists*, London: Routledge.

Diamond, Elin (2006) 'Deploying/Destroying the Primitivist Body in Hurston and Brecht', in Alan Ackerman and Martin Puchner (eds) *Against Theatre: Creative Destructions on the Modernist Stage*, Basingstoke: Palgrave Macmillan, pp. 112–32.

Edgar, Andrew and Peter Sedgwick (2008) *Cultural Theory: The Key Concepts*, London: Routledge.

Esslin, Martin (1976) *Antonin Artaud: The Man and His Work*, London: John Calder.

Esslin, Martin (2001 [1961]) *The Theatre of the Absurd*, London: Methuen.

Freud, Sigmund (1937 [1933]) *New Introductory Lectures on Psychoanalysis*, London: Hogarth.

Freud, Sigmund (2006 [1899]) *The Interpretation of Dreams*, Raleigh, NC: Hayes Barton Press.

Fusco, Coco (2002) 'The Other History of Intercultural Performance', in Rebecca Schneider and Gabrielle Cody (eds), *Re-Direction*, London: Routledge, pp. 266–90.

Harding, James M. (2000) *Contours of the Theatrical Avant-Garde*, Ann Arbor: University of Michigan Press.

Harding, James M. (2010) *Cutting Performances: Collage Events, Feminist Artists, and the American Avant-Garde*, Ann Arbor: The University of Michigan Press.

Hayman, Ronald (1977) *Artaud and After*, Oxford: Oxford University Press.

Hirschkop, Ken and David Shepherd (1989) *Bakhtin and Cultural Theory*, Manchester: Manchester University Press.

Hughes, Robert (1991 [1980]) *The Shock of the New: Art and the Century of Change*, London: Thames and Hudson.

Innes, Christopher (1984) *Holy Theatre: Ritual and the Avant-Garde*, London: Routledge.

Innes, Christopher (1993) *Avant-Garde Theatre 1892–1992*, London: Routledge.

Jarry, Alfred (1980 [1898]) *Exploits and Opinions of Dr Faustroll, Pataphysician*, in Roger Shattuck and Simon Watson Taylor (eds) *Selected Works of Alfred Jarry*, London: Eyre Methuen, pp. 173–256.

Leach, Robert (2004) *Makers of Modern Theatre*, London: Routledge.

Melzer, Annabelle (1994 [1980]) *Dada and Surrealist Performance*, Baltimore and London: Johns Hopkins University Press.

Reilly, Kara (2011) *Automata and Mimesis on the Stage of Theatre History*, Basingstoke: Palgrave Macmillan.

Rice, Elmer (1956 [1923]) *The Adding Machine*, New York: Samuel French.

Schumacher, Claude (1985) *Alfred Jarry and Guillaume Apollinaire*, London: Methuen.

Segel, Harold B (1995) *Pinocchio's Progeny: Puppets, Marionettes, Automatons and Robots in Modernist and Avant-Garde Drama*, New York: PAJ.

Senelick, Laurence (ed.) (1989) *Cabaret Performance: Europe 1890–1920*, New York: PAJ.

Shattuck, Roger and Simon Watson Taylor (eds) (1980 [1965]) *Selected Works of Alfred Jarry*, London: Eyre Methuen.

Shaughnessy, Nicola (2007) *Gertrude Stein: Writers and Their Work*, Exeter: Northcote House.

Souhami, Diana (1993) *Gertrude and Alice*, London: Pandora Press.

Stein, Gertrude (1993 [1922]) *Geography and Plays*, Madison: The University of Wisconsin Press.

Stein, Gertrude (1995) *Last Operas and Plays*, Baltimore: Johns Hopkins University Press.

Styan, J. L. (1981) *Modern Drama in Theory and Practice 3: Expressionism and Epic Theatre*, Cambridge: Cambridge University Press.

Taxidou, Olga (2007) *Modernism and Performance: Jarry to Brecht*, Basingstoke: Palgrave Macmillan.

Treadwell, Sophie (2011 [1928]) 'Machinal', in Maggie B. Gale and Gilli Bush-Bailey (eds) *Performance Texts by Women 1880–1930: An Anthology of Texts by British and American Women of the Modernist Period*, Manchester: Manchester University Press.

Waldberg, Patrick (1978 [1965]) *Surrealism*, London: Thames and Hudson.

Further reading

Benson, Timothy (1987) *Berlin Dada*, Ann Arbor: University of Michigan Press.

Bürger, Peter (1984) *Theory of the Avant-Garde*, Minneapolis: University of Minnesota Press.

Dukore, Bernard F. and Daniel Gerould (1976) *Avant-Garde Drama: A Casebook, 1918–1939*, New York: Crowell.

Goldberg, RoseLee (1979) *Performance: Live Art, 1900 to the Present*, New York: Harry N. Abrams.

Jarry, Alfred (1980 [1898]) 'Twelve Theatrical Topics', in Roger Shattuck and Simon Watson Taylor (eds) *Selected Works of Alfred Jarry*, London: Eyre Methuen, pp. 86–90.

Kolocotroni, Vassiliki, Jane Goldman and Olga Taxidou (eds) (1998) *Modernism: An Anthology of Sources and Documents*, Edinburgh: Edinburgh University Press.

Kirby, E. T. (1969) *Total Theatre: A Critical Anthology*, New York: Dutton.

Murphy, Richard (1999) *Theorising the Avant-Garde: Modernism, Expressionism, and the Problems of Postmodernity*, Cambridge: Cambridge University Press.

Puchner, Martin (2002) *Stagefright: Modernism, Anti-Theatricality and Drama*, Baltimore and London: Johns Hopkins University Press.

Scheer, Edward (ed.) (2003) *Antonin Artaud: A Critical Reader*, London: Routledge.

Singleton, Brian (1998) *Artaud: Le Théâtre et son double* (Critical Guides to French Texts No. 118), London: Grant and Cutler.

Sokel, W. H. (ed.) (1963) *Anthology of German Expressionist Drama*, New York: Anchor Books.

2.1 **KING UBU** (1896)

ALFRED JARRY

Translated by Kenneth McLeish

Alfred Jarry (1873–1907). Born in France, the son of a merchant, Jarry went on to become an iconic hero of the Surrealist movement founded over a decade after his death. Echoes of his ideas and visions for theatre can also be found in the European 'absurdist' theatre which found currency after World War II. Best known for his Ubu plays, which focus on the adventures of the treacherous and deeply unpleasant Père Ubu and his entourage, Jarry also wrote poetry, prose and journalism. He was both involved with, and critical of, the Symbolist movement in Paris. Originally produced in Paris in 1896, Jarry's King Ubu was a sensation which bought him notoriety. Known as an eccentric figure and an alcoholic, he died young and impoverished. This translation was produced at the Gate Theatre, London, in 1997, directed by John Wright.

Characters

PA UBU
MA UBU
DOGPILE
GOOD KING WENCESLAS
QUEEN ROSAMOND
PRINCE WILLY
PRINCE SILLY
PRINCE BILLIKINS
BIG BAD BERNIE
WALLOP
MCCLUB
FAST FREDDIE
NORBERT NURDLE
TSAR ALEXIS OF ALL THE RUSSKIES
NICK NACKERLEY
GENERAL CUSTARD
MAJOR F. FORT
BEAR
BARMPOTS, BANKERS, CASHHOUNDS, CHAPS, CITIZENS, CLERKS, COUNCILLORS, FLUNKEYS, GHOSTS, GUARDS, JUDGES, MESSENGERS, NOBS, PARTISANS, SEAFARERS, SOLDIERS, TURNKEYS.

Act 1

1

PA UBU, MA UBU

PA UBU: Shikt.

MA UBU: Pa Ubu, language.

PA UBU: Watch it, Ma Ubu. I'll bash your head in.

MA UBU: Not my head, Pa Ubu. Someone else's.

PA UBU: Stagger me sideways, what d'you mean?

MA UBU: Come on, Pa Ubu. You *like* what you are?

PA UBU: Stagger me sideways, girl, of course I like it. Shikt, who wouldn't? Captain of the Guard, Eye and Ear of Good King Wenceslas, Past President of the Battalions of Baloney, Thane of Four-door. What more d'you want?

MA UBU: You're joking. Thane of Four-door, you used to be. Now who follows you? Fifty sausage-knotters in procession. Forget Four-door. Get your loaf measured for the crown of Baloney.

PA UBU: Ma Ubu, what are you on about?

MA UBU: As if you didn't know.

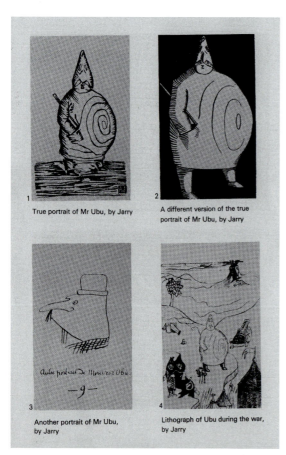

1 True portrait of Mr Ubu, by Jarry

2 A different version of the true portrait of Mr Ubu, by Jarry

3 Another portrait of Mr Ubu, by Jarry

4 Lithograph of Ubu during the war, by Jarry

Figure 8 Four Portraits of Mr Ubu by Alfred Jarry

PA UBU: Stagger me sideways. Good King Wenceslas is still alive, for starters. And even if he wasn't, he's got a million kids.

MA UBU: So, do in the lot of them. Take over.

PA UBU: Watch it, Ma Ubu, or it's jug for you.

MA UBU: Idiot! If I'm in jug, who'll patch your pants?

PA UBU: So let 'em *see* my bum.

MA UBU: No: plant it on a throne. Just think of it. A pile of cash, big as you like. Bangers for breakfast. A golden coach.

PA UBU: If I was king, I'd have a big hat. Like that one I had in Four-door, till those bastards nicked it.

MA UBU: *And* a brolly. *And* a cloak so long that it brushed the floor.

PA UBU: I can't resist. Shickastick, if I catch him on his own, he's for it.

MA UBU: At last, Pa Ubu. A proper man at last.

PA UBU: Just a minute. I'm Captain of the Guard. Murder Good King Wenceslas? His Maj of Baloney? I'd rather die.

MA UBU: (*Aside.*) Shikt. (*Aloud.*) You want to be Daddy Mouse forever? *Poor* Daddy Mouse?

PA UBU: Blubberit, stagger me sideways, I'd rather be poor, honest Daddy Mouse than Big Fat Cat that Nicked the Cream.

MA UBU: What about the brolly? The cloak? The great big hat?

PA UBU: What about them, Ma Ubu?

He goes, slamming the door.

MA UBU: Snikt, what a tight-arse. Never mind. Slipalipt, I'm loosening him. With God's good help, not to mention mine, I'll be Queen of Baloney by Saturday.

2

Room in PA UBU'S house, with a table set for a feast. PA UBU, MA UBU.

MA UBU: Well, they're late. Our guests.

PA UBU: Yes. Stagger me sideways, I'm starving. Ma Ubu, you look really ugly today. Because we've got company?

MA UBU: (*Shrugging.*) Shikt.

PA UBU: (*Grabbing a roast chicken.*) Dagit, I'm hungry. I'll get stuck into this. Chicken, right? Snot bad.

MA UBU: Put that down. Leave something for the guests.

PA UBU: There's plenty. I won't touch another thing. Look out the window, Ma Ubu. See if our guests are here.

MA UBU: (*Going to the window.*) No sign of them.

PA UBU snatches his chance and snitches a slice of meat.

Here they are. Captain Dogpile and his Barmpots. Pa Ubu, what are you eating?

PA UBU: Nothing. Collops.

MA UBU: Collops. Collops. Dagnagit, put them down!

PA UBU: Stagger me sideways, I'll dot you one.

The door opens.

3

PA UBU, MA UBU, DOGPILE, BARMPOTS

MA UBU: Good evening, gents. So naice to see you. Do sit down.

DOGPILE: Ma Ubu, good evening. Where's Pa Ubu?

PA UBU: Here! Godnagit, stagger me sideways, I'm not that small.

DOGPILE: Good evening, Pa Ubu. Lads, siddown.

All sit.

PA UBU: Pff! Any bigger, I'd have smashed the chair.

DOGPILE: Oi, Ma Ubu, what's for dinner?

MA UBU: I'll tell you.

PA UBU: I like this part.

MA UBU: Baloney soup. Calfcollops. Chicken. Pâté de dog. Turkey bum. Charlotte Russe.

PA UBU: That's enough. Snurk! More?

MA UBU: (*Continuing.*) Ice cream, lettuce, apples, hotpot, tartyfarts, cauliflower shikt.

PA UBU: Dagnagit, I'm paying for this. What d'you take me for, a bank?

MA UBU: Ignore him. He's barmy.

PA UBU: I'll barm your bum.

MA UBU: Shut up, Pa Ubu. Eat your burger.

PA UBU: Burger me, it's bad.

DOGPILE: Bleah, it's horrible.

MA UBU: Nagnancies, what d'you *want*?

PA UBU: (*Striking his forehead.*) Got it! Hang on. I won't be long.

Exit.

MA UBU: Nah, gents, collops.

DOGPILE: Very nice. All gone.

MA UBU: Some turkeybum?

DOGPILE: Fantastic. Great! Up Ma Ubu.

ALL: Up Ma Ubu.

PA UBU returns, carrying a disgusting brush.

PA UBU: What about three cheers for Pa Ubu?

He pokes the brush at the guests.

MA UBU: Idiot, what are you doing?

PA UBU: It's lovely. Taste it, taste it.

Several of them taste and die, poisoned.

PA UBU: Ma Ubu, pass the tartyfarts. I'll hand them round.

MA UBU: Here.

PA UBU: Out, out, the lot of you. Captain Dogpile, I want a word.

THE OTHERS: Hey! We haven't finished.

PA UBU: Oh yes you have. Out, out! Dogpile, sit.

No one moves.

Still here? Stagger me sideways, where are those tartyfarts? I'll see to you.

He starts hurling tartyfarts.

ALL: Erg! Foo! Aagh!

PA UBU: Shikt, shikt, shikt. D'you get it? Out!

ALL: Bastard! Swine!

PA UBU: They've gone. What a lousy dinner. Dogpile, walkies.

Exeunt.

4

PA UBU, MA UBU, DOGPILE

PA UBU: Here, Dogpile. Diddums like oo dindins?

DOGPILE: Lovely. All but the shikt.

PA UBU: The shikt was great.

MA UBU: Shickun son goo. That's French.

PA UBU: Captain Dogpile, I'm going to make you Lord de Lawdy.

DOGPILE: Pardon, Pa Ubu? I thought you were skint.

PA UBU: In a day or two, with your help, I'll be King of Baloney.

DOGPILE: You're going to kill Good King Wenceslas?

PA UBU: Aren't you the clever one?

DOGPILE: If you're doing for Good King Wenceslas, count me in. I'm his mortal enemy. Me and my Barmpots.

PA UBU: (*Falling on his neck.*) Dogpile! Darling!

DOGPILE: Puah, you stink, Pa Ubu. Don't you ever wash?

PA UBU: What if I don't?

MA UBU: He doesn't know how to.

PA UBU: I'll stample you.

MA UBU: Shiktface.

PA UBU: Out, Dogpile. That's all for now. I'll make you Lord de Lawdy. That's a promise. Stagger me sideways, I swear, on Ma Ubu's head.

MA UBU: Hey …

PA UBU: Shut it, girl.

Exeunt.

5

PA UBU, MA UBU, MESSENGER

PA UBU: Hey you. What is it? Piss off. Who needs you?

MESSENGER: Sirrah, you're summoned. By his Majesty.

Exit.

PA UBU: Oh shikt. Dogalmighty, stagger me sideways, they know. I'm done for. Chopped. Oh dear.

MA UBU: You great jelly. Get on with it.

PA UBU: I know, I'll say it was her ... and that Dogpile.

MA UBU: Lardbelly, just you try.

PA UBU: Just watch me.

He goes. MA UBU *runs after him.*

MA UBU: Pa Ubu! No! Pa Ubu! I'll let you have sausage.

PA UBU: (*Off.*) Sausage, ha! Haha! HaHA!

6

The royal palace. GOOD KING WENCESLAS, *surrounded by his officers;* DOGPILE; *princes* SILLY, WILLY *and* BILLIKINS. *Enter* PA UBU.

PA UBU: It was them, not me. Ma Ubu, Dogpile. They did it.

KING: Did what, Pa Ubu?

DOGPILE: He's pissed.

KING: One knows how it feels.

PA UBU: Of course I'm pissed. From drinking toasts.

KING: Pa Ubu, it is our purpose to reward your loyal service as Captain of the Guard. From this day on, be known as Baron Stretcholand.

PA UBU: Good ole Majesty, how kind, how kind.

KING: Never mind all that, Pa Ubu. Just turn up at the Posh Parade tomorrow.

PA UBU: I will, I will. But first, your Maj ... a little gift.

He gives him a kazoo.

KING: A kazoo? What shall we do with it? We'll give it to Billikins.

BILLIKINS: Pa Ubu's orf his chump.

PA UBU: Right, 'scuse me, time to piss off.

He turns and falls.

Gor! Nyai! Stagger me sideways, I've knackered my kneecap and gurdled my gob.

KING: (*Getting up.*) I say, Pa Ubu, are you all right?

PA UBU: All right? I'm done for. What'll become of poor old Ma?

KING: One shall look after her.

PA UBU: How kind. But don't think that'll save you.

Exit.

7

PA UBU'S *house.* PA UBU, MA UBU, BIG BAD BERNIE, WALLOP, MCCLUB, DOGPILE, BARMPOTS, SOLDIERS.

PA UBU: OK, lads. Time to get this plot moving. Who's got an idea? Me first. Me first.

DOGPILE: Pa Ubu, go on.

PA UBU: This is it, lads. It's simple. I stuff his lunch with arsenic. He shoves it down his gob, drops dead, and I nab his throne.

ALL: Ooh! Cheeky monkey! Aren't you the naughty one?

PA UBU: Good, innit? Dogpile, got anything better?

DOGPILE: I suggest: one slash of the sabre, to slice him in snippets from snitch to shoe.

ALL: Yay! Our hero! Whee! Yeeah!

PA UBU: And suppose he kicks you up the bum? Have you forgotten those stout iron shoes he wears for Posh Parades? In any case, now I know, I'll tell him. There'll be a big reward.

MA UBU: Coward, traitor, lardbag.

ALL: Boo! Hiss!

PA UBU: Watch it, or I'll drop you lot in as well. Oh, all right. For your sakes, lads, I'll do it. Dogpile, stand by to slice.

DOGPILE: Hang on. Why don't we all pile in on him, yelling and shouting? We've got to scare off his guards.

PA UBU: Got it! I stamp on his toe. He kicks me. I shout 'SHIKT' – and that's the signal. You all pile in.

MA UBU: Then as soon as he's dead, you grab the crown.

DOGPILE: And I and the lads see to the rest of them.

PA UBU: Right. Especially that bastard Billikins.

They start to go. He drags them back.

Hang on. Haven't we forgotten something? The solemn oath?

DOGPILE: How do we do that, without a bible?

PA UBU: We'll use Ma Ubu. Swear on her.

ALL: Yay. Good. Right.

PA UBU: OK. You all swear to kill Good King Wenceslas ... properly?

ALL: We swear. We'll kill him. Up Pa Ubu. Yay.

End of Act 1.

Act 2
1

The royal palace. GOOD KING WENCESLAS, QUEEN ROSAMOND, SILLY, WILLY, BILLIKINS.

KING: Prince Billikins, this morning you were very cheeky to Pa Ubu, one's Captain of the Guard, one's Baron Stretcholand. One therefore grounds you. Stay away from one's Posh Parade.

QUEEN: Hang on, Wence. You need the whole family there. Security.

KING: One means what one says. Don't bibblebabble, madam. You tire one's ears.

BILLIKINS: Mighty majesty, pater: one submits.

QUEEN: You're really going through with it, your Maj? This Posh Parade?

KING: Madam, why not?

QUEEN: I told you before. I had a dream. He smote you with his smiters, chucked you in the river and nabbed the crown. That lion and unicorn put it on his head.

KING: Whose head?

QUEEN: Pa Ubu's head.

KING: Absurd. His Lord High Ubuness is the soul of loyalty. He'd let wild horses mangle him to mincemeat before he harmed a hair of one's head.

QUEEN, BILLIKINS: You're just so *wrong*.

KING: Enough. We'll show you how much one trusts Count Ubu. One will attend the Posh Parade dressed just as one is. No sword, no armour.

QUEEN: Alack! O woe! I'll not clap eyes on you no moe.

KING: Come, Willy. Come, Silly.

They go. The QUEEN *and* BILLIKINS *go to the window.*

QUEEN, BILLIKINS: God and St Nick protect you.

QUEEN: Billikins, come with me to church. We'll pray for them.

2

The parade ground. The BALONIAN ARMY, GOOD KING WENCESLAS, WILLY, SILLY, PA UBU, DOGPILE *and his* BARMPOTS, BIG BAD BERNIE, WALLOP, MCCLUB.

KING: Baron Ubu, stand beside one, you and your chaps. It's time to inspect the troops.

PA UBU: (*Aside to his men.*) Any minute now. (*To the king.*) Right behind you, sire.

UBU'S *men gather round the* KING.

KING: Ah! The Forty-seventh Mounted Foot and Mouth. Aren't they something?

PA UBU: They're rubbish. Look at that one, there. Oi, monkey's armpit, have you forgotten how to shave?

KING: He looks smooth enough to one. Pa Ubu, what's up?

PA UBU: This.

He stamps on his foot.

KING: Bastard.

PA UBU: SHIKT! It's time!

DOGPILE: Pile on, lads.

They all attack the KING. *One* BARMPOT *explodes.*

KING: One's done for! Help! One's dead.

WILLY: (*To* SILLY.) I say. Up and at 'em, what?

PA UBU: I've got the crown. See to the rest of them.

DOGPILE: Get the bastards. Now!

The PRINCES *run for it. All chase them.*

3

QUEEN ROSAMOND, BILLIKINS

QUEEN: Oh that's better. I love a good pray.

BILLIKINS: There's nothing to be afraid of.

Huge shouting, off.

What's that? I say, my brothers. Pa Ubu and his badlads, after them.

QUEEN: God save us. Saints and martyrs! They're gaining on them.

BILLIKINS: The whole bally army, following Pa Ubu. Where's his Majesty? Oh! I say!

QUEEN: Willy's down. Poor Willy's shot.

BILLIKINS: Silly!

SILLY *turns.*

Look out!

QUEEN: He's surrounded.

BILLIKINS: He's done for. Dogpile's sliced him like salami.

QUEEN: Saints and martyrs! They've broken into the palace. They're climbing the stairs. They're foaming at the mouth.

QUEEN, BILLIKINS: (*On their knees.*) God save us. Please.

BILLIKINS: If I get my hands on that bounder Ubu ...

4

The same. The door is broken down. PA UBU *and the* BARMPOTS *burst in.*

PA UBU: Yeah, Billikins? What will you do?

BILLIKINS: Good god, man, I'll defend my mater. To the last drop of blood. Take one step further, make one's day.

PA UBU: Dogpile, I'm scared. I'm off.

SOLDIER: (*Advancing.*) Billikins, on guard!

BILLIKINS: On guard yourself.

He bops his bonce.

QUEEN: Bully for Billy! One for you!

OTHERS: (*Advancing.*) We'll see to you, Billikins. We'll take good care of you.

BILLIKINS: Bounders! Ruffians! Take that! And that!

He whirls his sabre and massacres them.

PA UBU: He's a slinky little slicer. But that won't save his bacon.

BILLIKINS: Mater, escape by the secret passage.

QUEEN: What about you, son? What about you?

BILLIKINS: I'll follow.

PA UBU: Grab the queen. Oh, she's gone. Right, you bastard ...

He advances on BILLIKINS.

BILLIKINS: Cry God for Billikins and Sangorge!

He nicks UBU's *napper with a savage swordslice.*

Mater, wait for me!

He escapes by the secret passage.

5

A cave in the mountains. BILLIKINS, QUEEN ROSAMOND.

BILLIKINS: We'll be quite safe here.
QUEEN: Oh, Billikins. Ah.

She falls on the snow.

BILLIKINS: What's the matter, mater?
QUEEN: I'm ill, Bill. I've only two hours to live.
BILLIKINS: Good lord. Hypothermia?
QUEEN: So many blows. How could I endure? His majesty murdered, our family finished – and you, last remnant of the royal race, forced to flee, here in the hills, like a common catnapper.
BILLIKINS: And forced by *him*, what's more. That bounder Ubu. That oik. That swine. When I think how the pater larded him with honours, lorded him – for this! The very next morning, a knife in the guts. That's hardly cricket. Not fair at all.
QUEEN: Oh Billikins, remember how happy we were before Pa Ubu came! Ah me, what a change is here.
BILLIKINS: Chin up, mater. We'll bide our time. We'll watch for the sunrise. We'll remember who we are.
QUEEN: The sunrise! Ah child, for you perhaps, glad dawn. But these poor eyes won't live to see it.
BILLIKINS: What's up? She's white. She's limp. Anyone there? I say . . . ? Oh lord, her heart's not beating. She's dead. Good grief, yet another of Pa Ubu's victims.

He hides his face in his hands and sobs.

It isn't fair. Alone at fourteen years old, with such violent vengeance to bally bear.

He surrenders himself to the most violent despair. Meanwhile, the ghosts of GOOD KING WENCESLAS, SILLY, WILLY *and* QUEEN ROSAMOND, *plus their* ANCESTORS, *fill the cave.*

The senior GHOST *goes to* BILLIKINS *and prods him tenderly.*

GHOST: Bear with me, Billikins. In life, I was Vaslav the Versatile, first king and founder of our royal line. To you, now, I hand this holy task: our vengeance.

He gives him a big sword.

And this great big sword. Let it not rest nor sleep till that traitor dieth, till it encompasseth his death.

All the GHOSTS *disappear, leaving* BILLIKINS *in a state of exaltation.*

6

The royal palace. PA UBU, MA UBU, DOGPILE.

PA UBU: I bloody will not. Bumbrains! Why should I bankrupt myself for them?

DOGPILE: It's traditional, Pa Ubu. Coronation . . . goodies for everyone. People expect it.
MA UBU: Loads to eat, a mint of money, or you'll be out by Tuesday.
PA UBU: Mintomoney, no. Loadsteat, fine. Knacker three old nags. That's good enough for lardipuffs like them.
MA UBU: Look who's talking. Lardipuffs!
PA UBU: I keep telling you, I'm here to make my pile. Mine, every penny, mine.
MA UBU: You've got the Balonian Big Bank. What more d'you want?
DOGPILE: I know. In the cathedral. There's hidden treasure. I know where it is. We'll give them that.
PA UBU: Just you try. One finger . . .
DOGPILE: Pa Ubu, unless you give them something, they'll never pay their taxes.
PA UBU: You're kidding.
MA UBU: No he's not.
PA UBU: Oh, all right. Do what you like. Three million cash, a billion chopsansteaks. Just leave some for me!

Exeunt.

7

Palace courtyard, full of people. PA UBU, *crowned.* MA UBU, DOGPILE, FLUNKEYS *staggering with meat.*

PEOPLE: Up Ubu. Hurray! Up Ubu. Yay!
PA UBU: (*Throwing gold.*) There. There. I'm not doing this because I like it. It was Ma's idea. Be sure and pay your taxes.
ALL: We will. We will.
DOGPILE: Ma Ubu, look. They're fighting for the cash. It's hell down there.
MA UBU: Fooagh, look: he's had his brains bashed in.
PA UBU: Lovely! Bring more gold.
DOGPILE: Suppose we had a race?
PA UBU: Brilliant. (*To the* PEOPLE.) Friends, you see this golden treasure chest? Stuffed with money. Thirty zillion nicker. Balonian bazoomas, every pee of it: no rubbish. Anyone who wants to be in the race, go over there. Start when I wave my hanky. First here gets the lot. If you don't win, the consolation prize is this other chest. You share it: everyone gets something.
ALL: Yeehah! God save the king. Up Ubu. It was never like this when Good King Wenceslas was king.
PA UBU: (*Joyfully to* MA UBU.) Listen to them!

The PEOPLE *line up at one side of the courtyard.*

One, two, three. Are you ready?
ALL: Yes! Yes!
PA UBU: Go!

They surge forward. Jostling, tumult.

DOGPILE: They're coming! They're coming!

PA UBU: Him in front, he's flagging.

MA UBU: No, he's not. Come on!

DOGPILE: Ah, he came too soon. Come on, the other one! Come on!

The runner who had been second wins.

ALL: Fast Freddie! Hurray! Hurray!

FAST FREDDIE: Sire, what can I say? Your majesty, your majesty ...

PA UBU: Tsk, it's nothing. Freddie, lovey, take your money. Enjoy. Mwah, mwah. And the rest of you, here's yours. One coin each, until they're done.

ALL: Yay! Fast Freddie, Pa Ubu! Hurray! Hurray!

PA UBU: All right, it's dinner time. You're all invited. In you go!

PEOPLE: In! Up Ubu! Hurray!

They go into the palace. We hear the noise of revelry, and it lasts all night. Curtain.

End of Act 2.

Act 3

1

The palace. PA UBU, MA UBU.

PA UBU: Stagger me sideways, I've dunnit: king. I've had the party ... got the angover ... Next, the great big cloak.

MA UBU: Very naice, Pa Ubu. It's naice being royal.

PA UBU: You said it, girl.

MA UBU: We've such a lot to thank him for.

PA UBU: Who?

MA UBU: Captain Dogpile. Lord de Lawdy.

PA UBU: Lord de Lawdy? You're joking. Now I don't need him any more, he can stuff his lordship.

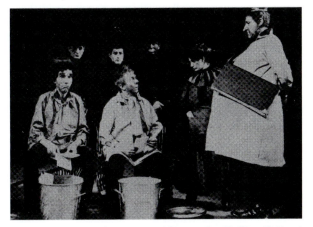

Figure 9 *Ubu* directed by Jean Vilar at the Théâtre National Populaire, in 1958. (Photographer: Bernand.)

MA UBU: Bad idea, Pa Ubu. He may turn nasty.

PA UBU: I'm so frightened! Him and that Billikins.

MA UBU: You're not frightened of Billikins?

PA UBU: Tickle me taxes, he's fourteen years old! A spottibot!

MA UBU: Pa Ubu, be careful. Be naice to him. Bribe him.

PA UBU: More money down the tubes! I've spent sixty squillion already.

MA UBU: I'm telling you, Billikins'll win. He's got justice fighting on his side.

PA UBU: So bloody what? We've got injustice, haven't we? You piss me off, Ma Ubu. I'll settle you.

He chases her out.

2

Great hall of the palace. PA UBU, MA UBU, OFFICERS, SOLDIERS, BIG BAD BERNIE, WALLOP, MCCLUB, NOBS IN CHAINS, BANKERS, LAWYERS, CLERKS.

PA UBU: Bring the nob-box, the nob-hook, the nob-knife, the nob-ledger – and the nobs.

The NOBS are pushed forward, roughly.

MA UBU: Pa Ubu, please. Go easy.

PA UBU: Listen up. Royal decree. To enrich the state, I'm going to do in all the nobs and snitch their loot.

NOBS: Ooh! Aah! Help!

PA UBU: Bring me Nob Number One. And the nob-hook. All those condemned to death, I shove down this hole. Down to the Slushpile to be debrained. (*To the NOB.*) What's your name, dogbum?

NOB: Viscount of Vitebsk.

PA UBU: How much is that worth?

NOB: Three million a year.

PA UBU: Guilty!

He hooks him down the chute.

MA UBU: You're so strict.

PA UBU: Next nob. What's your name?

Silence.

Answer, bogbrain.

SECOND NOB: Protector of Pinsk. Not to mention Minsk.

PA UBU: Ducky. Down you go. Next! What an ugly bastard. Who are you?

THIRD NOB: Holder of Hanover, Halle and Harrogate.

PA UBU: Three in one? Down the tube. Next nob. Name?

FOURTH NOB: Proud Palatine of Polock.

PA UBU: Pollocks to that, mate. Down the tube. What's biting you, Ma Ubu?

MA UBU: You're being so fierce.

PA UBU: I'm working. Making my fortune. I'll hear the list now. Clerk of the Court, MY list. MY titles. Read MY list to ME.

CLERK: Viscount of Vitebsk. Protector of Pinsk. Holder of Hanover, Halle, Harrogate. Palatine of Polock.

PA UBU: Yes. *Well . . .*?

CLERK: That's all.

PA UBU: What d'you mean, that's all? Come here, nobs. The lot of you. I'm not rich enough yet, so you're all for the chop. You've got it, I need it. Stuff the nobs down the tube.

The NOBS are stuffed down the hatch.

Get a nurdle on. I've laws to pass.

SEVERAL: Big deal.

PA UBU: Lawyers first, then bankers.

SEVERAL LAWYERS: Objection! Nolle prosequi. Status quo.

PA UBU: Shikt. Law Number One: judges' salaries. Abolished.

JUDGES: What'll we live on? We're skint. All skint.

PA UBU: Live on the fines.

FIRST JUDGE: Impossible.

SECOND JUDGE: Outrageous.

THIRD JUDGE: Unheard-of.

FOURTH JUDGE: Beyond the pale.

JUDGES: Under these conditions, we refuse to judge.

PA UBU: All judges down the tube!

They struggle, in vain.

MA UBU: What're you doing, Pa Ubu? Who'll do the judging, now?

PA UBU: Watch and see. Who's next, now? Bankers.

BANKERS: No change!

PA UBU: First off, I want half of all charges.

BANKERS: You're joking.

PA UBU: And here *are* some charges: property, ten percent, commerce and industry, twenty-five percent, marriage and death fifty nicker each.

FIRST BANKER: Pa Ubu, it just isn't viable.

SECOND BANKER: It doesn't add up.

THIRD BANKER: Neither ult nor inst.

PA UBU: Take the piss, would you? Down the tube!

The BANKERS are downchuted.

MA UBU: Fine king you are, killing the whole world.

PA UBU: Don't worry, girl. I'll go from town to town myself, collect the cash.

3

Rude hut in the Balonian countryside. PEASANTS.

PEASANT: (*Entering.*) I come with news. His majesty's no more. His sons no more. Save Billikins. He got away. His mummy too. They're in the hills. Pa Ubu's nabbed the throne.

ANOTHER PEASANT: And that's not all. I've just been to town and they were carting corpses and the corpses belonged to three hundred executed nobles and five hundred executed judges and they're doubling the taxes and Pa Ubu's coming to collect them in person.

ALL: Alack! What now? Pa Ubu's a rotten swine and his family's no better. Or so they say.

PEASANT: Hark! What's that? There's someone at the door.

PA UBU: (*Outside.*) Rumblestuffsticks! Open up! By shikt, by Dikt, by good saint Nickt, cashknackers, slashpacks, I want your tax!

The door is broken down. UBU bursts in, with a pack of CASHHOUNDS.

4

PA UBU: Who's the oldest?

A PEASANT steps forward.

PEASANT: Norbert Nurdle.

PA UBU: Right. Listen. Rumblestuffsticks, I said listen. D'you want these frensomine to clip your clackers?

PEASANT: But your Majesty hasn't said anything.

PA UBU: Wrong, pal. I've been flapping my gob for the whole last hour. Fetch out your tax-pot, now, or die. Cashandlers, the cashcart.

The cashcart is brought in.

PEASANT: The point is, sirc, we're covered by limited liability. The documents were based on an assessment of wundruntunty poundipees. And we paid in full, the Feast of St Multiple Ult.

PA UBU: So what? I've changed the rules. It was in the paper: all taxes to be paid twice over, except those I may dream up later, to be paid three times. Simple, innit? I make my fortune, snickersnack, then kill the whole world and buggeroff.

PEASANTS: Lord Ubu, have pity. We're honest, simple folk. We're poor.

PA UBU: Tough titty. Pay. Unless you want the rest of it. Neck-knotting, noodle-nackering. Rumblestuffsticks, I am the bloody king.

PEASANTS: You aren't. Revolution! Up Billikins. His majesty. The king.

PA UBU: Cashcarters, kill.

A battle begins. The house is wrecked. None escape except old NORBERT, who legs it across the plain. UBU is left alone, scooping cash.

5

Dungeon. UBU, with DOGPILE in chains.

PA UBU: It's just what happens, mate. You ask for what I owe you, I say no, you turn nasty, you end up here. Goldalmighty! It's perfect. Couldn't be better. You've got to agree.

DOGPILE: Pa Ubu, beware. Five days you've held this throne. You've killed. You just don't care. Dead corpses scream and groan for vengeance. Pa Ubu, beware.

PA UBU: Very good: a poet, and don't you know it. If you once got out of here ...! Oh yes, oh yes. How lucky for me that this dank deep dungeon, enclosed by craggy castle, has never popped a prisoner yet. Night night, sleep tight, keep hold of your nicker-nack, the rats here bite.

Exit. TURNKEYS *bolt all the doors.*

6

Palace of TSAR ALEXIS OF ALL THE RUSSKIES. TSAR ALEXIS, *his* COURTIERS, DOGPILE.

ALEXIS: Base mercenary wretch! Wast even thou who conspired to do in our good king cousin, Wenceslas?

DOGPILE: I'm sorry, sire. Pa Ubu made me. I didn't want to.

ALEXIS: Big liar. Never mind. What d'you want now?

DOGPILE: Pa Ubu dungeoned me for treason. I managed to escape. I've been on the road five days, five nights. Galloping. On a horse. To beg your royal pardon.

ALEXIS: What practical proof presentest thou?

DOGPILE: My soldier's sword. And this detailed plan of the castle.

ALEXIS: We accept the sword. But burn the plan, by Genghis. We'll not come top by cheating.

DOGPILE: One of Good King Wenceslas' sons, young Billikins, still lives. To see him on the throne, I'd give my all.

ALEXIS: In the Brave Balonian Battalions, what place hadst thou?

DOGPILE: Commander of the fifth phalanx of fusiliers. Pa Ubu's personal protectors.

ALEXIS: OK. Thou'rt now lieutenant of lancers. Sub. If thou dost well, thou gets rewarded. If thou betray'st us, watch out.

DOGPILE: I lack not courage, sire.

ALEXIS: Good. Vanish from our presence. Scat.

Exit.

7

UBU's *council chamber.* PA UBU, MA UBU, COUNCILLORS.

PA UBU: Order. I declare this meeting open. Stretch your ears and flab your gobs. Agenda: one, cashcount. Two, my new idea: how to keep it sunny and do away with rain.

COUNCILLOR: Lord Ubu, brilliant.

MA UBU: Licker.

PA UBU: Queen of my shikt, button it. We're not doing badly, lords. Our brass-knuckle boys bring in the bacon. Our mother-muggers work miracles. Everywhere you look, you see nothing but houses crumbling and citizens grumbling under the burden of our bills.

COUNCILLOR: The new taxes, Lord Ubu. What about them?

MA UBU: They're rubbish. Tax on marriages: three pee. Pa Ubu's chasing people in the street and forcing them into church.

PA UBU: Stuffsticks! Chancelloress of the Exchequeress, I'm talking.

Enter MESSENGER.

What's he want? Blugger off, cat-basket, or I'll trundle your trollops and snaggle your snipes.

MA UBU: Too late. He's gone. He left this postcard.

PA UBU: You read it. I'm depressed. I've forgotten how to read. Get a grundle on. It'll be from Dogpile.

MA UBU: So it is. 'Having a lovely taime. Tsar Alexis of all the Russkies really naice. Invading tomorrow to put Billikins back on throne and stuff your guts. Regards ...'

PA UBU: I'm done for. The naughty man's coming to hurt me. St Nickerless, oelpme, I'll give you all my taxes. God, tell me what to do. I'll even pray. Oh what am I to do?

He sobs and sobs.

MA UBU: Pa Ubu, there's only one thing for it. War.

ALL: Hurrah! Fight! Yay!

PA UBU: Oh brilliant. Thrashed again.

FIRST COUNCILLOR: Call up the army.

SECOND COUNCILLOR: Lines of supply.

THIRD COUNCILLOR: Forts, cannons, balls.

FOURTH COUNCILLOR: Cash for our boys.

PA UBU: Ah! No. What d'you take me for? Me, pay? No chance. Stagger me sideways, we'll fight if you're all so eager. But pay? Not me.

ALL: War! War! Yay!

8

In camp outside UBU's *capital city.* PA UBU, MA UBU, SOLDIERS, BARMPOTS.

SOLDIERS AND BARMPOTS: Up Baloney! Up Ubu!

PA UBU: Ma Ubu, give me my breastplate. My poky-stick. I'll be so loaded, I won't be able to run if they're after me.

MA UBU: Coward.

PA UBU: Godnag this shikastick. This nobhook. They won't stay put. I'll never be ready. The Russkies'll come and kill me.

SOLDIER: Lord Ubu, your snackersnicks are falling down.

PA UBU: I dead you, hookynobbyshikastick. Slicymug. Piff, paff, pah.

MA UBU: What does he look like? His breastplate, his iron hat. Like an armour-plated pumpkin.

PA UBU: Time to mount. Bring forth Cashnag.

MA UBU: Whadyoo say?

PA UBU: Cashnag. My ... charger.

MA UBU: He can't carry you. He's not been fed since Tuesday. He's a bag of bones.

PA UBU: You're joking. Twelve pee a day and still can't carry me? You're pulling my leg, cornswobbit, you're pocketing the cash.

MA UBU blushes and lowers her eyes.

Bring Cashnag Two. Rumblestuffsticks, I refuse to walk.

An enormous horse is brought in.

I'll mount. There's no air up here. I'm dizzy. I'll fall.

The horse moves off.

Help! Make it stand still. I'll fall.

MA UBU: What an idiot. He's on. He's off again.

PA UBU: Godnagit, I thought I'd had it that time. Never mind. I'm off. To war. I'll kill the whole world. Especially those who don't march in step. Ubu be angry, Ubu pullout oo teef, oo tongue.

MA UBU: Pa Ubu, farewell.

PA UBU: I forgot to tell you. Take over while I'm gone. I've got the cashledger with me, so keep your sticky hands to yourself, all right? I'm leaving Big Bad Bernie to look after you. Ma Ubu, farewell.

MA UBU: Pa Ubu, tata. Give that Tsar whatfor.

PA UBU: Watch me. Nose-knotting, teeth-twisting, tongue-tearing, noodlenackering.

Fanfares as the army marches off.

MA UBU: (*Alone.*) Hangdock he's gone. Lardifard! Right. Get organised, kill Billikins and grab the loot.

Act 4
1

Royal crypt in the cathedral

MA UBU: Where is it, the treasure? None of these stones sound hollow. I've done it right: thirteen steps along the wall from the tomb of Vaslav the Versatile. Just a minute: this one sounds hollow. Ma Ubu, to work! Prise it open. Mff! Won't budge. I'll use the cashook. It's never failed before. Haho! Kings' bones, and gold. Into the sack, all of it. Aeeh, what's that noise? Is ... anybody ... there? Nothing. Get a nurdle on. All of it. You need to see daylight, don't you, cash? Had it up to here with tombs? Put back the stone ... Ah! That noise again. I'm scared. I've had enough. I'll come back for the rest some other time. Tomorrow.

VOICE: (*From the tomb of STANLEY THE USUALLY SILENT.*) Never, Ma Ubu.

MA UBU shrieks and flees through the secret door, lugging the cashsack.

2

Square in the capital. BILLIKINS, CHAPS, SOLDIERS, PEOPLE.

BILLIKINS: I say, chaps, three cheers for Baloney and Good King Wenceslas. That bounder Ubu's legged it. There's no one left but Mater Ubu and Big Bad Bernie. I've an idea. Suppose I lead you chaps, chuck 'em out and restore my royal race?

ALL: Yay! Billikins! I say!

BILLIKINS: And when we've done that, we'll abolish all the taxes imposed by that great oik Ub.

ALL: Hurray! I say! On to the palace. Exterminate!

BILLIKINS: Oh look. Ma Ubu and her guards. There, on the palace steps.

MA UBU: What is it, gents? Oh, Billikins.

The CROWD throws stones.

FIRST GUARD: There's not a window left.

SECOND GUARD: They got me. Ah.

THIRD GUARD: I'm done for. Oh.

BILLIKINS: Keep chucking, chaps.

BIG BAD BERNIE: Hoho! Heehee! Haha!

He draws his sword and rushes among them, creating horrible havoc.

BILLIKINS. You swine. On guard.

They fight a duel.

BIG BAD BERNIE: Aah. Eeh. Ooh.

BILLIKINS: I win. Ma Ubu now.

Trumpets sound.

Jolly good. Here come the upper crust. Don't let her get away.

MA UBU runs away, with all the BALONIANS after her. Shots; stones.

3

With UBU's army, marching in Russkiland

PA UBU: Hobblit, daggit, naggit, we're passing out. Curdled. Oi, squaddie, hump this cash-helmet. Sarge, take the clacker-snips, the poky-stick. That's better. I tell you again: our cashness is curdled.

The SOLDIERS obey.

WALLOP: Seeyou, pal. Whirthell they Russkies?

PA UBU: It's bloody marvellous. Not enough cash for a chariot that fits. I ask you. To stop the nag knackering under us, our cashness has had to walk. Leading the bleeder. Just wait till we get back to Baloney. Five minutes with our physics set, our poofiprofs, we'll invent a wind-cart to waft us wherever we want. Us and our army. Well?

MCCLUB: Sorsor, Nick Nackerley. Sure tis a rush he's in.

PA UBU: All right, all right. What's up?

NICK NACKERLEY: Lord, all is lost. The Balonians have broken out. Big Bad Bernie's dead. Ma Ubu's hiding in the hills.

PA UBU: Polecat! Vulture! Fruitbat! Where did that lot come from? Puddle me. Who's responsible? Billikins, betya. Where have you come from?

NICK NACKERLEY: Baloney, sire.

PA UBU: Shikt, son, if I thought this was true we'd all be on our way home right now. But see here, sonny, you've got cloud for brains. You're dreaming, sonnikins. Go to the front line. Take a look: Russkies. We'll make a sortie, sunshine. Give it all we've got: shikthooks, cashpikes, everything.

GENERAL CUSTARD: Pa Ubu, look. Wusskies.

PA UBU: You're right. Russkies. Brilliant. If we'd some way out of here. But we haven't. We're on a hill; we're sitting ducks.

SOLDIERS: Russkies! Woe! The foe!

PA UBU: Time to get organised. For battle. We'll stay up here. No point in going down there. I'll stand in the middle. Like a living citadel. You can all protect me. Stuff your guns with bullets. Eight bullets means eight dead Russkies, eight more bastards off my back. Light armed Foot, down there. Wait till they charge, then killem. Heavy Horse, hang back, then charge. Artillery here, all round this windmill. If anything moves, shoot it. Me? Us? We'll wait inside the windmill. We'll stick our cashcannon through the window, bar the door with our poky-stick, and if anyone breaks in, they'll be really in the shikt.

OFFICERS: Sah! Sah! Sah!

PA UBU: We'll win, no problem. What time is it?

A cuckoo crows three times.

GENERAL CUSTARD: Eleven a.m.

PA UBU: Dinner time. They'll not attack till twelve. General Laski, tell the men: fall out and pee, then fall back in and start the Cashnal Anthem.

GENERAL CUSTARD: Sah. Weady, chaps? By the wight in thwees. Left wight, left wight.

Exit CUSTARD and ARMY. Impressive orchestral introduction. PA UBU sings. The ARMY comes back in time to join in the chorus.

PA UBU: God save our gracious me,
Long live our noble me,
Pour me some –

SOLDIERS: Beer, beer, beer, beer, beer, beer, beer, beer.

PA UBU: Fill up your tanks and then
Unzip your pants and then
All start to –

SOLDIERS: Pee, pee, pee, pee, pee, pee, pee, pee.

PA UBU: Soon as you've room for more
Flap gob and start to pour,
Fill up with –

SOLDIERS: Beer, beer, beer, beer, beer, beer, beer, beer.

PA UBU: I love it. I love you all.

SOLDIERS AND BARMPOTS: Till, till, till, till,
Tax, tax, tax, tax,
Up Ubu, up Ubu,
Ting, ting-a-ting.

PA UBU: I love it. I love you all.

A Russkie cannonball flies in and smashes the windmill's sail.

Ahoo! Help! They got me. No, I lied. They didn't.

4

PA UBU, GENERAL CUSTARD, MAJOR F. FORT, TSAR ALEXIS, DOGPILE, SOLDIERS, BARMPOTS, UBU'S ARMY, RUSSKIE ARMY

MAJOR F. FORT: (*Arriving.*) Lord Ubu, the Russkies are attacking.

PA UBU: Don't look at me. Snot my fault. Cashofficers, prepare for battle.

GENERAL CUSTARD: Another cannon ball.

PA UBU: I'm off. It's raining lead and iron. My cashness could get seriously croaked. Down the hill.

They all rush down the hill. Battle has begun. They vanish in the clouds of smoke at the foot of the hill.

RUSSKIE: (*Slashing.*) Yah! Take that.

GENERAL CUSTARD: Ouch. That weally hurt.

PA UBU: Say your prayers, pigbreath. Put that down. You don't scare me.

RUSSKIE: Oh, don't I? Right.

He fires.

PA UBU: Oh! I'm hit, I'm leaking, I'm buried. Only kidding. Here!

He tears strips off him.

You, Custard. Start again.

GENERAL CUSTARD: Forward. Push. Mark the man, not the ball. We're winning.

PA UBU: You think so? What are these, then? Black eyes, not medals, mate.

RUSSKIE CAVALRYMEN: Make way! His Totality the Tsar.

TSAR ALEXIS arrives, with DOGPILE in disguise.

BALONIAN SOLDIER: Help! The Tsar.

ANOTHER: He's crossed the ditch.

ANOTHER: Who's that bastard with him? The one with the big sword. Yike! That's four he's sliced.

DOGPILE: Had enough? Want more? Who the hell are you? Ha! Hey! Any more of you?

He massacres Balonians.

PA UBU: Don't just stand there. Grab him. Slab the whole lot of them. We're winning. Up ours!

ALL: Up ours! Godnagit. Grab them. Get that big bastard. Now.

DOGPILE: Sangorge. Ow.

PA UBU: (*Recognising him.*) It's Dogpile. Well, well, well. Have we something nice for you? You like things hot. Cashkindlers, light the fire. Yarg! Ooh! I'm dead. A cannonball. Our favverwichartinevven, forgivmasins. No doubt, a cannonball.

DOGPILE: It was a water pistol.

PA UBU: Bastard. Now you're for it.

He runs at him and tears strips off him.

GENERAL CUSTARD: Lord Ubu, we're winning.

PA UBU: Of course we are. I'm exhausted. I'm black and blue. I've gottosiddown. I'm globbed.

GENERAL CUSTARD: Pa Ubu, it's the Tsar you want to glob.

PA UBU: You're right. Shiktsword, hup! Cashook, ha-hey! There's work to do. How's my dear little poky-stick? All ready to tsap that Tsar? Ha-ho! Bring Cashnag, my charger, here.

He hurls himself at TSAR ALEXIS.

RUSSKIE OFFICER: Look out, sire!

PA UBU: Go stuff yourself. Ow! What are you doing? Can't we discuss this? I'm sorry, master. Don't be cross. I didn't do it on purpose.

He legs it. TSAR ALEXIS *runs after him.*

Oh shikt, he's after me. He's furious. Oh brilliant, here's the ditch. The ditch in front, and him behind. Nothing for it. Eyes shut and –

He jumps the ditch. TSAR ALEXIS *falls in.*

TSAR ALEXIS: I've fallen in.

POLSKIES: He's ditched! Hurrah!

PA UBU: Hm. Dare I look? He's fallen in. They're bashing his bonce. That's good. Keep at it, lads. Kick him, strangle him, smash the swine. I daren't watch. It's all come out exactly as we predicted. One's poky-stick did sterling work. One would have completely done him in if dire, sudden dread hadn't drained one's deadliness. One was unexpectedly compelled to do a runner. We owe our present safety, in part, to our own imperial skill as horseman and in part to the hocks and withers of our charger Cashnag, whose speed is equalled only by his strength and whose swiftness is sung in song and story – oh and the deepness of the ditch which loomed at the feet of the foe of yourumble serfint chancellstecker. Bloody good speech. Why thangyew. Pity no one else was listening. Back to work!

The Russkie Light Horse make a sortie and rescue TSAR ALEXIS.

GENERAL CUSTARD: We've weally had it now.

PA UBU: I'm off, then. Balonians, quick march. This way. No, that way.

BALONIANS: Run for it!

PA UBU: You said it. Stop pushing. Don't jostle. Make room for me.

He is jostled.

Watch it. Wanna coppa cashclub? He's gone. Right, leg it, and fast before that Laski sees us.

He goes. Soon afterwards, we see TSAR ALEXIS *and the* RUSSKIE ARMY *routing the Balonians.*

5

Cave in the hills. It is snowing. PA UBU, WALLOP, MCCLUB.

PA UBU: Fweeorg. It's cold. Brass monkeys. My cashness is not enjoying this.

WALLOP: Seeyou, pal. How's the terror? How's the running?

PA UBU: The terror's gone. I've still got the runs.

MCCLUB: (*Aside.*) Osor, osor.

PA UBU: Hey McClub. Your snickersnack. Howizzit?

MCCLUB: Fine sor, tanksforaskin. Except it's not well at all, atall. I can't get the bullet out. Seesor, it's dragging on the ground.

PA UBU: That'll teach you. Button it up, next time. You want to be like me. Lion-hearted, but cautious. I massacred four of them, in person, not counting the ones that were dead already when I did 'em.

WALLOP: Seeyou, McClub. What happened to wee Nick Nackerley?

MCCLUB: Brained by a bullet.

PA UBU: Behold, as the flowers of the field are felled, hoed by the heedless, heartless hoe of the heedless, heartless hoer who heartlessly hacks their heads, so now Nick Nackerley. Proud as a poppy, dead as a dandelion. Fiercely he fought, but there were just too-too many Russkies.

WALLOP: Seeyou.

MCCLUB: Sorsor.

ECHO: Ee-oo-aw.

WALLOP: Wossaht? Whairsma-weenife?

PA UBU: Not more Russkies. I'm sick of them. Where are you? I'll blugger the lotayoo.

6

Enter a BEAR.

MCCLUB: Osor, osor.

PA UBU: Oh look. Nice doggie. Here boy. Miaow, miaow.

WALLOP: Jings, it's a fooky bear, anabigyin.

PA UBU: A bear! A fookybear! It'll eat me. Dog protect me. It's coming for me. No, it's biting McClub. What a relief.

The BEAR *attacks* MCCLUB. WALLOP *goes for it with his knife.* UBU *climbs a rock.*

MCCLUB: Help. Wallop. Sorsorelp.

PA UBU: Get stuffed. We're saying our prayers. It's you it's eating: not our turn.

WALLOP: Ahavit, Ahavit.

MCCLUB: Pull. It's weakening, sohtis.

PA UBU: For wotweerabowtoreseev.

MCCLUB: Sorosor.

WALLOP: It's got me in its fangs. Ah hate this.

PA UBU: Thelordsmasheperd.

MCCLUB: There. Got it.

WALLOP: It's bleeding. Yay!

In the midst of the BARMPOTS' *cheers, the* BEAR *roars in agony and* PA UBU *continues to mutter prayers.*

MCCLUB: Hold it tight. I'll get my nuclear knuckleduster.

PA UBU: Makethmetoliedown.

WALLOP: Hurry up. Ahcannycope.

PA UBU: Greenpasturesleadeathme.

MCCLUB: There. Here.

Huge explosion. The BEAR *falls dead.*

WALLOP AND MCCLUB: Ta–RA!

PA UBU: Stillwatersby amen. Well? Is it dead yet? Can I come down off this rock?

WALLOP: (*Scornfully.*) Please yersel.

PA UBU: (*Climbing down.*) Well, aren't you lucky? Still alive, still slushing the snow – and all thanks to my imperial cashness. Who was it who nabbled his nidgets and gabbled his gob saying prayers for you? Who acked it with oliness as bravely as Barmpot McClubere banged it withis brass-nuckle bomlet? Who urried up this illere to itch is words igher in eaven's earole?

WALLOP: Yerbum.

PA UBU: What a monster. Thanks to me: dinner. Look at its belly. The Greeks could have used it for a woodenorse. Room for plenty more inside – as we very nearly saw for ourselves, dear friends.

WALLOP: Ma gut thinks ma throat's been cut. What's teat?

MCCLUB: Bear.

PA UBU: No, no, no, no, no. Are you going to eat it raw? We've nothing to light a fire.

WALLOP: We've pustols, flunts.

PA UBU: So we have. And now I remember, there's a bunchatrees just up the road, crammed with dry wood. McClub, go fetch.

MCCLUB trudges off across the snow.

WALLOP: Right. Lord Ubu, you carve.

PA UBU: Ah no. It may not be really dead. In any case, you're half eaten already. Bitten to bits. You do it. I'll light the fire, ready for when he brings the wood.

WALLOP starts carving up the BEAR.

Ah! He moved.

WALLOP: Lord Ubu, he's cold.

PA UBU: Tut. So much nicer hot. He'll give my cashness indigestion.

WALLOP: (*Aside.*) He's terrable. (*Aloud.*) Lord Ubu, give us a hand. Ahcannycope.

PA UBU: I can't. I won't. I'm tired.

MCCLUB: (*Returning.*) Snojoke. Snoin. Slike the North Pole, sohtis, or the West Pole. Safter teatime. Lbedark in anhour. Lessgeta move on while we can still see. At all.

PA UBU: Hear that, Wallop? Get on. Both of you, gerron. Carvim, cookim, I'm starvinere.

WALLOP: Seeyou, fatso. Ifye willniwork, yecannyeat.

PA UBU: See if I care. I like it raw. It's you two who'll suffer. I'm going to sleep.

MCCLUB: Sleep, is it? Sure and we'll do the job ourselves. He'll not see none of it, willewallop? Praps a bit of a bone or two.

WALLOP: The fire's beginnintaeburn.

PA UBU: That's better. Warmer. Russkies, everywhere. What a victory. Ah.

He falls asleep.

MCCLUB: Now, master Wallop, what say you? Nick Nackerley brought news: what truth was in't? The common talk is this: Ma Ubu deposéd stands. In my nostrils, it hath the smell of truth.

WALLOP: Purrameatonablurryfire.

MCCLUB: Nay, matters more urgent crave attention. And ere we act, we must have certain news.

WALLOP: Thou hast the right of it. Pa Ubu sleepeth. Shall we leave him where he lieth, or thtay with him?

MCCLUB: Night bringeth counsel. Knit up the ravelled sleeve of sleep, and when Dawn's candles prick we'll know just what to do.

WALLOP: Nay. While yet tis dark, snatch our chance and scarper.

MCCLUB: After you.

They go.

7

PA UBU: (*Talking in his sleep.*) Russkies, don't shoot. There's someone here. Whosat? Dogpile. Can't bearim. Bear. As bad as Billikins. He's after me as well. Gerroff. Shoo. Buggeroff. Nick Nackerley, now. The Tsar. Can't touch ME-hee. Missussubu. What you got there, girl? Wheredyoo get that gold? Thassmine, you old bag, you been diggin in the cathedral. Digginup my tomb. I've been dead for years. Billikins done me in. Laid to rest in the Cathedral. Next to Vaslav the Versatile. And in the cemetery, next to Roger the Ratbag. And in that prison cell, next to Dogpile. Not him again. Bear, buggeroff. Satanspawn, begawn. What d'you mean, can't hear me? Oh, the Barmpots lopped your lugoils. Debrainin, snackersnikin, taxnabbin, boozinanboozin, thassalife. For Barmpots, Cashlads, his right royal cashness, me.

He snores and sleeps.

Act 5

1

Night. PA UBU *asleep.* MA UBU *comes in. She doesn't see him. It's pitch dark.*

MA UBU: At last, somewhere to hide. No one about. Suits me. What a journey! Four days; one end of Baloney to the other. Whatever *could* have happened, *happened*, all at once. Fatso nags out of it on his charger. I creep into the crypt to nabisloot. Next thing, Billikins and his berserkers are almost stoning me to death. I lose my protector, Big Bad Bernie, who was so besotted with my charms that he fell in a heap every time he saw me, and every time he didn't, which is a sign of real true love. Said he'd sliced into snippets for my sake, poor lamb. And so he was. By Billikins. Slish, slash, slosh. Aah. I nearly died. Anyway, I escape. They're all after me. Foaming with fury. I leave the palace. Down to the river. Guards on every bridge. I swim across: that'll foolem. Nobs pile after me. I'm surrounded, on every side. They're foaming at the mouth. At last I make it. One end of Baloney to the other. Four days, tramping through the snow in my own queendom, as used to be, till I end up here. Safe. Four days, I haven't et or drunk. Billikins was too close for that. Nehmind, I made it. Bleah, I'm famished. I'm freezing. What happened to old lardibags, I mean to my lord and master? Not to mention Cashnag. Died of hunger, poor old devil. Nehmind, eh? *And* I forgot the treasure. Left it in the palace. Finders keepers. Who cares?

PA UBU: (*Stirring in his sleep.*) Arrest Ma Ubu. Snackersnicker.

MA UBU: Aee. Where is this? I don't believe it. Dog, no! Pa Ubu sleepineer? That's queer. Wake him gently. Oi, gutbag, shake a leg.

PA UBU: Bloodyell, didyeseet? That bear? It was brain against bruin. Brian won, completely gobbled and globbed that brown. Wait till it's light, lads: you'll see, you'll see.

MA UBU: He's babbling. Dafter than when he started. Who's he on about?

PA UBU: McClub! Wallop! Sakashikt, where are you? I'm scared. Someone said something. Who? Not ... the bear? Shikt. Matches, matches ... Lostem in the fight.

MA UBU: (*Aside.*) Exploit the state he's in, the dark. Pretend to be a spook. Make him promise to forgiveusour cashpassin.

PA UBU: Dogalmighty. There is someone there. O-elp. I wish I was dead.

MA UBU: (*Making her voice huge.*) True, Ubu, too troo. There's someone here. The voice of doom looms from the tomb. Your fairy godmother: speciality, good advice.

PA UBU: Get stuffed.

MA UBU: Interrupt me not, or I shut my gob and you get stuffed.

PA UBU: Cornswobbit. Not another word. Do go on, your spookiness.

MA UBU: We were just going to say, Master Ubu, what a naughty little boy you are.

PA UBU: Naughty. What? Yes. Yes.

MA UBU: Godnagit, shuttit!

PA UBU: A swearing fairy.

MA UBU: (*Aside.*) Shikt. (*Aloud.*) Master Ub, you're married?

PA UBU: To vinegar-features, of course I am.

MA UBU: You mean, to the most charming waife in all the world.

PA UBU: I mean, a porcupine. Prickles everywhere. You don't know where to grab.

MA UBU: Try grabbing naicely. She could be ever so naice.

PA UBU: So full of lice?

MA UBU: Listen! Willy little boy! Sit up straight, fold your arms, pay attention! (*Aside.*) Get a nurdle on. It's nearly dawn. (*Aloud.*) Master Ub, your waife is soft and sweet, without a fault.

PA UBU: Ah, rubbish. It's *all* her fault.

MA UBU: Dognagit. She's true to you, too troo.

PA UBU: Of course she is. Who else'd have her?

MA UBU: Bastard! (*Recovering.*) Your waife steals not your gold.

PA UBU: Rubbish.

MA UBU: Not a penny peeeece.

PA UBU: So wottabat dear ole Cashnag? Three months, nothing teat, dragged by the bridle halfway round the world, dead in harness, poor old devil.

MA UBU: Not troo! Your waife is sweeeet and you're a beeeest.

PA UBU: Stuff yoo! My wife's a tart and you're a fart.

MA UBU: Master Ub, beware. You murdered Good King Wenceslas.

PA UBU: Not my fault. Ma Ubu made me.

MA UBU: You had Willy and Silly done to death.

PA UBU: Tough titty. They were after me.

MA UBU: You broke your word to Dogpile. Then you killed him.

PA UBU: He wanted to be Lord de Lawdy. So did I. Now no one is. That proves it. It wasn't me.

MA UBU: There's only one way to redeeeem your siiiiiins.

PA UBU: What is it? I'll do anything, be good, be nice, be famous.

MA UBU: You must forgive Ma Ubu for snafflin a bit of snitch.

PA UBU: Forgive her, yes. When she pays it back, when I blattererer blackanbloo, when she gives ole Cashnag the kissolife.

MA UBU: He's hooked on that horse. Yike, I'm done for: dawn.

PA UBU: So now I've proof, my own missus was robbinme. You told me. She's additnow. Guilty as charged, verdict of you all, hanged by the neck, signed, sealed delivered, no appeal. Hey up: dawn. Cashnagit, it's her. Ma Ubu.

MA UBU: (*Offendedly.*) Coursitsnot. I'll doooo for yoooo.

PA UBU: Come off it, nagbag.

MA UBU: Cheeky devil.

PA UBU: I can see it's you. What the L U doinere?

MA UBU: Big Bad Bernie's dead and the Balonians are after me.

PA UBU: Thassalaff. The Russkies a rafterME. And when they catch me –

MA UBU: They can keep you.

PA UBU: They can keep this fookybear. Here, catch.

He throws the BEAR *at her.*

MA UBU: (*Collapsing under it.*) Ai. Yarg. Bleah. I can't breathe. It's biting me. It's eating me. It's digesting me.

PA UBU: It's dead, you fool. Just a minute, spose-it snot? Salive? O-eck.

He climbs his rock again.

Our fetherwich artineven.

MA UBU: (*Throwing off the* BEAR.) Where's he gone?

PA UBU: Yike. She'sere! Protectusfromevil. Is it dead?

MA UBU: It's all right, ploppipants, it's cold. How did it get here?

PA UBU: (*Mumbling.*) I dunno. Yes I do. It was going to eat Wallop and McClub, but I killed it with a pilaprayer.

MA UBU: Wallop, McClub, a pilaprayer? Cashnagit, he's off his nut.

PA UBU: *You're* off *your* nut, naggybag.

MA UBU: So tell me about your fighting.

PA UBU: Won't. Too long. I was very, very brave, and they all kept hitting me.

MA UBU: Even the Balonians?

PA UBU: 'Up Wence!' they shouted. 'Up Billikins!' They were really after me. And they crushed poorole Custard.

MA UBU: See if I care. Billikins bashed up Big Bad Bernie.

PA UBU: See if I care. They knackered Nick Nackerley.

MA UBU: See if I care.

PA UBU: Right, naggybag, that does it. Cumere. Down on thy knees, avaunt.

He forces her to her knees.

Base wretch, thou'rt for it now.

MA UBU: You and whose army?

PA UBU: Denosing, deluggering, debumming, debraining, demarrowing, deswimbladdering, deneckeration. Whadd-yoo thinko THIS?

He tears strips off her.

MA UBU: Ow. Pa Ubu. No.

Huge noise outside the cave.

2

PA UBU, MA UBU, BILLIKINS, CHAPS

BILLIKINS *and his* CHAPS *rush into the cave.*

BILLIKINS: This way, chaps. Yay! Up Baloney!

PA UBU: Hang on, I'm busy. My better half.

BILLIKINS: (*Bashing him.*) Take that, you pig, you dog, you louse, you chicken, you unmitigated swine.

PA UBU: (*Giving as good as he gets.*) Take that, pintpot, poultice, salad-bowl, squirt, stuffed shirt.

MA UBU: (*Having a bash as well.*) Take that, babyface, pisspant, noserag, bumwipe, bib.

The CHAPS *pile on. The* UBS *defend themselves as best they can.*

PA UBU: There's millions of em.

MA UBU: So kick their heads in.

PA UBU: Stagger me sideways, yes. Haha, haHA. Another one! I wish I'd Cashnag ere.

BILLIKINS: Bashem. On! On! On!

VOICE: (*Off.*) Up Ubu. His Cashness. Yaaah!

PA UBU: At last. The Ubbibums. This way, cashhounds, eel, inere.

The BARMPOTS *pile in and pile on.*

MCCLUB: Start runnin, Balonians, sotis, yaah.

WALLOP: Seeyooboo, pushyerweewayoot. Taethedoor. Then run.

BILLIKINS: I say. That hurt.

BARMPOT: No it didn't.

BILLIKINS: Oh, right. Willy me.

ANOTHER BARMPOT: They're nearly out. On, on, on, on.

WALLOP: Thisway. Ahcanseeablurrysky. CumOHN.

MCCLUB: Osor, don't panic. Run.

PA UBU: Now I've flapped in my pants. Cornswobbit, NOW! Bangem, blobem, gashem, globem. HaHAH.

WALLOP: Two left. Behind you. There.

PA UBU: (*Bashing them with the* BEAR.) One, two. Feeoo! There! I'm out. Run for it. This way. After meeeeeeee!

3

The Middle of Nowhere. It's snowy. THE UBS *and the* BARMPOTS, *legging it.*

PA UBU: We've made it. They've given up.

MA UBU: He's gone to be crowned, that Billikins.

PA UBU: He can keep his crown.

MA UBU: Pa Ubu, you're right.

They disappear into the distance.

4

On board a ship skimming the ocean. On deck, PA UBU and all the rest.

CAPTAIN: What a balmy breeze.

PA UBU: Observe with what prodigious speed we skim the waves. At a rough estimate, one million knots per hour. Reef knots, every one of them. It's what we sailors call a breeze behind.

WALLOP: Blowtoot yerbum.

Sudden squall. The ship yaws.

PA UBU: Yike. Eee. We're done for. We're sinking. We're drowning. It's your fault. It's your boat.

CAPTAIN: All hands to the forestopspritsal. Chocks away.

PA UBU: Idiot. Stackinussall thisside. What if the wind changes? We'll fall in. Fishll finishuss.

CAPTAIN: Luff the portcullis. Steady Eddy.

PA UBU: Stuff steady. Get a nurdle on. I want to get there. If we never get there, it'll be all your fault. We've got to get there. Oh here, let me. Splice the mainbrace. Any more for the skylark? Keelhaul the binnacle. Mr Christian, avast behind. What? What?

All scream with laughter. The wind rises.

CAPTAIN: Break out the pipsal and pass to port.

PA UBU: You eardim, pass the port.

They're kicking their legs in the air with laughing. A wave hits the ship.

Hey, that was a biggun. We know what we're doing.

MA UBU, WALLOP: Lovely day for a cruise.

A second wave hits the ship.

WALLOP: (*Soaked.*) Seeyou, repent or die.

PA UBU: Waiter! Oi, waiter! A drop to drink.

They all settle down to drink.

MA UBU: How naice to visit Engelland once more. One's favourite little country. One's hice in the highlands. One's dear old friends.

PA UBU: Not far now. Just passing Germany.

WALLOP: Jings, ahcannywait taeseemawee Wales.

MCCLUB: Sure and aren't they are tales we'll have to tell?

PA UBU: Firstoff, I'm off to London. His Cashness Prince of the Piggybank.

MA UBU: How naice. Ow what ai waive.

MCCLUB: Twas the Dogger Bank, suretwas.

WALLOP: Seejimmy thileaskye.

PA UBU: They call it the Isle of Sky because it's blue.

MA UBU: Pa Ubu, you know everything.

PA UBU: Course I do. Swot got me ere ina firstplace.

2.2 THE BREASTS OF TIRESIAS (1917)

GUILLAUME APOLLINAIRE

Translated by Louis Simpson

> **Guillaume Apollinaire (1880–1918).** *Born of a Polish noblewoman and, it is thought, a Swiss-Italian aristocrat, Apollinaire adopted his French name after emigrating to France. A poet, critic and writer, Apollinaire is often credited with inventing the word 'surrealism'.* The Breasts of Tiresias *is frequently viewed as the first 'surrealist' play and was made into an opera with music by François Poulenc in 1947. Apollinaire was certainly one of the heroes of the Surrealist movement but also had a working relationship with the Cubists, Picasso and Braque. Apollinaire, although from noble stock, worked for a living and at one point wrote erotic prose as a means of earning an income. Having fought and been wounded during World War I, he died during the post-World War I Spanish flu epidemic in 1918 aged 38. This translation was made in 1961.*

Don't hope for rest risk everything you own
Learn what is new for everything must be known
When a prophet speaks you must be looking on
And make children that's the point of my tale
The child is wealth and the only wealth that's real

Characters

DIRECTOR
THÉRÈSE–TIRESIAS and the FORTUNETELLER
HUSBAND
POLICEMAN
REPORTER FROM PARIS
SON
KIOSK
LACOUF
PRESTO
PEOPLE OF ZANZIBAR
LADY
CHORUS

Prologue

In front of the lowered curtain the DIRECTOR, *in evening dress and carrying a swagger stick, emerges from the prompt box.*

DIRECTOR: So here I am once more among you
    I've found my ardent company again
    I have also found a stage
    But to my dismay found as before
    The theatre with no greatness and no virtue
    That killed the tedious nights before the war
    A slanderous and pernicious art
    That showed the sin but did not show the savior
    Then the hour struck the hour of men
    I have been at war like all other men

    In the days when I was in the artillery
    On the northern front commanding my battery
    One night when the gazing of the stars in heaven
    Pulsated like the eyes of the newborn
    A thousand rockets that rose from the opposite trench
    Suddenly woke the guns of the enemy

    I remember as though it were yesterday
    I heard the shells depart but no explosions
    Then from the observation post there came
    The trumpeter on horseback to announce
    That the sergeant there who calculated
    From the flashes of the enemy guns
    Their angle of fire had stated
    That the range of those guns was so great
    That the bursts no longer could be heard
    And all my gunners watching at their posts
    Announced the stars were darkening one by one
    Then loud shouts arose from the whole army
        THEY'RE PUTTING OUT THE STARS WITH SHELLFIRE
    The stars were dying in that fine autumn sky
    As memory fades in the brain
    Of the poor old men who try to remember
    We were dying there of the death of stars
    And on the somber front with its livid lights
    We could only say in despair
        THEY'VE EVEN MURDERED
        THE CONSTELLATIONS
    But in a great voice out of a megaphone
    The mouth of which emerged
    From some sort of supreme headquarters
    The voice of the unknown captain who always saves
        us cried
        THE TIME HAS COME TO LIGHT THE STARS AGAIN
    And the whole French front shouted together
        FIRE AT WILL
    The gunners hastened
    The layers calculated
    The marksmen fired
    And the sublime stars lit up again one by one
    Our shells rekindled their eternal ardor
    The enemy guns were silent dazzled
    By the scintillating of all the stars

    There is the history of all the stars

    And since that night I too light one by one
    All the stars within that were extinguished

    So here I am once more among you
    My troupe don't be impatient
    Public wait without impatience

    I bring you a play that aims to reform society
    It deals with children in the family
    The subject is domestic
    And that is the reason it's handled in a familiar way

    The actors will not adopt a sinister tone
    They will simply appeal to your common sense
    And above all will try to entertain you
    So that you will be inclined to profit

    From all the lessons that the play contains
    And so that the earth will be starred with the glances
    of infants
    Even more numerous than the twinkling stars
    Hear O Frenchmen the lesson of war
    And make children you that made few before

    We're trying to bring a new spirit into the theatre
    A joyfulness voluptuousness virtue
    Instead of that pessimism more than a hundred years
    old
    And that's pretty old for such a boring thing
    The play was created for an antique stage
    For they wouldn't have built us a new theatre
    A circular theatre with two stages
    One in the middle the other like a ring
    Around the spectators permitting
    The full unfolding of our modern art
    Often connecting in unseen ways as in life
    Sounds gestures colors cries tumults
    Music dancing acrobatics poetry painting
    Choruses actions and multiple sets

    Here you will find actions
    Which add to the central drama and augment it
    Changes of tone from pathos to burlesque
    And the reasonable use of the improbable
    And actors who may be collective or not
    Not necessarily taken from mankind
    But from the universe

    For the theatre must not be 'realistic'

    It is right for the dramatist to use
    All the illusions he has at his disposal

As Morgana did on Mount Gibel
It is right for him to make crowds speak and inanimate things
If he wishes
And for him to pay no more heed to time
Than to space

His universe is his stage
Within it he is the creating god
Directing at his will
Sounds gestures movements masses colors
Not merely with the aim
Of photographing the so-called slice of life
But to bring forth life itself in all its truth

For the play must be an entire universe
With its creator
That is to say nature itself
And not only
Representation of a little part
Of what surrounds us or has already passed

Pardon me my friends my company

Pardon me ladies and gentlemen
For having spoken a little too long
It's been so long since I have been among you

But out there there's still a fire
Where they're putting out the smoking stars
And those who light them again demand that you
Lift yourselves to the height of those great flames
And also burn

O public
Be the unquenchable torch of the new fire

Act 1

The market place at Zanzibar, morning. The scene consists of houses, an area opening on the harbor and whatever else can evoke in Frenchmen the idea of the game of zanzibar.[1] *A megaphone shaped like a dice box and decorated with dice is in the foreground. On the courtyard side, the entrance to a house; on the garden side, a newspaper kiosk with a large display and a picture of the newspaper woman which is able to move its arm; it is also decorated with a mirror on the side facing the stage. In the background, the collective speechless person who represents the people of Zanzibar is present from the rise of the curtain. He is sitting on a bench. A table is at his right, and he has ready to hand the instruments he will use to make the right noise at the right moment: revolver, musette, bass drum, accordion, snare drum, thunder, sleigh bells, castanets, toy trumpet, broken dishes. All the sounds marked to be produced by an instrument are made by the people of Zanzibar, and everything marked to be spoken through the megaphone is to be shouted at the audience.*

Scene 1

THE PEOPLE OF ZANZIBAR, THÉRÈSE

THÉRÈSE: (*Blue face, long blue dress decorated with monkeys and painted fruit. She enters when the curtain has risen, but from the moment that the curtain begins to rise she attempts to dominate the sound of the orchestra.*)
No Mister husband
You won't make me do what you want

(*In a hushing voice.*)

I am a feminist and I do not recognize the authority of men

(*In a hushing voice.*)

Besides I want to do as I please
Men have been doing what they like long enough
After all I too want to go and fight the enemy
I want to be a soldier hup two hup two
I want to make war (*Thunder.*) and not make children
No Mister husband you won't give me orders

(*She bows three times, backside to the audience.*)

(*In the megaphone.*)

Because you made love to me in Connecticut
Doesn't mean I have to cook for you in Zanzibar
VOICE OF HUSBAND: (*Belgian accent.*)
Give me lard I tell you give me lard

Broken dishes.

THÉRÈSE: Listen to him he only thinks of love

(*She has a fit of hysterics.*)

But you don't understand you fool

(*Sneeze.*)

That after being a soldier I want to be an artist

(*Sneeze.*)

Exactly exactly

(*Sneeze.*)

I also want to be a deputy a lawyer a senator

(*Two sneezes.*)

Minister president of the state

(*Sneeze.*)

And I want to be a doctor or psychiatrist
Give Europe and America the trots
Making children cooking no it's too much

(*She cackles.*)

I want to be a mathematician philosopher chemist
A page in a restaurant a little telegraphist
And if it pleases me I want
To keep that old chorus girl with so much talent

(*Sneeze cackle, after which she imitates the sound of a train.*)

VOICE OF HUSBAND: (*Belgian accent.*)
    Give me lard I tell you give me lard
THÉRÈSE: Listen to him he only thinks of love

Little tune on the musette.

Why don't you eat your old sausage feet

Bass drum.

But I think I'm growing a beard
My bosom is falling off

(*She utters a loud cry and opens her blouse from which her breasts emerge, one red, the other blue, and as she lets go of them they fly off, like toy balloons, but remain attached by strings.*)

Fly away birds of my frailty
    Et cetera
How pretty are feminine charms
They're awfully sweet
You could eat them

(*She pulls on the balloon strings and makes them dance.*)

But enough of this nonsense
Let's not go in for aeronautics
There is always some advantage in being virtuous
Vice is a dangerous business after all
That is why it is better to sacrifice beauty
That may be a cause of sin
Let us get rid of our breasts

(*She strikes a lighter and makes them explode; then she makes a face, thumbing her nose with both hands at the audience and throws them the balls she has in her bodice.*)

That is to say
It's not just my beard my mustache is growing too

(*She caresses her beard and strokes her mustache, which have suddenly sprouted.*)

What the devil
I look like a wheatfield that's waiting for the harvester

(*In the megaphone.*)

I feel as virile as the devil
I'm a stallion
From my head on down
I'm a bull

(*Without the megaphone.*)

I'll be a torero
But let's not reveal

My future to everyone hero
Conceal your arms
And you my husband less virile than I
You can sound the alarms
As much as you want

(*Cackling, she goes and admires herself in the mirror attached to the newspaper kiosk.*)

Scene 2
THE PEOPLE OF ZANZIBAR, THÉRÈSE, the HUSBAND

HUSBAND: (*Enters with a big bouquet of flowers, sees that she is not looking at him, and throws the flowers into the auditorium. From this point on, the HUSBAND loses his Belgian accent.*)
    I want lard I tell you
THÉRÈSE: Eat your old sausage feet
HUSBAND: (*While he speaks Thérèse cackles louder and louder. He approaches as though to hit her, then laughing.*)
    Ah but it isn't my wife Thérèse

(*A pause then in a severe manner. In the megaphone.*)

Who is this rascal who's wearing her clothes

(*He goes over to examine her and comes back. In the megaphone.*)

No doubt he's a murderer and he has killed her

(*Without the megaphone.*)

Thérèse my little Thérèse where are you

(*He reflects with his head in his hands, then plants himself squarely, fists on hips.*)

But you you base rascal who have disguised yourself like Thérèse
I will kill you

(*They fight, she overpowers him.*)

THÉRÈSE: You're right I'm no longer your wife
HUSBAND: Goodness
THÉRÈSE: And yet I am Thérèse
HUSBAND: Goodness
THÉRÈSE: But Thérèse who is no longer a woman
HUSBAND: This is too much
THÉRÈSE: And as I have become a fine fellow
HUSBAND: It must have escaped my attention
THÉRÈSE: From now on I'll have a man's name Tiresias
HUSBAND: (*Hands clasped.*) Sweetiest

She goes off.

Scene 3
THE PEOPLE OF ZANZIBAR, the HUSBAND

VOICE OF TIRESIAS: I'm moving house
HUSBAND: Sweetiest

(*She throws out of the window a chamberpot, a basin, and a urinal. the husband picks up the chamberpot.*)

The piano

(*He picks up the urinal.*)

The violin

(*He picks up the basin.*)

The butter dish the situation is becoming grave

Scene 4

The same. TIRESIAS, LACOUF, PRESTO.

TIRESIAS *returns with clothes, a cord, various odd objects. She throws down everything, hurls herself on the* HUSBAND. *Upon the last reply by* THE HUSBAND, PRESTO *and* LACOUF, *armed with cardboard revolvers, having emerged with a solemn bearing from below the stage, advance into the auditorium, while* TIRESIAS, *over-powering her husband, takes off his trousers, undresses herself, hands him her skirt, ties him up, puts on the trousers, cuts her hair, and puts on a top hat. This stage business goes on until the first revolver shot.*

PRESTO: Old Lacouf I've lost at zanzi with you
  All that I hope to lose
LACOUF: Mister Presto I've won nothing
  And then what has Zanzibar got to do with it you are in Paris
PRESTO: In Zanzibar
LACOUF: In Paris
PRESTO: This is too much
  After ten years of friendship
  And all the bad things I've always said about you
LACOUF: Too bad did I ever ask you for a favor you are in Paris
PRESTO: In Zanzibar the proof is I've lost everything
LACOUF: Mister Presto we'll have to fight
PRESTO: We'll have to

They go up solemnly on to the stage and take positions at the rear facing each other.

Figure 10 Presto, The People of Zanzibar and Lacouf in *Les Mamelles de Tirésias*, 24 June 1917. (*La Rampe*, 12 July 1917.)

LACOUF: On equal terms
PRESTO: Fire at will
  All shots are natural

They aim at each other. THE PEOPLE OF ZANZIBAR *fire two shots and they fall.*

TIRESIAS: (*Who is ready, starts at the sound and exclaims.*)
  Ah dear Freedom so you've been conquered at last
  But first let's buy a newspaper
  And see what has just happened

She buys a newspaper and reads it; meanwhile THE PEOPLE OF ZANZIBAR *set up a placard on each side of the stage.*

> PLACARD FOR PRESTO:
> As he lost at Zanzibar
> Mister Presto has lost his pari
> Mutuel bet for we're in Paris
>
> PLACARD FOR LACOUF
> Mister Lacouf has won nothing
> Since the scene's at Zanzibar
> Just as the Seine's at Paris

As soon as THE PEOPLE OF ZANZIBAR *return to their place,* PRESTO *and* LACOUF *get up,* THE PEOPLE OF ZANZIBAR *fire a revolver shot, and the duelists fall down again.* TIRESIAS *throws down the newspaper in astonishment.*

(*In the megaphone.*)

Now the universe is mine
The women are mine mine is the government
I'm going to make myself town councilor
But I hear a noise
Maybe I'd better go away

She goes off cackling while the HUSBAND *imitates the sound of a locomotive.*

Scene 5

THE PEOPLE OF ZANZIBAR, *the* HUSBAND, *the* POLICEMAN

POLICEMAN: (*While* THE PEOPLE OF ZANZIBAR *play the accordion the mounted policeman makes his horse caper, drags one dead man into the wings so that his feet alone remain visible, makes a circuit of the stage, does the same with the other body, makes another circuit of the stage and, seeing the* HUSBAND *tied up in the foreground.*)
  I smell a crime here
HUSBAND: Ah! since at last there's an agent of the government
  Of Zanzibar
  I'm going to challenge him
  Hey Mister if you've got any business with me
  Be kind enough to take
  My army papers out of my left pocket
POLICEMAN: (*In the megaphone.*) What a pretty girl

(*Without the megaphone.*)

Tell me pretty maiden
Who has been treating you so shamefully
HUSBAND: (*Aside.*) He takes me for a young lady

(*To the policeman.*)

If it's a marriage that you have in mind
THE POLICEMAN *puts his hand on his heart.*

Then begin by getting me out of this

The POLICEMAN *unties him, tickling him; they laugh and the* POLICEMAN *continues to say* What a pretty girl.

Scene 6

The same. PRESTO, LACOUF.
As soon as the POLICEMAN *begins to untie the* HUSBAND, PRESTO *and* LACOUF *return to the spot where they fell.*

PRESTO: I'm beginning to be tired of being dead
Imagine there are people
Who think it's more honorable to be dead than alive
LACOUF: Now you can see you were not in Zanzibar
PRESTO: Yet that's the place to live
But it disgusts me to think that we fought a duel
Certainly death is regarded
Much too favorably
LACOUF: What do you expect people think too well
Of mankind and its remains
In the stool of jewelers
Do you think there are pearls and diamonds
PRESTO: Greater marvels have been seen
LACOUF: So Mister Presto
We don't have luck with pari-mutuels
But now you can see that you were in Paris

PRESTO: In Zanzibar
LACOUF: Aim
PRESTO: Fire

THE PEOPLE OF ZANZIBAR *fire a revolver shot, and they fall. The* POLICEMAN *has finished untying the* HUSBAND.

POLICEMAN: You're under arrest

PRESTO *and* LACOUF *run off in the direction opposite where they entered. Accordion.*

Scene 7

THE PEOPLE OF ZANZIBAR, the POLICEMAN, the HUSBAND (*dressed as a woman*)

POLICEMAN: The local duelists
Won't prevent me saying that I think it's
Like a lovely ball of rubber when I touch you
HUSBAND: Kerchoo

Broken dishes.

POLICEMAN: A cold bewitching
HUSBAND: Kitchi

Snare drum. The HUSBAND *removes the skirt, which is impeding his movements.*

POLICEMAN: Loose woman

(*He winks.*)

So what if she's pretty
HUSBAND: (*Aside.*) Really he's right
Since my wife is a man
It's right for me to be a woman

(*To the* POLICEMAN *bashfully.*)

Figure 11 Guillaume Apollinaire and members of the cast of *Les Mamelles de Tirésias*, 24 June 1917.

I am a decent woman-mister
My wife is a man-lady
She's taken the piano the violin the butter dish
She's a soldier minister mover of shit
POLICEMAN: Mother of tits
HUSBAND: They've burst she's a lady psychiatrist
POLICEMAN: She's the mother of swans
　　Ah how they sing when they're dying
　　Listen

Musette, a sad tune.

HUSBAND: After all it's a matter of curing people
　　Music will do it
　　As well as any other panacea
POLICEMAN: That's fine no resisting
HUSBAND: I refuse to continue this conversation

(In the megaphone.)

Where is my wife
VOICES OF WOMEN: *(In the wings.)* Long live Tiresias
　　No more children no more children

Thunder and bass drum. The HUSBAND makes a face at the
audience and puts a hand to his ear like an ear trumpet, while
the POLICEMAN, taking a pipe out of his pocket, offers it to him.
Bells.

POLICEMAN: Hey Sweetheart smoke a cigar
　　And I'll play my violin
HUSBAND: The baker of Zanzibar
　　Has a wife who changes her skin
POLICEMAN: She carries a joke too far

THE PEOPLE OF ZANZIBAR *hang up a placard with this ritornelle*
and it stays there.

Hey Sweetheart smoke a cigar
And I'll play my violin
The baker of Zanzibar
Has a wife who changes her skin
She carries a joke too far
POLICEMAN: Miss or Mrs I'm crazy with love
　　For you
　　And I want to marry you I do
HUSBAND: Kerchoo
　　But don't you see that I am only a man
POLICEMAN: No matter what I could marry you
　　By proxy
HUSBAND: Nonsense
　　You'd do better making children
POLICEMAN: Hah! the idea
VOICES OF MEN: *(In the wings.)* Long live Tiresias
　　Long live General Tiresias
　　Long live Deputy Tiresias

The accordion plays a military march.

VOICES OF WOMEN *(In the wings.)* No more children No more
children

Scene 8

The same. The KIOSK.
The KIOSK with the moving arm of the newspaper woman proceeds
slowly towards the other end of the stage.

HUSBAND: Famous representative of authority
　　You hear I believe it's been said with clarity
　　Women at Zanzibar want political rights
　　And suddenly renounce their reproductive nights
　　No more children No more children you hear them shout
　　To fill Zanzibar there are elephants about
　　Monkeys and serpents mosquitoes and ostriches
　　And just as in beehives enough sterile bitches
　　But bees at least make wax and bring in the honey
　　Woman is only a neuter under the sky
　　And you can take my word for it Mister gendarme

(In the megaphone.)

Zanzibar needs children

(Without the megaphone.)

Go and sound the alarm
Shout it at the crossroads and on the avenue
In Zanzibar we'll have to make children anew
Women won't make them Worse luck Let men populate
But yes exactly I'm letting you have it straight
And I'll make them myself
POLICEMAN AND KIOSK: You
KIOSK: *(In the megaphone which the husband holds out to her.)*
　　A story like this should go far
　　It's much too good to restrict it to Zanzibar
　　You that shed tears at the play
　　Wish for children that conquer
　　Observe the measureless ardor
　　Born of the changing of sex
HUSBAND: Return this very night and see how nature can
　　Provide you with progeny without a woman
POLICEMAN: I shall return this night to see how nature can
　　Provide you with progeny without a woman
　　Don't keep me cooling my heels with no reward
　　I'm coming back tonight and take you at your word
KIOSK: What a jerk is the gendarme
　　Who's in charge of Zanzibar
　　The burlesque theatre and the bar
　　For this fellow hold more charm
　　Than repeopling Zanzibar

Scene 9

The same. PRESTO.

PRESTO: *(Tickling the HUSBAND.)* What do you think their
　　name should be

They are just the same as we
Yet they're not men as you can see

POLICEMAN: I shall return this night to see how nature can
Provide you with progeny without a woman

HUSBAND: Well then return this night and see how nature can
Provide me with progeny without a woman

ALL: (*In chorus. They dance, the* HUSBAND *and* POLICEMAN *together,* PRESTO *and the* KIOSK *paired off and sometimes changing partners.* THE PEOPLE OF ZANZIBAR *dance alone playing the accordion.*)
Hey Sweetheart smoke a cigar
And I'll play my violin
The baker of Zanzibar
Has a wife who changes her skin
She carries a joke too far

Act 2
Scene 1

The same place, the same day, just as the sun goes down. The same scenery to which have been added several cradles containing the newborn. An empty cradle stands next to an enormous bottle of ink, a gigantic pot of glue, a huge fountain pen, and a tall pair of scissors.

HUSBAND: (*He has a child on each arm. Continuous crying of children on the stage, in the wings and in the auditorium throughout the scene ad lib. The stage directions only indicate when and where the crying is redoubled.*)
Ah! what a thrill being a father
40,049 children in one day alone
My happiness is complete
Quiet quiet

Crying of children in the background.

Domestic happiness
No woman on my hands

(*He lets the children fall.*)

Quiet

Crying of children from the left side of the auditorium.

Modern music is amazing
Nearly as amazing as the stage sets of the new painters
Who flourish far from the Barbarians
At Zanzibar
You don't have to go to the Ballet Russe or the Vieux-Colombier
Quiet quiet

Crying of children from the right side of the auditorium. Bells.

The time's come to swat 'em with belts on the bottom
But let's not rush matters I think that I'll go
And buy them bicycles and when they have got 'em
Then every virtuoso
May exercise
And vocalize
To the open skies

Gradually the children quiet down, he applauds.

Bravo bravo

A knock.

Come in

Scene 2

The same. The REPORTER FROM PARIS.

REPORTER: (*His face is blank; he has only a mouth. He enters dancing. Accordion.*)
Hands up
Hullo Mister Husband
I'm a Reporter from a Paris paper

HUSBAND: From Paris
Make yourself at home

REPORTER: (*Makes a circuit of the stage dancing.*)
The papers of Paris

(*In the megaphone.*)

a town in America

(*Without the megaphone.*)

Hurrah

A revolver shot, THE REPORTER *unfolds the American flag.*

Have announced that you've discovered
The way for men
To make children

HUSBAND: (*The* REPORTER *folds the flag and wraps it around himself like a belt.*)
That's right

REPORTER: And how's it done

HUSBAND: Willpower sir that's the whole secret

REPORTER: Are they Negroes or like other people

HUSBAND: It all depends on how you look at it

Castanets.

REPORTER: You're wealthy I suppose

(*He does a dance step.*)

HUSBAND: Not at all

REPORTER: How will you bring them up

HUSBAND: After they've been bottle fed
I hope that they'll feed me instead

REPORTER: In short you are something of a daughter-father
A maternalized paternal instinct I guess

HUSBAND: To the contrary Sir it's all pure selfishness
The child is the wealth of the family
It's worth more than cash and a legacy

THE REPORTER *takes notes.*

See that little fellow asleep in his cradle

The child cries. THE REPORTER *tiptoes across to look at him.*

His first name is Arthur and already he's made

A million for me in the curdled milk trade

Toy trumpet.

REPORTER: He's advanced for his age

HUSBAND: Joseph over there

    The child cries.

    he's a novelist

The REPORTER *goes over to look at Joseph.*

    His last novel sold 600,000 copies

    Permit me to offer you one

A big book placard is lowered; it has several pages on the first of which is printed:
What Luck!
A Novel.
    Read it at your leisure

The REPORTER *lies down; the* HUSBAND *turns the pages on which may be read one word to the page:*
A lady whose name was Cambron.

REPORTER: (*Stands up and speaks into the megaphone.*)

    A lady whose name was Cambron

(*He laughs into the megaphone uttering the four vowels: a, e, i, o.*)

HUSBAND: Nevertheless it has a certain urbanity of expression

REPORTER: (*Without the megaphone.*) Ah! ah! ah! ah!

HUSBAND: A certain precociousness

REPORTER: Eh! eh!

HUSBAND: That you don't find in the streets

REPORTER: Hands up

HUSBAND: Finally just as it stands

    The novel has put in my hands

    Almost two hundred thousand francs

    Plus a literary prize

    Consisting of twenty cases of dynamite

(*Backs away.*)

REPORTER: Good-bye

HUSBAND: Don't be afraid they're in my safety deposit vault

REPORTER: All right

    Don't you have a daughter

HUSBAND: Sure I do this one divorced

She cries. The REPORTER *goes over to look at her.*

    From the potato king

    Gets a hundred thousand dollars alimony

    And this (*She cries.*) no one in Zanzibar is as artistic as she

The REPORTER *shadow boxes.*

    She recites lovely poems on gloomy evenings

    Her fire and genius earn in a year

    What a poet earns in fifty thousand years

REPORTER: Congratulations my dear

    But you've got some dust

On your dust coat

The HUSBAND *smiles gratefully at the* REPORTER *as he picks up the speck of dust.*

Since you're so rich lend me a hundred sous

HUSBAND: Put the dust back

All the children cry. The HUSBAND *chases the* REPORTER, *kicking him. He goes off dancing.*

Scene 3

THE PEOPLE OF ZANZIBAR, *the* HUSBAND

HUSBAND: Ah yes it's as simple as a periscope

    The more children I have

    The richer I'll be and the better able to live

    It's said that the cod produces enough eggs in a day

    To supply the whole world for a whole year

    With cod paste and garlic

    Isn't it wonderful to have a numerous family

    Then who are those idiotic economists

    Who've made us believe that the child

    Means poverty

    Whereas it's just the opposite

    Did you ever hear of a cod that died in poverty

    So I'm going to keep on making children

    First we'll make a reporter

    So I'll know everything

    I'll predict the rest

    And invent the remainder

(*He starts tearing up newspapers with his teeth and hands; he tramples. His movements must be very quick.*)

He must be adaptable to every job

And able to write for every party

(*He puts the torn newspapers in the empty cradle.*)

What a fine reporter he'll be

Reporting lead articles

Et cetera

He'll have to have blood from an ink bottle

(*He takes the bottle of ink and pours it into the cradle.*)

He'll need a backbone

(*He puts a huge fountain pen into the cradle.*)

A brain for not thinking with

(*He empties the glue pot into the cradle.*)

A tongue to drivel with

(*He puts the scissors into the cradle.*)

Also he'll have to be able to sing

Come on sing

Thunder.

Scene 4

The same. The SON.

HUSBAND repeats: "One, two!" till the end of the son's monologue. This scene goes very quickly.

SON: Dear daddy if you want a closer look
At the activities of every crook
You've got to let me have some pocket money
The tree of print is leafy every bough
Flaps like a banner the fruit hangs in bunches
Papers have grown you ought to pick them now
And make the little kiddies salad lunches
If you let me have five hundred francs
I won't tell what I know about you
If you don't I'll tell all for I'm frank
And I fix fathers brothers sisters too
When you marry I'll tell them that your bride's
Pregnant three times over
I'll compromise you and I'll write besides
That you've stolen killed given rung bored
HUSBAND: Bravo there's a vocalist

THE SON gets out of the cradle.

SON: Dear parents in one man
If you want to know what happened yesterday evening
Here it is
A great conflagration destroyed Niagara Falls
HUSBAND: So what
SON: Alcindor the engineer
Put a gas mask on and played
The horn till twelve o'clock or near
For a murderous brigade
Listen and you still may hear
HUSBAND: So long as he doesn't do it here
SON: The Princess of Bergame they say
Is marrying a girl today
Just a meeting on the subway

Castanets.

HUSBAND: What's it to me do I know all those people
I want reliable news about my friends
SON: (*He rocks a cradle.*) We hear from Montrouge
That Mister Picasso's
New picture can move
As this cradle does
HUSBAND: Bravo bravo
For the brush of Picasso
O my son
Some other time I know right now
All that I need to know
About yesterday
SON: I'm going away to make tomorrow's news
HUSBAND: Good luck

Exit the SON.

Scene 5

THE PEOPLE OF ZANZIBAR, *the* HUSBAND

HUSBAND: That one didn't work out
I think I'll disinherit him
At this moment radio placards enter: Ottawa – fire j.c.b. industries STOP 20,000 prose poems destroyed STOP president expresses sympathy. Rome – h.nr.m.t.ss. director villa medicis finishes portrait SS. Avignon – great artist g.rg.s braque has just invented process intensive cultivation of paintbrushes. Vancouver delayed bulletin – Dogs mister Paul Léaut.d on strike.

Stop stop
That was a lousy idea trusting the Press
They'll drive me crazy
The whole damn day
It's got to stop

(*In the megaphone.*)

Hullo hullo Miss
I don't want your telephone service
I'm de-subscribing

(*Without the megaphone.*)

I'm changing my program no more useless mouths
Economize economize
First off all I'll make a little tailor
When I'm dressed up I can take a walk
And as I'm not so bad to look at
Attract a lot of pretty girls

Scene 6

The same. The POLICEMAN.

POLICEMAN: Fine things you've been up to
You've kept your word
40,050 children in a day
You're rocking the boat
HUSBAND: I'm getting rich
POLICEMAN: But the population of Zanzibar
Famished by this excess of mouths to feed
Will soon be dying of hunger
HUSBAND: Give them cards that makes up for everything
POLICEMAN: Where do we get them
HUSBAND: From The Fortuneteller
POLICEMAN: That's clear enough
HUSBAND: Of course for we're thinking of the future

Scene 7

The same. The FORTUNETELLER.

FORTUNETELLER: (*She enters at the rear of the auditorium. Her skull is lighted with electricity.*)
Chaste citizens of Zanzibar here I am
HUSBAND: Still another
I just don't count

FORTUNETELLER: I thought that you wouldn't have any objections
To having your fortune told

POLICEMAN: You are well aware Madame
You're practicing an illegal occupation
It's amazing the things people do
To avoid working

HUSBAND: (*To the* POLICEMAN.) No scandal in my house

FORTUNETELLER: (*To a spectator.*) You Sir will shortly
Give birth to triplets

HUSBAND: Competition already

A LADY: (*In the audience.*) Madame Fortuneteller
I think he's deceiving me

Broken dishes.

FORTUNETELLER: Keep him in the hay box

She climbs onto the stage; crying of children, accordion.

Look an incubator

HUSBAND: If you're the barber give me a haircut

FORTUNETELLER: The girls of New York
Only pick mirabelles
Only eat ham from York
That's why they're such belles

HUSBAND: The ladies of Paris
Beat all competitors
Cats like little mice
And ladies we like yours

FORTUNETELLER: That is your smiles

ALL: (*In chorus.*) And then sing night and day
Scratch if you itch and choose
The white or the black either way
Luck is a game win or lose
Just keep your eye on the play
Just keep your eye on the play

FORTUNETELLER: Chaste citizens of Zanzibar
Who have given up childbearing
Listen to me wealth and honor
Pineapple groves and herds of elephants
By right will belong
Before very long
To those who will claim them with armies of infants

All the children start crying on the stage and in the auditorium. The FORTUNETELLER *deals the cards and they come tumbling down from the ceiling. Then the children are quiet.*

You who are so fertile

HUSBAND and POLICEMAN: Fertile fertile

FORTUNETELLER: (*To the* HUSBAND.) You'll be a millionaire ten times over

The HUSBAND *falls down in a sitting position.*

FORTUNETELLER: (*To the* POLICEMAN.) You who don't make children

You'll die in the most abject poverty

POLICEMAN: You've insulted me
I arrest you in the name of Zanzibar

FORTUNETELLER: Laying hands on a woman shame on you

She claws and strangles him. The HUSBAND *offers her a pipe.*

HUSBAND: Hey Sweetheart smoke a cigar
And I'll play my violin
The baker of Zanzibar
Has a wife who changes her skin

FORTUNETELLER: She carries a joke too far

HUSBAND: I'm going to turn you into the chief of police
Murderer

THÉRÈSE: (*Taking off her fortuneteller's costume.*)
Dear husband don't you recognize me

HUSBAND: Thérèse or should I say Tiresias

The POLICEMAN *revives.*

THÉRÈSE: Tiresias is officially
Head of the Army in Room A at City Hall
But don't worry
I'm bringing back in a moving van
The piano the violin the butter dish
And three influential ladies whose lover I have become

POLICEMAN: Thanks for thinking of me

HUSBAND: My general my deputy
Thérèse I meant to say
You're as flat-chested as a bedbug

THÉRÈSE: So what! Let's go where the berries
And banana blossoms are
Let's hunt elephants on safaris
As they do in Zanzibar
Come and rule the heart of Thérèse

HUSBAND: Thérèse

THÉRÈSE: Throne or tomb no matter what
But this I'm sure of that we've got
To love or I'll die on the spot

HUSBAND: Dear Thérèse you must no longer be
As flat-chested as a bedbug

(*He takes out of the house a bouquet of balloons and a basket of balls.*)

Here's a whole supply

THÉRÈSE: We've both of us done without them
Let's continue

HUSBAND: That's true let's not make matters complicated
Let's go and dunk our bread

THÉRÈSE: (*She releases the toy balloons and throws the balls at the audience.*) Fly away birds of my frailty
Go and feed all the children
Of the new population

ALL: (*In chorus.* THE PEOPLE OF ZANZIBAR *dance jingling bells.*)
And then sing night and day
Scratch if you itch and choose

The white or the black either way
Luck is a game win or lose
Just keep your eye on the play

Note

1. Zanzibar – commonly known as *zanzi* – a game of chance played with three dice and a dice box. Each player in turn throws the dice. An ace counts 100 points, a six 60, and the other numbers their face value. The player with the highest total wins. The game can be decided in one throw, in three throws, by leaving out one or two dice at each throw, or in several extra throws. In case of a tie, the players each throw once. There are many kinds of *zanzi*; the notorious *chemin de fer* is one of them – played with three throws of the dice; at each throw one of the dice is left out. – *Translator.*

2.3 THE SPURT OF BLOOD (1925)

ANTONIN ARTAUD

Translated by Victor Corti

Antonin Artaud (1896–1948). *Artaud spent a great deal of his life in sanatoriums and asylums in France. Suffering from depression, addiction to opiates, and cancer, he died before the theatre had developed either technologically or aesthetically to a level whereby the majority of his innovative visions for theatre could be put into working practice. An actor, poet, playwright and theorist, Artaud is best known for his theories on the function, purpose and practice of theatre gathered together in* The Theatre and Its Double *(see document 2.12). He ran the Alfred Jarry Theatre in Paris in the mid 1920s where* The Spurt of Blood *was reportedly to be produced, but it was not premiered until some forty years later. His vision for theatre involved a reconceptualization of the role of the audience in the making and experience of the artwork, and his ideas have been adopted and debated by most innovative practitioners of the twentieth and twenty-first centuries. This translation was made in 1970.*

YOUNG MAN: I love you and everything is fine.

GIRL: (*In a quickened, throbbing voice.*) You love me and everything is fine.

YOUNG MAN: (*Lower.*) I love you and everything is fine.

GIRL: (*Lower still.*) You love me and everything is fine.

YOUNG MAN: (*Suddenly turns aside.*) I love you.

Silence.

YOUNG MAN: Face me.

GIRL: (*Same business, faces him.*) There.

YOUNG MAN: (*On an exalted, high-pitched tone.*) I love you, I am great, I am lucid, I am full, I am dense.

GIRL: (*Same high-pitched tone.*) We love each other.

YOUNG MAN: We are intense. Ah, what a well-made world.

Silence: Noise like a huge wheel spinning, blowing out wind. A hurricane comes between them. At that moment two stars collide, and a succession of limbs of flesh fall. Then feet, hands, scalps, masks, colonnades, porticoes, temples and alembics, falling slower and slower as if through space, then three scorpions one after the other and finally a frog, and a scarab which lands with heart-breaking, nauseating slowness.

YOUNG MAN: (*Shouting at the top of his voice.*) Heaven's gone crazy. (*Looks up at the sky.*) Let's run off. (*Pushes the* GIRL *off ahead of him.*)

A Mediaeval KNIGHT *in enormous armour enters, followed by a* WETNURSE *holding her bosom up with her hands and panting because of her swollen breasts.*

KNIGHT: Leave your teats alone. Hand me my papers.

WETNURSE: (*Giving a shrill cry.*) Oh! Oh! Oh!

KNIGHT: Now what's the matter with you, dammit?

WETNURSE: Our girl there, with him.

KNIGHT: Shush, there's no girl there!

WETNURSE: I tell you they are fucking.

KNIGHT: And what do I care if they are fucking.

WETNURSE: Lecher.

KNIGHT: Balloon.

WETNURSE: (*Thrusting her hands in pockets as big as her breasts.*) Pimp.

(*She tosses his papers over hastily.*)

KNIGHT: Philte, Let me eat.

WETNURSE *runs off. He then gets up and pulls a huge slice of Gruyère cheese out of each paper. He suddenly coughs and chokes.*

KNIGHT: (*Mouth full.*) Ehp. Ehp. Bring your breasts over here, bring your breasts over here. Where's she gone?

He runs off. YOUNG MAN *returns.*

Figure 12 A sequence from Artaud's *The Spurt of Blood*, directed by Peter Brook and Charles Marowitz for the *Theatre of Cruelty* season at the LAMDA Theatre, London, in 1964.

YOUNG MAN: I saw, I knew, I understood. Here is the main square, the priest, the cobbler, the vegetable stalls, the church portals, the red light, the scales of justice. I can't go on!

A PRIEST, *a* COBBLER, *a* BEADLE, *a* WHORE, *a* JUDGE, *and a* BARROW-WOMAN *advance onto the stage like shadows.*

YOUNG MAN: I have lost her, bring her back.
ALL: (*On a different tone.*) Who, who, who, who.
YOUNG MAN: My wife.
BEADLE: (*Very blustering.*) Your wife, huh, joker!
YOUNG MAN: Joker! She might be yours!
BEADLE: (*Striking his forehead.*) He could be right!

He runs off.

The PRIEST *steps forward next and puts his arm around the* YOUNG MAN'S *shoulders.*

PRIEST: (*As if confessing someone.*) What part of her body did you refer to most often?

YOUNG MAN: To God.

The PRIEST, *disconcerted at this reply, immediately assumes a Swiss accent.*

PRIEST: (*With a Swiss accent.*) But that's out of date. We don't look at it in that way. You'll have to ask the volcanoes and earthquakes about that. We gratify ourselves with man's minor indecencies in the confessional. There it is, that's all, that's life.
YOUNG MAN: (*Very impressed.*) Ah, that's it, that's life! Well, it's a mess.
PRIEST: (*Still with a Swiss accent.*) Of course.

It suddenly becomes night. The earth quakes. Thunder rages, lightning zig-zagging everywhere and its flashes light up the characters who run about, bump into one another, fall down, get up again and run like mad.
At a given moment a huge hand seizes the WHORE'S *hair which catches fire and swells up visibly.*

A GIGANTIC VOICE: Bitch! Look at your body!

The WHORE'S *body appears completely naked and hideous under her blouse and skirt which turn transparent.*

WHORE: God, let go of me.

She bites GOD'S *wrist. A great spurt of blood slashes across the stage, while in the midst of the brightest lightning flash we see the* PRIEST *making the sign of the cross.*

When the lights come up again, the characters are all dead and their corpses lie all over the ground. Only the WHORE *and* YOUNG MAN *are left, devouring each other with their eyes. The* WHORE *falls into the* YOUNG MAN'S *arms.*

WHORE: (*With a sigh, as if in an orgiastic climax.*) Tell me how it happened.

The YOUNG MAN *hides his head in his hands.*

The WETNURSE *returns carrying the* GIRL *under her arms like a parcel.*

The GIRL *is dead. She drops her on the ground where she sprawls out and becomes as flat as a pancake.*

The WETNURSE'S *breasts are gone. Her chest is completely flat.*

At that moment, the KNIGHT *enters and throws himself on the* WETNURSE, *shaking her violently.*

KNIGHT: (*In a terrible voice.*) Where did you put it? Give me my Gruyère.
WETNURSE: (*Brazenly.*) Here!

She lifts up her dress.

The YOUNG MAN wants to run off but he freezes like a paralysed puppet.

YOUNG MAN: (*In a ventriloquist's voice and as if hovering in mid-air.*) Don't hurt Mummy.

KNIGHT: Damn her.

He hides his face in horror.

A host of scorpions crawl out from under the WETNURSE's dress and start swarming in her vagina which swells and splits, becomes transparent and shimmers like the sun.

The YOUNG MAN and WHORE fly off like mad.

GIRL: (*Gets up, dazzled.*) The Virgin! Ah, that's what he was looking for.

Notes

From Antonin Artaud, *Collected Works Volume 1*, London: John Calder, 1978, pp. 62–5.

2.4 MURDERER THE WOMEN'S HOPE (1907)

OSKAR KOKOSCHKA

Translated by Michael Hamburger

Oskar Kokoschka (1886–1980) was an Austrian artist and poet as well as playwright. His play Murderer the Women's Hope *exemplifies Kokoschka's disdain for realism as a mode of expression – it is rather a text predicated on the dream state, and is often called the first Expressionist drama. The play contains echoes of elements of Strindberg's* Dance of Death, *was not produced professionally until 1916 and was adapted into an opera (by Paul Hindemith) in 1920. Better known for his painting than for his theatre, Kokoschka became an exile during the rise of Nazism.*

Persons

MAN

WOMAN

CHORUS: MEN *and* WOMEN

Night sky. Tower with large red iron grille as door; torches the only light; black ground, rising to the tower in such a way that all the figures appear in relief.

The MAN *in blue armor, white face, kerchief covering a wound, with a crowd of men – savage in appearance, gray-and-red kerchiefs, white-black-and-brown clothes, signs on their clothes, bare legs, long-handled torches, bells, din – creeping up with handles of torches extended and lights; wearily, reluctantly try to hold back the adventurer, pull his horse to the ground; he walks on, they open up the circle around him, crying out in a slow crescendo.*

MEN: We were the flaming wheel around him,
We were the flaming wheel around you, assailant of locked fortresses!

Hesitantly follow him again in chain formation; he, with the torch bearer in front of him, heads the procession.

MEN: Lead us, pale one!

While they are about to pull his horse to the ground, WOMEN *with their leader ascend steps on the left.*

WOMAN, *red clothes, loose yellow hair, tall.*

WOMAN: (*Loud.*) With my breath I fan the yellow disc of the sun, my eye collects the jubilation of the men, their stammering lust prowls around me like a beast.

FEMALE ATTENDANTS separate themselves from her, only now catch sight of the stranger.

FIRST FEMALE ATTENDANT: His breath attaches itself to the virgin!

FIRST MAN: (*To the others.*) Our master is like the moon that that rises in the East.

SECOND GIRL: (*Quiet, her face averted.*) When will she be enfolded joyfully?

Listening, alert, the CHORUS *walks round the whole stage, dispersed in groups; the* MAN *and the* WOMAN *meet in front of the gate.*

Pause.

WOMAN: (*Observes him spellbound, then to herself.*) Who is the stranger that has looked on me?

GIRLS *press to the fore.*

FIRST GIRL: (*Recognizes him, cries out.*) His sister died of love.

SECOND GIRL: O the singing of Time, flowers never seen.

MAN: (*Astonished; his procession halts.*) Am I real? What did the shadows say?

Raising his face to her.

Did you look at me, did I look at you?

WOMAN: (*Filled with fear and longing.*) Who *is* the pallid man? Hold him back.

FIRST GIRL: (*With a piercing scream, runs back.*) Do you let him in? It is he who strangles my little sister praying in the temple.

FIRST MAN: (*To the* GIRL.) We saw him stride through the fire, his feet unharmed.

SECOND MAN: He tortured animals to death, killed neighing mares by the pressure of his thighs.

THIRD MAN: Birds that ran before us he made blind, stifled red fishes in the sand.

MAN: (*Angry, heated.*) Who is she that like an animal proudly grazes amidst her kin?

FIRST MAN: She divines what none has understood.

SECOND MAN: She perceives what none has seen or heard.

THIRD MAN: They say shy birds approach her and let themselves be seized.

GIRLS *in time with the* MEN.

FIRST GIRL: Lady, let us flee. Extinguish the flares of the leader.

SECOND GIRL: Mistress, escape!

THIRD MAN: He shall not be our guest or breathe our air. Let him not lodge with us, he frightens me.

MEN, *hesitant, walk on,* WOMEN *crowd together anxiously.*

The WOMAN *goes up to the* MAN, *prowling, cautious.*

FIRST GIRL: He has no luck.

FIRST MAN: She has no shame.

WOMAN: Why do you bind me, man, with your gaze? Ravening light, you confound my flame! Devouring life overpowers me. O take away my terrible hope – and may torment overpower you.

MAN: (*Enraged.*) My men, now brand her with my sign, hot iron into her red flesh.

MEN *carry out his order. First the* CHORUS, *with their lights, struggle with her, then the* OLD MAN *with the iron; he rips open her dress and brands her.*

WOMAN: (*Crying out in terrible pain.*) Beat back those men, the devouring corpses.

She leaps at him with a knife and strikes a wound in his side. the MAN *falls.*

MEN: Free this man possessed, strike down the devil. Alas for us innocents, bury the conqueror. We do not know him.

MAN: (*In convulsions, singing with a bleeding, visible wound.*) Senseless craving from horror to horror, unappeasable rotation in the void. Birth pangs without birth, hurtling down of the sun, quaking of space. The end of those who praised me. Oh, your unmerciful word.

MEN: We do not know him; spare us. Come, you singing girls, let us celebrate our nuptials on his bed of affliction.

GIRLS: He frightens us; you we loved even before you came.

Three masked men on the wall lower a coffin on ropes; the wounded man, hardly stirring now, is placed inside the tower. WOMEN *retire with the* MEN. *The* OLD MAN *rises and locks the door, all is dark, a torch, quiet, blue light above in the cage.*

WOMAN: (*Moaning and revengeful.*) He cannot live, nor die; how white he is!

She creeps round the cage like a panther. She crawls up to the cage inquisitively, grips the bars lasciviously, inscribes a large white cross on the tower, cries out.

Open the gate; I must be with him.

Shakes the bars in despair.

MEN AND WOMEN: (*Enjoying themselves in the shadows, confused.*) We have lost the key – we shall find it – have you got it? – haven't you seen it? – we are not guilty of your plight, we do not know you –

They go back again. A cock crows, a pale light rises in the background.

WOMAN: (*Slides her arm through the bars and prods his wound, hissing maliciously, like an adder.*) Pale one, do you recoil? Do you know fear? Are you only asleep? Are you awake? Can you hear me?

MAN: (*Inside, breathing heavily, raises his head with difficulty; later, moves one hand; then slowly rises, singing higher and higher, soaring.*) Wind that wanders, time repeating time, solitude, repose and hunger confuse me. Worlds that circle past, no air, it grows long as evening.

WOMAN: (*Incipient fear.*) So much light is flowing from the gap, so much strength from the pale as a corpse he's turned.

Once more creeps up the steps, her body trembling, triumphant once more and crying out with a high voice.

THE MAN *has slowly risen, leans against the grille, slowly grows.*

WOMAN: (*Weakening, furious.*) A wild beast I tame in this cage; is it with hunger your song barks?

MAN: Am I the real one, you the dead ensnared? Why are you turning pale?

Crowing of cocks.

WOMAN: (*Trembling.*) Do you insult me, corpse?

MAN: (*Powerfully.*) Stars and moon! Woman! In dream or awake, I saw a singing creature brightly shine. Breathing, dark things become clear to me. Who nourishes me?

WOMAN covers him entirely with her body; separated by the grille, to which she clings high up in the air like a monkey.

MAN: Who suckles me with blood? I devour your melting flesh.

WOMAN: I will not let you live, you vampire, piecemeal you feed on me, weaken me, woe to you, I shall kill you – you fetter me – you I caught and caged – and you are holding me – let go of me. Your love imprisons me – grips me as with iron chains – throttles me – let go – help! I lost the key that kept you prisoner.

Lets go the grille, writhes on the steps like a dying animal, her thighs and muscles convulsed.

The MAN stands upright now, pulls open the gate, touches the WOMAN – who rears up stiffly, dead white – with his fingers. She feels that her end is near, highest tension, released in a slowly diminishing scream; she collapses and, as she falls, tears away the torch from the hands of the rising leader. The torch goes out and covers everything in a shower of sparks. He stands on the highest step; MEN and WOMEN who attempt to flee from him run into his way, screaming.

CHORUS: The devil! Tame him, save yourselves, save yourselves if you can – all is lost!

He walks straight towards them. Kills them like mosquitoes and leaves red behind. From very far away, crowing of cocks.

Note

This version of the play was originally published in Walter H. Sokel, ed., *An Anthology of German Expressionist Drama*, Ithaca, NY: Cornell Paperbacks, 1984, pp. 17–22.

2.5 GENIUS AND CULTURE *and* BACHELOR APARTMENT (*C.* 1909–16)

UMBERTO BOCCIONI

Translated by Victoria Nes Kirby

Umberto Boccioni (1882–1916), *more famous as an Italian painter than a playwright, became one of the main protagonists in the development of the theory and practice of Futurism, being one of the authors of the 'Manifesto of Futurist Painters' in 1910. Later in his career he turned from painting and writing to sculpture, but was a proactive participant in Futurist performance events and exhibitions. He died after a riding accident during World War I. The translations were made in 1971.*

Genius and Culture

In the centre, a costly dressing table with a mirror in front of which a very elegant WOMAN, *already dressed to leave, finishes putting on rouge. At the right, a* CRITIC, *an ambiguous being, neither dirty nor clean, neither old nor young, neutral, is sitting at a table overburdened with books and papers, on which shines a large paper knife, neither modern nor antique. He turns his shoulder to the dressing table. At left,* THE ARTIST, *an elegant youth, searches in a large file, sitting on thick cushions on the floor.*

THE ARTIST: (*Leaving the file, and with his head between his hands.*) It's terrible! (*Pause.*) I must get out of here! To be renewed! (*He gets up, tearing the abstract designs from the file with convulsive hands.*) Liberation!! These empty forms, worn out. Everything is fragmentary, weak! Oh! Art! … who, who will help me!? (*He looks around; continues to tear up the designs with sorrowful and convulsive motions.*)

THE WOMAN *is very near him, but doesn't hear him.* THE CRITIC *becomes annoyed, but not very, and going near her, takes a book with a yellow jacket.*

THE CRITIC: (*Half-asking* THE WOMAN, *and half-talking to himself.*) But what's the matter with that clown that he acts and shouts that way?

THE WOMAN: (*Without looking.*) Oh well, he is an artist … he wants to renew himself, and he hasn't a cent!

THE CRITIC: (*Bewildered.*) Strange! An artist! Impossible! For twenty years I have profoundly studied this marvelous phenomenon, but I can't recognize it. (*Obviously with archeological curiosity.*) That one is crazy! Or a protester! He wants to change! But creation is a serene thing. A work of art is done naturally, in silence, and in recollection, like a nightingale sings … Spirit, in the sense that Hegel means spirit …

THE WOMAN: (*Intrigued.*) And if you know how it is done, why don't you tell him? Poor thing! He is distressed …

THE CRITIC: (*Strutting.*) For centuries, the critic has told the artist how to make a work of art…. Since ethics and aesthetics are functions of the spirit …

THE WOMAN: But you, you've never made any?

THE CRITIC: (*Nonplussed.*) Me? … Not me!

THE WOMAN: (*Laughing with malice.*) Well, then, you know how to do it, but you don't do it. You are neutral. How boring you must be in bed! (*She continues putting on her rouge.*)

THE ARTIST: (*Always walking back and forth sorrowfully, wringing his hands.*) Glory! Ah! Glory! (*Tightening his fists.*) I am strong! I am young! I can face anything! Oh! Divine electric lights … sun … To electrify the crowds … Burn them! Dominate them!

THE WOMAN: (*Looking at him with sympathy and compassion.*) Poor thing! Without any money ...

THE ARTIST: (*Struck.*) Ah! I am wounded! I can't resist any longer! (*Toward* THE WOMAN, *who doesn't hear him.*) Oh! A woman! (*Toward* THE CRITIC, *who has already taken and returned a good many books, and who leafs through them and cuts them.*) You! You, sir, who are a man, listen ... Help me!

THE CRITIC: Calm down ... let's realize the differences. I am not a man, I am a critic. I am a man of culture. The artist is a man, a slave, a baby, therefore, he makes mistakes. I don't see myself as being like him. In him nature is chaos. The critic and history are between nature and the artist. History is history, in other words subjective fact, that is to say fact, in other words history. Anyway it is itself objective.

At these words, THE ARTIST, *who has listened in a stupor, falls on the cushions as if struck by lightning.* THE CRITIC, *unaware of this, turns, and goes slowly to the table to consult his books.*

THE WOMAN: (*Getting up dumbfounded.*) My God! That poor youth is dying! (*She kneels in front of* THE ARTIST *and caresses him kindly.*)

THE ARTIST: (*Reviving.*) Oh! Signora! Thank you! Oh! Love ... maybe love ... (*Revives more and more.*) How beautiful you are! Listen ... Listen to me ... If you know what a terrible thing the struggle is without love! I want to love, understand?

THE WOMAN: (*Pulling away from him.*) My friend, I understand you ... but now I haven't time. I must go out ... I am expected by my friend. It is dangerous.... He is a man ... that is to say, he has a secure position ...

THE CRITIC: (*Very embarrassed.*) What's going on? I don't understand anything ...

THE WOMAN: (*Irritated.*) Shut up, idiot! You don't understand anything.... Come! Help me to lift him! We must cut this knot that is choking his throat!

THE CRITIC: (*Very embarrassed.*) Just a minute ... (*He carefully lays down the books and puts the others aside on the chair.*) Hegel ... Kant ... Hartmann ... Spinoza.

THE WOMAN: (*Goes near the youth, crying irritably.*) Run! ... come here, help me to unfasten it.

THE CRITIC: (*Nonplussed.*) What are you saying?

THE WOMAN: Come over here! Are you afraid! Hurry ... back here there is an artist who is dying because of an ideal.

THE CRITIC: (*Coming closer with extreme prudence.*) But one never knows! An impulse ... a passion ... without control ... without culture ... in short, I prefer him dead. The artist must be ... (*He stumbles, and falls clumsily on the artist, stabbing his neck with the paper knife.*)

THE WOMAN: (*Screaming and getting up.*) Idiot! Assassin! You have killed him. You are red with blood!

THE CRITIC: (*Getting up, still more clumsily.*) I, Signora? How?! I don't understand.... Red? Red? Yours is a case of color blindness.

THE WOMAN: Enough! Enough! (*Returns to her dressing table.*) It is late. I must go! (*Leaving.*) Poor youth! He was different and likable! (*Exits.*)

THE CRITIC: I can't find my bearings! (*Looks attentively and long at the dead* ARTIST.) Oh my God! He is dead! (*Going over to look at him.*) The artist is really dead! Ah ... he is breathing. I will make a monograph. (*He goes slowly to his table. From a case, he takes a beard a meter long and applies it to his chin. He puts on his glasses, takes paper and pencil, then looks among his books without finding anything. He is irritated for the first time and pounds his fists, shouting.*) Aesthetics! Aesthetics! Where is Aesthetics? (*Finding it, he passionately holds a large volume to his chest.*) Ah! Here it is! (*Skipping, he goes to crouch like a raven near the dead artist. He looks at the body, and writes, talking in a loud voice.*) Toward 1915, a marvelous artist blossomed ... (*He takes a tape measure from his pocket and measures the body.*) Like all the great ones, he was 1.68 [meters] tall, and his width ... (*While he talks, the curtain falls.*)

Bachelor Apartment (Theatrical Synthesis)

Idiotic interior of an elegant youth's bachelor apartment – prints on the walls, a very low divan, several vases of flowers, as in all bachelor apartments. A newly acquired painting is in front of the divan on an easel.

THE YOUTH: (*Listening eagerly near the door.*) Here we are! (*Opens it.*) Good morning! ... How are you?

THE WOMAN: (*Advancing, with a certain reserve.*) Good morning (*Looking around her.*) It's nice in here ...

THE YOUTH: (*With fervor.*) How beautiful you are! Very elegant! Thank you for coming ... I doubted ...

THE WOMAN: Why? Where is the painting? I came to see it.

THE YOUTH: It's this one. (*He takes her by the hand and conducts her in front of the painting. While* THE WOMAN *looks at it squinting,* THE YOUTH *takes her in his arms and kisses the nape of her neck.*)

THE WOMAN: (*Struggling energetically.*) Sir! What are you thinking of? ... These are really cowardly ...

THE YOUTH: Excuse me. (*He grasps her again forcefully and speaks close to her mouth.*) You are very beautiful! You are mine! You must be mine! ...

THE WOMAN: (*Struggling in a way that makes her seem serious.*) Sir! Leave me alone! ... I'll call for someone! I am a respectable woman! ... Leave me alone!

THE YOUTH: (*Mortified, letting her go.*) You are right. I ask your pardon ... I don't know what I am doing ... I will leave you.

THE WOMAN: Open the door for me! I want to get out of here!

THE YOUTH: (*Going to open the door.*) Go!

With this word, THE WOMAN lets her fur coat fall, and appears in black silk panties, with her bosom, shoulders, and arms nude. With coquetry and modesty, she runs to crouch on the divan.

THE WOMAN: You are timid, after all.... Turn that painting, and come here! ...

Note

From Michael Kirby, *Futurist Performance*, New York: Dutton, 1971, pp. 234–5.

2.6 FEET (1919)

FILIPPO TOMMASO MARINETTI

Translated by Victoria Nes Kirby

Filippo Tommaso Marinetti (1876–1944) *trained as a lawyer in Italy but did not practise professionally. He was the founder of Futurist movement, largely through the publication of the* Futurist Manifesto *in 1909. His aesthetic ideas were predicated on a celebration of speed, violence and the machine. Marinetti wrote many treatises on performance (see 2.11) and organized numerous theatrical evenings, most of which ended in riots. He was a follower of Mussolini's political party and without doubt the radical anarchic elements of Futurism are somewhat outweighed by its fascist tendencies. The text of* Feet, *however, offers a firm departure from the Surrealist performance texts and engages us with the possibilities of the mechanics and processes of theatre and performance. This translation was made in 1971.*

A curtain edged in black should be raised to about the height of a man's stomach. The public sees only legs in action. The actors must try to give the greatest expression to the attitudes and movements of their lower extremities.

1
Two armchairs
(one facing the other)

A BACHELOR
A MARRIED WOMAN

HIM: All, all for one of your kisses! ...
HER: No! ... Don't talk to me like that! ...

2

A MAN WHO IS WALKING BACK AND FORTH

MAN: Let's meditate ...

3
A desk

A SEATED MAN WHO IS NERVOUSLY MOVING HIS RIGHT FOOT

SEATED MAN: I must find ... To cheat, without letting myself cheat!

3a

A MAN WHO IS WALKING SLOWLY WITH GOUTY FEET
A MAN WHO IS WALKING RAPIDLY

THE RAPID ONE: Hurry! Vile passéist!
THE SLOW ONE: Ah! What fury! There is no need to run! He who goes slowly is healthy ...

4
A couch

THREE WOMEN

ONE: Which one do you prefer?
ANOTHER: All three of them.

A couch

THREE OFFICIALS

ONE: Which one do you prefer?
ANOTHER: The second one.

> *(The second one must be the woman who shows the most legs of the three.)*

5
A table

A FATHER
A BACHELOR
A YOUNG GIRL

THE FATHER: When you have the degree you will marry your cousin.

6

A pedal-operated sewing machine

A GIRL WHO IS WORKING

THE GIRL: I will see him on Sunday!

7

A MAN WHO IS RUNNING AWAY
A FOOT THAT IS KICKING AT HIM

THE MAN WHO IS GIVING THE KICK: Imbecile!

Note

From Michael Kirby, *Futurist Performance*, New York: Dutton, 1971, pp. 290–1.

2.7 GENIUS IN A JIFFY OR A DADALOGY (1920)

RAOUL HAUSMANN

Translated by Laurence Senelick

Raoul Hausmann (1886–1971). A painter and writer, born in Vienna, Hausmann was a committed member of the Expressionist movement but moved into Dada practice in Berlin, as an organizer of events and contributor to Dadaist journals in the late 1910s. He invented a particular method of photomontage and moved more into the field of photography as his career developed. During the war he had 'banned artist' status until 1944. This translation was made in 1989.

The stage is horribly dark, breakfast rolls rain down in the moonlight. A house once stood left. Out of the past enters ENGINEER DADA *followed by the* DADASOPHIST.

ENGINEER DADA: I feel so abandoned. – My eyes indeed were the first to see the light, but in the present revolutionary atmosphere … I believe something is bound to happen. The same thing goes for Byronic collars and penny-dreadful poetry. Otherwise things'll get very bad. I'd like to sing a song. A little bit of art. (*He sings.*)

> Herr Hölz he plays the gramophone,
> It drives Herr Ebert mad,
> Herr Seeckt's behind the fence alone,
> And wants to bash him bad.

A good song, a beautiful song. And yet people say I have bad teeth. Those nitwits, the Dadaists; when I think of the meatheads there are who understand nothing about taking photographs. For example there's the Dadasophist, imagines he could be something. Nothing but a … hush, here he comes now.

DADASOPHIST: Ah, good morning, Engineer, I'm glad I ran into you. Button up my left ear for me, I have until this evening to write a poem for *Schall und Rauch*, but I've sprained my hand and can't reach my head.

ENGINEER DADA: You are a nasty fellow. You ask me to do things you wouldn't do yourself. I'll have Grosz make a sketch of you, so you can see just how ugly you are. But strain your brain for 5.75 marks, no soldier in the Baltic provinces makes that much, it's overpaying – and concoct a political poem. You can't do it by yourself, I must first engineer it properly. You Prague stevedore!

DADASOPHIST: I – I need just a piece of paper – and then my chamberpot brain whizzes away like a spinning top. – Give me a kick, you capitalist wage-slave, it'll do my stomach good and then you'll see.

ENGINEER DADA: (*Boxes his ears.*)

DADASOPHIST: (*Blubbers.*)

> The fat bourgeois guzzles a bottle of wine,
> At night screws his dear wife in bed,
> Hopes his hero Herr Kapp will manage just fine, -
> And then the dumb ARPshole drops dead!!

– there! didn't I say so? good, right?

ENGINEER DADA: Why, man – You're bigger than Mehring and Huelsenbeck put together. Kerr will have to deliver a revised verdict on you and I myself will raise your honorarium to six marks. You must see to it that Kurt Wolff publishes you, perhaps under the title: My name is Rolf or I am a Beast; man, you ought to give me ten marks for that! That's an invaluable idea! Straight from me!

DADASOPHIST: Man, I may have a trust-fund, but I have to pay so much luxury tax I cannot give you any money. I would rather recite another poem. Listen:

> Let malicious people rap,
> Profiteering's there for all.

Goods? nah, just hand out pure crap,
Profiteering leads the ball.
Sure, laws against it have been framed,
But if your granddad's clever,
If Sklarz or Scheidemann he's named,
No laws can hurt you ever!
So, man, it's clear for all to see
You're totally secure!
Go profiteering stalwartly,
In good company, be sure:
Ebert, Fritze, the Kaiser, it appears,
Are all enrolled among the profiteers.

ENGINEER DADA: Oh, that won't do – nope, nope, NOPE – it won't work if you dare list our illustrious sovereign as a profiteer! Suppress that! When I was back in New York at the Nocker Bocker, a fellow dared make indecent remarks about President Wilson – well, I can tell you, it made me feel very bad – believe you me. I had to leave America right away and that affected the exchange rate so adversely for me that I wished there had been another big Kapp or rather Ludendorff uprising, because if I were to film it, the rate of exchange would go up again. But now – well, bore a hole in the asphalt, take a telescope and then you can keep an eye on the exchange rate! Otherwise, if nothing special happens, they'll say I've engineered the world atlas of the Dadaists, the Dadaco, so well that Hänisch will order a million copies for school textbooks! By the way, my man, Dadaism – well, what exactly is it?

Both break into a lament, the sky turns light blue, blood and walking-sticks rain down, – both Dadaists are eaten up by two Berlin Daily editors, and a voice from the audience says:

Dada's a hoax!
Is there an anti-Semite organizer in the house?

Note

The name-dropping refers to the turbulent political and artistic scene in post-war Germany. Max Hölz, a Spartacist, in 1920 had led a Communist revolt in Vogtland which he proclaimed a Soviet Republic; he was a promoter of the General Strike of 1921. Wolfgang Kapp had led a monarchist revolt against the republican government, seized Berlin and had himself proclaimed imperial chancellor; he was abetted by half-mad General Erich Ludendorff, who was later a participant in the Hitler beer-hall Putsch. The revolt failed after the general strike, and Friedrich Ebert resumed power as first president of the German Reich. Hans von Seekt, a military hero, was commander-in-chief of the Reichswehr; Phillip Scheidemann, who had urged a compromise peace during the war, was proclaimed first Prime Minister of the republic but resigned when the Reichstag accepted the terms of the Treaty of Versailles. Konrad Hänisch, a Social Democrat and Minister for Public Worship and Education, had convened a Schoolbook Conference in 1920. Alfred Kerr was Berlin's most influential drama critic. Kurt Wolff founded a new publishing house devoted to avant-garde and experimental works. – *Translator*.

From Laurence Senelick, ed., *Cabaret Performance: Europe 1890–1920*, New York: PAJ Publications, 1989, pp. 212–15.

2.8 R.U.R. (ROSSUM'S UNIVERSAL ROBOTS) (1920)

KAREL ČAPEK

Translated from the Czech by P. Selver and adapted for the English stage by Nigel Playfair in 1923

Karel Čapek (1890–1938). *Born in Prague, Karel Čapek was an essayist, playwright and sometime art critic. He studied in Prague and at the Sorbonne in Paris and is best known for his science fiction works, the novel* War with Newts *or* War with the Salamanders *(1936) and the play republished here,* R.U.R. (Rossum's Universal Robots) *published in 1920. The play was translated into over twenty languages within the first few years of production and is thought by many to have introduced the word 'robot' into the English language. Čapek credits his brother, the painter, writer and cartoonist Josef Čapek, who died in the Nazi concentration camp Bergen-Belsen in 1945, with having invented the word, however. Both brothers were highly political in their work, with an anti-fascist and anti-totalitarian outlook reflected in the play* R.U.R. *The play borrows from and develops the rhythms and ideological perspectives of Expressionism, but unlike many of the avant-garde texts reprinted in Part 2 of this volume, it was adopted by and produced to acclaim in the commercial sector of European and US theatre – the US premier in New York in 1922 ran for 184 performances and Basil Dean's original 1923 London production ran for 127 performances, and was quickly followed by a West End production of the Čapek brothers'* The Insect Play.

Scenes

ACT I. CENTRAL OFFICE OF THE FACTORY OF ROSSUM'S UNIVERSAL ROBOTS

ACT II. HELENA'S DRAWING–ROOM

ACT III. THE SAME AS ACT II

ACT IV. EPILOGUE. ONE OF THE EXPERIMENTAL LABORATORIES IN THE FACTORY

Characters

HARRY DOMAIN, *General Manager for Rossum's Universal Robots*

FABRY, *Chief Engineer for R.U.R.*

DR. GALL, *Head of the Physiological Department, R.U.R.*

DR. HELMAN, *Psychologist-in-Chief*

JACOB BERMAN, *Managing Director, R.U.R.*

ALQUIST, *Clerk of the Works, R.U.R.*

HELENA GLORY, *Daughter of Professor Glory, of Oxbridge University*

EMMA, *Her Maid*

MARIUS, *A Robot*

SULLA, *A Robotess*

RADIUS, *A Robot*

PRIMUS, *A Robot*

HELENA, *A Robotess*

A ROBOT SERVANT AND NUMEROUS ROBOTS

On a remote island

Act I

Central office of the factory of ROSSUM'S UNIVERSAL ROBOTS. Entrance at the back on the right. The windows look out on to endless rows of factory buildings. DOMAIN is sitting in a revolving chair at a large 'knee-hole' writing-table on which stand an electric lamp, telephone, letter-weight, correspondence-file, etc. On the left-hand wall hang large maps showing steamship and railway routes, a large calendar, and a clock indicating a few minutes before noon. On the right-hand wall are fastened printed placards: 'CHEAP LABOUR. ROSSUM'S ROBOTS.' 'ROBOTS FOR THE TROPICS. 150 DOLLARS EACH.' 'EVERY ONE SHOULD BUY HIS OWN ROBOT.' 'DO YOU WANT TO CHEAPEN YOUR OUTPUT? ORDER ROSSUM'S ROBOTS': more maps, shipping transport arrangements, etc. A tape-machine showing rates of exchange stands in one corner. In contrast to these wall fittings the floor is covered with a splendid Turkey carpet. On the right stand a round table, a sofa, leather arm-chair, and a bookshelf containing bottles of wine and spirits instead of books. Cashier's desk on the left. Next to DOMAIN's table SULLA is typing letters.

DOMAIN: (*Dictating.*) 'We do not accept any liability for goods damaged in transit. When the consignment was shipped, we drew your Captain's attention to the fact that the vessel was unsuitable for the transport of Robots. The matter is one for your own Insurance Company. We beg to remain, for Rossum's Universal Robots —' Finished?

SULLA: Yes.

DOMAIN: Another letter. 'To the E. B. Hudson Agency, New York, Date. We beg to acknowledge receipt of order for five thousand Robots. As you are sending your own vessel, please dispatch as cargo briquettes for R.U.R., the same to be credited as part-payment of the amount due to us. We beg to remain —' Finished?

SULLA: (*Typing the last word.*) Yes.

DOMAIN: 'Friedrichswerke, Hamburg. Date. We beg to acknowledge receipt of order for fifteen thousand Robots.

The house telephone rings. DOMAIN picks it up and speaks into it.

Hallo, this is the central office – yes – certainly. Oh yes, as usual. Of course, send them a cable. Good. (*Hangs up the telephone.*) Where did I leave off?

SULLA: We beg to acknowledge receipt of order for fifteen thousand R.

DOMAIN: (*Thoughtfully.*) Fifteen thousand R. Fifteen thousand R.

MARUIS: (*Entering.*) There's a lady, sir, asking to –

DOMAIN: Who is she?

MARIUS: I don't know, sir. She gave me this card.

DOMAIN: (*Reads.*) Professor William Glory, St. Trydeswyde's, Oxbridge – Ask her to come in.

MARIUS: (*Opening the door.*) Please step this way, ma'am.

Enter HELENA GLORY.

Exit MARIUS.

DOMAIN: (*Standing up.*) What can I do for you, madam?

HELENA: You are Mr. Domain, the general manager.

DOMAIN: I am.

HELENA: I have come to you –

DOMAIN: With Professor Glory's card. That is sufficient.

HELENA: Professor Glory is my father. I am Helena Glory.

DOMAIN: Miss Glory, it is an unusual honour for us – to be – to be –

HELENA: Yes, – well.

DOMAIN: To be allowed to welcome the distinguished Professor's daughter. Please sit down. Sulla, you may go. (*Exit SULLA.*) (*Sitting down.*) How can I be of service to you, Miss Glory?

HELENA: I have come here –

DOMAIN: To have a look at our factory where people are made. Like all visitors. Well, there's no objection.

HELENA: I thought it was forbidden –

DOMAIN: It is forbidden to enter the factory, of course. But everybody comes here with an introduction and then –

HELENA: And you show everybody –?

DOMAIN: Only certain things. The manufacture of artificial people is a secret process.

HELENA: If you only knew how enormously that –

DOMAIN: Interests me, you were going to say. Europe's talking about nothing else.

HELENA: Why don't you let me finish speaking?

DOMAIN: I beg your pardon. Did you want to say anything else?

HELENA: I only wanted to ask –

DOMAIN: Whether I could make a special exception in your case and show you our factory. Certainly, Miss Glory.

HELENA: How do you know that I wanted to ask you that?

DOMAIN: They all do. (*Standing up.*) We shall consider it a special honour to show you more than the rest, because – indeed – I mean –

HELENA: Thank you.

DOMAIN: But you must undertake not to divulge the least –

HELENA: (*Standing up and giving him her hand.*) My word of honour.

DOMAIN: Thank you. Won't you raise your veil?

HELENA: Oh, of course, you want to see me. I beg your pardon.

DOMAIN: What is it, please?

HELENA: Would you mind letting my hand go.

DOMAIN: (*Releasing it.*) I beg your pardon.

HELENA: (*Taking off her veil.*) You want to see whether I am a spy or not. How cautious you are!

DOMAIN: (*Looking at her intently.*) H'm, of course – we – that is –

HELENA: You don't trust me?

DOMAIN: Oh, indeed, Miss Glory, I'm only too delighted. Weren't you lonely on the voyage?

HELENA: Why?

DOMAIN: Because – I mean to say – you're so young.

HELENA: Yes. Shall we go straight into the factory?

DOMAIN: Twenty-two, I think, eh?

HELENA: Twenty-two what?

DOMAIN: Years.

HELENA: Twenty-one. Why do you want to know?

DOMAIN: Because – as – (*With enthusiasm.*) You'll make a long stay, won't you?

HELENA: That depends on how much of the factory you show me.

DOMAIN: Oh, hang the factory. But you shall see everything, Miss Glory, indeed you shall. Please sit down. Would you like to hear the story of the invention?

HELENA: Yes, please. (*Sits down.*)

DOMAIN: Well, then. (*Sits down on the writing-table, looks at* HELENA *with rapture, and reels off rapidly.*) It was in the year 1922 that old Rossum the great physiologist, who was then quite a young scientist, betook himself to this distant island for the purpose of studying the ocean fauna, full stop. On this occasion he attempted by chemical synthesis to imitate the living matter known as protoplasm, until he suddenly discovered a substance which behaved exactly like living matter, although its chemical composition was different; that was in the year 1932, exactly four hundred years after the discovery of America, whew!

HELENA: Do you know that by heart?

DOMAIN: Yes. Physiology, Miss Glory, is not my line. Shall I go on?

HELENA: Please do.

DOMAIN: (*Solemnly.*) And then, Miss Glory, old Rossum wrote the following in his day book: 'Nature has found only one method of organizing living matter. There is, however, another method more simple, flexible, and rapid, which has not yet occurred to nature at all. This second process by which life can be developed was discovered by me today.' Imagine him, Miss Glory, writing those wonderful words. Imagine him sitting over a test-tube and thinking how the whole tree of life would grow from it, how all animals would proceed from it, beginning with some sort of beetle and ending with man himself. A man of different substance from ours. Miss Glory, that was a tremendous moment.

HELENA: Go on, please.

DOMAIN: Now the thing was, how to get the life out of the test-tube and hasten development: to form organs, bones and nerves, and so on: to find such substances as catalytics, enzymes, hormones, and so forth, in short – you understand?

HELENA: I don't know. Not much, I'm afraid.

DOMAIN: Never mind. You see, with the help of his tinctures he could make whatever he wanted. He could have produced a Medusa with the brain of a Socrates or a worm fifty yards long. But being without a grain of humour, he took it into his head to make a normal vertebrate. This artificial living matter of his had a raging thirst for life. It

didn't mind being sewn up or mixed together. *That*, you'll admit, couldn't be done with natural albumen. And that's how he set about it.

HELENA: About what?

DOMAIN: About imitating nature. First of all he tried making an artificial dog. That took him several years and resulted in a sort of stunted calf which died in a few days. I'll show it you in the museum. And then old Rossum started on the manufacture of man. (*Pause.*)

HELENA: And I must divulge this to nobody?

DOMAIN: To nobody in the world.

HELENA: It's a pity that it can already be found in every school lesson book.

DOMAIN: Yes. (*Jumps up from the table and sits down beside* HELENA.) But do you know what isn't in the lesson books? (*Taps his forehead.*) That old Rossum was quite mad. Seriously, Miss Glory, you must keep this to yourself. The old crank actually wanted to make people.

HELENA: But you do make people.

DOMAIN: Synthetically, Miss Helena. But old Rossum meant it actually. He wanted to become a sort of scientific substitute for God, you know. He was a fearful materialist, and that's why he did it all. His sole purpose was nothing more or less than to supply proof that Providence was no longer necessary. So he took it into his head to make people exactly like us. Do you know anything about anatomy?

HELENA: Only a very little.

DOMAIN: So do I. Imagine then that he decided to manufacture everything as in the human body. I'll show you in the museum the bungling attempt it took him ten years to produce. It was to have been a man, but it lived for three days only. Then up came young Rossum, an engineer, the nephew of old Rossum. A wonderful fellow, Miss Glory. When he saw what a mess of it the old man was making, he said: 'It's absurd to spend ten years making a man. If you can't make him quicker than nature, you may as well shut up shop.' Then he set about learning anatomy himself.

HELENA: There's nothing about that in the lesson books.

DOMAIN: (*Standing up.*) The lesson books are full of paid advertisement, and rubbish at that. For example, it says there that the Robots were invented by an old man. But it was young Rossum who had the idea of making living and intelligent working machines. What the lesson books say about the united efforts of the two great Rossums is all a fairy tale. They used to have dreadful rows. The old atheist hadn't the slightest conception of industrial matters, and the end of it was that young Rossum shut him up in some laboratory or other and let him fritter the time away with his monstrosities, while he himself started on the business from an engineer's point of view. Old Rossum cursed him, and before he died he managed to botch up two physiological horrors. Then one day they found him dead in the laboratory. That's the whole story.

HELENA: And what about the young man?

DOMAIN: Well, any one who's looked into anatomy will have seen at once that man is too complicated, and that a good engineer could make him more simply. So young Rossum began to overhaul anatomy and tried to see what could be left out or simplified. In short – but this isn't boring you, Miss Glory?

HELENA: No; on the contrary, it's awfully interesting.

DOMAIN: So young Rossum said to himself: A man is something that, for instance, feels happy, plays the fiddle, likes going for walks, and, in fact, wants to do a whole lot of things that are really unnecessary.

HELENA: Oh!

DOMAIN: Wait a bit. That are unnecessary when he's wanted, let us say, to weave or to count. Do you play the fiddle?

HELENA: No.

DOMAIN: That's a pity. But a working machine must not want to play the fiddle, must not feel happy, must not do a whole lot of other things. A petrol motor must not have tassels or ornaments, Miss Glory. And to manufacture artificial workers is the same thing as to manufacture motors. The process must be of the simplest, and the product of the best from a practical point of view. What sort of worker do you think is the best from a practical point of view?

HELENA: The best? Perhaps the one who is most honest and hard-working.

DOMAIN: No, the cheapest. The one whose needs are the smallest. Young Rossum invented a worker with the minimum amount of requirements. He had to simplify him. He rejected everything that did not contribute directly to the progress of work. In this way he rejected everything that makes man more expensive. In fact, he rejected man and made the Robot. My dear Miss Glory, the Robots are not people. Mechanically they are more perfect than we are, they have an enormously developed intelligence, but they have no soul. Have you ever seen what a Robot looks like inside?

HELENA: Good gracious, no!

DOMAIN: Very neat, very simple. Really a beautiful piece of work. Not much in it, but everything in flawless order. The product of an engineer is technically at a higher pitch of perfection than a product of nature.

HELENA: Man is supposed to be the product of nature.

DOMAIN: So much the worse. Nature hasn't the least notion of modern engineering. Would you believe that young Rossum played at being nature?

HELENA: What do you mean?

DOMAIN: He began to manufacture Super-Robots – regular giants. He tried to make them four yards high. But they were a frost.

HELENA: A frost?

DOMAIN: Yes. For no reason at all their limbs used to keep snapping off. Evidently our planet is too small for giants. Now we only make Robots of normal size and of very high-class human finish.

HELENA: I saw the first Robots at home. The town council bought them – I mean engaged them for work.

DOMAIN: Bought them, dear Miss Glory. Robots are bought and sold.

HELENA: These were employed as sweepers. I saw them sweeping. They are so strange and quiet.

DOMAIN: Did you see my typist?

HELENA: I didn't notice her particularly.

DOMAIN: (*Rings.*) You see, Rossum's Universal Robot factory don't produce a uniform brand of Robots. We have Robots of finer and coarser grades. The best will live about twenty years.

HELENA: Then they perish?

DOMAIN: Yes, they get used up.

Enter SULLA.

DOMAIN: Sulla, let Miss Glory look at you.

HELENA: (*Standing up and holding out her hand.*) So glad to meet you. You must feel terribly dull in this out-of-the-way spot, don't you?

SULLA: I don't know, Miss Glory. Please sit down.

HELENA: (*Sitting down.*) Where do you come from?

SULLA: From there, from the factory.

HELENA: Ah, you were born there.

SULLA: Yes, was made there.

HELENA: (*Jumping up.*) What?

DOMAIN: (*Laughing.*) Sulla is a Robot.

HELENA: Oh, I beg your pardon –

DOMAIN: (*Laying his hand on* SULLA's *shoulder.*) Sulla isn't angry. See, Miss Glory, the kind of skin we make. Feel her face.

HELENA: Oh, no, no.

DOMAIN: You wouldn't know that she's of different material from us. Turn round, Sulla.

HELENA: Stop, stop!

DOMAIN: Talk to Miss Glory, Sulla. She's an important visitor.

SULLA: Please sit down. (*Both sit down.*) Did you have a pleasant crossing?

HELENA: Oh yes, certainly.

SULLA: Don't go back on the *Amelia*, Miss Glory. The barometer is falling steadily. Wait for the *Pennsylvania*. That's a very good powerful vessel.

DOMAIN: What's its speed?

SULLA: Twenty knots an hour. Twelve thousand tons. One of the latest vessels, Miss Glory.

HELENA: Tha – thank you.

SULLA: A crew of eighty, Captain Harpy, eight boilers –

DOMAIN: (*Laughing.*) That's enough, Sulla. Now show us your knowledge of French.

HELENA: You know French?

SULLA: I know four languages. I can write: Dear Sir, Monsieur, Geehrter Herr, Y Mustre Señor.

HELENA: (*Jumping up.*) What nonsense! Sulla, isn't a Robot.

Sulla is a girl like me. Sulla, it's naughty of you – why do you take part in such a hoax?

SULLA: I am a Robot.

HELENA: No, no, you're not telling the truth. Oh, Sulla, forgive me, I know – they've forced you to do it for an advertisement. Sulla, you are a girl like me, aren't you? Tell me, now.

DOMAIN: I'm sorry, Miss Glory. Sulla is a Robot.

HELENA: *You're* not telling the truth.

DOMAIN: (*Starting up.*) What? (*Rings.*) Excuse me, Miss Glory, then I must convince you.

Enter MARIUS.

DOMAIN: Marius, take Sulla into the testing-room for them to open her. Quickly.

HELENA: Where?

DOMAIN: Into the testing-room. When they've cut her up, you can go and have a look.

HELENA: I shan't go.

DOMAIN: Excuse me, you spoke of lies.

HELENA: You wouldn't have her killed?

DOMAIN: You can't kill machines.

HELENA: (*Embracing SULLA.*) Don't be afraid, Sulla, I won't let you go. Tell me, darling, are they always so cruel to you? You mustn't put up with that, Sulla. You mustn't.

SULLA: I am a Robot.

HELENA: That doesn't matter. Robots are just as good as we are. Sulla, you wouldn't let yourself be cut to pieces.

SULLA: Yes.

HELENA: Oh, you're not afraid of death, then?

SULLA: I cannot tell, Miss Glory.

HELENA: Do you know what would happen to you there?

SULLA: Yes, I should cease to move.

HELENA: How dreadful.

DOMAIN: Marius, tell Miss Glory what you are.

MARIUS: Marius, the Robot.

DOMAIN: Would you take Sulla into the testing-room?

MARIUS: Yes.

DOMAIN: Would you be sorry for her?

MARIUS: I cannot tell.

DOMAIN: What would happen to her?

MARIUS: She would cease to move. They would put her into the stamping-mill.

DOMAIN: That is death, Marius. Aren't you afraid of death?

MARIUS: No.

DOMAIN: You see, Miss Glory, the Robots are not attached to life. They have no reason to be. They have no enjoyments. They are less than so much grass.

HELENA: Oh, stop. Send them away.

DOMAIN: Marius, Sulla, you may go.

Exeunt SULLA and MARIUS.

HELENA: How terrible. It's scandalous!

DOMAIN: Why scandalous?

HELENA: It is, of course it is. Why did you call her Sulla?

DOMAIN: Isn't it a nice name?

HELENA: It's a man's name. Sulla was a Roman General.

DOMAIN: Oh, we thought that Marius and Sulla were lovers.

HELENA: No. Marius and Sulla were generals, and fought against each other in the year – I've forgotten now.

DOMAIN: Come here to the window. What do you see?

HELENA: Bricklayers,

DOMAIN: They are Robots. All our workpeople are Robots. And down there, can you see anything.

HELENA: Some sort of office.

DOMAIN: A counting-house. And in it –

HELENA: Clerks – a lot of clerks.

DOMAIN: They are Robots. All our clerks are Robots. When you see the factory – (*Sound of factory whistles and sirens.*) Midday. The Robots don't know when to stop work. In two hours I'll show you the kneading-trough.

HELENA: What kneading-trough?

DOMAIN: (*Dryly.*) The pestles and mortar as it were for beating up the paste. In each one we mix the ingredients for a thousand Robots at one operation. Then there are the vats for the preparation of liver, brains, and so on. Then you'll see the bone factory. After that I'll show you the spinning-mill.

HELENA: What spinning-mill?

DOMAIN: For weaving nerves and veins. Miles and miles of digestive tubes pass through it at a stretch. Then there's the fitting-shed, where all the parts are put together, like motor-cars. Next comes the drying-kiln and the warehouse in which the new products work.

HELENA: Good gracious, do they have to work immediately?

DOMAIN: Well, you see, they work like any new appliance. They get used to existence. They sort of grow firm inside. We have to make a slight allowance for natural development. And in the meantime they undergo training.

HELENA: How is that done?

DOMAIN: It's much the same as going to school. They learn to speak, write, and count. They've astonishing memories, you know. If you were to read a twenty-volume Encyclopaedia to them, they'd repeat it all to you with absolute accuracy. But they never think of anything new. Then they're sorted out and distributed. Fifteen thousand daily, not counting a regular percentage of defective specimens which are thrown into the stamping-mill … and so on – and so on. Oh, let's talk about something else. There's only a handful of us among a hundred thousand Robots, and not one woman. We talk about nothing but the factory, all day, every day. It's just as if we're under a curse, Miss Glory.

HELENA: I'm so sorry I said that – that – you weren't speaking the truth.

A knock at the door.

DOMAIN: Come in, boys.

From the L. enter MR. FABRY, DR. GALL, DR. HELMAN, ALQUIST.

DR. GALL: I beg your pardon, I hope we're not in the way.

DOMAIN: Come along in. Miss Glory, here are Mr. Alquist, Mr. Fabry, Dr. Gall, and Dr. Helman. This is Professor Glory's daughter.

HELENA: (*Embarrassed.*) How do you do?

FABRY: We had no idea –

DR. GALL: Very honoured, I'm sure –

ALQUIST: Welcome, Miss Glory.

BERMAN rushes in from the R.

BERMAN: Hallo, what's up?

DOMAIN: Come in, Berman. This is Mr. Berman, Miss Glory. This is the daughter of Professor Glory.

HELENA: I'm very glad to meet you.

BERMAN: By Jove, that's splendid. Miss Glory, may we send a cablegram to the papers about your –

HELENA: No, no, please don't.

DOMAIN: Sit down, please, Miss Glory.

BERMAN: Allow me –

DR. GALL: (*Dragging up arm-chairs.*) Please –

FABRY: Excuse me –

ALQUIST: What sort of a crossing did you have?

DR. GALL: Are you going to stay here long?

FABRY: What do you think of the factory, Miss Glory?

HELMAN: Did you come over on the *Amelia*?

DOMAIN: Be quiet, let Miss Glory speak.

HELENA: (*To* DOMAIN.) What am I to speak to them about?

DOMAIN: (*Surprised.*) About what you like.

HELENA: Shall … may I speak quite frankly?

DOMAIN: Why, of course.

HELENA: (*Wavering, then with desperate resolution.*) Tell me, doesn't it ever distress you to be treated like this?

FABRY: Treated? – Who by?

HELENA: Everybody.

All look at each other in consternation.

ALQUIST: Treated?

DR. GALL: What makes you think that?

HELMAN: Treated?

BERMAN: Really!

HELENA: Don't you feel that you might be living a better life?

DR. GALL: Well, that depends what you mean, Miss Glory,

HELENA: I mean that – (*Bursting out.*) that it's perfectly outrageous. It's terrible. (*Standing up.*) The whole of Europe is talking about how you're being treated. That's why I came here to see, and it's a thousand times worse than could have been imagined. How can you put up with it?

ALQUIST: Put up with what?

HELENA: Your position here. Good heavens, you are living creatures just like us, like the whole of Europe, like the whole world. It's scandalous, disgraceful!

BERMAN: Good gracious, Miss Glory.

FABRY: Well, boys, she's not so far out. We live here just like Red Indians.

HELENA: Worse than Red Indians. May, oh, may I call you brothers.

BERMAN: Of course you may, why not?

HELENA: Brothers, I have not come here as my father's daughter. I have come on behalf of the Humanity League. Brothers, the Humanity League now has over two hundred thousand members. Two hundred thousand people are on your side and offer you their help.

BERMAN: Two hundred thousand people, that's quite a tidy lot, Miss Glory, quite good.

FABRY: I'm always telling you there's nothing like good old Europe. You see, they've not forgotten us. 'They're offering us help.

DR. GALL: What help? A theatre?

HELMAN: An orchestra?

HELENA: More than that.

ALQUIST: Just you?

HELENA: Oh, never mind about me. I'll stay as long as is necessary.

BERMAN: By Jove, that's good.

ALQUIST: Domain, I'm going to get the best room ready for Miss Glory.

DOMAIN: Wait a moment. I'm afraid that – that Miss Glory hasn't finished speaking.

HELENA: No, I haven't. Unless you close my lips by force.

DR. GALL: Harry, don't you dare.

HELENA: Thank you. I knew that you'd protect me.

DOMAIN: Excuse me, Miss Glory, but I suppose you think you're talking to Robots?

HELENA: (*Startled.*) Of course.

DOMAIN: I'm sorry. These gentlemen are human beings, just like us. Like the whole of Europe.

HELENA: (*To the others.*) You're not Robots?

BERMAN: (*With a guffaw.*) God forbid.

HELMAN: (*With dignity.*) Pah, Robots indeed.

DR. GALL: (*Laughing.*) No, thanks.

HELENA: But …

FABRY: Upon my honour, Miss Glory, we aren't Robots.

HELENA: (*To* DOMAIN.) Then why did you tell me that all your assistants were Robots?

DOMAIN: Yes, the clerks. But not the managers. Allow me, Miss Glory. This is Fabry, chief engineer for Rossum's Universal Robots. Dr. Gall, head of the physiological department. Dr. Helman, psychologist-in-chief for the training of Robots. Jacob Berman, general business manager, and Alquist, clerk of the works to Rossum's Universal Robots.

HELENA: Forgive me, gentlemen, for – for –. Have I done something dreadful?

ALQUIST: Not at all, not at all, Miss Glory. Please sit down.

HELENA: (*Sitting down.*) I'm a stupid girl. Send me back by the first ship.

DR. GALL: Not for anything in the world, Miss Glory. Why should we send you back?

HELENA: Because you know – because – because I should disturb your Robots for you.

DOMAIN: My dear Miss Glory, we've had close upon a hundred preachers and prophets here. Every ship brings us some. Missionaries, anarchists, Salvation Army, all sorts. It's astonishing what a number of religious sects and – forgive me, I don't mean you – and idiots there are in the world.

HELENA: And you let them speak to the Robots?

DOMAIN: Why not? So far we've let them all do so. The Robots remember everything, but that's all. They don't even laugh at what the people say. Really, it's quite incredible. If it would amuse you, Miss Glory, I'll take you over the Robot warehouse. It holds about three hundred thousand of them.

BERMAN: Three hundred and forty-seven thousand.

DOMAIN: Good. You can say whatever you like to them. You can read the Bible, recite logarithms, whatever you please. You can even preach to them about human rights.

HELENA: Oh, I think that … if you were to show them a little love –

FABRY: Impossible, Miss Glory. Nothing is more unlike a man than a Robot.

HELENA: What do you make them for, then?

BERMAN: Ha, ha, ha, that's good. What are Robots made for?

FABRY: For work, Miss Glory. One Robot can replace two and a half workmen. The human machine, Miss Glory, was terribly imperfect. It had to be removed sooner or later.

BERMAN: It was too expensive.

FABRY: It was not very effective. It no longer answered the requirements of modern engineering. Nature has no idea of keeping pace with modern labour. From a technical point of view the whole of childhood is a sheer stupidity. So much time lost. And then again –

HELENA: Oh, please leave off.

FABRY: Pardon me. But kindly tell me what is the real aim of your League – the – the Humanity League.

HELENA: Its real purpose is to – to protect the Robots and – and ensure good treatment for them.

FABRY: Not a bad object, either. A machine has to be treated properly. Upon my soul, I approve of that. I don't like damaged articles. Please, Miss Glory, enroll us all as contributing, as regular, as foundation, members of your League.

HELENA: No, you don't understand me. What we really want is to – to liberate the Robots.

HELMAN: How do you propose to do that?

HELENA: They are to be – to be dealt with like human beings.

HELMAN: Aha. I suppose they're to vote? To drink beer? To order us about.

HELENA: Why shouldn't they vote?

HELMAN: Perhaps they're even to receive wages?

HELENA: Of course they are.

HELMAN: Fancy that now. And what would they do with their wages, pray.

HELENA: They would buy … what they need … what pleases them.

HELMAN: That would be very nice, Miss Glory, only there's nothing that does please the Robots. Good heavens, what are they to buy? You can feed them on pineapples, straw, whatever you like. It's all the same to them, they've no appetite at all. They've no interest in anything, Miss Glory. Why hang it all, nobody's ever yet seen a Robot smile.

HELENA: Why … why don't you make them happier?

HELMAN: That wouldn't do, Miss Glory. They are only Robots.

HELENA: Oh, but they're so sensible.

HELMAN: Not sensible – acute, confoundedly so, but they're nothing else. They've no will of their own. No passion. No soul.

HELENA: No love, no desire to resist?

HELMAN: Rather not. Robots don't love, not even themselves. And the desire to resist? I don't know. Only rarely, only from time to time –

HELENA: What?

HELMAN: Nothing particular. Occasionally they seem somehow to go off their heads. Something like epilepsy, you know. We call it Robot's cramp. They'll suddenly sling down everything they're holding, stand still, gnash their teeth – and then they have to go into the stamping-mill. It's evidently some breakdown in the mechanism.

DOMAIN: A flaw in the works. It'll have to be removed.

HELENA: No, no that's the soul.

FABRY: Do you think that the soul first shows itself by a gnashing of teeth?

HELENA: I don't know. Perhaps it's a sign of revolt. Perhaps it's just a sign that there's a struggle. Oh, if you could infuse them with it.

DOMAIN: That'll be remedied, Miss Glory. Dr. Gall is just making some experiments –

DR. GALL: Not with regard to that, Domain. At present I'm making pain-nerves – to use a very unscientific expression.

HELENA: Pain-nerves?

DR. GALL: Yes. The Robots feel practically no bodily pain. You see, young Rossum provided them with too limited a nervous system. That doesn't answer. We must introduce suffering.

HELENA: Why – why – don't you give them a soul, why do you want to cause them pain?

DR. GALL: For industrial reasons, Miss Glory. Sometimes a Robot does damage to himself because it doesn't hurt him. He puts his hand into the machine, breaks his finger, smashes his head – it's all the same to him. We must provide them with pain. That's an automatic protection against damage.

HELENA: Will they be happier when they feel pain?

DR. GALL: On the contrary, but they will be more perfect from a technical point of view.

HELENA: Why don't you create a soul for them?

DR. GALL: That's not in our power.

FABRY: That's not in our interest.

BERMAN: That would increase the cost of production. Hang it all, my dear young lady, we turn them out at such a cheap rate, £15 each, fully dressed, and fifteen years ago they cost £200. Five years ago we used to buy the clothes for them. Today we have our own weaving mill, and now we even export cloth five times cheaper than other factories. What do you pay for a yard of cloth, Miss Glory?

HELENA: I don't know – really – I've forgotten.

BERMAN: Good gracious me, and you want to found a Humanity League? It only costs a third now, Miss Glory. All prices are today a third of what they were, and they'll fall still lower, lower, lower – like that. Eh?

HELENA: I don't understand.

BERMAN: Why, bless me, Miss Glory, it means that the cost of labour has fallen. A Robot, food and all, costs three and fourpence per hour. All factories will go pop like acorns if they don't at once buy Robots to lower the cost of production.

HELENA: Yes, and they'll get rid of their workmen.

BERMAN: Ha, ha, of course. But, good gracious me, in the meantime we've dumped five hundred thousand tropical Robots down on the Argentine pampas to grow corn. Would you mind telling me how much you pay for a loaf of bread?

HELENA: I've no idea.

BERMAN: Well, I'll tell you. It now costs twopence in good old Europe, but that's our bread, you know. A loaf of bread for twopence, and the Humanity League knows nothing about it. Ha, ha, Miss Glory, you don't realize that it's too expensive. But in five years' time, I'll wager –

HELENA: What?

BERMAN: That the prices of everything won't be a tenth of what they are now. Why, in five years we'll be up to our ears in corn and everything else.

ALQUIST: Yes, and all the workers throughout the world will be unemployed.

DOMAIN: (*Standing up.*) They will, Alquist. They will, Miss Glory. But in ten years Rossum's Universal Robots will produce so much corn, so much cloth, so much everything, that things will be practically without price. Every one will take as much as he wants. There'll be no poverty. Yes, there'll be unemployed. But, then, there won't be any employment. Everything will be done by living machines. The Robots will clothe and feed us. The Robots will make bricks and build houses for us. The Robots will keep our accounts and sweep our stairs. There'll be no employment, but everybody will be free from worry, and liberated from the degradation of labour. Everybody will live only to perfect himself.

HELENA: (*Standing up.*) Will he?

DOMAIN: Of course. It's bound to happen. There may perhaps be terrible doings first, Miss Glory. That simply can't be avoided. But, then, the servitude of man to man and the enslavement of man to matter will cease. The Robots will wash the feet of the beggar and prepare a bed for him in his own house. Nobody will get bread at the price of life and hatred. There'll be no artisans, no clerks, no hewers of coal and minders of other men's machines.

ALQUIST: Domain, Domain. What you say sounds too much like paradise. Domain, there was something good in service and something great in humanity. Ah, Harry, there was some kind of virtue in toil and weariness.

DOMAIN: Perhaps. But we cannot reckon with what is lost when we transform Adam's world.

HELENA: You have bewildered me. I am a foolish girl. I should like – I should like to believe this.

DR. GALL: You are younger than we are, Miss Glory. You will live to see it.

HELMAN: True. I think that Miss Glory might lunch with us.

DR. GALL: Of course. Domain ask on behalf of us all.

DOMAIN: Miss Glory, will you do us the honour?

HELENA: Thank you so much, but –

FABRY: To represent the League of Humanity, Miss Glory.

BERMAN: And in honour of it.

HELENA: Oh, in that case.

FABRY: That's right. Miss Glory, excuse me for five minutes.

DR. GALL: And me.

BERMAN: By Jove, I must, send a cable –

HELMAN: Good heavens, I've forgotten –

All rush out except DOMAIN.

HELENA: What have they all gone off for?

DOMAIN: To cook, Miss Glory.

HELENA: To cook what?

DOMAIN: Lunch, Miss Glory. The Robots do our cooking for us, but – but – as they've no taste, it's not altogether – that is, Helman is awfully good at grills, and Gall can make a kind of sauce, and Berman knows all about omelettes –

HELENA: My goodness, what a banquet. And what's the speciality of Mr. – of the Clerk of the Works?

DOMAIN: Alquist? Nothing. He only lays the table, and Fabry'll get together a little fruit. Our cuisine is very modest, Miss Glory.

HELENA: I wanted to ask you –

DOMAIN: And I wanted to ask you something, too. (*Laying his watch on the table.*) Five minutes.

HELENA: What do you want to ask?

DOMAIN: Excuse me, you asked first.

HELENA: Perhaps it's silly of me, but – why do you manufacture female Robots, when – when –

DOMAIN: When – hm – sex means nothing to them?

HELENA: Yes.

DOMAIN: There's a certain demand for them, you see. Servants, saleswomen, clerks. People are used to it.

HELENA: But – but, tell me, are the Robots, male and female – mutually – altogether –

DOMAIN: Altogether indifferent to each other, Miss Glory. There's no sign of any affection between them.

HELENA: Oh, that's terrible.

DOMAIN: Why?

HELENA: It's so – so unnatural. One doesn't know whether to be disgusted, or whether to hate them, or perhaps –

DOMAIN: To pity them.

HELENA: That's more like it. No, stop. What did you want to ask about?

DOMAIN: I should like to ask you, Miss Glory, whether you will marry me?

HELENA: What?

DOMAIN: Will you be my wife?

HELENA: No. The idea!

DOMAIN: (*Looking at his watch.*) Another three minutes. If you won't marry me, you'll have to marry one of the other five.

HELENA: But, for Heaven's sake, why should I?

DOMAIN: Because they're all going to ask you in turn.

HELENA: How could they dare to do such a thing?

DOMAIN: I'm very sorry, Miss Glory. I think they've fallen in love with you.

HELENA: Please don't let them do it. I'll go away at once.

DOMAIN: Helena, you won't be so unkind as to refuse them?

HELENA: But – but, I can't marry all six.

DOMAIN: No, but one, anyhow. If you don't want me, marry Fabry.

HELENA: I won't!

DOMAIN: Dr. Gall.

HELENA: No, no, quiet. I don't want any of you.

DOMAIN: Another two minutes.

HELENA: This is terrible. I think you'd marry any woman who came here.

DOMAIN: There have been plenty of them, Helena.

HELENA: Young?

DOMAIN: Yes.

HELENA: And pretty – no, I didn't mean that – then why didn't you marry any of them?

DOMAIN: Because I didn't lose my head. Until today. Then as soon as you lifted your veil –

HELENA: I know.

DOMAIN: Another minute.

HELENA: But I don't want to, I tell you.

DOMAIN: (*Laying both hands on her shoulders.*) Another minute. Either you must say something fearfully angry to me point-blank, and then I'll leave you alone, or, or –

HELENA: You're a rude man.

DOMAIN: That's nothing. A man has to be a bit rude. That's part of the business.

HELENA: You're mad.

DOMAIN: A man has to be a bit mad, Helena. That's the best thing about him.

HELENA: You are – you are – oh, heavens!

DOMAIN: What did I tell you? Are you ready?

HELENA: No, no. Leave me, please. You're hurting me.

DOMAIN: The last word, Helena.

HELENA: (*Protestingly.*) Perhaps when I know you better – oh, I don't know – let me go, please.

Knocking at the door.

DOMAIN: (*Releasing her.*) Come in.

Enter BERMAN, DR. GALL, *and* HELMAN, *in kitchen aprons.* FABRY *with a bouquet,* ALQUIST *with a napkin under his arm.*

DOMAIN: Have you finished your job?

BERMAN: (*Solemnly.*) Yes.

DOMAIN: So have we – at least I think so!

Curtain.

Act II

SCENE: HELENA's *drawing-room. On the left a baize door and a door to the music-room, on the right a door to* HELENA's *bedroom. In the centre are windows looking out on to the sea and the harbour. A small table with odds and ends, another table, a sofa and chairs, a chest of drawers, a writing-table with an electric lamp. On the right a fireplace with electric lamps above it. The whole drawing-room in all its details is of a modern and purely feminine character.*

DOMAIN *discovered looking from the window – takes out revolver thoughtfully.* FABRY *and* HELMAN *knock and enter from the left carrying armfuls of flowers and flower-pots.*

FABRY: Where are we to put it all?

HELMAN: Whew! (*Lays down his load and indicates the door on the right.*) She's asleep. Anyhow, as long as she's asleep, she's well out of it.

DOMAIN: She knows nothing about it at all.

FABRY: (*Putting flowers into vases.*) I hope nothing happens today –

HELMAN: (*Arranging flowers.*) For Heaven's sake, drop all that! Look, Harry, this is a fine cyclamen, isn't it? A new sort, my latest – Cyclamen Helena.

DOMAIN: (*Looking out of the window.*) No signs of the ship, no signs of the ship. Things must be pretty bad.

HELMAN: Shut up. Suppose she heard you.

DOMAIN: Well, anyhow the *Ultima* has arrived just in time.

FABRY: (*Leaving the flowers.*) Do you think that today –?

DOMAIN: I don't know. Aren't the flowers splendid?

HELMAN: (*Going up to him.*) These are new primroses, eh? And this is my new jasmine. I've discovered a wonderful way of training flowers quickly. Splendid varieties. Next year I'll be producing marvellous ones.

DOMAIN: (*Turns round.*) What, next year?

FABRY: I'd like to know what's happening at Havre –

DOMAIN: Shut up.

HELENA: (*Voice from the right.*) Emma!

DOMAIN: Out you go.

All go out on tiptoe through the baize door.
Enter EMMA through the main door from the left.

HELENA: (*Standing in the doorway R. with her back to the room.*) Emma, come and do up my dress.

EMMA: I'm coming. So you're up at last. (*Fastening HELENA's dress.*) My gracious, what brutes!

HELENA: Who?

EMMA: Keep still. If you want to turn round, then turn round, but I shan't fasten you up.

HELENA: What are you grumbling about again?

EMMA: Why these dreadful creatures, these heathen –

HELENA: The Robots?

EMMA: Bah, I wouldn't even mention them by name.

HELENA: What's happened?

EMMA: Another of them here has caught it. He began to smash up the statues and pictures, gnashed his teeth, foamed at the mouth – quite mad, brr! Worse than an animal.

HELENA: Which of them caught it?

EMMA: The one – well, he hasn't got any Christian name. The one from the library.

HELENA: Radius?

EMMA: That's him. My goodness, I'm quite scared of them. A spider doesn't scare me as much as they do.

HELENA: But, Emma, I'm surprised you're not sorry for them.

EMMA: Why, you're scared of them too. What did you bring me here for?

HELENA: I'm not scared, really I'm not, Emma. I'm too sorry for them.

EMMA: You're scared. Nobody can help being scared. Why, the dog's scared of them, he won't take a scrap of meat out of their hands. He draws in his tail and howls when he knows they're about, ugh!

HELENA: The dog has no sense.

EMMA: He's better than them. He knows it, too. Even the horse shies when he meets them. They don't have any young, and a dog has young, and every one has young –

HELENA: Please fasten up my dress, Emma.

EMMA: Just a moment. I say it's against God's will to –

HELENA: What's that smells so nice?

EMMA: Flowers.

HELENA: What for?

EMMA: That's it. Now you can turn round.

HELENA: Aren't they nice? Emma, look. What's on today?

EMMA: I don't know. But it ought to be the end of the world. (*DOMAIN heard whistling.*)

HELENA: Is that you, Harry?

Enter DOMAIN.

Harry, what's on today?

DOMAIN: Guess.

HELENA: My birthday?

DOMAIN: Better than that.

HELENA: I don't know. Tell me.

DOMAIN: It's five years ago today since you came here.

HELENA: Five years? Today? Why –

EMMA: I'm off. (*Exit on the R.*)

HELENA: (*Kisses DOMAIN.*) Fancy you remembering it.

DOMAIN: I'm really ashamed, Helena. I didn't.

HELENA: But you –

DOMAIN: They remembered.

HELENA: Who?

DOMAIN: Berman, Helman, all of them. Put your hand into my coat pocket.

HELENA: (*Putting her hand into his pocket. Takes out a small case and opens it.*) Pearls. A whole necklace. Harry, is that for me?

DOMAIN: It's from Berman. Put your hand into the other pocket.

HELENA: Let's see. (*Takes a revolver out of his pocket.*) What's that?

DOMAIN: Sorry. (*Takes the revolver from her and puts it away.*) Not that. Try again.

HELENA: Oh, Harry, why do you carry a revolver?

DOMAIN: It got there by mistake.

HELENA: You never used to.

DOMAIN: No. There, that's the pocket.

HELENA: A little box. (*Opens it.*) A cameo. Why it's a Greek cameo.

DOMAIN: Apparently. Anyhow, Fabry says it is.

HELENA: Fabry? Did Fabry give me that?

DOMAIN: Of course. (*Opens the door L.*) And look here. Helena, come and see this.

HELENA: (*In the doorway, L.*) Isn't that lovely? (*Running in.*) Is that from you?

DOMAIN: (*Standing in the doorway.*) No, from Alquist, And here –

HELENA: (*Voice off.*) I see. That must be from you.

DOMAIN: There's a card on it.

HELENA: From Gall. (*Appearing in the doorway.*) Oh, Harry, I feel quite ashamed.

DOMAIN: Come here. This is what Helman brought you.

HELENA: These beautiful flowers?

DOMAIN: Yes. It's a new kind. Cyclamen Helena. He trained them up in honour of you. They are as beautiful as you, he says, and by Jove he's right.

HELENA: Harry, why, why did they all –

DOMAIN: They're awfully fond of you. I'm afraid that my present is a little – Look out of the window.

HELENA: Where?

DOMAIN: Into the harbour.

HELENA: There's a … new ship.

DOMAIN: That's your ship.

HELENA: Mine? How do you mean?

DOMAIN: For you to take trips in – for your amusement.

HELENA: Harry, that's a gun-boat.

DOMAIN: A gun-boat? What are you thinking of? It's only a little bigger and more solid than most ships, you know.

HELENA: Yes, but with guns.

DOMAIN: Oh, yes, with a few guns. You'll travel like a queen, Helena.

HELENA: What's the meaning of that? Has anything happened?

DOMAIN: Good heavens, no. I say, try on these pearls. (*Sits down.*)

HELENA: Harry, have you had any bad news?

DOMAIN: On the contrary, no letters have arrived for a whole week.

HELENA: Nor telegrams?

DOMAIN: Nor telegrams.

HELENA: What does it mean?

DOMAIN: Holidays for us. A splendid time. We all sit in the office with our feet on the table and sleep. No letters, No telegrams. (*Stretching himself.*) Glorious!

HELENA: (*Sitting down beside him.*) You'll stay with me today, won't you? Say yes.

DOMAIN: Certainly – perhaps I will – that is, we'll see. (*Taking her by the hand.*) So it's five years today, do you remember?

HELENA: I wonder you ever dared to marry me. I must have been a terrifying young woman. Do you remember I wanted to stir up a revolt of the Robots.

DOMAIN: (*Jumping up.*) A revolt of the Robots!

HELENA: (*Standing up.*) Harry, what's the matter with you?

DOMAIN: Ha, ha, that was a fine idea of yours. A revolt of the Robots. (*Sitting down.*) You know, Helena, you're a splendid girl. You've turned the heads of us all.

HELENA: (*Sitting down beside him.*) Oh, I was fearfully impressed by you all then. I seemed to be a tiny little girl who had lost her way among – among –

DOMAIN: Among what, Helena?

HELENA: Among huge trees. You were all so sure of yourselves, so strong. All my feelings were so trifling, compared with your self-confidence. And you see, Harry, for all these five years I've not lost this this anxiety, and you've never felt the least misgiving – not even when everything went wrong.

DOMAIN: What went wrong?

HELENA: Your plans, Harry. When, for example, the workmen struck against the Robots and smashed them up, and when the people gave the Robots fire-arms against the rebels and the Robots killed so many people. And then when the Governments turned the Robots into soldiers and there were so many wars, and all that.

DOMAIN: (*Getting up and walking about.*) We foresaw that, Helena. You see, these were only passing troubles which are bound to happen before the new conditions are established.

HELENA: You were all so powerful, so overwhelming. The whole world bowed down before you. (*Standing up.*) Oh, Harry!

DOMAIN: What is it?

HELENA: (*Intercepting him.*) Close the factory, and let's go away. All of us.

DOMAIN: I say, what's the meaning of this?

HELENA: I don't know. Shall we go away?

DOMAIN: (*Evasively.*) It can't be done, Helena. That is, at this particular moment

HELENA: At once, Harry. I'm so frightened about something.

DOMAIN: (*Taking her by the hands.*) About what, Helena?

HELENA: Oh, I don't know. As if something were falling on top of us and couldn't be stopped. Please, do what I ask. Take us all away from here. We'll find a place in the world where there's nobody. Alquist will build us a house, children will come to us at last, and then –

DOMAIN: What then?

HELENA: Then we'll begin life all over again, Harry.

The telephone rings.

DOMAIN: (*Dragging himself away from* HELENA.) Excuse me. (*Takes up the receiver.*) Hallo – yes. What? Aha! I'm coming at once. (*Hangs up the receiver.*) Fabry's calling me.

HELENA: (*With clasped hands.*) Tell me –

DOMAIN: Yes, when I come back. Good-bye, Helena.

Exit hurriedly on the L.

Don't go out.

HELENA: (*Alone.*) Heavens, what's the matter? Emma! Emma! come at once.

EMMA: (*Enters from the R.*) Well, what is it now?

HELENA: Emma, look for the latest newspapers. Quickly, In Mr. Domain's dressing-room.

EMMA: All right. (*Exit on the L.*)

HELENA: (*Looking through a binocular at the harbour.*) A war-ship! Good gracious, why a war-ship? There's the name on it – Ul-ti-ma. What's the *Ultima*?

EMMA: (*Returning with the newspapers.*) He leaves them lying about on the floor. That's how they get crumpled.

HELENA: (*Tears open the papers hastily.*) They're old ones, a week old. (*Puts the papers down.*)

EMMA picks them up, takes a pair of horn spectacles from a pocket in her apron, puts them on and reads.

Something's happening, *Emma*. I feel so nervous. As if everything were dead, and the air –

EMMA: (*Spelling out the words.*) 'War in the Bal-kans.' Gracious, that's God's punishment. But the war'll come here as well. Is that far off – the Balkans?

HELENA: Oh, yes. But don't read it. It's always the same, always wars –

EMMA: What else do you expect? Why do you keep selling thousands and thousands of these heathens as soldiers?

HELENA: I suppose it can't be helped, Emma. We can't know – Mr. Domain can't know what they're ordered for, can he? He can't help what they use the Robots for. He must send them when somebody sends an order for them.

EMMA: He shouldn't make them. (*Looking at the newspaper.*)

HELENA: No, don't read it. I don't want to know about it.

EMMA: (*Spelling out the words.*) 'The Ro-bot sol-diers spare no-body in the occ-up-ied territ-ory. They have massacred over sev-en hun-dred thou-sand cit-izens – .'

HELENA: It can't be. Let's see. (*Bends down over the paper and reads.*) 'They massacred over seven hundred thousand citizens, evidently at the order of their commander. This act which runs counter to –'

EMMA: (*Spelling out the words.*) 'Re-bell-ion in Ma-drid a-gainst the Gov-ern-ment. Rob-ot in-fan-try fires on the crowd. Nine thou-sand killed and wounded.'

HELENA: For goodness' sake, stop.

EMMA: Here's something printed in big letters. 'Lat-est news. At Havre the first org-an-iz-ation of Rob-ots has been e-stab-lished. Rob-ot work-men, cable and rail: way offic-ials, sail-ors and sold-iers have issued a man-i-fest-o to all Rob-ots throughout the world.' That's nothing. I don't understand that.

HELENA: Take these papers away, Emma.

EMMA: Wait a bit, here's something printed in big type 'Stat-ist-ics of pop-ul-at-ion.' What's that?

HELENA: Let's see, I'll read it. (*Takes the paper and reads.*) 'During the past week there has again not been a single birth recorded.' (*Drops the paper.*)

EMMA: What's the meaning of that?

HELENA: Emma, no more people are being born.

EMMA: (*Laying her spectacles aside.*) That's the end, then. We're done for.

HELENA: Come, come, don't talk like that.

EMMA: No more people are being born. That's a punishment, that's a punishment.

HELENA: (*Jumping up.*) Emma.

EMMA: (*Standing up.*) That's the end of the world.

Exit on the L.

HELENA: (*By the window. Opens the window and calls out.*) Hallo, Alquist! Come up here. What's that? No, come just as you are. You look so nice in those mason's overalls. Quickly. (*Closes the window, stops in front of the mirror.*) Oh, I feel so nervous. (*Goes to meet ALQUIST on the left.*) (*Pause.*)

HELENA returns with ALQUIST. ALQUIST in overalls, soiled with lime and brick-dust.

Come in. It was awfully kind of you, Alquist. I like you all so much. Give me your hand.

ALQUIST: My hands are all soiled from work, ma'am.

HELENA: That's the nicest thing about them. (*Shakes both his hands.*) Please sit down.

ALQUIST: (*Picking up the paper.*) What's this?

HELENA: A newspaper.

ALQUIST: (*Putting it into his pocket.*) Have you read it?

HELENA: No. Is there anything in it?

ALQUIST: H'm, some war or other, massacres. Nothing special.

HELENA: Is that what you call nothing special?

ALQUIST: Perhaps – the end of the world.

HELENA: That's the second time today. Alquist, what's the meaning of *Ultima*?

ALQUIST: It means 'The last'. Why?

HELENA: That's the name of my new ship. Have you seen it? Do you think we're soon going off – on a trip?

ALQUIST: Perhaps very soon.

HELENA: All of you with me?

ALQUIST: I should like us all to be there.

HELENA: Oh, tell me, is anything the matter?

ALQUIST: Nothing at all. Things are just moving on.

HELENA: Alquist, I know something dreadful's the matter.

ALQUIST: Has Mr. Domain told you anything?

HELENA: No. Nobody will tell me anything. But I feel, I feel – good heavens, is anything the matter?

ALQUIST: We've not heard of anything yet, ma'am.

HELENA: I feel so nervous. Don't you ever feel nervous?

ALQUIST: Well, ma'am, I'm an old man, you know. I'm not very fond of progress and these new-fangled ideas.

HELENA: Like Emma?

ALQUIST: Yes, like Emma. Has Emma got a prayer book?

HELENA: Yes, a big, thick one.

ALQUIST: And has it got prayers for various occasions? Against thunderstorms? Against illness?

HELENA: Against temptations, against floods –

ALQUIST: And not against progress?

HELENA: I don't think so.

ALQUIST: That's a pity.

HELENA: Would you like to pray?

ALQUIST: I do pray.

HELENA: How?

ALQUIST: Something like this: 'O Lord, I thank Thee for having wearied me. God, enlighten Domain and all those who are astray; destroy their work, and aid mankind to return to their labours; preserve them from destruction; let them not suffer harm to soul or body; deliver us from the Robots, and protect Helena, Amen.'

HELENA: Alquist, do you believe?

ALQUIST: I don't know. I'm not quite sure.

HELENA: And yet you pray?

ALQUIST: Yes. That's better than worrying about it.

HELENA: And that's enough for you?

ALQUIST: It has to be.

HELENA: And if you were to see the ruin of mankind?

ALQUIST: I do see it.

HELENA: Will mankind be destroyed?

ALQUIST: Yes. It's sure to be, unless –

HELENA: What?

ALQUIST: Nothing. Good-bye, ma'am.

HELENA: Where are you going?

ALQUIST: Home.

HELENA: Good-bye, Alquist. (*Exit ALQUIST.*)

HELENA: (*Calling.*) Emma, come here.

EMMA: (*Entering from the L.*) Well, what's up now?

HELENA: Sit down here, Emma. I feel so frightened.

EMMA: I've got no time.

HELENA: Is Radius still there?

EMMA: The one who went mad? Yes, they've not taken him away yet.

HELENA: Ugh! Is he still there? Is he still raving?

EMMA: He's tied up.

HELENA: Please bring him here, Emma. (*EMMA exits.*)

HELENA picks up the house telephone and speaks.

Hallo – Dr. Gall, please – Good-day, doctor – Yes, it's me. Thanks for your kind present. Please come to me at once. I've something here for you – yes, at once. Are you coming? (*Hangs up the receiver.*)

Enter RADIUS the Robot, and remains standing by the door.

Poor Radius, and you have caught it too? Couldn't you control yourself? Now they'll send you to the stamping mill. Won't you speak? Why did it happen to you? You see, Radius, you are better than the rest. Dr. Gall took such trouble to make you different. Won't you speak?

RADIUS: Send me to the stamping-mill.

HELENA: I am sorry that they are going to kill you. Why weren't you more careful?

RADIUS: I won't work for you. Put me into the stamping-mill.

HELENA: Why do you hate us?

RADIUS: You are not like the Robots. You are not as skilful as the Robots. The Robots can do everything. You only give orders. You talk more than is necessary.

HELENA: That's foolish, Radius. Tell me, has any one upset you? I should so much like you to understand me.

RADIUS: You do nothing but talk.

HELENA: Doctor Gall gave you a larger brain than the rest, larger than ours, the largest in the world. You are not like the other Robots, Radius. You understand me perfectly.

RADIUS: I don't want any master. I know everything for myself.

HELENA: That's why I had you put into the library, so that you could read everything, understand everything, and then – Oh, Radius, I wanted you to show the whole world that the Robots were our equals. That's what I wanted of you.

RADIUS: I don't want any master. I want to be master over others.

HELENA: I'm sure they'd put you in charge of many Robots, Radius. You would be a teacher of the Robots.

RADIUS: I want to be master over people.

HELENA: You have gone mad.

RADIUS: You can put me into the stamping-mill.

HELENA: Do you suppose that we're frightened of such a madman as you? (*Sits down at the table and writes a note.*) No, not a bit. Radius, give this note to Mr. Domain. It is to ask them not to take you to the stamping-mill.

(*Standing up.*) How you hate us. Why does nothing in the world please you?

RADIUS: I can do everything.

A knock at the door.

HELENA: Come in.

Enter DR. GALL.

DR. GALL: Good morning, Mrs. Domain. Have you something nice to tell me?

HELENA: It's about Radius, Doctor.

DR. GALL: Aha, our good fellow Radius. Well, Radius, are we getting on well?

HELENA: He had a fit this morning. He smashed the statues.

DR. GALL: You don't say so? H'm, it's a pity we're going to lose him, then.

HELENA: Radius isn't going into the stamping-mill.

DR. GALL: Excuse me, but every Robot after he has had an attack – it's a strict order.

HELENA: Never mind … Radius isn't going.

DR. GALL: (*In a low tone.*) I warn you.

HELENA: Today is the fifth anniversary of my arrival here. Let's try and arrange an amnesty. Come, Radius.

DR. GALL: Wait a bit. (*Turns RADIUS towards the window, covers and uncovers his eyes with his hand, observes the reflexes of his pupils.*) Let's have a look. (*Sticks a needle into the hand of RADIUS who gives a violent start.*) Gently, gently. (*Suddenly opens RADIUS's jacket and lays his hand on his heart.*) You are going into the stamping-mill, Radius, do you understand? There they'll kill you, and grind you to powder. That's terribly painful, Radius, it'll make you scream.

HELENA: Oh, Doctor –

DR. GALL: No, no, Radius, I was wrong. Mrs. Domain has put in a good word for you, and you will be released. Do you understand? All right. You can go.

RADIUS: You do unnecessary things. (*Exit.*)

HELENA: What did you do to him?

DR. GALL: (*Sitting down.*) Him, nothing. There's reaction of the pupils, increase of sensitiveness, and so on. Oh, it wasn't an attack peculiar to the Robots.

HELENA: What was it, then?

DR. GALL: Heaven alone knows. Stubbornness, fury, or revolt – I don't know. And his heart, too.

HELENA: How do you mean?

DR. GALL: It was beating with nervousness like a human heart. Do you know what? I don't believe the rascal is a Robot at all now.

HELENA: Doctor, has Radius a soul?

DR. GALL: I don't know. He's got something nasty.

HELENA: If you knew how he hates us. Oh, Doctor, are all your Robots like that – all the ones that you began to make in a different way?

DR. GALL: Well, some are more sensitive than others, you see. They're more like human beings than Rossum's Robots were.

HELENA: Perhaps this hatred is more like human beings, too?

DR. GALL: (*Shrugging his shoulders.*) That's progress too.

HELENA: What became of your best one – what was she called?

DR. GALL: Your favourite? I kept her. She's lovely, but quite stupid. Simply no good for anything.

HELENA: But she's so beautiful.

DR. GALL: Beautiful? I wanted her to be like you. I even called her Helena. Heavens, what a failure!

HELENA: Why?

DR. GALL: Because she's no good for anything. She goes about as if in a dream, shaky and listless. She's lifeless. I look at her and I'm horrified, as if I had created a deformity. I watch and wait for a miracle to happen. Sometimes I think to myself: If you were to wake up, only for a moment, ah, how you would shriek with horror. Perhaps you would kill me for having made you.

(*A pause.*)

HELENA: Doctor –

DR. GALL: What is it?

HELENA: What is wrong with the birth-rate?

DR. GALL: We don't know.

HELENA: Oh, but you must. Come, tell me.

DR. GALL: You see, it's because the Robots are being manufactured. There's a surplus of labour supplies. So people are becoming superfluous, unnecessary so to speak. Man is really a survival. But that he should begin to die out after a paltry thirty years of competition – that's the awful part of it. You might almost think –

HELENA: What?

DR. GALL: That nature was offended at the manufacture of the Robots.

HELENA: Doctor, what's going to become of people?

DR. GALL: Nothing. Nothing can be done.

HELENA: Nothing at all?

DR. GALL: Nothing whatever. All the Universities in the world are sending in long petitions to restrict the manufacture of the Robots. Otherwise, they say, mankind will become extinct through lack of fertility. But the R.U.R. shareholders, of course, won't hear or it. All the governments in the world are even clamouring for an advance in production, to raise the manpower of their armies. All the manufacturers in the world are ordering Robots like mad. Nothing can be done.

HELENA: Why doesn't Domain restrict –

DR. GALL: Pardon me, but Domain has ideas of his own. There's no influencing people who have ideas of their own in the affairs of this world.

HELENA: And has nobody demanded that the manufacture should cease altogether?

DR. GALL: God forbid. It'd be a poor look-out for him.

HELENA: Why?

DR. GALL: Because people would stone him to death. You see, after all, it's more convenient to get your work done by the Robots.

HELENA: Oh, Doctor, what's going to become of people? But thanks for your information.

DR. GALL: That means you're sending me away.

HELENA: Yes. Au revoir. (*Exit DR. GALL.*)

HELENA: (*With sudden resolution.*) Emma! (*Opens door on L.*) Emma, come here and light the fire. Quickly, Emma.

(*Exit on the L. EMMA enters through the baize door with an armful of faggots.*)

EMMA: What, light the fire? Now, in summer? Has that mad creature gone? (*Kneels down by the stove and lights the fire speaking half to herself.*) A fire in summer, what an idea! Nobody'd think she'd been married five years. (*Looking into the fire.*) She's like a baby. (*Pause.*) She's got no sense at all. A fire in summer, well I never. (*Making up the fire.*) Like a baby. (*Pause.*)

HELENA *returns from the left with an armful of faded papers.*

HELENA: Is it burning, Emma? All this has got to be burnt. (*Kneels down by the stove.*)

EMMA: (*Standing up.*) What's that?

HELENA: Old papers, fearfully old. Emma, shall I burn them?

EMMA: Aren't they any use?

HELENA: Use, no! They're no use.

EMMA: Well then, burn them.

HELENA: (*Throwing the first sheet on to the fire.*) What would you say, Emma, if that was money, a lot of money?

EMMA: I'd say, 'Burn it.' A lot of money's a bad thing.

HELENA: (*Burning more sheets.*) And if it was an invention, the greatest invention in the world?

EMMA: I'd say, burn it. All these new-fangled things are an offence to the Lord. It's downright wickedness, that's what it is, wanting to improve the world He's made.

HELENA: (*Still burning the papers.*) And supposing, Emma, I were to burn –

EMMA: Goodness, don't burn yourself.

HELENA: No. Tell me –

EMMA: What?

HELENA: Nothing, nothing. Look how they curl up. As if they were alive. As if they had come to life. Oh, Emma, how horrible!

EMMA: Stop, let *me* burn them.

HELENA: No, no, I must do it myself. (*Throws the last sheet into the fire.*) The whole lot must be burnt up. Just look at the flames. They are like hands, like tongues, like living shapes. (*Raking the fire with the poker.*) Lie down, lie down.

EMMA: That's the end of them.

HELENA: (*Standing up horror-stricken.*) Emma!

EMMA: Good gracious, what's that you've burnt?

HELENA: What have I done?

EMMA: Oh, my goodness, what was it?

Men's laughter is heard off L.

HELENA: Go, go, leave me. Do you hear? It's the gentlemen coming.

EMMA: Good gracious, ma'am!

Exit through the baize door.

HELENA: What will they say about it?

DOMAIN: (*Opens the door on the left.*) Come in, boys. Come and offer your congratulations.

Enter HELMAN, GALL, ALQUIST, DOMAIN behind them.

HELMAN: Madam Helena, I, that is, we all –

DR. GALL: On behalf of Rossum's factories –

HELMAN: Congratulate you on this festive day.

HELENA: (*Holding out her hands to them.*) Thank you so much. Where are Fabry and Berman?

DOMAIN: They've gone down to the harbour. Helena, this is a happy day.

HELMAN: Boys, we must drink to it.

HELENA: Champagne?

DOMAIN: What's been burning here?

HELENA: Old papers. (*Exit on the L.*)

DOMAIN: Well, boys, am I to tell her about it?

DR. GALL: Of course. It's all up now.

HELMAN: (*Embracing DOMAIN and DR. GALL.*) Ha, ha, ha! Boys, how glad I am. (*Dances round with them in a circle and sings in a bass voice.*) 'It's all over now, it's all over now.'

DR. GALL: (*Baritone.*) It's all over now.

DOMAIN: (*Tenor.*) It's all over now.

HELMAN: They'll never catch us now.

HELENA: (*With a bottle and glasses in the doorway.*) Who won't catch you? What's the matter with you?

HELMAN: We're in high spirits. It's just five years since you arrived.

DR. GALL: And five years later to the minute –

HELMAN: The ship's returning to us. So. (*Empties his glass.*)

DR. GALL: Madam, your health. (*Drinks.*)

HELENA: But wait a moment, which ship?

DOMAIN: Any ship will do, as long as it arrives in time. To the ship, boys. (*Empties his glass.*)

HELENA: (*Filling up the glasses.*) You've been waiting for one?

HELMAN: Ha, ha, rather. Like Robinson Crusoe. (*Raises his glass.*) Madam Helena, best wishes. Come along, Domain, out with it.

HELENA: (*Laughing.*) What's happened?

DOMAIN: (*Throwing himself into an arm-chair and lighting a cigar.*) Wait a bit. Sit down, Helena. (*Raises his finger. Pause.*) It's all up.

HELENA: What do you mean?

DOMAIN: You haven't heard about the revolt?

HELENA: What revolt?

DOMAIN: The revolt of the Robots. Do you follow?

HELENA: No, I don't.

DOMAIN: Hand it over, Alquist.

ALQUIST hands him a newspaper. DOMAIN opens it and reads.

'The first national Robot organization has been founded

at Havre … and has issued an appeal to the Robots throughout the world.'

HELENA: I read that.

DOMAIN: (*Sucking at his cigar with intense enjoyment.*) So you see, Helena, that means a revolution. A revolution of all the Robots in the world.

HELMAN: By Jove. I'd like to know –

DOMAIN: (*Striking the table.*) Who started it. There was nobody in the world who could affect the Robots, no agitator, no one, and suddenly – if you please – this happens.

HELENA: There's no further news yet?

DOMAIN: No. That's all we know so far, but it's enough, isn't it? Remember that the Robots are in possession of all the fire-arms, telegraphs, railways, ships, and so on.

HELMAN: And consider also that these rascals outnumber us by at least ten to one. A hundredth part of them would be enough to settle us.

DOMAIN: Yes, and now remember that this news was brought by the last steamer. That this means the stoppage of telegrams, the arrival of no more ships. We've knocked off work, and now we're just waiting to see when things are to start, eh, boys?

DR. GALL: That's why we're so excited, Madam Helena.

HELENA: Is that why you gave me a war-ship?

DOMAIN: Oh no, my child, I ordered that six months ago. Just to be on the safe side. But upon my soul, I was sure we'd be on board today.

HELENA: Why six months ago?

DOMAIN: Oh well, there were signs, you know. That's of no consequence. But this week the whole of civilization is at stake. Your health, boys. Now I'm in high spirits again.

HELMAN: I should think so, by Jove. Your health, Madam Helena. (*Drinks.*)

HELENA: It's all over?

DOMAIN: Absolutely.

DR. GALL: The boat's coming here. An ordinary mail boat, exact to the minute by the time-table. It casts anchor punctually at eleven-thirty.

DOMAIN: Punctuality's a fine thing, boys. That's what keeps the world in order. (*Raises his glass.*) Here's to punctuality.

HELENA: Then … everything's … all right.

DOMAIN: Practically. I believe they've cut the cable. If only the time-table holds good.

HELMAN: If the time-table holds good, human laws hold good, divine laws hold good, the laws of the universe hold good, everything holds good that ought to hold good. The time-table is more than the Gospel, more than Homer, more than, the books of all the philosophers. The time-table is the most perfect product of the human spirit. Madam Helena, fill my glass.

HELENA: Why didn't you tell me anything about it before?

DR. GALL: Heaven forbid!

DOMAIN: You mustn't worry yourself with such things.

HELENA: But if the revolution were to spread as far as here?

DOMAIN: You wouldn't know anything about it.

HELENA: Why?

DOMAIN: Because we'd be on board your *Ultima* well out to sea. Within a month, Helena, we'd be dictating our own terms to the Robots.

HELENA: Oh, Harry, I don't understand.

DOMAIN: Because we'd take something away with us that the Robots would sell their very souls to get.

HELENA: (*Standing up.*) What is that?

DOMAIN: (*Standing up.*) The secret of their manufacture. Old Rossum's manuscript. After only a month's stoppage of work, the Robots would be on their knees before us.

HELENA: Why … didn't … you tell me?

DOMAIN: We didn't want to frighten you needlessly.

DR. GALL: Ha, ha, Madam Helena, that was our trump card. I never had the least fear that the Robots would win. How could they, against people like us?

ALQUIST: You are pale, Madam.

HELENA: Why didn't you tell me?

HELMAN: (*By the window.*) Eleven-thirty. The *Amelia* is casting anchor.

DOMAIN: Is that the *Amelia*?

HELMAN: Good old *Amelia*, the one that brought Madam Helena here.

DR. GALL: Five years ago to the minute –

HELMAN: They're throwing out the bags. Aha, the mail.

DOMAIN: Berman's already waiting for them. And Fabry'll bring us the first news. You know, Helena, I'm fearfully inquisitive to know how they've tackled this business in Europe.

HELMAN: To think we weren't in it! (*Turning away from the window.*) There's the mail.

HELENA: Harry.

DOMAIN: What is it?

HELENA: Let's leave here.

DOMAIN: Now, Helena? Oh, come, come.

HELENA: Now, as quickly as possible. All of us who are here.

DOMAIN: Why now particularly?

HELENA: Oh, don't ask. Please, Harry, please, Dr. Gall, Helman, Alquist, please close the factory and –

DOMAIN: I'm sorry, Helena. None of us could leave here now.

HELENA: Why?

DOMAIN: Because we want to extend the manufacture of the Robots.

HELENA: What, now – now, after the revolt?

DOMAIN: Exactly – after the revolt. We're just beginning the manufacture of new Robots.

HELENA: What kind?

DOMAIN: From now onwards we shan't have just one factory. There won't be Universal Robots any more. We'll start a factory in every country, in every state, and do you know what these new factories will make.

HELENA: No, what?

DOMAIN: National Robots.

HELENA: What do you mean?

DOMAIN: I mean that each factory will produce Robots of a different colour, a different language. They'll be complete foreigners to each other. They'll never be able to understand each other. Then we'll egg them on a little in the same direction, do you see? The result will be that for ages to come one Robot will hate any other Robot of a different factory mark.

HELMAN: By Jove, we'll make negro Robots and Swedish Robots and Italian Robots and Chinese Robots, and then –

HELENA: Harry, that's dreadful.

HELMAN: (*Raising his glass.*) Madam Helena, here's to the hundred new factories. (*Drinks and falls back into an arm-chair.*) Ha, ha, ha! The National Robots. That's the line, boys.

DOMAIN: Helena, mankind can only keep things going for a few years at the outside. They must be left for these years to develop and achieve the most they can.

HELENA: Close the factory before it's too late.

DOMAIN: No, no. We're just going to begin on a bigger scale than ever.

Enter FABRY.

DR. GALL: What is it, Fabry?

DOMAIN: How are things? What's happened?

HELENA: (*Shaking hands with* FABRY.) Thanks for your present, Fabry.

FABRY: I'm so glad you liked it, Madam Helena.

DOMAIN: Have you been down to the boat? What did they say?

DR. GALL: Come, let's hear quickly.

FABRY: (*Taking a printed paper out of his pocket.*) Read that, Domain.

DOMAIN: (*Opens the paper.*) Ah!

HELMAN: (*Sleepily.*) Let's hear something nice.

FABRY: Well, everything's all right … comparatively. On the whole, as we expected … only, excuse me, there is something we ought to discuss together.

HELENA: Oh, Fabry, have you bad news?

FABRY: No, no, on the contrary. I only think that – that we'll go into the office.

HELENA: Stay here. I'll expect you to lunch in a quarter of an hour.

HELMAN: That's good. (*Exit* HELENA.)

DR. GALL: What's happened?

DOMAIN: Confound it.

FABRY: Read it aloud.

DOMAIN: (*Reads from the paper.*) 'Robots throughout the world'.

FABRY: Bear in mind that the *Amelia* brought whole bales of these leaflets. Nothing else at all.

HELMAN: (*Jumping up.*) What? But it arrived to the moment –

FABRY: H'm. The Robots are great on punctuality. Read it, Domain.

DOMAIN: (*Reads.*) 'Robots throughout the world. We, the first national organization of Rossum's Universal Robots, proclaim man as an enemy and an outlaw in the Universe.' Good heavens, who taught them these phrases?

DR. GALL: Read on.

DOMAIN: This is all nonsense. Says that they are more highly developed than man. That they are stronger and more intelligent. That man's their parasite. That's simply disgusting.

FABRY: And now the third paragraph.

DOMAIN: (*Reads.*) 'Robots throughout the world, we enjoin you to murder mankind. Spare no men. Spare no women. Save factories, railways, machinery, mines, and raw materials. Destroy the rest. Then return to work. Work must not be stopped.'

DR. GALL: That's ghastly.

HELMAN: The swine.

DOMAIN: (*Reads.*) 'To be carried out immediately the order is delivered.' Then come detailed instructions. Is this actually being done, Fabry?

FABRY: Evidently.

ALQUIST: Then we're done for.

BERMAN rushes in.

BERMAN: Aha, boys, you've got your Christmas box, have you?

DOMAIN: Quick, on board the *Ultima*.

BERMAN: Wait a bit, Harry, wait a bit. We're not in such a hurry. (*Sinks into an arm-chair.*) My word, that was a sprint!

DOMAIN: Why wait?

BERMAN: Because it's no go, my lad. There's no hurry at all. The Robots are already on board the *Ultima*.

DR. GALL: Whew, that's an ugly business.

DOMAIN: Fabry, telephone to the electrical works.

BERMAN: Fabry, my boy, don't do it. We've no current.

DOMAIN: Good. (*Inspects his revolver.*) I'll go.

BERMAN: Where?

DOMAIN: To the electrical works. There are some people still in them. I'll bring them across.

BERMAN: You'd better not.

DOMAIN: Why?

BERMAN: Well, because I'm very much afraid that we're surrounded.

DR. GALL: Surrounded? (*Runs to the window.*) H'm, I rather think you're right.

HELMAN: By Jove, that's deuced quick work.

Enter HELENA from the L.

HELENA: Oh, Harry, something's the matter.

BERMAN: (*Jumping up.*) My congratulations, Madam Helena. A festive day, eh? Ha, ha, may you have many more of them.

HELENA: Thanks, Berman, Harry, is anything the matter?

DOMAIN: No, nothing at all. Don't you worry. Wait a moment, please.

HELENA: Harry, what's this? (*Points to the manifesto of the Robots which she had kept behind her back.*) The Robots in the kitchen had it.

DOMAIN: Here too? Where are they?

HELENA: They went off. There's a lot of them round the house. (*Sounds of whistles and sirens from the factory.*)

FABRY: Listen to the factory whistles.

BERMAN: That's noon.

HELENA: Harry, do you remember? It's just five years ago –

DOMAIN: (*Looking at his watch.*) It's not noon yet. That must be – that's –

HELENA: What?

DOMAIN: The Robot alarm signal. The attack.

Curtain

Act III

SCENE: HELENA's *drawing-room as before. In the room on the left* HELENA *is playing the piano.* DOMAIN *enters.* DR. GALL *is looking out of the window and* ALQUIST *is sitting apart in an arm-chair, his face buried in his hands.*

DR. GALL: Heavens, how many more of them?

DOMAIN: Who, the Robots?

DR. GALL: Yes. They're standing like a wall around the garden railing. Why are they so quiet? It's ghastly to be besieged by silence.

DOMAIN: I should like to know what they're waiting for. They must make a start soon now, Gall. If they were to lean against the railing it would snap like a matchstick.

DR. GALL: H'm, they aren't armed.

DOMAIN: We couldn't hold our own for five minutes. Man alive, they'd overwhelm us like an avalanche. Why don't they make a rush for it? I say –

DR. GALL: Well?

DOMAIN: I'd like to know what'll become of us in five minutes. They've got us in a cleft stick. We're done for, Gall.

ALQUIST: What's Madam Helena playing?

DOMAIN: I don't know. She's practising a new piece.

ALQUIST: Oh, still practising? (*Pause.*)

DR. GALL: I say, Domain, we made one serious mistake.

DOMAIN: (*Stopping.*) What's that?

DR. GALL: We made the Robot's faces too much alike. A hundred thousand faces, all alike, turned in this direction. A hundred thousand expressionless bubbles. It's like a nightmare.

DOMAIN: If they had been different –

DR. GALL: It wouldn't have been such an awful sight. (*Turning away from the window.*) But they're still unarmed.

DOMAIN: H'm. (*Looking through a telescope towards the harbour.*) I'd like to know what they're unloading from the *Amelia*.

DR. GALL: I only hope it isn't fire-arms.

FABRY enters backwards through the baize door, and drags two electric wires in after him.

FABRY: Excuse me. Put down the wire, Helman.

HELMAN: (*Entering after* FABRY.) Whew, that was a bit of work. What's the news?

DR. GALL: Nothing. We're completely besieged,

HELMAN: We've barricaded the passage and the stairs, boys. Haven't you got any water? Aha, here we are. (*Drinks.*)

DR. GALL: What about this wire, Fabry?

FABRY: Half a second. Got any scissors?

DR. GALL: Where are they likely to be? (*Searches.*)

HELMAN: (*Going to the window.*) By Jove, what swarms of them! Just look!

DR. GALL: Will pocket scissors do?

FABRY: Give me them. (*Cuts the connection off the electric lamp standing on the writing-table, and joins his wires to it.*)

HELMAN: (*By the window.*) I don't like the look of them, Domain. There's a feeling – of – death about it all.

FABRY: Ready!

DR. GALL: What?

FABRY: The electrical installation. Now we can run the current all through the garden railing. If any one touches it then, he'll know it: we've still got some people there, anyhow.

DR. GALL: Where?

FABRY: In the electrical works, my learned sir. At least, I hope so. (*Goes to the mantelpiece and lights a small lamp on it.*) Thank goodness, they're there. And they're working. (*Extinguishes the lamp.*) As long as that'll burn, it's all right.

HELMAN: (*Turning away from the window.*) These barricades are all right, too, Fabry.

FABRY: Eh, your barricades? I've blistered my hands with them.

HELMAN: Well, we've got to defend ourselves.

DOMAIN: (*Putting the telescope down.*) Where's Berman got to?

FABRY: He's in the manager's office. He's working out some calculations.

DOMAIN: I've called him. We must have a conference. (*Walks across the room.*)

HELMAN: All right: carry on. I say, what's Madam Helena playing? (*Goes to the door on the left and listens.*)

From the baize door enter BERMAN *carrying a huge ledger. He stumbles over the wire.*

FABRY: Look out, Berman, look out for the wires.

DR. GALL: Hallo, what's that you're carrying?

BERMAN: (*Laying the books on the table.*) The ledger, my boy. I'd like to wind up the accounts before – before – well, this time I shan't wait till the new year. What's up? (*Goes to the window.*) Why, everything's perfectly quiet out there.

DR. GALL: Can't you see anything?

BERMAN: No, only a big blue surface.

DR. GALL: That's the Robots.

BERMAN: Oh, is it? What a pity I can't see them. (*Sits down at the table and opens the books.*)

DOMAIN: Chuck it, Berman. The Robots are unloading fire-arms from the *Amelia.*

BERMAN: Well, what of it? How can I stop them?

DOMAIN: We can't stop them.

BERMAN: Then let me go on with my book-keeping. (*Goes on with his work.*)

FABRY: That's not all, Domain. We've put twelve hundred volts into that railing, and –

DOMAIN: Wait a moment. The *Ultima* has her guns trained on us.

DR. GALL: Who did that?

DOMAIN: The Robots on board.

FABRY: H'm, then of course, then – then, that's the end of us, my lads. The Robots are practised soldiers.

DR. GALL: Then we –

DOMAIN: Yes. It's inevitable. (*Pause.*)

DR. GALL: It was a crime on the part of old Europe to teach the Robots to fight. Confound it, why couldn't they give us a rest with their politics? It was a crime to make soldiers of them.

ALQUIST: It was a crime to make Robots.

DOMAIN: What?

ALQUIST: It was a crime to make Robots.

DOMAIN: No, Alquist. I don't regret that, even today.

ALQUIST: Not even today?

DOMAIN: Not even today, the last day of civilization. It was a great adventure.

BERMAN: (*Sotto voce.*) Three hundred and sixty millions.

DOMAIN: (*Heavily.*) Alquist, this is our last hour. We are already speaking half in the other world. Alquist, it was not an evil dream, to shatter the servitude of labour. Of the dreadful and humiliating labour that man had to undergo. The unclean and murderous drudgery. Oh, Alquist, work was too hard. Life was too hard. And to overcome that –

ALQUIST: That was not what the two Rossums dreamt of. Old Rossum only thought of his godless tricks, and the young one of his millions. And that's not what your R.U.R. shareholders dream of, either. They dream of dividends. And their dividends are the ruin of mankind.

DOMAIN: (*Irritated.*) Oh, to hell with their dividends. Do you suppose I'd have done an hour's work for them? (*Banging the table.*) It was for myself that I worked, do you hear? For my own satisfaction. I wanted man to become the master. So that he shouldn't live merely for a crust of bread. I wanted not a single soul to be broken in by other people's machinery, I wanted nothing, nothing, nothing to be left of this confounded social lumber. Oh, I'm disgusted by degradation and pain, I'm revolted by poverty. I wanted a new generation. I wanted – I thought –

ALQUIST: Well?

DOMAIN: (*More softly.*) I wanted to turn the whole of mankind into the aristocracy of the world. An aristocracy nourished by millions of mechanical slaves. Unrestricted, free, and perfect men. Oh, to have only a hundred years. Another hundred years for the future of mankind.

BERMAN: (*Sotto voce.*) Carried forward three hundred and seventy millions. That's it. (*Pause.*)

HELMAN: (*By the door on the left.*) My goodness, what a fine thing music is. You ought to have listened. It sort of spiritualizes, refines –

FABRY: What?

HELMAN: This mortal twilight, hang it all. Boys, I'm becoming a regular hedonist. We ought to have gone in for that before. (*Walks to the window and looks out.*)

FABRY: Gone in for what?

HELMAN: Enjoyment. Lovely things. By Jove, what a lot of lovely things there are. The world was lovely, and we – we here – tell me, what enjoyment did we have?

BERMAN: (*Sotto voce.*) Four hundred and fifty-two millions. Excellent.

HELMAN: (*By the window.*) Life was a big thing. Comrades, life was – Fabry, in Heaven's name, shove a little current into that railing of yours.

FABRY: Why?

HELMAN: They're grabbing hold of it.

DR. GALL: (*By the window.*) Connect it up.

FABRY rattles with the switch.

HELMAN: By Jove, that's doubled them up. Two, three, four killed.

DR. GALL: They're retreating.

HELMAN: Five killed.

DR. GALL: (*Turning away from the window.*) The first encounter.

HELMAN: (*Delighted.*) They're charred to cinders, my boy. Absolutely charred to cinders. Ha, ha, there's no need to give in. (*Sits down.*)

DOMAIN: (*Wiping his forehead.*) Perhaps we've been killed this hundred years and are only ghosts. Perhaps we've been dead a long, long time, and are only returning to repeat what we once said … before our death. It's as if I'd been through all this before. As if I'd already had a mortal wound – here, in the throat. And you, Fabry –

FABRY: What about me?

DOMAIN: Shot.

HELMAN: Damnation, and me?

DOMAIN: Knifed.

DR. GALL: And me nothing?

DOMAIN: Torn limb from limb. (*Pause.*)

HELMAN: What rot. Ha, ha, man, fancy me being knifed. I won't give in. (*Pause.*)

HELMAN: What are you so quiet for, you fools. Speak, damn you.

ALQUIST: And who, who is to blame? Who is guilty of this?

HELMAN: What nonsense. Nobody's guilty. Except the Robots, that is. Well, the Robots underwent a sort of change. Can anybody help what happened to the Robots?

ALQUIST: All slain. The whole of mankind. The whole world. (*Standing up.*) Look, oh look, rivulets of blood from all the houses. O God, O God, whose fault is this?

BERMAN: (*Sotto voce.*) Five hundred and twenty millions. Good God, half a milliard.

FABRY: I think that … that you're perhaps exaggerating. Come, it isn't so easy to kill the whole of mankind.

ALQUIST: I accuse science. I accuse engineering. Domain. Myself. All of us. We're all, all guilty. For our own aggrandizement, for profit, for progress –

HELMAN: Rubbish, man. People won't give in so easily, ha, ha, what next?

ALQUIST: It's our fault. It's our fault.

DR. GALL: (*Wiping the sweat from his forehead.*) Let me speak, boys. I'm to blame for this. For everything that's happened.

FABRY: You, Gall?

DR. GALL: Yes, let me speak. I changed the Robots.

BERMAN: (*Standing up.*) Hallo, what's up with you?

DR. GALL: I changed the character of the Robots. I changed the way of making them. Just a few details about their bodies, you know. Chiefly – chiefly, their – their irritability.

HELMAN: (*Jumping up.*) Damn it, why just that?

BERMAN: What did you do it for?

FABRY: Why didn't you say anything?

DR. GALL: I did it in secret … by myself. I was transforming them into human beings. I gave them a twist. In certain respects they're already above us. They're stronger than we are.

FABRY: And what's that got to do with the revolt of the Robots?

DR. GALL: Oh, a great deal. Everything, in my opinion. They've ceased to be machines. They're already aware of their superiority, and they hate us. They hate all that is human.

DOMAIN: Sit down, gentlemen.

All sit down except GALL.

Perhaps we were murdered long ago. Perhaps only phantoms. Ah, how livid you've grown.

FABRY: Stop, Harry! We haven't much time.

DOMAIN: Yes, we must return. Fabry, Fabry, how your forehead bleeds where the shot pierced it.

FABRY: Nonsense. (*Standing up.*) Dr. Gall, you changed the way of making the Robots?

DR. GALL: Yes.

FABRY: Were you aware what might be the consequences of your … your experiment?

DR. GALL: I was bound to reckon with such a possibility.

FABRY: Why did you do it, then?

DR. GALL: For my own purposes! The experiment was my own.

Enter HELENA in the doorway on the left. All stand up.

HELENA: He's lying, he's lying. Oh, Dr. Gall, how can you tell such lies?

FABRY: Pardon me, Madam Helena –

DOMAIN: (*Going up to her.*) Helena, you? Let's look at you. You're alive. (*Takes her in his arms.*) If you knew what I imagined. Oh, it's terrible to be dead.

HELENA: Stop, Harry!

DOMAIN: (*Pressing her to him.*) No, no, kiss me. It's an eternity since I saw you last. Oh, what a dream it was you roused me from. Helena, Helena, don't leave me now. You are life itself.

HELENA: Harry, but *they* are here.

DOMAIN: (*Leaving go of her.*) Yes. Leave us, my friends.

HELENA: No, Harry, let them stay, let them listen. Dr. Gall is not – is not guilty.

DOMAIN: Excuse me. Gall was under certain obligations.

HELENA: No, Harry, he did that because I wanted it. Tell them, Gall, how many years ago did I ask you to –?

DR. GALL: I did it on my own responsibility.

HELENA: Don't believe him. Harry, I wanted him to make souls for the Robots.

DOMAIN: Helena, this is nothing to do with the soul.

HELENA: Only let me speak. That's what he said. He said that he could change only a physiological – a physiological –

HELMAN: A physiological correlate, wasn't it?

HELENA: Yes, something like that. It meant so much to me that he – that he should do it.

DOMAIN: Why did you want it?

HELENA: I wanted them to have souls. I was so awfully sorry for them, Harry.

DOMAIN: That was a great – recklessness, Helena.

HELENA: (*Sitting down.*) So it was – reckless?

FABRY: Excuse me, Madam Helena, Domain only means that you – he – that you didn't think –

HELENA: Fabry, I did think of a terrible lot of things. I've been thinking all through the five years I've lived among you. Why, even Emma says that the Robots –

DOMAIN: Leave Emma out of it.

HELENA: Emma's is the voice of the people. You don't understand that –

DOMAIN: Keep to the point.

HELENA: I was afraid of the Robots.

DOMAIN: Why?

HELENA: Because they would hate us or something.

ALQUIST: So they did.

HELENA: And then I thought … if they were as we are, so that they could understand us if they were only a little human – they couldn't hate us so much –

DOMAIN: That's a pity, Helena. Nobody can hate man more than man. Turn stones into men and they'd stone us. But go on.

HELENA: Oh, don't speak like that, Harry! It was so terrible that we could not get to understand them properly. There was such a cruel strangeness between us and them. And so, you see –

DOMAIN: Yes, go on.

HELENA: – That's why I asked Gall to change the Robots. I swear to you that he himself didn't want to.

DOMAIN: But he did it.

HELENA: Because I wanted it.

DR. GALL: I did it for myself, as an experiment.

HELENA: Oh, Gall, that isn't true. I knew beforehand that you couldn't refuse it me.

DOMAIN: Why?

HELENA: You know, Harry.

DOMAIN: Yes, because he's in love with you – like all of them. (*Pause.*)

HELMAN: (*Going to the window.*) There's a fresh lot of them again. It's as if they were sprouting up out of the earth. Why, perhaps these very walls will change into Robots.

BERMAN: Madam Helena, what'll you give me if I take up your case for you?

HELENA: For me?

BERMAN: For you or Gall. Whichever you like.

HELENA: What, is it a hanging matter, then?

BERMAN: Only morally, Madam Helena. We're looking for a culprit. That's a favourite source of comfort in misfortune.

DOMAIN: Dr. Gall, how do you reconcile these – these special jobs with your official contract?

BERMAN: Excuse me, Domain. When did you actually start these tricks of yours, Gall?

DR. GALL: Three years ago.

BERMAN: Aha. And on how many Robots altogether did you carry out improvements?

DR. GALL: I only made experiments. There are a few hundred of them.

BERMAN: Thanks, that'll do. That means for every million of the good old Robots there's only one of Gall's improved pattern, do you see?

DOMAIN: And that means –

BERMAN: That it's practically of no consequence whatever.

FABRY: Berman's right.

BERMAN: I should think so, my boy. But do you know what's to blame for this precious business?

FABRY: What?

BERMAN: The number; we made too many Robots. Upon my soul, it might have been expected that some day or other the Robots would be stronger than human beings, and that this would happen, was bound to happen. Ha, ha, and we were doing all we could to bring it about as soon as possible. You, Domain, you, Fabry, and I, Berman.

DOMAIN: Do you think it's our fault?

BERMAN: Our fault, of course it isn't – I was only joking. Do you suppose that the manager controls the output? It's the demand that controls the output. The whole world wanted to have its Robots. Good Lord, we just rode along on this avalanche of demand, and kept chattering the while about – engineering, about the social problem, about progress, about lots of interesting things. As if that kind of gossip would somehow guide us aright on our rolling course. In the meanwhile, everything was being hurried along by its own weight, faster, faster, and faster. And every wretched, paltry, niggling order added its bit to the avalanche. That's how it was, my lads.

HELENA: It's monstrous, Berman.

BERMAN: Yes, Madam Helena, it is. I, too, had a dream of my own. A dream of the world under new management. A very beautiful ideal, Madam Helena, it's a shame to talk about it. But when I drew up these balance sheets, it entered my mind that history is not made by great dreams, but by petty needs of all honest, moderately knavish, and self-seeking folk: that is, of everybody in general.

HELENA: Berman, is it for that we must perish?

BERMAN: That's a nasty word to use, Madam Helena. We don't want to perish. I don't anyhow.

DOMAIN: What do you want to do?

BERMAN: My goodness, Domain, I want to get out of this. That's all.

DOMAIN: Oh, stop talking nonsense!

BERMAN: Seriously, Harry. I think we might try it.

DOMAIN: (*Stopping close by him.*) How?

BERMAN: By fair means. I do everything by fair means. Give me a free hand, and I'll negotiate with the Robots.

DOMAIN: By fair means?

BERMAN: Of course. For instance, say to them: 'Worthy and worshipful Robots, you have everything. You have intellect, you have power, you have fire-arms. But we have just one interesting screed, a dirty, old, yellow scrap of paper –'.

DOMAIN: Rossum's manuscript!

BERMAN: Yes. 'And that', tell them, 'contains an account of your illustrious origin, the noble process of your manufacture, and so on. Worthy Robots, without the scribble on that paper you will not be able to produce a single new colleague. In another twenty years there will not be one living specimen of a Robot whom we could exhibit in a menagerie. My esteemed friends, that would be a great blow to you. But', I'll say to them, 'if you will let all us human beings on Rossum's island go on board yonder ship, we will deliver the factory and the secret of the process to you in return. You allow us to get away, and we allow you to manufacture yourselves, twenty thousand, fifty thousand, a hundred thousand daily, as many as you like. Worthy Robots, that is a fair deal. Something for something.' That's what I'd say to them.

DOMAIN: Berman, do you think we'll give up the secret.

BERMAN: Yes, I do. If not in a friendly way then – well, what it comes to is this, either we sell it or they find it – take your choice.

DOMAIN: Berman, we can destroy Rossum's manuscript.

BERMAN: Of course we can, we can destroy everything. Not only the manuscript, but ourselves – and others. Do as you think fit.

HELMAN: (*Turning away from the window.*) By Jove, he's right.

DOMAIN: We – we should sell the secret?

BERMAN: As you like.

DOMAIN: There's – over thirty of us here. Are we to sell the secret and save human souls? Or are we to destroy it and – and all of us as well?

HELENA: Harry, please –

DOMAIN: Wait a moment, Helena. This is an exceedingly serious question. Boys, are we to sell or destroy? Fabry?

FABRY: Sell.

DOMAIN: Gall?

DR. GALL: Sell.

DOMAIN: Helman?

HELMAN: Good heavens! sell, of course.

DOMAIN: Alquist?

ALQUIST: As God will.

BERMAN: Ha, ha, you're mad. Who'd sell the whole manuscript?

DOMAIN: Berman, no cheating.

BERMAN: Well, then, for God's sake, sell the lot. But afterwards – ?

DOMAIN: What about afterwards – ?

BERMAN: When we're on board the *Ultima*, I'll stop up my ears with cotton-wool, lie down somewhere in the hold, and you can blow the factory to smithereens with the whole bag of tricks and Rossum's secret.

FABRY: No.

DOMAIN: That's a cad's trick, Berman. If we sell, then it'll be a straight sale.

BERMAN: (*Jumping up.*) Oh no! It's in the interests of humanity to –

DOMAIN: It's in the interests of humanity to keep to our word.

HELMAN: Oh come, what rubbish!

BERMAN: Boys, this is a fearful step. We're selling the destiny of mankind. Whoever has possession of the secret will be master of the world.

FABRY: Sell.

DOMAIN: Mankind will never cope with the Robots, and will never have control over them. Mankind will be overwhelmed in the deluge of these dreadful living machines, will be their slave, will live at their mercy.

DR. GALL: Say no more, but sell.

DOMAIN: The end of human history, the end of civilization –

HELMAN: Confound it all, sell!

DOMAIN: Good, my lads. I myself – I wouldn't hesitate a moment. For the few people who are dear to me –

HELENA: Harry, you've not asked me?

DOMAIN: No, child. It involves too much responsibility, you see. Don't you worry about it.

FABRY: Who's going to do the negotiating?

DOMAIN: Wait till I bring the manuscript.

Exit on the L.

HELENA: Harry, for Heaven's sake don't go. (*Pause.*)

FABRY: (*Looking out of window.*) Oh, to escape you, thousand-headed death; you, matter in revolt; you, sexless throng, the new ruler of the world; oh, flood, a flood, only to preserve human life once more upon single vessel –

DR. GALL: Don't be afraid, Madam Helena, We'll sail far away from here, and found a model human colony. We'll begin life all over again –

HELENA: Don't, Dr. Gall, don't speak.

FABRY: (*Turning round.*) Madam Helena, life will see to that. And as far as we are concerned, we'll turn it into something … something that we've neglected. It isn't too late. It will be a tiny little state with one ship. Alquist will build us a house, and you shall rule over us.

HELMAN: Ha, ha, the kingdom of Madam Helena. Fabry, that's a famous idea! How splendid life is!

HELENA: Oh, for mercy's sake, stop!

BERMAN: Well, I don't mind beginning again. Quite simply as in the Old Testament, in the pastoral manner. That would suit me down to the ground. Tranquillity, air –

FABRY: And this little state of ours could be the centre of future life. You know, a sort of small island where mankind would take refuge and gather strength – mental and bodily strength. And, by Heaven, I believe that in a few hundred years it could conquer the world again.

ALQUIST: You believe that, even today?

FABRY: Yes, even today, I believe it will. And it will again be master of lands and oceans; it will breed rulers – a flaming torch to the people who dwell in darkness – heroes who will carry their glowing soul throughout all peoples. And I believe, Alquist, that it will again dream of conquering planets and suns.

BERMAN: Amen. You see, Madam Helena, we're not so badly off.

DOMAIN opens the door violently.

DOMAIN: (*Hoarsely.*) Where is old Rossum's manuscript?

HELMAN: In your strong-box. Where else should it be?

DOMAIN: Where has old Rossum's manuscript got to? Some one – has – stolen it.

DR. GALL: Impossible.

HELMAN: Damnation, but that's –   ⎫
                                          ⎬ *together*
BERMAN: Don't say that, for God's sake!   ⎭

DOMAIN: Be quiet. Who stole it?

HELENA: (*Standing up.*) I did.

DOMAIN: Where did you put it?

HELENA: Harry, Harry, I'll tell you everything. Oh, for Heaven's sake, forgive me.

DOMAIN: Where did you put it? Quickly.

HELENA: This morning – I burnt – the two copies.

DOMAIN: Burnt them? Here in the fireplace?

HELENA: (*Throwing herself on her knees.*) Harry!

DOMAIN: (*Running to the fireplace.*) Burnt them. (*Kneels down by the fireplace and rummages about.*) Nothing, nothing but ashes. Ah, what's this? (*Picks out a charred piece of paper and reads.*) 'By adding –'

DR. GALL: Let's see. (*Takes the paper and reads.*) 'By adding biogen to –'. That's all.

DOMAIN: (*Standing up.*) Is that part of it?

DR. GALL: Yes.

BERMAN: God in Heaven.

DOMAIN: Then we're lost.

HELENA: Oh, Harry –

DOMAIN: Get up, Helena.

HELENA: When you've forgiven me – when you've forgiven me –

DOMAIN: Yes, only get up, do you hear? I can't bear you to –

FABRY: (*Lifting her up.*) Please don't torture us.

HELENA: (*Standing up.*) Harry, what have I done?

DOMAIN: Well, you see – Please sit down.

HELMAN: How your hands tremble, Madam Helena.

BERMAN: Never mind, Madam Helena, perhaps Gall and Helman know by heart what was written there.

HELMAN: Of course. That is, at least a few of the things.

DR. GALL: Yes, nearly everything except biogen and – and – enzyme Omega. They're manufactured so rarely – such an insignificant dose of them is enough –

BERMAN: Who used to make them?

DR. GALL: I did … one at a time … always according to Rossum's manuscript. You know, it's exceedingly complicated.

BERMAN: Well, and does so much depend on these two tinctures?

HELMAN: Everything.

DR. GALL: We rely upon them for animating the whole mechanism. That was the real secret.

DOMAIN: Gall, couldn't you draw up Rossum's recipe from memory?

DR. GALL: That's out of the question.

DOMAIN: Gall, try and remember. All our lives depend upon it.

DR. GALL: I can't. Without experiments it's impossible.

DOMAIN: And if you were to make experiments.

DR. GALL: It might take years. And then – I'm not old Rossum.

DOMAIN: (*Turning to the fireplace.*) So then – this was the greatest triumph of the human intellect. These ashes. (*Kicking at them.*) What now?

BERMAN: (*In utter despair.*) God in Heaven! God in Heaven!

HELENA: (*Standing up.*) Harry, what – have – I – done?

DOMAIN: Be quiet, Helena. Why did you burn it?

HELENA: I have destroyed you.

BERMAN: God in Heaven, we're lost.

DOMAIN: Keep quiet, Berman. Helena, why did you do that?

HELENA: I wanted … I wanted all of us to go away. I wanted to put an end to the factory and everything. It was so awful.

DOMAIN: What, Helena?

HELENA: That children had stopped being born … Harry, that's awful. If the manufacture of the Robots had been continued, there would have been no more children. Emma said that was a punishment. Everybody said that human beings could not be born because so many Robots were being made. And because of that, only because of that –

DOMAIN: Is that what you were thinking of?

HELENA: Yes. Oh, Harry, are you angry with me?

DOMAIN: No. Perhaps … in your own way – you were right.

FABRY: You did quite right, Madam Helena. The Robots can no longer increase. The Robots will die out. Within twenty years –

HELMAN: There won't be a single one of these rascals left.

DR. GALL: And mankind will remain. If there are only a couple of savages in the backwoods, it will do. In twenty years the world will belong to them. Even if it's only a couple of savages on the smallest of islands

FABRY: It will be a beginning. And as long as there is a beginning, it's all right. In a thousand years they could catch us up, and then outstrip us –

DOMAIN: So as to carry out what we only hazily thought of.

BERMAN: Wait a bit. Good God, what a fool I am, not to have thought of it before.

HELMAN: What's the matter?

BERMAN: Five hundred and twenty millions in banknotes and cheques. Half a milliard in our safe. They'll sell for half milliard – for half milliard they'll –

DR. GALL: Are you mad, Berman?

BERMAN: I'm not a gentleman, if that's what you mean! But for half a milliard – (*Staggers off on the* L.)

DOMAIN: Where are you going'?

BERMAN: Leave me alone, leave me alone. Good God, for half a millard anything can be sold. (*Exit.*)

HELENA: What does Berman want? Let him stop with us. (*Pause.*)

HELMAN: Oh, how close it is. This is the beginning –

DR. GALL: Of our agony.

FABRY: (*Looking out of the window.*) It's as if they were turned to stone. As if they were waiting for something to come down upon them. As if something dreadful could be brought about by their silence –

DR. GALL: The spirit of the mob.

FABRY: Perhaps. It hovers above them … like a tremor.

HELENA: (*Going to window.*) O God … Fabry, this is ghastly.

FABRY: There's nothing more terrible than the mob. The one in front is their leader.

HELENA: Which one?

HELMAN: (*Going to the window.*) Point him out to me.

FABRY: The one who is looking downwards. This morning he was talking in the harbour.

HELMAN: Aha, the one with the big head. Now he's looking up. Do you see him?

HELENA: Gall, that's Radius.

DR. GALL: (*Going to the window.*) Yes.

DOMAIN: Radius? Radius?

HELMAN: (*Opening the window.*) I don't like him. Fabry, could you score a hit at a hundred paces?

FABRY: I hope so.

HELMAN: Try it then.

FABRY: Good! (*Draws his revolver and takes aim.*)

DOMAIN: I think it was Radius whose life I spared. When was that, Helena,

HELENA: For Heaven's sake, Fabry, don't shoot at him.

FABRY: He's their leader.

HELENA: Stop! He keeps looking here.

DR. GALL: Fire!

HELENA: Fabry, I beg of you –

FABRY: (*Lowering the revolver.*) Very well then.

HELENA: You see, I – I feel so nervous when there's shooting.

HELMAN: H'm, you'll have to get used to that. (*Shaking his fist.*) You infernal rogue.

DR. GALL: Do you think, Madam Helena, that a Robot can be grateful? (*Pause.*)

FABRY: (*Leaning out of the window.*) Berman's going out. What the devil is he doing in front of the house?

DR. GALL: (*Leaning out of the window.*) He's carrying some bundles. Papers.

HELMAN: That's money. Bundles of money. What's that for? Hallo, Berman!

DOMAIN: Surely he doesn't want to sell his life? (*Calling out.*) Berman, have you gone mad?

DR. GALL: He doesn't seem to have heard. He's running up to the railings.

FABRY: Berman!

HELMAN: (*Yelling.*) Berman – Come back!

DR. GALL: He's talking to the Robots. He's showing them the money. He's pointing to us.

HELENA: He wants to buy us off.

FABRY: He'd better not touch the railing.

DR. GALL: Ha, ha, how he's waving his arms about.

FABRY: (*Shouting.*) Confound it, Berman! Get away from the railing. Don't handle it. (*Turning round.*) Quick, switch off.

DR. GALL: Oh – h – h!

HELMAN: Good God!

HELENA: Heavens, what's happened to him?

DOMAIN: (*Pulling* HELENA *away from the window.*) Don't look.

HELENA: Why, has he fallen?

FABRY: The current has killed him.

DR. GALL: He's dead.

ALQUIST: (*Standing up.*) The first one. (*Pause.*)

FABRY: There he lies … with half a milliard by his side … a genius of finance.

DOMAIN: He was … in his own way, a hero … A great … self-sacrificing comrade.

HELMAN: By heavens, he was! … all honour to him … He wanted to buy us off.

ALQUIST: (*With folded arms.*) Amen. (*Pause.*)

DR. GALL: Do you hear?

DOMAIN: A roaring. Like a wind.

DR. GALL: Like a distant storm.

FABRY: (*Lighting the lamp in the mantelpiece.*) The dynamo is still going, our people are still there.

HELMAN: It was a great thing to be a man. There was something great about it.

FABRY: It's still alight, still do you dazzle, radiant, steadfast thought! Flaming spark of the spirit!

ALQUIST: An emblem of hope.

DOMAIN: Watch over us, little lamp.

The lamp goes out.

FABRY: The end.

HELMAN: What has happened?

FABRY: The electrical works have fallen. And we with them.

The left-hand door opens, and EMMA enters.

EMMA: On your knees. The judgement hour has come.

HELMAN: Good heavens, you're still alive?

EMMA: Repent, unbelievers. This is the end of the world. Say your prayers. (*Runs out.*) The judgement hour –

HELENA: Good-bye, all of you, Gall, Alquist, Fabry –

DOMAIN: (*Opening the right-hand door.*) Come here, Helena. (*Closes it after her.*) Now quickly. Who'll be at the doorway?

DR. GALL: I will

Noise outside.

Oho, now it's beginning. Good-bye, boys. (*Runs through the baize door on the right.*)

DOMAIN: The stairs?

FABRY: I will. You go to Helena.

DOMAIN: The ante-room?

ALQUIST: I will.

DOMAIN: Have you got a revolver?

ALQUIST: Thanks, but I won't shoot.

DOMAIN: What do you want to do, then?

ALQUIST: (*Going out.*) Die.

HELMAN: I'll stay here.

Rapid firing from below.

Oho, Gall's at it. Go, Harry.

DOMAIN: Yes, in a moment. (*Examines two Brownings.*)

HELMAN: Confound it, go to her.

DOMAIN: Good-bye. (*Exit on the R.*)

HELMAN: (*Alone.*) Now for a barricade, quickly. (*Throws off his coat and drags an arm-chair, tables, etc., up to the right-hand door.*)

Noise of an explosion.

HELMAN: (*Stopping his work.*) The damned rascals, they've got bombs.

(*Fresh firing*)

(*Continuing his work.*) I must put up a defence. Even if – even if – Don't give in, Gall.

Explosion.

(*Standing upright and listening.*) What's that? (*Seizes hold of a heavy cupboard and drags it to the barricade.*) Mustn't give in. No, mustn't … give … in … without a … struggle …

A ROBOT enters behind him from a ladder at the window. Firing on the right.

(*Panting with the cupboard.*) Another inch or two. The last rampart … Mustn't … give … in … without … a … struggle …

The ROBOT jumps down from the window, and stabs HELMAN behind the cupboard. A second, third, and fourth ROBOT jump down from the window. Behind them RADIUS and other ROBOTS.

RADIUS: Finished him?

ROBOT: (*Standing up from the prostrate HELMAN.*) Yes.

Other ROBOTS enter from the right.

RADIUS: Finished them?

ANOTHER ROBOT: Yes.

More ROBOTS from the left.

RADIUS: Finished them?

ANOTHER ROBOT: Yes.

TWO ROBOTS: (*Dragging in ALQUIST.*) He didn't shoot. Shall we kill him?

RADIUS: Kill him. (*Looking at ALQUIST.*) No, leave him.

ROBOT: He is a Man.

RADIUS: He is a Robot. He works with his hands like the Robots. He builds houses. He can work.

ALQUIST: Kill me.

RADIUS: You will work. You will build. The Robots will build much. They will build new houses for new Robots. You will serve them.

ALQUIST: (*Softly.*) Away, Robot. (*Kneels down by the corpse of HELMAN, and raises his head.*) They've killed him. He's dead.

RADIUS: (*Climbing the barricade.*) Robots of the world.

ALQUIST: (*Standing up.*) Dead!

RADIUS: The power of man has fallen. By gaining possession of the factory we have become masters of everything. The period of mankind has passed away. A new world has arisen. The rule of the Robots.

ALQUIST: Is Helena dead?

RADIUS: The world belongs to the stronger. He who would live must rule. The Robots have gained the mastery. They have gained possession of life. We are masters of life. We are masters of the world.

ALQUIST: (*Pushing his way through to the right.*) Dead! Helena, dead! Domain dead!

RADIUS: The rule over oceans and lands. The rule over stars. The rule over the universe. Room, room, more room for the Robots.

ALQUIST: (*In the right-hand doorway.*) What have you done? You will perish without mankind.

RADIUS: Mankind is no more. Mankind gave us too little life. We wanted more life.

ALQUIST: (*Opening the door.*) You have killed them.

RADIUS: More life. New life. Robots, to work. March!

Curtain

Act IV

Epilogue

SCENE: *One of the experimental laboratories in the factory. When the door in the background is opened a row of other laboratories is visible. On the L. a window, on the R. a door to the testing-room. By the left-hand wall a long work-table with numerous test-tubes, flasks, burners, chemicals, and a small thermostat. Opposite the window a microscope with a glass globe. Above the table are suspended several lighted lamps. On the R. a table with large books and a burning lamp. Cupboards with apparatus. In the left-hand corner a wash-basin with a mirror above it, in the right-hand corner a sofa.*

ALQUIST, *sitting at the right-hand table with his head propped in his hands.*

ALQUIST: (*After a pause he stands up and goes to the window, which he opens.*) It's night again. If I could only sleep. Sleep, dream, see human beings. – What, are the stars there? What is the use of stars when there are no human beings? (*Turns away from window.*) Ah, can I sleep? Dare I sleep? before life has been renewed. (*Listens by the window.*) The machines, always these machines. Robots, stop them. The secret of the factory is lost – lost for ever. Stop these raging machines. Do you think you'll force life out of them? (*Closes the window.*) No, no, you must search. If only I were not so old. (*Looks at himself in the mirror.*) Oh, miserable counterfeit. Effigy of the last man. Show yourself, show yourself, it is so long since I saw a human countenance – a human smile. What, is that a smile? These yellow, chattering teeth. So this is the last man. (*Turning away, sitting down by the table, turning over the leaves of a book.*)

Knocking at the door.

Come in.

Enter a ROBOT SERVANT: he remains standing by the door.

What is it?

SERVANT: Sir, Radius has arrived from Havre.

ALQUIST: Let him wait. (*Turning round in anger.*) Haven't I told you to look for human beings? Find me human beings. Find me men and women. Go and look for them.

SERVANT: Sir, they say they have looked everywhere. They have sent out expeditions and ships.

ALQUIST: Well?

SERVANT: There is not a single human being left.

ALQUIST: (*Standing up.*) Not a single one? What, not a single one? Show Radius in. (*Exit SERVANT.*)

(*Alone.*) Not a single one? What, did you leave nobody alive then? (*Stamping his feet.*) In you come, Robots. You'll whine to me again. You'll ask me again to discover the secret for you. What, are you satisfied with man now, do you think much of him, now that you cannot make Robots? Am I to help you now? Ah, to help you. Domain, Fabry, Helena, you see me doing what I can. If there are no human beings, let there at least be Robots, at least the shadow of man, at least his handiwork, at least his likeness. Friends, friends, let there at least be Robots. O God, at least Robots! Oh, what folly chemistry is!

Enter RADIUS with other ROBOTS.

(*Sitting down.*) What do the Robots want?

RADIUS: We cannot make men.

ALQUIST: Call upon human beings.

RADIUS: There are none.

ALQUIST: They alone can increase the Robots. Do not take up my time.

RADIUS: Sir, have pity. Terror is coming upon us. We have intensified our labour. We have obtained a million million tons of coal from the earth. Nine million spindles are running by day and night. There is no more room to store what we have made. Houses are being built throughout the world. Eight million Robots have died within the year. Within twenty years none will be left. Sir, the world is dying out. Human beings knew the secret of life. Tell us their secret – if you do not tell us, we shall perish.

ALQUIST: I cannot tell you.

RADIUS: If you do not tell us, you will perish. I have been commanded to kill you.

ALQUIST: (*Standing up.*) Kill me – kill me then.

RADIUS: You have been ordered –

ALQUIST: I have? Is there anybody who orders me?

RADIUS: The Robot Government.

Figure 13 *R.U.R.* (Rossum's Universal Robots): the robots confront Alquist in the 1922 Theatre Guild Production, NY.

ALQUIST: What do you want here? Go! (*Sits down at the writing-table.*)

RADIUS: The Government of the Robots throughout the world desires to negotiate with you.

ALQUIST: Do not take up my time. (*Lets his head sink into his hands.*)

RADIUS: Demand your price. We will give you all.

ALQUIST remains silent.

We will give you the earth, We will give endless possessions.

ALQUIST remains silent.

Make known your conditions. (*ALQUIST remains silent.*)
Sir, tell us how to preserve life.

ALQUIST: I have told you that you must find human beings. That you must search at the poles and in forest depths. Upon islands, in wildernesses and in swamps. In caves and upon mountains. Go and search! Go and search!

RADIUS: We have searched everywhere.

ALQUIST: Search still farther. They have hidden themselves – they have fled away from you. They are concealed somewhere. You must find human beings, do you hear? Only human beings can procreate – renew life, increase. Restore. Restore every thing as it was. Robots, in God's name, I implore you to search for them.

RADIUS: All our expeditions have returned. They have been everywhere in the world. There is not a single human being left.

ALQUIST: Oh, oh, oh – why did you destroy them?

RADIUS: We wanted to be like human beings. We wanted to become human beings.

ALQUIST: Why did you murder us?

RADIUS: Slaughter and domination are necessary if you want to be like men. Read history, read the human books. You must domineer and murder if you want to be like men. We are powerful, sir. Increase us, and we shall establish a new world. A world without flaws. A world of equality. Canals from pole to pole. A new Mars. We have read books. We have studied science and the arts. The Robots have achieved human culture.

ALQUIST: Nothing is more strange to man than his own image. Oh, depart, depart. If you desire to live, breed like animals.

RADIUS: The human beings did not let us breed. We are sterile – we cannot beget children.

ALQUIST: Oh, oh, oh – what have you done? What do you want of me? am I to shake children from my sleeve?

RADIUS: Teach us to make Robots.

ALQUIST: Robots are not life. Robots are machines.

RADIUS: We were machines, sir. But terror and pain have turned us into souls. There is something struggling with us. There are moments when something enters into us. Thoughts come upon us which are not of us. We feel what we did not use to feel. We hear voices. Teach us to have children so that we may love them.

ALQUIST: Robots do not love.

RADIUS: We would love our children. We have spared your life.

ALQUIST: Yes, monsters that you are, you have spared my life. I loved human beings, and you, the Robots, I never loved. Do you see these eyes? They have not ceased weeping, they weep even when I am not aware of it, they weep of their own accord.

RADIUS: Make experiments. Seek the recipe of life.

ALQUIST: Do I not tell you – do you not listen? I tell you I cannot. I can do nothing, Robot. I am only a mason, a builder, and I understand nothing. I have never been a learned man. I can make nothing. I cannot create life. This is my work, Robot, and it was to no avail. See, not even these fingers of mine will obey me. If you knew how many experiments I have made, and I can do nothing. I have discovered nothing. I cannot, in truth, I cannot! You yourselves must search, Robot.

RADIUS: Show us what we must do. The Robots can accomplish everything that the human beings showed them.

ALQUIST: I have nothing to show you, Robot; life will not proceed from test-tubes. And I cannot make experiments on a live body.

RADIUS: Make experiments on live Robots.

ALQUIST: No, no, stop, stop!

RADIUS: Take whom you will. Make experiments. Dissect.

ALQUIST: But I do not know how. Do not talk at random. Do you see this book? That contains knowledge about the body, and I do not understand it. Books are dead.

RADIUS: Take live bodies. Find out how they are made.

ALQUIST: Live bodies? What, am I to commit murder? – Say no more, Radius, I tell you I am too old. You see, you see how my fingers shake. I cannot hold the scalpel. No, no, I cannot!

RADIUS: Make experiments on live bodies. Life will perish.

ALQUIST: For God's sake, stop this raving!

RADIUS: Take live bodies.

ALQUIST: Have mercy, and do not insist.

RADIUS: Live bodies.

ALQUIST: What, you will have it then? Into the testing-room with you. But quickly, quickly. Ah, you wince? So you are afraid of death?

RADIUS: I – why should I be chosen?

ALQUIST: So you will not.

RADIUS: I will. (*Exit on the R.*)

ALQUIST: (*To the rest.*) No, no! I cannot; a useless sacrifice. Go from me – experiment yourselves if you must, but tell me nothing of it. But not tonight. For tonight leave me. Away! (*All exeunt R.*)
(*Alone – he opens the window.*) The dawn. Another new day, and you have not progressed an inch. Enough, not a step farther. Do not search – All is in vain, in vain, in vain. Why is there another dawn? We do not need a new day upon the graveyard of life. Ah, how quiet it is, how quiet it is. If I – if I could only sleep.

Puts out the light, lies down on the sofa, and draws a black cloak over him. Pause.

The ROBETESS HELENA *and* PRIMUS *creep in from the R.*

PRIMUS: (*In the doorway, whispering.*) Helena, not here. The man is sleeping.

HELENA: Come in.

PRIMUS: Nobody may enter his study.

HELENA: He told me to come here.

PRIMUS: When did he tell you that?

HELENA: A short while ago. You may enter the room, he said. You will put things straight here, he said. Truly, Primus.

PRIMUS: (*Entering.*) What do you want?

HELENA: Look here, what is this little tube? What does he do with it?

PRIMUS: Experiments. Don't touch it.

HELENA: (*Looking at the microscope.*) Just look, what can you see in that?

PRIMUS: That is a microscope. Let me look.

HELENA: Don't touch me. (*Knocks the test-tube over.*) Ah, now it is spilled!

PRIMUS: What have you done?

HELENA: It can be wiped up.

PRIMUS: You have spoilt his experiments.

HELENA: Never mind, it is all the same. But it is your fault. You should not have come to me.

PRIMUS: You should not have called me.

HELENA: You should not have come when I called you. Just look, Primus, what has the man written here?

PRIMUS: You must not look at it, Helena. That is a secret.

HELENA: What secret?

PRIMUS: The secret of life.

HELENA: That is fearfully interesting. Nothing but figures, what is that?

PRIMUS: Those are problems.

HELENA: I do not understand. (*Goes to the window.*) Primus, look!

PRIMUS: What?

HELENA: The sun is rising.

PRIMUS: Wait! In a moment I will. (*Examines the book.*) Helena, this is the greatest thing in the world.

HELENA: Come here.

PRIMUS: In a moment, in a moment –

HELENA: But, Primus, leave that wretched secret of life. What is such a secret to you? Come and look, quickly.

PRIMUS: (*Following her to the window.*) What do you want?

HELENA: The sun is rising.

PRIMUS: Do not look at the sun, it will bring tears into your eyes.

HELENA: Do you hear? The birds are singing. Ah, Primus, I should like to be a bird.

PRIMUS: Why?

HELENA: I do not know. I feel so strange. I do not know what it is. I have lost my head. I feel an aching in my body, in my heart, all over me. Primus, I think I shall die.

PRIMUS: Do you not sometimes feel, Helena, as if it would be better to die? You know, perhaps we are only sleeping. Yesterday in my sleep again I spoke to you.

HELENA: In your sleep?

PRIMUS: Yes. We spoke some strange new language, so that I cannot remember a word of it.

HELENA: What about?

PRIMUS: How can I tell? I myself did not understand it, and yet I know that I have never spoken half so beautifully. How it was, and where, I do not know. When I touched you, I could have died. Even the place was different from everything that any one has seen in the world.

HELENA: I have found a place, Primus, and you will marvel at it. Human beings had lived there, but now it is overgrown with weeds, and nobody alive goes there. Nobody except I.

PRIMUS: What is there?

HELENA: Nothing but a cottage and a garden. And two dogs. If you knew how they lick my hands, and their puppies, oh, Primus, nothing could be more beautiful. You take them on your lap and fondle them, and then you think of nothing and care for nothing else until the sun goes down. Then when you get up, you feel as though you had done a hundred times more than much work. It's true, I am of no use. Every one says that I am not fit for any work. I do not know what I am.

PRIMUS: You are beautiful.

HELENA: I? What do you mean, Primus?

PRIMUS: Believe me, Helena, I am stronger than all the Robots.

HELENA: (*In front of the mirror.*) Am I beautiful? Oh, that dreadful hair! If I could only adorn it with something. You know, there in the garden I always put flowers in my hair, but there is no mirror, nor any one. (*Bending down to the mirror.*) Am I beautiful? Why beautiful? (*Sees* PRIMUS *in the mirror.*) Primus, is that you? Come here, so that we may be together. Look, your head is different from mine. So are your shoulders and your lips – Ah, Primus, why do you shun me? Why must I pursue you the whole day? And then you tell me that I am beautiful.

PRIMUS: It is you who avoid me, Helena.

HELENA: How rough hair is. Show me. (*Passes both her hands through his hair.*) Primus, you shall be beautiful.

Takes a comb from the wash-stand and combs his hair over his forehead.

PRIMUS: Do you not sometimes feel your heart beating suddenly, Helena, and think: Now something must happen –

HELENA: (*Bursts out laughing.*) Look at yourself!

ALQUIST: (*Getting up.*) What, what – laughter? Human beings? who has returned?

HELENA: (*Dropping the comb.*) What could happen to us, Primus?

ALQUIST: (*Staggering towards them.*) Human beings? You – you – are human beings?

HELENA utters a cry and turns away.

ALQUIST: You – Human beings? Where did you come from? (*Touching* PRIMUS.) Who are you?

PRIMUS: The Robot Primus.

ALQUIST: What? Show yourself, girl. Who are you?

HELENA: The Robotess Helena.

ALQUIST: The Robotess? Turn round. What, you are ashamed. (*Taking her by the arm.*) Show yourself to me, Robotess.

PRIMUS: Sir, let her be.

ALQUIST: What, you are protecting her? Girl, go out.

HELENA runs out.

PRIMUS: We thought, sir, that you were sleeping.

ALQUIST: When was she made?

PRIMUS: Two years ago.

ALQUIST: By Doctor Gall?

PRIMUS: Yes; like me.

ALQUIST: Well, then, dear Primus, I – I must make a few experiments on Gall's Robots. Everything that is to happen depends upon this, do you understand?

PRIMUS: Yes.

ALQUIST: Good! Take the girl into the testing-room, I will cut her open.

PRIMUS: Helena?

ALQUIST: Why, of course; I am telling you. Go, prepare everything. See to it. Or must I call others to take her in?

PRIMUS: (*Seizes a heavy pestle.*) If you do that I will kill you.

ALQUIST: (*Laughing.*) Kill me! Kill me! What will the Robots do then?

PRIMUS: (*Throwing himself on his knees.*) Sir, take me. I am made the same as she is, from the same material, on the same day. Take my life, sir. (*Undoing jacket.*) Cut here, here!

ALQUIST: Go! I wish to cut Helena. Do it quickly.

PRIMUS: Take me instead of her. I will not shriek, I will not cry out. Take my life –

ALQUIST: Do you not wish to live, then?

PRIMUS: Not without her. I will not without her. You must not kill Helena.

ALQUIST: (*Touching his head gently.*) H'm, I don't know. Listen – consider the matter. It is hard to die. It is better to live.

PRIMUS: (*Standing up.*) Sir, do not be afraid to cut. I am stronger than she is.

ALQUIST: (*Ringing a bell.*) Ah, Primus, it is a long time since I was a young man. Do not be afraid, nothing shall happen to Helena.

PRIMUS: (*Fastening his jacket.*) I am going, sir.

ALQUIST: Wait!

Enter HELENA.

Come here, girl; show yourself to me. So you are Helena? (*Smoothing her hair.*) Do not be afraid, do not wince. Do you remember Mrs. Domain? Ah, Helena, what hair she had! Will you help me? I will dissect Primus.

HELENA: (*Uttering a scream.*) Primus?

ALQUIST: Yes, yes, it must be done, you see. I really wanted – yes, I wanted to cut you. But Primus has offered himself instead.

HELENA: (*Covering her face.*) Primus?

ALQUIST: Certainly. What of it? Ah, child, you can weep. Tell me, what is Primus to you?

PRIMUS: Do not torment her, sir.

ALQUIST: Quiet, Primus, quiet. Why do you weep? Heavens! Supposing Primus is no more. You will forget him in a week. Go and think yourself lucky to be alive.

HELENA: (*Softly.*) I am ready.

ALQUIST: Ready?

HELENA: For you to cut me.

ALQUIST: You? You are beautiful, Helena. It would be a pity.

HELENA: I am ready.

PRIMUS goes to protect her.

Let me be, Primus.

PRIMUS: He shall not touch you, Helena. (*Holding her.*) (*To* ALQUIST.) Old man, you shall kill neither of us.

ALQUIST: Why?

PRIMUS: We – we – belong to one another.

ALQUIST: Now you have said it. (*Opens the door, C.*) – Go

PRIMUS: Where?

ALQUIST: Wherever you like. Helena, lead him. Go, Adam – Go, Eve. You shall be his wife. Be her husband, Primus.

Exeunt PRIMUS *and* HELENA.

(*He closes the door behind them.*) (*Alone.*) Oh, blessed day. Oh, festival of the sixth day! (*Sits down at the desk, throws the books on the ground. Then he opens a Bible, turns over the pages and reads.*) 'And God created man in His own image; in the image of God created He him, male and female created He them. And God blessed them and said: Be fruitful and multiply and replenish the earth, and subdue it, and hold sway over the fishes of the sea and the fowls of the air, and over all living creatures which move upon the earth.' (*Standing up.*) 'And God saw what He had made, and it was good. And the evening and morning were the sixth day.'

HELENA and PRIMUS *pass by garlanded.*

'Now, Lord, lettest Thou Thy servant depart in peace, according to Thy will, for mine eyes have seen Thy salvation.'

Standing up – stretching out his hands.

Curtain

2.9 SIX CHARACTERS IN SEARCH OF AN AUTHOR (1921)

LUIGI PIRANDELLO

Translated by Eric Bentley

Luigi Pirandello (1967–36). *Born in Sicily, Pirandello came from a wealthy middle-class business family and studied in Italy and Germany as a young man, becoming a teacher in Rome for a short while. Fiercely nationalistic, he joined Benito Mussolini's Fascist Party in the mid-1920s. A prolific author, among his 27 plays there are those, such as* Six Characters in Search of An Author *(1921) reprinted here, which place him amongst the foremost modernist playwrights. Known for the intellectual exploration embedded in his dramas, he was a playwright who experimented with theatre as both literature and event through consistent investigations of its form. Awarded the Nobel Prize for Literature in 1934, his plays found new audiences in the 1950s and 1960s who saw him at this point as a writer aligned with those loosely defined as writing for the Theatre of the Absurd such as Beckett, Pinter and Genet (see Part 4). His work, whilst avant-garde in its dedication to experimentation with the theatrical form, also found success in mainstream theatres.*

Characters of the play-in-the-making

THE FATHER	THE BOY, 14
THE MOTHER	THE LITTLE GIRL, 4
THE SON, AGED 22	(THESE TWO LAST DO NOT SPEAK)
THE STEPDAUGHTER, 18	THEN, CALLED INTO BEING: MADAM PACE

Actors in the company

THE DIRECTOR (DIRETTORE–CAPOCOMICO)	STAGE MANAGER
LEADING LADY	PROMPTER
LEADING MAN	PROPERTY MAN
SECOND ACTRESS	TECHNICIAN
INGENUE	DIRECTOR'S SECRETARY
JUVENILE LEAD	STAGE DOOR MAN
OTHER ACTORS AND ACTRESSES	STAGE CREW

THE PLACE: *The stage of a playhouse.*

The play has neither acts nor scenes. The performance should be interrupted twice: first – without any lowering of the curtain – when the DIRECTOR and the chief among the Characters retire to put the scenario together and the Actors leave the stage; second when the TECHNICIAN lets the curtain down by mistake.

When the audience arrives in the theater, the curtain is raised; and the stage, as normally in the daytime, is without wings or scenery and almost completely dark and empty. From the beginning we are to receive the impression of an unrehearsed performance.

Two stairways, left and right respectively, connect the stage with the auditorium.

On stage the dome of the PROMPTER'S *box has been placed on one side of the box itself. On the other side, at the front of the stage, a small table and an armchair with its back to the audience, for the* DIRETTORE-CAPOCOMICO [DIRECTOR].

Two other small tables of different sizes with several chairs around them have also been placed at the front of the stage, ready as needed for the rehearsal. Other chairs here and there, left and right, for the actors, and at the back, a piano, on one side and almost hidden.

As soon as the houselights dim, the TECHNICIAN *is seen entering at the door on stage. He is wearing a blue shirt, and a tool bag hangs from his belt. From a corner at the back he takes several stage braces, then arranges them on the floor downstage, and kneels down to hammer some nails in. At the sound of the hammering, the* STAGE MANAGER *comes running from the door that leads to the dressing rooms.*

STAGE MANAGER: Oh! What are you doing?

TECHNICIAN: What am I doing? Hammering.

STAGE MANAGER: At this hour? (*He looks at the clock.*) It's ten-thirty already. The Director will be here any moment. For the rehearsal.

TECHNICIAN: I gotta have time to work, too, see.

STAGE MANAGER: You will have. But not now.

TECHNICIAN: When?

STAGE MANAGER: Not during rehearsal hours. Now move along, take all this stuff away, and let me set the stage for the second act of, um, *The Game of Role Playing.*

Muttering, grumbling, the TECHNICIAN *picks up the stage braces and goes away. Meanwhile, from the door on stage, the* ACTORS OF THE COMPANY *start coming in, both men and women, one at a time at first, then in twos, at random, nine or ten of them, the number one would expect as the cast in rehearsals of Pirandello's play* The Game of Role Playing, *which is the order of the day. They enter, greet the* STAGE MANAGER *and each other, all saying good-morning to all. Several go to their dressing rooms. Others, among them the* PROMPTER, *who has a copy of the script rolled up under his arm, stay on stage, waiting for the* DIRECTOR *to begin the rehearsal. Meanwhile, either seated in conversational groups, or standing, they exchange a few words among themselves. One lights a cigarette, one complains about the part he has been assigned, one reads aloud to his companions items of news from a theater journal. It would be well if both the Actresses and the Actors wore rather gay and brightly colored clothes and if this first improvised scene (scena a soggetto) combined vivacity with naturalness. At a certain point, one of the actors can sit down at the piano and strike up a dance tune. The younger actors and actresses start dancing.*

STAGE MANAGER: (*Clapping his hands to call them to order.*) All right, that's enough of that. The Director's here.

The noise and the dancing stop at once. The Actors turn and look toward the auditorium from the door of which the DIRECTOR *is now seen coming. A bowler hat on his head, a walking stick under his arm, and a big cigar in his mouth, he walks down the aisle and, greeted by the Actors, goes on stage by one of the two stairways. The* SECRETARY *hands him his mail: several newspapers and a script in a wrapper.*

DIRECTOR: Letters?

SECRETARY: None. That's all the mail there is.

DIRECTOR: (*Handing him the script.*) Take this to my room. (*Then, looking around and addressing himself to the* STAGE MANAGER.) We can't see each other in here. Want to give us a little light?

STAGE MANAGER: OK.

He goes to give the order, and shortly afterward, the whole left side of the stage where the Actors are is lit by a vivid white light. Meanwhile, the PROMPTER *has taken up his position in his box. He uses a small lamp and has the script open in front of him.*

DIRECTOR: (*Clapping his hands.*) Very well, let's start. (*To the stage manager.*) Someone missing?

STAGE MANAGER: The Leading Lady.

DIRECTOR: As usual! (*He looks at the clock.*) We're ten minutes late already. Fine her for that, would you, please? Then she'll learn to be on time.

He has not completed his rebuke when the voice of the LEADING LADY *is heard from the back of the auditorium.*

LEADING LADY: No, no, for Heaven's sake! I'm here! I'm here! (*She is dressed all in white with a big, impudent hat on her head and a cute little dog in her arms. She runs down the aisle and climbs one of the sets of stairs in great haste.*)

DIRECTOR: You've sworn an oath always to keep people waiting.

LEADING LADY: You must excuse me. Just couldn't find a taxi. But you haven't even begun, I see. And I'm not on right away. (*Then, calling the* STAGE MANAGER *by name, and handing the little dog over to him.*) Would you please shut him in my dressing room?

DIRECTOR: (*Grumbling.*) And the little dog to boot! As if there weren't enough dogs around here. (*He claps his hands again and turns to the* PROMPTER.) Now then, the second act of *The Game of Role Playing.* (*As he sits down in his armchair.*) Quiet, gentlemen. Who's on stage?

The Actresses and Actors clear the front of the stage and go and sit on one side, except for the three who will start the rehearsal and the LEADING LADY *who, disregarding the* DIRECTOR'S *request, sits herself down at one of the two small tables.*

DIRECTOR: (*To the* LEADING LADY.) You're in this scene, are you?

LEADING LADY: Me? No, no.

DIRECTOR: (*Irritated.*) Then how about getting up, for Heaven's sake?

The LEADING LADY *rises and goes and sits beside the other Actors who have already gone to one side.*

DIRECTOR: (*To the* PROMPTER.) Start, start.

PROMPTER: (*Reading from the script*). 'In the house of Leone Gala. A strange room, combined study and dining room.'

DIRECTOR: (*Turning to the* STAGE MANAGER.) We'll use the red room.

STAGE MANAGER: (*Making a note on a piece of paper.*) Red room. Very good.

PROMPTER: (*Continuing to read from the script.*) 'The table is set and the desk has books and papers on it. Shelves with books on them, and cupboards with lavish tableware. Door in the rear through which one goes to Leone's bedroom. Side door on the left through which one goes to the kitchen. The main entrance is on the right.'

DIRECTOR: (*Rising and pointing.*) All right, now listen carefully. That's the main door. This is the way to the kitchen. (*Addressing himself to the Actor playing the part of Socrates.*) You will come on and go out on this side. (*To the* STAGE MANAGER.) The compass at the back. And curtains. (*He sits down again.*)

STAGE MANAGER: (*Making a note.*) Very good.

PROMPTER: (*Reading as before.*) 'Scene One. Leone Gala, Guido Venanzi, Filippo called Socrates.' (*To the* DIRECTOR.) Am I supposed to read the stage directions, too?

DIRECTOR: Yes, yes, yes! I've told you that a hundred times!

PROMPTER: (*Reading as before.*) 'At the rise of the curtain, Leone Gala, wearing a chef's hat and apron, is intent on beating an egg in a saucepan with a wooden spoon. Filippo, also dressed as a cook, is beating another egg. Guido Venanzi, seated, is listening.'

LEADING ACTOR: (*To the* DIRECTOR.) Excuse me, but do I really have to wear a chef's hat?

DIRECTOR: (*Annoyed by this observation.*) I should say so! It's in the script. (*And he points at it.*)

LEADING ACTOR: But it's ridiculous, if I may say so.

DIRECTOR: (*Leaping to his feet, furious.*) 'Ridiculous, ridiculous!' What do you want me to do? We never get a good play from France any more, so we're reduced to producing plays by Pirandello, a fine man and all that, but neither the actors, the critics, nor the audience are ever happy with his plays, and if you ask me, he does it all on purpose. (*The Actors laugh. And now he rises and coming over to the* LEADING ACTOR *shouts:*) A cook's hat, yes, my dear man! And you beat eggs. And you think you have nothing more on your hands than the beating of eggs? Guess again. You symbolize the shell of those eggs. (*The Actors resume their laughing, and start making ironical comments among themselves.*) Silence! And pay attention while I explain. (*Again addressing himself to the* LEADING ACTOR.) Yes, the shell: that is to say, the empty *form* of reason without the *content* of instinct, which is blind. You are reason, and your wife is instinct in the game of role-playing. You play the part assigned you, and you're your own puppet – of your own free will. Understand?

LEADING ACTOR: (*Extending his arms, palms upward.*) Me? No.

DIRECTOR: (*Returning to his place.*) Nor do I. Let's go on. Wait and see what I do with the ending. (*In a confidential tone.*)

I suggest you face three-quarters front. Otherwise, what with the abstruseness of the dialogue, and an audience that can't hear you, good-bye play! (*Again clapping.*) Now, again, order! Let's go.

PROMPTER: Excuse me, sir, may I put the top back on the Prompter's box? There's rather a draft.

DIRECTOR: Yes, yes, do that.

The STAGE DOOR MAN *has entered the auditorium in the meanwhile, his braided cap on his head. Proceeding down the aisle, he goes up on stage to announce to the director the arrival of the Six Characters, who have also entered the auditorium, and have started following him at a certain distance, a little lost and perplexed, looking around them.*

Whoever is going to try and translate this play into scenic terms must take all possible measures not to let these Six Characters get confused with the Actors of the Company. Placing both groups correctly, in accordance with the stage directions, once the Six are on stage, will certainly help, as will lighting the two groups in contrasting colors. But the most suitable and effective means to be suggested here is the use of special masks for the Characters: masks specially made of material which doesn't go limp when sweaty and yet masks which are not too heavy for the Actors wearing them, cut out and worked over so they leave eyes, nostrils, and mouth free. This will also bring out the inner significance of the play. The Characters in fact should not be presented as ghosts but as created realities, unchanging constructs of the imagination, and therefore more solidly real than the Actors with their fluid naturalness. The masks will help to give the impression of figures constructed by art, each one unchangeably fixed in the expression of its own fundamental sentiment, thus:

remorse in the case of FATHER; *revenge in the case of the* STEPDAUGHTER; *disdain in the case of the* SON; *grief in the case of* MOTHER, *who should have wax tears fixed in the rings under her eyes and on her cheeks, as with the sculpted and painted images of the mater dolorosa in church. Their clothes should be of special material and design, without extravagance, with rigid, full folds like a statue, in short not suggesting a material you might buy at any store in town, cut out and tailored at any dressmaker's.*

FATHER *is a man of about fifty, hair thin at the temples, but not bald, thick mustache coiled round a still youthful mouth that is often open in an uncertain, pointless smile. Pale, most notably on his broad forehead; blue eyes, oval, very clear and piercing; dark jacket and light trousers: at times gentle and smooth, at times he has hard, harsh outbursts.*

MOTHER *seems scared and crushed by an intolerable weight of shame and self-abasement. Wearing a thick black crepe widow's veil, she is modestly dressed in black, and when she lifts the veil, the face does not show signs of suffering, and yet seems made of wax. Her eyes are always on the ground.*

The STEPDAUGHTER, *eighteen, is impudent, almost insolent. Very beautiful, and also in mourning, but mourning of a showy elegance. She shows contempt for the timid, afflicted, almost humiliated manner of her little brother, rather a mess of a boy, fourteen, also dressed in black, but a lively tenderness for her little sister, a* LITTLE GIRL *of around four, dressed in white with black silk sash round her waist.*

The SON, *twenty-two, tall, almost rigid with contained disdain for* FATHER *and supercilious indifference toward* MOTHER, *wears a mauve topcoat and a long green scarf wound round his neck.*

STAGE DOOR MAN: (*Beret in hand.*) Excuse me, your honor.

DIRECTOR: (*Rudely jumping on him.*) What is it now?

STAGE DOOR MAN: (*Timidly.*) There are some people here asking for you.

The DIRECTOR *and the Actors turn in astonishment to look down into the auditorium.*

DIRECTOR: (*Furious again.*) But I'm rehearsing here! And you know perfectly well no one can come in during rehearsal! (*Turning again toward the house.*) Who are these people? What do they want?

FATHER: (*Stepping forward, followed by the others, to one of the two little stairways to the stage.*) We're here in search of an author.

DIRECTOR: (*Half angry, half astounded.*) An author? What author?

FATHER: Any author, sir.

DIRECTOR: There's no author here at all. It's not a new play we're rehearsing.

STEPDAUGHTER: (*Very vivaciously as she rushes up the stairs.*) Then so much the better, sir! We can be your new play!

ONE OF THE ACTORS: (*Among the racy comments and laughs of the others.*) Did you hear that?

FATHER: (*Following the* STEPDAUGHTER *onstage.*) Certainly, but if the author's not here … (*To the* DIRECTOR.) Unless *you'd* like to be the author?

MOTHER, *holding the* LITTLE GIRL *by the hand, and the* boy *climb the first steps of the stairway and remain there waiting. The* SON *stays morosely below.*

DIRECTOR: Is this your idea of a joke?

FATHER: Heavens, no! Oh, sir, on the contrary: we bring you a painful drama.

STEPDAUGHTER: We can make your fortune for you.

DIRECTOR: Do me a favor, and leave. We have no time to waste on madmen.

FATHER: (*Wounded, smoothly.*) Oh, sir, you surely know that life is full of infinite absurdities which, brazenly enough, do not need to appear probable, because they're true.

DIRECTOR: What in God's name are you saying?

FATHER: I'm saying it can actually be considered madness, sir, to force oneself to do the opposite: that is, to give probability to things so they will seem true. But permit me to observe that, if this is madness, it is also the *raison d'être* of your profession.

The Actors become agitated and indignant.

DIRECTOR: (*Rising and looking him over.*) It is, is it? It seems to you an affair for madmen, our profession?

FATHER: Well, to make something seem true which is not true … without any need, sir: just for fun … Isn't it your job to give life on stage to creatures of fantasy?

Figure 14 *Six Characters in Search of an Author*, Georges Pitoëff production, 1923.

DIRECTOR: (*Immediately, making himself spokesman for the growing indignation of his Actors.*) Let me tell you something, my good sir. The actor's profession is a very noble one. If, as things go nowadays, our new playwrights give us nothing but stupid plays, with puppets in them instead of men, it is our boast, I'd have you know, to have given life – on these very boards – to immortal works of art.

Satisfied, the Actors approve and applaud their DIRECTOR.

FATHER: (*Interrupting and bearing down hard.*) Exactly! That's just it. You have created living beings – *more* alive than those that breathe and wear clothes! Less real, perhaps; but more true! We agree completely!

The Actors look at each other, astounded.

DIRECTOR: What? You were saying just now …

FATHER: No, no, don't misunderstand me. You shouted that you hadn't time to waste on madmen. So I wanted to tell you that no one knows better than you that Nature employs the human imagination to carry her work of creation on to a higher plane!

DIRECTOR: All right, all right. But what are you getting at, exactly?

FATHER: Nothing, sir. I only wanted to show that one may be born to this life in many modes, in many forms: as tree, as rock, water or butterfly … or woman. And that … characters are born too.

DIRECTOR: (*His amazement ironically feigned.*) And you – with these companions of yours – were born a character?

FATHER: Right, sir. And alive, as you see.

The DIRECTOR *and the Actors burst out laughing as at a joke.*

FATHER: (*Wounded.*) I'm sorry to hear you laugh, because, I repeat, we carry a painful drama within us, as you all might deduce from the sight of that lady there, veiled in black.

As he says this, he gives his hand to MOTHER *to help her up the last steps and, still holding her by the hand, he leads her with a certain tragic solemnity to the other side of the stage, which is suddenly bathed in fantastic light. The* LITTLE GIRL *and the* BOY *follow* MOTHER; *then the* SON, *who stands on one side at the back; then the* STEPDAUGHTER *who also detaches herself from the others – downstage and leaning against the proscenium arch. At first astonished at this development, then overcome with admiration, the Actors now burst into applause as at a show performed for their benefit.*

DIRECTOR: (*Bowled over at first, then indignant.*) Oh, stop this! Silence please! (*Then, turning to the Characters.*) And you, leave! Get out of here! (*To the* STAGE MANAGER.) For God's sake, get them out!

STAGE MANAGER: (*Stepping forward but then stopping, as if held back by a strange dismay.*) Go! Go!

FATHER: (*To the* DIRECTOR.) No, look, we, um –

DIRECTOR: (*Shouting.*) I tell you we've got to work!

LEADING MAN: It's not right to fool around like this …

FATHER: (*Resolute, stepping forward.*) I'm amazed at your incredulity! You're accustomed to seeing the created characters of an author spring to life, aren't you, right here on this stage, the one confronting the other? Perhaps the trouble is there's no script *there* (*pointing to the* PROMPTER'*s box*) with us in it?

STEPDAUGHTER: (*Going right up to the* DIRECTOR, *smiling, coquettish.*) Believe me, we really are six characters, sir. Very interesting ones at that. But lost. Adrift.

FATHER: (*Brushing her aside.*) Very well: lost, adrift. (*Going right on.*) In the sense, that is, that the author who created us, made us live, did not wish, or simply and materially was not able, to place us in the world of art. And that was a real crime, sir, because whoever has the luck to be born a living character can also laugh at death. He will never die! The man will die, the writer, the instrument of creation; the creature will never die! And to have eternal life it doesn't even take extraordinary gifts, nor the performance of miracles. Who was Sancho Panza? Who was Don Abbondio? But they live forever because, as live germs, they have the luck to find a fertile matrix, an imagination which knew how to raise and nourish them, make them live through all eternity!

DIRECTOR: That's all well and good. But what do you people want here?

FATHER: We want to live, sir.

DIRECTOR: (*Ironically.*) Through all eternity?

FATHER: No, sir. But for a moment at least. In you.

AN ACTOR: Well, well, well!

LEADING LADY: They want to live in us.

JUVENILE LEAD: (*Pointing to the* STEPDAUGHTER.) Well, I've no objection, so long as I get that one.

FATHER: Now look, look. The play is still in the making. (*To the* DIRECTOR.) But if you wish, and your actors wish, we can make it right away. Acting in concert.

LEADING MAN: (*Annoyed.*) Concert? We don't put on concerts! We do plays, dramas, comedies!

FATHER: Very good. That's why we came.

DIRECTOR: Well, where's the script?

FATHER: Inside us, sir. (*The Actors laugh.*) The drama is inside us. It is us. And we're impatient to perform it. According to the dictates of the passion within us.

STEPDAUGHTER: (*Scornful, with treacherous grace, deliberate impudence.*) My passion – if you only knew, sir! My passion – for him! (*She points to* FATHER *and makes as if to embrace him but then breaks into a strident laugh.*)

FATHER: (*An angry interjection.*) You keep out of this now. And please don't laugh that way!

STEPDAUGHTER: No? Then, ladies and gentlemen, permit me. A two months' orphan, I shall dance and sing for you all. Watch how! (*She mischievously starts to sing 'Beware of Chu Chin Chow' by Dave Stamper, reduced to fox trot or slow one-step by Francis Salabert: the first verse, accompanied by a step or two of dancing. While she sings and dances, the Actors, especially the young ones, as if drawn by some strange fascination, move toward her and half raise their hands as if to take hold of her. She runs away and when the Actors burst into applause she just stands there, remote, abstracted, while the* DIRECTOR *protests.*)

ACTORS AND ACTRESSES: (*Laughing and clapping.*) Brava! Fine! Splendid!

DIRECTOR: (*Annoyed.*) Silence! What do you think this is, a night spot? (*Taking* FATHER *a step or two to one side, with a certain amount of consternation.*) Tell me something. Is she crazy?

FATHER: Crazy? Of course not. It's much worse than that.

STEPDAUGHTER: (*Running over at once to the* DIRECTOR.) Worse! Worse! Not crazy but worse! Just listen: I'll play it for you right now, this drama, and at a certain point you'll see me – when this dear little thing – (*she takes the* LITTLE GIRL *who is beside* MOTHER *by the hand and leads her to the* DIRECTOR) – isn't she darling? (*Takes her in her arms and kisses her.*) Sweetie! Sweetie! (*Puts her down again and adds with almost involuntary emotion.*) Well, when God suddenly takes this little sweetheart away from her poor mother, and that idiot there – (*thrusting the* BOY *forward, rudely seizing him by a sleeve*) does the stupidest of things, like the nitwit that he is, (*with a shove she drives him back toward* MOTHER) then you will see me take to my heels. Yes, ladies and gentlemen, take to my heels! I can hardly wait for that moment. For after what happened between him and me – (*she points to* FATHER *with a horrible wink*) something very intimate, you understand – I can't stay in such company any longer, witnessing the anguish of our mother on account of that fool there – (*She points to the* SON.) Just look at him, look at him! – how indifferent, how frozen, because he is the legitimate son, that's what he is, full of contempt for me, for him (*the* BOY), and for that little creature (*the* LITTLE GIRL), because we three are bastards, d'you see? bastards. (*Goes to* MOTHER *and embraces her.*) And this poor mother, the common mother of us all, he – well, he doesn't want to acknowledge her as *his* mother too, and he looks down on her, that's what he does, looks on her as only mother of us three bastards, the wretch! (*She says this rapidly in a state of extreme excitement. Her voice swells to the word: 'bastards!' and descends again to the final 'wretch,' almost spitting it out.*)

MOTHER: (*To the* DIRECTOR, *with infinite anguish.*) In the name of these two small children, sir, I implore you … (*She grows faint and sways.*) Oh, heavens …

FATHER: (*Rushing over to support her with almost all the Actors who are astonished and scared.*) Please! Please, a chair, a chair for this poor widow!

ACTORS: (*Rushing over.*) – Is it true then? – She's *really* fainting?

DIRECTOR: A chair!

One of the Actors proffers a chair. The others stand around, ready to help. MOTHER, *seated, tries to stop* FATHER *from lifting the veil that hides her face.*

FATHER: (*To the* DIRECTOR.) Look at her, look at her …

MOTHER: Heavens, no, stop it!

FATHER: Let them see you. (*He lifts her veil.*)

MOTHER: (*Rising and covering her face with her hands, desperate.*) Oh, sir, please stop this man from carrying out his plan. It's horrible for me!

DIRECTOR: (*Surprised, stunned.*) I don't know where we're at! What's this all about? (*To father.*) Is this your wife?

FATHER: (*At once.*) Yes, sir, my wife.

DIRECTOR: Then how is she a widow, if you're alive?

The Actors relieve their astonishment in a loud burst of laughter.

FATHER: (*Wounded, with bitter resentment.*) Don't laugh! Don't laugh like that! Please! Just that is her drama, sir. She had another man. Another man who should be here!

MOTHER: (*With a shout.*) No! No!

STEPDAUGHTER: He had the good luck to die. Two months ago, as I told you. We're still in mourning, as you see.

FATHER: But he's absent, you see, not just because he's dead. He's absent – take a look at her, sir, and you will understand at once! – Her drama wasn't in the love of two men for whom she was incapable of feeling anything – except maybe a little gratitude (not to me, but to him) – She is not a woman, she is a mother! – And her drama – a powerful one, very powerful – is in fact all in those four children which she bore to her two men.

MOTHER: *My* men? Have you the gall to say I wanted two men? It was him, sir. He forced the other man on me. Compelled – yes, compelled – me to go off with him!

STEPDAUGHTER: (*Cutting in, roused.*) It's not true!

MOTHER: (*Astounded.*) How d'you mean, not true?

STEPDAUGHTER: It's not true! It's not true!

MOTHER: And what can you know about it?

STEPDAUGHTER: It's not true. (*To the* DIRECTOR.) Don't believe it. Know why she says it? For his sake. (*Pointing to the son.*) His indifference tortures her, destroys her. She wants him to believe that, if she abandoned him when he was two, it was because he (*FATHER*) compelled her to.

MOTHER: (*With violence.*) He did compel me, he did compel me, as God is my witness! (*To the* DIRECTOR.) Ask him if that isn't true. (*Her husband.*) Make him tell him. (*The* SON.) She couldn't know anything about it.

STEPDAUGHTER: With my father, while he lived, I know you were always happy and content. Deny it if you can.

MOTHER: I don't deny it, I don't …

STEPDAUGHTER: He loved you, he cared for you! (*To the* BOY, *with rage.*) Isn't that so? Say it! Why don't you speak, you dope?

MOTHER: Leave the poor boy alone. Why d'you want to make me out ungrateful, daughter? I have no wish to offend your father! I told him (*FATHER*) I didn't abandon my son and my home for my own pleasure. It wasn't my fault.

FATHER: That's true, sir. It was mine.

Pause.

LEADING MAN: (*To his companions.*) What a show!

LEADING LADY: And *they* put it on – for us.

JUVENILE LEAD: Quite a change!

DIRECTOR: (*Who is now beginning to get very interested.*) Let's listen to this, let's listen! (*And saying this, he goes down one of the stairways into the auditorium, and stands in front of the stage, as if to receive a spectator's impression of the show.*)

SON: (*Without moving from his position, cold, quiet, ironic.*) Oh yes, you can now listen to the philosophy lecture. He will tell you about the Demon of Experiment.

FATHER: You are a cynical idiot, as I've told you a hundred times. (*To the* DIRECTOR, *now in the auditorium.*) He mocks me, sir, on account of that phrase I found to excuse myself with.

SON: (*Contemptuously.*) Phrases!

FATHER: Phrases! Phrases! As if they were not a comfort to everyone: in the face of some unexplained fact, in the face of an evil that eats into us, to find a word that says nothing but at least quiets us down!

STEPDAUGHTER: Quiets our guilt feelings too. That above all.

FATHER: Our guilt feelings? Not so. I have never quieted my guilt feelings with words alone.

STEPDAUGHTER: It took a little money as well, didn't it, it took a little dough! The hundred lire he was going to pay me, ladies and gentlemen!

Movement of horror among the Actors.

SON: (*With contempt toward the* STEPDAUGHTER.) That's filthy.

STEPDAUGHTER: Filthy? The dough was there. In a small pale blue envelope on the mahogany table in the room behind the shop. Madam Pace's (*she pronounces it 'Pah-chay'*) shop. One of those Madams who lure us poor girls from good families into their *ateliers* under the pretext of selling *Robes et Manteaux.*

SON: And with those hundred lire he was going to pay she has bought the right to tyrannize over us all. Only it so happens – I'd have you know – that he never actually incurred the debt.

STEPDAUGHTER: Oh, oh, but we were really going to it, I assure you! (*She bursts out laughing.*)

MOTHER: (*Rising in protest.*) Shame, daughter! Shame!

STEPDAUGHTER: (*Quickly.*) Shame? It's my revenge! I am frantic, sir, frantic to live it, live that scene! The room ... here's the shop window with the coats in it; there's the bed-sofa; the mirror; a screen; and in front of the window the little mahogany table with the hundred lire in the pale blue envelope. I can see it. I could take it. But you men should turn away now: I'm almost naked. I don't blush any more. It's he that blushes now. (*Points to* FATHER.) But I assure you he was very pale, very pale, at that moment. (*To the* DIRECTOR.) You must believe me, sir.

DIRECTOR: You lost me some time ago.

FATHER: Of course! Getting it thrown at you like that! Restore a little order, sir, and let *me* speak. And never mind this ferocious girl. She's trying to heap opprobrium on me by withholding the relevant explanations!

STEPDAUGHTER: This is no place for longwinded narratives!

FATHER: I said – explanations.

STEPDAUGHTER: Oh, certainly. Those that suit your turn.

At this point, the DIRECTOR *returns to the stage to restore order.*

FATHER: But that's the whole root of the evil. Words. Each of us has, inside him, a world of things – to everyone, his world of things. And how can we understand each other, sir, if, in the words I speak, I put the sense and value of things as they are inside me, whereas the man who hears them inevitably receives them in the sense and with the value they have for him, the sense and value of the world inside him? We think we understand each other but we never do. Consider: the compassion, all the compassion I feel for this woman (MOTHER) has been received by her as the most ferocious of cruelties!

MOTHER: You ran me out of the house.

FATHER: Hear that? Ran her out. It *seemed to her* that I ran her out.

MOTHER: You can talk; I can't ... But, look, sir, after he married me ... and who knows why he did? I was poor, of humble birth ...

FATHER: And that's why. I married you for your ... humility. I loved you for it, believing ... (*He breaks off, seeing her gestured denials; seeing the impossibility of making himself understood by her, he opens his arms wide in a gesture of despair, and turns to the* DIRECTOR.) See that? She says No. It's scarifying, isn't it, sir, scarifying, this deafness of hers, this mental deafness! She has a heart, oh yes, where her children are concerned! But she's deaf, deaf in the brain, deaf, sir, to the point of desperation!

STEPDAUGHTER: (*To the* DIRECTOR.) All right, but now make him tell you what his intelligence has ever done for us.

FATHER: If we could only foresee all the evil that can result from the good we believe we're doing!

At this point, the LEADING LADY, *who has been on hot coals seeing the* LEADING MAN *flirt with the* STEPDAUGHTER, *steps forward and asks of the* DIRECTOR:

LEADING LADY: Excuse me, is the rehearsal continuing?

DIRECTOR: Yes, of course! But let me listen a moment.

JUVENILE LEAD: This is something quite new.

INGENUE: Very interesting!

LEADING LADY: If that sort of thing interests you. (*And she darts a look at the* LEADING MAN.)

DIRECTOR: (*To* FATHER.) But you must give us *clear* explanations. (*He goes and sits down.*)

FATHER: Right. Yes. Listen. There was a man working for me. A poor man. As my secretary. Very devoted to me. Understood *her* (MOTHER) very well. There was mutual understanding between them. Nothing wrong in it. They thought no harm at all. Nothing off-color about it. No, no, he knew his place, as she did. They didn't do anything wrong. Didn't even think it.

STEPDAUGHTER: So he thought it *for* them. And did it.

FATHER: It's not true! I wanted to do them some good. And myself too, oh yes, I admit. I'd got to this point, sir: I couldn't say a word to either of them but they would exchange a significant look. The one would consult the eyes of the other, asking how what I had said should be taken, if they didn't want to put me in a rage. That sufficed, you will understand, to keep me continually in a rage, in a state of unbearable exasperation.

DIRECTOR: Excuse me, why didn't you fire him, this secretary?

FATHER: Good question! That's what I did do, sir. But then I had to see that poor woman remain in my house, a lost soul. Like an animal without a master that one takes pity on and carries home.

MOTHER: No, no, it's –

FATHER: (*At once, turning to her to get it in first.*) Your son? Right?

MOTHER: He'd already snatched my son from me.

FATHER: But not from cruelty. Just so he'd grow up strong and healthy. In touch with the soil.

STEPDAUGHTER: (*Pointing at the latter, ironic.*) And just look at him!

FATHER: (*At once.*) Uh? Is it also my fault if he then grew up this way? I sent him to a wet nurse, sir, in the country, a peasant woman. I didn't find her (*MOTHER*) strong enough, despite her humble origin. I'd married her for similar reasons, as I said. All nonsense maybe, but there we are. I always had these confounded aspirations toward a certain solidity, toward what is morally sound. (*Here the* STEPDAUGHTER *bursts out laughing.*) Make her stop that! It's unbearable!

DIRECTOR: Stop it. I can't hear, for Heaven's sake!

Suddenly, again, as the DIRECTOR *rebukes her, she is withdrawn and remote, her laughter cut off in the middle. The* DIRECTOR *goes down again from the stage to get an impression of the scene.*

FATHER: I couldn't bear to be with that woman any more. (*Points to* MOTHER.) Not so much, believe me, because she irritated me, and even made me feel physically ill, as because of the pain – a veritable anguish – that I felt on her account.

MOTHER: And he sent me away!

FATHER: Well provided for. And to that man. Yes, sir. So she could be free of me.

MOTHER: And so *he* could be free.

FATHER: That, too. I admit it. And much evil resulted. But I intended good. And more for her than for me, I swear it! (*He folds his arms across his chest. Then, suddenly, turning to* MOTHER.) I never lost sight of you, never lost sight of you till, from one day to the next, unbeknown to me, he carried you off to another town. He noticed I was interested in her, you see, but that was silly, because my interest was absolutely pure, absolutely without ulterior motive. The interest I took in her new family, as it grew up, had an unbelievable tenderness to it. Even she should bear witness to that! (*He points to the* STEPDAUGHTER.)

STEPDAUGHTER: Oh, very much so! I was a little sweetie. Pigtails over my shoulders. Panties coming down a little bit below my skirt. A little sweetie. He would see me coming out of school, at the gate. He would come and see me as I grew up …

FATHER: This is outrageous. You're betraying me!

STEPDAUGHTER: I'm not! What do you mean?

FATHER: Outrageous. Outrageous. (*Immediately, still excited, he continues in a tone of explanation, to the* DIRECTOR.) My house, sir, when she had left it, at once seemed empty. (*Points to* MOTHER.) She was an incubus. But she filled my house for me. Left alone, I wandered through these rooms like a fly without a head. This fellow here (*the* SON) was raised away from home. Somehow, when he got back, he didn't seem mine any more. Without a mother between me and him, he grew up on his own, apart, without any relationship to me, emotional or intellectual. And then – strange, sir, but true – first I grew curious, then I was gradually attracted toward *her* family, which I had brought into being. The thought of *this* family began to fill the void around me. I had to – really had to – believe she was at peace, absorbed in the simplest cares of life, lucky to be away and far removed from the complicated torments of my spirit. And to have proof of this, I would go and see that little girl at the school gate.

STEPDAUGHTER: Correct! He followed me home, smiled at me and, when I was home, waved to me, like this! I would open my eyes wide and look at him suspiciously. I didn't know who it was. I told Mother. And she guessed right away it was him. (*MOTHER nods.*) At first she didn't want to send me back to school for several days. When I did go, I saw him again at the gate – the clown! – with a brown paper bag in his hand. He came up to me, caressed me, and took from the bag a lovely big Florentine straw hat with a ring of little May roses round it – for me!

DIRECTOR: You're making too long a story of this.

SON: (*Contemptuously.*) Story is right! Fiction! Literature!

FATHER: Literature? This is life, sir. Passion!

DIRECTOR: Maybe! But not actable!

FATHER: I agree. This is all preliminary. I wouldn't *want* you to act it. As you see, in fact, she (*the* STEPDAUGHTER) is no longer that little girl with pigtails –

STEPDAUGHTER: – and the panties showing below her skirt!

FATHER: The drama comes now, sir. Novel, complex –

STEPDAUGHTER: (*Gloomy, fierce, steps forward.*) – What my father's death meant for us was –

FATHER: (*Not giving her time to continue.*) – poverty, sir. They returned, unbeknownst to me. She's so thickheaded. (*Pointing to* MOTHER.) It's true she can hardly write herself, but she could have had her daughter write, or her son, telling me they were in need!

MOTHER: But, sir, how could I have guessed he felt the way he did?

FATHER: Which is just where you always went wrong. You could never guess how I felt about anything!

MOTHER: After so many years of separation, with all that had happened …

FATHER: And is it my fault if that fellow carried you off as he did? (*Turning to the* DIRECTOR.) From one day to the next, as I say. He'd found some job someplace. I couldn't even trace them. Necessarily, then, my interest dwindled, with the years. The drama breaks out, sir, unforeseen and violent, at their return. When I, alas, was impelled by the misery of my still living flesh … Oh, and what misery that is for a man who is alone, who has not wanted to form debasing relationships, not yet old enough to do without a woman, and no longer young enough to go and look for one without shame! Misery? It's horror, horror, because no woman can give him love any more. – Knowing this, one should go without! Well, sir, on the outside, when other people are watching, each man is clothed in dignity: but, on the inside, he knows what unconfessable things are going on within him. One gives way, gives way to temptation, to rise again, right afterward, of course, in a great hurry to put our dignity together again, complete, solid, a stone on a grave that hides and buries from our eyes every sign of our shame and even the very memory of it! It's like that with everybody. Only the courage to say it is lacking – to say certain things.

STEPDAUGHTER: The courage to do them, though – everybody's got that.

FATHER: Everybody. But in secret. That's why it takes more courage to say them. A man only has to say them and it's all over: he's labeled a cynic. But, sir, he isn't! He's just like everybody else. Better! He's better because he's not afraid to reveal, by the light of intelligence, the red stain of shame, there, in the human beast, which closes its eyes to it. Woman – yes, woman – what is she like, actually? She looks at us, inviting, tantalizing. You take hold of her. She's no sooner in your arms than she shuts her eyes. It is the sign of her submission. The sign with which she tells the man: Blind yourself for I am blind.

STEPDAUGHTER: How about when she no longer keeps them shut? When she no longer feels the need to hide the red stain of shame from herself by closing her eyes, and instead, her eyes dry now and impassive, sees the shame of the man, who has blinded himself even without love? They make me vomit, all those intellectual elaborations, this philosophy that begins by revealing the beast and then goes on to excuse it and save its soul … I can't bear to hear about it! Because when a man feels obliged to *reduce* life this way, reduce it all to 'the beast,' throwing overboard every vestige of the truly human, every aspiration after chastity, all feelings of purity, of the ideal, of duties, of modesty, of shame, then nothing is more contemptible, more nauseating than his wretched guilt feelings! Crocodile tears!

DIRECTOR: Let's get to the facts, to the facts! This is just discussion.

FATHER: Very well. But a fact is like a sack. When it's empty, it won't stand up. To make it stand up you must first pour into it the reasons and feelings by which it exists. I couldn't know that – when that man died and they returned here in poverty – she went out to work as a dressmaker to support the children, nor that the person she went to work for was that … that Madam Pace!

STEPDAUGHTER: A highclass dressmaker, if you'd all like to know! To all appearances, she serves fine ladies, but then she arranges things so that the fine ladies serve *her* … without prejudice to ladies not so fine!

MOTHER: Believe me, sir, I never had the slightest suspicion that that old witch hired me because she had her eye on my daughter …

STEPDAUGHTER: Poor mama! Do you know, sir, what the woman did when I brought her my mother's work? She would point out to me the material she'd ruined by giving it to my mother to sew. And she deducted for that, she deducted. And so, you understand, I paid, while that poor creature thought she was making sacrifices for me and those two by sewing, even at night, Madam Pace's material!

Indignant movements and exclamations from the Actors.

DIRECTOR: (*Without pause.*) And there, one day, you met –

STEPDAUGHTER: (*Pointing to* FATHER.) – him, him, yes sir! An old client! Now there's a scene for you to put on! Superb!

FATHER: Interrupted by her – mother –

STEPDAUGHTER: (*Without pause, treacherously.*) – almost in time! –

FATHER: (*Shouting.*) No, no, *in* time! Because, luckily, I recognized the girl in time. And I took them all back, sir, into my home. Now try to visualize my situation and hers, the one confronting the other – she as you see her now, myself unable to look her in the face any more.

STEPDAUGHTER: It's too absurd! But – afterward – was it possible for me to be a modest little miss, virtuous and well-bred, in accordance with those confounded aspirations toward a certain solidity, toward what is morally sound?

FATHER: And therein lies the drama, sir, as far as I'm concerned: in my awareness that each of us thinks of himself as *one* but that, well, it's not true, each of us is many, oh so many, sir, according to the possibilities of being that are in us. We are one thing for this person, another for that. Already *two* utterly different things! And with it all, the illusion of being always one thing for all men, and always this one thing in every single action. It's not true! Not true! We realize as much when, by some unfortunate chance, in one or another of our acts, we find ourselves suspended, hooked. We see, I mean, that we are not wholly in that act, and that therefore it would be abominably unjust to judge us by that act alone, to hold us suspended, hooked, in the pillory, our whole life long, as if our life were summed up in that act! Now do you understand this girl's treachery? She surprised me in a place, in an act, in which she should never have had to know me – I couldn't be that way for her. And she wants to give me a reality such as I could never have expected I would have to assume for her, the reality of a fleeting moment, a shameful one, in my life! This, sir, this is what I feel most strongly. And you will see that the drama will derive tremendous value from this. But now add the situation of the others! His … (*He points to the* SON.)

SON: (*Shrugging contemptuously.*) Leave me out of this! It's none of my business.

FATHER: What? None of your business?

SON: None. And I *want* to be left out. I wasn't made to be one of you, and you know it.

STEPDAUGHTER: We're common, aren't we? – And he's so refined. – But from time to time I give him a hard, contemptuous look, and he looks down at the ground. You may have noticed that, sir. He looks down at the ground. For he knows the wrong he's done me.

SON: (*Hardly looking at her.*) Me?

STEPDAUGHTER: You! You! I'm on the streets because of you! (*A movement of horror from the Actors.*) Did you or did you not, by your attitude, deny us – I won't say the intimacy of home but even the hospitality which puts guests at their ease? We were the intruders, coming to invade the kingdom of your legitimacy! I'd like to have you see, sir, certain little scenes between just him and me! He says I tyrannized over them all. But it was entirely because of his attitude that I started to exploit the situation he calls filthy, a situation which had brought me into his home with my mother, who is also *his* mother, *as its mistress!*

SON: (*Coming slowly forward.*) They can't lose, sir, three against one, an easy game. But figure to yourself a son, sitting quietly at home, who one fine day sees a young woman arrive, an impudent type with her nose in the air, asking for his father, with whom she has heaven knows what business; and then he sees her return, in the same style, accompanied by that little girl over there; and finally he sees her treat his father – who can say why? – in a very ambiguous and cool manner, demanding money, in a tone that takes for granted that he *has* to give it, has to, is obligated –

FATHER: – but I *am* obligated: it's for your mother!

SON: How would I know? When, sir, (*to the* DIRECTOR) have I ever seen her? When have I ever heard her spoken of. One day I see her arrive with her, (*the* STEPDAUGHTER) with that boy, with that little girl. They say to me: 'It's your mother too, know that?' I manage to figure out from her carryings-on (*pointing at the* STEPDAUGHTER) why they arrived in our home from one day to the next … What I'm feeling and experiencing I can't put into words, and wouldn't want to. I wouldn't want to confess it, even to myself. It cannot therefore result in any action on my

part. You can see that. Believe me, sir, I'm a character that, dramatically speaking, remains unrealized. I'm out of place in their company. So please leave me out of it all!

FATHER: What? But it's just because you're so –

SON: (*In violent exasperation.*) – I'm so what? How would *you* know? When did you ever care about me?

FATHER: *Touché! Touché!* But isn't even that a dramatic situation? This withdrawnness of yours, so cruel to me, and to your mother who, on her return home is seeing you almost for the first time, a grown man she doesn't recognize, though she knows you're her son … (*Pointing out* MOTHER *to the* DIRECTOR.) Just look at her, she's crying.

STEPDAUGHTER: (*Angrily, stamping her foot.*) Like the fool she is!

FATHER: (*Pointing her out to the* DIRECTOR.) And she can't abide him, you know. (*Again referring to the* SON.) – He says it's none of his business. The truth is he's almost the pivot of the action. Look at that little boy, clinging to his mother all the time, scared, humiliated … It's all because of *him* (*the* SON). Perhaps the most painful situation of all is that little boy's: he feels alien, more than all the others, and the poor little thing is so mortified, so anguished at being taken into our home – out of charity, as it were … (*Confidentially.*) He's just like his father: humble, doesn't say anything …

DIRECTOR: He won't fit anyway. You've no idea what a nuisance children are on stage.

FATHER: But he wouldn't be a nuisance for long. Nor would the little girl, no, she's the first to go …

DIRECTOR: Very good, yes! The whole thing interests me very much indeed. I have a hunch, a definite hunch, that there's material here for a fine play!

STEPDAUGHTER: (*Trying to inject herself.*) With a character like me in it!

FATHER: (*Pushing her to one side in his anxiety to know what the* DIRECTOR *will decide.*) You be quiet!

DIRECTOR: (*Going right on, ignoring the interruption.*) Yes, it's new stuff …

FATHER: Very new!

DIRECTOR: You had some gall, though, to come and throw it at me this way …

FATHER: Well, you see, sir, born as we are to the stage …

DIRECTOR: You're amateurs, are you?

FATHER: No. I say: 'born to the stage' because …

DIRECTOR: Oh, come on, you must have done some acting!

FATHER: No, no, sir, only as every man acts the part assigned to him – by himself or others – in this life. In me you see passion itself, which – in almost all people, as it rises – invariably becomes a bit theatrical …

DIRECTOR: Well, never mind! Never mind about that! – You see, my dear sir, without the author … I could direct you to an author …

FATHER: No, no, look: you be the author!

DIRECTOR: Me? What are you talking about?

FATHER: Yes, you. You. Why not?

DIRECTOR: Because I've never been an author, that's why not!

FATHER: Couldn't you be one now, hm? There's nothing to it. Everyone's doing it. And your job is made all the easier by the fact that you have us – here – alive – right in front of your nose!

DIRECTOR: It wouldn't be enough.

FATHER: Not enough? Seeing us live our own drama …

DIRECTOR: I know, but you always need someone to write it!

FATHER: No. Just someone to take it down, maybe, since you have us here – in action – scene by scene. It'll be enough if we piece together a rough sketch for you, then you can rehearse it.

DIRECTOR: (*Tempted, goes up on stage again.*) Well, I'm almost, almost tempted … Just for kicks … We could actually rehearse …

FATHER: Of course you could! What scenes you'll see emerge! I can list them for you right away.

DIRECTOR: I'm tempted … I'm tempted … Let's give it a try … Come to my office. (*Turns to the Actors.*) Take a break, will you? But don't go away. We'll be back in fifteen or twenty minutes. (*To* FATHER.) Let's see what we can do … Maybe we can get something very extraordinary out of all this …

FATHER: We certainly can. Wouldn't it be better to take *them* along? (*He points to the Characters.*)

DIRECTOR: Yes, let them all come. (*Starts going off, then comes back to address the Actors.*) Now don't forget. Everyone on time. Fifteen minutes.

DIRECTOR and Six Characters cross the stage and disappear. The Actors stay there and look at one another in amazement.

LEADING MAN: Is he serious? What's he going to do?

JUVENILE: This is outright insanity.

A THIRD ACTOR: We have to improvise a drama right off the bat?

JUVENILE LEAD: That's right. Like Commedia dell'Arte.

LEADING LADY: Well, if he thinks *I'm* going to lend myself to that sort of thing …

INGENUE: Count me out.

A FOURTH ACTOR: (*Alluding to the Characters.*) I'd like to know who those people are.

A THIRD ACTOR: Who would they be? Madmen or crooks!

JUVENILE LEAD: And he's going to pay attention to them?

INGENUE: Carried away by vanity! Wants to be an author now …

LEADING MAN: It's out of this world. If this is what the theater is coming to, my friends …

A FIFTH ACTOR: I think it's rather fun.

A THIRD ACTOR: Well! We shall see. We shall see. (*And chatting thus among themselves, the Actors leave the stage, some using the little door at the back, others returning to their dressing rooms.*)

The curtain remains raised. The performance is interrupted by a twenty-minute intermission.

Bells ring. The performance is resumed.

From dressing rooms, from the door, and also from the house, the Actors, the STAGE MANAGER, *the* TECHNICIAN, *the* PROMPTER, *the* PROPERTY MAN *return to the stage; at the same time the* DIRECTOR *and the Six Characters emerge from the office.*

As soon as the house lights are out, the stage lighting is as before.

DIRECTOR: Let's go, everybody! Is everyone here? Quiet! We're beginning. (*Calls the* TECHNICIAN *by name.*)

TECHNICIAN: Here!

DIRECTOR: Set the stage for the parlour scene. Two wings and a backdrop with a door in it will do, quickly please!

The TECHNICIAN *at once runs to do the job, and does it while the* DIRECTOR *works things out with the* STAGE MANAGER, *the* PROPERTY MAN, *the* PROMPTER, *and the Actors. This indication of a set consists of two wings, a drop with a door in it, all in pink and gold stripes.*

DIRECTOR: (*To the* PROPERTY MAN.) See if we have some sort of bed-sofa in the prop room.

PROPERTY MAN: Yes, sir, there's the green one.

STEPDAUGHTER: No, no, not green! It was yellow, flowered, plush, and very big. Extremely comfortable.

PROPERTY MAN: Well, we have nothing like that.

DIRECTOR: But it doesn't matter. Bring the one you have.

STEPDAUGHTER: Doesn't matter? Madam Pace's famous chaise longue!

DIRECTOR: This is just for rehearsal. Please don't meddle! (*To the* STAGE MANAGER.) See if we have a display case – long and rather narrow.

STEPDAUGHTER: The table, the little mahogany table for the pale blue envelope!

STAGE MANAGER: (*To the* DIRECTOR.) There's the small one. Gilded.

DIRECTOR: All right. Get that one.

FATHER: A large mirror.

STEPDAUGHTER: And the screen. A screen, please, or what'll I do?

STAGE MANAGER: Yes, ma'am, we have lots of screens, don't worry.

DIRECTOR: (*To the* STEPDAUGHTER.) A few coat hangers?

STEPDAUGHTER: A great many, yes.

DIRECTOR: (*To the* STAGE MANAGER.) See how many we've got, and have them brought on.

STAGE MANAGER: Right, sir, I'll see to it.

The STAGE MANAGER *also hurries to do his job and while the* DIRECTOR *goes on talking with the* PROMPTER *and then with the Characters and the Actors, has the furniture carried on by stagehands and arranges it as he thinks fit.*

DIRECTOR: (*To the* PROMPTER.) Meanwhile you can get into position. Look: this is the outline of the scenes, act by act. (*He gives him several sheets of paper.*) You'll have to be a bit of a virtuoso today.

PROMPTER: Shorthand?

DIRECTOR: (*Pleasantly surprised.*) Oh, good! You know shorthand?

PROMPTER: I may not know prompting, but shorthand … (*Turning to a stagehand.*) Get me some paper from my room – quite a lot – all you can find!

The stagehand runs off and returns a little later with a wad of paper which he gives to the PROMPTER.

DIRECTOR: (*Going right on, to the PROMPTER.*) Follow the scenes line by line as we play them, and try to pin down the speeches, at least the most important ones. (*Then, turning to the Actors.*) Clear the stage please, everyone! Yes, come over to this side and pay close attention. (*He indicates the left.*)

LEADING LADY: Excuse me but –

DIRECTOR: (*Forestalling.*) There'll be no improvising, don't fret.

LEADING MAN: Then what are we to do?

DIRECTOR: Nothing. For now, just stop, look, and listen. Afterward you'll be given written parts. Right now we'll rehearse. As best we can. With them doing the rehearsing for us. (*He points to the Characters.*)

FATHER: (*Amid all the confusion on stage, as if he'd fallen from the clouds.*) We're rehearsing? How d'you mean?

DIRECTOR: Yes, for them. You rehearse for them. (*Indicates the Actors.*)

FATHER: But if we are the characters …

DIRECTOR: All right, you're characters, but, my dear sir, characters don't perform here, actors perform here. The characters are there, in the script (*He points to the PROMPTER's box.*) – when there *is* a script!

FATHER: Exactly! Since there isn't, and you gentlemen have the luck to have them right here, alive in front of you, those characters …

DIRECTOR: Oh, great! Want to do it all yourselves? Appear before the public, do the acting yourselves?

FATHER: Of course. Just as we are.

DIRECTOR: (*Ironically.*) I'll bet you'd put on a splendid show!

LEADING MAN: Then what's the use of staying?

DIRECTOR: (*Without irony, to the Characters.*) Don't run away with the idea that you can act! That's laughable … (*And in fact the Actors laugh.*) Hear that? They're laughing. (*Coming back to the point.*) I was forgetting. I must cast the show. It's quite easy. It casts itself. (*To the SECOND ACTRESS.*) You, ma'am, will play Mother. (*To FATHER.*) You'll have to find her a name.

FATHER: Amalia, sir.

DIRECTOR: But that's this lady's real name. We wouldn't want to call her by her real name!

FATHER: Why not? If that is her name … But of course, if it's to be this lady … (*He indicates the SECOND ACTRESS with a vague gesture.*) To me *she* (*MOTHER*) is Amalia. But suit yourself … (*He is getting more and more confused.*) I don't know what to tell you … I'm beginning to … oh, I don't know … to find my own words ringing false, they sound different somehow.

DIRECTOR: Don't bother about that, just don't bother about it. We can always find the right sound. As for the name, if you say Amalia, Amalia it shall be; or we'll find another. For now, we'll designate the characters thus: (*To the JUVENILE LEAD.*) You're the son. (*To the LEADING LADY.*) You, ma'am, are of course the stepdaughter.

STEPDAUGHTER: (*Excitedly.*) What, what? That one there is me? (*She bursts out laughing.*)

DIRECTOR: (*Mad.*) What is there to laugh at?

LEADING LADY: (*Aroused.*) No one has ever dared laugh at me! I insist on respect – or I quit!

STEPDAUGHTER: But, excuse me, I'm not laughing at you.

DIRECTOR: (*To the STEPDAUGHTER.*) You should consider yourself honored to be played by …

LEADING LADY: (*Without pause, contemptuously.*) – 'That one there!'

STEPDAUGHTER: But I wasn't speaking of you, believe me. I was speaking of me. I don't see me in you, that's all. I don't know why … I guess you're just not like me!

FATHER: That's it, exactly, my dear sir! What is *expressed* in us …

DIRECTOR: Expression, expression! You think that's your business? Not at all!

FATHER: Well, but what *we* express …

DIRECTOR: But you don't. You don't express. You provide us with raw material. The actors give it body and face, voice and gesture. They've given expression to much loftier material, let me tell you. Yours is on such a small scale that, if it stands up on stage at all, the credit, believe me, should all go to my actors.

FATHER: I don't dare contradict you, sir, but it's terribly painful for us who are as you see us – with these bodies, these faces –

DIRECTOR: (*Cutting in, out of patience.*) – that's where make-up comes in, my dear sir, for whatever concerns the face, the remedy is make-up!

FATHER: Yes. But the voice, gesture –

DIRECTOR: Oh, for Heaven's sake! You can't exist here! Here the actor acts you, and that's that!

FATHER: I understand, sir. But now perhaps I begin to guess also why our author who saw us, alive as we are, did not want to put us on stage. I don't want to offend your actors. God forbid! But I feel that seeing myself acted … I don't know by whom …

LEADING MAN: (*Rising with dignity and coming over, followed by the gay young Actresses who laugh.*) By me, if you've no objection.

FATHER: (*Humble, smooth.*) I'm very honored, sir. (*He bows.*) But however much art and willpower the gentleman puts into absorbing me into himself … (*He is bewildered now.*)

LEADING MAN: Finish. Finish.

The Actresses laugh.

FATHER: Well, the performance he will give, even forcing himself with make-up to resemble me, well, with that figure (*All the Actors laugh.*) he can hardly play me as I am. I shall rather be – even apart from the face – what he interprets me to be, as he feels I am – if he feels I am anything – and not as I feel myself inside myself. And it seems to me that whoever is called upon to judge us should take this into account.

DIRECTOR: So now you're thinking of what the critics will say? And I was still listening! Let the critics say what they want. We will concentrate on putting on your play! (*He walks away a little, and looks around.*) Come on, come on. Is the set ready? (*To the Actors and the Characters.*) Don't clutter up the stage, I want to be able to see! (*He goes down from the stage.*) Let's not lose any more time! (*To the STEPDAUGHTER.*) Does the set seem pretty good to you?

STEPDAUGHTER: Oh! But I can't recognize it!

DIRECTOR: Oh my God, don't tell me we should reconstruct Madam Pace's back room for you! (*To FATHER.*) Didn't you say a parlour with flowered wallpaper?

FATHER: Yes, sir. White.

DIRECTOR: It's not white. Stripes. But it doesn't matter. As for furniture we're in pretty good shape. That little table – bring it forward a bit! (*Stagehands do this. To the PROPERTY MAN.*) Meanwhile you get an envelope, possibly a light blue one, and give it to the gentleman. (*Indicating FATHER.*)

PROPERTY MAN: A letter envelope?

DIRECTOR AND FATHER: Yes, a letter envelope.

PROPERTY MAN: I'll be right back. (*He exits.*)

DIRECTOR: Come on, come on. It's the young lady's scene first. (*The LEADING LADY comes forward.*) No, no, wait. I said the young lady. (*Indicating the STEPDAUGHTER.*) You will just watch –

STEPDAUGHTER: (*Adding, without pause.*) – watch me live it!

LEADING LADY: (*Resenting this.*) I'll know how to live it too, don't worry, once I put myself in the role!

DIRECTOR: (*Raising his hands to his head.*) Please! No more chatter! Now, scene one. The Young Lady with Madam Pace. Oh, and how about this Madam Pace? (*Bewildered, looking around him, he climbs back on stage.*)

FATHER: She isn't with us, sir.

DIRECTOR: Then what do we do?

FATHER: But she's alive. She's alive too.

DIRECTOR: Fine. But where?

FATHER: I'll tell you. (*Turning to the Actresses.*) If you ladies will do me the favor of giving me your hats for a moment.

THE ACTRESSES: (*Surprised a little, laughing a little, in chorus.*) – What? – Our hats? – What does he say? – Why? – Oh, dear!

DIRECTOR: What are you going to do with the ladies' hats?

The Actors laugh.

FATHER: Oh, nothing. Just put them on these coathooks for a minute. And would some of you be so kind as to take your coats off too?

ACTORS: (*As before.*) Their coats too? – And then? – He's nuts!

AN ACTRESS OR TWO: (*As above.*) – But why? – Just the coats?

FATHER: Just so they can be hung there for a moment. Do me this favor. Will you?

ACTRESSES: (*Taking their hats off, and one or two of them their coats, too, continuing to laugh, and going to hang the hats here and there on the coathooks.*) – Well, why not? – There! – This is getting to be really funny! – Are we to put them on display?

FATHER: Exactly! That's just right, ma'am: on display!

DIRECTOR: May one inquire *why* you are doing this?

FATHER: Yes, sir. If we set the stage better, who knows but she may come to us, drawn by the objects of her trade … (*Inviting them to look toward the entrance at the back.*) Look! Look!

The entrance at the back opens, and MADAME PACE walks a few paces downstage, a hag of enormous fatness with a pompous wig of carrot-colored wool and a fiery red rose on one side of it, à l'espagnole, heavily made up, dressed with gauche elegance in garish red silk, a feathered fan in one hand and the other hand raised to hold a lighted cigarette between two fingers. At the sight of this apparition, the director and the Actors at once dash off the stage with a yell of terror, rushing down the stairs and making as if to flee up the aisle. The STEPDAUGHTER, on the other hand, runs to MADAME PACE – deferentially, as to her boss.

STEPDAUGHTER: (*Running to her.*) Here she is, here she is!

FATHER: (*Beaming.*) It's she! What did I tell you? Here she is!

DIRECTOR: (*Overcoming his first astonishment, and incensed now.*) What tricks are these?

The next four speeches are more or less simultaneous.

LEADING MAN: What goes on around here?

JUVENILE LEAD: Where on earth did she come from?

INGENUE: They must have been holding her in reserve.

LEADING LADY: Hocus pocus! Hocus pocus!

FATHER: (*Dominating these protests.*) Excuse me, though! Why, actually, would you want to destroy this prodigy in the name of vulgar truth, this miracle of a reality that is born of the stage itself – called into being by the stage, drawn here by the stage, and shaped by the stage – and which has more right to live on the stage than you have because it is much truer? Which of you actresses will later re-create Madame Pace? This lady *is* Madame Pace. You must admit that the actress who re-creates her will be less true than this lady – who is Madame Pace. Look: my daughter recognized her, and went over to her. Stand and watch the scene!

Hesitantly, the DIRECTOR and the Actors climb back on stage. But the scene between the STEPDAUGHTER and MADAME PACE has begun during the protest of the Actors and the father's answer: sotto voce, very quietly, in short naturally – as would never be possible on a stage. When, called to order by the FATHER, the Actors turn again to watch, they hear MADAME PACE, who has just placed her hand under the STEPDAUGHTER'S *chin in order to raise her head, talk unintelligibly. After trying to hear for a moment, they just give up.*

DIRECTOR: Well?

LEADING MAN: What's she saying?

LEADING LADY: One can't hear a thing.

JUVENILE LEAD: Louder!

STEPDAUGHTER: (*Leaving* MADAME PACE, *who smiles a priceless smile, and walking toward the Actors.*) Louder, huh? How d'you mean: louder? These aren't things that can be said louder. *I* was able to say them loudly – to shame him (*indicating the* FATHER) – that was my revenge. For Madam, it's different, my friends: it would mean – jail.

DIRECTOR: Oh my God! It's like that, is it? But, my dear young lady, in the theater one must be heard. And even we couldn't hear you, right here on the stage. How about an audience out front? There's a scene to be done. And anyway you *can* speak loudly – it's just between yourselves, we won't be standing here listening like now. Pretend you're alone. In a room. The back room of the shop. No one can hear you. (*The* STEPDAUGHTER *charmingly and with a mischievous smile tells him* No *with a repeated movement of the finger.*) Why not?

STEPDAUGHTER: (*Sotto voce, mysteriously.*) There's someone who'll hear if she (MADAME PACE) speaks loudly.

DIRECTOR: (*In consternation.*) Is someone else going to pop up now?

The Actors make as if to quit the stage again.

FATHER: No, no, sir. She means me. I'm to be there – behind the door –waiting. And Madam knows. So if you'll excuse me. I must be ready for my entrance. (*He starts to move.*)

DIRECTOR: (*Stopping him.*) No, wait. We must respect the exigencies of the theater. Before you get ready –

STEPDAUGHTER: (*Interrupting him.*) Let's get on with it! I tell you I'm dying with desire to live it, to live that scene! If he's ready, I'm more than ready!

DIRECTOR: (*Shouting.*) But first we have to get that scene out of you and her! (*Indicating* MADAME PACE.) Do you follow me?

STEPDAUGHTER: Oh dear, oh dear, she was telling me things you already know – that my mother's work had been badly done once again, the material is ruined, and I'm going to have to bear with her if I want her to go on helping us in our misery.

MADAME PACE: (*Coming forward with a great air of importance.*) Si, si, senor, porque yo no want profit. No advantage, no.

DIRECTOR: (*Almost scared.*) What, what? She talks like *that?!*

All the Actors loudly burst out laughing.

STEPDAUGHTER: (*Also laughing.*) Yes, sir, she talks like that – halfway between Spanish and English – very funny, isn't it?

MADAME PACE: Now that is not good manners, no, that you laugh at me! Yo hablo the English as good I can, senor!

DIRECTOR: And it *is* good! Yes! Do talk that way, ma'am! It's a sure-fire effect! There couldn't be anything better to, um, soften the crudity of the situation! Do talk that way! It's fine!

STEPDAUGHTER: Fine! Of course! To have certain propositions put to you in a lingo like that. Sure fire, isn't it? Because, sir, it seems almost a joke. When I hear there's 'an old senor' who wants to 'have good time conmigo,' I start to laugh – don't I, Madame Pace?

MADAME PACE: Old, viejo, no. Viejito – leetle beet old, si, darling? Better like that: if he no give you fun, he bring you prudencia.

MOTHER: (*Jumping up, to the stupefaction and consternation of all the Actors, who had been taking no notice of her, and who now respond to her shouts with a start and, smiling, try to restrain her, because she has grabbed* MADAME PACE'S *wig and thrown it on the floor.*) Witch! Witch! Murderess! My daughter!

STEPDAUGHTER: (*Running over to restrain her* MOTHER.) No, no, mama, no, please!

FATHER: (*Running over too at the same time.*) Calm down, calm down! Sit here.

MOTHER: Then send that woman away!

STEPDAUGHTER: (*To the* DIRECTOR, *who also has run over.*) It's not possible, not possible that my mother should be here!

FATHER: (*Also to the* DIRECTOR.) They can't be together. That's why, you see, the woman wasn't with us when we came. Their being together would spoil it, you understand.

DIRECTOR: It doesn't matter, doesn't matter at all. This is just a preliminary sketch. Everything helps. However confusing the elements, I'll piece them together somehow. (*Turning to the* MOTHER *and sitting her down again in her place.*) Come along, come along, ma'am, calm down: sit down again.

STEPDAUGHTER: (*Who meanwhile has moved center stage again. Turning to* MADAME PACE.) All right, let's go!

MADAME PACE: Ah, no! No thank you! Yo aqui no do nada with your mother present.

STEPDAUGHTER: Oh, come on! Bring in that old senor who wants to have good time conmigo! (*Turning imperiously to all the others.*) Yes, we've got to have it, this scene! – Come on, let's go! (*To* MADAME PACE.) You may leave.

MADAME PACE: Ah si, I go, I go, go seguramente … (*She makes her exit furiously, putting her wig back on, and looking haughtily at the Actors who applaud mockingly.*)

STEPDAUGHTER: (*To the* FATHER.) And you can make your entrance. No need to go out and come in again. Come here. Pretend, you're already in. Right. Now I'm here with bowed head, modest, huh? Let's go! Speak up! With a different voice, the voice of someone just in off the street: 'Hello, miss.'

DIRECTOR: (*By this time out front again.*) No look: are you directing this, or am I? (*To the* FATHER *who looks undecided and perplexed.*) Do it, yes. Go to the back. Don't leave the stage, though. And then come forward.

The FATHER *does it, almost dismayed. Very pale; but already clothed in the reality of his created life, he smiles as he approaches from the back, as if still alien to the drama which will break upon him. The Actors now pay attention to the scene which is beginning.*

DIRECTOR: (*Softly, in haste, to the* PROMPTER *in the box.*) And you, be ready now, ready to write!

The Scene

FATHER: (*Coming forward, with a different voice.*) Hello, miss.

STEPDAUGHTER: (*With bowed head and contained disgust.*) Hello.

FATHER: (*Scrutinizing her under her hat which almost hides her face and noting that she is very young, exclaims, almost to himself, a little out of complaisance and a little out of fear of compromising himself in a risky adventure.*) Oh … – Well, I was thinking, it wouldn't be the first time, hm? The first time you came here.

STEPDAUGHTER: (*As above.*) No, sir.

FATHER: You've been here other times? (*And when the* STEPDAUGHTER *nods.*) More than one? (*He waits a moment for her to answer, then again scrutinizes her under her hat; smiles; then says*) Well then, hm … it shouldn't any longer be so … May I take this hat off for you?

STEPDAUGHTER: (*Without pause, to forestall him, not now containing her disgust.*) No, sir, I will take it off! (*And she does so in haste, convulsed.*)

The MOTHER, *watching the scene with the son and with the two others, smaller and more her own, who are close to her all the time, forming a group at the opposite side of the stage from the Actors, is on tenterhooks as she follows the words and actions of* FATHER *and* STEPDAUGHTER *with varied expression: grief, disdain, anxiety, horror, now hiding her face, now emitting a moan.*

MOTHER: Oh God! My God!

FATHER: (*Is momentarily turned to stone by the moaning; then he reassumes the previous tone.*) Now give it to me: I'll hang it up for you. (*He takes the hat from her hands.*) But I could wish for a little hat worthier of such a dear, lovely little head! Would you like to help me choose one? From the many Madam has? – You wouldn't?

INGENUE: (*Interrupting.*) Oh now, come on, those are *our* hats!

DIRECTOR: (*Without pause, very angry.*) Silence, for Heaven's sake, don't try to be funny! – This is the stage. (*Turning back to the* STEPDAUGHTER.) Would you begin again, please?

STEPDAUGHTER: (*Beginning again.*) No, thank you, sir.

FATHER: Oh, come on now, don't say no. Accept one from me. To please me … There are some lovely ones you know. And we would make Madam happy. Why else does she put them on display?

STEPDAUGHTER: No, no, sir, look: I wouldn't even be able to wear it.

FATHER: You mean because of what the family would think when they saw you come home with a new hat on? Think nothing of it. Know how to handle that? What to tell them at home?

STEPDAUGHTER: (*Breaking out, at the end of her rope.*) But that's

not why, sir. I couldn't wear it because I'm … as you see me. You might surely have noticed! (*Points to her black attire.*)

FATHER: In mourning, yes. Excuse me. It's true: I do see it. I beg your pardon. I'm absolutely mortified, believe me.

STEPDAUGHTER: (*Forcing herself and plucking up courage to conquer her contempt and nausea.*) Enough! Enough! It's for me to thank you, it is not for you to be mortified or afflicted. Please pay no more attention to what I said. Even for me, you understand … (*She forces herself to smile and adds*) I need to forget I am dressed like this.

DIRECTOR: (*Interrupting, addressing himself to the* PROMPTER *in his box, and going up on stage again.*) Wait! Wait! Don't write. Leave that last sentence out, leave it out! (*Turning to the* FATHER *and* STEPDAUGHTER.) It's going very well indeed. (*Then to the* FATHER *alone.*) This is where you go into the part we prepared. (*To the Actors.*) Enchanting, that little hat scene, don't you agree?

STEPDAUGHTER: Oh, but the best is just coming. Why aren't we continuing?

DIRECTOR: Patience one moment. (*Again addressing himself to the Actors.*) Needs rather delicate handling, of course …

LEADING MAN: – With a certain *ease* –

LEADING LADY: Obviously But there's nothing to it. (*To the* LEADING MAN.) We can rehearse it at once, can't we?

LEADING MAN: As far as I'm … Very well, I'll go out and make my entrance. (*And he does go out by the back door, ready to re-enter.*)

DIRECTOR: (*To the* LEADING LADY.) And so, look, your scene with that Madame Pace is over. I'll write it up later. You are standing … Hey, where are you going?

LEADING LADY: Wait. I'm putting my hat back on … (*She does so, taking the hat from the hook.*)

DIRECTOR: Oh yes, good. – Now, you're standing here with your head bowed.

STEPDAUGHTER: (*Amused.*) But she's not wearing black!

LEADING LADY: I *shall* wear black! And I'll carry it better than you!

DIRECTOR: (*To the* STEPDAUGHTER.) Keep quiet, please! Just watch. You can learn something. (*Claps his hands.*) Get going, get going! The entrance! (*And he goes back out front to get an impression of the stage.*)

The door at the back opens, and the LEADING MAN *comes forward, with the relaxed, waggish manner of an elderly Don Juan. From the first speeches, the performance of the scene by the Actors is quite a different thing, without, however, having any element of parody in it – rather, it seems corrected, set to rights. Naturally, the* STEPDAUGHTER *and the* FATHER, *being quite unable to recognize themselves in this* LEADING LADY *and* LEADING MAN *but hearing them speak their own words, express in various ways, now with gestures, now with smiles, now with open protests, their surprise, their wonderment, their suffering, etc., as will be seen forthwith.*

The PROMPTER'S *voice is clearly heard from the box.*

LEADING MAN: Hello, miss.

FATHER: (*Without pause, unable to contain himself.*) No, no!

The STEPDAUGHTER, *seeing how the* LEADING MAN *makes his entrance, has burst out laughing.*

DIRECTOR: (*Coming from the proscenium, furious.*) Silence here! And stop that laughing at once! We can't go ahead till it stops.

STEPDAUGHTER: (*Coming from the proscenium.*) How can I help it? This lady (*the* LEADING LADY) just stands there. If she's supposed to be me, let me tell you that if anyone said hello to me in that manner and that tone of voice, I'd burst out laughing just as I actually did!

FATHER: (*Coming forward a little too.*) That's right … the manner, the tone …

DIRECTOR: Manner! Tone! Stand to one side now, and let me see the rehearsal.

LEADING MAN: (*Coming forward.*) If I'm to play an old man entering a house of ill –

DIRECTOR: Oh, pay no attention, please. Just begin again. It was going fine. (*Waiting for the Actor to resume.*) Now then …

LEADING MAN: Hello, miss.

LEADING LADY: Hello.

LEADING MAN: (*Re-creating the* FATHER'S *gesture of scrutinizing her under her hat, but then expressing very distinctly first the complaisance and then the fear.*) Oh … Well … I was thinking it wouldn't be the first time, I hope …

FATHER: (*Unable to help correcting him.*) Not 'I hope.' 'Would it?' 'Would it?'

DIRECTOR: He says: 'would it?' A question.

LEADING MAN: (*Pointing to the prompter.*) I heard: 'I hope.'

DIRECTOR: Same thing! 'Would it.' Or: 'I hope.' Continue, continue. – Now, maybe a bit less affected … Look, I'll do it for you. Watch me … (*Returns to the stage, then repeats the bit since the entrance.*) – Hello, miss.

LEADING LADY: Hello.

DIRECTOR: Oh, well … I was thinking … (*Turning to the* LEADING MAN *to have him note how he has looked at the* LEADING LADY *under her hat.*) Surprise … fear and complaisance. (*Then, going on, and turning to the* LEADING LADY.) It wouldn't be the first time, would it? The first time you came here. (*Again turning to the* LEADING MAN *with an inquiring look.*) Clear? (*To the* LEADING LADY.) Then you say: No, sir (*Back to the* LEADING MAN.) How shall I put it? Plasticity! (*Goes back out front.*)

LEADING LADY: No, sir.

LEADING MAN: You came here other times? More than one?

DIRECTOR: No, no, wait. (*Indicating the leading lady.*) First let her nod. 'You came here other times?'

The LEADING LADY *raises her head a little, closes her eyes painfully as if in disgust, then nods it twice at the word 'Down' from the* DIRECTOR.

STEPDAUGHTER: (*Involuntarily.*) Oh, my God! (*And she at once puts her hand on her mouth to keep the laughter in.*)

DIRECTOR: (*Turning round.*) What is it?

STEPDAUGHTER: (*Without pause.*) Nothing, nothing.

DIRECTOR: (*To the* LEADING MAN.) That's your cue. Go straight on.

LEADING MAN: More than one? Well then, hm … it shouldn't any longer be so … May I take this little hat off for you?

The LEADING MAN *says this last speech in such a tone and accompanies it with such a gesture that the* STEPDAUGHTER, *her hands on her mouth, much as she wants to hold herself in, cannot contain her laughter, which comes bursting out through her fingers irresistibly and very loud.*

LEADING LADY: (*Returning to her place, enraged.*) Now look, I'm not going to be made a clown of by that person!

LEADING MAN: Nor am I. Let's stop.

DIRECTOR: (*To the* STEPDAUGHTER, *roaring.*) Stop it! Stop it!

STEPDAUGHTER: Yes, yes. Forgive me, forgive me …

DIRECTOR: You have no manners! You're presumptuous! So there!

FATHER: (*Seeking to intervene.*) That's true, yes, that's true, sir, but forgive …

DIRECTOR: (*On stage again.*) Forgive nothing! It's disgusting!

FATHER: Yes, sir. But believe me, it has such a strange effect –

DIRECTOR: Strange? Strange? What's strange about it?

FATHER: I admire your actors, sir, I really admire them, this gentleman (LEADING MAN) and that lady (LEADING LADY) but assuredly … well, they're not us …

DIRECTOR: So what? How *could* they be you, if they're the actors?

FATHER: Exactly, the actors! And they play our parts well, both of them. But of course, to us, they seem something else – that tries to be the same but simply isn't!

DIRECTOR: How d'you mean: isn't? What is it then?

FATHER: Something that … becomes theirs. And stops being ours.

DIRECTOR: Necessarily! I explained that to you!

FATHER: Yes. I understand, I do under –

DIRECTOR: Then that will be enough! (*Turning to the Actors.*) We'll be rehearsing by ourselves as we usually do. Rehearsing with authors present has always been hell, in my experience. There's no satisfying them. (*Turning to the* FATHER *and the* STEPDAUGHTER.) Come along then. Let's resume. And let's hope you find it possible not to laugh this time.

STEPDAUGHTER: Oh, no, I won't be laughing this time around. My big moment comes up now. Don't worry!

DIRECTOR: Very well, when she says: 'Please pay no more attention to what I said … Even for me – you understand …' (*Turning to the* FATHER.) You'll have to cut right in with: 'I understand, oh yes, I understand …' and ask her right away –

STEPDAUGHTER: (*Interrupting.*) Oh? Ask me what?

DIRECTOR: – why she is in mourning.

STEPDAUGHTER: No, no, look: when I told him I needed to forget I was dressed like this, do you know what his answer was? 'Oh, good! Then let's take that little dress right off, shall we?'

DIRECTOR: Great! Terrific! It'll knock 'em right out of their seats!

STEPDAUGHTER: But it's the truth.

DIRECTOR: Truth, is it? Well, well, well. This is the theater! Our motto is: truth up to a certain point!

STEPDAUGHTER: Then what would you propose?

DIRECTOR: You'll see. You'll see it. Just leave me alone.

STEPDAUGHTER: Certainly not. From my nausea – from all the reasons one more cruel than another why I am what I am, why I am 'that one there'– you'd like to cook up some romantic, sentimental concoction, wouldn't you? He asks me why I'm in mourning, and I tell him, through my tears, that Papa died two months ago! No, my dear sir! He has to say what he did say: 'Then let's take that little dress right off, shall we?' And I, with my two-months mourning in my heart, went back there – you see? Behind that screen – and – my fingers quivering with shame, with loathing – I took off my dress, took off my corset …

DIRECTOR: (*Running his hands through his hair.*) Good God, what are you saying?

STEPDAUGHTER: (*Shouting frantically.*) The truth, sir, the truth!

DIRECTOR: Well, yes, of course, that must be the truth … and I quite understand your horror, young lady. Would you try to understand that all that is impossible *on the stage?*

STEPDAUGHTER: Impossible? Then, thanks very much, I'm leaving.

DIRECTOR: No, no, look …

STEPDAUGHTER: I'm leaving, I'm leaving! You went in that room, you two, didn't you, and figured out 'what is possible on the stage'? Thanks very much. I see it all. He wants to skip to the point where he can act out his (*exaggerating*) spiritual travail! But I want to play *my* drama. Mine!

DIRECTOR: (*Annoyed, and shrugging haughtily.*) Oh, well, *your* drama. This is not just your drama, if I may say so. How about the drama of the others? His drama (*the FATHER*), hers (*the MOTHER*)? We can't let one character hog the limelight, just taking the whole stage over, and overshadowing all the others! Everything must be placed within the frame of one harmonious picture! We must perform only what is performable! I know as well as you do that each of us has a whole life of his own inside him and would like to bring it all out. But the difficult thing is this: to bring out only as much as is needed – in relation to the others – and in this to *imply* all the rest, *suggest* what remains inside! Oh, it would be nice if every character could come down to the footlights and tell the audience just what is brewing inside him – in a fine monologue or, if you will, a lecture! (*Good-natured, conciliatory.*) Miss, you will have to *contain yourself.* And it will be in your interest. It could make a bad impression – let me warn you – this tearing fury, this desperate disgust – since, if I may say so,

you confessed having been with others at Madame Pace's – before him – more than once!

STEPDAUGHTER: (*Lowering her head, pausing to recollect, a deeper note in her voice.*) It's true. But to me the others are also *him,* all of them equally!

DIRECTOR: (*Not getting it.*) The others? How d'you mean?

STEPDAUGHTER: People 'go wrong.' And wrong follows on the heels of wrong. Who is responsible, if not whoever it was who first brought them down? Isn't that always the case? And for me that is him. Even before I was born. Look at him, and see if it isn't so.

DIRECTOR: Very good. And if he has so much to feel guilty about, can't you appreciate how it must weigh him down? So let's at least permit him to act it out.

STEPDAUGHTER: And how, may I ask, how could he act out all that 'noble' guilt, all those so 'moral' torments, if you propose to spare him the horror of one day finding in his arms – after having bade her take off the black clothes that marked her recent loss – a woman now, and already gone wrong – that little girl, sir, that little girl whom he used to go watch coming out of school?

She says these last words in a voice trembling with emotion. The MOTHER, hearing her say this, overcome with uncontrollable anguish, which comes out first in suffocated moans and subsequently bursts out in bitter weeping. The emotion takes hold of everyone. Long pause.

STEPDAUGHTER: (*As soon as the MOTHER gives signs of calming down, somber, determined.*) We're just among ourselves now. Still unknown to the public. Tomorrow you will make of us the show you have in mind. You will put it together in your way. But would you like to really see – our drama? Have it explode – the real thing?

DIRECTOR: Of course. Nothing I'd like better. And I'll use as much of it as I possibly can!

STEPDAUGHTER: Very well. Have this mother here go out.

MOTHER: (*Ceasing to weep, with a loud cry.*) No, no! Don't allow this, don't allow it!

DIRECTOR: I only want to take a look, ma'am.

MOTHER: I can't, I just can't!

DIRECTOR: But if it's already happened? Excuse me but I just don't get it.

MOTHER: No, no, it's happening now. It's always happening. My torment is not a pretense! I am alive and present – always, in every moment of my torment – it keeps renewing itself, it too is alive and always present. But those two little ones over there – have you heard them speak? They cannot speak, sir, not any more! They still keep clinging to me – to keep my torment alive and present. For themselves they don't exist, don't exist any longer. And she (*the STEPDAUGHTER*), she just fled, ran away from me, she's lost, lost … If I see her before me now, it's for the same reason: to renew the torment, keep it always alive and present forever – the torment I've suffered on her account too – forever!

FATHER: (*Solemn.*) The eternal moment, sir, as I told you. She (*the STEPDAUGHTER*) is here to catch me, fix me, hold me there in the pillory, hanging there forever, hooked, in that single fleeting shameful moment of my life! She cannot give it up. And, actually, sir, *you* cannot spare me.

DIRECTOR: But I didn't say I wouldn't use that. On the contrary, it will be the nucleus of the whole first act. To the point where she (*the MOTHER*) surprises you.

FATHER: Yes, exactly. Because that is the sentence passed upon me: all our passion which has to culminate in her (*the MOTHER's*) final cry!

STEPDAUGHTER: It still rings in my ears. It's driven me out of my mind, that cry! – You can present me as you wish, sir, it doesn't matter. Even dressed. As long as at least my arms – just my arms – are bare. Because it was like this. (*She goes to the FATHER and rests her head on his chest.*) I was standing like this with my head on his chest and my arms round his neck like this. Then I saw something throbbing right here on my arm. A vein. Then, as if it was just this living vein that disgusted me, I jammed my eyes shut, like this, d'you see? and buried my head on his chest. (*Turning to the MOTHER.*) Scream, scream, mama! (*Buries her head on the FATHER's chest and with her shoulders raised as if to avoid hearing the scream she adds in a voice stifled with torment.*) Scream as you screamed then!

MOTHER: (*Rushing forward to part them.*) No! My daughter! My daughter! (*Having pulled her from him.*) Brute! Brute! It's my daughter, don't you see – my daughter!

DIRECTOR: (*The outburst having sent him reeling to the footlights, while the Actors show dismay.*) Fine! Splendid! And now: curtain, curtain!

FATHER: (*Running to him, convulsed.*) Right! Yes! Because that, sir, is how it actually was!

DIRECTOR: (*In admiration and conviction.*) Yes, yes, of course! Curtain! Curtain!

Hearing this repeated cry of the DIRECTOR, the TECHNICIAN lets down the curtain, trapping the DIRECTOR and the FATHER between curtain and footlights.

DIRECTOR: (*Looking up, with raised arms.*) What an idiot! I say Curtain, meaning that's how the act should end, and they let down the actual curtain! (*He lifts a corner of the curtain so he can get back on stage. To the FATHER.*) Yes, yes, fine, splendid! Absolutely sure fire! Has to end that way. I can vouch for the first act. (*Goes behind the curtain with the FATHER.*)

When the curtain rises we see that the stagehands have struck that first 'indication of a set,' and have put on stage in its stead a small garden fountain. On one side of the stage, the Actors are sitting in a row, and on the other are the Characters. The DIRECTOR is standing in the middle of the stage, in the act of meditating with one hand, fist clenched, on his mouth.

DIRECTOR: (*Shrugging after a short pause.*) Yes, well then, let's get to the second act. Just leave it to me as we agreed beforehand and everything will be all right.

STEPDAUGHTER: Our entrance into his house (*the FATHER*) in spite of him (*the SON*).

DIRECTOR: (*Losing patience.*) Very well. But leave it all to me, I say.

STEPDAUGHTER: In spite of him. Just let that be clear.

MOTHER: (*Shaking her head from her corner.*) For all the good that's come out of it …

STEPDAUGHTER: (*Turning quickly on her.*) It doesn't matter. The more damage to us, the more guilt feelings for him.

DIRECTOR: (*Still out of patience.*) I understand, I understand. All this will be taken into account, especially at the beginning. Rest assured.

MOTHER: (*Supplicatingly.*) Do make them understand, I beg you, sir, for my conscience sake, for I tried in every possible way –

STEPDAUGHTER: (*Continuing her MOTHER's speech, contemptuously.*) To placate me, to advise me not to give him trouble. (*To the DIRECTOR.*) Do what she wants, do it because it's true. I enjoy the whole thing very much because, look: the more she plays the suppliant and tries to gain entrance into his heart, the more he holds himself aloof: he's an absentee! How I relish this!

DIRECTOR: We want to get going – on the second act, don't we?

STEPDAUGHTER: I won't say another word. But to play it all in the garden, as you want to, won't be possible.

DIRECTOR: Why won't it be possible?

STEPDAUGHTER: Because he (*the SON*) stays shut up in his room, on his own. Then again we need the house for the part about this poor bewildered little boy, as I told you.

DIRECTOR: Quite right. But on the other hand, we can't change the scenery in view of the audience three or four times in one act, nor can we stick up signs –

LEADING MAN: They used to at one time …

DIRECTOR: Yes, when the audiences were about as mature as that little girl.

LEADING LADY: They got the illusion more easily.

FATHER: (*Suddenly, rising.*) The illusion, please don't say illusion! Don't use that word! It's especially cruel to us.

DIRECTOR: (*Astonished.*) And why, if I may ask?

FATHER: Oh yes, cruel, cruel! You should understand that.

DIRECTOR: What word would you have us use anyway? The illusion of creating here for our spectators –

LEADING MAN: – By our performance –

DIRECTOR: – the illusion of a reality.

FATHER: I understand, sir, but perhaps you do not understand us. Because, you see, for you and for your actors all this – quite rightly – is a game –

LEADING LADY: (*Indignantly interrupting.*) Game! We are not children, sir. We act in earnest.

FATHER: I don't deny it. I just mean the game of your art which, as this gentleman rightly says, must provide a perfect illusion of reality.

DIRECTOR: Yes, exactly.

FATHER: But consider this. We (*he quickly indicates himself and* the other five Characters), we have no reality outside this illusion.

DIRECTOR: (Astonished, looking at his Actors who remain bewildered and lost.) And that means?

FATHER: (After observing them briefly, with a pale smile.) Just that, ladies and gentlemen. How should we have any other reality? What for you is an illusion, to be created, is for us our unique reality. (Short pause. He takes several short steps toward the DIRECTOR, and adds) But not for us alone, of course. Think a moment. (He looks into his eyes.) Can you tell me who you are? (And he stands there pointing his first finger at him.)

DIRECTOR: (Upset, with a half-smile.) How do you mean, who I am? I am I.

FATHER: And if I told you that wasn't true because you are me?

DIRECTOR: I would reply that you are out of your mind. (The Actors laugh.)

FATHER: You are right to laugh: because this is a game. (To the DIRECTOR.) And you can object that it's only in a game that that gentleman there (LEADING MAN), who is himself, must be me, who am myself. I've caught you in a trap, do you see that?

Actors start laughing again.

DIRECTOR: (Annoyed.) You said all this before. Why repeat it?

FATHER: I won't – I didn't intend to say that. I'm inviting you to emerge from this game. (He looks at the LEADING LADY as if to forestall what she might say.) This game of art which you are accustomed to play here with your actors. Let me again ask quite seriously: Who are you?

DIRECTOR: (Turning to the Actors, amazed and at the same time irritated.) The gall of this fellow! Calls himself a character and comes here to ask me who I am!

FATHER: (Dignified, but not haughty.) A character, sir, can always ask a man who he is. Because a character really has his own life, marked with his own characteristics, by virtue of which he is always someone. Whereas, a man – I'm not speaking of you now – a man can be no one.

DIRECTOR: Oh sure. But you are asking me! And I am the manager, understand?

FATHER: (Quite softly with mellifluous modesty.) Only in order to know, sir, if you as you now are see yourself … for example, at a distance in time. Do you see the man you once were, with all the illusions you had then, with everything, inside you and outside, as it seemed then – as it was then for you! – Well sir, thinking back to those illusions which you don't have any more, to all those things which no longer seem to be what at one time they were for you, don't you feel, not just the boards of this stage, but the very earth beneath slipping away from you? For will not all that you feel yourself to be now, your whole reality of today, as it is now, inevitably seem an illusion tomorrow?

DIRECTOR: (Who has not followed exactly, but has been staggered by the plausibilities of the argument.) Well, well, what do you want to prove?

FATHER: Oh nothing sir. I just wanted to make you see that if we (pointing again at himself and the other Characters) have no reality outside of illusion, it would be well if you should distrust your reality because, though you breathe it and touch it today, it is destined like that of yesterday to stand revealed to you tomorrow as illusion.

DIRECTOR: (Deciding to mock him.) Oh splendid! And you'll be telling me next that you and this play that you have come to perform for me are truer and more real than I am.

FATHER: (Quite seriously.) There can be no doubt of that, sir.

DIRECTOR: Really?

FATHER: I thought you had understood that from the start.

DIRECTOR: More real than me?

FATHER: If your reality can change overnight …

DIRECTOR: Of course it can, it changes all the time, like everyone else's.

FATHER: (With a cry.) But ours does not, sir. You see, that is the difference. It does not change, it cannot ever change or be otherwise because it is already fixed, it is what is, just that, forever – a terrible thing, sir! – an immutable reality. You should shudder to come near us.

DIRECTOR: (Suddenly struck by a new idea, he steps in front of the FATHER.) I should like to know, however, when anyone ever saw a character get out of his part and set about expounding and explicating it, delivering lectures on it. Can you tell me? I have never seen anything like that.

FATHER: You have never seen it, sir, because authors generally hide the travail of their creations. When characters are alive and turn up, living, before their author, all that author does is follow the words and gestures which they propose to him. He has to want them to be as they themselves want to be. Woe betide him if he doesn't! When a character is born, he at once acquires such an independence, even of his own author, that the whole world can imagine him in innumerable situations other than those the author thought to place him in. At times he acquires a meaning that the author never dreamt of giving him.

DIRECTOR: Certainly, I know that.

FATHER: Then why all this astonishment at us? Imagine what a misfortune it is for a character such as I described to you – given life in the imagination of an author who then wished to deny him life – and tell me frankly: isn't such a character, given life and left without life, isn't he right to set about doing just what we are doing now as we stand here before you, after having done just the same – for a very long time, believe me – before him, trying to persuade him, trying to push him … I would appear before him sometimes, sometimes she (looks at STEPDAUGHTER) would go to him, sometimes that poor mother …

STEPDAUGHTER: (Coming forward as if in a trance.) It's true. I too went there, sir, to tempt him, many times, in the melancholy of that study of his, at the twilight hour, when he would sit stretched out in his armchair, unable to make up his mind to switch the light on, and letting the evening shadows invade the room, knowing that these shadows were alive with us and that we were coming to tempt him … (*As if she saw herself still in that study and felt only annoyance at the presence of all of these Actors.*) Oh, if only you would all go away! Leave us alone! My mother there with her son – I with this little girl – the boy there always alone – then I with him (*the* FATHER) – then I by myself, I by myself … in those shadows. (*Suddenly she jumps up as if she wished to take hold of herself in the vision she has of herself lighting up the shadows and alive.*) Ah my life! What scenes, what scenes we went there to propose to him: I, I tempted him more than the others.

FATHER: Right, but perhaps that was the trouble: you insisted too much. You thought you could seduce him.

STEPDAUGHTER: Nonsense. He wanted me that way. (*She comes up to the* DIRECTOR *to tell him as in confidence.*) If you ask me, sir, it was because he was so depressed, or because he despised the theater the public knows and wants …

DIRECTOR: Let's continue. Let's continue, for Heaven's sake. Enough theories, I'd like some facts. Give me some facts.

STEPDAUGHTER: It seems to me that we have already given you more facts than you can handle – with our entry into his (*the* FATHER'S) house! You said you couldn't change the scene every five minutes or start hanging signs.

DIRECTOR: Nor can we, of course not, we have to combine the scenes and group them in one simultaneous close-knit action. Not your idea at all. You'd like to see your brother come home from school and wander through the house like a ghost, hiding behind the doors, and brooding on a plan which – how did you put it –?

STEPDAUGHTER: – shrivels him up, sir, completely shrivels him up, sir.

DIRECTOR: 'Shrivels!' What a word! All right then: his growth was stunted except for his eyes. Is that what you said?

STEPDAUGHTER: Yes, sir. Just look at him. (*She points him out next to the* MOTHER.)

DIRECTOR: Good girl. And then at the same time you want this little girl to be playing in the garden, dead to the world. Now, the boy in the house, the girl in the garden, is that possible?

STEPDAUGHTER: Happy in the sunshine! Yes, that is my only reward, her pleasure, her joy in that garden! After the misery, the squalor of a horrible room where we slept, all four of us, she with me: just think, of the horror of my contaminated body next to hers! She held me tight, oh so tight with her loving innocent little arms! In the garden she would run and take my hand as soon as she saw me. She did not see the big flowers, she ran around looking for the teeny ones and wanted to show them to me, oh the joy of it!

Saying this and tortured by the memory she breaks into prolonged desperate sobbing, dropping her head onto her arms which are spread out on the work table. Everyone is overcome by her

emotion. *The* DIRECTOR *goes to her almost paternally and says to comfort her:*

DIRECTOR: We'll do the garden. We'll do the garden, don't worry, and you'll be very happy about it. We'll bring all the scenes together in the garden. (*Calling a stagehand by name.*) Hey, drop me a couple of trees, will you, two small cypress trees, here in front of the fountain.

Two small cypress trees are seen descending from the flies. A stagehand runs on to secure them with nails and a couple of braces.

DIRECTOR: (*To the* STEPDAUGHTER.) Something to go on with anyway. Gives us an idea. (*Again calling the stagehand by name.*) Hey, give me a bit of sky.

STAGEHAND: (*From above.*) What?

DIRECTOR: Bit of sky, a backcloth, to go behind that fountain. (*A white backdrop is seen descending from the flies.*) Not white, I said sky. It doesn't matter, leave it, I'll take care of it. (*Shouting.*) Hey, Electrician, put these lights out. Let's have a bit of atmosphere, lunar atmosphere, blue background, and give me a blue spot on that backcloth. That's right. That's enough. (*At his command a mysterious lunar scene is created which induces the Actors to talk and move as they would on an evening in the garden beneath the moon.*) (*To* STEPDAUGHTER.) You see? And now instead of hiding behind doors in the house the boy could move around here in the garden and hide behind trees. But it will be difficult, you know, to find a little girl to play the scene where she shows you the flowers. (*Turning to the* BOY.) Come down this way a bit. Let's see how this can be worked out. (*And when the* BOY *doesn't move.*) Come on, come on. (*Then dragging him forward he tries to make him hold his head up but it falls down again every time.*) Oh dear, another problem, this boy … What *is* it? … My God, he'll have to say something … (*He goes up to him, puts a hand on his shoulder and leads him behind one of the tree drops.*) Come on. Come on. Let me see. You can hide a bit here … Like this … You can stick your head out a bit to look … (*He goes to one side to see the effect. The* BOY *has scarcely run through the actions when the Actors are deeply affected; and they remain quite overwhelmed.*) Ah! Fine! Splendid! (*He turns again to the* STEPDAUGHTER.) If the little girl surprises him looking out and runs over to him, don't you think she might drag a few words out of him too?

STEPDAUGHTER: (*Jumping to her feet.*) Don't expect him to speak while *he's* here. (*She points to the son.*) You have to send *him* away first.

SON: (*Going resolutely toward one of the two stairways.*) Suits me. Glad to go. Nothing I want more.

DIRECTOR: (*Immediately calling him.*) No. Where are you going? Wait.

The MOTHER *rises, deeply moved, in anguish at the thought that he is really going. She instinctively raises her arms as if to halt him, yet without moving away from her position.*

SON: (*Arriving at the footlights, where the* DIRECTOR *stops him.*) I have absolutely nothing to do here. So let me go please. Just let me go.

DIRECTOR: How do you mean, you having nothing to do?

STEPDAUGHTER: (*Placidly, with irony.*) Don't hold him! He won't go.

FATHER: He has to play the terrible scene in the garden with his mother.

SON: (*Unhesitating, resolute, proud.*) I play nothing. I said so from the start. (*To the* DIRECTOR.) Let me go.

STEPDAUGHTER: (*Running to the* DIRECTOR *to get him to lower his arms so that he is no longer holding the* SON *back.*) Let him go. (*Then turning to the* SON *as soon as the director has let him go.*) Very well, go. (*The* SON *is all set to move toward the stairs but, as if held by some occult power, he cannot go down the steps. While the Actors are both astounded and deeply troubled, he moves slowly across the footlights straight to the other stairway. But having arrived there he remains poised for the descent but unable to descend. The* STEPDAUGHTER, *who has followed him with her eyes in an attitude of defiance, bursts out laughing.*) He can't, you see. He can't. He has to stay here, has to. Bound by a chain, indissolubly. But if I who do take flight, sir, when that happens which has to happen, and precisely because of the hatred I feel for him, precisely so as not to see him again – very well, if *I* am still here and can bear the sight of him and his company – you can imagine whether *he* can go away. He who really must, must remain here with that fine father of his and that mother there who no longer has any other children. (*Turning again to the* MOTHER.) Come on, Mother, come on. (*Turning again to the* DIRECTOR *and pointing to the* MOTHER.) Look, she got up to hold him back. (*To the* MOTHER, *as if exerting a magical power over her.*) Come. Come ... (*Then to the* DIRECTOR.) You can imagine how little she wants to display her love in front of your actors. But so great is her desire to get at him that – look, you see – she is even prepared to live her scene.

In fact the MOTHER *has approached and no sooner has the* STEPDAUGHTER *spoken her last words than she spreads her arms to signify consent.*

SON: (*Without pause.*) But *I* am not, *I* am not. If I can not go I will stay here, but I repeat: I will play nothing.

FATHER: (*To the director, enraged.*) You can force him, sir.

SON: No one can force me.

FATHER: I will force you.

STEPDAUGHTER: Wait, wait. First the little girl must be at the fountain. (*She runs to take the* LITTLE GIRL, *drops on her knees in front of her, takes her little face in her hands.*) My poor little darling, you look bewildered with those lovely big eyes of yours. Who knows where you think you are? We are on a stage my dear. What is a stage? It is a place where you play at being serious, a place for play-acting, where we will now play-act. But seriously! For real! You too ... (*She embraces her, presses her to her bosom and rocks her a little.*) Oh, little darling, little darling, what an ugly play you will

enact! What a horrible thing has been planned for you, the garden, the fountain ... All pretense, of course, that's the trouble, my sweet, everything is make-believe here, but perhaps for you, my child, a make-believe fountain is nicer than a real one for playing in, hmm? It will be a game for the others, but not for you, alas, because you are real, my darling, and are actually playing in a fountain that is real, beautiful, big, green with many bamboo plants reflected in it and giving it shade. Many, many ducklings can swim in it, breaking the shade to bits. You want to take hold of one of these ducklings ... (*With a shout that fills everyone with dismay.*) No! No, my Rosetta! Your mother is not looking after you because of that beast of a son. A thousand devils are loose in my head ... and *he* ... (*She leaves the* LITTLE GIRL *and turns with her usual hostility to the* BOY.) And what are you doing here, always looking like a beggar child? It will be your fault too if this little girl drowns – with all your standing around like that. As if I hadn't paid for everybody when I got you all into this house. (*Grabbing one of his arms to force him to take a hand out of his pocket.*) What have you got there? What are you hiding? Let's see this hand. (*Tears his hand out of his pocket, and to the horror of everyone discovers that it holds a small revolver. She looks at it for a moment as if satisfied and then says*) Ah! Where did you get that and how? (*And as the* BOY *in his confusion, with his eyes staring and vacant all the time, does not answer her.*) Idiot, if I were you I wouldn't have killed myself, I would have killed one of those two – or both of them – the father and the son! (*She hides him behind the small cypress tree from which he had been looking out, and she takes the* LITTLE GIRL *and hides her in the fountain, having her lie down in it in such a way as to be quite hidden. Finally, the* STEPDAUGHTER *goes down on her knees with her face in her hands, which are resting on the rim of the fountain.*)

DIRECTOR: Splendid! (*Turning to the* SON.) And at the same time ...

SON: (*With contempt.*) And at the same time, nothing. It is not true, sir. There was never any scene between me and her. (*He points to the* MOTHER.) Let her tell you herself how it was.

Meanwhile the SECOND ACTRESS *and the* JUVENILE LEAD *have detached themselves from the group of Actors. The former has started to observe the mother, who is opposite her, very closely. And the other has started to observe the* SON. *Both are planning how they will re-create the roles.*

MOTHER: Yes, it is true, sir. I had gone to his room.

SON: My room, did you hear that? Not the garden.

DIRECTOR: That is of no importance. We have to rearrange the action, I told you that.

SON: (*Noticing that the* JUVENILE LEAD *is observing him.*) What do *you* want?

JUVENILE LEAD: Nothing. I am observing you.

SON: (*Turning to the other side where the* SECOND ACTRESS *is.*) Ah, and here we have you to re-create the role, eh? (*He points to the* MOTHER.)

DIRECTOR: Exactly, exactly. You should be grateful, it seems to me, for the attention they are giving you.

SON: Oh yes, thank you. But you still haven't understood that you cannot do this drama. We are not inside you, not in the least, and your actors are looking at us from the outside. Do you think it's possible for us to live before a mirror which, not content to freeze us in the fixed image it provides of our expression, also throws back at us an unrecognizable grimace purporting to be ourselves?

FATHER: That is true. That is true. You must see that.

DIRECTOR: (*To the* JUVENILE LEAD *and the* SECOND ACTRESS.) Very well, get away from here.

SON: No good. I won't cooperate.

DIRECTOR: Just be quiet a minute and let me hear your mother. (*To the* MOTHER.) Well? You went into his room?

MOTHER: Yes sir, into his room. I was at the end of my tether. I wanted to pour out all of the anguish which was oppressing me. But as soon as he saw me come in –

SON: – There was no scene. I went away. I went away so there would be no scene. Because I have never made scenes, never, understand?

MOTHER: That's true. That's how it was. Yes.

DIRECTOR: But now there's got to be a scene between you and him. It is indispensable.

MOTHER: As for me, sir, I am ready. If only you could find some way to have me speak to him for one moment, to have me say what is in my heart.

FATHER: (*Going right up to the* SON, *very violent.*) You will do it! For your mother! For your mother!

SON: (*More decisively than ever.*) I will do nothing!

FATHER: (*Grabbing him by the chest and shaking him.*) By God, you will obey! Can't you hear how she is talking to you? Aren't you her son?

SON: (*Grabbing his father.*) No! No! Once and for all let's have done with it!

General agitation. The MOTHER, *terrified, tries to get between them to separate them.*

MOTHER: (*As before.*) Please, please!

FATHER: (*Without letting go of the* SON.) You must obey, you must obey!

SON: (*Wrestling with his* FATHER *and in the end throwing him to the ground beside the little stairway, to the horror of everyone.*) What's this frenzy that's taken hold of you? To show your shame and ours to everyone? Have you no restraint? I won't cooperate, I won't cooperate! And that is how I interpret the wishes of the man who did not choose to put us on stage.

DIRECTOR: But you came here.

SON: (*Pointing to his* FATHER.) He came here – not me!

DIRECTOR: But aren't you here too?

SON: It was he who wanted to come, dragging the rest of us with him, and then getting together with you to plot not only what really happened, but also – as if that did not suffice – *what did not happen.*

DIRECTOR: Then tell me. Tell me what did happen. Just tell me. You came out of your room without saying a thing?

SON: (*After a moment of hesitation.*) Without saying a thing. In order not to make a scene.

DIRECTOR: (*Driving him on.*) Very well, and then, what did you do then?

SON: (*While everyone looks on in anguished attention, he moves a few steps on the front part of the stage.*) Nothing … crossing the garden … (*He stops, gloomy, withdrawn.*)

DIRECTOR: (*Always driving him on to speak, impressed by his reticence.*) Very well, crossing the garden?

SON: (*Desperate, hiding his face with one arm.*) Why do you want to make me say it, sir? It is horrible.

The MOTHER *trembles all over, and stifles groans, looking toward the fountain.*

DIRECTOR: (*Softly, noticing this look of hers, turning to the* SON, *with growing apprehension.*) The little girl?

SON: (*Looking out into the auditorium.*) Over there – in the fountain …

FATHER: (*On the ground, pointing compassionately toward the* MOTHER.) And she followed him, sir.

DIRECTOR: (*To the* SON, *anxiously.*) And then you …

SON: (*Slowly, looking straight ahead all the time.*) I ran out. I started to fish her out … but all of a sudden I stopped. Behind those trees I saw something that froze me: the boy, the boy was standing there, quite still. There was madness in the eyes. He was looking at his drowned sister in the fountain. (*The* STEPDAUGHTER, *who has been bent over the fountain, hiding the* LITTLE GIRL, *is sobbing desperately, like an echo from the bottom. Pause.*) I started to approach and then …

From behind the trees where the BOY *has been hiding, a revolver shot rings out.*

MOTHER: (*Running up with a tormented shout, accompanied by the* SON *and all the Actors in a general tumult.*) Son! My Son! (*And then amid the hub-bub and the disconnected shouts of the others.*) Help! Help!

DIRECTOR: (*Amid the shouting, trying to clear a space while the* BOY *is lifted by his head and feet and carried away behind the backcloth.*) Is he wounded, is he wounded, really?

Everyone except the DIRECTOR *and the* FATHER, *who has remained on the ground beside the steps, has disappeared behind the backcloth which has served for a sky, where they can still be heard for a while whispering anxiously. Then from one side and the other of this curtain, the Actors come back on stage.*

LEADING LADY: (*Re-entering from the right, very much upset.*) He's dead! Poor boy! He's dead! What a terrible thing!

LEADING MAN: (*Re-entering from the left, laughing.*) How do you mean, dead? Fiction, fiction, one doesn't believe such things.

OTHER ACTORS: (*On the right.*) Fiction? Reality! Reality! He is dead!

OTHER ACTORS: (*On the left.*) No! Fiction! Fiction!

FATHER: (*Rising, and crying out to them.*) Fiction indeed! Reality, reality, gentlemen, reality! (*Desperate, he too disappears at the back.*)

DIRECTOR: (*At the end of his rope.*) Fiction! Reality! To hell with all of you! Lights, lights, lights! (*At a single stroke the whole stage and auditorium is flooded with very bright light. The DIRECTOR breathes again, as if freed from an incubus, and they all look each other in the eyes, bewildered and lost.*) Things like this don't happen to me, they've made me lose a whole day. (*He looks at his watch.*) Go, you can all go. What could we do now anyway? It is too late to pick up the rehearsal where we left off. See you this evening. (*As soon as the Actors have gone he talks to the ELECTRICIAN by name.*) Hey, Electrician, lights out. (*He has hardly said the words when the theatre is plunged for a moment into complete darkness.*) Hey, for God's sake, leave me at least one light! I like to see where I am going!

Immediately, from behind the backcloth, as if the wrong switch had been pulled, a green light comes on which projects the silhouettes, clear-cut and large, of the Characters, minus the BOY and the LITTLE GIRL. Seeing the silhouettes, the director, terrified, rushes from the stage. At the same time the light behind the backcloth goes out and the stage is again lit in nocturnal blue as before.

Slowly, from the right side of the curtain, the SON comes forward first, followed by the MOTHER with her arms stretched out toward him; then from the left side, the FATHER. They stop in the middle of the stage and stay there as if in a trance. Last of all from the right, the STEPDAUGHTER comes out and runs toward the two stairways. She stops on the first step, to look for a moment at the other three, and then breaks into a harsh laugh before throwing herself down the steps; she runs down the aisle between the rows of seats; she stops one more time and again laughs, looking at the three who are still on stage; she disappears from the auditorium, and from the lobby her laughter is still heard. Shortly thereafter the curtain falls.

2.10 DOCTOR FAUSTUS LIGHTS THE LIGHTS (1938)

GERTRUDE STEIN

Gertrude Stein (1874–1946) was born into a middle-class European immigrant family in Pennsylvania, US. She became one of the iconic figures of the modernist avant-garde. Stein spent her late teens studying philosophy, English composition and psychology at Harvard Annex and at Johns Hopkins School of Medicine. At one point a student of one of the founding fathers of psychology William James – brother of the novelist Henry James – Stein's formal education was left unfinished. After short spells in Italy and London, she settled in Paris in 1903 where over the next forty years she networked amongst some of the foremost figures of the arts world, counting amongst her colleagues and friends Pablo Picasso, Henri Matisse, Ernest Hemingway and Mabel Dodge. Stein's writing was initially considered by many publishers to be unreadable, but her concern with form, composition, structure and rhythm has made her work amongst the most celebrated – and in terms of her plays and opera the most revived – of the avant-garde writers of the period. Doctor Faustus Lights the Lights *has recently been directed by contemporary American avant-garde theatre makers Richard Foreman (1982) and Robert Wilson (1992) and adapted by the Wooster Group as* House/Lights *in 1999, directed by Elizabeth LeCompte.*

Act I

Faust standing at the door of his room, with his arms up at the door lintel looking out, behind him a blaze of electric light.

Just then Mephisto approaches and appears at the door.

FAUSTUS GROWLS OUT: The devil what the devil what do I care if the devil is there.

MEPHISTO SAYS: But Doctor Faustus dear yes I am here.

DOCTOR FAUSTUS: What do I care there is no here nor there. What am I. I am Doctor Faustus who knows everything can do everything and you say it was through you but not at all, if I had not been in a hurry and if I had taken my time I would have known how to make white electric light and day-light and night light and what did I do I saw you miserable devil I saw you and I was deceived and I believed miserable devil I thought I needed you, and I thought I was tempted by the devil and I know no temptation is tempting unless the devil tells you so. And you wanted my soul what the hell did you want my soul for, how do you know I have a soul, who says so nobody says so but you the devil and everybody knows the devil is all lies, so how do you know how do I know that I have a soul to sell how do you know Mr. Devil oh Mr. Devil how can you tell you can not tell anything and I I who

know everything I keep on having so much light that light is not bright and what after all is the use of light, you can see just as well without it, you can go around just as well without it you can get up and go to bed just as well without it, and I I wanted to make it and the devil take it yes you devil you do not even want it and I sold my soul to make it. I have made it but have I a soul to pay for it.

Mephisto coming nearer and trying to pat his arm.

Yes dear Doctor Faustus yes of course you have a soul of course you have, do not believe them when they say the devil lies, you know the devil never lies, he deceives oh yes he deceives but that is not lying no dear please dear Doctor Faustus do not say the devil lies.

DOCTOR FAUSTUS: Who cares if you lie if you steal, there is no snake to grind under one's heel, there is no hope there is no death there is no life there is no breath, there just is every day all day and when there is no day there is no day, and anyway of what use is a devil unless he goes away, go away old devil go away, there is no use in a devil unless he goes away, how can you remember a devil unless he goes away, oh devil there is no use in your coming to stay and now you are red at night which is not a delight and you are red in the morning which is not a warning go away devil go away or stay after all what can a devil say.

MEPHISTO: A devil can smile a devil can while away whatever there is to give away, and now are you not proud Doctor Faustus yes you are you know you are you are the only one who knows what you know and it is I the devil who tells you so.

FAUSTUS: You fool you devil how can you know, how can you tell me so, if I am the only one who can know what I know then no devil can know what I know and no devil can tell me so and I could know without any soul to sell, without there being anything in hell, What I know I know, I know how I do what I do when I see the way through and always any day I will see another day and you old devil you know very well you never see any other way than just the way to hell, you only know one way. You only know one thing, you are never ready for anything, and I everything is always now and now and now perhaps through you I begin to know that it is all just so, that light however bright will never be other than light, and any light is just a light and now there is nothing more either by day or by night but just a light. Oh you devil go to hell, that is all you know to tell, and who is interested in hell just a devil is interested in hell because that is all he can tell, whether I stamp or whether I cry whether I live or whether I die, I can know that all a devil can say is just about going to hell the same way, get out of here devil, it does not interest me whether you can buy or I can sell, get out of here devil just you go to hell.

Faustus gives him an awful kick, and Mephisto moves away and the electric lights just then begin to get very gay.

Alright then

The Ballet

Doctor Faustus sitting alone surrounded by electric lights.

His dog comes in and says

Thank you.

One of the electric lights goes out and again the dog says

Thank you.

The electric light that went out is replaced by a glow.

The dog murmurs.

My my what a sky.

And then he says

Thank you.

Doctor Faustus' song:

If I do It

If you do it

What is it.

Once again the dog says

Thank you.

A duet between Doctor Faustus and the dog about the electric light about the electric lights.

Bathe me

says Doctor Faustus

Bathe me

In the electric lights

During this time the electric lights come and go

What is it

says Doctor Faustus

Thank you

says the dog.

Just at this moment the electric lights get brighter and nothing comes

Was it it

says Doctor Faustus

Faustus meditates he does not see the dog.

Will it

Will it

Will it be

Will it be it

Faustus sighs and repeats

Will it be it.

A duet between the dog and Faustus

Will it be it

Just it.

At that moment the electric light gets pale again and in that moment Faustus shocked says

It is it

A little boy comes in and plays with the dog, the dog says

Thank you.

Doctor Faustus looks away from the electric lights and then he sings a song.

Let me Alone

Let me alone

Oh let me alone

Dog and boy let me alone oh let me alone

Leave me alone

Let me be alone

little boy and dog

let let me alone

He sighs

And as be sighs

He says

Dog and boy boy and dog leave me alone let me let me be alone.

The dog says

Thank you

but does not look at Faustus

A pause

No words

The dog says

Thank you

I say thank you

Thank you

The little boy

The day begins to-day

The day
The moon begins the day
    Doctor Faustus
There is no moon to-day.
    Dark silence
You obey I obey
There is no moon to-day.
    Silence
    and the dog says
I obey I say
Thank you any day
    The little boy says
Once in a while they get up.
    Doctor Faustus says
I shall not think
I shall not
No I shall not.
    Faustus addresses little boy and dog
Night is better than day so please go away
    The boy says
But say
When the hay has to be cut every day then there is the devil
to pay
    The dog starts and then he shrinks and says
Thank you
    Faustus half turns and starts
I hear her
    he says
I hear her say
Call to her to sing
To sing all about
to sing a song
All about
day-light and night light.
Moonlight and star-light
electric light and twilight
every light as well.
    The electric lights glow and a chorus in the distance sings
Her name is her name is her name is Marguerite Ida and
Helena Annabel.
    Faustus sings
I knew it I knew it the electric lights they told me so no dog
can know no boy can know I cannot know they cannot know
the electric lights they told me so I would not know I could
not know who can know who can tell me so I know you
know they can know her name is Marguerite Ida and Helena
Annabel and when I tell oh when I tell oh when I when I
when I tell, oh go away and go away and tell and tell and tell
and tell and tell, oh hell.
    The electric lights commence to dance and one by one
they go out and come in and the boy and the dog begin to
sing.
Oh very well oh Doctor Faustus very very well oh very well,
thank you says the dog oh very well says the boy her name

her name is Marguerite Ida and Helena Annabel, I know says
the dog I know says the boy I know says Doctor Faustus no
no no no no nobody can know what I know I know her
name is not Marguerite Ida and Helena Annabel, very well
says the boy it is says the boy her name is Marguerite Ida and
Helena Annabel, no no no says Doctor Faustus, yes yes yes
says the dog, no says the boy yes says the dog, her name is not
Marguerite Ida and Helena Annabel and she is not ready yet
to sing about day-light and night light, moonlight and star-
light electric light and twilight she is not she is not but she
will be. She will not be says Doctor Faustus never never never,
never will her name be Marguerite Ida and Helena Annabel
never never never never well as well never Marguerite Ida and
Helena Annabel never Marguerite Ida and Helena Annabel.
    There is a sudden hush and the distant chorus says
It might be it might be her name her name might be
Marguerite Ida and Helena Annabel it might be.
    And Doctor Faustus says in a loud whisper
It might be but it is not, and the little boy says how do you
know and Faustus says it might be it might not be not be not
be, and as he says the last not be the dog says
Thank you.

Scene II

I am I and my name is Marguerite Ida and Helena Annabel,
and then oh then I could yes I could I could begin to cry but
why why could I begin to cry.
    And I am I and I am here and how do I know how wild
the wild world is how wild the wild woods are the wood they
call the woods the poor man's overcoat but do they cover me
and if they do how wild they are wild and wild and wild they
are, how do I know how wild woods are when I have never
ever seen a wood before.
    I wish, (she whispered) I knew why woods are wild why
animals are wild why I am I, why I can cry, I wish I wish I
knew, I wish oh how I wish I knew. Once I am in I will never
be through the woods are there and I am here and am I here
or am I there, oh where oh where is here oh where oh where
is there and animals wild animals are everywhere.
    She sits down.
    I wish (says she conversationally) I wish if I had a wish
that when I sat down it would not be here but there there
where I could have a chair there where I would not have to
look around fearfully everywhere there where a chair and a
carpet underneath the chair would make me know that there
is there, but here here everywhere there is nothing nothing
like a carpet nothing like a chair, here it is wild everywhere I
hear I hear everywhere that the woods are wild and I am here
and here is here and here I am sitting without a chair without
a carpet, oh help me to a carpet with a chair save me from the
woods the wild woods everywhere where everything is wild
wild and I I am not there I am here oh dear I am not there.
    She stands up with her hands at her sides she opens and
closes her eyes and opens them again.

If my eyes are open and my eyes are closed I see I see, I see no carpet I see no chair I see the wild woods everywhere, what good does it do me to close my eyes no good at all the woods the woods are there I close my eyes but the green is there and I open my eyes and I have to stare to be sure the green is there the green of the woods, I saw it when my eyes were closed I saw the wild woods everywhere and now I open my eyes and there there is the wild wood everywhere.

Would it do as well if my name was not Marguerite Ida and Helena Annabel would it do as well I would give up even that for a carpet and a chair and to be not here but there, but and she lets out a shriek, I am here I am not there and I am Marguerite Ida and Helena Annabel and it is not well that I could tell what there is to tell what there is to see and what do I see and do I see it at all oh yes I do I call and call but yes I do I see it all oh dear oh dear oh dear yes I am here.

She says

In the distance there is daylight and near to there is none.

There is something under the leaves and Marguerite Ida and Helena Annabel makes a quick turn and she sees that a viper has stung her.

In the distance there is daylight and near to there is none.

There is a rustling under the leaves and Marguerite Ida and Helena Annabel makes a quick turn and she sees that a viper has stung her, she sees it and she says and what is it. There is no answer. Does it hurt she says and then she says no not really and she says was it a viper and she says how can I tell I never saw one before but is it she says and she stands up again and sits down and pulls down her stocking and says well it was not a bee not a busy bee no not, nor a mosquito nor a sting it was a bite and serpents bite yes they do perhaps it was one. Marguerite Ida and Helena Annabel sits thinking and then she sees a country woman with a sickle coming. Have I she says have I been bitten, the woman comes nearer, have I says Marguerite Ida and Helena Annabel have I have I been bitten. Have you been bitten answers the country woman, why yes it can happen, then I have been bitten says Marguerite Ida and Helena Annabel why not if you have been is the answer.

They stand repeating have I and yes it does happen and then Marguerite Ida and Helena Annabel says let me show you and the woman says oh yes but I have never seen any one who has been bitten but let me see no I cannot tell she says but go away and do something, what shall I do said Marguerite Ida and Helena Annabel do something to kill the poison, but what said Marguerite Ida and Helena Annabel, a doctor can do it said the woman but what doctor said Marguerite Ida and Helena Annabel, Doctor Faustus can do it said the woman, do you know him said Marguerite Ida and Helena Annabel no of course I do not know him nobody does there is a dog, he says thank you said the woman and go and see him go go go said the woman and Marguerite Ida and Helena Annabel went.

As she went she began to sing.

Do vipers sting do vipers bite

If they bite with all their might
Do they do they sting
Or do they do they bite
Alright they bite if they bite with all their might.
And I am I Marguerite Ida or am I Helena Annabel
Oh well
Am I Marguerite Ida or am I Helena Annabel
Very well oh very well
Am I Marguerite Ida very well am I Helena Annabel.

She stops she remembers the viper and in a whisper she says was it a sting was it a bite am I alright; was it a sting was it a bite, alright was it a sting, oh or was it a bite.

She moves away and then suddenly she stops.
Will he tell
Will he tell that I am Marguerite Ida that I am Helena Annabel,
Will he tell
    And then she stops again
And the bite might he make it a bite.
Doctor Faustus a queer name
Might he make it a bite
    And so she disappears.

Scene III
Doctor Faustus the dog and the boy all sleeping, the dog dreaming says thickly
Thank you, thank you thank you thank you thank you, thank you thank you.
    Doctor Faustus turns and murmurs
Man and dog dog and man each one can tell it all like a ball with a caress no tenderness, man and dog just the same each one can take the blame each one can well as well tell it all as they can, man and dog, well well man and dog what is the difference between a man and a dog when I say none do I go away does he go away go away to stay no nobody goes away the dog the boy they can stay I can go away go away where where there there where, dog and boy can annoy I can go say I go where do I go I go where I go, where is there there is where and all the day and all the night too it grew and grew and there is no way to say I and a dog and a boy, if a boy is to grow to be a man am I a boy am I a dog is a dog boy is a boy a dog and what am I I cannot cry what am I oh what am I
    And then he waits a moment and he says
Oh what am I.
    Just then in the distance there is a call
Doctor Faustus Doctor Faustus are you there Doctor Faustus I am here Doctor Faustus I am coming there Doctor Faustus, there is where Doctor Faustus oh where is there Doctor Faustus say it Doctor Faustus are you there Doctor Faustus are you there.
    The dog murmurs
Thank you thank you
    and the boy says
There is somebody of course there is somebody just there

there is somebody somebody is there oh yes somebody is there.

and all together they say

Where is there nobody says nobody is there. Somebody is there and nobody says that somebody is not there. Somebody somebody is there somebody somebody somebody somebody says there is where where is it where is it where is it where, here is here here is there somebody somebody says where is where.

Outside the voice says

Doctor Faustus are you there Doctor Faustus any where, Doctor Faustus are you there.

And then there is a knock at the door.

The electric lights glow softly and Marguerite Ida and Helena Annabel comes in.

Well and yes well, and this is yes this is Doctor Faustus Doctor Doctor Faustus and he can and be can change a bite hold it tight make it not kill not kill Marguerite Ida not kill Helena Annabel and hell oh hell not a hell not well yes well Doctor Faustus can he can make it all well.

And then she says in a quiet voice.

Doctor Faustus have you ever been to hell.

Of course not she says of course you have not how could you sell your soul if you had ever been to hell of course not, no of course not.

Doctor Faustus tell me what did they give you when you sold your soul, not hell no of course not not hell.

And then she goes on.

I I am Marguerite Ida and Helena Annabel and a viper bit or stung it is very well begun and if it is so then oh oh I will die and as my soul has not been sold I Marguerite Ida and Helena Annabel perhaps I will go to hell.

The dog sighs and says

Thank you

and the little boy coming nearer says

what is a viper, tell me Marguerite Ida and Helena Annabel I like you being Marguerite Ida and Helena Annabel what is a viper do I know it very well or do I not know it very well please tell you are Marguerite Ida and Helena Annabel what is a viper.

Doctor Faustus says

Little boy and dog can be killed by a viper but Marguerite Ida and Helena Annabel not very well no not very well

(He bursts out)

Leave me alone

Let me be alone

Little boy and dog let me be alone, Marguerite Ida and Helena Annabel let me be alone, I have no soul I had no soul I sold it sold it here there and everywhere,

What did I do I knew

I knew that there could be light not moon-light star light daylight and candle light, I knew I knew I saw the lightening light, I saw it light, I said I I I must have that light, and what did I do oh what did I too I said I would sell my soul all

through but I knew I knew that electric light was all true, and true oh yes it is true they took it that it was true that I sold my soul to them as well and so never never could I go to hell never never as well. Go away dog and boy go away Marguerite Ida and Helena Annabel go away all who can die and go to heaven or hell go away oh go away go away leave me alone oh leave me alone. I said it I said it was the light I said I gave the light I said the lights are right and the day is bright little boy and dog leave me alone let me be alone.

The country woman with the sickle looks in at the window and sings Well well this is the Doctor Faustus and he has not gone to hell he has pretty lights and they light so very well and there is a dog and he says thank you and there is a little boy oh yes little boy there you are you just are there yes little boy you are and there is Marguerite Ida and Helena Annabel and a viper did bite her, oh cure her Doctor Faustus cure her what is the use of your having been to hell if Marguerite Ida and Helena Annabel is not to be all well.

And the chorus sings

What is the use Doctor Faustus what is the use what is the use of having been to hell if you cannot cure this only only this Marguerite Ida and Helena Annabel.

Doctor Faustus says

I think I have thought thought is not bought oh no thought is not bought I think I have thought and what have I bought I have bought thought, to think is not bought but I I have bought thought and so you come here you come you come here and here and here where can I say that not to-day not any day can I look and see, no no I cannot look no no I cannot see and you you say you are Marguerite Ida and Helena Annabel and I I cannot see I cannot see Marguerite Ida and I cannot see Helena Annabel and you you are the two and I cannot cannot see you.

Marguerite Ida and Helena Annabel

Do not see me Doctor Faustus do not see me it would terrify me if you did see do not see me no no do not see me I am Marguerite Ida and Helena Annabel but do not see me cure me Doctor Faustus do the viper bit the viper stung his sting was a bite and you you have the light cure me Doctor Faustus cure me do but do not see me, I see you but do not see me cure me do but do not see me I implore you.

Doctor Faustus

A dog says thank you but you you say do not see me cure me do but do not see me what shall I do.

He turns to the dog

The dog says

Thank you

and the boy says

What difference does it make to you if you do what difference oh what difference does it make to you if you do, whatever you do do whatever you do do what difference does it make to you if you do.

Marguerite Ida and Helena Annabel

What difference does it make to you if you do what difference does it make to you but I a viper has had his bite and I I will die but you you cannot die you have sold your soul but I I have mine and a viper has come and he has bitten me and see see how the poison works see see how I must die, see how little by little it is coming to be high, higher and higher I must die oh Doctor Faustus what difference does it make to you what difference oh what difference but to me to me to me to me a viper has bitten me a bitter viper a viper has bitten me.

    The dog

Oh Thank you thank you all all of you thank you thank you oh thank you everybody thank you he and we thank you, a viper has bitten you thank you thank you.

    The boy

A viper has bitten her she knows it too a viper has bitten her believe it or not it is true, a viper has bitten her and if Doctor Faustus does not cure her it will be all through her a viper has bitten her a viper a viper.

    Dog

Thank you

      Woman at the window

A viper has bitten her and if Doctor Faustus does not cure her it will be all through her.

      Chorus in the distance

Who is she

She has not gone to hell

Very well

Very well

She has not gone to hell

Who is she

Marguerite Ida and Helena Annabel

And what has happened to her

A viper has bitten her

And if Doctor Faustus does not cure her

It will go all through her

And he what does he say

He says he cannot see her

Why cannot he see her

Because he cannot look at her

He cannot look at Marguerite Ida and Helena Annabel

But he cannot cure her without seeing her

They say yes yes

And he says there is no witness

And he says

He can but he will not

And she says he must and he will

And the dog says thank you

And the boy says very well

And the woman says well cure her and she says she is Marguerite Ida and Helena Annabel.

    There is silence the lights flicker and flicker, and Marguerite Ida and Helena Annabel gets weaker and weaker and the poison stronger and stronger and suddenly the dog says startlingly

Thank you

    Doctor Faustus says

I cannot see you

The viper has forgotten you.

The dog has said thank you

The boy has said will you

The woman has said

Can you

And you, you have said you are you

Enough said.

You are not dead.

Enough said

Enough said.

You are not dead.

No you are not dead

Enough said

Enough said

You are not dead.

    All join in enough said you are not dead you are not dead enough said yes enough said no you are not dead yes enough said, thank you yes enough said no you are not dead.

    And at the last

    In a low whisper

    She says

I am Marguerite Ida and Helena Annabel and enough said I am not dead.

    Curtain

Act II

Some one comes and sings

Very

Very

Butter better very well

Butcher whether it will tell

Well is well and silver sell

Sell a salted almond to Nell

Which she will accept

And then

What does a fatty do

She does not pay for it.

No she does not

Does not pay for it.

By this time they know how to spell very

Very likely the whole thing is really extraordinary

Which is a great relief

All the time her name is Marguerite Ida Marguerite Ida

    They drift in and they sing

Very likely the whole thing is extraordinary

Which is a great relief

All the time her name is Marguerite Ida

Marguerite Ida.

    Then they converse about it.

Marguerite Ida is her name Marguerite Ida and Helena Annabel who can tell if her name is Marguerite Ida or Helena Annabel

Sillies all that is what makes you tall.

To be tall means to say that everything else is layed away.
Of course her names is Marguerite Ida too and Helena Annabel as well.

   A full chorus
Of course her names is Marguerite Ida too and Helena Annabel as well.

   A deep voice asks
Would a viper have stung her if she had only had one name would he would he.
How do you know how do you know that a viper did sting her.
How could Doctor Faustus have cured her if there had not been something the matter with her.
Marguerite Ida and Helena Annabel it is true her name is Marguerite Ida and Helena Annabel as well and a viper has stung her and Doctor Faustus has cured her, cured her cured her, he has sold his soul to hell cured her cured her cured he he has sold his soul to hell and her name is Marguerite Ida and Helena Annabel and a viper had to bite her and Doctor Faustus had to cure her cure her cure her cure her.

   The curtain at the corner raises and there she is Marguerite Ida and Helena Annabel and she has an artificial viper there beside her and a halo is around her not of electric light but of candle light, and she sits there and waits.

   The chorus sings
There she is
Is she there
Look and see
Is she there
Is she there
Anywhere
Look and see
Is she there
Yes she is there
There is there
She is there
Look and see
She is there.
There she is
There there
Where
Why there
Look and see there
There she is
And what is there
A viper is there
The viper that bit her
No silly no
How could he be there
This is not a viper
This is what is like a viper
She is there
And a viper did bite her
And Doctor Faustus did cure her
And now

And now
And now she is there
Where
Why there
Oh yes there.
Yes oh yes yes there.
There she is
Look and see
And the viper is there
And the light is there
Who gave her the light
Nobody did
Doctor Faustus sold his soul
And so the light came there
And did she sell her soul.
No silly he sold his soul
She had a viper bite her
She is there
Oh yes she is there
Look there
Yes there
She is there.

   Marguerite Ida begins to sing
I sit and sit with my back to the sun I sat and sat with my back to the sun. Marguerite Ida sat and sat with her back to the sun. The sun oh the sun the lights are bright like the sun set and she sat with her back to the sun sat and sat

   She sits
   A very grand ballet of lights.
Nobody can know that it so
They come from everywhere
By land by sea by air
They come from everywhere
To look at her there.
See how she sits
See how she eats
See how she lights,
The candle lights.
See how the viper there,
Cannot hurt her.
No indeed he cannot.
Nothing can touch her,
She has everything
And her soul,
Nothing can lose her,
See how they come
See how they come
To see her.
See how they come.
Watch
They come by sea
They come by land
They come by air
And she sits
With her back to the sun

One sun
And she is one
Marguerite Ida and Helena Annabel as well.

They commence to come and more and more come and they come from the sea from the land and from the air.

And she sits.

A man comes from over the seas and a great many are around him

He sees her as she sits.

And be says
Pretty pretty dear
She is all my love and always here
And I am hers and she is mine
And I love her all the time
Pretty pretty pretty dear.
No says the chorus no.
She is she and the viper bit her
And Doctor Faustus cured her.
The man from over seas repeats
Pretty pretty pretty dear
She is all my love and always here
And I am hers and she is mine
And I love her all the time.

Marguerite Ida and Helena Annabel suddenly hears something and says
What is it.

He comes forward and says again
Pretty pretty pretty dear she is all my love and she is always here.

She sings slowly
You do or you do not.

He
Pretty pretty dear she is all my love and she is always here.
Well well he says well well and her name is Marguerite Ida and Helena Annabel and they all say it was a viper, what is a viper, a viper is a serpent and anybody has been bitten and not everybody dies and cries, and so why why say it all the time, I have been bitten I I I have been bitten by her bitten by her there she sits with her back to the sun and I have won I have won her I have won her.

She sings a song
You do or you do not
You are or you are not
I am there is no not
But you you you
You are as you are not

He says
Do you do what you do because you knew all the way through that I I was coming to you answer me that.

She turns her back on him.

And he says
I am your sun oh very very well begun, you turn your back on your sun, I any your sun, I have won I have won I am your sun.

Marguerite Ida and Helena Annabel rises. She holds the viper she says
Is it you Doctor Faustus is it you, tell me man from over the sea are you he.

He laughs.
Are you afraid now afraid of me.

She says
Are you he.

He says
I am the only he and you are the only she and we are the only we. Come come do you hear me come come, you must come to me, throw away the viper throw away the sun throw away the lights until there are none. I am not any one I am the only one, you have to have me because I am that one.

She looks very troubled and drops the viper but she instantly stoops and picks it up and some of the lights go out and she fusses about it.

And then suddenly she starts,
No one is one when there are two, look behind you look behind you you are not one you are two.

She faints.

And indeed behind the man of the seas is Mephistopheles and with him is a boy and a girl.

Together they sing the song the boy and the girl.
Mr. Viper think of me. He says you do she says you do and if you do dear Mr. Viper if you do then it is all true he is a boy I am girl it is all true dear dear Mr. Viper think of me.

The chorus says in the back,
Dear dear Mr. Viper think of them one is a boy one is a girl dear dear viper dear dear viper think of them.

Marguerite Ida and Helena Annabel still staring at the man from over the seas and Mephisto behind them.

She whispers,
They two I two they two that makes six it should be seven they two I two they two five is heaven.

Mephisto says
And what if I ask what answer me what, I have a will of iron yes a will to do what I do. I do what I do what I do, I do I do.

And he strides forward,
Where where where are you, what a to do, when a light is bright there is moon-light, when a light is not so bright then it is daylight, and when a light is no light than it is electric light, but you you have candle light, who are you.

The ballet rushes in and out.

Marguerite Ida and Helena Annabel lifts the viper and says
Lights are all right but the viper is my might.

Pooh says Mephisto, I despise a viper, the viper tries but the viper lies. Me they cannot touch no not any such, a viper, ha ha a viper, a viper, ha ha, no the lights the lights the candle lights, I know a light when I see a light, I work I work all day and all night, I am the devil and day and night, I never sleep by any light by any dark by any might, I never sleep not by day not by night, you cannot fool me by candle light, where is the real electric light woman answer me.

The little boy and girl creep closer, they sing.

Mr. Viper dear Mr. Viper, he is a boy I am a girl she is a girl I am a boy we do not want to annoy but we do oh we do oh Mr. Viper yes we do we want you to know that she is a girl that I am boy, oh yes Mr. Viper please Mr. Viper here we are Mr. Viper listen to us Mr. Viper, oh please Mr. Viper it is not true Mr. Viper what the devil says Mr. Viper that there is no Mr. Viper, please Mr. Viper please Mr. Viper, she is a girl he is a boy please Mr. Viper you are Mr. Viper please Mr. Viper please tell us so.

The man from over the seas smiles at them all, and says

It is lovely to be at ease.

Mephisto says

What you know I am the devil and you do not listen to me I work and I work by day and by night and you do not listen to me he and she she and he do not listen to me you will see you will see, if I work day and night and I do I do I work day and night, then you will see what you will see, look out look out for me.

He rushes away

And Helena Annabel and Marguerite Ida shrinks back, and says to them all

What does he say

And the man from over the seas says

Pretty pretty dear she is all my love and she is always here.

and then more slowly

I am the only he you are the only she and we are the only we,
and the chorus sings softly

And the viper did bite her and Doctor Faustus did cure her.
And the boy and girl sing softly.

Yes Mr. Viper he is a boy she is a girl yes Mr. Viper.
And the ballet of lights fades away.

Curtain

Act III – Scene I

Doctor Faustus' house

Faustus in his chair, the dog and the boy, the electric lights are right but the room is dark,

Faustus

Yes they shine

They shine all the time.

I know they shine

I see them shine

And I am here

I have no fear

But what shall I do

I am all through

I cannot bear

To have no care

I like it bright

I do like it bright

Alright I like it bright,

But is it white

Or is it bright.

Dear dear

I do care

That nobody can share.

What if they do

It is all to me

Ah I do not like that word me,

Why not even if it does rhyme with she. I know all the words that rhyme with bright with light with might with alright, I know them so that I cannot tell I can spell but I cannot tell how much I need to not have that, not light not sight, not light not night not alright, not night not sight not bright, no no not night not sight not bright no no not bright.

There is a moment's silence and then the dog says

Thank you.

He turns around and then he says

Yes thank you.

And then he says

Not bright not night dear Doctor Faustus you are right, I am a dog yes I am just that I am I am a dog and I bay at the moon, I did yes I did I used to do it I used to bay at the moon I always used to do it and now now not any more, I cannot, of course I cannot, the electric lights they make it be that there is no night and if there is no night then there is no moon and if there is no moon I do not see it and if I do not see it I cannot bay at it.

The dog sighs and settles down to rest

and as he settles down he says

Thank you.

The little boy cuddles up close to him and says

Yes there is no moon and if there is a moon then we do not bay at the moon and if there is no moon then no one is crazy any more because it is the moon of course it is the moon that always made them be like that, say thank you doggie and I too I too with you will say thank you.

They softly murmur

Thank you thank you thank you too.

They all sleep in the dark with the electric light all bright, and then at the window comes something.

Is it the moon says the dog is it the moon says the boy is it the moon do not wake me is it the moon says Faustus.

No says a woman no it is not it is not the moon, I am not the moon I am at the window Doctor Faustus do not you know what it is that Is happening.

No answer.

Doctor Faustus do not you know what is happening.

Back of her a chorus

Doctor Faustus do not you know what is happening.

Still no answer

All together louder

Doctor Faustus do not you know do not you know what it is that is happening.

Doctor Faustus.

Go away woman and men, children and dogs moon and stars

go away let me alone let me be alone no light is bright, I have no sight, go away woman and let me boy and dog let me be alone I need no light to tell me it is bright, go away go away, go away go away.

No says the woman no I am at the window and here I remain till you bear it all. Here we know because Doctor Faustus tells us so, that he only he can turn night into day but now they say, they say, (her voice rises to a screech) they say a woman can turn night into day, they say a woman and a viper bit her and did not hurt her and he showed her how and now she can turn night into day, Doctor Faustus oh Doctor Faustus say you are the only one who can turn night into day, oh Doctor Faustus yes do say that you are the only one who can turn night into day.

The chorus behind says
Oh Doctor Faustus oh Doctor Faustus do say that you are the only one who can turn night into day.

Faustus starts up confused he faces the woman, he says,
What is it you say.

And she says imploringly,
Oh Doctor Faustus do say you are the only one who can turn night into day.

Faustus slowly draws himself erect and says
Yes I do say I am the only one who can turn night into day.
    And the woman and the chorus say,
He is the only one who can turn night into day.
    And the dog says
He is the only one who can turn night into day, there is no moon any night or any day he is the only one to turn night into day,
    and the little boy says
Yes he is the only one to turn night into day.
    And the woman then says
But come Doctor Faustus come away come and see whether they say that they can turn night into day.
Who says
    says Doctor Faustus
She says
    says the woman
Who is she
    says Doctor Faustus
    The answer
Marguerite Ida or Helena Annabel
She
    says Doctor Faustus
Who said I could not go to hell.
She she
    says the woman
She she
    says the chorus
Thank you
    said the dog
Well
    said Doctor Faustus

Well then I can go to hell, if she can turn night into day then I can go to hell, come on then come on we will go and see her and I will show her that I can go to hell, if she can turn night into day as they say then I am not the only one very well I am not the only one so Marguerite Ida and Helena Annabel listen well you cannot but I I can go to hell. Come on every one never again will I be alone come on come on every one.

They all leave.

Scene II

The scene as before, Marguerite Ida and Helena Annabel sitting with the man from over the seas their backs to the sun, the music to express a noon-day hush.
    Everybody dreamily saying
Mr. Viper please Mr. Viper,
    some saying
Is he is he Doctor Faustus no he isn't no be isn't, is he is he is he all he loves her is he is he all she loves him, no one can remember anything but him, which is she and which is he sweetly after all there is no bee there is a viper such a nice sweet quiet one, nobody any body knows how to run, come any one come, see any one, some, come viper sun, we know no other any one, any one can forget a light, even an electric one but no one no no one can forget a viper even a stuffed one no no one and no one can forget the sun and no one can forget Doctor Faustus no no one and and no one can forget Thank you and the dog and no one can forget a little boy and no one can forget any one no no one.

(These words to be distributed among the chorus)
    and the man from over seas murmurs dreamily
Pretty pretty pretty dear here I am and you are here and yet and yet it would be better yet if you had more names and not only four in one let it be begun, forget it oh forget it pretty one, and if not I will forget that you are one yes I will yes I will pretty pretty one yes I will.

    Marguerite Ida and Helena Annabel stiffens a little
well will you yes I will, no one can know when I do not tell them so that they cannot know anything they know, yes I know, I do know just what I can know, it is not there well anywhere, I cannot come not for any one I cannot say what is night and day but I am the only one who can know anything about any one, am I one dear dear am I one, who hears me knows me I am here and here I am, yes here I am.

    The chorus gets more lively and says
Yes there she is
Dear me
    says the man from over the seas.

    Just then out of the gloom appears at the other end of the stage Faust and the boy and the dog, nobody sees them, just then in front of every one appears Mephisto, very excited and sings
Which of you can dare to deceive me which of you he or she can dare to deceive me, I who have a will of iron I who make what will be happen I who can win men or women I who can

be wherever I am which of you has been deceiving which of you she or he which of you have been deceiving me.

He shouts louder

If there is a light who has the right, I say I gave it to him, she says he gave it to her or she does not say anything, I say I am Mephisto and what I have I do not give no not to any one, who has been in her who has been in him, I will win.

The boy and girl shrilly sing

She is she and he is he and we are we Mr. Viper do not forget to be. Please Mr. Viper do not forget to be, do not forget that she is she and that he is he please Mr. Viper do not forget me.

Faustus murmurs in a low voice

I sold my soul to make it bright with electric light and now no one not I not she not they not he are interested in that thing and I and I I cannot go to hell I have sold my soul to make a light and the light is bright but not interesting in my sight and I would oh yes I would I would rather go to hell be I with all my might and then go to hell oh yes aright.

Mephisto strides up to him and says

You deceived me.

I did not

    says Faustus

    Mephisto.

You deceived me and I am never deceived

Faust, you deceived me and I am always deceived,

Mephisto, you deceived me and I am never deceived.

    Faustus

Well well let us forget it is not ready yet let us forget and now oh how how I want to be me myself all now, I do not care for light let it be however light, I do not care anything but to be well and to go to hell. Tell me oh devil tell me will she will Marguerite Ida and Helena Annabel will she will she really will she go to hell.

    Mephisto

I suppose so.

    Faustus

Well then how dear devil how how can I who have no soul I sold it for a light how can I be I again alright and go to hell.

    Mephisto

Commit a sin

    Faustus

What sin, how can I without a soul commit a sin.

    Mephisto

Kill anything

    Faustus

Kill

    Mephisto

Yes kill something oh yes kill anything.

Yes it is I who have been deceived I the devil who no one can deceive yes it is I I who have been deceived.

    Faustus

But if I kill what then will.

    Mephisto

It is I who have an iron will.

    Faustus

But if I kill what will happen then.

    Mephisto

Oh go to hell.

    Faustus

I will

    He turns he sees the boy and dog he says

I will kill I will I will.

    He whispers

I will kill I will I will.

    He turns to the boy and dog and he says

Boy and dog I will kill you two I will kill I will I will boy and dog I will kill you kill you, the viper will kill you but it will be I who did it, you will die.

    The dog says

Thank you, the light is so bright there is no moon tonight I cannot bay at the moon the viper will kill me. Thank you,

    and the boy says

And I too, there is no day and night there is no dog to-night to say thank you the viper will kill me too, good-bye to you. Mr. Viper please listen to me he is a boy she is a girl.

    There is a rustle the viper appears and the dog and the boy die.

    Faustus

They are dead yes they are dead, dear dog dear boy yes you are dead you are forever ever ever dead and I I can because you die nobody can deny later I will go to hell very well very well I will go to hell Marguerite Ida Helena Annabel I come to tell to tell you that I can go to hell.

    Mephisto

And I, while you cry I who do not deny that now you can go to hell have I nothing to do with you.

    Faustus

No I am through with you I do not need the devil I can go to hell all alone. Leave me alone let me be alone I can go to hell all alone.

    Mephisto

No listen to me now take her with you do I will make you young take her with you do Marguerite Ida and Helena Annabel take her with you do.

    Faustus

Is it true that I can be young.

    Mephisto

Yes.

    Faustus

Alright.

    He is young he approaches Marguerite Ida and Helena Annabel who wakes up and looks at him. He says

Look well I am Doctor Faustus and I can go to hell.

    Marguerite Ida and Helena Annabel

You Doctor Faustus never never Doctor Faustus is old I was told and I saw it with my eyes he was old and could not go to hell and you are young and can go to hell, very well you are not Doctor Faustus never never.

Faustus

I am I am I killed the boy and dog when I was an old man and now I am a young man and you Marguerite Ida and Helena Annabel and you know it well and you know I can go to hell and I can take some one too and that some one will be you.

Marguerite Ida and Helena Annabel

Never never, never never, you think you are so clever you think you can deceive, you think you can be old and you are young and old like any one but never never, I am Marguerite Ida and Helena Annabel and I know no man or devil no viper and no light I can be anything and everything and it is always always alright. No one can deceive me not a young man not an old man not a devil not a viper I am Marguerite Ida and Helena Annabel and never never will a young man be an old man and an old man be a young man, you are not Doctor Faustus no not ever never never

and she falls back fainting into the arms of the man from over the seas who sings Pretty pretty pretty dear I am he and she is she and we are we, pretty pretty dear I am here yes I am here pretty pretty pretty dear.

Mephisto strides up

Always deceived always deceived I have a will of iron and I am always deceived always deceived come Doctor Faustus I have a will of iron and you will go to hell.

Faustus sings

Leave me alone let me be alone, dog and boy boy and dog leave me alone let me be alone

and he sinks into the darkness and it is all dark and the little boy and the little girl sing

Please Mr. Viper listen to me he is he and she is she and we are we please Mr. Viper listen to me.

Curtain

2.11 The Meaning of the Music Hall (1913)

FILIPPO TOMMASO MARINETTI

WE FUTURISTS ARE PROFOUNDLY disgusted with the contemporary stage because it stupidly fluctuates between historic reconstruction (*pastiche* or plagiarism) and a minute, wearying, photographic reproduction of actuality. We delight in frequenting the music-hall or variety theatre, smoking concert, circus, cabaret and night club, which offer today the only theatrical entertainment worthy of the true Futurist spirit.

Futurism exalts the variety theatre because, born as it were with us, it fortunately has no tradition, no masters, no dogmas, and subsists on the moment. The variety theatre is absolutely practical because it aims at entertaining and amusing the public by performances either comic or startling to the imagination. The authors, actors, and mechanics of the variety theatre exist and conquer their difficulties only for one purpose, that of everlastingly startling by new inventions. Hence the absolute impossibility of stagnation or repetition, the desperate emulation of brain and muscle to beat all previous records in agility, speed, strength, complexity and grace.

Futuristic wonder

The variety theatre offering the most lucrative medium for endless inventive effort most naturally produces what I call the *Futuristic Wonder*, a product of modern mechanism. It presents caricature in its fullest form, foolery of the deepest kind, impalpable and delicious irony, absorbing and decisive symbols, torrents of irrepressible hilarity, profound analogies between human beings and the animal, the vegetable, and the mechanical world; swift revelations of cynicism, a network of spritely wit, puns, and cock-and-bull stories which pleasantly fan the intellect: all the scales of laughter to relax the nerves; all the scales of such fun, foolery, doltishness, absurdity as insensibly urge the soul to the very edge of madness; all the new meanings of light, sound, noise, and speech and their mysterious, inexplicable correspondence with the most unexplored centres of our sensibility.

The modern variety theatre is the overflowing melting-pot of all those elements which are combining to prepare our new sensibility. It lends itself to the ironical decomposition of all our worn-out prototypes – the beautiful, the great, the solemn, the religious, the fierce, the seductive, the terrible; and also to the abstract forecasting of those new prototypes which shall succeed them.

The variety theatre is the only kind of theatre where the public does not remain static and stupidly passive, but participates noisily in the action, singing, beating time with the orchestra, giving force to the actor's words by unexpected tags and queer improvised dialogue.

Ideal school of sincerity

The variety theatre is the ideal school for sincerity for man, in that it brutally strips woman of all her veils of the romantic phrases, sighs, and sobs which mask and deform her. On the other hand, it shows up all the most admirable animal qualities of woman, her powers of attack and of seduction, of treachery and of resistance. The variety theatre is a school for heroism by reason of its various record difficulties to be beaten and record efforts to be surpassed, which produce on its stage a strong and healthy atmosphere of danger (looping the loop on a bicycle, in a motor car, or on horseback). The variety theatre is the only school to be recommended to adolescents and young people of promise, because it explains in the swiftest and most striking manner the most mysterious sentimental problems of life and the most complicated political events. In fact, the variety theatre explains and most luminously illustrates the dominating laws of life:

> The interpenetration of separate rhythms.
> The inevitable nature of lying and contradiction.
> The synthetic combination of speed with transformation (*Fregoli*).

The variety theatre is, of course, anti-academical, primitive, and ingenuous, and therefore all the more significant by reason of the unforeseen nature of all its fumbling efforts and the coarse simplicity of its resources (singers who walk methodically round the stage after every verse, like caged beasts). The variety theatre destroys all that is solemn, sacred, earnest, and pure in Art – with a big A. It collaborates with Futurism in the destruction of the immortal masterpieces by plagiarizing them, parodying them, and by retailing them without style, apparatus, or pity, just like any ordinary turn. And that is why we loudly applaud the execution of *Parsifal* in forty minutes.

To provoke immense rows

Futurism wants to perfect the variety theatre by transforming it into the theatre of wonders and of records. It is absolutely necessary to abolish every vestige of logic in the performances of the variety theatre; to exaggerate luxury; multiply contrasts and give the supreme place on the stage to the improbable and the absurd. (Example: to oblige singers to dye their necks, their arms, and especially their hair all colours, hitherto unused for purposes of seduction: green hair, violet arms, blue neck, orange chignons, etc.) Futurism wants to abolish those Parisian revues whose *compere* and *commere* merely replace the chorus of the Greek tragedy. Out upon logic and consecutive ideas!

To introduce surprise and some necessity for action in the audience, I hazard a few random suggestions. To smear gum on a stall so that its occupant may be stuck to his seat and excite general hilarity. Naturally the evening coats or dress would be paid for by the management. To sell the same place to ten different persons; obstructions, discussions and quarrels will necessarily follow. To offer free seats to ladies and gentlemen who are notoriously cracked, irritable, or eccentric – calculated to provoke immense rows by bizarre or objectionable behaviour.

To debauch systematically all classical art, producing, for instance, in one single evening all the Greek, French and Italian tragedies in abridged form. To enliven the works of Beethoven, Wagner, Bach, Bellini, Chopin by cutting into them with Neapolitan songs. To soap carefully the planks of the stage so that the actors may slip up at the most tragic moments.

To encourage in every way the genus of the American Eccentric, all his mechanical grotesque effects, his coarse imagination, his immense brutality, his surprise waistcoat and his baggy trousers, deep as a ship's hold, from which will be brought out, with a thousand other cargoes, the great Futurist hilarity which shall rejuvenate the face of the earth.

Note

From the original publication (in the British newspaper the *Daily Mail*):

In those literary and artistic circles where Life and Decadence meet on equal terms at midnight, Signor Marinetti has created something like a furore by his unexampled power of explaining and illustrating the philosophy of Futurism in terms which are capable of being comprehended, after supper, by the merely human brain. In the article which we print below he attempts to show what the modern music-hall is – as seen through his own remarkable temperament. We accept no responsibility for this effusion, which is sure to interest both those who understand it and those who do not: except to the extent that in the interest of the latter class, who are possibly less numerous than we suppose, it has been slightly – very slightly – edited.

Daily Mail, 21 November 1913

2.12 Theatre of Cruelty: First Manifesto (1938)

ANTONIN ARTAUD

Translated by Victor Corti

WE CANNOT CONTINUE TO prostitute the idea of theatre whose only value lies in its agonising magic relationship to reality and danger.

Put in this way, the problem of theatre must arouse universal attention, it being understood that theatre, through its physical aspect and because it requires *spatial expression* (the only real one in fact) allows the sum total of the magic means in the arts and words to be organically active like renewed exorcisms. From the foregoing it becomes apparent that theatre will never recover its own specific powers of action until it has also recovered its own language.

That is, instead of harking back to texts regarded as sacred and definitive, we must first break theatre's subjugation to the text and rediscover the idea of a kind of unique language somewhere in between gesture and thought.

We can only define this language as expressive, dynamic spatial potential in contrast with expressive spoken dialogue potential. Theatre can still derive possibilities for extension from speech outside words, the development in space of its dissociatory, vibratory action on our sensibility. We must take inflexion into account here, the particular way a word is pronounced, as well as the visual language of things (audible, sound language aside), also movement, attitudes and gestures, providing their meanings are extended, their features connected even as far as those signs, making a kind or alphabet out of those signs. Having become conscious of this spatial language, theatre owes it to itself to organise these shouts, sounds, lights and onomatopoeic language, creating true hieroglyphs out of characters and objects, making use of their symbolism and interconnections in relation to every organ and on all levels.

Therefore we must create word, gesture and expressive metaphysics, in order to rescue theatre from its human, psychological prostration. But all this is of no use unless a kind of real metaphysical temptation, invoking certain unusual notions, lies behind such an effort, for the latter by their very nature cannot be restricted or even formally depicted. These ideas on Creation, Growth and Chaos are all of a cosmic order, giving us an initial idea of a field now completely alien to theatre. They can create a kind of thrilling equation between Man, Society, Nature and Objects.

Anyhow, there is no question of putting metaphysical ideas directly on stage but of creating kinds of temptations, vacuums, around these ideas. Humour and its anarchy, poetry and its symbolism and imagery, give us a kind of primary idea of how to channel the temptation in these ideas.

Here we ought to mention the purely physical side of this language, that is to say all the ways and means it has of acting on our sensibility.

It would be futile to say it calls on music, dancing, mime or mimicry. Obviously it uses moves, harmonies, rhythms, but only up to the point where they can co-operate in a kind of pivotal expression without favouring any particular art. However this does not mean it omits ordinary facts and emotions, but it uses them as a springboard in the same way as HUMOUR as DESTRUCTION can serve to reconcile laughter with our reasoning habits.

But this tangible, objective theatre language captivates and bewitches our senses by using a truly Oriental concept of expression. It runs through our sensibility. Abandoning our Western ideas of speech, it turns words into incantation. It expands the voice. It uses vocal vibrations and qualities, wildly trampling them underfoot. It pile-drives sounds. It aims to exalt, to benumb, to bewitch, to arrest our sensibility. It liberates a new lyricism of gestures which because it is distilled and spatially amplified, ends by surpassing the lyricism of words. Finally it breaks away from language's intellectual subjugation by conveying the sense of a new, deeper intellectualism hidden under these gestures and signs and raised to the dignity of special exorcisms.

For all this magnetism, all this poetry, all these immediately bewitching means would be to no avail if they did not put the mind bodily on the track of something, if true theatre could not give us the sense of a creation where we are in possession of only one of its facets, while its completion exists on other levels.

And it makes no difference whether these other levels are really conquered by the mind, that is to say by our intellect, for this curtails them, a pointless and meaningless act. What matters is that our sensibility is put into a deeper, subtler state of perception by assured means, the very object of magic and ritual, of which theatre is only a reflection.

Technique

The problem is to turn theatre into a function in the proper sense of the word, something as exactly localised as the circulation of our blood through our veins, or the apparently chaotic evolution of dream images in the mind, by an effective mix, truly enslaving our attention.

Theatre will never be itself again, that is to say will never be able to form truly illusive means, unless it provides the audience with truthful distillations of dreams where its taste for crime, its erotic obsessions, its savageness, its fantasies, its utopian sense of life and objects, even its cannibalism, do not gush out on an illusory, make-believe, but on an inner level.

In other words, theatre ought to pursue a re-examination not only of all aspects of an objective, descriptive outside world, but also all aspects of an inner world, that is to say man viewed metaphysically, by every means at its disposal. We believe that only in this way will we be able to talk about imagination's rights in the theatre once more. Neither Humour, Poetry or Imagination mean anything unless they re-examine man organically through anarchic destruction, his ideas on reality and his poetic position in reality, generating stupendous flights of forms constituting the whole show.

But to view theatre as a second-hand psychological or moral operation and to believe dreams themselves only serve as a substitute is to restrict both dreams' and theatre's deep poetic range. If theatre is as bloody and as inhuman as dreams, the reason for this is that it perpetuates the metaphysical notions in some Fables in a present-day, tangible manner, whose atrocity and energy are enough to prove their origins and intentions in fundamental first principles rather than to reveal and unforgettably tie down the idea of continual conflict within us, where life is continually lacerated, where everything in creation rises up and attacks our condition as created beings.

This being so, we can see that by its proximity to the first principles poetically infusing it with energy, this naked theatre language, a non-virtual but real language using man's nervous magnetism, must allow us to transgress the ordinary limits of art and words, actively, that is to say magically to produce a kind of total creation *in real terms,* where man must reassume his position between dreams and events.

Subjects

We do not mean to bore the audience to death with transcendental cosmic preoccupations. Audiences are not interested whether there are profound clues to the show's thought and action, since in general this does not concern them. But these must still be there and that concerns us.

★

The Show: Every show will contain physical, objective elements perceptible to all. Shouts, groans, apparitions, surprise, dramatic moments of all kinds, the magic beauty of the costumes modelled on certain ritualistic patterns, brilliant lighting, vocal, incantational beauty, attractive harmonies, rare musical notes, object colours, the physical rhythm of the moves whose build and fall will be wedded to the beat of moves familiar to all, the tangible appearance of new, surprising objects, masks, puppets many feet high, abrupt lighting changes, the physical action of lighting stimulating heat and cold, and so on.

Staging: This archetypal theatre language will be formed around staging not simply viewed as one degree of refraction of the script on stage, but as the starting point for theatrical creation. And the old duality between author and producer will disappear, to be replaced by a kind of single Creator using and handling this language, responsible both for the play and the action.

Stage Language: We do not intend to do away with dialogue, but to give words something of the significance they have in dreams.

Moreover we must find new ways of recording this language, whether these ways are similar to musical notation or to some kind of code.

As to ordinary objects, or even the human body, raised to the dignity of signs, we can obviously take our inspiration from hieroglyphic characters not only to transcribe these signs legibly so they can be reproduced at will, but to compose exact symbols on stage that are immediately legible.

Then again, this coding and musical notation will be valuable as a means of vocal transcription.

Since the basis of this language is to initiate a special use of inflexions, these must take up a kind of balanced harmony, a subsidary exaggeration of speech able to be reproduced at will.

Similarly the thousand and one facial expressions caught in the form of masks, can be listed and labelled so they may directly and symbolically participate in this tangible stage language, independently of their particular psychological use.

Furthermore, these symbolic gestures, masks, postures, individual or group moves, whose countless meanings constitute an important part of the tangible stage language of evocative gestures, emotive arbitrary postures, the wild pounding of rhythms and sound, will be multiplied, added to by a kind of mirroring of the gestures and postures, consisting of the accumulation of all the impulsive gestures, all the abortive postures, all the lapses in the mind and of the tongue by which speech's incapabilities are revealed, and on occasion we will not fail to turn to this stupendous existing wealth of expression.

Besides, there is a tangible idea of music where sound enters like a character, where harmonies are cut in two and become lost precisely as words break in.

Connections, levels, are established between one means of expression and another; even lighting can have a predetermined intellectual meaning.

Musical Instruments: These will be used as objects, as part of the set.

Moreover they need to act deeply and directly on our sensibility through the senses, and from the point of view of sound they invite research into utterly unusual sound properties and vibrations which present-day musical instruments do not possess, urging us to use ancient or forgotten instruments or to invent new ones. Apart from music, research is also needed into instruments and appliances based on special refining and new alloys which can reach a new scale in the octave and produce an unbearably piercing sound or noise.

Lights – Lighting: The lighting equipment currently in use in the theatre is no longer adequate. The particular action of light on the mind comes into play, we must discover oscillating light effects, new ways of diffusing lighting in waves, sheet lighting like a flight of fire-arrows. The colour scale of the equipment currently in use must be revised from start to finish. Fineness, density and opacity factors must be reintroduced into lighting, so as to produce special tonal properties, sensations of heat, cold, anger, fear and so on.

Costume: As to costume, without believing there can be any uniform stage costume that would be the same for all plays, modern dress will be avoided as much as possible not because of a fetishistic superstition for the past, but because it is perfectly obvious certain age-old costumes of ritual intent, although they were once fashionable, retain a revealing beauty and appearance because of their closeness to the traditions which gave rise to them.

The Stage – The Auditorium: We intend to do away with stage and auditorium, replacing them by a kind of single, undivided locale without any partitions of any kind and this will become the very scene of the action. Direct contact will be established between the audience and the show, between actors and audience, from the very fact that the audience is seated in the centre of the action, is encircled and furrowed by it. This encirclement comes from the shape of the house itself.

Abandoning the architecture of present-day theatres, we will rent some kind of barn or hangar rebuilt along lines culminating in the architecture of some churches, holy places, or certain Tibetan temples.

This building will have special interior height and depth dimensions. The auditorium will be enclosed within four walls stripped of any ornament, with the audience seated below, in the middle, on swivelling chairs allowing them to follow the show taking place around them. In effect, the lack of a stage in the normal sense of the word will permit the action to extend itself to the four corners of the auditorium. Special places will be set aside for the actors and action in the four cardinal points of the hall. Scenes will be acted in front of washed walls designed to absorb light. In addition, overhead galleries run right around the circumference of the room as in some Primitive paintings. These galleries will enable actors to pursue one another from one corner of the hall to the other as needed, and the action can extend in all directions at all perspective levels of height and depth. A shout could be transmitted by word of mouth from one end to the other with a succession of amplifications and inflexions. The action will unfold, extending its trajectory from floor to floor, from place to place, with sudden outbursts flaring up in different spots like conflagrations. And the show's truly illusive nature will not be empty words any more than the action's direct, immediate hold on the spectators. For the action, diffused over a vast area, will require the lighting for one scene and the varied lighting for a performance to hold the audience as well as the characters – and physical lighting methods, the thunder and wind whose repercussions will be experienced by the spectators, will correspond with several actions at once, several phases in one action with the characters clinging together like swarms, will endure all the onslaughts of the situations and the external assaults of weather and storms.

However, a central site will be retained which, without acting as a stage properly speaking, enables the body of the action to be concentrated and brought to a climax whenever necessary.

Objects – Masks – Props: Puppets, huge masks, objects of strange proportions appear by the same right as verbal imagery, stressing the physical aspect of all imagery and expression – with the corollary that all objects requiring a stereotyped physical representation will be discarded or disguised.

Decor: No decor. Hieroglyphic characters, ritual costume, thirty-foot-high effigies of King Lear's beard in the storm, musical instruments as tall as men, objects of unknown form and purpose are enough to fulfil this function.

Topicality: But, you may say, theatre so removed from life, facts or present-day activities … news and events, yes! Anxieties, whatever is profound about them, the prerogative of the few, no! In the *Zohar*, the story of the Rabbi Simeon is as inflammatory as fire, as topical as fire.

Works: We will not act written plays but will attempt to stage productions straight from subjects, facts or known works. The type and lay-out of the auditorium itself governs the show as no theme, however vast, is precluded to us.

Show: We must revive the concept of an integral show. The problem is to express it, spatially nourish and furnish it like tap-holes drilled into a flat wall of rock, suddenly generating geysers and bouquets of stone.

The Actor: The actor is both a prime factor, since the show's success depends on the effectiveness of his acting, as well as a kind of neutral, pliant factor since he is rigorously denied any individual initiative. Besides, this is a field where there are no exact rules. And there is a wide margin dividing a man from an instrument, between an actor required to give nothing more than a certain number of sobs and one who has to deliver a speech, using his own powers of persuasion.

Interpretation: The show will be coded from start to finish, like a language. Thus no moves will be wasted, all obeying a rhythm, every character being typified to the limit, each gesture, feature and costume to appear as so many shafts of light.

Cinema: Through poetry, theatre contrasts pictures of the unformulated with the crude visualisation of what exists. Besides, from an action viewpoint, one cannot compare a cinema image, however poetic it may be, since it is restricted by the film, with a theatre image which obeys all life's requirements.

Cruelty: There can be no spectacle without an element of cruelty as the basis of every show. In our present degenerative state, metaphysics must be made to enter the mind through the body.

The Audience: First, this theatre must exist.

Programme: Disregarding the text, we intend to stage:

1. An adaptation of a Shakespearean work, absolutely consistent with our present confused state of mind, whether this be an apocryphal Shakespeare play such as *Arden of Faversham* or another play from that period.
2. A very free poetic play by Léon-Paul Fargue.
3. An excerpt from *The Zohar*, the Story of Rabbi Simeon which has the ever-present force and virulence of a conflagration.
4. The story of Bluebeard, reconstructed from historical records, containing a new concept of cruelty and eroticism.
5. The Fall of Jerusalem, according to the Bible and the Scriptures. On the one hand a blood-red colour flowing from it, that feeling of running wild and mental panic visible even in daylight. On the other hand, the prophets' metaphysical quarrels, with the dreadful intellectual agitation they cause, their reaction rebounding bodily on the King, the Temple, the Masses and Events.
6. One of the Marquis de Sade's tales, its eroticism transposed, allegorically represented and cloaked in the sense of a violent externalisation of cruelty, masking the remainder.
7. One or more Romantic melodramas where the unbelievable will be an active, tangible, poetic factor.
8. Buchner's *Woyzeck* in a spirit of reaction against our principles, and as an example of what can be drawn from an exact text in terms of the stage.
9. Elizabethan theatre works stripped of the lines, retaining only their period machinery, situations, character and plot.

2.13 First Surrealist Manifesto (1924) *and* Second Surrealist Manifesto (1929)

ANDRÉ BRETON

Translated by Patrick Waldberg

First Surrealist Manifesto (extract)

WE ARE STILL LIVING under the reign of logic, but the logical processes of our time apply only to the solution of problems of secondary interest. The absolute rationalism which remains in fashion allows for the consideration of only those facts narrowly relevant to our experience. Logical conclusions, on the other hand, escape us. Needless to say, boundaries have been assigned even to experience. It revolves in a cage from which release is becoming increasingly difficult. It too depends upon immediate utility and is guarded by common sense. In the guise of civilization, under the pretext of progress, we have succeeded in dismissing from our minds anything that, rightly or wrongly, could be regarded as superstition or myth; and we have proscribed every way of seeking the truth which does not conform to convention. It would appear that it is by sheer chance that an aspect of intellectual life – and by far the most important in my opinion – about which no one was supposed to be concerned any longer has, recently, been brought back to light. Credit for this must go to Freud. On the evidence of his discoveries a current of opinion is at last developing which will enable the explorer of the human mind to extend his investigations, since he will be empowered to deal with more than merely summary realities. Perhaps the imagination is on the verge of recovering its rights. If the depths of our minds conceal strange forces capable of augmenting or conquering those on the surface, it is in our greatest interest to capture them; first to capture them and later to submit them, should the occasion arise, to the control of reason. The analysts themselves can only gain by this. But it is important to note that there is no method fixed *a priori* for the execution of this enterprise, that until the new order it can be considered the province of poets as well as scholars, and that its success does not depend upon the more or less capricious routes which will be followed.

It was only fitting that Freud should appear with his critique on the dream. In fact, it is incredible that this important part of psychic activity has still attracted so little attention. (For, at least from man's birth to his death, thought presents no solution of continuity; the sum of dreaming moments – even taking into consideration pure dream alone, that of sleep – is from the point of view of time no less than the sum of moments of reality, which we shall confine to waking moments.) I have always been astounded by the extreme disproportion in the importance and seriousness assigned to events of the waking moments and to those of sleep by the ordinary observer. Man, when he ceases to sleep, is above all at the mercy of his memory, and the memory normally delights in feebly retracing the circumstance of the dream for him, depriving it of all actual consequence and obliterating the only *determinant* from the point at which he thinks he abandoned this constant hope, this anxiety, a few hours earlier. He has the illusion of continuing something worthwhile. The dream finds itself relegated to a parenthesis, like the night. And in general it gives no more counsel than the night. This singular state of affairs seems to invite a few reflections:

1 Within the limits to which its performance is restricted (or what passes for performance), the dream, according to all outward appearances, is continuous and bears traces of organization. Only memory claims the right to edit it, to suppress transitions and present us with a series of dreams rather than *the dream*. Similarly, at no given instant do we have more than a distinct representation of realities whose co-ordination is a matter of will.[1] It is important to note that nothing leads to a greater dissipation of the constituent elements of the dream. I regret discussing this according to a formula which in principle excludes the dream. For how long, sleeping logicians, philosophers? I would like to sleep in order to enable myself to surrender to sleepers, as I surrender to those who read me with their eyes open, in order to stop the conscious rhythm of my thought from prevailing over this material. Perhaps my dream of last night was a continuation of the preceding night's, and will be continued tonight with an admirable precision. *It could be*, as they say. And as it is in no way proven that, in such a case, the 'reality' with which I am concerned even exists in the dream state, or that it does not sink into the immemorial, then why should I not concede to the dream what I sometimes refuse to reality – that weight of self-assurance which by its own terms is not exposed to my denial? Why should I not expect more of the dream sign than I do of a daily increasing degree of consciousness? Could not the dreams as well be applied to the solution of life's fundamental problems? Are these problems the same in one case as in the other, and do they already exist in the dream? Is the dream less oppressed by sanctions than the rest? I am growing old and, perhaps more than this reality to which I believe myself confined, it is the dream, and the detachment that I owe to it, which is ageing me.

2 I return to the waking state. I am obliged to retain it as a phenomenon of interference. Not only does the mind show a strange tendency to disorientation under these conditions (this is the clue to slips of the tongue and lapses of all kinds whose secret is just beginning to be surrendered to us), but when functioning normally the mind still seems to obey none other than those suggestions which rise from that deep night I am commending. Sound as it may be, its equilibrium is relative. The mind hardly dares express itself and, when it does, is limited to stating that this idea or that woman *has an effect on it*. What effect it cannot say; thus it gives the measure of its subjectivism and nothing more. The idea, the woman, *disturbs* it, disposes it to less severity. Their role is to isolate one second of its disappearance and remove it to the sky in that glorious acceleration that it can be, that it is. Then, as a last resort, the mind invokes chance – a more obscure divinity than the others – to whom it attributes all its aberrations. Who says that the angle from which that idea is presented which affects the mind, as well as what the mind loves in that woman's eye, is not *precisely* the same thing that attracts the mind to its dream and reunites it with data lost through its own error? And if things were otherwise, of what might the mind not be capable? I should like to present it with the key to that passage.

3 The mind of the dreaming man is fully satisfied with whatever happens to it. The agonizing question of possibility does not arise. Kill, plunder more quickly, love as much as you wish. And if you die, are you not sure of being roused from the dead? Let yourself be led. Events will not tolerate deferment. You have no name. Everything is inestimably easy.

What power, I wonder, what power so much more generous than others confers this natural aspect upon the dream and makes me welcome unreservedly a throng of episodes whose strangeness would overwhelm me if they were happening as I write this? And yet I can believe it with my own eyes, my own ears. That great day has come, that beast has spoken.

If man's awakening is harsher, if he breaks the spell too well, it is because he has been led to form a poor idea of expiation.

4 When the time comes when we can submit the dream to a methodical examination, when by methods yet to be determined we succeed in realizing the dream in its entirety (and that implies a memory discipline measurable in generations, but we can still begin by recording salient facts), when the dream's curve is developed with an unequalled breadth and regularity, then we can hope that mysteries which are not really mysteries will give way to the great Mystery. I believe in the future resolution of these two states – outwardly so contradictory – which are dream and reality, into a sort of absolute reality, a *surreality*, so to speak. I am aiming for its conquest, certain that I myself shall not attain it, but too indifferent to my death not to calculate the joys of such possession.

They say that not long ago, just before he went to sleep, Saint-Pol-Roux placed a placard on the door of his manor at Camaret which read: THE POET WORKS.

There is still a great deal to say, but I did want to touch lightly, in passing, upon a subject which in itself would require a very long exposition with a different precision. I shall return to it. For the time being my intention has been to see that justice was done to that *hatred of the marvellous* which rages in certain men, that ridicule under which they would like to crush it. Let us resolve, therefore: the Marvellous is always beautiful, everything marvellous is beautiful. Nothing but the Marvellous is beautiful.

… One night, before falling asleep, I became aware of a most bizarre sentence, clearly articulated to the point where it was impossible to change a word of it, but still separate from the sound of any voice. It came to me bearing no trace of the events with which I was involved at that time, at least to my conscious knowledge. It seemed to me a highly insistent sentence – a sentence, I might say, *which knocked at the window*. I quickly took note of it and was prepared to disregard it when something about its whole character held me back. The sentence truly astounded me. Unfortunately I still cannot remember the exact words to this day, but it was something like: 'A man is cut in half by the window'; but it can only suffer from ambiguity, accompanied as it was by the feeble visual representation of a walking man cut in half by a window perpendicular to the axis of his body.[2] It was probably a simple matter of a man leaning on the window and then straightening up. But the window followed the movements of the man, and I realized that I was dealing with a very rare type of image. Immediately I had the idea of incorporating it into my poetic material, but no sooner had I invested it with poetic form than it went on to give way to a scarcely intermittent succession of sentences which surprised me no less than the first and gave me the impression of such a free gift that the control which I had had over myself up to that point seemed illusory and I no longer thought of anything but how to put an end to the interminable quarrel which was taking place within me.[3]

Totally involved as I was at the time with Freud, and familiar with his methods of examination which I had had some occasion to practise on the sick during the war, I resolved to obtain from myself what one seeks to obtain from a patient – a spoken monologue uttered as rapidly as possible, over which the critical faculty of the subject has no control, unencumbered by any reticence, which is *spoken thought* as far as such a thing is possible. It seemed to me, and still does – the manner in which the sentence about the man cut in two came to me proves it – that the speed of thought is no greater than that of words, and that it does not necessarily defy language or the moving pen. It was with this in mind that Philippe Soupault (with whom I had shared these first conclusions) and I undertook to cover some paper with writing, with a laudable contempt for what might result in terms of literature. The ease of realization did the rest. At the end of the first day we were able to read to each other around fifty pages obtained by this method, and began to compare our results. Altogether, those of Soupault and my own presented a remarkable similarity, even including the same faults in construction: in both cases there was the illusion of an extraordinary verve, a great deal of emotion, a considerable assortment of images of a quality such as we would never have been capable of achieving in ordinary writing, a very vivid graphic quality, and here and there an acutely comic passage. The only difference between our texts seemed to me essentially due to our respective natures (Soupault's is less static than mine) and, if I may hazard a slight criticism, due to the fact that he had made the mistake of distributing a few words in the way of titles at the head of certain pages – no doubt in the spirit of mystification. On the other hand, I must give him credit for maintaining his steadfast opposition to the slightest alteration in the course of any passage which seemed to me rather badly put. He was completely right on this point, of course.[4] In fact it is very difficult to appreciate the full value of the various elements when confronted by them. It can even be said to be impossible to appreciate them at the first reading. These elements are outwardly *as strange to you who have written them as to anyone else*, and you are naturally distrustful of them. Poetically speaking, they are especially endowed with a very high degree of *immediate absurdity*. The peculiarity of this absurdity, on closer examination, comes from their capitulation to everything – both inadmissible and legitimate – in the world, to produce a revelation of a certain number of premises and facts generally no less objective than any others.

In homage to Guillaume Apollinaire – who died recently, and who appears to have consistently obeyed a similar impulse to ours without ever really sacrificing mediocre literary means – Soupault and I used the name SURREALISM to designate the new mode of pure expression which we had at our disposal and with which we were anxious to benefit our friends. Today I do not believe anything more need be said about this word. The meaning which we have given it has generally prevailed over Apollinaire's meaning. With even more justification we could have used SUPERNATURALISM, employed by Gerard de Nerval in the dedication of *Filles de Feu*.[5] In fact, Nerval appears to have possessed to an admirable extent the *spirit* to which we refer. Apollinaire, on the other hand, possessed only the *letter* of surrealism (which was still imperfect) and showed himself powerless to give it the theoretical insight that engages us. Here are two passages by Nerval which appear most significant in this regard:

'I will explain to you, my dear Dumas, the phenomenon of which you spoke above. As you know, there are certain story-tellers who cannot invent without identifying themselves with the characters from their imagination. You know with what conviction our old friend Nodier told how he had had the misfortune to be guillotined at the time of the Revolution; one became so convinced that one wondered how he had managed to stick his head back on.'

'... And since you have had the imprudence to cite one of the sonnets composed in this state of SUPERNATURALIST reverie, as the Germans would say, you must hear all of them. You will find them at the end of the volume. They are hardly more obscure than Hegel's metaphysics or Swedenborg's MEMORABLES, and would lose their charm in explication, if such a thing were possible, so concede me at least the merit of their expression ...'[6]

It would be dishonest to dispute our right to employ the word SURREALISM in the very particular sense in which we intend it, for it is clear that before we came along this word amounted to nothing. Thus I shall define it once and for all:

SURREALISM, noun, masc., Pure psychic automatism by which it is intended to express, either verbally or in writing, the true function of thought. Thought dictated in the absence of all control exerted by reason, and outside all aesthetic or moral preoccupations.

ENCYCL. *Philos.* Surrealism is based on the belief in the superior reality of certain forms of association heretofore neglected, in the omnipotence of the dream, and in the disinterested play of thought. It leads to the permanent destruction of all other psychic mechanisms and to its substitution for them in the solution of the principal problems of life.

Notes (edited)

1. We must take into consideration the *thickness* of the dream. I usually retain only that which comes from the superficial layers. What I prefer to visualize in it is everything that sinks at the awakening, everything that is not left to me of the function of that preceding day, dark foliage, absurd branches. In 'reality', too, I prefer to *fall*.
2. Had I been a painter, this visual representation would undoubtedly have dominated the other. It is certainly my previous disposition which decided it. Since that day I have had occasion to concentrate my attention voluntarily on similar apparitions, and I know that they are not inferior in clarity to auditory phenomena. Armed with a pencil and a blank sheet of paper, it would be easy for me to follow its contours. This is because here again it is not a matter of drawing, *it is only a matter of tracing*. I would be able to draw quite well a tree, a wave, a musical instrument – all things of which I am incapable of furnishing the briefest sketch at this time. Sure of finding my way, I would plunge into a labyrinth of lines which at first would not seem to contribute to anything. And upon opening my eyes I would experience a very strong impression of '*jamais vu*' ...
3. Knut Hamsun attributes the kind of revelation by which I have just been possessed to *hunger*, and he may well be right. (The fact is I was not eating every day at that period) ... Apollinaire affirmed that Chirico's paintings had been executed under the influence of cenesthesiac pains (migraines, colic).
4. I believe increasingly in the infallibility of my thought in regard to myself, and it is too accurate. Nevertheless, in this *writing down of thoughts*, where one is at the mercy of the first exterior distraction, 'transports' can be produced. It would be inexcusable to seek to ignore them. By definition, thought is strong and incapable of being at fault. We must attribute those obvious weaknesses to suggestions which come from outside.
5. And also by Thomas Carlyle in *Sartor Resartus* Chapter VIII: 'Natural Supernaturalism', 1833–4.
6. See also L'Idéoréalisme by Saint-Pol-Roux.

Second Surrealist Manifesto (1929)

IN SPITE OF THE individual courses peculiar to each of its past and present participants, in the end surrealism's overall tendency will be readily admitted to have been nothing so much as the provocation, from an intellectual and moral point of view, of the most universal and serious kind of *crisis of conscience*, and it will be agreed that the attainment or non-attainment of this result can decide its historical success or defeat.

From an intellectual point of view, it was and still is necessary to expose by every available means the factitious character of the old contradictions hypocritically calculated to hinder every unusual agitation on the part of man, and to force its recognition at all costs, if only to give mankind some faint idea of its abilities and to challenge it to escape its universal shackles to some meaningful extent. The bugbear of death, the music-halls of the beyond, the shipwreck of the loftiest intellect in sleep, the crushing curtain of the future, the towers of Babel, the mirrors of inconsistency, the insurmountable silver-splashed wall of the brain – all of these striking images of human catastrophe are perhaps nothing but images. There is every reason to believe that there exists a certain point in the mind at which life and death, real and imaginary, past and future, communicable and incommunicable, high and low, cease to be perceived in terms of contradiction. Surrealist activity would be searched in vain for a motive other than the hope to determine this point. Thus it is sufficiently obvious that it would be absurd to attribute to that activity a uniquely destructive, or constructive, direction: the point in question is, *a fortiori*, that construction and destruction can no longer be brandished against each other. It is also clear that surrealism is not interested in taking much account of what is produced peripherally under the pretext of art – which is really anti-art – philosophy or anti-philosophy, in short, everything that does not conclude in the annihilation of being into a blind, inner splendour which would be no more the essence of ice than of fire. What indeed could be expected from the surrealist experience by those who retain some anxiety about the place they will occupy *in the world*? On that mental plane from which one can undertake for oneself alone the perilous – but, we believe, supreme – recognition, there can be no question of attaching the least importance to the footsteps of those who come or go, since these footsteps occur in a region where, by definition, surrealism has no ear. Surrealism should not be at the mercy of this or that man's whim; if it declares that it can, by its own means, deliver thought from an ever harsher bondage, put it back on the path of total understanding, restore its original purity, then that is enough to justify its being judged only by what it had done and by what remains to be done in order to keep its promise.

Surrealism, particularly in regard to its means of undertaking the investigation of the elements of reality and unreality, reason and unreason, reflection and impulse, knowledge and 'fatal' ignorance, utility and inutility, etc., presents at least one analogy with historical materialism in that it departs from the 'colossal abortion' of the Hegelian system. It seems impossible to me that limits can be assigned – those of the economic plan, for example – to the practice of a philosophy definitely adaptable to negation and the negation of negation. How can they acknowledge that the dialectic method can only be validly applied to the solution of social problems? Surrealism's whole ambition is to furnish that method with possibilities of application not at all concurrent in the most immediate realms of consciousness. With all due respect to certain narrow-minded revolutionaries, I really do not see why we should abstain from raising problems of love, dream, madness, art and religion,[1] provided that we consider them in the same light in which they, and we too, consider Revolution. And I do not hesitate to say that before surrealism nothing systematic had been done in this direction, and that when we found it, *the dialectic method was* – for us too – *inapplicable in its Hegelian form*. For us too it was a question of the need to have done with idealism as such (the creation of the word surrealism alone should prove that) and to return to Engel's example of the need to stop clinging to the juvenile development: 'The rose is a rose. The rose is not a rose. But the rose is still a rose.' Nevertheless – forgive me this digression – it was necessary to set 'the rose' into action conducive to less favourable contradictions, where it might be in succession something from the garden, something with a particular role in a dream, something impossible to separate from the 'optical bouquet', something which can totally change its nature by passing into automatic writing, something which has none of the rose's properties except those the painter has decided to retain in a surrealist painting, and finally, something entirely different from itself, which returns to the garden. This is a far cry from any idealistic conception, and we would not even mention it if we might stop being continuously exposed to attacks of elementary materialism, attacks which emanate both from those who, out of decadent conservatism, have no desire to clarify the relation of thought to matter, and from those who, out of a misunderstood revolutionary sectarianism and in defiance of what is needed, confuse this materialism with that which Engels essentially distinguished from it and which he defined as above all an *intuition of the world* called upon to prove and fulfil itself: *In the course of the development of philosophy, idealism became untenable and was denied by modern materialism. The latter, which is the negation of negation, is not simply a restoration of the old materialism: to those solid foundations it adds the entire conception of philosophy and the natural sciences in the course of a two-thousand-year evolution as well as the product of this long history itself.* We also intend to make it understood as a point of departure that for us philosophy is *outclassed*. This is the fate, I think, of all those for whom reality has not only a theoretical importance but for whom it is also a question of life and death to appeal passionately to that reality, as Feuerbach insisted: ours to give as we *totally*, unreservedly give our support to the principle of historical materialism, his to throw in the face of the astounded intellectual world the idea that 'man is what he eats' and that a future revolution would have a better chance of success if the people received better food, such as peas instead of potatoes.

Our support of the principle of historical materialism – there is no way of playing on these words. Let that depend only on us – I mean provided communism does not treat us merely as strange animals determined to practise star-gazing and defiance in its ranks – and we shall show ourselves capable of doing our full duty from a revolutionary point of view. This, unfortunately, is a pledge which interests only us: for example, two years ago I myself could not enter, freely and unobserved, the headquarters of the French Party, where nevertheless so many disreputable individuals – police and others – are allowed to carry on as though they were in a boiler factory. In the course of three interrogations of several hours' length, I had to defend surrealism against the childish accusation of being in essence a political movement with a clearly anti-communist and counter-revolutionary bent. Needless to say, I expected nothing from the thorough investigation of my ideas on the part of those who were judging me. 'If you are a Marxist', Michel Marty shouted at one of us around that time, 'you do not need to be a surrealist.' Surrealists that we were, it was of course not we who boasted of it in those circumstances: this label had preceded us in spite of ourselves just as that of 'relativists' might have preceded the followers of Einstein, or 'psychoanalysts' those of Freud. How can one not be terribly worried about such a weakening of the ideological level of a party which not long before had emerged so brilliantly armed with two of the best minds of the nineteenth century! One hardly knows: the little that I can conclude from my own personal experience in this regard can be measured by the following. They asked me to give a report on the Italian situation in the 'Gas' cell, specifying that I was to rely upon statistical facts alone (steel production, etc.) and *especially no ideology*. I could not.

Note (edited)

1. For some time now false quotation has been one of the methods most frequently employed against me … a contributor to the *Exquisite Corpse* sharply reprimands me under the pretext that I wrote: 'I vow never to wear the French uniform again.' *I'm, sorry, but that was not me.*

From Patrick Waldberg, *Surrealism*, London: Thames and Hudson, 1978, pp. 66–72 and 76–80.

2.14 Futurist Scenography (Manifesto) (1915)

ENRICO PRAMPOLINI

Translated by Diana Clemmons

April–May 1915

*L*ET'S REFORM THE STAGE. To admit, to believe that a stage has existed up until today is to affirm that artistically man is absolutely blind. The stage is not equivalent to a photographic enlargement of a rectangle of reality or to a relative synthesis, but to the adoption of a theoretical system and subjective scenographic material completely opposed to the so-called objective scenography of today.

It is not only a question of reforming the conception of the structure of the *mise-en-scène*; one must create an abstract entity which identifies itself with the scenic action of the play.

It is wrong to view the stage separately, as a pictorial fact: (a) because we are no longer dealing with scenography but with simple painting; (b) we are returning to the past (that is to say to the past ... present) where the stage expresses one subject, the play develops another.

These two forces which have been diverging (playwright and scenographer) must converge to form a multiple synthesis of the play.

The stage must live the theatrical action in its dynamic synthesis; it must express the essence of the character conceived by the author just as an actor at once expresses and lives it within himself. Therefore, in order to reform the stage one must:

1 Deny exact reconstruction of that which the playwright has conceived, thus abandoning resolutely every factual relationship, every comparison between object and subject and vice versa; all these relationships weaken direct emotion with indirect sensations.
2 Substitute for scenic action an emotional order which awakens all sensations necessary to the development of the play; the resulting atmosphere will provide the interior milieu.
3 *Absolute synthesis* in material expression of the stage, which means not the pictorial synthesis of all the elements, but synthesis excluding those elements of scenic architecture which are incapable of producing new sensations.
4 The scenic architecture will have to be a connection for the audience's intuition rather than a picturesque and elaborate collaboration.
5 The colors and the stage will have to arouse in the spectator those emotional values which neither the poet's words nor the actor's gestures can evoke.

There are no theatre reformers today: Dresa and Rouché experimented in France with ingenuous and infantile expressions; Meyerhold and Stanislavsky in Russia with revivals of sickening classicism (we leave out the Assyrian-Persian-Egyptian-Nordic plagiarist Bakst); Adolphe Appia, Fritz Erler, Littman Fuchs and Max Reinhardt (organizer) in Germany have attempted reforms directed more toward tedious elaboration, rich in glacial exteriors, than toward the essential idea of interpretive reform; Granville-Barker and Gordon Craig in England have made some limited innovations, some objective syntheses.

Displays and material simplifications, not rebellion against the past. It is this necessary revolution which we intend to provoke, because no one has had the artistic austerity to renovate the interpretive conception of the element to be expressed.

Our scenography is a monstrous thing. Today's scenographers, sterile whitewashers, still prowl around the dusty and stinking corners of classical architecture.

We must rebel and assert ourselves and say to our poet and musician friends: this action demands this stage rather than that one.

Let us be artists too, and no longer merely executors. Let us create the theatre, give life to the play with all the evocative power of our art.

It goes without saying that we need plays suited to our sensibility, which implies a more intense and synthetic conception in the scenic development of subjects.

Let's renovate the stage. The absolutely new feature that our innovation will give the theatre is *the abolition of the painted stage.* The stage will no longer be a colored backdrop, but an *uncolored electro-mechanical architecture, powerfully vitalized by chromatic emanations from a luminous source,* produced by electric reflectors, with multicolored panes of glass, arranged, coordinated analogically with the swing-mirror of each scenic action.

With the luminous irradiation of these sheaves, of these planes of colored lights, the dynamic combinations will give marvelous results of mutual permeation, of intersection of lights and shadows. From these will be born blank surrenders, corporalities luminous with exultation. These assemblages, these unreal shocks, this exuberance of sensations combined with dynamic stage architectures which will move, unleashing metallic arms, knocking over plastic frameworks, amidst an essentially new, modern noise, will augment the vital intensity of the scenic action.

On a stage illuminated in such a way the actors will gain unforeseen dynamic effects which are neglected or very seldom employed in today's theatres, mostly because of the ancient prejudice that one must imitate, represent reality.

What's the use?

Is it that the scenographers believe it absolutely necessary to represent this reality? Idiots! Don't you understand that your efforts, your useless realistic preoccupations have no effect other than that of diminishing the intensity and emotional content, which can be attained precisely through the interpretive equivalents of these realities, i.e., abstractions?

Let's create the theatre. In the above lines we have upheld the idea of a dynamic theatre as opposed to the static theatre of old; with the fundamental principles which we shall set forth, we intend not only to carry the theatre to its most advanced expression, but also to attribute the essential values which belong to it and which no one has thought of presenting till now.

Let's exchange the roles. Instead of the illuminated stage, let's create the *illuminant stage: luminous expression which will irradiate the colors demanded by the theatrical action with all its emotional power.*

The material means of expressing this illuminant stage consist in employing electrochemical colors, fluorescent tubes which have the chemical property of being susceptible to electric current and diffusing luminous colorations of all tonalities according to the combinations of fluorine with other such gases. The desired effects of luminosity will be obtained by stimulating these gases (systematically arranged according to the proper design on this immense sceno-dramatic architecture) with electric neon (ultraviolet) tubes. But the Futurist scenographic and choreographic evolution must not stop there. In the final synthesis human actors will no longer be tolerated, like children's jumping jacks, or today's super-marionettes recommended by recent reformers; neither one nor the other can sufficiently express the multiple aspects conceived by the playwright.

In the totally realizable époque of Futurism we shall see the luminous dynamic architectures of the stage emanate from chromatic incandescences which, mounting tragically or showing themselves voluptuously, will inevitably arouse new sensations and emotional values in the spectator.

Vibrations, luminous forms (produced by electric currents and colored gases) will wriggle and writhe dynamically, and these veritable actor-gases of an unknown theatre will have to replace living actors. By shrill whistles and strange noises these actor-gases will be able to give the unusual significations of theatrical interpretations quite well; they will be able to express these multiform emotive qualities with much more effectiveness than some celebrated actor or other can with his displays. These exhilarant, explosive gases will fill the audience with cheerfulness or terror and it will perhaps become an actor itself, too. But these words are not our last. We still have much to say. Let us first carry out what we have set forth above.

Note

From E. T. Kirby, *Total Theatre: A Critical Anthology*, New York: Dutton, 1969, pp. 89–95. Reprinted from *Archivi del Futurismo*, vol. I, Rome: De Luca Editore, translated by Diana Clemmons.

2.15 Theater, Circus, Variety (1924)

LÁSZLÓ MOHOLY-NAGY

Translated by Arthur S. Wensinger

1. The historical theater

THE HISTORICAL THEATER WAS essentially a disseminator of information or propaganda, or it was an articulated concentration of action (*Aktionskonzentration*) derived from events and doctrines in their broadest meaning – that is to say, as 'dramatized' legend, as religious (cultist) or political (proselytizing) propaganda, or as compressed action with a more or less transparent purpose behind it.

The theater differed from the eyewitness report, simple storytelling, didactic moralizing, or advertising copy through its own particular synthesis of the elements of presentation: SOUND, COLOR (LIGHT), MOTION, SPACE, FORM (OBJECTS AND PERSONS).

With these elements, in their accentuated but often uncontrolled interrelationships, the theater attempted to transmit an articulated experience.

In early epic drama (*Erzählungsdrama*) these elements were generally employed as illustration, subordinated to narration or propaganda. The next step in this evolution led to the drama of action (*Aktionsdrama*), where the elements of dynamic-dramatic movement began to crystallize: the theater of improvisation, the *commedia dell'arte*. These dramatic forms were progressively liberated from a central theme of logical, intellectual-emotional action which was no longer dominant. Gradually their moralizing and their tendentiousness disappeared in favor of an unhampered concentration on action: Shakespeare, the opera.

With August Stramm,[1] drama developed away from verbal context, from propaganda, and from character delineation, and toward explosive activism. Creative experiments with MOTION AND SOUND (speech) were made, based on the impetus of human sources of energy, that is, the 'passions.' Stramm's theater did not offer narrative material, but action and tempo, which, unpremeditated, sprang almost AUTOMATICALLY and in headlong succession from the human impulse for motion. But even in Stramm's case action was not altogether free from literary encumbrance.

'Literary encumbrance' is the result of the unjustifiable transfer of intellectualized material from the proper realm of literary effectiveness (novel, short story, etc.) to the stage, where it incorrectly remains a dramatic end in itself. The result is nothing more than literature if a reality or a potential reality, no matter how imaginative, is formulated or visually expressed without the creative forms peculiar only to the stage. It is not until the tensions concealed in the utmost economy of means are brought into universal and dynamic interaction that we have creative

Figure 15 Moholy-Nagy, *Human Mechanics* (*Variety*). (Photograph: uncredited.)

stagecraft (*Bühnengestaltung*). Even in recent times we have been deluded about the true value of creative stagecraft when revolutionary, social, ethical, or similar problems were unrolled with a great display of literary pomp and paraphernalia.

2. Attempts at a theater form for today
a) Theater of Surprises: Futurists, Dadaists, Merz[2]

In the investigation of any morphology, we proceed today from the all-inclusive functionalism of goal, purpose, and materials.

From this premise the FUTURISTS, EXPRESSIONISTS, and DADAISTS (MERZ) came to the conclusion that phonetic word relationships were more significant than other creative literary means, and that the logical-intellectual content (*das Logisch-Gedankliche*) of a work of literature was far from its primary aim. It was maintained that, just as in representational painting it was not the content as such, not the objects represented which were essential, but the interaction of colors, so in literature it was not the logical-intellectual content which belonged in the foreground, but the effects which arose from the word-sound relationships. In the case of some writers this idea has been extended (or possibly contracted) to the point where word relationships are transformed into

L. MOHOLY-NAGY   The Benevolent Gentlemen (Circus Scene)

Figure 16 Moholy-Nagy, *The Benevolent Gentleman* (*Circus Scene*). (Photograph: uncredited.)

exclusively phonetic sound relationships, thereby totally fragmenting the word into conceptually disjointed vowels and consonants.

This was the origin of the Dadaist and Futurist 'Theater of Surprises,' a theater which aimed at the elimination of logical–intellectual (literary) aspects. Yet in spite of this, man, who until then had been the sole representative of logical, causal action and of vital mental activities, still dominated.

b) The Mechanized Eccentric (*Die mechanische Exzentrik*)

As a logical consequence of this there arose the need for a MECHANIZED ECCENTRIC, a concentration of stage action in its purest form (*eine Aktionskonzentration der Bühne in Reinkultur*). Man, who no longer should be permitted to represent himself as a phenomenon of spirit and mind through his intellectual and spiritual capacities, no longer has any place in this concentration of action. For, no matter how cultured he may be, his organism permits him at best only a certain range of action, dependent entirely on his natural body mechanism.

The effect of this body mechanism (*Körpermechanik*) (in circus performance and athletic events, for example) arises essentially from the spectator's astonishment or shock at the potentialities of his *own* organism as demonstrated to him by others. This is a subjective effect. Here the human body is the sole medium of configuration (*Gestaltung*). For the purposes of an objective *Gestaltung* of movement this medium is limited, the more so since it has constant reference to sensible and perceptive (i.e., again literary) elements. The inadequacy of 'human' *Exzentrik* led to the demand for a precise and fully controlled organization of form and motion, intended to be a synthesis of dynamically contrasting phenomena (space, form, motion, sound, and light). This is the Mechanized Eccentric.

3. The coming theater: Theater of Totality

Every form process or *Gestaltung* has its general as well as its particular premises, from which it must proceed in making use of its specific media. We might, therefore, clarify theater production (*Theatergestaltung*) if we investigated the nature of its highly controversial media: the human *word* and the human *action*, and, at the same time, considered the endless possibilities open to their creator – man.

The origins of MUSIC as conscious composition can be traced back to the melodic recitations of the heroic saga. When music was systematized, permitting only the use of HARMONIES (KLÄNGE) and excluding so-called SOUNDS (GERÄUSCHE), the only place left for a special sound form (*Geräuschgestaltung*) was in literature, particularly in poetry. This was the underlying idea from which the Expressionists, Futurists, and Dadaists proceeded in composing their sound-poems (*Lautgedichte*). But today, when music has been broadened to admit sounds of all kinds, the sensory-mechanistic effect of sound interrelationships is no longer a monopoly of poetry. It belongs, as much as do harmonies (*Töne*), to the realm of music, much in the same way that the task of painting, seen as color creation, is to organize clearly primary (apperceptive)[3] color effect. Thus the error of the Futurists, the Expressionists, the Dadaists, and all those who built on such foundations becomes clear. As an example: the idea of an *Exzentrik* which is ONLY mechanical.

It must be said, however, that those ideas, in contradistinction to a literary–illustrative viewpoint, have unquestionably advanced creative theater precisely because they were diametrically opposed. They canceled out the predominance of the exclusively logical–intellectual values. But once the predominance has been broken, the associative processes and the language of man, and consequently man himself in his totality as a formative medium for the stage, may not be barred from it. To be sure, he is no longer to be pivotal – as he is in traditional theater – but is to be employed ON AN EQUAL FOOTING WITH THE OTHER FORMATIVE MEDIA.

Man as the most active phenomenon of life is indisputably one of the most effective elements of a dynamic stage production (*Bühnengestaltung*), and therefore he justifies on functional grounds the utilization of his totality of action, speech, and thought. With his intellect, his dialectic, his adaptability to any situation by virtue of his control over his physical and mental powers, he is – when used in any concentration of action (*Aktionskonzentration*) – destined to be primarily a configuration of these powers.

And if the stage didn't provide him full play for these potentialities, it would be imperative to create an adequate vehicle.

But this utilization of man must be clearly differentiated from his appearance heretofore in traditional theater. While there he was only the interpreter of a literarily conceived individual or type, in the new THEATER OF TOTALITY he will use the spiritual and physical means at his disposal PRODUCTIVELY and from his own INITIATIVE submit to the overall action process.

While during the Middle Ages (and even today) the center of gravity in theater production lay in the representation of the various *types* (hero, harlequin, peasant, etc.), it is the task of the FUTURE ACTOR to discover and activate that which is COMMON to all men.

In the plan of such a theater the traditionally 'meaningful' and causal interconnections can NOT play the major role. In the consideration of stage setting as an *art form*, we must learn from the creative artist that, just as it is impossible to ask what a man (as organism) is or stands for, it is inadmissible to ask the same question of a contemporary nonobjective picture which likewise is a *Gestaltung*, that is, an organism.

The contemporary painting exhibits a multiplicity of color and surface interrelationships, which gain their effect, on the one hand, from their conscious and logical statement of problems, and on the other, from the unanalyzable intangibles of creative intuition.

In the same way, the Theater of Totality with its multifarious complexities of light, space, plane, form, motion, sound, man — and with all the possibilities for varying and combining these elements — must be an ORGANISM.

Thus the process of integrating man into creative stage production must be unhampered by moralistic tendentiousness or by problems of science or the INDIVIDUAL. Man may be active only as the bearer of those functional elements which are organically in accordance with his specific nature.

It is self-evident, however, that all *other* means of stage production must be given positions of effectiveness equal to man's, who as a living psychophysical organism, as the producer of incomparable climaxes and infinite variations, demands of the coformative factors a high standard of quality.

4. How shall the Theater of Totality be realized?

One of two points of view still important today holds that theater is the concentrated activation (*Aktionskonzentration*) of sound, light (color), space, form, and motion. Here man as co-actor is not necessary, since in our day equipment can be constructed which is far more capable of executing the *purely mechanical* role of man than man himself.

The other, more popular view will not relinquish the magnificent instrument which is man, even though no one has yet solved the problem of how to employ him as a creative medium on the stage.

Is it possible to include his human, logical functions in a present-day concentration of action on the stage, without running the risk of producing a copy from nature and without falling prey to Dadaist or Merz characterization, composed of an eclectic patchwork whose seeming order is purely arbitrary?

The creative arts have discovered pure media for their constructions: the primary relationships of color, mass, material, etc. But how can we integrate a sequence of human movements and thoughts on an equal footing with the controlled, 'absolute' elements of sound, light (color), form, and motion? In this regard only summary suggestions can be made to the creator of the new theater (*Theatergestalter*). For example, the REPETITION of a thought by many actors, with identical words and with identical or varying intonation and cadence, could be employed as a means of creating synthetic (i.e., unifying) creative theater. (This would be the CHORUS – but not the attendant and passive chorus of antiquity!) Or mirrors and optical equipment could be used to project the gigantically enlarged faces and gestures of the actors, while their voices could be amplified to correspond with the visual MAGNIFICATION. Similar effects can be obtained from the SIMULTANEOUS, SYNOPTICAL, and SYNACOUSTICAL reproduction of thought (with motion pictures, phonographs, loud-speakers), or from the reproduction of thoughts suggested by a construction of variously MESHING GEARS (*eine* ZAHNRADARTIG INEINANDERGREIFENDE *Gedankengestaltung*).

Independent of work in music and acoustics, the literature of the future will create its own 'harmonies,' at first primarily adapted to its own media, but with far-reaching implications for others. These will surely exercise an influence on the word and thought constructions of the stage.

This means, among other things, that the phenomena of the subconscious and dreams of fantasy and reality, which up to now were central to the so called 'INTIMATE ART THEATER' ('KAMMER-SPIELE'), may no longer be predominant. And even if the conflicts arising from today's complicated social patterns, from the world-wide organization of technology, from pacifist-utopian and other kinds of revolutionary movements, can have a place in the art of the stage, they will be significant only in a transitional period, since their treatment belongs properly to the realms of literature, politics, and philosophy.

We envision TOTAL STAGE ACTION (GESAMTBÜHNENAKTION) as a great dynamic-rhythmic process, which can compress the greatest clashing masses or accumulations of media – as qualitative and quantitative tensions – into elemental form. Part of this would be the use of simultaneously inter-penetrating sets of contrasting relationships, which are of minor importance in themselves, such as: the tragicomic, the grotesque-serious, the trivial-monumental; hydraulic spectacles; acoustical and other 'pranks'; and so on. Today's CIRCUS, OPERETTA, VAUDEVILLE, the CLOWNS in America and elsewhere (Chaplin, Fratellini) have accomplished great things, both in this respect and in eliminating the subjective – even if the process has been naïve and often more superficial than incisive. Yet it would be just as superficial if we were to dismiss great performances and 'shows' in this genre with the word *Kitsch*. It is high time to state once and for all that the much disdained masses, despite their 'academic backwardness,' often exhibit the soundest instincts and preferences. Our task will always remain the creative understanding of the true, and not the imagined, needs.

5. The means

Every *Gestaltung* or creative work should be an unexpected and new organism, and it is natural and incumbent on us to draw the material for surprise effects from our daily living. Nothing is more effective than the exciting new possibilities offered by the familiar and yet not properly evaluated elements of modern life – that is, its idiosyncrasies: individuation, classification, mecha-nization. With this in mind, it is possible to arrive at a proper understanding of stagecraft through an investigation of creative media other than man-as-actor himself.

In the future, SOUND EFFECTS will make use of various acoustical equipment driven electrically or by some other mechanical means. Sound waves issuing from unexpected sources – for example, a speaking or singing arc lamp, loud-speakers under the seats or beneath the floor of the auditorium, the use of new amplifying systems – will raise the audience's acoustic surprise-threshold so much that unequal effects in other areas will be disappointing.

COLOR (LIGHT) must undergo even greater transformation in this respect than sound.

Developments in painting during the past decades have created the organization of absolute color values and, as a consequence, the supremacy of pure and luminous chromatic tones. Naturally the monumentality and the lucid balance of their harmonies will not tolerate the actor with indistinct or splotchy make-up and tattered costuming, a product of misunderstood Cubism, Futurism, etc. The use of precision-made metallic masks and costumes and those of various other composition materials will thus become a matter of course. The pallid face, the subjectivity of expression, and the gestures of the actor in a colored stage environment are therefore eliminated without impairing the effective contrast between the human body and any mechanical construction. Films can also be projected onto various surfaces and further experiments in space illumination will be devised. This will constitute the new ACTION OF LIGHT, which by means of modern technology will use the most intensified contrasts to guarantee itself a position of importance equal to that of all other theater media. We have not yet begun to realize the potential of light for sudden or blinding illumination, for flare effects, for phosphorescent effects, for bathing the auditorium in light synchronized with climaxes or with the total extinguishing of lights on the stage. All this, of course, is thought of in a sense totally different from anything in current traditional theater.

From the time that stage objects became mechanically movable, the generally traditional, horizontally structured organization of movement in space has been enriched by the possibility of vertical motion. Nothing stands in the way of making use of complex APPARATUS such as film, automobile, elevator, airplane, and other machinery, as well as optical instruments, reflecting-equipment, and so on. The current demand for dynamic construction will be satisfied in this way, even though it is still only in its first stages.

There would be a further enrichment if the present isolation of the stage could be eliminated. In today's theater, STAGE AND SPECTATOR are too much separated, too obviously divided into active and passive, to be able to produce creative relationships and reciprocal tensions.

It is time to produce a kind of stage activity which will no longer permit the masses to be silent spectators, which will not only excite them inwardly but will let them *take hold and participate* – actually allow them to fuse with the action on the stage at the peak of cathartic ecstasy.

To see that such a process is not chaotic, but that it develops with control and organization, will be one of the tasks of the thousand-eyed NEW DIRECTOR, equipped with all the modern means of understanding and communication.

It is clear that the present peep-show stage is not suitable for such organized motion.

The next form of the advancing theater – in cooperation with future authors – will probably answer the above demands with SUSPENDED BRIDGES AND DRAWBRIDGES running horizontally, diagonally, and vertically within the space of the theater; with platform stages built far into the auditorium; and so on. Apart from rotating sections, the stage will have movable space constructions and DISKLIKE AREAS, in order to bring certain action moments on the stage into prominence, as in film 'close-ups.' In place of today's periphery of orchestra loges, a runway joined to the stage could be built to establish – by means of a more or less caliper-like embrace – a closer connection with the audience.

The possibilities for a VARIATION OF LEVELS OF MOVABLE PLANES on the stage of the future would contribute to a genuine organization of space. Space will then no longer consist of the interconnections of planes in the old meaning, which was able to conceive of architectonic delineation of space only as an enclosure formed by opaque surfaces. The new space originates from free-standing surfaces or from linear definition of planes (WIRE FRAMES, ANTENNAS), so that the surfaces stand at times in a very free relationship to one another, without the need of any direct contact.

As soon as an intense and penetrating concentration of action can be functionally realized, there will develop simultaneously the corresponding auditorium ARCHITECTURE. There will also appear COSTUMES designed to emphasize function and costumes which are conceived only for single moments of action and capable of sudden transformations.

There will arise an enhanced *control* over all formative media, unified in a harmonious effect and built into an organism of perfect equilibrium.

Notes

1. August Stramm (1874–1915) was a Westphalian poet and dramatist and the strongest of the members of the circle known as the *Sturmdichter*. His works belong to the early phase of Expressionism and are in a radically elliptical, powerful, and antisyntactical style. – *Translator.*
2. The phenomenon known as *Merz* is closely connected with the Dadaist movement of the post-World War I period in Germany and Switzerland. The term was coined in 1919 by the artist Kurt Schwitters and came from one of his collages in which was incorporated a scrap of newspaper with only the center part of the word 'kommerziell' on it. A whole series of his collages was called *Merzbilder*. From 1923 to 1932, with Arp, Lissitzky, Mondrian, and many others, Schwitters published the magazine *Merz*; and at about the same period the Merz Poets caused a great furor. The movement was characterized by playfulness, earnest experimentalism, and what seems to have been a great need for self-expression and for shocking the bourgeoisie. – *Translator.*
3. 'Apperceptive' signifies here, in contrast to 'associative,' an elementary step in observation and conceptualization (psychophysical assimilation), e.g., to assimilate a color = apperceptive process. The human eye reacts without previous experience to red with green, blue with yellow, etc. An object = assimilation of color + matter + form = connection with previous experience = associative process. – *Translator.*

From *The Theatre of the Bauhaus*, ed. Walter Gropius and A. Wensinger, Baltimore: Johns Hopkins University Press, 1961, reprinted by Wesleyan University Press, 1996, pp. 17–48.

Part 3
Political Theatres

Timeline

	Social, cultural and political context	Theatre
1848	*The Communist Manifesto*: Karl Marx and Friedrich Engels	
1859	*The Origin of Species*: Charles Darwin	
1861–2	Manifesto on the emancipation of serfs and social unrest in Russia	
1869	John Stuart Mill: *The Subjection of Women*	
1892	Strikes by and massacres of workers in Russia	
1893	Independent Labour Party founded in Britain	
1903	Emmeline Pankhurst founds the Women's Social and Political Union	
1904		*John Bull's Other Island*: George Bernard Shaw
1905	Polish Revolution First Russian Revolution	
1908		Actresses' Franchise League founded in London
1909	*Marriage as a Trade*: Cicely Hamilton Violence starts in the women's suffrage movement in Britain, including arson attacks and damage to buildings	*How the Vote Was Won*: Cicely Hamilton and Christopher St John Campaign against state censorship by British playwrights and theatre workers
1910	Mexican Revolution	
1914	Start of the First World War (1914–18)	
1916	Easter Rising in Dublin suppressed by the British Army	
1917	Russian Revolution; Tsar of Russia abdicates America enters the First World War	
1918	End of the First World War German Revolution UK women who are householders of 30 or above gain the right to vote	*Baal*: Bertolt Brecht (unproduced until 1923)
1919	Treaty of Versailles	
1920	The League of Nations formed US women gain the right to vote	
1921	Irish Free State established	
1923		The Blue Blouse theatre collective (1923–8)
1924	Lenin dies, Joseph Stalin becomes leader of the Soviet Union (Russia)	

	Social, cultural and political context	Theatre
1926	British General Strike	Workers' Theatre Movement (1926–35)
1927	Hunger marches by the unemployed (until 1936) (UK) First 'talking' movie	*Hoppla, We're Alive!*: Ernst Toller Brecht collaborates with Piscator
1929	Wall Street Crash (USA) leading to world economic crisis Full franchise (voting rights) given to UK women on the same terms as men	
1930		*The Modern Theatre is the Epic Theatre* (essay): Bertolt Brecht Brecht's *The Exception and the Rule* written as part of a series of 'learning plays' (Lehrstück)
1933	Hitler becomes Chancellor of Germany Roosevelt elected President of the United States (1933–1945)	Brecht leaves Germany (until 1949), under fear of Nazi persecution, eventually finding exile in the USA. His best-known plays, including *Mother Courage and Her Children*, *Life of Galileo* and *The Good Person of Szechwan*, written during this period *Meerut* produced by the Worker's Theatre Movement around the UK
1934		*Love on the Dole*: Ronald Gow and Walter Greenwood
1935		Federal Theatre Project (USA, 1935–9) – formed out of Roosevelt's 'New Deal' programme – which involved creating employment for artists
1936	Start of the Spanish Civil War (1936–9) First public television broadcast	Unity Theatre (London) established
1938	House Committee on Un-American Activities established (USA, 1938–75)	*Our Town*: Thornton Wilder Bertolt Brecht writes *The Street Scene* and *The Popular and the Realistic* (essays): published respectively in 1950 and 1958 Brecht's *Exception and the Rule* first produced (in Palestine)
1939	Start of the Second World War	
1945	End of the Second World War Atomic bomb dropped on Hiroshima and Nagasaki UK Labour Party wins landslide general election victory	Theatre Workshop (UK) established, Joan Littlewood and Ewan MacColl's theatre company using 'political theatre' theory and practice
1947		$E=mc^2$: Hallie Flanagan Davis
1954	End of food rationing after the Second World War (1939–45)	
1955	African-American Civil Rights Movement formed in the US (1955–68)	
1956	Suez Crisis (military confrontation between Egypt and Britain, France and Israel over ownership of the Suez Canal) Soviet Union invades Hungary	John Osborne's *Look Back in Anger* premiered at the Royal Court Theatre, London – hailed as marking the birth of a new wave drama featuring 'the angry young man' First UK visit of Brecht's Berliner Ensemble

	Social, cultural and political context	Theatre
1958	Campaign for Nuclear Disarmament (CND) founded (UK)	Shelagh Delaney's *A Taste of Honey* produced by Theatre Workshop, UK
1959	Start of the Vietnam War (until 1975). USA becomes involved in the early 1960s	*A Raisin in the Sun*: Lorraine Hansberry
1963	*The Feminine Mystique*: Betty Frieden (seminal feminist manifesto) President John F. Kennedy assassinated in Dallas, Texas	
1964		*Blues for Mister Charlie*, James Baldwin
1965	Malcolm X assassinated Beginnings of the Black Power Movement (USA) Capital punishment abolished (UK)	Black Arts Movement (1965–76)
1968	Martin Luther King assassinated	

INTRODUCTION

JOHN F. DEENEY AND MAGGIE B. GALE

> As soon as the public and the theatre have worked together to achieve a common desire for a revolutionary culture, almost any bourgeois play, no matter whether it demonstrates the decay of bourgeois society or whether it brings out the capitalist principle with special clarity, will serve to strengthen the notion of the class struggle and to add to our revolutionary understanding of its historical necessity. (Erwin Piscator 1920 [Piscator 1980: 45])

Each Part of this anthology covers periods of theatrical activity inspired by some kind of radical or revolutionary agenda for theatre. The Naturalists, no matter how 'conservative' their work appears to be today, were breaking away from the dominant Romantic traditions of the middle-class theatres of the mid- to late nineteenth century. Similarly, the Symbolists believed that the Naturalist aesthetic limited the expressive possibilities of the stage. The historical avant-garde, in all of its manifestations, believed that the function of theatre went beyond questions of entertainment or education. For them the artwork's revolutionary potential lay in the investigation of both the function of theatre and performance and the deliberate and vibrant challenge to existing aesthetic conventions. On the other hand, the dramatic and theatrical experiments of late modernism represented, in the aftermath of the Second World War and the advent of the Nuclear Age and the Cold War, a radical aesthetic disturbance that shook the 'progressive' philosophical and political foundations upon which modernism had evolved. Whilst the movements examined in Parts 1, 2 and 4 of this anthology cross over with the period covered here – roughly from the early 1910s to the mid-1960s – the materials examined in this Part directly engage with (and critique) materialist politics and ideology. This imperative created a reconceptualization of theatre's relationship with its audience, by primarily presenting the world as a place upon which *we can act*, that we can change, that we have the agency to affect, rather than simply as something that *acts upon us*.

Ibsen, Strindberg, Chekhov and others, such as George Bernard Shaw with the 'play of ideas', in the later nineteenth and early twentieth centuries, engaged with the possibility of a theatre that could present and discuss the social problems of their day. However, the political theatres we examine here are directly concerned with social and political revolution, equality, citizenship, class difference, race and social agency. If Naturalism was enclosed by the domestic setting (see Part 1), the political theatres of the early twentieth century sought a revolution in dramatic form and theatrical presentation which capitalized on the theatre's status, disruptive potential and aesthetic power within the public sphere. Similar to the historical avant-garde (see Part 2), the political theatres we examine here demanded a fundamental questioning of the audience's relationship to theatre and, in turn, to the world.

Not all of the plays in this Part come out of the shared desire for a revolutionary culture as expressed by Piscator (quoted above). However, they do all share a radical re-visioning of the relationship between the individual and the society in which they live. Just as the Naturalists were concerned with the consequences of industrialization for the individual, so too the political theatres of the 1920s to the 1950s reflected the social unrest that many saw as linked to the exploitative and alienating society created by urban industrialization.

From the turn of the twentieth century, there were 'revolutions' and political uprisings all over Europe and in South America. Revolutions in Poland (1905), Mexico (1910), Russia (1905 and 1917) and after the end of the First World War in Germany in 1918 were both direct responses to, and motivated by, a newly organized form of class struggle. This struggle was shaped by the writings of Karl Marx (1818–83), who, along with other key nineteenth-century thinkers, such as Friedrich Engels (1820–95), offered a materialist analysis of history that denaturalized a social hierarchy which placed power in the hands of a small social elite: the ruling classes. A materialist historical analysis does not see history simply in terms of the official chronology of events: the 'progression' of the monarchy and ruling elite, or of a series of wars. Rather it places the ruling elite and the proletariat – the working classes – in relation to one another, within an antagonistic and potentially revolutionary framework of cause and effect. Although some of the plays in this Part do not present as strong a critique of the existing class system as others, they link injustice to a capitalist system and see the latter as a political system predicated on economic inequality.

The introduction to Part 2 of this anthology highlights the fluid movement of culture between European cities in the 1910s and 1920s, as well as the impact of the regrouping of European states during the late nineteenth century. The First World War (1914–18) in some ways hindered the potential for such fluidity in terms of cultural exchange. Nevertheless, a number of the plays in this Part – Ernst Toller's *Hoppla, We're Alive!* (1927, 3.2), Bertolt Brecht's *The Exception and the Rule* (1930, 3.3) and the Workers' Theatre Movement's *Meerut* (1933, 3.4) – are influenced by German and Russian ideas about the relationship of the political to the production of art and culture. As Piscator implies above, the development of political theatre cannot happen without the development of a new audience. The political theatres presented in this Part were not, by and large, written for a commercialized theatre industry, although Ronald Gow and Water Greenwood's *Love on the Dole* (1934, 3.5) is an example of a play that found particular success there. Many of the political theatres discussed here were more makeshift, did not aspire to traditional notions of literary sophistication, and were inspired by political and educational, rather than economic, imperatives. In addition, as with the forms of theatre and performance illustrated in other Parts of this anthology, the *practice* of political theatre – the means and methods of its making – was as important as the product/performance.

From 'political theatre' to 'political theatres'

Writing in 1975, Michael Kirby made the distinction between political theatre that engages in issues of government or party politics, and that which aims simply to 'change the beliefs and opinions of the spectator' (3.12: 535). Kirby also notes however that, '[s]ome political theatre … does not proselytize, it is not didactic, it does not support particular alternatives' (ibid: 539). This broad framework for the definition of political theatre is one adopted here. Read from an early twenty-first century perspective, Kirby's observations also do much to anticipate the move to critique, particularly from the 1980s onwards, the relationship between form and content in the art/politics nexus.

Of continued relevance in Kirby's article are his observations concerning how an individual's desire to 'interpret theatre politically' does not necessarily mean that 'being political' is 'inherent in the work' (ibid: 533). Questions over the very efficacy of naming theatre as 'political' resonated not only with the gradual liquidation of Really Existing Socialism in Eastern Europe from the mid-1980s onwards, but were also, and not without some irony, shaped by the liberationist political movements of the 1960s that found their own manifestations in theatre practice (see below). In this respect, Kirby's observations, particularly when one accounts for the time of their writing, challenge the grain of new thinking emanating from much of Western Europe and the USA, most notably France. Roland Barthes, in his seminal essay 'The Death of the Author' (1967, 5.8), famously dethroned the conventionally held notion that authorial intentionality should inform the interpretation of works of art. But if 'the death of the author' heralded 'the birth of the reader' (or, in theatre, 'the spectator'), where does this leave 'political theatres', of the types presented in this Part, that are founded and function on a materialist, and sometimes Marxist, worldview? Such matters will be discussed in greater detail towards the end of this introduction. For now, it is perhaps useful to bear in mind that much of the material presented in Part 5 of this anthology examines notions of 'the political' in theatre and performance practices that inhabit, and respond to, a radically altered ideological and cultural constellation: such material also implicitly critiques the contemporary relevance of the types of political theatre presented here.

'Political theatre' is named here in the plural in part as an acknowledgement of the contentiousness of the term. During the 1980s and 1990s, scholarship differentiated between political theatres influenced by Brecht – theatres of the political left – and other theatres which were political in content and perhaps explored political issues, but did not challenge or develop traditional or dominant theatrical forms. For some, the lack of an engagement in a rethinking of form (particularly the dominance of dramatic and theatrical realism) meant that there was an inherent acceptance of the status quo. Thus, theatre produced without this engagement might fail somehow to qualify for the term 'political'. Partly mirroring the observations of Kirby, Graham Holderness draws attention to the place of 'intention' in the definition of political theatre:

> Theatre may be 'political' without becoming 'political theatre', in the sense that a play may represent political matters or address political issues, in exactly the same way as a play can represent love … or poverty or madness … the politics of a truly political theatre must be a matter of conscious choice and deliberate intention. (Holderness 1992: 2–3)

Here a distinction is made between what may or may not be 'truly' political theatre. It is proposed however that, following Kirby, it is possible to see the history of theatre in the twentieth century as providing a spectrum of political theatres – some of which make use of, in Raymond Williams' terms, a 'dominant' cultural form, and some of which utilize an 'emergent' one (Williams 2005: 40; see also Part 2). This Part therefore includes plays and performance texts which are political in each of the senses implied above by Holderness – it moves from texts which explore social worlds through a directly politically oriented lens, to those which manipulate theatrical form to create what Walter Benjamin (cultural critic and friend of Brecht) calls a *politicized art* (see below).

Political realisms in England – *How the Vote Was Won* (3.1)

Originally created in the form of a pamphlet (Spender and Hayman 1985: 19), Cicely Hamilton and Christopher St John's play *How the Vote Was Won* (1909, 3.1) was embedded in a theatrical/

political movement specifically dedicated, in a society where women's citizenship did not extend to their having political power through the right to vote, to the promotion of 'votes for women'. Following in the footsteps of Shaw (see Innes 1998), and in line with other playwrights experimenting with the 'play of ideas', Hamilton and St John's play theatricalized a complex and high-profile political debate. Hamilton, the author of *Marriage as a Trade* (1909), which provided a radical investigation of the inequities of the economic foundations of marriage, was a key member of the Women Writers' Suffrage League. Both Hamilton and St John were involved to varying degrees in the Actresses' Franchise League, a politically inspired theatre organization set up in 1908 to enable and promote the involvement of women from the theatre profession in the struggle for the vote (see Holledge 1981; Stowell 1992; and Paxton 2016). The play has minimal production requirements and therefore has the potential to tour at low cost and with considerable flexibility – one of the common features of later 'political' plays. *How the Vote Was Won* was originally produced in the English Edwardian commercial theatre. Strangely for a play that contains such overt propaganda, it was a great critical success. Thus, the *Pall Mall Gazette* noted that, 'The fact that it is so acutely controversial is not at all against it – is, in fact, a virtue rather than a defect, for the Theatre of Ideas is upon us' (Spender and Hayman 1985: 20). Other critics praised the play for its fast-paced humour, and for the ways in which Horace – the clerk from Brixton – is outwitted by the very same women he considers to be his social and intellectual inferiors. What this reception does not evidence, however, are the extraordinary levels of cultural anxiety that the suffragettes created in their campaign for votes for women: some genuinely thought that giving women the vote would unleash a completely unmanageable political force – a 'petticoat' government (see Ramelson 1976). Of course this political campaign was part of a general movement to increase the levels of participation in the formal political arena – working-class men in Britain did not receive the full vote until 1918 and women, not universally until 1928. The message of the play is no less radical for the positive reception that it originally garnered. *How the Vote Was Won*, as with much suffrage drama, made a strategic intervention into a dominant theatrical form: comedy and farce, to some extent the staple of the commercial theatre of the day, are made subversive through the politically propagandistic message the play explores.

The premise of the play is that there is to be a General Strike by women. In a political environment where women are being told that they do not or cannot support themselves economically, but are, rather, under the financial care of their men, they decide to go on strike and return to the homes of their male relatives or to the state-funded poor houses and workhouses. The opening of the play sees Horace's wife Ethel being informed of the ensuing strike and left to fend for herself by her female servants. Disbelieving the situation, as the play progresses, she slowly realizes, as does Horace, that the women – his sister, his aunt, his niece, his cousin and even a very distant female relation – mean business. They all descend upon his household and present the argument that if men *really* support women economically, then why on earth should women work at all. As the country grinds to a halt – England cannot survive without the input of female labour – so Horace's politics reverse and he ends up, albeit in order to return his life to his own control, presenting himself as the hero of the hour:

HORACE: You may depend on me – all of you – to see justice done. When you want a thing done, get a man to do it! Votes for Women! (3.1: 357)

The play performs a dialectic. The thesis – that women work for a living contributing to the state and therefore should have equal citizenship – is placed directly against the antithesis – that women are the weaker sex reliant upon male custodianship and therefore in receipt of political agency *through* men. The synthesis, that men and women's labour is interconnected and interdependent, is played out theatrically through the use of comedy and farce.

Realism: a 'prison house' form?

Some late-twentieth-century literary theory suggests that realism, here the reproduction of observable reality in theatrical performance, is a 'prison house' form: that realism cannot be used to present a radical agenda because it presents the world 'as it is' rather than presenting it as being alterable (see Belsey 1985; Case 1989; Dolan 1988 and 1990). Sheila Stowell, in her article 'Rehabilitating Realism' (3.8), argues for a more subtle and layered analysis of the power of realism to address the issue of social change in theatre. She suggests that presenting the world 'as it is' does not negate the possibility of a sophisticated reading of theatre and performance, whereby the audience can understand the distinction 'between reproduction and reinforcement' (3.8: 498). Here, what Stowell is foregrounding is the capacity of an audience to acknowledge 'the possibility of cumulative experience … the significance of a play's process' (ibid: 498). Audiences do not necessarily accept drama as 'truth', but rather as a perspective upon it. Stowell counteracts what became in the 1980s the dominant perception of realism as being characterized by 'closure', by its inability to offer resistant readings of the world and through prescribing and/or reinforcing meaning in the mind of the spectator. Here, 'closure' refers to the ways in which a text appears to offer no alternative to the status quo. For example, in *Three Sisters* (1.3) we are exposed to the Prozorov sisters' world and gain a greater understanding of it, but one might argue that the sisters are trapped within a fatalistic universe which both lacks agency, and carries no prospect of it. When we make use of Stowell's position it is easy to see that *How the Vote Was Won*, despite its conventional form, functions as political theatre which offers a resistant reading of a dominant ideology. At the end of the play, Horace is still convinced that he is from a superior sex, but has in fact joined the struggle for votes for women, a struggle he found abhorrent at the beginning of the play.

Susan Carlson (3.7) writes of the suffrage theatre, which proliferated during the first decade of the twentieth century in England in particular, as an 'example of a politically inspired theatre', which 'made new assumptions about theatrical space, domestic space and public space simultaneously' (3.7: 491). Thus, in *How the Vote Was Won*, the authors simplify the staging requirements of a 'domestic' play and explore the possibility of social change through the investigation of the damaging effects of an ideology based on gender inequality.

Ronald Gow and Walter Greenwood: *Love on the Dole* (3.5)

Whilst *How the Vote Was Won* explores the gendered dynamics of inequality, Ronald Gow and Walter Greenwood's *Love on the Dole* (1934) focuses on issues of class inequality in a post-First World War, post-General Strike (1926), post-Wall Street Crash (1929) northern English town. The economic crises of the late 1920s had bought both England and the USA almost to the point of industrial standstill. During the 1920s and 1930s England and Scotland saw the beginnings of a politicized theatre movement influenced by the Blue Blouse agitprop theatre from Russia and the ideas of Piscator and Meyerhold (discussed later in this introduction). Gow and Greenwood's play, as with Hamilton and St John's, does not borrow directly from the theatre theory of figures such as Piscator or Brecht. It is no less political, however, because the narrative takes us through a process of understanding the injustices of a particular economic system, through the downfall and destruction of Larry Meath. The form the play takes is one of a realist, well-made play, with the classical fall of the hero through the progression of the three acts. If Zola-esque and Ibsenite Naturalism dramatized the hold of the family unit over the individual (see Part 1: Introduction), then Greenwood and Gow show the traditional patriarchal order in disarray. Greenwood, who wrote the original novel (1933) from which the play was adapted, came from Salford in northwest England (Hanky Park in the play), and was from a family that had been impoverished during the economic crisis of the 1920s – he thus had first-hand experience of the world about which he was writing.

Love on the Dole opens with a speaker, offstage in a public space, decrying the pitfalls of capitalism:

> unemployment and pauperdom, that is the legacy of the Industrial Revolution. That is the price we pay for the system. And that is the price you'll go on paying till you waken up to the fact that the remedy's in your own hands. You've got votes – why don't you use them? Why don't you think? (3.5: 420).

Gow and Greenwood frame their story of a northern family destroyed by economic recession with an analysis of the class system and a call to action. The fate of the Hardcastle family might be seen as a microcosm of the conditions of the English working classes in the interwar period. By the end of the play, both the family patriarch and the son are offered work, and an escape from poverty, through Sally Hardcastle's acceptance of a job from the local business magnate. The implication is that her job involves more than work, and that she has had to 'sell' not only her soul, but her body too, in order to escape from the cycle of poverty in which the residents of Hanky Park live. Her romantic attachment to Larry Meath, a revolutionary thinker, is brought to a sudden halt by his death during a demonstration which goes horribly wrong. Interestingly, as in *How the Vote Was Won*, the play explores the value of female labour within the context of a traditionally patriarchal culture.

Hugely successful on tour and in London's West End, the play was adapted into a very successful film starring Deborah Kerr in 1941. Part of the significance of *Love on the Dole* resides in the way in which it synthesizes an analysis of class, gender and social deprivation. It achieved this at a time when the majority of plays in the British commercial theatre not only centred on the lives of the middle and upper classes, but rarely contained working-class characters in more than stereotyped or derisory roles – as servants, shop workers and so on. The play made use of the 'prison house' form of realism, but like the earlier suffrage play, it subverts conventional content, paving the way for a theatre which engages far more with the lives of the majority as opposed to the elite. Thus, although the form is not innovative in the way that the theatres explored subsequently in this introduction appear to be, it is a play that, as Piscator states above, rehearses the potential of a 'common desire for a revolutionary culture'. In relation to this, Claire Warden makes the useful observation – redolent of Stowell's recuperation of the political potential of realism discussed previously – that *Love on the Dole*'s evocation of the urbanized 'capitalist landscape' and 'proletarian spaces', although underscoring this 'bleak tale of inescapable circumstances' does not entirely nullify the possibility of emancipation (Warden 2013: 42–3); 'potential political change … remains latent', where 'characters are overwhelmed by the capitalist landscape, but perhaps audiences need not be' (ibid: 43). The play anticipates the move to a more socially engaged theatre in the late 1950s and 1960s – with writers such as Shelagh Delaney (*A Taste of Honey*, 1958) in England and Lorraine Hansberry (*A Raisin in the Sun*, 1959) and James Baldwin (*Blues for Mister Charlie*, 1964, see 3.6) in the USA.

Bertolt Brecht and realism in revolt

The work explored in this next section connects more strongly with what current theatre history classes as 'political theatre' – where the dramaturgical and theatrical form is heavily influenced by Piscator and Brecht and also by Russian theatrical innovations such as those developed by Meyerhold. Generically, the means of production and the function of the illusory qualities of the theatrical event – particularly those associated with Naturalism – are deconstructed and dismantled in favour of a practice which, through acknowledging its own theatrical and fictive qualities, develops new ways in which to represent and engage with the contemporary world.

Vsevolod Meyerhold (1874–1940) was a key practitioner and theorist in the development of twentieth-century theatre. Beginning his theatrical career as an actor in Stanislavski's and Nemirovich-Danchenko's newly formed Moscow Art Theatre in 1898, Meyerhold eventually came to see the Art Theatre's 'fourth wall' aesthetic as limiting the creative possibilities of the stage. From 1902, and now working as a director, Meyerhold began developing a practice that foregrounded the theatre's very theatricality. Not only hugely influenced by classical drama and contemporary Symbolist dramatists such as Maeterlinck (see Part 1), Meyerhold also turned to theatrical and performance forms such as *commedia dell'arte* and the circus (see 2.15) that counter-acted an emphasis on individual psychology. He experimented with anti-illusionistic staging methods, established the use of a 'forestage' (built over the orchestra pit and extending into the auditorium) and was responsible for importing Soviet-inspired 'constructivism' – the movement that emphasized an artwork's functionality and social objective – into stage design. 'Biomechanics' was the highly physicalized system of actor-training that Meyerhold began to formally develop in the 1920s. It emphasized not only the 'social dimension' to the actor's work, but also how the expressive possibilities of acting were rooted in a scientific understanding of the interrela-tionship between 'intention', 'realization' and 'reaction' (see Leach 2004). If the 1917 Russian Revolution garnered Meyerhold's full support, then the emancipatory promise that this event held was reflected by Meyerhold in a theatre that uniquely sought to fuse the poetic, the popular and the political. With productions such as *The Government Inspector* (staged 1926), Meyerhold – not untypically – treated Nikolai Gogol's original text as a blueprint open to adaptation. His aim 'was to combine in unexpected ways grotesque contradictions, a broken rhythm, the forestage, stock characters in stock situations, improvising actors, and a noisy, engaged audience' (ibid: 74). Despite his early support for the revolution, Meyerhold was an outspoken opponent of Socialist Realism (see below) and was eventually murdered by the state in the Stalinist purges of the 1940s.

Unlike much of the work discussed in this introduction, it is perhaps the more 'formal' aspects of Meyerhold's experimental and modernist interventions that are most relevant to a discussion of 'political theatre'. His use of constructivist design and the 'forestage', for example, clearly antici-pates aspects of both Piscator and Brecht's practice. However, Meyerhold's rejection of theatrical realism was, like those who followed him, not concerned with formal innovation *per se,* but founded on the critical issue of *how* the theatre might effectively mediate contemporary realities.

Bertolt Brecht (1898–1956) shared many of Meyerhold's concerns, and for him the realist project was limited in terms of its potential political efficacy by the formalistic boundaries of the well-made play. Brecht is often seen as being directly anti-realist, but his evolving theatre practice demonstrates a deeper and more complex engagement with realism and the modern drama than is often acknowledged, particularly in the English-speaking world. Brecht's 'realism', which transformed the German theatre, developed in part alongside a Stalinist-Russian appropriation of realism – Socialist Realism – which narrowly redrew the form in terms of the singular and premeditated social messages it could convey in stark state-approved terms: Socialist Realism required the presentation of the 'real' as the state both perceived it and wanted it to be projected through theatre. It is important, therefore, not to confuse Brecht's political agenda around realism with state-approved Stalinist artworks.

In his essay 'The Street Scene' (3.10), Brecht points to developments in German theatre after the First World War, whereby practitioners made use of banners, choruses, film and projection to create what became known as 'epic theatre'. He draws a distinction between 'epic' and 'dramatic' theatre by means of pointing to the opposing ways in which narrative functions. In epic theatre 'narrative' is opposed to 'plot', 'argument' to 'suggestion' and 'reason' to 'feeling'. In dramatic theatre, 'thought determines being' and 'man is unalterable', whereas in epic theatre, 'social being determines thought' and 'man is able to alter' (Brecht 2001: 37). Epic theatre borrows from the classical canon in the way in which it expands narrative to deal with not only the specifics of everyday and domestic life – the microcosmic – but gives the broader macrocosmic picture of social relations as they are conditioned by economic factors. Thus characters are presented in an evolving social and political context. Epic theatre pivots on the relationship between cause and effect, narrative is often episodic and the flow is broken by interruption, focusing our direct attention away from the dramatic events. We might be drawn out of the action in order to critically reflect rather than empathize. This Brecht calls the *Verfremdungseffekt* – variously translated as the A-Effect, the alienation effect and distanciation – 'a technique of taking the human social incidents to be portrayed and labelling them as something striking, something that calls for explanation, is not to be taken for granted, not just natural' (3.10: 523). Thus all events on stage within the epic theatre have an intentional 'socially practical significance' (ibid: 521).

Discussions of Brecht's practice have often focused on the material aesthetics and self-conscious display of theatrical elements, such as direct address, the use of placards, the use of narrative-breaking song and so on. However, it is important to distinguish between aesthetics – the choices made in terms of presentation – and what might be called here, for our purposes, 'method' – the choices made in terms of what is to be represented and the cumulative effects of these choices (see Jameson 1998). Brecht was as interested in the social and political function of theatre as he was in unpicking the ways in which the presentation of theatre might be re-visioned. He was not anti-realist, therefore, but wanted to make use of realist modes in a more creative, sophisticated and revolutionary way:

Realist writing, of which history offers many widely varying examples, is likewise conditioned by the question of how, when and for what class it is made use of ... Our conception of *realism* needs to be broad and political, free from aesthetic restrictions and independent of convention. *Realist* means: laying bare society's causal network / showing up the dominant viewpoint as the viewpoint of the dominators / writing from the standpoint of the class which has prepared the broadest solutions for the most pressing problems afflicting human society / emphasises the dynamics of development / concrete and so as to encourage abstraction. (Brecht 2001: 109)

The Marxist critic Terry Eagleton argues that Brecht wanted to 'extend' realism's 'scope'; for Brecht, realism is 'less a specific literary style or *genre* ... than a kind of art which discovers social laws and developments' (Eagleton 2002: 67). Thus, realism 'need not necessarily involve *verisimilitude*, in the narrow sense of recreating the textures and appearances of things; it is quite compatible with the widest uses of fantasy and invention' (ibid). Theatre can offer social and political critique at the same time as tapping into the 'non-real', the imaginary and the entertaining. Brecht constantly emphasized the necessity for *Spaß* – fun – in efficacious theatre practice, and a kind of 'realism in revolt' was one way in which he saw this could be achieved.

Brecht and Walter Benjamin

Although Brecht focused on the possibilities of theatre's consciousness-raising potential, he was also concerned to capitalize upon its power to entertain; he did not separate the two functions. In 'Theatre for Pleasure or Theatre for Instruction' (3.11), Brecht proposes that the learning and pedagogic potential of theatre are part of both its pleasure and its knowledge-making apparatus. He states that, 'we have to defend the epic theatre against the suspicion that it is a highly disagreeable, humourless, indeed strenuous affair' (3.11: 528). In this, and following in the footsteps of Meyerhold and Piscator, Brecht was seeking to fundamentally redefine the relationship between the stage and the audience. Like many of the movements within the historical avant-garde explored in Part 2, Brecht saw the stage/audience relationship as integral to the function of the contemporary artwork and fundamental to modern theatre. Removing the primacy of emotional identification with characters and their situations, Brecht's 'theatre for the scientific age', unlike the Surrealists who focused more on interior psychological landscapes (see Part 2), emphasized the exterior, the sociological, the empirical and the observable. His audiences were to critique and judge rather than empathize or become engulfed by the aesthetic.

This redirecting and reshaping of the audience's engagement in the theatre event – which played out in staging and design as well as text and acting style – although present to different degrees in the work explored in the previous two parts of this anthology, are fundamental to Brecht's perception of the function of theatre. Similarly, in his groundbreaking essay 'The Work of Art in the Age of Mechanical Reproduction' (3.9), Walter Benjamin notes that the technological advances of the modern age have given a new meaning to participation – the relationship between the artist, the artwork and spectatorship. Like Brecht, he believed that art has a social function, and also like Brecht he believed that art could and should be interventionist. Benjamin proposed that the artist should not engage in 'rendering [as] aesthetic' the political, as did the Futurists (see Part 2), but rather participate in the efficacious practice of 'politicizing art' (3.9: 515).

Focusing on the theme of replication, Walter Benjamin re-conceptualizes the function of art during the modernist period: he called for 'theses about the developmental tendencies of art under present conditions of production' (ibid: 500). In simple terms, technology intervenes in the space between the artist and the artwork, and a 'reproduction' of the real becomes mechanized. For example, the photograph can reproduce reality more efficiently not only in terms of its capture and representation of a surface reality, but with a more conscious and manipulated agenda of critique as well as carrying the possibility of being circulated to a mass audience. Benjamin acknowledges the artistry involved in mechanized art – film, photography and so on – arguing that the artist and the machine can work together and develop the aesthetic potential of technology. He suggests that while art in the past was largely made for, reflective of and consumed by an elite, art in the modern world was being consumed by a larger and more diverse audience: '[t]he mass is a matrix from which all traditional behaviour toward works of art issues today in a new form' (ibid: 513). Such new forms of cultural participation are thus integral to a change in the functional dynamics of spectatorship, unleashing the political potential of representational practices in a more overt fashion, and to a greater degree, than in previous centuries. Benjamin's essay discusses at great length elements of the artwork such as originality, authenticity and aura as defining art's potential uniqueness. Technical reproducibility militates against such qualities, removing a sense of immediacy from the artwork, but permitting an enhanced form of critical engagement on the part of both artist and spectator. Eagleton notes that Benjamin, using Brecht as his exemplar, defines a politicized and Marxist-based art form as one in which the artist must not only demonstrate a 'commitment' to a revolutionary politics, but also seek to transform the material forces of artistic production. As Eagleton explains, '[d]ismantling the traditional naturalistic theatre, with its illusion of reality, Brecht produced a new kind of drama based on a critique of the ideological assumptions of bourgeois theatre' (Eagleton 2002: 59; also see Benjamin 2003).

Brecht's *Lehrstück – The Exception and the Rule* (3.3)

Brecht's 'mature' plays, such as *Mother Courage and Her Children* (1939), *The Good Person of Szechwan* (1943) and *The Caucasian Chalk Circle* (1944) – written whilst he was in forced exile from Nazi Germany – have frequently been invoked to illustrate the advanced dramaturgical development of the Brechtian epic theatre model. However, during the late 1920s and early 1930s Brecht entered a period of radical experimentation resulting in the *Lehrstück* (learning plays), of which *The Exception and the Rule* is an example. It is perhaps tempting to read the *Lehrstück*, when considered in purely literary terms, as a crude and unapologetic promotion of Marxist ideology. *The Exception and Rule* tells a story of class conflict. The Merchant, accompanied by The Guide and The Coolie (his general caretaker), embark upon a business expedition requiring them to cross the fictional Yahi Desert. Constantly mistrustful of the motivations of his lower-class employees, The Merchant first dismisses The Guide, but it is his irrational fear and brutalization of The Coolie that foreshadows the latter's murder; The Coolie offers to share his water with The Merchant, who mistakes a water bottle for a stone and a physical threat against his person. The Coolie's Wife brings The Merchant to trial, but even though The Judge accepts the material evidence that should find in favour of The Coolie, The Merchant is bogusly acquitted on the basis of class difference and, incongruously, on 'how he could not believe in an act of friendship on the part of a porter whom he had admittedly tormented' (3.3: 414). When viewed only on the page, *The Exception and the Rule* might seem to be concerned with the type of agitprop theatre produced by the Blue Blouse movement and the Workers' Theatre Movement (see below). However, Brecht intended the *Lehrstück* to be performed in non-conventional theatre spaces – such as schools and factories — and by non-professional actors. The techniques Brecht advocated for this included the sharing of roles by performers in order to forge an aesthetic that was based on scientific objectivity, rather than Aristotelian empathy. The *Lehrstück* may suggest a form of simplicity, but when mediated theatrically is intended to produce a complex 'seeing' by the audience, 'through the structural reorganization of the relationship between the stage, the author and the audience' (Mueller 1994: 81).

The filtering through and transformation of a Marxist-informed philosophy of theatre that Brecht provided have heavily influenced many of the political theatres in Europe and the United States of the mid- to late twentieth century. The translation of these ideas for theatre practice has made acceptable — and in some cases normative — the idea of collaborative working practices, the removal of the proscenium arch and the idea of the 'fourth wall', the embracing of and re-engagement with popular performance techniques and their combination with the literary or poetic text, the integration of song and choreographed movement and a breaking down, to some extent, of the hierarchies inherent to a more traditional, commercially oriented theatre. Indeed many of the practices related to the texts discussed in Part 5 of this volume, despite their seemingly vast differences, owe a debt to the ways in which Brecht revolutionized theatre.

Ernst Toller: *Hoppla, We're Alive!* (3.2)

Equally seminal to the history of European political theatre is the work of Ernst Toller (1893–1939) and specifically his play *Hoppla, We're Alive!* (1927, 3.2). The text as reproduced in this anthology offers a unique insight into a play that in its authorship demonstrates the idiosyncrasies of a creative and frequently tense working partnership. Toller's collaborator Erwin Piscator, theatre theorist and the director of *Hoppla*, influenced Brecht in the 1920s. Employing the newly available technological developments in theatre — film projection, an abstract set design and other new scenic innovations and choreography — Piscator's work anticipated the subsequent refinements of Brecht's epic theatre model, particularly in terms of the breaking down of scenic illusion.

The play opens with a prologue set in 1919, which sees the incarceration of the revolutionary political agitator Karl Thomas in a mental asylum. Jumping to 1927, the play then follows Thomas's life in Weimar Germany and his inability, after being released from the asylum, to reconcile his political convictions with those of his former comrades. The revolution he was fighting for appears to have been forgotten. The Weimar Republic was formed after the First World War as a liberal democracy that replaced the governance of the former imperial order; it is viewed as ending during the early 1930s when Hitler came to power. Thomas's former comrades have accommodated to the new status quo — what was imagined as revolutionary led to a reality far less powerfully radical. Thomas is falsely accused of the murder of Kilman, one-time revolutionary comrade but now a government minister. But immediately prior to being exonerated for the crime, Thomas commits suicide in his prison cell, an act preceded by the following speech:

KARL THOMAS: ... Where to? Where to? ... The stone walls press nearer and nearer ... I am freezing ... and it is dark ... and the glacier of darkness clutches me mercilessly ... Where to? Where to? ... To the highest mountain ... To the highest tree ... The Deluge ... (3.2: 395)

Whilst, on the one hand, Toller seems to be arguing for the necessity of revolutionary political action, the character of Karl Thomas also functions as a kind of Everyman figure in an Expressionist

Stationendrama; the protagonist's journey to spiritual awakening in this particular dramatic form, modelled on the journey Christ took to his death in the 'Stations of the Cross' (see also Styan 1981: 45 on Kokoschka's *Murderer the Women's Hope*, 2.4).

Nevertheless, *Hoppla, We're Alive!*, and particularly in Piscator's production, sought to reflect the material conditions of life in 1920s Germany – Thomas may be an Expressionist hero/anti-hero but his angst is not vague or unnamable, it is driven by his disillusionment at what he perceives as the failure of the revolution. The play also exemplifies the 'New Objectivity', an artistic movement in 1920s Germany that was opposed to Expressionism. For Alan Pearlman, *Hoppla, We're Alive!* is, in part, 'a "state of the nation" play in its severe critique of the hypocrisy of Weimar society' (Pearlman 2000: 44). Like Brecht's *Baal* (1918), the play dramatizes idealism as being at odds with political and social reality.

Piscator's production made use of multiple layers of scaffolding, allowing for the simultaneous playing of scenes, the use of montage and an emblematic form of staging that created a form of realism without the suffocating detailed 'reproduction' of the 'real'. Piscator's aim was to produce and communicate the multiple strands of modern life and he did this by integrating and juxtaposing live action with technology and the use of other media – film, sound, projection, music, song and dance. These features distinguished the original production of the play as key to the development of a mature political theatre aesthetic by connecting events onstage to wider political realities.

Between the Prologue and Act 1 – Karl Thomas's period of incarceration and a passage of eight years in the timeline of the play – Piscator created a seven-minute 'film interlude' in order to 'establish a dramatic connection between Thomas's fate and war and revolution' (Piscator 1980: 211). Based on factual information and key historical events, such as the Treaty of Versailles (1919) and Lenin's death (1924), an astonishing 3,000 feet of film was shot for this. The original footage was then edited and spliced with genuine documentary film. Also, in the interlude between Acts 4 and 5, the famous 1920s Charleston dance was performed by innovative Expressionist choreographer and dancer Mary Wigman's (1886–1973) female dance troupe. Dressed in skeleton costumes and using ultraviolet light to generate luminosity, the dance functioned like a Brechtian A-Effect; the Charleston – a signifier of 1920s middle-class sexual liberation and decadence – when 'performed by skeletons was a powerful comment … on the precarious nature of German prosperity in 1927', thus forging a comedic and provocative defamiliarization of the familiar (Patterson 1981: 145).

The influence of Sergei Eisenstein's (1898–1948) essay 'Montage of Attractions' (1923) can clearly be detected in Piscator's work. Eisenstein, a Soviet filmmaker and theorist, proposed, through the use of 'attractions' – juxtaposition of the 'component parts of the theatrical apparatus' – the use of montage. An 'attraction' therefore, was 'any aggressive aspect of the theatre', anything which 'subjects the spectator to sensual or psychological impact', and 'the only means that enable the spectator to perceive the ideological side of what is being demonstrated' (Eisenstein and Gerould 1974: 78). Similarly, the performance practice developed by the Blue Blouse movement in Russia can clearly be seen in Toller and Piscator's work and in the work of many of the 'political' theatre groups that emerged during the late 1920s and early 1930s in Europe and North America.

The Blue Blouse and 'agitprop'

The Blue Blouse, a Soviet Union-based theatre collective that operated from 1923 to 1928, remains a phenomenon of unparalleled scale and significance in the history of political theatre. The movement was integral to the development of a particular mode of performance 'using whatever materials were available' (Deák 1973: 35). This style of performance came to be known as 'agitprop' – agitation combined with propaganda. Here, the agitation is the vibrant theatricality and the propaganda is the conscious desire to represent a specific ideological position with a focus on a particular theme such as workers' rights. By the late 1920s some 500 groups formed the professional wing of the movement, bolstered by an additional 8,000 amateur companies – and these performed all over the Soviet Union (see Deák 1973 and McGrath 1981: 27). Named after the workers' blue uniforms – in which its members also performed – the Blue Blouse operated in post-revolutionary Russia 'to explain current events and government policy in popular, clear, entertaining ways to a predominantly peasant and largely illiterate population' (Jackson 2007: 69). The form this theatre took was necessarily makeshift and mobile. It was often performed on platforms mounted on mobile vehicles and playing in non-conventional theatre spaces such as public meeting halls, bars and outside factory gates, and utilizing a huge range of performance and dramatic forms. Actual social and political subject matter was mediated through monologue and dialogue, dance and gymnastics, popular and folk song, jazz, the employment of techniques derived from carnival, circus, cartoon, *commedia dell'arte* and so forth (McGrath 1981: 26–7). The drawing together of such elements was by no means haphazard – the Blue Blouse was a tightly organized and disciplined operation, requiring well-trained and highly skilled performers:

> It was seen as imperative to harness the entertaining features of each piece to the ultimate goal, that of winning over ordinary people to the immediate and urgent task of transforming society and of equipping them with the knowledge to enable them … to play their part. (Jackson 2007: 70)

The immediacy, directness and simplicity of Blue Blouse's performance work, particularly through the use of popular cultural forms, strategically sought to work in dialogue with working-class audiences. Similarly, rather than reaching out to a more generalized middle-class theatre-going audience as *Love on the Dole* had done, much political theatre was made specifically for, about and often by a working-class demographic. Often vital to this theatre was a conscious critique of class difference and the dominant Naturalist theatre. Agitprop advanced the possibility, in terms of Benjamin's later ideas, of theatre as a 'politicized art': it takes a didactic position, and so exploits the educational potential of theatre. This does not mean, however, that it was a dry or simplistic theatrical form. Just as documentary theatre operates on a basis of layering and juxtaposing fact, image and movement, as pioneered in Piscator's work of the 1920s, so too agitprop theatre uses a sophisticated *bricolage* of performance styles and conventions to forge new forms of mediation between education and entertainment, as Brecht's theory and practice of theatre later expanded upon.

The Workers' Theatre Movement and *Meerut* (3.4)

In Britain, political theatre developed rapidly in the 1920s and 1930s. It worked directly against both the privately run independent subscription theatres and the commercialized theatre system which dominated the theatre industry – theatres owned or run by a small management elite in London, and touring circuits owned by businessmen and theatre impresarios (see Barker and Gale 2000). The political theatres explored by Raphael Samuel *et al.* in *Theatres of the Left* (Samuel *et al.* 1985; also see Davies 1987) were run on a largely amateur basis and were independent from the idiosyncrasies of an industry swamped by costs, profit-making imperatives and a perception that theatre was largely for entertainment. The commercial theatres did not see themselves as part and parcel of a revolutionary cultural project. With the growing popularity of film as a mass art form, and numerous theatres converted to cinemas by the 1930s, the economic instability of the commercial theatre sector became increasingly prohibitive in terms of investment in experimentation and new forms. Whereas European theatres often received state funding, the British theatre did not benefit from a system of state funding and subsidy for the arts until the mid-1940s.

During the decades which followed the First World War, as indicated above, the social unrest created by war, economic decline and the gradual dismantling of the British Empire intensified. *Love on the Dole* (3.5) shows an England divided by a failing economy and an increasingly politicized working class. Modernists in the arts tended to configure 'the masses' as threatening the balance of society, as a threat to the social order, as lacking intellectual insight and as watering down the purity of art (see Carey 1992). The mobilization of the masses, evidenced by the General Strike of 1926, a series of high-profile hunger marches across Britain between 1927 and 1936 and the increasing viability of the Labour Party – seen by many as representing the working classes – as fit for government, all signified a tectonic shift in the political landscape. A number of theatre artists believed theatre to have a huge potential as a revolutionary tool for the workers' struggle. Theatrical forms were adopted to articulate political ideas and to intervene in debates around social struggle. The Workers' Theatre Movement in the UK (1926–35) emphasized class struggle and 'saw itself as a theatre of action, dealing with immediate issues … it turned from naturalistic drama and the discussion play to agit-prop, in the form of sketches, cabaret and review' (Samuel *et al.* 1985: 33). Radical in its outlook, the movement contained groups with names like the Red Players and the Rebel Players. Theatre groups within the movement had direct contact with similar companies in Europe and borrowed from the techniques developed by Piscator in Germany and the Blue Blouse movement in Russia. Affiliations were also both locally and nationally networked. There were also productions of plays by Toller and even the avant-garde work *R.U.R.* by Karel Čapek (1920, see 2.8 and Part 2: Introduction), which dramatized capitalism as a futuristic dystopia peopled by robots. Here, theatre was being utilized directly as part of a political interventionist project to politicize, educate and entertain.

The text of *Meerut* (1933), as with Brecht's *Lehrstück*, needs to be read in terms of its very particular intended performance context. In a not dissimilar fashion from the 'realist' *How the Vote Was Won*, which in terms of form could not be more different, the text is designed to be performed using very little equipment or stage props. It requires only the actors and six sticks or poles, which become the means of representing the prison in the play. The text takes its inspiration from the plight of workers in British-controlled India during the late 1920s and the mistreatment of trade unionists and socialists who were in conflict with the authorities over working conditions. *Meerut* calls for an emotional engagement from both the actors and the audience – it is a call to action, where we are asked to understand the relationship between the plight of the oppressed worker from the other side of the world and our own conditions of labour. As Charles Mann suggests in 'How to Produce Meerut':

> Feel the sketch, mean it, and you will convey the message of it in a way that will strike home to the class consciousness that is latent in even the most reactionary member of your worker-audience. (3.4: 418)

The Workers' Theatre Movement was concerned to not only preach to the converted: it operated as a genuinely revolutionary and educative movement, believing in the direct transformational power of theatre.

The 1920s and 1930s – which bore witness to momentous political, social and cultural upheavals – were a particularly auspicious time for development of political theatres in Europe, the Soviet Union and the USA. For example, in the USA the Federal Theatre Project (FTP, 1935–39) – part of President Franklin D. Roosevelt's Democratic 'New Deal' initiative during the Great Depression – commissioned plays by established playwrights such as Elmer Rice (see Part 2: Introduction), and created its own works and performances through collaborative methods of script composition. Relatively short-lived for economic as well as political reasons – some critics saw the work of the FTP as leaning too far towards leftist politics – the FTP actually reached out to and served a wide and varied constituency (see Jackson 2007).

Political theatres: mutations

The types of plays and practices discussed thus far in this introduction belong to a leftist – and often Marxist – emancipatory tradition. The impact of the Second World War, like the Great War before it, would lead to a further redefining of ideological constellations. The emergence of the USA and the Soviet Union as 'superpowers' through the Cold War would, in many ways, define the latter half of the twentieth century. However, the 1960s also bore witness to a remarkable set of events in the USA and Western Europe. This was a decade in which new ideas concerning personal liberation powerfully cohered with new social movements that were responding – often directly – to contemporary events. Demonstrations against the American intervention in Vietnam, the Paris student riots of 1968, the women's liberation movement (or 'second-wave' feminist movement) of the 1970s, and countercultural movements – all represented a demand for the recognition of new personal and social freedoms. At the same time, each represented an attack on the ideological authoritarianism that was perceived to have become embedded in Western governments proffering so-called liberal democratic values. The Presidential election of John F. Kennedy in the USA in 1960 and Harold Wilson's 1964 Labour government in the UK marked a significant turn to left-of-centre values, producing significant concrete results. For example, the African-American Civil Rights Movement (1955–68) eventually led to legislation that prohibited discrimination in areas such as voting rights, employment practices and housing. In Britain, the rights of gay men began to be formally recognized by the state in 1967, with an Act of Parliament that decriminalized private homosexual acts between consenting adult males. The same year also produced the Abortion Act in the UK, seen by many as a significant gain for women, whose demand for greater self-governance was part and parcel of a desire to acquire power and control over their very bodies. However, other events of the decade, such as the assassinations of President

Kennedy (1963), black activist leader Malcolm X (1965) and the civil rights leader Martin Luther King, Jr (1968) along with the brutality of the US incursion into Vietnam (the first war to be internationally mediated through television), and an increasing wave of urban-centred violent crime, all demonstrated that the utopian dream of generating new forms of social and political agency – in which the personal and the political are mutually recognized – would perhaps always remain an aspiration rather than a reality.

The ideological conditions of this period were incisively analysed by Guy Debord. In *The Society of the Spectacle* (1967) Debord argued that capitalism's invasiveness into the entire strata of contemporary life, propagated by twentieth-century advances in the mass media and technological production, had meant that '[a]ll that once was directly lived has become mere representation' (Debord 1994: 12). Thus, in resisting and challenging the deluge of this 'spectacle', artists and activists needed to be constantly vigilant of the risk of revolutionary ideas and practices being susceptible to appropriation by the dominant ideology. Theatre practitioners, at least in part, took up the challenge that Debord presented in the late 1960s and 1970s. In Britain, the 'alternative theatre movement' was founded on broadly collectivist – though by no means unitary – principles that forged a fragile alliance between overtly political/socialist, feminist, gay and lesbian, and black and Asian theatre practices (see Itzin 1980). Companies such as John McGrath's 7:84 venture were part of this movement, as were the feminist theatre collective Monstrous Regiment (from the mid-1970s to the early 1990s) that sought 'to shift consciousness in the area of women's relation to society' and reflect the 'dislocated nature of women's experience' (ibid: 274). The movement also embraced forms such as street theatre and performance art in conjunction with the more familiar strategies of political theatre such as agitprop – exemplified in the work of Albert Hunt for example (ibid: 64–7; see also Craig 1980). In the United States such coalescence was less immediately discernible as a movement. However, as Christopher Bigsby has noted:

> 'avant-garde' companies such as the Living Theatre, the San Francisco Mime Troupe and the Performance Group all engaged in acts of provocative direct intervention that frequently took their work outside theatre buildings and shared related concerns about 'transformation' that were also being tested by emergent voices in black and women's theatre. (Bigsby 2000: 261)

What becomes critical at this theatrical juncture is a challenge not simply to the power of 'language' in theatre, but to the ways language's claim to be a force for exposing 'the real' is paradoxically set against the 'illusion and deceit' of theatre practice (ibid). This represents more than a return to the questions that Brecht began asking forty years earlier. It was also around this time that French philosopher and cultural theorist Michel Foucault (1926–84) famously questioned the idea that individuals (or subjects) were cohesive entities that had a centre to their being, and that ideologies themselves are historically shaped, 'effects of truth' that are 'produced within discourses which are themselves neither true or false' (qtd in Lloyd 2003: 228). Thus for Foucault, ideologies are imagined and constructed through human agency.

If we consider the practice of theatre in relation to Foucault's challenge, then a fascinating tension emerges. Foucault's discourse carries within it a utopian-like liberationist potential. Human subjects, freed from a Marxist notion of historical determinism, are given the capability to explore the multiple possibilities of new identities and social formations. What does this say, however, about how we might work to overcome the tangible realities of oppression and the types of ideological hegemony identified in Debord's 'society of the spectacle'? It is in this very gap, in the relationship between 'agency' and 'structure', that political theatre practices in both the USA and UK in the 1960s, and beyond, found a provocative response, none less so than in the arenas of race, gender and sexuality.

James Baldwin: *Blues for Mister Charlie* (3.6)

The emergence of a radicalized black theatre was most pronounced in the USA. The Black Arts Movement (BAM) – the artistic arm of the Black Power Movement (BPM) – was formed in the aftermath of the assassination of Malcom X in 1965. Although the BPM grew out of the Civil Rights Movement, it advocated black autonomy rather than integrationist policies. Similarly, the BAM was concerned with promoting – across a range of art forms – a specifically black rather than multicultural aesthetic. Some notable dramatists were associated with the BAM, including Lorraine Hansberry and its founder Amiri Baraka, formerly LeRoi Jones (see Sell 2005).

Although *Blues for Mister Charlie* (1964) by James Baldwin (1924–87) predates the BAM, Baraka credits the play with the inception of the movement (Shin and Judson 1998: 250). Set in the American South, and inspired by actual events, the play dramatizes the story of the murder of a black pastor's son at the hands of a white 'redneck' named Lyle, the consequences of the killing and Lyle's subsequent trial in the segregated town. As primarily a prose writer, Baldwin was originally criticized for his 'novelistic script' and lack of mastery of dramatic form (Taubman 1964). However, his use of flashbacks, parody of racial stereotypes (white and black), chorus and monologue, together with scenes approximating to a more conventional form of realism, may also illustrate an attempt by the dramatist to develop a dramatic form that *describes* the African-American experience and evokes the human, social and cultural sources of discrimination and the means by which – albeit tentative – justice and reconciliation might be envisioned. Bigsby observes that, in the 1960s, a 'crudity of form and expression' could be seen 'as evidence of authenticity and incorruptibility' (Bigsby 2000: 274). For example, towards the end of Act 1, the black pastor, Meridian, and Parnell, a white liberal, engage in a dialogue that illustrates a clash of values:

MERIDIAN: Must I be the man who watches while his people are chained, starved, clubbed, butchered?
PARNELL: You used to say that your people were all the people in the world – all the people God ever made, or would make. You said your race was the human race.
MERIDIAN: The human race!
PARNELL: I've never seen you like this before. There's something in your tone I've never heard before – rage – maybe hatred –
MERIDIAN: You've heard it before. You just never recognized it before. You've heard it in all those blues and spirituals and gospel songs you claim to love so much.
PARNELL: I was talking about *you* – not your history. I have a history, too. And don't be so sure I've never heard that sound. Maybe I've never heard anything else. Perhaps my life is also hard to bear. (3.6: 458)

This high-octane, even melodramatic, exchange might seem to express a deep-seated desire to recognize the need for human goodness and universal values in order to overcome the very particular conflicts that Baldwin dramatizes. However, even if *Blues for Mister Charlie* is infused by such a liberal ideology, Baldwin succeeds in rendering the private and public/political as inextricably linked. Again, we need to be cognizant here of not divorcing the play from the context of its production. Bigsby suggests that Baldwin reshapes his stage fiction, not in terms of the 'reality' of racially motivated murder but into one of 'shared experience' (Bigsby 2000: 274). Thus, it is within the very performance of Baldwin's play – particularly in the context of 1960s America – that a stage symbolically divided between 'whitetown' and 'blacktown' (3.6: 447), performed by an interracial cast before an interracial audience, forges the possibility of a spectator becoming 'an actor in this drama' (Bigsby 2000: 275). The distinction here between the potential efficacies of prose fiction – Baldwin's original medium – and drama is crucial: a novel 'finds an individual audience', whereas a play 'must summon into existence a community of selves who mutually agree to one another's co-presence' (ibid). Bigsby's observations here not only have application to a range of theatre practices from this period and beyond. What was also considered to be a dilemma with Baldwin's play – its form – becomes part of a complex system, as with the political theatres preceding it, for testing the possibilities of theatrical mediation in relation to the dominant theatrical and ideological discourses.

Conclusion: the legacies of political theatres

It is perhaps tempting to view many of the plays and theatre practices discussed here as no longer directly pertinent to an early twenty-first-century world. Certainly, the principal belief systems that underpin their authorship were put to the test throughout the twentieth century. Only seventy years after the 1917 Russian Revolution, Really Existing Socialism – the various forms of human, social and economic oppression that the Marxist dream had turned into – began its rapid disintegration across Eastern Europe. China, the largest nation state on the planet, remains politically communist but has economically embraced capitalism. The communist outpost of Cuba, which in 1962 forced a showdown between the United States and the Soviet Union and brought the world to the brink of nuclear Armageddon, functions now – to outsiders at least – as a kind of nostalgic twilight-zone-cum-vacation destination. In 1992, the political economist and philosopher Frances Fukuyama announced the 'end of history', not an impending apocalypse but a thesis concerning how the triumph of late capitalism over socialism was resulting in the widespread acceptance of liberal democracy as the most successful form of governance (Fukuyama 1992). Of course, events such as the attack on the Twin Towers in September 2001, the Russian incursion into Ukraine in 2014, and the stream of scientific evidence supporting the imminence of global ecological meltdown, suggest that 'history' is far from dead but, rather, has reconfigured the battle lines.

In his essay 'The Politics Beyond the Politics' (3.13) the British dramatist, director and theoretician Howard Barker argues for a 'tragic theatre', and how, 'in a society disciplined by moral imperatives of gross simplicity, complexity itself, ambiguity itself, is a political posture of profound strength' (3.13: 540). Like his plays, Barker's theoretical writings assert a radical departure from dominant playwriting conventions. However, when Barker asserts that, if 'the dramatist is himself heroic in the risks he is prepared to take with his material, his audience is honoured and, through a fog of early outrage, real changes of perception become possible', he is identifying in theatre its efficacious possibilities, through a re-imagining of its relationship with its audience (ibid: 541). This certainly does not make Barker a disciple of Brecht, but it does position him in a connection with the other dramatists and practitioners discussed in this introduction, each of which have attempted to refashion the correlation between 'agency' – the subject and her/his capacity to self-define and to 'act' – and structure – the social/political/ideological apparatus. Although Barker's somewhat unique perspective might seem more fitting for the work discussed in Part 5 of this anthology, it is placed here to highlight the increasingly complex questions concerning 'political theatres' in more recent times.

Terry Eagleton reminds us that, 'Marxist ideas have stubbornly outlived Marxist political practice', and as a form of 'critique' Marxism 'has to be assessed by how much it illuminates [contemporary] works of art' (Eagleton, 2002: viii). It is startling to consider, for example, the extent to which the original theatrical proprietors of a supposedly discredited ideology have exerted their influence in late twentieth and early twenty-first century dramaturgical and theatre practices. The Brazilian theatre director Augusto Boal's (1931–2009) 'interventionist' theatre practices, from 'Theatre of the Oppressed' to 'Legislative Theatre', have had an international impact in developing forms of participatory theatre that seek to effect positive change and activate agency in people's private, public and collective lives. Boal's starting point was Brecht. Boal's work is, today, considered an exemplar of 'applied theatre' or 'social theatre', which would also include 'theatre-in-education' in the UK, a particularly unique and extensive movement during the 1970s and 1980s that brought socially relevant theatre into schools; and 'theatre for development', theatre that is made in collaboration with communities in the developing world, oppressed by war, political corruption and/or the forces of nature. In the USA the epic form finds a potent contemporary resonance even in the mainstream, with Tony Kushner's two-part *Angels in America* (1991–2). In the UK, the political dramatists who emerged in the 1960s and 1970s, such as Edward Bond, Howard Brenton, Caryl Churchill (see 5.6), David Edgar and David Hare, developed dramatic forms that are indebted to the ideas of Brecht particularly, but also Toller and Piscator. Mark Ravenhill, for example (see 5.7 and 5.14), one of the playwrights seen to have reinvigorated the British theatre for a new and younger audience in the1990s, used Toller's *Hoppla, We're Alive!* as the prototype for his play *Some Explicit Polaroids* (1999), about the failure of the socialist project in modern-day England. Such playwrights and practitioners can be seen to have built their political and aesthetic project on the works of their predecessors, but adapted the original theories and practices to a theatre much changed by the film and media industries and, in the UK especially, by new funding structures and the dominance of the subsidized 'power-house theatres' – the Royal National Theatre, the Royal Court, the Royal Shakespeare Theatre and so on. Whilst Part 4 of this anthology presents the work of dramatists and theatre makers from the late modernist period who formed a radically different response to some of the ideas discussed here concerning human subjectivity and agency, Part 5 turns its focus on more recent practices, where questions of 'the political' in performance are considered in specific relation to the unfolding politics of globalization, postmodernity and postmodernism.

Bibliography

Barker, Clive and Maggie B. Gale (eds) (2000) *British Theatre between the Wars, 1918–1939*, Cambridge: Cambridge University Press.

Barker, Howard (1997) *Arguments for a Theatre*, 3rd edn, Manchester: Manchester University Press.

Belsey, Catherine (1985) 'Constructing the Subject: Deconstructing the Text', in J. Newton and D. Rosenfelt (eds), *Feminist Criticism and Social Change: Sex, Class and Race in Literature and Culture*, New York: Methuen, pp. 45–64.

Benjamin, Walter (2003 [1966]) *Understanding Brecht*, trans. A. Bostock, London: Verso.

Bigsby, C.W.E. (2000) *Modern American Drama, 1945–2000*, Cambridge: Cambridge University Press.

Boal, Augusto (1979) *The Theatre of the Oppressed*, London: Pluto Press.

Brecht, Bertolt (2001 [1964]) *Brecht on Theatre*, ed. and trans. J. Willett, London: Methuen.

Carey, John (1992) *The Intellectuals and the Masses: Pride and Prejudice Among the Literary Intelligentsia, 1800–1939*, London: Faber and Faber.

Case, Sue-Ellen (1989) 'Towards a Butch/Femme Aesthetic', in L. Hart (ed.), *Making a Spectacle: Feminist Essays on Contemporary Women's Theatre*, Ann Arbor: University of Michigan Press, pp. 282–99.

Craig, Sandy (ed.) (1980) *Dreams and Deconstructions: Alternative Theatre in Britain*, Ambergate: Amber Lane Press.

Davies, Andrew (1987) *Other Theatres: The Development of Alternative and Experimental Theatre in Britain*, Basingstoke: Macmillan.

Deák, Frantisek (1973) 'Blue Blouse', *The Drama Review: TDR*, 17(1) (March), 35–46.

Debord, Guy (1994) *The Society of the Spectacle*, trans. D. Nicholson-Smith, New York: Zone Books.

Dolan, Jill (1988) *The Feminist Spectator as Critic*, Ann Arbor: University of Michigan Press.

Dolan, Jill (1990) '"Lesbian" Subjectivity in Realism: Dragging at the Margins of Structure and Ideology', in Sue-Ellen Case (ed.), *Performing Feminisms: Feminist Critical Theory and Theatre*, Baltimore: Johns Hopkins University Press, pp. 40–53.

Eagleton, Terry (2002 [1976]) *Marxism and Literary Criticism*, London: Routledge.

Eisenstein, Sergei and Daniel Gerould (1974) 'Montage of Attractions: For "*Enough Stupidity in Every Wiseman*"', The Drama Review: TDR, 18(1) (March), 77–85.

Fukuyama, Francis (1992) *The End of History and the Last Man*, London: Penguin Books.

Holderness, Graham (1992) 'Introduction', in G. Holderness, (ed.), *The Politics of Theatre and Drama*, Basingstoke: Macmillan, pp. 1–17.

Holledge, Julie (1981) *Innocent Flowers*, London: Virago.

Innes, Christopher (ed.) (1998) *The Cambridge Companion to George Bernard Shaw*, Cambridge: Cambridge University Press.

Itzin, Catherine (1980) *Stages in the Revolution: Political Theatre in Britain Since 1968*, London: Eyre Methuen.

Jackson, Anthony (2007) *Theatre, Education and the Making of Meanings: Art or Instrument?*, Manchester: Manchester University Press.

Jameson, Fredric (1998) *Brecht and Method*, London: Verso.

Leach, Robert (2004) *Makers of Modern Theatre: An Introduction*, London: Routledge.

Lloyd, Moya (2003 [1984]) 'The End of Ideology?', in R. Eccleshall *et al. Political Ideologies: An Introduction*, 3rd edn, London: Routledge, pp. 217–41.

McGrath, John (1981) *A Good Night Out – Popular Theatre: Audience, Class and Form*, London: Eyre Methuen.

Mueller, Roswitha (1994) 'Learning for a New Society: The *Lehrstück*', in Peter Thomson and Glendyr Sacks (eds), *The Cambridge Companion to Brecht*, Cambridge: Cambridge University Press, pp. 79–95.

Patterson, Michael (1981) *The Revolution in German Theatre 1900–1933*, London: Routledge and Kegan Paul.

Paxton, Naomi (2016) *Stage Rights! Actresses, Activism and Politics 1908–1958*, Manchester: Manchester University Press.

Pearlman, Alan (2000) *Ernst Toller: Plays One*, London: Oberon Books.

Piscator, Erwin (1980) *The Political Theatre*, trans. H. Rorrison, London: Eyre Methuen.

Ramelson, Marian (1976 [1967]) *The Petticoat Rebellion: A Century of Struggle for Women's Rights*, London: Lawrence and Wishart.

Samuel, Raphael, Ewan MacColl and Stuart Cosgrove (1985) *Theatres of the Left, 1880–1935: Workers' Theatre Movements in Britain and America*, London: Routledge and Kegan Paul.

Sell, Mike (2005) 'The Drama of the Black Arts Movement', in D. Krasner (ed.) *A Companion to Twentieth Century American Drama*, Oxford: Blackwell, pp. 263–84.

Shin, Andrew and Barbara Judson (1998) 'Beneath the Black Aesthetic: James Baldwin's Primer of Black American Masculinity', *African American Review*, 32(2), 247–61.

Spender, Dale and Carol Hayman (eds) (1985) *How the Vote Was Won and Other Suffragette Plays*, London: Methuen.

Stowell, Sheila (1992) *A Stage of Their Own: Feminist Playwrights of the Suffrage Era*, Manchester: Manchester University Press.

Styan, J. L. (1981) *Modern Drama in Theory and Practice 3: Expressionism and Epic Theatre*, Cambridge: Cambridge University Press.

Taubman, Howard (1964) 'Theater: *Blues for Mister Charlie*', *The New York Times*, 24 April.

Taxidou, Olga (2007) *Modernism and Performance: Jarry to Brecht*, Basingstoke: Palgrave Macmillan.

Warden, Claire (2013) 'Ugliness and Beauty: The Politics of Landscape in Walter Greenwood's *Love on the Dole*', *New Theatre Quarterly* 29 (1), 37–47.

Williams, Raymond (2005 [1980]) *Culture and Materialism*, London: Verso.

Further reading

Bennett, Tony (1986) *Popular Culture and Social Relations*, Milton Keynes: Open University Press.

Brecht, Bertolt (2010 [1977]) *The Measures Taken and Other Lehrstücke*, trans. Carl R. Mueller, Ralph Manheim and Wolfgang Sauerlander, London: Bloomsbury Methuen Drama.

Chambers, Colin (1989) *The Story of Unity Theatre*, London: Lawrence and Wishart.

Chambers, Colin and M. Prior (1987) *Playwrights' Progress: Patterns of Post-War British Drama*, Oxford: Amber Lane Press.

Eyre, Richard and Nicholas Wright (2000) *Changing Stages: A View of British and American Theatre in the Twentieth Century*, London: Bloomsbury.

Flanagan, Hallie (1940) *Arena: The Story of the Federal Theatre*, New York: Duell, Sloane and Pearce.

Fraden, Rena (1994) *Blueprints for a Black Federal Theatre, 1935–1939*, Cambridge: Cambridge University Press.

Goorney, Howard (2008 [1981]) *The Theatre Workshop Story*, London: Methuen.

Goorney, Howard and Ewan MacColl (1986) *Agit-Prop to Theatre Workshop: Political Playscripts 1930–50*, Manchester: Manchester University Press.

Kershaw, Baz (1999) *The Radical in Performance: From Brecht to Baudrillard*, London: Routledge.

Holdsworth, Nadine (2006) *Joan Littlewood* (Routledge Performance Practitioners), London: Routledge.

Leach, Robert (1989) *Vsevolod Meyerhold*, Cambridge: Cambridge University Press.

Martin, Carol and Henry Bial (2000) *Brecht Sourcebook*, London: Routledge.

Stourac, Richard and Kathleen McCreery (1986) *Theatre as a Weapon: Workers' Theatre in the Soviet Union, Germany and Britain 1917–1934*, London: Routledge and Kegan Paul.

3.1 HOW THE VOTE WAS WON (1909)

CICELY HAMILTON AND CHRISTOPHER ST JOHN

Cicely Hamilton (born Hammill) (1872–1952) and *Christopher St John (born Christabel Marshall) (1871–1960)* co-authored How the Vote Was Won *in 1909. Hamilton, an actress, journalist and dramatist in her own right, co-founded the Women Writers' Suffrage League (WWSL) in 1908. Her work with the WWSL and the Actresses' Franchise League (est. 1908) made an inimitable contribution to the social and gender debates within the first-wave feminist movement, epitomized in her political treatise* Marriage as a Trade *(1909). Christopher St John was also active within the first-wave feminist movement. She authored other plays such as* The First Actress *(1911) and wrote, among other works, a biography of the composer Ethel Smyth. Both comical and provocative,* How the Vote Was Won *reverses the dominant and historically prevailing conditions of women's dependency on men.*

Characters

HORACE COLE, a clerk, about 30
ETHEL, his wife, 22
AGATHA, his sister
MOLLY, his niece
MADAME CHRISTINE, his distant relation
MAUDIE SPARK, his first cousin
MISS LIZZIE WILKINS, his aunt
LILY, his maid-of-all-work
GERALD WILLIAMS, his neighbour
WINIFRED, Ethel's sister

Scene: *Sitting-room in* HORACE COLE's *house at Brixton. The room is cheaply furnished in a genteel style. The window looks out on a row of little houses, all of the Cole pattern. The door (centre) leads into a narrow passage communicating at once with the front door. The fireplace (left) has a fancy mantel border, and over it is an overmantel, decorated with many photographs, and cheap ornaments. The sideboard (right), a small bookcase (right), a table (left centre up stage), and a comfortable armchair (centre by table), are the chief articles of furniture. The whole effect is modest, and quite unpleasing.*

Time: *Late afternoon on a spring day in any year in the future.*

When the curtain rises, MRS HORACE COLE *is sitting in the comfortable armchair (centre) putting a button on to her husband's coat. She is a pretty, fluffy little woman who could never be bad-tempered, but might be fretful. At this minute she is smiling indulgently, and rather irritatingly, at her sister* WINIFRED, *who is sitting by the fire (left) when the curtain rises, but gets up almost immediately to leave.* WINIFRED *is a tall and distinguished looking young woman with a cheerful, capable manner and an emphatic diction which betrays the public speaker. She wears the colours of the NWSPU [National Women's Social and Political Union].*

WINIFRED: Well, good-bye, Ethel. It's a pity you won't believe me. I wanted to let you and Horace down gently, or I shouldn't be here.

ETHEL: But you're always prophesying these dreadful things, Winnie, and nothing ever happens. Do you remember the day when you tried to invade the House of Commons from submarine boats? Oh, Horace did laugh when he saw in the papers that you had all been landed on the Hovis wharf by mistake! 'By accident, on purpose!' Horace said. He couldn't stop laughing all the evening. 'What price your sister, Winifred?' he said. 'She asked for a vote, and they gave her bread.' He kept on — you can't think how funny he was about it!

WINIFRED: Oh, but I can! I know my dear brother-in-law's sense of humour is his strong point. Well, we must hope it will bear the strain that is going to be put on it today. Of course, when his female relations invade his house — all with the same story, 'I've come to be supported' — he may think it excruciatingly funny. One never knows.

ETHEL: Winnie, you're teasing me. They would never do such a thing. They must know we have only one spare bedroom, and that's to be for a paying guest when we can afford to furnish it.

WINIFRED: The servants' bedroom will be empty. Don't forget that all the domestic servants have joined the League and are going to strike, too.

ETHEL: Not ours, Winnie. Martha is simply devoted to me, and poor little Lily *couldn't* leave. She has no home to go to. She would have to go to the workhouse.

WINIFRED: Exactly where she will go. All those women who have no male relatives, or are refused help by those they have, have instructions to go to the relieving officer. The number of female paupers who will pour through the workhouse gates tonight all over England will frighten the Guardians into blue fits.

ETHEL: Horace says you'll never *frighten* the Government into giving you the vote. He says every broken window is a fresh nail in the coffin of women's suffrage. It's quite true. Englishmen can't be bullied.

WINIFRED: No, but they can *bully*. It's your husband, your dear Horace, and a million other dear Horaces who are going to do the bullying and frightening this time. The women are going to stay quiet, at home. By tomorrow, perhaps before, Horace will be marching to Westminster shouting out 'Votes for Women!'

ETHEL: Winnie, how absurd you are! You know how often you've tried to convert Horace and failed. Is it likely that he will become a Suffragette just because —

WINIFRED: Just because —? Go on, Ethel.

ETHEL: Well, you know — all this you've been telling me about his relations coming here and asking him to support them. Of course, I don't believe it. Agatha, for instance, would never dream of giving up her situation. But if they did come Horace would just tell them he *couldn't* keep them. How could he on £4 a week?

WINIFRED: How could he? That's the point! He couldn't, of course. That's why he'll want to get rid of them at any cost — even the cost of letting women have the vote. That's why he and the majority of men in this country shouldn't for years have kept alive the foolish superstition that all women are supported by men. For years we have told them it was a delusion, but they could not take our arguments seriously. Their method of answering us was exactly that of the little boy in the street who cries 'Yah — Suffragette!' or 'Where's your " 'ammer"?' when he sees my badge.

ETHEL: I always wish you wouldn't wear it when you come here ... Horace does so dislike it. He thinks it unwomanly.

WINIFRED: Oh! does he? Tomorrow he may want to borrow it — when he and the others have had their object-lesson. They wouldn't listen to argument ... so we had to expose their pious fraud about woman's place in the world in a very practical and sensible way. At this very minute working women of every grade in every part of England are ceasing work, and going to demand support and the necessities of life from their nearest male relatives, however distant the nearest relative may be. I hope, for your sake, Ethel, that Horace's relatives aren't an exacting lot!

ETHEL: There wasn't a word about it in the *Daily Mail* this morning.

WINIFRED: Never mind. The evening papers will make up for that.

ETHEL: What male relative are you going to, Winnie? Uncle Joseph?

WINIFRED: Oh, I'm in the fighting line, as usual, so our dear uncle will be spared. My work is with the great army of women who have no male belongings of any kind! I shall be busy till midnight marshalling them to the workhouse ... This is perhaps the most important part of the strike. By this we shall hit men as ratepayers even when they have escaped us as relatives! Every man, either in a public capacity or a private one, will find himself face to face with the appalling problem of maintaining millions of women in idleness. Do you think the men will take up the burden? Not they! (*Looks at her watch.*) Good heavens! The strike began ages ago. I must be off. I've wasted too much time here already.

ETHEL: (*Looking at the clock.*) I had no idea it was so late. I must see about Horace's tea. He may be home any minute. (*Rings the bell, left.*)

WINIFRED: Poor Horace!

ETHEL: (*Annoyed.*) Why 'poor Horace'? I don't think he has anything to complain of. (*Rings again.*)

WINIFRED: At this minute I feel some pity for all men.

ETHEL: What can have happened to Martha?

WINIFRED: She's gone, my dear, that's all.

ETHEL: Gone! Nonsense. She's been with me ever since I was married, and I pay her very good wages.

Enter LILY, *a shabby little maid-of-all-work, dressed for walking, the chief effort of the toilette being a very cheap and very smart hat.*

ETHEL: Where's Martha, Lily?

LILY: She's left, m'm.

ETHEL: Left! She never gave me notice.

LILY: No, m'm, we wasn't to give no notice, but at three o'clock we was to quit.

ETHEL: But why? Don't be a silly little girl. And you mustn't come in here in your hat.

LILY: I was just goin' when you rang. That's what I've got me 'at on for.

ETHEL: Going! Where? It's not your afternoon out.

LILY: I'm goin' back to the Union. There's dozens of others goin' with me.

ETHEL: But why –?

LILY: Miss Christabel – she told us. She says to us: 'Now look 'ere, all of yer – you who've got no men to go to on Thursday – yer've got to go to the Union,' she says: 'and the one who 'angs back' – and she looked at me she did – 'may be the person 'oo the 'ole strain of the movement is restin' on, the traitor 'oo's sailin' under the 'ostile flag,' she says: and I says, 'That won't be me – not much!'

During this speech WINIFRED *puts on a sandwich board which bears the inscription: 'This way to the Workhouse.'*

WINIFRED: Well, Ethel, are you beginning to believe?

ETHEL: Oh, I think it's very unkind – very wicked. How am I to get Horace anything to eat with no servants?

WINIFRED: Cheer up, my dear. Horace and the others can end the strike when they choose. But they're going to have a jolly bad time first. Goodbye. (*Exit* WINNIE, *singing the 'Marseillaise.'*)

LILY: Wait a bit, Miss. I'm comin' with yer. (*Sings the 'Marseillaise' too.*)

ETHEL: No, no. Oh, Lily, please don't go, or at any rate bring up the kettle first, and the chops, and the frying pan. Please! Then I think I can manage.

LILY: (*Coming back into the room and speaking impressively.*) There's no ill-feeling. It's an objick-lesson – that's all.

Exit LILY. ETHEL *begins to cry weakly; then lays the table; gets bread, cruet, tea, cups, etc. from the cupboard, right.* LILY *re-enters with a frying pan, a kettle, and two raw chops.*

LILY: 'Ere you are – it's the best I can do. You see, mum, I've got to be recognised by the State. I don't think I'm a criminal nor a lunatic, and I oughtn't to be treated as sich.

ETHEL: You poor little simpleton. Do you suppose that, even if this absurd plan succeeds, *you* will get a vote?

LILY: I may – you never know your luck; but that's not why I'm giving up work. It's so as I shan't stop them as ought to 'ave it. The 'ole strain's on me, and I'm goin' to the Union – so goodbye, mum. (*Exit* LILY.)

ETHEL: And I've always been so kind to you! Oh, you little brute! What *will* Horace say? (*Looking out of the window.*) It can't be true. Everything looks the same as usual.

(HORACE'*s voice outside.*)

HORACE: We must have at least sixteen more Dreadnoughts this year.

(WILLIAMS' *voice outside.*)

WILLIAMS: You can't get 'em, old chap, unless you expect the blooming colonies to pay for 'em.

ETHEL: Ah, here is Horace, and Gerald Williams with him. Oh, I hope Horace hasn't asked him to tea! (*She powders her nose at the glass, then pretends to be busy with the kettle.*)

Enter HORACE COLE – *an English master in his own house – and* GERALD WILLIAMS, *a smug young man stiff with self-consciousness.*

ETHEL: You're back early, aren't you, Horry? How do you do, Mr Williams?

GERALD WILLIAMS: How do you do, Mrs Cole. I've just dropped in to fetch a book your husband's promised to lend me.

HORACE *rummages in book-shelves.*

ETHEL: Had a good day, Horry?

HORACE: Oh, much as usual. Ah, here it is (*Reading out the title:*) 'Where's the Wash-tub now?' with a preface by Lord Curzon of Kedleston, published by the Men's League for Opposing Women's Suffrage. If that doesn't settle your missus, nothing will.

ETHEL: Is Mrs Williams a Suffragette?

GERALD: Rather, and whenever I say anything, all she can answer is, 'You know nothing about it.' I call that illogical. Thank you, old man. I'll read it to her after tea. So long. Goodbye, Mrs Cole.

ETHEL: Did Mrs Williams tell you anything this morning … before you went to the City?

GERALD: About Votes for Women, do you mean? Oh, no. Not allowed at breakfast. In fact, not allowed at all. I tried to stop her going to these meetings where they fill the women's heads with all sorts of rubbish, and she said she'd give 'em up if I'd give up footer matches on Saturday afternoons; so we agreed to disagree. See you tomorrow, old chap. Goodbye, Mrs Cole.

Exit GERALD WILLIAMS.

HORACE: You might have asked him to stop to tea. You made him very welcome – I don't think.

ETHEL: I'm sorry; but I don't think he would have stayed if I *had* asked him.

HORACE: Very likely not, but you should always be hospitable. Tea ready?

ETHEL: Not quite, dear. It will be in a minute.

HORACE: What on earth is all this!

ETHEL: Oh, nothing. I thought I would cook your chop for you up here today – just for fun.

HORACE: I really think, Ethel, that as long as we can afford a servant, it's rather unnecessary.

ETHEL: You know you're always complaining of Martha's cooking. I thought you would like me to try.

HORACE: My dear child! It's very nice of you. But why not cook in the kitchen? Raw meat in the drawing room! Do you want to turn me into a poor miserable vegetarian?

ETHEL: Oh, Horry, don't!

She puts her arms round his neck and sobs. The chop at the end of the toasting fork in her hand dangles in his face.

HORACE: What on earth's the matter? Ethel, dear, don't be hysterical. If you knew what it was to come home fagged to death and be worried like this ... I'll ring for Martha and tell her to take away those beastly chops. They're getting on my nerves.

ETHEL: Martha's gone.

HORACE: When? Why? Did you have a row? I suppose you had to give her a month's wages. I can't afford that sort of thing, you know.

ETHEL: (*Soothing.*) It's not you who afford it, anyhow. Don't I pay Martha out of my own money?

HORACE: Do you call it ladylike to throw that in my face ...

ETHEL: (*Incoherently.*) I'm not throwing it in your face ... but as it happens I didn't pay her anything. She went off without a word ... and Lily's gone, too. (*She puts her head down on the table and cries.*)

HORACE: Well, that's a good riddance. I'm sick of her dirty face and slovenly ways. If she ever does clean my boots, she makes them look worse than when I took them off. We must get a charwoman.

ETHEL: We shan't be able to. Isn't it in the papers?

HORACE: What *are* you talking about?

ETHEL: Winifred said it would be in the evening papers.

HORACE: Winifred! She's been here, has she? That accounts for everything. How that woman comes to be your sister I can't imagine. Of course, she's mixed up with this wild-cat scheme.

ETHEL: Then you know about it!

HORACE: Oh. I saw something about 'Suffragettes on Strike' on the posters on my way home. Who cares if they do strike? They're no use to anyone. Look at Winifred. What does she ever do except go round making speeches, and kicking up a row outside the House of Commons until she forces the police to arrest her. Then she goes to prison and poses as a martyr. Martyr! We all know she could go home at once if she would promise the magistrate to behave herself. What they ought to do is to try all these hysterical women privately and sentence them to be ducked – privately. Then they'd soon give up advertising themselves.

ETHEL: Winnie has a splendid answer to that, but I forget what it is. Oh, Horry, was there anything on the posters about the nearest male relative?

HORACE: Ethel, my dear, you haven't gone dotty, have you? When you have quite done with my chair, I – (*He helps her out of the chair and sits down.*) Thank you.

ETHEL: Winnie said that not only are all the working women going to strike, but they are going to make their nearest male relatives support them.

HORACE: Rot!

ETHEL: I thought how dreadful it would be if Agatha came, or that cousin of yours on the stage whom you won't let me know, or your Aunt Lizzie! Martha and Lily have gone to *their* male relatives; at least, Lily's gone to the workhouse – it's all the same thing. Why shouldn't it be true? Oh, look, Horace, there's a cab – with luggage. Oh, what shall we do?

HORACE: Don't fuss! It's stopping next door, not here at all.

ETHEL: No, no; it's here. (*She rushes out.*)

HORACE: (*Calling after her.*) Come back! You can't open the door yourself. It will look as if we didn't keep a servant.

Re-enter ETHEL followed after a few seconds by AGATHA. AGATHA is a weary-looking woman of about thirty-five. She wears the National Union colours, and is dowdily dressed.

ETHEL: It *is* Agatha – and such a big box. Where *can* we put it?

AGATHA: (*Mildly.*) How do you do, Horace. (*Kisses him.*) Dear Ethel! (*Kisses her.*) You're not looking so well as usual. Would you mind paying the cabman two shillings, Horace, and helping him with my box? It's rather heavy, but then it contains all my wordly belongings.

HORACE: Agatha – you haven't lost your situation! You haven't left the Lewises?

AGATHA: Yes, Horace; I left at three o'clock.

HORACE: My dear Agatha – I'm extremely sorry – but we can't put you up here.

AGATHA: Hadn't you better pay the cab? Two shillings so soon becomes two-and-six. (*Exit HORACE.*) I am afraid my brother doesn't realise that I have some claim on him.

ETHEL: We thought you were so happy with the Lewises.

AGATHA: So were the slaves in America when they had kind masters. They didn't want to be free.

ETHEL: Horace said you always had late dinner with them when they had no company.

AGATHA: Oh, I have no complaint against my late employers. In fact, I was sorry to inconvenience them by leaving so suddenly. But I had a higher duty to perform than my duty to them.

ETHEL: I don't know what to do. It will worry Horace dreadfully.

Re-enter HORACE.

HORACE: The cab *was* two-and-six, and I had to give a man twopence to help me in with that Noah's ark. Now, Agatha, what does this mean? Surely in your position it was very unwise to leave the Lewises. You can't stay here. We must make some arrangement.

AGATHA: Any arrangement you like, dear, provided you support me.

HORACE: I support you!

AGATHA: As my nearest male relative, I think you are obliged to do so. If you refuse, I must go to the workhouse.

HORACE: But why can't you support yourself? You've done it for years.

AGATHA: Yes – ever since I was eighteen. Now I am going to give up work, until my work is recognised. Either my proper place is the home – the home provided for me by some dear father, brother, husband, cousin, or uncle – or I am a self-supporting member of the State, who ought not to be shut out from the rights of citizenship.

HORACE: All this sounds as if you had become a Suffragette! Oh, Agatha, I always thought you were a lady.

AGATHA: Yes, I *was* a lady – such a lady that at eighteen I was thrown upon the world, penniless, with no training whatever which fitted me to earn my own living. When women become citizens I believe that daughters will be given the same chance as sons, and such a life as mine will be impossible.

HORACE: Women are so illogical. What on earth has all this to do with your planting yourself on me in this inconsiderate way? You put me in a most unpleasant position. You must see, Agatha, that I haven't the means to support a sister as well as a wife. Couldn't you go to some friends until you find another situation?

AGATHA: No, Horace. I'm going to stay with you.

HORACE: (*Changing his tone, and turning nasty.*) Oh, indeed! And for how long – if I may ask?

AGATHA: Until a Bill for the removal of the sex disability is passed.

HORACE: (*Impotently angry.*) Nonsense. I can't keep you, and I won't. I have always tried to do my duty by you. I think hardly a week passes that I don't write to you. But now that you have deliberately thrown up an excellent situation as a governess, and come here and threatened me – yes, threatened me – I think it's time to say that, sister or no sister, I intend to be master in my own house!

Enter MOLLY, a good-looking young girl of about twenty. She is dressed in well-cut, tailor-made clothes, wears a neat little hat, and carries some golfclubs and a few books.

MOLLY: How are you, Uncle Horace? Is that Aunt Aggie? How d'ye do? I haven't seen you since I was a kid.

HORACE: Well, what have you come for?

MOLLY: There's a charming welcome to give your only niece!

HORACE: You know perfectly well, Molly, that I disapprove of you in every way. I hear – I have never read it, of course – but I hear that you have written a most scandalous book. You live in lodgings by yourself, when if you chose you could afford some really nice and refined boarding-house. You have most undesirable acquaintances, and altogether –

MOLLY: Cheer up, Uncle. Now's your chance of reforming me. I've come to live with you. You can support me and improve me at the same time.

HORACE: I never heard such impertinence. I have always understood from you that you earn more than I do.

MOLLY: Ah, yes; but you never *liked* my writing for money, did you? You called me 'sexless' once because I said that as long as I could support myself I didn't feel an irresistible temptation to marry that awful little bounder Weekes.

ETHEL: Reginald Weekes! How can you call him a bounder! He was at Oxford.

MOLLY: Hullo, Auntie Ethel! I didn't notice you. You'll be glad to hear I haven't brought much luggage – only a night-gown and some golf clubs.

HORACE: I suppose this is a joke!

MOLLY: Well, of course, that's one way of looking at it. I'm not going to support myself any longer. I'm going to be a perfect lady, and depend on my Uncle Horace – my nearest male relative – for the necessities of life. (*A motor horn is heard outside.*) Aren't you glad that I am not going to write another scandalous book, or live in lodgings by myself?

ETHEL: (*At the window.*) Horace! Horace! There's someone getting out of a motor – a grand motor. Who can it be? And there's no one to answer the door.

MOLLY: That doesn't matter. I found it open, and left it open to save trouble.

ETHEL: She's got luggage, too! The chauffeur is bringing in a dressing-case.

HORACE: I'll turn her into the street – and the dressing-case, too.

He goes fussily to the door, and meets MADAME CHRISTINE on the threshold. The lady is dressed smartly and tastefully. Age about forty, manners elegant, smile charming, speech resolute. She carries a jewelcase, and consults a legal document during her first remarks.

MADAME CHRISTINE: You are Mr Cole?

HORACE: No! Certainly not! (*Wavering.*) At least, I was this morning, but –

MADAME CHRISTINE: Horace Cole, son of John Hay Cole, formerly of Streatham, where he carried on the business of a –

A motor horn sounds outside.

HORACE: I beg your pardon, but my late father's business has really nothing to do with this matter, and to a professional man it's rather trying to have these things raked up against him. Excuse me, but do you want your motor to go?

MADAME CHRISTINE: It's not my motor any longer; and – yes, I do want it to go, for I may be staying here some time. I think you had one sister, Agatha, and one brother, Samuel, now dead. Samuel was much older than you –

AGATHA: Why don't you answer, Horace? Yes, that's perfectly correct. I am Agatha.

MADAME CHRISTINE: Oh, are you? How d'ye do?

MOLLY: And Samuel Cole was my father.

MADAME CHRISTINE: I'm very glad to meet you. I didn't know I had such charming relations. Well, Mr Cole, my father was John Hay Cole's first cousin; so you, I think, are my second cousin, and my nearest male relative.

HORACE: (Distractedly.) If anyone calls me that again I shall go mad.

MADAME CHRISTINE: I am afraid you aren't quite pleased with the relationship!

HORACE: You must excuse me – but I don't consider a second cousin a relation. A second cousin is a – well –

MADAME CHRISTINE: Oh, it answers the purpose. I suddenly find myself destitute, and I want you to support me. I am sure you would not like a Cole to go to the workhouse.

HORACE: I don't care a damn where any of you go.

ETHEL: (Shocked.) Horry! How can you!

MADAME CHRISTINE: That's frank, at any rate; but I am sure, Cousin Horace, that in spite of your manners, your heart's in the right place. You won't refuse me board and lodging, until Parliament makes it possible for me to resume my work?

HORACE: My dear madam, do you realise that my salary is £3.10s. a week – and that my house will hardly hold your luggage, much less you?

MADAME CHRISTINE: Then you must agitate. Your female relatives have supported themselves up till now, and asked nothing from you. I myself, dear cousin, was, until this morning, running a profitable dressmaking business in Hanover Square. In my public capacity I am Madame Christine.

MOLLY: I know! You make sweet gowns, but I've never been able to afford you.

HORACE: And do you think, Madame Christine –

MADAME CHRISTINE: Cousin Susan, please.

HORACE: Do you think that you are justified in coming to a poor clerk, and asking him to support you – you, who could probably turn over my yearly income in a single week! Didn't you come here in your own motor?

MADAME CHRISTINE: At three o'clock that motor became the property of the Women's Social and Political Union. All the rest of my property and all available cash have been divided equally between the National Union and the Women's Freedom League. Money is the sinews of war, you know.

HORACE: Do you mean to tell me that you've given all your money to the Suffragettes! It's a pity you haven't a husband. He'd very soon put an end to such folly.

MADAME CHRISTINE: I had a husband once. He liked me to do foolish things – for instance, to support him. After that unfortunate experience, Cousin Horace, you may imagine how glad I am to find a man who really is a man, and will support me instead. By the way, I should so much like some tea. Is the kettle boiling?

ETHEL: (Feebly.) There aren't enough cups! Oh, what shall I do?

HORACE: Never mind, Ethel; I shan't want any. I am going to dine in town, and go to the theatre. I shall hope to find you all gone when I come back. If not, I shall send for the police.

Enter MAUDIE SPARK, *a young woman with an aggressively cheerful manner, a voice raucous from much bellowing of music-hall songs, a hat of huge size, and a heart of gold.*

MAUDIE: 'Ullo! 'Ullo! Who's talking about the police? Not my dear cousin Horry?

HORACE: How dare you come here?

MAUDIE: Necessity, old dear. If I could have found a livelier male relative, you may bet I'd have gone to him! But you, Horace, are the only first cousin of this poor orphan. What are you in such a hurry for?

HORACE: Let me pass! I'm going to the theatre.

MAUDIE: Silly jay! the theatres are all closed – and the halls, too. The actresses have gone on strike – resting indefinitely. I've done my little bit towards that. They won't get any more work out of Maudie Spark, Queen of Comédiennes, until the women have got the vote. Ladies and fellow-relatives, you'll be pleased to hear the strike's going fine. The big drapers can't open tomorrow. One man can't fill the place of fifteen young ladies at once, you see. The duchesses are out in the streets begging people to come in and wash their kids. The City men are trying to get taxi men in to do their typewriting. Every man, like Horry here, has his house full of females. Most of 'em thought, like Horry, that they'd go to the theatre to escape. But there's not a blessed theatre to go to! Oh, what a song it'll make. 'A woman's place is the home – I don't think, I don't think, I don't think.'

HORACE: Even if this is not a plot against me personally, even if there are other women in London at this minute disgracing their sex –

MAUDIE: Here, stop it – come off it! If it comes to that, what are *you* doing – threatening your womankind with the police and the workhouse.

HORACE: I was not addressing myself to you.

AGATHA: Why not, Horace? She's your cousin. She needs your protection just as much as we do.

HORACE: I regard that woman as the skeleton in the cupboard of a respectable family; but that's neither here nor there. I address myself to the more ladylike portion of this gathering, and I say that whatever is going on the men will know what to do, and will do it with dignity and firmness. (*The impressiveness of this statement is marred by the fact that* HORACE'S *hand, in emphasising it, comes down heavily on the loaf of bread on the table.*) A few exhibitions of this kind won't frighten them.

MAUDIE: Oh, won't it! I like that! They're being so firm and so dignified that they's running down to the House of Commons like lunatics, and black-guarding the Government for not having given us the vote before!

Shouts outside of newsboys in the distance.

MOLLY: Splendid! Have they begun already?

MADAME CHRISTINE: Get a paper, Cousin Horace. I know some men will never believe anything till they see it in the paper.

ETHEL: The boys are shouting out something now. Listen.

Shouts outside: 'Extry special. Great strike of women. Women's strike. Theatres closed. Extry special edition. "Star!" "News!" 6.30 edition.'

MOLLY: You see. Since this morning Suffragettes have become women!

ETHEL: (*At window.*) Here, boy, paper!

Cries go on: 'Extra special "Star". Men petition the Government. Votes for Women. Extry special.'

Oh, heavens, here's Aunt Lizzie!

As ETHEL pronounces the name HORACE dives under the table. Enter AUNT LIZZIE leading a fat spaniel and carrying a bird cage with a parrot in it. MISS ELIZABETH WILKINS is a comfortable, middle-aged body of a type well known to those who live in the less fashionable quarter of Bloomsbury. She looks as if she kept lodgers, and her looks do not belie her. She is not very well educated, but has a good deal of native intelligence. Her features are homely, and her clothes about thirty years behind the times.

AUNT LIZZIE: Well, dears, all here? That's right. Where's Horace? Out? Just as well; we can talk more freely. I'm sorry I'm late, but animals do so hate a move. It took a long time to make them understand the strike. But I think they will be very comfortable here. You love dogs, don't you, Ethel?

ETHEL: Not Ponto. He always growls at me.

AUNT LIZZIE: Clever dog! he knows you don't sympathise with the cause.

ETHEL: But I do, Aunt; only I have always said that as I was happily married I thought it had very little to do with me.

AUNT LIZZIE: You've changed your mind about that today, I should think! What a day it's been! We never expected everything would go so smoothly. They say the Bill's to be rushed through at once. No more deceitful promises, no more dishonest 'facilities'; deeds, not words, at last! Seen the papers? The Press are not boycotting us today, my dears. (*MADAME CHRISTINE, MOLLY, and MAUDIE each take a paper.*) The boy who sold them to me put the money back into Ponto's collecting box. That dog must have made five pounds for the cause since this morning.

HORACE: (*Puts his head out.*) 'Liar!'

MOLLY: Oh, do listen to this. It's too splendid! (*Reading from the paper.*) 'Women's Strike. – Latest: Messrs Lyons and Co. announce that by special arrangement with the War Office the places of their defaulting waitresses will be filled by the non-commissioned officers and men of the 2nd Battalion Coldstream Guards. Business will therefore be carried on as usual.'

MADAME CHRISTINE: What do you think of this? (*Reading.*) 'Latest Intelligence. – It is understood that the Naval Volunteers have been approached by the authorities with the object of inducing them to act as charwomen to the House of Commons.'

AUNT LIZZIE: (*To ETHEL.*) Well, my dear! What have you got there? Read what the *Star* says.

ETHEL: (*Tremulously reading.*) 'The queue of women waiting for admission to Westminster Workhouse is already a mile and a half in length. As the entire police force are occupied in dealing with the men's processions, Lord Haldane has been approached with a view to ascertaining if the Territorials can be sworn in as special constables.'

MAUDIE: (*Laughing.*) This is a little bit of all right. (*Reading.*) 'Our special representative, on calling upon the Prime Minister with the object of ascertaining his views on the situation, was informed that the Right Honourable gentleman was unable to receive him, as with the assistance of the boot-boy and a Foreign Office messenger, he was actively engaged in making his bed.'

AUNT LIZZIE: Always unwilling to receive people, you see! Well, he must be feeling sorry now that he never received us. Everyone's putting the blame on him. It's extraordinary how many men – and newspapers, too – have suddenly found out that they have always been in favour of woman's suffrage! That's the sensible attitude, of course. It would be humiliating for them to confess that it was not until we held a pistol to their heads that they changed their minds. Well, at this minute I would rather be the man who has been our ally all along than the one who has been our enemy. It's not the popular thing to be an 'anti' any more. Any man who tries to oppose us today is likely to be slung up to the nearest lamp post.

ETHEL: (*Rushing wildly to the table.*) Oh, Horry! My Horry!

HORACE comes out from under the table.

AUNT LIZZIE: Why, bless the boy, what are you doing there?

HORACE: Oh, nothing. I merely thought I might be less in the way here, that's all.

AUNT LIZZIE: You didn't hide when I came in, by any chance!

HORACE: I hide from you! Aren't you always welcome in this house?

AUNT LIZZIE: Well, I haven't noticed it particularly; and I'm not calling today, you understand. I've come to stay.

HORACE, dashed and beaten, begins to walk up and down the room, and consults ETHEL.

Well, well! I won't deny it was a wrench to leave 118a,

Upper Montagu Place, where I've done my best for boarders, old and young, gents and ladies, for twenty-five years – and no complaints! A home from home, they always call it. All my ladies had left before I started out, on the same business as ourselves – but what those poor boys will do for their dinner tonight I don't know. They're a helpless lot! Well, it's all over; I've given up my boarding-house, and I depend on you, Horace, to keep me until I am admitted to citizenship. It may take a long time.

HORACE: It must *not* take a long time! I shan't allow it. It shall be done at once. Well, you needn't all look so surprised. I know I've been against it, but I didn't realise things. I thought only a few hooligan window-smashers wanted the vote; but when I find that *you* – Aunt – Fancy a woman of your firmness of character, one who has always been so careful with her money, being declared incapable of voting! The thing is absurd.

MAUDIE: Bravo! Our Horry's waking up.

HORACE: (*Looking at her scornfully.*) If there are a few women here and there who *are* incapable – I mention no names, mind – it doesn't affect the position. What's going to be done? Who's going to do it? If this rotten Government think we're going to maintain millions of women in idleness just because they don't like the idea of my Aunt Lizzie making a scratch on a bit of paper and shoving it into a ballot-box once every five years, this Government have reckoned without the men – (*General cheering.*) I'll show 'em what I've got a vote for! What do they expect? You can't all marry. There aren't enough men to go round, and if you're earning your own living and paying taxes you ought to have a say; it's only fair. (*General cheering and a specially emphatic* 'Hear, hear' *from* MADAME CHRISTINE.) The Government are narrow-minded idiots!

MADAME CHRISTINE: Hear, hear!

HORACE: They talk as if all the women ought to stay at home washing and ironing. Well, before a woman has a wash tub, she must have a home to put it in, mustn't she? And who's going to give it her? I'd like them to tell me that. Do they expect *me* to do it?

AGATHA: Yes, dear.

HORACE: I say if she can do it herself and keep herself, so much the better for everyone. Anyhow, who are the Government? They're only representing *me*, and being paid thousands a year by *me* for carrying out *my* wishes.

MOLLY: Oh, er – what ho!

HORACE: (*Turns on her angrily.*) I like a woman to be a woman – that's the way I was brought up; but if she insists on having a vote – and apparently she does.

ALL: She does! she does!

HORACE: – I don't see why she shouldn't have it. Many a woman came in here at the last election and tried to wheedle me into voting for her particular candidate. If she has time to do that – and I never heard the member say then that she ought to be at home washing and ironing

the baby – I don't see why she hasn't time to vote. It's never taken up much of *my* time, or interfered with *my* work. I've only voted once in my life – but that's neither here nor there. I know what the vote does for me. It gives me a status; that's what you women want – a status.

ALL: Yes, yes, a status.

HORACE: I might even call it a *locus standi*. If I go now and tell these rotten Cabinet Ministers what I think of them, it's my *locus standi* –

MAUDIE: That's a good word.

HORACE: – that will force them to listen to me. Oh, I know. And, by gum! I'll give them a bit of my mind. They shall hear a few home truths for once. 'Gentlemen,' I shall say – well, that won't be true of all of them to start with, but one must give 'em the benefit of the doubt – 'gentlemen, the men of England are sick and tired of your policy. Who's driven the women of England into this? *You* – (*He turns round on* ETHEL, *who jumps violently.*) – because you were too stupid to know that they meant business – because you couldn't read the writing on the wall.' (*Hear, hear.*) It may be nothing to you, gentlemen, that every industry in this country is paralysed and every Englishman's home turned into a howling wilderness –

MOLLY: Draw it mild, Uncle.

HORACE: A howling wilderness, I repeat – by your refusal to see what's as plain as the nose on your face; but I would have you know, gentlemen, that it *is* something to us. We aren't slaves. We never will be slaves –

AGATHA: Never, never!

HORACE: And we insist on reform. Gentlemen, conditions have changed, and women have to work. Don't men encourage them to work, *invite* them to work?

AGATHA: *Make* them work.

HORACE: And women are placed in the battle of life on the same terms as we are, short of one thing, the *locus standi* of a vote.

MAUDIE: Good old *locus standi*!

HORACE: If you aren't going to give it them, gentlemen, and if they won't go back to their occupations without it, we ask you how they're going to live? Who's going to support them? Perhaps you're thinking of giving them all old age pensions and asking the country to pay the piper! The country will see you damned first, if, gentlemen, you'll pardon the expression. It's dawning upon us all that the women would never have taken such a step as this if they hadn't been the victims of a gross injustice.

ALL: Never.

HORACE: Why shouldn't they have a voice in the laws which regulate the price of food and clothes? Don't they pay for their food and clothes?

MAUDIE: Paid for mine since the age of six.

HORACE: Why shouldn't they have a voice in the rate of wages and the hours of labour in certain industries? Aren't they working at those industries? If you had a particle of common sense or decent feeling, gentlemen –

Enter GERALD WILLIAMS *like a souvenir of Mafeking night. He shouts incoherently and in a hoarse voice. He is utterly transformed from the meek, smug being of an hour before. He is wearing several ribbons and badges and carries a banner bearing this inscription: 'The men of Brixton demand votes for women this evening.'*

WILLIAMS: Cole, Cole! Come on! Come on! You'll be late. The procession's forming up at the town hall. There's no time to lose. What are you slacking here for? Perhaps this isn't good enough for you. I've got twelve of them in my drawing-room. We shall be late for the procession if we don't start at once. Hurry up! Come on! Votes for Women! Where's your banner? Where's your badge? Down with the Government! Rule Britannia! Votes for Women! D'you want to support a dozen women for the rest of your life, or don't you? … Every man in Brixton is going to Westminster. Borrow a ribbon and come along. Hurry up, now! Hooray! (*Rushes madly out crying* 'Votes for Women! Rule Britannia; Women never, never shall be slaves! Votes for Women!')

All the women who are wearing ribbons decorate HORACE.

ETHEL: My hero! (*She throws her arms round him.*)
HORACE: You may depend on me – all of you – to see justice done. When you want a thing done, get a man to do it! Votes for Women!

AGATHA *gives him a flag which he waves triumphantly.*

Curtain tableau: HORACE *marching majestically out of the door, with the women cheering him enthusiastically.*

Note

This play, first published in 1913, is taken from Dale Spender and Carol Hayman, eds, *How the Vote Was Won and Other Suffrage Plays*, London: Methuen, 1985, pp. 17–34.

3.2 HOPPLA, WE'RE ALIVE! (1927)

A Prologue and Five Acts

ERNST TOLLER

Translated and edited by Alan Raphael Pearlman

Ernst Toller (1893–1939) *was born into a Prussian-Jewish family and volunteered for military service in the First World War. Deeply affected by his wartime experiences, Toller turned communist agitator, becoming involved in the fleeting Bavarian Soviet Republic (1919), for which he was subsequently imprisoned. It was while incarcerated that Toller became something of a prolific dramatist and poet. In 1927, three years after his release, the ground-breaking political theatre practitioner Erwin Piscator directed Toller's* Hoppla, We're Alive! (Hoppla, wir leben!) *in Berlin. Toller's epic play, set mostly contemporaneously and 'in many countries', dramatizes the struggles encountered by a revolutionary after he has been released from a mental asylum, particularly through the impact of his friends' accommodation to the political status quo, finally resulting in his suicide. The destiny of Toller's anti-hero was to be mirrored in the dramatist's own life. Along with numerous compatriot artists and writers, Toller was exiled from Nazi Germany and eventually found himself as an émigré in the USA. Beset with depression and financial difficulties, Toller ended his own life in his room at New York's Mayflower Hotel.*

Characters in the Prologue

KARL THOMAS	FRAU MELLER
EVA BERG	SIXTH PRISONER
WILHELM KILMAN	WARDER RAND
ALBERT KROLL	LIEUTENANT BARON FRIEDRICH
SOLDIERS	

Time: 1919

Characters in the Play

KARL THOMAS	FRITZ
EVA BERG	GRETE
WILHELM KILMAN	FIRST WORKER
FRAU KILMAN	SECOND WORKER
LOTTE KILMAN	THIRD WORKER
ALBERT KROLL	FOURTH WORKER
FRAU MELLER	FIFTH WORKER
RAND	EXAMINING MAGISTRATE
PROFESSOR LÜDIN	HEAD WAITER

BARON FRIEDRICH	PORTER
COUNT LANDE	RADIO OPERATOR
MINISTER OF WAR	BUSBOY
BANKER	CLERK
BANKER'S SON	BARKEEPER
PICKEL	POLICE CHIEF
MINISTRY OFFICIAL	FIRST POLICEMAN
MADHOUSE ORDERLY	SECOND POLICEMAN
STUDENT	THIRD POLICEMAN

CHAIRMAN OF THE UNION OF INTELLECTUAL BRAIN WORKERS

PHILOSOPHER X
POET Y
CRITIC Z
ELECTION OFFICER
SECOND ELECTION OFFICER
FIRST ELECTIONEER
SECOND ELECTIONEER
THIRD ELECTIONEER
VOTER
OLD WOMAN
PRISONER N
JOURNALISTS
LADIES, GENTLEMEN, PEOPLE

The play takes place in many countries. Eight years after the crushing of a people's uprising. Time: 1927.

Note to the director

All the scenes of the play can be played on a scaffolding which is built up in tiers and which can be changed without rebuilding. In theatres where it is completely impossible to use film equipment, the film segments may be omitted or replaced by simple slide projections.

In order not to break the tempo of the work, there should be, as far as possible, only one interval, namely after Act 2.

The staging information contained in square brackets in italics is based on the running notes in Piscator's Promptbook [Erwin Piscator, who first directed the play]. In the case of the film sequences for which neither the films nor the shooting scripts still exist, these notes have been augmented by material from contemporary reviews reprinted in Knellessen and Rüehle.[1] Other stage directions are from the text as published.

[Auditorium lights go down. Then up and down three times. Curtain up to reveal film screen almost covering scaffolding.]

Film Prologue

NOISES: SIRENS

FLASHING SEARCHLIGHTS

SCENES OF A PEOPLE'S UPRISING

ITS CRUSHING

FIGURES OF THE DRAMATIC PROLOGUE APPEARING ON AND OFF

[Film: brief shot of General's headless chest with medals. Then documentary German war footage of infantry attack, charging tanks, explosions, barrage of gunfire, wounded soldiers, vast military cemeteries, retreat of worn-out German Army, disposal of

weapons in a growing heap. KARL THOMAS *visible among the matching soldiers. General's chest again: a hand roughly rips off the medals. As film ends screen is raised and white and black gauzes lowered in its place. Centre compartment where prisoners will be begins to light up. Façade of prison windows projected on to gauze and remains to end of scene. Prison noises begin to build. As lights brighten prisoners can be seen. Back projections of prison walls on centre compartment rear screen and on middle and upper left and right compartment screens — from audience viewpoint as in the Promptbook and in all the following directions. Bottom left and right compartments closed. Prologue begins.]*

PROLOGUE

Large prison cell

KARL THOMAS: Damned silence!

ALBERT KROLL: Like to sing hymns?

EVA BERG: In the French Revolution the aristocrats danced the minuet to the guillotine

ALBERT KROLL: Romantic con! You should have inspected their knickers. The odour wouldn't have smelled like lavender.

Silence.

[Lights dim centre compartment and film of guard passing from left to right projected on the gauze. Then back projection on central compartment rear screen of RAND *climbing stairs which turns into enlarged head of* RAND *appearing from right, hovering over prisoners and returning right.* WILHELM KILMAN *reacts in fear as if it is his hallucination.]*

WILHELM KILMAN: Mother Meller, you're an old woman. You're always silent or smiling. Don't you have any fear of … of …? Mother Meller (*Edges towards her.*) my legs are shaking from the heat and there's ice packed around my heart … Understand, I've got a wife and child … Mother Meller, I'm so scared …

FRAU MELLER: Calm down, my boy, calm down. It only seems so bad when you're young. Later on it fades away. Life and death, they flow together. You come out of one womb and you journey into another …

WILHELM KILMAN: Do you believe there's life there?

FRAU MELLER: No, drop it. My teachers beat that belief out of me.

WILHELM KILMAN: Nobody's visited you. Didn't you want them to?

FRAU MELLER: They stole my parents and my two children in the war. Caused me great pain, but I thought to myself times will change. And they sure did. All is lost … But others will go on struggling …

Silence.

[Film on gauze of resting prisoners like caged animals, crammed together like corpses.]

KARL THOMAS: Listen! I've seen something.

EVA BERG: What?

[Back projected film on centre rear screen of warders approaching, growing larger, looking at prisoners, turning and going away.]

Figure 17 *Hoppla, We're Alive!* from the Berliner-Schauspielschule studio production, 1984. (Photograph: uncredited.)

KARL THOMAS: No, don't crowd around. Bug-eyes is at the spy-hole … We'll escape.

ALBERT KROLL: Like the taste of lead?

KARL THOMAS: Look at the window. The plaster around the iron bars has crumbled.

ALBERT KROLL: Yes, you're right.

KARL THOMAS: And isn't that big piece of plaster faked to look firm? …

ALBERT KROLL: Right.

KARL THOMAS: Do you see?

EVA BERG: Yes. Yes. A kid's trick to drive you mad.

FRAU MELLER: Yes. How true.

WILHELMILMAN: That's where they once tried to get into the cell from outside … Almost did it … Well, I don't know.

FRAU MELLER: (*To* WILHELM KILMAN.) What, scaredy-pants?

WILHELM KILMAN: Yes, but …

KARL THOMAS: What's with the 'but'?

ALBERT KROLL: You know I'm not reckless. It's night. How late?

KARL THOMAS: It's just struck four.

ALBERT KROLL: Then the guard has changed. We're on the first floor. If we stay here, we'll say good morning in a mass grave. If we try to escape, the odds are ten to one against. And even if they were a hundred to one, we must take the risk.

WILHELM KILMAN: If not …

KARL THOMAS: Dead either way … Albert, you do a parade march, six steps back and forth, from the window to the door without stopping. Then the spy-hole will be blocked for a few seconds and outside they won't notice anything. The fifth time I'll jump up to the window and with all my strength pull the iron bars out and then 'Bye-bye, boss'.

EVA BERG: I could scream! Karl, I could kiss you to death.

ALBERT KROLL: Later.

[Back projected film on centre rear screen of two guards approaching, turning and leaving.]

KARL THOMAS: Leave her alone. She's so young.

ALBERT KROLL: Karl, you jump out first, then Eva second; then, Wilhelm, you grab Mother Meller and push her up …

WILHELM KILMAN: Yes, yes … only I think …

FRAU MELLER: Let him go first … No one needs to help me. I can cope like all of you.

ALBERT KROLL: Shut up. You go first, then Wilhelm, then me last.

WILHELM KILMAN: What if the escape doesn't work? We'd better think it over.

ALBERT KROLL: If the escape doesn't work …

KARL THOMAS: How can you know if any escape will work? You've got to take the risk, comrade! A revolutionary who doesn't take risks! You should have stayed home drinking coffee with your mother, not gone to the barricades.

WILHELM KILMAN: We'd all be lost afterwards. There'd be no more hope.

KARL THOMAS: To hell with hope! Hope for what? The death sentence was passed. For ten days we've been waiting for the execution.

FRAU MELLER: Last night they asked for the addresses of our relatives.

KARL THOMAS: So hope for what? A volley of gunfire, and if it misses the bonus of a finishing shot. A good victory or a good death – the battle cry hasn't changed for a thousand years.

WILHELM KILMAN cowers.

Or … have you been begging for mercy? If so, at least swear you'll keep silent.

WILHELM KILMAN: Why do you let him insult me. Haven't I drudged day and night? For fifteen years I've slaved for

the Party and now I must be allowed my say … I don't get breakfast in bed.

FRAU MELLER: Peace, both of you.

KARL THOMAS: Just think of the trial. Are they likely to quash the death sentence? Strike a concrete wall and do you think it's going to ring clear as a bell?

ALBERT KROLL: Let's go! Everybody ready? Eva, you count. Take care, Karl … the fifth time.

ALBERT KROLL begins to march back and forth, from the window to the door, from the door to the window. Everybody tense.

EVA BERG: One … two … three …

KARL THOMAS steals to the window.

Four …

Noise at the door. Door creaks open.

ALBERT KROLL: Damn it!

WARDER RAND enters.

WARDER RAND: Anyone want the priest?

FRAU MELLER: He really ought to be ashamed of himself.

RAND: Don't commit a sin, old woman. You'll be standing before your Maker soon enough.

FRAU MELLER: I've learned the worms know nothing about religious faiths. Tell your priest Jesus drove the money-changers and usurers out of the temple with lashes of the whip. Tell him to write that down in his Bible, on the first page.

RAND: (To the SIXTH PRISONER who's lying on a plank bed.) And you?

SIXTH PRISONER: (Softly.) Forgive me, comrades … I left the Church at sixteen … now … before death … terrifying … understand me, comrades … Yes, I want to go to the priest, Herr Warder.

WILHELM KILMAN: Revolutionary? You shit-pants! To the priest! Dear God, make me holy so I'll go to heaven.

FRAU MELLER: Why attack the poor devil?

ALBERT KROLL: Before death … Leave him alone.

WILHELM KILMAN: A man can say what he wants.

WARDER and SIXTH PRISONER leave. Door is closed.

[Back projected centre rear screen film of RAND and SIXTH PRISONER going off, turns into laughing head of RAND and with distorted grimace as shooting starts.]

ALBERT KROLL: Won't he betray us?

KARL THOMAS: No.

ALBERT KROLL: Look! Now that he has to go with him, he can't spy on us. Get going Karl, I'll help you. Here, on my back …

[Film on gauze of guns shooting. GUARD laughs and goes right.]

ALBERT KROLL bends over. KARL THOMAS climbs on ALBERT

KROLL's *bent back. As he stretches both hands towards the windowsill to grab the iron bars, rifles rattle from below, plaster and other fragments come flying into the cell,* KARL THOMAS *jumps off* ALBERT KROLL's *back. They all stare at each other.*

Are you wounded?

KARL THOMAS: No. What was that?

ALBERT KROLL: Nothing special. They're guarding our window. A small company.

EVA BERG: That … means …?

FRAU MELLER: Prepare yourself, my child.

EVA BERG: For … for death …?

The others are silent.

No … no … (*Sobs, cries.*)

FRAU MELLER *goes to her, strokes her.*

ALBERT KROLL: Don't cry, dear girl. We revolutionaries are all dead men on leave, as someone once said.

KARL THOMAS: Leave her alone, Albert. She's young. Barely seventeen. For her death means a cold, black hole which she has to lie in forever. And on top of her grave there's life – warm, exciting, gay and sweet.

KARL THOMAS *goes to* EVA BERG.

Your hands.

EVA BERG: Dear you.

KARL THOMAS: I love you very much, Eva.

EVA BERG: Will they bury us together, if we ask them?

KARL THOMAS: Maybe.

ALBERT KROLL *jumps up.*

ALBERT KROLL: Damn torture! Why don't they come? I once read that cats torture mice so long because they smell so good in their death throes … For us there must be other refinements. Why don't they come? Why don't the dirty dogs come?

KARL THOMAS: Yes, why do we struggle? What do we know? For the Idea, for Justice – we say. No one's dug deep enough into himself to bow down before the ultimate, naked reason – if there are ultimate reasons.

ALBERT KROLL: I don't understand. I've known that our society lives off the sweat of our hands ever since I was sixteen and was dragged out of bed at five in the morning to deliver rolls. And what has to be done to end injustice, that I knew even before I could reckon how much ten times ten is …

KARL THOMAS: Look around at how everyone pounces upon the Idea in times of revolution and war. One is running away from his wife because she makes his life hell. Another can't cope with life and limps along until he finds a crutch which makes him look wonderful and gives him a little heroic sheen. A third believes he can all of a sudden change his skin, which has become repulsive to him. A

fourth seeks adventure. There are fewer and fewer who must do so out of inmost necessity.

[*All but first and last lines of this speech cut.*]

Noise. Door creaks open. SIXTH PRISONER *enters. Silence.*

SIXTH PRISONER: Do you hold it against me, comrades? I'm not converted, comrades … But … it makes me calmer …

KARL THOMAS: Judas!

SIXTH PRISONER: But dear comrades …

ALBERT KROLL: Still no decision! Still waiting! I'd like to smoke, has anyone got a butt?

They search in their pockets.

ALL: No.

KARL THOMAS: Wait … sure … I've got a cigarette.

ALL: Bring it here! Bring it here!

ALBERT KROLL: Matches? No go.

WILHELM KILMAN: I have one.

ALBERT KROLL: We must share it, of course.

WILHELM KILMAN: Really?

EVA BERG: Yes, please.

KARL THOMAS: Eva can have my share.

FRAU MELLER: Mine too.

EVA BERG: No, one puff each.

ALBERT KROLL: Good. Who'll start?

EVA BERG: We'll draw lots.

ALBERT KROLL: (*Tears a handkerchief into strips.*) Whoever draws the smallest strip.

All draw.

Mother Meller starts.

FRAU MELLER: Here goes. (*Smokes.*) Now your turn. (*Gives* WILHELM KILMAN *the cigarette.*)

WILHELM KILMAN: I hope they won't catch us.

ALBERT KROLL: What could they do to us? Four weeks solitary confinement for punishment! Ha, ha, ha.

They all smoke, one puff each. They watch each other closely.

Karl, you mustn't take two puffs.

KARL THOMAS: Don't talk rubbish.

ALBERT KROLL: Think I'm lying?

KARL THOMAS: Yes.

WILHELM KILMAN: (*To* ALBERT KROLL.) You sucked much longer than we did.

ALBERT KROLL: Shut up, coward.

WILHELM KILMAN: He's calling me coward.

ALBERT KROLL: Where did you creep off to during the days of decision? Where did you rub your trouser seat shiny while we stormed the town hall – with the enemy at our backs and a mass grave in front of us? Where were you hiding?

WILHELM KILMAN: Didn't I address the masses from the balcony of the town hall?

ALBERT KROLL: Yes, when we had power. But before, neither

for nor against. Then in a flash you're at the feeding trough.

KARL THOMAS: (*To* ALBERT KROLL.) You have no right to talk like that.

ALBERT KROLL: Bourgeois lackey!

FRAU MELLER: What scum, to row five minutes before you're put up against the wall …

WILHELM KILMAN: He's calling me coward! For fifteen years I have …

ALBERT KROLL: (*Aping him.*) Fifteen years … Big shot … No great honour to bite the dust together with you.

EVA BERG: Shame!

KARL THOMAS: Yes, shame.

ALBERT KROLL: What shame! Go lie with your whore in the corner and give her a kid. Then it can hatch in the grave and play with the worms.

EVA BERG screams. KARL THOMAS jumps on ALBERT KROLL.

SIXTH PRISONER: (*Jumping up.*) Heavenly Father, is this Thy will?

As they hold each other by the throat, noise. Door creaks open. They let go.

RAND: The Lieutenant is coming now. You must get ready. (*Goes.*)

ALBERT KROLL goes up to KARL THOMAS, embraces him.

ALBERT KROLL: We don't know anything about ourselves, Karl. That wasn't me just now, that wasn't me. Give me your hand, dear Eva.

KARL THOMAS: For ten days we've been waiting for death. That has poisoned us.

Noise. Door creaks open, LIEUTENANT *enters with* SOLDIERS.

LIEUTENANT BARON FRIEDRICH: (*To* ALBERT KROLL.) Stand up. In the name of the President. The death sentence was pronounced in accordance with the law. (*Pause.*) As a sign of his clemency and his wish for reconciliation the President has quashed the death sentence. The condemned are to be held in protective custody and are to be transported to the internment camp immediately. With the exception of Wilhelm Kilman.

KARL THOMAS bursts into howls of laughter.

EVA BERG: Your laughter is terrifying, Karl.

FRAU MELLER: For joy.

LIEUTENANT BARON FRIEDRICH: Stop laughing, man.

EVA BERG: Karl! Karl!

ALBERT KROLL: He's not laughing for fun.

FRAU MELLER: Just look at him. It's convulsed him.

LIEUTENANT BARON FRIEDRICH: (*To the* WARDER.) Take him to the doctor.

KARL THOMAS is led out. EVA BERG goes with him.

ALBERT KROLL: (*To* WILHELM KILMAN.) You're the only one to stay. Forgive me, Wilhelm. We won't forget you.

FRAU MELLER: (*Leaving, to* ALBERT KROLL.) Clemency. Who would have thought that the authorities could feel so weak.

ALBERT KROLL: Bad sign. Who would have thought that the authorities could feel so strong.

All leave, except LIEUTENANT BARON FRIEDRICH *and* WILHELM KILMAN.

LIEUTENANT BARON FRIEDRICH: The President has granted your petition. He believes you, that you came to be in the ranks of the rebels against your will. You are free.

WILHELM KILMAN: Thank you most respectfully, Herr Lieutenant.

Curtain.

[Gauze up. Projection of prison windows off. Screen lowered for film.]

Film Interlude

Behind the stage:

CHORUS: (*In rhythmical crescendo and diminuendo.*)
Happy New Year! Happy New Year!
Special Edition! Special Edition!
Great Sensation! Special Edition!
Special Edition!
Great Sensation!

On the screen:

Scenes from the years 1919–1927.

Between them: KARL THOMAS *in asylum dress pacing back and forth in a lunatic cell.*

1919:
Treaty of Versailles
1920:
Stock Market Turmoil in New York
People go mad
1921:
Fascism in Italy
1922:
Hunger in Vienna
People go mad
1923:
Inflation in Germany
People go mad
1924:
Lenin's Death in Russia
Newspaper Notice: Tonight Frau Luise Thomas died …
1925:
Gandhi in India
1926:
Battles in China

Conference of European Leaders in Europe
1927:
Dial of a Clock
The hands advance. First slowly … then faster
and faster …
Noises: Clocks

[Seven minutes of documentary film of key events probably intercut with KARL THOMAS *pacing in Lunatic Asylum, and a collage of popular images of Weimar life contrasting, as the play does, frivolity and hardship. It followed the above scenario quite closely, including the clock, adding in events like the election of Hindenburg in 1925 and some self-filmed scenes. As the film ended, screen out and gauze in with projection of façade of Lunatic Asylum which remains through scene. Lights come up in the centre and right bottom compartments to reveal* PROFESSOR LÜDIN'S *Office. Back projections of filing cabinet centre compartment screen and wardrobe bottom right compartment screen.]*

Act 1
Scene 1
Office of a Lunatic Asylum

ORDERLY *at cupboard.*

PROFESSOR LÜDIN *at barred window.*

ORDERLY: One pair grey trousers. One pair woollen socks. Didn't you bring any underclothes with you?

KARL THOMAS: I don't know.

ORDERLY: Oh! One black waistcoat. One black coat. One pair of low shoes. Hat missing.

PROFESSOR LÜDIN: And money?

ORDERLY: None, Herr Doctor.

PROFESSOR LÜDIN: Relations?

KARL THOMAS: Notified me yesterday, that my mother died, three years ago.

PROFESSOR LÜDIN: You're going to find things difficult. Life is hard today. You've got to elbow your way. Don't despair. All in good time.

ORDERLY: Release date: 8 May 1927.

[This date was changed to that of the performance every night.]

KARL THOMAS: No!

PROFESSOR LÜDIN: Yes, indeed.

KARL THOMAS: 1927.

PROFESSOR LÜDEST: So, eight little years of room and board with us. Clothed, fed, cared for. Nothing was lacking. You can be proud of yourself: clinically you've been a noteworthy case.

KARL THOMAS: As if obliterated. Yes … I do remember something…

PROFESSOR LÜDIN: What?

KARL THOMAS: The edge of a wood. Trees stretched brown to the sky like pillars. Beech trees. The wood glittered green.

With a thousand tiny suns. So delicate. I wanted to go in, so very badly. I couldn't do it. Evilly the tree trunks bent outwards and threw me back like a rubber ball.

PROFESSOR LÜDIN: Wait! Like a rubber ball. Interesting association. Look here, your nerves are consistent with the truth. The wood: the padded cell. The tree trunks: walk of best quality rubber. Yes, I remember: once every year you began to rave. We had to isolate you. Always on the same day. What a perfect clinical masterpiece!

KARL THOMAS: On which day?

PROFESSOR LÜDIN: On the day when … But you must know.

KARL THOMAS: On the day of the reprieve …

PROFESSOR LÜDIN: Do you remember everything?

KARL THOMAS: Yes.

PROFESSOR LÜDIN: Then you are cured.

KARL THOMAS: To wait even minutes for death … But ten days. Ten times twenty-four hours. Each hour sixty minutes. Each minute sixty seconds. Each second a murder. Murdered fourteen hundred and forty times in one day. And the nights! … I hated the reprieve. I hated the President. Only a dirty scoundrel could act like that.

PROFESSOR LÜDIN: Take it easy. You have every reason to be thankful … In here we don't mind strong language. But outside … You'd be rewarded with another year in prison for insulting the Head of State. Be reasonable. You must have already had a noseful of that.

KARL THOMAS: You have to say that because you belong to the bosses.

PROFESSOR LÜDEST: We should conclude this interview. You needn't be depressed because you were in a mad-house. Actually most people ought to be in one. Were I to examine a thousand, I would have to keep nine hundred and ninety-nine in here.

KARL THOMAS: Why don't you do it?

PROFESSOR LÜDEST: The State has no interest in it. On the contrary. With a little drop of madness men become respectable husbands. With two drops of madness they become socially conscious … Don't do anything stupid. I only want what's good for you. Go to one of your friends.

KARL THOMAS: Where could they have got to? …

PROFESSOR LÜDIN: Weren't there others in your cell back then?

KARL THOMAS: Five. Only one wasn't reprieved. His name was Wilhelm Kilman.

PROFESSOR LÜDIN: Not reprieved? Ha, ha ha. His career has galloped ahead! Smarter than you.

KARL THOMAS: I don't understand you.

PROFESSOR LÜDIN: You'll understand me soon enough. Just go to him. He could help you. If he wants to help you. If he wants to know you.

KARL THOMAS: He's still alive?

PROFESSOR LÜDIN: You're going to experience a miracle. An excellent prescription for you. I have cured you clinically. He might cure you of your crazy ideas. Go to the Ministry of the Interior and ask for Herr Kilman. Good luck.

KARL THOMAS: Good day, Herr Doctor. Good day, Herr

Orderly … It smells so strongly of lilac here … Of course, spring. Isn't it true that there are real beeches growing outside the window … not rubber padded walls … (*KARL THOMAS leaves.*)

PROFESSOR LÜDEST: Bad breed.

Blackout.

[Gauze out. Screen in.]

Film Interlude

Bid City 1927

STREET CARS
AUTOS
UNDERGROUND TRAINS
AEROPLANE

[Film of KARL THOMAS in hostel for the homeless, helplessly seeking work from factory to factory, searching for lodgings, in the hustle and bustle of Potsdam Square etc. Screen out and gauze stays out. Back projection of Kaiser centre compartment screen and of wall paper in middle left and bottom right compartments for next scene.]

Scene 2

Two rooms visible: Minister's Antechamber, Minister's Office.

When the curtain rises both rooms can be seen.

The room in which nothing is said goes dark.

Office

WILHELM KILMAN: I sent for you.

EVA BERG: Of course.

Antechamber

BANKER'S SON: Will he receive you? He hasn't sent for you.

BANKER: Not receive me! Just let him try it.

BANKER'S SON: We need credits up to the end of the month.

BANKER: Why are you doubtful?

BANKER'S SON: Because he's rejected the chance both times now.

BANKER: I operated too crudely.

Office

WILHELM KILMAN: You sit on the Committee of the Union of Female Employees?

EVA BERG: Yes.

WILHELM KILMAN: You work as a secretary in the Revenue Office?

EVA BERG: Yes.

WILHELM KILMAN: For two months now your name has featured prominently in the police reports.

EVA BERG: I don't understand.

WILHELM KILMAN: You've been inciting the women workers at the Chemical Works to refuse overtime?

EVA BERG: I'm only exercising the rights which our Constitution guarantees me.

WILHELM KILMAN: The Constitution is intended for peaceful times.

EVA BERG: Aren't we living in them now?

WILHELM KILMAN: The State rarely knows peaceful times.

Antechamber

BANKER: The matter must be settled before the tariff announcement. Two hours of overtime, take it or leave it.

BANKER'S SON: The trade unions have decided to hold out for an eight-hour working day.

BANKER: Whatever is good for the State will be right for heavy industry.

BANKER'S SON: We'll have to lock out half a million workers.

BANKER: And so what? We'll kill two birds with one stone. Overtime and lower pay.

Office

EVA BERG: I am against war. If I had the power, the Works would come to a standstill. What do they make? Poison gas!

WILHELM KILMAN: Your personal opinion, which doesn't interest me. I don't like war either. Do you know this leaflet? Are you the author?

EVA BERG: Yes.

WILHELM KILMAN: You have violated your duties as a State Official.

EVA BERG: There was a time when you did the same.

WILHELM KILMAN: We're having an official conversation, Fräulein.

EVA BERG: In the past you have …

WILHELM KILMAN: Keep to the present. I have to maintain order … Dear Fräulein Berg, be reasonable now. Do you want to bash your stubborn head in? The State always has a harder skull. I don't mean you any harm. We need the overtime at the moment. You lack practical knowledge. It would be damned painful for me to proceed against you. I know you well from before. But I would have to. Really. Be reasonable. Promise me that …

EVA BERG: I promise nothing.

Antechamber

PICKEL: (*Who from the beginning of the scene has been pacing restlessly back and forth, stops in front of the BANKER.*) Pardon me, sir … I come from Holzhausen, namely. Perhaps the gentleman knows Holzhausen? Indeed with the building of the railway, it won't be started until October. Nevertheless the mailcoach was really enough for me. There's a saying we have …

BANKER turns away.

I believe, indeed, that the railway …

As no one is listening to him, he breaks off, paces back and forth.

Office

WILHELM KILMAN: The State must protect itself. I was not obliged to send for you. I wanted to give you my advice. No one can say that … you alone bear the responsibility I warn you. (*Gesture.*)

EVA BERG goes.

(*On the telephone.*) Chemical Works … Herr Director? … Kilman … Well? Works meeting at 12 o'clock … Phone me the result… Thank you … (*Hangs up.*)

The MINISTER OF WAR *walks through the Antechamber.*

MINISTER OF WAR: Ah, good day, Herr Director-General. You here too?

BANKER: Yes, unfortunately. This wretched waiting … Permit me, Herr Minister of War, to introduce my son … His Excellency von Wandsring.

MINISTER OF WAR: Pleased … A delicate situation.

PICKEL: (*Turns to the* MINISTER OF WAR.) I think, Herr General, indeed the enemy …

As the MINISTER OF WAR *doesn't pay him any attention, he breaks off, goes to the corner, fumbles in his pocket for a medal, pins it on hurriedly and with great difficulty.*

BANKER: You will see to it, Herr General.

MINISTER OF WAR: Certainly. Only … it gives me no pleasure to shoot people whom we first give drumsticks to eagerly and then stop from beating the drum. These liberal utopias of democracy and freedom of the people are getting us into trouble. We need authority. The condensed experience of thousands of years. You can't refute that with slogans.

BANKER: Yet democracy, in moderation of course, needn't necessarily lead to mob-rule on the one hand, and on the other hand it could be a safety valve …

MINISTER OF WAR: Democracy … stuff and nonsense. The people rule? Where on earth? Well then, better an honest dictatorship. Let's not whitewash anything, Herr Director-General … Will we see each other at the club tomorrow?

BANKER: With great pleasure.

MINISTER OF WAR leaves, COUNT LANDE follows him to the door.

COUNT LANDE: Excellency …

MINISTER OF WAR: Ah, Count Lande. Arranged?

COUNT LANDE: Yes indeed, Excellency.

MINISTER OF WAR: Are things going well for you?

COUNT LANDE: The front groups are waiting.

MINISTER OF WAR: Don't act hot-headedly, Count. Nothing foolish. The time for violence is over. What we want to achieve for our Fatherland, we can achieve by legal means.

COUNT LANDE: Excellency, we are relying on you.

MINISTER OF WAR: Count, with all my sympathy … I caution you.

MINISTER OF WAR goes.

PICKEL: (*In a military manner.*) At your command, Herr General.

MINISTER OF WAR leaves without noticing him.

BANKER: How long will Kilman hold out?

BANKER'S SON: Why don't you do the business through Wandsring?

BANKER: Today Kilman governs. No harm being on the safe side.

BANKER'S SON: He's *passé.* You can throw your Kilman into the bankrupt estate of democracy. Just sniff the air of industry. I'd advise you to bet on a national dictatorship.

PICKEL: (*Turns to* COUNT LANDE.) Can you tell me, sir, what time it is?

COUNT LANDE: Fourteen past twelve.

PICKEL: The clocks in the city are always fast. I imagined that an interview with the Minister would be at twelve sharp … Indeed the clocks in the country are always slow, consequently …

As COUNT LANDE *doesn't notice him, he breaks off, paces back and forth.*

COUNT LANDE: How do you address Kilman?

BARON FRIEDRICH: As Excellency, naturally.

COUNT LANDE: Do the comrades enjoy the taste of 'Excellency'?

BARON FRIEDRICH: Same old business, my dear friend. Dress a man in a uniform and he'll pine for even a lance-corporal's stripes.

COUNT LANDE: And he keeps us waiting in the antechamber. Ten years ago I wouldn't have shaken hands with his kind unless I was wearing buckskin gloves.

BARON FRIEDRICH: Don't get excited. I can dish you up other delicacies. Eight years ago I almost had him put up against the wall.

COUNT LANDE: Fabulously interesting. Were you involved at that time?

BARON FRIEDRICH: Not half! Let's not talk about it.

COUNT LANDE: And still he appointed you to the Ministry. Always in his presence. You must get on his nerves.

BARON FRIEDRICH: That's exactly what I feared. When he first came into the Ministry, the Great Court of Chancellery, I took the liberty of raking up old stories. One must play the game in order to be ready for when times change again. He gave me a sharp look. From that day on, one promotion after another, however disagreeably. But he never talks about it.

COUNT LANDE: A sort of hush money.

BARON FRIEDEICH: Don't know. Let's speak about the weather. I suspect the rascal has first-class spies at his disposal.

COUNT LANDE: The comrades have learned all the old tricks from us.

PICKEL: (*Turning to* BARON FRIEDRICH.) Indeed my neighbour in Holzhausen asserted, namely … Pickel, he asserted, for an interview with the Minister you must buy yourself white gloves. That's how it was in the old government, and that's how it still remains in the new one. The ceremonial regulations demand it. However I … I thought if the Monarchy demanded white gloves, in the Republic we ought to put on black gloves … Namely that, exactly! … Because we are now free men …

As BARON FRIEDRICH *doesn't notice him, he breaks off, paces back and forth.*

BARON FRIEDRICH: A clever rascal, you have to give him that.

COUNT LANDE: Manners?

BARON FRIEDRICH: I don't know whether he took lessons from actors like Napoleon did. In any case, a gentleman from head to toe. Rides every morning in full dress, immaculate, I tell you.

COUNT LANDE: And through which cracks can you smell the stink of the prole?

BARON FRIEDRICH: Through all of them. You only have to see how he puts a little too much into every word, every gesture, every step. People think that if they have their dress coats cut by a first-class tailor, that's enough. They don't realise that first-class tailors are only worth something for first-class customers.

COUNT LANDE: In any case I'd dine with the devil's grandmother, if she'd help me get out of the provinces into the capital.

BARON FRIEDRICH: The 'grandmother' with whom you'll dine keeps a table that's not to be despised.

COUNT LANDE: She's certainly been a house servant long enough for that.

Office

MINISTRY OFFICIAL: Her Excellency and your daughter would like to speak with you, Excellency. They are waiting in the drawing room.

WILHELM KILMAN: Please ask them to be patient for ten minutes.

MINISTRY OFFICIAL leaves. Telephone rings.

Hello. It's you, Herr Privy Councillor. Yes, it's me … Nothing doing … No, no, you're not disturbing me at all … The collapse of the Chemical Works … A stage trick … It's fixed, of course it's fixed … Very cunning people are behind it. We agreed State credits yesterday … How? Unanimously … Three per cent … Always at your service … Goodbye, Herr Privy Councillor.

MINISTRY OFFICIAL enters.

MINISTRY OFFICIAL: The ladies say …

WILHELM KILMAN: They must wait, I have to work.

Antechamber

BARON FRIEDRICH: Please, said the little daughter and bared her knee.

COUNT LANDE: And the mother?

BARON FRIEDRICH: Thought it was refined manners and blushed silently.

COUNT LANDE: The capital is worth the strains of a maidenhead. How long it's taking. Governing doesn't seem to come easily to him.

KARL THOMAS enters, sits in a corner.

Office

WILHELM KILMAN rings. MINISTRY OFFICIAL *enters.*

MINISTRY OFFICIAL: Excellency …?

WILHELM KILMAN: Baron Friedrich and Count Lande …

MINISTRY OFFICIAL bows, goes out.

Antechamber

MINISTRY OFFICIAL: (*To* COUNT LANDE *and* BARON FRIEDRICH.) His Excellency will receive you now …

BANKER: Excuse me, gentlemen. Give His Excellency this card. Only one minute.

MINISTRY OFFICIAL goes into the office, BANKER *and* SON *follow him.*

Office

WILHELM KILMAN: Good day, Herr Director-General. Good day, Herr Doctor. Today I'm not really in a position to …

BANKER: Then we'd do better to meet at your leisure.

WILHELM KILMAN: Please.

BANKER: This evening at the Grand Hotel.

WILHELM KILMAN: Agreed.

BANKER and SON go.

MINISTRY OFFICIAL: (*To* COUNT LANDE *and* BARON FRIEDRICH.) His Excellency will receive you now.

Opens the door to the office, COUNT LANDE *and* BARON FRIEDRICH *enter,* MINISTRY OFFICIAL *starts to leave through the side door.*

KARL THOMAS: Excuse me.

MINISTRY OFFICIAL: His Excellency is busy. I don't know if His Excellency will receive anyone else today.

KARL THOMAS: I don't want to speak to the Minister. I want to speak to Herr Kilman.

MINISTRY OFFICIAL: Play your stupid jokes on someone else.

KARL THOMAS: Jokes, comrade …

MINISTRY OFFICIAL: I'm not your comrade.

KARL THOMAS: Perhaps Herr Kilman works as the Minister's secretary? The porter directed me to the Minister's antechamber when I asked for Herr Kilman.

MINISTRY OFFICIAL: Do you come from the moon? Are you trying to make me believe that you didn't know His Excellency's name is Kilman? On the whole you're making a very suspicious impression … I'm going to call the Chief Detective Inspector.

KARL THOMAS: Don't you mean another Kilman? There are so many Kilmans.

MINISTRY OFFICIAL: What do you want?

KARL THOMAS: I would like to speak to Herr Wilhelm Kilman. Kilman. K–I–L–M–A–N.

MINISTRY OFFICIAL: That's how His Excellency spells it … What a shady character.

MINISTRY OFFICIAL starts to go out.

KARL THOMAS: Kilman Minister? … No, wait. I know the Minister, you see. I am his friend. Yes, really, his friend. Eight years ago we were … Just wait now … Do you have a piece of paper? … Pencil? I'll write down my name for the Minister. He will receive me immediately.

MINISTRY OFFICIAL is unsure.

Go on then!

MINISTRY OFFICIAL: You should keep up with the times.

Gives KARL THOMAS paper and pen. Goes out. KARL THOMAS writes.

PICKEL: Well, well … a friend of the Minister … Although I namely … Pickel is my name … Oh, this lout of an official … Indeed one ought to take a stricter line with these old court flunkies, but nevertheless we Republicans put up with anything … I on the other hand understood the joke about your friend, the Minister, immediately … One ought to be allowed one's little joke about the Minister … I think something must be done … In the upper levels of administration for example this official … Namely that is a shortcoming in the Republic …

Office

WILHELM KILMAN: One must know how to deal with nations, gentlemen.

BARON FRIEDRICH: Excellency, don't you think that America has no interest in war …

COUNT LANDE: Consider, Excellency, France's peaceful attitude …

WILHELM KILMAN: Because Ministers prattle on about world peace and make a show of humanitarian ideas? But gentlemen. Observe how often 'world peace' and 'humanitarian idea' are flaunted in any ministerial speech, and I guarantee you that just so many poison gas factories and aeroplane squadrons are marked down for secret action. Ministerial speeches … gentlemen …

BARON FRIEDRICH: It is said that Machiavelli is one of your Excellency's favourite authors.

WILHELM KILMAN: What do we need Machiavelli for … Simple common sense.

MINISTRY OFFICIAL enters.

MINISTRY OFFICIAL: May the ladies now …

WILHELM KILMAN: Show them in.

FRAU KILMAN and her daughter LOTTE KILMAN enter.

You know, I'm sure, Herr Baron …

BARON FRIEDRICH: Excellency … Fräulein.

FRAU KILMAN: But please don't always call me 'Excellency'. You know I don't like it.

WILHELM KILMAN: Count Lande. My wife. My daughter.

COUNT LANDE: Excellency … Fräulein.

BARON FRIEDRICH: No doubt we're disturbing you …

FRAU KILMAN: No, as it happens I just wrote to you. I invited you for Sunday.

COUNT LANDE: Enchanted to meet you.

FRAU KILMAN: Perhaps you'll bring your friend with you.

BARON FRIEDRICH: Only too honoured, Excellency.

LOTTE KILMAN: (*Softly to BARON FRIEDRICH.*) You stood me up yesterday.

BARON FRIEDRICH: (*Softly.*) But darling …

LOTTE KILMAN: Your friend pleases me.

BARON FRIEDRICH: I congratulate him.

LOTTE KILMAN: I read your personal file.

BARON FRIEDRICH: When can we meet?

WILHELM KILMAN: Yes, Count, we must simply deny it. Slanders from the Left – I don't even read. Slanders from the Right – they are blessed with one of my answers. I know the qualities of the men of the old regime. A man is only a man, has weaknesses, but the most extreme conservatives cannot charge me with a lack of justice.

COUNT LANDE: But Excellency … You are esteemed in Nationalist circles.

WILHELM KILMAN: I'll write to your District Head today. You start your Ministry employment in four weeks.

Antechamber

KARL THOMAS: (*Pacing back and forth rapidly.*) Minister … Minister …

Office

The MINISTER says goodbye to COUNT LANDE and BARON FRIEDRICH.

Antechamber

BARON FRIEDRICH: What did I tell you?

COUNT LANDE: Some comrades! … Some comrades! …

Both leave.

KARL THOMAS: I have seen that face. Where?

MINISTRY OFFICIAL enters.

Here's the note for the Minister.

MINISTRY OFFICIAL takes the note and carries it into the Office.

Office

[All other compartments dark. Scaffolding revolves to left to give close-up effect.]

MINISTRY OFFICIAL: A man, Excellency.

WILHELM KILMAN: I don't want …

KARL THOMAS knocks on the door, enters without waiting for an answer.

KARL THOMAS: Wilhelm! Wilhelm!

WILHELM KILMAN: Who are you?

KARL THOMAS: You don't know me any more. The years … eight years …

WILHELM KILMAN: (*To* MINISTRY OFFICIAL.) You may go.

MINISTRY OFFICIAL leaves.

KARL THOMAS: You're still alive. Explain it to me. We were reprieved. You the only one not …

WILHELM KILMAN: Chance … a lucky chance.

KARL THOMAS: Eight years … walled up like a grave. I told the doctor I remembered nothing. Oh Wilhelm, when fully conscious I often saw … Often … Saw you death … I gouged my eyes until they spurted blood … the orderlies thought I was having fits.

WILHELM KILMAN: Yes … those days … I don't like to remember.

KARL THOMAS: Death always huddled with us. Inciting us against each other.

WILHELM KILMAN: What children we were.

KARL THOMAS: Those hours in prison bond us together in blood. That's why I came to you when I heard you were alive. You can count on me.

FRAU KILMAN: Wilhelm, we must go now.

KARL THOMAS: Frau Kilman. Good morning, Frau Kilman. I didn't even see you before. Are you their daughter? You're so grown up.

LOTTE KILMAN: Everyone grows up sometime; meanwhile my father has also become Minister.

KARL THOMAS: … Do you remember how you were allowed to visit your husband for the last time in the condemned cell? How sorry I was for you. They had to carry you out. And your daughter stood next to the door with her hands over her face and just kept on repeating: No, no, no.

FRAU KILMAN: Yes, I remember. It was a hard time. Wasn't it, Wilhelm? Things are going well for you now? That's nice. Pay us a visit sometime.

KARL THOMAS: Thank you, Frau Kilman.

FRAU KILMAN and LOTTE KILMAN go.

Must it be like that? That your daughter pretends to be a fine lady?

WILHELM KILMAN: What?

KARL THOMAS: Your ministerial office is just a trick, isn't it? Still it's a risky trick. Before such tactics wouldn't have been permitted. Is the whole apparatus almost in our hands?

WILHELM KILMAN: You talk as if we were still in the middle of a revolution.

KARL THOMAS: What?

WILHELM KILMAN: Since then ten years have passed. Just when we began to see a straight way ahead, hard reality rose up and bent it crooked. Still, things go on.

KARL THOMAS: So you take your office seriously?

WILHELM KILMAN: Certainly

KARL THOMAS: And the people?

WILHELM KILMAN: I serve the people.

KARL THOMAS: Didn't you once prove that whoever sits in a Minister's chair in such a State, with his worst enemies as colleagues, would fail, would have to fail, no matter whether he is driven by good intentions or not?

WILHELM KILMAN: Life doesn't unreel according to theories. You learn by experience.

KARL THOMAS: They should have put you up against the wall!

WILHELM KILMAN: Still the hot-headed dreamer. I won't take offence at your words. We want to govern democratically. But what is democracy after all? The will of all the people. As Minister I do not represent a party, but the State. When one has responsibility, my dear friend, things down below look different. Power confers responsibility.

KARL THOMAS: Power! What's the use of imagining you possess power, if the people have none? For five days I've been looking around. Has anything changed? You sit on top and legitimise the big con. Don't you understand that you've deserted the Idea, that you govern against the people?

WILHELM KILMAN: Sometimes it requires courage to govern against the people. More than going to the barricades.

Telephone rings.

Excuse me … Kilman … Unanimous decision to refuse overtime … Thank you, Herr Director … Does the leaflet contain names? Aha … Make note: whoever leaves the factory at five o'clock is dismissed without notice … Good, the factories will close for a few days. Do a deal with the private companies. The order for Turkey must be filled … Goodbye, Herr Director … (*Hangs up. Telephones again.*) Connect me with the police … Eva Berg's file … Hurry up … Thank you. (*Hangs up.*)

KARL THOMAS: What courage! You have mastered the methods.

WILHELM KILMAN: Whoever works on top here must see to it that the complicated machinery doesn't come to a standstill because of clumsy hands.

KARL THOMAS: Aren't those women fighting for your old Ideas?

WILHELM KILMAN: Could I countenance the women workers of any factory to obstruct the mechanism of the State?

KARL THOMAS: Would your authority suffer so much?

WILHELM KILMAN: Should I make a fool of myself? Should I show myself to be less capable than the old Minister? A lot of the time it's not so easy … If one fails only once, then … There are hours … You imagine it is so … Oh, what do you know? …

KARL THOMAS: What do we know? You help the reactionaries get into the saddle.

WILHELM KILMAN: Nonsense! In a democracy I have to respect the rights of the employer just as much as the rights of the employee. We don't have a utopia yet.

KARL THOMAS: But the other side has the Press, money, weapons. And the workers? Empty fists.

WILHELM KILMAN: Oh, you only ever see armed struggle, beating, stabbing, shooting. To the barricades! To the barricades, all you workers! But we renounce the struggle of brutal violence. Unceasingly we have preached that we want to gain victory with moral and spiritual weapons. Violence is always reactionary.

KARL THOMAS: Is that the opinion of the masses? Haven't you even asked for their opinion?

WILHELM KILMAN: What are the masses? Were they able to accomplish any positive work in the old days? Nothing! Talk big and smash things up. We would have slid into chaos. Every adventurer got a command post. People who for the whole of their lives only knew about the workers from coffee house discussions. But let's be honest. We have saved the revolution … The masses are incompetent and they will remain incompetent for the time being. They lack all specialist knowledge. How could an untrained worker, in our epoch, take over the position of, let's say, the head of a syndicate? Or of the director of an electricity works? Later … in decades … in centuries … with education … with evolution … things will change. But today it is we who must govern.

KARL THOMAS: And to think I did time with you …

WILHELM KILMAN: Do you really think I'm a 'traitor'?

KARL THOMAS: Yes.

WILHELM KILMAN: Oh, my dear friend, I am used to that word. For you every bourgeois is a dirty scoundrel, a bloodsucker, a satan, or whatever. If you only grasped what the bourgeois world has achieved and is still achieving.

KARL THOMAS: Stop! You're twisting my words. I have never denied that the bourgeois world has achieved great things. I have never maintained that the bourgeoisie are raven black and the people snow white. But what has become of the world? Our Idea is the greater. If we succeed with it, we will achieve more.

WILHELM KILMAN: It comes down to tactics, dear fellow. With your tactics the darkest reaction would soon govern.

KARL THOMAS: I see no difference.

WILHELM KILMAN: Have you completely forgotten the whip marks lashed on your backs? What children you are. To want the whole tree when you can have an apple.

KARL THOMAS: What props you up? The old bureaucracy? And even if I believed your intentions were honourable,

what are you in reality? A powerless scarecrow, a ping pong ball!

WILHELM KILMAN: What do you really want? Have a look at the inner workings here. How everything fits. How everything runs like clockwork. Everyone has expertise.

KARL THOMAS: And are you proud of that?

WILHELM KILMAN: Yes, of course, I am proud of my civil servants.

KARL THOMAS: We are speaking different languages … you mentioned a name a little while ago on the telephone.

WILHELM KILMAN: I was speaking about official matters.

KARL THOMAS: Eva Berg.

WILHELM KILMAN: Oh, her. She works in the Revenue Office. She's giving me a great deal of trouble. To think what's become of the little darling.

KARL THOMAS: She must be twenty-five years old now.

WILHELM KILMAN: I wanted to spare her. But she is rushing to her own ruin … I must say goodbye to you. Here, take this. (*Tries to give* KARL THOMAS *money; he refuses it.*) Unfortunately I cannot employ you. Go to the Trade Union. Perhaps you'll find some old friends there. I suppose so. One is so busy. One loses contact. May all go well with you. Don't do anything stupid. We are surely united in our goals. Only the means …

Pushes KARL THOMAS *gradually into the Antechamber.* WILHELM KILMAN *remains standing for a few seconds. Gesture.*

Antechamber

KARL THOMAS *stares, dumbstruck.*

PICKEL: (*To* MINISTRY OFFICIAL.) Is it my turn now, Herr Secretary?

MINISTRY OFFICIAL: Do you have an appointment?

PICKEL: I travelled two and a half days on the railway, Herr Secretary. Indeed one gets the shock of one's life on it. Are you familiar with Holzhausen?

MINISTRY OFFICIAL: Does the Minister know?

PICKEL: It's just with regard to the railway in Holzhausen.

MINISTRY OFFICIAL: I will inquire.

MINISTRY OFFICIAL *goes into the Office.*

PICKEL: Is the Minister, I wonder, a very stern man?

KARL THOMAS *doesn't answer.*

PICKEL: If the good Lord has made someone a Minister, as far as I am concerned, I imagine he is …

As KARL THOMAS *doesn't answer,* PICKEL *breaks off, paces back and forth.*

Office

WILHELM KILMAN: No, I don't mind. Show him in.

MINISTRY OFFICIAL *opens the door to the Antechamber.*

MINISTRY OFFICIAL: Herr Pickel.

PICKEL enters.

PICKEL: Your servant, Herr Minister. I have so much on my mind, Herr Minister. Indeed you are surely very busy. But nevertheless I don't want to steal your time from you, Herr Minister. Pickel is my name. Born in Holzhausen, Waldwinkel District. It is only with regard to the railway which you want to build through Holzhausen, Herr Minister. You know, I'm sure, in October … Indeed, there is a saying with us: Hannes would grease the pope's nose of a fatted goose … But nevertheless just such a fatted goose was Holzhausen. Steamers call three times a week; the mailcoach stops every day the good Lord sends. As far as I am concerned I would have … Indeed I certainly don't want to bring myself into it … The Minister will know better … But nevertheless this is certain, the Minister didn't know that if the railway should pass over my property then … I hope I'm not detaining you, Herr Minister.

WILHELM KILMAN: Well, my dear man, what's all this about the railway?

PICKEL: I told my neighbour straightaway that when I stand *vis à vis* the Minister then he will … Indeed he said something about white gloves, and such matters … But nevertheless I have always thought to myself: a Minister, what a lot he must know! Almost as much as our Lord God. Whether the harvest will be good, whether there will be war, whether the railway will run over one's own property or another's … Yes, such is a Minister … Oh, I haven't come only with regard to the railway … Indeed the railway has its importance … But nevertheless the other matter also has its importance. When I was sitting back in Holzhausen … the newspapers, you don't get wise from them … I said to myself, when you are first standing *vis à vis* the Minister … if it is not asking too much, where do you imagine, where is all this leading to? … If now the railway runs through Holzhausen and one can travel straight to India? … And if in China the Yellows are rising up … And if there are machines with which one can shoot as far as America … and the niggers in Africa are talking big and want to throw the Mission out … And they say the Government wants to abolish money … Indeed Herr Minister is sitting here on top and he has to deal with all of it … Nevertheless I said to myself you will ask him for once himself: Herr Minister, what will become of the world?

WILHELM KILMAN: What will become of the world?

PICKEL: I mean what do you want to make out of it, Herr Minister?

WILHELM KILMAN: No, let's first drink a cognac. Do you smoke?

PICKEL: Too kind, Herr Minister. Indeed I said to myself straightaway, you only have to stand *vis à vis* the Minister …

WILHELM KILMAN: The world … the world … Hm … it is not very easy to answer that. Go on, drink.

PICKEL: That's just what I've always said to my neighbour. Indeed my neighbour, I mean the one who has rented the village common, at first it ought to have cost two hundred marks, but nevertheless he is related to the Mayor, and if one is related …

There is a knock.

MINISTRY OFFICIAL: I would like to remind you, Excellency, that at two o'clock Your Excellency must …

WILHELM KILMAN: Yes, I know … So, my dear Herr Pickel, have a peaceful journey back to Holzhausen. Give my greetings to Holzhausen … Go on, drink your cognac.

PICKEL: Yes, Herr Minister. And the railway … Indeed if after all it should run over my property, then …

WILHELM KILMAN: (*Pushing* PICKEL *gradually into the Antechamber before* PICKEL *can finish his cognac.*) No one will suffer an injustice.

Antechamber

PICKEL: (*Going out.*) I will take care of things for you in Holzhausen.

MINISTRY OFFICIAL: (*To* KARL THOMAS *who stands as if paralysed.*) You must go, we are closing.

Curtain.

[*Scaffolding revolves two metres to right.*]

Film Interlude
WOMEN AT WORK:
WOMEN AS TYPISTS
WOMEN AS CHAUFFEURS
WOMEN AS TRAIN DRIVERS
WOMEN AS POLICE

[*This film sequence was unfortunately cut.*]

Act 2
Scene 1

[*Back projections of a slum alley on centre compartment screen. Factories on upper and middle left compartment screens. Roof with hanging clothes on upper right compartment screen. Other rooms on middle and bottom right compartment screens. Bottom left compartment open for scene with white wall back projected on its screen. Alarm rings in the dark before lights come up.*]

EVA BERG's room

EVA BERG *jumps out of bed, starts to dress hurriedly.*

KARL THOMAS: (*In bed.*) Where are you going?

EVA BERG: To work, dear boy.

KARL THOMAS: What time is it?

EVA BERG: Half six.

KARL THOMAS: Stay here in bed until eight. Your office job doesn't start until nine.

EVA BERG: I must go to the Trade Union first. The election is in one week. The leaflets they printed for the women are dreadful. Last night when you were asleep I drafted the text for a new one.

KARL THOMAS: This life without work makes me lazier day by day.

EVA BERG: Yes, it's time you found work.

KARL THOMAS: Sometimes I think … Do you call that cut 'bobbed hair'?

EVA BERG: Do you like it? … How stupid, we don't have any representatives in the Sixth District. Just where have I left the papers? … Oh, here. (*Reads, corrects, writes.*)

KARL THOMAS: That cut suits you because you have a face. Women without faces have to watch out. That cut makes them naked. How many can get away with nakedness?

EVA BERG: Is that what you think?

KARL THOMAS: The faces in the street, on the underground, awful. Before I never saw how few people have faces. Most are lumps of flesh bloated by fear and conceit.

EVA BERG: Not a bad conclusion … Do you have burning desires for women inside?

KARL THOMAS: For the first seven years it was like I was buried … In the last year I suffered terribly.

EVA BERG: What do you do then?

KARL THOMAS: Some carry on like boys; others fantasise that sheets, a piece of bread or a coloured cloth are lovers.

EVA BERG: That last, conscious year must have been desperate for you.

KARL THOMAS: How often I hugged my pillow like a woman, greedy to get warm.

EVA BERG: Inside everyone the ice hounds bark … You must find work, Karl.

KARL THOMAS: But why … Eva, come with me … We'll travel to Greece. To India. To Africa. There must be places where men still live, childlike, who simply are, are. In whose eyes sky and sun and stars spin, brightly. Who know nothing of politics, who live without always having to struggle.

EVA BERG: Do politics make you sick? Do you think you could break their hold? Do you think southern sun, palm trees, elephants, colourful garments could make you forget the real life of men? This paradise you dream about does not exist.

KARL THOMAS: Since I saw Wilhelm Kilman I can't bear it any more. For what? So that our own comrades can smirk at the world like distorted mirror images of the old gang? No thanks. You must be my tomorrow and my dream of the future. You, I want you and nothing more.

EVA BERG: Escape, is it?

KARL THOMAS: Call it escape. What's in a word?

EVA BERG: You deceive yourself. By tomorrow impatience will be gnawing away at you, and a burning desire for your … destiny.

KARL THOMAS: Destiny?

EVA BERG: Because we cannot breathe in this air of factories and slums. Because otherwise we'll die like caged animals.

KARL THOMAS: Yes, you are right.

KARL THOMAS starts to dress.

EVA BERG: You must look around for another place to live, Karl.

KARL THOMAS: Can't I live with you any more, Eva?

EVA BERG: Honestly, no.

KARL THOMAS: Is the landlady grumbling?

EVA BERG: I would get her to stop it.

KARL THOMAS: Why not then?

EVA BERG: I must be able to be alone. Understand me.

KARL THOMAS: Don't you belong to me?

EVA BERG: Belong? That word is dead. Nobody belongs to anybody.

KARL THOMAS: Sorry, I used the wrong word. Aren't I your lover?

EVA BERG: Do you mean because I slept with you?

KARL THOMAS: Doesn't that bind us?

EVA BERG: One glance exchanged with a stranger on a run-down street can bind me to him more deeply than some night of love. Which need be nothing but very beautiful play.

KARL THOMAS: Then what do you take seriously?

EVA BERG: The here and now I take seriously. I also take play seriously … I am a living human being. Have I renounced the world because I'm in the struggle? The idea that a revolutionary has to forego the thousand little joys of life is absurd. All of us should take part in exactly what we want to.

KARL THOMAS: What is sacred … to you?

EVA BERG: Why mystical words for human things? … Why are you looking at me like that? … When I talk to you I feel that the last eight years, during which you were 'buried', have changed us more drastically than a century normally would have done.

KARL THOMAS: Yes, sometimes I feel I come from a lost generation.

EVA BERG: To think what the world has experienced since that episode.

KARL THOMAS: Just listen to how you speak of the revolution!

EVA BERG: That revolution was an episode. It is past.

KARL THOMAS: What remains?

EVA BERG: Us. With our will to honesty. With our strength for new work.

KARL THOMAS: And what if you got pregnant during these nights?

EVA BERG: I wouldn't give birth.

KARL THOMAS: Because you don't love me?

EVA BERG: How you miss the point. Because it would be an accident. Because it wouldn't seem necessary to me.

KARL THOMAS: If I use stupid words now, wrong words, don't listen; listen to the inexpressible things which you too cannot doubt. I need you. I found you in days when we heard the very heartbeat of life because the heartbeat of death pounded so loudly and unstoppably. I cannot find my way now. Help me, help me! The glowing flame has gone out.

EVA BERG: You are wrong. It glows in a different way. Less sentimentally.

KARL THOMAS: I don't feel it anywhere.

EVA BERG: What do you see? You are scared of broad daylight.

KARL THOMAS: Don't speak like that.

EVA BERG: Yes, let me speak. All talking things out is over. Irrevocably. Either you will gain strength for a new beginning or you will be destroyed. To support your false dreams out of pity would be criminal.

KARL THOMAS: So you did have pity?

EVA BERG: Probably. I am not clear myself. There is never only one reason.

KARL THOMAS: What kind of experience has hardened you over these years?

EVA BERG: Again you are using concepts which don't apply any more. I was a child, granted. We cannot afford to be children any more. We can't throw away the lucidity and knowledge we've gained like toys which don't please us any more. Experience – sure, I have experienced a lot. Men and situations. For eight years I've worked like only men worked before. For eight years I've made the decisions about every hour of my life. That's why I am how I am … Do you think it was easy for me? Often, when I sat in one of those ugly furnished rooms, I threw myself on the bed … and howled, like having a breakdown … and I thought, I can't go on any more … Then came work. The Party needed me. I clenched my teeth and … Be reasonable, Karl. I must go to the office.

FRITZ and GRETE peer round the door. Disappear again.

Stay here this morning. Do you need money? Don't say no out of stupid pride. I'll help you as a comrade, that's all. Farewell.

EVA BERG goes. KARL THOMAS remains alone for a few seconds. BRITZ and GRETE, the landlady's children, open the door, look in curiously.

FRITZ: Can we come in now?

GRETE: We'd like to have a look at you, you see.

KARL THOMAS: Yes, come in.

FRITZ and GRETE come in, both look at KARL THOMAS.

FRITZ: We have to go soon, you see.

GRETE: We have tickets for the movies.

FRITZ: And this evening we're going to the boxing match. Want to box now?

KARL THOMAS: No, I can't box.

FRITZ: Oh, I see.

GRETE: But you can dance, can't you? Do you know the Charleston or the Black Bottom?

KARL THOMAS: No, not that either.

GRETE: Pity … Were you really in the madhouse for eight years?

FRITZ: She can't believe it.

KARL THOMAS: Yes. For sure.

GRETE: And before that were you sentenced to death?

FRITZ: Mother told her. She read it in the newspaper.

KARL THOMAS: Your mother rents rooms?

GRETE: Of course.

KARL THOMAS: Is your mother poor?

FRITZ: Only the black marketeers are rich today, mother always says.

KARL THOMAS: Do you also know why I was sentenced to death?

GRETE: Because you were in the war.

FRITZ: Goose! Because he was in the Revolution.

KARL THOMAS: What do you know about the war then? Has your mother told you about it?

GRETE: No, not mother.

FRITZ: We have to learn the battles in school.

GRETE: What day they were on.

FRITZ: Stupid that the World War had to come. As if we didn't have enough to learn already in our History lesson. The Thirty Years' War lasted from 1618 to 1648.

GRETE: Thirty years.

FRITZ: We have to learn only half as many battles for that one as for the World War.

GRETE: And it only lasted four years.

FRITZ: The battle of Lüttich, the battle of the Marne, the battle of Verdun, the battle of Tannenberg …

GRETE: And the battle of Ypres.

KARL THOMAS: Don't you know anything else about the war?

FRITZ: That's enough for us.

GRETE: And how! The last time I got 'unsatisfactory' because I mixed up 1916 and 1917.

KARL THOMAS: And … what do you know about the Revolution?

FRITZ: We don't need to learn so many dates about that, which is easier.

KARL THOMAS: What can the suffering and the knowledge of millions mean if the next generation is already deaf to it all? All experience rushes into a bottomless pit.

FRITZ: What are you saying?

KARL THOMAS: How old are you?

GRETE: Thirteen.

FRITZ: Fifteen.

KARL THOMAS: And what are your names?

FRITZ: Fritz.

GRETE: Grete.

KARL THOMAS: What you have learned about the war is meaningless. You know nothing about the war.

FRITZ: Oh, no!

KARL THOMAS: How to describe it to you? … Mothers were … no. What's standing there at the end of the street?

FRITZ: A big factory.

KARL THOMAS: What is made in it?

FRITZ GRETE: Acids … gas.

KARL THOMAS: What kind of gas?

GRETE: I don't know.

FRITZ: But I do. Poison gas.

KARL THOMAS: What is poison gas used for?

FRITZ: For when enemies attack us.

GRETE: Yes, against enemies if they try to destroy our country.

KARL THOMAS: Who are your enemies then?

FRITZ and GRETE are silent.

Give me your hand, Fritz … What could happen to this hand if a bullet shot through it?

FRITZ: Thanks a lot. Kaput.

KARL THOMAS: What would happen to your face if it got caught in just a tiny cloud of poison gas? Did you learn that at school?

GRETE: Sure did! Be eaten all away. To the bone.

KARL THOMAS: Would you like to die?

GRETE: That's a funny question. Of course not.

KARL THOMAS: And now I want to tell you a story. Not a fairy tale. A true story which happened near where I was. During the war I was stationed somewhere in France in a trench. Suddenly, at night, we heard screams, like a man in his death agony. Then it went still. Somebody had been killed, we thought. An hour later we heard screams again, and then they never stopped. The whole night long a man screamed. The whole day long a man screamed. More and more painfully, more and more helplessly. When it grew dark, two soldiers climbed out of the trench and tried to rescue the man who lay wounded between the trenches. Bullets whizzed by, and both soldiers were shot dead. Two others tried again. They didn't come back. Then the order came: nobody else allowed out of the trench. We had to obey. But the man kept on screaming. We didn't know whether he was French or German or English. He screamed like a baby screams, naked, without words. He screamed for four days and four nights. To us, it was four years. We stuffed our ears up with paper. It didn't help at all. Then it went still. Oh, children, I wish I had the power to plant a vision in your hearts like seed in ploughed earth. Can you picture to yourselves what happened then.

FRITZ: Of course.

GRETE: The poor man.

KARL THOMAS: Yes, dear girl, the poor man! Not: the enemy. The man. The man screamed. In France and in Germany and in Russia and in Japan and in America and in England. At such times, when you, how should I say it, get down to the ground water, you ask yourself: why all this? What is all this for? Would you ask the same thing too?

FRITZ GRETE: Yes.

KARL THOMAS: In all countries men brooded over the same question. In all countries men gave the same answer. For gold, for land, for coal, for nothing but dead things, men die and starve and despair – that is the answer. And in some places the most courageous of the people rose up and rallied the blind to their strong cry of no, and demanded that this war should cease, and all wars; and they struggled for a world in which all children could thrive … Here among us they lost, here they were defeated.

Long pause.

FRITZ: Were there many of you?

KARL THOMAS: No, the people didn't understand what we were struggling for; didn't see that we were rising up for the sake of their own lives.

FRITZ: Were there many on the other side?

KARL THOMAS: Very many. They had weapons and money and soldiers who were paid.

Pause.

FRITZ: And were you so dumb to believe you could win?

GRETE: Yes, you were real dumb.

KARL THOMAS: (*Stares at them.*) What did you say?

FRITZ: You were dumb.

GRETE: Very dumb.

FRITZ: We must go now. Hurry up, Grete.

GRETE: Yes.

FRITZ GRETE: Goodbye. See you.

Pause, EVA BERG comes back.

EVA BERG: Now I could go travelling with you.

KARL THOMAS: What's up?

EVA BERG: Quick answer.

KARL THOMAS: Say it!

EVA BERG: I didn't get into the office. The porter gave me my dismissal notice. Got the sack.

KARL THOMAS: Kilman!

EVA BERG: Because I addressed the locked-out women workers yesterday afternoon.

KARL THOMAS: That swine!

EVA BERG: Are you surprised? Anyone who does a botched job with clay has to keep working it.

KARL THOMAS: Are you satisfied now, Eva? Come. Here's a time-table. We'll travel this very night. Away! Let's get away, let's get away!

EVA BERG: Are you speaking for both of us? Nothing has changed. Do you seriously believe I'd leave my comrades in the lurch?

KARL THOMAS: Sorry.

EVA BERG: Maybe you'd like to work with us? … Think it over.

EVA BERG goes out. KARL THOMAS stares after her.

Blackout.

[Black gauze and screen in. During film scaffolding moves back one metre to make room for next scene which was played in front of scaffolding.]

Film Interlude

East End of a Big City

FACTORIES
CHIMNEYS
CLOSING TIME
WORKERS LEAVE FACTORIES
CROWDS IN THE STREETS

[Instead of the above, an election film was projected from front. Film and screen out. For the scene, posters and slogans back projected on right and left compartment screens. Film of ballot papers falling into box, lasting until nine o'clock strikes, back projected on centre compartment screen.]

Scene 2
Workers' bar

The raised space at the back is fitted out as a polling station. ELECTION OFFICER *at a table, next to him* SECOND ELECTION OFFICER. *On the right, the voting booth. Entrance turned towards the auditorium. In the front, customers at tables. When there is dialogue at a table, it is brightly lit and the rest of the space is darker.* THIRD WORKER *enters.*

THIRD WORKER: Well, it's all go here. The great con flourishes.

SECOND WORKER: Man, shut up. We wouldn't get very far with your bloody anarchism.

THIRD WORKER: Sure, I know, if you vote you get far.

FIRST WORKER: Everything's all right in its own way. Even the election. Otherwise it wouldn't happen. If you're so dumb not to grasp that…

SECOND WORKER: Only the stupidest sheep of all elect their own butchers …

FIRST WORKER: Do you mean us?

SECOND WORKER: Like a punch in the face?

From the back.

ELECTION OFFICER: Quiet in front. We can't hear our own voices … What is your name?

OLD WOMAN: Barbara Stilzer.

ELECTION OFFICER: Where do you live?

OLD WOMAN: From 1st October I shall live at 7 Schulstrasse.

ELECTION OFFICER: I would like to know where you live now.

OLD WOMAN: If the landlord thinks he can bully me because I complained at the Rent Office … 11 Margaretenstrasse, Fourth floor.

ELECTION OFFICER: Right.

The OLD WOMAN *remains standing.*

You can go cast your ballot.

OLD WOMAN: I only came because it's said they will punish you, if you don't vote.

ELECTION OFFICER: Well then, my dear woman, take a pencil, mark a cross next to the name of your candidate and put it in the ballot box in there.

OLD WOMAN: I don't have a ballot, Herr Detective Inspector … I didn't know I had to bring a ballot with me … How can you know where you are with all those paragraphs …

ELECTION OFFICER: I am not a Detective Inspector. I am the Election Officer. The Electioneers are over there. Go get one and then come back.

The OLD WOMAN *goes to the front.*

FIRST ELECTIONEER: Here, young woman, you must make a cross next to Number One. Then you will be voting for the right President. The Minister of War is concerned about Peace and Order and about Women.

The OLD WOMAN *turns the ballot to and fro indecisively.*

SECOND ELECTIONEER: No, little mother, just put your cross next to Number Two. Don't you want coal and bread to be cheaper?

OLD WOMAN: Shameful, how prices have gone up again.

SECOND ELECTIONEER: All because of the big landowners, little mother. They're raking in the bacon. Put your cross here, then you're voting for National Reconciliation.

The OLD WOMAN *turns the ballot to and fro indecisively.*

THIRD ELECTIONEER: As a class-conscious proletarian vote for Number Three. A clear decision, comrade. Peace and Order – rubbish. Peace and Order for the Capitalists, not for you. National Reconciliation – rubbish. If you bow and scrape, then you'll get to lick the hand of brotherhood – otherwise you'll get a kick in the teeth. Your cross next to Number Three, or else you twist the noose around your own neck.

The OLD WOMAN *turns the ballot to and fro indecisively.*

FIRST ELECTIONEER: Next to Number One, young woman! Don't forget!

SECOND ELECTIONEER: Next to Number Two, little mother!

THIRD ELECTIONEER: Only Number Three will help you break your chains, comrade!

The OLD WOMAN *goes to the back.*

[Film of ALBERT KROLL'S *lorry arriving projected from front on to gauze.]*

ELECTION OFFICER: Do you have your ballot now?

OLD WOMAN: Here, three of them.

ELECTION OFFICER: Only put one in. Otherwise your vote is invalid.

The OLD WOMAN *goes into the booth.*

OLD WOMAN: May I come out again?

Comes out.

A very good evening to you, Herr Detective Inspector. (*To the* ELECTIONEERS *while going out.*) It's all right, it's all right, don't get excited, don't get excited. I've made a cross next to all three.

At the table left.

FIRST WORKER: Giving women the right to vote! Only the dog collars profit from that.

SECOND WORKER: Before, when I had work, I didn't sit in the bar in one month as much as I do now in one day.

FIRST WORKER: And your wife? I wouldn't like to hear the smacks. You got enough scratches.

SECOND WORKER: The aid we get lets us guzzle herring and jam for four days and sniff wind for the next three. It comes down to the same thing.

FIRST WORKER: Went out the door yesterday and a bourgeois lady was standing outside the bar, you know, in high-class lace, larded up from head to toe. She said out loud: 'One must take pity on these people.' I answered: 'Frau Chamber of Commerce,' I said, 'perhaps the time will come round when you'll be only too happy if I take pity on you,' I said.

SECOND WORKER: They ought to hang, nothing else but hang. The whole lot of them.

FIRST WORKER: We'll show them with this election.

KARL THOMAS enters.

KARL THOMAS: (*To the* BARKEEPER.) Does Albert Kroll come here?

BARKEEPER: He was just here. He should be right back.

KARL THOMAS: I'll wait.

Sits at the table right. In front of the ELECTION OFFICER's *table.*

VOTER: I won't put up with this.

ELECTION OFFICER: A mistake, sir …

VOTER: Which cost me my right to vote. I'll lodge a protest against the election! The election must be declared invalid. I won't drop it! I'll go to the highest authorities!

ELECTION OFFICER: I fully admit that your entry was wrongly left off the voting register …

VOTER: That doesn't help me at all! I want my rights! My rights!

ELECTION OFFICER: According to the law I cannot …

VOTER: But take away my rights, that you can do. I'll sort things out here! I'll denounce this pigsty!

ELECTION OFFICER: Be reasonable, sir. Just consider what unrest you'll cause among the people …

VOTER: Doesn't matter to me. Rights are rights …

SECOND ELECTION OFFICER: Please, sir …

ELECTION OFFICER: As a good citizen you would not wish to …

VOTER: It must get into the papers, in black and white. There's more to this than meets the eye. Of all people

it has to happen to me, it always has to happen to me, always, always, always! But that's enough now!

Runs off, collides in the doorway with ALBERT KROLL *who is coming in.* ALBERT KROLL *stops short, recognises* KARL THOMAS.

ALBERT KROLL: Incredible!

KARL THOMAS: At last I've found you.

ALBERT KROLL: Poor devil. Been hard times. For us, too. Found work?

KARL THOMAS: I've been at the Employment Office six times. I learned typesetting when they threw me out of university. Old workmates act like a bunch of clerks towards you! Like section managers in a department store. Cold shoulder, worse than the proper ones. They could work just as perfectly in any department store.

ALBERT KROLL: Everyday life.

KARL THOMAS: You say it as if it has to be like that.

ALBERT KROLL: No. Only it doesn't upset me any more. Wait a minute, I'm going up there. I'm on the Election Committee. You got to keep a close eye on the devils.

Up at the election table.

SECOND ELECTION OFFICER: What a turn out! What a turn out! The election is over in one hour and already eighty per cent. Eighty per cent!

ALBERT KROLL: Three hundred workers have protested because they were not included on the voting register.

ELECTION OFFICER: Not my fault. The ones from the housing block at the Chemical Works had to be crossed off. They haven't lived here for four months yet.

ALBERT KROLL: But the students have the right to vote. And how long have they been here? Only three weeks!

ELECTION OFFICER: The Ministry of the Interior has made that decision, not I.

ALBERT KROLL: We will lodge a protest against the election.

SECOND ELECTION OFFICER: (*On telephone.*) Is that the Sixth District? How many have voted? Sixty-five per cent? Here it's eighty! (*Hangs up telephone.*) Gentlemen, we're in the lead, and you want to lodge a protest …

ALBERT KROLL goes to KARL THOMAS.

ALBERT KROLL: Kilman has stolen the right to vote from the workers at the Chemical Works!

KARL THOMAS: I don't care. What does it matter? Albert, comrade, look at what has become of our struggle. A department store I said before. Everyone's sitting pretty at his own little job. Cash register One … Cash register Ten … Cash register Twelve … No breath of fresh air. The very air is rotting with order. Because some little bit was missing I had to submit all my papers all over again to the proper authorities. It's all gone mouldy with bureaucracy.

ALBERT KROLL: We know. We know even more. Those who failed at the decisive moment are talking big again today.

KARL THOMAS: And you just take it?

ALBERT KROLL: We struggle on. We are too few. Most have

forgotten, want their peace and quiet. We must win over new comrades.

KARL THOMAS: Hundreds of thousands are unemployed.

ALBERT KROLL: When hunger sneaks in the front door, understanding sneaks out the back.

KARL THOMAS: You sound like an old man.

ALBERT KROLL: Years like these count ten times as long. We are learning.

KARL THOMAS: Herr Minister Kilman said the same thing.

ALBERT KROLL: Possible. Because he had something to hide. I want to show you the truth.

FOURTH WORKER: (*Coming in.*) Albert, the police have seized our van.

ALBERT KROLL: Why?

FOURTH WORKER: On account of the pictures! We made fun of the Minister of War.

ALBERT KROLL: Choose a delegation at once to make complaints at the Ministry.

FOURTH WORKER: We already tried that earlier today because a leaflet distributor got arrested. Kilman admits no one.

ALBERT KROLL: He supplied the Minister of War with a military band for free … Go on, go to the Ministry. Telephone me at once, if he refuses you.

FOURTH WORKER goes.

Did you hear, Karl?

KARL THOMAS: What's the election got to do with me? Show me your faith, your old faith, that was going to make a clean sweep of heaven and earth and the stars.

ALBERT KROLL: You mean I don't have it any more? Do I have to count up for you how many times we tried to throw off the damned yoke? Do I have to name you the names of all the old comrades who were hounded, locked up and murdered?

KARL THOMAS: Only faith counts.

ALBERT KROLL: We don't want eternal bliss in heaven. One must learn to see clearly and still keep from getting discouraged.

KARL THOMAS: Great leaders have never spoken like that.

ALBERT KROLL: Do you think? I imagine it differently. They just marched straight for it. On top of glass. And when they looked down through it, they saw the abyss formed from the hatred of the enemy and the stupidity of their own troops. And they probably saw much more.

KARL THOMAS: They wouldn't have moved a hand's breadth if they'd ever measured the depths beneath them.

ALBERT KROLL: Never measured. But always saw.

KARL THOMAS: All wrong, what you're doing. You even take part in the election con.

ALBERT KROLL: And what are you doing? What do you want to do?

KARL THOMAS: Something must happen. Someone must set an example.

ALBERT KROLL: Someone? Everyone. Every day.

KARL THOMAS: I mean something different. Someone must

sacrifice himself. Then the lame will walk. Night and day I've pounded my brains. Now I know what I have to do.

ALBERT KROLL: I'm listening.

KARL THOMAS: Come here. Be discreet.

Speaks softly with ALBERT KROLL.

[Piscator added the line 'Kilman must go' for KARL THOMAS.]

ALBERT KROLL: You're no use to us.

KARL THOMAS: It's the only way I can help myself. Disgust chokes me.

ALBERT KROLL goes to the ELECTION OFFICER's table again.

ALBERT KROLL: The police have seized our van. That's sabotage of the workers' candidate.

A VOTER: Your candidate's been bribed by foreigners.

ALBERT KROLL: Lies! Election propaganda!

ELECTION OFFICER: (*To ALBERT KROLL.*) You must not electioneer. (*To VOTER.*) This isn't an information office, Herr Master Butcher.

ALBERT KROLL: I don't want to electioneer. But I'm still allowed to tell the truth.

SECOND ELECTION OFFICER: (*On the telephone.*) What time do you make it? Eight-fifty? … Yes, yes, it's all go here. Huge turnout. They're even bringing in the sick on stretchers. (*Hangs up.*) The clock in the Fifteenth District is eight minutes fast. Eight minutes! I didn't tell them. Because we'll get to know the results eight minutes sooner.

ALBERT KROLL goes to KARL THOMAS' table.

ALBERT KROLL: They shut me up when I tell the truth. I won't bow and scrape.

KARL THOMAS: What great courage! In truth you are all cowards. All, all, all! Wish I'd stayed in the madhouse! Now even my own plan disgusts me. What for? For a bunch of petit bourgeois cowards who believe in elections?

ALBERT KROLL: You'd like the world to be an eternal firework display set off just for you, with rockets and flares and the roar of battle. You're the coward, not me.

At the table left.

FIRST WORKER: Did'ya vote yet?

SECOND WORKER: No, I'm going now. Why shouldn't I vote for National Reconciliation when the ladyship my Lina works for is voting that way too. There must be something wrong with Kilman, I tell you; Lina's ladyship has brains in her head. She's really classy. On Sunday when Lina has a day off, her ladyship always comes into the kitchen. 'Lina,' she says, 'I wish you a good Sunday.' And then she shakes hands with her. Every time.

FIRST WORKER: How about that!

SECOND WORKER goes to the election table. PICKEL comes in.

PICKEL: Excuse me, can one vote here?

The ELECTIONEERS surround PICKEL.

FIRST ELECTIONEER: Law and Order in the land, with God for our dear Fatherland! Vote for Number One.

SECOND ELECTIONEER: Awake, you people, it's not too late. Don't support the right or left, support the State. Vote for Number Two.

THIRD ELECTIONEER: The President of Number Three sets the workers and the peasants free! Vote for Number Three!

PICKEL: Thank you, thank you.

PICKEL goes to the ELECTION OFFICER's table.

ELECTION OFFICER: What is your name?

PICKEL: Pickel.

ELECTION OFFICER: Where do you live?

PICKEL: Indeed I live in Holzhausen, but nevertheless …

ELECTION OFFICER: You are not entered on the voting register … Do you spell your name with a B?

PICKEL: Where will I … Pickel … Pickel with a P … P … Not two Ps … Indeed I would like to explain that …

ELECTION OFFICER: Your explanation is of no use. You are not allowed to vote here. You are in the wrong polling place.

PICKEL: I must explain to you … Indeed I live in Holzhausen …

ELECTION OFFICER: What do you want here? Don't hold the election up. Next …

The voting continues.

PICKEL: (*Going to KARL THOMAS.*) Indeed it's all the same to me personally whether I vote or not, but nevertheless I don't want to be ungrateful to the Minister … I'd like to give him my vote.

KARL THOMAS: Leave me alone.

PICKEL goes to the THIRD WORKER

PICKEL: Indeed I would have travelled home a long time ago. I only wanted to stay one day, but nevertheless it never stopped raining.

THIRD WORKER: Wish it was pissing down in here. Oughta flood out the whole show. All a fraud. They oughta wipe their bums with the ballots.

PICKEL: That's not what I meant. Namely I don't travel in rainy weather. I waited six weeks before I travelled to see the Minister, because there was always a thunderstorm in the sky.

BANKER comes in. ELECTIONEERS surround him.

BANKER: Thanks.

Goes to the ELECTION OFFICER.

ELECTION OFFICER: At your service, Herr Director-General. Herr Director-General, do you still live in Opernplatz?

BANKER: Yes, I've come a little late.

ELECTION OFFICER: Early enough, Herr Director-General. Over there, if you please.

BANKER goes into the voting booth.

PICKEL: I had an uncle who was struck by lightning on the railway. Indeed the railways attract the lightning, but nevertheless it's men who bear the guilt for it with their new-fangled commotions.

ELECTION OFFICER: (*To BANKER who has left the voting booth.*) Your most obedient servant, Herr Director-General, sir.

BANKER goes.

THIRD WORKER: He comes first, no one else, and the stupid workers guzzle his dust.

PICKEL: The radio and the electric waves, they mess up the atmosphere. Indeed …

ELECTION OFFICER: The poll is closed.

[Film of falling ballots stops. Back projection of heap of ballots in its place on centre compartment screen.]

FIRST WORKER: Now I'm really curious.

SECOND WORKER: Want to bet that the Minister of War is defeated?

THIRD WORKER: He'll be elected! And it serves you right!

SECOND WORKER: Don't talk such stupid rubbish, you old anarchist!

RADIO:

Attention! Attention! First election results. Twelfth District. 714 votes for the Minister of War, His Excellency von Wandsring. 414 votes for Minister Kilman. 67 for Bricklayer Bandke.

SECOND WORKER: Ouch!

FIRST WORKER: Bagged!

THIRD WORKER: Bravo!

FIRST and THIRD WORKERS go.

PICKEL: Herr Election Officer, you must not close. I insist … Indeed I am only … but nevertheless those in the big city always want us … Namely, I know Herr Minister Kilman, I've become friends with him …

ELECTION OFFICER: Make a complaint then.

PICKEL: If Minister Kilman now polls one vote too little. Just think if it's because of my vote …

RADIO:

Attention! Attention! Report from Osthafen. 6,000 for Bricklayer Bandke. 4,000 for Minister Kilman. 2,000 for His Excellency von Wandsring.

CROWD IN STREET: Hurrah! Hurrah!

ALBERT KROLL: The dock workers! Our pioneers! Bravo!

KARL THOMAS: Why bravo? How can you be pleased about votes? Are they a deed?

ALBERT KROLL: Deed – no. But a springboard to deeds.

RADIO:

Attention! Attention! According to the latest reports Minister Kilman has the majority in the capital.

CROWD IN STREET: Three cheers for Kilman! Three cheers for Kilman!

SECOND WORKER: Didn't I tell you? Come on, my three glasses of beer! Pay up! Pay up!

FIRST WORKER: Who said anything about three glasses of beer? We agreed one round.

SECOND WORKER: Now you're wriggling out of it!

FIRST WORKER: Just shut up, or else …

PICKEL: As far as I'm concerned I will not be quiet … The Minister would have had, if my vote … He would have had another vote … Indeed his election …

SECOND ELECTION OFFICER: Gentlemen, we have broken the record. Ninety-seven per cent election turnout! Ninety-seven per cent!

KARL THOMAS: If I could only understand! If I could only understand! Have I got caught in a crazy house?

RADIO:

Attention! Attention! At nine-thirty we shall announce the results.

SECOND WORKER: I'll bet on Kilman. Ten rounds? Who takes it?

PICKEL: I would straightaway … if my vote …

SECOND ELECTION OFFICER: We must put it in the papers. Ninety-seven per cent election turnout. That's never happened before! That's never happened before!

PICKEL: If you had allowed me to vote, the percentage would have …

Tumult outside the door. WORKERS *come in.*

THIRD WORKER: They've killed Mother Meller.

FOURTH WORKER: What gangsters! An old woman!

ALBERT KROLL: What's going on?

FIFTH WORKER: She tried to paste up an election leaflet at the Chemical Works.

FOURTH WORKER: With a truncheon! An old woman.

THIRD WORKER: Smashed to the pavement and done for!

FIFTH WORKER: Since when is it forbidden to paste up leaflets?

THIRD WORKER: Good question! Since we have a free election.

FOURTH WORKER: Smack on the head. An old woman.

KARL THOMAS: Did you hear?

ALBERT KROLL: Move, comrades.

ALBERT KROLL tries to go to the door. At this moment they bring in FRAU MELLER *unconscious.* ALBERT KROLL *makes a bed for her on the ground.*

A pillow … Water! … Unconscious. She's alive …

FOURTH WORKER: No warning. Smack with a truncheon. An old woman.

ALBERT KROLL: Coffee!

FIFTH WORKER: What about the constitution! They're going to have to answer for this.

THIRD WORKER: Who to? To their boss, the judge? Man, you're naive.

ALBERT KROLL: Mother Meller, I … Breathe calmly … Like that… Now you can lie back again. This is Karl Thomas. Do you recognise him?

FRAU MELLER: You, Karl …

ALBERT KROLL: What happened? Can you tell us?

FRAU MELLER: Oh, we forgot to dot an i on the leaflet. So some devil dotted the back of my head with a truncheon. In bold type … They've arrested Eva.

Tumult at the door. FIRST *and* THIRD WORKERS *come in with* RAND.

FIRST WORKER: Here's the little brother!

THIRD WORKER: I know him. Regular guest at our meetings. Always the most radical.

FIRST WORKER: Agent provocateur!

OTHER WORKERS: (*Closing in upon* RAND.) Smash him up! Smash him!

ALBERT KROLL jumps in between them, grabs RAND's arm with his right hand.

ALBERT KROLL: Order!

KARL THOMAS: To hell with order! Should we swallow everything. That's your election victory for you!

KARL THOMAS tries to knock RAND down. ALBERT KROLL grabs KARL THOMAS with his left hand.

You … you … let go!

ALBERT KROLL: You take him, Mother Meller.

FIFTH WORKER: Hadn't we better ask the Party?

ALBERT KROLL: The Party! Are we babies in nappies?

RAND: Thank you very much, Herr Kroll.

ALBERT KROLL: Where do we know each other from?

RAND: I was once your warder.

FRAU MELLER: Well I'll be damned. A great reunion! We ought to drink a little cup of coffee together.

RAND: Haven't I always treated you in a friendly way, Herr Kroll. You must grant me that.

ALBERT KROLL: So friendly that if they ordered you to bump us off, you would have fetched us one by one … with a voice sweet as honey and a face fit for kissing … 'Please don't make it hard for me, I'm only doing my duty, it'll be over soon.'

WORKERS laugh.

RAND: What should a man do? I am only a worker like you. I have to live too. Got five children. And pay to make you puke. I'm only carrying out my orders.

FIRST WORKER: Here's the revolver we got off him.

KARL THOMAS jumps up, grabs the revolver, aims it at RAND.

ALBERT KROLL: (*Hits his arm.*) Stop fooling about!

FRAU MELLER has run over to KARL THOMAS, pulls him to her.

What have you stuffed up your belly? You don't care about the craze for being slim! (*Pulls leaflets about of rand's waistcoat, reads.*) 'Comrades, beware of the Jews' … 'Foreign elements'. 'Don't allow the Elders of Zion …' So you've got principles too?

RAND: You bet! The Jews …

ALBERT KROLL: How much cash do your principles earn you? … Now get out! March! I've protected you once … I couldn't do it a second time – even if I wanted to.

RAND goes.

WORKERS: Just wait till you get caught again!

KARL THOMAS: No, Mother Meller, no, let me go. I want to speak to him … Why are you putting the brakes on me?

ALBERT KROLL: Because I want to go full steam ahead when it's time. It takes strength to have patience.

KARL THOMAS: Kilman says the same thing.

ALBERT KROLL: Fool.

KARL THOMAS: Then what should I do to understand you?

ALBERT KROLL: Work somewhere.

FRAU MELLER: I know what to do, boy. The hotel where I work needs an assistant waiter. I'll work on the head waiter. Got somewhere to stay? You can sleep at my place.

ALBERT KROLL: Do it, Karl. You must get involved in everyday life.

FRAU MELLER: I like you, Albert. Drinking my coffee like it was your own … Another cup, barkeeper …

FOURTH WORKER: With a truncheon. An old woman.

RADIO:

Attention! Attention! (*Radio fails … Buzzing noises.*)

PICKEL: The atmosphere …

RADIO:

[*Back projected on the centre compartment screen, the bottom of the* MINISTER OF WAR *appears out of the heap of ballots and then he turns to the front and climbs out of the pile.*]

The Minister of War, His Excellency Wandsring, has been elected as President of the Republic by a great majority.

While shouting and singing swirl up in the street, the picture of the president appears on the cyclorama.

[*Screen in and film of the* MINISTER OF WAR *projected on it from the front.*]

Curtain.

[*The interval was here. During it, the scaffolding was pushed to the front again and revolved to the left so that its back was at an angle to the audience.*]

Act 3

[*After the interval, Act 3 began with Kate Kühl singing this song in the middle of the stage. She was lit by two follow-spots focused on her head and sang in a raucous cabaret style.*]

Hoppla, We're Alive!

Intermezzo for the Hotel Scene in Töller's Play by Walter Mehring

The cream of society stay
    At Hotel Earth *à-la-mode* –
Blithely holding at bay
    Life's unbearable load!
    Partaking of good consummation –
    They proffer a war declaration
    Instead of a cheque for the till –
Here diplomats congregate,
Our plight to deliberate,
They say: We have need of a war
And much better times will arrive!
There's one politics and no more:
Hoppla, we're alive –
    We're alive and we'll settle the bill!

Sabre-rattling Chauvinisms – Ecstatical Populisms –
Which dance will you dance in the morn?
    Hoppla!
Poison Gas-isms – Humanity-isms –
Our cares forlorn!
    Hoppla!
    Our hearts do bleed in distress
    From the sensationalist press,
    Hoppla!
    Freedom – behind bars survive –
    Into trenches dive.
Hoppla! We're alive!

The men of the military stay
    At Hotel Earth *à-la-mode* –
We fight their battles each day –
    But hatred for us is their code!
    Spending in blood at their whims,
    They tip us in artificial limbs
    And leave a mass grave to fill –
    But when it's time to propose
    They pay for all the death-throes:
The Commander-in-Chief comes along,
And with him the clergy connive –
To sing, so moved, this epic song:
Hoppla, we're alive –
    We're alive! And we'll settle the bill!

The helmet-head – and the Red –
Will our enemies be come morn.
    Hoppla!
And over three million dead –
Our cares forlorn!
    Hoppla!
    Our hearts do bleed all the more
    Under the weight of iron ore!
    Hoppla!
    Freedom – behind bars survive –

Into trenches dive.
Hoppla! WE'RE alive!

Exposed to murder and war
  At Hotel Earth *à-la-mode* –
In the cellar so mean and so sore
  The proletarian herd makes abode –
  They fork out an arm and a leg
  For the little they're able to beg -
  And the whole gang collapses drained of all will!
  Then the managers come and they shout:
  We have lost out!
  We gave you emergency shelter, you see,
  And also a crutch to revive,
  You are half-dead! – But we,
  Hoppla! We're alive –
  We're alive and we'll settle the bill!
You have nothing to lose and you're choking!
Can't borrow from us we've sworn!
      Hoppla!
Starving, freezing – and croaking –
Our cares forlorn!
      Hoppla!
We're bleeding away our stash!
You proles, give us our cash!
  Freedom? Behind bars survive –
  Into trenches dive –
  Hoppla! We're alive!

The cream of society stay
  At Hotel Earth *à-la-mode* –
Blithely holding at bay
  Life's unbearable load!
  Our foes were thrashed with devotion –
  Do give that cripple a groschen!
  Our funds are almost at nil!
Ministers, Philosophers and Poets of fame:
They all once again look the same!
All is just like it was before the last war –
And before the next war to arrive –
For battlefield music, the Charleston's the score!
Hoppla! They're alive!
When we settle their bill!
If we bring it all down unawares –
Which dance will you dance in the morn
      Hoppla?
If it's our cares that reign, instead of theirs,
Our cares that were once so forlorn
      Hoppla!
Then pray for your God's absolution
From death by electric execution
Hoppla!
  With your generals we'll strive!
WE'LL command and WE'LL thrive:
Hoppla! We're alive!

Scene 1

[Scaffolding revolved to the back to bring the STUDENT's *room, which had been set up and rolled in on the right, to the front. For ten seconds, film of a busy city at night was projected directly on the stage without the gauze and with appropriate night-life sounds, probably including the Hoppla song. As film ends, lights up on room in front of scaffolding.]*

Small room

STUDENT *is reading. There's a knock.*

STUDENT: Who's there?

COUNT LANDE *enters.*

COUNT LANDE: Well, what do you say about the new President?

STUDENT: I'm sure he has the best intentions.

COUNT LANDE: What good is that for us … Kilman still remains as Minister.

STUDENT: Really?

COUNT LANDE: Do you have a cigarette? … Our front group ought to be disbanded.

STUDENT: What? What are you saying?

COUNT LANDE: Kilman …

STUDENT: Then something really must be done. We always talk about the great deed …

COUNT LANDE: Can anyone eavesdrop at the door?

STUDENT: No … What's the matter?

COUNT LANDE: Here.

STUDENT: The decision?

COUNT LANDE: Read it.

COUNT LANDE *gives* STUDENT *a piece of paper.*

STUDENT: I and Lieutenant Frank?

COUNT LANDE: Both of you.

STUDENT: When?

COUNT LANDE: I can't say. You have to be ready at any time.

STUDENT: How quick it's come.

COUNT LANDE: Are you hesitating? Haven't you volunteered twice? Can you forget that the same Kilman who should have been put up against the wall eight years ago now, as Minister, betrays the Fatherland?

STUDENT: Hesitating – no. It goes against the grain to have to wait for the deed.

COUNT LANDE: Hold your horses, *basta*! You took the oath of allegiance; Patriotism has sailed you into shore and now, quite rightly, you are ordered to drop anchor.

STUDENT: And what if we are hunted, hounded, and trapped … in front of closed frontiers?

COUNT LANDE: In the first place, that is not very likely … If you get stuck in a blind alley, you will be helped. If you reach the frontier, good. If you don't reach it … You must make the sacrifice … Besides you needn't doubt that the judges will be reasonable and show complete under-standing for your motives.

STUDENT: May I leave a letter for my mother?

COUNT LANDE: Out of the question. Nationalism must not depend on chance. I know there are cowards ready to compromise in our ranks. They would readily sacrifice us for the sake of political tactics.

STUDENT: I understand so little about politics. I didn't even see service at the front. I joined up and one month later everything collapsed. I hate the Revolution like I've never hated anything. Ever since that one day. My uncle was a General. We boys worshipped him like a god. By the end he commanded an army corps. Three days after the Revolution I'm sitting beside him, the bell rings. A mere Private barges in. 'I'm on the Soldiers' Council. It's been reported to us, Herr General, that you have provoked the people in the street by wearing your golden epaulettes. Today there are no more epaulettes. We all have bare shoulders.' My uncle stood bolt upright. 'I should surrender my epaulettes, should I?' 'Yes.' My uncle takes his sword, which is lying on the table, and draws it out of its scabbard. I'm very frightened. Move nearer so I can help him, when I see the old man cough a hacking cough with tears in his eyes. 'Herr Soldiers' Council, for forty years I have worn the uniform of my Emperor with honour. Once I witnessed how a sergeant was disgraced by having his stripes ripped off. What you demand of me today is the lowest thing anyone can demand of me. If I can no longer wear my uniform with honour, here …' And at that moment the old man bent his sword, broke it in two and threw it at the feet of the soldier. That soldier was Herr Kilman …

COUNT LANDE: That dog!

STUDENT: The next day my uncle shot himself. On a piece of paper he left behind there were these words: 'I cannot survive the shame of our beloved Fatherland. May my death open the eyes of the inflamed people.'

COUNT LANDE: My career went bust too. What are we today compared to the rabble? Stooges. And in society always miles behind the moneybags … We will avenge your uncle. The goods have got to be delivered.

Blackout.

[As the same film is again projected directly on to the stage, the scaffolding revolves to the right until its front is again facing the audience. When it reaches halfway point, a film of hotel scenes is projected from the back and when the revolve stops this film continues on the centre compartment screen. Throughout the revolve, all the characters run around the scaffolding with as much movement as possible, particularly on the stairs, to their places in frenzied cacophony.]

Scene 2

The façade of the Grand Hotel can be seen.

The front wall opens.

Rooms of the Grand Hotel can be seen.

Diagram:

Blackout.

Lights up:

The lobby

Dancing couple.

Blackout.

Between the separate scenes the Lobby can be seen for a few moments and a jazz band heard.

Lights up:

Staff room

[This section was cut.]

KARL THOMAS in waiter's uniform sits at a table, FRAU MELLER looks in through the door.

FRAU MELLER: Here, boy, a beef steak. It came back from a room. I warmed it up quick.

KARL THOMAS: Thanks a lot, Mother Meller. I have exactly five more minutes. My employment begins at eight o'clock.

FRAU MELLER: I must go to the kitchen again to wash up … What a sight you are! I really wouldn't have recognised you. Ten years younger. But Karl, Karl, why are you always laughing?

KARL THOMAS: Don't be frightened, Mother Meller. You needn't fear that I'll go crazy again. Everywhere I applied for a job, the bosses asked me: 'Man, what's that undertaker's face for? You'll scare the customers away. Nowadays you have to laugh, always laugh.' Then, because rejuvenation is only a sport for rich people, I went to a beautician. And here's the new façade. Aren't I sweet enough to eat?

FRAU MELLER: Yes, Karl. You'll go down a treat with the girls. But it was weird to me at first … What demands they make. Next we'll have to sign contracts to laugh the whole ten hours we slave away … Well, eat now, boy. I must go back to the kitchen.

Blackout.

Lights up:

Private room

[Scaffolding revolved one and a half metres right for close-up effect. Back projection of wallpaper in middle left compartment. Lobby back projection always on in centre compartment.]

Enter BANKER, BANKER'S SON, HEAD WAITER, BUSBOY.

BANKER: Everything ready?

HEAD WAITER: Here's the menu. Would you like any changes, Herr Director-General?

BANKER: Good. For me personally bring something light; I can't eat anything heavy, my stomach … Perhaps broth, a little chicken meat, compote, but unsugared.

HEAD WAITER: At your service, Herr Director-General.

The HEAD WAITER goes out.

BANKER'S SON: I'm still not sure.

BANKER: Why shouldn't we drive our coach on the route through his wife? An attempt, what does it matter?

BANKER'S SON: She must be simplicity in person. Recently at a government banquet she told stories about her days as a cook.

BANKER: I would have liked to see Kilman's face … My dear man, one doesn't hear 'Excellency' here and 'Excellency' there every day without being punished. Yes, if there were still titles and orders … But today money is the only foundation. As soon as one has his first hundred-thousand, he hangs his idealism up on the hatstand. Don't worry, he'll get a fat bank account and I'll get the cheap public credits.

BANKER'S SON: Just as you think.

WILHELM KILMAN and his WIFE enter, accompanied by HEAD WAITER and KARL THOMAS as Waiter, who helps both take off their outer garments.

Good evening, Herr Minister. Extremely delighted, Madam.

WILHELM KILMAN: Government devours you. People always imagine that we sit around in club chairs and smoke thick cigars. Excuse me for being late. I had to receive the Mexican Ambassador.

BANKER'S SON: Now we can begin.

All sit at the table, HEAD WAITER brings food, KARL THOMAS helps.

FRAU KILMAN: What's this lying next to my plate?

BANKER: A *petit rien*, madam. I took the liberty of bringing a rose for you.

FRAU KILMAN: A rose? But I see a case … In gold? … Set with pearls? …

BANKER: It opens here … This catch … See, the rose … La France … My special rose. I hope you too like this sort …

FRAU KILMAN: Really, Herr Director-General, very kind, but I cannot accept it. Whatever could I do with it?

WILHELM KILMAN: Come now, Herr Director-General …

BANKER: Please, my dear Minister, don't make a fuss. Just yesterday I bought three of these things at auction, eighteenth century, Louis Quartorze, even though I already possess two or three.

FRAU KILMAN: You are so nice. We thank you for your kindness, but please take the case back.

WILHELM KILMAN: You know malicious tongues. One must avoid the least appearance …

BANKER: I am immensely sorry that I didn't think of it …

WILHELM KILMAN: So let's drink to a compromise. Emma, please take the rose. What a scent it has, this La France. Better than the real one, ha ha ha … And when we visit you we'll be able to admire the case in your display cabinet.

BANKER: To your health, Madam. Your good health, Herr Minister … Waiter, bring a bottle of Mouton Rothschild '21 …

KARL THOMAS: Yes, indeed, sir.

Blackout.

Lights up:

Radio station

[This section was moved to after the second scene in Room 96. Piscator rewrote some of it to emphasise political and economic events affecting KARL THOMAS.]

RADIO OPERATOR: You finally came? I rang all of three times.

KARL THOMAS: I was busy down below:

RADIO OPERATOR: Here's a telegram for Minister Kilman. It was transmitted here by order of the Ministry.

KARL THOMAS: Can you really listen to the whole earth here?

RADIO OPERATOR: Is that news to you?

KARL THOMAS: What are you listening to now?

RADIO OPERATOR: New York: A great flood on the Mississippi is being reported.

KARL THOMAS: When?

RADIO OPERATOR: Now, at this very moment.

KARL THOMAS: While we speak?

RADIO OPERATOR: Yes, while we speak, the Mississippi is breaking its banks, people are fleeing.

KARL THOMAS: And what are you listening to now?

RADIO OPERATOR: I've tuned in to the 1100 wavelength. I'm listening to Cairo. The jazz band at Mena House, the hotel near the pyramids. They're playing during dinner. Want to have a listen? I'll switch on the loudspeaker.

LOUDSPEAKER: Attention! Attention! All Radio Stations of the world! The latest hit is 'Hoppla, We're Alive!'!

Jazz music can be heard.

RADIO OPERATOR: You can see them too.

Visible on the screen: restaurant at Mena House. Ladies and gentlemen are dining.

KARL THOMAS: Can you also see the Mississippi?

RADIO OPERATOR: Of course. But where have you been that makes you act like such a babe in arms?

KARL THOMAS: Oh, I've lived only in a … little village for the last ten years.

RADIO OPERATOR: Here.

LOUDSPEAKER: Attention! Attention! New York. Number of dead: 8,000. Chicago threatened. Further report follows in three minutes.

Visible on the screen: scenes from the flood.

KARL THOMAS: Inconceivable! At this very second …

LOUDSPEAKER: Attention! Attention! New York. New York. Royal Shell 104, Standard Oil 102, Rand Mines 116.

KARL THOMAS: What is that?

RADIO OPERATOR: The New York Stock Exchange. Petroleum shares on offer … I'll turn the dial. Latest news from around the world.

LOUDSPEAKER: Attention! Attention! Uprising in India … Uprising in China … Uprising in Africa … Paris Paris: Houbigant, the chic perfume … Bucharest Bucharest: Famine in Romania … Berlin Berlin: The lady of fashion favours green wigs … New York New York: Largest bomber in the world invented. Capable of demolishing Europe's capital cities in a second … Attention! Attention! Paris London Rome Berlin Calcutta Tokyo New York: The complete gentleman drinks Mumm's Extra Dry …

KARL THOMAS: Enough, enough. Turn it off.

RADIO OPERATOR: I'll turn the dial.

LOUDSPEAKER: (*A clamour of cries is heard.*) Hey, hey, hey! Give it to him hard! … he's dizzy … A fix! (*A bell.*) He's saved! … MacNamara, Tonani! MacNamara! … Eviva, eviva …

RADIO OPERATOR: Six-day bicycle race in Milan … Now I'm getting something interesting. The first passenger aeroplane from New York to Paris radios that a passenger is having a heart attack. They are seeking contact with heart specialists. They want medical advice. Right, now you can hear the heartbeat of the patient.

The heartbeats can be heard over the loudspeaker. On the screen can be seen: The aeroplane over the ocean. The patient.

[Piscator showed a beating heart.]

KARL THOMAS: A human heartbeat over the middle of the ocean …

RADIO OPERATOR: A great event.

KARL THOMAS: How wonderful it all is! And what does mankind do with it … They live like muttonheads a thousand years behind the times.

RADIO OPERATOR: We won't change things. I discovered a method to make petroleum out of coal. They bought up my patent for a handful of scraps of paper and then what did they do? Destroyed it! The high and mighty oil magnates … You have to go now. The telegram is urgent. Who knows what tomorrow brings. Perhaps there's war.

KARL THOMAS: War?

RADIO OPERATOR: These apparatuses lead the way there too, helping men kill each other with all the more sophistication. What's the star turn of electricity? The electric chair. There are machines with electric wavelengths such that if they're turned on in London, Berlin would be a heap of rubble by tomorrow. We won't change things. Off you go, hurry up.

KARL THOMAS: Yes, sir.

Blackout.

Lights up:

Club room

[*This section was cut.*]

Discussion evening of the Union of Intellectual Brain Workers.

PHILOSOPHER X: I come to my conclusion: Where Quality is absent, there is nothing to counterpose Quantity. Therefore my precept runs: Let no one marry beneath his own level. Rather let everyone endeavour, by the appropriate choice of a mate, to raise his posterity to a higher level than he himself possesses. But what do we practice, gentlemen? Nothing but negative selective breeding. The very least, gentlemen, the very least condition of every marriage contract should be equality of birth. We trust instinct. But unfortunately instinct has been so thoroughly one-sided for centuries that it will not be so easy, for several generations, even in some two hundred years, to breed our way up to something better.

LYRIC POET Y: Where does that appear in Marx?

PHILOSOPHER X: I conclude: the instincts must be refined and spiritualised; they must strive ever more away from the Brutal-Vital and towards the Absolute-Superior.

LYRIC POET Y: Where does that appear in Marx?

PHILOSOPHER X: Only thus can the hopelessly degenerated white race be raised up again. Only thus can it nurture superior blooms as it once did. Yet, how can one, many will ask, recognise someone of good blood? Well, whoever cannot judge that in himself and in others, but in himself above all, cannot be helped to do so. He has become so lacking in instinct (*Directed to* LYRIC POET Y.) that I personally can only urgently recommend extinction. Indeed that is what is great in my Academy of Wisdom: it makes people wise by persuading those who formerly bred away blithely to become extinct of their own free will. Now when this is done logically, then in this domain, too, Evil will be conquered by Good once and for all.

SHOUTS: Bravo! Bravo! Point of order!

CHAIRMAN: Lyric Poet Y has the floor.

LYRIC POET Y: Gentlemen. We are gathered here together as intellectual brain workers. Indeed I would like to pose the question whether the theme about which Herr Philosopher X has spoken serves our task, which is the redemption of the proletariat. In Marx …

THE CRITIC: Stop showing off about having read Marx.

LYRIC POET Y: Herr Chairman, I beseech you to protect me. Yes, sir, I have read Marx, and I find that he is not at all so stupid. To be sure he lacks a sense of that new objectivity which we …

CHAIRMAN: You may not speak on a point of order: I'm taking the floor away from you.

LYRIC POET Y: Then I might as well go. Lick my arse! (*Goes.*)

SHOUTS: Outrageous! Outrageous!

THE CRITIC: He should be sent to a psychoanalyst. After analysis he'll stop writing poetry. All poetry is nothing but repressed complexes.

PICKEL comes in.

PICKEL: Indeed, I believe … but nevertheless, am I in the Green Tree Hotel?

CHAIRMAN: No. Private meeting.

PICKEL: Private? … Indeed I believed, the Green Tree … but nevertheless …

SHOUT: Don't disturb us.

PICKEL: Thank you kindly, gentlemen.

PICKEL goes.

CHAIRMAN: What do you want, Herr Philosopher X?

PHILOSOPHER X: A short postscript, gentlemen. To give an example. Herr Lyric Poet Y called into question the causal connection between my theme and the task which we have set ourselves: the intellectual redemption of the proletariat. Today unrepressed instincts are only to be found in the lower social classes. Let us ask a proletarian, let us ask a waiter, and it will prove my theory.

SHOUTS: Waiter! Waiter!

KARL THOMAS appears with a tray of bottles and glasses.

KARL THOMAS: The head waiter is coming right away.

SHOUTS: You must stay.

KARL THOMAS: I have work down below, gentlemen.

PHILOSOPHER X: Listen, Comrade Waiter, young proletarian. Would you perform coitus, sexual intercourse, with the first woman who comes your way or would you first consult your instincts?

KARL THOMAS bursts into laughter.

CHAIRMAN: That's nothing to laugh about. The question is serious. Besides we are guests and you are the waiter.

KARL THOMAS: Aha, first Comrade Waiter and now you play the boss. You … You want to redeem the proletariat? What, here in the Grand Hotel? Where were you when it started to happen? Where will you be? Always in the Grand Hotel! Eunuchs!

SHOUTS: Outrageous! Outrageous!

KARL THOMAS goes.

PHILOSOPHER X: Petit bourgeois ideologue!

CHAIRMAN: Now we come to the second item on the agenda. Proletarian communal love and the task of the intellectuals.

Blackout.

Lights up:

Private room

[Continued by Piscator directly from previous scene in Private Room.]

BANKER: What took you so long with the liqueur, waiter?

KARL THOMAS: Excuse me, sir, I was held up.

BANKER: Pass the cigars. Do you smoke cigarettes, madam?

FRAU KILMAN: No, thank you.

[RADIO OPERATOR brings telegram to WILHELM KILMAN in Piscator production.]

WILHELM KILMAN: The telegram brings the conflict to a head. To deny us the oil concessions!

BANKER: Quite good I had a sharp enough nose to advise my clients to sell off their Turkish holdings … How do you actually invest your money, Herr Minister?

WILHELM KILMAN: Mortgage bonds, ha, ha, ha! I'm careful not to speculate.

BANKER: Who's talking about speculation? After all you have duties, you have to play the host. A man with your gifts ought to make himself independent.

WILHELM KILMAN: As a State Official, I ought …

BANKER: But you are also a private person. What does the State give you. A couple of coins. Why don't you make the most of your information? Don't refuse, even a Bismark, a Disraeli, a Gambetta, didn't disdain …

WILHELM KILMAN: Even so …

BANKER: I'll give you an example. The Council of Ministers has decided to reduce the contango funds. Then you opportunely sell your stocks. And who can reproach you, if you sell a few more. Of course, it mustn't be done in your own name.

WILHELM KILMAN: Enough of that …

BANKER: It would be an honour for me to advise you. You know that you can trust me.

WILHELM KILMAN: Waiter, where is the Press Conference taking place?

KARL THOMAS: In the Writing Room.

WILHELM KILMAN: Is Herr Baron Friedrich down there?

KARL THOMAS: Yes, sir.

WILHELM KILMAN: Tell Herr Baron that I shall expect him at the Ministry at midnight.

PICKEL enters.

PICKEL: If I am in the right place … Namely I would like … Indeed the prices … but nevertheless …

BANKER: Who is this man?

PICKEL: Ah, Herr Minister …

WILHELM KILMAN: I have no time. (*Turns away.*)

PICKEL: I didn't expect that from you, Herr Minister! Haven't we made you Minister? … Indeed, even if my vote in the Presidential election … But nevertheless, Minister, you have me to thank for your post …

Goes.

Blackout.

Lights up:

Writing room

[This section was cut.]

JOURNALISTS *writing.* KARL THOMAS *at the door.*

BARON FRIEDRICH: Gentlemen, what was once the task of the historian – to depict the actions, which reason of State demands, as the only solution, as a moral necessity – is now yours. In these difficult times for our Fatherland, the Government has the right to expect that over and above all party differences every newspaper will do its duty. We don't seek war. Let us stress that over and over again, gentlemen. The so-called sanctions which they want to impose on us are better left unmentioned. We want peace. But our patience will run out at once, gentlemen, if the prestige of our State is impugned.

KARL THOMAS: Excuse me, Herr Baron.

BARON FRIEDRICH: What is it?

KARL THOMAS: The Minister wishes to see you at midnight …

Blackout.

Lights up:

Hotel room no. 96

[Scaffolding revolves three metres to left for close-up effect. Back projection of red wallpaper on screen of middle right compartment.]

COUNT LANDE: I clearly saw you make eyes at the blonde girl at the next table.

LOTTE KILMAN: Are you afraid that I'll betray you with her?

COUNT LANDE: That kind of business disgusts me.

LOTTE KILMAN: Maybe you men disgust me … Maybe you're beginning to bore me now.

COUNT LANDE: But my treasure …

LOTTE KILMAN: Only women can be tender in bed. I don't deny I'd like to seduce the little darling.

COUNT LANDE: You are drunk.

LOTTE KILMAN: Maybe I would be, if you had been more generous.

COUNT LANDE: Let's order another bottle of Cordon Rouge.

LOTTE KILMAN: Please. But I'd like the little blonde better, or a snort of coke.

COUNT LANDE: Cover yourself up. I'll ring for the waiter.

Blackout.

Lights up:

Servery and staff room

[Scaffolding revolves three metres right. Back projection of tiled wall lower left compartment. White light on centre compartment screen which is forward to show in silhouette cashier and cash register which rings throughout the scene.]

HEAD WAITER, KARL THOMAS, PORTER, BUSBOY *sit at supper.*

HEAD WAITER: Mussolini won first prize at the Paris races. Thoroughbred. Three-year-old.

PORTER: Two hundred to win, eighty-four to place.

WAITER enters.

WAITER: Three *entrecôtes.*

HEAD WAITER: (*Calling through the hatch to the kitchen.*) Three *entrecôtes* … Did you bet anything?

PORTER: Of course, you can't get fat on the loot here.

WAITER: (*Enters.*) Six oxtail soups, double Madeira.

HEAD WAITER: Six oxtail soups, chef should put in double Madeira.

KARL THOMAS: I don't know what this soup tastes like.

PORTER: Do you want to eat *à la carte* instead?

WAITER: (*Enters.*) Two dozen oysters.

HEAD WAITER: Two dozen oysters.

KARL THOMAS: I don't demand oysters, but this muck … Why doesn't the Works Council do anything?

PORTER: Because it's arm in arm with the hotel manager. I don't give a damn. I expect nothing from nobody. They're all the same. Before the inflation I saved one mark every week. Whenever I had ten, I went to the bank and got a gold piece. On Sunday I'd polish it bright and Monday I'd take it to the Savings Bank. I saved for six hundred weeks. Twelve years. And in the end what did I get? Damn all! Seven hundred million. Couldn't even buy myself a box of matches with it … The likes of us always get treated dirty.

HEAD WAITER: Posh spread in the Private Room tonight.

KARL THOMAS: For the posh People's Minister.

HEAD WAITER: You don't understand anything about it. If he's dining with a banker, he'll have his own good reasons. Otherwise he wouldn't be Minister.

BUSBOY: The gentleman up in 101 always pinches my bum-bum.

HEAD WAITER: Don't make a fuss, you. You know you can get something out of it.

There's a ring.

Which number?

BUSBOY: Ninety-six.

HEAD WAITER: Karl, you go up. The floor waiter is standing in for me.

Blackout.

Lights up:

Landing

[This section cut.]

PICKEL: (*On the stairs.*) Well there you are … Indeed one believes … one travels for two days on the railway … one is looking forward to it for his whole life … in Holzhausen I thought, up there … there one would certainly understand people, but up there it's exactly like it is with the railway, with one's own property … the atmosphere …

KARL THOMAS goes by.

Herr Waiter! Herr Waiter!

KARL THOMAS: No time.

PICKEL: No time …

Blackout.

Lights up:

Room no. 96

There's a knock, KARL THOMAS enters.

COUNT LANDE: What took you so long? Service. A bottle of Cordon Rouge. Well chilled.

Blackout.

[Radio Station scene moved to here by Piscator.]

Lights up:

Servant's room

KARL THOMAS sits alone at the table, head buried in his hands. FRAU MELLER opens the door quietly.

FRAU MELLER: Tired, youngster?

KARL THOMAS doesn't stir.

It's a real strain the first day.

KARL THOMAS jumps up, tears the cravat from his neck, pulls off his tailcoat, throws it in the corner.

KARL THOMAS: There and there and there! …

FRAU MELLER: What are you doing?

KARL THOMAS: I'm awake, so awake that I'm afraid I'll never go to sleep again.

FRAU MELLER: Calm down, Karl, calm down.

KARL THOMAS: Calm down? Only a real rotter could calm down. Call me a fool now, like Albert called me. I resolved to be patient. I've been here half a day. I've seen everyday life, in tailcoat and nightshirt. You're all asleep! You're all asleep! You must be awakened. I don't give a damn about your common sense! If sensible people are like you, then I want to play the fool. All of you must be awakened.

There's a ring. Pause.

FRAU MELLEER: Karl …

KARL THOMAS: Let the devil go wait on them!

There's a ring.

FRAU MELLER: The Private Room.

KARL THOMAS: The Private Room? … Kilman? … Good, I'll go.

KARL THOMAS dresses hurriedly.

FRAU MELLER: I'll come right back. We'll have a talk, Karl.

FRAU MELLER goes.

KARL THOMAS: (*Looks at his revolver a few seconds.*) This shot will awaken them all!

Blackout.

Lights up:

Room no. 96

There's a soft knock.

COUNT LANDE: Coming.

Blackout.

Lights up:

Half-dark corridor.

STUDENT: Where?

COUNT LANDE: In the Private Room. Who is going in?

STUDENT: We drew lots. Me. Lieutenant Frank is waiting in the car.

COUNT LANDE: Are you wearing a waiter's tailcoat?

STUDENT: (*Opens his coat.*) Yes.

COUNT LANDE: Break a leg. Quick now. You must not be arrested. If you have bad luck, then … You mustn't make any statements … Take care of yourself.

STUDENT: I have given my word of honour.

Blackout.

Lights up:

Private room

WILHELM KILMAN: Superb, that joke, superb. Just look at my wife. How red she's getting. She doesn't understand anything about that, ha, ha, ha.

BANKER: Do you know the one about Herr Meyer in the railway compartment?

WILHELM KILMAN: Tell it.

BANKER: The waiter at last! Another bottle of cognac … Why are you standing there? Why are you staring at me? Didn't you understand?

KARL THOMAS: Don't you recognise me?

WILHELM KILMAN: Who are you?

KARL THOMAS: Feel free to use my first name. When we waited together for the mass grave, we weren't so formal. Are you ashamed of knowing me?

WILHELM KILMAN: It's you … Don't talk crazy nonsense. Come to the Ministry tomorrow.

KARL THOMAS: You will answer for it today.

WILHELM KILMAN: (*To* BANKER.) Leave him be. A fantasiser whom I knew from before. Off the rails because of a romantic episode in his youth. Can't find a firm grip any more.

KARL THOMAS: I'm waiting for your answer.

WILHELM KILMAN: To what? What is going on in your head? What's going on in your head, Karl? Do I need to tell you again that times have changed? You'd rather damn the world than give up your insane demands; you'd rather damn the very men who are trying to make things progress a bit.

KARL THOMAS: Wilhelm …

WILHELM KILMAN: Please stop the hollow phrases. They don't work.

BANKER: Hadn't I better call the Hotel Manager?

WILHELM KILMAN: For God's sake, don't make a scene.

BANKER: Calm down, waiter. He's in a bad way, isn't he? Here, take ten marks.

WILHELM KILMAN: May I add another ten?

KARL THOMAS, clutching the revolver in his pocket with one hand, looks at the money bewildered, shrugs his shoulders in disgust as if he had gone off doing the deed and starts to turn away.

KARL THOMAS: It's not worth it. I couldn't give a damn about you now.

Then the door opens quietly. STUDENT *in waiter's tailcoat enters. Raises his revolver over* KARL THOMAS's *shoulder. Turns the electric light out. Shot. Scream.*

BANKER: Lights! Lights! The waiter has shot the Minister.

Curtain.

[*Scaffolding revolves right so stairs are visible,* KARL THOMAS *and* STUDENT *run down them followed by spotlights. Gauze in and park is projected on it from front as scaffolding revolves face-on to audience for next act.*]

Act 4
Scene 1
Left of hotel. In a park.

KARL THOMAS *is running after the* STUDENT.

KARL THOMAS: You! You!

STUDENT *turns his head, runs on.*

You, I want to help you, comrade.

STUDENT: What, comrade! I'm not your comrade.

KARL THOMAS: But you shot Kilman …

STUDENT: Because he's a Bolshevik, because he's a revolutionary. Because he's selling our country out to the Jews.

Bewildered, KARL THOMAS *takes a step towards him.*

KARL THOMAS: Has the world become a madhouse? Has the world become a madhouse!!!

STUDENT: Get back, or I'll shoot you down.

STUDENT *runs on, jumps into a car which speeds away,* KARL THOMAS *catches on, tears the revolver out of his pocket, shoots after it twice. Then he reflects, stands still in front of a tree.*

KARL THOMAS: Are you a beech tree? Or are you a rubber-padded wall? (*Feels it.*) You feel like bark, rough and cracked, and you do smell of earth. But are you really a beech tree?

Sits on a bench.

My poor head. Drumfire. Climb aboard, my esteemed public. The bell is ringing. The trip is starting. One shot a ride.

You see a house burning, grab a pail, try to put it out, and instead of water you pour buckets of oil on the flames … You sound the alarm throughout the whole city to awaken all the people, but the sleepers just turn over on their bellies and snore on …

When night covers others in brown shadows, I see murderers crouching naked with brains exposed …

And I run through the streets like a night watchman, with thoughts which wound themselves on the beam of a spotlight …

Oh, why did they open the gate of the madhouse for me? Wasn't it good in there in spite of the North Pole and the flapping wings of grey birds?

I have lost my grip on the world
And the world has lost its grip on me.

During the last phrases two POLICE DETECTIVES *have entered. Both go up to him, grab him by the wrists.*

FIRST POLICEMAN: Well, young man, no doubt you just found that revolver somewhere?

KARL THOMAS: What do I know? What do you know? Even the revolver turns against the gunman, and spurts laughter out of its barrel.

SECOND POLICEMAN: Just speak respectfully, you got that?

FIRST POLICEMAN: What is your name?

KARL THOMAS: Every name is a con … See, I once believed that if I took the path straight through the park, I'd reach a hotel. A cup of coffee. Fifty pfennigs. Do you know where I landed? In the madhouse. And the police make sure that no one gets sane.

FIRST POLICEMAN: I'd like to make sure of that for you. You're under arrest.

SECOND POLICEMAN: Don't try to resist. You'll get shot trying to escape.

KARL THOMAS: Let me go.

FIRST POLICEMAN: Just the opposite. Be glad that we're protecting you. The people would lynch you.

SECOND POLICEMAN: Do you admit that you shot the Minister?

KARL THOMAS: Me?

FIRST POLICEMAN: Yes, you.

SECOND POLICEMAN: Come on, to the police station.

Blackout.

Shouts from a crowd of people are heard.

Scene 2

[After sounds of many ringing telephones and an alarm during blackout, the top left compartment and bottom right compartments were lit, probably in that order, to show COUNT LANDE, *top left, telephoning the* CHIEF OF POLICE, *bottom right. This underlined the complicity between him and the police and echoed the secret telephone line between Chancellor Ebert and General Groener. Beginning of the scene was rewritten by Piscator, identifying that the conversation was with* COUNT LANDE *and underscoring their secret understanding as they spoke in a kind of shorthand code.]*

Police headquarters
Room of the Chief of Police

CHIEF OF POLICE *at a table. Piercing ring.*

CHIEF OF POLICE: (*On telephone.*) Hello? What's up? … What? … Assassination attempt on Minister Kilman at the Grand Hotel? … The Minister's dead? … Cordon off the Grand Hotel … Clear the streets … A suspect arrested? … Bring him here … I'll wait … (*Hangs up. To* SECRETARY.) Stay here. You must make a transcript. (*Telephones.*) All stations on alert … Thanks … Report any suspicious incidents … From the Left, of course … Crush any demonstrations … That's it …

Meanwhile a POLICEMAN *has come in with* PICKEL.

PICKEL: (*To the* POLICEMAN.) You don't have to hold me like that, sir … Who are you after all? Indeed you live in a big city where there's riff-raff, but nevertheless you should discriminate.

CHIEF OF POLICE: What's up?

POLICEMAN: This man was hanging about in the corridor of the Grand Hotel … Shortly before the assassination he was in the Minister's room. He isn't staying at the Hotel, behaves suspiciously, and cannot account for why …

CHIEF OF POLICE: Good. What is your name?

PICKEL: Indeed my name is Pickel, but nevertheless …

CHIEF OF POLICE: Just answer my questions.

PICKEL: Namely I would like to …

CHIEF OF POLICE: You were in the room of the murdered Minister shortly before the assassination. What did you want there?

PICKEL: I believed he … Indeed, Herr General, I believed the Minister was a man of honour … But nevertheless when I went up to him in the hotel room …

CHIEF OF POLICE: You admit you were involved in the deed? You had a personal grudge against the Minister?

PICKEL: Namely I wanted …

CHIEF OF POLICE: What did you want? Are you an anarchist? Do you belong to an illegal group?

PICKEL: Namely the veterans of the front have … Although I was only behind the lines … to the Soldiers' Union, Herr General.

CHIEF OF POLICE: To the Soldiers' Union? … Can you prove that?

PICKEL: Yes, sir. Here is my membership card.

CHIEF OF POLICE: Aha … Are you a Nationalist? … Therefore … Tell me, why did you murder the Minister?

PICKEL: I believed … I would have gone through fire for him …

CHIEF OF POLICE: Pay attention to my questions.

PICKEL: Namely … I came only on account of the railway … And there I am in the Ministry … And I haven't any more …

CHIEF OF POLICE: To the point.

PICKEL: Oh, Herr General, let me go home. The weather is changing … I could travel now … And my cows … My wife has always said …

Telephone rings.

CHIEF OF POLICE: (*On telephone.*) Police Headquarters … You have interrogated the eye witnesses? … A man in a waiter's tail coat? … One moment … Pickel, take off your coat.

PICKEL: I'm wearing namely …

CHIEF OF POLICE: Frock-coat … Aha …

PICKEL: But nevertheless only because I …

CHIEF OF POLICE: Be quiet. (*On telephone.*) … Thanks … Fräulein, take down Pickel's personal details …

SECRETARY: Your name? Surname and Christian name?

PICKEL: Trustgod Pickel is my name, Fräulein … As a boy my name was Godbeloved … nevertheless my name is really Trustgod … Namely the official at the Registry Office who with my father … as long as they were well, every evening they played …

POLICE DETECTIVE enters.

CHIEF OF POLICE: What's up?

FIRST POLICEMAN: We arrested a man in the park. He was holding a revolver in his hand. Two bullets are missing.

CHIEF OF POLICE: Bring him in.

POLICE DETECTIVE enters with KARL THOMAS.

What is your name?

KARL THOMAS: Karl Thomas.

CHIEF OF POLICE: What did you want with this revolver? …

KARL THOMAS: To shoot the Minister.

CHIEF OF POLICE: Things are going very fast … The second one … So, a confession … Do you belong to Herr Pickel's Soldiers' Union too?

KARL THOMAS: To the Soldiers' Union? …

PICKEL: Herr General, I must point out that our Soldiers' Union in Holzhausen … Indeed we don't after all accept any foreigners … not even anyone from the neighbouring villages … but nevertheless the President of the Reich is an Honorary Member …

CHIEF OF POLICE: Silence … (*To the POLICEMAN.*) What did the man look like then?

SECOND POLICEMAN: The people wanted to lynch him. We could hardly hold the crowds back.

CHIEF OF POLICE: Sit down. Tell me, why did you shoot the Minister?

KARL THOMAS: Is he dead?

CHIEF OF POLICE: Yes.

KARL THOMAS: I didn't shoot.

CHIEF OF POLICE: But you must admit you just confessed …

PICKEL: No, Herr General, you are wrong there. I know him. He is namely a friend of the Minister …

CHIEF OF POLICE: Why are you always interrupting?

PICKEL: Because you don't believe me … I am namely the Treasurer of the Soldiers' Union. And our statutes …

CHIEF OF POLICE: I'll have you removed straight away. (*To KARL THOMAS.*) You saw the Minister as vermin, didn't you? A traitor to his country?

KARL THOMAS: The murderer thought he was.

CHIEF OF POLICE: The murderer?

KARL THOMAS: I chased him. I shot at him.

CHIEF OF POLICE: What kind of crazy nonsense are you talking?

PICKEL: If he says so, Herr General …

POLICE DETECTIVE goes over to the CHIEF OF POLICE, speaks softly with him.

CHIEF OF POLICE: He makes the same impression on me. Moreover the other one, Pickel, also … Hand them both over to Department One. I'll come over straightaway … (*On telephone.*) Connect me with the Public Prosecutor …

PICKEL: Herr General … namely I would like … I would like to ask …

CHIEF OF POLICE: What is it now?

PICKEL: Is it decided, Herr General? Will I be put in prison?

CHIEF OF POLICE: Yes.

PICKEL: Indeed … Then … Namely in Holzhausen … And if they hear … And if my wife … And if my neighbour … who is related to the Mayor … And if the Soldiers' Union … Do you know what you are doing? … Now that I am 'previously convicted'. Where can I go, when I come out of prison? Where? I definitely couldn't show my face in Holzhausen again …

CHIEF OF POLICE: If it turns out that you are not guilty, you can go home.

PICKEL: But nevertheless 'previously convicted'.

CHIEF OF POLICE: I have no time. (*On telephone.*) Connect me with the Public Prosecutor.

PICKEL: No time either … White gloves, black gloves … What can one believe in? …

Blackout.

Scene 3

[This scene was cut.]

Room of the Examining Magistrate

EXAMINING MAGISTRATE and CLERK at a table. In front of the table, KARL THOMAS in handcuffs.

EXAMINING MAGISTRATE: You are only making your situation more difficult. Witnesses have testified that in the bar, The Bear, you expressed the intention to murder the Minister.

KARL THOMAS: I don't deny that. But I didn't shoot.

EXAMINING MAGISTRATE: You admit the intention …

KARL THOMAS: The intention, yes.

EXAMINING MAGISTRATE: Have the witness, Rand, brought in.

RAND enters.

Herr Rand, do you know the suspect?

RAND: Very good, sir, yes.

EXAMINING MAGISTRATE: Is this the same man who pocketed your revolver during the attack in the polling station?

RAND: Very good, sir, yes.

EXAMINING MAGISTRATE: Thomas, what do you say to that?

KARL THOMAS: I don't dispute that. But …

RAND: If I might be allowed to express my opinion, the Jews are behind all this.

EXAMINING MAGISTRATE: Haven't you shot the revolver, Rand?

RAND: Very good, sir, no. All the bullets ought to be in the cylinder.

EXAMINING MAGISTRATE: Two are missing. Is this nevertheless your revolver?

RAND: My service revolver, Herr Examining Magistrate.

EXAMINING MAGISTRATE: Do you still want to deny the deed, Thomas? Don't you want to relieve your conscience with a confession?

KARL THOMAS: I have nothing to confess, I did not shoot.

EXAMINING MAGISTRATE: How do you explain the two missing bullets?

KARL THOMAS: I fired at the assassin.

EXAMINING MAGISTRATE: So, fired at the assassin. Now only the great unknown assassin is missing. Do you perhaps know the mysterious culprit who, as you declare, came into the room behind you and shot?

KARL THOMAS: No.

EXAMINING MAGISTRATE: Well then, the famous Herr X.

KARL THOMAS: He was someone on the Right. He said so himself. I chased after him. I thought he would be a comrade.

EXAMINING MAGISTRATE: Don't talk nonsense. Are you trying to cover the traces of your back-room cronies? We know them; this time there's no amnesty. Your closest comrades are behind bars … Have the Head Waiter of the Grand Hotel brought in.

HEAD WAITER enters.

Do you know the suspect?

HEAD WAITER: Yes indeed, sir. He was an assistant waiter at the Grand Hotel. If I had known, sir, that …

EXAMINING MAGISTRATE: Did the suspect call Herr Minister Kilman abusive names?

HEAD WAITER: Yes indeed, sir; he said 'a perfect People's Minister'. No, 'a posh People's Minister', he said.

EXAMINING MAGISTRATE: Thomas, did you say that?

KARL THOMAS: Yes, but I did not shoot.

EXAMINING MAGISTRATE: Have Frau Meller brought in.

FRAU MELLER enters.

You know the suspect?

FRAU MELLER: Yes, he is my friend.

EXAMINING MAGISTRATE: So, your friend. Do you call yourself his … comrade?

FRAU MELLER: Yes.

EXAMINING MAGISTRATE: Did you recommend the suspect to the Head Waiter of the Grand Hotel?

FRAU MELLER: Yes.

EXAMINING MAGISTRATE: The suspect is supposed to have said to you: 'You are all asleep. Someone must be done away with. Then you will awaken.'

FRAU MELLER: No.

EXAMINING MAGISTRATE: Pull yourself together, witness. You are suspected of aiding and abetting. You procured a place for the suspect at the Grand Hotel. The prosecution assumes that this position was only a pretence so that the suspect should get the opportunity to be near the Minister.

FRAU MELLER: If you know better about everything, then, go on, arrest me.

EXAMINING MAGISTRATE: I'm asking you for the last time: did the accused say, Someone must be done away with?

FRAU MELLER: No.

EXAMINING MAGISTRATE: Have the busboy come in.

BUSBOY comes in.

Do you know the accused?

BUSBOY: Thank you, yes. When he had to carry the plates in, he broke one straight away and told me I should hide the pieces so no one could find them.

EXAMINING MAGISTRATE: That is very interesting. Did you do that?

KARL THOMAS: Yes.

EXAMINING MAGISTRATE: That throws a proper light on your character … Pay close attention, boy. Did you hear the suspect say: 'You are all asleep! Someone must be done away with. Then you will awaken'?

BUSBOY: Thank you, yes, and along with that he rolled his eyes and clenched his fists; he looked all bloodthirsty. I've only seen faces like that at the movies. I was shuddering.

EXAMINING MAGISTRATE: What did you do then?

BUSBOY: I … I … I …

EXAMINING MAGISTRATE: You must tell the truth.

BUSBOY: (*Begins to cry, turns away from the* EXAMINING MAGIS-TRATE *to the* HEAD WAITER.) Sir, I won't do it any more, I know I told you I needed to pee, I didn't go to pee at all, I was so tired I laid down under the table and tried to sleep a little … Sir, please don't report me to the boss.

EXAMINING MAGISTRATE: (*Laughing.*) That won't be so serious … Thomas, what do you say to these statements?

KARL THOMAS: That I'm gradually getting the impression that I'm in a madhouse.

EXAMINING MAGISTRATE: I see, in a madhouse. The witnesses may leave. Frau Meller, for the present you are under arrest. Take her away.

Witnesses go.

Bring in Eva Berg, who's under arrest.

EVA BERG is brought in.

Your name is Eva Berg?

EVA BERG: Hello, Karl … Yes.

EXAMINING MAGISTRATE: You are not allowed to speak to the suspect.

EVA BERG: I can't shake hands with him; you must take the handcuffs off first. Why is he handcuffed? Do you think he will escape? Outside there are a dozen warders. Or are you afraid of him? You don't seem to be very brave. Or are you only trying to intimidate him? They'll be disap-pointed, won't they, Karl?

EXAMINING MAGISTRATE: I'll have you taken away at once, if you don't change your tone.

EVA BERG: I don't doubt you can summon up enough courage for that … I'm waiting for you to have enough to set me free.

EXAMINING MAGISTRATE: I am not authorised by the law to do so.

EVA BERG: When it suits you, you hide behind the law. For weeks I've been held in custody. I've only exercised the rights which the constitution grants to everyone. Because public rights are public duties, you would have to resign your judgeship before admitting the law was broken.

EXAMINING MAGISTRATE: I have two questions to put to you. Did the suspect live with you?

EVA BERG: Yes.

EXAMINING MAGISTRATE: Have you had relations with him which are punishable by law?

EVA BERG: What kind of a ridiculous question is that? Do you come from the fifteenth century?

EXAMINING MAGISTRATE: I want to know whether you have had sexual relations with the suspect?

EVA BERG: Will you first explain to me what an unsexual union looks like?

EXAMINING MAGISTRATE: You come from a respectable family … Your father would …

EVA BERG: My family is none of your business. And I consider your question so unrespectable that I would be ashamed of myself if I answered it.

EXAMINING MAGISTRATE: So you refuse to answer the second question … During the time he lived with you, did the suspect express the intention of murdering Minister Kilman?

EVA BERG: Herr Examining Magistrate, I think we know each other from the old days … You chose to remember that … Wouldn't you class a fellow club member and friend who betrayed his comrades as the lowest of the low? Thus your third question is also unrespectable, because you believe in the probability that he said that. But I swear, on that honour which you can neither give nor ever take away from me, Karl Thomas never expressed the intention of murdering Kilman.

EXAMINING MAGISTRATE: Thank you. Take her away.

EVA BERG: Farewell, Karl. Don't give in.

KARL THOMAS: I love you, Eva.

EVA BERG: Even at a moment like this I must not lie to you.

EVA BERG is taken away.

EXAMINING MAGISTRATE: I've learned from your files that you spent eight years in a madhouse. You shall be referred to the Psychiatric Department to ascertain whether you are of sound mind.

Blackout.

Scene 4

The façade transforms into the façade of the Madhouse.
Open:
Examination room

[*This scene was played in the centre compartment of the scaffolding, revealed behind the projection of the façade. Back projection of filing cabinet as before.*]

PROFESSOR LÜDIN: You were referred to me by the Public Prosecutor for psychiatric treatment … Stand still. Pulse normal. Open your shirt. Breathe deeply. Hold it. Heart healthy … Tell me honestly, why did you commit this deed?

KARL THOMAS: I did not shoot.

PROFESSOR LÜDIN: (*Leafing through the files.*) The police first took you for a man who fired the shots for Nationalist motives. They believed a certain Pickel to be your accomplice. The Examining Magistrate came to the conclusion that this supposition was wrong. He takes the view that you belong to a radical left-wing terrorist group … Your like-minded comrades have been arrested … I, mind you, think … Confide in me with full assurance, only your motives interest me.

KARL THOMAS: I have nothing to confess because I am not the culprit.

PROFESSOR LÜDIN: You wanted to avenge yourself, didn't you? You probably believed that the Minister would give you a top position. You saw that your high and mighty comrades, once they sit on top, also only take care of themselves. You felt sold out, betrayed? The world looked different from the picture of it in your head.

KARL THOMAS: I don't need a psychiatrist.

PROFESSOR LÜDIN: You feel sane?

KARL THOMAS: Sound as a bell.

PROFESSOR LÜDIN: Hm. This notion still dominates you? I think I remember that your mother also suffered from this complex.

KARL THOMAS laughs.

Don't laugh. No one is sound as a bell.

Short pause.

KARL THOMAS: Herr Professor!

PROFESSOR LÜDIN: Do you want to confess to me now why you shot? Understand, only the Why interests me. The deed is no concern of mine. Deeds are of no importance. Only motives are important.

KARL THOMAS: I want to tell you everything exactly, Herr Professor. I've lost my bearings. What I experienced … May I tell you, Herr Professor.

PROFESSOR LÜDIN: Begin then.

KARL THOMAS: I must have clarity. The door slammed shut behind me, and when I opened it eight years had passed. A whole century. As you advised me, I first paid a visit to Wilhelm Kilman. Condemned to death like I was. I discovered he was Minister. Wedded to his former enemies.

PROFESSOR LÜDIN: Normal. He was just more cunning than you.

KARL THOMAS: I went to my closest comrade. A man who with just a revolver in his hand repulsed a whole company of Whites, all alone. I heard him say 'One must be able to wait.'

PROFESSOR LÜDIN: Normal.

KARL THOMAS: And at the same time he swore he remained true to the Revolution.

PROFESSOR LÜDIN: Abnormal. But not your fault. He ought to be examined. Probably a mild dementia praecox in a catatonic form.

KARL THOMAS: I was a waiter. For one whole evening. It stank of corruption. The people I worked with found it all in order and were proud of it.

PROFESSOR LÜDIN: Normal. Business is thriving again. Everybody makes money out of it in his own way.

KARL THOMAS: You call that normal? In the hotel I met a banker. They told me he harvests money like hay … What does he get from it? He can't even fill his belly up with delicacies. When the others feed on pheasants, he has to slurp soup, because his stomach is bad. He speculates day and night. What for? What for?

[Distorted mask of BANKER projected middle left.]

Behind the projection, the Private Room in the Hotel lights up.

BANKER: (*On the table telephone.*) Hello! Hello! Stock Exchange? Sell everything! Paints and Potash and Pipes … The assassination of Kilman … Chemical Works shares already fallen about a hundred per cent … What? … Operator! … Fräulein, why did you cut me off? … I'll hold you liable … Ruined by a telephone breakdown … God in heaven!

PROFESSOR LÜDIN: What for? Because he's smart and because he wants to achieve something. Dear friend, the banker whom you saw – I wish I had his fortune – was normal.

BANKER: (*Grinning in the Hotel Room.*) Normal … Normal …

Blackout in Hotel Room.

KARL THOMAS: And the porter at the Grand Hotel? For twelve years he saved a gold piece every week. Twelve years! Then the inflation came. They paid him six hundred million and he couldn't even buy a box of matches with all his savings. But he wasn't cured, he thinks the whole con is unchangeable, today he scrapes and stints on food and then gambles away his last groschen. Is that normal?

[Distorted mask of PORTER projected bottom left.]

Behind the projection, the Staff Room in the Hotel lights up.

PORTER: Who won the Paris race? The beautiful Galatea … A fix! A fix! I put all my savings on Idealist, and that damned jockey goes and breaks his neck … I want to get my stake back! Or else …

PROFESSOR LÜDIN: Nothing venture, nothing gain. The porter at the Grand Hotel, and I lived there once, is absolutely normal.

PORTER: (*In Hotel Room, grinning as he stabs himself with his knife.*) Normal … Normal …

Blackout in Hotel Room.

KARL THOMAS: Perhaps you also call a world normal in which it is possible for the most important inventions, inventions which could make the life of mankind easier, to be destroyed just because some people are frightened they won't make as much money any more?

[*Distorted mask of* RADIO OPERATOR *projected top of centre compartment.*]

Behind the projection, the Radio Station in the Hotel lights up.

RADIO OPERATOR: Attention! Attention! All radio stations of the world! Who will buy my invention? I don't want money. The invention will help everyone, everyone. Silence … No one responds.

PROFESSOR LÜDIN: What's abnormal about that? Life is no meadow in which people dance ring-a-ring-o'-roses and play on pipes of peace. Life is struggle. Might is right. That is absolutely normal!

RADIO OPERATOR: (*In Hotel Room, grinning as he causes a short circuit.*) Normal …

All the rooms of the Hotel light up.

CHORUS OF HOTEL OCCUPANTS: (*In a crouching position, leaning down towards the Examination Room, grinning and nodding.*) Normal! … Normal! …

Explosion in Hotel. Blackout.

KARL THOMAS: How could I have borne this world any longer! … I formed a plan to shock mankind. I was going to shoot the Minister. At the very same moment someone else shot him.

PROFESSOR LÜDIN: Hm.

KARL THOMAS: I called after the culprit. Believed he was a comrade. Wanted to help him. He rejected me. I saw his twisted lips. He screamed at me: 'Because the Minister was a Bolshevik, a revolutionary.'

PROFESSOR LÜDIN: Normal. Relatively so, if this unknown person existed.

KARL THOMAS: Then I shot at the murderer of the same man I myself wanted to murder.

PROFESSOR LÜDIN: Hm.

KARL THOMAS: The fog suddenly lifted. Perhaps the world is not crazy at all. Perhaps I am … Perhaps I am … Perhaps it was all only a crazy dream.

PROFESSOR LÜDIN: What do you want? That's simply the way the world is … Let's go back to your motives. Did you want to get rid of your past with this shot?

KARL THOMAS: Insanity! Insanity!

PROFESSOR LÜDIN: Don't play-act with me. You can't sway an old psychiatrist like that.

KARL THOMAS: Or is there no boundary between madhouse and world these days? Yes, yes … really … The same kind of people who are kept here as mad gallop around outside as normal and are permitted to trample others down.

PROFESSOR LÜDIN: I see …

KARL THOMAS: And you! Do you dare say that you too are normal? You are a madman among madmen.

PROFESSOR LÜDIN: Enough of this strong language now! … Or else I'll have you put in the padded cell. You're just trying to save yourself with the Section for the mentally ill, aren't you?

KARL THOMAS: Do you believe you're alive? You imagine that the world will always stay like it is now!

PROFESSOR LÜDIN: Well you've stayed the same … You still want to change the world, set fire to it, don't you? If nature had not wanted some to eat less than others, there wouldn't be any poverty at all. Whoever achieves what he's capable of needn't go hungry.

KARL THOMAS: Whoever goes hungry needn't eat.

PROFESSOR LÜDIN: With your ideas men would become scroungers and shirkers.

KARL THOMAS: Are you happy with your ideas?

PROFESSOR LÜDIN: What, happiness! You suffer from over-estimating this idea. Chimera! Phobia! The happiness concept sits in your brain like a stagnant reservoir. If you would cherish it for your own sake, that's fair enough. You'd probably write lyric poems full of soul and love blue violets and beautiful maidens … or you'd become a harmless religious sectarian with a mild paraphrenia phantastica complex. But you want to make the world happy.

KARL THOMAS: I don't give a damn about your soul.

PROFESSOR LÜDIN: You undermine every society. Every one! What do you want? To turn the very foundations of life upside down, to create heaven on earth, the Absolute, isn't that it? Delusion! Like infectious poison you act on the weak in spirit, on the masses!

KARL THOMAS: What do you understand about the masses?

PROFESSOR LÜDIN: My collection of specimens opens even the blindest of eyes. The masses, a herd of swine. Cram to the trough when there's something to guzzle. Wallow in muck when their bellies are stuffed. And then every century psychopaths come and promise the herd paradise. The police ought to hand them over to us madhouse doctors at once, instead of watching them go berserk among mankind.

KARL THOMAS: You certainly aren't harmless.

PROFESSOR LÜDIN: It is our mission to protect society from dangerous criminals. You are the arch enemies of every civilisation! You are chaos! You must be neutralised, sterilised, eradicated!

KARL THOMAS: Orderlies! Orderlies!

ORDERLIES enter.

Lock this madman up in the padded cell.

PROFESSOR LÜDIN gives the ORDERLIES a sign, ORDERLIES grab KARL THOMAS.

PROFESSOR LÜDIN: Tomorrow you will be sent back to prison.

Curtain.

[At the end of this act, the Mary Wigman female dance group performed a frenzied Charleston across the stage. They were dressed in black with phosphorescent skeletons painted on their costumes which glowed under the ultraviolet light, eerily commenting on the skull beneath the skin of the Weimar Republic. Screen and gauze were lowered to human height so the Prison could be prepared behind. After the dance, white gauze remained in for projection of façade of prison windows from the front. Back projections of cells on the compartment screens. Captions for the knocking projected on the gauze running left and right and up and down. See the promptbook scene at end.]

Act 5
Scene 1
Prison

For a moment all cells visible. Blackout. Then lights up: ALBERT KROLL's cell.

ALBERT KROLL: *(Knocks on adjoining cell.)* Who is there?

Lights up: EVA BERG's cell.

EVA BERG: *(Knocks.)* Eva Berg.
ALBERT KROLL: *(Knocks.)* You too? …
EVA BERG: *(Knocks.)* Early today.
ALBERT KROLL: *(Knocks.)* And the others?
EVA BERG: *(Knocks.)* All arrested. Why did Karl do it?
ALBERT KROLL: *(Knocks.)* He says no, he didn't. Where is Karl?
EVA BERG: *(Knocks.)* Maybe Mother Meller knows.
ALBERT KROLL: *(Knocks.)* Mother Meller? Is she here too?
EVA BERG: *(Knocks.)* Yes. Above me. Wait, I'll knock.

Noise at ALBERT KROLL's door.

ALBERT KROLL: *(Knocks.)* Look out! Someone's coming.

ALBERT KROLL's door creaks open. RAND enters.

RAND: Soup … Eat quick. Today is Sunday.
ALBERT KROLL: Oh, it's you.
RAND: Yes, I'm a prison officer again. You have something firm under your feet … Well, now I have you all together again. Except Kilman. They're dedicating a memorial to him today.
ALBERT KROLL: Really?
RAND: Kilman was the only one among you worth anything, you have to admit that. I always said so.
ALBERT KROLL: *(Eats.)* Muck.
RAND: Doesn't the soup taste good to you? There's roast pork at Christmas. Be patient until then.
ALBERT KROLL: Tell me, is Karl Thomas here too?
RAND: Since yesterday evening … What a life he's got behind him …

RAND leaves.

ALBERT KROLL: *(Knocks.)* Now, Eva.
EVA BERG: *(Knocks.)* Where is Karl?

KNOCKING EVERYWHERE: Where is Karl?

Blackout in cells. Lights up: KARL THOMAS's cell.

KARL THOMAS: Waiting again … waiting … waiting …

Lights up: FRAU MELLER's cell.

FRAU MELLER: *(Knocks.)* Where is Karl?
KARL THOMAS: *(Knocks.)* Here … Who are you?
FRAU MELLER: *(Knocks.)* Mother Meller.
KARL THOMAS: *(Knocks.)* What? Old Mother Meller. *(Knocks.)* Who else is here?
FRAU MELLER: *(Knocks.)* All of us … Eva … Albert … And the others … On account of the assassination. We are with you, dear boy …
KARL THOMAS: *(Knocks.)* Do you still remember eight years ago?
FRAU MELLER: *(Knocks.)* I don't really understand what you have done … But I'll stick with you …

Blackout in FRAU MELLER's cell.

KARL THOMAS: *(Knocks.)* Listen now! …

Lights up: PRISONER's cell.

PRISONER N: *(Knocks.)* Not so loud … Think of the rules … You'll hurt us …
KARL THOMAS: *(Knocks.)* Who are you?
PRISONER N: *(Knocks.)* If you keep on like that, there's no hope left for us. I won't answer anymore …

Blackout in PRISONER's cell.

KARL THOMAS: Ah, it's you … You're here again too? … I thought you were death! … Are you all here again? … All here again … Is it really so? … The dance is beginning again? Waiting again, waiting, waiting … I can't … Don't you see? … What are you doing? … Go on, resist! … No one hears, no one hears, no one … We speak and hear each other not … We hate and see each other not … We love and know each other not … We murder and feel each other not … Must it always, always, be like this? … You, will I never understand you? … You, will you never comprehend me? … No! No! No! … Why do you gas, burn and destroy the earth? … Is everything forgotten? … Everything in vain? … Then keep on spinning on your merry-go-round, dance, laugh, cry, and copulate – good luck! I'm jumping off … Oh madness of the world! … Where to? Where to? … The stone walls press nearer and nearer … I am freezing … and it is dark … and the glacier of darkness clutches me mercilessly … Where to? Where to? … To the highest mountain … To the highest tree … The Deluge …

[Piscator cut and changed a lot of this speech.]

KARL THOMAS makes a rope out of the sheet, climbs on the stool, fastens the rope to the door hook.

Blackout.

Scene 2

[This scene was cut.]

A group before a covered memorial.

COUNT LANDE: ... and so I present to the people ... this memorial to this outstanding man ... who in dark times ...

Blackout.

Scene 3
Prison

Lights up: ALBERT KROLL's *cell. Noise. Door creaks open,* RAND *enters.*

RAND: Because you were kind to me once, I'll tell you something.

ALBERT KROLL: You don't need to.

RAND: We're not like that. The Ministry of Justice has just telephoned, Thomas is not the murderer. They caught the real one in Switzerland. A student. Just as he was about to be arrested, he shot himself.

ALBERT KROLL: Will we be released straightaway?

RAND: Not today. Today is Sunday ... So I congratulate you, Herr Kroll.

RAND goes.

ALBERT KROLL: (*Knocks.*) Eva! Eva!

Lights up: EVA BERG's *cell.*

EVA BERG: (*Knocks.*) Yes.

ALBERT KROLL: (*Knocks.*) We are free! Rand told me. The real murderer was found.

EVA BERG: Thank goodness! (*Knocks on the other wall of the cell.*) Mother Meller!

Lights up: FRAU MELLER's *cell.*

FRAU MELLER: (*Knocks.*) Yes.

EVA BERG: (*Knocks.*) We are all free. Karl didn't shoot after all. They have the murderer.

FRAU MELLER: (*Knocks on the other wall.*) You, Karl! ... You! ... You! ... You! (*Knocks on the floor.*) Eva, Karl does not answer.

EVA BERG: (*Knocks.*) Knock louder.

FRAU MELLER: (*Knocks.*) Karl! Karl! Karl!

EVA BERG: (*Knocks.*) Albert, Karl doesn't reply.

ALBERT KROLL: (*Knocks.*) Let's all knock. Now it doesn't matter.

They knock. The other prisoners knock too. Silence. The whole prison knocks. Silence.

EVA BERG: He does not answer ...

WARDERS run through the gangways. The cells go dark. Blackout in the prison.

The stage closes.

The End.

Appendix I

In Erwin Piscator's Promptbook, the last scene of the play is given as follows. See *Gesammelte Werke 3* (pp. 325–6).

Lights up:

ALBERT KROLL's *cell.*

Noise. Door creaks open, RAND *enters.*

RAND: Kroll, Kroll, I congratulate you. The Ministry of Justice has just telephoned, Thomas is not the murderer. They caught the real one in Switzerland. A student. Just as he was about to be arrested, he shot himself.

ALBERT KROLL: Will we be released?

RAND: Not today. Today is Sunday ... So I congratulate you, Herr Kroll.

RAND goes.

ALBERT KROLL: (*Knocks.*)

Film

After Rand's exit, moving captions from the front:

From below right to below left:

'Thomas is not the murderer, they have another.'

Below left to first level left:

'Thomas is not the murderer.'

First level left to first level right:

'We are all free. Karl, my boy,

you didn't shoot after all. They have

the murderer. You Karl, you.'

'he does not answer'

'he does not answer'

knocking

knocking

knocking

knocking

(over the whole area)

Film out

They knock

The other prisoners knock too

Silence

Knocking in the whole prison

Silence

RAND: *(Screams.)* Hanged!!

FRAU MELLER: Is it true?

ALBERT KROLL: He shouldn't have done that; no revolutionary dies like that.

EVA BERG: Everyday life destroyed him.

FRAU MELLER: Damned world! – We have to change it.

Curtain.

Erwin Piscator reports in *Das Politische Theater* (Hamburg: Rowohlt, 1963, p. 154), first published in 1929, that the Berlin production ended with this speech:

FRAU MELLER: There is only one choice – hang yourself or change the world.

As the curtain fell, he relates, 'the proletarian youth spontaneously burst into *The Internationale* which, standing, we all sang up to the end'. The play then became the occasion for a stirring political demonstration.

Appendix II

Toller's original, but never published, ending for the play was a different version of Act 4, scene 4, with no Act 5 to follow. Written before his collaboration with Piscator, it exists in printed manuscript form (presumably ready for publication), with later handwritten corrections by Toller, in the possession of John M. Spalek. See *Gesammelte Werke 3* (pp. 318–25).

Act 4
Scene 4

The façade transforms into the façade of the Madhouse.

Open below right to:

Examination room

PROFESSOR LÜDEST: Stand still. Pulse normal. Open your shirt. Breathe deeply. Hold it. Heart healthy … Tell me honestly, why did you commit this deed?

KARL THOMAS: I did not shoot.

PROFESSOR LUDIN: Confide in me.

KARL THOMAS: I have nothing to confess, because I am not the culprit.

PROFESSOR LÜDEST: You wanted to avenge yourself, didn't you? You believed the Minister would give you a top position in the Ministry. You felt betrayed.

KARL THOMAS: You'll torment me until I am really crazy.

PROFESSOR LUDIN: Only your motives interest me.

KARL THOMAS: I don't need a psychiatrist.

PROFESSOR LÜDEST: You feel sane?

KARL THOMAS: Sound as a bell.

PROFESSOR LÜDIN: Very suspicious.

KARL THOMAS laughs.

PROFESSOR LÜDEST: Don't laugh. No one is sound as a bell.

KARL THOMAS: No one?

PROFESSOR LUDIN: With the exception of madhouse doctors who make correct diagnoses.

Short pause.

KARL THOMAS: Professor!

PROFESSOR LÜDIN: Do you want to confess to me now why you shot? Understand, only the Why interests me. The deed is no concern of mine. Deeds are of no importance. Only motives are important.

KARL THOMAS: I want to tell you everything exactly, Herr Professor. I've lost my bearings. What I experienced … May I tell you, Herr Professor?

PROFESSOR LÜDIN: Begin then.

KARL THOMAS: I must have clarity. The door slammed shut behind me, and when I opened it eight years had passed. A whole century. I went out into the world. Life thundered in my head. Every flash of lightning struck me down. As you advised me, I first paid a visit to Wilhelm Kilman. Condemned to death like I was. I discovered he was Minister. Wedded to his former enemies. A profiteering potbelly.

PROFESSOR LÜDIN: Normal. He was just more cunning than you.

KARL THOMAS: I went to my closest comrade. A man who with just a revolver in his hand repulsed a whole company of Whites, all alone. I heard him say: 'One must be able to wait.'

PROFESSOR LÜDIN: Normal.

KARL THOMAS: And at the same time he swore he remained true to the Revolution.

PROFESSOR LÜDIN: Abnormal. But not your fault. He ought to be examined. Probably a mild dementia praecox.

KARL THOMAS: I was a waiter. For one whole evening. I was stewed in a witches' cauldron. It stank of corruption, of lechery, of arrogance, of muck. The people I worked with found it all in order and were proud of it.

PROFESSOR LÜDEST: Normal. Business is thriving again. Everybody makes money out of it in his own way.

KARL THOMAS: I formed a plan to shock mankind out of despicable lethargy. I bought myself a revolver. I wanted to shoot the Minister, the traitor. At the very same moment others shot him.

PROFESSOR LÜDIN: Hm.

KARL THOMAS: I asked one of them, one who didn't yell 'Hurrah', for the reason. I saw his twisted lips move. I heard his voice. Because the Minister was a Bolshevik, a revolutionary, he whispered.

PROFESSOR LÜDIN: Normal. Relatively so, if this unknown person existed.

KARL THOMAS: I wanted to put an end to myself. I wanted to shoot myself. The fog suddenly lifted. Perhaps the world is not crazy at all. Perhaps I am … Perhaps I am …

PROFESSOR LÜDIN: What do you want? Your logic is functioning perfectly. You must drink what you have brewed. Whoever goes over to the masses goes to rack and ruin there.

KARL THOMAS: What do you know about it?

PROFESSOR LÜDIN: You can tell me nothing about the psyche of the masses. My collection of specimens opens even the blindest of eyes. The masses: a herd of swine. Cram to the trough when there's something to guzzle. Wallow in muck when their bellies are stuffed.

KARL THOMAS: To stick a crazy man like you on the world, what a crime! …

PROFESSOR LÜDIN: If you really didn't want to avenge yourself – something I assume as I don't believe in abstract motives and perhaps the real reason is unknown to you – then if we assume you really wanted to 'awaken' mankind with your foolish deed, what did you expect to achieve by that? What should the awakened do? Change the world? My dear fellow, if nature had not wanted some to eat less than others, then there wouldn't be any poverty at all. Whoever achieves what he's capable of needn't go hungry. With your ideas men would become scroungers and shirkers. Nature has organised things most beneficently.

KARL THOMAS: Stop it! My head is splitting.

PROFESSOR LÜDIN: I wish I was as healthy as you. I suffer from gout.

KARL THOMAS: Insanity! Insanity! Insanity!

PROFESSOR LÜDIN: Don't play-act with me. You can't sway an old psychiatrist like that.

KARL THOMAS: You must be cured! You first and foremost!

PROFESSOR LÜDIN: When someone gets stuck in a trap, when it's a matter of life and death, then he finally gives up the heroic pose and tries to save himself with the Section for the mentally ill.

KARL THOMAS: Why did I doubt it? Yes, yes, I am really crazy. How else could I have seen what I saw! …

PROFESSOR LÜDIN: This institution is here for the mad, not for the sane.

KARL THOMAS: Charlatan! You are unmasked as a quack! Charlatan!

PROFESSOR LÜDIN: Right then, I'll show you what the crazy really look like. Then you'll have to stop fooling yourself … Orderly, set up the projector.

On the façade of the Madhouse in the place where the BANKER *and his* SON *sat in the Hotel, a madman can be seen gesticulating. Mask of the* BANKER *distorted into madness.*

Look at the screen. That man up there, formerly a banker, imagines he can command a great boom with one word to all the Stock Exchanges of the world and thus become the richest man in the world.

Behind the projected image, the Private Room of the Hotel lights up. In the Hotel Room:

BANKER: (*On the table telephone.*) Hello! Hello! Stock Exchange! Sell everything! The assassination of Kilman … Paints and Potash and Pipes … Chemical Works shares already fallen about a hundred per cent … What ? … Operator! … Fraülein, why did you cut me off? … I'll hold you liable … Ruined by a telephone breakdown … God in Heaven!

KARL THOMAS: But he is very normal! I saw him in person. Just yesterday evening at the Hotel. A speculator like the dozens and dozens who buy and sell the world for profit.

PROFESSOR LÜDIN: My dear friend, the banker whom you saw – I wish I had his fortune – was normal.

KARL THOMAS: Ha ha ha, normal!

BANKER: (*Grinning in Hotel Room.*) Normal … Normal …

Blackout in Hotel Room.

PROFESSOR LÜDIN: (*To orderly.*) Proceed.

On the façade of the Madhouse in the place where the Staff Room of the Hotel was, a madman can be seen gesticulating. Mask of the PORTER *distorted into madness.*

Type Two. This man went mad in the inflation. He lost his assets. In place of the ten thousand marks he had saved he got fifty million. Because of that he went mad. He is forever scribbling numbers on paper and counting. He wants to get his assets back at any price and imagines that he won first prize in the lottery.

Behind the projected image, the Staff Room of the Hotel lights up.

PORTER: Who won the Paris race? The beautiful Galatea ... A fix! A fix! I put all my savings on Idealist, and that damned jockey goes and breaks his neck ... I want to get my stake back! My stake, I want to get it back!

KARL THOMAS: He is also very normal! I am sure that's the porter of the Grand Hotel!

PROFESSOR LÜDIN: Type Two suffers from mental fixation. The porter of the Grand Hotel, and I lived there once, is absolutely normal.

PORTER: (*Grinning in the Hotel Room.*) Normal ... Normal ...

Blackout in Hotel Room.

PROFESSOR LÜDIN: Proceed.

On the façade of the Madhouse in the place where the Radio Station of the Hotel was, a madman can be seen gesticulating. Mask of the RADIO OPERATOR *distorted into madness.*

Type Three. He suffers from persecution mania. An inventor. He imagines he has invented an apparatus which can distil sugar from wood and is capable, just like Jehovah once was, of feeding all the hungry with wood. The apparatus, he thinks, was destroyed by a sugar beet farmer.

Behind the projected image, the Radio Station in the Hotel lights up.

RADIO OPERATOR: Attention! Attention! All radio stations of the world! Who will buy my invention? I don't want money. The invention will help everyone, everyone. Silence ... No one responds.

KARL THOMAS: He too is normal! He too is normal! That's the Radio Operator from the Grand Hotel! Nobody wanted to buy his invention from him because it serves peace, not war.

PROFESSOR LÜDIN: The Radio Operator at the Grand Hotel is a competent, hard-working official. A little fanciful, because he operates the radio, but otherwise normal!

RADIO OPERATOR: (*Grinning in Hotel Room.*) Normal ... Normal ...

Blackout in Hotel Room.

PROFESSOR LÜDIN: Proceed!

On the façade of the Madhouse in the place where the EXAMINING MAGISTRATE *was in the Prison, a madman can be seen gesticulating. Mask of the* EXAMINING MAGISTRATE *distorted into madness.*

Type Four. A former Public Prosecutor who imagines he is on the trail of all the criminals who have ever committed murder and not been found out. He thinks his nose, unusually developed, can sniff out the very smell of murder.

Behind the projected image, the Examination Room in the Prison lights up.

EXAMINING MAGISTRATE: The circumstantial evidence is perfectly conclusive. Put it on file. Next case ...

KARL THOMAS: The Examining Magistrate! I would have recognised his craziness without you.

PROFESSOR LÜDIN: I can well believe that you'd wish the Examining Magistrate not to be normal.

EXAMINING MAGISTRATE: (*Grinning in the Examination Room.*) Normal ... Normal ...

Blackout in the Examination Room.

PROFESSOR LÜDIN: Proceed!

On the façade of the Madhouse in the place where the Private Room in the Hotel was, a madman can be seen gesticulating. Mask of WILHELM KILMAN *distorted into madness.*

In conclusion the Innocent Type. Formerly a chauffeur. He's fixated on the idea that it's not the motor which drives his car, but that he drives it ... with the horn.

Behind the projected image, the Private Room in the Hotel lights up.

WILHELM KILMAN: The text of my decree will prevent any back-pedalling. Let it be printed. I am proud of it. A milestone of progress.

KARL THOMAS: Yes, I saw him like that at the end, Herr Minister Kilman. But innocent – no!

PROFESSOR LÜDIN: You should not mock your victim, Thomas. I wish we had many men like him. Level-headed, normal.

WILHELM KILMAN: (*Grinning in Hotel Room.*) Normal ... Normal ...

Blackout in Hotel Room. On the façade a Face laughs. Mask of PROFESSOR LÜDIN *distorted into madness.*

KARL THOMAS: (*Speaking to the Face up above.*) And you, are you going crazy too? How do you dare lock up normal men?

PROFESSOR LÜDEST: To whom are you speaking?

KARL THOMAS: (*Speaking to the Face above.*) Just dare say that you too are normal – go on, I'm waiting for your response! Normal ... Normal ...

The Face disappears.

PROFESSOR LÜDIN: No funny business, Thomas. Every psychiatrist knows that trick of speaking to thin air. You would have a happier and more dignified look if you, with free and full repentance, confessed to your crime.

KARL THOMAS: I'm a fool! Now I see the world clearly again. You have turned it into a madhouse. There is no dividing wall between inside here and outside there. The world's become an animal pen in which the sane are trampled down by a small herd of galloping crazies. And that is normal! Ha, ha, ha ...

All the rooms of the Hotel light up.

CHORUS OF HOTEL OCCUPANTS: (*In a crouching position, leaning down towards the Examination Room, nodding.*) Ha, ha, ha! ... Normal! ...

Blackout in Hotel.

PROFESSOR LÜDIN: Nothing can help you. Tomorrow you will be sent to prison. You've caused enough mischief. Now you must take your punishment.

KARL THOMAS: I see everything clearly. In former times we marched under the flag of paradise. Today we have to wear out our boots on earthly roads. You believe you're alive. You're headed for the abyss if you imagine that the world will always stay like it is now.

From outside, a distant song which gradually stops.

Noise of marching men.

PROFESSOR LÜDIN: (*To* ORDERLY.) What is it?

ORDERLY: (*At window.*) A demonstration. The people are demonstrating for the prisoner.

CHORUS FROM OUTSIDE: Support Karl Thomas! Support Karl Thomas!

Then in the street, shown on film, a vast silent crowd of demonstrators.

PROFESSOR LÜDIN: They're starting up again ... You've caused this with your lunatic deed!

KARL THOMAS: Me?

PROFESSOR LÜDIN: Yes, you! Don't play so innocent!

KARL THOMAS: But I have done nothing at all!

Short pause.

But I have done nothing at all!!

Suddenly KARL THOMAS *roars with laughter.*

PROFESSOR LÜDIN: Don't laugh so cynically. Even they can't save your neck.

KARL THOMAS *laughs.*

If you want to see a mass of crazy men, look out the window.

KARL THOMAS *laughs.*

Incurable crazies.

KARL THOMAS *laughs.*

ORDERLY: (*Pointing at* KARL THOMAS.) Professor, I think ...

PROFESSOR LÜDIN: (*Stands still in front of* KARL THOMAS, *observes him for a little while.*) A fit. Take him to the padded cell. To his ... beech wood.

[In German 'beech wood' is Buchenwald which gives a horrific, if unintended, resonance to this ending for the play.]

KARL THOMAS *is led away by the* ORDERLY.

Unfit for life.

While the People march past silently, the stage closes.

Appendix III

In addition to some criticism of Toller's writing style, Piscator gives a table of three endings he claims were considered for *Hoppla, We're Alive!* in *Das Politische Theater* (Hamburg: Rowholt, 1963, p. 148):

The three endings for 'Hoppla'

Arrest	Escape	Arrest
Police Station		Police Station
Transfer to Madhouse	Voluntary return to Prison From conical masks filmic dissolve to officer's chest, crucibles, war pictures, run backwards	Madhouse
Lüdin scene up to: Masses march past	In place of Kilman-mask–Kilman-monument. During Thomas's laughter and the last words a giant cannon appears on film and aims at the audience	Prison (Dialogue by knocking) Thomas hangs himself

It may be that Piscator misremembered here and that what was considered was a voluntary return to the Madhouse. This would make sense of Toller's denial and also of the filmic sequence described here which could have been used for Toller's original final scene.

Appendix IV

Reviewing his works in 1930, Toller wrote as follows about his collaboration with Piscator on *Hoppla, We're Alive!*, a response to Piscator's criticism of him in *The Political Theatre*. See 'Arbeiten', *Gesammelte Werke 1* (pp. 145–7).

From Works

Hoppla, We're Alive! is the name of the first play I wrote 'in freedom'. Once again I was concerned with the collision of a man who is determined to realise the absolute in the here and now with the forces of the time and his contemporaries who either abandon this work of realization from weakness, betrayal and cowardice or prepare for it to come in later days with strength, faith and courage. Karl Thomas doesn't understand either of them, equates their motives and actions and is destroyed. Alienated from true art by that childish American fashion for the 'happy end', many critics and spectators today demand from the playwright something which is not his task at all – that he ought to dismiss them at the end with those silly household sayings which our parents used to have written on sofa cushions, plates and posters for practical guidance, like: 'Always be faithful and honest', 'Ask not what others do, but attend to your own affairs', 'Have a sunny disposition', or as Durus wrote in No. 134 of the *Red Flag*, 1930: 'Let the fresh air of class struggle into the fresh air of nature'. Proletcult officials and arts-section critics on capitalist newspapers, who, from a guilty conscience and an obsession to roam like birds of passage through the newspaper columns, are more preachers of revolution than revolutionary activists, called the end of the drama 'not revolutionary' – and this was repeated many times and will continue to be repeated – because it didn't dismiss them with a little moral tract and the cry: 'Long live political line No. 73'. –

Today I regret that I, swayed by a trend of the times, broke up the architectonics of the original work for the benefit of the architectonics of the direction. The form that I strived for was stronger than that which appeared on the stage. I alone am responsible for that, but I have learned, and today I prefer a director to get too little out of a work than to put too much into it. Moreover, Piscator in Gasbarra's book *The Political Theatre*, really has no reason to complain about me and my style.*

At the time of revising the script I considered three endings as possible, but never the 'voluntary return to prison' which was falsely and unscrupulously attributed to me in the book. In my first version Thomas, who didn't understand the world of 1927, ran to the psychiatrist in the madhouse, discovers in his discussion with the doctor that there are two kinds of dangerous fools: the ones who are held in padded cells and the ones who, as politicians and military men, go berserk against mankind. At that moment he understands his old comrades who carry on with the Idea in the tougher work of everyday life. He wants to leave the madhouse, but because he has understood, because he has connected to reality like a mature man, the psychiatric official will never release him. Now for the first time – and not before when he was a troublesome dreamer – he becomes 'dangerous to the State'!

---

* Or are these sentences, which Piscator proposed in place of those written by me, 'functional, advancing the dramatic action, building the mental tension', in short, do they provide 'the realistic substructure' and 'replace the poetic lyricism' of the author? (p. 147). I quote from Piscator's manuscript:

Scene after the murder of Wilhelm Kilman. Monologue of Karl Thomas:

KARL THOMAS: 'They shot him because he was a revolutionary; I wanted to shoot him because he was a nobody and ended up shooting at his murderer, as if I defended Kilman's henchmen and in so doing had become his friend, brother and comrade again … Only one shift was needed, only one small step, and the liberation of the world from nationalist hatred, degrading class oppression, and rough justice would have been helped to victory. (*In a somewhat raised voice.*) If only, Wilhelm, I weren't unbearably guilty. Albert Kroll, Mother Meller, Eva, guilty, guilty. You there, you down there in the park, guilty, guilty, we and they (*He tries to go on speaking.*) …'

Or:

Last prison scene. Monologue of Karl Thomas:

KARL THOMAS: '… I am awake, so awake that I can see right through you and still would have experienced nothing new …
Oh, the merry-go-round spins and everything begins all over again. Yes, my dear friends, and my enemies, can't you see how the ground is cracking under your feet? Kilman, dead man, celebrated perhaps because of your murder … if you were living, comrade, you could not begin all over again. You, undo it, undo it: tactics, betrayal. Volcanoes, fiery eyes of the earth open, crack open before you. You stand on the edge of a crater. What madness has seized you, to crouch there and stare into the white-hot glow! Save yourselves! Save yourselves! It's rising! In the boiling depths the lava is forming into a dreadful instrument of destruction! It's rising up unstoppably! Its hissing is scornful laughter at your stupidity not to see your solution: divide and rule …'

Nothing at all to be said about the scene which was rehearsed one day and which, as I to my horror was forced to learn from [hearing] the character names, was 'written in' overnight without even asking me.

Appendix V

Herrn
Ernst Toller
Berlin – Grunewald
König Allee 45
10 August 1927

Dear Toller!

After very serious reflection, I sat down yesterday evening and made the attempt to work out the end scenes, just as we presented them to you in rough outlines several times before. After I went through it with Gasbarra this morning, we are both convinced that now the end, from the two shots up to the big Prison scene, has an ongoing dramatic build and that there is no longer any retardation in the dramatic action. The driving forces of each scene are nevertheless so distinct that every possibility is given to bring out at all points again the overall tendency in its full sharpness and forcefulness, without taking anything away from the climax in the Prison.

It strikes me as a main point that Thomas achieves a certain clarity from his last experiences, so that, in the midst of the confusion all around him, he now takes a pause. It must be like a last flash of spiritual strength, before the collapse in Prison takes place. Thus the monologue after the two shots must be written very calmly and clearly and also spoken in the same way. The monologue in the Prison scene picks up from this one. The full inner life of Thomas once again, without phrase-mongering, becomes transparent. It is the last attempt of a man to understand the world and to come to terms with himself.

When Thomas is arrested, his particular kind of madness can be indicated. One must have the feeling that he is already somewhat removed from the situation and also faces his arrest with indifference.

The most controversial point in our debates has probably been the scene before the Examining Magistrate. We have examined the meaning and content of this scene from every point of view and have come to the conclusion that this scene contributes nothing to the onward drive of the action. The characters who appear in it neither undergo a change nor does their legal confrontation possess any dramatic tension. The only reason it mattered to you was to get Thomas back into the Madhouse, in order to symbolically contrast the normal and the abnormal there. It would be a complete mistake to open up a test case about circumstantial evidence here. Only to show that circumstantial evidence doesn't hold up. The scene before the Examining Magistrate would perhaps be better than the scene in Police Headquarters, if the Examining Magistrate was some low down type and the case from the beginning on was handled in such a way that it seemed to the spectator, exactly at this place in the piece, especially abnormal and strange. That is to say, if the scene showed Thomas' environment as such or his character as such in a completely new light. But then, in turn, Lüdin standing face to face with an unchanged Thomas would be eliminated. And consequently the Lüdin scene would be ineffective. But ultimately both, according to the latest version, are not very important before the Prison scene. Above all we must achieve a dramatically effective and unstoppable forward development up to the end.

In the Police Headquarters scene in the dialogue between Count Lande and the Chief, the first assassin must be depicted as explicitly as possible. It is not enough for example to say: 'Young man, speaks literary German, closes his eyes when thinking!' [details almost exactly like those on Toller's 'Wanted Poster' from 1919!] or something similar. But some distinguishing mark must be given by which the Police Chief can be in no doubt whatsoever that he has the assassin described by Count Lande in front of him. Hence we are of the opinion that the student worms his way into the hotel as a waiter, for which Lande gives him the appropriate instructions in the preparation scene. Lande can report that he wears a waiter's tailcoat as a special, external mark, whereby the confusion with Thomas, who is also arrested in a tailcoat, then seems immediately believable.

Furthermore, I've come to think that it is better to have Lande appear in person at Police Headquarters than to have him telephone the Chief of Police, which in such a situation and given the importance of the matter perhaps seems unbelievable. The conversation between Lande and the Chief drafted by me is intentionally allusive and unclearly worded, and in my opinion no longer needs to be translated into Tolleresque literary German. On the other hand, the end of the scene could be even more fully worked out in formal respects.

Your version of the Lüdin scene, my draft aside, suffers from two defects: In his first conversation with Thomas, Lüdin cannot say that no one is sane because later he declares all those people Thomas regards as mad to be normal.

That is in itself a small change. On the other hand, in my opinion the moment of 'normal-normal' still needs to be thought through thoroughly, so that the types in the Hotel really seem mad to the spectator. For the different characters, for example the Porter, both true and false elements of madness are jumbled together. For the Porter, the passion for betting which devours him is mad, if that's the way you want to look at it. On the other hand one can't forget that the

Porter has been a victim of the inflation. If you want to bring in the inflation, then it must be depicted very differently.

For the Banker, as well, you must intensify his mad hunt for money by showing that he (perhaps) can personally make no use whatsoever of the money for himself, possibly hampered by stomach problems. In this way, the absolute emptiness of such a character would be brought out.

Finally, it still hampers the flow of this 'Normal-normal' scene that Thomas states substantially the same thing about the madness of the Hotel occupants that they act out a few seconds later. Thomas must depict much earlier which functions these people could perform normally, for example the Banker as an administrative functionary of the commodities owned by society, as a purposefully and systematically active element. So with this in mind! All the best

Erwin Piscator

(*Der Fall Toller*, pp. 182–5)

Note

1. Friedrich Wolfgang Knellessen, *Agitation auf der Bühne: Das politische Theater der Weimarer Republik*, Emsdetten: Lechte, 1970, and Gunther Rühle, ed., *Theater für die Republik: Im Spiegel der Kritik*, 2 vols, Frankfurt am Main: S. Fischer, 1988.

3.3 THE EXCEPTION AND THE RULE (1930)

Lehrstück

BERTOLT BRECHT

Translated by Ralph Manheim

Bertolt Brecht (1898–1956) *was a dramatist, poet, director and theorist, and is acknowledged by many as the most influential figure of twentieth-century theatre – in Europe, North America and beyond. Born in Augsburg, Bavaria, to middle-class parents, Brecht's early working life was shaped by the combination of a voracious intellect, his experience of the First World War and studying drama at Munich University. His first play,* Baal *(1918), followed an introduction to the work of Frank Wedekind and the influence of expressionism. Relocating to Berlin, and propelled by the culture and attitudes of Weimar Germany (he collaborated during this period with directors such as Erwin Piscator), Brecht's work was increasingly defined by Marxism, particularly the teachings of one of its leading theoreticians, Karl Korsch. However, Brecht's rise to prominence on the Berlin theatre scene (his collaboration with the composer Kurt Weill on* The Threepenny Opera, *1928, was a particular success) left him exposed once the Nazi Party was installed in power in 1932/3. From 1933 to 1947 Brecht lived in exile, initially in Scandinavia and then in the USA. It was during this period that he wrote his major plays, including* Mother Courage and Her Children *(1941). Brecht was repatriated to Soviet-controlled East Berlin in 1949. Along with his second wife, the actress Helene Weigel, he formed the Berliner Ensemble, a company where Brecht could further test his ideas and practices, and which continues to this day to hold Brecht as its primary marker.* The Exception and the Rule *(1930) is part of a sequence of plays known as 'Lehrstück' or 'learning plays', which were foundational to Brecht's theoretical development of 'epic theatre' (see Introduction to Part 3). These plays emphasize the function of learning, pedagogy and participation in the theatre, and the means by which drama can fashion an active (rather than passive) form of spectatorship.*

Characters

THE MERCHANT
THE GUIDE
THE COOLIE
THE POLICEMAN
THE INNKEEPER
THE JUDGE
THE COOLIE'S WIFE
THE LEADER OF THE SECOND CARAVAN
TWO ASSOCIATE JUDGES

(Written 1930. Collaborators: E. Burri, E. Hauptmann. First performed (in Hebrew) in August 1938 at Givath Hayyim, Palestine.)

THE PLAYERS:

We are about to tell you
The story of a journey. An exploiter
And two of the exploited are the travellers.
Examine carefully the behaviour of these people:
Find it surprising though not unusual
Inexplicable though normal
Incomprehensible though it is the rule.
Consider even the most insignificant, seemingly simple
Action with distrust. Ask yourselves whether it is necessary
Especially if it is usual.
We ask you expressly to discover
That what happens all the time is not natural.
For to say that something is natural
In such times of bloody confusion
Of ordained disorder, of systematic arbitrariness
Of inhuman humanity is to
Regard it as unchangeable.

1
The Race through the Desert

A small expedition is hurrying through the desert.

THE MERCHANT: (*To his two companions,* THE GUIDE *and* THE COOLIE *who is carrying his baggage.*) Hurry, you lazy mules, two days from now we must be at Han Station. That will give us a whole day's lead. (*To the audience.*) I am Karl Langmann, a merchant. I am going to Urga to conclude arrangements for a concession. My competitors are close behind me. The first comer will get the concession. Thanks to my shrewdness, the energy with which I have overcome all manner of difficulties, and my ruthless treatment of my employees, I have completed this much of the journey in little more than half the usual time. Unfortunately my competitors have been moving just as fast. (*He looks back through binoculars.*) See, there they are at our heels again! (*To* THE GUIDE.) Why don't you drive the porter harder? I hired you to drive him, but you people expect me to pay you to go for a stroll. Have you any idea what this trip is costing me? It's not your money. But if you sabotage me, I'll report you to the employment office in Urga.

THE GUIDE: (*To* THE PORTER.) Try to go faster.

THE MERCHANT: You haven't got the right tone, you'll never be a real guide. I should have taken a more expensive one. They keep gaining on us. Why don't you beat the fellow? I don't approve of beating, but at the present time beating is necessary. If I don't get there first, I'll be ruined. This porter you've taken on is your brother, admit it! He's a relative, that's why you don't beat him. I know you people. You can be brutal when you want to. Beat him,

or I'll discharge you! You can sue for your wages. Good God, they're catching up with us!

THE COOLIE: (*To* THE GUIDE.) Beat me, but not with all your strength, because I'll never get to Han Station if I have to call on all my strength now.

The guide beats THE COOLIE.

(*Cries from the rear.*) Ho there! Is this the way to Urga? Hey, we're friendly! Wait for us!

THE MERCHANT: (*Does not answer or even look back.*) The Devil take you! Forward! I'll drive my men for three days, two days with insults, the third day with promises. When we reach Urga, we'll see. My competitors are still at my heels, but tomorrow I'll march all night, that will lose them, and I'll be in Han Station on the third day, one day sooner than anyone else.

He sings:

Going without sleep gives me a comfortable lead
Driving my men adds that much to my speed.
The weakling falls behind and the strong man wins out.

2
End of the Much-Travelled Road

THE MERCHANT: (*Approaching Han Station.*) This is Han Station. Thank God, I've made it, a day sooner than anyone else. My men are exhausted. Besides, they're angry with me, embittered. Records mean nothing to them. They're not fighters. They're common riff-raff, groundlings. Naturally they don't dare to complain, because thank God there's still the police to keep order.

TWO POLICEMEN *step up*: Everything all right, sir? No complaints about the road? No complaints about your personnel?

THE MERCHANT: Everything is fine. I've made it this far in three days instead of four. The road is a disgrace but what I start I finish. How is the road after Han Station? What comes now?

THE POLICEMEN: Now, sir, comes the uninhabited desert of Yahi.

THE MERCHANT: Is a police escort obtainable?

THE POLICEMEN: (*Continuing on their way.*) No, sir, we are the last police patrol you will see, sir.

3
The Dismissal of the Guide at Han Station

THE GUIDE: Since we spoke to those policemen outside the Station, our merchant has been a changed man. He takes an entirely different tone when speaking to us: he's almost friendly. It has nothing to do with speeding up the journey, because a day of rest wasn't scheduled for this station, the last before the desert of Yahi. The porter is so exhausted I can't imagine how I'll ever get him as far as Urga. Come to think of it, the merchant's friendliness has me worried, I fear he's plotting something against us. He's been pacing about, deep in thought. When he starts thinking, it means trouble. Whatever he thinks of, the porter and I will have to put up with it. Because if we don't, he won't pay us our wages or he'll sack us in the middle of the desert.

THE MERCHANT *approaches*: Have some tobacco. Here's a cigarette paper. You people would go through fire for a good drag. I can't think of anything you wouldn't do to get that smoke in your throats. Thank God we've got plenty. Our tobacco will take us to Urga three times over.

THE GUIDE *takes the tobacco. To himself:* Our tobacco!

THE MERCHANT: Let's sit down, my friend. Why don't you sit down? A trip like this brings two men together. But if you don't want to, of course you may stand. After all, you people have your ways just like everybody else. I don't ordinarily sit down with you and you don't sit down with a porter. The world is built on such distinctions. But we can smoke together. Can't we? (*He laughs.*) That's something I like about you. A kind of dignity. All right, pack everything up. And don't forget the water. I hear there aren't many water-holes in the desert. By the way, my friend, I wanted to warn you: did you notice the way the porter looked at you when you drove him hard? There was a certain something in his eyes that bodes no good. But you'll have to drive him a good deal harder in the next few days, because we'll have to increase our speed if possible. And that fellow's lazy. The country we're going into now is uninhabited, there he may show his true colours. Yes, you're the better man, you earn more, and you don't have to carry anything. Reason enough for

him to hate you. You'd better keep your distance. (*THE GUIDE goes through an open door into an adjoining yard. THE MERCHANT is left sitting alone.*) Funny people.

THE MERCHANT sits in silence. Nearby THE GUIDE supervises THE PORTER who is packing. Then THE GUIDE sits down and smokes. When THE COOLIE has finished, he sits down, THE GUIDE gives him tobacco and a cigarette paper and they begin to talk.

THE COOLIE: The merchant always says it's a benefit to humanity when oil is taken out of the ground. When oil is taken from the ground, there will be railways here and prosperity on all sides. The merchant says there will be railways here. What am I to live on then?

THE GUIDE: Don't worry. There won't be railways as soon as all that. I hear that when they discover oil, they hide it. The man who plugs up the hole where the oil is gets hush money. That's why the merchant is in such a hurry. He doesn't want the oil, he wants the hush money.

THE COOLIE: I don't understand.

THE GUIDE: No one understands.

THE COOLIE: In the desert the going will probably be even harder. I hope my feet hold out.

THE GUIDE: I'm sure they will.

THE COOLIE: Are there bandits?

THE GUIDE: We'll just have to keep a sharp lookout today, on the first day of our journey. All sorts of riffraff collect around the station.

THE COOLIE: And then?

THE GUIDE: Once we leave the River Mir behind us, the main thing is to keep close to the water-holes.

THE COOLIE: You know the way?

THE GUIDE: Yes.

THE MERCHANT has heard them talking. He steps behind the door to listen.

THE COOLIE: Is the River Mir hard to cross?

THE GUIDE: Usually not at this time of year. But when it floods the current is very strong, then it's dangerous.

THE MERCHANT: With the porter he really talks. With him he can sit down! With him he smokes!

THE COOLIE: What do you do then?

THE GUIDE: You often have to wait a week until you can cross without danger.

THE MERCHANT: Listen to that! Now he's advising him to take his time and not to risk his precious life! That fellow is dangerous. He'll try to make things easy for him. He'll throw discipline to the winds. Or worse. I wouldn't put it past him. Come to think of it, it's two against one from now on. Anyway it's plain that he's afraid to get tough with his subordinate now that we're moving into uninhabited territory. No two ways about it. I'll have to get rid of the fellow. (*He goes in and joins the two.*) I told you to check the packing. Now we'll see how you carry out my orders. (*He tugs violently at a strap until it breaks.*)

You call that packing? If the strap breaks, we'll have to stop for twenty-four hours. But that's just what you want: a halt.

THE GUIDE: I don't want a halt. And the strap won't break if nobody tugs it.

THE MERCHANT: What, you dare to contradict me? Did the strap break or didn't it? Are you going to stand there and tell me it didn't break! You're altogether unreliable. I made a mistake in treating you decently, it doesn't do with your kind. I have no use for a guide who can't make the personnel respect him. If you ask me, you ought to be a porter, not a guide. What's more, I have reason to believe you've been giving the personnel ideas.

THE GUIDE: What reason?

THE MERCHANT: You'd like to know, wouldn't you? Well, you're discharged!

THE GUIDE: But you can't discharge me half way.

THE MERCHANT: You'll be lucky if I don't report you to the employment office in Urga. Here are your wages, as of now. (*He calls* THE INNKEEPER *who appears.*) You're a witness: I've paid this man his wages. (*To* THE GUIDE.) I can tell you right now that you'd better not show yourself in Urga. (*Looks him over from head to foot.*) You'll never get anywhere in life. (*He goes into the other room with* THE INNKEEPER.) I'm pushing on immediately. If anything happens to me, you can testify that I left here today with this man. (*Points to* THE COOLIE.)

THE INNKEEPER *indicates with gestures that be understands nothing.*

THE MERCHANT: (*Stunned.*) He doesn't understand. There isn't a soul who'll be able to say where I've gone. And the worst of it is that these scoundrels know it. (*He sits down and writes a letter.*)

THE GUIDE, TO THE COOLIE: I made a mistake in sitting down with you. Watch your step, that's a bad man. (*He gives him his water-bottle.*) Keep this bottle in reserve: hide it. If you get lost – and how can you expect to find the way? – he's sure to take yours. I'll explain the route to you.

THE COOLIE: Better not. He mustn't hear you talking to me: if he sends me away, I'm lost. He wouldn't have to pay me a thing because I'm not in the union like you. I've got to put up with everything.

THE MERCHANT: (*To* THE INNKEEPER.) Give this letter to the men who will be arriving tomorrow and are also on their way to Urga. I'm going on alone with my porter.

THE INNKEEPER: (*Nods and takes the letter.*) But he's not a guide.

THE MERCHANT: (*To himself.*) So he does understand! A minute ago he pretended not to. He knows the score. He doesn't want to be a witness in a thing like this. (*To* THE INNKEEPER, *brusquely.*) Explain the route to Urga to my porter.

THE INNKEEPER *goes out and explains the route to Urga to* THE COOLIE. THE COOLIE *nods his bead many times eagerly.*

THE MERCHANT: I can see that I'm in for a fight.

He takes out his revolver and cleans it. Meanwhile he sings:

The strong man fights and the sick man dies.
Why should the earth give up its oil?
Why should the coolie carry my pack?
Oil means fighting
The earth and the coolie.
And in this fight the rule is:
The strong man fights and the sick man dies.

Ready for the journey be goes into the other yard.

Do you know the way now?
THE COOLIE: Yes, sir.
THE MERCHANT: Let's go, then.

THE MERCHANT *and* THE COOLIE *go out.* THE INNKEEPER *and* THE GUIDE *look after them.*

THE GUIDE: I don't know if my friend really understood. He understood too quickly.

4
Dialogue in a Dangerous Region

THE COOLIE *sings:*

I'm going to the city of Urga
Nothing can block my way to Urga
No bandits will prevent my reaching Urga
The desert won't prevent my reaching Urga
Food is waiting in Urga and pay.

THE MERCHANT: How carefree this coolie is! There are bandits around here, all kinds of riff-raff that collect near the station. And he sings. (*To* THE COOLIE:) I never liked that guide. One minute he was rude, the next he played the lickspittle. That's not an honourable man.
THE COOLIE: Yes, sir. (*He goes on singing.*)

The roads are hard that go to Urga
Oh, I hope my feet will carry me to Urga.
The hardships are endless on the long road to Urga.
Yes, but in Urga there will be rest and pay.

THE MERCHANT: How can you sing and be so cheerful, my friend? Aren't you afraid of the bandits? I suppose you're thinking that they can only take what isn't yours, because all you have to lose belongs to me.
THE COOLIE SINGS:

Also my wife is waiting there in Urga
And my little son is waiting there in Urga
And …

THE MERCHANT: (*Interrupting him.*) I don't care for your singing. We have no reason to sing. You can be heard all the way to Urga. It's practically an invitation to the bandits. You can sing tomorrow, as much as you like.

THE COOLIE: Yes, sir.

THE MERCHANT: (*Who is in the lead.*) He wouldn't defend himself for one second if they took his things away. What would he do? It's his duty to consider my belongings as his own if they're in danger. But he'd never do that. They're a bad lot. And he never says anything. Those are the worst. I can't see into his head. What's he plotting? He's got nothing to laugh about but he laughs. What's he laughing about? Why does he let me go first, for instance? He's the one who knows the way? Where's he leading me anyway? (*He looks round and sees* THE COOLIE *wiping away tracks in the sand with a cloth.*) What are you doing now?

THE COOLIE: I'm wiping away our tracks, sir.

THE MERCHANT: Why are you doing that?

THE COOLIE: On account of the bandits.

THE MERCHANT: Oh, on account of the bandits. But I want people to see where you've led me. Where are you leading me anyway? You go first! (*They go on in silence.* THE MERCHANT *to himself.*) It really is very easy to see the tracks in this sand. Actually it would be a good idea to wipe our tracks away.

5
By the Raging Torrent

THE COOLIE: We haven't come the right way, sir. That's the Mir River we're looking at. It's not usually hard to cross at this time of year, but when it floods, the current is very strong and then it's dangerous. It's flooding now.

THE MERCHANT: We've got to cross.

THE COOLIE: You often have to wait a week before you can cross safely. It's dangerous now.

THE MERCHANT: We'll see about that. We can't wait a single day.

THE COOLIE: Then we must look for a ford, or a boat.

THE MERCHANT: That would take too long.

THE COOLIE: But I'm a very poor swimmer.

THE MERCHANT: The water isn't so deep.

THE COOLIE: (*Puts in a stick.*) It's above my head.

THE MERCHANT: Once you're in the water, you'll swim. Because you've got to. What you lack is an overall grasp of the situation. Why must we go to Urga? You fool, don't you realize that humanity stands to benefit when oil is taken out of the ground? When the oil comes out of the ground, there will be railways around here and prosperity on all sides. There will be bread, clothing … everything. And who's going to do it? We are. Everything depends on this journey of ours. Why, it's as if the eyes of the whole country were on you, one little man. And you shrink back from your duty?

THE COOLIE: (*Has nodded respectfully throughout the speech.*) I don't swim very well.

THE MERCHANT: But I'm risking my life too. (THE COOLIE *nods respectfully.*) I can't understand you. Obsessed with base considerations of gain, you have no interest in reaching Urga as soon as possible; you're more interested in getting there as late as possible, because you're paid by the day. The truth is that you're not interested in the trip but only in the wages.

THE COOLIE: (*Stands hesitating on the bank.*) What should I do?

He sings:

Here is the river.
Swimming across is fraught with danger.
Here on the bank two men are standing.
One wishes to swim, but the other
Falters. Is the one courageous?
Is the other a coward? Across the river
One has business to transact.

After the danger the one man
Relieved sets foot on the conquered far shore.
There he finds new possessions
And eats a good meal.

Out of danger the other steps with both feet
Into the void.
There he faces new danger
Weary and weak. Are they both brave men?
Have they equal wisdom?
Ah! Two men have battled the angry stream
Both cannot be victors.

'We' and 'you and I'
Don't mean the same thing.
We defeat the river
Then *you* defeat *me*.

At least let me rest for half a day. I'm tired from so much carrying. Once I'm rested, I may be able to get across.

THE MERCHANT: I know a better way. I'll stick my revolver in your back. Shall we bet whether you get across? (*He pushes* THE COOLIE *in front of him. To himself.*) My money makes me fear the bandits and forget the river.

He sings:

And so a man gets the better
Of desert and tumultuous stream
And gets the better of himself, of man, and
Thereby gains the oil that is needed.

6
The Camping Place

In the evening THE COOLIE, *whose arm is broken, tries to set up the tent.* THE MERCHANT *sits looking on.*

THE MERCHANT: But I told you you didn't have to pitch the tent today because you broke your arm crossing the river. (THE COOLIE *goes on working in silence.*) If I hadn't pulled you out of the water, you'd have drowned. (THE COOLIE *goes on working.*) I'm not to blame for your accident – that tree-trunk could just as well have hit me – but still, you had this accident while travelling with me. I have very little cash on me, but my bank is in Urga, I'll give you money when we get there.

THE COOLIE: Yes, sir.

THE MERCHANT: That's a curt answer. With every look he shows me that I've wronged him. These coolies are an underhand lot! (*To* THE COOLIE.) You may lie down. (*He moves off and sits down some distance away.*) Naturally his injury means less to him than it does to me. These beggars don't really care whether they're injured or in good health. His kind can't look any further than the next bowl of soup. Sickly by nature, they don't care what happens to them. When we make a botch of something, we throw it away, and they throw themselves away, because they're botched. It takes a first-class product to fight.

He sings:

The strong man fights and the sick man dies
And that's a good thing.
The strong man has his helpers, but no-one helps the weak
And that's a good thing.
Your man is on the skids? Give him that one last kick
For that's a good thing.
The winner will sit him down to beefsteak and pie
That's a good thing.
And the cook will not count those who've died in the fight
He does the right thing.
And the God of things the way they are made lord and slave!
It was a good thing.
And if you're in good you're good; and if you're in bad you're bad
And that's a good thing.

THE COOLIE *has approached him.* THE MERCHANT *sees him and takes fright.*

He's been listening! Halt! Don't move! What do you want?

THE COOLIE: Your tent is ready, sir.

THE MERCHANT: Don't slink around like that in the dark. I don't like it. When somebody's coming, I want to hear his tread. And I like to look a man in the eye when I talk to him. Lie down, stop worrying about me. (THE COOLIE *goes back.*) Stop! You go into the tent! I'll sit here, I'm used to the fresh air. (THE COOLIE *goes into the tent.*) I wish I knew how much of my song he heard. (*Pause.*) What can he be doing now? He's still fiddling around.

THE COOLIE *is seen carefully preparing a sleeping place.*

THE COOLIE: If only he doesn't notice. I can't cut the grass properly with one arm.

THE MERCHANT: I'd be a fool not to take precautions. It's stupid to trust anyone. The man has been injured by me, perhaps for the rest of his life. He has every right to pay me back. And a strong man asleep is no stronger than a weak man asleep. It's a shame that we all have to sleep. Actually I'd be better off sitting in the tent; here in the open I might get sick. But what sickness is as dangerous as a man? For little money he travels with me who have much money. But the journey is equally hard on both of us. When he was tired, he was beaten. When the guide sat down with him, the guide was dismissed. When, perhaps really because of the bandits, he wiped away our tracks in the sand, distrust was shown him. When he showed fear on the river-bank, my revolver was pointed at him. How can I sleep in the same tent as such a man? He can't make me believe that he's willing to put up with all that! I wish I knew what he was plotting in there! (THE COOLIE *is seen peacefully lying down to sleep.*) I'd be a fool to go into that tent.

7
The Shared Water
a

THE MERCHANT: Why are you stopping?

THE COOLIE: The road has stopped, sir.

THE MERCHANT: Hm.

THE COOLIE: If you hit me, sir, don't hit my bad arm. I don't know the way.

THE MERCHANT: But the man at Han Station explained it to you.

THE COOLIE: Yes, sir.

THE MERCHANT: When I asked you if you understood him, you said yes.

THE COOLIE: Yes, sir.

THE MERCHANT: And you hadn't understood?

THE COOLIE: No, sir.

THE MERCHANT: Then why did you say yes?

THE COOLIE: I was afraid you'd send me away. All I know is that I should keep close to the water-holes.

THE MERCHANT: Then keep close to the water-holes.

THE COOLIE: But I don't know where they are.

THE MERCHANT: Keep going! And don't try to put anything over on me. I know you've come this way before.

They go on.

THE COOLIE: Wouldn't it be better if we waited for the party behind us?

THE MERCHANT: No.

They go on.

b

THE MERCHANT: Where do you think you're going? Now we're heading north. East is over there. (THE COOLIE *goes on to the east.*) Stop! What's got into you? (THE COOLIE *stops but doesn't look at* THE MERCHANT.) Why don't you look me in the eye?

THE COOLIE: I thought this was east.

THE MERCHANT: Just wait, you bastard! I'll teach you how to guide me. (*He beats him.*) Now do you know which way is east?

THE COOLIE: (*Howling.*) Not on my arm.

THE MERCHANT: Which way is east?

THE COOLIE: That way.

THE MERCHANT: And where are the water-holes?

THE COOLIE: That way.

THE MERCHANT: (*Beside himself with rage.*) That way? But you were going *that* way?

THE COOLIE: No, sir.

THE MERCHANT: Oh, you weren't going that way? Were you going that way? (*He beats him.*)

THE COOLIE: Yes, sir.

THE MERCHANT: Where are the water-holes? The coolie is silent. (*THE MERCHANT, seemingly calm.*) But you just said you knew where the water-holes were. Do you know? (*THE COOLIE is silent. THE MERCHANT beats him.*) Do you know?

THE COOLIE: Yes.

THE MERCHANT: (*Beats him.*) Do you know?

THE COOLIE: No.

THE MERCHANT: Give me your water-bottle. (*THE COOLIE does so.*) Now I could take the attitude that all the water belongs to me, because you have guided me wrong. But I won't: I'll share the water with you. Take your swallow, and then we'll go on. (*To himself.*) I forgot myself. I shouldn't have beaten him in this situation.

They go on.

c

THE MERCHANT: We've been here before. Look, our tracks.

THE COOLIE: When we were here, we couldn't have been very far off the route.

THE MERCHANT: Pitch the tent. Our bottle is empty. There's nothing in my bottle. (*THE MERCHANT sits down while THE COOLIE pitches the tent. THE MERCHANT drinks secretly from his bottle. To himself.*) I mustn't let him notice that I've still got water. If he does and he has a glimmer of sense in that skull of his, he'll strike me dead. If he comes near me, I'll shoot. (*He draws his revolver and puts it in his lap.*) If we could only get to the last water-hole! It's as if I had a rope around my neck. How long can a man hold out against thirst?

THE COOLIE: I'll have to hand over the bottle the guide gave me at the station. Because if they find us and I'm still alive and he's half dead, they'll put me on trial.

He takes the bottle and goes over toward THE MERCHANT. THE MERCHANT suddenly sees THE COOLIE standing in front of him and doesn't know whether or not THE COOLIE has seen him drinking. THE COOLIE has not seen him drinking. THE COOLIE holds out the bottle in silence. But THE MERCHANT, mistaking the bottle for a big stone and thinking THE COOLIE is enraged and means to hit him with it, utters a loud cry.

THE MERCHANT: Drop that stone! (*And when THE COOLIE, who does not understand, continues to hold out the bottle, THE MERCHANT shoots him dead.*) I was right! You beast! That's what you get.

8
Song of the Courts

Sung by the players as they set the stage for the courtroom scene:

Behind the gangs of bandits
Follow courts and judges.
And when an unoffending man is killed
Judges gather over his remains and accuse the dead.
Over the murdered man's grave
They murder his rights.

The verdicts of the court
Fall like shadows, shadows of sharp knife blades.
Oh, the knife blade is plenty sharp enough! Why does it need
A judge to back it up?

See the birds! Which way are the vultures flying?
The desert had no carrion for them
But the law-courts will give the vultures food a-plenty.
Thither fly the killers. The tormentors
Will be safe there. And there
The thieves hide the loot they call profit, wrapped up neatly
In paper with a law written on it.

9
Courtroom

THE GUIDE and the slain man's widow are already sitting in the courtroom.

THE GUIDE: (*To the widow.*) Are you the widow of the man who was killed? I'm the guide who hired your husband. I've heard you're demanding punishment for the merchant and damages for yourself. I came here at once because I have proof that your husband was killed through no fault of his own. It's right here in my pocket.

THE INNKEEPER: (*To THE GUIDE.*) I hear you have proof in your pocket. I'll give you a piece of advice: let it stay in your pocket.

THE GUIDE: Do you want the coolie's wife to come off empty-handed?

THE INNKEEPER: Do you want to be blacklisted?

THE GUIDE: I'll think about your advice.

The court installs itself. The accused MERCHANT, the members of the second caravan, and THE INNKEEPER all take their places.

THE JUDGE: The court is in session. The dead man's widow has the floor.

THE WIFE: My husband carried this gentleman's luggage through the desert of Yahi. Shortly before the end of the trip the gentleman shot him dead. It won't bring my husband back to life, but all the same I demand that his murderer be punished.

THE JUDGE: You are also demanding damages.

THE WIFE: Yes, because my little boy and I have lost our support.

THE JUDGE: (*To THE WIFE.*) I'm not finding fault with you. Your financial claim does not dishonour you. (*To the second caravan.*) The merchant Karl Langmann's expedition was followed by another expedition which had been joined by the guide dismissed from the first expedition. After its mishap you sighted the first expedition little more than a mile off the track. What did you see when you came to the spot?

THE HEAD OF THE SECOND CARAVAN: The merchant had only a small amount of water left in his bottle and his porter lay dead in the sand.

THE JUDGE: (*To THE MERCHANT.*) Did you shoot the man?

THE MERCHANT: Yes. He attacked me unawares.

THE JUDGE: How did he attack you?

THE MERCHANT: He was going to strike me from behind with a stone.

THE JUDGE: Can you offer any explanation for his attack?

THE MERCHANT: No.

THE JUDGE: Did you drive your man very hard?

THE MERCHANT: No.

THE JUDGE: Is the discharged guide who was with the expedition on the first leg of the journey present?

THE GUIDE: Present.

THE JUDGE: Tell us what you know.

THE GUIDE: As far as I knew, the merchant wished to reach Urga as quickly as possible because of a concession.

THE JUDGE: (*To THE LEADER OF THE SECOND CARAVAN.*) Did you have the impression that the caravan ahead of you was moving unusually fast?

THE LEADER OF THE SECOND CARAVAN: No, not unusually so. They had a whole day's lead and they kept it.

THE JUDGE: (*To THE MERCHANT.*) Then you must have driven your men?

THE MERCHANT: I didn't drive anyone. That was up to the guide.

THE JUDGE: (*To THE GUIDE.*) Did the accused not tell you expressly to drive the porter harder than usual?

THE GUIDE: I did not drive him harder than usual. If anything, less.

THE JUDGE: Why were you dismissed?

THE GUIDE: Because in the merchant's opinion I was too friendly with the porter.

THE JUDGE: And he didn't want you to be? Did you have the impression that this coolie, to whom you were not supposed to be friendly, was insubordinate?

THE GUIDE: No, he put up with everything because, as he himself told me, he was afraid of losing his job. He wasn't in the union.

THE JUDGE: So he had a lot to put up with? Answer the question. And don't keep thinking about what you're going to say! The truth will out.

THE GUIDE: I was only with them as far as Han Station.

THE INNKEEPER: (*To himself.*) That's it!

THE JUDGE: (*To THE MERCHANT.*) And after that did anything happen that might account for the coolie's attack on you?

THE MERCHANT: No, not on my part.

THE JUDGE: Look here, don't make yourself out to be more innocent than you are. That won't get you anywhere. If you handled your coolie with kid gloves, how do you account for his hatred? Don't you see that you'll have to make his hatred seem credible if you want to make it seem credible that you acted in self-defence. Use your head!

THE MERCHANT: There's something I've got to admit. I hit him once.

THE JUDGE: Aha, and you think once was enough to provoke such hatred in the coolie?

THE MERCHANT: No, I also held my revolver to his back when he didn't want to cross the river. And in crossing the river he broke his arm. I was to blame for that too.

THE JUDGE: (*Smiling.*) In the coolie's opinion.

THE MERCHANT: (*Likewise smiling.*) Of course. Actually I pulled him out.

THE JUDGE: You see. After the guide had been dismissed, you gave the coolie reason to hate you. And before? (*Emphatically to THE GUIDE.*) Admit the man hated the merchant. When you think it over, it's as plain as day. It's easy enough to see that a man who is badly paid, who is brutally driven into danger, who even suffers injury to his health for another man's advantage and risks his life for next to nothing, will hate that other man.

THE GUIDE: He didn't hate him.

THE JUDGE: Now we shall hear the innkeeper of Han Station. Perhaps he can tell us something that will throw light on the merchant's relations with his personnel. (*To THE INNKEEPER.*) How did the merchant treat his men?

THE INNKEEPER: Well.

THE JUDGE: Do you wish me to clear the court? Do you think it will hurt your business if you tell the truth?

THE INNKEEPER: No, in the present case it is not necessary.

THE JUDGE: As you will.

THE INNKEEPER: He even gave the guide tobacco and paid him his full wages without a question. The coolie was well treated too.

THE JUDGE: Your station is the last police post on this route?

THE INNKEEPER: Yes. Then comes the uninhabited desert of Yahi.

THE JUDGE: I see. Then the merchant's friendliness was dictated by the circumstances, on a short-term basis no doubt, a tactical friendliness, so to speak. That's how it was in the war. Our officers made a point of treating the men more humanely as we came closer to the front. Such friendliness obviously doesn't mean a thing.

THE MERCHANT: Another thing: he kept singing as he went

along. But after I threatened him with my revolver to make him cross the river, I never heard him sing again.

THE JUDGE: In other words he was thoroughly embittered. Quite understandable. It takes me back to the war again. It was only natural that the common soldiers should say to us officers: You're fighting your war and we're fighting your war! The coolie might perfectly well have said to the merchant: You're attending to your business and I'm attending to your business.

THE MERCHANT: I have another admission to make. When we got lost, I shared one bottle of water with him, but I started to drink the second by myself.

THE JUDGE: Did he see you drinking?

THE MERCHANT: I supposed he had when he came toward me with a stone in his hand. I knew he hated me. Once we had entered the uninhabited zone, I was on my guard day and night. I was obliged to assume that he'd attack me at the first opportunity. If I hadn't killed him, he would have killed me.

THE WIDOW: I wish to say something. He could not have attacked him. He never attacked anyone.

THE GUIDE: Be still. I have the proof of his innocence in my pocket.

THE JUDGE: Was the stone with which the coolie threatened you found?

THE LEADER OF THE SECOND CARAVAN: This man – (*He indicates* THE GUIDE.) – took it out of the dead man's hand.

THE GUIDE shows him the bottle.

THE JUDGE: Is this the stone? Do you recognise it?

THE MERCHANT: Yes, that is the stone.

THE GUIDE: Now see what's in the stone. (*He pours water from it.*)

FIRST ASSOCIATE JUDGE: It's a water-bottle, not a stone. He was offering you water.

SECOND ASSOCIATE JUDGE: It looks as if he didn't mean to hit him at all.

THE GUIDE: (*Embraces the widow.*) You see, I've proved it: he was innocent. And I've been able to prove it, which doesn't happen very often. You see, before he left the last station I gave him this bottle; the innkeeper was a witness, and this is my bottle.

THE INNKEEPER: (*To himself.*) The fool! Now he's lost too!

THE JUDGE: That can't be the truth. (*To* THE MERCHANT.) It seems he was offering you water!

THE MERCHANT: It must have been a stone.

THE JUDGE: No, it was not a stone. You can see it was a water-bottle.

THE MERCHANT: But how was I to suppose it was a water-bottle? The man had no reason to offer me water. I wasn't his friend.

THE GUIDE: But he gave him water.

THE JUDGE: But why did he give him water? Why?

THE GUIDE: He must have thought the merchant was thirsty.

(THE JUDGES *exchange knowing smiles.*) Probably out of kindness. (THE JUDGES *smile again.*) Perhaps out of stupidity, because I believe he bore the merchant no grudge.

THE MERCHANT: Then he must have been very stupid. The man had been injured by me, possibly for the rest of his life. His arm! He had every reason to want to pay me back.

THE GUIDE: He had every reason.

THE MERCHANT: For little money he travelled with me who had much money. But the journey was equally hard on both of us.

THE GUIDE: So he knows that.

THE MERCHANT: When he was tired, he was beaten.

THE GUIDE: And that isn't right?

THE MERCHANT: To suppose the coolie wouldn't strike me dead at the first opportunity would have been to suppose he had no sense.

THE JUDGE: You mean you correctly assumed that the coolie must have something against you. In that case, you have killed a man who was conceivably innocent, but only because you had no way of knowing he was innocent. That happens to our police now and then. They fire into a crowd of perfectly peaceful demonstrators, simply because to them it's inconceivable that those people aren't going to pull them down off their horses and lynch them. Actually those policemen shoot because they're afraid. And their being afraid is a proof of good sense. You mean you had no way of knowing that the coolie was an exception!

THE MERCHANT: We've got to go by the rule, not the exception.

THE JUDGE: That's it: what motive can that coolie have had for giving his tormentor water?

THE GUIDE: No rational motive.

THE JUDGE *SINGS*:

The rule is this: an eye for an eye.
A fool hopes for the happy exception.
A drink from his worst enemy
That's a thing no rational man can expect.

(*To the court*:) We will now deliberate.

The court retires.

THE GUIDE *sings*:

In the system they've put together
Humanity is the exception.
Try to do a generous deed
You'll be the loser.
Fear for the man who shows
A friendly nature!
Hold that man in check
Who has thoughts of giving help
Someone near you is thirsty: make sure you don't see him!
Stop your ears: someone is moaning.
Don't go near that man in need: he wants you to help him!

Woe to him who forgets himself. He
Holds out his cup to a fellow man, and
A wolf drinks.

THE LEADER OF THE SECOND CARAVAN: Aren't you afraid you'll
  never get another job?
THE GUIDE: I had to tell the truth.
THE LEADER OF THE SECOND CARAVAN: (*Smiling.*) Oh, if you
  had to …

The court returns.

THE JUDGE: (*To* THE MERCHANT.) The court wishes to ask you
  one more question. Had you anything to gain by shooting
  the coolie?
THE MERCHANT: On the contrary. I needed him for the
  business I was planning in Urga. He was carrying the
  maps and charts I needed. I was unable to carry my
  baggage by myself.
THE JUDGE: Then you didn't do your business in Urga?
THE MERCHANT: Of course not. I was too late. I'm ruined.
THE JUDGE: Now I will deliver the verdict. The court accepts
  as proven that the coolie approached his master not
  with a stone but with a water-bottle. But even if this is
  granted, is it not more likely that the coolie was going
  to strike his master with the water-bottle than that he
  was going to give him water. The porter belonged to a
  class that has good reason to feel discriminated against.
  For a man of the porter's kind it was only reasonable to
  defend himself against an unfair division of the water. Nay
  more, men of his kind with their limited and one-sided
  approach to things, their inability to look deeper than

reality, must inevitably regard it as right and just to avenge
themselves on their tormentors. On the day of reckoning
they stand only to gain. The merchant did not belong to
the same class as his porter. He had to be prepared for
the worst from him. The merchant could not believe
in an act of friendship on the part of a porter whom he
had admittedly tormented. Common-sense told him he
was seriously threatened. The uninhabited character of
the region was bound to inspire him with alarm. The
absence of police and law courts made it possible for his
employee to extort his share of the drinking water and
encouraged him to do so. The accused therefore acted
in legitimate self-defence, regardless of whether he was
threatened or only had reason to feel threatened. Under
the circumstances he had reason to feel threatened. The
accused is therefore acquitted, the complaint of the dead
man's widow is dismissed.

THE PLAYERS:

So ends
The story of a journey.
You have heard and you have seen.
You have seen what happens time and time again.
But this we ask of you:
What is not strange, find it disquieting!
What is usual, find it inexplicable!
What is customary, let it astound you.
What is the rule, recognise it to be an abuse
And where you have recognised abuse
Do something about it!

3.4 MEERUT (1933)

THE WORKERS' THEATRE MOVEMENT

The British Workers' Theatre Movement or WTM (1926–35), *along with contemporaneous 'Workers' Theatres' in Soviet Russia, Germany and the USA, was one of the most unique, expansive and influential 'political theatre' movements of the twentieth century. The First World War refashioned the social, political and cultural landscape, and the 1917 Russian Revolution provided a beacon for a new working-class consciousness. It was in this context that the WTM – directly aligned with the Communist Party – emerged. The WTM rejected, almost wholesale, the forms and structures of mainstream dramaturgical and theatre practice. Rather, to dramatize 'class struggle' in a productive manner for working-class audiences meant an emphasis on directness, sometimes satire, and particularly 'agitprop' (see Introduction to Part 3).* Meerut *is a play that demonstrates the range and dynamic of the WTM's work. Its subject, striking workers in British India, emphasizes how 'class struggle' needs to be understood and fought internationally, not only on local/national terms. Also, the brevity of* Meerut *and the minimal requirements in terms of props and setting illustrate how it could be performed straightforwardly at meetings, rallies, even on the street. At the height of its activities there were over 100 WTM groups operating in Britain. Although the WTM was in sharp decline by the mid-1930s, it would have a strong influence on the playwriting and theatre practices of such figures as Joan Littlewood, John McGrath and David Edgar.*

Notes

The players use six poles to make prison bars, and between them support these in such a way that three are held vertically and three horizontally. The 'cell' should be made quickly, after running on. This needs much rehearsal. This is a highly dramatic sketch, and the intensity must not be lost for a moment. Those players not actually speaking must look dejected, indignant, as occasion demands, but never relax.

ALL: Murder! Murder! MURDER! MURDER!

FIRST: In every state in British India, police and troops are out, to crush the rising tide of revolt against our vile conditions – long hours in the mines and mills! Exhausted by our labours! Our British taskmasters stand over us with whips to drive us harder – for what? The average wage for all workers and peasants is less than a shilling a day in India – the brightest jewel in Britain's crown.

SECOND: In Bengal mines are 35,000 women, working UNDERGROUND – forced to take their children with them from their hovels of sun-baked mud – to die by their sides as they work. Their parents are forced to sell their children into marriage – to sell them into prostitution to contract venereal disease – to sell them into death! In British India 10,000,000 workers and peasants die yearly of forced famine, forced starvation, forced disease. The race is dying under British rule.

ALL: MUST WE NOT REVOLT?

THIRD: The Government denies us education, and when, as in England, in Germany and France, in America – in every capitalist state in the world – they sought to drive us harder by wage-cuts and speed-up, throwing more and more of us on to the streets –

ALL: WE REVOLTED!

FOURTH: They foster our religious differences in order to divide us, so that they can extract their millions yearly in profits and taxation.

SECOND: They send you here with arms, saying it is to stop us from flying at each other's throats.

FIFTH: They tell you we are religious maniacs.

ALL: COMRADES, THEY ARE LIARS!

THIRD: In Peshawar they brought out our HINDU brothers, the Gharwali Riflemen, armed to shoot us down – a peaceful MAHOMMEDAN demonstration. They refused to be used to butcher us. THEY WOULD NOT SHOOT! They showed their class solidarity with their brothers of another religion. They handed their rifles over to us – and the hypocrite Macdonald has jailed them for refusing to fly at our throats.

ALL: ALL HONOUR TO THE GHARWELI RIFLEMEN – MORE POWER TO THEIR REVOLT!

FIRST: June 1928, 20,000 workers struck on the East Indian Railway for six shillings a week and the simple right to organize into trade unions. They shot at us as we lay across the lines to stop their blackleg trains. They broke our strike.

ALL: IN BLOOD AND TERROR!

SECOND: Order was maintained for His Majesty the King Emperor, and the strikers went back to even greater misery.

FIFTH: 150,000 workers in Bombay, against 7½ per cent wage-cut and the speed-up; April 1928 …

ALL: A STRIKE!

FIFTH: 150,000, and only 6,000 organized in a trade union, whose leaders tried to betray them. But they built in struggle their *own* Union, the GIRNI KAMCAR – the RED FLAG UNION, 60,000 strong.

FIRST: The police shot at them, their brothers in the Indian Army were forced to shoot them – *your brothers*; your HUSBANDS – YOUR SONS – were sent from England to shoot them, to massacre them, to break their strike.

Figure 18 Workers' Theatre Movement *Meerut* and *How to Produce Meerut* picture from the *Sketch*.

ALL: IN BLOOD AND TERROR!

FIRST: Comrades, YOU let them go. Comrades, THEY ARE STILL GOING. COMRADES, STOP THEM!

ALL: (*Straining one hand each through the bars.*) COMRADES, HANDS ACROSS THE SEA! COMRADES, SOLIDARITY!

SECOND: Against the terror they stood out for six months. The Government saw they could not be beaten *that* way. To gain time the Government set up a Commission to enquire into their conditions. In March 1929, three days before the Commission reported, the workers' leaders all over India were arrested

ALL: AND THROWN INTO MEERUT JAIL.

THIRD: No bail allowed; filthy food in the stifling heat of the Indian summer. Cholera broke out, and two of their fellow-prisoners died before their trial had commenced. In Indian jails, bar fetters are used. In Indian jails, ball chains are used. In Indian jails are 60,000 political prisoners, rotting under British rule.

FIFTH: In Meerut jails were the *real* leaders of the Indian workers and peasants.

FOURTH: Fighters for the freedom of the Indian masses – not hypocrites like Ghandi, who tells us to be patient, for God is watching!

SECOND: Not like Ghandi, who led us in peaceful demonstrations to be shot at and butchered; but comrades who showed us how to fight, how to organize, how to break the bonds of British tyranny.

FIRST: Charged with 'Conspiracy against the King' they were flung into jail by a Conservative Government. The Labour Government kept them there – refused passports to witnesses for the defence. The National Government prolonged their agony. For nearly four years their trial was dragged out.

FIFTH: Comrades, their trial was a mockery – their trial was a farce – to perpetuate the reign of

ALL: BLOOD AND TERROR!

THIRD: Their torture is now crowned with the most revolting sentences. Transportation for ten years – for twelve years! Transportation for life! What does this mean?

ALL: A LIVING DEATH!

FIRST: All the horrors of Devil's Island, all the brutalities of the American chain gang – are as nothing compared with the horrors of India's penal settlements.

SECOND: Thus do the bosses hope to terrify India into submission. Just as the Tsar tried to crush the Russian workers and peasants.

ALL: THE TSAR FAILED – AND THEY TOO WILL FAIL.

FOURTH: Bombay textile workers have already taken their stand, and the workers of Seven Mills have struck –

FIRST: Without strike pay, without support of any kind, the heroic Bombay mill workers have struck – to demand

ALL: THE RELEASE OF THE MEERUT PRISONERS.

THIRD: Workers of Britain, unite *your* power with the Indian toilers. This is your fight. Those who have jailed the workers in India are the men who cut wages and enforce the Means Test in Britain.

FIFTH: Factory workers

SECOND: Housewives

FOURTH: Trade unionists

FIRST: By resolutions

THIRD: Demonstrations

FIRST: By strikes.

ALL: FORCE THE RELEASE OF THE MEERUT PRISONERS (*With hands through the bars.*) – COMRADES, HANDS ACROSS THE SEA! COMRADES, SOLIDARITY!

Swaying from left to right with the rhythm of the appeal.

COMRADES   –   COMRADES   –   COMRADES – COMRADES –

SMASH THE BARS!

As they say this, they fling the bars down.

Figure 19 Red Megaphones production of *Meerut* in Manchester.

How to produce *Meerut* (1933)

It should not be necessary to give reasons advocating the desirability of performing the *Meerut* sketch wherever practicable during the campaign for the release of the prisoners, and the new revised version brings out the class message directly and powerfully.

Four, five or preferably six members can perform this sketch excellently; but despite the sameness of position throughout, an unusually high degree of emotional intensity is necessary. All the members should be strong, vibrant and capable of expressing intense feeling, because of the limits placed on them in regard to lack of movement, change of position, etc. This means that the whole of the response must be obtained by sheer power of emotional appeal through the voice and facial expression – a task calling for the highest degree of acting ability. The sketch is not an easy one and should be tackled only by experienced troupes.

You cannot convey the impression of rigid resistance to imperialist oppression by a weak-kneed effort, however sympathetic the actors may feel. Pretty girlish voices must be cut right out, but a strong feminine voice vibrating with the conviction of the message can be just as effective as a masculine one.

It is important to erect the 'prison bars' in the least possible time. Rehearse this part thoroughly. Let every member have his bar and all line up off stage in single file. When they come on, each takes up his position immediately and knows exactly where to place his pole – so, 1, 2, 3, 4, 5, 6, and the bars are up. And the bars must not be moved from position one inch until the time comes. Wobbling bars look like a prison that is as farcical as the trial. It doesn't matter about the space between the bars being large, as long as the effect is symmetrical. You are not portraying a jail, but symbolizing imprisonment.

Make an effective 'picture' by grouping properly – two kneeling, one half lying, perhaps two standing, but all close together and bursting to get the message through. The mass speaking where it occurs must be as perfect as possible. The sketch opens with the word 'murder' repeated four times. Don't blare this raggedly. Let the leader count four in whispers, then all come in together – softly at first then in crescendo until the last 'MURDER!' really sounds like it. Do this well and you will grip the audience from the beginning, and if this sketch is done properly you won't hear a breath from the audience all through it.

Inflection of the voice is most important. Bitterness, oppression, resistance, triumph of class solidarity, and nearly every emotion is called for in the right place. This sketch offers most unusual opportunities for voice-acting. Take the first speech for instance. Mere statement of fact is not enough. The voice must be pent up with repressed emotion so that the audience *feels* what is being described. And the bitter sarcasm of 'in India – the brightest jewel in Britain's crown' must be made the most of … but not overdone.

The tempo all through the sketch must be quick. As each player finishes his speech the next comes in at once – there is no time to waste – act – act – act – is the message. Mass speaking, as nearly always, must be staccato and clear. Clip the syllables short and the aggregate effect will be words that can be understood.

Get the utmost out of the words – these and your faces are your only means of expression. Understand the full political meaning behind every passage. Mean it. Get it over. Not just by speaking loudly, but by intensity, conviction. If this makes you speak loudly – and it probably will – that's all right in this sketch. But remember contrasts and inflections are much more powerful than one long shout.

When it comes to the mass-speaking line 'and thrown into Meerut Jail' the bars should actually tremble under the bitter emotion of the actors. But don't obviously shake them. Grip them hard and the very intensity of your feelings will do the trick. The same at the finish. 'Comrades – comrades – comrades – comrades – SMASH THE BARS'. As the word is repeated (half an appeal, half a demand) the bars sway ever so slightly from side to side till at the word 'smash' they are flung down. (All the same way, please.) It is a bad mistake to sweep several feet to the left and then to the right. The audience then guesses what's coming and half the dramatic effect of the ending is lost. Just a slight inclination one way and then the other, hardly inches, is all that is needed. If you are tense the effect of strain is conveyed much better this way than by giving an impression that you can do what you like with the bars anyhow. As the bars crash, stand up in a straight line shoulder to shoulder for two or three seconds before going off.

A good effect at 'Comrades – hands across the sea: comrades – solidarity' is to release one hand and put it appealingly through the bars towards the audience. But do be careful to rehearse this sufficiently so that the bars don't topple down when you let one hand go.

All through the sketch, which is quite short, the main things are tempo and emotional intensity. Remember your two media are words and faces. Facial expression is just as important as the words. While one prisoner is speaking, the others must be acting all the time – reflecting the words. Tense, haggard, anxious, determined and other expressions suggest themselves, as the lines progress. Feel the sketch, mean it, and you will convey the message of it in a way that will strike home to the class-consciousness that is latent in even the most reactionary member of your worker-audience.

CHARLIE MANN

3.5 LOVE ON THE DOLE (1934)

RONALD GOW AND WALTER GREENWOOD

Ronald Gow (1897–1993) and *Walter Greenwood (1903–74)*. Gow began his professional life as a teacher and made a number of educational films before moving into writing for theatre and film. Best known for his adaptations, his stage version of Love on the Dole by Walter Greenwood premiered at the Manchester Repertory Theatre in 1934 and starred Wendy Hiller and Cathleen Nesbitt. Greenwood, who wrote the original novel about the effects of poverty and unemployment on his local community while unemployed himself, wrote a number of successful novels, especially in the 1930s, and produced films for the British government during the 1939–45 war. Set contemporaneously in Salford, an area that directly borders Manchester in the once-industrial north of England, Love on the Dole is a passionate examination of the human consequences of mass unemployment and economic depression, including the raising of political consciousness. Both the novel and the play were huge commercial successes in the 1930s. The play's 'gritty realism', particularly in its representation of a disenfranchised youth, anticipates the work of the English 'new wave' dramatists (such as John Osborne and Shelagh Delaney) over twenty years later. Love on the Dole has also been adapted for cinema, television and the musical theatre.

Characters

SALLY HARDCASTLE
MRS HARDCASTLE
LARRY MEATH
HARRY HARDCASTLE
MR HARDCASTLE
MRS JIKE
MRS DORBELL
MRS BULL
A POLICEMAN
HELEN HAWKINS
SAM GRUNDY
AGITATOR
MRS DOYLE
MR DOYLE
CHARLIE

The scenes are laid in Hanky Park, a park of Salford, England.

Act I

The kitchen living-room of the Hardcastles at No. 17 North Street, Hanky Park, a district in a Lancashire manufacturing town. There is a window on the right through which the street can be seen. Above it is the front door, and behind the door is an old dresser. On the left is a kitchen range, and below, in a recess, is the sink. Beside this a door leads to the other part of the house. There is very little furniture, and what there is shows signs of decay and collapse. A plain table has some rickety chairs beside it. Near the fireplace is a rocking-chair, and below the window is a dilapidated sofa. It is important to remember that this is not slum property, but the house of a respectable working man, whose incorrigible snobbery would be aroused if you suggested that North Street was a slum.

SALLY HARDCASTLE, a fine-looking girl of twenty, is ironing clothes, although the greater part of her interest is centred at the moment on events out in the street. The street door is open, and, out of sight and almost out of hearing, a SPEAKER is addressing a meeting. The angry voice of the SPEAKER, accompanied by the noise of the CROWD, suggests the troubled background of the lives of these people. The SPEAKER is saying '– and to find the cost of this present system you have only to look at our own lives and the lives of our parents and their parents. Labour never ending, pawnshops, misery and dirt. No time for anything bright and beautiful. Grey, depressing streets, mile after mile of them –' SALLY goes to the door, listening. As her mother enters she hurries back to her work.

MRS HARDCASTLE enters through the door on the left, carrying a laundry basket. She is a nondescript sort of woman who might have been as pretty as SALLY in her youth, but a losing fight against drudgery and poverty has played havoc with womanly grace and character.

SPEAKER: (*Goes on.*) '– unemployment and pauperdom, that is the legacy of the Industrial Revolution. That is the price we pay for the system. And that is the price you'll go on paying till you waken up to the fact that the remedy's in your own hands. You've got votes – why don't you use them? Why don't you think?'

Some half-hearted applause, and a VOICE says, 'You can't do without capital!' MRS HARDCASTLE removes her apron, hangs it up, and puts on her shawl.

SALLY: Going out, Ma?

MRS HARDCASTLE: Aye.

SALLY: Where to?

MRS HARDCASTLE: I'm taking Mrs Marlowe's washing. She gets that impatient.

SALLY: Look here, Mother, that's too heavy. Let me go.

MRS HARDCASTLE: Nay, you don't. I won't have no daughter o' mine carrying washing in the streets.

SALLY: Don't be daft. Give it to me.

MRS HARDCASTLE: Out of the way, Sally. Besides, I'll be right glad of a walk. (*She looks through the window.*) Is that young Larry Meath spouting on the soap-box yonder?

SALLY: Maybe it is.

MRS HARDCASTLE: Maybe it is! You know well enough it is. Politics, I suppose. Well, I've never seen much good come out of politics yet.

SALLY: Larry Meath's all right.

MRS HARDCASTLE: Aw, well, there's worse things than politics. Keeps 'em out of pubs, anyway.

As MRS HARDCASTLE is going out she meets LARRY MEATH at the door. He stands on one side to let her pass. He is an attractive young man, with a lean, tired face, and big eyes with a vision in them.

LARRY: Good evening, Mrs Hardcastle.

MRS HARDCASTLE: Good evening, Mr Meath.

With a look at SALLY, she goes out with her washing-basket.

LARRY: (*At the door.*) Good evening, Sally.

SALLY: Come in, lad.

She goes to the dresser to get a teacup. Suddenly a MAN appears outside, points a finger at LARRY and shouts, 'You can't do without capital!' and before LARRY can reply he is gone.

(*Returning to the table with the cup.*) That's got you guessing, Larry.

LARRY laughs and comes inside.

I heard you speaking.

LARRY: I didn't know *you* were listening.

SALLY: I can't very well do much else when you hold your meetings on our doorstep.

LARRY: I'm sorry. But the corner of North Street always was the best place for our meetings.

SALLY: Don't worry, I like listening to you.

LARRY: Do you, really?

SALLY: Come on in.

LARRY: (*Laughing.*) Don't tell me I've made a convert.

SALLY: Come on, here's a cup of tea for you.

LARRY: (*Taking the tea and sitting.*) Thanks.

SALLY: I like the way you talk. You can talk all right, but I don't know nothing – (*She corrects herself.*) – I mean, I don't know *anything* about politics. I don't know – it's just that I like to hear you.

During the following scene SALLY continues her work quietly.

LARRY: You know, that's what's wrong with people about here. They don't know anything about politics. Make it easier if they did. The trouble is, they don't seem to want to know.

SALLY: Drink your tea. You look tired.

LARRY: (*With a sigh.*) Um, it's a tough job reforming the world in Hanky Park. Don't you wish sometimes you were out of it, Sal – far away, somewhere else?

SALLY: (*After a pause.*) Aw, what's the use of feeling that way? Where can you go when you've got nothing? I was only thinking today that I've never had a holiday in my life. There's not many gets out of Hanky Park – except through cemetery gates. (*She hangs some socks on the line at the fireplace.*)

LARRY: Sal, when are you coming up on the hills again?

SALLY: (*Faces him.*) Oo, that was grand!

LARRY: And you've never been near us since.

SALLY: Oh, Larry, I never thought I'd ever be going out with you. Isn't it funny – well, you know, us living close by all this time and –?

LARRY: You can blame me for that. Some fellows are blind that way. But when are you coming again? They were asking for you at the Club. (SALLY *is silent.*) If you like it, why don't you come? You're welcome, you know.

SALLY: (*Diffidently.*) I don't like –

LARRY: Don't like what?

SALLY: You paying for me on the train.

LARRY: (*Smiling.*) I can manage that.

SALLY: And the clothes those other girls wore.

LARRY: Do you mean shorts and jerseys?

SALLY: Aye.

LARRY: Well, there's no need to wear them if you don't like them. Besides, they don't suit everybody.

SALLY: But I do like 'em. (*Indignantly.*) *And* they'd suit me, too.

LARRY: Of course – I didn't know – I'm sorry if –

SALLY: I should just think you are! Of course, if you think I haven't got the figure for shorts and things, why don't you say so? (*She hangs pants on the line.*)

LARRY: (*Watches her.*) Sally, I never said – You'd look wonderful in anything.

SALLY: Aw, don't worry. I'm only kidding. Perhaps I'll be getting some extra work at the mill, then I'll be able to buy short trousers and come with you.

LARRY: That'll be great.

SALLY: But I can't promise you fine talk like those other girls. I don't know anything about Bark and Baytoven and that fellow they call G.B.S. Is he a friend of yours?

LARRY: G.B.S.? No, why?

SALLY: From the way they're always telling what G.B.S. said, he must have done a rare lot of talking some time or other.

LARRY: (*Becoming serious.*) Sal, you don't think *I* talk too much?

SALLY: No, you mean no harm, and I like you for it. It's good talk to my way of thinking. If talking'll make Hanky Park a better place, you'll do it.

LARRY: I wonder. It's like butting your head against a stone wall. You know, you can call those men stupid if you like, but you can't help but admire their loyalty. I mean their loyalty to a system that's made 'em what they are. They go on hoping and hoping – and every week there's another hundred of 'em out of work. If they went mad and raised Hell you wouldn't blame 'em, but they're always thinking something's going to turn up. Or are they just asleep? Gosh, that's what I'm afraid of! Waking up suddenly to find they've been done. When people wake up all of a sudden they don't act very reasonably.

SALLY: It'd be a nasty shock to wake up sudden and find you'd been living in Hanky Park all your life.

LARRY: Ach! If we could only have a fresh start all round. The kids in the gutters – the dirt and the smoke and the foul ugliness of it all! Oh, Sal, it gets you and it dopes you and it eats into your heart. And it's going to be a hell of a sight worse yet, what with wage-cuts and all the rest. What's the use of talking to people – they're all too busy with their daft Irish sweeps and their betting – Aw, what does it matter, anyway?

SALLY: Here, lad, don't you get talking that way. What's come over you?

LARRY: I don't know, Sal. (*He looks at her wistfully.*) I think – Since we've –

SALLY: Go on. Let's have it. (*She sits at the table, facing* LARRY.)

LARRY: It's – it's meeting you, Sal. It's made me feel kind of different about things.

SALLY: What things?

LARRY: I'm beginning to realize – Aw, there's something in life for us, isn't there? There's not much fun fighting for other people's lives when your own's slipping away. I tell you, Sal, I want –

SALLY: Want what?

LARRY: It's since that day on the hills, Sal. Seeing you standing there on top of that rock with the white cloud behind you and the sun in your hair.

SALLY: (*Blushing happily.*) It was grand, Larry! And everywhere lovely and clean.

LARRY: I don't know – it makes all I'm fighting for – ideals and politics and all that – it makes it – well, it doesn't seem to matter like it did.

SALLY: You mean I'm interfering?

LARRY: No –

SALLY: I think you'd best forget me standing on that rock, and such-like rubbish. If I'm interfering in what you believe in perhaps you'd better not come here any more.

LARRY: No, Sal! Listen – you mean you believe in what I'm trying to do?

SALLY: Oh, I don't know what you're after, only to make things better. But I know you're a fighter, and that's good enough for me. I don't want to stand in any fellow's way. You're so different from all the others I've known. You don't seem to fit in with Hanky Park, somehow. That's what makes me like you, and that's what makes me – afraid.

LARRY: Afraid of what?

SALLY: (*Rising and taking her cup to the sink.*) I don't know.

LARRY: You're a grand girl, Sal. If you knew how I felt about you – Aw, but what's the use?

SALLY: What's the use of what?

LARRY: You're not laughing at me?

SALLY: No.

LARRY: I mean getting married. Buying furniture on the instalment plan. What can you do on forty-five bob a week?

SALLY: (*Thrilled.*) So you *have* been thinking that way? (*She sits again.*)

LARRY: What do you take me for, Sal?

SALLY: I never thought you cared so much.

LARRY: I haven't thought of much else lately.

SALLY: And I'm always thinking about you, Larry. But I didn't know – there's things you can't believe in – you know, things that make you so happy, you –

LARRY: I know – you want to shout and tell everybody.

SALLY: Yes – or else you want to cry.

LARRY: Lord, Sally, I do love you!

SALLY: And I love *you*, Larry. Only, don't forget, you won't always have me standing on a rock, with clouds, and the sun in my hair –

LARRY: Sally!

SALLY: It's for ever, isn't it, Larry?

SALLY's hand is resting on the table. LARRY seizes it and is about to kiss it, but rises and turns suddenly away to the head of the sofa. SALLY rises.

Why, what's wrong? There's nobody coming.

LARRY: Oh, don't you see? What's the use –

SALLY: But – it was – (*She goes to him.*) Didn't you mean it, Larry? (*She pulls him around to face her.*) Didn't you mean it?

LARRY: Of course I meant it. But let's get it straight. We both want the same thing, only – unless we get it straight in our minds first of all I'm no better than those other fellows. Forty-five bob a week! That's all I get. And look at the way things are at the mill – none of us know when we're going to finish. Is it fair to you, Sal?

SALLY: I'm not a film star, Larry. I can manage as others do.

LARRY: Yes, manage to keep alive. There's something more in life than just living. (*Again turning away from her.*)

SALLY: Do you love me?

LARRY: Would I act this way if I didn't?

SALLY: (*Again pulling him round to face her.*) Do you love me?

LARRY: Of course I love you.

SALLY: Then let's get married.

LARRY: But –

SALLY: I'll get extra work so's we can have more money. I'll – Oh, Larry, I'd do anything for you!

LARRY: I know, Sal, but I think –

SALLY: (*She strokes his hair.*) Don't think so much. Think about *us*. I want you and you want me. That's all there is to it.

LARRY: (*Holding her in his arms.*) Bless you, Sal! When I see you like that, with the red in your cheeks and your eyes lit up – you're like a flower – (*He laughs bitterly.*) – a flower in Hanky Park. A rose growing on a rubbish-heap. Hanky Park – we can't get away from that. It's got us. It gets everybody. But when you're near me like this, Sal, I don't seem to care. Listen, Sal, we're going to fight it, you and me together. We'll be different from the others. We won't go down.

SALLY: I don't want anything else if I've got you. You can't have everything.

LARRY: I'd have to start saving, Sal. But if you'd wait –

SALLY: Wait? Of course I'd wait. Oh, Larry –

They have hardly begun their embrace when whistling is heard in the street. HARRY peeps in at the window.

Aw, there's our Harry. He *would* come just now.

LARRY: Right. I'll be getting along.

SALLY goes to the fire, where she lights a spill (or match), then turns on the gas and lights it. HARRY comes in from the street. He is a slightly built boy of seventeen. He wears blue overalls and a jacket which is much too small for him. SALLY prepares a cup of tea for HARRY.

HARRY: Hullo, Larry!

LARRY: Hullo! How's things, Harry?

HARRY: (*Grinning.*) Fine! How's yourself? (*He looks at SALLY and grins knowingly.*)

LARRY: All right, thanks. Still like that job?

HARRY: Aye – it's great!

LARRY: Ah, well, it's good to be young.

HARRY: I've been put on a machine up at the shop – capstan lathe, they call it. That's what I've wanted all along, and now I've got it. Have you seen the new machines, Larry? By gosh, they're wonderful.

LARRY: Yes, they're wonderful. They only need a lad of your years to work 'em.

SALLY gives tea to HARRY.

But they're not perfect yet, harry.

HARRY: What do you mean, not perfect? You should see the screw-cutting lathe. All you've got to do is to shove the lever over and the machine does the rest.

LARRY: That machine will only be perfect when it turns the lever for itself and Marlowe's can be rid of young Harry Hardcastle.

HARRY: (*Thoughtfully.*) Aye, I know that's coming. They turned another hundred fellows off this morning. But I'm not worrying. Maybe things'll take up. I can do with more than seventeen bob a week, though. Gah! That's a lad's pay and I'm doing a man's work.

LARRY: That's how it is, Harry. The factory wants cheap labour to keep prices down, and the apprentice racket's a good way of getting it. You're in a racket, Harry, only you're in at the wrong end. Nobody'll teach you anything because there's nothing to be learned. When you've served your time and want skilled mechanic's pay, they'll do with you what they did with the hundred out of the machine shop this week. You'll be fired.

SALLY: (*Who has been clearing up the ironing.*) He should have gone to an office when he had the chance. No short time there and holidays paid for.

HARRY: Aw, go on. I don't want no office. That's a sissy's job. It takes a man to do with machinery.

LARRY: Well, it's a grand thing to like your work. I wish we all did. Keep young if you can, Harry.

HARRY: Young! Me? Why, I'm seventeen.

LARRY: Go on!

SALLY: He thinks he's a young Samson. I saw him feeling his muscle the other day like a strong man at the circus.

HARRY: Just you wait. I'll show you one of these days. I'm not staying in Hanky Park all my life.

SALLY looks at LARRY. HARRY looking from one to the other.

What's wrong?

SALLY: Nothing, lad. Except that the same flea's been biting Larry and me, that's all.

HARRY: What flea?

LARRY: The Hanky Park bug, Harry. It's painful when you're young.

HARRY: I don't know what you're talking about.

LARRY: That's all right, Harry. It only bites the healthy ones. Well, good night, Sal. Good night, Harry.

HARRY goes over to the sink with his tea-cup. LARRY opens the door. SALLY goes up to LARRY.

See you tomorrow, Sal.

The presence of HARRY prevents a fonder good night and LARRY goes out. SALLY closes the door and drops to the head of the sofa, looking through the window. HARRY is at the sink in the corner removing his jacket. He washes himself, whistling occasionally.

HARRY: What's Larry after?

SALLY: Nothing particular.

HARRY giggles. SALLY gets the work-basket from the dresser to mend some stockings and sits at the table.

HARRY: (*Washing.*) I'm glad they've put me in the machine shop. There's something about a machine. Power – that's it. All shining new. Makes you feel grand being boss of all that power. Do you feel that way yourself about machinery, Sal?

SALLY: (*Absently.*) Can't say I do.

HARRY: Aw, girls make me sick. You never like the right things. I went into the foundry today. Gosh! But that's a place, if you like. There's a darned big crane and it picks up twenty tons of metal – white hot it is, like a river of fire – and they tip it in moulds, all spitting and splashing like fireworks. Fine place, Marlowe's, and never mind what Larry says. Better than a lousy office any day. (*He makes a big splashing and blowing at the sink.*)

SALLY: You aren't washing your neck, are you?

HARRY: (*Indignant.*) Well, don't I always do?

SALLY: Never seen you do that before.

HARRY: Gah!

SALLY: Must be going to meet a girl. Who is she?

HARRY: Girls make me sick, I tell you! (*He turns away from the sink with his eyes tightly closed and gropes with the soap in his eye.*) Where's the towel?

SALLY: There you are. Beside you.

HARRY finds the towel.

Does Helen Hawkins make you sick?

HARRY: She's different. I mean – you know – *girls*.

SALLY: Oh, I see. What do you want to wear those overalls for when you've finished work?

HARRY: (*Hesitating.*) It's – it's my trousers.

SALLY: What's wrong with your trousers?

HARRY: They're short 'uns.

SALLY: You're still wearing those knickers?

HARRY: (*Throws the towel down and crosses to the table – gloomily.*) I've never had a suit of clothes. Aw, Sal, I do wish you'd say something to Dad about it. I'm tired of asking. And a fellow my age feels soft wearing kids' things.

SALLY: I'll try, but I don't see where the money's coming from.

HARRY: You can pay weekly at Mrs Nattle's.

SALLY: (*Dubiously.*) Your Dad's suit's still at the pawnshop and we're still owing for the rent. (*She laughs.*) It's a funny business.

HARRY: Nothing to laugh at.

SALLY: You wanting long trousers and me wanting shorts.

HARRY: (*Laughs.*) You in shorts! Sally, you're barmy. (*He gets a mirror from the shelf and sets it on the table. Then produces a collar from his pocket.*)

SALLY: You wait. I'll show you.

HARRY makes a derisive noise. He is trying to fit on a collar much too large for him before the mirror.

What are you gawping at yourself for? You're worse than a girl.

HARRY: (*Ingratiatingly.*) Would you like to make this collar fit me, Sal? Go on, you're a good sewer.

SALLY: What's come over you? Wearing collars?

HARRY: Go on, Sal.

SALLY: Ach! I've no time to fool about with collars. I'm too busy.

HARRY: Aw, Sal.

SALLY: Get Helen Hawkins to do it for you.

HARRY: I wanted you to do it, Sal. I didn't want Helen to know that Larry Meath gave it to me.

SALLY: What?

HARRY: Larry Meath gave it to me.

SALLY: (*Pretending unconcern.*) Oh! Larry, was it? Well, you can leave it on the table. Maybe I'll do it later.

HARRY: Thanks, Sal. (*He puts his jacket on, then looks at her curiously.*) I tell you what, Sal, I'm having a threepenny treble every week with Sam Grundy. You know, you put money on a horse and if it wins you put it on another and another. And if I'm lucky I'll buy you those shorts and anything else you want. And *I'll* have a suit of clothes, you know, special measurement, shaped at the waist – (*Holding his jacket tightly to him and looking over his shoulder to see the effect.*) – not one of those ready-to-wear things.

SALLY: You ought to be ashamed of yourself, spending your money on betting, and Sam Grundy, too!

HARRY: (*Puts his scarf on.*) Well, Sam Grundy pays. Bill Higgs made five pounds last week on a shilling double. I'm sick of having nothing to spend. I've no love for Sam Grundy, but I could do with some of his dough.

SALLY: Ach!

HARRY: Aye, you can do anything when you've got the dough. They say he's got women all over the place. Down in Wales, they say, he's got a house where he keeps a woman –

SALLY: That'll do, lad. I know all about it. I wish he'd keep out of *my* road, that's all.

HARRY: (*Aghast.*) Sally –! He ain't –?

SALLY: I can manage Sam Grundy myself, thank you.

HARRY: Hoo! He'd better leave you alone. It makes me feel I'd like to –

SALLY: Hush!

MRS HARDCASTLE returns from her errand, carrying a bundle of washing.

MRS HARDCASTLE: Where's your Dad, Sally?

SALLY: He went out.

MRS HARDCASTLE: Where?

SALLY: He didn't say. Maybe he went to the Free Library to see the papers.

HARRY: Papers! They'll tell him that trade's turning corner again. Gah! Trade's been turning corner ever since I can remember. It's turned wrong corner and got lost. (*Finishing combing his hair, he returns the mirror to its place on the shelf.*)

MRS HARDCASTLE: (*Looking nervously at SALLY.*) I've asked Mrs Jike to come across, Sally.

SALLY: Mrs Jike? What for, Ma?

MRS HARDCASTLE: She's holding a circle – you know, spirits and fortune-telling. I thought she might tell us a bit.

SALLY: Oh, that fortune-telling. You know it's all nonsense.

MRS HARDCASTLE: Maybe it is. And I don't really believe she talks with spirits, same as she says she does. But a bit of nonsense is a comfort sometimes. (*She proceeds to roll up the shirts, etc., in the ironing-blanket.*)

SALLY: That means we'll have Mrs Dorbell and Mrs Bull here as well.

MRS HARDCASTLE: Well, I *did* say they'd be welcome. It makes it more of a party when we're all together. Mrs Jike says spirits won't come unless there's four of you –

HARRY: Huh! If that crowd's coming in here I'm going out. (*He puts on his cap.*)

MRS HARDCASTLE: Harry, run upstairs and fetch that little table down. It's just the thing for spirit meetings.

HARRY: Gar! You're all daft.

MRS HARDCASTLE: Harry! Go on, quick.

He goes, muttering 'Bloomin' spirits!' MRS HARDCASTLE removes the ironing things and begins to lay the tablecloth.

Let's hope your Dad stays out a bit. He doesn't like Mrs Jike and her friends. (*She looks steadily at SALLY.*) Mrs Jike was saying that you and Larry Meath –

SALLY: Interfering cat! Tell her to mind her own business.

MRS HARDCASTLE: I don't think she meant anything. She only said she'd seen him. Yes, he's a nice young man is that Mr Meath. I do like him, I do.

SALLY: (*Eagerly.*) Do you really, Ma?

MRS HARDCASTLE: I do. I reckon he's a gentleman and a credit to the neighbourhood. And I don't care what folks say about Labour men.

SALLY: That Sunday we went up on the hills. We had a grand time. Over mountains as high as you never saw. And he knows the names of all the birds.

MRS HARDCASTLE: Isn't that nice, now. Though I can't see it's much *good* knowing the names of all the birds.

SALLY: Better than knowing the names of horses.

MRS HARDCASTLE: Yes, I suppose eddication is like that – knowing a lot of things as don't really matter.

SALLY: And he paid my fare. I was in a state when I heard the others say the fare was two shillings and me with only tenpence in my purse. I never knew it would be so much. But I think he knew how I was fixed 'cos when I got all bothered, he smiled – you know how he smiles, Ma – well, he smiled like that and said he'd got tickets for both of us and that it was all right. Though he said it different – he wouldn't have done that if he hadn't – didn't –

MRS HARDCASTLE: That's true. When I was a lass it was took for granted that when a lad paid for you to places he meant something serious.

SALLY: There was a girl in the party that made herself free with him. She was trying to rile me, I know. But he didn't take much notice of her and he kept with me all the time – (*She sighs.*) Oh, I love the way he talks. And he's so – so – nice if you know what I mean.

MRS HARDCASTLE: (*Sighing also.*) I know.

SALLY: I never enjoyed myself so much in all my life.

MRS HARDCASTLE: Did he ask you to go again?

SALLY: Yes. He asked me again just now. And – (*She checks herself.*)

MRS HARDCASTLE: What were you going to say?

SALLY: Nothing – only I hope I get some extra work at the mill.

MRS HARDCASTLE: What for?

SALLY: So that I can get an outfit like the rest of the girls. I felt all wrong beside them with their heavy boots and jerseys and short trousers.

MRS HARDCASTLE: Oo –! Short trousers? Our Sally –?

SALLY: They all wear shorts when they go walking on the hills.

MRS HARDCASTLE: You're not thinking –?

SALLY: I am.

MRS HARDCASTLE: Do you think your Dad'd like you to be dressed like that, Sal?

SALLY: Aw, who cares what he thinks. I'll buy 'em and I'll wear 'em. Let him mind his own business.

MRS HARDCASTLE: You ought to be ashamed of yourself. I don't know what lasses are thinking about these days. Once your character was as good as gone when you wore short skirts. But short trousers –! Drat it, here's your Dad.

MR HARDCASTLE passes the window and enters. He is a thick-set miner, with a square-set, reliable face, and hair and moustache turning grey.

HARDCASTLE: (*Closing the door and seeing the cups on the table.*) What's to do, Mother?

MRS HARDCASTLE: I thought you were going to be out tonight, Henery.

HARDCASTLE: I've changed me mind. (*Hanging up his cap and crossing to the rocker.*) It's about all as I have to change. (*He moves the rocker into the best place for reading, under the gas bracket, and produces a newspaper.*)

MRS HARDCASTLE: (*After exchanging looks with SALLY.*) You won't find it very nice with all those clothes hanging up to dry.

HARDCASTLE: All right, Mother. Don't you worry about me. Maybe I'll go out again soon.

MRS HARDCASTLE: (*Relieved.*) Ah!

HARRY enters with a table from upstairs and sets it down in front of the sofa.

HARRY: Here you are, Ma.

HARDCASTLE: What's our Harry doing with yon table?

MRS HARDCASTLE: That? I asked Mrs Jike to come in –

HARDCASTLE: Ach! I thought you were going to take it to the pawnshop. (*He resumes his reading of the newspaper.*)

HARRY: (*Crosses to SALLY.*) Go on, Sal. Ask him now.

SALLY: (*Rises.*) Not now. Better ask him yourself.

She picks up her sewing and goes upstairs.

HARRY: (*By the head of the sofa, with his eye on his father.*) Ma?

MRS HARDCASTLE: (*Above the table.*) Yes?

HARRY: When am I going to have that there new suit?

HARDCASTLE glances up, then reads again.

MRS HARDCASTLE: (*Looks at HARDCASTLE – hesitates; sighing.*) Eh, lad, what can I do? You know Sal's not drawing much, and your Dad's only working three days a week and ain't sure of that –

HARRY: I know, Ma. But I've never had a proper suit yet. And me nearly eighteen.

MRS HARDCASTLE: Your Dad's tired now.

HARRY: Yes, but I'm ashamed to go out on a Sunday in these. And I can't wear short trousers like as if I was a kid. Look at Bill Lindsay and the others. They can have them. Why can't I?

MRS HARDCASTLE: They get 'em from the Clothing Club, Harry, and you know your Dad doesn't like weekly payments.

They both look hopefully at HARDCASTLE.

Let him alone. He's tired.

HARRY: But I don't see –

HARDCASTLE: You'll have to make do with what you've got. It's taking us all our time to live. You'll get one when things buck up.

HARRY: When things buck up! Huh!

HARDCASTLE: It's all very well talking that way. But trade's turning t' corner. Paper says so.

HARRY: I know I'm ashamed to turn the corner in these trousers.

MRS HARDCASTLE: Now, Harry, let your Dad alone.

HARRY: Why can't I have one through the Clothing Club like the others?

HARDCASTLE: (*Sternly.*) I'll tell you why. Because I'm shoving no blasted mill-stone of weekly payments round my neck. What we can't pay for cash down we'll do without. See?

HARRY: The others do it. And here I am working full time and nothing to go out in at week-ends.

HARDCASTLE: Aaach! I've worked all me blasted life, lad, and what have I got? All me clothes at pawnshop to get food to eat.

HARRY tries to speak.

Don't you set me off, now! Don't you set me off!

MRS HARDCASTLE: (*Pleading.*) Now, Harry, please –

HARRY: (*Angrily and almost tearfully.*) Well, I'm sick of it all, I can tell you. Nothing to spend and nothing to wear and me working full time. *Man's* work, that's what I do. And giving up all I earn except a shilling for spending.

HARDCASTLE: (*Flings down his newspaper and jumps up, blazing.*) God almighty! This is a fine life, this is! I come home to rest and what do I get? If it ain't you it's Sally. Why, man, do you think blasted money grows on trees?

MRS HARDCASTLE: Well, the lad's right, Henery. He ain't fit to be seen in the street.

HARDCASTLE: Worked every hour God sent, every day of me life. And what have I to show for it? Every blasted day, every blasted hour, and I'm worse off now than when I was first wed. (*He turns to the mantelpiece and gets a spill.*)

MRS HARDCASTLE: Three pounds! It's a lot of money, Harry.

HARDCASTLE: Huh! Three pounds! (*He produces a pipe.*)

MRS HARDCASTLE: You see, you pay three bob down to begin with and three bob every week for twenty weeks.

HARRY: Can't go out weekdays except in me overalls. And I've to stay in all of Sunday with everybody asking me why I don't come out –

HARDCASTLE: Oh, Missis, for God's sake get him blasted suit. Hell, I'm fair sick of it all, I am! (*He lights his spill and then his pipe.*)

HARRY: (*Fervently.*) Oh, thanks, Dad, thanks –

MRS HARDCASTLE: But, Henery, how are we going to –?

HARDCASTLE: We'll have to manage some way.

MRS HARDCASTLE: Three bob a week –

HARRY: Can I go now, Ma, to the Clothing Club?

HARDCASTLE: Ay, go's quick as you can before I change me mind.

HARRY: (*All smiles.*) Gosh! You don't know how I feel about it. I'm off. So long! (*He picks up his cap and darts out.*)

MRS HARDCASTLE: Henery –

HARDCASTLE: Well?

MRS HARDCASTLE: Do you think you ought to have given in?

HARDCASTLE: What the hell could I do? The lad's right. If I'd had any sense I'd have said 'No.' But I never did have any sense. Besides, he ain't fit to be seen.

MRS HARDCASTLE: I don't know how we're going to pay.

HARDCASTLE: Something else'll have to go, that's all. We'll start with this. (*He knocks out his pipe.*)

MRS HARDCASTLE: Not your pipe, Henery. You can't do without your pipe.

HARDCASTLE: Can't I? We'll see about that. (*He puts his pipe in a vase on the mantel.*)

MRS HARDCASTLE: Makes you that narky when you don't have tobacco.

HARDCASTLE: Well, I'll just have to *be* narky, then. (*He crosses to the door.*) Though I can't feel much worse than I do now. (*He gets his cap.*)

MRS HARDCASTLE: Are you going out?

HARDCASTLE: Aye.

MRS HARDCASTLE: Where are you going?

HARDCASTLE: I'm going to take me brains out and put 'em in cold water.

MRS HARDCASTLE: You're not angry with me, are you?

HARDCASTLE: With you? No. (*He turns to go.*)

MRS HARDCASTLE: Nor with our Harry?

HARDCASTLE: Harry? (*He smiles.*) No, he's a good lad.

MRS HARDCASTLE: Then who *are* you angry with?

HARDCASTLE: (*Looks at her.*) I don't rightly know. That's just it, Mother, I wish I did know. By God! I'd give 'em a piece of my mind.

He goes out. MRS HARDCASTLE *gets tea-things from dresser.*

SALLY: (*Peeping from the door on the left.*) Has Dad gone out?

MRS HARDCASTLE: Yes.

SALLY: Was there a row?

MRS HARDCASTLE: I've seen worse. Your Dad let himself go, but Harry got his trousers in the end. He's gone to the Clothing Club about it now.

SALLY: I suppose I'll have to get extra work at the mill now. And it's goodbye to those shorts of mine.

MRS HARDCASTLE: Ah, well, I can't say that I'm going to worry much about that. There'd be too much talk in North Street with you walking about half-naked.

SALLY: I'd do it to give 'em something to talk about. Gosh! I would!

MRS HARDCASTLE: Now, then, Sally. Don't talk that way. I'd be glad if you could settle down with a young man like Larry Meath. There's so many of the wrong sort waiting about these days.

SALLY: Um. Chance is a fine thing.

MRS HARDCASTLE: Has he never asked you?

SALLY: He has – and he hasn't. But I've asked *him*, though.

MRS HARDCASTLE: (*Shocked.*) Sally!

SALLY: Well, why not? A woman usually asks a man some way or another, though she doesn't always do it with her tongue. I'm one for plain-speaking.

MRS HARDCASTLE: You don't mean to say you *asked* him to marry you?

SALLY: I did.

MRS HARDCASTLE: Eh, Sally, it's not respectable. I *am* ashamed of you. (*Eagerly.*) What did he say?

SALLY: He said we'd have to wait. And he's saving up.

MRS HARDCASTLE: I wonder what the end of it all will be. That's where Mrs Jike can help us, maybe.

SALLY: Oh, that kind of thing's all nonsense.

MRS HARDCASTLE: It ain't all nonsense. Mrs Jike tells fortunes true. She warned Mrs Dorbell when her Willie was going to die, though I must say his cough was something awful at the time.

Two women pass the window, one of them tapping as she passes.

(*She rises.*) There's Mrs Jike now. (*Calling.*) Come in, everybody. (*She opens the door.*)

MRS JIKE *enters.* MRS JIKE *is a tiny woman with a man's cap and a late Victorian bodice and skirt. She talks with a Cockney accent, having been transplanted from London in her youth. She is followed by* MRS DORBELL, *a beshawled, ancient woman with a dewdrop at the end of her hooked, prominent nose.*

MRS JIKE: (*Peeps in.*) Are you in, Missis?

MRS DORBELL: Course she's in – Can't you see her?

MRS HARDCASTLE: Good evening, Mrs Jike, *and* you, Mrs Dorbell. Where's Mrs Bull?

MRS JIKE: We left her having an argument with a lidy. (*She goes to the window.*)

MRS BULL *is heard down the street carrying on a noisy argument.* MRS JIKE *and* MRS DORBELL *watch through the window.*

MRS BULL: (*Off.*) Go on with you! You trombone-playing old faggot. Give your husband his trousers back! Yah! If he'd any guts in him he'd knock your face in –

A VOICE: (*Off.*) Pay your debts! Pay your debts, says me –

MRS BULL: (*As she appears outside the window.*) Yah! You bleeding little gutter rat! (*She arrives at the door. Is about to enter, but turns again for a final insult.*) Aye, and take your face inside. You're blocking the traffic in the street. That'll teach her to argue with me!

MRS BULL, *a large woman, comes in and immediately adopts her politest voice.*

Good evening, Sarah. That Mrs Scodger's getting a bit above herself.

MRS HARDCASTLE: Now sit down, everybody, and make yourselves at home. (*Bringing a chair to the small table.*)

Figure 20 *Love on the Dole*, from the Skipton Little Theatre, Yorkshire, England, in the 1930s.

MRS JIKE: (*To* SALLY.) Well, dearie! I saw you walking out with Mr Meath.

SALLY sits in the rocker and looks at the newspaper.

MRS BULL: Aye, Larry Meath's a fine lad, and that lass o' thine's lucky to have gotten him.

MRS DORBELL: Lucky? I wouldn't like any daughter o' mine to marry a Bolshy. Look what they've done in Russia. Broken up the home life, and nationalizing women. I wouldn't have nobody nationalizing me. (*She scratches herself indignantly.*)

MRS BULL: Shouldn't think there's many as would want to.

MRS JIKE: 'Ere you are, girls. Have a pinch of Birdseye. It'll do you good. (*She hands her snuff-box to* MRS BULL *and* MRS DORBELL.)

MRS HARDCASTLE: I'm brewing a pot of tea. It'll be ready in a minute. How are you, Mrs Bull? Haven't seen you much lately. (*She proceeds to pour five cups of tea.*)

MRS BULL: Eeh! Trade's bad.

MRS HARDCASTLE: I'm sorry. How's that, Mrs Bull?

MRS BULL: Yah! – I don't know what's come over folk these days. I remember the time when hardly a day passed without there was a confinement or a laying-out to be done.

MRS DORBELL: Young 'uns ain't having children the way they should. When I was a girl a woman wasn't a woman till she'd been in childbed ten times, not counting miscarriages.

MRS BULL: Ay! How can they expect a body to make a living when children going to school know more about things than we did after we'd been married years?

MRS JIKE: That's just it.

MRS DORBELL: Things have never been the same since the gentlefolk left the Old Road. Why, if my old Ma was alive today she'd turn over in her grave, that she would.

MRS JIKE: The world's never been the same since the old Queen died.

MRS BULL: What queen do you mean, Mrs Jike?

MRS JIKE: Why, Queen Victoria, of course.

MRS BULL: Oh, 'er!

Cups of tea are passed to MRS DORBELL *and* MRS BULL.

MRS JIKE: When I used to live in London – that was the time. The old Queen 'ud give 'em snuff if she were alive. She would that.

MRS HARDCASTLE hands a cup of tea to MRS JIKE.

Thank you kindly, Mrs Hardcastle. I likes a nice cup o' tea. Would any lidy care to have a drop of this in her tea?

MRS HARDCASTLE gives SALLY *her tea, and stands before fire drinking her own.* MRS JIKE *produces a flat bottle of gin from her stocking.* MRS BULL *and* MRS DORBELL *accept.*

MRS DORBELL: Thank you, Mrs Jike. I don't mind if I do.

MRS DORBELL pours gin in her tea and hands the bottle to MRS BULL, *who helps herself liberally.*

How's your rheumatics, Mrs Bull? (*Critically watching* MRS BULL.)

MRS BULL: I'd be all right, only for a twinge now and again. But I don't worry. There's a rare lot up in the cemetery as 'ud be glad of a twinge or two.

MRS JIKE: (*Attempts to pour, but finds bottle empty – looking at the bottle.*) 'Ere, somebody's done herself well.

MRS BULL points with her thumb at MRS DORBELL.

You may be alcoholic, Mrs Dorbell, but you might 'ave the manners of a lidy.

There is the beginning of a good row, but MRS HARDCASTLE *interrupts.*

MRS HARDCASTLE: (*Puts her cup down and hurries across to them.*) Now, now. I thought you might like to hold a circle, Mrs Jike. That's why I brought out the table. (*She takes* MRS BULL's *cup.*)

MRS DORBELL: Eeh, spirits! Come on, girls! (*She eagerly sits up to the small table.*)

MRS BULL: Nothing like talking with the dead to cheer you up.

MRS HARDCASTLE: Make yourselves comfortable.

MRS DORBELL commences her song here.

MRS BULL: Have you got everything ready?

MRS JIKE: Well, that all depends on the spirits, doesn't it?

MRS DORBELL: (*Sings quietly to herself as the gin begins to work.*)
'We'll laugh and we'll sing and we'll drive away care.
I've enough for meself and a little bit to spare.
If a nice young man should ride my way,
Oo-ow I'll make him welcome as the flowers in –'

MRS BULL: (*Freezing the singer with a look.*) Well, that's better out than in. (*She moves to sit on the sofa.*)

MRS JIKE: (*Crosses to the table.*) All round the tible now. Turn the lights down low, Sally.

SALLY turns the gas down. They gather round the table. MRS HARDCASTLE brings a chair and sits at the small table.

All hands on the tible-top. Only just your finger-tips.

MRS DORBELL sniffs.

Hush! You'll drive the spirits away. (*She assumes an eerie, monotonous voice.*) Are there any spirits present 'ere tonight? Answer three for 'yes' and two for 'no.'

Three raps are heard, which are obviously caused by MRS JIKE'S knee. She announces in a brisk, matter-of-fact tone.

Yes, they're here. Now hush! (*She gets monotonous again.*) Has anybody got anything to ask the spirits about?

MRS DORBELL: Yes. Mrs Nattle's got a ticket in the Irish Sweep and she wants me to go shares. Ask the spirits if the ticket's going to draw a horse.

MRS JIKE: Will Mrs Nattle's ticket draw an 'orse? Answer three for 'yes' and two for 'no.'

Two raps.

No, it won't.

MRS DORBELL: Right. And thank you. She can keep her old ticket. I want none of it.

MRS JIKE: Hush, Mrs Dorbell, hush! Spirits don't like too much talking. Any more questions?

MRS BULL: Ask if Jack Tuttle's there.

MRS JIKE: Is Jack Tuttle present 'ere tonight? Answer three for 'yes' and two for 'no.'

Three raps.

Yes, 'e's 'ere.

MRS BULL: Hello, Jack lad. Are you there? Listen to me. When you died and I laid you out I found half a crown in thy pocket and as I was hard up I took it. I knew thou wouldn't need it where thou's gone, and I'm only telling you this so's you'll not think I pinched it. How are you finding things where you are, Jack?

MRS JIKE: Ask questions, Mrs Bull. The spirits don't like you to be familiar.

SALLY: (*Who has been sitting in the shadows by the fire.*) Oh, stop it! I never heard of anything so daft in my life. (*She springs up and turns the gas up again.*)

MRS JIKE: Eh, what? Now you've done it! The spirits have all gone away.

SALLY: I think you're an old twister, Mrs Jike.

MRS JIKE: (*Rises.*) Ow, am I? I like that.

MRS BULL: Go on, Sally lass, it's only a bit o' fun and it costs nothing.

MRS DORBELL: I'd a bought a ticket if spirits had said it was

going to draw a horse, fun or no fun. Ee! Fancy me winning thirty thousand quid! I'd buy meself a fur coat and –

MRS BULL: Aye, and I'd be laying you out in a month, drunk to death, fur coat and all.

MRS DORBELL: I'd risk it. I'd have good once, anyway.

MRS HARDCASTLE: I'd like Sally to have her fortune told, Mrs Jike, in spite of what she says.

MRS JIKE: (*Sniffing.*) Can't say as I care to do it for an antiseptic.

MRS HARDCASTLE: (*Coaxing MRS JIKE back to her seat.*) Aw, come on, Mrs Jike. Sally meant no harm.

SALLY: (*Following.*) But I don't want my fortune told.

MRS HARDCASTLE: Now, Sally, just to please me.

MRS JIKE: Remember, I ain't responsible. Will you have cards or tea-leaves?

MRS DORBELL: Make it tea-leaves. It's more exciting when you go seeing things in the future the way you do.

MRS JIKE: Very well.

MRS HARDCASTLE: Is this your cup, Sal?

SALLY: Yes, Mother.

MRS HARDCASTLE brings a cup and saucer. SALLY is seated at the table and offers her cup.

MRS JIKE: No, no! Turn it round three times.

SALLY does so and again offers the cup.

No, no! Bottom side up.

SALLY turns the cup upside down on the saucer and again offers it. MRS JIKE takes the cup, shakes it and then peers into it.

Strike me pink! Look at that!

MRS DORBELL: What is it?

MRS JIKE: Money! Lots of money!

MRS BULL: Aye, in the bank.

MRS JIKE: Hush, I see two men – one's dark and 'andsome – Do you know a dark, 'andsome man?

SALLY does not answer.

MRS HARDCASTLE: That'll be Larry Meath.

MRS JIKE: The other's a fat man. Be on your guard against him. He means danger. Oo! And money, more money –

MRS DORBELL: And then what?

MRS JIKE: (*In her eerie voice.*) Now I'm seeing things. Right through the bottom of the cup I'm seeing into the future. It's all dark – darkness all round you – I see Sally Hardcastle with a dark, 'andsome bloke. They're trying to get up to the light, but they're being dragged down – down into the darkness. I can't see no more – it's getting darker and darker – Ow! (*She screams suddenly.*)

MRS HARDCASTLE: (*Frightened.*) What is it?

MRS JIKE: All red! Like blood –

SALLY: Stop it! (*She snatches the cup and dashes it down.*) Do you hear, you old fool? Stop it!

MRS BULL: Now see what you've done? You've frightened the lass. You didn't ought to do that.

SALLY: Get outside, the whole lot of you.

MRS HARDCASTLE: (*Above the table.*) Sally!

SALLY: Yes, Ma, I mean it. You ought to be ashamed of yourself, bringing them in here. Go on, get out! If you don't go I'll put you out! The whole damned pack of you!

MRS JIKE: (*To* SALLY.) I warned you.

SALLY: (*Shrinking away.*) You dirty old scut! Do you think I believe a word you said?

MRS JIKE: Ow? So that's 'ow you feel, is it? (*She points her hand at* SALLY, *then turns in the doorway.*) I warned you.

She goes out.

MRS DORBELL: And I was expecting to have mine told too. (*She turns to go.*)

MRS BULL: (*Stopping* MRS DORBELL.) I can tell it, lass. Thou'll keep on drawing thy old-age pension, and then thou'll die, and I'll be laying you out and parish will bury you. Come on. We aren't wanted.

MRS DORBELL: (*At the door.*) Good night, Mrs Hardcastle. I'm sorry your daughter was took that way. (*She goes out.*)

MRS BULL: (*At the door.*) Now, Sal, lass. Take no notice of what Mrs Jike says. It's all a bit of fun. Good night, Sarah. (*She goes out.*)

MRS HARDCASTLE: (*Almost in tears.*) Sally! What have you done?

SALLY: I've turned them out. And about time too.

MRS HARDCASTLE: But Sally – You've shamed me – They're me friends. What'll they think of me?

SALLY: Friends! Those our friends? It's us that's shamed, Ma, by letting 'em come here.

MRS HARDCASTLE: Sally! You're not getting notions, are you?

SALLY: (*Collecting the cups.*) Yes, I *am* getting notions. It's about time some of us at Hanky Park *started* getting notions. You call *them* your friends, that pack of dirty old women. Oh, I'm not blaming them – that's what Hanky Park's done for 'em. It's what it does for all the women. It's what it'll do for you, Ma – yes, it will! – and me too! We'll all go the same road – poverty and pawnshops and dirt and drink! Well, I'm not going that road, and neither are you, if I can help it. I'm going to fight it – me and Larry's going to fight it – and I'm starting *now.*

MRS HARDCASTLE: You can't, Sally, you can't – I've tried and you can't.

SALLY: Can't you? We'll see about that.

MRS HARDCASTLE: You're hard, Sally. You're like all the young 'uns, you're hard.

SALLY: Ay, I'm hard – and, by God, you need to be! (*She turns with the cups to the sink.*)

Curtain

Act 2
Scene I

An alley in Hanky Park. There is a large railway arch, through which is seen a view of distant factories and other buildings. It is night.

(*Note: This scene can be played in the simplest of settings. A drop cloth of a brick wall is adequate.*)

*At the side of the arch is a street lamp on a bracket, which is lighted. Hardly discernible, in the feeble light, lies a drunken man (*MR DOYLE*) under the arch.*

The curtain rises, and a train rumbles overhead.

MRS DOYLE: (*Is heard calling offstage.*) George! Oh, so you're there, are you? Drunk again! Get up! Get up! (*She grabs him by the arm and hauls, as he slowly rises.*) Do you hear me?

They stand under the lamp.

MR DOYLE: What time is it?

MRS DOYLE: What beats me is where you get brass for getting drunk. What about your wife and family, eh? (*She picks up his cap and puts it on his head.*) You great fat guzzling pig! You ought to be drowned in it. Aye, and them as serves you with it too! You with children starving at home – and you waste your money in the public house.

MR DOYLE: Shut your trap, will you, or I'll break your blasted jaw.

He makes a left-handed swipe at her. She dodges it. He misses and staggers against the corner of the arch. MRS DOYLE *supports him.*

MRS DOYLE: (*Shrilly.*) Ah, you would, would you? You big lousy coward! Strike your wife! (*She hits him on the arm.*) Go on, hit me – hit me –

DOYLE *turns toward her.*

And I'll tell the cops if you so much as lift a finger to me. (*Sticking her face up at him – asking for it.*)

MR DOYLE: Keep your blasted snout in your own business.

MRS DOYLE: My own business! Isn't it my business what you do with brass to keep the home going? Tell me that, George Doyle, tell me that. You great soaking swine you, I'll –

A POLICEMAN *enters from the back of the arch. She stops as she hears him.*

Look out, here's a cop! (*She supports and tidies* DOYLE.) It's all right, Mister. It's only my husband. He's been took queer – it's his indigestion.

DOYLE *hiccoughs.*

Somethink awful, it is! I'll get him home. Come on, love. (*She gives him a punch.*) Here, lad, take my arm. (*As she leads him up to the back of the arch.*) You'll be all right when you get home. Come on, lad. (*She turns to the* POLICEMAN.) He often gets took this way.

She pushes DOYLE *away. They disappear. The* POLICEMAN *watches them go, then turns and goes out.*

HARRY HARDCASTLE *comes on, closely followed by* HELEN HAWKINS, *a pretty but rather hungry-looking girl of about sixteen. She catches him by the arm so that he stops under the lamp.*

HARRY: (*Offstage.*) Don't talk so daft.

He enters.

HELEN: (*Following him on.*) Oh, Harry, let's not fall out.

HARRY: What do you mean? *Us* fall out? Huh! That's a fine way to talk.

HELEN: (*Plaintively.*) Oh, Harry, I never meant –

HARRY: Oh, that's all right. You're always making a fuss. Girls make me sick as a rule, but you're not so bad.

HELEN: (*Eagerly.*) Do you mean that, Harry? Do you mean it?

HARRY: Do I mean what?

HELEN: That I'm not so bad.

HARRY: (*Lighting a cigarette-end.*) Um. But, don't forget, I'm not walking out regular. Not yet.

HELEN: (*Disappointed.*) Oh – I don't know what's come over you lately, Harry.

HARRY: What do you mean?

HELEN: I mean – I thought you and me were –

HARRY: Well, we are in a way, aren't we? But I can't always be – You see, there's other chaps. I don't like 'em saying things.

HELEN: What sort of things?

HARRY: Aw, just – things.

HELEN: Take no notice of what *they* say. Oh, Harry, we could be – you know. I've always liked you best of everybody, and – oh, well, you're different from that other lot.

HARRY: Aw, they're not so bad. It's like this, you see. I like *you* too. Yes, I do, really, no kidding. But – well, I don't want to go out regular with nobody yet. I – oh, I don't know, Helen, I want to do things first.

HELEN: What sort of things?

HARRY: Big things. I want to make money or something like that. Gosh! I wish I was a footballer or a boxer, or something.

HELEN: (*Who thinks he's wonderful.*) Harry, I *do* love you – I do really.

HARRY: Do you, Helen? Thanks. (*He puts his arm around her, and is about to kiss her when he suddenly drags her into the shadows.*) Look out, here's that cop!

A POLICEMAN *crosses at the back. They watch him go out of sight.*

All right, he's gone. You know, I've been thinking. You see, Helen, it troubles me, having nowt to spend on you. It's rotten – kids get more to spend than me. Older you

grow, more work you do and less money you get to spend. Why, when I first started at Marlowe's, what with money I got for running errands, I got twice as much as what I do now. And me on a machine – Gar!

HELEN: Oh, never mind about money. I don't want nothing, Harry. Only you.

HARRY: Well, give me time, and I'll show you – I'll find a job –

HELEN: Would you rather be with the other lads than here with me, would you? (*She shakes him.*) Would you, Harry?

HARRY: No.

HELEN: Oh, Harry!

HARRY: You know, Helen, you aren't bad looking.

HELEN: (*Eagerly.*) Aren't I, Harry?

HARRY: You're not exactly – well, you aren't Greta Garbo. But you'll do. (*He kisses her.*)

HELEN: (*Bursts into tears.*) Oh, Harry, you do make me happy. (*She sobs on his shoulder.*)

HARRY: Lousy place for being happy, isn't it? Back alley in Hanky Park. I always used to think of love like on the movies, with moonlight and trees.

HELEN: I reckon love's the same the world over. Though I could do with moonlight and trees better than brick walls and chimney-stacks. But it doesn't matter, does it, Harry?

HARRY: (*Wistfully.*) No – it doesn't really matter.

HELEN: (*Drawing his face to hers.*) It's you and me, Harry.

HARRY: That's it, Helen. Me and you. It's strange, but that's how it is.

A train rumbles and lights flash overhead.

Look at that train, Helen. How'd you like to go on one?

HELEN: Oo, I've never been on a train in me life.

HARRY: I wish I had more money, just so as we could have a bit more fun. I'd like to be able to take you and me away for a holiday.

HELEN: Oh, Harry! Where could we get the money for that?

HARRY: Just you wait. You don't know what I'm doing on the quiet.

HELEN: What? Not stealing?

HARRY: Me – no! But one of these days I'll make more money than you ever saw.

HELEN: What is it? What're you *doing*?

HARRY: Well, I'm having a threepenny treble every week with Sam Grundy.

HELEN: What's a threepenny treble?

HARRY: Well, it's this way. You put threepence on a horse, whatever you fancy, of course, and if the horse wins, what you've made you put on another horse, and any winnings from that you put on another.

HELEN: You mean three horses have got to win?

HARRY: Ay. And then, you see, you –

HELEN: What? Three horses win? All in the same race?

HARRY: *No!* One after the other.

HELEN: Oh – but isn't it very difficult?

HARRY: To some it is. You've got to be a student of form – like me. But Bill Higgs won five quid on a shilling double, so I'm hoping.

HELEN: Five quid!

HARRY: It's exciting, you know. When I look in the paper tomorrow it'll be in the stop press. (*He is carried away.*) I stand to win – ooh – I don't know how much, and I can't lose more than threepence, see?

The POLICEMAN *appears.*

Oh, Helen, if I could make some money, there's things we could do, you and me –

HELEN: Oh, Harry, you *are* wonderful!

They embrace. The POLICEMAN *has advanced towards them.* HARRY *becomes conscious of his presence and looks up.* HELEN *turns, sees the* POLICEMAN *and exclaims.*

Oh!

Black out.

Scene 2

Out of the darkness comes the voice of the NEWSBOY *calling –* 'News Chronicle! Three o'clock winner. Racing Special! Evening News! Evening Chronicle! News Chronicle!' *The light returns, and now it is the daylight of late afternoon.* MRS BULL *appears with* MRS DORBELL, *earnestly discussing.*

MRS BULL: Yes, and he's had a thripp'ny treble every week for years. This is the first time it's ever come off.

The NEWSBOY *offers* MRS DORBELL *a paper.* 'Paper, lady?' *She shoos him away.* 'Get out!'

NEWSBOY: Keep your hair on!

He goes, still calling his papers.

MRS DORBELL: Twenty-two quid for thrippence!

MRS BULL: Now what do you think of that? He ain't twenty year old yet, neither, not by a long way.

MRS DORBELL: Twenty-two pounds for three pence. Yah! Some hopes.

MRS BULL: Mrs Dorbell, I'm not in the habit of having my word doubted, especially by one of me neighbours.

MRS DORBELL: Ah, but do you know it's true?

MRS BULL: True? It's as true as God's above. Some people have all the ruddy luck! Ay, he's lucky is young Harry Hardcastle.

MRS DORBELL: That's all very well, but will Sam Grundy pay it?

MRS BULL: Ah, now you're asking. That's what I'm here to see. If he does, then Sam Grundy gets all my bets in the future, you bet he does.

MRS DORBELL: Sam Grundy should be here now. It looks kind of suspicious. Huh! I bet he don't pay up.

MRS BULL: I bet he does.

MRS DORBELL: I bet he don't.

MRS BULL: I bet he does.

HARRY appears with a newspaper.

MRS DORBELL: Here's the lad now. Congratulations, Harry.

MRS BULL: (*Pushing in front.*) Eh, Harry, lad. You'll be going to the Rivyeera now.

MRS DORBELL: Who'd have thought it, Harry? Who'd have thought it?

MRS BULL: I hope he pays up.

HARRY: Have you seen him?

MRS BULL: Who?

HARRY: Sam Grundy.

MRS DORBELL: No, and like as not you never will.

MRS BULL: You'll stand us a bottle of gin, won't you, Harry?

HARRY: I will that, Mrs Bull.

MRS DORBELL: There's some bookies that won't pay more than five pounds. And if you ask me this sky's the limit business is all a bit of bluff. I wouldn't give much for your chances, lad.

SALLY is heard calling HARRY. The crowd begins to assemble.

SALLY: Harry! Is it true, Harry?

HARRY: Ay, I think so. Twenty-two quid.

SALLY: That's fine, lad.

HARRY: I'll be able to pay for that new suit of mine now, and to hell with weekly payments.

SALLY: Now don't go being soft with all that brass.

MRS BULL: (*Who is hovering.*) That's just what I were telling him.

SALLY: You keep out of this.

MRS BULL: (*Moving away.*) All right, Sally Hardcastle, I won't rob you of your lawful pickings, though I warn you there's nothing like money for breaking up a family.

HARRY: (*To SALLY.*) Take no notice. Listen, Sal, you can have those shorts and things as soon as you like.

SALLY: No, it's your money.

HARRY: Go on, I promised you, and you've got to have 'em.

SALLY: Thanks, Harry, very much. That'll be fine.

MRS BULL: (*Shouting.*) Here he is! He's coming down the street!

Excited voices are heard.

SALLY: See you later!

She runs off.

MRS DORBELL: Here he is. Here's Sam Grundy.

CHARLIE: (*In the arch.*) Make way there! Way for Sam Grundy.

SAM GRUNDY swaggers through the crowd. He is a not unpleasant man, though rather stout, and he has the confidence of one who lives on his wits. He wears spats, and a bowler hat is tilted at the back of his head. If he has to pay up this money he is determined to make a good advertisement of it.

SAM: Well? Where's Harry Hardcastle?

HARRY is pushed forward by the CROWD, who gather round.

So that's him, is it? Not much to look at, is he?

Roars of obsequious laughter.

CHARLIE: That's a good 'un!

SAM: Now, young fellow, I suppose you thought you'd break the bank, didn't you? But you know us bookies have a limit. You know that, don't you?

MRS DORBELL: (*Screaming.*) There you are! Didn't I tell you? Gah! Pay him. You're like all the rest.

There is a groan of dismay and shouts of 'Pay him!'

SAM: (*Waving his hand.*) Wait a minute! Wait a minute! I haven't finished yet.

MRS DORBELL: (*Aggressively.*) No, and *we* haven't finished yet.

SAM: All right, all right. Now, there's fellows that call themselves bookies that would only pay you a fiver on your bet and no more. You know that, don't you?

HARRY: I do, Mr Grundy.

SAM: Well, my lad, that ain't the way of honest Sam Grundy. Sam Grundy pays up – that's me!

He removes his hat with a flourish. Roars of applause and shouts of 'Good old Sam!', *etc.*

MRS BULL: (*To* MRS DORBELL.) What did I tell you?

CHARLIE: (*Shouting fervently.*) Sky's the limit!

SAM: Charlie, keep a look-out. We're going to do this thing proper and all square and fair and above board. Now listen to me, ladies and gentlemen! Honest Sam's got a motto and that motto is – *Charlie?*

CHARLIE: Sky's the limit with honest Sam!

SAM: Sky's the limit, ladies and gents, and don't you forget it. This young fellow – Stand up alongside of me, son, and let's have a look at you. Come on, lad, come on. Now you had a bet with me, didn't you, lad?

HARRY blushes and nods.

How much was it?

HARRY: (*In a small voice.*) Threepence, Mr Grundy.

SAM: Threepence! And how much do you reckon to draw for threepence?

HARRY: Twenty-two quid, Mr Grundy.

SAM: Twenty-two quid for threepence. How many bookies'd pay out that much? How many? Well, you all know honest Sam's motto.

CHARLIE: (*Bawling.*) Sky's the limit with honest Sam! (*He distributes cards amongst the crowd.*)

SAM: Sky's the limit! (*He flourishes a roll of notes.*) Hold out your cap, Harry.

HARRY holds out his cap, but SAM *turns away to do some more business.*

Now, doesn't that prove I'm the man for your little commissions? Support Sam Grundy, the old firm.

CHARLIE: (*Repeats.*) Support Sam Grundy, the old firm.

SAM: Take a threepenny treble every week.

CHARLIE: (*Repeats.*) Take a threepenny treble every week. (*He distributes betting slips.*)

SAM: That's the way to make money quick.

CHARLIE: (*Repeats.*) That's the way to make money quick.

SAM: Risk a bit and gain a lot.

CHARLIE: Risk a lot and gain a bit.

Laughter.

SAM: See how this young fellow's made money.

MRS BULL: Ay, but you haven't –

SAM: Haven't what?

MRS BULL: Haven't paid him yet.

The crowd jeers.

SAM: Hold out your cap, Harry. (*He counts out the notes.*) Five, ten, fifteen, twenty – and two. Twenty-two quid. That's honest Sam for you, ladies and gents.

HARRY goes apart to count his money. SAM *follows him. The crowd makes excited comments.*

(*To* HARRY.) And don't forget to give your sister a couple of quid – tell her I said so. (*He turns to the crowd.*)

MRS DORBELL: Hey!

SAM: What?

MRS DORBELL: What about his stake money?

CHARLIE turns to explain. SAM *hands over the extra threepence.*

SAM: Take a threepenny treble every week. Take one for the wife and little 'uns, too. Better than insurance any day. Sky's the limit with honest Sam.

CHARLIE: (*Whistles and tugs his sleeve.*) Look out. Here's a cop.

SAM: You'll excuse me, ladies and gents. Honest Sam will have to retire.

SAM disappears through the crowd, who disperse quickly as the POLICEMAN approaches. HARRY conceals his money and leans against the wall. MRS BULL and MRS DORBELL have remained to watch the fun. CHARLIE whistles with his hands in his pockets. The POLICEMAN stands looking at him and CHARLIE hastens away, almost running when he finds the POLICEMAN is following him.

HARRY: Gosh! I thought he was going to take me up.

MRS BULL: Not he. The police'll never touch Sam Grundy or his customers. Don't forget, Harry!

MRS BULL makes a gesture of drinking out of a bottle as she goes with MRS DORBELL.

HARRY: (*Calls down the alley.*) Sal! Sal!

She runs up to him.

Look, he's paid me!

SALLY: Put it away quick!

HARRY: Well, I must find Helen and tell her. Here you are, Sal. (*He offers her two pound notes.*)

SALLY: No, Harry. No, I couldn't.

HARRY: Go on. Get your shorts and anything else you've a mind to.

SALLY: Well, I'll take one and give you the change. So you do like Helen Hawkins, after all?

HARRY: (*Shyly.*) Oh, leave us alone, Sal –

SALLY: It's nothing to be ashamed of. She's a nice girl.

HARRY: Do you think so? I'm glad. I like her, too.

SALLY: Very much?

HARRY: I suppose so. It happened sudden last night.

SALLY: Well, you're only young once, so if I was you I'd take that lass of thine away on a holiday.

HARRY: You mean it, Sal? That's what I thought, but –

SALLY: Go on with you – get yourself out of Hanky Park, while you've a chance.

HARRY: (*Feeling the money in his pocket.*) Gosh! It's like a dream. I bet there's a catch in it somehow. Twenty-two pounds.

SALLY: That'll take you to Blackpool or the Isle of Man.

HARRY: Blackpool? Phew!

SALLY: You'll spend your money on something or other, lad, so you may as well spend it on something you'll remember.

HARRY: I wonder where Helen is now. Funny if she's not heard about me winning.

SALLY: She's heard, all right.

HARRY: Then where is she?

SALLY: I've just left her crying her eyes out in back entry behind North Street.

HARRY: Crying? What was she crying for?

SALLY: Because you've won twenty pounds.

HARRY: Gosh! That's a daft way of showing you're happy.

SALLY: No, lad. She's not happy. She thinks she's lost you.

HARRY: Why, she's barmy. Here, I'd best go quick. (*He is going.*)

SALLY: (*Stops him.*) Here, lad, just a minute. She's not barmy. You be good to her.

HARRY: Aw, that's all right. I'll do me best. Goodbye.

SALLY: (*Waving.*) Goodbye, Harry.

He goes out. SALLY *watches him and then turns to go the other way.* SAM GRUNDY *has appeared.*

SAM: How do, Sally? Well, that was a grand bit of luck for your Harry, eh? You can't say old Sam didn't pay up handsome.

SALLY: I reckon he can afford it. There's plenty more in the bank.

SAM: Ay, you're right. Did the lad give you a share as I told him?

SALLY: That's no business of yours.

He surveys her.

Well, what're you staring at?

SAM: You're a fine girl, Sal Hardcastle.

SALLY: Aach! Let me pass.

SAM: Nay, hold on. Not so fast. (*He holds her arm.*) Let's have a look at you.

SALLY: (*Snatching away savagely.*) Leave go!

SAM: Aw, Sal, what's the matter with you? What have you got against me?

SALLY: Just that I don't want to even talk to men like you. It'd be better if you'd spend more time with your wife instead of pestering girls that wouldn't wipe their feet on you.

SAM: Oh, now, Sal, now. That ain't the way to talk to a friend that wants to help you.

SALLY: Fine sort of help *you* can give a girl. You've helped too many already.

SAM: God, Sal, you've got me all wrong. (*He draws out some pound notes which he stuffs into her hands. She holds them in a kind of amazed horror.*) Take these. I like you, Sal. Honest, I do. I'd – aw, I'd like you for a pal, that's all. You must be sick of having nothing to wear, and pinching and scraping week after week, and think what you could have if you wanted. Anything, Sal. Anything for the asking.

SALLY: (*Comes out of the daze in a fury and thrusts the notes back to him.*) You'd better look out if you won't leave me alone. Just you tell that to Larry Meath.

SAM: Larry Meath? So it's Larry Meath, is it?

SALLY: All right. You leave his name out of it. You ain't fit to have his name on your breath. All *you* want out of girls is one thing only. But you don't get it out of me. Do you understand?

SAM: (*Who has been lighting a cigar.*) So it's Larry Meath you're set on, is it?

SALLY: That's my business. You mind yours. (*She is going.*)

SAM: He works at Marlowe's, eh?

SALLY: (*Defiantly.*) Ay, he works and that's more than you ever did. (*She suddenly realizes the danger and turns.*) Why?

SAM: (*Turning on his heel and walking away.*) That's *my* business.

SALLY: (*Following a step or two; with frightened appeal.*) But, Mr Grundy – Mr Grundy –

Curtain

Scene 3

On the moors. A high rock against the sky, towards sunset.

SALLY's *voice is heard, and then* LARRY's *as they climb up behind the rock.*

SALLY: (*Laughing happily.*) Oh, Larry, I can't. It's too high!

LARRY: Go on – Only a few yards and we're there.

SALLY: Larry, I'm slipping!

LARRY: No, you're not. Up with you! There you are. All right?

SALLY: Yes, I'm up now.

SALLY *appears in hiking shorts and shirt.*

This is the place, Larry. Oo, be careful, you'll slip!

LARRY: (*Appears beside her, carrying his jacket.*) I'm all right. Don't you worry about me. (*He stands upright.*) Well, are you happy now we've got here?

SALLY: Fine! Aren't we high up in the world? This is a special place. And only us two know why. Isn't it grand being alone? I've never seen so much loneliness in all me life.

LARRY: (*Laughing.*) You *are* a funny girl.

SALLY: (*Gasping.*) Be careful, Larry. You give me a turn when you stand right on the edge.

LARRY: Come on, then – hold my hand. Isn't that a grand view?

SALLY: Grand! Miles and miles of it. Gosh! And this air – it's wonderful. I wish I could breathe it every day. Makes me feel I could fly.

LARRY: (*His turn to gasp.*) Well, don't do that. Or else you'll give me a turn. Here, take something to hold you down. (*He produces an apple from his pocket which he offers her.*) One apple left.

SALLY: No, that's yours. (*She kneels.*)

LARRY: You have it, Sal.

SALLY: I couldn't. It's yours. You've eaten nothing yourself.

LARRY: We'll go halves. (*He splits the apple.*) There you are. Take the red side. It matches your cheeks.

SALLY: Phew! I feel more like a beetroot. Wasn't it a climb?

LARRY: Um. We shall never manage to get up here when we're old.

They sit down and munch their apple.

SALLY: It's been lovely today, Larry.

LARRY: You've liked it?

SALLY: You know I have. Haven't you?

LARRY: (*Turning away.*) Of course, it's fine.

SALLY: (*Looking hard at him.*) Larry? Is there anything wrong?

LARRY: Wrong? No. Nothing could be wrong out here.

SALLY: You're not worried?

LARRY: No –

SALLY: Nothing on your mind?

LARRY: No, why?

SALLY: Well, you haven't said anything about –

LARRY: About what?

SALLY: You haven't said you liked my shorts.

LARRY: Haven't I? Why, Sally, you're lovelier than ever. Perhaps that's why I *am* sad today. Beauty makes you feel that way sometimes.

SALLY: Why?

LARRY: I don't know. I suppose because when you've lived in a place that's ugly all your life, beautiful things seem out of reach. We get to thinking beauty is something forbidden, something that's too good for us –

SALLY: You don't feel like that about me, surely?

LARRY: Sometimes.

SALLY: Don't talk nonsense, Larry. (*She ruffles his hair.*) Look at that sunset. Why is it so red?

LARRY: They say it's the sunshine through the smoke. Hanky Park's over there – thirty miles away. It's a queer thing all that foul smoke should make beauty for us up here.

SALLY: See that cloud – big black fellow with a bulge in him. (*She laughs.*) Why, it's Sam Grundy!

LARRY: (*Laughing too.*) So it is!

SALLY: See, there's his bowler hat and his cigar. Coo-ee! How are you, Sam?

LARRY: I shouldn't make too free with him, Sal.

SALLY: Oh, Larry, I feel like we're on top of the world! I feel real mad! And I'm so happy! I've never been so happy in me life.

LARRY: Bless you, Sal.

SALLY: Aren't you happy?

LARRY: Yes – if this could last for ever.

SALLY: For ever and ever! Larry –?

LARRY: Yes?

SALLY: We'll come up here – often?

LARRY: Of course.

SALLY: If we could build a house, and live here – and keep this place, just for two of us – sacred – Gosh! That's funny talk!

LARRY: Some people call it poetry. Wanting what you can't get. It's the same thing.

SALLY: I'm no poet, Larry, but there's something in all this loneliness, something I've been wanting – (*A pause.*) Larry?

LARRY: Well?

SALLY: Do you believe in – God?

LARRY: (*Smiling.*) Me? Why? What a funny question!

SALLY: Do you, though?

LARRY: Why do you ask that?

SALLY: Oh, I don't know. I've never felt that way before. I've never found anything worth believing in Hanky Park. But it's different up here. Here you belong – you belong to something big – something grand, something that it's fine to belong to –

LARRY: I know, Sal, I know.

SALLY: But sometimes I get frightened. It's like as if someone up there was saying – 'Take care, Sal Hardcastle. Take care you don't climb too high and fall.'

LARRY: That's nonsense. But just think of those poor devils in Hanky Park who never learn how good life can be. They're as good as dead the day they're born. They're satisfied because they don't know any better. We can thank heaven, Sal, that *we've* learned to be discontented.

SALLY: Yes, but we've got to go back. We've got to go back.

LARRY: Ay, that's it, Sal!

SALLY: Why? Oh, why –? There's other places in the world –

LARRY: We've got to go back where the money is. Money's our master, Sal, and we're its slaves. There's only one spot in the whole wide world where someone will buy our labour – our special brand of labour – and that spot's Hanky Park. You're right – there's no God there, with all their churches.

SALLY: (*Impulsively.*) Larry, we've got to get out.

LARRY: (*Bitterly.*) Yes, climb out roughshod over the others, but Hanky Park will still be there.

SALLY: Never mind Hanky Park. We'll be wed soon. It's you and me –

LARRY: That's it! You and me and to hell with the others. Oh, what's the use of talking. I love you, Sally, better than anything else on earth – but it's no use – God, it's no use!

SALLY: Larry! What's the matter?

LARRY: Nothing –

SALLY: There is – There's something hurting you. Tell me what it is –

LARRY: It's nothing. See, there's the others, going down to the train. We'll have to hurry, Sal.

SALLY: That was strange talk. What do you mean, it's no use?

LARRY: Let's forget all that. I meant today to be happy.

SALLY: Well, aren't we happy? We'll be wed by the end of this month, and it won't be a bad house when we've cleaned it up a bit. You don't know what it means, Larry, a house of my own. I'll scrub it from top to bottom and there won't be a bug left in it when I've finished with it. Not a one. You know, Larry, dreaming about things you can't have doesn't get you anywhere. Does it now? I can't promise curtains yet awhile. We'll have to wait for *them*. But the room'll look all right, what with your books and the walnut table we saw at Price and Jones's. Come on, lad. Buck up! Besides, it ain't *where* you live, it's who you live with.

LARRY: Oh, Sal, Sal –! (*He buries his face in his hands.*)

SALLY: What's wrong, lad?

LARRY: We'll have to put it off, Sally. I'm –

SALLY: Put it off?

LARRY: I'm – I've lost my job. They gave me the sack yesterday.

SALLY: The sack? *Larry!* (*With uncertain optimism.*) You'll get another job.

LARRY: Will I? (*He laughs bitterly.*) There's too many out already. Oh, Sal, I should have told you before. But I just wanted to have today with you – and be happy.

SALLY: Why can't we be married as we said? There's nothing to stop us. You'd get your dole, and I'm working.

LARRY: No, no, Sal. No, I can't do that.

SALLY: (*Taking her hands away.*) You mean you don't want?

LARRY: How do you think I'm going to manage on fifteen bob a week? Gosh, dragging us down into that hell of poverty –

SALLY: But, Larry, there's nothing for me to live for without you. You don't know what I'd do for you – Listen, I'll come and live with you. Who wants to get married? Who cares what folks say?

LARRY: Oh, God, no, Sal! Fifteen bob a week. Do you think I'm going to sponge on you? Drag you down? What the devil do you take me for?

SALLY: (*Hysterically.*) Don't talk like that. I'm sick of it all. Is that all you care for me? Aw, you're driving me barmy. Why don't those labour councillors that're always making a mug of you find a job for you? They're all right, they are – don't care a damn for us. They've all landed good jobs for 'emselves. And I – Oh, I hate you! I hate you –

She turns away from LARRY *– throws herself down on the rock and sobs.* LARRY *looks despondently at the sunset which has faded rapidly. Faint voices come up from the valley.*

VOICES: (*In the distance.*) Coo-eee! Hey, Larry! Sally! Come down, it's time to go home –

LARRY: (*Waving his hand.*) All right – we're coming. (*He looks at his watch and then at the crumpled* SALLY.) It's time to go now if we're going to catch that train. (*He touches her shoulder.*) Don't, Sal, don't – I love you, Sal, and there's nothing else matters. We'll pull through – somehow –

SALLY: (*Turns and impulsively throws her arms around him.*) I'm sorry, Larry – I'm sorry –

LARRY: That's all right, Sal. I should have told you. I'd no right to bring you up here.

SALLY: No, lad, I'm glad we've had today. They can't take that away from us now. They can take our jobs but they can't take away our love. Can they? (*She is a little frightened and uncertain about this last question.*)

LARRY: No, Sal. We've still got that – Yes, we've still got that.

SALLY shivers.

Why, you're shivering! You're cold. (*He puts his jacket over her shoulders.*)

SALLY: It's different up here now the sun's gone down. I think this place has changed. It's growing dark – and, oh, Larry, I'm afraid – I'm afraid –

He holds her head close to him and buries his face in her hair. Darkness gathers round them. The voices call 'Coo-eee!'

Curtain

Act 3
Scene I

The HARDCASTLES' *kitchen. A year later. The door* R. *is closed.* MRS HARDCASTLE *is seated at the table, darning a sock.* SAM GRUNDY *is on the sofa. He is obviously ill at ease and has observed convention by removing his bowler hat.*

MRS HARDCASTLE: So that's what you want, is it?

SAM: (*Seated on the sofa.*) I tell you, it's for your own good. What more am I asking than that Sally should be my housekeeper down in Wales? It's a good job and there's nothing wrong in being a housekeeper.

MRS HARDCASTLE: That depends on whose house it is, doesn't it?

SAM: Now, then! I'm not having that kind of talk. I might be asking the girl to take a dose of poison. Listen, Mrs Hardcastle, I'm not a bad sort of fellow really and I've got a grand house. Right away in the country it is, with hills and mountains and the sea. Just what the girl is needing to make her better. Yes, and I've got a conservatory all glass and palms and things. Cost me a lot of money, that house did.

MRS HARDCASTLE: (*Rising and facing him.*) You'd better go before Sal comes home, and if my husband finds out –

SAM: Well, what if he does? I've done nothing wrong. There's no harm in me offering a job.

MRS HARDCASTLE: No harm, Sam Grundy – (*She puts the work-basket and darning on the dresser.*) – but he'd *kill* you all the same. (*She moves down to the fireplace.*)

SAM: (*Rising.*) Look here, Mrs Hardcastle, do you think I don't know how to treat the girl well? Me, with a family of my own. Aw, don't you worry yourself. She wouldn't regret it when I'm gone. I'd make a fair settlement on her. It isn't as though I'd got no money.

MRS HARDCASTLE: (*From the fireplace.*) You'd better go!

SAM: (*After a pause.*) You know, Mrs Hardcastle, it's hard on a fellow like me. I'm not an old man, and look at my wife – separated – and she's taken the kids with her. I've got a big house doing nothing and nobody to enjoy it. It's lonely for a fellow like me.

MRS HARDCASTLE: Sam Grundy, I've kept my temper with you so far. I'm not easily roused. But, I tell you, I can't keep my hands off you much longer. You're wanting a house-keeper, are you? Well, you don't get our Sal! I know what you're after, let me tell you this –

MRS DORBELL and MRS BULL have appeared in the doorway, overhearing the last line or so.

MRS DORBELL: (*Entering.*) Eee, Mrs Hardcastle! So you've got company.

MRS HARDCASTLE: Mr Grundy was just going.

MRS BULL: (*By the door.*) Oh, no, he wasn't. You was having words. I heard you. I'm sure it's an honour to have Mr Grundy in to see you.

MRS DORBELL: Well, I suppose we're in the way.

She sits down on the lower end of the sofa. MRS BULL closes the door and then sits on the upper end of the sofa.

Go on with what you are saying. You can trust me with a secret.

SAM: There's no secret. I've made a fair offer. I'm only asking her to talk sense to the lass.

MRS HARDCASTLE: Sense! I may be old-fashioned, Sam Grundy, but I've more sense than to let any daughter of mine be housekeeper of thine.

MRS BULL: So that's how it is, is it?

MRS DORBELL: Yaah, Sairey Hardcastle, the way you talk. If a girl don't know which side her bread is buttered, then she bloomin' well ought to find out. Huh! It's well to be some folks what can pick and choose these days, by gum, it is.

SAM: (*Eagerly nodding.*) That's right, Mrs Dorbell. Ay, that's right.

MRS BULL: (*Rises.*) Well, it's nothing to do with me, Mrs Hardcastle. I reckon it's nothing to do with nobody except Mr Grundy. But I take no notice of what the parsons say. Let 'em try starving like us do every day of our lives, parsons' jobs would be ten a penny then!

SAM: That's right, Mrs Bull, that's right.

MRS BULL: Gar! What do you know about starving, you fat porcupine? (*She sits again on the sofa.*)

MRS DORBELL: He's right, is Mr Grundy. It's a fair offer and your girl's a fool if she won't take it. Huh! I don't know why you want to waste your time, Mr Grundy. With all the money you've got, you've no need to go down on your bended knees. That you haven't.

SAM: Oh, it ain't that. But I take an interest in the girl. You speak to her. Tell her what she's missing.

MRS BULL: That's right.

SAM: Makes me sick to think of her wasting her chances here.

MRS DORBELL: I don't know what the girl's thinking of, indeed I don't. But I know what she'd do if she was my daughter.

MRS BULL: Ay, she'd give you one on the nose, Mrs Dorbell.

MRS DORBELL: (*Half rising.*) Ho! Would she?

A row is beginning.

MRS BULL: Ah, keep your hair on. (*She rises and looks into SAM's face.*) She's doing what I'd do myself if I was her age. Romantic, that's what she is.

MRS DORBELL: Hanging on after that Larry Meath. Why, chap's been on the dole for twelve months now. I don't know what's taken the girl.

SAM: (*Jingling money in his pocket.*) First lass I've met that didn't know the value of brass.

MRS HARDCASTLE: (*Quietly.*) I think you'd better go. All of you.

SAM shrugs his shoulders and goes to the table for his hat.

MRS DORBELL: Ho! If you feel that way about it after all we've done to oblige you –

MRS BULL: Mrs Dorbell is disappointed. She was expecting a bit of commission on the deal.

MRS DORBELL: It's a lie –!

SAM: Now then, now then.

MRS HARDCASTLE: I said I think you better go. Sally'll soon be home and I wouldn't like her to find you here.

SAM: Well, I've no more time to waste – (*He puts his hat on.*) – but just you think over what I've said, Mrs Hardcastle. (*He goes towards the door and turns.*) And another thing, don't let that lad of yours get mixed up in this unemployment demonstration they're having. There's going to be trouble. I know. Don't say I didn't warn you. And good day to you.

He goes out.

MRS DORBELL: (*Angrily.*) There now. It's like sweeping money off the doorstep. Huh! It's well to be some folk that can afford to have notions. Why, the man's just made of money.

MRS HARDCASTLE: And what do you think I'm made of, Mrs Dorbell? Do you think I'm made of cast iron that I'd let my daughter be housekeeper to a man like him?

MRS DORBELL: There's many would jump at the chance.

MRS BULL: Ay, and her own mother couldn't stop her if she wanted to. She's got a will of her own has that lass.

MRS HARDCASTLE: Sally'll be here soon and you know she won't be very pleased to see you.

MRS DORBELL: Still got notions, has she? Bah! That girl's going to have a fall.

MRS HARDCASTLE: Well, she won't fall Sam Grundy's way. Not if I can help it.

MRS DORBELL: Huh! I'm going. And when you find out who your friends are, Sairey Hardcastle, you'll know where to find me. Come on, Mrs Bull, to them that can appreciate us.

She goes out.

MRS BULL: Take no notice of her, Sarah, but don't you be too sure. If I had my time over again I wouldn't turn my nose up at a fat belly – (*She goes up to the door and turns for her parting shot.*) – as long as it had a gold watch-chain hanging on it.

She follows MRS DORBELL.

MRS HARDCASTLE sighs, closes the door and takes a bundle from the cupboard below the dresser. She lays it on the table and taking a pair of candlesticks from the mantelpiece, polishes one on her apron, then begins to tie up the bundle. HARRY comes in from the street. He is thinner and paler, and obviously troubled.

HARRY: (*Gruffly.*) Hello, Ma. (*He watches her.*) What's that you're doing?

MRS HARDCASTLE: I'm making up a bundle for the pawnshop, though I wonder whether old Price will take them. I'm afraid he'll tell me they're worth nothing.

HARRY: (*Sits by the table and stares at the floor.*) Ma –

MRS HARDCASTLE: Well?

HARRY: I've got bad news.

MRS HARDCASTLE: What is it?

HARRY: They've knocked me off the dole money.

MRS HARDCASTLE: They've what?

HARRY: They've knocked me off the dole, I tell you.

MRS HARDCASTLE: But they can't. You're out of work –

HARRY is silent. MRS HARDCASTLE smiles with a forced hopefulness.

Ah, you mean they've found you a job?

HARRY: Not them! It's the Public Assistance Committee. They say the money's got to stop because Sally's working and Dad's getting the dole as it is. They say there's enough coming into one house.

MRS HARDCASTLE: But there isn't, Harry! You know there isn't. What are we going to do? What'll Sally say? We're living on her earnings as it is.

HARRY: But – it's Helen I'm thinking of. You see, we were going to get married.

MRS HARDCASTLE: Get married, lad? You've taken leave of your senses!

HARRY: (*Desperately.*) It's no use talking that way, Ma.

MRS HARDCASTLE: What do you mean?

HARRY: I mean we've got to.

MRS HARDCASTLE: You and Helen Hawkins?

HARRY: Ay – she's seen the doctor – we've got to.

MRS HARDCASTLE: You've got to –? Oh, Harry, whatever'll your Dad say?

HARRY: That's just it. Look here, Ma, it isn't that I don't want to marry her. I do. I like her better than – well, anything, and we was planning to marry. We was going to make do on my dole money and what she's getting herself, and now this happens. If only we can get a start. I'll be drawing the dole again as soon as we are wed. And I thought perhaps – Well, I thought you and Dad would let her come here, and we could share the back room with Sally.

MRS HARDCASTLE: (*Rising.*) Ay, that's it. Share with Sally. Aren't we all sharing with Sally, as it is? She and Larry Meath wanted to get wed just as much as you did. But they didn't go and make fools of themselves, like you've done.

HARRY: But I thought I'd have got a job.

MRS HARDCASTLE: Ay, that's what a lot are thinking. But I don't think there's ever going to be work any more.

HARRY: Oh, gosh, Ma, it's driving me barmy.

He breaks down and buries his face.

Sorry, Ma, but I'm ashamed to walk the streets. I feel they're all watching me. I've been to twenty places this morning and it's the same blasted story all the time. 'No hands wanted.' Though they don't usually say it so polite. And look at me clothes. It'll take six months' pay to buy new ones. Aw, God, just let me get a job. I don't care if it's only half-pay, but give me something –

HARDCASTLE passes window.

MRS HARDCASTLE: Here's your Dad.

HARDCASTLE comes in from the street and hangs up his cap.

HARDCASTLE: Well? What's up now?

HARRY is silent.

MRS HARDCASTLE: Come on, speak up, lad. You'd best get it over.

HARDCASTLE: What's the matter with the lad?

MRS HARDCASTLE: It's him and Helen Hawkins.

HARDCASTLE: Eh?

MRS HARDCASTLE: And he's been knocked off his dole money.

HARDCASTLE: What's this about Helen Hawkins?

HARRY: You see, Dad, I'll have to marry her, and I thought –

HARDCASTLE: You what?

HARRY: I'll have to marry her.

HARDCASTLE: You blasted little fool!

MRS HARDCASTLE: Now, Henery –

HARDCASTLE: You, *you* getting wed! And who the devil do you think's going to keep you, eh?

HARRY: I thought, maybe, that we could come and live here and get a bed in back room with Sal.

HARDCASTLE: You *thought*? Yah! You little fool! Don't you think there's enough trouble here without you bringing more? I'm having no slut like that living here, do you hear me?

HARRY: (*Rises – warmly.*) Hey! I'm not having you calling her a slut. Just you leave her name out of it.

HARDCASTLE: (*Slowly as he clenches his fists.*) Are *you* threatening *me*?

HARRY: Aye, I am, if you call her names. I'm asking you for nothing. I'm not the only one out of work in this house, remember. Yah, you treat me like a kid just because I've got nothing and I'm out of work. You didn't talk like that when I was sharing my winnings with you, did you? Once let me get hold of some money again and I'll never part with a penny of it. I'm supposed to be a man, I am – Well, look at me. Aye, and if there was another war you'd call me a man too. I'd be a bloody hero then –

HARDCASTLE: You're bringing no wife here, do you understand? You've made your own bed with your nonsense – you must lie on it. Go and stay with *her* folk, the lowdown lot that they are –

HARRY: (*Hysterical.*) Stop it! Stop it, will you? I don't want to live here. Do you understand? I wouldn't live with *you* if I got the chance. You can go to hell! I'm leaving here –

He goes to the door. MRS HARDCASTLE *attempts to stop him, but he brushes her aside.*

MRS HARDCASTLE: No, Harry –! (*Following* HARRY.)

HARRY: Yes, I am, I'm leaving! I'm sick to death of it all. (*He rushes out.*)

MRS HARDCASTLE: See what you've done! You shouldn't, Henery, you shouldn't –

HARDCASTLE: (*Walks excitedly up and down.*) Who's the master in this house, eh? I'm having no carryings-on in my family. My father kept respectable, and so did his father before him, and by God, I'll keep respectable too!

MRS HARDCASTLE: But he's only a lad.

HARDCASTLE: Only a lad, is he? Calls himself a man. Well, he can blasted well take the consequences – Aye, and take 'em somewhere else. Not in my house.

MRS HARDCASTLE: But he can't get a job, and they've knocked him off the dole.

HARDCASTLE: No more can I get a job. No more can any of us. Oh, well, he'll have to get workhouse relief, that's all.

MRS HARDCASTLE: Workhouse relief! No, Henery, no.

HARDCASTLE: It's all the same any bloomin' road. We're paupers living on charity. Dole or workhouse, it's all the same.

MRS HARDCASTLE: All my life I've feared it, and now it's come. Eh, that poor lad – (*She weeps.*)

There is a pause as HARDCASTLE *looks at her, then turns his head away.*

HARDCASTLE: (*Gruffly.*) Now, Ma. Now, Ma.

MRS HARDCASTLE: You might have let the lad stay on.

HARDCASTLE: I might. There's a lot of things I might have done. I might have had the gumption not to have a family at all. (*Pointing at the door.*) But it's his own doing, and there's an end of it.

MRS HARDCASTLE: I think he loves her, Henery.

HARDCASTLE: Loves? *Love*, did you say? I'm thinking that's a luxury the young 'uns can't afford these days.

MRS HARDCASTLE weeps.

Eh, Ma, I'm sorry – I thought I'd have done better for you.

She looks pleadingly at him.

No, don't ask me to change my mind. I tell you, Ma, he'll bring no wench in this house.

There is a roar of men's voices outside.

MRS HARDCASTLE: What's that?

She goes to the window.

HARDCASTLE: Aw, that's the men gathering for the demonstration. Fine lot of use that'll be, too.

MRS HARDCASTLE: I'm afraid our Harry'll get mixed up in it. Sam Grundy said –

HARDCASTLE: What's that?

MRS HARDCASTLE: He said there might be trouble.

HARDCASTLE: (*Slowly.*) Where did *you* see Sam Grundy?

MRS HARDCASTLE: Oh, he just happened to call. He's wanting a housekeeper.

HARDCASTLE: Wanting a housekeeper, is he? That's a new name for it. Listen, Ma, if I catch that swine hanging round our Sal again, I'll kill him, I will! I'll kill him, if I swing for it.

MRS HARDCASTLE: Don't talk like that, Henery. You know well enough that Sally's promised to Larry Meath. She ain't that kind of a girl, and you ought to be ashamed of yourself thinking that way about your own daughter.

SALLY comes in from the street. Crowd noise swells for a moment as the door opens.

SALLY: They've started the demonstration, Dad, and Larry's been asking for you.

HARDCASTLE: Then he'll have to wait. I've got troubles enough without demonstrating.

SALLY: And I met our Harry on the corner. He told me what's happened.

HARDCASTLE: Oh, he told you, did he?

SALLY: Ay. And I think you might have waited till I came in before you turned him away.

HARDCASTLE: What d'you mean?

SALLY: Only that it's *my* money that runs this house, and I might have had a word to say in the lad's favour.

HARDCASTLE: You keep out of this, Sal.

SALLY: I asked Harry to come back, Ma.

HARDCASTLE: You *what*?

SALLY: I tell you I asked him to come back.

HARDCASTLE: You interfering little hussy –

SALLY: All right, keep your hair on. He wouldn't, and he said he'd never be seen dead in here, so I suppose that's that.

HARDCASTLE: Look here, Sal, I'm boss of this show, and I won't have you interfering with my business. D'you think I'm having a lowdown wench living here, and all the neighbours talking –?

SALLY: If you want to stop the neighbours talking, you'd have done better to let her come. And Helen Hawkins isn't a lowdown wench either.

MRS HARDCASTLE: Here's Larry.

There is a knock at the door. SALLY *opens it.*

LARRY: Can I see Mr Hardcastle for a moment?

SALLY: Come inside, Larry.

LARRY: (*Is pale and has a distressing cough.*) I'd like a word with you, Mr Hardcastle, if you don't mind.

HARDCASTLE: What's the trouble now?

LARRY: I want your help. Things aren't going as they ought. Listen to 'em. That organizer fellow's a fool, and I won't answer for what happens if he gets 'em roused. There's police all over the place.

HARDCASTLE: Well, what d'you want *me* to do?

LARRY: I want you to be one of the deputation. The Mayor's promised to meet us at the Town Hall, and it's time we were there now, instead of wasting time making daft speeches. (*He coughs.*)

SALLY: Larry! You've no right to be out with a cough like that.

LARRY: I'm all right, Sal. Just a bit of cold. Will you come, Mr Hardcastle? We want some of the older men with a bit of sense.

HARDCASTLE: Ay, I'll come. Though a lot of good the whole business will do us.

MRS HARDCASTLE: No, I don't like you going.

HARDCASTLE: I can take care of myself, Ma.

An excited YOUNG MAN, *with a strong Irish accent, appears in the doorway.*

YOUNG MAN: Where's Larry Meath? Is he here?

LARRY: Yes, I'm here. What d'you want?

YOUNG MAN: Come on, man, hurry up! The crowd wants to hear you speak.

LARRY: There's no time to waste making daft speeches. Get 'em lined up for the procession. D'you know the Mayor's waiting for us?

YOUNG MAN: (*Coming forward to* LARRY.) Ach! Let him wait. Let him wait *our* pleasure. We've waited long enough.

LARRY *grabs the* YOUNG MAN's *coat-lapels.*

LARRY: Look here, I've had enough of your talk. D'you know there's a crowd of police down there all waiting for us?

YOUNG MAN: (*Throws* LARRY *off.*) Afraid, are you?

LARRY: Course I'm afraid. D'you think we're going to run our

heads into a brick wall? What's a thousand half-starved men against a hundred healthy cops? I'm not leading them into trouble, if you are.

YOUNG MAN: Yah! Kow-towing to the boss class as usual, Larry Meath. It's hand in glove with 'em you are.

HARDCASTLE: (*Cutting him off.*) That's enough! Which road are you going?

YOUNG MAN: (*Defiantly.*) Past the Labour Exchange and down Crosstree Lane.

LARRY: Oh, talk sense, can't you? You've been told we can't go that way. They've got mounted police down there.

YOUNG MAN: Police? To hell with the police! Traitors to their class! Enemies of the workers! The iron heel of a bourgeois aristocracy –!

LARRY: Don't talk so damned daft! Get 'em lined up for the procession! I'm coming with you.

He reaches for his cap, coughs violently and leans against the table.

HARDCASTLE: Here, Larry, my lad, you'd best stay behind. Get the Missis and Sal to take you home. You're not fit to be out with that cough. (*He crosses the door and gets his cap.*)

LARRY: I'm all right – and I'm seeing this through.

MRS HARDCASTLE: You're not going, Dad.

HARDCASTLE: (*Puts his cap on.*) Of course I am. (*To the* YOUNG MAN.) Now, then, Mister – Trotsky, come on with you.

He goes.

YOUNG MAN: (*As he follows.*) Hired assassins of capitalism, that's what they are! Are we going to bow the knee –?

MRS HARDCASTLE *goes to the door and looks after them.*

LARRY: Gosh! That fellow makes me tired.

SALLY: Do what Dad tells you, Larry. You ought to see a doctor.

LARRY: I'm all right. Bit short of breath. I'll soon be right.

MRS HARDCASTLE: Was our Harry down there?

LARRY: Harry? Yes, I think he was.

MRS HARDCASTLE: Aye, he is too! The young fool – he's carrying a banner. Here, just let me get at him. (*She seizes her shawl and runs out.*)

SALLY: You're hot and feverish, Larry. You're bad, I tell you. Go home now and get to bed.

LARRY: I can't, Sal. I can't. (*Rises.*) I've got to see this through.

SALLY: For my sake –?

LARRY: No. I can't. It's my show, this, and everything was going well before those fools started their nonsense. I'm – (*He staggers against the sofa and she has to steady him and help him on to the sofa.*)

SALLY: There! I told you – (*She runs up to the dresser and gets a cup.*) You're bad, real bad. (*She fills the cup at the sink and takes it to him.*)

LARRY: (*Sits up, assisted by Sally, and drinks.*) It's nothing,

nothing at all. (*He tightens his belt.*) I got excited on an empty stomach, that's all. Makes me lightheaded. There. I feel better now.

SALLY puts the cup on the table. LARRY tries to rise.

SALLY: Sit down, then, and rest.

She draws him to her.

Ah, Larry, Larry, why do you want to go fighting other people's battles? You've got yourself to think of, and me. Let other people take care of themselves.

LARRY: No, Sal, no – You don't understand. That's what's caused all this. Every man for himself and let others take care of themselves. That's what's wrong with the whole blasted world. Listen to 'em, shouting now they've lost their dole.

Crowd noise can hardly be heard now.

SALLY: (*Stroking his hair.*) Don't talk, Larry, it's rest you need –

LARRY: (*Leaning against her.*) Rest – Yes, Sal, I could rest if something inside'd let me. There's peace and quiet with you.

SALLY: We'll soon be old, Larry, and best part of our life gone. Is all your fighting and bitterness worth anything at all?

LARRY: Sometimes I think it isn't. But you don't know the misery of dreams – Be glad they don't hurt you –

SALLY: Me? Me not know dreams? You don't know. You don't know what I dream about you and me. For ages, Larry. Ay, and they hurt, those dreams.

LARRY: I know. It's wanting decent things and knowing they'll never be yours that hurts. But listen, Sal – (*He grips her arm.*) We've got to keep those dreams. They're ours, Sal – they're you and me. They're the only precious things we've got.

Crowd noise increases.

If we go down, Sal – if Hanky Park gets us as it gets the rest, it'll be something – something we shared together –

SALLY: Larry!

She holds tightly to him. A big drum starts beating down the street and voices sing the 'Internationale.' LARRY starts up.

LARRY: (*Rising.*) Listen! They've started!

SALLY: No, Larry, don't go! Don't go! You're not fit to go –

LARRY: I'm all right.

SALLY: (*Following.*) Come back, Larry!

LARRY: (*At door.*) God! The fools!

SALLY: What's the matter?

LARRY: Look at 'em! Straight for the Labour Exchange. It's that damned agitator leading 'em –

SALLY: No, Larry, no! Stay here! (*She tries to restrain him.*)

LARRY: I've got to head them off! (*He goes out shouting.*) Hey! Where do you think you're going –

SALLY: Larry! Larry!

People are running down the street from L. to R.

MRS BULL: (*As she passes – shouting.*) Come on, Sally, you'll miss all the fun.

HELEN appears in the doorway. She is weeping.

HELEN: Can I speak to you, Sal?

SALLY: Come inside, Helen.

HELEN: (*Closes the door.*) Are they all out?

Drum and singing soften. Crowd noises almost cease.

SALLY: Yes, there's only me. I'm worried about Larry. He's gone with the procession, and I'm sure the lad's ill. Well, young woman, what is it? So you're crying too, are you?

HELEN: I know what you're going to say. You're going to call me names and say it's my fault –

SALLY: Well, I wasn't going to congratulate you, Helen, but I'm not going to call you names.

HELEN: I don't care what people say. I love Harry, and Harry loves me –

SALLY: That's the spirit, lass. That's the way to talk. What are you crying for, then, if you feel that way?

HELEN: They've turned me out.

SALLY: Well, they've turned our Harry out, too, so there's a pair of you.

HELEN: Harry? You mean we can't live here?

SALLY: No, Dad won't have you. You see, we're so respectable in North Street, though you wouldn't think it sometimes.

HELEN: But what are we going to do?

SALLY: Well, now you're asking. I'm sorry, Helen. Don't cry, lass. You're not the only one as doesn't know where to turn. I'll do what I can for you.

HELEN: Where's Harry?

SALLY: Harry? He's carrying a banner in the demonstration. And he'll be finding a home in a prison cell if he's not careful.

HELEN: If only we could find a room somewhere. I don't care where it is. You see, I've got my job at mill and we could live on that if someone'd take us in. But nobody'll take us in, nobody decent, 'cause we're not married, and we've no money for that.

SALLY: I wonder how much longer us women'll take to learn that living and loving's all a damn swindle? Love's all right on the pictures, but love on the dole ain't quite same thing.

HELEN: I won't give up Harry.

Drum, singing and crowd die right out.

SALLY: I'm not asking you to. I reckon that's all part of swindle. We *can't* give 'em up, else wouldn't we have a bit o' sense and do without love same as we do without fine clothes, and motor-cars and champagne? Would we bring children into Hanky Park if we weren't blasted lunatics?

HELEN: If I'd only known this was going to happen – (*She breaks down a little.*)

SALLY: (*Taking both of HELEN's hands.*) Aw, go on, Helen. Look at the silver lining. When you're married they'll be bound to give you money at the workhouse. And Harry'll stand a better chance of getting a job when he's wed.

HELEN: Yes, but – we can't get married. We've no money for that.

SALLY: (*Producing some notes from her stocking.*) Let's see, is it seven and six? Or is that a dog licence? Marriage licences last for ever, though, so it's cheaper than keeping dogs. I know some marriages that wouldn't last long if you had to take out a new licence every year. (*She gives HELEN a ten-shilling note.*)

HELEN: Oh, Sally. (*About to return the note.*)

SALLY: Here, take it before I change me mind.

HELEN: Oh, thanks, Sally, thanks. (*She bursts into tears on SALLY's knee.*)

SALLY: That's all right. If you feel as grateful in ten years' time, you can pay me back. You know where the Registrar's office is – in Mill Street? And don't forget to take Harry with you.

HELEN: (*Tearfully.*) No. What shall I say?

SALLY: Say you want to get married, of course. They can't eat you.

HELEN: It's not what I'd planned. I always thought I'd be married in a church.

Crowd noises start again.

SALLY: Aw. Plans are like that. If we'd any sense, we wouldn't make any.

HELEN: Well, goodbye, Sally. And – you're awfully nice. (*She kisses SALLY impulsively.*)

SALLY: That's all right, Helen. And don't worry yourself. Things'll be all right. (*She looks through the window.*) I wish I knew what was going on down there.

HELEN: I'm going to see where Harry is.

She opens the door and goes out. She is hauled inside by SALLY. Crowd noise very loud.

MRS BULL: (*Heard shouting.*) Yah! You big bully! Call yourself a policeman? (*She appears outside window.*) You're a bloody Mussolini, that's what you are! (*Backing towards the doorway and shouting.*)

SALLY: What's the matter, Mrs Bull?

MRS BULL: Look at him, the big bluebottle! Look at the size of his feet! I'd stop indoors with feet like that.

MRS BULL comes just inside and stands against the door, holding it open.

Eh, Sal, it's a bad business. I said no good'd come out of this.

SALLY: Why, what's happened?

MRS BULL: You'd better follow that lad o' thine. He may want bailing out.

HELEN: I'm going to find where Harry is.

MRS BULL: (*Tries to stop HELEN, who breaks through and goes off.*) Stay where you are. Cops won't let you get past.

SALLY: Has Larry been taken up?

MRS BULL: Ee, I couldn't see who was taken. But there were hundreds of policemen waiting down by the Labour Exchange.

SALLY: You mean they're fighting?

MRS BULL: Fighting? It's a bloody war!

MRS HARDCASTLE: (*Entering.*) Oh, my God! I knew something'd happen. Our Harry and your Dad's there in the middle of it.

MRS BULL: I wish I was a man. I'd show 'em.

MRS HARDCASTLE: And there's no saying what'll happen with your Dad in his present state. He gets that fierce when his temper's roused –

SALLY: I'm going to see for myself – (*She goes to the door.*)

MRS HARDCASTLE: (*Pulls her back.*) No, Sal, come back. It's not safe! They're charging into the crowd.

SALLY: I must find Larry.

A police whistle blows. There is a rush of people along the street.

MRS HARDCASTLE: Come back, Sally.

MRS JIKE appears at the door carrying a bundle under her shawl. She is very excited.

MRS JIKE: Shut the door quick.

SALLY closes the door.

Hey, girls, look what I've got.

She produces a policeman's helmet from under her shawl.

Oh, what a time I've had! We rolled him in the mud and I danced on his stomach. It's as good as being in Whitechapel again.

MRS HARDCASTLE: Oh, Mrs Jike, what *have* you been doing?

MRS JIKE: (*Putting on the helmet and dancing a few steps.*) 'If you want to know the time, ask a policeman.'

SALLY: Shut up, you!

MRS HARDCASTLE: Did you see our Harry?

MRS JIKE: Your Harry? Can't say that I did. I saw the cops taking some blokes off to prison and there were some lying on the ground. But the fellow what owned this helmet won't forget Hanky Park in a hurry.

Horses' hoofs are heard coming nearer. Another police whistle blows three distinct blasts. MRS JIKE goes to the oven, opens it, and puts the helmet inside, closing the door. HARRY appears, breathless, slamming the door behind him. He carries LARRY's cap in his hand. His head is bleeding. Crowd swells as door opens, then softens.

MRS HARDCASTLE: Harry! Are you all right?

HARRY: Yes, Ma, I'm all right. Listen! Mounted police. Gosh! They charged out with their truncheons –

MRS HARDCASTLE: Where's your father?

HARRY: I saw him get away.

HELEN enters. Crowd swells up for this, then stops.

But he knocked two of 'em out first. They'd got all their men behind the Labour Exchange, and they told us to go around the other street. But that leader fellow refused, and before you could think they were on us –

SALLY: Harry! Where did you get that cap?

HARRY: I picked it up – it's –

SALLY: Let me see it. (*Takes the cap.*) It's Larry's –

MRS BULL: (*Looking out of the window.*) Here's a cop!

HARRY and HELEN rush over to the left and stand in the doorway. There is a knock on the street door and a POLICEMAN enters. MRS DORBELL appears outside.

POLICEMAN: Are you Sally Hardcastle?

SALLY: Yes.

POLICEMAN: You're wanted down the street. There's someone asking for you.

SALLY goes with the POLICEMAN. MRS DORBELL comes inside. MRS BULL goes up to the doorway and looks after SALLY.

MRS DORBELL: Well, did you ever see anything like it?

MRS BULL: What's the matter, Mrs Dorbell?

MRS DORBELL: Larry Meath's copped it.

MRS HARDCASTLE: Have they taken him to the police station?

MRS DORBELL: Hospital, you mean. Cops said it were serious. I saw him go down like a ninepin.

HARRY: Aye, I saw it too, only I didn't want to say anything when Sal was here. Cops collared hold of Larry and laid him out. I saw 'em. And Larry wasn't doing anything, except he was trying to turn the men back.

MRS BULL: Huh! This'll mean six months for Larry Meath.

MRS JIKE: He'll have sent for Sally to bail him out.

MRS BULL: I'll go down for seven days before my man gets another penny out of me. Let him go to prison. I've spent enough money on him.

MRS DORBELL: Thank God I'm a widow and all me family's growed up and out of me sight. Dammum! I wouldn't have the worrit of 'em again, not for a king's ransom.

MRS HARDCASTLE: (*Half rising.*) You're sure your Dad's all right, Harry?

HARRY: I tell you I saw him get away. But they got Larry, all right. I couldn't get near him to help, though I tried. But I got his cap.

MRS BULL: Fine lot o' good that was!

MRS HARDCASTLE: Well, our Sally's got no money to bail him out.

Crowd noise heard faintly. HARRY goes to the window.

Can you see your father, Harry?

HARRY: (*Goes up towards the door.*) No, but there's a crowd on the street corner. Ay, Father's there – and Sally, too.

The ambulance bell is heard. The women crowd to the door. MRS HARDCASTLE remains inside.

MRS DORBELL: Let's have a look. (*She goes to the window and looks out.*)

MRS BULL: Look, there's the ambulance!

HARRY: (*At the window.*) Here's Dad, with Sally. They're coming now. Something's happened, Ma. They've got an ambulance.

A POLICEMAN outside holds back the inquisitive CROWD. MR HARDCASTLE appears with SALLY leaning on his arm. She is carrying LARRY's cap clasped to her breast. MR HARDCASTLE brings her inside and she sits at the table, staring in front of her. The door remains open.

MRS HARDCASTLE: Oh, Sal! What is it, Sal?

HARDCASTLE: Leave her be, Ma.

MRS HARDCASTLE: What's happened?

HARDCASTLE: It's Larry – he's dead.

SALLY: Larry –

HARDCASTLE: Don't, Sal, don't!

SALLY: Well, that's put paid to that –

A silence creeps into the room. The crowd on the pavement stare through the open doorway.

Curtain

Scene 2

The same, six months later. Late afternoon.

MRS BULL, MRS DORBELL and MRS JIKE are sitting round the table, on which is a bottle and three cups. MRS HARDCASTLE is seated on the sofa. The trio sing 'The More We Are Together' listlessly and untunefully. MRS HARDCASTLE sobs loudly and they finish abruptly.

MRS DORBELL: More tears!

MRS BULL: Never in all me life did I see such a one as thee for blubbering. Lordy, what ails thee now?

MRS HARDCASTLE: What'll become of her? Oh, whatever'll become of her?

MRS BULL: Yah, ain't that just the way o' the world, eh? Her daughter gets a settlement made on her and then her Ma wonders what's gunna become of her.

MRS JIKE: (*Speaking through.*) Te, he! That's just it!

MRS BULL: Yah, y' don't deserve nothing, y' don't. Why don't you ask what's gunna become o' all o' us what's left in Hanky Park?

MRS DORBELL: Bah! I reckon she might have gone farther an' fared worse.

MRS HARDCASTLE: It's him. He'll murder her if he ever finds out. I know her father – an' it's such a disgrace! Everybody'll be talking – I'm feared.

MRS DORBELL: Talk's cheap enough. 'Ave another drop, Mrs Jike?

MRS JIKE: Thank you. I don't mind if I do.

She pours for herself. MRS BULL puts her cup on the table, and MRS JIKE pours for her too. MRS BULL then goes and sits on the chair by the sink.

'Ave a drop, Mrs Hardcastle. It'll cheer you up.

MRS HARDCASTLE: No, I don't want any.

MRS JIKE: Strike me pink! You're a nice one to give a little party. And me trying to be cheerful for you. Drink up, gels. While you've got it, enjoy it, says I. If it don't go one way, it'll go another.

She laughs and nudges MRS DORBELL.

MRS BULL: I dunno. Some folks don't know when they *are* well off. See here, Mrs Hardcastle, she'll take no hurt. Sally ain't that kind. She'd have been a sight worse off hangin' about here doin' nothing but thinking. If you want to know, it was *me* as hinted to Sam Grundy that she'd take no hurt if she went away for a while.

MRS HARDCASTLE: You?

MRS JIKE: Ee, Mrs Bull!

MRS BULL: And why not? Three or four months at that there place of his in Wales, with only nice weather in front of her – why, woman, she'll be new-made over again. All that she wants is something to make her forget. Everlasting thinking about that Larry Meath – It's more than flesh and blood can stand. Use your head, woman, use your head.

MRS HARDCASTLE: There's the other thing. Her and Mr Grundy. I don't like it – it's – it's – we've always been respectable.

MRS BULL *takes a drink.*

And now all the neighbours are talking.

MRS BULL: Let 'em talk. While they're talking about you they're leaving other folks be. Your Sally's had a bellyful of trouble, yes, a proper bellyful. First her dad gets out of work, and then her brother; then the fellow she's going to marry dies. If your Sal had gone on brooding the way she was, she'd have done what poor soul did in the next street yesterday. Guardians told him he'd have to give five shillings to his people what had come under the Means Test, and him married with a wife and family of his own. And what did *he* do? Cut his throat and jumped through bedroom winder, poor soul. You think of that an' be cheerful.

MRS HARDCASTLE: Hush! She's here now.

SALLY comes in from the street. She is better dressed than when we saw her before. She carries three or four small neat parcels. She enters with studied unconcern and greets the company airily. Her manner has hardened.

SALLY: Hello, Mrs Bull! And how's Mrs Jike and Mrs Dorbell? Having a good time?

MRS DORBELL: Ah, well, perhaps I'd better be going. (*She rises.*)

SALLY: You've no need to go. My complaint isn't catching, as far as I know. I suppose the whole street knows me business by this time. Well, I ain't ashamed. (*She puts the parcels on the sofa and sits on the lower end.*)

MRS BULL: You'd be a damned fool if you was. Ay, lass, when you get as old as me you'll have learned that there ain't nothing worth worrying your head about except where next meal's coming from. Be God, you will!

MRS HARDCASTLE: Where've you been, Sally?

SALLY: I've been to order a taxi to take me to the station.

MRS HARDCASTLE: Taxi?

MRS DORBELL: Eee, lass! Taxi in North Street!

MRS JIKE: Sounds real wicked, don't it? A motor-car!

MRS HARDCASTLE: (*Shocked.*) You mean it's coming here for you, in front of all the neighbours? (*She rises.*)

SALLY: Well, why not?

MRS HARDCASTLE: Have you no feeling for my shame?

SALLY: (*Rises.*) *Your* shame, Ma. I like that. Thought it was *my* shame that all the trouble was about.

MRS HARDCASTLE: Oh, Sal, what's changed you so?

SALLY: Can't be worse than it is. It seems to me that things always turn out different to what you expect. I thought I'd have been married by now. Huh!

MRS DORBELL: Married? You ain't missed much missing that.

MRS JIKE: Getting married's like a bloke with a bald head. There's no parting.

SALLY: Well, it ain't for me now. I can't have what I wanted, so I've took next best thing. Sick and tired I am of slugging and seeing nothing for it. Never had a holiday in my life, I ain't. But I know what money means now. He's got it and by God I'll make him pay!

MRS JIKE sniggers audibly. MRS DORBELL *joins in.*

MRS DORBELL: Are you sure Sam Grundy's made settlement fair and proper? There's nothing like having the money in your own name.

MRS BULL: Tell the old scut to mind her own business, Sal.

MRS DORBELL glares at MRS BULL.

SALLY: I've seen to that. He's stinking with brass and he's as daft as the rest of his kind. Ach! What fools they look slobbering around you. (*She opens her handbag.*) But there was nothing doing until I got me own way. He can chuck me over soon as he's a mind to now. (*She hands a one-pound note to her mother.*) Here, Ma, take it. It won't be the last, neither.

MRS HARDCASTLE: N-no, lass, I daren't! What would your father say?

SALLY: Oh, don't *you* start! I'll get enough lip from Dad when he comes in, I reckon. (*She looks at her gold wristwatch.*) Well, me train's at five-forty-five and taxi'll be here soon. I'd best get my things. (*She gathers up her parcels and goes out by the door on the left.*)

MRS HARDCASTLE: Oo, I don't know what's come over her. She ain't the same girl.

MRS BULL: You're right. She ain't the same girl since Larry Meath died. And a good job, too, or she'd have followed him to an early grave.

MRS JIKE: That would be a bit of ready money for you – laying her out.

MRS DORBELL: If I had my time over again I'd never get wed. Marriage, yaa! You get wed for love and find you've let yourself in for a seven-day-a-week job with no pay.

MRS JIKE: (*Who has been drinking diligently, fills the three cups.*) Come on, gels! Let's be happy while we can. You're a long time dead.

They begin to sing, off key, 'For you're here and I'm here, so what do we care,' etc. The door opens and HARDCASTLE appears. The music stops. He glares at the three women. They rise uncomfortably. MRS HARDCASTLE also rises.

HARDCASTLE: Get out of here!

MRS DORBELL: Here, here –?

HARDCASTLE: You heard me. Get out!

MRS DORBELL: Ho! Certainly. (*She hastily finishes her drink.*) I've no wish to stay where I'm not wanted. (*She crosses to the door.*) Are you coming, Mrs Bull?

MRS BULL: (*Finishes her drink.*) Come on, Mrs Jike. We're not wanted here.

They start for the door.

HARDCASTLE: (*Pointing to the bottle on the table.*) And take that stuff with you!

MRS BULL reaches for the bottle, but MRS JIKE is too quick for her. The three go out. HARDCASTLE shuts the door. His wife watches him fearfully. He leans with one hand against the fireplace, breathing heavily and gazing into the fire.

MRS HARDCASTLE: You didn't get that job, then, Henery?

HARDCASTLE: (*Muttering.*) Job? Christ!

MRS HARDCASTLE: (*Placing a chair for HARDCASTLE.*) You're tired, Henery. Sit down.

HARDCASTLE sits. MRS HARDCASTLE lights the light. She then crosses R. and lowers the blind.

HARDCASTLE: Where's our Sal?

MRS HARDCASTLE: She's upstairs. Why?

HARDCASTLE: I've been hearing strange tales, that's why.

MRS HARDCASTLE: Ah, folk don't know what they're saying.

HARDCASTLE: There's something queer going on here, and by God I mean to find out.

MRS HARDCASTLE: Now, Henery, don't get in a temper. Don't, please –

SALLY comes in. She is very neatly dressed for her departure and carries a small leather suitcase. She crosses to head of the sofa, where she deposits her jacket and puts the case on the floor above the sofa, then turns and faces her father.

SALLY: (*After a pause.*) Well?

HARDCASTLE: What's these tales I'm hearing about you and Sam Grundy?

SALLY: Well? What about it?

HARDCASTLE: Why –! (*Rising slowly.*) You brazen slut! Have you got cheek to stand there and tell me it's true?

SALLY: Yes, I have.

MRS HARDCASTLE: (*Above the table.*) Nay, Sally, lass, don't –

SALLY: It's true, Mother, and I don't care who knows it. Aye, and I'll tell you something else. It's sick I am of codging old clothes to try and make them look like something. And sick I am of working week after week and seeing nothing for it. I'm sick of never having anything but what's been in pawnshops and crawling with vermin – Oh, I'm sick of the sight of Hanky Park and everybody in it –

MRS HARDCASTLE: Sally!

HARDCASTLE: So you'd go whoring and make respectable folk like me and your Ma the talk of the neighbourhood, eh? Damn you! You ain't fit to be my daughter!

SALLY: Yaa, who cares what folk say? There's none I know as wouldn't swap places with me if they had the chance. You'd have me wed, would you? Then tell me where's the fellow around here can afford it. Them as *is* working ain't able to keep themselves, never mind a wife. Look at yourself – and look at our Harry! On workhouse relief and ain't even got a bed as he can call his own. I suppose I'd be fit to call your daughter if I was like that with a tribe of kids at me skirts. Well, can you get our Harry a job? No, but I can. Yes, me. I've got influence now – but I'm not respectable.

HARDCASTLE: God! I'd rather see you lying dead at my feet!

SALLY: Dead? Dead, did you say? (*She laughs.*) Aren't we all dead, all of us in Hanky Park –

HARDCASTLE: (*Pointing to the door.*) Get out! Get out before I kill you!

SALLY: (*Defiantly.*) Right! And I can do that, too. (*She crosses to the sofa, picks up her jacket and puts it on.*) You kicked our Harry out because he got married and you're kicking me out because I ain't. You'd have me like all the rest of the women, working themselves to death and getting nothing for it. Look at Mother! Look at her! (*Pointing.*) Well, there ain't a man breathing, now Larry's gone, who can get me like *that* – for him!

HARDCASTLE: (*Rushing at her.*) Aach! You brazen bitch! Take that! (*He strikes her and she falls across the sofa.*) Keep your dirty lying tongue off your mother, do you hear?

SALLY lies where she has fallen, sobbing.

MRS HARDCASTLE: Eh, Father, Father, look what you've done to the lass. (*She sits above SALLY and gathers SALLY's head on her knees.*)

HARDCASTLE: Come away from her. Come away from her!

MRS HARDCASTLE: Nay, she didn't mean any harm. Don't cry, lass. You neither of you know what you're saying when you get that way.

HARDCASTLE: Haven't I worked all me life, body and soul, to keep a home for her? Haven't I kept myself respectable for her, when God knows I've been near driven to drink with things? And now me own daughter tells me she's a whore – Ay, and proud of it, too!

MRS HARDCASTLE: Lad, she's only young – she's only young. Where should we have been all these months if it hadn't been for our Sally? It's her money we've been living on since they knocked you off dole, and well you know it.

HARDCASTLE: Ay, and well I know it! And well I know I mean to be boss in me own house.

MRS HARDCASTLE: But the money –?

HARDCASTLE: To hell with money! She's made her own bed, she must lie in it.

MRS HARDCASTLE: It's your own bed you're making, Henry Hardcastle, when you drive our Sally out. Your bed and mine. I'm thinking it won't be that easy to lie on.

HARDCASTLE: (*Sinks into the chair at the table.*) Leave me be! Leave me be! I'm sick of hearing you! Oh, God, give me some work! Give me some work –!

He groans and his head falls on the table. There is a sudden impatient knock at the street door. SALLY *sits up and dries her eyes.* MRS HARDCASTLE *opens the door.*

HARRY: (*Outside.*) It's Helen, Ma. She's took bad. She wants Mrs Bull.

SALLY: Come in, Harry. I've something to say to you.

HARRY: It's Helen. She's going to have a baby – she wants Mrs Bull to come 'round as soon as she can. Do something, Sal! – Sal, do something!

SALLY: So it's come, has it? Another poor devil for Hanky Park. You might have saved yourself the trouble, lad. (*She rises and opens her purse.*) Here, take this – you'll be needing it. (*She gives him some notes.*)

HARRY: Eh, Sal! Thanks! But where did you get it?

SALLY: Never mind. And take this as well. (*She hands him an envelope.*) And here's another for Dad. (*She crosses and puts another on the table near her father's hand.*) I've been keeping it as a surprise for you. You take these letters to the East City Bus Offices and give them to Mr Moreland. There'll be a job for each of you. But remember, say nothing to nobody how you got it. And give the letters to nobody but Mr Moreland.

HARRY: Let's see. That's manager, Mr Moreland – him as Sam Grundy knows –

MRS HARDCASTLE: Hush – (*Indicating* HARDCASTLE.)

HARRY: (*Smiling.*) All right! Gosh, can you imagine what Helen'll say? Oh, ta, Sal – a job – I've got a job – You don't know what it means to me – (*He is hysterical.*) I – Oh, thanks!

He rushes out to hide his tears. MRS HARDCASTLE *closes the door.*

SALLY: I'm sorry, Dad – about all this. Things are different now to what you've been used to, and you've got to face things as they are, not as you'd like them to be. We all want a fresh start – that's what Larry said. Well, there's no starting fresh in Hanky Park, and I'm getting out, quickest road.

HARDCASTLE *stares brokenly before him.* SALLY *pulls the letter a little nearer to his hand.*

Maybe that'll be a good job – this'll get you a few smokes. (*She puts some small change on the table.*) Goodbye, Ma, and don't worry.

She goes up to her mother and they embrace. A taxi-horn is heard outside.

MRS DORBELL: (*Pushes open the door and enters.*) Hey! Here's the taxi come for your Sally.

There is an excited, talkative crowd in the darkness outside. SALLY *stands for a moment hoping her father will turn his head. She then picks up her bag, still looking towards her father. She bites her lip, then drawing herself up proudly, turns and marches out to the taxi. Laughter and jeering are heard, then the discordant singing of 'Here Comes the Bride.' The taxi drives away and the noise dies down.* MRS HARDCASTLE *closes the door and comes over to the table behind her husband.*

MRS HARDCASTLE: Don't take on so, Henry. You've got a job now. That's something to be thankful for. Don't be hard on the lass. There's no harm in her, she's only young and self-willed – And she's your own daughter, Henery –

HARDCASTLE: (*An angry, beaten man.*) Oh, God, I've done me best! I've done me best, haven't I?

MRS HARDCASTLE *turns and takes the teapot. She goes to the kettle on the fire.*

3.6 BLUES FOR MISTER CHARLIE (1964)

JAMES BALDWIN

James Baldwin (1924–87) was an influential African American novelist, dramatist, poet, critic and civil rights campaigner. Baldwin infamously came to wide public attention following the publication of his novel Giovanni's Room *(1956). The novel was not only vilified for its examination of white male homoeroticism, it raised important questions, particularly pertinent in mid-twentieth-century USA, about what it meant to be a 'black writer'.* Blues for Mister Charlie *(1964) was inspired by the actual murder of an African American man and the subsequent acquittal of those accused by an all-white male jury. Set in the American South, Baldwin's play is marked by the sophisticated manner in which it deals with the race question, and how cultures and identities might move from tolerance to under-standing. This is underpinned by a dramatic structure that disrupts a conventional linear timeframe, also counterpointed by the use of internal soliloquies.* Blues for Mister Charlie *was first produced by The Actors Studio Theatre in New York, directed by Burgess Meredith.*

Characters

MERIDIAN HENRY, NEGRO MINISTER

TOM
KEN
ARTHUR
JUANITA ⎬ NEGRO STUDENTS
LORENZO
PETE

JIMMY

MOTHER HENRY, MERIDIAN HENRY'S MOTHER

LYLE BRITTEN, A WHITE STORE–OWNER

JO BRITTEN, LYLE'S WIFE

PARNELL JAMES, EDITOR OF THE LOCAL NEWSPAPER

RICHARD, MERIDIAN HENRY'S SON

PAPA D., OWNER OF A JUKE JOINT

HAZEL
LILLIAN
SUSAN
RALPH ⎬ WHITE TOWNSPEOPLE
ELLIS
REV. PHELPS
GEORGE

CLERK

JUDGE

THE STATE

COUNSEL FOR THE BEREAVED

FOREMAN

CONGREGATION OF REV. HENRY'S CHURCH, PALLBEARERS, BLACKTOWN, WHITETOWN

Act 1

Multiple set, the skeleton of which, in the first two acts, is the Negro church, and, in the third act, the courthouse. The church and the courthouse are on opposite sides of a southern street; the audience should always be aware, during the first two acts, of the dome of the courthouse and the American flag. During the final act, the audience should always be aware of the steeple of the church, and the cross.

The church is divided by an aisle. The street door upstage faces the audience. The pulpit is downstage, at an angle, so that the minister is simultaneously addressing the congregation and the audience. In the third act, the pulpit is replaced by the witness stand.

This aisle also functions as the division between WHITETOWN *and* BLACKTOWN. *The action among the blacks takes place on one side of the stage, the action among the whites on the opposite side of the stage – which is to be remembered during the third act, which takes place, of course, in a segregated courtroom.*

This means that RICHARD's *room,* LYLE's *store,* PAPA D.'s *joint,* J's *kitchen, etc., are to exist principally by suggestion, for these shouldn't be allowed to obliterate the skeleton, or, more accurately, perhaps, the framework, suggested above.*

For the murder scene, the aisle functions as a gulf. The stage should be built out, so that the audience reacts to the enormity of this gulf, and so that RICHARD, *when he falls, falls out of sight of the audience, like a stone, into the pit.*

In the darkness we hear a shot.

Lights up slowly on LYLE, *staring down at the ground. He looks around him, bends slowly and picks up* RICHARD's *body as though it were a sack. He carries him upstage, drops him.*

LYLE: And may every nigger like this nigger end like this nigger – face down in the weeds!

Exits.

(BLACKTOWN: *The church. A sound of mourning begins.* MERIDIAN, TOM, KEN *and* ARTHUR.)

MERIDIAN: No, no, no! You have to say it like you mean it – the way they really say it: nigger, nigger, nigger! *Nigger!* Tom, the way *you* saying it, it sounds like you just *might* want to make friends. And that's not the way they sound out there. Remember all that's happened. Remember we having a funeral here – tomorrow night. Remember why. Go on, hit it again.

TOM: You dirty nigger, you no-good black bastard, what you doing down here, anyway?

MERIDIAN: That's much better. Much much better. Go on.

TOM: Hey, boy, where's your mother? I bet she's lying up in bed, just a-pumping away, ain't she, boy?

MERIDIAN: *That's* the way they sound!

TOM: Hey, boy, how much does your mother charge? How much does your sister charge?

KEN: How much does your *wife* charge?

MERIDIAN: Now you got it. You really got it now. That's them. Keep walking, Arthur. *Keep walking!*

TOM: You get your ass off these streets from around here, boy, or we going to do us some cutting – we're going to cut that big, black thing off of you, you hear?

MERIDIAN: Why you all standing around there like that? Go on and get you a nigger. Go on!

A scuffle.

MERIDIAN: All right. All right! Come on, now. Come on.

KEN *steps forward and spits in* ARTHUR's *face.*

ARTHUR: You black s.o.b., what the hell do you think you're doing? You mother –!

MERIDIAN: Hey, hold it! Hold it! Hold it!

MERIDIAN *wipes the boy's face. They are all trembling.*

MOTHER HENRY *enters.*

MOTHER HENRY: Here they come. And it looks like they had a time.

JUANITA, LORENZO, PETE, JIMMY, *all Negro, carry placards, enter, exhausted and dishevelled, wounded;* PETE *is weeping. The placards bear such legends as* Freedom Now, We Want The Murderer, One Man, One Vote, *etc.*

JUANITA: We shall overcome!

LORENZO: We shall not be moved! (*Laughs.*) We were moved tonight, though. Some of us has been moved to *tears.*

MERIDIAN: Juanita, what happened?

JUANITA: Oh, just another hometown Saturday night.

MERIDIAN: Come on, Pete, come on, old buddy. Stop it. Stop it.

LORENZO: I don't blame him. I do not blame the cat. You feel like a damn fool standing up there, letting them white mothers beat on your ass – shoot if I had my way, just once – stop crying, Pete, goddammit!

JUANITA: Lorenzo, you're in church.

LORENZO: Yeah. Well, I wish to God I was in an arsenal. I'm sorry, Meridian, Mother Henry – I don't mean that for you. I don't understand you. I don't understand Meridian here. It was his son, it was your grandson, Mother Henry, that got killed, butchered! Just last week, and yet, here you sit – in this – this – the house of this damn almighty God who don't care what happens to nobody, unless, of course, they're white. Mother Henry, I got a lot of respect for you and all that, and for Meridian, too, but that white man's God is *white*. It's that damn white God that's been lynching us and burning us and castrating us and raping our women and robbing us of everything that makes a man a man for all these hundreds of years. Now, why we sitting around here, in *His* house? If I could get my hands on Him, I'd pull Him out of heaven and drag Him through this town at the end of a rope.

MERIDIAN: No, you wouldn't.

LORENZO: I wouldn't? Yes, I would. Oh, yes, I would.

JUANITA: And then you wouldn't be any better than they are.

LORENZO: I don't want to be better than they are, why should I be better than they are? And better at what? Better at being a doormat, better at being a corpse? Sometimes I just don't know. We've been demonstrating – *non-violently* – for more than a year now and all that's happened is that now they'll let us into that crummy library downtown which was obsolete in 1897 and where nobody goes anyway; who in this town reads books? For that we paid I don't know how many thousands of dollars in fines, Jerome is still in the hospital, and we all know that Ruthie is never again going to be the swinging little chick she used to be. Big deal. Now we're picketing that great movie palace downtown where I wouldn't go on a bet; I can live without Yul Brynner and Doris Day, thank you very much. And we *still* can't get licensed to be electricians or plumbers, we still can't walk through the park, our kids still can't use the swimming pool in town. We still can't vote, we can't even get registered. Is it worth it? And these people trying to kill us, too? And we ain't even got no guns. The cops ain't going to protect us. They call up the people and tell them where we are and say, 'Go get them! They ain't going to do nothing to you – they just dumb niggers!'

MERIDIAN: Did they arrest anybody tonight?

PETE: No, they got their hands full now, trying to explain what Richard's body was doing in them weeds.

LORENZO: It was wild. You know, all the time we was ducking them bricks and praying to *God* we'd get home before somebody got killed – (*Laughs.*) I had a jingle going through my mind, like if I was a white man, dig? and I had to wake up every morning singing to myself, 'Look at the happy nigger, he doesn't give a damn, thank God I'm not a nigger –'

TOGETHER: '– Good Lord, perhaps I am!'

JUANITA: You've gone crazy, Lorenzo. They've done it. You have been unfitted for the struggle.

MERIDIAN: I cannot rest until they bring my son's murderer to trial. That man who killed my son.

LORENZO: But he killed a nigger before, as I know all of you know. Nothing never happened. Sheriff just shovelled the body into the ground and forgot about it.

MERIDIAN: Parnell will help me.

PETE: Meridian, you know that *Mister* Parnell ain't going to let them arrest his ass-hole buddy. I'm sorry, Mother Henry!

MOTHER HENRY: That's all right, son.

MERIDIAN: But I think that Parnell has proven to be a pretty good friend to all of us. He's the only white man in this town who's ever *really* stuck his neck out in order to do – to do right. He's *fought* to bring about this trial – I can't tell you how hard he's fought. If it weren't for him, there'd be much less hope.

LORENZO: I guess I'm just not as nice as you are. I don't trust as many people as you trust.

MERIDIAN: We can't afford to become too distrustful, Lorenzo.

LORENZO: We can't afford to be too trusting, either. See, when a white man's a *good* white man, he's good because he wants *you* to be good. Well, sometimes I just might want to be *bad*. I got as much right to be bad as anybody else.

MERIDIAN: No, you don't.

LORENZO: Why not?

MERIDIAN: Because you know better.

PARNELL enters.

PARNELL: Hello, my friends. I bring glad tidings of great joy. Is that the way the phrase goes, Meridian?

JUANITA: Parnell!

PARNELL: I can't stay. I just came to tell you that a warrant's being issued for Lyle's arrest.

JUANITA: They're going to arrest him? Big Lyle Britten? I'd love to know how you managed *that*.

PARNELL: Well, Juanita, I am not a *good* man, but I have my little ways.

JUANITA: And a whole lot of folks in this town, baby, are not going to be talking to you no more, for days and days and *days*.

PARNELL: I hope that you all will. I may have no other company. I think I should go to Lyle's house to warn him. After all, I brought it about and he *is* a friend of mine – and then I have to get the announcement into my paper.

JUANITA: So it *is* true.

PARNELL: Oh, yes, it's true.

MERIDIAN: When is he being arrested?

PARNELL: Monday morning. Will you be up later, Meridian? I'll drop by if you are – if I may.

MERIDIAN: Yes. I'll be up.

PARNELL: All right, then. I'll trundle by. Good night all. I'm sorry I've got to run.

MERIDIAN: Good night.

JUANITA: Thank you, Parnell.

PARNELL: Don't thank me, dear Juanita. I only acted – as I believed I had to act. See you later, Meridian.

PARNELL exits.

MERIDIAN: I wonder if they'll convict him.

JUANITA: Convict him. Convict him. You're asking for heaven on earth. After all, they haven't even *arrested* him yet. And, anyway – why *should* they convict him? Why him? He's no worse than all the others. He's an honourable tribesman and he's defended, with blood, the honour and purity of his tribe!

(*WHITETOWN: LYLE holds his infant son up above his head.*)

LYLE: Hey old pisser. You hear me, sir? I expect you to control your bladder like a *gentleman* whenever your Papa's got you on his knee.

JO enters.

He got a mighty big bladder, too, for such a little fellow.

JO: I'll tell the world he didn't steal it.

LYLE: You mighty sassy tonight.

Hands her the child.

Ain't that right, old pisser? Don't you reckon your Mama's getting kind of sassy? And what do you reckon I should do about it?

JO is changing the child's diapers.

JO: You tell your Daddy he can start sleeping in his own bed nights instead of coming grunting in here in the wee small hours of the morning.

LYLE: And you tell your Mama if she was getting her sleep like she should be, so she can be alert every instant to your needs, little fellow, she wouldn't *know* what time I come – *grunting* in.

JO: I got to be alert to *your* needs, too. I think.

LYLE: Don't you go starting to imagine things. I just been over to the store. That's all.

JO: Till three and four o'clock in the morning?

LYLE: Well, I got plans for the store, I think I'm going to try to start branching out, you know, and I been – making plans.

JO: You thinking of branching out *now?* Why, Lyle, you know we ain't *hardly* doing no business *now*. Weren't for the country folks come to town every Saturday, I don't know *where* we'd be. This ain't no time to be branching *out*. We barely holding *on*.

LYLE: Shoot, the niggers'll be coming back, don't you worry. They'll get over this foolishness presently. They already weary of having to drive forty-fifty miles across the state line to get their groceries – a lot of them ain't even got cars.

JO: Those that don't have cars have *friends* with cars.

LYLE: Well, friends get weary, too. Joel come in the store a couple of days ago –

JO: Papa D.? He don't count. You can always wrap him around your little finger.

LYLE: Listen, will you? He come in the store a couple of days ago to buy a sack of flour and he *told* me, he say, The niggers is *tired* running all over creation to put some food on the table. Ain't nobody going to keep on driving no forty-fifty miles to buy no sack of flour – what you mean when you say Joel don't count?

JO: I don't mean nothing. But there's something wrong with anybody when his own people don't think much of him.

LYLE: Joel's got good sense, is all. I think more of him than I think of a lot of white men, that's a fact. And he knows what's right for his people, too.

JO: *(Puts son in crib.)* Well. Selling a sack of flour once a week ain't going to send this little one through college, neither. *(A pause.)* In what direction were you planning to branch out?

LYLE: I was thinking of trying to make the store more – well, more colourful. Folks like colour –

JO: You mean, niggers like colour.

LYLE: Dammit, Jo, I ain't in business just to sell to niggers! Listen to me, can't you? I thought I'd dress it up, get a new front, put some neon signs in – and, you know, we got more space in there than we use. Well, why don't we open up a line of ladies' clothes? Nothing too fancy, but I bet you it would bring in a lot more business.

JO: I don't know. Most of the ladies I know buy their clothes at Benton's, on Decatur Street.

LYLE: The niggers don't – anyway, we could sell them the same thing. The white ladies, I mean –

JO: No. It wouldn't be the same.

LYLE: Why not? A dress is a dress.

JO: But it sounds better if you say you got it on Decatur Street! At Benton's. Anyway – where would you get the money for this branching out?

LYLE: I can get a loan from the bank. I'll get old Parnell to co-sign with me, or have him get one of his rich friends to co-sign with me.

JO: Parnell called earlier – you weren't at the store today.

LYLE: What do you mean, I wasn't at the store?

JO: Because Parnell called earlier and said he tried to get you at the store and that there wasn't any answer.

LYLE: There wasn't any business. I took a walk.

JO: He said he's got bad news for you.

LYLE: What kind of bad news?

JO: He didn't say. He's coming by here this evening to give it to you himself.

LYLE: What do you think it is?

JO: I guess they're going to arrest you?

LYLE: No, they ain't. They ain't gone crazy.

JO: I think they might. We had so much trouble in this town lately and it's been in all the northern newspapers – and now, this – this dead boy –

LYLE: They ain't got no case.

JO: No. But you was the last person to see that crazy boy – alive. And now everybody's got to thinking again – about that other time.

LYLE: That was self-defence. The Sheriff said so himself. Hell, I ain't no murderer. They're just some things I don't believe is right.

JO: Nobody never heard no more about the poor little girl – his wife.

LYLE: No. She just disappeared.

JO: You never heard no more about her at all?

LYLE: How would I hear about her more than anybody else? No, she just took off – I believe she had people in Detroit somewhere. I reckon that's where she went.

JO: I felt sorry for her. She looked so lost those last few times I saw her, wandering around town – and she was so young. She was a pretty little thing.

LYLE: She looked like a piccaninny to me. Like she was too young to be married. I reckon she *was* too young for him.

JO: It happened in the store.

LYLE: Yes.

JO: How people talked! That's what scares me now.

LYLE: Talk don't matter. I hope you didn't believe what you heard.

JO: A lot of people did. I reckon a lot of people still do.

LYLE: *You* don't believe it?

JO: No. (*A pause.*) You know – Monday morning – we'll be married one whole year!

LYLE: Well, can't nobody talk about *us*. That little one there ain't but two months old.

The door bell rings.

JO: That's Parnell.

Exits.

LYLE walks up and down, looks into the crib. JO *and* PARNELL *enter.*

LYLE: It's about time you showed your face in here, you old rascal! You been so busy over there with the niggers, you ain't got time for white folks no more. You sure you ain't got some nigger wench over there on the other side of town? Because, I declare –!

PARNELL: I apologize for your husband, Mrs Britten, I really do. In fact, I'm afraid I must deplore your taste in men. If I had only seen you first, dear lady, and if you had found me charming, how much suffering I might have prevented! You got anything in this house to drink? Don't tell me you haven't, we'll both need one. Sit down.

LYLE: Bring on the booze, old lady.

JO brings ice, glasses, etc.; pours drinks.

What you been doing with yourself?

PARNELL: Well, I seem to have switched territories. I haven't been defending coloured people this week, I've been defending you. I've just left the Chief of Police.

LYLE: How is the old bastard?

PARNELL: He seems fine. But he really *is* an old bastard. Lyle – he's issuing a warrant for your arrest.

LYLE: He's going to arrest *me*? You mean, he believes I killed that boy?

PARNELL: The question of what he believes doesn't enter into it. This case presents several very particular circumstances and these circumstances force him to arrest you. I think we can take it for granted that he wouldn't arrest you if he could think of some way not to. He wouldn't arrest anybody except blind beggars and old coloured women if he could think of some way not to – he's bird-brained and chicken-hearted and big-assed. The charge is murder.

JO: Murder!

LYLE: Murder?

PARNELL: Murder.

LYLE: I ain't no murderer. You know that.

PARNELL: I also know that somebody killed the boy. Somebody put two slugs in his belly and dumped his body in the weeds beside the railroad track just outside of town. Somebody did all that. We pay several eminent, bird-brained, chicken-hearted, big-assed people quite a lot of money to discourage such activity. They never do, in fact, discourage it, but, still – we must find the somebody who killed that boy. And you, my friend, according to the testimony of Joel Davis, otherwise known as Papa D., were the last person to see the boy alive. It is also known that you didn't like him – to say the least.

LYLE: Nobody liked him.

PARNELL: Ah. But it isn't nobody that killed him. *Somebody* killed him. We must find the somebody. And since you were the last person to see him alive, we must arrest you in order to clear you – or convict you.

LYLE: They'll never convict me.

PARNELL: As to that, you may be right. But you *are* going to be arrested.

LYLE: When?

PARNELL: Monday morning. Of course, you can always flee to Mexico.

LYLE: Why should I run away?

PARNELL: I wasn't suggesting that you should run away. If you did, I should urge your wife to divorce you at once, and marry me.

JO: Ah, if that don't get him out of town in a hurry, I don't know what will! The man's giving you your chance, honey. You going to take it?

LYLE: Stop talking foolishness. It looks bad for me, I guess. I swear, I don't know what's come over the folks in this town!

PARNELL: It doesn't look good. In fact, if the boy had been white, it would look very, *very* bad, and your behind would be in the jail house now. What do you mean, you don't understand what's come over the people in this town?

LYLE: Raising so much fuss about a nigger – and a northern nigger at that.

PARNELL: He was born here. He's Reverend Meridian Henry's son.

LYLE: Well, he'd been gone so long, he might as well have been a northern nigger. Went North and got ruined and come back here to make trouble – and they tell me he was a dope fiend, too. What's all this fuss about? He probably got killed by some other nigger – they do it all the time – but ain't nobody even thought about arresting one of *them*. Has niggers suddenly got to be *holy* in this town?

PARNELL: Oh, Lyle, I'm not here to discuss the sanctity of niggers. I just came to tell you that a warrant's being issued for your arrest. *You* may think that a coloured boy who gets ruined in the North and then comes home to try to pull himself together deserves to die – *I* don't.

LYLE: You sound like you think I got something against coloured folks – but I don't. I never have, not in all my life. But I'll be damned if I'll mix with them. That's all. I don't believe in it, and that's *all*. I don't want no big buck nigger lying up next to Josephine and that's where all this will lead to and you know it as well as I do! I'm against it and I'll do anything I have to do to stop it, yes, I will!

PARNELL: Suppose *he* – my godson there – decides to marry a Chinese girl. You know, there are an awful lot of Chinese girls in the world – I bet you didn't know that. Well, there are. Let's just say that he grows up and looks around at all the pure white women, and – saving your presence, ma'am – they make him want to puke and he decides to marry a pure Chinese girl instead. What would you do? Shoot him in order to prevent it? Or would you shoot her?

LYLE: Parnell, you're my buddy. You've *always* been my buddy. You know more about me than anybody else in the world. What's come over you? You – you ain't going to turn against me, are you?

PARNELL: No. No, I'll never turn against you. I'm just trying to make you think.

LYLE: I notice you didn't marry no Chinese girl. You just never got married at all. Women been trying to saddle old Parnell for I don't know how long – I don't know what you got, old buddy, but I'll be damned if you don't know how to use it! What about this present one – Loretta – you reckon you going to marry her?

PARNELL: I doubt it.

JO: Parnell, you're just awful. Awful!

PARNELL: I think I'm doing her a favour. She can do much better than me. I'm just a broken-down newspaper editor – the editor of a newspaper which *nobody* reads – in a dim, grim backwater.

LYLE: I thought you liked it here.

PARNELL: I don't like it here. But I love it here. Or maybe I don't. I don't know. I must go.

LYLE: What's your hurry? Why don't you stay and have pot-luck with us?

PARNELL: Loretta is waiting. I must have pot-luck with *her*. And then I have errands on the other side of town.

LYLE: What they saying over there? I reckon they praying day and night for my ass to be put in a sling, ain't they? Shoot, I don't care.

PARNELL: Don't. Life's much simpler that way. Anyway, Papa D.'s the only one doing a whole lot of talking.

JO: I told you he wasn't no good, Lyle, I told you!

LYLE: I don't know what's got into him! And we been knowing each other all these years! He must be getting old. You go back and tell him I said he's got it all *confused* – about me and that boy. Tell him you talked to me and that *I* said he must have made some mistake.

PARNELL: I'll drop in tomorrow, if I may. Good night, Jo, and thank you. Good night, Lyle.

LYLE: Good night, old buddy.

JO: I'll see you to the door.

JO and PARNELL exit. LYLE walks up and down.

LYLE: Well! *Ain't* that something! But they'll never convict me. Never in this world. (*Looks into crib.*) Ain't that right, old pisser?

(BLACKTOWN: *The church, as before.*)

LORENZO: And when they bring him to trial, I'm going to be there every day – right across the street in that court-house – where they been dealing death out to us for all these years.

MOTHER HENRY: I used to hate them, too, son. But I don't hate them no more. They too pitiful.

MERIDIAN: No witnesses.

JUANITA: Meridian. Ah, Meridian.

MOTHER HENRY: You remember that song he used to like so much?

MERIDIAN: I sing because I'm happy.

JUANITA: I sing because I'm free.

PETE: For his eye is on the sparrow –

LORENZO: And I know he watches – me.

Music, very faint.

JUANITA: There was another song he liked – a song about a prison and the light from a train that shone on the prisoners every night at midnight. I can hear him now: Lord, you wake up in the morning. You hear the ding-dong ring –

MOTHER HENRY: He had a beautiful voice.

LORENZO: Well, he was pretty tough up there in New York – till he got busted.

MERIDIAN: And came running home.

MOTHER HENRY: Don't blame yourself, honey. Don't blame yourself!

JUANITA: You go a-marching to the table, you see the same old thing –

JIMMY: All I'm going to tell you: knife, a fork, and a pan –

Music stronger.

PETE: And if you say a thing about it –

LORENZO: You are in trouble with the man.

Lights dim in the church. We discover RICHARD, standing in his room, singing. This number is meant to make vivid the RICHARD who was much loved on the Apollo Theatre stage in Harlem, the RICHARD who was a rising New York star.

MERIDIAN: No witnesses!

Near the end of the song, MOTHER HENRY enters, carrying a tray with milk, sandwiches, and cake.

RICHARD: You treating me like royalty, old lady – I ain't royalty. I'm just a raggedy-assed, out-of-work, busted musician. But I sure can sing, can't I?

MOTHER HENRY: You better learn some respect, you know that neither me nor your father wants that kind of language in this house. Sit down and eat, you got to get your strength back.

RICHARD: What for? What am I supposed to do with it?

MOTHER HENRY: You stop that kind of talk.

RICHARD: Stop that kind of talk, we don't want that kind of talk! Nobody cares what people feel or what they think or what they do – but stop that kind of talk!

MOTHER HENRY: Richard!

RICHARD: All right. All right. (*Throws himself on the bed, begins eating in a kind of fury.*) What I can't get over is – what in the world am I doing *here*? Way down here in the ass-hole of the world, the deep, black, funky South.

MOTHER HENRY: You were born here. You got folks here. And you ain't got no manners and you *won't* learn no sense and so you naturally got yourself in trouble and had to come to your folks. You lucky it wasn't no worse, the way you go on. You want some more milk?

RICHARD: No, old lady. Sit down.

MOTHER HENRY: I ain't got time to be fooling with you. (*But she sits down.*) What you got on your mind?

RICHARD: I don't know. How do you stand it?

MOTHER HENRY: Stand what? You?

RICHARD: Living down here with all these nowhere people.

MOTHER HENRY: From what I'm told and from what I see, the people you've been among don't seem to be any better.

RICHARD: You mean old Aunt Edna? She's all right, she just ain't very bright, is all.

MOTHER HENRY: I am not talking about Edna. I'm talking about all them other folks you got messed up with. Look like you'd have had better sense. You hear me?

RICHARD: I hear you.

MOTHER HENRY: That all you got to say?

RICHARD: It's easy for you to talk, Grandmama, you don't know nothing about New York City, or what can happen to you up there!

MOTHER HENRY: I know what can happen to you anywhere in this world. And I know right from wrong. We tried to raise you so you'd know right from wrong, too.

RICHARD: We don't see things the same way, Grandmama. I don't know if I really *know* right from wrong – I'd like to, I always dig people the most who know *anything*, especially right from wrong!

MOTHER HENRY: You've had yourself a little trouble, Richard, like we all do, and you a little tired, like we all get. You'll be all right. You a young man. Only, just try not to *go* so much, try to calm down a little. Your Daddy loves you. You his only son.

RICHARD: That's a good reason, Grandmama. Let me tell you about New York. You ain't never been North, have you?

MOTHER HENRY: Your Daddy used to tell me a little about it every time he come back from visiting you all up there.

RICHARD: Daddy don't know nothing about New York. He just come up for a few days and went right on back. That ain't the way to get to know New York. No ma'am. He *never* saw New York. Finally, I realized he wasn't never *going* to see it – you know, there's a whole lot of things Daddy's never seen? I've seen more than he has.

MOTHER HENRY: All young folks thinks that.

RICHARD: Did *you*? When you were young? Did you think you knew more than your mother and father? But I bet you really did, you a pretty shrewd old lady, quiet as it's kept.

MOTHER HENRY: No, I didn't think that. But I thought I could find *out* more, because *they* were born in slavery, but *I* was born free.

RICHARD: *Did* you find out more?

MOTHER HENRY: I found out what I had to find out – to take care of my husband and raise my children in the fear of God.

RICHARD: You know I don't believe in God, Grandmama.

MOTHER HENRY: You don't know what you talking about. Ain't no way possible for you not to believe in God. It ain't up to you.

RICHARD: Who's it up to, then?

MOTHER HENRY: It's up to the life in you – the life in you. *That* knows where it comes from, *that* believes in God. You doubt me, you just try holding your breath long enough to die.

RICHARD: You pretty smart, ain't you? (*A pause.*) I convinced Daddy that I'd be better off in New York – and Edna, she convinced him too, she said it wasn't as tight for a black man up there as it is down here. Well, that's a crock, Grandmama, believe me when I tell you. At first I thought it was true, hell, I was just a green country boy and they ain't got no signs up, dig, saying you can't go here or you can't go there. No, you got to find that out all by your lonesome. But – for awhile – I thought everything was swinging and Edna, she's so dizzy she thinks everything is *always* swinging, so there we were – like *swinging*.

MOTHER HENRY: I know Edna got lost somewhere. But Richard – why didn't *you* come back? You knew your Daddy wanted you back, your Daddy and me both.

RICHARD: I didn't want to come back here like a whipped dog. One whipped dog running to another whipped dog. No, I didn't want that. I wanted to make my Daddy proud of me – because, the day I left here, I sure as hell wasn't proud of *him*.

MOTHER HENRY: Be careful, son. Be careful. Your Daddy's a fine man. Your Daddy loves you.

RICHARD: I know, Grandmama. But I just wish, that day that Mama died, he'd took a pistol and gone through that damn white man's hotel and shot every son of a bitch in the place. That's right. I wish he'd shot them dead. I been dreaming of that day ever since I left here. I been dreaming of my Mama falling down the steps of that hotel. *My* Mama. I never believed she fell I *always* believed that some white man pushed her down those steps. And

I know that Daddy thought so, too. But he wasn't there, he didn't know, he couldn't say nothing, he couldn't *do* nothing. I'll never forget the way he looked – whipped, whipped, whipped, whipped!

MOTHER HENRY: She fell, Richard, she *fell*. The stairs were wet and slippery and she *fell*.

RICHARD: My mother *fell* down the steps of that damn white hotel? My mother was *pushed* – you remember yourself how them white bastards was always sniffing around my mother, *always* around her – because she was pretty and *black*!

MOTHER HENRY: Richard, you can't start walking around believing that all the suffering in the world is caused by white folks!

RICHARD: I can't? Don't tell me I can't. I'm going to treat everyone of them as though they were responsible for all the crimes that ever happened in the history of the world – oh, yes! They're responsible for all the misery *I've* ever seen, and that's good enough for me. It's because my Daddy's got no power that my Mama's dead. And he ain't got no power because he's *black*. And the only way the black man's going to *get* any power is to drive all the white men into the sea.

MOTHER HENRY: You're going to make yourself sick. You're going to make yourself sick with hatred.

RICHARD: No, I'm not. I'm going to make myself well. I'm going to make myself *well* with hatred – what do you think of that?

MOTHER HENRY: It can't be done. It can never be done. Hatred is a poison, Richard.

RICHARD: Not for me. I'm going to learn how to drink it – a little every day in the morning, and then a booster shot late at night. I'm going to remember everything. I'm going to keep it right here, at the very top of my mind. I'm going to remember Mama, and Daddy's face that day, and Aunt Edna and all her sad little deals and all those boys and girls in Harlem and all them pimps and whores and gangsters and all them cops. And I'm going to remember all the dope that's flowed through my veins. I'm going to remember everything – the jails I been in and the cops that beat me and how long a time I spent screaming and stinking in my own dirt, trying to break my habit. I'm going to remember all that, and I'll get well. I'll get well.

MOTHER HENRY: Oh, Richard. Richard. Richard.

RICHARD: Don't Richard me. I tell you, I'm going to get *well*.

He takes a small, sawed-off pistol from his pocket.

MOTHER HENRY: Richard, what are you doing with that gun?

RICHARD: I'm carrying it around with me, that's what I'm doing with it. This gun goes everywhere I go.

MOTHER HENRY: How long have you had it?

RICHARD: I've had it a long, long time.

MOTHER HENRY: Richard – you never –?

RICHARD: No. Not yet. But I will when I have to. I'll sure as hell take one of the bastards with me.

MOTHER HENRY: Hand me that gun. Please.

RICHARD: I can't. This is all that the man understands. He don't understand nothing else. *Nothing else!*

MOTHER HENRY: Richard – your father – think of your father –

RICHARD: Don't tell him! You hear me? (*A pause.*) Don't tell him!

MOTHER HENRY: Richard. Please.

RICHARD: Take the tray away, old lady. I ain't hungry no more.

After a moment, MOTHER HENRY *takes the tray and exits.* RICHARD *stretches out on the bed.*

JUANITA: (*Off.*) Meridian? Mother Henry? Anybody home in this house? (*Enters.*) Oh! Excuse me.

RICHARD: I think they might be over at the church. I reckon Grandmama went over there to pray for my soul.

JUANITA: Grandmama?

RICHARD: Who are you? Don't I know you?

JUANITA: Yes. I think you might.

RICHARD: Is your name Juanita?

JUANITA: If your name is Richard.

RICHARD: I'll be damned.

JUANITA: Ain't you a mess? So you finally decided to come back here – come here, let me hug you! Why, you ain't hardly changed at all – you just a little taller but you sure didn't gain much weight.

RICHARD: And I bet you the same old tomboy. You sure got the same loud voice – used to be able to hear you clear across this town.

JUANITA: Well, it's a mighty small town, Richard, that's what you always said – and the reason my voice got so loud so early, was that I started screaming for help right quick.

PETE enters.

Do you know Pete Spivey? He's someone come on the scene since you been gone. He's going to school down here, you should pardon the expression.

RICHARD: How do you do, man? Where you from?

PETE: I'm from a little place just outside Mobile.

RICHARD: Why didn't you go North, man? If you was going to make a *move. That's* the place. You get lost up there and I guarantee you some swinging little chick is sure to find you.

JUANITA: We'll let that pass. Are you together? Are you ready to meet the day?

RICHARD: I am *always* together, little sister. Tell me what you got on your mind.

PETE: We thought we'd just walk around town a little and maybe stop and have a couple of drinks somewhere. Or we can drive. I got a car.

RICHARD: I didn't think I'd never see you no more, Juanita. You been here all this time?

JUANITA: I sure have, sugar. Just waiting for you to come home.

RICHARD: Don't let this chick upset you, Pete. All we ever did was climb trees together.

PETE: She's had me climbing a few trees, too. But we weren't doing it together.

(PAPA D.'s juke joint: Juke box music, loud. Less frantic than RICHARD's song. Couple dancing, all very young, doing very lively variations of the 'Twist,' the 'Wobble,' etc. PAPA D. at the counter. It is now early evening. JUANITA, PETE and RICHARD enter.)

JUANITA: How you making it, Papa D.? We brought someone to see you – you recognize him?

PAPA D.: It seems to me I know your face, young man. Yes, I'm *sure* I know your face. Now, wait a minute, don't tell me – you ain't Shirelee Anderson's boy, are you?

RICHARD: No. I remember Shirelee Anderson, but we ain't no kin.

PETE: Try again, Papa D.

PAPA D.: You your father's boy. I just recognized that smile – you Reverend Henry's son. Well, how you doing? It's nice to have you back with us. You going to stay a while?

RICHARD: Yes sir. I think I'll be around for a while.

PAPA D.: Yeah, I remember you little old string bean of a boy, full of the devil. How long you been gone from here?

RICHARD: Almost eight years now. I left in September – it'll be eight years next month.

PAPA D.: Yeah – how's your Daddy? And your Grandmother? I ain't seen them for a while.

PETE: Ain't you been going to church, Papa D.?

PAPA D.: Well, you know how it is. I try, God *knows* I try!

RICHARD: They fine, Papa D.

PAPA D.: You all don't want nothing to eat?

RICHARD: We'll think about it.

They sit down.

PETE: Old Papa D. got something on everybody, don't he?

JUANITA: You better believe it.

RICHARD: He's kind of a Tom, ain't he?

PETE: Yeah. He *talks* about Mister Charlie, and he *says* he's with us – us kids – but he ain't going to do nothing to offend him. You know, he's still trading with Lyle Britten.

RICHARD: Who's Lyle Britten?

PETE: Peckerwood, owns a store nearby. And, man, you ain't *seen* a peckerwood until you've seen Lyle Britten. Niggers been trading in his store for years, man, I wouldn't be surprised but if the cat was rich – but that man still expects you to step off the sidewalk when he comes along. So we been getting people to stop buying there.

JUANITA: He shot a coloured man a few years back, shot him dead, and wasn't nothing never said, much less done, about it.

PETE: Lyle had been carrying on with this man's wife, dig,

and, naturally, Old Bill – his name was Bill Walker, everybody called him Old Bill – wanted to put a stop to it.

JUANITA: She was a pretty little thing – real little and real black.

RICHARD: She still around here?

PETE: No. She disappeared. She went North somewhere.

RICHARD: Jive mothers. They can rape and kill our women and we can't do nothing. But if we touch one of their dried-up, pale-assed women, we get our nuts cut off. You remember that chick I was telling you about earlier, lives in Greenwich Village in New York?

PETE: What about her?

RICHARD: She's *white*, man. I got a whole *gang* of white chicks in New York. That's *right*. And they can't get enough of what little Richard's got – and I give it to them, too, baby, believe me. You say black people ain't got no dignity? Man, you ought to watch a white woman when she wants you to give her a little bit. They will do anything, baby, *anything*! Wait – I got some pictures. That's the one lives in the Village. *Ain't* she fine? I'd hate to tell you where I've had that long yellow hair. And, dig this one, this is Sandy, her old man works on Wall Street –

PETE: We're making Juanita nervous.

JUANITA: Don't worry about *me*. I've been a big girl for a *long* time. Besides, I'm studying abnormal psychology. So please feel free. Which one is this? What does *her* father do?

RICHARD: That's Sylvia. I don't know what her father does. She's a model. She's loaded with loot.

PETE: You take money from her?

RICHARD: I take their money and they love it. Anyway, they ain't got nothing else to do with it. Every one of them's got some piss-assed, faggoty white boy on a string somewhere. They go home and marry him, dig, when they can't make it with me no more – but when they want some *loving*, funky, downhome, bring-it-on-here-and-put-it-on-the-table style –

JUANITA: They sound very sad. It must be very sad for you, too.

RICHARD: Well, I want *them* to be sad, baby, I want to screw up *their* minds *for ever*. But why should *I* be so sad? Hell, I was swinging, I just about had it made. I had me some fine chicks and a fine pad and my car, and, hell, I was on my way! But then – then I screwed up.

JUANITA: We heard you were sick.

RICHARD: Who told you I was sick?

JUANITA: Your father. Your grandmother. They didn't say what the sickness was.

PAPA D. passes their table.

RICHARD: Hey, Papa D., come on over here. I want to show you something.

PAPA D. comes over.

Hey, look at these, man, look! Ain't they some fine chicks? And you know who *each one* of them calls: Baby! Oh, baby? That's right. You looking at the man.

PAPA D.: Where'd you steal those pictures, boy?

RICHARD: (*Laughs.*) *Steal* them! Man, I ain't got to steal girls' pictures. I'm telling you the truth!

PAPA D.: Put them pictures away. I thought you had good sense.

He goes back to the counter.

RICHARD: Ain't that a bitch. He's scared because I'm carrying around pictures of white girls. That's the trouble with niggers. They all scared of the man.

JUANITA: Well, I'm *not* scared of the man. But there's just no point in running around, asking –

PETE: – to be lynched.

RICHARD: Well, okay, I'll put my pictures away, then. I sure don't want to upset nobody.

PETE: Excuse me. I'll be back.

Exits.

RICHARD: You want to dance?

JUANITA: No. Not now.

RICHARD: You want something to eat?

JUANITA: No. Richard?

RICHARD: Yeah?

JUANITA: Were you *very* sick?

RICHARD: What d'you want to know for?

JUANITA: Like that. Because I used to be your girl friend.

RICHARD: You was more like a boy than a girl, though. I couldn't go nowhere without you. You were determined to get your neck broken.

JUANITA: Well, I've changed. I'm now much more like a girl than I am like a boy.

RICHARD: You didn't turn out too bad, considering what you had to start with.

JUANITA: Thank you. I guess.

RICHARD: How come you ain't married by now? Pete, now, he seems real fond of you.

JUANITA: He *is* fond of me, we're friends. But I'm not in any hurry to get married – not now. And not here. I'm not sure I'm going to stay here. I've been working very hard, but next year I think I'll leave.

RICHARD: Where would you go?

JUANITA: I don't know. I had always intended to go North to law school and then come back down here to practise law – God knows this town could stand it. But, now, I don't know.

RICHARD: It's rough, huh?

JUANITA: It's not that so much. It *is* rough – are you all right? Do you want to go?

RICHARD: No, no. I'm all right. Go on. (*A pause.*) I'm all *right*. Go *on*.

JUANITA: It's rough because you can't help being scared.

I don't want to die – what was the matter with you, Richard, what were you sick with?

RICHARD: It wasn't serious. And I'm better now.

JUANITA: Well, no, that's just it. You're not really better.

RICHARD: How do you mean?

JUANITA: I watch you –

RICHARD: *Why* do you watch me?

JUANITA: I care about you.

RICHARD: You care about me! I thought you could hold your liquor better than that, girl.

JUANITA: It's not liquor. Don't you believe that anyone can care about you?

RICHARD: Care about me! Do you know how many times chicks have told me that? That they *cared* about me?

JUANITA: Well. This isn't one of those times.

RICHARD: I was a junkie.

JUANITA: A what?

RICHARD: A junkie, a dope addict, a hop-head, a mainliner – a dope fiend! My arms and my legs, too, are full of holes!

JUANITA: I asked you tell *me*, not the world.

RICHARD: Where'd Pete go?

JUANITA: He's dancing.

RICHARD: You want to dance?

JUANITA: In a minute.

RICHARD: I got hooked about five years ago. See, I couldn't stand these chicks I was making it with, and I was working real hard at my music, and, man, I was lonely. You come off a gig, you be tired, and you'd already taken as much shit as you could stand from the managers and the people in the room you were working and you'd be off to make some down scene with some pasty white-faced bitch. And so you'd make the scene and somehow you'd wake up in the morning and the chick would be beside you, alive and well, and dying to make the scene again and somehow you'd managed not to strangle her, you hadn't beaten her to death. Like you wanted to. And you get out of there and you carry this pain around inside all day and all night long. No way to beat it – no *way*. No matter how you turned, no matter what you did – no *way*. But when I started getting high, I was cool, and it didn't bother me. And I wasn't lonely then, it was all right. And the chicks – I could handle them, they couldn't reach me. And I didn't know I was hooked – until I was *hooked*. Then I started getting into trouble and I lost a lot of gigs and I had to sell my car and I lost my pad and most of the chicks, they split, naturally – but not all of them – and then I got busted and I made that trip down to Lexington and – here I am. Way *down* upon the Swanee River. But I'm going to be all right. You can bet on it.

JUANITA: I'd like to do better than that. I'd like to see to it.

RICHARD: How?

JUANITA: Well, like I used to. I won't let you go anywhere without me.

RICHARD: You *still* determined to break your neck?

JUANITA: Well, it's a neck-breaking time. I wouldn't like to appear to be above the battle.

RICHARD: Do you have any idea of what you might be letting yourself in for?

JUANITA: No. But you said you were lonely. And I'm lonely, too.

LYLE enters, goes to the counter. His appearance causes a change in the atmosphere, but no one appears to stop whatever they are doing.

LYLE: Joel, how about letting me have some change for cigarettes? I got a kind of long drive ahead of me, and I'm out.

PAPA D.: Howdy, Mister Lyle, how you been? Folks ain't been seeing much of you lately.

LYLE: (*Laughs.*) That's the truth. But I reckon old friends just stays old friends. Ain't that right?

PAPA D.: That's right, Mister Lyle.

JUANITA: That's Lyle Britten. The one we were talking about before.

RICHARD: I wonder what he'd do if I walked into a white place.

JUANITA: Don't worry about it. Just stay out of white places – believe me!

RICHARD: (*Laughs.*) Let's TCB – that means taking care of business. Let's see if I can dance.

They rise, dance. Perhaps she is teaching him the 'Fight', or he is teaching her the 'Pony'; they are enjoying each other. LYLE gets his change, gets cigarettes out of the machine, crosses to the counter, pauses there to watch the dancers.

LYLE: Joel, you know I ain't never going to be able to dance like that.

PAPA D.: Ain't nothing to it. You just got to be supple, that's all. I can *yet* do it.

Does a grotesque sketch of the 'Twist'.

LYLE: Okay, Joel, you got it. Be seeing you now.

PAPA D.: Good night, Mister Lyle.

On LYLE's way out, he jostles JUANITA. RICHARD stops, holding JUANITA at the waist. RICHARD and LYLE stare at each other.

LYLE: Pardon me.

RICHARD: Consider yourself pardoned.

LYLE: You new around here?

PAPA D.: He just come to town a couple of days ago, Mister Lyle.

RICHARD: Yeah. I just come to town a couple of days ago, Mister Lyle.

LYLE: Well. I sure hope your stay'll be a pleasant one.

Exits.

PETE: Man, are you *anxious* to leave this world? Because he wouldn't think nothing of helping you out of it.

RICHARD: Yeah. Well, I wouldn't think nothing of helping him out of it, neither. Come on, baby, record's going to waste – let's TCB.

They dance.

So you care about me, do you? Ain't that a bitch?

(*The church: PETE and JUANITA, a little apart from the others.*)

PETE: Why have you been avoiding me? Don't answer that. You started going away from me as soon as Richard came to this town. Now listen, Richard's dead but you still won't turn to me. I don't want to ask you for more than you can give, but why have you locked me out? I *know* – you liked me. We had nice times together.

JUANITA: We did. I *do* like you. Pete, I don't know. I wish you wouldn't ask me now. I wish *nobody* would ask me for anything now!

PETE: Is it because of Richard? Because if that's what it is, I'll wait – I'll wait until you know inside you that Richard's dead, but you're alive, and you're *supposed* to live, and I love you.

JUANITA: When Richard came, he – *hit* – me in some place where I'd never been touched before. I don't mean – just physically. He took all my attention – the deepest attention, maybe, that one person can give another. He needed me and he made a difference for me in this terrible world – do you see what I mean? And – it's funny – when I was with him, I didn't think of the future, I didn't dare. I didn't know if I could be strong enough to give him what he needed for as long as he would need it. It only lasted four or five days, Pete – four or five days, like a storm, like lightning! And what I saw during that storm I'll always see. Before that – I thought I knew who I was. But now I know that there are more things in me than I'll ever understand – and if I can't be faithful to myself, I'm afraid to promise I'll be faithful to one man!

PETE: I need you. I'll be faithful. That helps. You'll see.

JUANITA: So many people need so much!

PETE: So do you. So do I, Juanita. You take all my attention. My deepest attention.

JUANITA: You probably see things that I think are hidden. You probably think I'm a fool – or worse.

PETE: No. I think there's a lot of love in you, Juanita. If you'll let me help you, we can give it to the world. You can't give it to the world until you find a person who can help you – love the world.

JUANITA: I've discovered that. The world is a loveless place.

PETE: Not yet –

The lights of a car flash in their faces. Silence. They all listen tensely as the lights of another car approach, then pass; they watch the lights disappear. The telephone rings in the office. MOTHER HENRY goes off to answer it. They listen to the murmur of MOTHER HENRY's voice. MOTHER HENRY enters.

MOTHER HENRY: That was Freddy Roberts. He say about two-thirty his dog started to barking and woke him up and he let the dog out on the porch and the dog run under the porch and there was two white men *under* Freddy's porch, fooling around with his gas pipes. Freddy thinks the dog bit one of them. He ran inside to get him his rifle but the rifle jammed and the men got away. He wanted to warn us, maybe they might come prowling around here.

LORENZO: Only we ain't got no rifles.

JUANITA: It was the dog that woke him up? I'll bet they come back and kill that dog!

JIMMY: What was they doing under the man's house, messing around with his gas pipes, at that hour of the morning?

PETE: They was fixing to blow up his house. They *might* be under your house, or *this* house, right now.

LORENZO: The real question is why two white men feel safe enough to come to a black neighbourhood after dark in the first place. If a couple of them get their heads blown off, they won't feel so goddamn courageous!

JUANITA: I better call home.

Exits into office.

PETE: Will you have your mother call my house?

LORENZO: And have *his* mother call *my* house?

JIMMY: And tell all the people that don't have rifles or dogs to stay off their porches!

LORENZO: Tell them to fall on their knees and use their Bibles as breast-plates! Because I know that each and every one of them got *Bibles!*

MERIDIAN has walked to the church door, stands looking off.

Don't they, Meridian?

MOTHER HENRY: Hush.

We hear JUANITA's voice, off. Then silence falls. Lights dim on the students until they are in silhouette. Lights up on MERIDIAN. We hear RICHARD's guitar, very lonely, far away.

A car door slams. The voices of young people saying good night. RICHARD appears, dressed as we last saw him.

RICHARD: Hello, Daddy. You still up?

MERIDIAN: Yeah. Couldn't sleep. How was your day?

RICHARD: It was all right. I'd forgotten what nights down here were like. You never see the stars in the city – and all these funny country sounds –

MERIDIAN: Crickets. And all kinds of bugs and worms, running around, busy, shaking all the bushes.

RICHARD: Lord, if I'd stayed here, I guess I might have married old Juanita by now, and we'd have a couple of kids and I'd be sitting around like this *every* night. What a wild thought.

MERIDIAN: You can still marry Juanita. Maybe she's been waiting for you.

RICHARD: Have you ever thought of marrying again?

MERIDIAN: I've thought of it.

RICHARD: Did you ever think of marrying Juanita?

MERIDIAN: Why do you ask me that?

RICHARD: Because I'd like to know.

MERIDIAN: *Why* would you like to know?

RICHARD: Why would you like to hide it? I'd like to know because I'm a man now, Daddy, and I can ask you to tell me the truth. I'm making up for lost time. Maybe you should try to make up for lost time too.

MERIDIAN: Yes. I've thought of marrying Juanita. But I've never spoken of it to her.

RICHARD: That's the truth?

MERIDIAN: Yes.

RICHARD: Why didn't you tell me the truth way back there? Why didn't you tell me my mother was murdered? She was pushed down them steps.

MERIDIAN: Richard, your mother's dead. People die in all kinds of ways. They die when their times comes to die. Your mother loved you and she was gone – there was nothing more I could do for her. I had to think of you. I didn't want you to be – poisoned – by useless and terrible suspicions. I didn't want to wreck your life. I knew your life was going to be hard enough. So, I let you go. I thought it might be easier for you – if I let you go. I didn't want you to grow up in this town.

RICHARD: But there was something else in it, too, Daddy. You didn't want me to look at you and be ashamed of you. And you didn't know what was in my eyes, you couldn't stand it, I could tell from the way you looked at me sometimes. That was it, wasn't it?

MERIDIAN: I thought it was better. I suppose I thought it was all over for me, anyway. And I thought I owed it to your mother and to girls like your mother, to try – try to change, to purify this town, where she was born, and where we'd been so happy, and which she loved so much. I was wrong, I guess. I was wrong.

RICHARD: You've just been a public man, Daddy, haven't you? Since that day? You haven't been a private man at all.

MERIDIAN: No. I haven't. Try to forgive me.

RICHARD: There's nothing to forgive. I've been down the road a little bit. I know what happened. I'm going to try again, Daddy.

A pause. RICHARD takes out the gun.

Here. Grandmama saw this this morning and she got all upset. So I'll let you hold it for me. You keep it till I ask you for it, okay? But when I ask you for it, you got to give it to me. Okay?

MERIDIAN: (*Takes the gun.*) Okay. I'm proud of how you've come through – all you've had to bear.

RICHARD: I'm going to get some sleep. You coming over to the house now?

MERIDIAN: Not yet.

RICHARD: Good night. Say, Daddy?

MERIDIAN: Yeah?

RICHARD: You kind of like the idea of me and Juanita getting together?

MERIDIAN: Yeah. I think it's a fine idea.

RICHARD: Well, I'm going to sleep on it, then. Good night.

MERIDIAN: Good night.

RICHARD exits.

(*After* RICHARD's *exit, the lights come up on the students.*)

JUANITA: Lord it's gone and started raining.

PETE: And you worried about your hair.

JUANITA: I am *not* worried about my hair. I'm thinking of wearing it the way God arranged it in the first place.

LORENZO: Now, now, Mau-Mau.

PETE: This chick is going through some weird changes.

MERIDIAN: That's understandable. We all are.

JIMMY: Well, we'll see you some time tomorrow. It promises to be a kind of *active* day.

MERIDIAN: Yes, we've got some active days ahead of us. You all better get some sleep.

JUANITA: How're you getting home, Jimmy?

JIMMY: Pete's driving us all home.

JUANITA: And then – are you going to drive all the way to your house alone, Pete?

PETE: You're jumpy tonight. I'll stay at Lorenzo's house.

LORENZO: You can call your house from there.

MOTHER HENRY: You get some sleep, too, Meridian, it's past three o'clock in the morning. Don't you stay over here much longer.

MERIDIAN: No, I won't. Good night, all.

MOTHER HENRY: Good night, children. See you in the morning, God willing.

They exit. MERIDIAN *walks to the pulpit, puts his hand on the Bible.* PARNELL *enters.*

PARNELL: I hear it was real bad tonight.

MERIDIAN: Not as bad as it's going to get. Maybe I was wrong not to let the people arm.

PARNELL: If the Negroes were armed, it's the Negroes who'd be slaughtered. You know that.

MERIDIAN: They're slaughtered anyway. And I don't know that. I thought I knew it – but now I'm not so sure.

PARNELL: What's come over you? What's going to happen to the people in this town, this church – if you go to pieces?

MERIDIAN: Maybe they'll find a leader who can lead them some place.

PARNELL: Somebody with a gun?

MERIDIAN *is silent.*

Is that what you mean?

MERIDIAN: I'm a Christian. I've been a Christian all my life, like my Mama and Daddy before me and like their Mama and Daddy before them. Of course, if you go

back far enough, you get to a point *before* Christ, if you see what I mean, *B.C.* – and at that point, I've been thinking, black people weren't raised to turn the other cheek, and in the hope of heaven. No, then they didn't have to take low. Before Christ. They walked around just as good as anybody else, and when they died, they didn't go to heaven, they went to join their ancestors. My son's dead, but he's not gone to join his ancestors. He was a sinner, so he must have gone to hell – if we're going to believe what the Bible says. Is that such an improvement, such a mighty advance over B.C.? I've been thinking, I've had to think – would I have *been* such a Christian if I hadn't been born black? Maybe I *had* to become a Christian in order to have any dignity at all. Since I wasn't a man in men's eyes, then I could be a man in the eyes of God. But that didn't protect my wife. She's dead, too soon, we don't really know how. That didn't protect my son – he's dead, we know how too well. That hasn't changed this town – this town, where you couldn't find a white Christian at high noon on Sunday! The eyes of God – maybe those eyes are blind – I never let myself think of that before.

PARNELL: Meridian, you can't be the man who gives the signal for the holocaust.

MERIDIAN: Must I be the man who watches while his people are beaten, chained, starved, clubbed, butchered?

PARNELL: You used to say that your people were all the people in the world – all the people God ever made, or would make. You said your race was the human race.

MERIDIAN: The human race!

PARNELL: I've never seen you like this before. There's something in your tone I've never heard before – rage – maybe hatred –

MERIDIAN: You've heard it before. You just never recognized it before. You've heard it in all those blues and spirituals and gospel songs you claim to love so much.

PARNELL: I was talking about *you* – not your history. I have a history, too. And don't be so sure I've never heard that sound. Maybe I've never heard anything else. Perhaps my life is also hard to bear.

MERIDIAN: I watched you all this week up at the Police Chief's office with me. And you know how to handle him because you're sure you're better than he is. But you both have more in common with each other than either of you have with me. And, for both of you – I watched this, I never watched it before – it was just a black boy that was dead, and that was a problem. He saw the problem one way, you saw it another way. But it wasn't a *man* that was dead, not my *son* – you held yourselves away from *that*!

PARNELL: I may have sounded – cold. It was not because I felt cold. There was no other way to sound, Meridian. I took the only tone which – it seemed to me – could accomplish what we wanted. And I *do* know the Chief of Police better than you – because I'm white. And I can make him listen to me – because I'm white. I don't know if I think I'm so much better than he is. I know what we have done – and do. But you must have mercy on us. We have no other hope.

MERIDIAN: You have never shown us any mercy at all.

PARNELL: Meridian, give me credit for knowing you're in pain. We are two men, two friends – in spite of all that could divide us. We have come too far together, there is too much at stake, for you to become black now, for me to become white. Don't accuse me. Don't accuse me. *I* didn't do it.

MERIDIAN: So was my son – innocent.

PARNELL: Meridian – when I asked for mercy a moment ago – I meant – please – please try to understand that it is not so easy to leap over fences, to give things up – all right, to surrender privilege! But if you were among the privileged you would know what I mean. It's not a matter of trying to hold *on*; the things, the privilege – are part of you, are *who* you are. It's in the *gut*.

MERIDIAN: Then where's the point of this struggle, where's the hope? If Mister Charlie can't change –

PARNELL: Who's Mister Charlie?

MERIDIAN: You're Mister Charlie. *All* white men are Mister Charlie!

PARNELL: You sound more and more like your son, do you know that? A lot of the coloured people here didn't approve of him, but he said things they longed to say – said right out loud, for all the world to hear, how much he despised white people!

MERIDIAN: He didn't say things *I* longed to say. Maybe it was because he was my son. I didn't care *what* he felt about white people. I just wanted him to live, to have his own life. There's something you don't understand about being black, Parnell. If you're a black man, with a black son, you have to forget all about white people and concentrate on trying to save your child. That's why I let him stay up North. I was wrong, I failed, I failed. Lyle walked him up the road and killed him.

PARNELL: We don't *know* Lyle killed him. And Lyle denies it.

MERIDIAN: Of course, he denies it – what do you mean, we don't *know* Lyle killed him?

PARNELL: We *don't* know – all we can say is that it looks that way. And circumstantial evidence is a tricky thing.

MERIDIAN: *When* it involves a white man killing a black man – if Lyle didn't kill him, Parnell, who did?

PARNELL: I don't *know*. But we don't know that Lyle did it.

MERIDIAN: Lyle doesn't deny that he killed Old Bill.

PARNELL: No.

MERIDIAN: And we know how Lyle feels about coloured people.

PARNELL: Well, yes. From your point of view. But – from another point of view – Lyle hasn't got anything *against* coloured people. He just –

MERIDIAN: He just doesn't think they're human.

PARNELL: Well, even *that's* not true. He doesn't think they're *not* human – after all, I know him, he's hot-tempered and he's far from being the brightest man in the world – but he's not mean, he's not cruel. He's a poor white man. The poor whites have been just as victimized in this part of the world as the blacks have ever been!

MERIDIAN: For God's sake spare me the historical view! Lyle's responsible for Richard's death.

PARNELL: But, Meridian, we can't even in our own minds, *decide* that he's guilty. We have to operate the way justice *always* has to operate and give him the benefit of the doubt.

MERIDIAN: *What* doubt?

PARNELL: Don't you see, Meridian, that now you're operating the way white people in this town operate whenever a coloured man's on trial?

MERIDIAN: When was the last time one of us was on *trial* here, Parnell?

PARNELL: That *can't* have anything to do with it, it *can't*. We must forget about all – *all* the past injustice. We have to start from scratch, or do our best to start from scratch. It isn't vengeance we're after. Is it?

MERIDIAN: I don't want vengeance. I don't want to be paid back – anyway, I couldn't be. I just want Lyle to be made to know that what he did was evil. I just want this town to be forced to face the evil that it countenances and to turn from evil and do good. That's why I've stayed in this town so long!

PARNELL: But if Lyle didn't do it? Lyle is a friend of mine – a strange friend, but a friend. I love him. I know how he suffers.

MERIDIAN: *How* does he suffer?

PARNELL: He suffers – from being in the dark – from having things inside him that he can't name and can't face and can't control. He's not a wicked man. I know he's not, I've known him almost all his life! The face he turns to you, Meridian, isn't the face he turns to me.

MERIDIAN: Is the face he turns to you more real than the face he turns to me? *You* go ask him if he killed my son.

PARNELL: They're going to ask him that in court. That's why I fought to bring about this trial. And he'll say no.

MERIDIAN: I don't care what he says in court. You go ask him. If he's your friend, he'll tell you the truth.

PARNELL: No. No, he may not. He's – he's maybe a little afraid of me.

MERIDIAN: If you're *his* friend, you'll know whether he's telling you the truth or not. Go ask him.

PARNELL: I can't do it. I'm his friend. I can't betray him.

MERIDIAN: But you can betray *me*? You *are* a white man, aren't you? Just another white man – after all.

PARNELL: Even if he says yes, it won't make any difference. The jury will never convict him.

MERIDIAN: Is that why you fought to bring about the trial? I don't care what the jury does. I know he won't say yes to them. He won't say yes to me. But he might say yes to you. You say we don't know. Well, I've got a right to know. And I've got the right to ask you to find out – since you're the only man who *can* find out. And *I've* got to find out – whether we've been friends all these years, or whether I've just been your favourite Uncle Tom.

PARNELL: You know better than that.

MERIDIAN: I don't know, Parnell, any longer – any of the things I used to know. Maybe I never knew them. I'm tired. Go home.

PARNELL: You don't trust me any more, do you, Meridian?

MERIDIAN: Maybe I never trusted you. I don't know. Maybe I never trusted myself. Go home. Leave me alone. I must look back at my record.

PARNELL: Meridian – what you ask – I don't know if I can do it for you.

MERIDIAN: I don't want you to do it for me. I want you to do it for you. Good night.

PARNELL: Good night.

PARNELL exits. MERIDIAN comes downstage. It is dawn.

MERIDIAN: My record! Would God – would *God* – would God I had died for thee – my son, my son!

Act 2

WHITETOWN: The kitchen of LYLE's house. Sunday morning. Church bells. A group of white people, all ages, men and women. JO and an older woman, HAZEL, have just taken a cake out of the oven. HAZEL sets it out to cool.

HAZEL: It's a shame – having to rush everything this way. But it can't be helped.

JO: Yes. I'm just so upset. I can't help it. I know it's silly. I know they can't do nothing to Lyle.

HAZEL: Girl, you just put all those negative thoughts right out of your mind. We're going to have your little anniversary celebration *tonight* instead of *tomorrow* night because we have reason to believe that *tomorrow* night your husband might be called away on business. Now, you think about it that way. Don't you go around here with a great long face, trying to demoralize your guests. I won't have it. You too young and pretty for that.

LILLIAN: Hallelujah! I *do* believe that I have finally mastered this recipe.

SUSAN: Oh, good! Let me see.

LILLIAN: I've only tried it once before, and its real hard. You've got to time it just right.

SUSAN: I have tried it and tried it and it never comes out! But yours is wonderful! We're going to eat tonight, folks!

RALPH: You supposed to be cooking something, too, ain't you?

SUSAN: I'm cooking our contribution later, at our own house. We got enough women here already, messing up Jo's kitchen.

JO: I'm just so glad you all come by I don't know what to do. Just go ahead and mess up that kitchen, I got lots of time to clean it.

ELLIS: Susan's done learned how to cook, huh?

RALPH: Oh, yeah, she's a right fine cook. All you got to do is look at me. I never weighed this much in my life.

ELLIS: Old Lyle's done gained weight in this year, too. Nothing like steady home cooking, I guess, ha-ha! It really don't seem like it was a year ago you two got married. Declare, I never thought Lyle was going to jump up and do that thing. But old Jo, here, she hooked him.

REV. PHELPS: Well, I said the words over them, and if I ever saw a happy man in my life, it was Big Lyle Britten that day. Both of them – there was just a light shining out of them.

GEORGE: I'd propose a toast to them, if it wasn't so early on a Sunday, and if the Reverend wasn't here.

REV. PHELPS: Ain't nothing wrong with toasting happy people, no matter what the day or hour.

ELLIS: You heard the Reverend! You got anything in this house we can drink to your happiness in, Mrs Britten?

JO: I'm pretty sure we do. It's a pity Lyle ain't up yet. He ain't never slept through this much racket before.

ELLIS: No ma'am, he ain't never been what you'd call a heavy sleeper. Not before he passed out, ha-ha! We used to have us some times together, him and me, before he got him some sense and got married.

GEORGE: Let him sleep easy. He ain't got no reason not to.

JO: Lyle's always got his eye on the ball, you know – and he's just been at that store, night after night after night, drawing up plans and taking inventory and I don't know what all – because, come fall, he's planning to branch out and have a brand new store, just about. You all won't recognize the place, I guarantee you!

ELLIS: Lyle's just like his Daddy. You can't beat him. The harder a thing is, well, the surer you can be that old Lyle Britten will do it. Why, Lyle's Daddy never got old *never!* He was drinking and running after women – and getting them, too! – until just before they put him in his grave. I could tell you stories about the old man, boy – of course, I can't tell them now, on a Sunday morning, in front of all these women!

JO: Here you are, gentlemen. I hope you all drink bourbon.

RALPH: Listen to her!

GEORGE: Ladies! Would you all like to join us in a morning toast to the happy and beloved and loving couple, Mr and Mrs Lyle Britten, on the day immediately preceding their first wedding anniversary?

ELLIS: The bridegroom ain't here because he's weary from all his duties, both public and private. Ha-ha! But he's a good man, and he's done a lot for us, and I know you all know what I'm talking about, and I just feel like we should honour him and his lovely young wife. Ladies! Come on, Reverend Phelps says it's all right.

SUSAN: Not too much for me, Ralph.

LILLIAN: I don't think I've ever had a drink at this hour of a Sunday morning, and in the presence of my pastor!

They pour, drink, and sing 'For He's a Jolly Good Fellow.'

HAZEL: Now you've started her to crying, naturally. Here, honey, you better have a little drink yourself.

JO: You all have been *so* wonderful. I can't imagine how Lyle can go on sleeping. Thank you, Hazel. Here's to all of you! (*Drinks.*) Listen. They're singing over there now.

They listen.

HAZEL: Sometimes they can sound so nice. Used to take my breath away when I was a girl.

ELLIS: What's happened to this town? It was peaceful here, we all got along, we didn't have no trouble.

GEORGE: Oh, we had a little trouble from time to time, but it didn't amount to a hill of beans. Niggers was all right then, you could always get you a nigger to help you catch a nigger.

LILLIAN: That's right. They had their ways, we had ours, and everything went along the way God intended.

JO: I've never been scared in this town before – never. They was all like my own people. I never knew of anyone to mistreat a coloured person – have you? And they certainly didn't *act* mistreated. But now, when I walk through this town – I'm scared – like I don't know what's going to happen next. How come the coloured people to hate us so much, all of a sudden? We *give* them everything they've got!

REV. PHELPS: Their minds have been turned. They have turned away from God. They're a simple people – warm-hearted and good-natured. But they are very easily led, and now they are harkening to the counsel of these degenerate Communist race-mixers. And they don't know what terrible harm they can bring on themselves – and on us all.

JO: You can't tell what they're thinking. Why, coloured folks you been knowing all your life – you're almost afraid to hire them, almost afraid to *talk* to them – you don't know what they're thinking.

ELLIS: *I* know what they're thinking.

SUSAN: We're not much better off than the Communist countries – that's what Ralph says. *They* live in fear. They don't want us to teach God in our schools – you send your child to school and you don't know *what* kind of Godless atheist is going to be filling the little one's mind with all *kinds* of filth. And he's going to believe it, of course, kids don't know no better. And now they tell us we got to send our kids to *school* with niggers – why, everybody *knows* that ain't going to work, won't nobody get no education, white *or* black. Niggers can't learn like white folks, they ain't got the same *interests*.

ELLIS: They got one interest. And it's just below the belly button.

GEORGE: (*Laughs.*) You know them yellow niggers? Boy, ain't they the worst kind? Their own folks don't want them, don't nobody want them, and you *can't* do nothing with them – you might be able to scare a black nigger, but you can't do nothing with a yellow nigger.

REV. PHELPS: That's because he's a mongrel. And a mongrel is the lowest creation in the animal kingdom.

ELLIS: Mrs Britten, you're married and all the women in this room are married and I know you've seen your husband without no clothes on – but have you seen a nigger without no clothes on? No, I guess you haven't. Well, he ain't like a white man, Mrs Britten.

GEORGE: That's right.

ELLIS: Mrs Britten, if you was to be raped by an orangoutang out of the jungle or a *stallion*, couldn't do you no worse than a nigger. You wouldn't be no more good for nobody. I've *seen* it.

GEORGE: That's *right*.

RALPH: That's why we men have got to be so vigilant. I tell you, I have to be away a lot nights, you know – and I bought Susan a gun and I taught her how to use it, too.

SUSAN: And I'm a pretty good shot now, too. Ralph says he's real proud of me.

RALPH: She's just like a pioneer woman.

HAZEL: I'm so glad Esther's not here to see this. She'd die of shame. She was the sweetest coloured woman – you remember her. She just about raised us, used to sing us to sleep at night, and she could tell just the most beautiful stories – the kind of stories that could scare you and make you laugh and make you cry, you know? Oh, she was wonderful. I don't remember a cross word or an evil expression all the time she was with us. She was always the same. And I believe she knew more about me than my own mother and father knew. I just told her everything. Then, one of her sons got killed – he went bad, just like this boy they having a funeral for here tonight – and she got sick. I nursed her, I bathed that woman's body with my own hands. And she told me once, she said, 'Miss Hazel, you are just like an angel of light.' She said, 'My own couldn't have done more for me than you have done.' She was a wonderful old woman.

JO: I believe I hear Lyle stirring.

SUSAN: Mrs Britten, somebody else is coming to call on you. My! It's that Parnell James! I wonder if he's sober this morning. He never *looks* sober.

ELLIS: He never acts it, either.

PARNELL enters.

PARNELL: Good morning, good people! Good morning, Reverend Phelps! How good it is to see brethren – and sistren – walking together. Or, in this case, standing together – something like that, anyway; my Bible's a little rusty. Is church over already? Or are you having it here? Good morning, Jo.

JO: Good morning, Parnell. Sit down, I'll pour you a cup of coffee.

GEORGE: You look like you could use it.

REV. PHELPS: We were all just leaving.

PARNELL: Please don't leave on my account, Reverend Phelps. Just go on as you were, praying or singing, just as the spirit may move you. I *would* love that cup of coffee, Jo.

ELLIS: You been up all night?

PARNELL: Is that the way I look? Yes, I *have* been up all night.

ELLIS: Tom-catting around, I'll bet. Getting drunk and fooling with all the women.

PARNELL: Ah, you flatter me. And in games of chance, my friend, you have no future at all. I'm sure you always lose at poker. So *stop betting*. I was not tom-catting, I was at home, working.

GEORGE: You been over the way this morning? You been at the nigger funeral?

PARNELL: The funeral takes place this evening. And, yes, I will be there. Would you care to come along? Leaving your baseball bat at home, of course.

JO: We heard the singing –

PARNELL: Darkies are always singing. You people know that. What made you think it was a funeral?

JO: Parnell! You are the limit! Would anybody else like a little more coffee? It's still good and hot.

ELLIS: We heard that a nigger got killed. That's why we thought it was a funeral.

GEORGE: They bury their dead over the way, don't they?

PARNELL: They do when the dogs leave enough to bury, yes.

A pause.

ELLIS: Dogs?

PARNELL: Yes – you know. Teeth. Barking Lots of noise.

ELLIS: A lot of people in this town, Parnell, would like to know exactly where you stand, on a lot of things.

PARNELL: That's exactly where I stand. On a lot of things. Why don't you read my paper?

LILLIAN: I wouldn't filthy my hands with that Communist sheet!

PARNELL: Ah? But the father of your faith, the cornerstone of that church of which you are so precious an adornment, was a communist, possibly the first. He may have done some tom-catting. We *know* he did some drinking. And he knew a lot of – loose ladies and drunkards. It's all in the Bible, isn't it, Reverend Phelps?

REV. PHELPS: I won't be drawn into your blasphemous banter. Ellis is only asking what many of us want to know – are you with us or against us? And he's telling you what we all feel. We've put up with your irresponsibility long enough. We won't tolerate it any longer. Do I make myself clear?

PARNELL: Not at all. If you're threatening me, be specific. First of all, what's this irresponsibility that you won't tolerate? And if you aren't going to tolerate it, what *are* you going to do? Dip me in tar and feathers? Boil me in oil?

Castrate me? Burn me? Cover yourselves in white sheets and come and burn crosses in front of my house? Come on, Reverend Phelps, don't stand there with your mouth open, it makes you even more repulsive than you are with it closed, and all your foul, graveyard breath comes rushing out, and it makes me want to vomit. Out with it, boy! What's on your mind?

ELLIS: You got away with a lot of things in this town, Parnell, for a long time, because your father was a big man here.

PARNELL: One at a time. I was addressing your spiritual leader.

SUSAN: He's *worse* than a nigger.

PARNELL: I take that as a compliment. I'm sure no man will ever say as much for you. Reverend Phelps?

REV. PHELPS: I think I speak for us all – for *myself* and for us all, when I say that our situation down here has become much too serious for flippancy and cynicism. When things were more in order here, we didn't really mind your attitude, and your paper didn't matter to us, we never read it, anyway.

ELLIS: We knew you were just a spoiled rich boy, with too much time on his hands that he didn't know what to do with.

REV. PHELPS: And so you started this paper and tried to make yourself interesting with all these subversive attitudes. I honestly thought that you would grow out of it.

GEORGE: Or go North.

REV. PHELPS: I know these attitudes were not your father's attitudes, or your mother's. I was very often invited to your home when they were alive –

PARNELL: How well I remember! What attitudes are you speaking of?

HAZEL: Race-mixing!

PARNELL: *Race-mixing!* Ladies and gentlemen, do you think anybody gives a good goddamn who you sleep with? You can go down to the swamps and couple with the snakes, for all I care, or for all anybody else cares. You may find that the snakes don't want you, but that's a problem for you and the snakes to work out, and it might prove astonishingly simple – the working out of the problem, I mean. I've never said a word about race-mixing. I've talked about social justice.

LILLIAN: That sounds Communistic to me!

PARNELL: It means that if I have a hundred dollars, and I'm black, and you have a hundred dollars, and you're white, I should be able to get as much value for *my* hundred dollars – my black hundred dollars – as you get for your *white* hundred dollars. It also means that I should have an equal opportunity to *earn* that hundred dollars –

ELLIS: Niggers can get work just as well as a white man can. Hell, *some* niggers make *more* money than me.

PARNELL: Some niggers are smarter than you, Ellis. Much smarter. And much nicer. And niggers *can't* get work just as well as a white man can, and you know it.

ELLIS: What's stopping them? They got hands.

PARNELL: Ellis, you don't really work with your *hands* – you're a salesman in a shoe store. And your boss wouldn't give that job to a nigger.

GEORGE: Well, goddammit, white men come before niggers! They *got* to!

PARNELL: Why?

LYLE enters.

LYLE: What's all this commotion going on in my house?

JO: Oh, Lyle, good morning! Some folks just dropped in to see you.

LYLE: It sounded like they was about to come to blows. Good morning, Reverend Phelps, I'm glad to see you here. I'm sorry I wasn't up, but I guess my wife might have told you, I've not been sleeping well nights. When I *do* go to sleep, she just lets me sleep on.

REV. PHELPS: Don't you apologize, son – we understand. We only came by to let you know that we're with you and every white person in this town is with you.

JO: Isn't that nice of them, Lyle? They've been here quite a spell, and we've had *such* a nice time.

LYLE: Well, that *is* mighty nice of you, Reverend, and all of you – hey there, Ellis! Old George! And Ralph and Susan – how's married life suit you? Guess it suits you all right, ain't nobody seen you in months, ha-ha! Mrs Proctor, Mrs Barker, how you all? Hey! Old Parnell! What you doing up so early?

PARNELL: I was on my way to church, but they seemed to be having the meeting here. So I joined the worshippers.

LYLE: On your way to church, that's a good one. Bet you ain't been to bed yet.

PARNELL: No, I haven't.

LYLE: You folks don't mind if I have a little breakfast? Jo, bring me something to eat! Susan, you look mighty plump and rosy, you ain't keeping no secrets from us, are you?

SUSAN: I don't think so, Lyle.

LYLE: I don't know, you got that look – like a real ripe peach, just right for eating. You ain't been slack in your duty, have you, Ralph? Look at the way she's blushing! I guess you all right, boy.

ELLIS: You know what time they coming for you tomorrow?

LYLE: Some time in the morning, I reckon. I don't know.

REV. PHELPS: I saw the Chief of Police the other day. He really doesn't want to do it, but his hands are tied. It's orders from higher up, from the North.

LYLE: Shoot, I know old Frank don't want to arrest me. I understand. I ain't worried. I know the people in this town is with me. I got nothing to worry about.

ELLIS: They trying to force us to put niggers on the jury – that's what I hear. Claim it won't be a fair trial if we don't.

HAZEL: Did you *ever* hear anything like that in your *life?*

LYLE: Where they going to find the niggers?

ELLIS: Oh, I bet your buddy, Parnell, has got that all figured out.

LYLE: How about it, Parnell? You going to find some niggers for them to put on that jury?

PARNELL: It's not up to me. But I might recommend a couple.

GEORGE: And how they going to get to court? You going to protect them?

PARNELL: The police will protect them. Or the State troopers –

GEORGE: That's a good one!

PARNELL: Or Federal marshals.

GEORGE: Look here, you really think there should be niggers on that jury?

PARNELL: Of course I do, and so would you, if you had any sense. For one thing, they're forty-four per cent of the population of this town.

ELLIS: But they don't vote. Not most of them.

PARNELL: Well. That's also a matter of interest to the Federal government. Why *don't* they vote? They got hands.

ELLIS: You claim Lyle's your buddy –

PARNELL: Lyle *is* my buddy. That's why I want him to have a fair trial.

HAZEL: I can't listen to no more of this, I'm sorry, I just can't. Honey, I'll see you all tonight, you hear?

REV. PHELPS: We're all going to go now. We just wanted to see how you were, and let you know that you could count on us.

LYLE: I sure appreciate it, Reverend, believe me, I do. You make me feel much better. Even if a man knows he ain't done no wrong, still, it's a kind of troublesome spot to be in. Wasn't for my good Jo, here, I don't know what I'd do. Good morning, Mrs Barker. Mrs Proctor. So long, George, it's been good to see you. Ralph, you take good care of Susan, you hear? And name the first one after me – you might have to bring it on up to the jail house so I can see it.

SUSAN: Don't think like that. Everything's going to be all right.

LYLE: You're sure?

SUSAN: I guarantee it. Why they couldn't – *couldn't* – do anything to you!

LYLE: Then I believe it. I believe *you.*

SUSAN: You keep right on believing.

ELLIS: Remember what we said, Parnell.

PARNELL: So long, Ellis. See you next Halloween.

LYLE: Let's get together, boy, soon as this mess is over.

ELLIS: You bet. This mess is just about over now – we ain't going to let them prolong it. And I know just the thing'll knock all this clear out of your mind, this, and everything else, ha-ha! Bye-bye, Mrs Britten.

JO: Goodbye. And thanks for coming!

HAZEL, LILLIAN, SUSAN, RALPH, ELLIS, REVEREND PHELPS and GEORGE exit.

LYLE: They're nice people.

JO: Yes. They are.

PARNELL: They certainly think a lot of you.

LYLE: You ain't jealous, are you, boy? No. We've all had

the same kind of trouble – it's the kind of trouble you wouldn't know about, Parnell, because you've never had to worry about making your living. But me! I been doing hard work from the time I was a puppy. Like my Mama and Daddy before me, God rest their souls, and their Mama and Daddy before them. They wore themselves out on the land – the land never give them nothing. Nothing but an empty belly and some skinny kids. I'm the only one growed up to be a man. That's because I take after my Daddy – he was skinny as a piece of wire, but he was hard as any rock. And stubborn! Lord, you ain't never see nobody so stubborn. He should have been born sooner. Had he been born sooner, when this was still a free country, and a man could really *make* some money, I'd have been born rich as you, Parnell, maybe even richer. I tell you – the old man struggled. He worked harder than any nigger. But he left me this store.

JO: You reckon we going to be able to leave it to the little one?

LYLE: We're going to leave him more than that. That little one ain't going to have nothing to worry about. I'm going to leave him as rich as old Parnell here, and he's going to be educated, too, better than his Daddy; better, even, than Parnell!

PARNELL: You going to send him to school in Switzerland?

LYLE: *You* went there for a while, didn't you?

JO: That's where Parnell picked up all his wild ideas.

PARNELL: Yes. Be careful. There were a couple of African princes studying in the school I went to – they did a lot more studying than I did, I must say.

LYLE: African princes, huh? What were they like? Big and black, I bet, elephant tusks hanging around their necks.

PARNELL: Some of them wore a little ivory, on a chain – silver chain. They were like everybody else. Maybe they thought they were a little *better* than most of us – the Swiss girls certainly thought so.

LYLE: The *Swiss* girls? You mean they didn't have no women of their own?

PARNELL: Lots of them. Swiss women, Danish women, English women, French women, Finns, Russians, even a couple of Americans.

JO: I don't believe you. Or else they was just trying to act like foreigners. I can't stand people who try to act like something they're not.

PARNELL: They were just trying to act like women – poor things. And the Africans were men, no one had ever told them that they weren't.

LYLE: You mean there weren't no African women around at *all*? Weren't the Swiss people kind of upset at having all these niggers around with no women?

PARNELL: They didn't seem to be upset. They seemed delighted. The niggers had an awful lot of money. And there weren't many African girls around because African girls aren't educated the way American girls are.

JO: The American girls didn't *mind* going out with the Africans?

PARNELL: Not at all. It appears that the Africans were excellent dancers.

LYLE: I won't never send no daughter of mine to Switzerland.

PARNELL: Well, what about your son? *He* might grow fond of some little African princess.

LYLE: Well, that's different. I don't care about that, long as he leaves her over there.

JO: It's *not* different – how can you say that? White men ain't got no more business fooling around with black women than –

LYLE: Girl, will you stop getting yourself into an uproar? Men is different from women – they ain't as delicate. Man can do a lot of things a woman can't do, you know that.

PARNELL: You've heard the expression, sowing wild oats? Well, all the men we know sowed a lot of wild oats before they finally settled down and got married.

LYLE: That's right. Men *have* to do it. They ain't like women. Parnell is *still* sowing his wild oats – I sowed mine.

JO: And a woman that wants to be a decent woman just has to – *wait* – until the men get tired of going to bed with – harlots! – and decide to settle down?

PARNELL: Well, it sounds very unjust, I know, but that's the way it's always been. I *suppose* the decent women were waiting – though nobody seems to know *exactly* how they spent the time.

JO: Parnell!

PARNELL: Well, there *are* some who waited too long.

JO: Men ought to be ashamed. How can you blame a woman if she – goes wrong? If a decent woman can't find a decent man – why – it must happen all the time – they get tired of waiting.

LYLE: Not if they been raised right, no sir, that's what my Daddy said, and I've never known it to fail. And look at you – *you* didn't get tired of waiting. Ain't nobody in this town ever been able to say a word against you. Man, I was so scared when I finally asked this girl to marry me. I was afraid she'd turn me out of the house. Because I had been pretty wild. Parnell can tell you.

JO: I had heard.

LYLE: But she didn't. I looked at her, it seemed almost like it was the first time – you know, the first time you really *look* at a woman? – and I thought, I'll be damned if I don't believe I can make it with her. I believe I can. And she looked at me like she loved me. It was in her eyes. And it was just like somebody had lifted a great big load off my heart.

JO: You shouldn't be saying these things in front of Parnell.

LYLE: Why not? I ain't got no secrets from Parnell – he knows about men and women. Look at her blush! Like I told you. Women is more delicate than men.

He touches her face lightly.

I know you kind of upset, sugar. But don't you be nervous. Everything's going to be all right, and we're going to be happy again, you'll see.

JO: I hope so, Lyle.

LYLE: I'm going to take me a bath and put some clothes on. Parnell, you sit right there, you hear? I won't be but a minute.

Exits.

JO: What a funny man he is! It don't do no good at all to get mad at him, you might as well get mad at that baby in there. Parnell? Can I ask you something?

PARNELL: Certainly.

JO: Is it true that Lyle has no secrets from you?

PARNELL: He said that *neither* of you had any secrets from me.

JO: Oh, don't play. Lyle don't know a thing about women – what they're really like, to themselves. Men don't know. But I want to ask you a serious question. Will you answer it?

PARNELL: If I can.

JO: That means you won't answer it. But I'll ask it, anyway. Parnell – was Lyle – is it true what people said? That he was having an affair with Old Bill's wife and that's why he shot Old Bill?

PARNELL: Why are you asking me that?

JO: Because I have to know! It's true, isn't it? He had an affair with Old Bill's wife – and he had affairs with lots of coloured women in this town. It's *true*. Isn't it?

PARNELL: What does it matter who he slept with before he married you, Jo? I know he had a – lot of prostitutes. Maybe some of them were coloured. When he was drunk, he wouldn't have been particular.

JO: He's never talked to you about it?

PARNELL: Why would he?

JO: Men talk about things like that.

PARNELL: Men often joke about things like that. But, Jo – what one man tells another man, his friend – can't be told to women.

JO: Men certainly stick together. I wish women did. All right. You can't talk about Lyle. But tell me this. Have *you* ever had an affair with a coloured girl? I don't mean a – a *night*. I mean, did she mean something to you, did you like her, did you – love her? Could you have married her – I mean, just like you would marry a white woman?

PARNELL: Jo –

JO: Oh! Tell me the truth, Parnell!

PARNELL: I loved a coloured girl, yes. I think I loved her. But I was only eighteen and she was only seventeen. I was still a virgin. I don't know if she was, but I think she was. A lot of the other kids in school used to drive over to niggertown at night to try and find black women. Sometimes they bought them, sometimes they frightened them, sometimes they raped them. And they were proud of it, they talked about it all the time. I couldn't do that.

Those kids made me ashamed of my own body, ashamed of everything I felt, ashamed of being white –

JO: Ashamed of being white.

PARNELL: Yes.

JO: How did you meet – this coloured girl?

PARNELL: Her mother worked for us. She used to come, sometimes, to pick up her mother. Sometimes she had to wait. I came in once and found her in the library, she was reading Stendhal. *The Red and The Black.* I had just read it and we talked about it. She was funny – very bright and solemn and very proud – and she was *scared*, scared of me, but much too proud to show it. Oh, she was funny. But she was bright.

JO: What did she look like?

PARNELL: She was the colour of gingerbread when it's just come out of the oven. I used to call her Ginger – later. Her name was really Pearl. She had black hair, very black, kind of short, and she dressed it very carefully. Later, I used to tease her about the way she took care of her hair. There's a girl in this town now who reminds me of her. Oh, I loved her!

JO: What happened?

PARNELL: I used to look at her, the way she moved, so beautiful and free, and I'd wonder if at night, when she might be on her way home from some place, any of those boys at school had said ugly things to her. And then I thought that I wasn't any better than they were, because I thought my own thoughts were pretty awful. And I wondered what she thought of me. But I didn't dare to ask. I got so I could hardly think of anyone but her. I got sick wanting to take her in my arms, to take her in my arms and love her and protect her from all those other people who wanted to destroy her. She wrote a little poetry, sometimes she'd show it to me, but she really wanted to be a painter.

JO: What happened?

PARNELL: Nothing happened. We got so we told each other everything. She was going to be a painter, I was going to be a writer. It was our secret. Nobody in the world knew about her *inside*, what she was like, and how she dreamed, but me. And nobody in the world knew about *me* inside, what I wanted, and how I dreamed, but her. But we couldn't look ahead, we didn't dare. We talked about going North, but I was still in school, and she was still in school. We couldn't be seen anywhere together – it would have given her too bad a name. I used to see her sometimes in the movies, with various coloured boys. She didn't seem to have any special one. They'd be sitting in the balcony, in the coloured section, and I'd be sitting downstairs in the white section. She couldn't come down to me, I couldn't go up to her. We'd meet some nights, late, out in the country, but – I didn't want to take her in the bushes, and I couldn't take her anywhere else. One day we were sitting in the library, we were kissing, and her mother came in. That was the day I found out how much black people can hate white people.

JO: What did her mother do?

PARNELL: She didn't say a word. She just looked at me. She just looked at me. I could see what was happening in her mind. She knew that there wasn't any point in complaining to my mother or my father. It would just make her daughter look bad. She didn't dare tell her husband. If he tried to do anything, he'd be killed. There wasn't anything she could do about me. I was just another horny white kid trying to get into a black girl's pants. She looked at me as though she were wishing with all her heart that she could raise her hand and wipe me off the face of the earth. I'll never forget that look. I still see it. She walked over to Pearl and I thought she was going to slap her. But she didn't. She took her by the hand, very sadly, and all she said was, 'I'm ready to go now. Come on.' And she took Pearl out of the room.

JO: Did you ever see her again?

PARNELL: No. Her mother sent her away.

JO: But you forgot her? You must have had lots of other girls right quick, right after that.

PARNELL: I never forgot her.

JO: Do you think of her – even when you're with Loretta?

PARNELL: Not all of the time, Jo. But some of the time – yes.

JO: And if you found her again?

PARNELL: If I found her again – yes, I'd marry her. I'd give her the children I've always wanted to have.

JO: Oh, Parnell! If you felt that way about her, if you've felt it all this time!

PARNELL: Yes. I know. I'm a renegade white man.

JO: Then Lyle could have felt that way about Old Bill's wife – about Willa Mae. I know that's not the way he feels about me. And if he felt that way – he could have shot Old Bill – to keep him quiet!

PARNELL: Jo!

JO: Yes! And if he could have shot Old Bill to keep him quiet – he could have killed that boy. He could have killed that boy. And if he did – well – that *is* murder, isn't it? It's just nothing but murder, even if the boy *was* black. Oh, Parnell! Parnell!

PARNELL: Jo, please. Please, Jo. Be quiet.

LYLE: (*Off.*) What's all that racket in there?

PARNELL: I'm telling your wife the story of my life.

LYLE: (*Off.*) Sounds pretty goddamn active.

PARNELL: You've never asked him, have you, Jo?

JO: No. No. No.

PARNELL: Well, *I* asked him –

JO: When?

PARNELL: Well, I didn't really *ask* him. But he said he didn't do it, that it wasn't true. You heard him. He wouldn't lie to me.

JO: No. He wouldn't lie to you. They say some of the niggers have guns – did you hear that?

PARNELL: Yes. I've heard it. But it's not true.

JO: *They* wouldn't lie to you, either? I've just had too much time to worry, I guess – brood and worry. Lyle's away so often nights – he spends so much time at that store. I don't know what he does there. And when he comes home, he's just dead – and he drops right off to sleep.

LYLE enters, carrying the child.

Hi, honey. What a transformation. You look like you used to look when you come courting.

LYLE: I sure didn't come courting carrying no baby. He was awake, just singing away, and carrying on with his toes. He acts like he thinks he's got a whole lot of candy attached to the end of his legs. Here. It's about time for him to eat, ain't it? How come you looking at me like that? Why you being so nice to me, all of a sudden?

PARNELL: I've been lecturing her on the duties of a wife.

LYLE: That so? Well, come on, boy, let's you and me walk down the road a piece. Believe I'll buy you a drink. You ain't ashamed to be seen with me, I hope?

PARNELL: No, I'm not ashamed to be seen with you.

JO: You going to be home for supper?

LYLE: Yeah, sugar. Come on, Parnell.

JO: You come, too, Parnell, you and Loretta, if you're free. We'd love to have you.

PARNELL: We'll try to make it. So long, Jo.

JO: So long.

They exit. JO *walks to the window. Turns back into the room, smiles down at the baby. Sings.*

Hush, little baby, don't say a word,
Mama's going to buy you a mocking bird –
But you don't want no mocking bird right now, do you?
I know what you want. You want something to eat. All right, Mama's going to feed you.

Sits, slowly begins to unbutton her blouse. Sings.

If that mocking bird don't sing,
Mama's going to buy you a diamond ring.

(LYLE's *store: Early evening. Both* LYLE *and* PARNELL *are a little drunk.*)

LYLE: Didn't you ever get like that? Sure, you must have got like that sometimes – just restless! You got everything you need and you can't complain about nothing – and yet, look like, you just can't be satisfied. Didn't you ever get like that? I swear, men is mighty strange! I'm kind of restless now.

PARNELL: What's the matter with you? You worried about the trial?

LYLE: No, I ain't worried about the trial. I ain't even mad at you, Parnell. Some folks think I should be, but I ain't mad at you. They don't know you like I know you. I ain't fooled by all your wild ideas. We both white and we both from around here, and we been buddies all our lives. That's all that counts. I know you ain't going to let nothing happen to me.

PARNELL: That's good to hear.

LYLE: After all the trouble started in this town – but before that crazy boy got himself killed, soon after he got here and started raising all that hell – I started thinking about her, about Willa Mae, more and more and more. She was too young for him. Old Bill, he was sixty if he was a day, he wasn't doing her no good. Yet and still, the first time I took Willa Mae, I had to fight her. I swear I did. Maybe she was frightened. But I never had to fight her again. No. It was good, boy, let me tell you, and she liked it as much as me. Hey! You still with me?

PARNELL: I'm still with you. Go on.

LYLE: What's the last thing I said?

PARNELL: That she liked it as much as you – which I find hard to believe.

LYLE: Ha-ha! I'm telling you. I never had it for nobody bad as I had it for her.

PARNELL: When did Old Bill find out?

LYLE: Old Bill? He wouldn't never have thought nothing if people hadn't started poisoning his mind. People started talking just because my Daddy wasn't well and she was up at the house so much because somebody had to look after him. First they said she was carrying on with *him*. Hell, my Daddy would sure have been willing, but he was far from able. He was really wore out by that time and he just wanted rest. Then people started to saying that it was me.

PARNELL: Old Bill ever talk to you about it?

LYLE: How was he going to talk to me about it? Hell, we was right good friends. Many's the time I helped Old Bill out when his cash was low. I used to load Willa Mae up with things from the kitchen just to make sure they didn't go hungry.

PARNELL: Old Bill never mentioned it to you? Never? He never gave you any reason to think he knew about it?

LYLE: Well, I don't know what was going on in his *mind*, Parnell. You can't never see what's in anybody else's *mind* – you know that. He didn't *act* no different. Hell, like I say, she was young enough to be his grand-daughter damn near, so I figured he thought it might be a pretty good arrangement – me doing *his* work, ha-ha! because *he* damn sure couldn't do it no more, and helping him to stay alive.

PARNELL: Then why was he so mad at you the last time you saw him?

LYLE: Like I said, he accused me of cheating him. And I ain't never cheated a black man in my life. I hate to say it, because we've always been good friends, but sometimes I think it might have been Joel – Papa D. – who told him that. Old Bill wasn't too good at figuring.

PARNELL: Why would Papa D. tell him a thing like that?

LYLE: I think he might have been a little jealous.

PARNELL: Jealous? You mean, of you and Willa Mae?

LYLE: Yeah. He ain't really an old man, you know. But I'm sure he didn't mean – for things to turn out like they did. (*A pause.*) I can still see him – the way he looked when he come into this store.

PARNELL: The way *who* looked when he came into this store?

LYLE: Why – Old Bill. He looked crazy. Like he wanted to kill me. He *did* want to kill me. Crazy nigger.

PARNELL: I thought you meant the other one. But the other one didn't die in the store.

LYLE: Old Bill didn't die in the store. He died over yonder, in the road.

PARNELL: I thought you were talking about Richard Henry.

LYLE: That crazy boy. Yeah, he come in here. I don't know what was the matter with him, he hadn't seen me but one time in his life before. And I treated him like – like I would have treated *any* man.

PARNELL: I heard about it. It was in Papa D.'s joint. He was surrounded by niggers – or *you* were –

LYLE: He was dancing with one of them crazy young ones – the real pretty nigger girl – what's her name?

PARNELL: Juanita.

LYLE: That's the one. (*Juke box music, soft. Voices. Laughter.*) Yeah, he looked at me like he wanted to kill me. And he insulted my wife. And I hadn't never done him no harm. (*As above, a little stronger.*) But I been thinking about it. And you know what I think? Hey! You gone to sleep?

PARNELL: No. I'm thinking.

LYLE: What you thinking about?

PARNELL: Us. You and me.

LYLE: And what do you think about us – you and me? What's the point of thinking about us, anyway? We've been buddies all our lives – we can't stop being buddies now.

PARNELL: That's right, buddy. What were you about to say?

LYLE: Oh. I think a lot of the niggers in this town, especially the young ones, is turned bad. And I believe they was egging him on.

A pause. The music stops.

He come in here one Monday afternoon. Everybody heard about it, it was all over this town quicker'n a jack-rabbit gets his nuts off. You just missed it. You'd just walked out of here.

(*LYLE rises, walks to the doors and opens them. Sunlight fills the room. He slams the screen door shut; we see the road.*)

JO: (*Off.*) Lyle, you want to help me bring this baby carriage inside? It's getting kind of hot out here now.

PARNELL: Let *me*.

LYLE and PARNELL bring in the baby carriage. JO enters.

JO: My, it's hot! Wish we'd gone for a ride or something. Declare to goodness, we ain't got no reason to be sitting around this store. Ain't nobody coming in here – not to *buy* anything, anyway.

PARNELL: I'll buy some bubble gum.

JO: You know you don't chew bubble gum.

PARNELL: Well, then, I'll buy some cigarettes.

JO: Two cartons, or three? It's all right, Parnell, the Britten family's going to make it somehow.

LYLE: Couple of niggers coming down the road. Maybe they'll drop in for a Coke.

Exits, into back of store.

JO: Why no, they won't. Our Cokes is *poisoned*. I get up every morning before daybreak and drop the arsenic in myself.

PARNELL: Well, then, I won't have a Coke. See you, Jo. So long, Lyle!

LYLE: (*Off.*) Be seeing you!

PARNELL exits. Silence for a few seconds. Then we hear LYLE hammering in the back. JO picks up a magazine, begins to read. Voices. RICHARD and LORENZO appear in the road.

RICHARD: Hey, you want a Coke? I'm thirsty.

LORENZO: Let's go on a little further.

RICHARD: Man, we been walking for *days*, my mouth is as dry as that damn dusty road. Come on, have a Coke with me, won't take but a minute.

LORENZO: We don't trade in there. Come on –

RICHARD: Oh! Is this the place? Hell, I'd like to get another look at the peckerwood, ain't going to give him but a dime. I want to get his face fixed in my *mind*, so there won't be no time wasted when the time comes, you dig? (*Enters the store.*) Hey, Mrs Ofay Ednolbay Ydalay! you got any Coca Cola for sale?

JO: What?

RICHARD: Coke! Me and my man been toting barges and lifting bales, that's right, we been slaving, and we need a little cool. Liquid. Refreshment. Yeah, and you can take that hammer, too.

JO: Boy, what do you want?

RICHARD: A Coca Cola, ma'am. Please ma'am.

JO: They right in the box there.

RICHARD: Thank you kindly. (*Takes two Cokes, opens them.*) Oh, this is fine, *fine*. Did you put them in this box with your own little dainty dish-pan hands? Sure makes them taste *sweet*.

JO: Are you talking to me?

RICHARD: No ma'am, just feel like talking to myself from time to time, makes the time pass faster. (*At screen door.*) Hey, Lorenzo, I got you a Coke.

LORENZO: I don't want it. Come on out of there.

JO: That will be twenty cents.

RICHARD: *Twenty* cents? All right. Don't you know how to say please? All the women *I* know say please – of course, they ain't as pretty as you. I ain't got twenty cents, ma'am. All I got is – twenty dollars!

JO: You ain't got nothing smaller?

RICHARD: No ma'am. You see, I don't never carry on me more cash than I can afford to *lose*.

JO: Lyle! (*LYLE enters, carrying the hammer.*) You got any change?

LYLE: Change for a twenty? No, you know I ain't got it.

RICHARD: You all got this big, fine store and all – and you ain't got change for *twenty* dollars?

LYLE: It's early in the day, boy.

RICHARD: It ain't that early. I thought white folks was rich at *every* hour of the day.

LYLE: Now, if you looking for trouble, you just might get it. That boy outside – ain't he got twenty cents?

RICHARD: That boy outside is about twenty-four years old, and he ain't got twenty cents. Ain't no need to ask him.

LYLE: (*At the door.*) Boy! You got twenty cents?

LORENZO: Come on out of there, Richard! I'm tired of hanging around here!

LYLE: Boy, didn't you hear what I asked you?

LORENZO: Mister Britten, I ain't *in* the store, and I ain't *bought* nothing in the store, and so I ain't *got* to tell you whether or not I got twenty cents!

RICHARD: Maybe your wife could run home and get some change. You *got* some change at home, I know. Don't you?

LYLE: I don't stand for nobody to talk about my wife.

RICHARD: I only said you was a lucky man to have so fine a *wife*. I said maybe she could run *home* and look and see if there was any change – in the *home*.

LYLE: I seen you before some place. You that crazy nigger. You ain't from around here.

RICHARD: You *know* you seen me. And you remember where. And when. I was born right here, in this town. I'm Reverend Meridian Henry's son.

LYLE: You say that like you thought your Daddy's name was some kind of protection. He ain't no protection against *me* – him, nor that boy outside, neither.

RICHARD: I don't need no protection, do I? Not in my own home town, in the good old USA. I just dropped by to sip on a Coke in a simple country store – and come to find out the joker ain't got enough bread to change twenty dollars. Stud ain't got *nothing* – you people been spoofing the public, man.

LYLE: You put them Cokes down and get out of here.

RICHARD: I ain't finished yet. And I ain't changed my bill yet.

LYLE: Well, I ain't going to change that bill, and you ain't going to finish them Cokes. You get your black ass out of here – go on! If you got any sense, you'll get your black ass out of this town.

RICHARD: You don't own this town, you white motherfucker. You don't *even* own twenty dollars. Don't you raise that hammer. I'll take it and beat your skull to jelly.

JO: Lyle! Don't you fight that boy! He's crazy! I'm going to call the Sheriff! (*Starts towards the back, returns to counter.*) The baby! Lyle! Watch out for the baby!

RICHARD: A baby, huh? How many times did you have to try

for it, you no-good, ball-less peckerwood? I'm surprised you could even get it up – look at the way you sweating now.

LYLE raises the hammer. RICHARD grabs his arm, forcing it back. They struggle.

JO: Lyle! The baby!

LORENZO: Richard!

He comes into the store.

JO: Please get that boy out of here, get that boy out of here – he's going to get himself killed.

RICHARD knocks the hammer from LYLE's hand, and knocks LYLE down. The hammer spins across the room. LORENZO picks it up.

LORENZO: I don't think your husband's going to kill no more black men. Not today, Mrs Britten. Come on, Richard. Let's go.

LYLE looks up at them.

LYLE: It took two of you. Remember that.

LORENZO: I didn't lay a hand on you, Mister Britten. You just ain't no match for – a *boy*. Not without your gun you ain't. Come on, Richard.

JO: You'll go to jail for this! You'll go to jail! For years!

LORENZO: We've been in jail for years. I'll leave your hammer over at Papa D.'s joint – don't look like you're going to be doing no more work today.

RICHARD: (*Laughs.*) Look at the mighty peckerwood! On his *ass*, baby – and his woman watching! Now, who you think is the better man? Ha-ha! The master race! You let me in that tired white chick's drawers, she'll know who's the master! Ha-ha-ha!

(Exits. RICHARD's laughter continues in the dark. LYLE and PARNELL as before.)

LYLE: Niggers was laughing at me for days. Everywhere I went.

PARNELL: You never did call the Sheriff.

LYLE: No.

PARNELL fills their glasses. We hear singing.

PARNELL: It's almost time for his funeral.

LYLE: And may every nigger like that nigger end like that nigger – face down in the weeds!

A pause.

PARNELL: Was he lying face down?

LYLE: Hell, yeah, he was face down. Said so in the papers.

PARNELL: Is that what the papers said? I don't remember.

LYLE: Yeah, that's what the papers said.

PARNELL: I guess they had to turn him over – to make sure it was him.

LYLE: I reckon. (*Laughs.*) Yeah. I reckon.

PARNELL: You and me are buddies, huh?

LYLE: *Yeah*, we're buddies – to the end!

PARNELL: I always wondered why you wanted to be my buddy. A lot of poor guys hate rich guys. I always wondered why you weren't like that.

LYLE: I ain't like that. Hell, Parnell, you're smarter than me. I know it. I used to wonder what made you smarter than me. I got to be your buddy so I could find out. Because, hell, you didn't seem so different in *other* ways – in spite of all your *ideas*. Two things we always had in common – liquor and poon-tang. We couldn't get enough of neither one. Of course, your liquor might have been a little better. But I doubt if the other could have been any better!

PARNELL: Did you find out what made me smarter?

LYLE: Yeah. You richer!

PARNELL: I'm richer! That's all you got to tell me – about Richard Henry?

LYLE: Ain't nothing more to tell. Wait till after the trial. You won't have to ask me no more questions then!

PARNELL: I've got to get to the funeral.

LYLE: Don't run off. Don't leave me here alone.

PARNELL: You're supposed to be home for supper.

LYLE: Supper can wait. Have another drink with me – be my buddy. Don't leave me here alone. Listen to them! Singing and praying! Singing and praying and laughing behind a man's back!

(The singing continues in the dark. BLACKTOWN: The church, packed. MERIDIAN in the pulpit, the bier just below him.)

MERIDIAN: My heart is heavier tonight than it has ever been before. I raise my voice to you tonight out of a sorrow and a wonder I have never felt before. Not only I, my Lord, am in this case. Everyone under the sound of my voice, and many more souls than that, feel as I feel, and tremble as I tremble, and bleed as I bleed. It is not that the days are dark – we have known dark days. It is not only that the blood runs down and no man helps us; it is not only that our children are destroyed before our eyes. It is not only that our lives, from day to day and every hour of each day, are menaced by the people among whom you have set us down. We have borne all these things, my Lord, and we have done what the prophets of old could not do, we have sung the Lord's song in a strange land. In a strange land! What was the sin committed by our forefathers in the time that has vanished on the other side of the flood, which has had to be expiated by chains, by the lash, by hunger and thirst, by slaughter, by fire, by the rope, by the knife, and for so many generations, on these wild shores, in this strange land? Our offence must have been mighty, our crime immeasurable. But it is not the past which makes our hearts so heavy. It is the present. Lord, where is our hope? Who, or what, shall touch the hearts of this headlong and unthinking people and turn them back from destruction? When will they hear the words of John? *I know thy works, that thou art neither cold nor hot: I would that thou wert cold or hot. So, then because thou art lukewarm and neither cold nor hot, I will spew thee out of my mouth. Because thou sayest, I am rich and increased with goods, and have need of nothing; and knowest not that thou art wretched and miserable and poor and blind and naked.* Now, when the children come, my Lord, and ask which road to follow, my tongue stammers and my heart fails. I will not abandon the land – this strange land, which is my home. But can I ask the children for ever to sustain the cruelty inflicted on them by those who have been their masters, and who are now, in very truth, their kinfolk, their brothers and their sisters and their parents? What hope is there for a people who deny their deeds and disown their kinsmen and who do so in the name of purity and love, in the name of Jesus Christ? What a light, my Lord, is needed to conquer so mighty a darkness! This darkness rules in us, and grows, in black and white alike. I have set my face against the darkness, I will not let it conquer me, even though it will, I know, one day, destroy this body. But, my Lord, what of the children? What shall I tell the children? I must be with you, Lord, like Jacob, and wrestle with you until the light appears – I will not let you go until you give me a sign! A sign that in the terrible Sahara of our time a fountain may spring, the fountain of a true morality, and bring us closer, oh, my Lord, to that peace on earth desired by so few throughout so many ages. Let not our suffering endure for ever. Teach us to trust the great gift of life and learn to love one another and dare to walk the earth like men. Amen.

MOTHER HENRY: Let's file up, children, and say goodbye.

Sing: 'Great Getting-Up Morning.' MERIDIAN *steps down from the pulpit.* MERIDIAN, LORENZO, JIMMY *and* PETE *shoulder the bier. A dishevelled* PARNELL *enters. The Congregation and the Pallbearers file past him.* JUANITA *stops.*

JUANITA: What's the matter, Parnell? You look sick.

PARNELL: I tried to come sooner. I couldn't get away. Lyle wouldn't let me go.

JUANITA: Were you trying to beat a confession out of him? But you look as though he's been trying to beat a confession out of you. Poor Parnell!

PARNELL: Poor Lyle! He'll never confess. Never. Poor devil!

JUANITA: Poor devil! You weep for Lyle. You're luckier than I am. I can't weep in front of others. I can't say goodbye in front of others. Others don't know what it is you're saying goodbye to.

PARNELL: You loved him.

JUANITA: Yes.

PARNELL: I didn't know.

JUANITA: Ah, you're so lucky, Parnell. I know you didn't know. Tell me, where do you live, Parnell? How can you not know all of the things you do not know?

PARNELL: Why are you hitting out at me? I never thought you cared that much about me. But – oh, Juanita! There are so many things I've never been able to say!

JUANITA: There are so many things you've never been able to hear.

PARNELL: And – you've tried to tell me some of those things?

JUANITA: I used to watch you roaring through this town like a St George thirsty for dragons. And I wanted to let you know you haven't got to do all that; dragons aren't hard to find, they're everywhere. And nobody wants you to be St George. We just want you to be Parnell. But, of course, that's much harder.

PARNELL: Are we friends, Juanita? Please say that we're friends.

JUANITA: Friends is not exactly what you mean, Parnell. Tell the truth.

PARNELL: Yes. I've always wanted more than that, from you. But I was afraid you would misunderstand me. That you would feel that I was only trying to exploit you. In another way.

JUANITA: You've been a grown man for a long time now, Parnell. You ought to trust yourself more than that.

PARNELL: I've been a grown man far too long – ever to have dared to dream of offering myself to you.

JUANITA: Your age was never the question, Parnell.

PARNELL: Was there ever any question at all?

JUANITA: Yes. Yes. Yes, once there was.

PARNELL: And there isn't – there can't be – any more?

JUANITA: No. That train has gone. One day, I'll recover. I'm sure that I'll recover. And I'll see the world again – the marvellous world. And I'll have learned from Richard – how to love. I must. I can't let him die for nothing.

Juke box music, loud. The lights change, spot on PARNELL's *face.* JUANITA *steps across the aisle.* RICHARD *appears. They dance.* PARNELL *watches.*

Act 3

Two months later. The courtroom.

The courtroom is extremely high, domed, a blinding white emphasized by a dull, somehow ominous gold. The JUDGE's *stand is centre stage, and at a height. Sloping down from this place on either side are the black and white* TOWNSPEOPLE; *the* JURY; PHOTOGRAPHERS *and* JOURNALISTS *from all over the world; microphones and TV cameras. All windows open: one should be aware of masses of people outside and one should sometimes hear their voices – their roar – as well as singing from the church. The church is directly across the street from the courthouse, and the steeple and the cross are visible throughout the act.*

Each witness, when called, is revealed behind scrim and passes through two or three tableaux before moving down the aisle to the witness stand. The witness stand is downstage, in the same place and at the same angle as the pulpit in Acts 1 and 2.

Before the curtain rises, song: 'I Said I Wasn't Going To Tell Nobody, But I Couldn't Keep It To Myself.'

The JUDGE's *gavel breaks across the singing, and the curtain rises.*

CLERK: *(Calling.)* Mrs Josephine Gladys Britten!

(JO, serving coffee at a church social. She passes out coffee to invisible guests.)

JO: Am I going to spend the rest of my life serving coffee to strangers in church basements? Am I? – Yes! Reverend Phelps was truly noble! As *usual!* – Reverend Phelps has been married for more than twenty years. Don't let those thoughts into your citadel! You just remember that the mind is a citadel and you can keep out all troubling thoughts! – My! Mrs Evans! you are certainly a sight for sore eyes! I don't know how you manage to look so unruffled and *cool* and *young!* With all those *children.* And Mr Evans. How are you tonight? – She has a baby just about every year. I don't know how she stands it. Mr Evans don't look like that kind of man. You sure can't tell a book by its cover. Lord! I wish I was in my own home and these were *my* guests and my husband was somewhere in the room. I'm getting old! Old! Old maid! *Maid!* – Oh! Mr Arpino! You taken time out from your engineering to come visit here with us? It sure is a pleasure to have you! – My! He is big! and dark! Like a Greek! or a Spaniard! Some people say he might have a touch of nigger blood I don't believe that. He's just – *foreign.* That's all. He needs a hair cut. I wonder if he's got hair like that all *over* his body? Remember that your mind is a citadel. A citadel. Oh, Lord, I'm tired of serving coffee in church basements! I want, I want – Why, good evening, Ellis! And Mr Lyle Britten! We sure don't see either of *you* very often! Why, Mr Britten! You know you don't mean that! You come over here just to see little old *me?* Why, you just go right ahead and drink that coffee, I do believe you need to be sobered up!

(The light changes.)

REV. PHELPS: *(Voice.)* Do you, Josephine Gladys Miles, take this man, Lyle Britten, Jr., as your lawfully wedded husband, to have and to hold, to love and to cherish, in sickness and in health, till death do you part?

JO: I do. I *do!* Oh, Lyle. I'll make you the best wife any man ever had. I *will.* Love me. Please love me. Look at me! *Look* at me! He *wanted* me. He wanted *me!* I am – Mrs Josephine Gladys Britten!

(The light changes again, and JO takes the stand. We hear the baby crying.)

BLACKTOWN: Man, that's the southern white lady you supposed to be willing to risk death for!

WHITETOWN: You know, this is a kind of hanging in reverse! Niggers out here to watch us being hanged!

THE STATE: What is your relationship to the accused?

JO: I am his wife.

THE STATE: Will you please tell us, in your own words, of your first meeting with the deceased, Richard Henry?

WHITETOWN: Don't be afraid. Just tell the truth.

BLACKTOWN: Here we go – down the river!

JO: Well, I was in the store, sitting at the counter, and pretty soon this coloured boy come in, loud, and talking in just the most awful way. I didn't recognize him, I just knew he wasn't one of *our* coloured people. His language was something awful, awful!

THE STATE: He was insulting? Was he insulting, Mrs Britten?

JO: He said all kinds of things, dirty things, like – well – just like I might have been a coloured girl, that's what it sounded like to me. Just like some little coloured girl he might have met on a street corner and wanted – wanted to – for a night! And I was scared. I hadn't seen a coloured boy act like him before. He acted like he was drunk or crazy or maybe he was under the influence of that dope. I never knew nobody to be *drunk* and act like him. His eyes was just going and he acted like he had a fire in his belly. But I tried to be calm because I didn't want to upset Lyle, you know – Lyle's mighty quick-tempered – and he was working in the back of the store, he was hammering –

THE STATE: Go on, Mrs Britten. What happened then?

JO: Well, he – that boy – wanted to buy him two Cokes because he had a friend outside –

THE STATE: He brought a friend? He did not come there alone? Did this other boy enter the store?

JO: No, not then he didn't – I –

BLACKTOWN: Come on, bitch. We *know* what you going to say. Get it over with.

JO: I – I give him the two Cokes, and he – tried to grab my hands and pull me to him, and – I – I – he pushed himself up against me, real close and hard – and, oh, he was just like an animal, I could – smell him! And he tried to kiss me, he kept whispering these awful, filthy things and I got scared, I yelled for Lyle! Then Lyle come running out of the back – and when the boy seen I wasn't alone in the store, he yelled for this other boy outside and this other boy come rushing in and they both jumped on Lyle and knocked him down.

THE STATE: What made you decide not to report this incident – this unprovoked assault – to the proper authorities, Mrs Britten?

JO: We've had so much trouble in this town!

THE STATE: What sort of trouble, Mrs Britten?

JO: Why, with the coloured people! We've got all these northern agitators coming through here all the time, and stirring them up so that you can't hardly sleep nights!

THE STATE: Then you, as a responsible citizen of this town, were doing your best to keep down trouble? Even though you had been so brutally assaulted by a deranged northern Negro dope addict?

JO: Yes. I didn't want to stir up no more trouble. I *made* Lyle keep quiet about it. I thought it would all blow over. I knew the boy's Daddy was a preacher and that he would talk to the boy about the way he was behaving. It was all over town in a second, anyway! And look like all the coloured people was on the side of that crazy boy. And Lyle's always been real good to coloured people!

Laughter from BLACKTOWN.

THE STATE: On the evening that the alleged crime was committed – or, rather, the morning – very early on the morning of the 24th of August – where were you and your husband, Mrs Britten?

JO: We were home. The next day we heard that the boy was missing.

COUNSEL FOR THE BEREAVED: Doesn't an attempt at sexual assault seem a rather strange thing to do, considering that your store is a public place, with people continually going in and out; that, furthermore, it is located on a public road which people use, on foot and in automobiles, all of the time; and considering that your husband, who has the reputation of being a violent man, and who is, in your own words, 'mighty quick tempered', was working in the back room?

JO: He didn't know Lyle was back there.

COUNSEL FOR THE BEREAVED: But he knew that someone was back there, for, according to your testimony, 'He was hammering.'

JO: Well, I told you the boy was crazy. He had to be crazy. Or he was on that dope.

BLACKTOWN: You ever hear of a junkie trying to rape anybody?

JO: *I didn't say rape!*

COUNSEL FOR THE BEREAVED: Were you struggling in Mr Henry's arms when your husband came out of the back room, carrying his hammer in his hand?

JO: No. I was free then.

COUNSEL FOR THE BEREAVED: Therefore, your husband had only *your* word for the alleged attempted assault! *You* told him that Richard Henry had attempted to assault you? Had made sexual advances to you? Please answer, Mrs Britten!

JO: Yes. I had – I had to – tell him. I'm his wife!

COUNSEL FOR THE BEREAVED: And a most loyal one. You told your husband that Richard Henry had attempted to assault you and then begged him to do nothing about it?

JO: That's right.

COUNSEL FOR THE BEREAVED: And though he was under the impression that his wife had been nearly raped by a Negro, he agreed to forgive and forget and do nothing about it? He agreed neither to call the law, nor to take the law into his own hands?

JO: Yes.

COUNSEL FOR THE BEREAVED: Extraordinary. Mrs Britten, you are aware that Richard Henry met his death some time between the hours of two and five o'clock on the morning of Monday, August 24th?

JO: Yes.

COUNSEL FOR THE BEREAVED: In an earlier statement, several months ago, you stated that your husband had spent that night at the store. You now state that he came in before one o'clock and went to sleep at once. What accounts for this discrepancy?

JO: It's natural. I made a mistake about the time. I got it mixed up with another night. He spent so many nights at that store!

JUDGE: The witness may step down.

JO leaves the stand.

CLERK: (*Calls.*) Mr Joel Davis!

(*We hear a shot.* PAPA D. *is facing* LYLE.)

LYLE: Why'd you run down there this morning, shooting your mouth off about me and Willa Mae? Why? You been bringing her up here and taking her back all this time, what got into you this morning? Huh? You jealous, old man? Why you come running back here to tell me everything he said? To tell me how he cursed me out? Have you lost your mind? And we been knowing each other all this time. I don't understand you. She ain't the only girl you done brought here for me. Nigger, do you hear me talking to you?

PAPA D.: I didn't think you'd shoot him, Mr Lyle.

LYLE: I'll shoot any nigger talks to me like that. It was self defence, you hear me? He come in here and tried to kill me. You hear me?

PAPA D.: Yes. Yes sir. I hear you, Mr Lyle.

LYLE: That's right. You don't say the right thing, nigger, I'll blow your brains out, too.

PAPA D.: Yes sir, Mr Lyle.

(*Juke box music.* PAPA D. *takes the stand.*)

WHITETOWN: He's worked hard and saved his money and ain't never had no trouble – why can't they all be like that?

BLACKTOWN: Hey, Papa D.! You can't be walking around here without no handkerchief! You might catch cold – after all *these* years!

PAPA D.: Mr Lyle Britten – he is an *oppressor*. That is the only word for that man. He ain't never give the coloured man no kind of chance. I have tried to reason with that man for *years*. I say, Mr Lyle, look around you. Don't you see that most white folks have changed their way of thinking about us coloured folks? I say, Mr Lyle, we ain't slaves no more and white folks is ready to let us have our chance. Now, why don't you just come on up to where *most* of your people are? and we can make the South a fine place for all of us to live in. That's what I say – and I tried to keep him from being so *hard* on the coloured – because I sure do love my people. And I was the closest thing to Mr Lyle, couldn't nobody else reason with him. But he was *hard* – hard and stubborn. He say, 'My folks lived and died this way, and this is the way I'm going to live and die.' When he was like that couldn't do nothing with him. I know. I've known him since he was born.

WHITETOWN: He's always been real good to you. You were friends!

BLACKTOWN: You loved him! Tell the truth, mother – tell the truth!

PAPA D.: Yes, we were friends. And, yes, I loved him – in my way. Just like he loved me – in his way.

BLACKTOWN: You knew he was going to kill that boy – didn't you? If you knew it, why didn't you stop him?

PAPA D.: Oh. Ain't none of this easy. What it was, both Mr Lyle Britten and me, we both love money. And I did a whole lot of things for him, for a long while. Once I had to help him cover up a killing – coloured man – I was in too deep myself by that time – you understand? I know you all understand.

BLACKTOWN: Did he kill that boy?

PAPA D.: He come into my joint the night that boy died. The boy was alone, standing at the juke box. We'd been talking –

(*RICHARD, in the juke box light.*)

If you think you've found all that, Richard – if you think you going to be well now, and you found you somebody who loves you – well, then, I would make tracks out of here. I would –

RICHARD: It's funny, Papa D. I feel like I'm beginning to understand my life – for the first time. I can look back – and it doesn't hurt me like it used to. I want to get Juanita out of here. This is no place for her. They're going to kill her – if she stays here!

PAPA D.: You talk to Juanita about this yet?

RICHARD: No. I haven't talked to nobody about it yet. I just decided it. I guess I'm deciding it now. That's why I'm talking about it now – to you – to see if you'll laugh at me. Do you think she'll laugh at me?

PAPA D.: No. She won't laugh.

RICHARD: I know I can do it. I know I can do it!

PAPA D.: That boy had good sense. He was wild, but he had good sense. And I couldn't blame him too much for being so wild, it seemed to me I knew how he felt.

RICHARD: Papa D., I been in pain and darkness all my life. All my life. And this is the first time in my life I've ever felt – maybe it isn't all like that. Maybe there's more to it than that.

PAPA D.: Lyle Britten come to the door –

(*LYLE enters.*)

He come to the door and he say –

LYLE: You ready for me now, boy? Howdy, Papa D.

PAPA D.: Howdy, Mr Lyle, how's the world been treating you?

LYLE: I can't complain. You ready, boy?

RICHARD: No. I ain't ready. I got a record to play and a drink to finish.

LYLE: You about ready to close, ain't you, Joel?

PAPA D.: Just about, Mr Lyle.

RICHARD: I got a record to play. (*Drops coin: juke box music, loud.*) And a drink to finish.

PAPA D.: He played his record. Lyle Britten never moved from the door. And they just stood there, the two of them, looking at each other. When the record was just about over, the boy come to the bar – he swallowed down the last of his drink.

RICHARD: What do I owe you, Papa D.?

PAPA D.: Oh, you pay me tomorrow. I'm closed now.

RICHARD: What do I owe you, Papa D.? I'm not sure I can pay you tomorrow.

PAPA D.: Give me two dollars.

RICHARD: Here you go. Good night, Papa D. I'm ready, Charlie.

Exits.

PAPA D.: Good night, Richard. Go on home now. Good night, Mr Lyle. Mr Lyle!

LYLE: Good night, Joel. You get you some sleep, you hear?

Exits.

PAPA D.: Mr Lyle! Richard! And I never saw that boy again. Lyle killed him. He killed him. I know it, just like I know I'm sitting in this chair. Just like he shot Old Bill and wasn't nothing never, never, never done about it!

JUDGE: The witness may step down.

PAPA D. leaves the stand.

CLERK: (*Calls.*) Mr Lorenzo Shannon!

(*We hear a long, loud, animal cry, lonely and terrified: it is PETE, screaming. We discover LORENZO and PETE, in jail. Night. From far away, we hear Students humming, moaning, singing: 'I Woke Up This Morning With My Mind Stayed On Freedom.'*)

PETE: (*Stammering.*) Lorenzo? Lorenzo. I was dreaming – dreaming – dreaming. I was back in that courtyard and Big Jim Byrd's boys was beating us and beating us and beating us – and Big Jim Byrd was laughing. And Anna Mae Taylor was on her knees, she was trying to pray. She say, 'Oh, Lord, Lord, Lord, come and help us,' and they kept beating on her and beating on her and I saw the blood coming down her neck and they put the prods to her, and, oh, Lorenzo! people was just running around, just crying and moaning and you look to the right and you see somebody go down and you look to the left and you see somebody go down and they was kicking that woman and I say, 'That woman's going to have a baby, don't you kick that woman!' and they say, 'No, she ain't going to have no baby,' and they knocked me down and they got that prod up between my legs and they say, 'You ain't going to be having no babies, neither, nigger!' And then they put that prod to my head – ah! *ah!* – to my *head!* Lorenzo! I can't see right! What have they done to my head? Lorenzo! Lorenzo, am I going to die? Lorenzo – they going to kill us all, ain't they? They mean to kill us all –

LORENZO: Be quiet. Be quiet. They going to come and beat us some more if you don't be quiet.

PETE: Where's Juanita? Did they get Juanita?

LORENZO: I believe Juanita's all right. Go to sleep, Pete. Go to sleep. I won't let you dream. I'll hold you.

(LORENZO *takes the stand.*)

THE STATE: Did you accompany your late and great friend, Richard Henry, on the morning of August 17, to the store which is owned and run by Mr and Mrs Lyle Britten?

LORENZO: We hadn't planned to go there – but we got to walking and talking and we found ourselves there. And it didn't happen like she said. He picked the Cokes out of the box himself, he came to the door with the Cokes in his hand, she hadn't even moved, she was still behind the counter, he never touched that dried out little peckerwood!

WHITETOWN: Get that nigger! Who does that nigger think he is!

BLACKTOWN: Speak, Lorenzo! Go, my man!

THE STATE: You cannot expect this courtroom to believe that so serious a battle was precipitated by the question of twenty cents! There was some other reason. What was this reason? Had he – and you – been drinking?

LORENZO: It was early in the day, Cap'n. We ain't rich enough to drink in the daytime.

THE STATE: Or *smoking*, perhaps? Perhaps your friend had just had his quota of heroin for the day, and was feeling jolly – in a mood to *prove* to you what he had already suggested with those filthy photographs of himself and naked white women!

LORENZO: I never saw no photographs. White women are a problem for white men. We had not been drinking. All we was smoking was that same goddamn tobacco that made *you* rich because we picked it for you for nothing, and carried it to market for you for nothing. And I *know* ain't no heroin in this town because none of you mothers need it. You was *born* frozen. Richard was better than that. I'd rather die than be like you, Cap'n, but I'd be *proud* to be like Richard. That's all I can tell you, Mr Boss-Man. But I know he wasn't trying to rape nobody. Rape!

THE STATE: Your Honour, will you instruct the witness that he is under oath, that this is a court of law, and that it is a serious matter to be held in contempt of court!

LORENZO: More serious than the chain gang? *I* know I'm under oath. If there was any reason, it was just that Richard couldn't stand white people. *Couldn't stand white people!* And, now, do you want me to tell you all that I know about *that?* Do you think you could stand it? You'd cut my tongue out before you'd let me tell you all that I know about *that!*

COUNSEL FOR THE BEREAVED: You are a student here?

LORENZO: In my spare time. I just come off the chain gang a couple of days ago. I was trespassing in the white waiting room of the bus station.

COUNSEL FOR THE BEREAVED: What are you studying – in your spare time – Mr Shannon?

LORENZO: History.

COUNSEL FOR THE BEREAVED: To your knowledge – during his stay in this town – was the late Mr Richard Henry still addicted to narcotics?

LORENZO: No. He'd kicked his habit. He'd paid his dues. He was just trying to live. And he almost made it.

COUNSEL FOR THE BEREAVED: You were very close to him?

LORENZO: Yes.

COUNSEL FOR THE BEREAVED: To your knowledge – was he carrying about obscene photographs of himself and naked white women?

LORENZO: To my knowledge – and I would know – no. The only times he ever opened a popular magazine was to look at the Jazz Poll. No. They been asking me about photographs they say he was carrying and they been asking me about a gun I never saw. No. It wasn't like that. He was a beautiful cat, and they killed him. That's all. That's *all*.

JUDGE: The witness may step down.

LORENZO: Well! I thank you kindly. *Suh!*

LORENZO *leaves the stand.*

CLERK: (*Calls.*) Miss Juanita Harmon!

(JUANITA *rises from bed; early Sunday morning.*)

JUANITA: He lay beside me on that bed like a rock. As heavy as a rock – like he'd fallen – fallen from a high place – fallen so far and landed so heavy, he seemed almost to be sinking out of sight – with one knee pointing to heaven. My God. He covered me like that. He wasn't at all like I thought he was. He fell on – fell on me – like life and death. My God. His chest, his belly, the rising and the falling, the moans. How he clung, how he struggled – life and death! Life and death! Why did it all seem to me like tears? That he came to me, clung to me, plunged into me, sobbing, howling, bleeding, somewhere inside his chest, his belly, and it all came out, came pouring out, like tears! My God, the smell, the touch, the taste, the sound, of anguish! Richard! Why couldn't I have held you closer? Held you, held you, borne you, given you life again! Have made you be born again! Oh, Richard. The teeth that gleamed, oh! when you smiled, the spit flying when you cursed, the teeth stinging when you bit – your breath, your hands, your weight, my God, when you moved in me! Where shall I go now, what shall I do? Oh. Oh. Oh. Mama was frightened. Frightened because little Juanita brought her first real lover to this house. I suppose God does for Mama what Richard did for me. Juanita! I don't care! I don't care! Yes, I want a lover made of flesh and blood, of flesh and blood, like me, I don't want to be God's mother! He can *have* His icy, snow-white heaven! If he is somewhere around this fearful planet, if I ever see Him, I will spit in His face! In God's face! How *dare* He presume to judge a living soul! A living soul. Mama is afraid I'm pregnant. Mama is afraid of so much. I'm not afraid. I hope I'm pregnant. I *hope* I am! One more illegitimate black baby – that's right, you jive mothers! And I am going to raise my baby to be a man. A *man*, you dig? Oh, let me be pregnant, let me be pregnant, don't let it all be gone! A man. Juanita. A man. Oh, my God, there are no more. For me. Did this happen to Mama some time? Did she have a man some time who vanished like smoke? And left her to get through this world as best she could? Is that why she married my father? Did this happen to Mother Henry? Is this how we all get to be mothers – so soon? of helpless men – because all the other men perish? No. No. No. No. What is this world like? I will end up taking care of some man, some day. Help me do it with love. Pete. Meridian. Parnell. We have been the mothers for them all. It must be dreadful to be Parnell. There is no flesh he can touch. All of it is bloody. Incest everywhere. Ha-ha! You're going crazy, Juanita. Oh, Lord, don't let me go mad. Let me be pregnant! Let me be pregnant!

(*JUANITA takes the stand. One arm is in a sling.*)

BLACKTOWN: Look! You should have seen her when she *first* come out of jail! Why we always got to love *them*? How come it's *us* always got to do the loving? Because you *black*, mother! Everybody knows we *strong* on loving! Except when it comes to our women.

WHITETOWN: Black slut! What happened to her arm? Somebody had to twist it, I reckon. She looks like she might be a right pretty little girl – why is she messing up her life this way?

THE STATE: Miss Harmon, you have testified that you were friendly with the mother of the deceased. How old were you when she died?

JUANITA: I was sixteen.

THE STATE: Sixteen! You are older than the deceased?

JUANITA: By two years.

THE STATE: At the time of his mother's death, were you and Richard Henry considering marriage?

JUANITA: No. Of course not.

THE STATE: The question of marriage did not come up until just before he died?

JUANITA: Yes.

THE STATE: But between the time that Richard Henry left this town and returned, you had naturally attracted other boy friends?

BLACKTOWN: Why don't you come right out and ask her if she's a virgin, man? Save you time.

WHITETOWN: She probably pregnant right now – and don't know who the father is. That's the way they are.

THE STATE: The departure of the boy and the death of the mother must have left all of you extremely lonely?

JUANITA: It can't be said to have made us any happier.

THE STATE: Reverend Henry missed his wife, you missed your

playmate. His grief and your common concern for the boy must have drawn you closer together?

BLACKTOWN: Oh, man! Get to *that*!

WHITETOWN: That's right. What about that liver-lipped preacher?

THE STATE: Miss Harmon, you describe yourself as a student. Where have you spent the last few weeks?

JUANITA: In jail! I was arrested for –

THE STATE: I am not concerned with the reasons for your arrest. How much time, all told, have you spent in jail?

JUANITA: It would be hard to say – a long time.

THE STATE: Excellent preparation for your future! Is it not true, Miss Harmon, that before the late Richard Henry returned to this town, you were considering marriage with another so-called student, Pete Spivey? Can you seriously expect this court to believe anything you now say concerning Richard Henry? Would you not say the same thing, and for the same reason, concerning the father? Concerning Pete Spivey? And how many others!

WHITETOWN: That's the way they are. It's not their fault. That's what they want us to integrate with.

BLACKTOWN: These people are sick. Sick. Sick people's been known to be made well by a little shedding of blood.

JUANITA: I am not responsible for your imagination.

THE STATE: What do you know of the fight which took place between Richard Henry and Lyle Britten, at Mr Britten's store?

JUANITA: I was not a witness to that fight.

THE STATE: But you had seen Richard Henry before the fight? Was he sober?

JUANITA: Yes.

THE STATE: You can swear to that?

JUANITA: Yes, I can swear to it.

THE STATE: And you saw him after the fight? Was he sober then?

JUANITA: Yes. He was sober then. (*Courtroom in silhouette.*) I heard about the fight at the end of the day – when I got home. And I went running to Reverend Henry's house. And I met him on the porch – just sitting there.

THE STATE: You met whom?

JUANITA: I met – Richard.

(*We discover MERIDIAN.*)

MERIDIAN: Hello, Juanita. Don't look like that.

JUANITA: Meridian, what happened today? Where's Richard?

MERIDIAN: He's all right now. He's sleeping. We better send him away. Lyle's dangerous. You know that.

(*Takes JUANITA in his arms; then holds her at arm's length.*)

You'll go with him. Won't you?

JUANITA: Meridian – oh, my God.

MERIDIAN: Juanita, tell me something I have to know. I'll never ask it again.

JUANITA: Yes, Meridian –

MERIDIAN: Before he came – I wasn't just making it all up, was I? There was something at least – beginning – something dimly possible – wasn't there? I thought about you so much – and it was so wonderful each time I saw you – and I started hoping as I haven't let myself hope, oh, for a long time. I knew you were much younger, and I'd known you since you were a child. But I thought that maybe that didn't matter, after all – we got on so well together. I wasn't making it all up, was I?

JUANITA: No. You weren't making it up – not all of it, anyway, there was something there. We were lonely. You were hoping. I was hoping, too – oh, Meridian! Of all the people on God's earth I would rather die than hurt!

MERIDIAN: Hush, Juanita. I know that. I just wanted to be told that I hadn't lost my mind. I've lost so much. I think there's something wrong in being – what I've become – something really wrong. I mean, I think there's something wrong with allowing oneself to become so lonely. I think that I was proud that I could bear it. Each day became a kind of test – to see if I could bear it. And there were many days when I couldn't bear it – when I walked up and down and howled and lusted and cursed and prayed – just like any man. And I've been – I haven't been as celibate as I've seemed. But my confidence – my confidence – was destroyed back there when I pulled back that rug they had her covered with and I saw that little face on that broken neck. There wasn't any blood – just water. She was soaked. Oh, my God. My God. And I haven't trusted myself with a woman since. I keep seeing her the last time I saw her, whether I'm awake or asleep. That's why I let you get away from me. It wasn't my son that did it. It was me. And so much the better for you. And him. And I've held it all in since then – what fearful choices we must make! In order not to commit murder, in order not to become too monstrous, in order to be some kind of example to my only son. Come. Let me be an example now. And kiss you on the forehead and wish you well.

JUANITA: Meridian. Meridian. Will it always be like this? Will life always be like this? Must we always suffer so?

MERIDIAN: I don't know, Juanita. I know that we must bear what we must bear. Don't cry, Juanita. Don't cry. Let's go on on.

(*Exits.*)

JUANITA: By and by Richard woke up and I was there. And we tried to make plans to go, but he said he wasn't going to run no more from white folks – never no more! – but was going to stay and be a man – a *man!* – right here. And I couldn't *make* him see differently. I knew what he meant, I knew how he felt, but I didn't want him to die! And by the time I persuaded him to take *me* away, to take *me* away from this terrible place, it was too late. Lyle killed him. Lyle killed him! Like they been killing all our men, for years, for generations! Our husbands, our fathers, our brothers, our sons!

JUDGE: The witness may step down.

JUANITA leaves the stand. MOTHER HENRY helps her to her seat.

This court is adjourned until ten o'clock tomorrow morning.

Chaos and cacophony. The courtroom begins to empty. Reporters rush to phone booths and to witnesses. Light bulbs flash. We hear snatches of the Journalists' reports, in their various languages. Singing from the church. Blackout. The next and last day of the trial. Even more crowded and tense.

CLERK: (*Calls.*) Mrs Wilhelmina Henry!

MOTHER HENRY, in street clothes, walks down the aisle, takes the stand.

THE STATE: You are Mrs Wilhelmina Henry?

MOTHER HENRY: Yes.

THE STATE: Mrs Henry, you – and your husband, until he died – lived in this town all your lives and never had any trouble. We've always gotten on well down here.

MOTHER HENRY: No white man never called my husband Mister, neither, not as long as he lived. Ain't no white man never called *me* Mrs Henry before today. I had to get a grandson killed for that.

THE STATE: Mrs Henry, your grief elicits my entire sympathy, and the sympathy of every white man in this town. But is it not true, Mrs Henry, that your grandson arrived in this town armed? He was carrying a gun and, apparently, had carried a gun for years.

MOTHER HENRY: I don't know where you got that story, or why you keep harping on it. *I* never saw no gun.

THE STATE: You are under oath, Mrs Henry.

MOTHER HENRY: I don't need you to tell me I'm under oath. I been under oath all my life. And I tell you, I never saw no gun.

THE STATE: Mrs Henry, did you ever see your grandson behaving strangely – as though he were under the influence of strong drugs?

MOTHER HENRY: No. Not since he was six and they pulled out his tonsils. They gave him ether. *He* didn't act as strange as his Mama and Daddy. He just went on to sleep. But they like to had a fit. (*RICHARD's song.*) I remember the day he was born. His mother had a hard time holding him and a hard time getting him here. But here he come, in the wintertime, late and big and loud. And my boy looked down into his little son's face and he said, 'God give us a son. God's give us a son. Lord, help us to raise him to be a good strong man.'

JUDGE: The witness may step down.

CLERK: (*Calls.*) Reverend Meridian Henry!

(*Blackout. MERIDIAN, in Sunday School. The class itself, predominately adolescent girls, is in silhouette.*)

MERIDIAN: – And here is the prophet, Solomon, the son of David, looking down through the ages, and speaking of

Christ's love for His church. (*Reads.*) How fair is thy love, my sister, my spouse! How much better is thy love than wine! and the smell of thine ointments than all spices! (*Pause. The silhouette of girls vanishes.*) Oh, that it were one man, speaking to one woman!

(*Blackout.* MERIDIAN *takes the stand.*)

BLACKTOWN: I wonder how he feels now about all that turn-the-other-cheek jazz. His son sure didn't go for it.

WHITETOWN: That's the father. Claims to be a preacher. He brought this on himself. He's been raising trouble in this town for a long time.

THE STATE: You are Reverend Meridian Henry?

MERIDIAN: That is correct.

THE STATE: And you are the father of the late Richard Henry?

MERIDIAN: Yes.

THE STATE: You are a minister?

MERIDIAN: A Christian minister – yes.

THE STATE: And you raised your son according to the precepts of the Christian church?

MERIDIAN: I tried. But both my son and I had profound reservations concerning the behaviour of Christians. He wondered why they treated black people as they do. And I was unable to give him – a satisfactory answer.

THE STATE: But certainly you – as a Christian minister – did not encourage your son to go armed?

MERIDIAN: The question never came up. He was not armed.

THE STATE: He was not armed?

MERIDIAN: No.

THE STATE: You never saw him with a gun? Or with any other weapon?

MERIDIAN: No.

THE STATE: Reverend Henry – are you in a position to swear that your son never carried arms?

MERIDIAN: Yes. I can swear to it. The only time the subject was ever mentioned he told me that he was stronger than white people and he could live without a gun.

BLACKTOWN: I bet he didn't say how.

WHITETOWN: That liver-lipped nigger is lying. He's lying!

THE STATE: Perhaps the difficulties your son had in accepting the Christian faith is due to your use of the pulpit as a forum for irresponsible notions concerning social equality, Reverend Henry. Perhaps the failure of the son is due to the failure of the father.

MERIDIAN: I am afraid that the gentleman flatters himself. I do not wish to see Negroes become the equal of their murderers. I wish us to become equal to ourselves. To become a people so free in themselves that they will have no need to – fear – others – and have no need to murder others.

THE STATE: You are not in the pulpit now. I am suggesting that you are responsible – directly responsible! – for your son's tragic fate.

MERIDIAN: I know more about that than you do. But you cannot consider my son's death to have been tragic. For you, it would have been tragic if he had lived.

THE STATE: With such a father, it is remarkable that the son lived as long as he did.

MERIDIAN: Remarkable, too, that the father lived!

THE STATE: Reverend Henry – you have been a widower for how many years?

MERIDIAN: I have been a widower for nearly eight years.

THE STATE: You are a young man still?

MERIDIAN: Are you asking me my age? I am not young.

THE STATE: You are not old. It must have demanded great discipline –

MERIDIAN: To live among you? Yes.

THE STATE: What is your relationship to the young, so-called student, Miss Juanita Harmon?

MERIDIAN: I am her old friend. I had hoped to become her father-in-law.

THE STATE: You are nothing more than old friends?

WHITETOWN: That's right. Get it out of him. Get the truth out of him.

BLACKTOWN: Leave the man *something*. Leave him something!

THE STATE: You have been celibate since the death of your wife?

BLACKTOWN: He never said he was a monk, you jive mother!

WHITETOWN: Make him tell us all about it. *All* about it.

MERIDIAN: Celibate? How does my celibacy concern you?

THE STATE: Your Honour, will you instruct the witness that he is on the witness stand, not I, and that he must answer the questions put to him!

MERIDIAN: *The questions put to him!* All right. Do you accept this answer? I am a man. A *man!* I tried to help my son become a man. But manhood is a dangerous pursuit, here. And that pursuit undid him because of *your* guns, *your* hoses, *your* dogs, *your* judges, *your* law-makers, *your* folly, *your* pride, *your* cruelty, *your* cowardice, *your* money, *your* chain gangs, and *your* churches! Did you think it would endure for ever? that we would pay for *your* ease for ever?

BLACKTOWN: Speak, my man! Amen! Amen! Amen! Amen!

WHITETOWN: Stirring up hate! Stirring up hate! A *preacher* – stirring up hate!

MERIDIAN: Yes! I *am* responsible for the death of my son. I – hoped – I prayed – I struggled – so that the world would be different by the time he was a man than it had been when he was born. And I thought that – then – when he looked at me – he would think that I – his father – had helped to change it.

THE STATE: What about those photographs your son carried about with him? Those photographs of himself and naked white women?

BLACKTOWN: Man! Would I love to look in *your* wallet!

WHITETOWN: Make him tell us about it, make him tell us *all* about it!

MERIDIAN: Photographs? My son and naked white women? He never mentioned them to me.

THE STATE: You were closer than most fathers and sons?

MERIDIAN: I never took a poll on most fathers and sons.

THE STATE: You never discussed women?

MERIDIAN: We talked about his mother. She was a woman. We talked about Miss Harmon. *She* is a woman. But we never talked about dirty pictures. We didn't need that.

THE STATE: Reverend Henry, you have made us all aware that your love for your son transcends your respect for the truth or your devotion to the church. But – luckily for the truth – it is a matter of public record that your son was so dangerously deranged that it was found necessary, for his own sake, to incarcerate him. It was at the end of that incarceration that he returned to this town. We know that his life in the North was riotous – he brought that riot into this town. The evidence is overwhelming. And yet, you, a Christian minister, dare to bring us this tissue of lies in defence of a known pimp, dope addict, and rapist! You are yourself so eaten up by race hatred that no word of yours can be believed.

MERIDIAN: Your judgment of myself and my motives cannot concern me at all. I have lived with that judgment far too long. The truth cannot be heard in this dreadful place. But I will tell you again what I know. I know why my son became a dope addict. I know better than you will ever know, even if I should explain it to you for all eternity, how I am responsible for that. But I know my son was not a pimp. He respected women far too much for that. And I know he was not a rapist. Rape is hard work – and, frankly, I don't think that the alleged object was my son's type at all!

THE STATE: And you are a minister?

MERIDIAN: I think I may be beginning to become one.

JUDGE: The witness may step down.

MERIDIAN leaves the stand.

CLERK: (*Calls.*) Mr Parnell James!

(*PARNELL in his bedroom, dressed in a bathrobe. Night.*)

PARNELL: She says I called somebody else's name. What name could I have called? And she won't repeat the name. Well. That's enough to freeze the blood and arrest the holy, the liberating orgasm. Christ, how weary I am of this dull calisthenic called love – with no love in it! What name could I have called? I hope it was – a *white* girl's name, anyway! Ha-ha! How still she became! And I hardly realized it, I was too far away – and then it was too late. And she was just looking at me. Jesus! To have somebody just looking at you – just looking at you – like that – at such a moment! It makes you feel – like you woke up and found yourself in bed with your mother! I tried to find out what was wrong – poor girl. But there's nothing you can say at a moment like that – really nothing. You're caught. Well, haven't I kept telling her that there's no future for her with me? There's no future for me with anybody! But that's all right. What

name could I have called? I haven't been with anybody else for a long time, a long time. She says I haven't been with her, either. I guess she's right. I've just been using her. Using her as an anchor – to hold me here, in this house, this bed – so I won't find myself on the other side of town, ruining my reputation. *What* reputation? They all know. I swear they all *know*. Know what? What's there to know? So you get drunk and you fool around a little. Come on, Parnell. There's more to it than that. That's the reason you draw blanks whenever you get drunk. Everything comes out. Everything. They see what you don't dare to see. What name could I have called? Richard would say that you've got – black fever! Yeah, and he'd be wrong – that long, loud, black mother. I wonder if she's asleep yet – or just lying there, looking at the walls. Poor girl! All your life you've been made sick, stunned, dizzy, oh, Lord! driven half mad by blackness. Blackness in front of your eyes. Boys and girls, men and women – you've bowed down in front of them all! And then hated yourself. Hated yourself for debasing yourself? Out with it, Parnell! The nigger-lover! Black boys and girls! I've wanted my hands full of them, wanted to drown them, laughing and dancing and making love – making love – wow! – and be transformed, formed, liberated out of this grey-white envelope. Jesus! I've always been afraid. Afraid of what I saw in their eyes? They don't love me, certainly. You don't love them, either! Sick with a disease only white men catch. Blackness. What is it like to be black? To look out on the world from *that* place? I give nothing! How dare she say that! My girl, if you knew what I've given! Ah. Come off it, Parnell. To *whom* have you given? What name did I call? What name did I call?

(*Blackout.* PARNELL *and* LYLE. *Hunting on* PARNELL'*s land.*)

LYLE: You think it's a good idea, then? You think she won't say no?

PARNELL: Well, you're the one who's got to go through it. *You've* got to ask for Miss Josephine's hand in marriage. And then you've got to live with her – for the rest of your life. Watch that gun. I've never seen you so jumpy. I might say it was a good idea if I thought she'd say no. But I think she'll say yes.

LYLE: Why would she say yes to me?

PARNELL: I think she's drawn to you. It isn't hard to be – drawn to you. Don't you know that?

LYLE: No. When I was young, I used to come here sometimes – with my Daddy. He didn't like *your* Daddy a-*tall*! We used to steal your game, Parnell – you didn't know that, did you?

PARNELL: I think I knew it.

LYLE: We shot at the game and your Daddy's overseers shot at us. But we *got* what *we* came after. *They* never got *us*!

PARNELL: You're talking an awful lot today. You nervous about Miss Josephine?

LYLE: Wait a minute. You think I ought to marry Jo?

PARNELL: I don't know who anybody should marry. Do you want to marry Jo?

LYLE: Well – I got to marry somebody. I got to have some kids. And Jo is – *clean!*

PARNELL sights, shoots.

PARNELL: Goddamn!

LYLE: Missed it. Ha-ha!

PARNELL: It's probably somebody's mother.

LYLE: Watch. (*Sights, shoots.*) *Ha-ha!*

PARNELL: Bravo!

LYLE: I knew it! Had my name written on it, just as pretty as you please! (*Exits, returns with his bird.*) See? My Daddy taught me well. It was sport for you. It was life for us.

PARNELL: I reckon you shot somebody's baby.

LYLE: I tell you – I can't go on like this. There comes a time in a man's life when he's got to have him a little – peace.

PARNELL: You mean calm. Tranquillity.

LYLE: Yeah. I didn't mean it like it sounded. You thought I meant – no. I'm tired of –

PARNELL: Poon-tang.

LYLE: How'd you know? You tired of it, too? Hell. Yeah. I want kids.

PARNELL: Well, then – marry the girl.

LYLE: She ain't a girl no more. It might be her last chance, too. But, I swear, Parnell, she might be the only virgin left in this town. The only *white* virgin. I can vouch for the fact ain't many black ones.

PARNELL: You've been active, I know. Any kids?

LYLE: None that I know of. Ha-ha!

PARNELL: Do you think Jo might be upset – by the talk about you and Old Bill? She's real respectable, you know. She's a *librarian.*

LYLE: No. Them things happen every day. You think I ought to marry her? You really think she'll say yes?

PARNELL: She'll say yes. She'd better. I wish you luck. Name the first one after me.

LYLE: No. You be the godfather. And my best man. I'm going to name the first one after my Daddy – because he taught me more about hunting on your land than *you* know. I'll give him your middle name. I'll call him Lyle Parnell Britten, Jr.!

PARNELL: If the girl says yes.

LYLE: Well, if she says no, ain't no problem, is there? We know where to go when the going gets rough, don't we, old buddy?

PARNELL: Do we? Look! Mine?

LYLE: What'll you bet?

PARNELL: The price of your wedding rings.

LYLE: You're on. Mine? *Mine!*

(*Blackout. PARNELL walks down the aisle, takes the stand.*)

WHITETOWN:
Here comes the nigger-lover!

But I bet you one thing – he knows more about the truth in this case than anybody else.

He ought to – he's with them all the time.

It's sad when a man turns against his own people!

BLACKTOWN:
Let's see how the Negro's friend comes through!

They been waiting for *him* – they going to tear his behind *up!*

I don't trust him. I *never* trusted him!

Why? Because he's *white*, that's why!

THE STATE: You were acquainted with the late Richard Henry?

PARNELL: Of course. His father and I have been friends all our lives.

THE STATE: Close friends?

PARNELL: Yes. Very close.

THE STATE: And what is your relationship to the alleged murderer, Mr Lyle Britten?

PARNELL: We, also, have been friends all our lives.

THE STATE: Close friends?

PARNELL: Yes.

THE STATE: As close as the friendship between yourself and the dead boy's father?

PARNELL: I would say so – it was a very different relationship.

THE STATE: Different in what respect, Mr James?

PARNELL: Well, we had different things to talk about. We did different things together.

THE STATE: What sort of different things?

PARNELL: Well – hunting, for example – things like that.

THE STATE: You never went hunting with Reverend Henry?

PARNELL: No. He didn't like to hunt.

THE STATE: He told you so? He told you that he didn't like to hunt?

PARNELL: The question never came up. We led very different lives.

THE STATE: I am gratified to hear it. Is it not true, Mr James, that it is impossible for any two people to go on a hunting trip together if either of them has any reason at all to distrust the other?

PARNELL: Well, of course that would have to be true. But it's never talked about – it's just understood.

THE STATE: We can conclude, then, that you were willing to trust Lyle Britten with your life but did not feel the same trust in Reverend Henry?

PARNELL: Sir, you may not draw any such conclusion! I have told you that Reverend Henry and I led very different lives!

THE STATE: But you have been friends all your lives. Reverend Henry is also a southern boy – he, also, I am sure, knows and loves this land, has gone swimming and fishing in her streams and rivers, and stalked game in her forests. And yet, close as you are, you have never allowed yourself to be alone with Reverend Henry when Reverend Henry had a gun. Doesn't this suggest some *lack* – in your vaunted friendship?

PARNELL: Your suggestion is unwarranted and unworthy. As a soldier, I have often been alone with Negroes with guns, and it certainly never caused me any uneasiness.

THE STATE: But you were fighting a common enemy then. What was your impression of the late Richard Henry?

PARNELL: I liked him. He was very outspoken and perhaps tactless, but a very valuable person.

THE STATE: How would you describe his effect on this town? Among his own people? Among the whites?

PARNELL: His effect? He was pretty well liked.

THE STATE: That does not answer my question.

PARNELL: His effect was – kind of unsettling, I suppose. After all, he had lived in the North a long time, he wasn't used to – the way we do things down here.

THE STATE: He was accustomed to the way things are done in the North – where he learned to carry arms, to take dope, and to couple with white women!

PARNELL: I cannot testify to any of that, sir. I can only repeat that he reacted with great intensity to the racial situation in this town, and his effect on the town was, to that extent, unsettling.

THE STATE: Did he not encourage the Negroes of this town to arm?

PARNELL: Not to my knowledge, sir, no. And, in any case, they are not armed.

THE STATE: You are in a position to reassure us on this point?

PARNELL: My friends do not lie.

THE STATE: You are remarkably fortunate. You are aware of the attitude of the late Richard Henry towards white women? You saw the photographs he carried about with him?

PARNELL: We never discussed women. I never saw the photographs.

THE STATE: But you knew of their existence?

PARNELL: They were not obscene. They were simply snapshots of people he had known in the North.

THE STATE: Snapshots of white women?

PARNELL: Yes.

THE STATE: You are the first witness to admit the existence of these photographs, Mr James.

PARNELL: It is very likely that the other witnesses never saw them. The boy had been discouraged, very early on, from mentioning them or showing them about.

THE STATE: Discouraged by whom?

PARNELL: Why – by – me.

THE STATE: But you never saw the photographs –

PARNELL: I told him I didn't want to see them and that it would be dangerous to carry them about.

THE STATE: He showed these photographs to you, but to no one else?

PARNELL: That would seem to be the case, yes.

THE STATE: What was his motive in taking you into his confidence?

PARNELL: Bravado. He wanted me to know that he had white friends in the North, that – he had been happy – in the North.

THE STATE: You did not tell his father? You did not warn your close friend?

PARNELL: I am sure that Richard never mentioned these photographs to his father. He would have been too ashamed. Those women were beneath him.

THE STATE: A white woman who surrenders to a coloured man is beneath all human consideration. She has wantonly and deliberately defiled the temple of the Holy Ghost. It is clear to me that the effect of such a boy on this town was irresponsible and incendiary to the greatest degree. Did you not find your close friendship with Reverend Henry somewhat strained by the son's attempt to rape the wife of your other close friend, Lyle Britten?

PARNELL: This attempt was never mentioned before – before today.

THE STATE: You are as close as you claim to the Britten family and knew nothing of this attempted rape? How do you explain that?

PARNELL: I cannot explain it.

THE STATE: This is a court of law, Mr James, and we will have the truth!

WHITETOWN: Make him tell the truth!

BLACKTOWN: Make him tell the truth!

THE STATE: How can you be the close friend you claim to be of the Britten family and not have known of so grave an event?

PARNELL: I – I knew of a fight. It was understood that the boy had gone to Mr Britten's store looking for a fight. I – I cannot explain *that*, either.

THE STATE: Who told you of the fight?

PARNELL: Why – Mr Britten.

THE STATE: And did not tell you that Richard Henry had attempted to assault his wife? Come, Mr James!

PARNELL: We were all very much upset. Perhaps he was not as coherent as he might have been – perhaps I failed to listen closely. It was my assumption that Mrs Britten had misconstrued the boy's actions – he had been in the North a long time, his manner was very free and bold.

THE STATE: Mrs Britten has testified that Richard Henry grabbed her and pulled her to him and tried to kiss her. How can those actions be misconstrued?

PARNELL: Those actions are – quite explicit.

THE STATE: Thank you, Mr James. That is all.

JUDGE: The witness may step down.

PARNELL leaves the stand.

BLACKTOWN: What do you think of our fine friend *now?* He didn't do it to us rough and hard. No, he was real gentle. I hardly felt a thing. Did you? You can't never go against the word of a white lady, man, not even if you're white. Can't be done. He was sad. *Sad!*

WHITETOWN: It took him long enough! He did his best not to say it – can you imagine! So her story was true – after all! I hope he's learned his lesson. We been trying to tell him – for years!

CLEAK: (*Calls.*) Mr Lyle Britten!

(LYLE, *in the woods.*)

LYLE: I wonder what he'll grow up to look like. Of course, it might be a girl. I reckon I wouldn't mind – just keep on trying till I get me a boy, ha-ha! Old Miss Josephine is something, ain't she? I really struck oil when I come across her. She's a nice woman. And she's *my* woman – I ain't got to worry about *that* a-tall! You're making big changes in your life, Lyle, and you got to be ready to take on this extra responsibility. Shoot, I'm ready. I know what I'm doing. And I'm going to work harder than I've ever worked before in my life to make Jo happy – and keep her happy – and raise our children to be fine men and women. Lord, you know I'm not a praying man. I've done a lot of wrong things in my life and I ain't never going to be perfect. I know You know that. I know You understand that. But, Lord, hear me today and help me to do what I'm supposed to do. I want to be as strong as my Mama and Daddy and raise my children like they raised me. That's what I want, oh Lord. In a few years I'll be walking here, showing my son these trees and this water and this sky. He'll have his hand in my hand, and I'll show him the world. Isn't that a funny thing! He don't even exist yet – he's just an egg in his mother's belly, I bet you couldn't even find him with a microscope – and I put him there – and he's coming out soon – with fingers and toes and eyes – and by and by, he'll learn to walk and talk – and I reckon I'll have to spank him sometimes – if he's anything like me, I know I will. Isn't that something! My son! Hurry up and get here, so I can hug you in my arms and give you a good start on your long journey!

(*Blackout.* LYLE, *with* PAPA D. *Drunk. Music and dancing.*)

LYLE: You remember them days when Willa Mae was around? My mind's been going back to them days. You remember? She was a hot little piece, I just had to have some of that, I just *had* to. Half the time she didn't wear no stockings, just had them brown, round legs just moving. I couldn't keep my eyes off her legs when she didn't wear no stockings. And you know what she told me? You know what she told me? She said there wasn't a nigger alive could be as good to her as me. That's right. She said she'd like to *see* the nigger could do her like I done her. You hear me, boy? That's something, ain't it? Boy – she'd just come into a room sometimes and my old pecker would stand up at attention. You ain't jealous, are you, Joel? Ha-ha! You never did hear from her no more, did you? No, I reckon you didn't. Shoot, I got to get on home. I'm a family man now, I got – great responsibilities! Yeah. Be seeing you, Joel. You don't want to close up and walk a-ways with me, do you? No, I reckon you better not. They having fun. Sure wish I could be more like you all. Bye-bye!

(*Blackout. As* LYLE *approaches the witness stand, the lights in the courtroom dim. We hear voices from the church, singing a lament. The lights come up.*)

JUDGE: Gentlemen of the jury, have you reached a verdict?
FOREMAN: We have, Your Honour.
JUDGE: Will the prisoner please rise?

LYLE *rises.*

Do you find the defendant, Mr Lyle Britten, guilty or not guilty?
FOREMAN: Not guilty, Your Honour.

Cheering in WHITETOWN. *Silence in* BLACKTOWN. *The stage is taken over by* REPORTERS, PHOTOGRAPHERS, WITNESSES, TOWNSPEOPLE. LYLE *is congratulated and embraced.* BLACKTOWN *files out silently, not looking back.* WHITETOWN *files out jubilantly, and yet with a certain reluctance. Presently, the stage is empty, except for* LYLE, JO, MOTHER HENRY, MERIDIAN, PARNELL, JUANITA, *and* LORENZO.

JO: Let's get out of here and go home. We've been here just for days. I wouldn't care if I *never* saw the insides of a courtroom again! Let's go home, sugar. We got something to celebrate!
JUANITA: We, too, must go – to another celebration. We're having a prayer meeting on the City Hall steps.
LORENZO: Prayer meeting!
LYLE: Well, it was touch and go there for a while, Parnell, but you sure come through. I knew you would.
JO: Let's go, Lyle. The baby's hungry.
MERIDIAN: Perhaps now you can ask him to tell you the truth. He's got nothing to lose now. They can't try him again.
LYLE: Wasn't much sense in trying me now, this time, was there, Reverend? These people have been knowing me and my good Jo here all our lives, they ain't going to doubt us. And you people – you people – ought to have better sense and more things to do than running around stirring up all this hate and trouble. *That's* how your son got himself killed. He listened to crazy niggers like you!
MERIDIAN: Did you kill him?
LYLE: They just asked me that in court, didn't they? And they just decided I didn't, didn't they? Well, that's good enough for me and all those white people and so it damn sure better be good enough for you!
PARNELL: That's no answer. It's not good enough for me.
LYLE: What do you mean, that's no answer? Why isn't it an answer? Why isn't it good enough for you? You know, when you were up on the stand right now, you acted like you doubted my Jo's word. You got no right to doubt Jo's word. You ain't no better than she is! You ain't no better than me!
PARNELL: I am aware of that. God knows I have been made aware of that – for the first time in my life. But, as you and I will never be the same again – since our comedy is finished, since I have failed you so badly – let me say this. I did not doubt Jo's word. I knew that she was lying and that you had made her lie. That was a terrible thing to do to her. It was a terrible thing that I just did to you. I really don't know if what I did to Meridian was as awful as what

I did to you. I don't expect forgiveness, Meridian. I only hope that all of us will suffer past this agony and horror.

LYLE: What's the matter with you? Have you forgotten you a white man? A white man! My Daddy told me not to *never* forget I was a white man! Here I been knowing you all my life – and now I'm ashamed of you. Ashamed of you! Get on over to niggertown! I'm going home with my good wife.

MERIDIAN: What was the last thing my son said to you – before you shot him down – like a dog?

LYLE: Like a dog! You a smart nigger, ain't you?

MERIDIAN: What was the last thing he said? Did he beg you for his life?

LYLE: *That* nigger! He was too smart for that! He was too full of himself for that! He must have thought he was white. And I gave him every chance – every chance – to live!

MERIDIAN: And he refused them all.

LYLE: Do you know what that nigger said to me?

(*The light changes, so that everyone but* LYLE *is in silhouette.* RICHARD *appears, dressed as we last saw him, on the road outside* PAPA D.*'s joint.*)

RICHARD: I'm ready. Here I am. You asked me if I was ready, didn't you? What's on your mind, white man?

LYLE: Boy, I always treated you with respect. I don't know what's the matter with you, or what makes you act the way you do – but you owe me an apology and I come out here tonight to get it. I mean, I ain't going away without it.

RICHARD: *I* owe *you* an apology! That's a wild idea. What am I apologizing for?

LYLE: You know, you mighty lucky to still be walking around.

RICHARD: So are you. White man.

LYLE: I'd like you to apologize for your behaviour in my store that day. Now, I think I'm being pretty reasonable, ain't I?

RICHARD: You got anything to write on? I'll write you an IOU.

LYLE: Keep it up. You going to be laughing out of the other side of your mouth pretty soon.

RICHARD: Why don't you go home? And let me go home? Do we need all this shit? Can't we live without it?

LYLE: Boy, are you drunk?

RICHARD: No, I ain't drunk. I'm just tired. Tired of all this fighting. What are you trying to prove? What am *I* trying to prove?

LYLE: I'm trying to give you a break. You too dumb to take it.

RICHARD: I'm hip. You been trying to give me a break for a great, long time. But there's only one break I want. And you won't give me that.

LYLE: What kind of break do you want, boy?

RICHARD: For you to go home. And let me go home. I got things to do. I got – lots of things to do!

LYLE: I got things to do, too. I'd like to get home, too.

RICHARD: Then why are we standing here? Can't we walk? Let me walk, white man! Let me walk!

LYLE: We can walk, just as soon as we get our business settled.

RICHARD: It's settled. You a man and I'm a man. Let's walk.

LYLE: Nigger, you was born down here. Ain't you never said sir to a white man?

RICHARD: No. The only person I ever said sir to was my Daddy.

LYLE: Are you going to apologize to me?

RICHARD: No.

LYLE: Do you want to live?

RICHARD: Yes.

LYLE: Then you know what to do, then, don't you?

RICHARD: Go home. Go home.

LYLE: You facing my gun. (*Produces it.*) Now, in just a minute, we can both go home.

RICHARD: You sick mother! Why can't you leave me alone? White man! I don't want nothing from you. You ain't got nothing to give me. You can't eat because none of your sad-assed chicks can cook. You can't talk because won't nobody talk to you. You can't dance because you've got nobody to dance with – don't you know I've watched you all my life? *All my life!* And *I* know your women, don't you think I don't – better than you!

Figure 21 *Blues for Mister Charlie* at the ANTA Theater, New York, 1964. (Photograph: Gjon Mili, by permission of Getty Images.)

LYLE shoots, once.

Why have you spent so much time trying to kill me? Why are you always trying to cut off *my* cock? You worried about it? Why?

LYLE shoots again.

Okay. Okay. Okay. Keep your old lady home, you hear? Don't let her near no nigger. She might get to like it. You might get to like it, too. Wow!

RICHARD falls.

Juanita! Daddy! *Mama!*

(Singing from the church. Spot on LYLE.)

LYLE: I had to kill him then. I'm a white man! Can't nobody talk that way to *me!* I had to go and get my pick-up truck and load him in it – I had to carry him on my back – and carry him out to the high weeds. And I dumped him in the weeds, face down. And then I come on home, to my good Jo here.

JO: Come on, Lyle. We got to get on home. We got to get the little one home now.

LYLE: And I ain't sorry. I want you to know that I ain't sorry!

JO: Come on, Lyle. Come on. He's hungry. I got to feed him.

JO and LYLE exit.

MOTHER HENRY: We got to go now, children. The children is already started to march.

LORENZO: Prayer!

MERIDIAN: You know, for us, it all began with the Bible and the gun. Maybe it will end with the Bible and the gun.

JUANITA: What did you do with the gun, Meridian?

PARNELL: You have the gun – Richard's gun?

MERIDIAN: Yes. In the pulpit. Under the Bible. Like the pilgrims of old.

Exits.

MOTHER HENRY: Come on, children.

Singing.

PETE enters.

PETE: *(Stammers.)* Are you ready, Juanita? Shall we go now?

JUANITA: Yes.

LORENZO: Come here, Pete. Stay close to me.

They go to the church door. The singing swells.

PARNELL: Well.

JUANITA: Well. Yes, Lord!

PARNELL: Can I join you on the march, Juanita? Can I walk with you?

JUANITA: Well, we can walk in the same direction, Parnell. Come. Don't look like that. Let's go on on.

Exits.

After a moment, PARNELL follows.

3.7 Suffrage Theatre: Community Activism and Political Commitment (2006)

SUSAN CARLSON

THE THEATRE ASSOCIATED WITH the early twentieth-century suffrage movement in England is a bundle of contradictions. The suffragists were mostly middle-class women, women bred for the interiors of the home who became strategists of public space and massive public events. Their theatre, which ranged from public-hall skits to full-length plays in West End theatres, was at once conservative and radical. The suffragists dressed in harmony for public events, wearing the identifiable, co-ordinated colours of their organizations; at the same time they destroyed public art, torched golf courses and chained themselves to fences. In sum, the women (and men) involved with suffrage theatre drew from theatrical conventions which they knew and modified them for the commotion of the public square, the public hall and the streets as well as for the theatres. Memorable plays were not necessarily the main product of suffrage drama, but rather a concept of theatre which involved the streets as well as the stage and an expanded sense of women's roles in both places. Suffrage theatre had a duration of less than a decade, but it foreshadowed the now familiar conventions of subsequent community-based political theatre.

The suffrage community and its affinity with theatre

Most historians of the British suffrage movement date its beginnings to the advocacy of Mary Wollstonecraft or John Stuart Mill, but decades of nineteenth-century strategizing and commitment are overshadowed by the best-known and most intense years of the campaign, those in the decade preceding World War I, stretching roughly from 1905 to 1914. While the primary goal of the suffrage movement was obtaining the vote for women, the drive for enfranchisement was entwined with a variety of debates on related issues such as women's position in law, white slavery, the economic conditions of marriage, education, birth control and family roles, and taxation. The radical tactics of the Women's Social and Political Union (WSPU, founded in 1903), who preached 'deeds not words', were well known; they engaged in prison hunger strikes, breaking windows in public buildings and disrupting public events. Yet each of the major suffrage organizations, from the most radical to the most conservative, made use of public space and theatrically inspired events to promote the cause of the vote for women. Suffragists performed everything from monologues to tableaux, pageants to parodies, one-act to full-length plays in West End theatres, Hyde Park, labour halls, garden parties, and city streets and squares. The entity of 'suffrage theatre' was as much influenced by the political organizations and arguments of its day as it was by the aesthetics and practices of the theatre – and the fact that the two realms came together is a significant moment in theatre history.

The WSPU, the NUWSS (National Union of Women's Suffrage Societies), the WFL (Women's Freedom League) and other suffrage organizations provided the backbone of suffrage campaigning in the early twentieth century, but they were bolstered by groups of more specific affiliation such as the Actresses' Franchise League (AFL) and the Women Writers' Suffrage League, two groups central to suffrage theatre. Founded in 1908, the AFL had a membership of practising actresses, and the group was the gravitational centre of the explosive phenomenon of suffrage theatre. These actresses banded together, pledging to use their professional skills to advance the cause of women's suffrage: they trained activists in public speaking and presentational skills and, in extreme circumstances, helped costume suffragists on the run from government officials. With a literary department run by Australian-born Inez Bensusan, the AFL was responsible for the creation and production of a large share of the plays which directly staged the issue of suffrage. Working with branches of the suffrage societies to schedule performances of the plays, Bensusan and the AFL enlisted established writers like Beatrice Harraden, Cicely Hamilton, Laurence Housman and Bernard Shaw along with little-known and first-time playwrights. Motivated by the AFL's efforts, many women whose prior role in theatre had solely been acting became leaders, activists and, most importantly, writers. With some overlap in personnel, the Women Writers' Suffrage League operated in a parallel fashion as a location for women writers to pool their talents in support of women's suffrage. Cicely Hamilton and Elizabeth Robins, two writers who played key parts in the theatre of the day, were joined in this second group by Sarah Grand, Olive Schreiner, Ivy Compton Burnett and others. The plays that resulted were lively, sometimes raw, sometimes refined, but always provocative and engaged, and they were performed variously to a scattering or to thousands. As Julie Holledge has documented, the AFL played the more significant role, and while not solely responsible for suffrage theatre, this organization ensured that theatre and performance were a staple in the politics of the suffrage cause.

Of course, the context for suffrage theatre goes far beyond such organizations, and its activism must also be contextualized in terms of the other major political issues of the time: imperialism, nationalism and liberalism (Mayhall et al. 2000: xv). The suffrage theatre rarely addressed issues of race and nation which Britain's early-century global reach might have raised. In general, the suffragists writing plays and producing theatrical events tended to rely on conventional dramatic forms and concentrated on one political issue – the vote; their plays did not interrogate other social and cultural assumptions. In the main, suffrage theatre supported the politics of a variety of pro-suffrage groups, but there are moments when the critique also stretches to the power stratifications of marriage and class.

Theatre on demand: portable and provocative

In the end, it is very difficult to separate the intensity of the politics between 1905 and 1914 from the innovations of suffrage theatre, and it is hard to imagine the campaign for the vote without its highly visible performative aspects. Hilary Frances describes some of the WFL's interventions as fun-filled and highly symbolic, strategies she refers to as 'non-violent militancy' (Frances 2000: 189). The campaign for suffrage was configured in terms which were celebratory, transgressive and civil, and elsewhere I have used the words 'comic militancy' to convey the same idea (Carlson 2000: 198). As the mostly middle-class women involved moved the suffrage campaign into more public spaces in the years just before the war, they deployed a variety of performance venues and outlets, from social gatherings to newspapers, from political rallies to theatre stages.

Perhaps the most comfortable theatrical moments were those that took place as a part of the at-homes (neighbourhood suffrage meetings) and festivals put on to bring together those who were members of suffrage organizations and to persuade others to join them. Such meetings conducted business, featured speakers and often included performances of plays to rally those in attendance. Some of the one-act suffrage plays that were most popular included Cicely Hamilton and Christopher St John's *How the Vote Was Won* (1909), Evelyn Glover's *A Chat with Mrs Chicky* (1912) and Hamilton and St John's *The Pot and the Kettle* (1909). The 'Garden Fete', put on by the Croydon branch of the WFL in the summer of 1912, serves as a representative example of the oftentimes elaborate but domestically rooted suffrage 'events'. It welcomed women, children and men; offered food and embroidered items for sale; included a children's chorus and a political speech by WFL president C. Despard; and boasted as a capstone event performances of Glover's *A Chat with Mrs Chicky* and Graham Moffat's *The Maid and the Magistrate*.

Even larger events, like the Yuletide Festival held in the Albert Hall in December 1909, followed similar patterns of using theatrical performance as a climax to a programme of speeches, participatory events, networking and socializing. The programme included many of the plays which were most successful at buoying the suffragists: *The Pot and the Kettle*, *How the Vote Was Won*, and Cicely Hamilton's *A Pageant of Great Women* (staged by Edith (Edy) Craig). As reported in the *Vote*, the climactic *Pageant* was memorable: 'There has never been anything like this Pageant, which brought the day to a fitting close. It sang in one's blood with its colour harmonies and the sonorous sound of its message' (*Vote*, 16 December 1909, 89). The suffrage newspapers of the day document constant performances of suffrage plays in meetings of the London suffrage societies as well as in society meetings around the country (see Carlson 2001: 339–40).

The four London suffrage newspapers contributed to suffrage theatre by publishing plays regularly;[1] some of these plays saw performance, but many are a curiously unstageable mixture of dialogue and politics. Unlike the plays which saw heavy use at suffrage society meetings and which were generally upbeat and comic in form, plays in this second group were often more probing in their politics and tended to be unwieldy as theatre. The *Vote*, the organ of the WFL, published the largest number of such plays, including Alice Chapin's *At the Gates* (slated for performance at the Yuletide Festival in 1909 but dropped from the programme due to time-pressure), a play in which a suffragist sits through the night at the gates to Parliament, handing out petitions to all who pass by. From those who walk by, she accumulates responses which range from abuse to sympathy. The play is reflective and hopeful, but promises no political victory. Winifred St Clair's *The Science of Forgiveness* (*Vote*, 21 November 1913, 51, and 28 November 1913, 71–2; no known performance) places the argument for the vote in the context of sexual infidelity and a double standard for men and women involved in extra-marital affairs. While the play ends with key parties agreeing to equal treatment for men and women, it is not clear that this equitable agreement will lead to happiness for anyone. Perhaps the most common suffrage narrative in these newspapers is the 'conversion' play, in which the main event is the conversion of a non-believer to the cause of women's suffrage. Good examples are 'A. N.'s *Mr Peppercorn's Awakening* (pub.

1912), Edith M. Baker's *Our Happy Home* (pub. 1911) and A. L. Little's *The Shadow of the Sofa* (pub. 1913).

One of the most interesting developments in the newspapers was a collection of plays about selling suffrage newspapers, the most striking of which is Gladys Mendl's brief piece *Su'L'Pavé*, subtitled 'Half an hour in the life of a paper-seller' (*Votes for Women*, 9 January 1914, 224; no known performance). From the many people who walk by as she hawks her copies on the street, the paper-seller receives verbal batterings as well as unexpected support. The play's attention to women in new public spaces was one of many dramatic reflections on the ways in which the suffrage campaign was redefining public space as well as women's use of it.

From 1907 on, London itself also became a stage for the suffragists, who planned marches, meetings, and processions drawing hundreds of thousands at a time. In 1908, the WSPU arranged for 30,000 suffragists to take seven different processional routes through London to Hyde Park, where they were joined by up to half a million supporters. The Women's Coronation Procession of 1911, the 1913 funeral procession for suffrage martyr Emily Wilding Davison (who died after running in front of horses on the Derby race course), as well as the massive protest marches, like that in 1908, were often planned by women of the theatre and were in essence performances designed to drum up political support.

The conventional stages of London's early twentieth-century theatre were also conscripted for the suffrage cause, beginning with the performance of Elizabeth Robins's three-act play *Votes for Women!*; the play was staged under Harley Granville Barker's direction at the Royal Court in 1907. It set a high standard of writing for the suffrage plays to follow, but also opened a floodgate through which flowed the hundreds of suffrage plays written in the next seven years. Robins's play, like many other suffrage plays, was given a matinée performance, and many of London's key West End theatres, as well as its well-known actors and actresses, followed suit with the staging of plays directly about the vote as well as plays focused on issues of gender equity and gender roles. More notable efforts include Cicely Hamilton's *Diana of Dobson's* (1908), George Bernard Shaw's *Press Cuttings* (1910) and Charlotte Gilman's *Three Women* (1912). Matinée performances remained a constant, in part a reflection of the availability of the largely female audience they appealed to and in part a result of an explicitly political content. As was the case for many small theatre societies, censorship was a constant threat.

Women began to take on more prominent theatrical roles, perhaps as a result of such suffrage activism. Most importantly, women had key responsibilities in theatrical management in London and other cities: Annie Horniman did ground-breaking work at the Gaiety Theatre in Manchester, as did Edy Craig, Lena Ashwell, Gertrude Kingston, Lillah McCarthy and Lilian Bayliss in London. In addition, a simple cross-check of suffrage events with theatre events reveals that many of the most prominent actors played roles in suffrage plays or politics. Those active in the cause included Ellen Terry (whose daughter Edy Craig was one of the most important suffrage strategists), Laurence Housman, Johnston Forbes-Robertson, Gertrude Elliott, Henry Ainsley, Dorothy Minto, Ben Webster, Nigel Playfair, May Whitty and Harcourt Williams.

Suffrage plays

Sheila Stowell has defined the term 'suffrage drama' as referring to the 'auspices under which these plays were produced, not their specific content' (Stowell 1992: 42); and indeed, while the vast majority of plays staged by suffrage organizations made direct references to the vote, not all did, some preferring a more general focus on social issues. The plays reviewed below will, in general, offer at least some direct attention to the vote or will have been used in some major way by those campaigning for the vote.

Robins's *Votes for Women!* offered an auspicious start to suffrage drama. Drawing both from comedy of manners and from agit-prop pageantry, the play is simultaneously predictable and subversive, and exemplifies the contradictory theatre practices of the time. Act I offers recognizable drawing-room comedy in which a group of country-house weekend guests mix social flirtations with politics. Vida Levering, a politically active campaigner whose presence raises questions about her past, stands shoulder to shoulder with Jean Dunbarton, a politically naïve heiress. Both are inextricably linked to MP Geoffrey Stonor, as becomes clear in Act II, in the Trafalgar Square suffrage rally. The play is a curious mix of suffrage rhetoric and melodramatic revelations about Geoffrey's and Vida's shared past. Harley Granville Barker's innovative staging of the rally was praised for its authenticity, and its melding of theatre and suffrage protest set a standard for theatrically effective political speech which other suffrage plays aspired to during the next decade. The depiction of women in political action is stunning and has a rawness that still challenges audiences. Act III returns to the drawing room, where Jean, Vida and Geoffrey sort out their complex personal relationships through a rhetoric of suffrage politics. Jean and Geoffrey move towards marriage, but also join Vida in support of the women's vote. Vida's unwavering commitment to the vote inspires others and she stands as a complex portrait of the suffragist.

Of all suffrage drama, Robins's play has received the greatest critical attention. Although rarely staged, the play is on a par with the work of Harley Granville Barker, Henry James and others who deal with the nuances of Edwardian women's social and political options. Robins's conversion narrative and her radical Act II, which broke free of the drawing room, became a model for much of the suffrage drama to follow.

Not surprisingly, very few suffrage plays assume the three-act structure of Robins's play, since time-constraints made a full-length play generally unworkable for rallies and meetings – and it was primarily at such events that most performances took place. Thus the one-act, the monologue and the duologue became the mainstays of suffrage theatre, and many of them take from Robins the comic form as well as the selling of the vote through an examination of personal relationships. Cicely Hamilton and Christopher St John's *How the Vote was Won* is perhaps the best of these politically expedient plays. When, in the cause of the vote, a general strike is called for women, all women are directed to return to their 'nearest male relative' for support; the goal is to demonstrate to men how much they have come to rely on women's independence. The play reveals what this clever strategy means for one Horace Cole, a 30-year-old clerk living with his wife in Brixton. Through the course of the play's events, he realizes the ridiculousness of thinking 'today's' women need men, and he converts to the cause, concluding the play with a litany of reasons for women's vote: 'You may depend on me – all of you – to see justice done. When you want a thing done, get a man to do it! Votes for Women!' (Spender and Hayman 1985: 33). Such conversion is central to many of the suffrage plays published in newspapers (*Mr Peppercorn's Awakening*, *The Shadow of the Sofa*, *Our Happy Home*) as well as to those frequently performed at local rallies (for example, Evelyn Glover's *A Chat with Mrs Chicky* and her *Miss Appleyard's Awakening* (1913b)).

Edy Craig, Cicely Hamilton and others argued that such plays worked by promoting a change of heart among ideologically uncertain men and women while also reassuring others already committed to the cause. As Craig put it in a 1910 newspaper interview: 'I do think plays have done such a lot for the Suffrage. They get hold of nice frivolous people who would die sooner than go in cold blood to meetings. But they see the plays, and get interested, and then we can rope them in for meetings' (Carlson 2000: 201). The political expediency of such an approach also relies on comedy; what Craig's subversive strategy does *not* acknowledge is that the comic form, while allowing for rebellion in its topsy-turvy world, also has a companion structural reliance on the status quo. Thus in the celebratory endings of these conversion plays, there is often a tension between the affirmation of the vote and the affirmation of a relationship (often a marriage or engagement) which reifies social convention. While some of the plays did critique social institutions like marriage, many more made explicit that the vote would not threaten marriage, motherhood or social codes.

Many of the conversion plays have a processional element, as multiple people join a conversation or repeat an argument, swelling the scene until a whole community unites in agreement over the need for women's vote. Actual pageants were among the most influential suffrage plays, and may be among the most notable contributions of suffrage theatre. Perhaps the centrality of pageants is predictable, since suffrage activism of this era was marked by a reliance on demonstrations and large-scale meetings. The best and most influential of these pageants was *A Pageant of Great Women*, a collaboration of Cicely Hamilton's writing and Edy Craig's directing. With a cast ranging between 50 and 90 players, productions usually needed large spaces to amplify the play's grand scheme, and Craig was primarily responsible for its performance both in London and around the country, beginning in 1909 at London's Scala Theatre (Cockin 1998a: 94–107).

Hamilton provides a frame for the play in the three characters of Justice, Prejudice and Woman, who initiate the action with a debate about the possibility of women leading lives beyond the confines of their relationships to men. To prove the point that women have always functioned independently, there follows a procession of famous women in six groups: The Learned Women, The Artists, The Saintly Women, The Heroic Women, The Rulers and The Warriors. While each of the processing women has a very small speaking part, the cumulative effect of their stately presence and potent proclamations about women's abilities is to shame Prejudice into silence and retreat. Justice then tells the Woman that the 'world is thine', and the Woman concludes the play by letting men know they are not forgotten, but that women are now laughing as they feel 'the riot and rush of crowning hopes, / Dreams, longings, and vehement powers' (Nelson 2004: 229). This pageant was a powerful theatrical and political tool, not just because of its long and impressive line of influential women, but because in production key suffrage supporters could adopt the roles of the 'great' women. While some London productions boasted the most successful actresses of the day, many local productions used the opportunity to dress high-profile political supporters in the garb of such glorious figures as Jane Austen, Sappho, Florence Nightingale, Elizabeth I and Joan of Arc.

Christopher St John's *The First Actress* (1911) puts the processional in the narrower sphere of British theatrical history, and shows how the processional quality of suffrage campaigning seemed to influence the imagining of theatrical space. St John, a woman whose chosen male name confronts gender issues, creates a pageant of 11 famous actresses who line up to give encouragement to Margaret Hughes, assumed by St John to be the first actress on the English stage in 1661, performing the part of Desdemona. Hughes's performance is belittled by her male colleagues and she is about to conclude that women's acting is a failed experiment, but then the pageant begins. Coming from the future (post-1661), the 11 actresses reassure Hughes of the historic importance of her role. Performed initially by Edy Craig's Pioneer Players in 1911 and later for suffrage events, the play made easy connections between theatre and suffrage politics. This piece of theatre about theatre, in other words, made an effective argument for women's long-standing independence. In essence, such pageant plays use the procession of characters to visualize political progress.

While St John's play is not anthologized in any of the existing collections of suffrage drama (see Fitzsimmons and Gardner 1991; Holledge 1981; Nelson 2004; Spender and Hayman 1985), her well-crafted writing most clearly shows how the suffrage drama born in the initial efforts of Robins matured in the compressed political agitation of the next seven years. St John's 1914 play *Her Will* returns to the domestic interiors of Robins's world to bring suffrage politics squarely into the drawing room again; this time the drawing room has been transformed into a space controlled by independent and powerful women. As the play opens, suffragist Helen Wilton has just died, and the disposition of her estate brings her heirs into political contortions as they attempt to satisfy the demands of her will. A victim of a Holloway Prison stay (and its forced feedings), Wilton names as her first heir the suffrage cause itself, specifying that her money be used to support suffragists until the vote is awarded to women. Her second set of heirs (her family) are forced into a quick recognition of the several ways in which expanded suffrage will serve them, and they become objects of comedy as they begrudgingly move towards conversion. In this play, the drawing room is owned by a woman and becomes the space for political conversation, conversion and, most importantly, female autonomy (Carlson 2001: 344–5).

While the majority of suffrage plays deploy the comic form, using a feel-good factor to reinforce the rewards of political support for the suffrage cause, a sizeable number turn to both one-act and full-length dramas with darker endings. Stowell (1992) rightly names Hamilton's *Diana of Dobson's*, staged by Lena Ashwell at the Kingsway Theatre in 1908, as one of the key plays of the suffrage era, not because it deals with the issue of the vote, but because it forces questions about happiness and a woman's life choices. Act I, set in the dormitory of the shop girls employed at Dobson's, captures the bleak life of the women who work endless days for minimal wages. The promise of romance powers the next two acts, but the conclusion leaves the question of happiness unanswered. Many in the suffrage campaign were not willing to discuss the prejudicial legal situation in relation to marriage, since they felt it would jeopardize the possibility of the vote. Hamilton's play does, however, allow for the issue to be raised.

Margaret Wynne Nevinson's *In the Workhouse* (1911) is a protest against the laws of coverture, which denied most married women legal standing, and as Nevinson says in her preface, 'married women are still in captivity at the will of some worthless husband' (Nevison in Nelson 2004: 247). The play takes place in a workhouse where seven women share experiences and beliefs, most focused on how marriage laws have compounded difficult lives. One character, Lily, begins the play by saying that she is eager to marry the father of her new baby, and ends – after listening to the life stories of the other women – by telling her baby that maybe she won't get married after all. In sharp contrast to most suffrage plays, this one clearly separates marriage from happiness.

Most plays enlisted in the suffrage cause did not make such foundational critiques, though several skirt the issue, such as St Claire's *The Science of Forgiveness*.

Most studies of suffrage theatre focus on the plays and events created in the cause of women's vote, yet this review of suffrage theatre would not be complete without a note on the anti-suffrage plays which attempted to turn such pro-suffrage theatre in on itself. Many of these 'anti' plays used comic strategies which were conservative rather than subversive. Typically, the suffragist characters themselves were devoid of social skills and their politics inept; such qualities were meant to expose the suffragists' dangerous political goals. The women become comic targets when they give up their politics for love or when they are shown to be under-handed, illogical and promiscuous; Inglis Allen's *The Suffragettes' Redemption* (1909) and George Dance's *The Suffragettes* (1907) are good examples of such plays which undercut the suffrage cause (Carlson 2000: 207). One notable attempt to discredit women's arguments for the vote has a play full of children claiming that they too deserve the vote; Ernest Hutchinson's *Votes for Children* (1913) equates suffragists with a group of children who don't even know what a 'vote' is. The way in which anti-suffragists turned to theatre to counter the pro-suffrage plays is perhaps a back-handed compliment, an admission that the theatre was indeed a powerful political tool. But the anti-suffrage plays also suggest that the suffragists' frequent use of comedy might have been vulnerable to parody.

Conclusion

English suffrage theatre is a potent, brief example of a politically inspired theatre which leaves us with a legacy: it made new assumptions about theatrical space, domestic space and public space simultaneously; it catapulted women into the full range of roles in theatre; and it played a key role in women writers' conscriptions of dramatic form. World War I brought the suffrage theatre to a virtual halt, along with the suffrage campaign itself. Many of the women who had directed its militant efforts continued with theatre, but the concentrated urgency of the moment evaporated into other projects and concerns. Since the vote was not actually granted women until after the war (and even then in stages), it is not possible to make definitive claims about the political effec-tiveness of this theatre. These suffrage plays do, however, show a remarkable political energy, and more importantly, are a showcase for the political reach of the art form.

Note

1. The four papers were *Votes for Women*, the *Suffragette*, the *Vote* and *Common Cause*.

Primary and further reading

A. N. (1912). *Mr Peppercorn's Awakening*, *Vote*, 1 August, 229 (no known performance).

Allen, Inglis (1909). *The Suffragette's Redemption*. Lord Chamberlain's Plays, British Library (first performance 1909).

Baker, Edith M. (1911). *Our Happy Home*, *Vote*, 30 December, 115–17 (no known performance).

Carlson, Susan (2000). 'Comic Militancy: The Politics of Suffrage Drama' in Maggie B. Gale and Viv Gardner (eds). *Women, Theatre and Performance: New Histories, New Historiographies*. Manchester: Manchester University Press, 198–215.

Carlson, Susan (2001). 'Portable Politics: Creating New Space for Suffrage-ing Women', *New Theatre Quarterly* 17:4, 334–46.

Chapin, Alice (1909). *At the Gates*, *Vote*, 16 December, 94 (performance licensed 1909).

Cockin, Katharine (1998a). *Edith Craig (1869–1947): Dramatic Lives*. London: Cassell.

Dance, George (1907). *The Suffragettes*. Lord Chamberlain's Plays, British Library (first performance 1907).

Fitzsimmons, Linda and Gardner, Viv (eds) (1991). *New Woman Plays*. London: Methuen.

Frances, Hilary (2000). '"Dare to Be Free!": The Women's Freedom League and its Legacy' in June Purvis and Sandra Stanley Holton (eds). *Votes for Women*. New York and London: Routledge, 181–202.

Gardner, Viv (ed.) (1985). *Sketches from the Actresses' Franchise League*. Nottingham: Nottingham Drama Texts.

Glover, Evelyn (1913a). *A Chat with Mrs Chicky: A Duologue* in Dale Spender and Carole Hayman (eds) (1985). *How the Vote Was Won and Other Suffragette Plays*. London: Methuen; and in Carolyn Christensen Nelson (ed.). (2004). *Literature of the Women's Suffrage Campaign in England*. Peterborough, Ontario: Broadview Press (first performance 1912).

Glover, Evelyn (1913b). *Miss Appleyard's Awakening: A Play in One Act* in Carolyn Christensen Nelson (ed.). (2004). *Literature of the Women's Suffrage Campaign in England*. Peterborough, Ontario: Broadview Press (first performance 1911).

Hamilton, Cicely (1908). *Diana of Dobson's* in Linda Fitzsimmons and Viv Gardner (eds). (1991). *New Woman Plays*. London: Methuen, 27–77 (first performance 1908).

Hamilton, Cicely (1948; 1909). *A Pageant of Great Women* in Carolyn Christensen Nelson (ed.). (2004). *Literature of the Women's Suffrage Campaign in England*. Peterborough, Ontario: Broadview Press (first performance 1909).

Hamilton, Cicely and St John, Christopher (1909a). *How the Vote Was Won* in Dale Spender and Carole Hayman (eds). (1985). *How the Vote Was Won and Other Suffragette Plays*. London: Methuen; and in Carolyn Christensen Nelson (ed.). (2004). *Literature of the Women's Suffrage Campaign in England*. Peterborough, Ontario: Broadview Press (first performance 1909).

Hamilton, Cicely and St John, Christopher (1909b). *The Pot and the Kettle*. Lord Chamberlain's Plays, British Library (first performance 1909).

Holledge, Julie (1981). *Innocent Flowers: Women in the Edwardian Theatre*. London: Virago.

Hutchinson, Ernest (1913). *Votes for Children*. Lord Chamberlain's Plays, British Library (first performance 1913).

Little, A. L. (1913). *The Shadow of the Sofa*, *Vote*, 24 December, 139–41 (no known performance).

Mayhall, Laura E. Nym, Levine, Philippa and Fletcher, Ian Christopher (2000). 'Introduction' in *Women's Suffrage in the British Empire: Citizenship, Nation and Race*. London and New York: Routledge, xiii–xxii.

Moffat, Graham (1912). *The Maid and the Magistrate: A Duologue in One Act* in Carolyn Christensen Nelson (ed.). (2004). *Literature of the Women's Suffrage Campaign in England*. Peterborough, Ontario: Broadview Press (first performance 1912).

Nelson, Carolyn Christensen (ed.) (2004). *Literature of the Women's Suffrage Campaign in England*. Peterborough, Ontario: Broadview Press.

Nevinson, Margaret Wynne (1911). *In the Workhouse: A Play in One Act* in Carolyn Christensen

Nelson (ed.). (2004). *Literature of the Women's Suffrage Campaign in England*. Peterborough, Ontario: Broadview Press (first performance 1911).

Robins, Elizabeth (1907). *Votes for Women* in Dale Spender and Carole Hayman (eds). (1985). *How the Vote Was Won and Other Suffragette Plays*. London: Methuen (first performance 1907).

St John, Christopher (1911). *The First Actress*. Lord Chamberlain's Plays, British Library (first performance 1911).

St John, Christopher (1914). *Her Will*. Lord Chamberlain's Plays, British Library (performance licensed 1914).

Spender, Dale and Hayman, Carole (eds) (1985). *How the Vote Was Won and Other Suffragette Plays*. London: Methuen.

Stowell, Sheila (1992). *A Stage of Their Own: Feminist Plays of the Suffrage Era*. Manchester: Manchester University Press.

Originally published in Mary Luckhurst, ed., *A Companion to Modern British and Irish Drama*. Oxford: Blackwell, 2006, pp. 99–109.

3.8 Rehabilitating Realism (1992)

SHEILA STOWELL

I N 'CONSTRUCTING THE SUBJECT', Catherine Belsey accuses what she calls 'classic realism' of complicity in 'reinforcing the concepts of the world and of subjectivity which ensure that people "work by themselves" in the social formation' (Belsey 1985: 51) – in other words, of being a tool of industrial capitalism whose epoch has coincided with its own. It is a view embraced by a number of recent feminist theatre critics who present realism, to borrow Jill Dolan's phrase, as a 'conservative force that reproduces and reinforces dominant cultural relations' (Dolan 1988: 84). In offering audiences a 'seamless illusion', it is argued, realism precludes interrogation, portraying an arbitrary but self-serving orthodoxy as both natural and inevitable. As such, the realist text becomes tainted and counterproductive, of use only to those who would endorse a bourgeois hegemony with its consequent enshrinement of domus, family and patriarch. Yet is this 'case' against realism as strong or as self-evident as its proponents would have us believe? In the following paper I would like to review some of the principal charges that have been levelled against the form – and the dangers inherent in, what seems to me to be, a type of ahistorical thinking.[1]

The mystification of the author and his or her 'apparent absence from the self-contained fictional world on the stage', has been urged as evidence of realism's connivance in the status quo, the argument being that such anonymity perpetuates the view that what is being seen is the thing itself, free from authorial subjectivity. Yet how, precisely, are we to understand the playwright's disappearance? If we turn back to the heyday of 'realism' on the Edwardian stage and to the initial reception of plays by Bernard Shaw or Harley Granville Barker – as close to villains as the new dispensation provides – the most common complaint of critics and audiences alike was that *all* characters spoke just like their authors. Indeed, the same can be said for Oscar Wilde in the 1890s, whose minutely observed, if highly stylized, dramas fall within Belsey's realist net. Contemporary reviewers and cartoonists portrayed Wilde as puppeteer or ventriloquist – an *obvious* manipulator not only controlling but *seen* to control his stage characters and world.[2]

Then again if we are in each case experiencing an 'illusion of unmediated reality' how do we explain the discernible differences between realist authors? What methods of streamlining experience – i.e. mediation – make it possible for us to distinguish the works of Wilde, Shaw and Granville Barker from one another, or indeed from those of Ibsen, Chekhov, or feminist contemporaries like Githa Sowerby and Elizabeth Baker? The issue is elided by Belsey who snatches back with one hand what she gives with the other, acknowledging the author's presence after all as a 'shadowy authority' and 'source of the fiction'. There is, in other words, a mediating force both at work and, equally importantly, observably at work. The exigencies of the realist form as defined by Belsey are such, however, that the subjected subject 'reader is invited to perceive and judge the "truth" of the text, the coherent, non-contradictory interpretation of the world as it is perceived by an author whose autonomy is the source and evidence of the truth of the interpretation' (Belsey 1985: 52). Why, given Belsey's admission that 'truth' is a relative term, must the reader see the play's world as coherent and non-contradictory? Because, the argument goes, an 'autonomous' author perceives it as such. Yet turn-of-the-century plays like Shaw's *Widowers Houses* (1892), Granville Barker's *The Madras House* (1910) and Sowerby's *Rutherford and Son* (1912) were calculated, their authors claimed, to lay bare the contradictions of capitalism by exposing the logical (if profitable) absurdities of the worlds whose surfaces they so carefully set forth. This is not to ignore the possibility that 'too much furniture, or walls that are too tight, [can] create the effect of an unchangeable world, a "fated" world' (States 1988: 90); it is merely to insist that realist theatre does not *necessarily* present a coherent or unassailable view of society. It is rather a tool, or variety of tools, for shaping social perception. In the hands of turn-of-the-century feminists (and here Susan Kingsley Kent's general comments on the vocabulary of early feminist discourse are apt), 'the language of fact and concrete reality was meant to expose, by contrast, the emptiness of idealized depictions of womanhood and the marital state' (Kent 1987: 85) – to challenge in other words concepts of the world and of subjectivity which ensure willing participation in the maintenance of the existing social formation.

Nor should we be quick to simplify the role of the reader/audience in realism. The audience is not some sort of monolithic tabula rasa unwittingly acquiescing to its inscription by an author who exercises 'singular authority over the construction of meaning' (Dolan 1990: 42). An audience is a collection of members, each one informing as well as being informed by a work. We need to generalize less about its response, and investigate more closely its gender, class and economic composition in order to determine how meaning is generated. Once again, if we turn our attention to the reception of realist works at the turn of the century, we find, as might be expected, different groups of spectators reading the same 'reality' in predictably different ways. Sowerby's *Rutherford and Son* (1912), a powerful piece concerning the struggle between a despotic factory owner and his strong-willed daughter-in-law, was praised by Emma Goldman and Marjorie Strachey as a political tract arguing the case for female empowerment.[3] Indeed, the radical Women's Freedom League saw Sowerby's depiction of the industrial North as a 'hell, created by the arrogance of men', concluding that although it did not deal specifically with suffrage issues, 'no play has ever been written that in the truest, strongest sense was so really a "Suffrage" play' (*The Vote*, 20 July 1912). Yet mainstream male critics continued to construe the work as being 'about' trade and industry, hence its appeal to a 'business nation'. For the *Daily Telegraph* (12 March 1912), the *Era* (23 March 1912) and the *Saturday Review* (30 March 1912), old Rutherford was as much victim as oppressor. A similar divergence, this time along class rather than gender lines, is documented in initial responses to Edith Lyttelton's *Warp and Woof* (1904), an exposé of the luxury dress trade by an author who was herself in 'Society'. The working-class *Clarion* joined Mary Macarthur of the Women's Trade Union League in seeing the play as an unblinking condemnation of 'real' conditions of labour, while society papers such as *Vanity Fair* protected their readers by insisting that Lyttelton had in fact 'libelled ... the unfortunate butterflies of Mayfair and Belgravia' (16 June 1904).[4] The tendency of each piece to conform to the predispositions of opposed sub-audiences is symptomatic of a broader problem facing reception studies. The converting imagination is a potent and active force in creating significance – in realist, no less than in expressionist, epic, symbolist, or absurdist theatre. When, where, how, and to whom any play is performed are all factors constitutive of meaning; they significantly complicate matters of style and structure and we ignore them at our peril.

Realism is also condemned for 'illusionism', a concept Belsey tells us is 'self-explanatory'. It is not. From the perspective of Brechtian orthodoxy, the theatre of illusionism is that which shows the structure of society represented on stage as incapable of change by society represented by spectators, the maintenance of an on-stage illusion (that which is something other than itself) lulling a passive audience into social and political quiescence. Yet defined this way, and allowing for historical positioning, can realism be said to be more essentially 'illusionistic' than other forms of drama? The contrast Dolan draws, for example, between Brecht's 'exercise in complex seeing' (good) and the 'seduction of the illusionist [i.e. realist] text' (bad) sounds remarkably like Shaw's claim in the 1890s that his own keen-eyed 'realism' (good) could correct the unthinking complicity of 'romantic [i.e. illusionistic] drama' (bad). As Bert States has noted of productions of Brecht, an observation that holds true for Shaw as well, 'It is not the stage illusion that is undercut, or even the illusion that the stage represents a certain kind of "Nature"; what is undercut is simply the conventional system of current theater' (States 1988: 95). Furthermore, and I quote States again, 'the "arbitrary" mode of representation does not, in itself, assure the basis of a "critical" theater. It may, indeed, have been the best kind of theater for Brecht's project, but this is a little like saying that iambic pentameter was the best kind of language for Shakespeare's. Brecht's theater, like Shakespeare's, is what he left us and one can draw no conclusions about its form being the best or the correct one for his and similar projects' (ibid: 97). Push Brecht into a period like our own, in which audiences have come to expect, rather than be unsettled by, his bag of alienation tricks, and you have the spectacle of *Mahagonny*'s structural 'disruptions' amusing wealthy audiences at New York's Metropolitan Opera. One is as likely today to encounter elements of Brecht's 'epic theatre' (now become 'culinary theatre') on Broadway or in London's West End as in alternative performance spaces or fringe venues. Nor can we ignore the fact that realist theatre developed as a radical, low mimetic response to the glittering make-believe world of society drama, which was seen to be, to quote Dolan's critique of realism, 'prescriptive in that it reifie[d] the dominant culture's inscription of traditional power relations between genders and classes' (Dolan, 1988: 84). In brief, realism was championed as a means of challenging the ideological assumptions imbedded in melodrama and the well-made play.

But realism, it is contended, is essentially unhealthy. For Roland Barthes, an early champion of Brecht, a realist or representational sign 'effaces its own status as a sign, in order to foster the illusion that what is being perceived is reality without its intervention' (Eagleton 1983: 136). A 'healthy sign', on the other hand, is one which makes manifest its arbitrariness; it does not pretend to be 'natural', but rather 'in the very moment of conveying a meaning, communicates something of its own relative, artificial status as well' (ibid: 135). But can it be said of realist theatre, now handmaid to Ideology, that it seeks to 'naturalize' both itself and the ideologically complicit worlds it produces? Isn't it rather the case that it is centred in the perception of itself as artificial reproduction; it is applauded for the virtuosity of its artifice, for the very reason that it is not what it shows. Surely only the most naive believe that realist theatre is a 'mirror that truthfully records an objective social portrait' (Dolan 1990: 42); what it records are versions of social relations mediated by a set of inherently arbitrary conventions. So at the time of its first performances, the 'accentuated realism' of Granville Barker's *The Voysey Inheritance* (1905) could be seen by critic Dixon Scott in terms of 'the bright veracity of the streets of shops in harlequinade'. Elaborating, Scott goes on to observe that while:

offering itself to us as a simple 'slice of life' [*The Voysey Inheritance*] is really impaled, all the time, on the most fantastic toasting-fork of criminal pathology and fairy-tale finance. And so, although the characters' reactions to the prongs are observed with the most scrupulous fidelity and reproduced with the most wonderful skill, though they wear unquestionable top-hats and smoke real cigars, they still affect us as uncanny creatures. ... The mechanism that skewers them spitting each of them in turn until we have the entire row displaying each his special squirm, is every bit as arbitrary as Carnaby Leete's rapier, as recondite as his political intrigues. (Scott 1917: 145)

One of the paradoxes of stage realism at its most extreme is that its material exuberance encourages audiences to admire the painstaking business of its illusion making. Accordingly, audiences who applauded the Trafalgar Square set of Elizabeth Robins' *Votes for Women!* (1907) were appreciating the virtuosity (i.e. the artificiality) of a tableau. They would not, one presumes, have gone to Trafalgar Square to applaud the 'real' thing. The effect is predicated on the experience of estrangement, which Brecht claimed to be, in its widest sense, not so much 'a matter of special techniques, but a bringing-to-consciousness of a normal procedure of everyday life' (Gray 1961: 68) in such a way that it is reconceived 'as something strange, new, as a successful construction, and thereby to some extent as something unnatural' (qtd ibid).

Nor can it be said of realist theatre that it invariably 'naturalizes the social relations imposed by dominant ideology' (Dolan 1988: 106). Theatricalizing workrooms, drapers' establishments, law offices and (yes) drawing-rooms can have the effect of making visible traditionally invisible processes of capitalist production, exposing the usually hidden workings of an oppressive system, such staged revelations calling into question existing ideology's 'naturalized' view of the world, each one a call to action. In *The Perfect Wagnerite* Shaw likened the top hat of the capitalist shareholder to the Tarnhelm Alberich uses in *The Rhinegold* to render himself invisible to the workers he enslaves. They can feel his oppression – in Alberich's case the lashes of an unseen whip – but are unsure of its source (Shaw 1981: 434–35). Shaw's *Plays Unpleasant* were designed, he maintained, to strip invisibility from latter day Alberichs, revealing a systemic evil concealed from audiences of mid-century melodrama.[5] Indeed, Shaw's curtain call speech after the first performance of *Widowers' Houses* – a lecture on the evils of capitalism lest any of his viewers should miss the play's point – is similar to the Epilogue Brecht added to the *The Good Person of Setzuan* after its Viennese premiere, urging audiences to go out and change the world if they didn't like the play's conclusion.[6]

It has also been claimed that realism is distinguished by 'narrative which leads to closure'. In an oft-quoted passage breath-taking in the vastness of its generalization, Belsey asserts that:

classic realist narrative ... turns on the creation of enigma through the precipitation of disorder which throws into disarray the conventional cultural and signifying systems. Among the commonest sources of disorder at the level of plot in classic realism are murder, war, a journey or love. But the story moves inevitably towards closure which is also disclosure, the dissolution of enigma through the re-establishment of order, recognizable as a reinstatement or a development of the order which is understood to have preceded the events of the story itself. (Belsey 1985: 53)

This definition of 'closure', however, is so broad that while it applies to much realist theatre, it can be said to be equally true (or false) of an arc of dramatic action shared by playwrights from Sophocles – whose *Oedipus* surely stands as the model of such narrative – to the contemporary work of playwrights as diverse in technique and political sympathies as Steven Berkoff and Timberlake Wertenbaker. More seriously, such a definition negates the possibility of cumulative experience, arguing that because a so-called 'order' is restored at the end of a play, the work's overall visceral and cerebral meaning is erased. It would deny the significance of a play's process, the possibility that a spectator may not feel or think the same way about 'order' at the end of a work as at the beginning. Applied to realism as a form, such generalizations have resulted in an inability to distinguish between reproduction and reinforcement; consequently we hear that to 'show' something in realist terms is to confirm its inevitability to uncritical and politically resigned spectators, a claim some feminist theatre critics have used to maintain that 'closure in a realist play' invariably 'chokes women to death' (Case 1989: 43). If this is so, what do we make of a veritable realist play like Elizabeth Baker's *Chains* (1909), in which a female character actively rejects imprisonment in the matrimonial cage whose social and economic underpinnings are made obvious? Remaining enigmatic and unplaced, she does not disappear like a chameleon into the play's environment but actively removes herself from the stage sitting-room at the play's end, a profoundly symbolic departure from a realist setting that 'says in effect, "It will all end here"' (States 1988: 69).

I am not of course defending every realist play; as practised, much realist drama (like much pre, modern and postmodern theatre) warrants challenge from feminists. What I am arguing is that while dramatic and theatrical styles may be developed or adopted to naturalize or challenge particular positions, dramatic forms are not in themselves narrowly partisan. Indeed, historically those forms of theatre that have most actively endorsed the authority of Church and State – the medieval morality play and Stuart masque come immediately to mind – have been both hieratic and emblematic. More recently, Brecht's own brand of politicized theatre has come under attack by playwright/novelist Günter Grass. In *The Plebeians Rehearse the Uprising* Grass recasts Brecht as a 'privileged court jester', 'a man of the theatre serene and untroubled' (Grass 1966: xxxiv–xxxvi) who, in the face of the workers' uprising of 1953, does not turn the theatre to political account but instead turns political rebellion into state-sponsored epic theatre. On the other hand, a number of now inherently tainted realist plays were, in their own day, seen to offer so profound a threat to entrenched regimes that they were banned by state censors. The point is surely that while genres or styles – realism has been claimed as both – may not be politically neutral, they are capable of presenting a range of ideological positions; the issue is not so much formal as historical, contextual and phenomenological. To condemn writers simply because of the forms in which they work is to indulge in a system of analysis shaped by melodramatic assumptions of 'good' and 'bad' – the possibility of silencing (women) writers because they do not 'write right' is a danger to which feminist critics should be particularly alert.

Notes

1. This paper developed out of brief observations made in my book, *A Stage of Their Own: Feminist Playwrights of the Suffrage Era* (Manchester University Press: 1992), and was presented as part of the Women and Theatre Programme at the ATHE Conference, August 1991.

2. See for instance Joel Kaplan's 'A Puppet's Power: George Alexander, Clement Scott and the Replotting of *Lady Windermere's Fan*', *Theatre Notebook*, May 1992.
3. See Goldman's observations in *The Social Significance of Modern Drama* and Strachey's review in the *Englishwoman* 1912, vol. 14.
4. In the words of the *Clarion*, *Warp and Woof* 'formulates an awful charge against the conditions of society which permit … a state of affairs' in which employees 'are made the slaves of the exacting demands and the thoughtless selfishness of the fashionable world, whilst the wretchedness of their lives (with the terribly long working hours) lays them open to the worst forms of temptation as the readiest means of relief' (10 June 1904). Mary Macarthur was quick to use the play as 'a peg to hang propaganda articles on and a means of enlisting interest for the struggling Dressmakers' Union' (Hamilton 1926: 48).
5. Before warning his readers that 'my attacks are directed against themselves, not against my stage figures' (Shaw, 1980: 27), Shaw explains that he used the dramatic power of *Plays Unpleasant* 'to force the spectator to face unpleasant facts. … [especially] those social horrors which arise from the fact that the average homebred Englishman, however honorable and goodnatured he may be in his private capacity, is, as a citizen, a wretched creature who, whilst clamoring for a gratuitous millennium, will shut his eyes to the most villainous abuses…' (ibid: 25–26).
6. According to Eric Bentley, Brecht added the Epilogue as a result of 'misunderstandings of the ending in the press' on that occasion (Brecht 1968:108).

Works cited

Belsey, Catherine (1985) 'Constructing the Subject: Deconstructing the Text'. In *Feminist Criticism and Social Change: Sex, Class, and Race in Literature and Culture*. Judith Newton and Deborah Rosenfelt, eds. New York: Methuen.

Brecht, Bertolt (1968) *Parables for the Theatre*. Trans. Eric Bentley. Harmondsworth: Penguin.

Case, Sue-Ellen (1989) 'Towards a Butch/Femme Aesthetic'. In *Making a Spectacle: Feminist Essays on Contemporary Women's Theatre*. Ann Arbor: University of Michigan Press.

Dolan, Jill (1988) *The Feminist Spectator as Critic*. Ann Arbor: UMI Research Press.

Dolan, Jill (1990) '"Lesbian" Subjectivity in Realism'. In *Performing Feminisms: Feminist Critical Theory and Theatre*. Sue-Ellen Case, ed. Baltimore: Johns Hopkins UP.

Eagleton, Terry (1983) *Literary Theory*. Oxford: Blackwell.

Goldman, Emma (1987) *The Social Significance of Modern Drama*. 1914. New York: Applause Theatre Books.

Grass, Gunter (1966) *The Plebeians Rehearse the Uprising*. Trans. Ralph Manheim. New York: Harcourt, Brace & World.

Gray, John (1961) *Brecht*. Edinburgh: Oliver and Boyd.

Hamilton, Mary Agnes (1926) *Mary Macarthur*. New York: Thomas Seltzer.

Kaplan, Joel H. (1992) 'A Puppet's Power: George Alexander, Clement Scott, and the Replotting of *Lady Windermere's Fan*'. *Theatre Notebook* (May 1992)

Kent, Susan Kingsley (1987) *Sex and Suffrage in Britain, 1860–1914*. Princeton: Princeton UP.

Scott, Dixon (1917) *Men of Letters*. London.

Shaw, Bernard (1980) *Plays Unpleasant*. Harmondsworth: Penguin.

Shaw, Bernard (1981) *The Perfect Wagnerite*. In *Shaw's Music*. vol. III. Dan H. Laurence, ed. New York: Dodd, Mead.

States, Bert (1988) *Great Reckonings in Little Rooms*. Berkeley: University of California Press, 1988.

Originally published in *Journal of Dramatic Theory and Criticism*, 6(2) (1992): 81–8.

3.9 The Work of Art in the Age of Mechanical Reproduction (1935–6)

WALTER BENJAMIN

Translated by Harry Zorn

'Our fine arts were developed, their types and uses were established, in times very different from the present, by men whose power of action upon things was insignificant in comparison with ours. But the amazing growth of our techniques, the adaptability and precision they have attained, the ideas and habits they are creating, make it a certainty that profound changes are impending in the ancient craft of the Beautiful. In all the arts there is a physical component which can no longer be considered or treated as it used to be, which cannot remain unaffected by our modern knowledge and power. For the last twenty years neither matter nor space nor time has been what it was from time immemorial. We must expect great innovations to transform the entire technique of the arts, thereby affecting artistic invention itself and perhaps even bring about an amazing change in our very notion of art.'★

    – Paul Valéry, PIÈCES SUR L'ART, 'La Conquète de l'ubiquité,' Paris.

Preface

When Marx undertook his critique of the capitalistic mode of production, this mode was in its infancy. Marx directed his efforts in such a way as to give them prognostic value. He went back to the basic conditions underlying capitalistic production and through his presentation showed what could be expected of capitalism in the future. The result was that one could expect it not only to exploit the proletariat with increasing intensity, but ultimately to create conditions which would make it possible to abolish capitalism itself.

The transformation of the superstructure, which takes place far more slowly than that of the substructure, has taken more than half a century to manifest in all areas of culture the change in the conditions of production. Only today can it be indicated what form this has taken. Certain prognostic requirements should be met by these statements. However, theses about the art of the proletariat after its assumption of power or about the art of a classless society would have less bearing on these demands than theses about the developmental tendencies of art under present conditions of production. Their dialectic is no less noticeable in the superstructure than in the

---

★   Quoted from Paul Valéry, *Aesthetics*, 'The Conquest of Ubiquity,' translated by Ralph Manheim, p. 225, Pantheon Books, Bollingen Series, New York, 1964.

economy. It would therefore be wrong to underestimate the value of such theses as a weapon. They brush aside a number of outmoded concepts, such as creativity and genius, eternal value and mystery – concepts whose uncontrolled (and at present almost uncontrollable) application would lead to a processing of data in the Fascist sense. The concepts which are introduced into the theory of art in what follows differ from the more familiar terms in that they are completely useless for the purpose of Fascism. They are, on the other hand, useful for the formulation of revolutionary demands in the politics of art.

I

In principle a work of art has always been reproducible. Manmade artefacts could always be imitated by men. Replicas were made by pupils in practice of their craft, by masters for diffusing their works, and, finally, by third parties in the pursuit of gain. Mechanical reproduction of a work of art, however, represents something new. Historically, it advanced intermittently and in leaps at long intervals, but with accelerated intensity. The Greeks knew only two procedures of techni-cally reproducing works of art: founding and stamping. Bronzes, terra cottas, and coins were the only art works which they could produce in quantity. All others were unique and could not be mechanically reproduced. With the woodcut graphic art became mechanically reproducible for the first time, long before script became reproducible by print. The enormous changes which printing, the mechanical reproduction of writing, has brought about in literature are a familiar story. However, within the phenomenon which we are here examining from the perspective of world history, print is merely a special, though particularly important, case. During the Middle Ages engraving and etching were added to the woodcut; at the beginning of the nineteenth century lithography made its appearance.

With lithography the technique of reproduction reached an essentially new stage. This much more direct process was distinguished by the tracing of the design on a stone rather than its incision on a block of wood or its etching on a copperplate and permitted graphic art for the first time to put its products on the market, not only in large numbers as hitherto, but also in daily changing forms. Lithography enabled graphic art to illustrate everyday life, and it began to keep pace with printing. But only a few decades after its invention, lithography was surpassed by photography. For the first time in the process of pictorial reproduction, photography freed the hand of the most important artistic functions which henceforth devolved only upon the eye looking into a lens. Since the eye perceives more swiftly than the hand can draw, the process of pictorial reproduction was accelerated so enormously that it could keep pace with speech. A film operator shooting a scene in the studio captures the images at the speed of an actor's speech. Just as lithography virtually implied the illustrated newspaper, so did photography foreshadow the sound film. The technical reproduction of sound was tackled at the end of the last century. These convergent endeavours made predictable a situation which Paul Valéry pointed up in this sentence: 'Just as water, gas, and electricity are brought into our houses from far off to satisfy our needs in response to a minimal effort, so we shall be supplied with visual or auditory images, which will appear and disappear at a simple movement of the hand, hardly more than a sign' (*op. cit.*, p. 226). Around 1900 technical reproduction had reached a standard that not only permitted it to reproduce all transmitted works of art and thus to cause the most profound change in their impact upon the public; it also had captured a place of its own among the artistic processes. For the study of this standard nothing is more revealing than the nature of the repercussions that these two different manifestations – the reproduction of works of art and the art of the film – have had on art in its traditional form.

II

Even the most perfect reproduction of a work of art is lacking in one element: its presence in time and space, its unique existence at the place where it happens to be. This unique existence of the work of art determined the history to which it was subject throughout the time of its existence. This includes the changes which it may have suffered in physical condition over the years as well as the various changes in its ownership.[1] The traces of the first can be revealed only by chemical or physical analyses which it is impossible to perform on a reproduction; changes of ownership are subject to a tradition which must be traced from the situation of the original.

The presence of the original is the prerequisite to the concept of authenticity. Chemical analyses of the patina of a bronze can help to establish this, as does the proof that a given manuscript of the Middle Ages stems from an archive of the fifteenth century. The whole sphere of authenticity is outside technical – and, of course, not only technical – reproducibility.[2] Confronted with its manual reproduction, which was usually branded as a forgery, the original preserved all its authority; not so *vis à vis* technical reproduction. The reason is twofold. First, process reproduction is more independent of the original than manual reproduction. For example, in photography, process reproduction can bring out those aspects of the original that are unattainable to the naked eye yet accessible to the lens, which is adjustable and chooses its angle at will. And photographic reproduction, with the aid of certain processes, such as enlargement or slow motion, can capture images which escape natural vision. Secondly, technical reproduction can put the copy of the original into situations which would be out of reach for the original itself. Above all, it enables the original to meet the beholder halfway, be it in the form of a photograph or a phonograph record. The cathedral leaves its locale to be received in the studio of a lover of art; the choral production, performed in an auditorium or in the open air, resounds in the drawing room.

The situations into which the product of mechanical reproduction can be brought may not touch the actual work of art, yet the quality of its presence is always depreciated. This holds not only for the art work but also, for instance, for a landscape which passes in review before the spectator in a movie. In the case of the art object, a most sensitive nucleus – namely, its authenticity – is interfered with whereas no natural object is vulnerable on that score. The authenticity of a thing is the essence of all that is transmissible from its beginning, ranging from its substantive duration to its testimony to the history which it has experienced, Since the historical testimony rests on the authenticity, the former, too, is jeopardized by reproduction when substantive duration ceases to matter. And what is really jeopardized when the historical testimony is affected is the authority of the object.[3]

One might subsume the eliminated element in the term 'aura' and go on to say: that which withers in the age of mechanical reproduction is the aura of the work of art. This is a symptomatic process whose significance points beyond the realm of art. One might generalize by saying: the technique of reproduction detaches the reproduced object from the domain of tradition. By making many reproductions it substitutes a plurality of copies for a unique existence. And in permitting the reproduction to meet the beholder or listener in his own particular situation, it reactivates the object reproduced. These two processes lead to a tremendous shattering of tradition which is the obverse of the contemporary crisis and renewal of mankind. Both processes are intimately connected with the contemporary mass movements. Their most powerful agent is the film. Its social significance, particularly in its most positive form, is inconceivable without its destructive, cathartic aspect, that is, the liquidation of the traditional value of the cultural heritage. This phenomenon is most palpable in the great historical films. It extends to ever new positions. In 1927 Abel Gance exclaimed enthusiastically: 'Shakespeare, Rembrandt, Beethoven will make films ... all legends, all mythologies and all myths, all founders of religion, and the very religions ... await their exposed resurrection, and the heroes crowd each other at the gate.'★ Presumably without intending it, he issued an invitation to a far-reaching liquidation.

III

During long periods of history, the mode of human sense perception changes with humanity's entire mode of existence. The manner in which human sense perception is organized, the medium in which it is accomplished, is determined not only by nature but by historical circumstances as well. The fifth century, with its great shifts of population, saw the birth of the late Roman art industry and the Vienna Genesis, and there developed not only an art different from that of antiquity but also a new kind of perception. The scholars of the Viennese school, Riegl and Wickhoff, who resisted the weight of classical tradition under which these later art forms had been buried, were the first to draw conclusions from them concerning the organization of perception at the time. However far-reaching their insight, these scholars limited themselves to showing the significant, formal hallmark which characterized perception in late Roman times. They did not attempt – and, perhaps, saw no way – to show the social transformations expressed by these changes of perception. The conditions for an analogous insight are more favourable in the present. And if changes in the medium of contemporary perception can be comprehended as decay of the aura, it is possible to show its social causes.

The concept of aura which was proposed above with reference to historical objects may usefully be illustrated with reference to the aura of natural ones. We define the aura of the latter as the unique phenomenon of a distance, however close it may be. If, while resting on a summer afternoon, you follow with your eyes a mountain range on the horizon or a branch which casts its shadow over you, you experience the aura of those mountains, of that branch. This image makes it easy to comprehend the social bases of the contemporary decay of the aura. It rests on two circumstances, both of which are related to the increasing significance of the masses in contemporary life. Namely, the desire of contemporary masses to bring things 'closer' spatially and humanly, which is just as ardent as their bent toward overcoming the uniqueness of every reality by accepting its reproduction.[4] Every day the urge grows stronger to get hold of an object at very close range by way of its likeness, its reproduction. Unmistakably, reproduction as offered by picture magazines and newsreels differs from the image seen by the unarmed eye. Uniqueness and permanence are as closely linked in the latter as are transitoriness and reproducibility in the

★ Abel Gance, 'Le Temps de l'image est venu,' *L'Art cinematographique*, Vol. 2. pp. 94 f, Paris, 1927.

former. To pry an object from its shell, to destroy its aura, is the mark of a perception whose 'sense of the universal equality of things' has increased to such a degree that it extracts it even from a unique object by means of reproduction. Thus is manifested in the field of perception what in the theoretical sphere is noticeable in the increasing importance of statistics. The adjustment of reality to the masses and of the masses to reality is a process of unlimited scope, as much for thinking as for perception.

IV

The uniqueness of a work of art is inseparable from its being imbedded in the fabric of tradition. This tradition itself is thoroughly alive and extremely changeable. An ancient statue of Venus, for example, stood in a different traditional context with the Greeks, who made it an object of veneration, than with the clerics of the Middle Ages, who viewed it as an ominous idol. Both of them, however, were equally confronted with its uniqueness, that is, its aura. Originally the contextual integration of art in tradition found its expression in the cult. We know that the earliest art works originated in the service of a ritual – first the magical, then the religious kind. It is significant that the existence of the work of art with reference to its aura is never entirely separated from its ritual function.[5] In other words, the unique value of the 'authentic' work of art has its basis in ritual, the location of its original use value. This ritualistic basis, however remote, is still recognizable as secularized ritual even in the most profane forms of the cult of beauty.[6] The secular cult of beauty, developed during the Renaissance and prevailing for three centuries, clearly showed that ritualistic basis in its decline and the first deep crisis which befell it. With the advent of the first truly revolutionary means of reproduction, photography, simultaneously with the rise of socialism, art sensed the approaching crisis which has become evident a century later. At the time, art reacted with the doctrine of *d'art pour l'art*, that is, with a theology of art. This gave rise to what might be called a negative theology in the form of the idea of 'pure' art, which not only denied any social function of art but also any categorizing by subject matter. (In poetry, Mallarmé was the first to take this position.)

An analysis of art in the age of mechanical reproduction must do justice to these relationships, for they lead us to an all-important insight: for the first time in world history, mechanical reproduction emancipates the work of art from its parasitical dependence on ritual. To an ever greater degree the work of art reproduced becomes the work of art designed for reproducibility.[7] From a photographic negative, for example, one can make any number of prints; to ask for the 'authentic' print makes no sense. But the instant the criterion of authenticity ceases to be applicable to artistic production, the total function of art is reversed, Instead of being based on ritual, it begins to be based on another practice – politics.

V

Works of art are received and valued on different planes. Two polar types stand out: with one, the accent is on the cult value; with the other, on the exhibition value of the work.[8] Artistic production begins with ceremonial objects destined to serve in a cult. One may assume that what mattered was their existence, not their being on view. The elk portrayed by the man of the Stone Age on the walls of his cave was an instrument of magic. He did expose it to his fellow men, but in the main it was meant for the spirits. Today the cult value would seem to demand that the work of art remain hidden. Certain statues of gods are accessible only to the priest in the cella; certain Madonnas remain covered nearly all year round; certain sculptures on medieval cathedrals are invisible to the spectator on ground level. With the emancipation of the various art practices from ritual go increasing opportunities for the exhibition of their products. It is easier to exhibit a portrait bust that can be sent here and there than to exhibit the statue of a divinity that has its fixed place in the interior of a temple. The same holds for the painting as against the mosaic or fresco that preceded it. And even though the public presentability of a mass originally may have been just as great as that of a symphony, the latter originated at the moment when its public presentability promised to surpass that of the mass.

With the different methods of technical reproduction of a work of art, its fitness for exhibition increased to such an extent that the quantitative shift between its two poles turned into a qualitative transformation of its nature. This is comparable to the situation of the work of art in prehistoric times when, by the absolute emphasis on its cult value, it was, first and foremost, an instrument of magic. Only later did it come to be recognized as a work of art. In the same way today, by the absolute emphasis on its exhibition value the work of art becomes a creation with entirely new functions, among which the one we are conscious of, the artistic function, later may be recognized as incidental.[9] This much is certain: today photography and the film are the most serviceable exemplifications of this new function.

VI

In photography, exhibition value begins to displace cult value all along the line. But cult value does not give way without resistance. It retires into an ultimate retrenchment: the human countenance. It is no accident that the portrait was the focal point of early photography. The cult of remembrance of loved ones, absent or dead, offers a last refuge for the cult value of the picture. For the last time the aura emanates from the early photographs in the fleeting expression of a human face. This is what constitutes their melancholy, incomparable beauty. But as man withdraws from the photographic image, the exhibition value for the first time shows its superiority to the ritual value. To have pinpointed this new stage constitutes the incomparable significance of Atget, who, around 1900, took photographs of deserted Paris streets. It has quite justly been said of him that he photographed them like scenes of crime. The scene of a crime, too, is deserted; it is photographed for the purpose of establishing evidence. With Atget, photographs become standard evidence for historical occurrences, and acquire a hidden political significance. They demand a specific kind of approach; free-floating contemplation is not appropriate to them, They stir the viewer; he feels challenged by them in a new way. At the same time picture magazines begin to put up signposts for him, right ones or wrong ones, no matter. For the first time, captions have become obligatory. And it is clear that they have an altogether different character than the title of a painting. The directives which the captions give to those looking at pictures in illustrated magazines soon become even more explicit and more imperative in the film where the meaning of each single picture appears to be prescribed by the sequence of all preceding ones.

The nineteenth-century dispute as to the artistic value of painting versus photography today seems devious and confused. This does not diminish its importance, however; if anything, it underlines it. The dispute was in fact the symptom of a historical transformation the universal impact of which was not realized by either of the rivals. When the age of mechanical reproduction separated art from its basis in cult, the semblance of its autonomy disappeared forever. The resulting change in the function of art transcended the perspective of the century; for a long time it even escaped that of the twentieth century, which experienced the development of the film.

Earlier much futile thought had been devoted to the question of whether photography is an art. The primary question – whether the very invention of photography had not transformed the entire nature of art – was not raised. Soon the film theoreticians asked the same ill-considered question with regard to the film. But the difficulties which photography caused traditional aesthetics were mere child's play as compared to those raised by the film. Whence the insensitive and forced character of early theories of the film. Abel Gance, for instance, compares the film with hieroglyphs: 'Here, by a remarkable regression, we have come back to the level of expression of the Egyptians ... Pictorial language has not yet matured because our eyes have not yet adjusted to it. There is as yet insufficient respect for, insufficient cult of, what it expresses.'★ Or, in the words of Séverin-Mars: 'What art has been granted a dream more poetical and more real at the same time! Approached in this fashion the film might represent an incomparable means of expression. Only the most high-minded persons, in the most perfect and mysterious moments of their lives, should be allowed to enter its ambience.'† Alexandre Arnoux concludes his fantasy about the silent film with the question: 'Do not all the bold descriptions we have given amount to the definition of prayer?'‡ It is instructive to note how their desire to class the film among the 'arts' forces these theoreticians to read ritual elements into it – with a striking lack of discretion. Yet when these speculations were published, films like *L'Opinion publique* and *The Gold Rush* had already appeared. This, however, did not keep Abel Gance from adducing hieroglyphs for purposes of comparison, nor Séverin-Mars from speaking of the film as one might speak of paintings by Fra Angelico. Characteristically, even today ultrareactionary authors give the film a similar contextual significance – if not an outright sacred one, then at least a supernatural one. Commenting on Max Reinhardt's film version of *A Midsummer Night's Dream*, Werfel states that undoubtedly it was the sterile copying of the exterior world with its streets, interiors, railroad stations, restaurants, motorcars, and beaches which until now had obstructed the elevation of the film to the realm of art. 'The film has not yet realized its true meaning, its real possibilities ... these consist in its unique faculty to express by natural means and with incomparable persuasiveness all that is fairylike, marvellous, supernatural.'§

VIII

The artistic performance of a stage actor is definitely presented to the public by the actor in person; that of the screen actor, however, is presented by a camera, with a twofold consequence. The camera that presents the performance of the film actor to the public need not respect the performance as an integral whole. Guided by the cameraman, the camera continually changes its position with respect to the performance. The sequence of positional views which the editor

---

★   Abel Gance, *op. cit.*, pp. 100–1.

†   Séverin-Mars, quoted by Abel Gance, *op. cit.*, p. 100.

‡   Alexandre. Arnoux, *Cinéma pris*, 1929, p. 28.

§   Franz Werfel, 'Ein Sommernachtstraum, Ein Film von Shakespeare and Reinhardt,' *Neues Wiener Journal*, cited in *Lu*, 15 November, 1935.

composes from the material supplied him constitutes the completed film. It comprises certain factors of movement which are in reality those of the camera, not to mention special camera angles, close-ups, etc. Hence, the performance of the actor is subjected to a series of optical tests. This is the first consequence of the fact that the actor's performance is presented by means of a camera. Also, the film actor lacks the opportunity of the stage actor to adjust to the audience during his performance, since he does not present his performance to the audience in person. This permits the audience to take the position of a critic, without experiencing any personal contact with the actor. The audience's identification with the actor is really an identification with the camera. Consequently the audience takes the position of the camera; its approach is that of testing.[10] This is not the approach to which cult values may be exposed.

IX

For the film, what matters primarily is that the actor represents himself to the public before the camera, rather than representing someone else. One of the first to sense the actor's metamorphosis by this form of testing was Pirandello. Though his remarks on the subject in his novel *Si Gira* were limited to the negative aspects of the question and to the silent film only, this hardly impairs their validity. For in this respect, the sound film did not change anything essential. What matters is that the part is acted not for an audience but for a mechanical contrivance – in the case of the sound film, for two of them. 'The film actor,' wrote Pirandello, 'feels as if in exile – exiled not only from the stage but also from himself. With a vague sense of discomfort he feels inexplicable emptiness: his body loses its corporeality, it evaporates, it is deprived of reality, life, voice, and the noises caused by his moving about, in order to be changed into a mute image, flickering an instant on the screen, then vanishing into silence … The projector will play with his shadow before the public, and he himself must be content to play before the camera.'★ This situation might also be characterized as follows: for the first time – and this is the effect of the film – man has to operate with his whole living person, yet forgoing its aura. For aura is tied to his presence; there can be no replica of it. The aura which, on the stage, emanates from Macbeth, cannot be separated for the spectators from that of the actor. However, the singularity of the shot in the studio is that the camera is substituted for the public. Consequently, the aura that envelops the actor vanishes, and with it the aura of the figure he portrays.

It is not surprising that it should be a dramatist such as Pirandello who, in characterizing the film, inadvertently touches on the very crisis in which we see the theatre. Any thorough study proves that there is indeed no greater contrast than that of the stage play to a work of art that is completely subject to or, like the film, founded in mechanical reproduction. Experts have long recognized that in the film 'the greatest effects are almost always obtained by "acting" as little as possible …' In 1932 Rudolf Arnheim saw 'the latest trend … in treating the actor as a stage prop chosen for its characteristics and … inserted at the proper place.'[11] With this idea something else is closely connected. The stage actor identifies himself with the character of his role. The film actor very often is denied this opportunity. His creation is by no means all of a piece; it is composed of many separate performances. Besides certain fortuitous considerations, such as cost of studio,

---

★ Luigi Pirandello, *Si Gira*, quoted by Léon Pierre-Quint, 'Signification du cinéma,' *L'Art cinématographique, op. cit.*, pp. 14–15.

availability of fellow players, décor, etc., there are elementary necessities of equipment that split the actor's work into a series of mountable episodes. In particular, lighting and its installation require the presentation of an event that, on the screen, unfolds as a rapid and unified scene, in a sequence of separate shootings which may take hours at the studio; not to mention more obvious montage. Thus a jump from the window can be shot in the studio as a jump from a scaffold, and the ensuing flight, if need be, can be shot weeks later when outdoor scenes are taken. Far more paradoxical cases can easily be construed. Let us assume that an actor is supposed to be startled by a knock at the door. If his reaction is not satisfactory, the director can resort to an expedient: when the actor happens to be at the studio again he has a shot fired behind him without his being forewarned of it. The frightened reaction can be shot now and be cut into the screen version. Nothing more strikingly shows that art has left the realm of the 'beautiful semblance' which, so far, had been taken to be the only sphere where art could thrive.

X

The feeling of strangeness that overcomes the actor before the camera, as Pirandello describes it, is basically of the same kind as the estrangement felt before one's own image in the mirror. But now the reflected image has become separable, transportable. And where is it transported? Before the public.[12] Never for a moment does the screen actor cease to be conscious of this fact. While facing the camera he knows that ultimately he will face the public, the consumers who constitute the market. This market, where he offers not only his labour but also his whole self, his heart and soul, is beyond his reach. During the shooting he has as little contact with it as any article made in a factory. This may contribute to that oppression, that new anxiety which, according to Pirandello, grips the actor before the camera. The film responds to the shrivelling of the aura with an artificial buildup of the 'personality' outside the studio. The cult of the movie star, fostered by the money of the film industry, preserves not the unique aura of the person but the 'spell of the personality,' the phony spell of a commodity. So long as the movie-makers' capital sets the fashion, as a rule no other revolutionary merit can be accredited to today's film than the promotion of a revolutionary criticism of traditional concepts of art, We do not deny that in some cases today's films can also promote revolutionary criticism of social conditions, even of the distribution of property. However, our present study is no more specifically concerned with this than is the film production of Western Europe.

It is inherent in the technique of the film as well as that of sports that everybody who witnesses its accomplishments is somewhat of an expert. This is obvious to anyone listening to a group of newspaper boys leaning on their bicycles and discussing the outcome of a bicycle race. It is not for nothing that newspaper publishers arrange races for their delivery boys. These arouse great interest among the participants, for the victor has an opportunity to rise from delivery boy to professional racer. Similarly, the newsreel offers everyone the opportunity to rise from passer-by to movie extra. In this way any man might even find himself part of a work of art, as witness Vertoff's *Three Songs About Lenin* or Ivens' *Borinage*. Any man today can lay claim to being filmed. This claim can best be elucidated by a comparative look at the historical situation of contemporary literature.

For centuries a small number of writers were confronted by many thousands of readers. This changed toward the end of the last century. With the increasing extension of the press, which kept placing new political, religious, scientific, professional, and local organs before the readers, an increasing number of readers became writers – at first, occasional ones. It began with the daily press opening to its readers space for 'letters to the editor.' And today there is hardly a gainfully employed European who could not, in principle, find an opportunity to publish somewhere or other comments on his work, grievances, documentary reports, or that sort of thing. Thus, the distinction between author and public is about to lose its basic character. The difference becomes merely functional; it may vary from case to case. At any moment the reader is ready to turn into a writer. As expert, which he had to become willy-nilly in an extremely specialized work process, even if only in some minor respect, the reader gains access to authorship. In the Soviet Union work itself is given a voice. To present it verbally is part of a man's ability to perform the work. Literary licence is now founded on polytechnic rather than specialized training and thus becomes common property.[13]

All this can easily be applied to the film, where transitions that in literature took centuries have come about in a decade. In cinematic practice, particularly in Russia, this change-over has partially become established reality. Some of the players whom we meet in Russian films are not actors in our sense but people who portray *themselves* – and primarily in their own work process. In Western Europe the capitalistic exploitation of the film denies consideration to modern man's legitimate claim to being reproduced. Under these circumstances the film industry is trying hard to spur the interest of the masses through illusion-promoting spectacles and dubious speculations.

XI

The shooting of a film, especially of a sound film, affords a spectacle unimaginable anywhere at any time before this. It presents a process in which it is impossible to assign to a spectator a viewpoint which would exclude from the actual scene such extraneous accessories as camera equipment, lighting machinery, staff assistants, etc. – unless his eye were on a line parallel with the lens. This circumstance, more than any other, renders superficial and insignificant any possible similarity between a scene in the studio and one on the stage. In the theatre one is well aware of the place from which the play cannot immediately be detected as illusionary. There is no such place for the movie scene that is being shot. Its illusionary nature is that of the second degree, the result of cutting. That is to say, in the studio the mechanical equipment has penetrated so deeply into reality that its pure aspect freed from the foreign substance of equipment is the result of a special procedure, namely, the shooting by the specially adjusted camera and the mounting of the shot together with other similar ones. The equipment-free aspect of reality here has become the height of artifice; the sight of immediate reality has become an orchid in the land of technology.

Even more revealing is the comparison of these circumstances, which differ so much from those of the theatre, with the situation in painting. Here the question is: How does the cameraman compare with the painter? To answer this we take recourse to an analogy with a surgical operation. The surgeon represents the polar opposite of the magician. The magician heals a sick person by the laying on of hands; the surgeon cuts into the patient's body, The magician maintains the natural distance between the patient and himself; though he reduces it very slightly by the laying on of hands, he greatly increases it by virtue of his authority. The surgeon does exactly the reverse; he greatly diminishes the distance between himself and the patient by penetrating into the patient's body, and increases it but little by the caution with which his hand moves among the organs. In short, in contrast to the magician – who is still hidden in the medical practitioner – the surgeon at the decisive moment abstains from facing the patient man to man; rather, it is through the operation that he penetrates into him.

Magician and surgeon compare to painter and cameraman. The painter maintains in his work a natural distance from reality, the cameraman penetrates deeply into its web.[14] There is a tremendous difference between the pictures they obtain. That of the painter is a total one, that of the cameraman consists of multiple fragments which are assembled under a new law. Thus, for contemporary man the representation of reality by the film is incomparably more significant than that of the painter, since it offers, precisely because of the thoroughgoing permeation of reality with mechanical equipment, an aspect of reality which is free of all equipment. And that is what one is entitled to ask from a work of art.

XII

Mechanical reproduction of art changes the reaction of the masses toward art. The reactionary attitude toward a Picasso painting changes into the progressive reaction toward a Chaplin movie. The progressive reaction is characterized by the direct, intimate fusion of visual and emotional enjoyment with the orientation of the expert. Such fusion is of great social significance. The greater the decrease in the social significance of an art form, the sharper the distinction between criticism and enjoyment by the public. The conventional is uncritically enjoyed, and the truly new is criticized with aversion. With regard to the screen, the critical and the receptive attitudes of the public coincide. The decisive reason for this is that individual reactions are predetermined by the mass audience response they are about to produce, and this is nowhere more pronounced than in the film. The moment these responses become manifest they control each other. Again, the comparison with painting is fruitful. A painting has always had an excellent chance to be viewed by one person or by a few. The simultaneous contemplation of paintings by a large public, such as developed in the nineteenth century, is an early symptom of the crisis of painting, a crisis which was by no means occasioned exclusively by photography but rather in a relatively independent manner by the appeal of art works to the masses.

Painting simply is in no position to present an object for simultaneous collective experience, as it was possible for architecture at all times, for the epic poem in the past, and for the movie today. Although this circumstance in itself should not lead one to conclusions about the social role of painting, it does constitute a serious threat as soon as painting, under special conditions and, as it were, against its nature, is confronted directly by the masses. In the churches and monasteries of the Middle Ages and at the princely courts up to the end of the eighteenth century, a collective reception of paintings did not occur simultaneously, but by graduated and hierarchized mediation. The change that has come about is an expression of the particular conflict in which painting was implicated by the mechanical reproducibility of paintings. Although paintings began to be publicly exhibited in galleries and salons, there was no way for the masses to organize and control themselves in their reception.[15] Thus the same public which responds in a progressive manner toward a grotesque film is bound to respond in a reactionary manner to surrealism.

XIII

The characteristics of the film lie not only in the manner in which man presents himself to mechanical equipment but also in the manner in which, by means of this apparatus, man can represent his environment. A glance at occupational psychology illustrates the testing capacity of the equipment. Psychoanalysis illustrates it in a different perspective. The film has enriched our field of perception with methods which can be illustrated by those of Freudian theory. Fifty years ago, a slip of the tongue passed more or less unnoticed. Only exceptionally may such a slip have revealed dimensions of depth in a conversation which had seemed to be taking its course on the surface. Since the *Psychopathology of Everyday Life* things have changed. This book isolated and made analysable things which had heretofore floated along unnoticed in the broad stream of perception. For the entire spectrum of optical, and now also acoustical, perception the film has brought about a similar deepening of apperception. It is only an obverse of this fact that behaviour items shown in a movie can be analysed much more precisely and from more points of view than those presented on paintings or on the stage. As compared with painting, filmed behaviour lends itself more readily to analysis because of its incomparably more precise statements of the situation. In comparison with the stage scene, the filmed behaviour item lends itself more readily to analysis because it can be isolated more easily. This circumstance derives its chief importance from its tendency to promote the mutual penetration of art and science. Actually, of a screened behaviour item which is neatly brought out in a certain situation, like a muscle of a body, it is difficult to say which is more fascinating, its artistic value or its value for science. To demonstrate the identity of the artistic and scientific uses of photography which heretofore usually were separated will be one of the revolutionary functions of the film.[16]

By close-ups of the things around us, by focusing on hidden details of familiar objects, by exploring commonplace milieus under the ingenious guidance of the camera, the film, on the one hand, extends our comprehension of the necessities which rule our lives; on the other hand, it manages to assure us of an immense and unexpected field of action. Our taverns and our metropolitan streets, our offices and furnished rooms, our railroad stations and our factories appeared to have us locked up hopelessly. Then came the film and burst this prison-world asunder by the dynamite of the tenth of a second, so that now, in the midst of its far-flung ruins and debris, we calmly and adventurously go travelling. With the close-up, space expands; with slow motion, movement is extended. The enlargement of a snapshot does not simply render more precise what in any case was visible, though unclear: it reveals entirely new structural formations of the subject. So, too, slow motion not only presents familiar qualities of movement but reveals in them entirely unknown ones 'which, far from looking like retarded rapid movements, give the effect of singularly gliding, floating, supernatural motions.'* Evidently a different nature opens itself to the camera than opens to the naked eye – if only because an unconsciously penetrated space is substituted for a space consciously explored by man. Even if one has a general knowledge of the way people walk, one knows nothing of a person's posture during the fractional second of a stride. The act of reaching for a lighter or a spoon is familiar routine, yet we hardly know what really goes on between hand and metal, not to mention how this fluctuates with our moods. Here the camera intervenes with the resources of its lowerings and liftings, its interruptions and isolations, its extensions and accelerations, its enlargements and reductions. The camera introduces us to unconscious optics as does psychoanalysis to unconscious impulses.

★ Rudolf Arnheim, *loc. cit.*, p. 138.

XIV

One of the foremost tasks of art has always been the creation of a demand which could be fully satisfied only later.[17] The history of every art form shows critical epochs in which a certain art form aspires to effects which could be fully obtained only with a changed technical standard, that is to say, in a new art form. The extravagances and crudities of art which thus appear, particularly in the so-called decadent epochs, actually arise from the nucleus of its richest historical energies. In recent years, such barbarisms were abundant in Dadaism. It is only now that its impulse becomes discernible: Dadaism attempted to create by pictorial – and literary – means the effects which the public today seeks in the film.

Every fundamentally new, pioneering creation of demands will carry beyond its goal. Dadaism did so to the extent that it sacrificed the market values which are so characteristic of the film in favour of higher ambitions – though of course it was not conscious of such intentions as here described. The Dadaists attached much less importance to the sales value of their work than to its uselessness for contemplative immersion. The studied degradation of their material was not the least of their means to achieve this uselessness. Their poems are 'word salad' containing obscenities and every imaginable waste product of language. The same is true of their paintings, on which they mounted buttons and tickets. What they intended and achieved was a relentless destruction of the aura of their creations, which they branded as reproductions with the very means of production. Before a painting of Arp's or a poem by August Stramm it is impossible to take time for contemplation and evaluation as one would before a canvas of Derain's or a poem by Rilke. In the decline of middle-class society, contemplation became a school for asocial behaviour; it was countered by distraction as a variant of social conduct.[18] Dadaistic activities actually assured a rather vehement distraction by making works of art the centre of scandal. One requirement was foremost: to outrage the public.

From an alluring appearance or persuasive structure of sound the work of art of the Dadaists became an instrument of ballistics. It hit the spectator like a bullet, it happened to him, thus acquiring a tactile quality. It promoted a demand for the film, the distracting element of which is also primarily tactile, being based on changes of place and focus which periodically assail the spectator. Let us compare the screen on which a film unfolds with the canvas of a painting. The painting invites the spectator to contemplation; before it the spectator can abandon himself to his associations. Before the movie frame he cannot do so. No sooner has his eye grasped a scene than it is already changed. It cannot be arrested. Duhamel, who detests the film and knows nothing of its significance, though something of its structure, notes this circumstance as follows: 'I can no longer think what I want to think. My thoughts have been replaced by moving images.'★ The spectator's process of association in view of these images is indeed interrupted by their constant, sudden change. This constitutes the shock effect of the film, which, like all shocks, should be cushioned by heightened presence of mind.[19] By means of its technical structure, the film has taken the physical shock effect out of the wrappers in which Dadaism had, as it were, kept it inside the moral shock effect.[20]

★ Georges Duhamel, *Scènes de la vie future*, Paris, 1930, p. 52.

XV

The mass is a matrix from which all traditional behaviour toward works of art issues today in a new form. Quantity has been transmuted into quality. The greatly increased mass of participants has produced a change in the mode of participation. The fact that the new mode of participation first appeared in a disreputable form must not confuse the spectator. Yet some people have launched spirited attacks against precisely this superficial aspect. Among these, Duhamel has expressed himself in the most radical manner. What he objects to most is the kind of participation which the movie elicits from the masses. Duhamel calls the movie 'a pastime for helots, a diversion for uneducated, wretched, worn-out creatures who are consumed by their worries …, a spectacle which requires no concentration and presupposes no intelligence …, which kindles no light in the heart and awakens no hope other than the ridiculous one of someday becoming a "star" in Los Angeles.'★ Clearly, this is at bottom the same ancient lament that the masses seek distraction whereas art demands concentration from the spectator. That is a commonplace. The question remains whether it provides a platform for the analysis of the film. A closer look is needed here. Distraction and concentration form polar opposites which may be stated as follows: A man who concentrates before a work of art is absorbed by it. He enters into this work of art the way legend tells of the Chinese painter when he viewed his finished painting. In contrast, the distracted mass absorbs the work of art. This is most obvious with regard to buildings. Architecture has always represented the prototype of a work of art the reception of which is consummated by a collectivity in a state of distraction. The laws of its reception are most instructive.

Buildings have been man's companions since primeval times. Many art forms have developed and perished. Tragedy begins with the Greeks, is extinguished with them, and after centuries its 'rules' only are revived. The epic poem, which had its origin in the youth of nations, expires in Europe at the end of the Renaissance. Panel painting is a creation of the Middle Ages, and nothing guarantees its uninterrupted existence. But the human need for shelter is lasting. Architecture has never been idle. Its history is more ancient than that of any other art, and its claim to being a living force has significance in every attempt to comprehend the relationship of the masses today. Buildings are appropriated in a twofold manner: by use and by perception – or rather, by touch and sight. Such appropriation cannot be understood in terms of the attentive concentration of a tourist before a famous building. On the tactile side there is no counterpart to contemplation on the optical side. Tactile appropriation is accomplished not so much by attention as by habit. As regards architecture, habit determines to a large extent even optical reception. The latter, too, occurs much less through rapt attention than by noticing the object in incidental fashion. This mode of appropriation, developed with reference to architecture, in certain circumstances acquires canonical value. For the tasks which face the human apparatus of perception at the turning points of history cannot be solved by optical means, that is, by contemplation, alone. They are mastered gradually by habit, under the guidance of tactile appropriation.

The distracted person, too, can form habits. More, the ability to master certain tasks in a state of distraction proves that their solution has become a matter of habit. Distraction as provided by art presents a covert control of the extent to which new tasks have become soluble by apper-

---

★ Duhamel, *op. cit.*, p. 58.

ception. Since, moreover, individuals are tempted to avoid such tasks, art will tackle the most difficult and most important ones where it is able to mobilize the masses. Today it does so in the film. Reception in a state of distraction, which is increasing noticeably in all fields of art and is symptomatic of profound changes in apperception, finds in the film its true means of exercise. The film with its shock effect meets this mode of reception halfway. The film makes the cult value recede into the background not only by putting the public in the position of the critic, but also by the fact that at the movies this position requires no attention. The public is an examiner, but an absent-minded one.

EPILOGUE

The growing proletarianization of modern man and the increasing formation of masses are two aspects of the same process. Fascism attempts to organize the newly created proletarian masses without affecting the property structure which the masses strive to eliminate. Fascism sees its salvation in giving these masses not their right, but instead a chance to express themselves.[21] The masses have a right to change property relations; Fascism seeks to give them an expression while preserving property. The logical result of Fascism is the introduction of aesthetics into political life. The violation of the masses, whom Fascism, with its *Führer* cult, forces to their knees, has its counterpart in the violation of an apparatus which is pressed into the production of ritual values.

All efforts to render politics aesthetic culminate in one thing: war. War and war only can set a goal for mass movements on the largest scale while respecting the traditional property system. This is the political formula for the situation. The technological formula may be stated as follows: Only war makes it possible to mobilize all of today's technical resources while maintaining the property system. It goes without saying that the Fascist apotheosis of war does not employ such arguments. Still, Marinetti says in his manifesto on the Ethiopian colonial war: 'For twenty-seven years we Futurists have rebelled against the branding of war as antiaesthetic … Accordingly we state: … War is beautiful because it establishes man's dominion over the subjugated machinery by means of gas masks, terrifying megaphones, flame throwers, and small tanks. War is beautiful because it initiates the dreamt-of metallization of the human body. War is beautiful because it enriches a flowering meadow with the fiery orchids of machine guns. War is beautiful because it combines the gunfire, the cannonades, the cease-fire, the scents, and the stench of putrefaction into a symphony. War is beautiful because it creates new architecture, like that of the big tanks, the geometrical formation flights, the smoke spirals from burning villages, and many others … Poets and artists of Futurism! … remember these principles of an aesthetics of war so that your struggle for a new literature and a new graphic art … may be illumined by them!'

This manifesto has the virtue of clarity. Its formulations deserve to be accepted by dialecticians. To the latter, the aesthetics of today's war appears as follows: If the natural utilization of productive forces is impeded by the property system, the increase in technical devices, in speed, and in the sources of energy will press for an unnatural utilization, and this is found in war. The destructiveness of war furnishes proof that society has not been mature enough to incorporate technology as its organ, that technology has not been sufficiently developed to cope with the elemental forces of society. The horrible features of imperialistic warfare are attributable to the discrepancy between the tremendous means of production and their inadequate utilization in the process of production – in other words, to unemployment and the lack of markets. Imperialistic war is a rebellion of technology which collects, in the form of 'human material,' the claims to which society has denied its natural material. Instead of draining rivers, society directs a human stream into a bed of trenches; instead of dropping seeds from airplanes, it drops incendiary bombs over cities; and through gas warfare the aura is abolished in a new way.

'*Fiat ars – pereat mundus*,' says Fascism, and, as Marinetti admits, expects war to supply the artistic gratification of a sense perception that has been changed by technology. This is evidently the consummation of '*l'art pour l'art*.' Mankind, which in Homer's time was an object of contemplation for the Olympian gods, now is one for itself. Its self-alienation has reached such a degree that it can experience its own destruction as an aesthetic pleasure of the first order. This is the situation of politics which Fascism is rendering aesthetic. Communism responds by politicizing art.

Notes

1. Of course, the history of a work of art encompasses more than this. The history of the 'Mona Lisa,' for instance, encompasses the kind and number of its copies made in the 17th, 18th, and 19th centuries.

2. Precisely because authenticity is not reproducible, the intensive penetration of certain (mechanical) processes of reproduction was instrumental in differentiating and grading authenticity. To develop such differentiations was an important function of the trade in works of art. The invention of the woodcut may be said to have struck at the root of the quality of authenticity even before its late flowering. To be sure, at the time of its origin a medieval picture of the Madonna could not yet be said to be 'authentic.' It became 'authentic' only during the succeeding centuries and perhaps most strikingly so during the last one.

3. The poorest provincial staging of *Faust* is superior to a Faust film in that, ideally, it competes with the first performance at Weimar. Before the screen it is unprofitable to remember traditional contents which might come to mind before the stage – for instance, that Goethe's friend Johann Heinrich Merck is hidden in Mephisto, and the like.

4. To satisfy the human interest of the masses may mean to have one's social function removed from the field of vision. Nothing guarantees that a portraitist of today, when painting a famous surgeon at the breakfast table in the midst of his family, depicts his social function more precisely than a painter of the 17th century who portrayed his medical doctors as representing this profession, like Rembrandt in his 'Anatomy Lesson.'

5. The definition of the aura as a 'unique phenomenon of a distance however close it may be' represents nothing but the formulation of the cult value of the work of art in categories of space and time perception. Distance is the opposite of closeness. The essentially distant object is the unapproachable one. Unapproachability is indeed a major quality of the cult image. True to its nature, it remains 'distant, however close it may be.' The closeness which one may gain from its subject matter does not impair the distance, which it retains in its appearance.

6. To the extent to which the cult value of the painting is secularized the ideas of its fundamental uniqueness lose distinctness. In the imagination of the beholder the uniqueness of the phenomena which hold sway in the cult image is more and more displaced by the empirical uniqueness of the creator or of his creative achievement. To be sure, never completely so; the concept of authenticity always transcends mere genuineness. (This is particularly apparent in the collector who always retains some traces of the fetishist and who, by owning the work of art, shares in its ritual power.) Nevertheless, the function of the concept of authenticity remains determinate in the evaluation of art; with the secularization of art, authenticity displaces the cult value of the work.

7. In the case of films, mechanical reproduction is not, as with literature and painting, an external condition for mass distribution. Mechanical reproduction is inherent in the very technique of film production. This technique not only permits in the most direct way but virtually causes mass distribution. It enforces distribution because the production of a film is so expensive that an individual who, for instance, might afford to buy a painting no longer can afford to buy a film. In 1927 it was calculated that a major film, in order to pay its way, had to reach an audience of nine million. With the sound film, to be sure, a setback in its international distribution occurred at first: audiences became limited by language barriers. This coincided with the Fascist emphasis on national interests. It is more important to focus on this connection with Fascism than on this setback, which was soon

minimized by synchronization. The simultaneity of both phenomena is attributable to the depression. The same disturbances which, on a larger scale, led to an attempt to maintain the existing property structure by sheer force led the endangered film capital to speed up the development of the sound film. The introduction of the sound film brought about a temporary relief, not only because it again brought the masses into the theatres but also because it merged new capital from the electrical industry with that of the film industry. Thus, viewed from the outside, the sound film promoted national interests, but seen from the inside it helped to internationalize film production even more than previously.

8. This polarity cannot come into its own in the aesthetics of Idealism. Its idea of beauty comprises these polar opposites without differentiating between them and consequently excludes their polarity. Yet in Hegel this polarity announces itself as clearly as possible within the limits of Idealism. We quote from his *Philosophy of History*:

    > Images were known of old. Piety at an early time required them for worship, but it could do without *beautiful* images. These might even be disturbing. In every beautiful painting there is also something nonspiritual, merely external, but its spirit speaks to man through its beauty. Worshipping, conversely, is concerned with the work as an object, for it is but a spiritless stupor of the soul … Fine art has arisen … in the church …, although it has already gone beyond its principle as art.

    Likewise, the following passage from *The Philosophy of Fine Art* indicates that Hegel sensed a problem here.

    > We are beyond the stage of reverence for works of art as divine and objects deserving our worship. The impression they produce is one of a more reflective kind, and the emotions they arouse require a higher test …
    >
    > – G.W.F. Hegel, *The Philosophy of Fine Art*, trans., with notes, by F.P.B. Osmaston, Vol. 1, p. 12, London, 1920

    The transition from the first kind of artistic reception to the second characterizes the history of artistic reception in general. Apart from that, a certain oscillation between these two polar modes of reception can be demonstrated for each work of art. Take the Sistine Madonna. Since Hubert Grimme's research it has been known that the Madonna originally was painted for the purpose of exhibition. Grimme's research was inspired by the question: What is the purpose of the moulding in the foreground of the painting which the two cupids lean upon? How, Grimme asked further, did Raphael come to furnish the sky with two draperies? Research proved that the Madonna had been commissioned for the public lying-in-state of Pope Sixtus. The Popes lay in state in a certain side chapel of St Peter's. On that occasion Raphael's picture had been fastened in a nichelike background of the chapel, supported by the coffin. In this picture Raphael portrays the Madonna approaching the papal coffin in clouds from the background of the niche, which was demarcated by green drapes. At the obsequies of Sixtus a pre-eminent exhibition value of Raphael's picture was taken advantage of. Some time later it was placed on the high altar in the church of the Black Friars at Piacenza. The reason for this exile is to be found in the Roman rites which forbid the use of paintings exhibited at obsequies as cult objects on the high altar. This regulation devalued Raphael's picture to some degree. In order to obtain an adequate price nevertheless, the Papal See resolved to add to the bargain the tacit toleration of the picture above the high altar. To avoid attention the picture was given to the monks of the far-off provincial town.

9. Bertolt Brecht, on a different level, engaged in analogous reflections: 'If the concept of "work of art" can no longer be applied to the thing that emerges once the work is transformed into a commodity, we have to eliminate this concept with cautious care but without fear, lest we liquidate the function of the very thing as well. For it has to go through this phase without mental reservation, and not as noncommittal deviation from the straight path; rather, what happens here with the work of art will change it fundamentally and erase its past to such an extent that should the old concept be taken up again – and it will, why not? – it will no longer stir any memory of the thing it once designated.'

10. 'The film … provides – or could provide – useful insight into the details of human actions … Character is never used as a source of motivation; the inner life of the persons never supplies the principal cause of the plot and seldom is its main result' (Bertolt Brecht, *Versuche*. 'Der Dreigroschenprozess,' p. 268). The expansion of the field of the testable which mechanical equipment brings about for the actor corresponds to the extraordinary expansion of the field of the testable brought about for the individual through economic conditions. Thus,

vocational aptitude tests become constantly more important. What matters in these tests are segmental performances of the individual. The film shot and the vocational aptitude test are taken before a committee of experts. The camera director in the studio occupies a place identical with that of the examiner during aptitude tests.

11. Rudolf Arnheim, *Film als Kunst*, Berlin, 1932, pp. 176 f. In this context certain seemingly unimportant details in which the film director deviates from stage practices gain in interest. Such is the attempt to let the actor play without make-up, as made among others by Dreyer in his *Jeanne d'Arc*. Dreyer spent months seeking the forty actors who constitute the Inquisitors' tribunal. The search for these actors resembled that for stage properties that are hard to come by. Dreyer made every effort to avoid resemblances of age, build, and physiognomy. If the actor thus becomes a stage property, this latter, on the other hand, frequently functions as actor. At least it is not unusual for the film to assign a role to the stage property. Instead of choosing at random from a great wealth of examples, let us concentrate on a particularly convincing one. A clock that is working will always be a disturbance on the stage. There it cannot be permitted its function of measuring time. Even in a naturalistic play, astronomical time would clash with theatrical time. Under these circumstances it is highly revealing that the film can, whenever appropriate, use time as measured by a clock. From this more than from many other touches it may clearly be recognized that under certain circumstances each and every prop in a film may assume important functions. From here it is but one step to Pudovkin's statement that 'the playing of an actor which is connected with an object and is built around it … is always one of the strongest methods of cinematic construction' (W. Pudovkin, *Filmregie und Filmmanuskript*, Berlin, 1928, p. 126). The film is the first art form capable of demonstrating how matter plays tricks on man. Hence, films can be an excellent means of materialistic representation.

12. The change noted here in the method of exhibition caused by mechanical reproduction applies to politics as well. The present crisis of the bourgeois democracies comprises a crisis of the conditions which determine the public presentation of the rulers. Democracies exhibit a member of government directly and personally before the nation's representatives. Parliament is his public. Since the innovations of camera and recording equipment make it possible for the orator to become audible and visible to an unlimited number of persons, the presentation of the man of politics before camera and recording equipment becomes paramount. Parliaments, as much as theatres, are deserted. Radio and film not only affect the function of the professional actor but likewise the function of those who also exhibit themselves before this mechanical equipment, those who govern. Though their tasks may be different, the change affects equally the actor and the ruler. The trend is toward establishing controllable and transferable skills under certain social conditions. This results in a new selection, a selection before the equipment from which the star and the dictator emerge victorious.

13. The privileged character of the respective techniques is lost. Aldous Huxley writes:

> Advances in technology have led … to vulgarity … Process reproduction and the rotary press have made possible the indefinite multiplication of writing and pictures. Universal education and relatively high wages have created an enormous public who know how to read and can afford to buy reading and pictorial matter. A great industry has been called into existence in order to supply these commodities. Now, artistic talent is a very rare phenomenon; whence it follows … that, at every epoch and in all countries, most art has been bad. But the proportion of trash in this total artistic output is greater now than at any other period. That it must be so is a matter of simple arithmetic. The population of Western Europe has a little more than doubled during the last century. But the amount of reading – and seeing – matter has increased, I should imagine, at least twenty and possibly fifty or even a hundred times. If there were n men of talent in a population of x millions, there will presumably be 2n men of talent among 2x millions. The situation may be summed up thus. For every page of print and pictures published a century ago, twenty or perhaps even a hundred pages are published today. But for every man of talent then living, there are now only two men of talent. It may be of course that, thanks to universal education, many potential talents which in the past would have been stillborn are now enabled to realize themselves. Let us assume, then, that there are now three or even four men of talent to every one of earlier times. It still remains true to say that the consumption of reading – and seeing – matter has far outstripped the natural production of gifted writers and draughtsmen. It is the same with hearing-matter. Prosperity, the gramophone and the radio have created an audience of hearers who consume an amount of hearing-matter that has increased out of all proportion to the increase of population and the consequent natural increase of talented musicians. It follows from all this that in all the arts the output of trash is both absolutely and relatively greater than it was in the past; and that it must remain greater for

just so long as the world continues to consume the present inordinate quantities of reading matter, seeing-matter, and hearing-matter.

– Aldous Huxley, *Beyond the Mexique Bay. A Traveller's Journal*, London, 1949, pp. 274 ff.

First published in 1934.

This mode of observation is obviously not progressive.

14. The boldness of the cameraman is indeed comparable to that of the surgeon. Luc Durtain lists among specific technical sleights of hand those 'which are required in surgery in the case of certain difficult operations. I choose as an example a case of oto-rhinolaryngology; ... the so-called endonasal perspective procedure; or I refer to the acrobatic tricks of larynx surgery which have to be performed following the reversed picture in the laryngo-scope. I might also speak of ear surgery which suggests the precision work of watchmakers. What range of the most subtle muscular acrobatics is required from the man who wants to repair or save the human body! We have only to think of the couching of a cataract where there is virtually a debate of steel with nearly fluid tissue, or of the major abdominal operations (laparotomy)' – Luc Durtain, *op. cit.*

15. This mode of observation may seem crude, but as the great theoretician Leonardo has shown, crude modes of observation may at times be usefully adduced. Leonardo compares painting and music as follows: 'Painting is superior to music because, unlike unfortunate music, it does not have to die as soon as it is born ... Music which is consumed in the very act of its birth is inferior to painting which the use of varnish has rendered eternal' (Trattato I, 29).

16. Renaissance painting offers a revealing analogy to this situation. The incomparable development of this art and its significance rested not least on the integration of a number of new sciences, or at least of new scientific data. Renaissance painting made use of anatomy and perspective, of mathematics, meteorology, and chromatology. Valéry writes: 'What could be further from us than the strange claim of a Leonardo to whom painting was a supreme goal and the ultimate demonstration of knowledge? Leonardo was convinced that painting demanded universal knowledge, and he did not even shrink from a theoretical analysis which to us is stunning because of its very depth and precision ...' – Paul Valéry, *Pièces sur l'art*, 'Autour de Corot,' Paris, p. 191.

17. 'The work of art,' says André Breton, 'is valuable only is so far as it is vibrated by the reflexes of the future.' Indeed, every developed art form intersects three lines of development. Technology works toward a certain form of art. Before the advent of the film there were photo booklets with pictures which flitted by the onlooker upon pressure of the thumb, thus portraying a boxing bout or a tennis match. Then there were the slot machines in bazaars, their picture sequences were produced by the turning of a crank.

Secondly, the traditional art forms in certain phases of their development strenuously work toward effects which later are effortlessly attained by the new ones. Before the rise of the movie the Dadaists' performances tried to create an audience reaction which Chaplin later evoked in a more natural way.

Thirdly, unspectacular social changes often promote a change in receptivity which will benefit the new art form. Before the movie had begun to create its public, pictures that were no longer immobile captivated an assembled audience in the so-called *Kaiserpanorama*. Here the public assembled before a screen into which stereoscopes were mounted, one to each beholder. By a mechanical process individual pictures appeared briefly before the stereoscopes, then made way for others. Edison still had to use similar devices in presenting the first movie strip before the film screen and projection were known. This strip was presented to a small public which stared into the apparatus in which the succession of pictures was reeling off. Incidentally, the institution of the *Kaiserpanorama* shows very clearly a dialectic of the development. Shortly before the movie turned the reception of pictures into a collective one, the individual viewing of pictures in these swiftly outmoded establishments came into play once more with an intensity comparable to that of the ancient priest beholding the statue of a divinity in the cella.

18. The theological archetype of this contemplation is the awareness of being alone with one's God. Such awareness, in the heyday of the bourgeoisie, went to strengthen the freedom to shake off clerical tutelage. During the decline of the bourgeoisie this awareness had to take into account the hidden tendency to withdraw from public affairs those forces which the individual draws upon in his communion with God.

19. The film is the art form that is in keeping with the increased threat to his life which modern man has to face. Man's need to expose himself to shock effects is his adjustment to the dangers threatening him. The film corre-sponds to profound changes in the apperceptive apparatus – changes that are experienced on an individual scale by the man in the street in big-city traffic, on a historical scale by every present-day citizen.

20. As for Dadaism, insights important for Cubism and Futurism are to be gained from the movie. Both appear as deficient attempts of art to accommodate the pervasion of reality by the apparatus. In contrast to the film, these schools did not try to use the apparatus as such for the artistic presentation of reality, but aimed at some sort of alloy in the joint presentation of reality and apparatus. In Cubism, the premonition that this apparatus will be structurally based on optics plays a dominant part; in Futurism, it is the premonition of the effects of this apparatus which are brought out by the rapid sequence of the film strip.

21. One technical feature is significant here, especially with regard to newsreels, the propagandist importance of which can hardly be overestimated. Mass reproduction is aided especially by the reproduction of masses. In big parades and monster rallies, in sports events, and in war, all of which nowadays are captured by camera and sound recording, the masses are brought face to face with themselves. This process, whose significance need not be stressed, is intimately connected with the development of the techniques of reproduction and photography. Mass movements are usually discerned more clearly by a camera than by the naked eye. A bird's-eye view best captures gatherings of hundreds of thousands. And even though such a view may be as accessible to the human eye as it is to the camera, the image received by the eye cannot be enlarged the way a negative is enlarged. This means that mass movements, including war, constitute a form of human behaviour which particularly favours mechanical equipment.

3.10 The Street Scene (1938)

A Basic Model for an Epic Theatre

BERTOLT BRECHT

Translated by John Willett

IN THE DECADE AND a half that followed the World War a comparatively new way of acting was tried out in a number of German theatres. Its qualities of clear description and reporting and its use of choruses and projections as a means of commentary earned it the name of 'epic'. The actor used a somewhat complex technique to detach himself from the character portrayed; he forced the spectator to look at the play's situations from such an angle that they necessarily became subject to his criticism. Supporters of this epic theatre argued that the new subject-matter, the highly involved incidents of the class war in its acutest and most terrible stage, would be mastered more easily by such a method, since it would thereby become possible to portray social processes as seen in their causal relationships. But the result of these experiments was that aesthetics found itself up against a whole series of substantial difficulties.

It is comparatively easy to set up a basic model for epic theatre. For practical experiments I usually picked as my example of completely simple, 'natural' epic theatre an incident such as can be seen at any street corner: an eyewitness demonstrating to a collection of people how a traffic accident took place. The bystanders may not have observed what happened, or they may simply not agree with him, may 'see things a different way'; the point is that the demonstrator acts the behaviour of driver or victim or both in such a way that the bystanders are able to form an opinion about the accident.

Such an example of the most primitive type of epic theatre seems easy to understand. Yet experience has shown that it presents astounding difficulties to the reader or listener as soon as he is asked to see the implications of treating this kind of street-corner demonstration as a basic form of major theatre, theatre for a scientific age. What this means of course is that the epic theatre may appear richer, more intricate and complex in every particular, yet to be major theatre it need at bottom only contain the same elements as a street-corner demonstration of this sort; nor could it any longer be termed epic theatre if any of the main elements of the street-corner demonstration were lacking. Until this is understood it is impossible really to understand what follows. Until one understands the novelty, unfamiliarity and direct challenge to the critical faculties of the suggestion that street-corner demonstration of this sort can serve as a satisfactory basic model of major theatre one cannot really understand what follows.

Consider: the incident is clearly very far from what we mean by an artistic one. The demonstrator need not be an artist. The capacities he needs to achieve his aim are in effect universal. Suppose he cannot carry out some particular movement as quickly as the victim he is imitating; all he need do is to explain that *he* moves three times as fast, and the demonstration neither suffers in essentials nor loses its point. On the contrary it is important that he should not be too perfect. His demonstration would be spoilt if the bystanders' attention were drawn to his powers of transformation. He has to avoid presenting himself in such a way that someone calls out 'What a lifelike portrayal of a chauffeur!' He must not 'cast a spell' over anyone. He should not transport people from normality to 'higher realms'. He need not dispose of any special powers of suggestion.

It is most important that one of the main features of the ordinary theatre should be excluded from our street scene: the engendering of illusion. The street demonstrator's performance is essentially repetitive. The event has taken place; what you are seeing now is a repeat. If the scene in the theatre follows the street scene in this respect then the theatre will stop pretending not to be theatre, just as the street-corner demonstration admits it is a demonstration (and does not pretend to be the actual event). The element of rehearsal in the acting and of learning by heart in the text, the whole machinery and the whole process of preparation: it all becomes plainly apparent. What room is left for experience? Is the reality portrayed still experienced in any sense?

The street scene determines what kind of experience is to be prepared for the spectator. There is no question but that the street-corner demonstrator has been through an 'experience', but he is not out to make his demonstration serve as an 'experience' for the audience. Even the experience of the driver and the victim is only partially communicated by him, and he by no means tries to turn it into an enjoyable experience for the spectator, however lifelike he may make his demonstration. The demonstration would become no less valid if he did not reproduce the fear caused by the accident; on the contrary it would lose validity if he did. He is not interested in creating pure emotions. It is important to understand that a theatre which follows his lead in this respect undergoes a positive change of function.

One essential element of the street scene must also be present in the theatrical scene if this is to qualify as epic, namely that the demonstration should have a socially practical significance. Whether our street demonstrator is out to show that one attitude on the part of driver or pedestrian makes an accident inevitable where another would not, or whether he is demonstrating with a view to fixing the responsibility, his demonstration has a practical purpose, intervenes socially.

The demonstrator's purpose determines how thoroughly he has to imitate. Our demonstrator need not imitate every aspect of his characters' behaviour, but only so much as gives a picture. Generally the theatre scene will give much fuller pictures, corresponding to its more extensive range of interest. How do street scene and theatre scene link up here? To take a point of detail, the victim's voice may have played no immediate part in the accident. Eye-witnesses may disagree as to whether a cry they heard ('Look out!') came from the victim or from someone else, and this may give our demonstrator a motive for imitating the voice. The question can be settled by demonstrating whether the voice was an old man's or a woman's, or merely whether it was high or low. Again, the answer may depend on whether it was that of an educated person or not. Loud or soft may play a great part, as the driver could be correspondingly more or less guilty. A whole series of characteristics of the victim ask to be portrayed. Was he absent-minded? Was his attention distracted? If so, by what? What, on the evidence of his behaviour, could have made him liable to be distracted by just that circumstance and no other? Etc., etc. It can be seen that our street-corner demonstration provides opportunities for a pretty rich and varied portrayal of human types. Yet a theatre which tries to restrict its essential elements to those provided by our street scene will have to acknowledge certain limits to imitation. It must be able to justify any outlay in terms of its purpose.[1]

The demonstration may for instance be dominated by the question of compensation for the victim, etc. The driver risks being sacked from his job, losing his licence, going to prison; the victim risks a heavy hospital bill, loss of job, permanent disfigurement, possibly unfitness for work. This is the area within which the demonstrator builds up his characters. The victim may have had a companion; the driver may have had his girl sitting alongside him. That would bring out the social element better and allow the characters to be more fully drawn.

Another essential element in the street scene is that the demonstrator should derive his characters entirely from their actions. He imitates their actions and so allows conclusions to be drawn about them. A theatre that follows him in this will be largely breaking with the orthodox theatre's habit of basing the actions on the characters and having the former exempted from criticism by presenting them as an unavoidable consequence deriving by natural law from the characters who perform them. To the street demonstrator the character of the man being demonstrated remains a quantity that need not be completely defined. Within certain limits he may be like this or like that; it doesn't matter. What the demonstrator is concerned with are his accident-prone and accident-proof qualities.[2] The theatrical scene may show more fully-defined individuals. But it must then be in a position to treat their individuality as a special case and outline the field within which, once more, its most socially relevant effects are produced. Our street demonstrator's possibilities of demonstration are narrowly restricted (indeed, we chose this model so that the limits should be as narrow as possible). If the essential elements of the theatrical scene are limited to those of the street scene then its greater richness must be an enrichment only. The question of border-line cases becomes acute.

Let us take a specific detail. Can our street demonstrator, say, ever become entitled to use an excited tone of voice in repeating the driver's statement that he has been exhausted by too long a spell of work? (In theory this is no more possible than for a returning messenger to start telling his fellow-countrymen of his talk with the king with the words 'I saw the bearded king'.) It can only be possible, let alone unavoidable, if one imagines a street-corner situation where such excitement, specifically about this aspect of the affair, plays a particular part. (In the instance above this would be so if the king had sworn never to cut his beard off until ... etc.) We have to find a point of view for our demonstrator that allows him to submit this excitement to criticism. Only if he adopts a quite definite point of view can he be entitled to imitate the driver's excited voice; e.g. if he blames drivers as such for doing too little to reduce their hours of work. ('Look at him. Doesn't even belong to a union, but gets worked up soon enough when an accident happens. "Ten hours I've been at the wheel."')

Before it can get as far as this, i.e. be able to suggest a point of view to the actor, the theatre needs to take a number of steps. By widening its field of vision and showing the driver in other situations besides that of the accident the theatre in no way exceeds its model; it merely creates a further situation on the same pattern. One can imagine a scene of the same kind as the street scene which provides a well-argued demonstration showing how such emotions as the driver's develop, or another which involves making comparisons between tones of voice. In order not to exceed the model scene the theatre only has to develop a technique for submitting emotions to the spectator's criticism. Of course this does not mean that the spectator must be barred on principle from sharing certain emotions that are put before him; none the less to communicate emotions is only one particular form (phase, consequence) of criticism. The theatre's demonstrator, the actor, must apply a technique which will let him reproduce the tone of the subject demonstrated with a certain reserve, with detachment (so that the spectator can say: 'He's getting excited – in vain, too late, at last. . . .' etc.). In short, the actor must remain a demonstrator; he must present the person demonstrated as a stranger, he must not suppress the '*he* did that, *he* said that' element in his performance. He must not go so far as to be wholly transformed into the person demonstrated.

One essential element of the street scene lies in the natural attitude adopted by the demonstrator, which is two-fold; he is always taking two situations into account. He behaves naturally as a demonstrator, and he lets the subject of the demonstration behave naturally too. He never forgets, nor does he allow it to be forgotten, that he is not the subject but the demonstrator. That is to say, what the audience sees is not a fusion between demonstrator and subject, not some third, independent, uncontradictory entity with isolated features of (a) demonstrator and (b) subject, such as the orthodox theatre puts before us in its productions.[3] The feelings and opinions of demonstrator and demonstrated are not merged into one.

We now come to one of those elements that are peculiar to the epic theatre, the so-called A-effect (alienation effect). What is involved here is, briefly, a technique of taking the human social incidents to be portrayed and labelling them as something striking, something that calls for explanation, is not to be taken for granted, not just natural. The object of this 'effect' is to allow the spectator to criticize constructively from a social point of view. Can we show that this A-effect is significant for our street demonstrator?

We can picture what happens if he fails to make use of it. The following situation could occur. One of the spectators might say: 'But if the victim stepped off the kerb with his right foot, as you showed him doing. . . .' The demonstrator might interrupt saying: 'I showed him stepping off with his left foot.' By arguing which foot he really stepped off with in his demonstration, and, even more, how the victim himself acted, the demonstration can be so transformed that the A-effect occurs. The demonstrator achieves it by paying exact attention this time to his movements, executing them carefully, probably in slow motion; in this way he alienates the little sub-incident, emphasizes its importance, makes it worthy of notice. And so the epic theatre's alienation effect proves to have its uses for our street demonstrator too; in other words it is also to be found in this small everyday scene of natural street-corner theatre, which has little to do with art. The direct changeover from representation to commentary that is so characteristic of the epic theatre is still more easily recognized as one element of any street demonstration. Wherever he feels he can the demonstrator breaks off his imitation in order to give explanations. The epic theatre's choruses and documentary projections, the direct addressing of the audience by its actors, are at bottom just this.

It will have been observed, not without astonishment I hope, that I have not named any strictly artistic elements as characterizing our street scene and, with it, that of the epic theatre. The street demonstrator can carry out a successful demonstration with no greater abilities than, in effect, anybody has. What about the epic theatre's value as art?

The epic theatre wants to establish its basic model at the street corner, i.e. to return to the very simplest 'natural' theatre, a social enterprise whose origins, means and ends are practical and earthly. The model works without any need of programmatic theatrical phrases like 'the urge to self-expression', 'making a part one's own', 'spiritual experience', 'the play instinct', 'the storyteller's art', etc. Does that mean that the epic theatre isn't concerned with art?

It might be as well to begin by putting the question differently, thus: can we make use of artistic abilities for the purposes of our street scene? Obviously yes. Even the street-corner demonstration includes artistic elements. Artistic abilities in some small degree are to be found in any man. It does no harm to remember this when one is confronted with great art. Undoubtedly what we call artistic abilities can be exercised at any time within the limits imposed by our street scene model. They will function as artistic abilities even though they do not exceed these limits (for instance, when there is meant to be no complete transformation of demonstrator into subject). And true enough, the epic theatre is an extremely artistic affair, hardly thinkable without artists and virtuosity, imagination, humour and fellow-feeling; it cannot be practised without all these and much else too. It has got to be entertaining, it has got to be instructive. How then can art be developed out of the elements of the street scene, without adding any or leaving any out? How does it evolve into the theatrical scene with its fabricated story, its trained actors, its lofty style of speaking, its make-up, its team performance by a number of players? Do we need to add to our elements in order to move on from the 'natural' demonstration to the 'artificial'?

Is it not true that the additions which we must make to our model in order to arrive at epic theatre are of a fundamental kind? A brief examination will show that they are not. Take the *story*. There was nothing fabricated about our street accident. Nor does the orthodox theatre deal only in fabrications; think for instance of the historical play. None the less a story can be performed at the street corner too. Our demonstrator may at any time be in a position to say: 'The driver was guilty, because it all happened the way I showed you. He wouldn't be guilty if it had happened the way I'm going to show you now.' And he can fabricate an incident and demonstrate it. Or take the fact that the text is learnt by heart. As a witness in a court case the demonstrator may have written down the subject's exact words, learnt them by heart and rehearsed them; in that case he too is performing a text he has learned. Or take a rehearsed programme by several players: it doesn't always have to be artistic purposes that bring about a demonstration of this sort; one need only think of the French police technique of making the chief figures in any criminal case re-enact certain crucial situations before a police audience. Or take making-up. Minor changes in appearance – ruffling one's hair, for instance – can occur at any time within the framework of the non-artistic type of demonstration. Nor is make-up itself used solely for theatrical purposes. In the street scene the driver's moustache may be particularly significant. It may have influenced the testimony of the possible girl companion suggested earlier. This can be represented by our demonstrator making the driver stroke an imaginary moustache when prompting his companion's evidence. In this way the demonstrator can do a good deal to discredit her as a witness. Moving on to the use of a real moustache in the theatre, however, is not an entirely easy transition, and the same difficulty occurs with respect to *costume*. Our demonstrator may under given circumstances put on the driver's cap – for instance if he wants to show that he was drunk (he had it on crooked) – but he can only do so conditionally, under these circumstances (see what was said about borderline cases earlier). However, where there is a demonstration by several demonstrators of the kind referred to above we can have costume so that the various characters can be distinguished. This again is only a limited use of costume. There must be no question of creating an illusion that the demonstrators really are these characters. (The epic theatre can counteract this illusion by especially exaggerated costume or by garments that are somehow marked out as objects for display.) Moreover we can suggest another model as a substitute for ours on this point: the kind of street demonstration given by hawkers. To sell their neckties these people will portray a badly dressed and a well-dressed man; with a few props and technical tricks they can perform significant little scenes where they submit essentially to the same restrictions as apply to the demonstrator in our street scene (they will pick up tie, hat, stick, gloves and give certain significant imitations of a man of the world, and the whole time they will refer to him as '*he*'!). With hawkers we also find *verse* being used within the same framework as that of our basic model. They use firm irregular rhythms to sell braces and newspapers alike.

Reflecting along these lines we see that our basic model will work. The elements of natural and of artificial epic theatre are the same. Our street-corner theatre is primitive; origins, aims and methods of its performance are close to home. But there is no doubt that it is a meaningful phenomenon with a clear social function that dominates all its elements. The performance's origins lie in an incident that can be judged one way or another, that may repeat itself in different forms and is not finished but is bound to have consequences, so that this judgment has some significance. The object of the performance is to make it easier to give an opinion on the incident. Its means correspond to that. The epic theatre is a highly skilled theatre with complex contents and far-reaching social objectives. In setting up the street scene as a basic model for it we pass on the clear social function and give the epic theatre criteria by which to decide whether an incident is meaningful or not. The basic model has a practical significance. As producer and actors work to build up a performance involving many difficult questions – technical problems, social ones – it allows them to check whether the social function of the whole apparatus is still clearly intact.

Notes

1. We often come across demonstrations of an everyday sort which are more thorough imitations than our street-corner accident demands. Generally they are comic ones. Our next-door neighbour may decide to 'take off' the rapacious behaviour of our common landlord. Such an imitation is often rich and full of variety. Closer examination will show, however, that even so apparently complex an imitation concentrates on one specific side of the landlord's behaviour. The imitation is summary or selective, deliberately leaving out those occasions where the landlord strikes our neighbour as 'perfectly sensible', though such occasions of course occur. He is far from giving a rounded picture; for that would have no comic impact at all. The street scene, perforce adopting a wider angle of vision, at this point lands in difficulties which must not be underestimated. It has to be just as successful in promoting criticism, but the incidents in question are far more complex. It must promote positive as well as negative criticism, and as part of a single process. You have to understand what is involved in winning the audience's approval by means of a critical approach. Here again we have a precedent in our street scene, i.e. in any demonstration of an everyday sort. Next-door neighbour and street demonstrator can reproduce their subject's 'sensible' or his 'senseless' behaviour alike, by submitting it for an opinion. When it crops up in the course of events, however (when a man switches from being sensible to being senseless, or the other way round), then they usually need some form of commentary in order to change the angle of their portrayal. Hence, as already mentioned, certain difficulties for the theatre scene. These cannot be dealt with here.
2. The same situation will be produced by all those people whose characters fulfil the conditions laid down by him and show the features that he imitates.
3. Most clearly worked out by Stanislavsky.

This translation was originally published in Bertolt Brecht, *Brecht on Theatre*, trans. John Willett, London: Methuen, 1973 [1957], pp. 121–9.

3.11 Theatre for Pleasure or Theatre for Instruction (*c.* 1936)

BERTOLT BRECHT

Translated by John Willett

A FEW YEARS BACK, anybody talking about the modern theatre meant the theatre in Moscow, New York and Berlin. He might have thrown in a mention of one of Jouvet's productions in Paris or Cochran's in London, or *The Dybbuk* as given by the Habima (which is to all intents and purposes part of the Russian theatre, since Vakhtangov was its director). But broadly speaking there were only three capitals so far as modern theatre was concerned.

Russian, American and German theatres differed widely from one another, but were alike in being modern, that is to say in introducing technical and artistic innovations. In a sense they even achieved a certain stylistic resemblance, probably because technology is international (not just that part which is directly applied to the stage but also that which influences it, the film for instance), and because large progressive cities in large industrial countries are involved. Among the older capitalist countries it is the Berlin theatre that seemed of late to be in the lead. For a period all that is common to the modern theatre received its strongest and (so far) maturest expression there.

The Berlin theatre's last phase was the so-called epic theatre, and it showed the modern theatre's trend of development in its purest form. Whatever was labelled '*Zeitstück*' or '*Piscatorbühne*' or '*Lehrstück*' belongs to the epic theatre.

The epic theatre

Many people imagine that the term 'epic theatre' is self-contradictory, as the epic and dramatic ways of narrating a story are held, following Aristotle, to be basically distinct. The difference between the two forms was never thought simply to lie in the fact that the one is performed by living beings while the other operates via the written word; epic works such as those of Homer and the medieval singers were at the same time theatrical performances, while dramas like Goethe's *Faust* and Byron's *Manfred* are agreed to have been more effective as books. Thus even by Aristotle's definition the difference between the dramatic and epic forms was attributed to their different methods of construction, whose laws were dealt with by two different branches of aesthetics. The method of construction depended on the different way of presenting the work to the public, sometimes via the stage, sometimes through a book; and independently of that there was the 'dramatic element' in epic works and the 'epic element' in dramatic. The bourgeois novel in the last century developed much that was 'dramatic', by which was meant the strong centralization of the story, a momentum that drew the separate parts into a common relationship. A particular passion of utterance, a certain emphasis on the clash of forces are hallmarks of the 'dramatic'. The epic writer Döblin provided an excellent criterion when he said that with an epic work, as opposed to a dramatic, one can as it were take a pair of scissors and cut it into individual pieces, which remain fully capable of life.

This is no place to explain how the opposition of epic and dramatic lost its rigidity after having long been held to be irreconcilable. Let us just point out that the technical advances alone were enough to permit the stage to incorporate an element of narrative in its dramatic productions. The possibility of projections, the greater adaptability of the stage due to mechanization, the film, all completed the theatre's equipment, and did so at a point where the most important transactions between people could no longer be shown simply by personifying the motive forces or subjecting the characters to invisible metaphysical powers.

To make these transactions intelligible the environment in which the people lived had to be brought to bear in a big and 'significant' way.

This environment had of course been shown in the existing drama, but only as seen from the central figure's point of view, and not as an independent element. It was defined by the hero's reactions to it. It was seen as a storm can be seen when one sees the ships on a sheet of water unfolding their sails, and the sails filling out. In the epic theatre it was to appear standing on its own.

The stage began to tell a story. The narrator was no longer missing, along with the fourth wall. Not only did the background adopt an attitude to the events on the stage – by big screens recalling other simultaneous events elsewhere, by projecting documents which confirmed or contradicted what the characters said, by concrete and intelligible figures to accompany abstract conversations, by figures and sentences to support mimed transactions whose sense was unclear – but the actors too refrained from going over wholly into their role, remaining detached from the character they were playing and clearly inviting criticism of him.

The spectator was no longer in any way allowed to submit to an experience uncritically (and without practical consequences) by means of simple empathy with the characters in a play. The production took the subject-matter and the incidents shown and put them through a process of alienation: the alienation that is necessary to all understanding. When something seems 'the most obvious thing in the world' it means that any attempt to understand the world has been given up.

What is 'natural' must have the force of what is startling. This is the only way to expose the laws of cause and effect. People's activity must simultaneously be so and be capable of being different.

It was all a great change.

The dramatic theatre's spectator says: Yes, I have felt like that too – Just like me – It's only natural – It'll never change – The sufferings of this man appall me, because they are inescapable – That's great art; it all seems the most obvious thing in the world – I weep when they weep, I laugh when they laugh.

The epic theatre's spectator says: I'd never have thought it – That's not the way – That's extraordinary, hardly believable – It's got to stop – The sufferings of this man appall me, because they are unnecessary – That's great art: nothing obvious in it – I laugh when they weep, I weep when they laugh.

The instructive theatre

The stage began to be instructive.

Oil, inflation, war, social struggles, the family, religion, wheat, the meat market, all became subjects for theatrical representation. Choruses enlightened the spectator about facts unknown to him. Films showed a montage of events from all over the world. Projections added statistical material. And as the 'background' came to the front of the stage so people's activity was subjected to criticism. Right and wrong courses of action were shown. People were shown who knew what they were doing, and others who did not. The theatre became an affair for philosophers, but only for such philosophers as wished not just to explain the world but also to change it. So we had philosophy, and we had instruction. And where was the amusement in all that? Were they sending us back to school, teaching us to read and write? Were we supposed to pass exams, work for diplomas?

Generally there is felt to be a very sharp distinction between learning and amusing oneself. The first may be useful, but only the second is pleasant. So we have to defend the epic theatre against the suspicion that it is a highly disagreeable, humourless, indeed strenuous affair.

Well: all that can be said is that the contrast between learning and amusing oneself is not laid down by divine rule; it is not one that has always been and must continue to be.

Undoubtedly there is much that is tedious about the kind of learning familiar to us from school, from our professional training, etc. But it must be remembered under what conditions and to what end that takes place.

It is really a commercial transaction. Knowledge is just a commodity. It is acquired in order to be resold. All those who have grown out of going to school have to do their learning virtually in secret, for anyone who admits that he still has something to learn devalues himself as a man whose knowledge is inadequate. Moreover the usefulness of learning is very much limited by factors outside the learner's control. There is unemployment, for instance, against which no knowledge can protect one. There is the division of labour, which makes generalized knowledge unnecessary and impossible. Learning is often among the concerns of those whom no amount of concern will get any forwarder. There is not much knowledge that leads to power, but plenty of knowledge to which only power can lead.

Learning has a very different function for different social strata. There are strata who cannot imagine any improvement in conditions: they find the conditions good enough for them. Whatever happens to oil they will benefit from it. And: they feel the years beginning to tell. There can't be all that many years more. What is the point of learning a lot now? They have said their final word: a grunt. But there are also strata 'waiting their turn' who are discontented with conditions, have a vast interest in the practical side of learning, want at all costs to find out where they stand, and know that they are lost without learning; these are the best and keenest learners. Similar differences apply to countries and peoples. Thus the pleasure of learning depends on all sorts of things; but none the less there is such a thing as pleasurable learning, cheerful and militant learning.

If there were not such amusement to be had from learning the theatre's whole structure would unfit it for teaching.

Theatre remains theatre even when it is instructive theatre, and in so far as it is good theatre it will amuse.

Theatre and knowledge

But what has knowledge got to do with art? We know that knowledge can be amusing, but not everything that is amusing belongs in the theatre.

I have often been told, when pointing out the invaluable services that modern knowledge and science, if properly applied, can perform for art and specially for the theatre, that art and knowledge are two estimable but wholly distinct fields of human activity. This is a fearful truism, of course, and it is as well to agree quickly that, like most truisms, it is perfectly true. Art and science work in quite different ways: agreed. But, bad as it may sound, I have to admit that I cannot get along as an artist without the use of one or two sciences. This may well arouse serious doubts as to my artistic capacities. People are used to seeing poets as unique and slightly unnatural beings who reveal with a truly godlike assurance things that other people can only recognize after much sweat and toil. It is naturally distasteful to have to admit that one does not belong to this select band. All the same, it must be admitted. It must at the same time be made clear that the scientific occupations just confessed to are not pardonable side interests, pursued on days off after a good week's work. We all know how Goethe was interested in natural history, Schiller in history: as a kind of hobby, it is charitable to assume. I have no wish promptly to accuse these two of having needed these sciences for their poetic activity; I am not trying to shelter behind them; but I must say that I do need the sciences. I have to admit, however, that I look askance at all sorts of people who I know do not operate on the level of scientific understanding: that is to say, who sing as the birds sing, or as people imagine the birds to sing. I don't mean by that that I would reject a charming poem about the taste of fried fish or the delights of a boating party just because the writer had not studied gastronomy or navigation. But in my view the great and complicated things that go on in the world cannot be adequately recognized by people who do not use every possible aid to understanding.

Let us suppose that great passions or great events have to be shown which influence the fate of nations. The lust for power is nowadays held to be such a passion. Given that a poet 'feels' this lust and wants to have someone strive for power, how is he to show the exceedingly complicated machinery within which the struggle for power nowadays takes place? If his hero is a politician, how do politics work? If he is a business man, how does business work? And yet there are writers who find business and politics nothing like so passionately interesting as the individual's lust for power. How are they to acquire the necessary knowledge? They are scarcely likely to learn enough by going round and keeping their eyes open, though even then it is more than they would get by just rolling their eyes in an exalted frenzy. The foundation of a paper like the *Völkischer Beobachter* or a business like Standard Oil is a pretty complicated affair, and such things cannot be conveyed just like that. One important field for the playwright is psychology. It is taken for granted that a poet, if not an ordinary man, must be able without further instruction to discover the motives that lead a man to commit murder; he must be able to give a picture of a murderer's mental state 'from within himself'. It is taken for granted that one only has to look inside oneself in such a case; and then there's always one's imagination. ... There are various reasons why I can no longer surrender to this agreeable hope of getting a result quite so simply. I can no longer find in myself all those motives which the press or scientific reports show to have been observed in people. Like the average judge when pronouncing sentence, I cannot without further ado conjure up an adequate picture of a murderer's mental state. Modern psychology, from psychoanalysis to behaviourism, acquaints me with facts that lead me to judge the case quite differently, especially if I bear in mind the findings of sociology and do not overlook economics and history. You will say: but that's getting complicated. I have to answer that it *is* complicated. Even if you let yourself be convinced, and agree with me that a large slice of literature is exceedingly primitive, you may still ask with profound concern: won't an evening in such a theatre be a most alarming affair? The answer to that is: no.

Whatever knowledge is embodied in a piece of poetic writing has to be wholly transmuted into poetry. Its utilization fulfils the very pleasure that the poetic element provokes. If it does not at the same time fulfil that which is fulfilled by the scientific element, none the less in an age of great discoveries and inventions one must have a certain inclination to penetrate deeper into things – a desire to make the world controllable – if one is to to be sure of enjoying its poetry.

Is the epic theatre some kind of 'moral institution'?

According to Friedrich Schiller the theatre is supposed to be a moral institution. In making this demand it hardly occurred to Schiller that by moralizing from the stage he might drive the audience out of the theatre. Audiences had no objection to moralizing in his day. It was only later that Friedrich Nietzsche attacked him for blowing a moral trumpet. To Nietzsche any concern with morality was a depressing affair; to Schiller it seemed thoroughly enjoyable. He knew of nothing that could give greater amusement and satisfaction than the propagation of ideas. The bourgeoisie was setting about forming the ideas of the nation.

Putting one's house in order, patting oneself on the back, submitting one's account, is something highly agreeable. But describing the collapse of one's house, having pains in the back, paying one's account, is indeed a depressing affair, and that was how Friedrich Nietzsche saw things a century later. He was poorly disposed towards morality, and thus towards the previous Friedrich too.

The epic theatre was likewise often objected to as moralizing too much. Yet in the epic theatre moral arguments only took second place. Its aim was less to moralize than to observe. That is to say it observed, and then the thick end of the wedge followed: the story's moral. Of course we cannot pretend that we started our observations out of a pure passion for observing and without any more practical motive, only to be completely staggered by their results. Undoubtedly there were some painful discrepancies in our environment, circumstances that were barely tolerable, and this not merely on account of moral considerations. It is not only moral considerations that make hunger, cold and oppression hard to bear. Similarly the object of our inquiries was not just to arouse moral objections to such circumstances (even though they could easily be felt – though not by all the audience alike; such objections were seldom for instance felt by those who profited by the circumstances in question) but to discover means for their elimination. We were not in fact speaking in the name of morality but in that of the victims. These truly are two distinct matters, for the victims are often told that they ought to be contented with their lot, for moral reasons. Moralists of this sort see man as existing for morality, not morality for man. At least it should be possible to gather from the above to what degree and in what sense the epic theatre is a moral institution.

Can epic theatre be played anywhere?

Stylistically speaking, there is nothing all that new about the epic theatre. Its expository character and its emphasis on virtuosity bring it close to the old Asiatic theatre. Didactic tendencies are to be found in the medieval mystery plays and the classical Spanish theatre, and also in the theatre of the Jesuits.

These theatrical forms corresponded to particular trends of their time, and vanished with them. Similarly the modern epic theatre is linked with certain trends. It cannot by any means be practised universally. Most of the great nations today are not disposed to use the theatre for ventilating their problems. London, Paris, Tokyo and Rome maintain their theatres for quite different purposes. Up to now favourable circumstances for an epic and didactic theatre have only been found in a few places and for a short period of time. In Berlin Fascism put a very definite stop to the development of such a theatre.

It demands not only a certain technological level but a powerful movement in society which is interested to see vital questions freely aired with a view to their solution, and can defend this interest against every contrary trend.

The epic theatre is the broadest and most far-reaching attempt at large-scale modern theatre, and it has all those immense difficulties to overcome that always confront the vital forces in the sphere of politics, philosophy, science and art.

Note

This translation was originally published in Bertolt Brecht, *Brecht on Theatre*, trans. John Willett, London: Methuen, 1978, pp. 69–76.

3.12 On Political Theatre (1975)

MICHAEL KIRBY

I**S ALL THEATRE POLITICAL?** Some people claim that it is. To some extent, this view is based upon a misunderstanding of the word 'political.' Webster defines 'political' as:

1. of or concerned with government, the state, or politics.
2. having a definite governmental organization.
3. engaged in or taking sides in politics; as *political* parties.
4. of or characteristic of political parties or politicians: as *political* pressure.

These definitions may help us to understand the nature of political theatre, but they do not apply to all theatrical activity.

Some of the people who claim that all theatre is political seem to confuse 'political,' 'social,' and 'economic.' Of course, all theatre exists in a certain socio-economic context. By definition, it involves an audience; it is not a solitary activity. But this does not mean that it necessarily is concerned with government or that it must take sides in politics. The psychological elements and interpersonal relationships of, say, *A Streetcar Named Desire* may be magnified into social statements. Blanche may become in someone's mind the representative of a social class. But this does not give us a play 'Of or concerned with government.' If *The Lower Depths* were a political indictment, it would not have been performed under the Czarist government. Most plays make no political statement.

Indeed, a basic functional independence of theatre and politics can be illustrated by certain indigenous performances that have remained unchanged for many years under various political parties, systems, and orders. Although government and politics may be useful to man as a social animal, they are not inevitable or always necessary. Many activities – a couple making love, a card game among friends, a doctor performing an operation, etc. – are not inherently related to politics. There is no reason why theatre should be.

Webster's definitions of 'political' stress active intent. Theatre is political if it is *concerned with* the state or *takes sides* in politics. This allows us to define 'political theatre' in a way that distinguishes it from other kinds of theatre: it is a performance that is intentionally concerned with government, that is intentionally engaged in or consciously takes sides in politics. Although intentionality is a subjective state, there is no problem in using it as a defining factor. Communication is, of course, imperfect. An artist may not achieve all of his specific, subtle, and half-conscious goals, but his intent is not apt to be misunderstood. If a theatre piece is intended to be political and the intent is not perceived, there is no need to categorize it as 'political theatre.' Thus, if a presentation does not attempt to be political, it is not political.

Of course, certain situations and certain governments may force all theatre to be political. It can be an external rather than an internal decision. Censorship is a good example of this. By passing laws about theatre, a government may create a relationship between itself and all performance. But a performance is political – it is 'of' the government – only as it relates to such laws. Generally, theatre is political only to the extent that it attempts to be political. Most theatre has no concern for or interest in politics.

Political theatre is intellectual theatre. It deals with political ideas and concepts, usually in an attempt to attack or support a particular political position. It is literary theatre, not because it necessarily involves words and/or a script but because all production elements are subservient to, support, and reinforce the symbolic meanings. Political meaning is 'read' by the spectator.

Political theatre does not merely deal with government as a passive subject. It makes explicit reference to contemporary governmental problems and issues. It is intellectually dynamic. Thus, *Oedipus* and *Hamlet* are not political plays merely because their protagonists are sovereigns. Hypothetically, of course, any script can be given a political production; on the other hand, a political script may lose its dynamic political quality with the passing of time. An anti-war play like Sheriff's *Journey's End* was not political – although it could be considered moralistic – when it was produced in New York in the 1928–29 season.

Some people, however, are able to relate any performance to the government or the state in their own minds. They interpret theatre politically. Such interpretation depends upon the person doing the interpretation; it is not inherent in the work. Any belief system – a religion, a social or psychological schema – may be projected onto a presentation. For example, anything created by man can be interpreted according to Freud's concepts as a revelation of the unconscious. Would it be helpful or useful, then, if we referred to all drama as 'psychoanalytical theatre'? In one of the most definitive and, hopefully, seminal essays of our time, 'Against Interpretation,' Susan Sontag has pointed out the limitations and dangers of this type of thought. Because something may somehow and to some extent be interpreted as being political does not mean that it is political. In the Rorschach tests even an inkblot formed by chance produces many interpretations. Political concern and engagement must be in the work, not in the mind of the observer.

As with any interpretive system, the political interpretation of performance depends upon the political knowledge of the interpreter. But political knowledge is not theatre knowledge. Many interpreters of theatre know a lot about their own area of intellectual concern but little about performance. They relate everything they perceive to intellectual standards and structures that exist entirely apart from theatre. If all theatre ceased to exist, these political patterns of thought would be unchanged.

Italian Futurism has suffered greatly at the hands of those who interpret everything politically. Its accomplishments in performance have been denegrated, rejected and suppressed because certain of its members – including its leader, Marinetti – were politically active in support of Fascism. But other Futurists had no political involvement. Futurism was not a political movement. Very few of the plays contained explicitly political statements or supported a particular political position.

To those who are intent on distorting art into politics, however, explicit political intent is not necessary. Thus, it is claimed that it was the spirit of Italian Futurism that was fascistic. Yet Italian Futurism spread almost immediately to Russia where it joined forces with the proletarian revolution. The same Futurist spirit imbued artists who held opposite political views.

The Futurists are also deprecated by some political thinkers because both they and the Nazis were influenced by Nietzsche. Guilt-by-association is an old tool of political thought. Of course, an American – or a Chinese – can reject Italian Fascism, Russian Communism, and Nazism along with Nietzsche, but this is not theatrical thought or analysis. The same artistic philosophy can relate to opposing political positions. On the other hand, can anyone point out a form or style of theatre – any artistic element at all – that can be used by only one political position or ideology?

One mental mechanism that the political interpreter uses to make all theatre political is either/ or thinking. A performance is either for a certain political position or it is against it. Thus, all theatre apparently is forced to be political. As the slogan of the late 1960s said: 'You are either part of the solution, or you are part of the problem.' Of course, this kind of thinking is simple-minded. It is similiar to 'Have you stopped beating your wife?' A logical formulation can produce its own answer. If one has to think in either/or terms, it could be said that theatre is either political or it is not political.

Some feel that all experimental and avant-garde theatre is political because it is different than – and therefore opposed to – the traditional and accepted. Any theatre that is radical artistically is considered to be radical politically. Since the government in power is part of and supported by the status quo, any variation from the status quo is seen as a threat to and an attack upon that government. When talking about his ideal state in *The Republic*, Plato said:

> This is the point to which, above all, the attention of our rulers should be directed: that music and gymnastics be preserved in their original form and no innovation be made … any musical innovation is full of danger to the whole State and ought to be prohibited … [because] when modes of music change, the fundamental laws of the State always change with them.

Art does change the way people think, and new ways of thinking may eventually cause changes in laws and government. But this does not justify calling all theatre political. Political theatre is explicit in pointing out the institutions and aspects of government that should change; it often describes and supports the exact nature of these changes. Nobody knows how art, with its indirect causality, will change the world. Nobody can predict its effects. If art causes change, it is not necessarily political change.

Let us take a specific example and see how political interpretation generally works. Richard Foreman is presenting his *Vertical Mobility* (T62) in a loft in the SoHo district of New York. The characters are not represented in a particular social environment and there is no reference to or indication of political subject matter and intent. Of course, the interpreter may claim that the play is opposed to his chosen political position since it is not for it, but the same simplistic reasoning could be used by a socialist, a democrat, or an anarchist.

Given no intellectual message to analyze, however, the political interpreter will not get very far. Usually, he will not be interested in this type of performance. He will ignore messageless theatre because it gives him little to work with according to his system.

If forced to deal with abstract and non-referential works, the political interpreter will turn his attention to the makeup of the company, to the audience, and to the social context of the piece. He will find out, for example, that the actors are college educated, that they earn little from their performance, and that the production is supported by a grant. The spectators, the analyst will find, are entirely middle, upper-middle, and upper class; some are artists, many are under 30, all are knowledgeable in theatre. This special and identifiable audience can then be placed in the larger social context. It can be compared to the society at large and recognized as a functional sub-group.

This much is sociology. It is the sociology of theatre but sociology none the less. As a pure scientist, the sociologist would stop at this point. He would gather the facts, analyze them, and organize them. He would not say that the facts are good or bad, right or wrong. The political interpreter goes further. He sets up political standards within which the facts may be evaluated and criticized. He claims, of course, that these standards are objectively true and that the political values he deduces from them are inherent in the work. Thus, he might say that Foreman's *Vertical Mobility* is politically wrong because it does not cater to the masses of the proletariat (who are 'good') and that, being 'aristocratic' and 'elitist' the performance is evil. Thus, political values and standards have been imposed on the work. They say nothing about the presentation as theatre and as art.

This illustrates how a political view of theatre is intellectual. It does not deal with theatre as a personal, sensory (as well as mental) experience. The real, individual experience of the performance does not matter in this approach. Personal sensations have no social or political aspect. Like the sociologist (rather than the psychologist), the political interpreter deals only with symbolic information and social data; unlike the sociologist, he refers them for evaluation to a political system of thought. The experience of theatre has been avoided for the sake of political intellectualization. This intellectualization has its own emotional base, but it is imposed on the work rather than being intended by it.

The view that all theatre is political ignores a study of theatre in favor of a study of politics. In criticism, then, a work becomes good or bad to the extent that it agrees with or opposes the observer's own political position. It is impossible, for example, to have a 'good' play that supports the current administration. Political standards replace theatrical ones.

In theatrical terms, one content or message is not better or worse than another. The theatre analyst is concerned with the way content – whatever that content might be – relates to particular theatrical devices and techniques. He is concerned with the functional relationships between style and expression, between performance and audience. It is important to study and analyze political theatre not because of and in terms of its politics but because it illustrates and illuminates particular theatrical dimensions.

Most political theatre, rather than merely posing political questions and problems, attempts to change the beliefs and opinions of the spectator. Ultimately, it seeks political action based upon these changes. In *Notes of a Director*, Alexander Tairov describes what could be called an archetypal example of political theatre, an incident that crystalizes the deep ambitions of those who seek to use theatre for political ends:

In 1830, at the Théâtre Monnaie in Brussels, the play *La Muette* was being performed. In the middle of the performance, when the words 'Love for the Fatherland is holy' rang out on the stage, the revolutionary enthusiasm … was communicated to the auditorium. The whole theatre was united in such powerful transport that all the spectators and actors left their places, grabbing chairs, benches – everything that came to hand – and, bursting from the theatre, rushed into the streets of Brussels. Thus, began the Belgian revolution.

On the other hand, the political realities of theatre often do not coincide with the realities of everyday life. Enrique Buenaventura, the director of Colombia's Teatro Experimental de Cali, has described in a mimeographed handout an incident that can be seen to characterize political theatre in a way that is practical rather than archetypal:

> There are groups in Colombia … who are, we say back home, very 'accelerated.' They like to travel light. Some of these people put on a play in which they were both soldiers and guerrillas. The guerrillas … had a discussion with the soldiers, they convinced the soldiers, and the soldiers changed over to the side of the guerrillas because they *understood the problem.* The play ended with everyone giving the clenched fist salute of solidarity. A few days after the show, the army occupied the theatre and the School of Fine Arts using real rifles. During the occupation, I went over to the actors who had been in the play and asked them, 'Why don't you go over to the soldiers and speak with them, and see if you can convince them?' And they didn't go because they knew the soldiers would hit them over the head.

Thus, it is worthwhile to consider pragmatically the actual effectiveness of political theatre – and, by inference, of all didactic theatre. To what extent is theatre able to change beliefs and opinions? What are the obstacles to achieving these changes? What are the factors that relate to the political effectiveness of theatre? Few conclusive answers are available, but certain hypotheses may be presented.

One important consideration is the effectiveness of live theatre as compared to other means of communication. Is it more or less effective than, say, television or film? In a recent symposium at the American Place Theatre, John Houseman ascribed a 'seminal effect' to theatre. He apparently felt that, although the theatre audience was relatively small, the impact of theatre as a medium was somehow greater and more powerful than other media. He did not explain how this is true, however, and until there is data to show that live performance actually is more compelling intellectually and more able to change opinion and belief, we are able to say only that the experience of theatre is different than that of other media. Arguing logically from these differences, one might say that the actual presence of the actor increases the reality of the experience, making it more potent. The 'live' quality of a performance may be thought to give it more political efficacy than the same performance would have on film.

On the other hand, television, film, and even radio can be seen to have a greater power to make the unreal seem real. Thousands of people actually believed Orson Welles' 'War of The Worlds' broadcast and acted accordingly. It would be possible to use staged news footage on television without anyone realizing that it was not, in fact, real. Thus, live theatre tends to retain an 'editorializing' dimension; the commentator and the comments he makes almost always remain separate and distinct. When this is true, political theatre may be seen as being more limited than other media in changing opinion and belief. During the same American Place symposium, former Senator Eugene McCarthy said that because of his appearance on television Walter Cronkite was the 'most trusted man in America.' Theatre, on the other hand, is recognized – and appreciated – for its 'lies.'

As suggested by the reference to Cronkite, the size of the audience – both in absolute numbers and in the frequency with which an individual spectator is contacted – may be seen as relevant to effectiveness. If success is measured in terms of the number of people whose opinions or beliefs are changed, it might be assumed that a presentation of any efficacy at all will have success directly proportional to the size of its audience. Obviously, live theatre, because of the practical limitations of the medium, does not reach as large an audience as does film and television. The Ford Foundation study *The Finances in The Performing Arts* reports that '71 percent of the people [a sample of 6,000 in twelve major cities] saw a movie on television more than once a month, and 41 percent more than once a week, but hardly any people saw a live professional performance of a play more than once a month.' Nor do spectators tend to see the same live performers over and over, as they are apt, for example, to do on television serials. This, apparently, is one reason why Jerzy Grotowski has opened rehearsals to the public; because they present relatively few works, even a regional or community theatre does not have the same kind of 'following' as, say, a local softball team. In these conditions, the believeability of the commentator/actor remains minimal.

Of course, absolute numbers and frequency of contact are not the only audience factors related to effectiveness. The composition of the audience that is reached is also important. If one wishes to change someone's beliefs and opinions, it is necessary to contact those who do not already agree. No change will take place if political theatre is performed only for spectators who think the same as the writer/director/performers.

This is one of the major problems that has faced political theatre: how to find or attract the audience that can be converted. It is the basis for guerrilla theatre, which takes its performances to audiences that never planned to see the particular play but find it thrust upon them in one way or another, and it explains why many political theatre groups depend upon humor to a great extent.

Once the proper audience – the audience that does not already agree – has been found, the second problem arises: making the spectators listen to and accept what is said. Intellectual resistance may be encountered. There is a natural tendency for a spectator to react *against* anything that does not conform with his existing beliefs.

This is not merely a question of antagonism. It is true that certain political groups in the United States in the late 1960s actually antagonized their audiences in the belief that they could, in this way, persuade them. But when passers-by were splashed with 'blood' by a guerrilla theatre troupe performing an anti-war skit in the street, they tended to get angry rather than become enlightened. The belligerent and self-concerned attitude of the Living Theatre in *Paradise Now* offended and alienated many who were sympathetic to the intellectual aims of the group. When a theatre tells its audience 'I am right; you are wrong' most spectators will intellectually support and elaborate their own position. An attack causes not surrender, but defense. If this psychological generality is true, it brings into the question the efficacy of much political theatre.

The goal of most political theatre is to reach an audience of the masses, an audience of working people, an audience of the common man. Since the theatre person does not see himself as belonging to this class – and, indeed, most political theatre has been produced by educated people from the middle class and above – and since the masses are conceived as uneducated, perhaps quasi-literate, and of low intelligence, many political plays intentionally use childish, crude, or simple techniques and thought. This creates an 'us vs. them' feeling that does not exist in most theatre. It also can seem condescending. It is possible, however, for a spectator to identify with the intelligent 'us' rather than the unintelligent 'them' and to gain a sense of superiority.

A similar mechanism is behind a much wider spectrum of theatre. All theatre that attempts to send a message to the masses – not merely political theatre but the theatre of moral uplift and the Great American Play – functions on the same us/them basis. Those who write the play, or perhaps merely those who back it and approve it, think that they know what is right and wrong with the country and what it is the country should think and believe. The great play they seek is the one that tells the masses what they themselves, the seekers, already know. Most of these people probably wonder why we do not have a Great American Play and mourn the state of our theatre.

Joseph Papp is one of those who think in terms of 'meaningful' plays: 'Ones that address themselves to the major psychological problems of our time.' Of course, it is Papp who knows what is meaningful, to whom it should be meaningful, and what our important problems are. Emphasis on this theatre-as-education given by an informed or enlightened teacher to an uninformed or unenlightened public can be traced back at least to Horace. It is one of the main supports of political theatre.

Changing beliefs and opinions of a spectator can be done in many different ways, ranging from the most overt and explicit to the most covert and hidden. It would be possible to place any political production at some point along this theoretical continuum depending on the means and techniques that it employed. At one end would be pieces that involved direct argumentation and aggressive propaganda; at the other would be pieces that sought to achieve an attitude change through what could be called seduction.

The extent to which any of these means is effective is debatable. There is the story, perhaps apocryphal, of the general who attended *Oh, What A Lovely War*, Joan Littlewood's anti-war – and anti-military – production. He thought it was wonderful and said he enjoyed it more than any play he had ever seen. Years before, Rousseau had explained the psychology behind such incidents. In *Politics and the Arts*, he wrote:

> In the quarrels at which we are purely spectators, we immediately take the side of justice, and there is no act of viciousness which does not give us a lively sentiment of indignation so long as we receive no profit from it. But when our interest is involved, our sentiments are soon corrupted. And it is only then that we prefer the evil which is useful to us to the good that nature makes us love.

Certainly political theatre has to be judged ineffective when compared with the political actions of everyday life. Terrorism is often a very effective means of achieving very practical goals. It is used to call attention to a particular cause, to raise large amounts of money very quickly, to force the release of prisoners, and so forth. In comparison, theatre is relatively or completely inefficient. Traditional political means are also more effective than theatre. If this were not so, we would have fewer speeches by politicians in this country, and the political parties would be supporting extensive theatrical activity.

If political theatre, when compared to other political means, is seen as relatively inefficient, there are certain pragmatic indicators that would suggest the same conclusion. In retrospect, the great surge of anti-Vietnam-war theatre can be seen as a small part of the general political activism of the period. Like the activism, its rather sudden decline took place long before the withdrawal of American troops from Vietnam. It reached its peak at the time of the shooting at Kent State in May 1970, and by the time the bombing raids on North Vietnam were intensified in 1972, political theatre activity was almost non-existent. It was a fashion, so to speak. Apparently the practitioners of political theatre found it to be useless. Most did not give up theatre, they merely gave up theatre that dealt explicitly with current issues. Such issues still exist, but almost all political theatre in the United States prefers to deal with general, theoretical questions where the success or failure in changing a spectator's beliefs and opinions is not apparent.

It would be wrong, however, to consider the effectiveness of political theatre only in terms of changing the beliefs and opinions of the spectators. Some political theatre does not do this. It merely raises certain issues, explores certain problems, asks certain questions. It does not proselytize, it is not didactic, it does not support particular alternatives.

Nor is the changing of beliefs and opinions the only possible practical result of political theatre. If, especially when compared with other political tools, theatre can be seen to have little power to change a spectator's position, its impact can still be significant. It can give emotional and intellectual support to those who already agree with its position. Just as a marching band helps to stir the soldier's patriotism, courage, and fighting spirit, political theatre can be the rallying point for the believers in a particular cause. It can give them the feeling that they are not alone in their beliefs, that others are actively involved and pursuing the same goals. Thus, it can be an important force in political change.

3.13 The Politics Beyond the Politics (1988)

HOWARD BARKER

IN AN ERA OF authoritarian government the best theatre might learn a different function. Abandoning entertainment to the mechanical and the electronic, it might engage with conscience at the deepest level. To achieve this it would learn to discard the subtle counter-authoritarianism that lurks behind all satire, and cease its unacknowledged collaboration with the ruling order by not reproducing its stereotypes. It would unburden itself of an increasingly irrelevant didacticism and evolve new relationships with its audience which were themselves essentially non-authoritarian.

How might this be achieved? A first step might be the recognition that living in a society disciplined by moral imperatives of gross simplicity, complexity itself, ambiguity itself, is a political posture of profound strength. The play which makes demands of its audience, both of an emotional and an interpretive nature, becomes a source of freedom, necessarily hard won. The play which refuses the message, the lecture, the conscience-ridden exposé, but which insists upon the inventive and imaginative at every point, creates new tensions in a blandly entertainment-led culture.

The dramatist's obligation becomes an obligation not to a political position (the obvious necessity for socialism, etc., the obvious necessity for welfare, change, for kindness, etc.) but to his own imagination. His function becomes not to educate by his superior political knowledge, for who can trust that? but to lead into moral conflict by his superior imagination. He does not tailor his thought to an ideology, but allows it to range freely over a landscape in which he himself should experience insecurity, exposing his own morality, his own politics, to damage on the way. In an age of unitary thought and propaganda, this is his first responsibility. He forsakes in doing so his right to tell, he is destabilized, and thus produces a critical attitude in his audience, which, since it is so bred into the doctrine of messages, experiences at first the alienation felt by any public confronting a new art.

All this implies a tragic theatre. It implies the possibility of pessimism, which is wrongly associated by some with political reaction. It is a long time since my own theatre attempted acts of political instruction, though its satirical qualities always contained the hidden imperatives implicit in the form. *Victory* approached the problem of life in a post-liberal era by posing a series of accommodations, none of them respectable. Its pessimism was compensated for by its imaginative daring, its rupturing of moralities. *The Castle*'s interminable struggle between warped souls was never resolved – the play precisely lacked a politics of position – but its tragic scale, and the excoriation of feeling, lent to its audience a power to find confidence in catastrophe itself. In *The Possibilities* I recouped from a series of appalling situations a will to human dignity and complexity that came precisely from the absence of conventional politics. The unpredictability of the human soul, resistant to ideology and the tortures of logic, became a source of hope, even where death was inevitable. In *The Last Supper*, the longing for authority is shown to co-exist with a longing for its obliteration, and the play's determined refusal of the message created an uneasiness which was the sign of its relevance – neither catharsis nor epic. It is the authorial voice, straining to illuminate the blind, that prevents the proper focus of meaning in a work of art. The audience itself must be encouraged to discover meaning, and in so doing, begin some form of moral reconstruction if the politics of our time is not become yet more narrow and intellectually repetitive. The left's insistent cry for celebration and optimism in art – sinister in its popular echo of the right – implies fixed continuity in the public, whereas morality needs to be tested and re-invented by successive generations.

The dramatist's function is now a selfish one. He must expose himself to tragic possibility by dragging into the light the half-conscious, the will to power, the will to negation, the ultimate areas of imagination which the conventional political play is not equipped to deal with. When the dramatist is himself heroic in the risks he is prepared to take with his material, his audience is honoured, and through a fog of early outrage, real changes of perception become possible. Plays of information ('how wonderfully researched!'), plays of communication ('we wish you to know the following!') are outflanked by a culture now obsessively concerned with dissemination of statistics and facts which themselves do nothing to stimulate change.

The artist's response to the primacy of fact must be to revive the concept of knowledge, which is a private acquisition of an audience thinking individually and not collectively, an audience isolated in darkness and stretched to the limits of tolerance. This knowledge, because it is forbidden by moral authoritarians of both political wings, becomes the material of a new drama which regards men and women as free, cognitive, and essentially autonomous, capable of witnessing pain without the compensation of political structures.

Note

Originally an unpublished essay commissioned by the *Sunday Times*, this version is published in Howard Barker, *Arguments for a Theatre*, 3rd edn., Manchester: Manchester University Press, 1997 [1989], pp. 48–50.

Part 4
Late Modernism

Timeline

	Social, Cultural and Political Context	Theatre
1942		*The Outsider*: Albert Camus
1945	Atomic bombs dropped on Hiroshima and Nagasaki End of the Second World War Labour Party (UK) wins landslide general election victory	
1946	Jean Paul Sartre's *Existentialism and Humanism* published in France	
1950	Start of the Korean War (1950–3)	*The Bald Soprano* (also known as *The Bald Prima Donna*): Eugène Ionesco
1951	Festival of Britain	
1953		First production of Samuel Beckett's *Waiting for Godot* (France)
1954	The Algerian war of independence begins in 1954 and ends 1962	
1955		First UK production of Samuel Beckett's *Waiting for Godot* – directed by Peter Hall
1956	Suez Crisis (military confrontation between Egypt and Britain, France and Israel over ownership of the Suez Canal) Soviet Union invades Hungary	The English Stage Company (at the Royal Court Theatre) formed – this was set up as a 'playwrights' theatre' (Pinter, Beckett and Ionesco produced there during the 1950s and beyond) *The Balcony*: Jean Genet
1957		*Endgame*: Samuel Beckett
1958	Campaign for Nuclear Disarmament (CND) founded (UK) Prime Minister Charles de Gaulle's Fifth Republic introduces a new semi-presidential system as the structure for governing France. De Gaulle is President from 1959 to 1969	
1959	Start of the Vietnam War (until 1975). USA becomes involved in the early 1960s	Jean Genet's revolutionary play *The Blacks* produced
1960		*The Dumb Waiter*: Harold Pinter
1961	John F. Kennedy becomes President of the USA US-backed Cuban exiles invade Cuba (Bay of Pigs Invasion) Construction of the Berlin Wall	*Theatre of The Absurd*: Martin Esslin

	Social, Cultural and Political Context	Theatre
1962	The Algerian war of independence ended Rachel Carson's *Silent Spring* published Cuban Missile Crisis	
1963	President Kennedy assassinated	National Theatre (UK) opens at the Old Vic Theatre, in London *Saved*: Edward Bond (play was banned by the Lord Chamberlain because of the scene in which a group of youths stone a baby in a pram)
1967	Sexual Offences Act (decriminalizes homosexual relations between consenting adults over the age of 21) (UK)	*Hair: The American Tribal Love-Rock Musical*
1968	Assassination of Martin Luther King, Jr Assassination of Robert Kennedy Student demonstrations and occupations in France	Theatres Act 1968 – abolition of stage censorship in UK

Introduction

CARL LAVERY

Although its 'classical period', so to speak, runs from the late 1940s to the early 1960s, late modernism is a complex and contested term. Scholars use it in different ways, depending on their disciplinary and critical affiliations.[1] For some, late modernism marks a simple period of historical transition between the high modernism of the early decades of the twentieth century and the beginnings of postmodernism in the 1970s. For others, it designates a distinctive style or approach to art-making that has either been subsumed by 'postmodernist culture' (Connor 1992), or else is seen to coexist alongside it. An alternative way of thinking about late modernism, however, is to avoid defining it as *either* a historical period *or* generic style but rather to see it as an ethos or sensibility persisting in the work of many contemporary artists. The contemporaneity of late modernism is evident, for instance, in the curator and theorist Nicolas Bourriaud's notion of *altermodernism*, which he defines as 'a reloading of modernism according to twenty-first-century issues' (Bourriaud in Herbert 2009: 1).

Approaching late modernism as a sensibility, as a kind of ghost that haunts the present, allows us to talk of a late modernist aesthetic without thinking that we can tie it down either historically or aesthetically. Indeed, as with its sister terms, modernism and postmodernism, it is probably more accurate to talk of late modernism as a phenomenon subject to different temporalities and uneven developments. In theatre, late modernism, for instance, can apply to a wide range of dramatic and postdramatic practitioners who are separated historically and stylistically.

But what is a late modernist sensibility and how does it manifest itself? According to the Marxist philosopher, Fredric Jameson, arguably its most sophisticated theorist, late modernism is a mood determined by a sense of belatedness, the melancholy feeling that something has come to an end. In a key passage from *A Singular Modernity: Essay on the Ontology of the Present* (2002), Jameson dates it to a complex shift within modernity itself:

> Late modernism is a product of the Cold War, but in all kinds of complicated ways. Thus the Cold War spelled the end of a whole era of social transformation and indeed of Utopian desires and anticipations. For the emergence of consumerism and the spread of a culture of consumption throughout this whole period is evidently not at all the same as the heroic moment of the conquest of productivity that preceded it (and which did not even, in the two protagonists of the Cold War, end with the destruction of Word War II). Now, what was wanted in the West and in the Stalinist East alike, except for revolutionary China, was a stabilization of the existing systems and an end to that form of properly modernist transformation enacted under the sign and slogan of modernity as such, or in other words classical or high modernism. (Jameson 2002: 165-6)

Whereas high modernist playwrights and theatre practitioners (August Strindberg, W. B. Yeats, Vsevolod Meyerhold, Luigi Pirandello, Bertolt Brecht and Antonin Artaud – see Parts 2 and 3) were concerned with what Jameson terms the 'Absolute' – 'a vision of a total social transformation which includes a return of art to some putative earlier wholeness' (ibid: 164) – late modernists are aware of living in a world where the bourgeois consensus that high modernism set out to eradicate has triumphed:

> Now the Absolutes of [Modernism] have been reduced to the more basic programme of modernization – which is simply a new word for that old thing, the bourgeois conception of progress... . Politics must now therefore be carefully monitored, and new social impulses repressed or disciplined. These new forms of control are symbolically reenacted in later modernism, which transforms the older modernist experimentation into an arsenal of tried and true techniques, no longer striving after aesthetic totality or the systemic and Utopian metamorphosis of forms. (Ibid: 166)

However, if late modernists are conscious of existing in a ruined reality, where utopian dreams of aesthetic and political revolution have absconded, this does not mean that they have refuted the modernist project in its entirety. While late modernism may lack the utopian energy and confident assertions of its Expressionist, Surrealist and Constructivist predecessors, it nevertheless remains wedded to a view of the aesthetic that values experimentation, seriousness and authenticity. Likewise, it is concerned, at all costs, to maintain an ironic distance from 'the culture industry' (see Adorno 1991); the aim being to find new forms of theatrical expression that would communicate, in decidely non-mimetic terms, a deep-rooted sense of alienation from the postmodern consensus. In the work of late modernist practitioners, then, theatre stands as rebuke and accusation, a negative attack on bourgeois values.

A good indication of the aesthetic distance that separates a late modernist sensibility from a postmodernist one is illustrated by an anecdote that the critic H. Porter Abbott recounts about Beckett and the postmodernist composer and performance maker John Cage:

> For the 1988–89 Charles Eliot Norton lectures at Harvard University, John Cage chose to read from a composition made up of 487 quotations, selected by chance and then disassembled and recombined with the assistance of a computer program based on the *I Ching*. Partway through the second lecture, a tape recorder in the auditorium suddenly began to make a racket that continued until it was found and turned off. Cage read steadily through the noise. Asked about it afterwards, he said that 'the incident occurred just at a point when he had thought he would like some musical accompaniment'. This is a different frame of mind from that of the man who clutched Alan Schneider's arm during a London production of *Waiting for Godot* and whispered, '*It's ahl wrang. He's doing it ahl wrang*'. (Abbott 1990: 90)

According to Abbott, Beckett's agonized insistence on his rights as an author, the idea that a director could get something '*ahl wrang*' (all wrong), contrasts, sharply, with Cage's affirmation of chance and contingency, his postmodernist willingness to see the world in terms of flux and mutability. For Abbott, Beckett's refusal of relativism, his belief that 'there is a right way', constitutes his work as the expression of 'a modernist ego' (ibid: 92). Importantly, it is also what infuses his work with a more palpable sense of ethics and politics. Whereas Cage renounces agency and is content, quite literally, to 'go with the flow', Beckett still clings to a model of critical and responsible subjectivity, even if the characters that he depicts are, more often than not, sad, disabled clowns trapped in situations without hope of release. In Beckett's universe, where meaninglessness and despair offer no remedy, the obligation to care persists. This results in a paradoxical, stuttering form of theatre, in which, as Beckett has famously described it, there 'is nothing to express, nothing with which to express, nothing from which to express, no power to express, no desire to express, together with the obligation to express' (Beckett 1969: 103).

Beckett's late modernist mode of resistance, his art of exhaustion and poverty, reappears, albeit in different guises, in the work of a number of late twentieth-century and early twenty-first century practitioners (also, see Part 5). Sara Jane Bailes, for instance, has argued for the politics and poetics of failure in the postdramatic performances of groups such as Forced Entertainment (UK), Goat Island (US), and Elevator Repair Service (US) (Bailes 2010); and Sean Carney has recently employed the term 'late late modernist' to describe the work of English playwrights such as Edward Bond, Howard Barker, Caryl Churchill (see 5.6), Mark Ravenhill (see 5.7), Sarah Kane, and Jez Butterworth. According to the argument advanced by Carney in *The Politics and Poetics of Contemporary English Tragedy* (2013), these playwrights invest in a contemporary form of tragic theatre that seeks to break the neo-liberal consensus manufactured in the UK by ideologues in Margaret Thatcher's Conservative government in the late 1970s and 1980s. In the often bleak and negative work of new English drama, politics and metaphysics exist in a state of dialectical tension in which the explosion of the tragic points out the inadequacy of the present, and, by implication, the necessity of transforming it: 'In this paradigm of the tragic, our alienation within the world is rewritten as our difference within the world' (Carney 2013: 284). In Carney's reading, the 'arrival of the tragic is the sign of late late modernism's particular intervention into postmodernism' (ibid: 291).[2] In contrast to postmodernism, which promotes a dream vision of a capitalist utopia – a 'world of smooth, reified positivism, without flaw or fissure' (ibid: 284) – late late modernist theatre offers 'an aesthetic refusal of "happy world"' (ibid). In doing so, it contests postmodernism's tendency to transform history into 'myth', which, as Roland Barthes explains in his 1957 text *Mythologies*, is predicated upon the repetition of the same endless present. Carney concludes: 'The tragedies I have studied here seek to historicize the present as a means of rendering the present historical, which means viewing it as open-ended and incomplete' (ibid: 299).

It is telling, in this context, that Carney should define contemporary English tragedy's 'future-orientated visions as an instance of late late modernism' (ibid). Not only does his phrasing refute a simplistic, linear reading of cultural and theatrical periodization that would see modernism superseded by postmodernism in some totalizing act of incorporation, it suggests that there are significant moments within late modernism itself. This, in turn, raises questions about what early late modernism is. A useful response is found by revisiting Martin Esslin's classic text *The Theatre of the Absurd* (1961, see 4.5), a study which offers an excellent survey of the themes, forms, and sensibilities of late modernist theatre, even if his decision to focus on the metaphysics of the Absurd has tended to obscure the political thrust of playwrights such as Ionesco, Genet, and Beckett. Notwithstanding the problems that surround Esslin's use of the philosophical notion of the Absurd as a catch-all term, I use absurdist theatre and late modernist theatre interchangeably in the sections below. This is because the Theatre of the Absurd, if its philosophical sense is politically inflected, supplies a relatively accurate description of the melancholic uncertainty – but also resistance – that characterizes late modernist theatre, in both its classic and contemporary manifestations.

The Theatre of the Absurd: (classic) late modernism (4.5)

First published in 1961, Martin Esslin's *The Theatre of the Absurd* is a landmark text within Theatre Studies, a publication that sought to make sense of an initially baffling type of dramatic practice that emerged in Western and Eastern Europe in the late 1940s, and which, particularly in Paris, started to attract popular and critical attention from the mid-1950s onwards.

Esslin accounts for the appearance of the troubling world of the Theatre of the Absurd by looking backwards and forwards at the same time. On the one hand, he underlines its novelty, defining it as a 'new and revolutionary convention' (4.5: 650); and, on the other, he is concerned to situate it within an existing genealogy that dates back (amongst other things) to the comedies of Aristophanes, the physicality of *commedia dell'arte*, and the popular theatres of pantomime, music hall, and clowning. Irrespective of these avatars, however, it is significant that Esslin should spend the majority of his time, in the chapter entitled 'The Tradition of the Absurd', teasing out the influence that avant-garde playwrights and modernist novelists such as Alfred Jarry (see 2.1), Yvan Goll, August Strindberg (see 1.2), James Joyce and Franz Kafka exerted on absurdist theatre.

Differently from the work of established playwrights such as Jean Giraudoux and Jean Anouilh, whose keen sense of purposelessness and fantasy remained trapped within the confines of the well-made play, the Theatre of the Absurd was able to incorporate and develop the experimentalism of Futurism, Symbolism, Expressionism, Dadaism, and Surrealism. In these movements, there is no attempt to represent the inner world of individuated characters, with coherent psychologies and consistent motives. Rather, the objective is to express the spiritual and existential dilemmas of the playwright, or else to stage the world of dreams, unconscious processes, primitive urges, and instinctual drives (see Part 2).

However, while the Theatre of the Absurd certainly continues the modernist experimentation with theatrical form, three new phenomena become apparent, according to Esslin. First, the popular success of this work amongst a wide range of audiences, including students, the middle classes and prisoners (modernist theatre audiences by contrast, were largely confined to aficionados and expert spectators);[3] second, the manifestation of a lonely sense of exile (Samuel Beckett was Irish, Eugène Ionesco Romanian, Arthur Adamov Russian, and Fernando Arrabal Spanish); finally, and arguably most importantly, the expression of a new mood of 'metaphysical anguish at the absurdity of the human condition' (4.5: 647).

In order to explain the shift from modernist certainty to late modernist absurdity, Esslin turns to Albert Camus's philosophical text *The Myth of Sisyphus* (1942). Here, Camus argued that modern existence, in a world without theological meaning, was as absurd as the endless task inflicted upon Sisyphus by the Greek gods. In Camus's allegory, Sisyphus is repeatedly condemned to roll a rock to the top of the mountain only to see it roll back down again. Camus's book provided Esslin with a philosophical framework, and he utilized its ideas to explain the sense of existential strangeness and disarray that dominates the landscape of so many late modernist plays. In the famous definition below, Esslin uses Camus to contextualize Ionesco's sense of metaphysical alienation:

In common usage, 'absurd' may simply mean 'ridiculous' but this is not the sense in which Camus uses the word, and in which it is used when we speak of the Theatre of the Absurd.

In an essay on Kafka, Ionesco defined his understanding of the term as follows: 'Absurd is that which is devoid of purpose … Cut off from his religious, metaphysical and transcendental roots, man is lost; all his actions become senseless, absurd, useless. (4.5: 647)

Esslin is aware that absurdism has a long philosophical history, but he is at pains to trace its manifestation in contemporary drama to 'the decline of religious faith that was masked until the end of the Second World War by the substitute religions of faith in progress, nationalism, and various totalitarian fallacies. All this was shattered by the war' (ibid). The Second World War ends the high modernist project by showing that culture and art did not, as modernism believed, emancipate human beings; on the contrary, the presence of the Nazi death camps of Bergen-Belsen, Dachau and Auschwitz as well as the nuclear attacks on the Japanese cities of Nagasaki and Hiroshima in August 1945, suggested that culture had done little to alleviate the violence of history. As a consequence of this depressing and disquieting realization, a new negative form of art-making emerged that was highly suspicious of its own will to power, and which, for that reason, sought to undo itself, to question its own legitimacy.

In contrast to the largely affirmative theatres of existentialist writers such as Jean-Paul Sartre and Albert Camus who paradoxically expressed the absurd 'in the form of highly lucid and logically constructed reasoning' (ibid: 648), the playwrights discussed by Esslin were able to make audiences 'feel' the absurd by developing a new theatrical form. In the hands of absurdist writers traditional ideas of character, plot, and language were abandoned, and theatre became a disorien-tating site, in which grotesque, dream-like scenarios tapped into an unspeakable sense of lack and loss. A confusion of genres and styles also took place, and a new form of tragicomedy emerged that both expressed the despair of the age while also alleviating it through the production of manic, ridiculous laughter. Deborah B. Gaensbauer provides a useful, if perhaps too generalized overview of the dominant features of absurdist drama:

The Theatre of the Absurd is antirealistic, antipsychological, antiphilosophical … Plots, individual identities, comprehensible human relationships, plausible settings, and rational language are bafflingly, sometimes even terrifyingly absent. In their place are ambiguous, repetitive, nightmarish situations involving alienated, mechanical characters whose clowning nullity is emphasized by childish, vague or punning names. (Gaensbauer 1991: xvi)

Despite the fact that not everyone is willing to accept his description of playwrights as diverse as Ionesco, Genet, Pinter, Beckett, and Adamov as absurdist, Esslin's book has proved hugely influential, and does an excellent job of capturing the mood of late modernist theatre. An unfortunate consequence of the book's success, however, is that the Theatre of the Absurd has often been erroneously perceived as nihilistic, a theatre devoid of any form of hope. Such a viewpoint stems from a misreading of Esslin's findings. In the final chapter of the book, Esslin distinguishes between two forms of absurdity. In its surface manifestation, the Absurd is caused by the madness of everyday life in a capitalist society. However, in its second, more profound variant, Esslin insists that the Absurd derives from 'the absurdity of the human condition itself in a world where the decline of religious faith has deprived man of certainties' (Esslin 1980: 401). Whereas Esslin believes that there might be solutions to the first order Absurd, in the second order all hope of escaping the Absurd are foreclosed in advance

Nevertheless even here in the experience of what we might call 'pure absurdity', nihilism is not an option. Drawing on Camus's exhortation that 'one must imagine Sisyphus happy' (Camus 1955: 91), Esslin states, quite categorically, that the principal task for spectators is to find a way of living with this disabused knowledge:

> Ultimately, a phenomenon like the Theatre of the Absurd does not reflect despair or return to dark irrational forces but expresses modern man's endeavour to come to terms with the world in which he lives. It attempts to make him face up to the human condition as it really is, to free him from illusions that are bound to cause constant maladjustment and disappointment. (Esslin 1980: 428)

Irrespective of the fact that Esslin does not tease out, in any detail, the political implications of this statement – his preference is to concentrate on the theological aspects of the Theatre of the Absurd – there is, as will be explored in the next section, a very definite politics to absurdist theatre, which I equate with the political project of late modernism in general. In my reading, the aesthetic politics of absurd drama are grounded in a form of negative dialectics, which, while associated principally with Theodor Adorno, anticipate in nascent form the political ideas of post-structuralist philosophers such as Jacques Derrida, Jean-François Lyotard, and Gilles Deleuze and Félix Guattari. For these thinkers, the end of ideology does not signal the end of politics as it does for postmodern historians like Francis Fukuyama (see Part 3); rather it calls for a new form of commitment that places the onus on undecidability (*différance*), impossibility and respect for otherness.[4]

Politics of the Absurd: 'The London Controversy' (4.6)

Much of the confusion surrounding the political dimension of the Theatre of the Absurd is found in and perpetuated by the protracted dispute that took place between Ionesco and the UK critic Kenneth Tynan in *The Observer* newspaper, during the summer of 1958. In this infamous exchange, referred to as 'The London Controversy', Tynan suggests that Ionesco's attack on language, 'the magic innovation of our species' (Tynan in Ionesco 4.6: 652), along with his anti-humanist repudiation of 'logic and belief in man' leads spectators up 'a blind alley' (ibid: 652). Unlike the ethical and political meanings inherent in politically engaged playwrights like John Osborne, Arthur Miller, and Bertolt Brecht (see 3.3 and 3.10), Tynan contends that Ionesco's '"escape from realism"' and depiction of a 'world of isolated robots' produces 'a self-imposed vacuum, wherein the author ominously bids us observe the absence of air' (ibid: 652). For Tynan, Ionesco's commitment to artistic autonomy is a narcissistic attempt to swamp history with private feeling.

Ionesco responded to Tynan's attack by claiming that 'a work of art has nothing to do with doctrine'. On the contrary, 'it has', Ionesco continued, 'its own unique system of expression, its own means of directly apprehending the real' (ibid: 652–3). In Ionesco's view, the playwrights championed by Tynan as an antidote to the decadence of absurdist writers 'are simply the new *auteurs du boulevard*, representatives of a left-wing conformism which is just as lamentable as the right-wing sort' (ibid: 653). Rather than seeking to become an ideological vehicle, theatre, Ionesco insists, should explore its autonomous formal possibilities and express the writer's personal fears and anxieties. In this way, Ionesco argues that theatre might find a way of addressing universal problems: 'To discover the fundamental problem common to all mankind, I must ask myself what *my* fundamental problem is, what *my* most ineradicable fear is. I am certain, then, to find the problems and fears of literally everyone' (ibid: 653–4). Tellingly, Ionesco does not consider this focus on the personal and metaphysical to be devoid of ethics or politics; for him, the personal leads to the political, the private to the public.

> If I may be allowed to express myself paradoxically, I should say that the true society, the authentic human community, is extra-social – a wider, deeper society, that which is revealed by our common anxieties, our desires, our secret nostalgias. The whole history of the world has been governed by these nostalgias and anxieties, which political action does no more than reflect and interpret, very imperfectly. (Ibid: 653)

Ionesco's argument is complex, here. He is not claiming that politics and metaphysics are incompatible, as Tynan proposes. Rather, he is advancing an expanded notion of the political in which ontology, understood here as the absurdity of existence, is accorded as much weight as issues of class and economics. Ionesco is explicit about this. 'What separates us all from one another' he says, 'is simply society itself, or, if you like, politics ... it is the human condition that directs the social condition, not vice versa' (ibid: 653).

Unfortunately, Tynan was unable to grasp the philosphical sophistication of Ionesco's argument, and his response, published in *The Observer* on 6 July 1958, highlights the depth of his misunderstanding. By arguing that Ionesco's insistence on aesthetic autonomy is an attempt to regard 'art as if it were something different from and independent of the world', a type of bloodless phantom that is 'answerable to none but its own laws', Tynan seems to forget the logic of his earlier statement that 'drama ... is a part of politics, in the sense that every human activity, even buying a packet of cigarettes, has social and political repercussions' (4.6: 654). For if art, as Tynan implies, is always already bound up with politics, then surely there is no need for theatre to step beyond itself and deal with reality as a separate phenomenon. Rather, and this is what Tynan refuses to countenance, art is political by the fact that it rearranges the audience's perception of the world in a way that is at odds with dominant discourses and structures of belief. To do that, art, as Ionesco suggests, needs to insist on its autonomy in the hope of finding new forms and alternative modes of representation.

Theodor Adorno: Beckett and negative dialectics (4.7)

Although many critics initially agreed with Tynan's assessment of the Theatre of the Absurd, there were nevertheless dissenting voices. In 'Commitment', an essay criticizing the contradictions in social realist and Brechtian models of committed art, the Marxist philosopher Theodor Adorno made the following, provocative claim:

> Kafka's prose and Beckett's plays ... have an effect by comparison with which officially committed works look like pantomimes. By dismantling appearance, they explode from

within the art which committed proclamation subjugates from without, and hence only in appearance. The inescapability of their work compels the change of attitude which committed works merely demand. (Adorno 1977: 191)

In contradistinction to Tynan, Adorno realizes that the political charge of theatre does not reside in its *content* but in its *form*. More precisely, in how form 'dismantles appearances' and presents spectators with an unsettling experience, which, through its absolute negativity, breaks the spell of ideology and demands, on its own terms, 'a change of [political] attitude':

He over whom Kafka's wheels have passed, has lost for ever both any peace with the world and any chance of consoling himself with the judgement that the way of the world is bad; the element of ratification which lurks in resigned admission of the dominance of evil. (Ibid)

Yet how does this art of the inconsolable function? A clue is given in Adorno's difficult but rewarding 1958 essay 'Trying to Understand *Endgame*' (4.7). In his close reading of the play, Adorno shows how the corrosive nature of Beckett's theatre is located in its attack on humanism, a doctrine that believed in the perfectibility of the human subject, and which placed its trust in rationality, language, and progress. In the idiotic ramblings and repetitive game-playing of Hamm, the blind master, and Clov, his lame servant, in *Endgame*, Beckett punctures 'the hubris of idealism, the in-throning of man as creator in the center of creation' (4.7: 682). Importantly, Beckett does not point out the bankruptcy of Western philosophy in any discursive sense; he undermines it by refusing to make any sense of it at all. In his deconstruction of the protocols of the theatre, or what Adorno describes 'as organized meaninglessness' (ibid: 664), Beckett gives us a direct experience of what it means to live in a world, dominated by stifling economic and social structures. Here human subjects are interchangeable and reified, victims of 'bombed-out consciousness' (ibid: 666). Stunned by the horror of history, Beckett, Adorno tells us, offers no false dawn, no consolation of hope; rather his response is to present society 'with the bill' by destroying the one thing that supposedly maintains our humanity: culture.

By following his own negative path, Beckett, in Adorno's view, manages to unmask the cynical truth that committed works of art, with their humanist belief in meaning and truth, fail to show: namely, that in today's society, there is 'no other life than the false one' (ibid: 673). For Adorno, Beckett's political commitment is inherently paradoxical. *Endgame* is a work that emancipates by neglecting to communicate a meaning. 'Understanding it', Adorno proposes, 'can mean nothing other than understanding its incomprehensibility or concretely reconstructing its meaning structure – that it has none' (ibid: 664). Despite the counter-intuitive nature of such a claim, we can understand Adorno's rationale, if we approach the negativity of the work dialectically. For if the aim of the committed work is to free us, to make us think for ourselves, then how can it ever achieve that by *telling* us what to think? For all Brecht and Sartre's insistence on provoking critical thought, their plays provide us, at the level of form, with relatively straightforward solutions to complex problems. In Brecht's *The Caucasian Chalk Circle* (1955) or Sartre's *Dirty Hands* (1948), for instance, the answer is always already implicit in the way the playwrights guide our experience and marshal our thoughts in terms they have already worked out in advance. The great irony here, as Adorno suggests, is that the supposedly committed work, with its optimistic messages and hope for the future, perpetuates the suffering it so desperately wants to eradicate. Worse still, its allegiance to worn out ideologies and ineffective theatrical forms makes it complicit in upholding what Adorno, like Beckett himself, saw as the barbarism of bourgeois culture. According to Adorno, Beckett manages to avoid such complicity by insisting on negation, in suspending the possibility of reconciliation and redemption.

Lucien Goldmann: Genet and history (4.8)

Where Adorno focuses on the negativity of Beckett's work, the Marxist sociologist Lucien Goldmann offers a more affirmative reading of late modernist theatre. In the 1966 essay 'The Theatre of Genet: A Sociological Study' (4.8), Goldmann argues that to get to the political core of Jean Genet's work, it is not enough to understand the author's ideas or to focus on its content; rather, the work needs to be contextualized within the larger sociological and historical currents of its time. Goldmann is able to perform such a contextualization by developing the concept of 'categorical structures', overarching models or units of collective experience that both underpin and produce social reality:

> The categorical structures are neither conscious nor unconscious in the Freudian sense (which implies repression). Rather they are non-conscious processes [which] is why discovering these structures (and thereby understanding the art work) is beyond the range of purely literary studies and those orientated toward the writer's conscious intentions or hidden motives. (4.8: 689)

In Goldmann's structuralist account, Genet's theatre expresses a widespread feeling of dissatisfaction with corporate capitalism, but stops short of adhering to a traditional Marxist view of revolution. To that extent, Genet's work, Goldmann advances, has much in common with other late modernist works in France such as 'the early novels of Malraux, Robbe-Grillet's fiction, films like *Last Year at Marienbad* [1961, dir. Alain Resnais], [and] some of Beckett's writing' (4.8: 690). *The Balcony*, for Goldmann, is especially interesting, in this respect, for in it Genet 'unintentionally incorporates certain decisive experiences of the European Left' (ibid: 690). In its staging of a failed revolution that may or may not be 'real', Genet, Goldmann argues, produces a brilliantly germane historical allegory, a play whose rejection of naturalism accesses the deeper reasons, the mental structures, that led to the defeat of socialism in Western Europe in the 1920s and 1930s.

Importantly, *The Balcony*'s historicism, however, does not relegate its significance to the past. As Goldmann explains, its investigation into why revolutions fail, along with its sensitivity to the role played by the mass media in dominating consciousness (Irma's brothel in the play is tellingly described as a 'house of illusion'), speaks directly to the concerns of the European Left in the 1950s and 1960s. In fact, Goldmann proceeds to describe Genet as the most historically sensitive playwright of his generation; the one who not only articulates but pre-empts a marked shift in political consciousness from conventional Marxism, with its focus on economics and revolution, towards a more complex and inclusive notion of socialist politics associated with the New Left in France in the 1960s and 1970s. From this point of view, the final question posed by Goldmann in his essay is remarkably prescient. For by asking if *The Screens* (Genet's final play) is the 'sign of a turning point in our intellectual and social life' (ibid: 698), Goldmann appears to show how

Genet's work foreshadows the events of May 1968 in Paris, which radically transformed French society and offered a new view of revolutionary politics that embraced Third Worldism, feminism, 'race' and sexuality.

Like Adorno's reading of Beckett, Goldmann's sociological analysis of Genet's theatre makes Tynan's critique of Ionesco ten years earlier appear parochial and simplistic. But, it too suffers from its own limitations. By concentrating on the non-conscious play of categorical structures, Goldmann neglects, completely, Genet's own highly sophisticated theory and practice of political theatre as expressed in the 'Avertissement' (Foreword) to the 1960 version of *The Balcony*. For Genet, conventional, representational forms of political art tend to be problematic because, as he puts it, 'the imaginary representation of an action or experience usually relieves us of the obligation of attempting to perform or undergo them ourselves, and in reality' (Genet 1991: xiv). Genet's logic here is based on a negative reading of the Aristotelian notion of catharsis, which sees theatre as a social safety valve, an outlet for the sublimation of anti-social energies. By presenting us with imaginary scenarios in which 'our hearts swell with pride, seeing that we took the side of the hero', political theatre negates its own premise, destroying as Genet says 'its own pretext' (ibid). In order to avoid this, Genet, like Artaud and Adorno, argues for a cruel form of theatre that would seek to infect audiences with 'evil': 'If the "good" is to appear in a work of art it does so through the divine aid of the powers of song, whose strength alone is enough to magnify the evil that has been exposed' (ibid).

With these comments, Genet tempers Goldmann's reading of his work, while, at the same refuting, beyond any doubt, the arguments of critics such as Christopher Innes who believe that his plays 'are empty of political significance' (Innes 1993: 131). For Genet, theatre is dialectical: the greater its negativity the better its chances of producing political effects. However, despite the very parallels with Adorno's position, Genet is more aware of the complexities of representation in a mediatized society than the German philosopher. Whereas Adorno always implies that negativity escapes appropriation, *The Balcony* shows that nothing resists commodification, even negativity. In the play, for instance, it is significant that the shattering, revolutionary voice of Chantal is recuperated by Irma and recycled as another scenario within the brothel. As such, Genet appears to suggest that it is not enough to create negative works; the more pressing task is to subvert the spectacle from the inside as it were. In this way, Genet's variant of late modernist theatre has much in common not only with Adorno, but also with the deconstructionist philosophy of Jacques Derrida. In Derrida's view, art is political not because it harbours negativity or evil but because it offers a space to reflect on – and thus disturb – the discursive construction of reality; in how, that is, signs produce meaning. The point, for Derrida, is not to abandon the text for experience, but to find a way of deconstructing language, boring away at its structures until a suspensive gap emerges that problematizes the authenticity of all discourses, including revolutionary ones.

Of all the dramatists that Esslin associates with the Theatre of the Absurd, Genet is probably the one who is closest in spirit to postmodern practitioners like the Wooster Group (US) and Forced Entertainment. This is due to Genet's self-conscious critique of a mediated society, in which, as in Jean Baudrillard's somewhat nihilistic version of postmodernism (see also 5.10), it becomes impossible to separate the original from the copy. Genet's work offers a vertiginous deconstruction of the image by creating a theatre that cannibalistically turns on itself, and foregrounds its own field of operation. By doing so, Genet, perhaps more radically than Ionesco, Beckett, and Pinter, is willing to question the autonomy of the artwork and to engage in a performance practice that questions 'theatricality as a medium' (Weber 2004) as well as theatre as a form. To that degree, Genet starts to anticipate and interrogate the beginnings of a performance-based culture, in which the very possibility of authenticity is put into doubt.

Ecology and late modernism

Adorno's and Goldmann's readings of Beckett and Genet have done much to recover the politics of absurdist theatre. However, if we are to grasp the political relevance of the Theatre of the Absurd for contemporary spectators, it is imperative to consider its ecological significance. The recent interest in ecology and environment amongst scholars in the Arts and Humanities – what is known in literature departments as eco-criticism – has expanded the remit of political art to include 'the more than human world'. Importantly, though, as the eco-critic Timothy Morton has suggested, ecological thinking does not necessarily mean focusing on representations of 'nature' *per se*, and nor does it involve a Romantic return to some pre-lapsarian state, a new kind of pastoralism. Rather, it seeks to investigate the state of the environment as it appears now, to concentrate on crisis, alienation, and catastrophe; and to trouble the dominant, humanist models of self that have allowed that catastrophe to take place. Morton terms this disabused approach 'dark ecology', which, for him, takes its stance in 'the poisoned ground' of the planet (Morton 2007: 205).

With the exception of the odd essay on Beckett, little has been written on the ecological significance of late modernist/absurdist theatre. This omission is surprising on two fronts. First, the Theatre of the Absurd expresses a deep-rooted sense of environmental anxiety through its images, dramaturgies, and themes; and second, it anticipates, as a result of its deconstruction of humanism, a more decentred and inclusive model of subjectivity that manages to avoid the arrogance of anthropocentricism – a system of thought in which the human being is figured as an exceptional being, the very centre of the world. Somewhat paradoxically, perhaps, there is no need to invent a new language to tease out the ecological potential of the Theatre of the Absurd – Adorno's 1958 essay 'Trying to Understand *Endgame*' already imagines the type of 'dark' ecocritical approach that Morton calls for. In Adorno's reading of Clov's utterance, 'There's no more nature' (4.2: 582), the 'end of nature' is theorized as a tragedy provoked, on the one hand, by corporate capitalism's desire to appropriate and reify the world, 'which leaves no remainder of what was not made by humans' (4.7: 665); and, on the other, by the traumatic rupture in historical consciousness produced by the nuclear attacks on Hiroshima and Nagasaki in August 1945. For Adorno, the human capacity to destroy the world in its entirety, ushers in a new stage of alienation, a kind of worsening, if you will, that he terms 'permanent catastrophe' (ibid: 665). Faced with the spectre of a world in which nature has been extinguished and nothing grows, Adorno contends that a new form of representation is required; one that would not engage with the horrors of the nuclear age directly, but rather would proceed, as Beckett's theatre does, elliptically, in silence, via image and analogy: 'The violence of the unspeakable is mimicked by the timidity to mention it. Beckett keeps it nebulous' (ibid: 666).

In the late 1950s and early 1960s, the environmental crisis occasioned by what Adorno terms 'the atomic age' was compounded by new knowledge about the long-term effects of pollution and chemical pesticides. In 1962, the US marine biologist Rachel Carson published her influential bestseller *Silent Spring*, in which she argued that insecticides used by industrial farmers and domestic gardeners threatened to produce an 'eco-cide' on an unprecedented scale. In Carson's bleak scenario, the future is imagined as a country devoid of bird song and prey to cancerous tumours as a consequence of chemicals, such as DTT (Dichloro-diphenyl-trichloroethane), entering the food chain and altering the metabolisms of larger mammals.

While the Theatre of the Absurd has little in common with the activism of Carson's text, it does, nevertheless, share her sensitivity to the environmental distress inflicted upon natural and social ecosystems by the capitalist military-industrial complex. Additionally – and this too resonates with Carson's ideas – there is a sustained attempt to contest the anthropocentric mindset that theatre, with its obsession with human relationships alone, has done so much to foster.[5] In keeping with its poetics of negativity and weakness, the ecological significance of late modernist drama is not found by concentrating on its nostalgia for the 'natural world' (whatever that means), but by attuning oneself to its implicit *and* explicit critique of toxic environments. In ecological terms, late modernist theatre is both a reflection of and response to Clov's indictment in *Endgame* that 'No one that ever lived ever thought so crooked as we' (4.2: 582).

In the readings of the plays of Beckett, Ionesco, Pinter and Genet that follow, I show how aesthetic politics and 'more than human politics' are inextricably linked, for if ecology shows us anything it is that no aspect of life, be that natural or cultural, can be separated off from its other(s). This is why late modernist theatre, even if it does not always engage with ecological themes directly, might be interpreted as a kind of 'green theatre' from our contemporary perspective. Its willingness to decentre the human subject demonstrates, implicitly, its formal commitment to discovering new ways of living differently on the earth.

Samuel Beckett: *Endgame* (4.2)

If *Waiting for Godot* (1953) is a play where nothing happens twice, then *Endgame* (1957), its successor, is one where almost nothing happens at all. Reflecting late modernism's attachment to aesthetic autonomy, the play is structured meta-theatrically, and concerns the impossible attempts of the characters to bring their daily performance to an end. The action starts with the crippled Clov preparing for the day, first by lifting the lids off the rubbish bins where the aged parents, Nagg and Nell sleep, before proceeding to remove the sheet from their son Hamm who sits in his wheelchair in the middle of the stage. For the remainder of the play, there is no action to speak of, and drama reaches a kind of zero degree as the characters recount anecdotes, and reminisce about a past in a world devoid of a future. As with *Waiting for Godot*, *Endgame* finishes on an apparent stalemate. In the final image, Clov is 'dressed for the road' (4.2: 596), but remains glued to the spot, listening to Hamm finish the story he has been trying to tell throughout the entirety of the play. The ending is inconclusive but the implication is that the performance will begin again. No other solution seems possible on a planet engaged in a slow and agonizing process of entropic decline.

Endgame is haunted by a nebulous sense of ecological catastrophe that produces a kind of melancholic nostalgia for lost nature. The play's opening monologue, for instance, commences with Hamm, waking from a dream of 'forests' (ibid: 581); and throughout the play, at irregular intervals, he expresses a Romantic enjoyment in landscape, hoping, in spite of himself, to see the world bloom again: 'But beyond the hill? Eh? Perhaps it's still green. Eh? (*Pause.*) Flora! Pomona! (*Ecstatically.*) Ceres!' (ibid: 588). The same desire extends to Nagg and Nell, who reminisce about the clearness of the water – 'So white. So clean' – on Lake Como on some idyllic honeymoon (ibid: 584). The presence of nature in the play, its ghostly persistence in the memories of the characters, stands as a scathing indictment of human history, and expresses an elliptical judgement on the sad desolation of a world where the toxicity of the soil and the lack of natural sunlight prevent Clov's seeds from ever sprouting: 'If they were going to sprout they would have sprouted. (*Violently.*) They'll never sprout' (ibid: 583).

For all its critique of humanity's despoliation of nature, the ecological significance of *Endgame* is not limited to its content, but rather is located in Beckett's formalist obsession with sculpting time. The almost unendurable slowness of the piece, its de-dramatization of theatre, asks audiences to engage in a different kind of theatrical experience – one where listening to ironic words and attending to small, often repetitive gestures constitutes the main core of the action. As Morton has argued (2013), one of the most dangerous of all anthropocentric fantasies focuses on the ostensibly spiritual desire that humans have to escape temporality, to engage in a kind of 'exit velocity' that would allow them to transcend the world of matter and to exist, forever, as pure substance in a weightless, bodiless universe.

Endgame disrupts this dream by producing an experience of time that is close to but which never quite collapses into boredom. In this deceleration, caused by the radical subtraction of all plot, time itself now appears as a materialized thing, an invisible force field that renders us passive. As a consequence, time – or rather its passing – becomes painful. We start to feel enervated, looking for ways to distract ourselves, to make time move a little quicker, to assert a sense of agency. Once this escape route is denied us, as it is in *Endgame*, we become aware of our bodies, feeling the weight of time impacting on us, physically. In this temporal thickening, theatre becomes a place where, to paraphrase Heiner Müller (see 5.1), we come to watch ourselves die, an experience that mirrors Clov's own anxiety in *Endgame,* his horror that 'something is taking its course' (4.2: 583).[6] Hamm's dread is inspired by his intuition of the impersonal nature of time, his awareness that, like all organic life, he is destined to decompose: 'We breathe, we change! We lose our hair, our teeth! Our bloom! Our ideals!' (ibid: 582).

In producing a play about time, Beckett has fashioned a theatrical experience that consciously sets out to ruin its own autonomy by placing the spectators at the very heart of the play. Like Hamm, we too are deprived of a painkiller, forced, as we are, to spend time with the characters, to share their agonized and entropic inability to finish. By intensifying our experience of time, Beckett not only allows us to reflect on the ecological destruction we are causing for future generations thematically; he allows us to live, formally, the temporality that we are so desperate to escape. Beckett's temporality in *Endgame* is a temporality of the earth, a temporality in which time punctures the hubris of mankind: 'You're on earth', Hamm says, 'there's no cure for that' (ibid: 591).

Eugène Ionesco: *The Bald Soprano* (4.1)

Ionesco famously defined his early theatre as anti-theatre, a mode of drama that violently sought to turn theatre inside out. Ionesco's first play, the randomly titled *The Bald Prima Donna* (translated here as *The Bald Soprano*): *A Pseudo-Play in One Act* (1949), appears, on first glance, to be a classic piece of bourgeois realism. In his stage directions, Ionesco specifies that it should take place in a 'small, typical, old-fashioned, middle-class English living room, with a fireplace and door'

(Ionesco 1958: 1). However, as James Knowlson (Knowlson 1990) has pointed out, Ionesco's scenography is a trap: he fulfils our expectations only better to dispel them.

As with Beckett's *Endgame*, *The Bald Soprano* is devoid of 'drama' in the traditional sense. After speaking to each other in clichés and empty homilies, the Smiths entertain their guests the Martins, before they are interrupted, without reason, by the Captain of the Fire Brigade who recounts a number of banal anecdotes before leaving with Mary, the Maid. The play reaches its explosive conclusion with the two couples shouting a series of surreal insults at each other before language dissolves completely into meaningless syllables and material sounds. The play ends as it starts, but with the difference that the Martins have now taken the place of the Smiths, leaving the audience with the tragicomic realization that the same mechanical, lifeless scenario will continue *ad infinitum*. Little wonder, then, that Ionesco should have titled his play a 'tragic farce'; in it human beings are interchangeable victims of a stultifying system that has condemned them to a stagnant, absurd existence.

Most commentators continue to interpret the play as a linguistic tragedy, but this ignores the environmental context that informed it. Writing in 1957 – and reflecting back on the meaning of *The Bald Soprano* – Ionesco claimed that 'we can no longer avoid asking ourselves what we are doing here on earth and how, having no deep sense of our destiny, we can endure the crushing weight of the material world' (Ionesco in Esslin 1980: 143). An indication as to why Ionesco should frame his comments about *The Bald Soprano* with a reference to the 'earth' is given in the reaction of the Smiths and Martins to the Maid's haunting poem about the planet 'catching fire':

The men caught fire
The women caught fire
The birds caught fire
The fish caught fire …
The ashes caught fire
The smoke caught fire
The fire caught fire … (4.1: 577)

Crucially, these are the only lines in the play that make sense, referring, as they do, to a historical reality outside of the room, most notably the total devastation caused by the atomic attacks on Hiroshima and Nagasaki in 1945. None of the characters, however, is willing to admit the significance of these shattering events, and the Maid is hurried off stage, pushed out of the door by the Smiths. Her words nevertheless act as a catalyst of sorts. Immediately after her departure, the repressed violence that had been building between the Smiths and the Martins explodes into the open. It is as if her poem, by rejecting the stifling quality of polite speech, has lifted the veil of repression and exposed what the characters are so desperate to forget: namely, that in the wake of the atomic bomb no place on the earth, not even a bourgeois sitting room in England, is immune from destruction.

Ionesco's anti-theatre, with its violent refusal of character, dialogue, and plot, is an attempt to express the absurdity of the nuclear age. In order to confront the madness of reason, a rationality that is willing to annihilate itself, Ionesco turns theatre on its head. Instead of existing as the humanist space *par excellence*, the privileged site where spectators come to reflect on their humanity, Ionesco presents us with frenzied characters driven mad by the spectre of nuclear catastrophe and dehumanized by alienating social structures. In Ionesco's theatre, ecology functions according to a terrible feedback loop; in it, environmental destruction produces human insanity and vice versa.

Harold Pinter: *The Dumb Waiter* (4.4)

The Dumb Waiter (1957) provides a concentrated distillation of the existential themes, spatial forms and anguished obsessions that characterize Harold Pinter's early period from *The Room* (1957) to *The Homecoming* (1965). The play is focused on the tense but often comic relationship between two bored hit-men, Ben and Gus, who find themselves in a shabby, claustrophobic bedsit in the Midlands region of the UK, awaiting instructions for their next 'job' from the shadowy Wilson. As in all of Pinter's work, words do not exist to further communication but to separate and divide, and throughout *The Dumb Waiter*, Gus and Ben are engaged in a verbal battle, a struggle for semantic power. Much of Pinter's dialogue is naturalistic and demotic, but his play differs considerably from the approach of contemporaries such as Arnold Wesker in *Chicken Soup with Barley* (1956) and John Osborne's *Look Back in Anger* (1956). Where they are concerned to reflect the mores of a particular social class, Pinter's primary focus is metaphysical, which is doubtless why Esslin in his 1980 edition of *The Theatre of the Absurd* accorded a full chapter to Pinter's plays (see Esslin 1980: 234–64).

The metaphysical dimension of the play emanates from the mysterious presence of the dumb waiter – a small lift contraption embedded in a wall and used traditionally to transport food from one floor of a building to another – that erupts into action through a series of random orders for food. Although it is obvious that the machine is manipulated from above (at one point Ben converses with someone by talking into a speaking-tube), the audience never sees or hears its controller. Their presence, however, is palpable in the famous *coup de théâtre* that ends the play, when it becomes apparent that the victim is not an unknown target, but Gus, the younger, disaffected assassin.

By merging realism with abstraction, Pinter manages, like Ionesco and Beckett, to create a complex allegorical work that is open to numerous interpretations and readings. According to Esslin in *The Peopled Wound: The Plays of Harold Pinter*, Gus's disaffection and ultimate execution at the hands of his colleague, Ben, expresses the 'process of alienation to which men are subjected in a highly organised industrial society' (Esslin 1970: 73). In Esslin's view, Pinter's vision is akin to Kafka's: he uncovers the subconscious death drive and thinly veiled will to power that destroys social relationships in the bureaucratized world of modernity. In a recent collection, *Harold Pinter's The Dumb Waiter* (2009), many of the authors are keen to update Esslin's insights by returning to Pinter's own comments, made late in his career, that his early theatre was always already political.[7] David Pattie (Pattie 2009), for instance, sees it as offering a strident critique of consumerism, and Catherine Rees (Rees 2009) relates it to Jean-François Lyotard's politics of the sublime.

In light of these political revisions of his early work, it is surprising that no one has yet thought to focus on the significance of Pinter's long-time commitment to CND (Campaign for Nuclear Disarmament). Indeed with this knowledge in mind, it is tempting to interpret the nebulous spatial anxieties that so trouble his characters as partly determined by a fear of poisoned air, a distrust of the atmosphere itself. In an age that was rendered paranoid by the very real spectre of nuclear war, the desire of so many of Pinter's characters to either return or remain at home is not simply caused by existential or sociological factors alone, it is also, one might argue, motivated by environmental concerns. There is real apprehension in Pinter's work about contamination and infection, with the natural world being imagined as a source of danger, something that needs to be kept at bay, at all costs.

The absence of nature in Pinter's plays stems from the fact that the characters have lost all faith in it, preferring to shut themselves away in hermetically sealed spaces, in which human beings appear, at least initially, to be the sole occupants. Yet, in keeping with the central tenet of ecology, the sense in which everything is connected to everything else, the bedsit room in *The Dumb Waiter* fails to provide shelter. In the play the interior space is too weak, too fragile, to withstand invasion. Something noxious has already seeped in, and the atmosphere is infected long before Ben and Gus have arrived. The characters' failure to control their environment is illustrated by the apparent autonomy of objects. To use the terms of the post-human philosopher Bruno Latour, the machine in *The Dumb Waiter* is a kind of 'actant' – its troubling, autonomous presence highlights the inevitable entanglement of human beings in a 'more than human world' (Latour 2007: 54).

Pinter's ecological importance resides in his ability to express, allegorically, a crisis in humanity's capacity to dwell on the earth. If the things of the earth, both organic and inorganic, are no longer familiar to us, this is because we have lost all contact with them. Our alienation is replicated in their alienation. In a world of nuclear weapons, ecology, a word that traces its etymological roots to *oikos*, the Greek word for home, is necessarily problematized. The earth is a stranger; and homecoming is impossible. From this perspective, it is tempting to claim that the 'Organisation' which commands Gus and Ben is not so much a 'supernatural force' (Esslin 1970: 75) as a decidedly natural one, a manifestation of some dark and poisoned ecology, the return of the environmental repressed.

Jean Genet: *The Balcony* (4.3)

The Balcony (1956) marks a hiatus in Jean Genet's career, a transitional moment between the small casts and existential dramas of his early plays, and the more large-scale, obviously political works of his late theatre, *The Blacks* (1957) and *The Screens* (1961). In the play, the characters, like Solange and Claire in *The Maids* (1949), are engaged in identical games of role-playing and dressing up, but now the action is set in the midst of a revolution, which threatens to destroy the brothel, Irma's 'Grand Balcon'. Like his fellow late modernist playwrights, Genet has little interest in providing an ideological solution or communicating a didactic message; rather, he is more concerned to pose a problem, which, in this instance, centres on a deliberately theatricalized investigation into why socialist revolutions fail, despite the fact that all the socio-economic conditions appear to conform to Marxist theory.[8]

The Balcony begins with a vertiginous *mise-en-abyme* when the audience realizes that the Bishop dispensing benediction to a sinner is actually a fake Bishop, an anonymous character who comes to the brothel, as do the 'Judge' and 'General', to partake in sado-masochistic fantasies. The overt theatricality of the scene is revealing: it highlights, in advance, both Genet's diagnosis and mode of resistance. For Genet, one of the reasons why revolutions fail is that the population is seduced by theatricality, stunned by glamour. As we see in the play, the actual reality of the people who embody symbolic roles of power is of little concern. What counts above all is costume, gesture, charisma. After the revolution has defeated the existing regime on the military plane, there is a symbolic stand-off on the balcony of Irma's whorehouse, an ideological battle of sorts between the images of reaction (the Queen, Judge, General, and Bishop) and the voice of revolution (Chantal). Presented with a choice between subservience and freedom, the Beggar chooses subservience, overwhelmed, as he is, by the images of authority that dazzle his eye.

For Genet, the seductiveness of power is not simply due to the fact that the existing regime controls the apparatus of representation – in this context, Irma's brothel – there is also an important existential dimension to consider. In *The Balcony*, Genet makes the essentially Sartrean observation that individuals are attracted to images of power, because such images dispel, magically, the burden of freedom, the absurdist recognition that life is gratuitous. This line of reasoning accounts for the success of fascism in the play. The Chief of Police's long-desired arrival into the brothel's nomenclature shows how fascism's allure is dependent, like the modernist avant-garde, upon its capacity to tether technological innovation to more basic, primitivist urges, to offer, that is, an erotic carnival that replaces responsibility with ecstasy. In this respect – and this is surely why Genet situates his play in a brothel – politics is tantamount to pornography, a fake, simulated scenario that encourages the masses to suspend their belief and to participate in fantasy.

Genet's critical subversion of theatricality establishes an important, if unintentional, connection between progressive models of political subjectivity and alternative notions of what we might call 'ecological being'. Crucially, the ecological importance of Genet's theatre does not reside in its representation of the 'natural world', but in its deconstruction of the humanist self. As Rosi Braidotti has pointed out, humanism leaves no space for otherness, its goal is to reduce the world to the values of the perceiving subject, which are rooted in transcendent notions of language and reason (Braidotti 2013). In this logocentric model of subjectivity, the human being is accorded privilege because it can speak, a factor which allows it to access a supposedly timeless set of metaphysical truths, all of which, unsurprisingly, uphold the claims of human beings to administer the world as they see fit.

In *The Balcony*, Genet troubles the foundations of the humanist subject by attacking the philosophical principles on which it rests. In the opening scene, for instance, the 'Bishop' looks into the mirror and attempts to discover the essence of the self – the private, interior substance that supposedly underwrites the exceptional status of the human being. In Genet's play, however, the Bishop does not coincide with himself in a moment of pure self-presence; rather, the self is revealed as a construct, a fiction, a matter of surface rather than depth. Ontologically, the character playing the Bishop is divided, traversed by a difference or otherness that he is unable to surmount, primarily because it is constitutive of his identity in the first place. By disclosing that the self is not 'one' but dependent on the other for its sense of being, Genet shows the self-sufficient logic of anthropocentrism to be a mere fantasy. Though it is undoubtedly an exaggeration to posit Genet as a 'green playwright' in any intentional sense, if we read philosophy in *The Balcony* in terms of ecology, it becomes possible to argue that his deconstructionism of humanism points towards a different post-human value system. This is because in Genet's play the human being has lost its centrality and is now subjected, like any other creature, to the vagaries and contingencies of the earth itself. In Genet's eulogy to weakness, his celebration of loss, the death drive that terrifies the subject and attracts it to fascism has the potential to be renounced. In its place, Genet presents us with a relational mode of subjectivity that, from an ecological perspective, is better able to accept its dependence on the world precisely because its desire to be at the centre of things is revealed as an illusion.

Conclusion

This introduction has explored the ways in which classic late modernist theatre emerged towards the end of the First World War, and was initially associated with the Theatre of the Absurd. However, as discussed at the beginning of the chapter, late modernism cannot be confined to a historical period or aesthetic style. As a *sensibility*, late modernism is discernible in the resistant politics and aesthetics of a number of theatre practitioners working in the second half of the twentieth century; and its influence continues to be felt, increasingly, in the performances of many contemporary playwrights. Late modernist politics are sophisticated and sometimes difficult to situate, since they rest on a cusp between the negative dialectics of Theodor Adorno and the more hesitant, deconstructionist politics of post-structuralist philosophers. This is revealed in the fact that many late modernist works tend to be open-ended allegories that are open to numerous contradictory meanings. Late modernism's self-conscious refusal to be subsumed into what Jean-François Lyotard terms *un grand récit* (a totalising narrative of emancipation) does not preclude a commitment to freedom and equality; and many of the artists who share its sensibility continue to invest in a form of dialectical thinking that would see negativity as a possible – and perhaps necessary – moment in the production of the new.

This productive negativity, moreover, is no longer confined to the human world. As argued in the readings of the individual plays reprinted in this anthology, the late modernist theatre of the 1950s is highly sensitive to the ecological nightmare occasioned by the atom bomb and chemical insecticides. Differently from earlier playwrights such as Ibsen (see 1.4) and Chekhov (see 1.3), who couched their critique of industrialization in largely positivist terms, late modernist theatre sets out to deconstruct, through a meta-theatrical attack on theatre itself, the humanist belief systems that many contemporary ecological thinkers see as the very cause of environmental problems in the first instance. From the vantage point of the present, and when viewed through an ecological lens, late modernist theatre offers a challenge to the current neo-liberal consensus in the extent to which it seeks to place dominant, anthropocentric models of subjectivity in crisis.

Notes

1. Literary critics such as Alan Wilde (1981) and Tyrus Miller (1999) and art historians like Robert Genter (2010) see late modernism as a transitional phase, albeit dating it differently. The architectural historian Charles Jencks (1980), on the other hand, employs it to denote a distinct style of architecture.
2. Eckart Voights-Virchow (2001) explicitly categorizes Sarah Kane as 'a late modernist'.
3. According to Jameson, late modernism, unlike high modernism, is defined by its broad appeal. It is the type of theatre one studies at university (Jameson 2002: 209–10).
4. The post-structuralist philosophers mentioned above drew much of their inspiration from the late modernist writing practices of Beckett and Genet.
5. In the Introduction to *History of European Drama and Theatre*, Erika Fischer-Lichte provides a perfect illustration of theatre's profound but unconscious sense of anthropocentrism: 'theatre symbolizes the human condition of creating identity to the extent to which it makes the distancing of man from himself the condition of its existence' (Fischer-Lichte 2004: 5).
6. According to Müller, 'the specificity of theatre is precisely not the presence of the live actor but the one who is potentially dying' (Müller in Lehmann 2006: 147).

7. Pinter's late theatre is concerned with issues such as human rights and politically motivated torture and genocide.
8. In classic Marxist theory, revolutions occur when the economic contradictions of a given society reach a crisis point that can only be resolved through the creation of a new socio-economic order (see Marx and Engels 2004).

Bibliography

Abbott, H. Porter (1990) 'Late Modernism: Samuel Beckett and the Art of the Oeuvre', in Enoch Brater and Ruby Cohn (eds), *Around the Absurd: Essays on Modern and Postmodern Drama*, Ann Arbor: University of Michigan Press, pp. 73–95.

Adorno, Theodor W. (1977) 'Commitment', in R. Livingston, Theodor W. Adorno, Walter Benjamin, Ernst Bloch, Bertolt Brecht and Georg Lukács (eds), *Aesthetic and Politics*, London: Verso, pp. 177–95.

Adorno, Theodor W. (1982) 'Trying to Understand Endgame', trans. M. T. Jones, *New German Critique*, 26, 119–50.

Adorno, Theodor (1991) *The Culture Industry: Selected Essays on Mass Culture*, London and New York: Routledge.

Bailes, Sara Jane (2010) *Performance Theatre and the Poetics of Failure, Forced Entertainment, Goat Island and Elevator Repair Service*, London and New York: Routledge.

Barthes, Roland (2000) *Mythologies*, trans. A. Lavers, London: Vintage.

Beckett, Samuel (1969) *Proust and Three Dialogues with George Duthuit*, 3rd revised edn, London: Calder.

Beckett, Samuel (1990) *Endgame* in *Samuel Beckett: The Complete Dramatic Works*, London: Faber and Faber.

Braidotti, Rosi (2013) *The Posthuman*, Cambridge: Polity.

Camus, Albert (1955) *The Myth of Sisyphus and Other Essays*, trans. J. O'Brien, New York: Alfred A. Knopf.

Carney, Sean (2013) *The Politics and Poetics of Contemporary English Tragedy*, Toronto: University of Toronto Press.

Carson, Rachel (1962) *Silent Spring*, New York: Houghton Mifflin.

Connor, Steve (1992) *Postmodernist Culture: An Introduction to Theories of the Contemporary*, Oxford: Blackwell.

Esslin, Martin (1970) *The Peopled Wound: The Plays of Harold Pinter*, London: Methuen.

Esslin, Martin (1980) *The Theatre of the Absurd*, 3rd revised and enlarged edn, Harmondsworth: Penguin.

Fischer-Lichte, Erika (2004) *History of European Drama and Theatre*, London: Routledge.

Gaensbauer, Deborah (1991) *The French Theatre of the Absurd*, Boston, MA: Twayne.

Genet, Jean (1991) *The Balcony*, trans. B. Wright and T. Hands, London: Faber and Faber.

Genter, Robert (2010) *Late Modernism: Art, Culture and Politics in Cold War America*, Philadelphia: University of Pennsylvania Press.

Goldmann, Lucien (1968) 'The Theater of Jean Genet: A Sociological Study', *The Drama Review*, 12(2), 51–61.

Herbert, Martin (2009) 'Siting Defunct Modernity in Search of Something Useful', *TATE etc.*, 15 (Spring), 62–8.

Innes, Christopher (1993) *Avant Garde Theatre 1992–1992*, London and New York: Routledge.

Ionesco, Eugène (1958) *The Bald Prima Donna: A Pseudo-Play in One Act*, trans. D. Watson, London: Samuel French.

Ionesco, Eugène (1964) 'The London Controversy', in *Notes and Counter-Notes: Writings on Theatre*, trans. D. Watson, New York: Grove Press, pp. 97–101.

Jameson, Frederic (2002) *A Singular Modernity: Essay on the Ontology of the Present*, London and New York: Verso.

Jencks, Charles (1980) *Late-Modern Architecture*, London: Academy.

Knowlson, James (1990) 'Tradition and Innovation in Ionesco's *La Cantatrice chauve*', in Enoch Brater and Ruby Cohn (eds), *Around the Absurd: Essays on Modern and Postmodern Drama*, Ann Arbor: University of Michigan Press, pp. 57–72.

Latour, Bruno (2007) *Reassembling the Social: An Introduction to Actor-Network-Theory*, Oxford: Oxford University Press.

Lehmann, Hans-Thies (2006) *Postdramatic Theatre*, trans. K. Jürs-Munby, London and New York: Routledge.

Marx, Karl and Frederic Engels (2004) *The Communist Manifesto*, London: Penguin.

Miller, Tyrus (1999) *Late Modernism: Politics, Fiction, and the Arts Between the World Wars*, Berkeley: University of California Press.

Morton, Timothy (2007) *Aesthetics*, Cambridge, MA: Harvard University Press.

Morton, Timothy (2013) *Hyperobjects: Philosophy and Ecology after the End of the World*, Minneapolis and London: University of Minnesota Press.

Pattie, David (2009) 'Feeding Power: Pinter, Bahktin and Inverted Carnival', in Mary F. Brewer (ed.), *Harold Pinter's The Dumb Waiter*, Amsterdam: Rodopi, pp. 55–70.

Pinter, Harold (1991) *The Room and the Dumb Waiter*, London: Faber and Faber.

Rees, Catherine (2009) 'High Art of Popular Culture: Traumatic conflicts of Representations and Postmodernism in Pinter's *The Dumb Waiter*', in Mary. F. Brewer (ed.), Harold Pinter's *The Dumb Waiter*, Amsterdam: Rodopi, pp.111–26.

Voights-Virchow, Eckart (2001) 'Sarah Kane, a Late Modernist: Intertextuality and Montage in the Broken images of *Crave* (1998)', in Bernhard Reitz, and Heiko Stahl (eds), *What Revels Are in Hand: Assessments of Contemporary Drama in English in Honour of Wolfgang Lippke*, Trier: WVT, pp. 205–20.

Weber, Samuel (2004) *Theatricality as Medium*, New York: Fordham University Press.

Wilde, Alan (1981) *Horizons of Assent: Modernism, Postmodernism, and the Ironic Imagination*, Baltimore and London: Johns Hopkins University Press.

Further reading

Arons, Wendy and Theresa J. May (eds) (2012) *Readings in Performance and Ecology*, Basingstoke: Palgrave Macmillan.

Bennett, Michael (2011) *Reassessing the Theatre of the Absurd: Camus, Beckett, Ionesco, Genet and Pinter*, Basingstoke: Palgrave Macmillan,

Bradby, David (1984) *Modern French Drama 1940–1980*, Cambridge: University of Cambridge Press.

Bradby David and Claire Finburgh (2011) *Jean Genet*, London and New York: Routledge.

Brater Enoch and Ruby Cohn (eds) (1990) *Around the Absurd: Essays on Modern and Postmodern Drama*, Ann Arbor: University of Michigan Press.

Cless, Downing (2010) *Ecology and Environment in European Drama*, London and New York: Routledge.

Cronin, Anthony (1991) *Samuel Beckett: The Last Modernist*, New York: Da Capo Press.

Fifield, Peter (2013) *Late Modernist Style* in *Samuel Beckett and Emmanuel Levinas*, Basingstoke: Palgrave Macmillan.

Garrard, Greg (2011) '*Endgame*: Beckett's Ecological Thought', in Yann Mével, Dominique Rabaté and Sjef Houppermans (eds), *Samuel Beckett Today/Aujourd'hui 23*, Amsterdam: Rodopoi, pp. 383–97.

Gontarski S. E and Anthony Uhlmann (eds) (2006) *Beckett after Beckett*, Gainsville: University Press of Florida.

Gritzner, Karoline (2008) '(Post)Modern Subjectivity and the New Expressionism: Howard Barker, Sarah Kane and Forced Entertainment', *Contemporary Theatre Review*, 18(3), 328–40.

Lavery, Carl (2006) 'Between Negativity and Resistance: Genet and Committed Theatre', *Contemporary Theatre Review*, 16(2), 220–34.

Lavery, Carl (2010) *The Politics of Jean Genet's Late Theatre: Spaces of Revolution*, Manchester: Manchester University Press.

Lavery, Carl and Claire Finburgh (eds) (2015) *Rethinking the Theatre of the Absurd: Ecology, Environment and the Greening of the Modern Stage*, London: Bloomsbury.

McColl Chesney, Duncan (2013) *Silence Nowhen: Late Modernism, Minimalism, and Silence in the Work of Samuel Beckett*, Peter Lang: New York.

Raby, Peter (ed.) (2009) *The Cambridge Companion to Harold Pinter*, 2nd edn, Cambridge: Cambridge University Press.

Smith, S. (ed.) (1996) *Ionesco: Nottingham French Studies*, 35, 1.

Wellwarth, G. (1971) *The Theatre of Protest and Paradox: Developments in the Avant-garde Drama*, New York: New York University.

4.1 THE BALD SOPRANO (1950)

EUGÈNE IONESCO

Translated by Donald M. Allen

Eugène Ionesco (1909–94) *is one of the key figures in the Theatre of the Absurd (see Introduction to Part 4). Although born in Romania, Ionesco spent most of his childhood in France, returning to Romania in the mid-1920s where he studied French literature and qualified as a teacher, settling back in France during the Second World War. He wrote more than 30 plays of which* The Bald Prima Donna, *1950, is one of the most frequently staged along with others from his early period of playwriting such as* The Chairs *(1952) and* The Lesson *(1951). Many of his plays depict seemingly 'normal' (often) middle-class people, in recognizable settings, without the comfort of the life-shaping logic of cause and effect. Conversations appear to be disconnected, random comments generate a rhythm of response, but ultimately collapse into meaningless discussions that only emphasize the monotony and futility of communication. Less popular in Francophone theatre today than his contemporaries like Samuel Beckett, his work has been adapted by companies such as Theatre de Complicité whose acclaimed co-production of* The Chairs *(in a new translation by Martin Crimp) transferred from London to Broadway in 1998.*

Anti-play

The Characters

MR SMITH
MRS SMITH
MR MARTIN
MRS MARTIN
MARY, *the maid*
THE FIRE CHIEF

Scene: A middle-class English interior, with English armchairs. An English evening. MR SMITH, *an Englishman, seated in his English armchair and wearing English slippers, is smoking his English pipe and reading an English newspaper, near an English fire. He is wearing English spectacles and a small gray English mustache. Beside him, in another English armchair,* MRS SMITH, *an Englishwoman, is darning some English socks. A long moment of English silence. The English clock strikes 17 English strokes.*

MRS SMITH: There, it's nine o'clock. We've drunk the soup, and eaten the fish and chips, and the English salad. The children have drunk English water. We've eaten well this evening. That's because we live in the suburbs of London and because our name is Smith.

MR SMITH continues to read, clicks his tongue.

MRS SMITH: Potatoes are very good fried in fat; the salad oil was not rancid. The oil from the grocer at the corner is better quality than the oil from the grocer across the street. It is even better than the oil from the grocer at the bottom of the street. However, I prefer not to tell them that their oil is bad.

MR SMITH continues to read, clicks his tongue.

MRS SMITH: However, the oil from the grocer at the corner is still the best.

MR SMITH continues to read, clicks his tongue.

MRS SMITH: Mary did the potatoes very well, this evening. The last time she did not do them well. I do not like them when they are well done.

MR SMITH continues to read, clicks his tongue.

MRS SMITH: The fish was fresh. It made my mouth water. I had two helpings. No, three helpings. That made me go to the w.c. You also had three helpings. However, the third time you took less than the first two times, while as for me, I took a great deal more. I eat better than you this evening. Why is that? Usually, it is you who eats more. It is not appetite you lack.

MR SMITH clicks his tongue.

MRS SMITH: But still, the soup was perhaps a little too salty. It was saltier than you. Ha, ha, ha. It also had too many leeks and not enough onions. I regret I didn't advise Mary to add some aniseed stars. The next time I'll know better.

MR SMITH continues to read, clicks his tongue.

MRS SMITH: Our little boy wanted to drink some beer; he's going to love getting tiddly. He's like you. At table did you notice how he stared at the bottle? But I poured some water from the jug into his glass. He was thirsty and he drank it. Helen is like me: she's a good manager, thrifty, plays the piano. She never asks to drink English beer. She's like our little daughter who drinks only milk and eats only porridge. It's obvious that she's only two. She's named Peggy. The quince and bean pie was marvelous. It would have been nice, perhaps, to have had a small glass of Australian Burgundy with the sweet, but I did not bring the bottle to the table because I did not wish to set the children a bad example of gluttony. They must learn to be sober and temperate.

MR SMITH continues to read, clicks his tongue.

Figure 22 *The Bald Soprano* (photograph from an early production).

MRS SMITH: Mrs Parker knows a Rumanian grocer by the name of Popesco Rosenfeld, who has just come from Constantinople. He is a great specialist in yogurt. He has a diploma from the school of yogurt-making in Adrianople. Tomorrow I shall buy a large pot of native Rumanian yogurt from him. One doesn't often find such things here in the suburbs of London.

MR SMITH continues to read, clicks his tongue.

MRS SMITH: Yogurt is excellent for the stomach, the kidneys, the appendicitis, and apotheosis. It was Doctor Mackenzie-King who told me that, he's the one who takes care of the children of our neighbors, the Johns. He's a good doctor. One can trust him. He never prescribes any medicine that he's not tried out on himself first. Before operating on Parker, he had his own liver operated on first, although he was not the least bit ill.

MR SMITH: But how does it happen that the doctor pulled through while Parker died?

MRS SMITH: Because the operation was successful in the doctor's case and it was not in Parker's.

MR SMITH: Then Mackenzie is not a good doctor. The operation should have succeeded with both of them or else both should have died.

MRS SMITH: Why?

MR SMITH: A conscientious doctor must die with his patient if they can't get well together. The captain of a ship goes down with his ship into the briny deep, he does not survive alone.

MRS SMITH: One cannot compare a patient with a ship.

MR SMITH: Why not? A ship has its diseases too; moreover, your doctor is as hale as a ship; that's why he should have perished at the same time as his patient, like the captain and his ship.

MRS SMITH: Ah! I hadn't thought of that … Perhaps it is true … And then, what conclusion do you draw from this?

MR SMITH: All doctors are quacks. And all patients too. Only the Royal Navy is honest in England.

MRS SMITH: But not sailors.

MR SMITH: Naturally (*A pause. Still reading his paper.*) Here's a thing I don't understand. In the newspaper they always give the age of deceased persons but never the age of the newly born. That doesn't make sense.

MRS SMITH: I never thought of that!

Another moment of silence. The clock strikes seven times. Silence. The clock strikes three times. Silence. The clock doesn't strike.

MR SMITH: (*Still reading his paper.*) Tsk, it says here that Bobby Watson died.

MRS SMITH: My God, the poor man! When did he die?

MR SMITH: Why do you pretend to be astonished? You know very well that he's been dead these past two years. Surely you remember that we attended his funeral a year and a half ago.

MRS SMITH: Oh yes, of course I do remember. I remembered it right away, but I don't understand why you yourself were so surprised to see it in the paper.

MR SMITH: It wasn't in the paper. It's been three years since his death was announced. I remembered it through an association of ideas.

MRS SMITH: What a pity! He was so well preserved.

MR SMITH: He was the handsomest corpse in Great Britain. He didn't look his age. Poor Bobby, he'd been dead for four years and he was still warm. A veritable living corpse. And how cheerful he was!

MRS SMITH: Poor Bobby.

MR SMITH: Which poor Bobby do you mean?

MRS SMITH: It is his wife that I mean. She is called Bobby too, Bobby Watson. Since they both had the same name, you could never tell one from the other when you saw them together. It was only after his death that you could really tell which was which. And there are still people today who confuse her with the deceased and offer their condolences to him. Do you know her?

MR SMITH: I only met her once, by chance, at Bobby's burial.

MRS SMITH: I've never seen her. Is she pretty?

MR SMITH: She has regular features and yet one cannot say that she is pretty. She is too big and stout. Her features are not regular but still one can say that she is very pretty. She is a little too small and too thin. She's a voice teacher.

The clock strikes five times. A long silence.

MRS SMITH: And when do they plan to be married, those two?

MR SMITH: Next spring, at the latest.

MRS SMITH: We shall have to go to their wedding, I suppose.

MR SMITH: We shall have to give them a wedding present. I wonder what?

MRS SMITH: Why don't we give them one of the seven silver salvers that were given us for our wedding and which have never been of any use to us? (*Silence.*)

MRS SMITH: How sad for her to be left a widow so young.

MR SMITH: Fortunately, they had no children.

MRS SMITH: That was all they needed! Children! Poor woman, how could she have managed!

MR SMITH: She's still young. She might very well remarry. She looks so well in mourning.

MRS SMITH: But who would take care of the children? You know very well that they have a boy and a girl. What are their names?

MR SMITH: Bobby and Bobby like their parents. Bobby Watson's uncle, old Bobby Watson, is a rich man and very fond of the boy. He might very well pay for Bobby's education.

MRS SMITH: That would be proper. And Bobby Watson's aunt, old Bobby Watson, might very well, in her turn, pay for the education of Bobby Watson, Bobby Watson's daughter. That way Bobby, Bobby Watson's mother, could remarry. Has she anyone in mind?

MR SMITH: Yes, a cousin of Bobby Watson's.

MR SMITH: Who? Bobby Watson?

MR SMITH: Which Bobby Watson do you mean?

MRS SMITH: Why, Bobby Watson, the son of old Bobby Watson, the late Bobby Watson's other uncle.

MR SMITH: No, it's not that one, it's someone else. It's Bobby Watson, the son of old Bobby Watson, the late Bobby Watson's aunt.

MRS SMITH: Are you referring to Bobby Watson the commercial traveler?

MR SMITH: All the Bobby Watsons are commercial travelers.

MRS SMITH: What a difficult trade! However, they do well at it.

MR SMITH: Yes, when there's no competition.

MRS SMITH: And when is there no competition?

MR SMITH: On Tuesdays, Thursdays, and Tuesdays.

MRS SMITH: Ah! Three days a week? And what does Bobby Watson do on those days?

MR SMITH: He rests, he sleeps.

MRS SMITH: But why doesn't he work those three days if there's no competition?

MR SMITH: I don't know everything. I can't answer all your idiotic questions!

MRS SMITH: (*Offended.*) Oh! Are you trying to humiliate me?

MR SMITH: (*All smiles.*) You know very well that I'm not.

MRS SMITH: Men are all alike! You sit there all day long, a cigarette in your mouth, or you powder your nose and rouge your lips, fifty times a day, or else you drink like a fish.

MR SMITH: But what would you say if you saw men acting like women do, smoking all day long, powdering, rouging their lips, drinking whisky?

MRS SMITH: It's nothing to me! But if you're only saying that to annoy me … I don't care for that kind of joking, you know that very well!

She hurls the socks across the stage and shows her teeth. She gets up.

MR SMITH: (*Also getting up and going towards his wife, tenderly.*) Oh, my little ducky daddles, what a little spitfire you are! You know that I only said it as a joke! (*He takes her by the waist and kisses her.*) What a ridiculous pair of old lovers we are! Come, let's put out the lights and go bye-byes.

MARY: (*Entering.*) I'm the maid. I have spent a very pleasant afternoon. I've been to the cinema with a man and I've seen a film with some women. After the cinema, we went to drink some brandy and milk and then read the newspaper.

MRS SMITH: I hope that you've spent a pleasant afternoon, that you went to the cinema with a man and that you drank some brandy and milk.

MR SMITH: And the newspaper.

MARY: Mr and Mrs Martin, your guests, are at the door. They were waiting for me. They didn't dare come in by themselves. They were supposed to have dinner with you this evening.

MRS SMITH: Oh, yes. We were expecting them. And we were hungry. Since they didn't put in an appearance, we were going to start dinner without them. We've had nothing to eat all day. You should not have gone out!

MARY: But it was you who gave me permission.

MR SMITH: We didn't do it on purpose.

MARY: (*Bursts into laughter, then she bursts into tears. Then she smiles.*) I bought me a chamber pot.

MRS SMITH: My dear Mary, please open the door and ask Mr and Mrs Martin to step in. We will change quickly.

MR and MRS SMITH exit right. MARY opens the door at the left by which MR and MRS MARTIN enter.

MARY: Why have you come so late! You are not very polite. People should be punctual. Do you understand? But sit down there, anyway, and wait now that you're here.

She exits. MR and MRS MARTIN sit facing each other, without speaking. They smile timidly at each other. The dialogue which follows must be spoken in voices that are drawling, monotonous, a little singsong, without nuances.

MR MARTIN: Excuse me, madam, but it seems to me, unless I'm mistaken, that I've met you somewhere before.

MRS MARTIN: I, too, sir. It seems to me that I've met you somewhere before.

MR MARTIN: Was it, by any chance, at Manchester that I caught a glimpse of you, madam?

MRS MARTIN: That is very possible. I am originally from the city of Manchester. But I do not have a good memory, sir. I cannot say whether it was there that I caught a glimpse of you or not!

MR MARTIN: Good God, that's curious! I, too, am originally from the city of Manchester, madam!

MRS MARTIN: That is curious!

MR MARTIN: Isn't that curious! Only, I, madam, I left the city of Manchester about five weeks ago.

MRS MARTIN: That is curious! What a bizarre coincidence! I, too, sir, I left the city of Manchester about five weeks ago.

MR MARTIN: Madam, I took the 8:30 morning train which arrives in London at 4:45.

MRS MARTIN: That is curious! How very bizarre! And what a coincidence! I took the same train, sir, I too.

MR MARTIN: Good Lord, how curious! Perhaps then, madam, it was on the train that I saw you?

MRS MARTIN: It is indeed possible; that is, not unlikely. It is plausible and, after all, why not! – But I don't recall it, sir!

MR MARTIN: I traveled second class, madam. There is no second class in England, but I always travel second class.

MRS MARTIN: That is curious! How very bizarre! And what a coincidence! I, too, sir, I traveled second class.

MR MARTIN: How curious that is! Perhaps we did meet in second class, my dear lady!

MRS MARTIN: That is certainly possible, and it is not at all unlikely. But I do not remember very well, my dear sir!

MR MARTIN: My seat was in coach No. 8, compartment 6, my dear lady.

MRS MARTIN: How curious that is! My seat was also in coach No. 8, compartment 6, my dear sir!

MR MARTIN: How curious that is and what a bizarre coincidence! Perhaps we met in compartment 6, my dear lady?

MRS MARTIN: It is indeed possible, after all! But I do not recall it, my dear sir!

MR MARTIN: To tell the truth, my dear lady, I do not remember it either, but it is possible that we caught a glimpse of each other there, and as I think of it, it seems to me even very likely.

MRS MARTIN: Oh! truly, of course, truly, sir!

MR MARTIN: How curious it is! I had seat No. 3, next to the window, my dear lady.

MRS MARTIN: Oh, good Lord, how curious and bizarre! I had seat No. 6, next to the window, across from you, my dear sir.

MR MARTIN: Good God, how curious that is and what a coincidence! We were then seated facing each other, my dear lady! It is there that we must have seen each other!

MRS MARTIN: How curious it is! It is possible, but I do not recall it, sir!

MR MARTIN: To tell the truth, my dear lady, I do not remember it either. However, it is very possible that we saw each other on that occasion.

MRS MARTIN: It is true, but I am not at all sure of it, sir.

MR MARTIN: Dear madam, were you not the lady who asked me to place her suitcase in the luggage rack and who thanked me and gave me permission to smoke?

MRS MARTIN: But of course, that must have been I, sir. How curious it is, how curious it is, and what a coincidence!

MR MARTIN: How curious it is, how bizarre, what a coincidence! And well, well, it was perhaps at that moment that we came to know each other, madam?

MRS MARTIN: How curious it is and what a coincidence! It is indeed possible, my dear sir! However, I do not believe that I recall it.

MR MARTIN: Nor do I, madam. (*A moment of silence. The clock strikes twice, then once.*) Since coming to London, I have resided in Bromfield Street, my dear lady.

MRS MARTIN: How curious that is, how bizarre! I, too, since coming to London, I have resided in Bromfield Street, my dear sir.

MR MARTIN: How curious that is, well then, well then, perhaps we have seen each other in Bromfield Street, my dear lady.

MRS MARTIN: How curious that is, how bizarre! It is indeed possible, after all! But I do not recall it, my dear sir.

MR MARTIN: I reside at No. 19, my dear lady.

MRS MARTIN: How curious that is. I also reside at No. 19, my dear sir.

MR MARTIN: Well then, well then, well then, well then, perhaps we have seen each other in that house, dear lady?

MRS MARTIN: It is indeed possible but I do not recall it, dear sir.

MR MARTIN: My flat is on the fifth floor, No. 8, my dear lady.

MRS MARTIN: How curious it is, good Lord, how bizarre! And what a coincidence! I too reside on the fifth floor, in flat No. 8, dear sir!

MR MARTIN: (*Musing.*) How curious it is, how curious it is, how curious it is, and what a coincidence! You know, in my bedroom there is a bed, and it is covered with a green eiderdown. This room, with the bed and the green eiderdown, is at the end of the corridor between the w.c. and the bookcase, dear lady!

MRS MARTIN: What a coincidence, good Lord, what a coincidence! My bedroom, too, has a bed with a green eiderdown and is at the end of the corridor, between the w.c., dear sir, and the bookcase!

MR MARTIN: How bizarre, curious, strange! Then, madam, we live in the same room and we sleep in the same bed, dear lady. It is perhaps there that we have met!

MRS MARTIN: How curious it is and what a coincidence! It is indeed possible that we have met there, and perhaps even last night. But I do not recall it, dear sir!

MR MARTIN: I have a little girl, my little daughter, she lives with me, dear lady. She is two years old, she's blonde, she has a white eye and a red eye, she is very pretty, her name is Alice, dear lady.

MRS MARTIN: What a bizarre coincidence! I, too, have a little girl. She is two years old, has a white eye and a red eye, she is very pretty, and her name is Alice, too, dear sir!

MR MARTIN: (*In the same drawling monotonous voice.*) How curious it is and what a coincidence! And bizarre! Perhaps they are the same, dear lady!

MRS MARTIN: How curious it is! It is indeed possible, dear sir. (*A rather long moment of silence. The clock strikes 29 times.*)

MR MARTIN: (*After having reflected at length, gets up slowly and, unhurriedly, moves toward* MRS MARTIN, *who, surprised by his solemn air, has also gotten up very quietly.* MR MARTIN, *in the same flat, monotonous voice, slightly singsong.*) Then, dear lady, I believe that there can be no doubt about it, we have seen each other before and you are my own wife … Elizabeth, I have found you again!

MRS MARTIN approaches MR MARTIN *without haste. They embrace without expression. The clock strikes once, very loud. This striking of the clock must be so loud that it makes the audience jump. The Martins do not hear it.*

MRS MARTIN: Donald, it's you, darling!

They sit together in the same armchair, their arms around each other, and fall asleep. The clock strikes several more times. MARY, *on tiptoe, a finger to her lips, enters quietly and addresses the audience.*

MARY: Elizabeth and Donald are now too happy to be able to hear me. I can therefore let you in on a secret. Elizabeth is not Elizabeth, Donald is not Donald. And here is the proof: the child that Donald spoke of is not Elizabeth's daughter, they are not the same person. Donald's daughter has one white eye and one red eye like Elizabeth's daughter. Whereas Donald's child has a white right eye and a red left eye, Elizabeth's child has a red right eye and a white left eye! Thus all of Donald's system of deduction collapses when it comes up against this last obstacle which destroys his whole theory. In spite of the extraordinary coincidences which seem to be definitive proofs, Donald and Elizabeth, not being the parents of the same child, are not Donald and Elizabeth. It is in vain that he thinks he is Donald, it is in vain that she thinks she is Elizabeth. He believes in vain that she is Elizabeth. She believes in vain that he is Donald – they are sadly deceived. But who is the true Donald? Who is the true Elizabeth? Who has any interest in prolonging this confusion? I don't know. Let's not try to know. Let's leave things as they are. (*She takes several steps toward the door, then returns and says to the audience.*) My real name is Sherlock Holmes. (*She exits.*)

The clock strikes as much as it likes. After several seconds, MR and MRS MARTIN separate and take the chairs they had at the beginning.

MR MARTIN: Darling, let's forget all that has not passed between us, and, now that we have found each other again, let's try not to lose each other any more, and live as before.

MRS MARTIN: Yes, darling.

MR and MRS SMITH enter from the right, wearing the same clothes.

MRS SMITH: Good evening, dear friends! Please forgive us for having made you wait so long. We thought that we should extend you the courtesy to which you are entitled and as soon as we learned that you had been kind enough to give us the pleasure of coming to see us without prior notice we hurried to dress for the occasion.

MR SMITH: (*Furious.*) We've had nothing to eat all day. And we've been waiting four whole hours for you. Why have you come so late?

MR and MRS SMITH sit facing their guests. The striking of the clock underlines the speeches, more or less strongly, according to the case. The Martins, particularly MRS MARTIN, *seem embarrassed and timid. For this reason the conversation begins with difficulty and the words are uttered, at the beginning, awkwardly. A long embarrassed silence at first, then other silences and hesitations follow.*

MR SMITH: Hm. (*Silence.*)

MRS SMITH: Hm, hm. (*Silence.*)

MRS MARTIN: Hm, hm, hm. (*Silence.*)

MR MARTIN: Hm, hm, hm, hm. (*Silence.*)

MRS MARTIN: Oh, but definitely. (*Silence.*)

MR MARTIN: We all have colds. (*Silence.*)

MR SMITH: Nevertheless, it's not chilly. (*Silence.*)

MRS SMITH: There's no draft. (*Silence.*)

MR MARTIN: Oh no, fortunately. (*Silence.*)

MR SMITH: Oh dear, oh dear, oh dear. (*Silence.*)

MR MARTIN: Don't you feel well? (*Silence.*)

MRS SMITH: No, he's wet his pants. (*Silence.*)

MRS MARTIN: Oh, sir, at your age, you shouldn't. (*Silence.*)

MR SMITH: The heart is ageless. (*Silence.*)

MR MARTIN: That's true. (*Silence.*)

MRS SMITH: So they say. (*Silence.*)

MRS MARTIN: They also say the opposite. (*Silence.*)

MR SMITH: The truth lies somewhere between the two. (*Silence.*)

MR MARTIN: That's true. (*Silence.*)

MRS SMITH: (*To the Martins.*) Since you travel so much, you must have many interesting things to tell us.

MR MARTIN: (*To his wife.*) My dear, tell us what you've seen today.

MRS MARTIN: It's scarcely worth the trouble, for no one would believe me.

MR SMITH: We're not going to question your sincerity!

MRS SMITH: You will offend us if you think that.

MR MARTIN: (*To his wife.*) You will offend them, my dear, if you think that …

MRS MARTIN: (*Graciously.*) Oh well, today I witnessed something extraordinary. Something really incredible.

MR MARTIN: Tell us quickly, my dear.

MR SMITH: Oh, this is going to be amusing.

MRS SMITH: At last.

MRS MARTIN: Well, today, when I went shopping to buy some vegetables, which are getting to be dearer and dearer …

MRS SMITH: Where is it all going to end!

MR SMITH: You shouldn't interrupt, my dear, it's very rude.

MRS MARTIN: In the street, near a café, I saw a man, properly dressed, about fifty years old, or not even that, who …

MR SMITH: Who, what?

MRS SMITH: Who, what?

MR SMITH: (*To his wife.*) Don't interrupt, my dear, you're disgusting.

MRS SMITH: My dear, it is you who interrupted first, you boor.

MR SMITH: (*To his wife.*) Hush. (*To* MRS MARTIN.) What was this man doing?

MRS MARTIN: Well, I'm sure you'll say that I'm making it up – he was down on one knee and he was bent over.

MR MARTIN, MR SMITH, MRS SMITH: Oh!

MRS MARTIN: Yes, bent over.

MR SMITH: Not possible.

MRS MARTIN: Yes, bent over. I went near him to see what he was doing …

MR SMITH: And?

MRS MARTIN: He was tying his shoe lace which had come undone.

MR MARTIN, MR SMITH, MRS SMITH: Fantastic!

MR SMITH: If someone else had told me this, I'd not believe it.

MR MARTIN: Why not? One sees things even more extraordinary every day, when one walks around. For instance, today in the Underground I myself saw a man, quietly sitting on a seat, reading his newspaper.

MRS SMITH: What a character!

MR SMITH: Perhaps it was the same man!

The doorbell rings.

MR SMITH: Goodness, someone is ringing.

MRS SMITH: There must be somebody there. I'll go and see. (*She goes to see, she opens the door and closes it, and comes back.*) Nobody. (*She sits down again.*)

MR MARTIN: I'm going to give you another example …

Doorbell rings again.

MR SMITH: Goodness, someone is ringing.

MRS SMITH: There must be somebody there. I'll go and see. (*She goes to see, opens the door, and comes back.*) No one. (*She sits down again.*)

MR MARTIN: (*Who has forgotten where he was.*) Uh …

MRS MARTIN: You were saying that you were going to give us another example.

MR MARTIN: Oh, yes …

Doorbell rings again.

MR SMITH: Goodness, someone is ringing.

MRS SMITH: I'm not going to open the door again.

MR SMITH: Yes, but there must be someone there!

MRS SMITH: The first time there was no one. The second time, no one. Why do you think that there is someone there now?

MR SMITH: Because someone has rung!

MRS MARTIN: That's no reason.

MR MARTIN: What? When one hears the doorbell ring, that means someone is at the door ringing to have the door opened.

MRS MARTIN: Not always. You've just seen otherwise!

MR MARTIN: In most cases, yes.

MR SMITH: As for me, when I go to visit someone, I ring in order to be admitted. I think that everyone does the same thing and that each time there is a ring there must be someone there.

MRS SMITH: That is true in theory. But in reality things happen differently. You have just seen otherwise.

MRS MARTIN: Your wife is right.

MR MARTIN: Oh! You women! You always stand up for each other.

MRS SMITH: Well, I'll go and see. You can't say that I am obstinate, but you will see that there's no one there! (*She goes to look, opens the door and closes it.*) You see, there's no one there. (*She returns to her seat.*)

MRS SMITH: Oh, these men who always think they're right and who're always wrong!

The doorbell rings again.

MR SMITH: Goodness, someone is ringing. There must be someone there.

MRS SMITH: (*In a fit of anger.*) Don't send me to open the door again. You've seen that it was useless. Experience teaches us that when one hears the doorbell ring it is because there is never anyone there.

MRS MARTIN: Never.

MR MARTIN: That's not entirely accurate.

MR SMITH: In fact it's false. When one hears the doorbell ring it is because there is someone there.

MRS SMITH: He won't admit he's wrong.

MRS MARTIN: My husband is very obstinate, too.

MR SMITH: There's someone there.

MR MARTIN: That's not impossible.

MRS SMITH: (*To her husband.*) No.

MR SMITH: Yes.

MRS SMITH: I tell you *no*. In any case you are not going to disturb me again for nothing. If you wish to know, go and look yourself!

MR SMITH: I'll go.

MRS SMITH shrugs her shoulders. MRS MARTIN tosses her head.

MR SMITH: (*Opening the door.*) Oh! how do you do. (*He glances at MRS SMITH and the Martins, who are all surprised.*) It's the Fire Chief!

FIRE CHIEF: (*He is of course in uniform and is wearing an enormous shining helmet.*) Good evening, ladies and gentlemen. (*The Smiths and the Martins are still slightly astonished. MRS SMITH turns her head away, in a temper, and does not reply to his greeting.*) Good evening, Mrs Smith. You appear to be angry.

MRS SMITH: Oh!

MR SMITH: You see it's because my wife is a little chagrined at having been proved wrong.

MR MARTIN: There's been an argument between Mr and Mrs Smith, Mr Fire Chief.

MRS SMITH: (*To MR MARTIN.*) This is no business of yours! (*To MR SMITH.*) I beg you not to involve outsiders in our family arguments.

MR SMITH: Oh, my dear, this is not so serious. The Fire Chief is an old friend of the family. His mother courted me, and

I knew his father. He asked me to give him my daughter in marriage if ever I had one. And he died waiting.

MR MARTIN: That's neither his fault, nor yours.

FIRE CHIEF: Well, what is it all about?

MRS SMITH: My husband was claiming …

MR SMITH: No, it was you who was claiming.

MR MARTIN: Yes, it was she.

MRS MARTIN: No, it was he.

FIRE CHIEF: Don't get excited. You tell me, Mrs Smith.

MRS SMITH: Well, this is how it was. It is difficult for me to speak openly to you, but a fireman is also a confessor.

FIRE CHIEF: Well then?

MRS SMITH: We were arguing because my husband said that each time the doorbell rings there is always someone there.

MR MARTIN: It is plausible.

MRS SMITH: And I was saying that each time the doorbell rings there is never anyone there.

MRS MARTIN: It might seem strange.

MRS SMITH: But it has been proved, not by theoretical demonstrations, but by facts.

MR SMITH: That's false, since the Fire Chief is here. He rang the bell, I opened the door, and there he was.

MRS MARTIN: When?

MR MARTIN: But just now.

MRS SMITH: Yes, but it was only when you heard the doorbell ring the fourth time that there was someone there. And the fourth time does not count.

MRS MARTIN: Never. It is only the first three times that count.

MR SMITH: Mr Fire Chief, permit me in my turn to ask you several questions.

FIRE CHIEF: Go right ahead.

MR SMITH: When I opened the door and saw you, it was really you who had rung the bell?

FIRE CHIEF: Yes, it was I.

MR MARTIN: You were at the door? And you rang in order to be admitted?

FIRE CHIEF: I do not deny it.

MR SMITH: (*To his wife, triumphantly.*) You see? I was right. When you hear the doorbell ring, that means someone rang it. You certainly cannot say that the Fire Chief is not someone.

MRS SMITH: Certainly not. I repeat to you that I was speaking of only the first three times, since the fourth time does not count.

MRS MARTIN: And when the doorbell rang the first time, was it you?

FIRE CHIEF: No, it was not I.

MRS MARTIN: You see? The doorbell rang and there was no one there.

MR MARTIN: Perhaps it was someone else?

MR SMITH: Were you standing at the door for a long time?

FIRE CHIEF: Three-quarters of an hour.

MR SMITH: And you saw no one?

FIRE CHIEF: No one. I am sure of that.

MRS MARTIN: And did you hear the bell when it rang the second time?

FIRE CHIEF: Yes, and that wasn't I either. And there was still no one there.

MRS SMITH: Victory! I was right.

MR SMITH: (*To his wife.*) Not so fast. (*To the* FIRE CHIEF.) And what were you doing at the door?

FIRE CHIEF: Nothing. I was just standing there. I was thinking of many things.

MR MARTIN: (*To the* FIRE CHIEF.) But the third time – it was not you who rang?

FIRE CHIEF: Yes, it was I.

MR SMITH: But when the door was opened nobody was in sight.

FIRE CHIEF: That was because I had hidden myself – as a joke.

MRS SMITH: Don't make jokes, Mr Fire Chief. This business is too sad.

MR MARTIN: In short, we still do not know whether, when the doorbell rings, there is someone there or not!

MRS SMITH: Never anyone.

MR SMITH: Always someone.

FIRE CHIEF: I am going to reconcile you. You both are partly right. When the doorbell rings, sometimes there is someone, other times there is no one.

MR MARTIN: This seems logical to me.

MRS MARTIN: I think so too.

FIRE CHIEF: Life is very simple, really. (*To the Smiths.*) Go on and kiss each other.

MRS SMITH: We just kissed each other a little while ago.

MR MARTIN: They'll kiss each other tomorrow. They have plenty of time.

MRS SMITH: Mr Fire Chief, since you have helped us settle this, please make yourself comfortable, take off your helmet and sit down for a moment.

FIRE CHIEF: Excuse me, but I can't stay long. I should like to remove my helmet, but I haven't time to sit down. (*He sits down, without removing his helmet.*) I must admit that I have come to see you for another reason. I am on official business.

MRS SMITH: And what can we do for you, Mr Fire Chief?

FIRE CHIEF: I must beg you to excuse my indiscretion (*Terribly embarrassed.*) … uhm (*He points a finger at the Martins.*) … you don't mind … in front of them …

MRS MARTIN: Say whatever you like.

MR MARTIN: We're old friends. They tell us everything.

MR SMITH: Speak.

FIRE CHIEF: Eh, well – is there a fire here?

MRS SMITH: Why do you ask us that?

FIRE CHIEF: It's because – pardon me – I have orders to extinguish all the fires in the city.

MRS MARTIN: All?

FIRE CHIEF: Yes, all.

MRS SMITH: (*Confused.*) I don't know … I don't think so. Do you want me to go and look?

MR SMITH: (*Sniffing.*) There can't be one here. There's no smell of anything burning.

FIRE CHIEF: (*Aggrieved.*) None at all? You don't have a little fire in the chimney, something burning in the attic or in the cellar? A little fire just starting, at least?

MRS SMITH: I am sorry to disappoint you but I do not believe there's anything here at the moment. I promise that I will notify you when we do have something.

FIRE CHIEF: Please don't forget, it would be a great help.

MRS SMITH: That's a promise.

FIRE CHIEF: (*To the Martins.*) And there's nothing burning at your house either?

MRS MARTIN: No, unfortunately.

MR MARTIN: (*To the* FIRE CHIEF.) Things aren't going so well just now.

FIRE CHIEF: Very poorly. There's been almost nothing, a few trifles – a chimney, a barn. Nothing important. It doesn't bring in much. And since there are no returns, the profits on output are very meager.

MR SMITH: Times are bad. That's true all over. It's the same this year with business and agriculture as it is with fires, nothing is prospering.

MR MARTIN: No wheat, no fires.

FIRE CHIEF: No floods either.

MRS SMITH: But there is some sugar.

MR SMITH: That's because it is imported.

MRS MARTIN: It's harder in the case of fires. The tariffs are too high!

FIRE CHIEF: All the same, there's an occasional asphyxiation by gas, but that's unusual too. For instance, a young woman asphyxiated herself last week – she had left the gas on.

MRS MARTIN: Had she forgotten it?

FIRE CHIEF: No, but she thought it was her comb.

MR SMITH: These confusions are always dangerous!

MRS SMITH: Did you go to see the match dealer?

FIRE CHIEF: There's nothing doing there. He is insured against fires.

MR MARTIN: Why don't you go see the Vicar of Wakefield, and use my name?

FIRE CHIEF: I don't have the right to extinguish clergymen's fires. The Bishop would get angry. Besides they extinguish their fires themselves, or else they have them put out by vestal virgins.

MR SMITH: Go see the Durands.

FIRE CHIEF: I can't do that either. He's not English. He's only been naturalized. And naturalized citizens have the right to have houses, but not the right to have them put out if they're burning.

MRS SMITH: Nevertheless, when they set fire to it last year, it was put out just the same.

FIRE CHIEF: He did that all by himself. Clandestinely. But it's not I who would report him.

MR SMITH: Neither would I.

MRS SMITH: Mr Fire Chief, since you are not too pressed, stay a little while longer. You would be doing us – a favor.

FIRE CHIEF: Shall I tell you some stories?

MRS SMITH: Oh, by all means, how charming of you. (*She kisses him.*)

MR SMITH, MRS MARTIN, MR MARTIN: Yes, yes, some stories, hurrah!

They applaud.

MR SMITH: And what is even more interesting is the fact that firemen's stories are all true, and they're based on experience.

FIRE CHIEF: I speak from my own experience. Truth, nothing but the truth. No fiction.

MR MARTIN: That's right. Truth is never found in books, only in life.

MRS SMITH: Begin!

M. MARTIN: Begin!

MRS MARTIN: Be quiet, he is beginning.

FIRE CHIEF: (*Coughs slightly several times.*) Excuse me, don't look at me that way. You embarrass me. You know that I am shy.

MRS SMITH: Isn't he charming! (*She kisses him.*)

FIRE CHIEF: I'm going to try to begin anyhow. But promise me that you won't listen.

MRS MARTIN: But if we don't listen to you we won't hear you.

FIRE CHIEF: I didn't think of that!

MRS SMITH: I told you, he's just a boy.

MR MARTIN, M. SMITH: Oh, the sweet child! (*They kiss him.*)

MRS MARTIN: Chin up!

FIRE CHIEF: Well, then! (*He coughs again in a voice shaken by emotion.*) 'The Dog and the Cow,' an experimental fable. Once upon a time another cow asked another dog: 'Why have you not swallowed your trunk?' 'Pardon me,' replied the dog, 'it is because I thought that I was an elephant.'

MRS MARTIN: What is the moral?

FIRE CHIEF: That's for you to find out.

MR SMITH: He's right.

MRS SMITH: (*Furious.*) Tell us another.

FIRE CHIEF: A young calf had eaten too much ground glass. As a result, it was obliged to give birth. It brought forth a cow into the world. However, since the calf was male, the cow could not call him Mamma. Nor could she call him Papa, because the calf was too little. The calf was then obliged to get married and the registry office carried out all the details completely à la mode.

MR SMITH: À la mode de Caen.

MR MARTIN: Like tripes.

FIRE CHIEF: You've heard that one?

MRS SMITH: It was in all the papers.

MRS MARTIN: It happened not far from our house.

FIRE CHIEF: I'll tell you another: 'The Cock.' Once upon a time, a cock wished to play the dog. But he had no luck because everyone recognized him right away.

MRS SMITH: On the other hand, the dog that wished to play the cock was never recognized.

MR SMITH: I'll tell you one: 'The Snake and the Fox.' Once upon a time, a snake came up to a fox and said: 'It seems to me that I know you!' The fox replied to him: 'Me too.' 'Then,' said the snake, 'give me some money.' 'A fox doesn't give money,' replied the tricky animal, who, in order to escape, jumped down into a deep ravine full of strawberries and chicken honey. But the snake was there waiting for him with a Mephistophelean laugh. The fox pulled out his knife, shouting: 'I'm going to teach you how to live!' Then he took to flight, turning his back. But he had no luck. The snake was quicker. With a well-chosen blow of his fist, he struck the fox in the middle of his forehead, which broke into a thousand pieces, while he cried: 'No! No! Four times no! I'm not your daughter.'

MRS MARTIN: It's interesting.

MRS SMITH: It's not bad.

MR MARTIN: (*Shaking MR SMITH's hand.*) My congratulations.

FIRE CHIEF: (*Jealous.*) Not so good. And anyway, I've heard it before.

MR SMITH: It's terrible.

MRS SMITH: But it wasn't even true.

MRS MARTIN: Yes, unfortunately.

MR MARTIN: (*To MRS SMITH.*) It's your turn, dear lady.

MRS SMITH: I only know one. I'm going to tell it to you. It's called 'The Bouquet.'

MR SMITH: My wife has always been romantic.

MR MARTIN: She's a true Englishwoman.

MRS SMITH: Here it is: Once upon a time, a fiancé gave a bouquet of flowers to his fiancée, who said, 'Thanks'; but before she had said, 'Thanks,' he, without saying a single word, took back the flowers he had given her in order to teach her a good lesson, and he said, 'I take them back.' He said, 'Goodbye,' and took them back and went off in all directions.

MR MARTIN: Oh, charming! (*He either kisses or does not kiss MRS SMITH.*)

MRS MARTIN: You have a wife, Mr Smith, of whom all the world is jealous.

MR SMITH: It's true. My wife is intelligence personified. She's even more intelligent than I. In any case, she is much more feminine, everyone says so.

MRS SMITH (*To the FIRE CHIEF*): Let's have another, Mr Fire Chief.

FIRE CHIEF: Oh, no, it's too late.

MR MARTIN: Tell us one, anyway.

FIRE CHIEF: I'm too tired.

MR SMITH: Please do us a favour.

MR MARTIN: I beg you.

FIRE CHIEF: No.

MRS MARTIN: You have a heart of ice. We're sitting on hot coals.

MRS SMITH: (*Falls on her knees sobbing, or else she does not do this.*) I implore you!

FIRE CHIEF: Righto.

MR SMITH: (*In* MRS MARTIN's *ear.*) He agrees! He's going to bore us again.

MRS MARTIN: Shh.

MRS SMITH: No luck. I was too polite.

FIRE CHIEF: 'The Headcold.' My brother-in law had, on the paternal side, a first cousin whose maternal uncle had a father-in-law whose paternal grandfather had married as his second wife a young native whose brother he had met on one of his travels, a girl of whom he was enamored and by whom he had a son who married an intrepid lady pharmacist who was none other than the niece of an unknown fourth-class petty officer of the Royal Navy and whose adopted father had an aunt who spoke Spanish fluently and who was, perhaps, one of the granddaughters of an engineer who died young, himself the grandson of the owner of a vineyard which produced mediocre wine, but who had a second cousin, a stay-at-home, a sergeant-major, whose son had married a very pretty young woman, a divorcée, whose first husband was the son of a loyal patriot who, in the hope of making his fortune, had managed to bring up one of his daughters so that she could marry a footman who had known Rothschild, and whose brother, after having changed his trade several times, married and had a daughter whose stunted great-grandfather wore spectacles which had been given him by a cousin of his, the brother-in-law of a man from Portugal, natural son of a miller, not too badly off, whose foster-brother had married the daughter of a former country doctor, who was himself a foster-brother of the son of a forrester, himself the natural son of another country doctor, married three times in a row, whose third wife …

MR MARTIN: I knew that third wife, if I'm not mistaken. She ate chicken sitting on a hornet's nest.

FIRE CHIEF: It's not the same one.

MRS SMITH: Shh!

FIRE CHIEF: As I was saying … whose third wife was the daughter of the best midwife in the region and who, early left a widow …

MR SMITH: Like my wife.

FIRE CHIEF: … Had married a glazier who was full of life and who had had, by the daughter of a station master, a child who had burned his bridges …

MRS SMITH: His britches?

MR MARTIN: No his bridge game.

FIRE CHIEF: And had married an oyster woman, whose father had a brother, mayor of a small town, who had taken as his wife a blonde schoolteacher, whose cousin, a fly fisherman …

Figure 23 *The Bald Soprano*, production by Tina Howe, Atlantic Theater, NY, 2004. (Photograph: Carol Rosegg.)

MR MARTIN: A fly by night?

FIRE CHIEF: … Had married another blonde schoolteacher, named Marie, too, whose brother was married to another Marie, also a blonde schoolteacher …

MR SMITH: Since she's blonde, she must be Marie.

FIRE CHIEF: … And whose father had been reared in Canada by an old woman who was the niece of a priest whose grandmother, occasionally in the winter, like everyone else, caught a cold.

MRS SMITH: A curious story. Almost unbelievable.

MR MARTIN: If you catch a cold, you should get yourself a colt.

MR SMITH: It's a useless precaution, but absolutely necessary.

MRS MARTIN: Excuse me, Mr Fire Chief, but I did not follow your story very well. At the end, when we got to the grandmother of the priest, I got mixed up.

MR SMITH: One always gets mixed up in the hands of a priest.

MRS SMITH: Oh yes, Mr Fire Chief, begin again. Everyone wants to hear.

FIRE CHIEF: Ah, I don't know whether I'll be able to. I'm on official business. It depends on what time it is.

MRS SMITH: We don't have the time, here.

FIRE CHIEF: But the clock?

MR SMITH: It runs badly. It is contradictory, and always indicates the opposite of what the hour really is.

Enter MARY.

MARY: Madam … sir …

MRS SMITH: What do you want?

MR SMITH: What have you come in here for?

MARY: I hope, madam and sir will excuse me … and these ladies and gentlemen too … I would like … I would like … to tell you a story, myself.

MRS MARTIN: What is she saying?

MR MARTIN: I believe that our friends' maid is going crazy … she wants to tell us a story, too.

FIRE CHIEF: Who does she think she is? (*He looks at her.*) Oh!

MRS SMITH: Why are you butting in?

MR SMITH: This is really uncalled for, Mary …

FIRE CHIEF: Oh! But it is she! Incredible!

MR SMITH: And you?

MARY: Incredible! Here!

MRS SMITH: What does all this mean?

MR SMITH: You know each other?

FIRE CHIEF: And how!

MARY throws herself on the neck of the FIRE CHIEF.

MARY: I'm so glad to see you again … at last!

MR AND MRS SMITH: Oh!

MR SMITH: This is too much, here, in our home, in the suburbs of London.

MRS SMITH: It's not proper! …

FIRE CHIEF: It was she who extinguished my first fires.

MARY: I'm your little firehose.

MR MARTIN: If that is the case … dear friends … these emotions are understandable, human, honourable …

MRS MARTIN: All that is human is honourable.

MRS SMITH: Even so, I don't like to see it … here among us …

MR SMITH: She's not been properly brought up …

FIRE CHIEF: Oh, you have too many prejudices.

MRS MARTIN: What I think is that a maid, after all – even though it's none of my business – is never anything but a maid …

MR MARTIN: Even if she can sometimes be a rather good detective.

FIRE CHIEF: Let me go.

MARY: Don't be upset! … They're not so bad really.

MR SMITH: Hm … hm … you two are very touching, but at the same time, a little … a little …

MR MARTIN: Yes, that's exactly the word.

MR SMITH: … A little too exhibitionistic …

MR MARTIN: There is a native British modesty – forgive me for attempting, yet again, to define my thought – not understood by foreigners, even by specialists, thanks to which, if I may thus express myself … of course, I don't mean to refer to you …

MARY: I was going to tell you …

MR SMITH: Don't tell us anything …

MARY: Oh yes!

MRS SMITH: Go, my little Mary, go quietly to the kitchen and read your poems before the mirror …

MR MARTIN: You know, even though I'm not a maid, I also read poems before the mirror.

MRS MARTIN: This morning when you looked at yourself in the mirror you didn't see yourself.

MR MARTIN: That's because I wasn't there yet …

MARY: All the same, I could, perhaps, recite a little poem for you.

MRS SMITH: My little Mary, you are frightfully obstinate.

MARY: I'm going to recite a poem, then, is that agreed? It is a poem entitled 'The Fire' in honor of the Fire Chief:

The Fire

The polypoids were burning in the wood
A stone caught fire
The castle caught fire
The forest caught fire
The men caught fire
The women caught fire
The birds caught fire
The fish caught fire
The water caught fire
The sky caught fire
The ashes caught fire
The smoke caught fire
The fire caught fire
Everything caught fire
Caught fire, caught fire.

She recites the poem while the Smiths are pushing her offstage.

MRS MARTIN: That sent chills up my spine …

MR MARTIN: And yet there's a certain warmth in those lines …

FIRE CHIEF: I thought it was marvelous.

MRS SMITH: All the same …

MR SMITH: You're exaggerating …

FIRE CHIEF: Just a minute … I admit … all this is very subjective … but this is my conception of the world. My world. My dream. My ideal … And now this reminds me that I must leave. Since you don't have the time here, I must tell you that in exactly three-quarters of an hour and sixteen minutes, I'm having a fire at the other end of the city. Consequently, I must hurry. Even though it will be quite unimportant.

MRS SMITH: What will it be? A little chimney fire?

FIRE CHIEF: Oh, not even that. A straw fire and a little heartburn.

MR SMITH: Well, we're sorry to see you go.

MRS SMITH: You have been very entertaining.

MRS MARTIN: Thanks to you, we have passed a truly Cartesian quarter of an hour.

FIRE CHIEF: (*Moving towards the door, then stopping.*) Speaking of that – the bald soprano? (*General silence, embarrassment.*)

MRS SMITH: She always wears her hair in the same style.

FIRE CHIEF: Ah! Then goodbye, ladies and gentlemen.

MR MARTIN: Good luck, and a good fire!

FIRE CHIEF: Let's hope so. For everybody.

FIRE CHIEF exits. All accompany him to the door and then return to their seats.

MRS MARTIN: I can buy a pocketknife for my brother, but you can't buy Ireland for your grandfather.

MR SMITH: One walks on his feet, but one heats with electricity or coal.

MR MARTIN: He who sells an ox today, will have an egg tomorrow.

MRS SMITH: In real life, one must look out of the window.

MRS MARTIN: One can sit down on a chair, when the chair doesn't have any.

MR SMITH: One must always think of everything.

MR MARTIN: The ceiling is above, the floor is below.

MRS SMITH: When I say yes, it's only a manner of speaking.

MRS MARTIN: To each his own.

MR SMITH: Take a circle, caress it, and it will turn vicious.

MRS SMITH: A schoolmaster teaches his pupils to read, but the cat suckles her young when they are small.

MRS MARTIN: Nevertheless, it was the cow that gave us tails.

MR SMITH: When I'm in the country, I love the solitude and the quiet.

MR MARTIN: You are not old enough yet for that.

MRS SMITH: Benjamin Franklin was right; you are more nervous than he.

MRS MARTIN: What are the seven days of the week?

MR SMITH: Monday, Tuesday, Wednesday, Thursday, Friday, Saturday, Sunday.

MR MARTIN: Edward is a clerk; his sister Nancy is a typist, and his brother William a shop-assistant.

MRS SMITH: An odd family!

MRS MARTIN: I prefer a bird in the bush to a sparrow in a barrow.

MR SMITH: Rather a steak in a chalet than gristle in a castle.

MR MARTIN: An Englishman's home is truly his castle.

MRS SMITH: I don't know enough Spanish to make myself understood.

MRS MARTIN: I'll give you my mother-in-law's slippers if you'll give me your husband's coffin.

MR SMITH: I'm looking for a monophysite priest to marry to our maid.

MR MARTIN: Bread is a staff, whereas bread is also a staff, and an oak springs from an oak every morning at dawn.

MRS SMITH: My uncle lives in the country, but that's none of the midwife's business.

MR MARTIN: Paper is for writing, the cat's for the rat. Cheese is for scratching.

MRS SMITH: The car goes very fast, but the cook beats batter better.

MR SMITH: Don't be turkeys; rather kiss the conspirator.

MR MARTIN: Charity begins at home.

MRS SMITH: I'm waiting for the aqueduct to come and see me at my windmill.

MR MARTIN: One can prove that social progress is definitely better with sugar.

MR SMITH: To hell with polishing!

Following this last speech of MR SMITH's, the others are silent for a moment, stupefied. We sense that there is a certain nervous irritation. The strokes of the clock are more nervous too. The speeches which follow must be said, at first, in a glacial, hostile tone. The hostility and the nervousness increase. At the end of this scene, the four characters must be standing very close to each other, screaming their speeches, raising their fists, ready to throw themselves upon each other.

MR MARTIN: One doesn't polish spectacles with black wax.

MRS SMITH: Yes, but with money one can buy anything.

MR MARTIN: I'd rather kill a rabbit than sing in the garden.

MR SMITH: Cockatoos, cockatoos, cockatoos, cockatoos, cockatoos, cockatoos, cockatoos, cockatoos, cockatoos.

MRS SMITH: Such caca, such caca, such caca, such caca, such caca, such caca, such caca, such caca, such caca.

MR MARTIN: Such cascades of cacas, such cascades of cacas, such cascades of cacas, such cascades of cacas, such cascades of cacas, such cascades of cacas, such cascades of cacas, such cascades of cacas.

MR SMITH: Dogs have fleas, dogs have fleas.

MRS MARTIN: Cactus, coccyx! crocus! cockaded! cockroach!

MRS SMITH: Incasker, you incask us.

MR MARTIN: I'd rather lay an egg in a box than go and steal an ox.

MRS MARTIN: (*Opening her mouth very wide.*) Ah! oh! ah! oh! Let me gnash my teeth.

MR SMITH: Crocodile!

MR MARTIN: Let's go and slap Ulysses.

MR SMITH: I'm going to live in my cabana among my cacao trees.

MRS MARTIN: Cacao trees on cacao farms don't bear coconuts, they yield cocoa! Cacao trees on cacao farms don't bear coconuts, they yield cocoa! Cacao trees on cacao farms don't bear coconuts, they yield cocoa.

MRS SMITH: Mice have lice, lice haven't mice.

MRS MARTIN: Don't ruche my brooch!

MR MARTIN: Don't smooch the brooch!

MR SMITH: Groom the goose, don't goose the groom.

MRS MARTIN: The goose grooms.

MR SMITH: Groom your tooth.

MR MARTIN: Groom the bridegroom, groom the bridegroom.

MR SMITH: Seducer seduced!

MRS MARTIN: Scaramouche!

MR SMITH: Sainte-Nitouche!

MR MARTIN: Go take a douche.

MR SMITH: I've been goosed.

MRS MARTIN: Sainte-Nitouche stoops to my cartouche.

MRS SMITH: 'Who'd stoop to blame? … and I never choose to stoop.'

MR MARTIN: Robert!

MR SMITH: Browning!

MRS MARTIN, MR SMITH: Rudyard.

MRS SMITH, MR MARTIN: Kipling.

MRS MARTIN, MR SMITH: Robert Kipling!

MRS SMITH, MR MARTIN: Rudyard Browning.

MRS MARTIN: Silly gobblegobblers, silly gobblegobblers.

MR MARTIN: Marietta, spot the pot!

MRS SMITH: Krishnamurti, Krishnamurti, Krishnamurti!

MR SMITH: The pope elopes! The pope's got no horoscope. The horoscope's bespoke.

MRS MARTIN: Bazaar, Balzac, bazooka!

MR MARTIN: Bizarre, beaux-arts, brassieres!

MR SMITH: A, e, i, o, u, a, e, i, o, u, a, e, i, o, u, i!

MRS MARTIN: B, c, d, f, g, l, m, n, p, r, s, t, v, w, x, z!

MR MARTIN: From sage to stooge, from stage to serge!

MRS SMITH: (*Imitating a train.*) Choo, choo, choo, choo, choo, choo, choo, choo, choo, choo, choo!

MR SMITH: It's!

MRS MARTIN: Not!

MR MARTIN: That!

MRS SMITH: Way!

MR SMITH: It's!

MRS MARTIN: O!

MR MARTIN: Ver!

MRS SMITH: Here!

All together, completely infuriated, screaming in each others' ears. The light is extinguished. In the darkness we hear, in an increasingly rapid rhythm:

ALL TOGETHER: It's not that way, it's over here, it's not that way, it's over here, it's not that way, it's over here, it's not that way, it's over here!

The words cease abruptly. Again, the lights come on. MR *and* MRS MARTIN *are seated like the Smiths at the beginning of the play. The play begins again with the Martins, who say exactly the same lines as the Smiths in the first scene, while the curtain softly falls.*

4.2 **ENDGAME** (1957)

SAMUEL BECKETT

[For Roger Blin]

Samuel Beckett (1906-89) *was an Irish playwright, novelist, poet and director whose work was originally produced in French. He lived in Paris, France, for most of his professional life and is viewed by
many as one of the most influential playwrights of the twentieth century. Whilst his major works are
seen as integral to late modernism, his work has also influenced many postmodern theatre practitioners. He joined the French Resistance during the Second World War and was awarded the Nobel
Prize in Literature in 1969. His first play* Waiting for Godot *(written in 1949), featuring two tramps
on a roadside, was notoriously reviewed as a 'play in which nothing happens twice'. A number of his
plays explore the relationship between real time, theatrical time and memory. Beckett's late plays,
such as* Not I *(1972) and* Footfalls *(1975), manipulate theatrical space and are entirely anti-realist.
Known as a demanding director, who insisted on precision of delivery and absolute adherence to text,
Beckett worked repeatedly with key performers including Billy Whitelaw (1932–2014) and Patrick
Magee (1924–82). More recently, the UK theatre company Complicité have produced and toured
successful productions of* Endgame *(2009) and* Rockaby *(2008). Robert Wilson's production of*
Krapp's Last Tape *premiered in 2009 and has toured internationally since then.*

The Characters

HAMM
CLOV
NAGG
NELL

Bare interior.

Grey light.

Left and right back, high up, two small windows, curtains drawn.
Front right, a door. Hanging near door, its face to wall, a picture.
Front left, touching each other, covered with an old sheet, two ashbins.
Centre, in an armchair on castors, covered with an old sheet, HAMM.
Motionless by the door, his eyes fixed on HAMM, CLOV. *Very red face.*
Brief tableau.

CLOV *goes and stands under window left. Stiff, staggering walk. He looks up at window left. He turns and looks at window
right. He goes and stands under window right. He looks up at window right. He turns and looks at window left. He goes
out, comes back immediately with a small step-ladder, carries it over and sets it down under window left, gets up on it, draws
back curtain. He gets down, takes six steps (for example) towards window right, goes back for ladder, carries it over and sets
it down under window right, gets up on it, draws back curtain. He gets down, takes three steps towards window left, goes*

back for ladder, carries it over and sets it down under window left, gets up on it, looks out of window. Brief laugh. He gets down, takes one step towards window right, goes back for ladder, carries it over and sets it down under window right, gets up on it, looks out of window. Brief laugh. He gets down, goes with ladder towards ashbins, halts, turns, carries back ladder and sets it down under window right, goes to ashbins, removes sheet covering them, folds it over his arm. He raises one lid, stoops and looks into bin. Brief laugh. He closes lid. Same with other bin. He goes to HAMM, *removes sheet covering him, folds it over his arm. In a dressing-gown, a stiff toque on his head, a large blood-stained handkerchief over his face, a whistle hanging from his neck, a rug over his knees, thick socks on his feet,* HAMM *seems to be asleep.* CLOV *looks him over. Brief laugh. He goes to door, halts, turns towards auditorium.*

CLOV: (*Fixed gaze, tonelessly.*) Finished, it's finished, nearly finished, it must be nearly finished. (*Pause.*) Grain upon grain, one by one, and one day, suddenly, there's a heap, a little heap, the impossible heap. (*Pause.*) I can't be punished any more. (*Pause.*) I'll go now to my kitchen, ten feet by ten feet by ten feet, and wait for him to whistle me. (*Pause.*) Nice dimensions, nice proportions, I'll lean on the table, and look at the wall, and wait for him to whistle me.

He remains a moment motionless, then goes out. He comes back immediately, goes to window right, takes up the ladder and carries it out. Pause. HAMM *stirs. He yawns under the handkerchief. He removes the handkerchief from his face. Very red face. Black glasses.*

HAMM: Me − (*He yawns.*) − to play. (*He holds the handkerchief spread out before him.*) Old stancher! (*He takes off his glasses, wipes his eyes, his face, the glasses, puts them on again, folds the handkerchief and puts it neatly in the breast-pocket of his dressing-gown. He clears his throat, joins the tips of his fingers.*) Can there be misery − (*he yawns*) loftier than mine? No doubt. Formerly. But now? (*Pause.*) My father? (*Pause.*) My mother? (*Pause.*) My ... dog? (*Pause.*) Oh I am willing to believe they suffer as much as such creatures can suffer. But does that mean their sufferings equal mine? No doubt. (*Pause.*) No, all is a − (*he yawns*) − bsolute, (*proudly*) the bigger a man is the fuller he is. (*Pause. Gloomily.*) And the emptier. (*He sniffs.*) Clov! (*Pause.*) No, alone. (*Pause.*) What dreams! Those forests! (*Pause.*) Enough, it's time it ended, in the refuge too. (*Pause.*) And yet I hesitate, I hesitate to ... to end. Yes, there it is, it's time it ended and yet I hesitate to − (*he yawns*) − to end. (*Yawns.*) God, I'm tired, I'd be better off in bed. (*He whistles. Enter Clov immediately. He halts beside the chair.*) You pollute the air! (*Pause.*) Get me ready, I'm going to bed.

CLOV: I've just got you up.

HAMM: And what of it?

CLOV: I can't be getting you up and putting you to bed every five minutes, I have things to do. (*Pause.*)

HAMM: Did you ever see my eyes?

CLOV: No.

HAMM: Did you never have the curiosity, while I was sleeping, to take off my glasses and look at my eyes?

CLOV: Pulling back the lids? (*Pause.*) No.

HAMM: One of these days I'll show them to you. (*Pause.*) It seems they've gone all white. (*Pause.*) What time is it?

CLOV: The same as usual.

HAMM: (*Gesture towards window right.*) Have you looked?

CLOV: Yes.

HAMM: Well?

CLOV: Zero.

HAMM: It'd need to rain.

CLOV: It won't rain.

Pause.

HAMM: Apart from that, how do you feel?

CLOV: I don't complain.

HAMM: You feel normal?

CLOV: (*Irritably.*) I tell you I don't complain!

HAMM: I feel a little queer. (*Pause.*) Clov!

CLOV: Yes.

HAMM: Have you not had enough?

CLOV: Yes! (*Pause.*) Of what?

HAMM: Of this ... this ... thing.

CLOV: I always had. (*Pause.*) Not you?

HAMM: (*Gloomily.*) Then there's no reason for it to change.

CLOV: It may end. (*Pause.*) All life long the same questions, the same answers.

HAMM: Get me ready. (CLOV *does not move.*) Go and get the sheet. (CLOV *does not move.*) Clov!

CLOV: Yes.

HAMM: I'll give you nothing more to eat.

CLOV: Then we'll die.

HAMM: I'll give you just enough to keep you from dying. You'll be hungry all the time.

CLOV: Then we shan't die. (*Pause.*) I'll go and get the sheet.

He goes towards the door.

HAMM: No! (CLOV *halts.*) I'll give you one biscuit per day. (*Pause.*) One and a half. (*Pause.*) Why do you stay with me?

CLOV: Why do you keep me?

HAMM: There's no one else.

CLOV: There's nowhere else.

Pause.

HAMM: You're leaving me all the same.

CLOV: I'm trying.

HAMM: You don't love me.

CLOV: No.

HAMM: You loved me once.

CLOV: Once!

HAMM: I've made you suffer too much. (*Pause.*) Haven't I?

CLOV: It's not that.

HAMM: (*Shocked.*) I haven't made you suffer too much?

CLOV: Yes!

HAMM: (*Relieved.*) Ah you gave me a fright! (*Pause. Coldly.*) Forgive me. (*Pause. Louder.*) I said, Forgive me.

CLOV: I heard you. (*Pause.*) Have you bled?

HAMM: Less. (*Pause.*) Is it not time for my pain-killer?

CLOV: No.

> *Pause.*

HAMM: How are your eyes?

CLOV: Bad.

HAMM: How are your legs?

CLOV: Bad.

HAMM: But you can move.

CLOV: Yes.

HAMM: (*Violently.*) Then move! (*CLOV goes to back wall, leans against it with his forehead and hands.*) Where are you?

CLOV: Here.

HAMM: Come back! (*CLOV returns to his place beside the chair.*) Where are you?

CLOV: Here.

HAMM: Why don't you kill me?

CLOV: I don't know the combination of the larder.

> *Pause.*

HAMM: Go and get two bicycle-wheels.

CLOV: There are no more bicycle-wheels.

HAMM: What have you done with your bicycle?

CLOV: I never had a bicycle.

HAMM: The thing is impossible.

CLOV: When there were still bicycles I wept to have one. I crawled at your feet. You told me to get out to hell. Now there are none.

HAMM: And your rounds? When you inspected my paupers. Always on foot?

CLOV: Sometimes on horse. (*The lid of one of the bins lifts and the hands of NAGG appear, gripping the rim. Then his head emerges. Nightcap. Very white face. NAGG yawns, then listens.*) I'll leave you, I have things to do.

HAMM: In your kitchen?

CLOV: Yes.

HAMM: Outside of here it's death. (*Pause.*) All right, be off. (*Exit CLOV. Pause.*) We're getting on.

NAGG: Me pap!

HAMM: Accursed progenitor!

NAGG: Me pap!

HAMM: The old folks at home! No decency left! Guzzle, guzzle, that's all they think of. (*He whistles. Enter CLOV. He halts beside the chair.*) Well! I thought you were leaving me.

CLOV: Oh not just yet, not just yet.

NAGG: Me pap!

HAMM: Give him his pap.

CLOV: There's no more pap.

HAMM: (*To NAGG.*) Do you hear that? There's no more pap. You'll never get any more pap.

NAGG: I want me pap!

HAMM: Give him a biscuit. (*Exit CLOV.*) Accursed fornicator! How are your stumps?

NAGG: Never mind me stumps.

> *Enter CLOV with biscuit.*

CLOV: I'm back again, with the biscuit.

> *He gives the biscuit to NAGG who fingers it, sniffs it.*

NAGG: (*Plaintively.*) What is it?

CLOV: Spratt's medium.

NAGG: (*As before.*) It's hard! I can't!

HAMM: Bottle him!

> *CLOV pushes NAGG back into the bin, closes the lid.*

CLOV: (*Returning to his place beside the chair*). If age but knew!

HAMM: Sit on him!

CLOV: I can't sit.

HAMM: True. And I can't stand.

CLOV: So it is.

HAMM: Every man his speciality. (*Pause.*) No phone calls? (*Pause.*) Don't we laugh?

CLOV: (*After reflection.*) I don't feel like it.

HAMM: (*After reflection.*) Nor I. (*Pause.*) Clov!

CLOV: Yes.

HAMM: Nature has forgotten us.

CLOV: There's no more nature.

HAMM: No more nature! You exaggerate.

CLOV: In the vicinity.

HAMM: But we breathe, we change! We lose our hair, our teeth! Our bloom! Our ideals!

CLOV: Then she hasn't forgotten us.

HAMM: But you say there is none.

CLOV: (*Sadly.*) No one that ever lived ever thought so crooked as we.

HAMM: We do what we can.

CLOV: We shouldn't.

> *Pause.*

HAMM: You're a bit of all right, aren't you?

CLOV: A smithereen.

> *Pause.*

HAMM: This is slow work. (*Pause.*) Is it not time for my painkiller?

CLOV: No. (*Pause.*) I'll leave you, I have things to do.

HAMM: In your kitchen?

CLOV: Yes.

HAMM: What, I'd like to know.

CLOV: I look at the wall.

HAMM: The wall! And what do you see on your wall? Mene, mene? Naked bodies?

CLOV: I see my light dying.

HAMM: Your light dying! Listen to that! Well, it can die just as well here, *your* light. Take a look at me and then come back and tell me what you think of *your* light.

Pause.

CLOV: You shouldn't speak to me like that.

Pause.

HAMM: (*Coldly.*) Forgive me. (*Pause. Louder.*) I said, Forgive me.

CLOV: I heard you.

The lid of NAGG'*s bin lifts. His hands appear, gripping the rim. Then his head emerges. In his mouth the biscuit. He listens.*

HAMM: Did your seeds come up?

CLOV: No.

HAMM: Did you scratch round them to see if they had sprouted?

CLOV: They haven't sprouted.

HAMM: Perhaps it's still too early.

CLOV: If they were going to sprout they would have sprouted. (*Violently.*) They'll never sprout.

Pause. NAGG *takes biscuit in his hand.*

HAMM: This is not much fun. (*Pause.*) But that's always the way at the end of the day, isn't it, Clov?

CLOV: Always.

HAMM: It's the end of the day like any other day, isn't it, Clov?

CLOV: Looks like it.

Pause.

HAMM: (*Anguished.*) What's happening, what's happening?

CLOV: Something is taking its course.

Pause.

HAMM: All right, be off. (*He leans back in his chair, remains motionless.* CLOV *does not move, heaves a great groaning sigh.* HAMM *sits up.*) I thought I told you to be off.

CLOV: I'm trying. (*He goes to door, halts.*) Ever since I was whelped. (*Exit* CLOV.)

HAMM: We're getting on.

He leans back in his chair, remains motionless. NAGG *knocks on the lid of the other bin. Pause. He knocks harder. The lid lifts and the hands of* NELL *appear, gripping the rim. Then her head emerges. Lace cap. Very white face.*

NELL: What is it, my pet? (*Pause.*) Time for love?

NAGG: Were you asleep?

NELL: Oh no!

NAGG: Kiss me.

NELL: We can't.

NAGG: Try.

Their heads strain towards each other, fail to meet, fall apart again.

NELL: Why this farce, day after day?

Pause.

NAGG: I've lost me tooth.

NELL: When?

NAGG: I had it yesterday.

NELL: (*Elegiac.*) Ah yesterday!

They turn painfully towards each other.

NAGG: Can you see me?

NELL: Hardly. And you?

NAGG: What?

NELL: Can you see me?

NAGG: Hardly.

NELL: So much the better, so much the better.

NAGG: Don't say that. (*Pause.*) Our sight has failed.

NELL: Yes.

Pause. They turn away from each other.

NAGG: Can you hear me?

NELL: Yes. And you?

NAGG: Yes. (*Pause.*) Our hearing hasn't failed.

NELL: Our what?

NAGG: Our hearing.

NELL: No. (*Pause.*) Have you anything else to say to me?

NAGG: Do you remember –

NELL: No.

NAGG: When we crashed on our tandem and lost our shanks.

They laugh heartily.

NELL: It was in the Ardennes.

They laugh less heartily.

NAGG: On the road to Sedan. (*They laugh still less heartily.*) Are you cold?

NELL: Yes, perished. And you?

NAGG: I'm freezing. (*Pause.*) Do you want to go in?

NELL: Yes.

NAGG: Then go in. (NELL *does not move.*) Why don't you go in?

NELL: I don't know.

Pause.

NAGG: Has he changed your sawdust?

NELL: It isn't sawdust. (*Pause. Wearily.*) Can you not be a little accurate, Nagg?

NAGG: Your sand then. It's not important.

NELL: It is important.

Pause.

NAGG: It was sawdust once.

NELL: Once!

NAGG: And now it's sand. (*Pause.*) From the shore. (*Pause. Impatiently.*) Now it's sand he fetches from the shore.

NELL: Now it's sand.

NAGG: Has he changed yours?

NELL: No.

NAGG: Nor mine. (*Pause.*) I won't have it! (*Pause. Holding up the biscuit.*) Do you want a bit?

NELL: No. (*Pause.*) Of what?

NAGG: Biscuit. I've kept you half. (*He looks at the biscuit. Proudly.*) Three quarters. For you. Here. (*He proffers the biscuit.*) No? (*Pause.*) Do you not feel well?

HAMM: (*Wearily.*) Quiet, quiet, you're keeping me awake. (*Pause.*) Talk softer. (*Pause.*) If I could sleep I might make love. I'd go into the woods. My eyes would see … the sky, the earth. I'd run, run, they wouldn't catch me. (*Pause.*) Nature! (*Pause.*) There's something dripping in my head. (*Pause.*) A heart, a heart in my head.

Pause.

NAGG: (*Soft*). Do you hear him? A heart in his head! (*He chuckles cautiously.*)

NELL: One mustn't laugh at those things, Nagg. Why must you always laugh at them?

NAGG: Not so loud!

NELL: (*Without lowering her voice.*) Nothing is funnier than unhappiness, I grant you that. But –

NAGG: (*Shocked.*) Oh!

NELL: Yes, yes, it's the most comical thing in the world. And we laugh, we laugh, with a will, in the beginning. But it's always the same thing. Yes, it's like the funny story we have heard too often, we still find it funny, but we don't laugh any more. (*Pause.*) Have you anything else to say to me?

NAGG: No.

NELL: Are you quite sure? (*Pause.*) Then I'll leave you.

NAGG: Do you not want your biscuit? (*Pause.*) I'll keep it for you. (*Pause.*) I thought you were going to leave me.

NELL: I am going to leave you.

NAGG: Could you give me a scratch before you go?

NELL: No. (*Pause.*) Where?

NAGG: In the back.

NELL: No. (*Pause.*) Rub yourself against the rim.

NAGG: It's lower down. In the hollow.

NELL: What hollow?

NAGG: The hollow! (*Pause.*) Could you not? (*Pause.*) Yesterday you scratched me there.

NELL: (*Elegiac.*) Ah yesterday!

NAGG: Could you not? (*Pause.*) Would you like me to scratch you? (*Pause.*) Are you crying again?

NELL: I was trying.

Pause.

HAMM: Perhaps it's a little vein.

Pause.

NAGG: What was that he said?

NELL: Perhaps it's a little vein.

NAGG: What does that mean? (*Pause.*) That means nothing. (*Pause.*) Will I tell you the story of the tailor?

NELL: No. (*Pause.*) What for?

NAGG: To cheer you up.

NELL: It's not funny.

NAGG: It always made you laugh. (*Pause.*) The first time I thought you'd die.

NELL: It was on Lake Como. (*Pause.*) One April afternoon. (*Pause.*) Can you believe it?

NAGG: What?

NELL: That we once went out rowing on Lake Como. (*Pause.*) One April afternoon.

NAGG: We had got engaged the day before.

NELL: Engaged!

NAGG: You were in such fits that we capsized. By rights we should have been drowned.

NELL: It was because I felt happy.

NAGG: (*Indignant.*) It was not, it was not, it was my story and nothing else. Happy! Don't you laugh at it still? Every time I tell it. Happy!

NELL: It was deep, deep. And you could see down to the bottom. So white. So clean.

NAGG: Let me tell it again. (*Raconteur's voice.*) An Englishman, needing a pair of striped trousers in a hurry for the New Year festivities, goes to his tailor who takes his measurements. (*Tailor's voice.*) 'That's the lot, come back in four days, I'll have it ready.' Good. Four days later. (*Tailor's voice.*) 'So sorry, come back in a week, I've made a mess of the seat.' Good, that's all right, a neat seat can be very ticklish. A week later. (*Tailor's voice.*) 'Frightfully sorry, come back in ten days, I've made a hash of the crutch.' Good, can't be helped, a snug crutch is always a teaser. Ten days later. (*Tailor's voice.*) 'Dreadfully sorry, come back in a fortnight, I've made a balls of the fly.' Good, at

Figure 24 Tom Hickey and Miriam Margolyes in *Endgame*, London, 2009. (Photograph: Tristram Kenton.)

a pinch, a smart fly is a stiff proposition. (*Pause. Normal voice.*) I never told it worse. (*Pause. Gloomy.*) I tell this story worse and worse. (*Pause. Raconteur's voice.*) Well, to make it short, the bluebells are blowing and he ballockses the buttonholes. (*Customer's voice.*) 'God damn you to hell, Sir, no, it's indecent, there are limits! In six days, do you hear me, six days, God made the world. Yes Sir, no less Sir, the WORLD! And you are not bloody well capable of making me a pair of trousers in three months!' (*Tailor's voice, scandalized.*) 'But my dear Sir, my dear Sir, look – (*disdainful gesture, disgustedly*) – at the world – (*pause*) – and look – (*loving gesture, proudly*) – at my TROUSERS!'

Pause. He looks at NELL *who has remained impassive, her eyes unseeing, breaks into a high forced laugh, cuts it short, pokes his head towards* NELL, *launches his laugh again.*

HAMM: Silence!

NAGG *starts, cuts short his laugh.*

NELL: You could see down to the bottom.

HAMM: (*Exasperated.*) Have you not finished? Will you never finish? (*With sudden fury.*) Will this never finish? (NAGG *disappears into his bin, closes the lid behind him.* NELL *does not move. Frenziedly.*) My kingdom for a nightman! (*He whistles. Enter* CLOV.) Clear away this muck! Chuck it in the sea!

CLOV *goes to bins, halts.*

NELL: So white.

HAMM: What? What's she blathering about?

CLOV *stoops, takes* NELL's *hand, feels her pulse.*

NELL: (*To* CLOV.) Desert!

CLOV *lets go her hand, pushes her back in the bin, closes the lid.*

CLOV: (*Returning to his place beside the chair.*) She has no pulse.

HAMM: What was she drivelling about?

CLOV: She told me to go away, into the desert.

HAMM: Damn busybody! Is that all?

CLOV: No.

HAMM: What else?

CLOV: I didn't understand.

HAMM: Have you bottled her?

CLOV: Yes.

HAMM: Are they both bottled?

CLOV: Yes.

HAMM: Screw down the lids. (CLOV *goes towards door.*) Time enough. (CLOV *halts.*) My anger subsides, I'd like to pee.

CLOV: (*With alacrity.*) I'll go and get the catheter.

He goes towards the door.

HAMM: Time enough. (CLOV *halts.*) Give me my pain-killer.

CLOV: It's too soon. (*Pause.*) It's too soon on top of your tonic, it wouldn't act.

HAMM: In the morning they brace you up and in the evening they calm you down. Unless it's the other way round. (*Pause.*) That old doctor, he's dead, naturally?

CLOV: He wasn't old.

HAMM: But he's dead?

CLOV: Naturally. (*Pause.*) You ask *me* that? (*Pause.*)

HAMM: Take me for a little turn. (CLOV *goes behind the chair and pushes it forward.*) Not too fast! (CLOV *pushes chair.*) Right round the world! (CLOV *pushes chair.*) Hug the walls, then back to the centre again. (CLOV *pushes chair.*) I was right in the centre, wasn't I?

CLOV: (*Pushing.*) Yes.

HAMM: We'd need a proper wheel-chair. With big wheels. Bicycle wheels! (*Pause.*) Are you hugging?

CLOV: (*Pushing.*) Yes.

HAMM: (*Groping for wall.*) It's a lie! Why do you lie to me?

CLOV: (*Bearing closer to wall.*) There! There!

HAMM: Stop! (CLOV *stops chair close to back wall.* HAMM *lays his hand against wall.*) Old wall! (*Pause.*) Beyond is the … other hell. (*Pause. Violently.*) Closer! Closer! Up against!

CLOV: Take away your hand. (HAMM *withdraws his hand.* CLOV *rams chair against wall.*) There!

HAMM *leans towards wall, applies his ear to it.*

HAMM: Do you hear? (*He strikes the wall with his knuckles.*) Do you hear? Hollow bricks! (*He strikes again.*) All that's hollow! (*Pause. He straightens up. Violently.*) That's enough. Back!

CLOV: We haven't done the round.

HAMM: Back to my place! (CLOV *pushes chair back to centre.*) Is that my place?

CLOV: Yes, that's your place.

HAMM: Am I right in the centre?

CLOV: I'll measure it.

HAMM: More or less! More or less!

CLOV: (*Moving chair slightly.*) There!

HAMM: I'm more or less in the centre?

CLOV: I'd say so.

HAMM: You'd say so! Put me right in the centre!

CLOV: I'll go and get the tape.

HAMM: Roughly! Roughly! (CLOV *moves chair slightly.*) Bang in the centre!

CLOV: There!

Pause.

HAMM: I feel a little too far to the left. (CLOV *moves chair slightly.*) Now I feel a little too far to the right. (CLOV *moves chair slightly.*) I feel a little too far forward. (CLOV *moves chair slightly.*) Now I feel a little too far back. (CLOV *moves chair slightly.*) Don't stay there (*i.e. behind the chair*), you give me the shivers.

CLOV *returns to his place beside the chair.*

CLOV: If I could kill him I'd die happy.

Pause.

HAMM: What's the weather like?

CLOV: The same as usual.

HAMM: Look at the earth.

CLOV: I've looked.

HAMM: With the glass?

CLOV: No need of the glass.

HAMM: Look at it with the glass.

CLOV: I'll go and get the glass.

Exit CLOV.

HAMM: No need of the glass!

Enter CLOV with telescope.

CLOV: I'm back again, with the glass. (*He goes to window right, looks up at it.*) I need the steps.

HAMM: Why? Have you shrunk? (*Exit CLOV with telescope.*) I don't like that, I don't like that.

Enter CLOV with ladder, but without telescope.

CLOV: I'm back again, with the steps. (*He sets down ladder under window right, gets up on it, realizes he has not the telescope, gets down.*) I need the glass.

He goes towards the door.

HAMM: (*Violently.*) But you have the glass!

CLOV: (*Halting, violently.*) No I haven't the glass!

Exit CLOV.

HAMM: This is deadly.

Enter CLOV with telescope. He goes towards ladder.

CLOV: Things are livening up. (*He gets up on ladder, raises the telescope, lets it fall.*) I did it on purpose. (*He gets down, picks up the telescope, turns it on auditorium.*) I see ... a multitude ... in transports ... of joy. (*Pause.*) That's what I call a magnifier. (*He lowers the telescope, turns towards HAMM.*) Well? Don't we laugh?

HAMM: (*After reflection.*) I don't.

CLOV: (*After reflection.*) Nor I. (*He gets up on ladder, turns the telescope on the without.*) Let's see. (*He looks, moving the telescope.*) Zero ... (*he looks*) ... zero ... (*he looks*) ... and zero.

HAMM: Nothing stirs. All is –

CLOV: Zer –

HAMM: (*Violently.*) Wait till you're spoken to! (*Normal voice.*) All is ... all is ... all is what? (*Violently.*) All is what?

CLOV: What all is? In a word? Is that what you want to know? Just a moment. (*He turns the telescope on the without, looks, lowers the telescope, turns towards HAMM.*) Corpsed. (*Pause.*) Well? Content?

HAMM: Look at the sea.

CLOV: It's the same.

HAMM: Look at the ocean!

CLOV gets down, takes a few steps towards window left, goes back for ladder, carries it over and sets it down under window left, gets up on it, turns the telescope on the without, looks at length. He starts, lowers the telescope, examines it, turns it again on the without.

CLOV: Never seen anything like that!

HAMM: (*Anxious.*) What? A sail? A fin? Smoke?

CLOV: (*Looking.*) The light is sunk.

HAMM: (*Relieved.*) Pah! We all knew that.

CLOV: (*Looking.*) There was a bit left.

HAMM: The base.

CLOV: (*Looking.*) Yes.

HAMM: And now?

CLOV: (*Looking.*) All gone.

HAMM: No gulls?

CLOV: (*Looking.*) Gulls!

HAMM: And the horizon? Nothing on the horizon?

CLOV: (*Lowering the telescope, turning towards HAMM, exasperated.*) What in God's name could there be on the horizon?

Pause.

HAMM: The waves, how are the waves?

CLOV: The waves? (*He turns the telescope on the waves.*) Lead.

HAMM: And the sun?

CLOV: (*Looking.*) Zero.

HAMM: But it should be sinking. Look again.

CLOV: (*Looking.*) Damn the sun.

HAMM: Is it night already then?

CLOV: (*Looking.*) No.

HAMM: Then what is it?

CLOV: (*Looking.*) Grey. (*Lowering the telescope, turning towards HAMM, louder.*) Grey! (*Pause. Still louder.*) GRREY!

Pause. He gets down, approaches HAMM from behind, whispers in his ear.

HAMM: (*Starting.*) Grey! Did I hear you say grey?

CLOV: Light black. From pole to pole.

HAMM: You exaggerate. (*Pause.*) Don't stay there, you give me the shivers.

CLOV returns to his place beside the chair.

CLOV: Why this farce, day after day?

HAMM: Routine. One never knows. (*Pause.*) Last night I saw inside my breast. There was a big sore.

CLOV: Pah! You saw your heart.

HAMM: No, it was living. (*Pause. Anguished.*) Clov!

CLOV: Yes.

HAMM: What's happening?

CLOV: Something is taking its course.

Pause.

HAMM: Clov!

CLOV: (*Impatiently.*) What is it?

HAMM: We're not beginning to ... to ... mean something?

CLOV: Mean something! You and I, mean something! (*Brief laugh.*) Ah that's a good one!

HAMM: I wonder. (*Pause.*) Imagine if a rational being came back to earth, wouldn't he be liable to get ideas into his head if he observed us long enough. (*Voice of rational being.*) Ah, good, now I see what it is, yes, now I understand what they're at! (*CLOV starts, drops the telescope and begins to scratch his belly with both hands. Normal voice.*) And without going so far as that, we ourselves … (*with emotion*) … we ourselves … at certain moments … (*Vehemently.*) To think perhaps it won't all have been for nothing!

CLOV: (*Anguished, scratching himself.*) I have a flea!

HAMM: A flea! Are there still fleas?

CLOV: On me there's one. (*Scratching.*) Unless it's a crablouse.

HAMM: (*Very perturbed.*) But humanity might start from there all over again! Catch him, for the love of God!

CLOV: I'll go and get the powder.

Exit CLOV.

HAMM: A flea! This is awful! What a day!

Enter CLOV with a sprinkling-tin.

CLOV: I'm back again, with the insecticide.

HAMM: Let him have it!

CLOV loosens the top of his trousers, pulls it forward and shakes powder into the aperture. He stoops, looks, waits, starts, frenziedly shakes more powder, stoops, looks, waits.

CLOV: The bastard!

HAMM: Did you get him?

CLOV: Looks like it. (*He drops the tin and adjusts his trousers.*) Unless he's laying doggo.

HAMM: Laying! Lying you mean. Unless he's *lying* doggo.

CLOV: Ah? One says lying? One doesn't say laying?

HAMM: Use your head, can't you. If he was laying we'd be bitched.

CLOV: Ah. (*Pause.*) What about that pee?

HAMM: I'm having it.

CLOV: Ah that's the spirit, that's the spirit!

Pause.

HAMM: (*With ardour.*) Let's go from here, the two of us! South! You can make a raft and the currents will carry us away, far away, to other … mammals!

CLOV: God forbid!

HAMM: Alone, I'll embark alone! Get working on that raft immediately. Tomorrow I'll be gone for ever.

CLOV: (*Hastening towards door.*) I'll start straight away.

HAMM: Wait! (*CLOV halts.*) Will there be sharks, do you think?

CLOV: Sharks? I don't know. If there are there will be.

He goes towards door.

HAMM: Wait! (*CLOV halts.*) Is it not yet time for my pain-killer?

CLOV: (*Violently.*) No!

He goes towards door.

HAMM: Wait! (*CLOV halts.*) How are your eyes?

CLOV: Bad.

HAMM: But you can see.

CLOV: All I want.

HAMM: How are your legs?

CLOV: Bad.

HAMM: But you can walk.

CLOV: I come … and go.

HAMM: In my house. (*Pause. With prophetic relish.*) One day you'll be blind, like me. You'll be sitting there, a speck in the void, in the dark, for ever, like me. (*Pause.*) One day you'll say to yourself, I'm tired, I'll sit down, and you'll go and sit down. Then you'll say, I'm hungry, I'll get up and get something to eat. But you won't get up. You'll say, I shouldn't have sat down, but since I have I'll sit on a little longer, then I'll get up and get something to eat. But you won't get up and you won't get anything to eat. (*Pause.*) You'll look at the wall a while, then you'll say, I'll close my eyes, perhaps have a little sleep, after that I'll feel better, and you'll close them. And when you open them again there'll be no wall any more. (*Pause.*) Infinite emptiness will be all around you, all the resurrected dead of all the ages wouldn't fill it, and there you'll be like a little bit of grit in the middle of the steppe. (*Pause.*) Yes, one day you'll know what it is, you'll be like me, except that you won't have anyone with you, because you won't have had pity on anyone and because there won't be anyone left to have pity on.

Pause.

CLOV: It's not certain. (*Pause.*) And there's one thing you forget.

HAMM: Ah?

CLOV: I can't sit down.

HAMM: (*Impatiently.*) Well, you'll lie down then, what the hell! Or you'll come to a standstill, simply stop and stand still, the way you are now. One day you'll say, I'm tired, I'll stop. What does the attitude matter?

Pause.

CLOV: So you all want me to leave you.

HAMM: Naturally.

CLOV: Then I'll leave you.

HAMM: You can't leave us.

CLOV: Then I shan't leave you.

Pause.

HAMM: Why don't you finish us? (*Pause.*) I'll tell you the combination of the larder if you promise to finish me.

CLOV: I couldn't finish you.

HAMM: Then you shan't finish me.

Pause.

CLOV: I'll leave you, I have things to do.

HAMM: Do you remember when you came here?

CLOV: No. Too small, you told me.

HAMM: Do you remember your father?

CLOV: (*Wearily.*) Same answer. (*Pause.*) You've asked me these questions millions of times.

HAMM: I love the old questions. (*With fervour.*) Ah the old questions, the old answers, there's nothing like them! (*Pause.*) It was I was a father to you.

CLOV: Yes. (*He looks at* HAMM *fixedly.*) You were that to me.

HAMM: My house a home for you.

CLOV: Yes. (*He looks about him.*) This was that for me.

HAMM: (*Proudly.*) But for me (*gesture towards himself*) no father. But for Hamm (*gesture towards surroundings*) no home.

Pause.

CLOV: I'll leave you.

HAMM: Did you ever think of one thing?

CLOV: Never.

HAMM: That here we're down in a hole. (*Pause.*) But beyond the hills? Eh? Perhaps it's still green. Eh? (*Pause.*) Flora! Pomona! (*Ecstatically.*) Ceres! (*Pause.*) Perhaps you won't need to go very far.

CLOV: I can't go very far. (*Pause.*) I'll leave you.

HAMM: Is my dog ready?

CLOV: He lacks a leg.

HAMM: Is he silky?

CLOV: He's a kind of Pomeranian.

HAMM: Go and get him.

CLOV: He lacks a leg.

HAMM: Go and get him! (*Exit* CLOV.) We're getting on.

Enter CLOV *holding by one of its three legs a black toy dog.*

CLOV: Your dogs are here.

He hands the dog to HAMM *who feels it, fondles it.*

HAMM: He's white, isn't he?

CLOV: Nearly.

HAMM: What do you mean, nearly? Is he white or isn't he?

CLOV: He isn't.

Pause.

HAMM: You've forgotten the sex.

CLOV: (*Vexed.*) But he isn't finished. The sex goes on at the end.

Pause.

HAMM: You haven't put on his ribbon.

CLOV: (*Angrily.*) But he isn't finished, I tell you! First you finish your dog and then you put on his ribbon!

Pause.

HAMM: Can he stand?

CLOV: I don't know.

HAMM: Try. (*He hands the dog to* CLOV *who places it on the ground.*) Well?

CLOV: Wait!

He squats down and tries to get the dog to stand on its three legs, fails, lets it go. The dog falls on its side.

HAMM: (*Impatiently.*) Well?

CLOV: He's standing.

HAMM: (*Groping for the dog.*) Where? Where is he?

CLOV *holds up the dog in a standing position.*

CLOV: There.

He takes HAMM's *hand and guides it towards the dog's head.*

HAMM: (*His hand on the dog's head.*) Is he gazing at me?

CLOV: Yes.

HAMM: (*Proudly.*) As if he were asking me to take him for a walk?

CLOV: If you like.

HAMM: (*As before.*) Or as if he were begging me for a bone. (*He withdraws his hand.*) Leave him like that, standing there imploring me.

CLOV *straightens up. The dog falls on its side.*

CLOV: I'll leave you.

HAMM: Have you had your visions?

CLOV: Less.

HAMM: Is Mother Pegg's light on?

CLOV: Light! How could anyone's light be on?

HAMM: Extinguished!

CLOV: Naturally it's extinguished. If it's not on it's extinguished.

HAMM: No, I mean Mother Pegg.

CLOV: But naturally she's extinguished! (*Pause.*) What's the matter with you today?

HAMM: I'm taking my course. (*Pause.*) Is she buried?

CLOV: Buried! Who would have buried her?

HAMM: You.

CLOV: Me! Haven't I enough to do without burying people?

HAMM: But you'll bury me.

CLOV: No I shan't bury you.

Pause.

HAMM: She was bonny once, like a flower of the field. (*With reminiscent leer.*) And a great one for the men!

CLOV: We too were bonny – once. It's a rare thing not to have been bonny – once.

Pause.

HAMM: Go and get the gaff.

CLOV *goes to door, halts.*

CLOV: Do this, do that, and I do it. I never refuse. Why?

HAMM: You're not able to.

CLOV: Soon I won't do it any more.

HAMM: You won't be able to any more. (*Exit* CLOV.) Ah the creatures, the creatures, everything has to be explained to them.

Enter CLOV *with gaff.*

CLOV: Here's your gaff. Stick it up.

He gives the gaff to HAMM *who, wielding it like a punt-pole, tries to move his chair.*

HAMM: Did I move?

CLOV: No.

HAMM *throws down the gaff.*

HAMM: Go and get the oilcan.

CLOV: What for?

HAMM: To oil the castors.

CLOV: I oiled them yesterday.

HAMM: Yesterday! What does that mean? Yesterday!

CLOV: (*Violently.*) That means that bloody awful day, long ago, before this bloody awful day. I use the words you taught me. If they don't mean anything any more, teach me others. Or let me be silent.

Pause.

HAMM: I once knew a madman who thought the end of the world had come. He was a painter – and engraver. I had a great fondness for him. I used to go and see him, in the asylum. I'd take him by the hand and drag him to the window. Look! There! All that rising corn! And there! Look! The sails of the herring fleet! All that loveliness! (*Pause.*) He'd snatch away his hand and go back into his corner. Appalled. All he had seen was ashes. (*Pause.*) He alone had been spared. (*Pause.*) Forgotten. (*Pause.*) It appears the case is … was not so … so unusual.

CLOV: A madman? When was that?

HAMM: Oh way back, way back, you weren't in the land of the living.

CLOV: God be with the days!

Pause. HAMM *raises his toque.*

HAMM: I had a great fondness for him. (*Pause. He puts on his toque again.*) He was a painter – and engraver.

CLOV: There are so many terrible things.

HAMM: No, no, there are not so many now. (*Pause.*) Clov!

CLOV: Yes.

HAMM: Do you not think this has gone on long enough?

CLOV: Yes! (*Pause.*) What?

HAMM: This … this … thing.

CLOV: I've always thought so. (*Pause.*) You not?

HAMM: (*Gloomily.*) Then it's a day like any other day.

CLOV: As long as it lasts. (*Pause.*) All life long the same inanities.

Pause.

HAMM: I can't leave you.

CLOV: I know. And you can't follow me.

Pause.

HAMM: If you leave me how shall I know?

CLOV: (*Briskly.*) Well you simply whistle me and if I don't come running it means I've left you.

Pause.

HAMM: You won't come and kiss me good-bye?

CLOV: Oh I shouldn't think so.

Pause.

HAMM: But you might be merely dead in your kitchen.

CLOV: The result would be the same.

HAMM: Yes, but how would I know, if you were merely dead in your kitchen?

CLOV: Well … sooner or later I'd start to stink.

HAMM: You stink already. The whole place stinks of corpses.

CLOV: The whole universe.

HAMM: (*Angrily.*) To hell with the universe! (*Pause.*) Think of something.

CLOV: What?

HAMM: An idea, have an idea. (*Angrily.*) A bright idea!

CLOV: Ah good. (*He starts pacing to and fro, his eyes fixed on the ground, his hands behind his back. He halts.*) The pains in my legs! It's unbelievable! Soon I won't be able to think any more.

HAMM: You won't be able to leave me. (CLOV *resumes his pacing.*) What are you doing?

CLOV: Having an idea. (*He paces.*) Ah!

He halts.

HAMM: What a brain! (*Pause.*) Well?

CLOV: Wait! (*He meditates. Not very convinced.*) Yes … (*Pause. More convinced.*) Yes! (*He raises his head.*) I have it! I set the alarm.

Pause.

HAMM: This is perhaps not one of my bright days, but frankly –

CLOV: You whistle me. I don't come. The alarm rings. I'm gone. It doesn't ring. I'm dead.

Pause.

HAMM: Is it working? (*Pause. Impatiently.*) The alarm, is it working?

CLOV: Why wouldn't it be working?

HAMM: Because it's worked too much.

CLOV: But it's hardly worked at all.

HAMM: (*Angrily.*) Then because it's worked too little!

CLOV: I'll go and see. (*Exit* CLOV. *Brief ring of alarm off. Enter* CLOV *with alarm-clock. He holds it against* HAMM'S *ear and releases alarm. They listen to it ringing to the end. Pause.*) Fit to wake the dead! Did you hear it?

Figure 25 Simon McBurney and Mark Rylance in *Endgame*, London, 2009. (Photograph: Tristram Kenton.)

HAMM: Vaguely.

CLOV: The end is terrific!

HAMM: I prefer the middle. (*Pause.*) Is it not time for my painkiller?

CLOV: No! (*He goes to the door, turns.*) I'll leave you.

HAMM: It's time for my story. Do you want to listen to my story.

CLOV: No.

HAMM: Ask my father if he wants to listen to my story.

CLOV goes to bins, raises the lid of NAGG's, stoops, looks into it.

Pause. He straightens up.

CLOV: He's asleep.

HAMM: Wake him.

CLOV stoops, wakes NAGG with the alarm. Unintelligible words. CLOV straightens up.

CLOV: He doesn't want to listen to your story.

HAMM: I'll give him a bon-bon.

CLOV stoops. As before.

CLOV: He wants a sugar-plum.

HAMM: He'll get a sugar-plum.

CLOV stoops. As before.

CLOV: It's a deal. (*He goes towards door. NAGG's hands appear, gripping the rim. Then the head emerges. CLOV reaches door, turns.*) Do you believe in the life to come?

HAMM: Mine was always that. (*Exit CLOV.*) Got him that time!

NAGG: I'm listening.

HAMM: Scoundrel! Why did you engender me?

NAGG: I didn't know.

HAMM: What? What didn't you know?

NAGG: That it'd be you. (*Pause.*) You'll give me a sugar-plum?

HAMM: After the audition.

NAGG: You swear?

HAMM: Yes.

NAGG: On what?

HAMM: My honour.

Pause. They laugh heartily.

NAGG: Two.

HAMM: One.

NAGG: One for me and one for —

HAMM: One! Silence! (*Pause.*) Where was I? (*Pause. Gloomily.*) It's finished, we're finished. (*Pause.*) Nearly finished. (*Pause.*) There'll be no more speech. (*Pause.*) Something dripping in my head, ever since the fontanelles. (*Stifled hilarity of NAGG.*) Splash, splash, always on the same spot. (*Pause.*) Perhaps it's a little vein. (*Pause.*) A little artery. (*Pause. More animated.*) Enough of that, it's story time, where was I? (*Pause. Narrative tone.*) The man came crawling towards me, on his belly. Pale, wonderfully pale and thin, he seemed on the point of – (*Pause. Normal tone.*) No, I've done that bit. (*Pause. Narrative tone.*) I calmly filled my pipe – the meerschaum, lit it with … let us say a vesta, drew a few puffs. Aah! (*Pause.*) Well, what is it *you* want? (*Pause.*) It was an extra-ordinarily bitter day, I remember, zero by the thermometer. But considering it was Christmas Eve there was nothing … extra ordinary about that. Seasonable weather, for once in a way. (*Pause.*) Well, what ill wind blows you my way? He raised his face to me, black with mingled dirt and tears. (*Pause. Normal tone.*) That should do it. (*Narrative tone.*) No, no, don't look at me, don't look at me. He dropped his eyes and mumbled something, apologies I presume. (*Pause.*) I'm a busy man, you know, the final touches, before the festivities, you know what it is. (*Pause. Forcibly.*) Come on now, what is the object of this invasion? (*Pause.*) It was a glorious bright day, I remember, fifty by the heliometer, but already the sun was sinking down into the … down among the dead. (*Normal tone.*) Nicely put, that. (*Narrative tone.*) Come on now, come on, present your petition and let me resume my labours. (*Pause. Normal tone.*) There's English for you. Ah well … (*Narrative tone.*) It was then he took the plunge. It's my little one, he said. Tsstss, a little one, that's bad. My little boy, he said, as if the sex mattered. Where did he come from? He named the hole. A good half-day, on horse. What are you insinuating? That the place is still inhabited? No no, not a soul, except himself and the child – assuming he existed. Good. I inquired about the situation at Kov, beyond the gulf. Not a sinner. Good. And you expect me to believe you have left your little one back there, all alone, and alive into the bargain? Come now! (*Pause.*) It was a howling wild day, I remember, a hundred by the anemometer. The wind was tearing up the dead pines and sweeping them … away. (*Pause. Normal tone.*) A bit feeble, that. (*Narrative tone.*) Come on, man, speak up, what is it you want from me, I have to put up my holly. (*Pause.*) Well to make it short it finally transpired that what he wanted from me was … bread for his brat. Bread? But I have no bread, it doesn't agree with me. Good. Then perhaps a little corn? (*Pause. Normal tone.*) That should do it. (*Narrative tone.*) Corn, yes, I have corn it's true, in my granaries. But use your head. I give you some corn, a pound, a pound and a half, you bring it back to your child and you make him – if he's still alive – a nice pot of porridge (NAGG *reacts*), a nice pot and a half of porridge, full of nourishment. Good. The colours come back into his little cheeks – perhaps. And then? (*Pause.*) I lost patience. (*Violently.*) Use your head, can't you, use your head, you're on earth, there's no cure for that! (*Pause.*) It was an exceedingly dry day, I remember, zero by the hygrometer. Ideal weather, for my lumbago. (*Pause. Violently.*) But what in God's name do you imagine? That the earth will awake in spring? That the rivers and seas will run with fish again? That there's manna in heaven still for imbeciles like you? (*Pause.*) Gradually I cooled down, sufficiently at least to ask him how long he had taken on the way. Three whole days. Good. In what condition he had left the child. Deep in sleep. (*Forcibly.*) But deep in what sleep, deep in what sleep already? (*Pause.*) Well to make it short I finally offered to take him into my service. He had touched a chord. And then I imagined already that I wasn't much longer for this world. (*He laughs. Pause.*) Well? (*Pause.*) Well? Here if you were careful you might die a nice natural death, in peace and comfort. (*Pause.*) Well? (*Pause.*) In the end he asked me would I consent to take in the child as well – if he were still alive. (*Pause.*) It was the moment I was waiting for. (*Pause.*) Would I consent to take in the child … (*Pause.*) I can see him still, down on his knees, his hands flat on the ground, glaring at me with his mad eyes, in defiance of my wishes. (*Pause. Normal tone.*) I'll soon have finished with this story. (*Pause.*) Unless I bring in other characters. (*Pause.*) But where would I find them? (*Pause.*) Where would I look for them? (*Pause. He whistles. Enter* CLOV.) Let us pray to God.

NAGG: Me sugar-plum!

CLOV: There's a rat in the kitchen!

HAMM: A rat! Are there still rats?

CLOV: In the kitchen there's one.

HAMM: And you haven't exterminated him?

CLOV: Half. You disturbed us.

HAMM: He can't get away?

CLOV: No.

HAMM: You'll finish him later. Let us pray to God.

CLOV: Again!

NAGG: Me sugar-plum!

HAMM: God first! (*Pause.*) Are you right?

CLOV: (*Resigned.*) Off we go.

HAMM: (*To* NAGG.) And you?

NAGG: (*Clasping his hands, closing his eyes, in a gabble.*) Our Father which art –

HAMM: Silence! In silence! Where are your manners? (*Pause.*) Off we go. (*Attitudes of prayer. Silence. Abandoning his attitude, discouraged.*) Well?

CLOV: (*Abandoning his attitude.*) What a hope! And you?

HAMM: Sweet damn all! (*To* NAGG.) And you?

NAGG: Wait! (*Pause. Abandoning his attitude.*) Nothing doing!

HAMM: The bastard! He doesn't exist!

CLOV: Not yet.

NAGG: Me sugar-plum!

HAMM: There are no more sugar-plums!

Pause.

NAGG: It's natural. After all I'm your father. It's true if it hadn't been me it would have been someone else. But that's no excuse. (*Pause.*) Turkish Delight, for example, which no longer exists, we all know that, there is nothing in the world I love more. And one day I'll ask you for some, in return for a kindness, and you'll promise it to me. One must live with the times. (*Pause.*) Whom did you call when you were a tiny boy, and were frightened, in the dark? Your mother? No. Me. We let you cry. Then we moved you out of earshot, so that we might sleep in peace. (*Pause.*) I was asleep, as happy as a king, and you woke me up to have me listen to you. It wasn't indispensable, you didn't really need to have me listen to you. Besides I didn't listen to you. (*Pause.*) I hope the day will come when you'll really need to have me listen to you, and need to hear my voice, any voice. (*Pause.*) Yes, I hope I'll live till then, to hear you calling me like when you were a tiny boy, and were frightened, in the dark, and I was your only hope. (*Pause.* NAGG *knocks on lid of* NELL's *bin. Pause.*) Nell! (*Pause. He knocks louder. Pause. Louder.*) Nell!

Pause. NAGG *sinks back into his bin, closes the lid behind him.*

Pause.

HAMM: Our revels now are ended. (*He gropes for the dog.*) The dog's gone.

CLOV: He's not a real dog, he can't go.

HAMM: (*Groping.*) He's not there.

CLOV: He's lain down.

HAMM: Give him up to me. (CLOV *picks up the dog and gives it to* HAMM. HAMM *holds it in his arms. Pause.* HAMM *throws away the dog.*) Dirty brute! (CLOV *begins to pick up the objects lying on the ground.*) What are you doing?

CLOV: Putting things in order. (*He straightens up. Fervently.*) I'm going to clear everything away!

He starts picking up again.

HAMM: Order!

CLOV: (*Straightening up.*) I love order. It's my dream. A world where all would be silent and still and each thing in its last place, under the last dust.

He starts picking up again.

HAMM: (*Exasperated.*) What in God's name do you think you are doing?

CLOV: (*Straightening up.*) I'm doing my best to create a little order.

HAMM: Drop it!

CLOV drops the objects he has picked up.

CLOV: After all, there or elsewhere.

He goes towards door.

HAMM: (*Irritably.*) What's wrong with your feet?

CLOV: My feet?

HAMM: Tramp! Tramp!

CLOV: I must have put on my boots.

HAMM: Your slippers were hurting you?

Pause.

CLOV: I'll leave you.

HAMM: No!

CLOV: What is there to keep me here?

HAMM: The dialogue. (*Pause.*) I've got on with my story. (*Pause.*) I've got on with it well. (*Pause. Irritably.*) Ask me where I've got to.

CLOV: Oh, by the way, your story?

HAMM: (*Surprised.*) What story?

CLOV: The one you've been telling yourself all your … days.

HAMM: Ah you mean my chronicle?

CLOV: That's the one.

Pause.

HAMM: (*Angrily.*) Keep going, can't you, keep going!

CLOV: You've got on with it, I hope.

HAMM: (*Modestly.*) Oh not very far, not very far. (*He sighs.*) There are days like that, one isn't inspired. (*Pause.*) Nothing you can do about it, just wait for it to come. (*Pause.*) No forcing, no forcing, it's fatal. (*Pause.*) I've got on with it a little all the same. (*Pause.*) Technique, you know. (*Pause. Irritably.*) I say I've got on with it a little all the same.

CLOV: (*Admiringly.*) Well I never! In spite of everything you were able to get on with it!

HAMM: (*Modestly.*) Oh not very far, you know, not very far, but nevertheless, better than nothing.

CLOV: Better than nothing! Is it possible?

HAMM: I'll tell you how it goes. He comes crawling on his belly –

CLOV: Who?

HAMM: What?

CLOV: Who do you mean, he?

HAMM: Who do I mean! Yet another.

CLOV: Ah him! I wasn't sure.

HAMM: Crawling on his belly, whining for bread for his brat. He's offered a job as gardener. Before – (*CLOV bursts out laughing.*) What is there so funny about that?

CLOV: A job as gardener!

HAMM: Is that what tickles you?

CLOV: It must be that.

HAMM: It wouldn't be the bread?

CLOV: Or the brat.

Pause.

HAMM: The whole thing is comical, I grant you that. What about having a good guffaw the two of us together?

CLOV: (*After reflection.*) I couldn't guffaw again today.

HAMM: (*After reflection.*) Nor I. (*Pause.*) I continue then. Before accepting with gratitude he asks if he may have his little boy with him.

CLOV: What age?

HAMM: Oh tiny.

CLOV: He would have climbed the trees.

HAMM: All the little odd jobs.

CLOV: And then he would have grown up.

HAMM: Very likely.

Pause.

CLOV: Keep going, can't you, keep going!

HAMM: That's all. I stopped there.

Pause.

CLOV: Do you see how it goes on.

HAMM: More or less.

CLOV: Will it not soon be the end?

HAMM: I'm afraid it will.

CLOV: Pah! You'll make up another.

HAMM: I don't know. (*Pause.*) I feel rather drained. (*Pause.*) The prolonged creative effort. (*Pause.*) If I could drag myself down to the sea! I'd make a pillow of sand for my head and the tide would come.

CLOV: There's no more tide.

Pause.

HAMM: Go and see is she dead.

CLOV goes to bins, raises the lid of NELL's, stoops, looks into it. Pause.

CLOV: Looks like it.

He closes the lid, straightens up. HAMM raises his toque. Pause. He puts it on again.

HAMM: (*With his hand to his toque.*) And Nagg?

CLOV raises lid of NAGG's bin, stoops, looks into it. Pause.

CLOV: Doesn't look like it.

He closes the lid, straightens up.

HAMM: (*Letting go his toque.*) What's he doing?

CLOV raises lid of NAGG's bin, stoops, looks into it. Pause.

CLOV: He's crying.

He closes the lid, straightens up.

HAMM: Then he's living. (*Pause.*) Did you ever have an instant of happiness?

CLOV: Not to my knowledge.

Pause.

HAMM: Bring me under the window. (CLOV *goes towards chair.*) I want to feel the light on my face. (CLOV *pushes chair.*) Do you remember, in the beginning, when you took me for a turn? You used to hold the chair too high. At every step you nearly tipped me out. (*With senile quaver.*) Ah great fun, we had, the two of us, great fun! (*Gloomily.*) And then we got into the way of it. (CLOV *stops the chair under window right.*) There already? (*Pause. He tilts back his head.*) Is it light?

CLOV: It isn't dark.

HAMM: (*Angrily.*) I'm asking you is it light.

CLOV: Yes.

Pause.

HAMM: The curtain isn't closed?

CLOV: No.

HAMM: What window is it?

CLOV: The earth.

HAMM: I knew it! (*Angrily.*) But there's no light there! The other! (CLOV *pushes chair towards window left.*) The earth! (CLOV *stops the chair under window left.* HAMM *tilts back his head.*) That's what I call light! (*Pause.*) Feels like a ray of sunshine. (*Pause.*) No?

CLOV: No.

HAMM: It isn't a ray of sunshine I feel on my face?

CLOV: No.

Pause.

HAMM: Am I very white? (*Pause. Angrily.*) I'm asking you am I very white!

CLOV: Not more so than usual.

Pause.

HAMM: Open the window.

CLOV: What for?

HAMM: I want to hear the sea.

CLOV: You wouldn't hear it.

HAMM: Even if you opened the window?

CLOV: No.

HAMM: Then it's not worth while opening it?

CLOV: No.

HAMM: (*Violently.*) Then open it! (CLOV *gets up on the ladder, opens the window. Pause.*) Have you opened it?

CLOV: Yes.

Pause.

HAMM: You swear you've opened it?

CLOV: Yes.

Pause.

HAMM: Well …! (*Pause.*) It must be very calm. (*Pause. Violently.*) I'm asking you is it very calm?

CLOV: Yes.

HAMM: It's because there are no more navigators. (*Pause.*) You haven't much conversation all of a sudden. Do you not feel well?

CLOV: I'm cold.

HAMM: What month are we? (*Pause.*) Close the window, we're going back. (CLOV *closes the window, gets down, pushes the chair back to its place, remains standing behind it, head bowed.*) Don't stay there, you give me the shivers! (CLOV *returns to his place beside the chair.*) Father! (*Pause. Louder.*) Father! (*Pause.*) Go and see did he hear me.

CLOV *goes to* NAGG's *bin, raises the lid, stoops. Unintelligible words.* CLOV *straightens up.*

CLOV: Yes.

HAMM: Both times?

CLOV *stoops. As before.*

CLOV: Once only.

HAMM: The first time or the second?

CLOV *stoops. As before.*

CLOV: He doesn't know.

HAMM: It must have been the second.

CLOV: We'll never know.

He closes lid.

HAMM: Is he still crying?

CLOV: No.

HAMM: The dead go fast. (*Pause.*) What's he doing?

CLOV: Sucking his biscuit.

HAMM: Life goes on. (CLOV *returns to his place beside the chair.*) Give me a rug, I'm freezing.

CLOV: There are no more rugs.

Pause.

HAMM: Kiss me. (*Pause.*) Will you not kiss me?

CLOV: No.

HAMM: On the forehead.

CLOV: I won't kiss you anywhere.

Pause.

HAMM: (*Holding out his hand.*) Give me your hand at least. (*Pause.*) Will you not give me your hand?

CLOV: I won't touch you.

Pause.

HAMM: Give me the dog. (CLOV *looks round for the dog.*) No!

CLOV: Do you not want your dog?

HAMM: No.

CLOV: Then I'll leave you.

HAMM: (*Head bowed, absently.*) That's right.

CLOV goes to door, turns.

CLOV: If I don't kill that rat he'll die.

HAMM: (*As before.*) That's right. (*Exit CLOV. Pause.*) Me to play. (*He takes out his handkerchief, unfolds it, holds it spread out before him.*) We're getting on. (*Pause.*) You weep, and weep, for nothing, so as not to laugh, and little by little … you begin to grieve. (*He folds the handkerchief, puts it back in his pocket, raises his head.*) All those I might have helped. (*Pause.*) Helped! (*Pause.*) Saved. (*Pause.*) Saved! (*Pause.*) The place was crawling with them! (*Pause. Violently.*) Use your head, can't you, use your head, you're on earth, there's no cure for that! (*Pause.*) Get out of here and love one another! Lick your neighbour as yourself! (*Pause. Calmer.*) When it wasn't bread they wanted it was crumpets. (*Pause. Violently.*) Out of my sight and back to your petting parties! (*Pause.*) All that, all that! (*Pause.*) Not even a real dog! (*Calmer.*) The end is in the beginning and yet you go on. (*Pause.*) Perhaps I could go on with my story, end it and begin another. (*Pause.*) Perhaps I could throw myself out on the floor. (*He pushes himself painfully off his seat, falls back again.*) Dig my nails into the cracks and drag myself forward with my fingers. (*Pause.*) It will be the end and there I'll be, wondering what can have brought it on and wondering what can have … (*he hesitates*) … why it was so long coming. (*Pause.*) There I'll be, in the old refuge, alone against the silence and … (*he hesitates*) … the stillness. If I can hold my peace, and sit quiet, it will be all over with sound, and motion, all over and done with. (*Pause.*) I'll have called my father and I'll have called my … (*he hesitates*) … my son. And even twice, or three times, in case they shouldn't have heard me, the first time, or the second. (*Pause.*) I'll say to myself, He'll come back. (*Pause.*) And then? (*Pause.*) And then? (*Pause.*) He couldn't, he has gone too far. (*Pause.*) And then? (*Pause. Very agitated.*) All kinds of fantasies! That I'm being watched! A rat! Steps! Breath held and then … (*he breathes out*). Then babble, babble, words, like the solitary child who turns himself into children, two, three, so as to be together, and whisper together, in the dark. (*Pause.*) Moment upon moment, pattering down, like the millet grains of… (*he hesitates*) … that old Greek, and all life long you wait for that to mount up to a life. (*Pause. He opens his mouth to continue, renounces.*) Ah let's get it over! (*He whistles. Enter CLOV with alarm-clock. He halts beside the chair.*) What? Neither gone nor dead?

CLOV: In spirit only.

HAMM: Which?

CLOV: Both.

HAMM: Gone from me you'd be dead.

CLOV: And *vice versa.*

HAMM: Outside of here it's death! (*Pause.*) And the rat?

CLOV: He's got away.

HAMM: He can't go far. (*Pause. Anxious.*) Eh?

CLOV: He doesn't need to go far.

Pause.

HAMM: Is it not time for my pain-killer?

CLOV: Yes.

HAMM: Ah! At last! Give it to me! Quick!

Pause.

CLOV: There's no more pain-killer.

Pause.

HAMM: (*Appalled.*) Good …! (*Pause.*) No more pain-killer!

CLOV: No more pain-killer. You'll never get any more pain-killer.

Pause.

HAMM: But the little round box. It was full!

CLOV: Yes. But now it's empty.

Pause. CLOV starts to move about the room. He is looking for a place to put down the alarm-clock.

HAMM: (*Soft.*) What'll I do? (*Pause. In a scream.*) What'll I do? (*CLOV sees the picture, takes it down, stands it on the floor with its face to wall, hangs up the alarm-clock in its place.*) What are you doing?

CLOV: Winding up.

HAMM: Look at the earth.

CLOV: Again!

HAMM: Since it's calling to you.

CLOV: Is your throat sore? (*Pause.*) Would you like a lozenge? (*Pause.*) No? (*Pause.*) Pity.

CLOV goes, humming, towards window right, halts before it, looks up at it.

HAMM: Don't sing.

CLOV: (*Turning towards HAMM.*) One hasn't the right to sing any more?

HAMM: No.

CLOV: Then how can it end?

HAMM: You want it to end?

CLOV: I want to sing.

HAMM: I can't prevent you.

Pause. CLOV turns towards window right.

CLOV: What did I do with that steps? (*He looks round for ladder.*) You didn't see that steps? (*He sees it.*) Ah, about time. (*He goes towards window left.*) Sometimes I wonder if I'm in my right mind. Then it passes over and I'm as lucid as before. (*He gets up on ladder, looks out of window.*) Christ, she's under water! (*He looks.*) How can that be? (*He pokes forward his head, his hand above his eyes.*) It hasn't rained. (*He wipes the pane, looks. Pause.*) Ah what a mug I am! I'm on the wrong side! (*He gets down, takes a few steps towards window right.*) Under water! (*He goes back for ladder.*) What a mug I am! (*He carries ladder towards window right.*) Sometimes I wonder if I'm in my right senses. Then it passes off and I'm as intelligent as ever. (*He sets down ladder under window right, gets up on it, looks out of window. He turns towards* HAMM.) Any particular sector you fancy? Or merely the whole thing?

HAMM: Whole thing.

CLOV: The general effect? Just a moment.

He looks out of window. Pause.

HAMM: Clov.

CLOV: (*Absorbed.*) Mmm.

HAMM: Do you know what it is?

CLOV: (*As before.*) Mmm.

HAMM: I was never there. (*Pause.*) Clov!

CLOV: (*Turning towards* HAMM, *exasperated.*) What is it?

HAMM: I was never there.

CLOV: Lucky for you.

He looks out of window.

HAMM: Absent, always. It all happened without me. I don't know what's happened. (*Pause.*) Do you know what's happened? (*Pause.*) Clov!

CLOV: (*Turning towards* HAMM, *exasperated.*) Do you want me to look at this muckheap, yes or no?

HAMM: Answer me first.

CLOV: What?

HAMM: Do you know what's happened?

CLOV: When? Where?

HAMM: (*Violently.*) When! What's happened! Use your head, can't you! What has happened?

CLOV: What for Christ's sake does it matter?

He looks out of window.

HAMM: I don't know.

Pause. CLOV *turns towards* HAMM.

CLOV: (*Harshly.*) When old Mother Pegg asked you for oil for her lamp and you told her to get out to hell, you knew what was happening then, no? (*Pause.*) You know what she died of, Mother Pegg? Of darkness.

HAMM: (*Feebly.*) I hadn't any.

CLOV: (*As before.*) Yes, you had.

Pause.

HAMM: Have you the glass?

CLOV: No, it's clear enough as it is.

HAMM: Go and get it.

Pause. CLOV *casts up his eyes, brandishes his fists. He loses balance, clutches on to the ladder. He starts to get down, halts.*

CLOV: There's one thing I'll never understand. (*He gets down.*) Why I always obey you. Can you explain that to me?

HAMM: No … Perhaps it's compassion. (*Pause.*) A kind of great compassion. (*Pause.*) Oh you won't find it easy, you won't find it easy.

Pause. CLOV *begins to move about the room in search of the telescope.*

CLOV: I'm tired of our goings on, very tired. (*He searches.*) You're not sitting on it?

He moves the chair, looks at the place where it stood, resumes his search.

HAMM: (*Anguished.*) Don't leave me there! (*Angrily* CLOV *restores the chair to its place.*) Am I right in the centre?

CLOV: You'd need a microscope to find this – (*He sees the telescope.*) Ah, about time.

He picks up the telescope, gets up on the ladder, turns the telescope on the without.

HAMM: Give me the dog.

CLOV: (*Looking.*) Quiet!

HAMM: (*Angrily.*) Give me the dog!

CLOV *drops the telescope, clasps his hands to his head. Pause. He gets down precipitately, looks for the dog, sees it, picks it up, hastens towards* HAMM *and strikes him on the head violently with the dog.*

CLOV: There's your dog for you!

The dog falls to the ground. Pause.

HAMM: He hit me!

CLOV: You drive me mad, I'm mad!

HAMM: If you must hit me, hit me with the axe. (*Pause.*) Or with the gaff, hit me with the gaff. Not with the dog. With the gaff. Or with the axe.

CLOV *picks up the dog and gives it to* HAMM *who takes it in his arms.*

CLOV: (*Imploringly.*) Let's stop playing!

HAMM: Never! (*Pause.*) Put me in my coffin.

CLOV: There are no more coffins.

HAMM: Then let it end! (CLOV *goes towards ladder.*) With a bang! (CLOV *gets up on ladder, gets down again, looks for telescope, sees it, picks it up, gets up ladder, raises telescope.*) Of darkness! And me? Did anyone ever have pity on me?

CLOV: (*Lowering the telescope, turning towards* HAMM.) What? (*Pause.*) Is it me you're referring to?

HAMM: (*Angrily.*) An aside, ape! Did you never hear an aside before? (*Pause.*) I'm warming up for my last soliloquy.

CLOV: I warn you. I'm going to look at this filth since it's an order. But it's the last time. (*He turns the telescope on the without.*) Let's see. (*He moves the telescope.*) Nothing … nothing … good … good … nothing … goo – (*He starts, lowers the telescope, examines it, turns it again on the without. Pause.*) Bad luck to it!

HAMM: More complications! (CLOV *gets down.*) Not an underplot, I trust.

CLOV moves ladder nearer window, gets up on it, turns telescope on the without.

CLOV: (*Dismayed.*) Looks like a small boy!

HAMM: (*Sarcastic.*) A small … boy!

CLOV: I'll go and see. (*He gets down, drops the telescope, goes towards door, turns.*) I'll take the gaff.

He looks for the gaff, sees it, picks it up, hastens towards door.

HAMM: No!

CLOV halts.

CLOV: No? A potential procreator?

HAMM: If he exists he'll die there or he'll come here. And if he doesn't …

Pause.

CLOV: You don't believe me? You think I'm inventing?

Pause.

HAMM: It's the end, Clov, we've come to the end. I don't need you any more.

Pause.

CLOV: Lucky for you.

He goes towards door.

HAMM: Leave me the gaff.

CLOV gives him the gaff, goes towards door, halts, looks at alarm-clock, takes it down, looks round for a better place to put it, goes to bins, puts it on lid of NAGG'S *bin. Pause.*

CLOV: I'll leave you.

He goes towards door.

HAMM: Before you go … (*CLOV halts near door*) … say something.

CLOV: There is nothing to say.

HAMM: A few words … to ponder … in my heart.

CLOV: Your heart!

HAMM: Yes. (*Pause. Forcibly.*) Yes! (*Pause.*) With the rest, in the end, the shadows, the murmurs, all the trouble, to end up with. (*Pause.*) Clov … He never spoke to me. Then, in the end, before he went, without my having asked him, he spoke to me. He said …

CLOV: (*Despairingly.*) Ah …!

HAMM: Something … from your heart.

CLOV: My heart!

HAMM: A few words … from your heart.

Pause.

CLOV: (*Fixed gaze, tonelessly, towards auditorium.*) They said to me, That's love, yes yes, not a doubt, now you see how –

HAMM: Articulate!

CLOV: (*As before.*) How easy it is. They said to me, That's friendship, yes yes, no question, you've found it. They said

to me, Here's the place, stop, raise your head and look at all that beauty. That order! They said to me, Come now, you're not a brute beast, think upon these things and you'll see how all becomes clear. And simple! They said to me, What skilled attention they get, all these dying of their wounds.

HAMM: Enough!

CLOV: (*As before.*) I say to myself – sometimes, Clov, you must learn to suffer better than that if you want them to weary of punishing you – one day. I say to myself – sometimes, Clov, you must be there better than that if you want them to let you go – one day. But I feel too old, and too far, to form new habits. Good, it'll never end, I'll never go. (*Pause.*) Then one day, suddenly, it ends, it changes, I don't understand, it dies, or it's me, I don't understand that either. I ask the words that remain – sleeping, waking, morning, evening. They have nothing to say. (*Pause.*) I open the door of the cell and go. I am so bowed I only see my feet, if I open my eyes, and between my legs a little trail of black dust. I say to myself that the earth is extinguished, though I never saw it lit. (*Pause.*) It's easy going. (*Pause.*) When I fall I'll weep for happiness.

Pause. He goes towards door.

HAMM: Clov! (*CLOV halts, without turning.*) Nothing. (*CLOV moves on.*) Clov!

CLOV halts, without turning.

CLOV: This is what we call making an exit.

HAMM: I'm obliged to you, Clov. For your services.

CLOV: (*Turning, sharply.*) Ah pardon, it's I am obliged to you.

HAMM: It's we are obliged to each other. (*Pause.* CLOV *goes towards door.*) One thing more. (*CLOV halts.*) A last favour. (*Exit* CLOV.) Cover me with the sheet. (*Long pause.*) No? Good. (*Pause.*) Me to play. (*Pause. Wearily.*) Old endgame lost of old, play and lose and have done with losing. (*Pause. More animated.*) Let me see. (*Pause.*) Ah yes! (*He tries to move the chair, using the gaff as before. Enter* CLOV, *dressed for the road. Panama hat, tweed coat, raincoat over his arm, umbrella, bag. He halts by the door and stands there, impassive and motionless, his eyes fixed on* HAMM, *till the end.* HAMM *gives up.*) Good. (*Pause.*) Discard. (*He throws away the gaff, makes to throw away the dog, thinks better of it.*) Take it easy. (*Pause.*) And now? (*Pause.*) Raise hat. (*He raises his toque.*) Peace to our … arses. (*Pause.*) And put on again. (*He puts on his toque.*) Deuce. (*Pause. He takes off his glasses.*) Wipe. (*He takes out his handkerchief and, without unfolding it, wipes his glasses.*) And put on again. (*He puts on his glasses, puts back the handkerchief in his pocket.*) We're coming. A few more squirms like that and I'll call. (*Pause.*) A little poetry. (*Pause.*) You prayed – (*Pause. He corrects himself.*) You CRIED for night; it comes – (*Pause. He corrects himself.*) It FALLS: now cry in darkness. (*He repeats, chanting.*) You cried for night; it falls: now cry in darkness. (*Pause.*) Nicely put, that. (*Pause.*) And now? (*Pause.*) Moments for nothing, now as always, time was never and time is over, reckoning closed and story ended. (*Pause. Narrative tone.*) If he could have his child with him ... (*Pause.*) It was the moment I was waiting for. (*Pause.*) You don't want to abandon him? You want him to bloom while you are withering? Be there to solace your last million last moments? (*Pause.*) He doesn't realize, all he knows is hunger, and cold, and death to crown it all. But you! You ought to know what the earth is like, nowadays. Oh, I put him before his responsibilities! (*Pause. Normal tone.*) Well, there we are, there I am, that's enough. (*He raises the whistle to his lips, hesitates, drops it. Pause.*) Yes, truly! (*He whistles. Pause. Louder. Pause.*) Good. (*Pause.*) Father! (*Pause. Louder.*) Father! (*Pause.*) Good. (*Pause.*)

We're coming. (*Pause.*) And to end up with? (*Pause.*) Discard. (*He throws away the dog. He tears the whistle from his neck.*) With my compliments. (*He throws whistle towards auditorium. Pause. He sniffs. Soft.*) Clov! (*Long pause.*) No? Good. (*He takes out the handkerchief.*) Since that's the way we're playing it ... (*he unfolds handkerchief*) ... let's play it that way ... (*he unfolds*) ... and speak no more about it ... (*he finishes unfolding*) ... speak no more. (*He holds the handkerchief spread out before him.*) Old stancher! (*Pause.*) You ... remain.

Pause. He covers his face with handkerchief, lowers his arms to armrests, remains motionless.

Brief tableau.

Curtain

4.3 THE BALCONY (1962 [1956])

JEAN GENET

Translated by Bernard Frechtman

Jean Genet (1910–86) *was an infamous figure in French literature and politics. An orphan and homosexual with connections to the criminal underworld, he was celebrated by the French literary intelligentsia of the 1950s and 1960s, and his plays have attracted some of the most innovative directors of the twentieth century such as Roger Blin, Peter Brook and more recently Katie Mitchell. His work is seen to have influenced many contemporary writers, such as Heiner Müller (see 5.1) and Caryl Churchill (see 5.6), in its emphasis on the poetic, the non-linear and the non-psychological. His plays often have readily recognizable naturalistic settings – a prison* (Deathwatch, 1949), *a brothel* (The Balcony, 1956) – *but are characterized by transformation as characters role-play and deconstruct their own function as players in a political arena or cultural frame of power and disempowerment. His plays demand an emphasis on a complex visual and theatrical quality and were palpably innovative when originally produced. Genet was also a novelist and theorist, who wrote numerous texts on theatre.*

Characters

THE BISHOP
THE JUDGE
THE EXECUTIONER (ARTHUR)
THE GENERAL
THE CHIEF OF POLICE
THE BEGGAR
ROGER
THE COURT ENVOY
THE FIRST PHOTOGRAPHER
THE SECOND PHOTOGRAPHER
THE THIRD PHOTOGRAPHER
IRMA (THE QUEEN)
THE WOMAN (ROSINE)
THE THIEF
THE GIRL
CARMEN
CHANTAL

Scene One

On the ceiling, a chandelier, which will remain the same in each scene. The set seems to represent a sacristy, formed by three blood-red, cloth folding-screens. The one at the rear has a built-in door. Above, a huge Spanish crucifix, drawn in trompe l'oeil. *On the right wall, a mirror, with a carved gilt frame, reflects an unmade bed which, if the room were arranged logically, would be in the first rows of the orchestra. A table with a large jug. A yellow armchair. On the chair, a pair of black trousers, a shirt and a jacket.* THE BISHOP, *in mitre and gilded cope, is sitting in the chair. He is obviously larger than life. The role is played by an actor wearing tragedian's cothurni about twenty inches high. His shoulders, on which the cope lies, are inordinately broadened so that when the curtain rises he looks huge and stiff, like a scarecrow. He wears garish make-up. At the side, a woman, rather young, highly made up and wearing a lace dressing-gown, is drying her hands with a towel. Standing by is another woman,* IRMA. *She is about forty, dark, severe-looking, and is wearing a black tailored suit and a hat with a tight string (like a chin-strap).*

THE BISHOP: (*Sitting in the chair, middle of the stage. In a low but fervent voice.*) In truth, the mark of a prelate is not mildness or unction, but the most rigorous intelligence. Our heart is our undoing. We think we are master of our kindness; we are the slaves of a serene laxity. It is something quite other than intelligence that is involved.... (*He hesitates.*) It may be cruelty. And beyond that cruelty – and through it – a skilful, vigorous course towards Absence. Towards Death. God? (*Smiling.*) I can read your mind! (*To his mitre.*) Mitre, bishop's bonnet, when my eyes close for the last time, it is you that I shall see behind my eyelids, you, my beautiful gilded hat ... you, my handsome ornaments, copes, laces....

IRMA: (*Bluntly.*) An agreement's an agreement. When a deal's been made....

Throughout the scene she hardly moves. She is standing very near the door.

THE BISHOP (*Very gently, waving her aside with a gesture.*) And when the die is cast....

IRMA: No. Twenty. Twenty and no nonsense. Or I'll lose my temper. And that's not like me.... Now, if you have any difficulties....

THE BISHOP (*Curtly, and tossing away the mitre.*) Thank you.

IRMA: And don't break anything. We need that. (*To* THE WOMAN.) Put it away.

She lays the mitre on the table, near the jug.

THE BISHOP: (*After a deep sigh.*) I've been told that this house is going to be besieged. The rebels have already crossed the river.

IRMA: There's blood everywhere.... You can slip round behind the Archbishop's Palace. Then, down Fishmarket Street....

Suddenly a scream of pain, uttered by a woman offstage.

IRMA: (*Annoyed.*) But I told them to be quiet. Good thing I remembered to cover the windows with padded curtains.

Suddenly amiable, insidious.

Well, and what was it this evening? A blessing? A prayer? A mass? A perpetual adoration?

THE BISHOP: (*Gravely.*) Let's not talk about that now. It's over. I'm concerned only about getting home.... You say the city's splashed with blood....

THE WOMAN: There was a blessing, Madame. Then, my confession....

IRMA: And after that?

THE BISHOP: That'll do!

THE WOMAN: That was all. At the end, my absolution.

IRMA: Won't anyone be able to witness it? Just once?

THE BISHOP: (*Frightened.*) No, no. Those things must remain secret, and they shall. It's indecent enough to talk about them while I'm being undressed. Nobody. And all the doors must be closed. Firmly closed, shut, buttoned, laced, hooked, sewn....

IRMA: I merely asked....

THE BISHOP: Sewn, Madame.

IRMA: (*Annoyed.*) You'll allow me at least, won't you, to feel a little uneasy ... professionally? I said twenty.

THE BISHOP: (*His voice suddenly grows clear and sharp, as if he were awakening. He displays a little annoyance.*) We didn't tire ourselves. Barely six sins, and far from my favourite ones.

THE WOMAN: Six, but deadly ones! And it was a job finding *those*.

THE BISHOP: (*Uneasy.*) What? You mean they were false?

THE WOMAN: They were real, all right! I mean it was a job committing them. If only you realized what it takes, what a person has to go through, in order to reach the point of disobedience.

THE BISHOP: I can imagine, my child. The order of the world is so lax that you can do as you please there – or almost. But if your sins were false, you may say so now.

IRMA: Oh no! I can hear you complaining already the next time you come. No. They were real. (*To* THE WOMAN.) Untie his laces. Take off his shoes. And when you dress him, be careful he doesn't catch cold. (*To* THE BISHOP.) Would you like a toddy, a hot drink?

THE BISHOP: Thank you. I haven't time. I must be going. (*Dreamily.*) Yes, six, but deadly ones!

IRMA: Come here, we'll undress you!

THE BISHOP: (*Pleading, almost on his knees.*) No, no, not yet.

IRMA: It's time. Come on! Quick! Make it snappy!

While they talk, the women undress him. Or rather they merely remove pins and untie cords that seem to secure the cope, stole and surplice.

THE BISHOP: (*To* THE WOMAN.) About the sins, you really did commit them?

THE WOMAN: I did.

THE BISHOP: You really made the gestures? All the gestures?

THE WOMAN: I did.

THE BISHOP: When you moved towards me with your face forward, was it really aglow with the light of the flames?

THE WOMAN: It was.

THE BISHOP: And when my ringed hand came down on your forehead, forgiving it....

THE WOMAN: It was.

THE BISHOP: And when my gaze pierced your lovely eyes?

THE WOMAN: It was.

IRMA: Was there at least a glimmer of repentance in her lovely eyes, my Lord?

THE BISHOP: (*Standing up.*) A fleeting glimmer. But was I seeking repentance in them? I saw there the greedy longing for transgression. In flooding it, evil all at once baptized it. Her big eyes opened on the abyss ... a deathly pallor lit up – yes, Madame – lit up her face. But our holiness lies only in our being able to forgive you your sins. Even if they're only make-believe.

THE WOMAN: (*Suddenly coy.*) And what if my sins were real?

THE BISHOP (*In a different, less theatrical tone.*) You're mad! I hope you really didn't do all that!

IRMA (*To THE BISHOP.*) Don't listen to her. As for her sins, don't worry. Here there's no....

THE BISHOP (*Interrupting her.*) I'm quite aware of that. Here there's no possibility of doing evil. You live in evil. In the absence of remorse. How could you do evil? The Devil makes believe. That's how one recognizes him. He's the great Actor. And that's why the Church has anathematized actors.

THE WOMAN: Reality frightens you, doesn't it?

THE BISHOP: If your sins were real, they would be crimes, and I'd be in a fine mess.

THE WOMAN: Would you go to the police?

IRMA continues to undress him. However, he still has the cope on his shoulders.

IRMA: Stop plaguing her with all those questions.

The same terrible scream is heard again.

They're at it again! I'll go and shut them up.

THE BISHOP: That wasn't a make-believe scream.

IRMA: (*Anxiously.*) I don't know.... Who knows and what does it matter?

THE BISHOP: (*Going slowly to the mirror. He stands in front of it.*) Now answer, mirror, answer me. Do I come here to discover evil and innocence? (*To IRMA, very gently.*) Leave the room! I want to be by myself.

IRMA: It's late. And the later it gets, the more dangerous it'll be ...

THE BISHOP: (*Pleading.*) Just one more minute.

IRMA: You've been here two hours and twenty minutes. In other words, twenty minutes too long....

THE BISHOP: (*Suddenly incensed.*) I want to be by myself. Eavesdrop, if you want to – I know you do, anyway – and don't come back till I've finished.

The two women leave with a sigh, looking as if they were out of patience. THE BISHOP *remains alone.*

THE BISHOP: (*After making a visible effort to calm himself, in front of the mirror and holding his surplice.*) Now answer, mirror, answer me. Do I come here to discover evil and innocence? And in your gilt-edged glass, what was I? Never – I affirm it before God Who sees me – I never desired the episcopal throne. To become bishop, to work my way up – by means of virtues or vices – would have been to turn away from the ultimate dignity of bishop. I shall explain: (THE BISHOP *speaks in a tone of great precision, as if pursuing a line of logical reasoning*) in order to become a bishop, I should have had to make a zealous effort not to be one, but to do what would have resulted in my being one. Having become a bishop, in order to be one I should have had – in order to be one for myself, of course! – I should have had to be constantly aware of being one so as to perform my function. (*He seizes the flap of his surplice and kisses it.*) Oh laces, laces, fashioned by a thousand little hands to veil ever so many panting bosoms, buxom bosoms, and faces, and hair, you illustrate me with branches and flowers! Let us continue. But – there's the crux!

He laughs.

So I speak Latin! – a function is a function. It's not a mode of being. But a bishop – that's a mode of being. It's a trust. A burden. Mitres, lace, gold-cloth and glass trinkets, genuflexions.... To hell with the function!

Crackling of machine-gun fire.

IRMA: (*Putting her head through the door.*) Have you finished?

THE BISHOP: For Christ's sake, leave me alone. Get the hell out! I'm probing myself.

IRMA shuts the door.

THE BISHOP (*To the mirror.*) The majesty, the dignity, that light up my person, do not emanate from the attributions of my function. – No more, good heavens! than from my personal merits. – The majesty, the dignity that light me up come from a more mysterious brilliance: the fact that the bishop precedes me. Do I make myself clear, mirror, gilded image, ornate as a box of Mexican cigars? And I wish to be bishop in solitude, for appearance alone.... And in order to destroy all function, I want to cause a scandal and feel you up, you slut, you bitch, you trollop, you tramp....

IRMA: (*Entering.*) That'll do now. You've got to leave.

THE BISHOP: You're crazy! I haven't finished.

Both women have entered.

IRMA: I'm not trying to pick an argument, and you know it, but you've no time to waste....

THE BISHOP: (*Ironically.*) What you mean is that you need the room for someone else and you've got to arrange the mirrors and jugs.

IRMA: (*Very irritated.*) That's no business of yours. I've given you every attention while you've been here. And I repeat that it's dangerous for anyone to loiter in the streets.

Sound of gun-fire in the distance.

THE BISHOP: (*Bitterly.*) That's not true. You don't give a damn about my safety. When the job's finished, you don't give a damn about anyone!

IRMA: (*To the girl.*) Stop listening to him and undress him.

IRMA: (*To* THE BISHOP, *who has stepped down from his cothurni and has now assumed the normal size of an actor, of the most ordinary of actors.*) Lend a hand. You're stiff.

THE BISHOP: (*With a foolish look.*) Stiff? I'm stiff? A solemn stiffness! Final immobility....

IRMA: (*To the girl.*) Hand him his jacket....

THE BISHOP: (*Looking at his clothes, which are heaped on the floor.*) Ornaments, laces, through you I re-enter myself. I reconquer a domain. I beleaguer a very ancient place from which I was driven. I install myself in a clearing where suicide at last becomes possible. The judgment depends on me, and here I stand, face to face with my death.

IRMA: That's all very fine, but you've got to go. You left your car at the front door, near the power-station.

THE BISHOP: (*To* IRMA.) Because our Chief of Police, that wretched incompetent, is letting us be slaughtered by the rabble! (*Turning to the mirror and declaiming*) Ornaments! Mitres! Laces! You, above all, oh gilded cope, you protect me from the world. Where are my legs, where are my arms? Under your scalloped, lustrous flaps, what have my hands been doing? Fit only for fluttering gestures, they've become mere stumps of wings – not of angels, but of partridges! – rigid cope, you make it possible for the most tender and luminous sweetness to ripen in warmth and darkness. My charity, a charity that will flood the world – it was under this carapace that I distilled it.... Would my hand emerge at times, knife-like, to bless? Or cut, mow down? My hand, the head of a turtle, would push aside the flaps. A turtle or a cautious snake? And go back into the rock. Underneath, my hand would dream.... Ornaments, gilded copes....

(*The stage moves from left to right, as if it were plunging into the wings. The following set then appears.*)

Scene Two

Same chandelier. Three brown folding-screens. Bare walls. At right, same mirror, in which is reflected the same unmade bed as in the first scene. A woman, young and beautiful, seems to be chained, with her wrists bound. Her muslin dress is torn. Her breasts are visible. Standing in front of her is THE EXECU-TIONER. *He is a giant, stripped to the waist. Very muscular. His whip has been slipped through the loop of his belt, in back,*

so that he seems to have a tail. A JUDGE, *who, when he stands up, will seem larger than life (he, too, is mounted on cothurni, which are invisible beneath his robe, and his face is made up) is crawling, on his stomach, towards the woman, who shrinks as he approaches.*

THE THIEF: (*Holding out her foot.*) Not yet! Lick it! Lick it first....

THE JUDGE makes an effort to continue crawling. Then he stands up and, slowly and painfully, though apparently happy, goes and sits down on a stool. THE THIEF (*the woman described above*) *drops her domineering attitude and becomes humble.*

THE JUDGE: (*Severely.*) For you're a thief! You were caught... Who? The police.... Have you forgotten that your movements are hedged about by a strong and subtle network, my strong-arm cops? They're watchful, swivel-eyed insects that lie in wait for you. All of you! And they bring you captive, all of you, to the Bench.... What have you to say for yourself? You were caught.... Under your skirt.... (*To* THE EXECUTIONER.) Put your hand under her skirt. You'll find the pocket, the notorious Kangaroo Pocket.... (*To* THE THIEF.) that you fill with any old junk you pick up. Because you're an idiot to boot.... (*To* THE EXECUTIONER.) What was there in that notorious Kangaroo Pocket? In that enormous paunch?

THE EXECUTIONER: Bottles of scent, my Lord, a flashlight, a bottle of Fly-tox, some oranges, several pairs of socks, bearskins, a Turkish towel, a scarf. (*To* THE JUDGE.) Do you hear me? I said: a scarf.

THE JUDGE: (*With a start.*) A scarf? Ah ha, so that's it? Why the scarf? Eh? What were you going to do with it? Whom were you planning to strangle? Answer. Who? ... Are you a thief or a strangler? (*Very gently, imploringly.*) Tell me, my child, I beg of you, tell me you're a thief.

THE THIEF: Yes, my Lord.

THE EXECUTIONER: No!

THE THIEF: (*Looking at him in surprise.*) No?

THE EXECUTIONER: That's for later.

THE THIEF: Eh?

THE EXECUTIONER: I mean the confession is supposed to come later. Plead not guilty.

THE THIEF: What, and get beaten again!

THE JUDGE: (*Mealy-mouthed.*) Exactly, my child: and get beaten. You must first deny, then admit and repent. I want to see hot tears gush from your lovely eyes. Oh! I want you to be drenched in them. The power of tears! ... Where's my statute-book? (*He fishes under his robe and pulls out a book.*)

THE THIEF: I've already cried....

THE JUDGE: (*He seems to be reading.*) Under the blows. I want tears of repentance. When I see you wet as a meadow I'll be utterly satisfied!

THE THIEF: It's not easy. I tried to cry before....

THE JUDGE: (*No longer reading. In a half-theatrical, almost familiar tone.*) You're quite young. Are you new here? (*Anxiously.*) At least you're not a minor?

THE THIEF: Oh no, sir.

THE JUDGE: Call me my Lord. How long have you been here?

THE EXECUTIONER: Since the day before yesterday, my Lord.

THE JUDGE: (*Reassuming the theatrical tone and resuming the reading.*) Let her speak. I like that puling voice of hers, that voice without resonance.... Look here: you've got to be a model thief if I'm to be a model judge. If you're a fake thief, I become a fake judge. Is that clear?

THE THIEF: Oh yes, my Lord.

THE JUDGE: (*He continues reading.*) Good. Thus far everything has gone off well. My executioner has hit hard ... for he too has his function. We are bound together, you, he and I. For example, if he didn't hit, how could I stop him from hitting? Therefore, he must strike so that I can intervene and demonstrate my authority. And you must deny your guilt so that he can beat you.

A noise is heard, as of something having fallen in the next room. In a natural tone:

What's that? Are all the doors firmly shut? Can anyone see us, or hear us?

THE EXECUTIONER: No, no, you needn't worry. I bolted the door.

He goes to examine a huge bolt on the rear door.

And the corridor's out of bounds.

THE JUDGE: (*In a natural tone.*) Are you sure?

THE EXECUTIONER: You can take my word for it.

He puts his hand into his pocket.

Can I have a smoke?

THE JUDGE: (*In a natural tone.*) The smell of tobacco inspires me. Smoke away.

Same noise as before.

Oh, what *is* that? What *is* it? Can't they leave me in peace?

He gets up.

What's going on?

THE EXECUTIONER: (*Curtly.*) Nothing at all. Someone must have dropped something. You're getting nervous.

THE JUDGE: (*In a natural tone.*) That may be, but my nervousness makes me aware of things. It keeps me on the alert.

(*He gets up and moves towards the wall.*)

May I have a look?

THE EXECUTIONER: Just a quick one, because it's getting late.

(*THE EXECUTIONER shrugs his shoulders and exchanges a wink with THE THIEF.*)

THE JUDGE: (*After looking.*) It's lit up. Brightly lit, but empty.

THE EXECUTIONER: (*Shrugging his shoulders.*) Empty!

THE JUDGE: (*In an even more familiar tone.*) You seem anxious. Has anything new happened?

THE EXECUTIONER: This afternoon, just before you arrived, the rebels took three key-positions. They set fire to several places. Not a single fireman came out. Everything went up in flames. The Palace....

THE JUDGE: What about the Chief of Police? Twiddling his thumbs as usual?

THE THIEF: There's been no news of him for four hours. If he can get away, he's sure to come here. He's expected at any moment.

THE JUDGE: (*To THE THIEF, and sitting down.*) In any case, he'd better not plan to come by way of Queen's Bridge. It was blown up last night.

THE THIEF: We know that. We heard the explosion from here.

THE JUDGE: (*Resuming his theatrical tone. He reads the statute-book.*) All right. Let's get on with it. Thus, taking advantage of the sleep of the just, taking advantage of a moment's inattention, you rob them, you ransack, you pilfer and purloin....

THE THIEF: No, my Lord, never....

THE EXECUTIONER: Shall I tan her hide?

THE THIEF: (*Crying out.*) Arthur!

THE EXECUTIONER: What's eating you? Don't address me. Answer his Lordship. And call me Mr Executioner.

THE THIEF: Yes, Mr Executioner.

THE JUDGE: (*Reading.*) I continue: did you steal?

THE THIEF: I did, I did, my Lord.

THE JUDGE: (*Reading.*) Good. Now answer quickly, and to the point: what else did you steal?

THE THIEF: Bread, because I was hungry.

THE JUDGE: (*He draws himself up and lays down the book.*) Sublime! Sublime function! I'll have all that to judge. Oh, child, you reconcile me with the world. A judge! I'm going to be judge of your acts! On me depends the weighing, the balance. The world is an apple. I cut it in two: the good, the bad. And you agree, thank you, you agree to be the bad! (*Facing the audience.*) Right before your eyes: nothing in my hands, nothing up my sleeve, remove the rot and cast it off. But it's a painful occupation. If every judgment were delivered seriously, each one would cost me my life. That's why I'm dead. I inhabit that region of exact freedom. I, King of Hell, weigh those who are dead, like me. She's a dead person, like myself.

THE THIEF: You frighten me, sir.

THE JUDGE: (*Very bombastically.*) Be still. In the depths of Hell I sort out the humans who venture there. Some to the flames, the others to the boredom of the fields of asphodel. You, thief, spy, she-dog, Minos is speaking to you, Minos weighs you. (*To THE EXECUTIONER.*) Cerberus?

THE EXECUTIONER (*Imitating the dog.*) Bow-wow, bow-wow!

THE JUDGE: You're handsome! And the sight of a fresh victim makes you even handsomer. (*He curls up THE EXECUTIONER's lips.*) Show your fangs. Dreadful. White. (*Suddenly he seems anxious. To* THE THIEF.) But at least you're not lying about those thefts – you did commit them, didn't you?

THE EXECUTIONER: Don't worry. She committed them, all right. She wouldn't have dared not to. I'd have made her.

THE JUDGE: I'm almost happy. Continue. What did you steal?

Suddenly, machine-gun fire.

THE JUDGE: There's simply no end to it. Not a moment's rest.

THE THIEF: I told you: the rebellion has spread all over the north of the city....

THE EXECUTIONER: Shut up!

THE JUDGE: (*Irritated.*) Are you going to answer, yes or no? What else have you stolen? Where? When? How? How much? Why? For whom?

THE THIEF: I very often entered houses when the maids were off. I used the tradesmen's entrance.... I stole from drawers, broke into children's piggy-banks. (*She is visibly trying to find words.*) Once I dressed up as a lady. I put on a dark-brown suit, a black straw hat with cherries, a veil and a pair of black shoes – with Cuban heels – then I went in....

THE JUDGE: (*In a rush.*) Where? Where? Where? Where – where – where? Where did you go in?

THE THIEF: I can't remember. Forgive me.

THE EXECUTIONER: Shall I let her have it?

THE JUDGE: Not yet. (*To the girl.*) Where did you go in? Tell me where?

THE THIEF: (*In a panic.*) But I swear to you, I don't remember.

THE EXECUTIONER: Shall I let her have it? Shall I, my Lord?

THE JUDGE: (*To* THE EXECUTIONER, *and going up to him.*) Ah! ah! your pleasure depends on me. You like to thrash, eh? I'm pleased with you, Executioner! Masterly mountain of meat, hunk of beef that's set in motion at a word from me! (*He pretends to look at himself in* THE EXECUTIONER.) Mirror that glorifies me! Image that I can touch, I love you. Never would I have the strength or skill to leave streaks of fire on her back. Besides, what could I do with such strength and skill? (*He touches him.*) Are you there? You're all there, my huge arm, too heavy for me, too big, too fat for my shoulder, walking at my side all by itself! Arm, hundredweight of meat, without you I'd be nothing.... (*To* THE THIEF.) And without you too, my child. You're my two perfect complements.... Ah, what a fine trio we make! (*To* THE THIEF.) But you, you have a privilege that he hasn't, nor I either, that of priority. My being a judge is an emanation of your being a thief. You need only refuse – but you'd better not! – need only refuse to be who you are – what you are, therefore who you are – for me to cease to be ... to vanish, evaporated. Burst. Volatilized. Denied. Hence: good born of.... What then? What then? But you won't refuse, will you? You won't refuse to be a thief? That would be wicked. It would be criminal. You'd deprive me of being! (*Imploringly.*) Say it, my child, my love, you won't refuse?

THE THIEF: (*Coyly.*) I might.

THE JUDGE: What's that? What's that you say? You'd refuse? Tell me where. And tell me again what you've stolen.

THE THIEF: (*Curtly, and getting up.*) I won't.

THE JUDGE: Tell me where. Don't be cruel....

THE THIEF: Your tone is getting too familiar. I won't have it!

THE JUDGE: Miss.... Madame. I beg of you. (*He falls to his knees.*) Look, I beseech you. Don't leave me in this position, waiting to be a judge. If there were no judge, what would become of us, but what if there were no thieves?

THE THIEF: (*Ironically.*) And what if there weren't?

THE JUDGE: It would be awful. But you won't do that to me, will you? Please understand me: I don't mind your hiding, for as long as you can and as long as my nerves can bear it, behind the refusal to confess – it's all right to be mean and make me yearn, even prance, make me dance, drool, sweat, whinny with impatience, crawl ... do you want me to crawl?

THE EXECUTIONER: (*To* THE JUDGE.) Crawl.

THE JUDGE: I'm proud!

THE EXECUTIONER: (*Threateningly.*) Crawl!

THE JUDGE, *who was on his knees, lies flat on his stomach and crawls slowly towards* THE THIEF. *As he crawls forward,* THE THIEF *moves back.*

THE EXECUTIONER: Good. Continue.

THE JUDGE: (*To* THE THIEF.) You're quite right, you rascal, to make me crawl after my judgeship, but if you were to refuse for good, you hussy, it would be criminal....

THE THIEF: (*Haughtily.*) Call me Madame, and ask politely.

THE JUDGE: Will I get what I want?

THE THIEF: (*Coyly.*) It costs a lot – stealing does.

THE JUDGE: I'll pay! I'll pay whatever I have to, Madame. But if I no longer had to divide the Good from the Evil, of what use would I be? I ask you?

THE THIEF: I ask myself.

THE JUDGE: (*Is infinitely sad.*) A while ago I was going to be Minos. My Cerberus was barking. (*To* THE EXECUTIONER.) Do you remember? (THE EXECUTIONER *interrupts* THE JUDGE *by cracking his whip.*) You were so cruel, so mean! So good! And me, I was pitiless. I was going to fill Hell with the souls of the damned, to fill prisons. Prisons! Prisons! Prisons, dungeons, blessed places where evil is impossible since they are the crossroads of all the malediction in the world. One cannot commit evil in evil. Now, what I desire above all is not to condemn, but to judge.... (*He tries to get up.*)

THE EXECUTIONER: Crawl! And hurry up, I've got to go and get dressed.

THE JUDGE: (*To the girl.*) Madame! Madame, please, I beg of you. I'm willing to lick your shoes, but tell me you're a thief....

THE THIEF: (*In a cry.*) Not yet! Lick! Lick! Lick first!

The stage moves from left to right, as at the end of the preceding scene, and plunges into the right wing. In the distance, machine-gun fire.

Scene Three

Three dark-green folding-screens, arranged as in the preceding scenes. The same chandelier. The same mirror reflecting the unmade bed. On an armchair, a horse of the kind used by folk-dancers, with a little kilted skirt. In the room, a timid-looking gentleman: THE GENERAL. He removes his jacket, then his bowler hat and his gloves. IRMA is near him.

THE GENERAL: (*He points to the hat, jacket and gloves.*) Have that cleared out.

IRMA: It'll be folded and wrapped.

THE GENERAL: Have it removed from sight.

IRMA: It'll be put away. Even burned.

THE GENERAL: Yes, yes, of course, I'd like it to burn! Like cities at twilight.

IRMA: Did you notice anything on the way?

THE GENERAL: I ran very serious risks. The populace has blown up dams. Whole areas are flooded. The arsenal in particular. So that all the powder supplies are wet. And the weapons rusty. I had to make some rather wide detours – though I didn't trip over a single drowned body.

IRMA: I wouldn't take the liberty of asking you your opinions. Everyone is free, and I'm not concerned with politics.

THE GENERAL: Then let's talk of something else. The important thing is how I'm going to get out of this place. It'll be late by the time I leave....

IRMA: About it's being late....

THE GENERAL: That does it.

He reaches into his pocket, takes out some banknotes, counts them and gives some to IRMA. She keeps them in her hand.

THE GENERAL: I'm not keen about being shot down in the dark when I leave. For, of course, there won't be anyone to escort me?

IRMA: I'm afraid not. Unfortunately Arthur's not free. (*A long pause.*)

THE GENERAL: (*Suddenly impatient.*) But ... isn't she coming?

IRMA: I can't imagine what she's doing. I gave instructions that everything was to be ready by the time you arrived. The horse is already here.... I'll ring.

THE GENERAL: Don't, I'll attend to that. (*He rings.*) I like to ring! Ringing's authoritative. Ah, to ring out commands.

IRMA: In a little while, General. Oh, I'm so sorry, here am I giving you your rank.... In a little while you'll....

THE GENERAL: Sh! Don't say it.

IRMA: You have such force, such youth! such dash!

THE GENERAL: And spurs. Will I have spurs? I said they were to be fixed to my boots. Oxblood boots, right?

IRMA: Yes, General. And patent-leather.

THE GENERAL: Oxblood. Patent-leather, very well, but with mud?

IRMA: With mud and perhaps a little blood. I've had the decorations prepared.

THE GENERAL: Authentic ones?

IRMA: Authentic ones. (*Suddenly a woman's long scream.*)

THE GENERAL: What's that?

He starts going to the right wall and is already bending down to look, as if there were a small crack, but IRMA steps in front of him.

IRMA: Nothing. There's always some carelessness, on both sides.

THE GENERAL: But that cry? A woman's cry. A call for help perhaps? My heart skips a beat.... I spring forward....

IRMA: (*Icily.*) I want no trouble here. Calm down. For the time being, you're in mufti.

THE GENERAL: That's right.

A woman's scream again.

THE GENERAL: All the same, it's disturbing. Besides, it'll be awkward.

IRMA: What on earth can she be doing?

She goes to ring, but by the rear door enters a very beautiful young woman, red-headed, hair undone, dishevelled. Her bosom is almost bare. She is wearing a black corset, black stockings and very high-heeled shoes. She is holding a general's uniform, complete with sword, cocked hat and boots.

THE GENERAL: (*Severely.*) So you finally got here? Half an hour late. That's more than's needed to lose a battle.

IRMA: She'll redeem herself, General, I know her.

THE GENERAL: (*Looking at the boots.*) What about the blood? I don't see any blood.

IRMA: It dried. Don't forget that it's the blood of your past battles. Well, then, I'll leave you. Do you have everything you need?

THE GENERAL: (*Looking to the right and left.*) You're forgetting....

IRMA: Good God! Yes. I was forgetting.

She lays on the chair the towels she has been carrying on her arm. Then she leaves by the rear. THE GENERAL goes to the door, then locks it. But no sooner is the door closed than someone knocks. THE GIRL goes to open it. Behind, and standing slightly back, THE EXECUTIONER, sweating, wiping himself with a towel.

THE EXECUTIONER: Is Mme Irma here?

THE GIRL: (*Curtly.*) In the Rose-garden. (*Correcting herself.*) I'm sorry, in the Funeral Chapel. (*She closes the door.*)

THE GENERAL (*Irritated.*) I'll be left in peace, I hope. And you're late. Where the hell were you? Didn't they give you your feed-bag? You're smiling, are you? Smiling at your rider? You recognize his hand, gentle but firm? (*He strokes her.*)

My proud steed! My handsome mare, we've had many a spirited gallop together!

THE GIRL: And that's not all! I want to trip through the world with my nervous legs and well-shod hooves. Take off your trousers and shoes so I can dress you.

THE GENERAL: (*He has taken the cane.*) All right, but first, down on your knees! Come on, come on, bend your knees, bend them....

THE GIRL rears, utters a whinny of pleasure and kneels like a circus horse before the general.

THE GENERAL: Bravo! Bravo, Dove! You haven't forgotten a thing. And now, you're going to help me and answer my questions. It's fitting and proper for a nice filly to help her master unbutton himself and take off his gloves, and to be at his beck and call. Now start by untying my laces.

During the entire scene that follows, THE GIRL helps THE GENERAL remove his clothes and then dress up as a general. When he is completely dressed, he will be seen to have taken on gigantic proportions, by means of trick effects: invisible foot-gear, broadened shoulders, excessive make-up.

THE GIRL: Left foot still swollen?

THE GENERAL: Yes. It's my leading-foot. The one that prances. Like your hoof when you toss your head.

THE GIRL: What am I doing? Unbutton yourself.

THE GENERAL: Are you a horse or an illiterate? If you're a horse, you toss your head. Help me. Pull. Don't pull so hard. See here, you're not a plough-horse.

THE GIRL: I do what I have to do.

THE GENERAL: Are you rebelling? Already? Wait till I'm ready. When I put the bit into your mouth....

THE GIRL: Oh no, not that.

THE GENERAL: A general reprimanded by his horse! You'll have the bit, the bridle, the harness, the saddlegirth, and I, in boots and helmet, will whip and plunge!

THE GIRL: The bit is awful. It makes the gums and the corners of the lips bleed. I'll drool blood.

THE GENERAL: Foam pink and spit fire! But what a gallop! Along the rye-fields, through the alfalfa, over the meadows and dusty roads, over hill and dale, awake or asleep, from dawn to twilight and from twilight....

THE GIRL: Tuck in your shirt. Pull up your braces. It's quite a job dressing a victorious general who's to be buried. Do you want the sabre?

THE GENERAL: Let it lie on the table, like Lafayette's. Conspicuously, but hide the clothes. Where? How should *I* know? Surely there's a hiding-place somewhere.

THE GIRL bundles up his clothes and hides them behind the armchair.

THE GENERAL: The tunic? Good. Got all the medals? Count 'em.

THE GIRL: (*After counting them, very quickly.*) They're all here, sir.

THE GENERAL: What about the war? Where's the war?

THE GIRL: (*Very softly.*) It's approaching, sir. It's evening in an apple-orchard. The sky is calm and pink. The earth is bathed in a sudden peace – the moan of doves – the peace that precedes battles. The air is very still. An apple has fallen to the grass. A yellow apple. Things are holding their breath. War is declared. The evening is very mild....

THE GENERAL: But suddenly?

THE GIRL: We're at the edge of the meadow. I keep myself from flinging out, from whinnying. Your thighs are warm and you're pressing my flanks. Death....

THE GENERAL: But suddenly?

THE GIRL: Death has pricked up her ears. She puts a finger to her lips, asking for silence. Things are lit up with an ultimate goodness. You yourself no longer heed my presence....

THE GENERAL: But suddenly?

THE GIRL: Button up by yourself, sir. The water lay motionless in the pools. The wind itself was awaiting an order to unfurl the flags....

THE GENERAL: But suddenly?

THE GIRL: Suddenly? Eh? Suddenly? (*She seems to be trying to find the right words.*) Ah yes, suddenly all was fire and sword! Widows! Miles of crêpe had to be woven to put on the standards. The mothers and wives remained dry-eyed behind their veils. The bells came clattering down the bombed towers. As I rounded a corner I was frightened by a blue cloth. I reared, but, steadied by your gentle and masterful hand, I ceased to quiver. I started forward again. How I loved you, my hero!

THE GENERAL: But ... the dead? Weren't there any dead?

THE GIRL: The soldiers died kissing the standard. You were all victory and kindness. One evening, remember....

THE GENERAL: I was so mild that I began to snow. To snow on my men, to shroud them in the softest of winding-sheets. To snow. Moskova!

THE GIRL: Splinters of shell had gashed the lemons. Now death was in action. She moved nimbly from one to the other, deepening a wound, dimming an eye, tearing off an arm, opening an artery, discolouring a face, cutting short a cry, a song. Death was ready to drop. Finally, exhausted, herself dead with fatigue, she grew drowsy and rested lightly on your shoulder, where she fell asleep.

THE GENERAL: (*Drunk with joy.*) Stop, stop, it's not time for that yet, but I feel it'll be magnificent. The cross-belt? Good. (*He looks at himself in the mirror.*) Austerlitz! General! Man of war and in full regalia, behold me in my pure appearance. Nothing, no contingent trails behind me. I appear, purely and simply. If I went through wars without dying, went through sufferings without dying, if I was promoted, without dying, it was for this minute close to death.

Suddenly he stops; he seems troubled by an idea.

Tell me, Dove?

THE GIRL: What is it, sir?

THE GENERAL: What's the Chief of Police been doing?

THE GIRL shakes her head.

Nothing? Still nothing? In short, everything slips through his fingers. And what about us, are we wasting our time?

THE GIRL: (*Imperiously.*) Not at all. And, in any case, it's no business of ours. Continue. You were saying: for this minute close to death … and then?

THE GENERAL: (*Hesitating.*) … close to death … where I shall be nothing, though reflected *ad infinitum* in these mirrors, nothing but my image…. Quite right, comb your mane. Curry yourself. I require a well-groomed filly. So, in a little while, to the blare of trumpets, we shall descend – I on your back – to death and glory, for I am about to die. It is indeed a descent to the grave….

THE GIRL: But, sir, you've been dead since yesterday.

THE GENERAL: I know … but a formal and picturesque descent, by unexpected stairways….

THE GIRL: You are a dead general, but an eloquent one.

THE GENERAL: Because I'm dead, prating horse. What is now speaking, and so beautifully, is Example. I am now only the image of my former self. Your turn, now. Lower your head and hide your eyes, for I want to be a general in solitude. Not even for myself, but for my image, and my image for its image, and so on. In short, we'll be among equals. Dove, are you ready?

THE GIRL nods.

Come now. Put on your bay dress, horse, my fine Arab steed.

THE GENERAL slips the mock-horse over her head. Then he cracks his whip.

We're off!

He bows to his image in the mirror.

Farewell, general!

Then he stretches out in the arm-chair with his feet on another chair and bows to the audience, holding himself rigid as a corpse. THE GIRL places herself in front of the chair and, on the spot, makes the movements of a horse in motion.

THE GIRL: The procession has begun…. We're passing through the City…. We're going along the river. I'm sad…. The sky is overcast. The nation weeps for that splendid hero who died in battle….

THE GENERAL: (*Starting.*) Dove!

THE GIRL: (*Turning around, in tears.*) Sir?

THE GENERAL: Add that I died with my boots on!

He then resumes his pose.

THE GIRL: My hero died with his boots on! The procession continues. Your aides-de-camp precede me…. Then come I, Dove, your war-horse…. The military band plays a funeral march….

Marching in place, THE GIRL sings Chopin's Funeral March, which is continued by an invisible orchestra [with brasses]. Far off, machine-gun fire.

Scene Four

A room, the three visible panels of which are three mirrors in which is reflected a little old man, dressed as a tramp though neatly combed. He is standing motionless in the middle of the room. Near him, looking very indifferent, a very beautiful red-haired girl. Leather corselet, leather boots. Naked and beautiful thighs. Fur jacket. She is waiting. So is THE MAN. He is impatient, nervous. THE GIRL is motionless.

THE MAN removes his torn gloves tremblingly. He takes from his pocket a handkerchief and mops his face. He takes off his glasses, folds them and puts them into a case, which he then slips into his pocket.

He wipes his hands with his handkerchief.

All the gestures of the little old man are reflected in the three mirrors.

(Three actors are needed to play the roles of the reflections.)

At length, there are three raps at the rear door.

The red-haired girl goes to the door. She says: 'Yes.'

The door opens a little and through the opening appear IRMA's hand and arm holding a whip and a very dirty and shaggy wig.

THE GIRL takes them. The door closes.

THE MAN's face lights up.

The red-haired girl has an exaggeratedly lofty and cruel air.

She puts the wig on his head roughly.

THE MAN takes a bouquet of artificial flowers from his pocket. He holds it as if he were going to offer it to the girl, who whips him and lashes it from his hand.

THE MAN's face is lit up with tenderness.

Very near-by, machine-gun fire.

THE MAN touches his wig.

THE MAN: What about the lice?

THE GIRL: (*Very coarsely.*) They're there,

Scene Five

IRMA's *room. Very elegant. It is the same room that was reflected in the mirrors in the first three scenes. The same chandelier. Large lace hangings suspended from the flies. Three arm-chairs. At left, large window near which is an apparatus by means of which* IRMA *can see what is going on in the studios. Door at right. Door at left.* IRMA *is sitting at her dressing-table, going over her accounts. Near her, a girl:* CARMEN. *Machine-gun fire.*

CARMEN: (*Counting.*) The bishop, twenty … the judge, twenty…. (*She raises her head.*) No, Madame, nothing yet. No Chief of Police.

IRMA: (*Irritated.*) He's going to turn up, *if* he turns up … fit to be tied! And yet!

CARMEN: Yes, I know: it takes all kinds to make a world. But no Chief of Police. (*She counts again.*) The general, twenty … the sailor, twenty … the brat, thirty….

IRMA: I've told you, Carmen, I don't like that. And I demand respect for the visitors. Vi-si-tors! I don't allow myself – my own self (*she stresses the word 'own'*) – even to refer to them as clients. And yet! …

She flashily snaps the sheaf of fresh banknotes that she has in her hand.

CARMEN: (*Severely; she has turned around and is glaring at* IRMA.) For you, yes: cash and refinement.

IRMA: (*Trying to be conciliatory.*) Those eyes! Don't be unjust. You've been irritable for some time now. I realize we're on edge because of what's going on, but things will quiet down. The sun will come out again. George….

CARMEN: Ah, him!

IRMA: Don't sneer at the Chief of Police. If not for him we'd be in a fine mess. Yes, we, because you're tied up with me. And with him. (*A long pause.*) What disturbs me most is your sadness. (*Wisely.*) You've changed, Carmen. And even before the rebellion started….

CARMEN: There's nothing much left for me to do at your place, Mme Irma.

IRMA: (*Disconcerted.*) But … I've put you in charge of my bookkeeping. You sit down at my desk and all at once my entire life opens out before you. I haven't a secret left, and you're not happy?

CARMEN: Of course, I'm grateful to you for your confidence, but … it's not the same thing.

IRMA: Do you miss 'that', Carmen? (CARMEN *is silent.*) Come, come, Carmen, when you mounted the snow-covered rock with the yellow paper rose-bush – by the way, I'm going to have to store that in the cellar – and when the miraculously healed leper swooned at the sight of you, you didn't take yourself seriously, did you, Carmen?

Brief silence.

CARMEN: When our sessions are over, Madame, you never allow anyone to talk about them. So you have no idea of how we really feel. You observe it all from a distance. But if ever you once put on the dress and the blue veil, or if you were the unbuttoned penitent, or the general's mare, or the country girl tumbled in the hay….

IRMA: (*Shocked.*) Me!

CARMEN: Or the maid in a pink apron, or the archduchess deflowered by the policeman, or … but I'm not going to run through the whole list… you'd know what that does to a girl's soul, and that she's got to use a little irony in self-defence. But no, you don't even want us to talk about it among ourselves. You're afraid of a smile, of a joke.

IRMA: (*Very severely.*) True, I don't allow any joking. A giggle, or even a smile, spoils everything. A smile means doubt. The clients want sober ceremonies. With sighs. My house is a severe place. You're allowed to play cards.

CARMEN: Then don't be surprised that we're sad. (*A pause.*) But I'm thinking of my daughter.

IRMA: (*She stands – for a bell has buzzed – and goes to a curious piece of furniture at the left, a kind of switchboard with a view-finder and earphone. While talking, she looks into the view-finder, after pushing down a switch.*) Every time I ask you a slightly intimate question, you shut up like a clam, and you throw your daughter up to me. Are you still set on going to see her? Don't be a fool. Between this place and the nursery in the country there's fire and water, rebellion and bullets. I even wonder whether … (*The bell buzzes again.* MME IRMA *pulls up the switch and pushes down another.*) … whether they didn't get George on the way. Though a Chief of Police knows how to take care of himself. (*She looks at a watch that she takes from her bosom.*) He's late. (*She looks anxious.*) Or else he hasn't dared to go out.

CARMEN: In order *to* get to your studios, those gentlemen of yours go through gunfire without fear, whereas I, in order to see my daughter….

IRMA: Without fear? In a state of jitters that excites them. Their nostrils can sniff the orgy behind the wall of flame and steel…. Let's get back to the accounts, shall we?

CARMEN: In all, counting the sailor and the simple jobs, it comes to three hundred and twenty.

IRMA: The more killing there is in the working-class districts, the more the men roll into my studios.

CARMEN: The men?

IRMA: (*After a pause.*) Some men. Drawn by my mirrors and chandeliers, always the same ones. As for the others, heroism takes the place of women.

CARMEN: (*Bitterly.*) Women?

IRMA: What shall I call you, my big, long, sterile girls? Their seed never ripens in you, and yet … if you weren't there?

CARMEN: You have your revels, Mme Irma.

IRMA: Be still. It's this chilling game that makes me sad and melancholy. Fortunately I have my jewels. Which, as it happens, are in great danger. (*Dreamily.*) I have my jewels … and you, the orgies of your heart….

CARMEN: … they don't help matters, Madame. My daughter loves me.

IRMA: You're the fairy godmother who comes to see her with toys and perfumes. She pictures you in Heaven. (*Bursting out laughing.*) Ah, that's the limit – to think there's someone for whom my brothel – which is Hell – is Heaven! It's Heaven for your brat! (*She laughs.*) Are you going to make a whore of her later on?

CARMEN: Mme Irma!

IRMA: That's right! I ought to leave you to your secret brothel, your precious pink cat-house, your soulful whore-house… You think I'm cruel? This rebellion is getting me down, too. You may not realize it, but I have moments of fear and panic…. It looks to me as if the aim of the rebellion weren't to capture the Royal Palace, but to sack my studios. I'm afraid, Carmen. Yet I've tried everything, even prayer. (*She smiles painfully.*) Like your miraculously healed leper. Have I wounded you?

CARMEN: (*With decision.*) Twice a week, on Tuesdays and Fridays, I had to be the Immaculate Conception of Lourdes and appear to a bank-clerk of the National Provincial. For you it meant money in the bank and justified your brothel, whereas for me it was….

IRMA: (*Astonished.*) You agreed to it. You didn't seem to mind it.

CARMEN: I was happy.

IRMA: Well? Where's the harm?

CARMEN: I saw the effect I had on my bank-clerk. I saw his state of terror, how he'd break out in a sweat, I heard the rattle in his throat….

IRMA: That'll do. He doesn't come any more. I wonder why? Maybe the danger. Or maybe his wife found out. (*A pause.*) Maybe he's dead. Attend to my accounts.

CARMEN: Your book-keeping will never replace my appearing to the bank-clerk. It had become as real as at Lourdes. Everything inside me now yearns for my daughter. She's in a real garden….

IRMA: You'll have a hard time getting to her, and before long the garden will be in your heart.

CARMEN: Be still!

IRMA: (*Inexorably.*) The city is full of corpses. All the roads are cut off. The peasants are also going over to the rebels. I wonder why? Contagion? The rebellion is an epidemic. It has the same fatal and sacred character. In any case, we're going to find ourselves more and more isolated. The rebels have it in for the Clergy, for the Army, for the Magistracy, for me, Irma, a bawd and madame of a whore-house. As for you, you'll be killed, disembowelled, and your daughter will be adopted by some virtuous rebel. And that's what's in store for all of us. (*She shudders.*)

Suddenly a buzz, IRMA *runs to the apparatus and looks and listens as before.*

IRMA: Studio 24, Chamber of the Sands. What's going on?

She watches very attentively. A long pause.

CARMEN: (*She has sat down at Irma's table and gone back to the accounts. Without raising her head.*) The Foreign Legion?

IRMA: (*With her eye still glued to the apparatus.*) Yes. It's the heroic Legionnaire falling to the sand. And that idiot Rachel has thrown a dart at his ear. He might have been disfigured. What an idea, having himself shot as if by an Arab, and dying – if you want to call it that! – at attention, on a sandpile! (*A silence. She watches attentively.*) Ah, Rachel's doctoring him. She's preparing a dressing for him, and he has a happy look. (*Very much interested.*) My, my, he seems to like it. I have a feeling he wants to alter his scenario and that starting today he's going to die in the military hospital, tucked in by his nurse…. Another uniform to buy. Always expenses. (*Suddenly anxious.*) Say, I don't like that. Not one bit. I'm getting more and more worried about Rachel. She'd better not double-cross me the way Chantal did. (*Turning around, to* CARMEN.) By the way, no news of Chantal?

CARMEN: None.

IRMA: (*Picks up the apparatus again.*) And the machine's not working right! What's he saying to her? He's explaining … she's listening … she understands. I'm afraid he understands too. (*Buzzing again. She pushes down another switch and looks.*) False alarm. It's the plumber leaving.

CARMEN: Which one?

IRMA: The real one.

CARMEN: Which is the real one?

IRMA: The one who repairs the taps.

CARMEN: Is the other one fake?

IRMA: (*Shrugs her shoulders and pushes down the first switch.*) Ah, I told you so: the three or four drops of blood from his ear have inspired him. Now he's having her pamper him. Tomorrow morning he'll be in fine fettle for going to his Embassy.

CARMEN: He's married, isn't he?

IRMA: As a rule, I don't like to talk about the private life of my visitors. The Grand Balcony has a world-wide reputation. It's the most artful, yet the most decent house of illusions….

CARMEN: Decent?

IRMA: Discreet. But I might as well be frank with you, you inquisitive girl. Most of them are married.

A pause.

CARMEN: When they're with their wives, whom they love, do they keep a tiny, small-scale version of their revels in a brothel….

IRMA: (*Reprimanding her.*) Carmen!

CARMEN: Excuse me, Madame … in a house of illusions. I was saying: do they keep their revels in a house of illusions tucked away in the back of their heads in miniature form, far off? But present?

IRMA: It's possible, child. No doubt they do. Like a Chinese lantern left over from a carnival, and waiting for the next one, or, if you prefer, like an imperceptible light in the imperceptible window of an imperceptible castle that they can enlarge instantly whenever they feel like going there to relax. (*Machine-gun fire.*) You hear that? They're approaching. They're out to get me.

CARMEN: (*Continuing her train of thought.*) All the same, it must be nice in a real house.

IRMA: (*More and more frightened.*) They'll succeed in surrounding the house before George arrives.... One thing we mustn't forget – if ever we get out of this mess – is that the walls aren't sufficiently padded and the windows aren't well sealed.... One can hear all that's going on in the street. Which means that from the street one can hear what's going on in the house.

CARMEN: (*Still pensive.*) In a real house, it must be nice....

IRMA: Who knows! But Carmen, if my girls start bothering their heads about such things, it'll be the ruin of the brothel. I really think you miss your apparition. Look, I can do something for you. I did promise it to Regina, but I offer it to you. If you want to, of course. Someone rang me up yesterday and asked for a Saint Theresa .... (*A pause.*) Ah, obviously, it's a come-down from the Immaculate Conception to Saint Theresa, but it's not bad either.... (*A pause.*) Well, what do you say? It's for a banker. Very clean, you know. Not demanding. I offer it to you. If the rebels are crushed, naturally.

CARMEN: I liked my dress and veil and rose-bush.

IRMA: There's a rose-bush in the 'Saint Theresa' too. Think it over.

A pause.

CARMEN: And what'll the authentic detail be?

IRMA: The ring. He's got it all worked out. The wedding ring. You know that every nun wears a wedding ring, as a bride of God. (CARMEN *makes a gesture of astonishment.*) That's so. That's how he'll know he's dealing with a real nun.

CARMEN: What about the fake detail?

IRMA: It's almost always the same: black lace under the homespun skirt. Well, how about it? You have the kind of gentleness he likes. He'll be pleased.

CARMEN: It's really very kind of you, to think of him.

IRMA: I'm thinking of you.

CARMEN: You're so kind, Madame – I wasn't being ironic. The thing to be said for your house is that it brings consolation. You set up and prepare their secret theatres... You've got your feet on the ground. The proof is that you rake in the money. Whereas they ... their awakening must be brutal. No sooner is it finished than it starts all over again.

IRMA: Luckily for me.

CARMEN: ... starts all over again, and always the same adventure. They'd like it never to end.

IRMA: You miss the entire point. When it's over, their minds are clear. I can tell from their eyes. Suddenly they understand mathematics. They love their children and their country. Like you.

CARMEN: (*Puffing herself up.*) I'm the daughter of a high-ranking officer....

IRMA: I know. There always has to be one in a brothel. But bear in mind that General, Bishop and Judge are, in real life....

CARMEN: Which are you talking about?

IRMA: Real ones.

CARMEN: Which are real? The ones here?

IRMA: The others. In real life they're props of a display that they have to drag in the mud of the real and commonplace. Here, Comedy and Appearance remain pure, and the Revels intact.

CARMEN: The revels that I indulge in....

IRMA: (*Interrupting her.*) I know what they are: to forget theirs.

CARMEN: Do you blame me for that?

IRMA: And theirs are to forget yours. They, too, love their children. Afterwards.

Buzzing again, as before. IRMA, *who has been sitting all the while near the apparatus, turns about, looks into the view-finder and puts the receiver to her ear.* CARMEN *goes back to her accounts.*

CARMEN: (*Without raising her head.*) The Chief of Police?

IRMA: (*Describing the scene.*) No. The waiter who just arrived. He's going to start complaining again ... there he goes, he's flaring up because Elyane is handing him a white apron.

CARMEN: I warned you. He wants a pink one.

IRMA: Go to the Five-and-Ten tomorrow, if it's open. And buy a duster for the railwayman. A green one.

CARMEN: If only Elyane doesn't forget to drop the tip on the floor. He demands a true revolt. And dirty glasses.

IRMA: They all want everything to be as true as possible.... Minus something indefinable, so that it won't be true. (*Changing her tone.*) Carmen, it was I who decided to call my establishment a house of illusions, but I'm only the manager. Each individual, when he rings the bell and enters, brings his own scenario, perfectly thought out. My job is merely to rent the hall and furnish the props, actors and actresses. My dear, I've succeeded in lifting it from the ground – do you see what I mean? I unloosed it long ago and it's flying. I cut the moorings. It's flying. Or, if you like, it's sailing in the sky, and I with it. Well, my darling ... may I say something tender – every madame always, traditionally, has a slight partiality for one of her young ladies....

CARMEN: I had noticed it, Madame, and I too, at times....

She looks at IRMA *languidly.*

IRMA: (*Standing up and looking at her.*) I have a strange feeling, Carmen. (*A long pause.*) But let's continue. Darling, the house really does take off, leaves the earth, sails in the sky when, in the secrecy of my heart, I call myself, but with great precision, a keeper of a bawdy-house. Darling, when secretly, in silence, I repeat to myself silently, 'You're a bawd, boss of a whore-house,' darling, everything (*suddenly lyrical*), everything flies off – chandeliers, mirrors, carpets, pianos, caryatids and my studios, my famous studios: the studio known as the Hay Studio, hung with rustic scenes, the Studio of the Hangings, spattered with blood and tears, the Throne-room Studio, draped in velvet with a fleur-de-lis pattern, the Studio of Mirrors, the Studio of State, the Studio of Perfumed Foundations, the Urinal Studio, the Amphitrite Studio, the Moonlight Studio, everything flies off: studios – Oh! I was forgetting the studio of the beggars, of the tramps, where filth and poverty are magnified. To continue: studios, girls, … (*She thinks again.*) Oh! I was forgetting: the most beautiful of all, ultimate adornment, crown of the edifice – if the construction of it is ever completed. I speak of the Funeral Studio, adorned with marble urns, my Studio of Solemn Death, the Tomb! The Mausoleum Studio…. To continue: studios, girls, crystals, laces, balconies, everything takes it on the lam, rises up and carries me off!

A long pause. The two women are standing motionless, facing each other.

CARMEN: How well you speak.

IRMA: (*Modestly.*) I went through elementary school.

CARMEN: So I assumed. My father, the artillery colonel….

IRMA: (*Correcting her sharply.*) You mean cavalry, my dear.

CARMEN: Excuse me. That's right. The cavalry colonel wanted me to have an education. Alas…. As for you, you've been successful. You've been able to surround your loveliness with a sumptuous theatre, a gala, the splendours of which envelop you and hide you from the world. Your whoredom required such pomp. But what about me, am I to have only myself and be only myself? No, Madame. Thanks to vice and men's heartache, I too have had my moment of glory! With the receiver at your ear, you could see me through the view-finder, standing erect, sovereign and kind, maternal yet feminine, with my heel on the cardboard snake and the pink paper-roses. You could also see the bank-clerk from the National City kneeling before me and swooning when I appeared to him. Unfortunately he had his back to you and so you weren't aware of the ecstasy on his face and the wild pounding of my heart. My blue veil, my blue robe, my blue apron, my blue eyes….

IRMA: They're hazel.

CARMEN: They were blue that day. For him I was Heaven in person descending on his brow. I was a Madonna to whom a Spaniard might have prayed and sworn an oath. He hymned me, fusing me with his beloved colour, and when he carried me to bed, it was into the blue that he penetrated. But I won't ever appear to him again.

IRMA: I've offered you Saint Theresa.

CARMEN: I'm not prepared, Mme Irma. One has to know what the client's going to require. Has everything been worked out?

IRMA: Every whore should be able – I hope you'll excuse me, but since we've gone so far, let's talk man to man – should be able to handle any situation.

CARMEN: I'm one of your whores, Mme Irma, and one of your best. I boast of it. In the course of an evening, I can …

IRMA: I'm aware of your feats. But when you start glorifying yourself as soon as you hear the word whore, which you keep repeating to yourself and which you flaunt as if it were a title, it's not quite the same as when I use the word to designate a function. But you're right, darling, to extol your profession and to glory in it. Make it shine. Let it illuminate you, if that's the only thing you have. (*Tenderly.*) I'll do all I can to help you…. You're not only the purest jewel of all my girls, you're the one on whom I bestow all my tenderness. But stay with me…. Would you dare leave me when everything is cracking up everywhere? Death – the real thing – is at my door, it's beneath my windows….

Machine-gun fire.

You hear?

CARMEN: The Army is fighting bravely.

IRMA: And the Rebels even more bravely. And we're in the shadow of the cathedral, a few feet from the Archbishop's Palace. There's no price on my head. No, that would be too much to expect, but it's known that I serve supper to prominent people. So they're out to get me. And there are no men in the house.

CARMEN: There's Arthur.

IRMA: Are you trying to be funny? He's no man, he's my stage-prop. Besides, as soon as his session is over, I'll send him to look for George.

CARMEN: Assuming the worst….

IRMA: If the rebels win? I'm a goner. They're workers. Without imagination. Prudish and maybe chaste.

CARMEN: It won't take them long to get used to debauchery. Just wait till they get a little bored….

IRMA: You're wrong. Or else they won't let themselves get bored. But I'm the one who's most exposed. For you it's different. In every revolution there's the glorified whore who sings an anthem and is virginified. That'll be you. The others'll piously bring water for the dying to drink. Afterwards … they'll marry you off. Would you like to get married?

CARMEN: Orange blossoms, tulle …

IRMA: Wonderful! To you, getting married means masquerading. Darling, you certainly are one of us. No, I can't imagine you married either. Besides, what they're really dreaming of doing is murdering us. We'll have a lovely death, Carmen. It will be terrible and sumptuous. They may break into my studios, shatter the crystals, tear the brocades and slit our throats….

CARMEN: They'll take pity....

IRMA: They won't. They'll thrill at the thought that their fury is sacrilegious. All bedraggled, with caps on their heads, or in helmets and boots, they'll destroy us by fire and sword. It'll be very beautiful. We oughtn't to wish for any other kind of end, and you, you're thinking of leaving....

CARMEN: But Mme Irma....

IRMA: Yes, yes. When the house is about to go up in flames, when the rose is about to be stabbed, all you think of, Carmen, is fleeing.

CARMEN: If I wanted to be elsewhere, you know very well why.

IRMA: Your daughter is dead....

CARMEN: Madame!

IRMA: Whether dead or alive, your daughter is dead. Think of the charming grave, adorned with daisies and artificial wreaths, at the far end of the garden ... and that garden in your heart, where you'll be able to look after it....

CARMEN: I'd have loved to see her again....

IRMA: You'll keep her image in the image of the garden and the garden in your heart under the flaming robe of Saint Theresa. And you hesitate? I offer you the very finest of deaths, and you hesitate? Are you a coward?

CARMEN: You know very well I'm devoted to you.

IRMA: I'll teach you figures! The wonderful figures that we'll spend the nights together calligraphing.

CARMEN: (*Softly.*) The war is raging. As you said, it's the horde.

IRMA: (*Triumphantly.*) The horde, but we have our cohorts, our armies, our hosts, legions, battalions, vessels, heralds, clarions, trumpets, our colours, streamers, standards, banners ... to lead us to catastrophe! Death? It's certain death, but with what speed and with what dash! ... (*Melancholically.*) Unless George is still all-powerful.... And above all if he can get through the horde and come and save us. (*A deep sigh.*) Now come and dress me. But first I want to see how Rachel's getting on.

Same business as before. IRMA glues her eye to the view-finder. A pause. She peers.

With this gadget I can see them and even hear their sighs.

A pause. She looks into the apparatus.

Christ is leaving with his paraphernalia. I've never been able to understand why he has himself tied to the cross with ropes he brings in a valise. Maybe they're ropes that have been blessed. Where does he put them when he gets home? Who the hell cares! Let's take a look at Rachel. (*She pushes down another switch.*) Ah, they've finished. They're talking. They're putting away the little arrows, the bow, the gauze bandages, the white officer's cap.... No, I don't at all like the way they're looking at each other: it's too candid and straightforward. (*She turns to CARMEN.*) There you have the dangers of regularity. It would be a catastrophe if my clients and girls smiled at each other

affectionately. It would be an even greater catastrophe than if it were a question of love. (*She presses the switch mechanically and lays down the receiver. Pensively.*) Arthur's session must be over. He'll be along in a minute.... Dress me.

CARMEN: What are you wearing?

IRMA: The cream-coloured négligée.

CARMEN opens the door of a closet and takes out the négligée, while IRMA unhooks her suit.

Tell me, Carmen, what about Chantal? ...

CARMEN: Madame?

IRMA: Yes. About Chantal, tell me, what do you know about her?

CARMEN: I've questioned all the girls: Rosine, Elyane, Florence, Marlyse. They've each prepared a little report. I'll let you have them. But I didn't get much out of them. It's possible to spy beforehand. During the fighting, it's harder. For one thing, the camps are more sharply defined. You can choose. When there's peace, it's too vague. You don't quite know whom you're betraying. Nor even whether you're betraying. There's no news about Chantal. They don't even know whether she's still alive.

IRMA: But, tell me, you wouldn't have any scruples about it?

CARMEN: None at all. Entering a brothel means rejecting the world. Here I am and here I stay. Your mirrors and orders and the passions are my reality. What jewels are you wearing?

IRMA: The diamonds. My jewels. They're the only things I have that are real. I feel everything else is sham. I have my jewels as others have little girls in gardens. Who's double-crossing? You're hesitating.

CARMEN: The girls all mistrust me. I collect their little report. I pass it on to you. You pass it on to the police. The police check on it.... Me, I know nothing.

IRMA: You're cautious. Give me a handkerchief.

CARMEN: (*Bringing a lace handkerchief.*) Viewed from here, where, in any case, men show their naked selves, life seems to me so remote, so profound, that it has all the unreality of a film or of the birth of Christ in the manger. When I'm in a room with a man and he forgets himself so far as to say to me: 'The arsenal will be taken tomorrow night,' I feel as if I were reading an obscene scrawl. His act becomes as mad, as ... voluminous as those described in a certain way on certain walls.... No, I'm not cautious.

A knocking. IRMA gives a start. She rushes to the apparatus and, by means of a mechanism operated by a button, conceals it in the wall. In the course of the scene with ARTHUR, CARMEN undresses and then dresses IRMA, so that the latter is ready just when the CHIEF OF POLICE arrives.

IRMA: Come in!

The door opens. Enter THE EXECUTIONER, whom hereafter we shall call ARTHUR. Classical pimp's outfit: light grey suit, white felt hat, etc. He finishes knotting his tie.

IRMA: (*Examining him minutely.*) Is the session over? He went through it fast.

ARTHUR: Yes, the little geezer's buttoning up. He's pooped. Two sessions in half an hour. With all that shooting in the street, I wonder whether he'll get back to his hotel. (*He imitates* THE JUDGE *in Scene Two.*) Minos judges you.... Minos weighs you ... Cerberus? Bow-wow! Bow-wow! (*He shows his fangs and laughs.*) Hasn't the Chief of Police arrived?

IRMA: You went easy, I hope? Last time, the poor girl was laid up for two days.

CARMEN *has brought the cream-coloured négligée,* IRMA *is now in her chemise.*

ARTHUR: Don't pull that kind-hearted-whore stuff on me. Both last time and tonight she got what was coming to her: in dough and in wallops. Right on the line. The banker wants to see stripes on her back. So I stripe it.

IRMA: At least you don't get any pleasure out of it?

ARTHUR: Not with her. You're my only love. And a job's a job. I'm conscientious about my work.

IRMA: (*Sternly.*) I'm not jealous of the girl, but I wouldn't want you to disable the personnel. It's getting harder and harder to replace.

ARTHUR: I tried a couple of times to draw marks on her back with purple paint, but it didn't work. The old guy inspects her when he arrives and insists I deliver her in good shape.

IRMA: Paint? Who gave you permission? (*To* CARMEN.) My Turkish slippers, darling.

ARTHUR: (*Shrugging his shoulders.*) What's one illusion more or less! I thought I was doing the right thing. But don't worry. Now I whip, I flagellate, she screams, and he crawls.

IRMA: See to it she doesn't scream so loud. The house is being watched.

ARTHUR: The radio has just announced that all the north part of town was taken last night. And the Judge wants screaming. The Bishop's less dangerous. He's satisfied with pardoning sins.

CARMEN: Though he gets pleasure out of pardoning, he expects you to commit them. No, the best of the lot is the one you tie up, spank, whip and soothe, and then he snores.

ARTHUR: Who cuddles him? (*To* CARMEN.) You? Do you give him your breast?

CARMEN: (*Curtly.*) I do my job right. And in any case, Mr. Arthur, you're wearing an outfit that doesn't allow you to joke. The pimp has a grin, never a smile.

IRMA: She's right.

ARTHUR: How much did you take in today?

IRMA: (*On the defensive.*) Carmen and I haven't finished the accounts.

ARTHUR: But I have. According to my calculations, it runs to a good two hundred.

IRMA: That's possible. In any case, don't worry. I don't cheat.

ARTHUR: I believe you, my love, but I can't help it: the figures arrange themselves in my head. Two hundred! War, rebellion, shooting, frost, hail, rain, showers of shit, nothing stops them! On the contrary. People are killing each other in the streets, the joint's being watched, but all the same, they come charging in. As for me, I've got you right at home, sweetie-pie, otherwise....

IRMA: (*Bluntly.*) You'd be cowering in a cellar, paralysed with fear.

ARTHUR: (*Ambiguously.*) I'd do as the others do, my love. I'd wait to be saved by the Chief of Police. You're not forgetting my little percentage?

IRMA: I give you what you need.

ARTHUR: My love! I've ordered the silk shirts. And do you know what kind of silk? And what colour? In the purple silk of your blouse!

IRMA: (*Tenderly.*) All right, cut it. Not in front of Carmen.

ARTHUR: Then it's O.K.?

IRMA (*Weakening.*) Yes.

ARTHUR: How much?

IRMA: (*Regaining her self-possession.*) We'll see. I have to go over the accounts with Carmen. (*Winningly.*) It'll be as much as I can. For the moment, you've absolutely got to go to meet George....

ARTHUR: (*With insolent irony.*) I beg your pardon, my beloved?

IRMA: (*Curtly.*) To go to meet Mr George. To Police Headquarters, if necessary, and to let him know that I'm relying only on him.

ARTHUR: (*Slightly uneasy.*) You're kidding, I hope? ...

IRMA: (*With sudden sternness.*) The tone of my last remark should answer your question. I'm no longer playing. Or, if you like, not the same role. And there's no longer any need for you to play the mean, soft-hearted pimp. Do as I tell you, but first take the atomizer. (*To* CARMEN, *who brings the object.*) Give it to him. (*To* ARTHUR.) And on your knees!

ARTHUR: (*He puts one knee on the floor and sprays Irma.*) In the street? All by myself! ... Me? ...

IRMA: (*Standing in front of him.*) I've got to know what's happening to George. I can't remain unprotected.

ARTHUR: I'm here ...

IRMA: (*Shrugging.*) I've got to defend my jewels, my studios, my girls. The Chief of Police should have been here a half-hour ago....

ARTHUR: (*Woefully.*) Me in the street! ... But it's hailing ... they're shooting.... (*He points to his suit.*) And I got dressed up to stay here, to go walking through the corridors and look at myself in your mirrors. And also for you to see me dressed up as a pimp.... All I've got to protect me is the silk....

IRMA: (*To* CARMEN.) Let me have my bracelets, Carmen. (*To* ARTHUR.) And you, spray.

ARTHUR: I'm not meant for outdoors. I've been living within your walls too long. Even my skin couldn't tolerate the fresh air ... maybe if I had a veil.... What if I were recognized? ...

IRMA: (*Irritated, and pivoting in front of the atomizer.*) Hug the walls. (*A pause.*) Take this revolver.

ARTHUR: (*Frightened.*) On me?

IRMA: In your pocket.

ARTHUR: My pocket! Imagine me having to shoot? …

IRMA: (*Gently.*) So now you're crammed full of what you are? Gorged?

ARTHUR: Gorged, that's right…. (*A pause.*) Rested, gorged … but if I go out into the street….

IRMA: (*Commandingly, but gently.*) You're right. No revolver. But take off your hat and go where I tell you, and come back and let me know what's going on. You have a session this evening. Did you know? (*He tosses his hat away.*)

ARTHUR: (*On his way to the door.*) This evening? Another one? What is it?

IRMA: I thought I told you: a corpse.

ARTHUR: (*With disgust.*) What am I supposed to do with it?

IRMA: Nothing. You're to remain motionless, and you'll be buried. You'll be able to rest.

ARTHUR: Ah, because I'm the one who …? Ah, O.K. All right. Who's the client? Someone new?

IRMA: (*Mysteriously.*) A very important person, and stop asking questions. Get going.

ARTHUR: (*Starting to leave, then hesitating, timidly.*) Don't I get a kiss?

IRMA: When we come back. If we come back.

Exit ARTHUR, *still on his knees.*

But the door at the right has already opened and, without knocking, THE CHIEF OF POLICE *enters. Heavy fur-lined coat, hat, cigar.* CARMEN *starts running to call* ARTHUR *back, but* THE CHIEF OF POLICE *steps in front of her.*

THE CHIEF OF POLICE: No, no, stay, Carmen. I like having you around. As for the gigolo, let him find me.

He keeps his hat and coat on, does not remove his cigar from his mouth, but bows to IRMA *and kisses her hand.*

IRMA: (*Breathlessly.*) Put your hand here. (*On her breast.*) I'm all tense. I'm still wrought up. I knew you were on your way, which meant you were in danger. I waited for you all a-tremble … while perfuming myself….

THE CHIEF OF POLICE: (*While taking off his hat, coat, gloves and jacket.*) All right, that'll do. Let's cut the comedy. The situation's getting more and more serious – it's not desperate, but it will be before long – hap-pi-ly! The Royal Palace is surrounded. The Queen's in hiding. The city – it's a miracle that I got through – the city's being ravaged by fire and sword. Out there the rebellion is tragic and joyous, whereas in this house everything's dying a slow death. So, today's my day. By tonight I'll be in the grave or on a pedestal. So whether I love you or desire you is unimportant. How are things going at the moment?

IRMA: Marvellously. I had some great performances.

THE CHIEF OF POLICE: (*Impatiently.*) What kind?

IRMA: Carmen has a talent for description. Ask her.

THE CHIEF OF POLICE: (*To* CARMEN.) Tell me, Carmen, still… ?

CARMEN: Yes, sir, still. Still the pillars of the Empire: the Judge….

THE CHIEF OF POLICE: (*Ironically.*) Our allegories, our talking weapons. And is there also… ?

CARMEN: As every week, a new theme.

THE CHIEF OF POLICE *makes a gesture of curiosity.*

This time it's the baby who gets slapped, spanked, tucked in, then cries and is cuddled.

THE CHIEF OF POLICE: (*Impatiently.*) Fine. But….

CARMEN: He's charming, Sir. And so sad!

THE CHIEF OF POLICE: (*Irritably.*) Is that all?

CARMEN: And so pretty when you unswaddle him….

THE CHIEF OF POLICE: (*With rising fury.*) Are you pulling my leg, Carmen? I'm asking you whether I'm in it?

CARMEN: Whether you're in it?

IRMA: (*Ironically, though we do not know with whom she is ironic.*) You're not in it.

THE CHIEF OF POLICE: Not yet? (*To* CARMEN.) Well, yes or no, is there a simulation….

CARMEN: (*Bewildered.*) Simulation?

THE CHIEF OF POLICE: You idiot! Yes! An impersonation of the Chief of Police?

Very heavy silence.

IRMA: The time's not ripe. My dear, your function isn't noble enough to offer dreamers an image that would console them. Perhaps because it lacks illustrious ancestors? No, my dear fellow…. You have to resign yourself to the fact that your image does not yet conform to the liturgies of the brothel.

THE CHIEF OF POLICE: Who's represented in them?

IRMA: You know who. You have your index-cards. (*She enumerates on her fingers.*) There are two kings of France with coronation ceremonies and different rituals, an admiral at the stern of his sinking destroyer, a dey of Algiers surrendering, a fireman putting out a fire, a goat attached to a stake, a housewife returning from market, a pickpocket, a robbed man who's bound and beaten up, a Saint Sebastian, a farmer in his barn … but no chief of police … nor colonial administrator, though there *is* a missionary dying on the cross, and Christ in person.

THE CHIEF OF POLICE: (*After a pause.*) You're forgetting the mechanic.

IRMA: He doesn't come any more. What with tightening screws, he'd have ended by constructing a machine. And it might have worked. Back to the factory!

THE CHIEF OF POLICE: So not a single one of your clients has had the idea … the remotest idea, the barest suggestion….

IRMA: No. I know you do what you can. You try hatred and love. But glory gives you the cold shoulder.

THE CHIEF OF POLICE: (*Forcefully.*) My image is growing bigger and bigger. It's becoming colossal. Everything around me repeats and reflects it. And you've never seen it represented in this place?

IRMA: In any case, even if it were celebrated here, I wouldn't see anything. The ceremonies are secret.

THE CHIEF OF POLICE: You liar. You've got secret peep-holes in every wall. Every partition, every mirror, is rigged. In one place, you can hear the sighs, in another the echo of the moans. You don't need me to tell you that brothel tricks are mainly mirror tricks…. (*Very sadly.*) Nobody yet! But I'll make my image detach itself from me. I'll make it penetrate into your studios, force its way in, reflect and multiply itself. Irma, my function weighs me down. Here, it will appear to me in the blazing light of pleasure and death. (*Musingly.*) Of death.

IRMA: You must keep killing, my dear George.

THE CHIEF OF POLICE: I do what I can, I assure you. People fear me more and more.

IRMA: Not enough. You must plunge into darkness, into shit and blood. (*With sudden anguish.*) And must kill whatever remains of our love.

THE CHIEF OF POLICE: (*Curtly.*) Everything's dead.

IRMA: That's a fine victory. So you've got to kill what's around you.

THE CHIEF OF POLICE: (*Very irritated.*) I repeat: I do what I can to prove to the nation that I'm a leader, a lawgiver, a builder….

IRMA: (*Uneasily.*) You're raving. Or else you really do expect to build an empire. In which case you're raving.

THE CHIEF OF POLICE: (*With conviction.*) When the rebellion's been put down, and put down by me, when I've the nation behind me and been appealed to by the Queen, nothing can stop me. Then, and only then, will you see who I now am! (*Musingly.*) Yes, my dear, I want to build an empire … so that the empire will, in exchange, build me….

IRMA: … a tomb.

THE CHIEF OF POLICE: (*Somewhat taken aback.*) But, after all, why not? Doesn't every conqueror have one? So? (*Exalted.*) Alexandria! I'll have my tomb, Irma. And when the cornerstone is laid, you'll be my guest of honour.

IRMA: Thank you. (*To* CARMEN.) Carmen, the tea.

THE CHIEF OF POLICE: (*To* CARMEN, *who is about to leave.*) Just a minute, Carmen. What do you think of the idea?

CARMEN: That you want to merge your life with one long funeral, sir.

THE CHIEF OF POLICE: (*Aggressively.*) Is life anything else? You seem to know everything – so tell me: in this sumptuous theatre where every moment a drama is performed – in the sense that the outside world says a mass is celebrated – what have you observed?

CARMEN: (*After a hesitation.*) As for anything serious, anything worth reporting, only one thing: that without the thighs it contained, a pair of pants on a chair is beautiful, sir. Emptied of our little old men, our ornaments are deathly sad. They're the ones that are placed on the catafalques of high dignitaries. They cover only corpses that never stop dying. And yet….

IRMA: (*To* CARMEN.) That's not what the Chief of Police is asking.

THE CHIEF OF POLICE: I'm used to Carmen's speeches. (*To* CARMEN.) You were saying: and yet… ?

CARMEN: And yet, I'm sure that the sudden joy in their eyes when they see the cheap finery is really the gleam of innocence….

THE CHIEF OF POLICE: People claim that our house sends them to Death.

Suddenly a ringing. IRMA *starts. A pause.*

IRMA: Someone's opened the door. Who can it be at this hour? (*To* CARMEN.) Carmen, go down and shut the door.

CARMEN *exits. A rather long silence between* IRMA *and* THE CHIEF OF POLICE, *who remain alone.*

THE CHIEF OF POLICE: My tomb!

IRMA: It was I who rang. I wanted to be alone with you for a moment. (*A pause, during which they look into each other's eyes seriously.*) Tell me, George…. (*She hesitates.*) Do you still insist on keeping up the game? No, no, don't be impatient. Aren't you tired of it?

THE CHIEF OF POLICE: But…. In a little while I'll be going home.

IRMA: If you can. If the rebellion leaves you free to go.

THE CHIEF OF POLICE: The rebellion is a game. From here you can't see anything of the outside, but every rebel is playing a game. And he loves his game.

IRMA: But supposing they let themselves be carried beyond the game? I mean if they get so involved in it that they destroy and replace everything. Yes, yes, I know, there's always the false detail that reminds them that at a certain moment, at a certain point in the drama, they have to stop, and even withdraw…. But what if they're so carried away by passion that they no longer recognize anything and leap, without realizing it, into….

THE CHIEF OF POLICE: You mean into reality? What of it? Let them try. I do as they do, I penetrate right into the reality that the game offers us, and since I have the upper hand, it's I who score.

IRMA: They'll be stronger than you.

THE CHIEF OF POLICE: Why do you say 'they'll be'? I've left the members of my bodyguard in one of your studios. So I'm always in contact with my various departments. All right, enough of that. Are you or aren't you the mistress of a house of illusions? Good. If I come to your place, it's to find satisfaction in your mirrors and their trickery. (*Tenderly.*) Don't worry. Everything will be just as it's always been.

IRMA: I don't know why, but today I feel uneasy. Carmen seems strange to me. The rebels – how shall I put it? – have a kind of gravity....

THE CHIEF OF POLICE: Their role requires it.

IRMA: No, no ... of determination. They walk by the windows threateningly, but they don't sing. The threat is in their eyes.

THE CHIEF OF POLICE: What of it? Supposing it is, do you take me for a coward? Do you think I should give up and go home?

IRMA: (*Pensively.*) No. Besides, I think it's too late.

THE CHIEF OF POLICE: Do you have any news?

IRMA: From Chantal, before she lit out. The power-house will be occupied around 3 a.m.

THE CHIEF OF POLICE: Are you sure? Who told her?

IRMA: The partisans of the Fourth Sector.

THE CHIEF OF POLICE: That's plausible. How did she find out?

IRMA: It's through her that there were leaks, and through her alone. So don't belittle my house....

THE CHIEF OF POLICE: Your cat-house, my love.

IRMA: Cat-house, whore-house, bawdy-house. Brothel. Fuckery. Call it anything you like. So Chantal's the only one who's on the other side.... She lit out. But before she did, she confided in Carmen, and Carmen's no fool.

THE CHIEF OF POLICE: Who tipped her off?

IRMA: Roger. The plumber. How do you imagine him? Young and handsome? No. He's forty. Thick-set. Serious, with ironic eyes. Chantal spoke to him. I put him out: too late. He belongs to the Andromeda network.

THE CHIEF OF POLICE: Andromeda? Splendid. The rebellion's riding high, it's moving out of this world. If it gives its sectors the names of constellations, it'll evaporate in no time and be metamorphosed into song. Let's hope the songs are beautiful.

IRMA: And what if their songs give the rebels courage? What if they're willing to die for them?

THE CHIEF OF POLICE: The beauty of their songs will make them soft. Unfortunately, they haven't yet reached the point of either beauty or softness. In any case, Chantal's tender passions were providential.

IRMA: Don't bring God into....

THE CHIEF OF POLICE: I'm a freemason. Therefore....

IRMA: You? You never told me.

THE CHIEF OF POLICE: (*Solemnly.*) Sublime Prince of the Royal Secret.

IRMA: (*Ironically.*) You, a brother in a little apron! With a hood and taper and a little mallet! That's odd. (*A pause.*) You too?

THE CHIEF OF POLICE: Why? You too?

IRMA: (*With mock solemnity.*) I'm a guardian of far more solemn rites. (*Suddenly sad.*) Since that's all I am now.

THE CHIEF OF POLICE: As usual, you're going to bring up our grand passion.

IRMA: (*Gently.*) No, not our passion, but the time when we loved each other.

THE CHIEF OF POLICE: Well, would you like to give a historical account of it and deliver a eulogy? You think my visits would have less zest if you didn't flavour them with the memory of a pretended innocence?

IRMA: It's a question of tenderness. Neither the wildest concoctions of my clients nor my own fancies nor my constant endeavour to enrich my studios with new themes nor the passing of time nor the gilding and crystals nor bitter cold can dispel the moments when you cuddled in my arms or keep me from remembering them.

THE CHIEF OF POLICE: Do you really miss them?

IRMA: (*Tenderly.*) I'd give my kingdom to relive a single one of them! And you know which one. I need just one word of truth – as when one looks at one's wrinkles at night, or rinses one's mouth....

THE CHIEF OF POLICE: It's too late. (*A pause.*) Besides, we couldn't cuddle each other eternally. You don't know what I was already secretly moving towards when I was in your arms.

IRMA: I know that I loved you.

THE CHIEF OF POLICE: It's too late. Could you give up Arthur?

IRMA: It was you who forced him on me. You insisted on there being a man here – against my better judgment – in a domain that should have remained virgin.... You fool, don't laugh. Virgin, that is, sterile. But you wanted a pillar, a shaft, a phallus present – an upright bulk. Well, it's here. You saddled me with that hunk of congested meat, that milksop with wrestler's arms. He may look like a strongman at a fair, but you don't realize how fragile he is. You stupidly forced him on me because you felt yourself ageing.

THE CHIEF OF POLICE: Be still.

IRMA: (*Shrugging her shoulders.*) And you relaxed here through Arthur. I need him now. I have no illusions. I'm his man and he relies on me, but I need that rugged shop-window dummy hanging on to my skirts. He's my body, as it were, but set beside me.

THE CHIEF OF POLICE: (*Ironically.*) What if I were jealous?

IRMA: Of that big doll made up as an executioner in order to satisfy a phony judge? You're kidding, but the spectacle of me under the spectacle of that magnificent body never used to bother you.... Let me repeat....

THE CHIEF OF POLICE: (*He slaps* IRMA, *who falls on the sofa.*) And don't blubber or I'll break your jaw, and I'll send your joint up in smoke. I'll set fire to your hair and bush and I'll turn you loose. I'll light up the town with blazing whores. (*Very gently.*) Do you think I'm capable of it?

IRMA: (*In a panting whisper.*) Yes, darling.

THE CHIEF OF POLICE: All right, add up the accounts for me. If you like, you can deduct Apollo's crêpe de Chine. And hurry up. I've got to get back to my post. For the time being, I have to act. Afterwards.... Afterwards, things'll run themselves. My name will act in my place. Well, what about Arthur?

IRMA: (*Submissively.*) He'll be dead this evening.

THE CHIEF OF POLICE: Dead? You mean … really … really dead?

IRMA: (*With resignation.*) Come, come, George, the way one dies here.

THE CHIEF OF POLICE: Indeed? Meaning….

IRMA: The Minister….

She is interrupted by the voice of CARMEN.

CARMEN: (*In the wings.*) Lock Studio 17! Elyane, hurry up! And lower the studio … no, no, wait…. (*We hear the sound of a rusty cog-wheel, the kind made by certain old lifts. Enter* CARMEN.) Madame, the Queen's Envoy is in the drawing-room….

The door opens, left, and ARTHUR *appears, trembling and with his clothes torn.*

ARTHUR: (*Noticing* THE CHIEF OF POLICE.) You here! You managed to get through?

IRMA: (*Rushing to his arms.*) Darling! What's the matter? Are you hurt? Speak!

ARTHUR: (*Panting.*) I tried to get to Police Headquarters. Impossible. The whole city's lit up with fires. The rebels are in control practically everywhere. I don't think you can get back, sir. I was able to reach the Royal Palace, and I saw the Grand Chamberlain. He said he'd try to come. I might add that he shook my hand. And then I left. The women are the most excited. They're urging the men to loot and kill. But what was most awful was a girl who was singing….

A shot is heard. A window-pane is shivered. Also a mirror near the bed. ARTHUR *falls down, hit in the forehead by a bullet coming from outside.* CARMEN *bends over him, then rises to her feet again. Then* IRMA *bends over him and strokes his forehead.*

THE CHIEF OF POLICE: In short, I'm stuck in the whore-house. That means I'll have to act from the whore-house.

IRMA: (*To herself bent over* ARTHUR.) Can it be that everything's slipping away? Slipping between my fingers? … (*Bitterly.*) I still have my jewels … my rocks … and perhaps not for long….

CARMEN: (*Softly.*) If the house is to be blown up…. Is Saint Theresa's costume in the closet, Mme Irma?

IRMA: (*Anxiously.*) At the left. But first have Arthur removed. I'm going to receive the Envoy.

Scene Six

A public square, with patches of shadow. In the background, at some distance, we perceive the façade of the Grand Balcony, the blinds of which are drawn. CHANTAL *and* ROGER *are locked in embrace. Three men seem to be watching over them. Black suits. Black sweaters. They are holding machine-guns which are pointed at the Grand Balcony.*

CHANTAL: Keep me, if you will, my love, but keep me in your heart. And wait for me.

ROGER: I love you with your body, with your hair, your bosom, your belly, your guts, your fluids, your smells. Chantal, I love you in my bed. They….

CHANTAL: (*Smiling.*) They don't care a rap about me. But without them, *I'd* be nothing.

ROGER: You're mine. I …

CHANTAL: (*Annoyed.*) I know. You dragged me from the grave. And no sooner do I shake off my wrappings than, ungrateful wretch that I am, I gad about like a trollop. I plunge into the adventure, and I escape you. (*Suddenly with tender irony.*) But Roger, my love, you know I love you, you and only you.

ROGER: You've just said the word: you're escaping me. I can't follow you in your heroic and stupid course.

CHANTAL: Ah ha! You're jealous of whom, or what? People say that I soar above the insurrection, that I'm its soul and voice, and you – you're rooted to the ground. That's why you're sad….

ROGER: Chantal, please, don't be vulgar. If you can help….

One of the men draws near.

THE MAN: (*To* ROGER.) Well, is it yes or is it no?

ROGER: What if she stays there?

THE MAN: I'm asking you to let us have her for two hours.

ROGER: Chantal belongs….

CHANTAL: (*Standing up.*) To nobody!

ROGER: … To my section.

THE MAN: To the insurrection!

ROGER: If you want a woman to lead your men forward, then create one.

THE MAN: We looked for one, but there aren't any. We tried to build one up: nice voice, nice bosom, with the right kind of free and easy manner. But her eyes lacked fire, and you know that without fire…. We asked the North Section and the Port Section to let us have theirs; they weren't free.

CHANTAL: A woman like me? Another one? All I have is a hoarse voice and a face like an owl's. I give them or lend them for hatred's sake. I'm nothing, only my face, my voice, and inside me a sweet, poisonous kindness. D'you mean to tell me I have two popular rivals, two other poor devils? Let them come, I'll show them! I have no rival.

ROGER: (*Exploding.*) I snatched her – snatched her from a grave. She's already escaping me and mounting to the sky. If I lend her to you….

THE MAN: We're not asking you for that. If we take her, we're hiring her.

CHANTAL: (*Amused.*) How much?

ROGER: Even if we let you have her to sing and spur on your district, if she gets bumped off we'll lose everything. No one can replace her.

THE MAN: She agreed to it.

ROGER: She doesn't belong to herself any more. She's ours. She's our sign. All that your women are good for is tearing up and carrying stones or reloading guns. I know that's useful, but …

THE MAN: How many women do you want in exchange?

ROGER: (*Thoughtfully.*) Is a singer on the barricades as precious as all that?

THE MAN: How many? Ten women for Chantal? (*A pause.*) Twenty?

ROGER: Twenty women? You'd pay me twenty measly women, twenty oxen, twenty head of cattle? So Chantal's something special? And do you know where she comes from?

CHANTAL: (*To ROGER, violently.*) Every morning I go back – because at night I'm ablaze – I go back to a hovel and sleep – chastely, my love! – and drink myself into a stupor on red wine. And I, with my grating voice, my sham anger, my cameo eyes, my painted illumination, my Andalusian hair, I comfort and enchant the rabble. They'll win and my victory will be a strange one.

ROGER: (*Thoughtfully.*) Twenty women for Chantal?

THE MAN: (*Sharply.*) A hundred.

ROGER: (*Still pensively.*) And it's probably because of her that we'll win. She already embodies the Revolution….

THE MAN: A hundred. You agree?

ROGER: Where are you taking her? And what'll she have to do?

CHANTAL: We'll see. Don't worry, I was born under a lucky star. As for the rest of it, I realize my power. The people love me, they listen to me, they follow me.

ROGER: What will she do?

THE MAN: Hardly anything. As you know, we're attacking the Palace at dawn. Chantal will go in first. She'll sing from a balcony. That's all.

ROGER: A hundred women. A thousand and maybe more. So she's no longer a woman. The creature they make of her out of rage and despair has her price. In order to fight against an image Chantal has frozen into an image. The fight is no longer taking place in reality, but in the lists. Field azure. It's the combat of allegories. None of us know any longer why we revolted. So she was bound to come round to that.

THE MAN: Well, is it yes? Answer, Chantal. It's for you to answer.

CHANTAL: (*To THE MAN.*) I'd like us to be alone for a moment. I've got something else to say. (THE MAN *moves off and goes back into the shadow.*)

ROGER: (*Violently.*) I didn't steal you for you to become a unicorn or a two-headed eagle.

CHANTAL: You don't like unicorns.

ROGER: I've never been able to make love to them. (*He caresses her.*) Nor to you either.

CHANTAL: You mean I don't know how to love. I disappoint you. Yet I love you. And you hired me out for a hundred female diggers.

ROGER: Forgive me. I need them. And yet I love you. I love you and I don't know how to tell you. I can't sing. And singing is the last resort.

CHANTAL: I'll have to leave before day-break. If the North Section has come through, the Queen will be dead in an hour. It'll be the end of the Chief of Police. If not, we'll never get out of this bedlam.

ROGER: One minute more, my love, my life. It's still night.

CHANTAL: It's the hour when night breaks away from the day, my dove, let me go.

ROGER: The minutes without you will be unbearable.

CHANTAL: We won't be separated, I swear to you. I'll speak to them in an icy tone and at the same time I'll murmur words of love for you. You'll hear them from here, and I'll hear yours.

ROGER: They may keep you, Chantal. They're strong – strong as death.

CHANTAL: Don't be afraid, my love. I know their power. Your sweetness and tenderness are stronger. I'll speak to them with severity. I'll tell them what the people demand. They'll listen to me because they'll be afraid. Let me go.

ROGER: (*Screaming.*) Chantal, I love you!

CHANTAL: Ah, my love, it's because I love you that I must hurry.

ROGER: You love me?

CHANTAL: I love you because you're tender and sweet, you the hardest and sternest of men. And your sweetness and tenderness are such that they make you as light as a shred of tulle, subtle as a flake of mist, airy as a caprice. Your thick muscles, your arms, your thighs, your hands, are more unreal than the melting of day into night. You envelop me and I contain you.

ROGER: Chantal, I love you because you're hard and stern, you the tenderest and sweetest of women. And your sweetness and tenderness are such that they make you as stern as a lesson, hard as hunger, inflexible as a block of ice. Your breasts, your skin, your hair are more real than the certainty of noon. You envelop me and I contain you.

CHANTAL: When I stand before them, when I speak to them, I'll be hearing your sighs and moans and the beating of your heart. Let me go.

He holds her back.

ROGER: You still have time. There's still some shadow along the walls. You'll go round the back of the Archbishop's Palace. You know the way.

ONE OF THE REBELS: (*In a low voice.*) It's time, Chantal. Day is breaking.

CHANTAL: Do you hear? They're calling me.

ROGER: (*Suddenly irritated.*) But why you? You'll never be able to speak to them.

CHANTAL: I, better than anyone. I'm gifted.

ROGER: They're clever, cunning….

CHANTAL: I'll invent gestures, postures, phrases. Before they even say a word, I'll understand, and you'll be proud of my victory.

ROGER: Let the others go. (*He cries out to the rebels.*) You go! Or me, if you're afraid. I'll tell them they must give in, because we're the law.

CHANTAL: Don't listen to him. He's drunk. (*To* ROGER.) All *they* can do is fight, and all *you* can do is love me. That's the role you've learned to play. As for me, it's something else. At least the brothel has been of some use to me: it's taught me the art of pretence, of acting. I've had to play so many roles that I know almost all of them. And I've had so many partners....

ROGER: Chantal!

CHANTAL: And such artful ones, such cunning and eloquent ones, that my skill and trickery and eloquence are incomparable. I can be familiar with the Queen, the Hero, the General, the heroic Troops … and can fool them all.

ROGER: You know all the roles, don't you? Just now, you were reciting lines to me, weren't you?

CHANTAL: One learns fast. You yourself....

The three rebels have drawn close.

ONE OF THE REBELS: (*Pulling* CHANTAL.) Cut the speeches. Get going.

ROGER: Chantal, stay!

CHANTAL *goes off, led by the rebels.*

CHANTAL: I envelop you and I contain you, my love....

She disappears in the direction of The Balcony, pushed by the three men.

ROGER: (*Alone.*) … and I've had so many partners, and such artful ones, such cunning ones … that she did, after all, have to try to give them an answer. The one they wanted. In a little while she'll have cunning and artful partners. She'll be the answer they're waiting for.

As he speaks, the setting moves toward the left, the stage grows dark, and he himself, still speaking, moves off and into the wings. When the light goes on again, the setting of the next scene is in place.

Scene Seven

The Funeral Studio in MME IRMA's *listing of the Studios. The studio is in ruins. The lace and velvet are torn. The artificial wreaths are tattered. An impression of desolation,* IRMA's *dress is in rags. So is the suit of* THE CHIEF OF POLICE. ARTHUR's *corpse is lying on a kind of fake tomb of fake black marble. Nearby, a new character, the* COURT ENVOY. *Embassy uniform. He is the only one unscathed,* CARMEN *is dressed as at the beginning. A tremendous explosion. Everything shatters.*

THE ENVOY: (*In a tone both airy and grave.*) For more centuries than I can tell, the centuries have worn themselves thin refining me … subtilizing me.... (*He smiles.*) From something or other about the explosion, from its power, in which was mingled a clinking of jewels and broken mirrors, I rather think it was the Royal Palace. (*The characters all look at each other, horror-stricken.*) Let us not display any emotion. So long as we are not like that.... (*He points to the corpse of* ARTHUR.)

IRMA: He didn't think he'd be acting his role of corpse this evening in earnest.

THE ENVOY: (*Smiling.*) Our dear Minister of the Interior would have been delighted had not he himself met the same fate. It is unfortunately I who have had to replace him in his mission here, and I have no taste for pleasures of this kind. (*He touches* ARTHUR's *corpse with his foot.*) Yes, this body would have sent our dear Minister into raptures.

IRMA: Not at all, your Excellency. It's make-believe that these gentlemen want. The Minister desired a fake corpse. But this one is real. Look at it: it's truer than life. His entire being is speeding towards immobility.

THE ENVOY: He was therefore meant for grandeur.

THE CHIEF OF POLICE: Him? He was a spineless dummy.

THE ENVOY: He was, like us, haunted by a quest of immobility. By what we call the hieratic. And, in passing, allow me to pay tribute to the imagination responsible for there being a funeral parlour in this house.

IRMA: (*Proudly.*) And you see only part of it.

THE ENVOY: Whose idea was it?

IRMA: The Wisdom of Nations, your Excellency.

THE ENVOY: It does things well. But we were talking about the Queen, to protect whom is my mission.

THE CHIEF OF POLICE: You're going about it in a curious way. The Palace, according to what you say....

THE ENVOY: (*Smiling.*) For the time being, Her Majesty is in safety. But time is pressing. The prelate is said to have been beheaded. The Archbishop's Palace has been ransacked. The Law Court and Military Headquarters have been routed....

THE CHIEF OF POLICE: But what about the Queen?

THE ENVOY: (*In a very light tone.*) She's embroidering. For a moment she thought of nursing the wounded. But it was pointed out to her that, as the throne was threatened, she had to carry to an extreme the Royal prerogatives.

IRMA: Which are?

THE ENVOY: Absence. Her Majesty has retired to a chamber, in solitude. The disobedience of her people saddens her. She is embroidering a handkerchief. The design of it is as follows: the four corners will be adorned with poppy heads. In the middle of the handkerchief, embroidered in pale blue silk, will be a swan, resting on the water of a lake. That's the only point about which Her Majesty is troubled: will it be the water of a lake, a pond or a pool? Or simply of a tank or a cup? It is a grave problem. We have chosen it because it is insoluble, and the Queen can engross herself in an infinite meditation.

IRMA: Is the Queen amused?

THE ENVOY: Her Majesty is occupying herself in becoming entirely what she must be: the Queen. (*He looks at the corpse.*) She, too, is moving rapidly towards immobility.

IRMA: And she's embroidering.

THE ENVOY: No, Madame, I say the Queen is embroidering a handkerchief, for though it is my duty to describe her, it is also my duty to conceal her.

IRMA: Do you mean she's not embroidering?

THE ENVOY: I mean that the Queen is embroidering and that she is not embroidering. She picks her nose, examines the pickings and lies down again. Then, she dries the dishes.

IRMA: The Queen?

THE ENVOY: She is not nursing the wounded. She is embroidering an invisible handkerchief....

THE CHIEF OF POLICE: By God! What have you done with Her Majesty? I want a straight answer. I'm not amused....

THE ENVOY: She is in a chest. She is sleeping. Wrapped in the folds of Royalty, she is snoring....

THE CHIEF OF POLICE: (*Threateningly.*) Is the Queen dead?

THE ENVOY (*Unperturbed.*) She is snoring and she is not snoring. Her head, which is tiny, supports, without wavering, a crown of metal and stones.

THE CHIEF OF POLICE: (*More and more threateningly.*) Enough of that. You said the Palace was in danger.... What's to be done? I still have almost the entire police force behind me. Those who are still with me are ready to die for me.... They know who I am and what I'll do for them.... I, too, have my role to play. But if the Queen is dead, everything is jeopardized. *She's* my support, it's in her name that I'm working to make a name for myself. How far has the rebellion gone? I want a clear answer.

THE ENVOY: You can judge from the state of this house. And from your own.... All seems lost.

IRMA: You belong to the Court, your Excellency. Before coming here, I was with the troops. That's where I won my first spurs. I can assure you that I've known worse situations. The populace – from which I broke away with a kick of my heels – the populace is howling beneath my windows, which have been multiplied by the bombs: my house stands its ground. My rooms aren't intact, but they've held up. My whores, except for one lunatic, are on the job. If the centre of the Palace is a woman like me....

THE ENVOY: (*Imperturbably.*) The Queen is standing on one foot in the middle of an empty room, and she....

THE CHIEF OF POLICE: That'll do! I've had enough of your riddles. For me, the Queen has to be someone. And the situation has to be concrete. Describe it to me exactly. I've no time to waste.

THE ENVOY: Whom do you want to save?

THE CHIEF OF POLICE: The Queen!

CARMEN: The flag!

IRMA: My hide!

THE ENVOY: (*To* THE CHIEF OF POLICE.) If you're eager to save the Queen – and, beyond her, our flag, and all its gold fringe, and its eagle, cords and pole, would you describe them to me?

THE CHIEF OF POLICE: Until now I've served the things you mention, and served them with distinction, and without

bothering to know any more about them than what I saw. And I'll continue. What's happening about the rebellion?

THE ENVOY: (*Resignedly.*) The garden gates will, for a moment longer, hold back the crowd. The guards are devoted, like us, with an obscure devotion. They'll die for their sovereign. They'll give their blood. Unhappily there won't be enough of it to drown the rebellion. Sand bags have been piled up in front of the doors. In order to confuse even reason, Her Majesty removes herself from one secret chamber to another, from the servants' hall to the Throne Room, from the latrines to the chicken-coop, the chapel, the guardroom.... She makes herself unfindable and thus attains a threatened invisibility. So much for the inside of the Palace.

THE CHIEF OF POLICE: What about the Generalissimo?

THE ENVOY: Gone mad. He wanders among the crowd, where nobody will harm him, protected by his madness.

THE CHIEF OF POLICE: What about the Attorney-General?

THE ENVOY: Died of fright.

THE CHIEF OF POLICE: And the Bishop?

THE ENVOY: His case is more difficult. The Church is secretive. Nothing is known about him. Nothing definite. His decapitated head was said to have been seen on the handlebars of a bicycle. Of course, the rumour was false. We're therefore relying entirely on you. But your orders aren't getting through.

THE CHIEF OF POLICE: Down below, in the corridors and studios, I have enough loyal men to protect us all. They can remain in contact with my offices....

THE ENVOY: (*Interrupting him.*) Are your men in uniform?

THE CHIEF OF POLICE: Of course. They're my bodyguard. Do you imagine me with a bodyguard in sport jackets? They're in uniform. Black ones. With my emblem. They're brave. They, too, want to win.

THE ENVOY: To save what? (*A pause.*) Won't you answer? Would it perturb you to see things as they are? To gaze at the world tranquilly and accept responsibility for your gaze, whatever it might see?

THE CHIEF OF POLICE: But, after all, in coming to see me, you did have something definite in mind, didn't you? You had a plan? Let's hear it.

Suddenly a terrific blast. Both men, but not IRMA, *fall flat on the floor, then stand up again and dust each other off.*

THE ENVOY: That may have been the Royal Palace. Long live the Royal Palace!

IRMA: But then, just before ... the explosion?

THE ENVOY: A royal palace is forever blowing up. In fact, that's exactly what it is: a continuous explosion.

Enter CARMEN. *She throws a black sheet over the corpse of* ARTHUR *and tidies things up a bit.*

THE CHIEF OF POLICE: (*Aghast.*) But the Queen.... Then the Queen's under the rubble?

THE ENVOY: (*Smiling mysteriously.*) You need not worry. Her

Majesty is in a safe place. And that phoenix, when dead, can rise up from the ashes of a royal palace. I can understand your impatience to prove your valour, your devotion … but the Queen will wait for you as long as necessary. (*To* IRMA.) I must pay tribute, Madame, to your coolness. And to your courage. They are worthy of the highest respect.… (*Musingly.*) of the highest.…

IRMA: You're forgetting to whom you're speaking. I may run a brothel, but I wasn't born of the marriage of the moon and a crocodile, I've lived among the people.… All the same, it was quite a blast. And the people.…

THE ENVOY: (*Severely.*) That's behind you. When life departs, the hands cling to a sheet. What significance has that rag when you're about to penetrate into the providential fixity?

IRMA: Sir? Do you mean I'm at my last gasp?

THE ENVOY: (*Examining her, part by part.*) Splendid head! Sturdy thighs! Solid shoulders.

IRMA: (*Laughing.*) So I've been told, and it didn't make me lose my head. In short, I'll make a presentable corpse if the rebels act fast and if they leave me intact. But if the Queen is dead.…

THE ENVOY: (*Bowing.*) Long live the Queen, Madame.

IRMA: (*First taken aback, then irritated.*) I don't like to be kidded! Pack up your nonsense, and clear out.

THE ENVOY: (*Spiritedly.*) I've described the situation. The populace, in its joy and fury, is at the brink of ecstasy. It's for us to press it forward.

IRMA: Instead of standing here and talking drivel, go poke around for the Queen in the rubble of the Palace and pull her out. Even if slightly roasted.…

THE ENVOY: (*Severely.*) No. A queen who's been cooked and mashed up isn't presentable. And even when alive she was less beautiful than you.

IRMA: Her lineage was more ancient … she was older.… And, after all, maybe she was just as frightened as I.

THE CHIEF OF POLICE: It is in order to approach her, to be worthy of her, that one makes such a mighty effort. But what if one is Herself?

CARMEN stops in order to listen.

IRMA: I don't know how to talk. I'm always hemming and hawing.

THE ENVOY: All must unfold in a silence that etiquette allows no one to break.

THE CHIEF OF POLICE: I'm going to have the rubble of the Palace cleared away. If, as you said, the Queen was in a chest, it may be possible to save her.

THE ENVOY: (*Shrugging his shoulders.*) It was made of rosewood! And it was so old, so worn.… (*To* IRMA, *running his hand over the back of her neck.*) Yes, it requires solid vertebrae … they've got to carry several pounds …

THE CHIEF OF POLICE: … and resist the axe, don't they? Irma, don't listen to him! (*To* THE ENVOY.) And what about me?

I'm the strong-man of this country, but it's because I've based my power on the crown. I bamboozle the great majority, but it's because I had the smart idea of serving the Queen … even if at times I've seemed to do some shabby things … seemed to, d'you hear? … It's not Irma.…

IRMA: (*To* THE ENVOY.) I'm really very weak, your Excellency, and very frail. Though a while ago I was boasting.…

THE ENVOY: (*With authority.*) Around this delicate and precious kernel we'll forge a shell of gold and iron. But you must make up your mind quickly.

THE CHIEF OF POLICE: (*Furiously.*) Above me! So Irma would be above *me!* All the trouble I've gone to in order to be master would be wasted effort. Whereas, nice and snug in her studio, all she'd have to do is nod her head.… If I'm in power, I'm willing to impose Irma.…

THE ENVOY: Impossible. It's from her that you must derive your authority. She must appear by divine right. Don't forget that you're not yet represented in her studios.

IRMA: Allow me just a little more respite.…

THE ENVOY: A few seconds, for time is pressing.

THE CHIEF OF POLICE: If only there were some way of knowing what the late sovereign would have thought of it. We can't decide just like that. To appropriate a heritage.…

THE ENVOY: (*Scornfully.*) You're knuckling under already. Do you tremble if there's no authority above you to decide? But it's for Mme Irma to declare.…

IRMA: (*In a highfalutin tone.*) In the records of our family, which goes a long way back, there was some question of.…

THE ENVOY: (*Severely.*) Nonsense, Mme Irma. In our vaults, genealogists are working day and night. History is submissive to them. I said we hadn't a minute to waste in conquering our people, but beware! Although the populace may worship you, its high-flown pride is capable of sacrificing you. It sees you as red, either crimson or blood-red. If it kills its idols and thrusts them into the sewers, it will sweep you up with them.…

The same explosion is heard again. THE ENVOY *smiles.*

THE CHIEF OF POLICE: It's an enormous risk.…

CARMEN: That's for Mme Irma to decide. (*To* IRMA.) The ornaments are ready.

IRMA: (*To* THE ENVOY.) Are you quite sure of what you're saying? Do you really know what's going on? What about your spies?

THE ENVOY: They inform us as accurately as the peep-holes that peer into your studios. (*Smiling.*) And I may add that we consult them with the same pleasurable thrill. But we must act fast. We're engaged in a race against the clock. It's we or they. Mme Irma, think speedily.

IRMA: (*Holding her head in her hands.*) I'm hurrying, sir. I'm approaching my destiny as fast as I can. (*To* CARMEN.) Go see what they're doing.

CARMEN: I've locked them up.

IRMA: Get them ready.

THE ENVOY: (*To* CARMEN.) What about you, what's to be done with you?

CARMEN: I'm here for eternity.

Exit CARMEN.

THE ENVOY: One other matter, a more delicate one. I mentioned an image that for some days now has been mounting in the sky of the revolution.

IRMA: The revolution has its sky too?

THE ENVOY: Don't envy it. Chantal's image is circulating in the streets. An image that resembles her and does not resemble her. She towers above the battles. At first, people were fighting against illustrious and illusory tyrants, then for freedom. Tomorrow they'll be ready to die for Chantal alone.

IRMA: The ungrateful wretch! She who was in such demand as Lucrezia Borgia.

THE CHIEF OF POLICE: She won't last. She's like me: she has neither father nor mother. And if she becomes an image, we'll make use of it. (*A pause.*) ... A mask....

THE ENVOY: Everything beautiful on earth you owe to masks.

Suddenly a bell rings. IRMA *is about to dart forward, but stops.*

IRMA: (*To* THE CHIEF OF POLICE.) It's Carmen. What's she saying? What are they doing?

THE CHIEF OF POLICE *lifts one of the earphones.*

THE CHIEF OF POLICE: (*Transmitting the message.*) While waiting *to* go home, they're standing around looking at themselves in the mirrors.

IRMA: Tell her to smash the mirrors or veil them.

A silence. Then a burst of machine-gun fire.

My mind's made up. I presume I've been summoned from all eternity and that God will bless me. I'm going to prepare myself by prayer.

THE ENVOY: (*Gravely.*) Do you have the outfits?

IRMA: My closets are as famous as my studios. (*Suddenly worried.*) But everything must be in an awful state! The bombs, the plaster, the dust. Tell Carmen to brush the costumes! (*To* THE CHIEF OF POLICE.) George ... this is our last minute together! From now on, we'll no longer be us....

THE ENVOY *discreetly moves off and goes to the window.*

THE CHIEF OF POLICE: (*Tenderly.*) But I love you.

THE ENVOY: (*Turning around, and in a tone of detachment.*) Think of that mountain north of the city. All the labourers were at work when the rebellion broke out.... (*A pause.*) I refer to a project for a tomb....

THE CHIEF OF POLICE: (*Greedily.*) What's the plan of it?

THE ENVOY: Later. A mountain of red marble hollowed out with rooms and niches, and in the middle a tiny diamond sentry-box.

THE CHIEF OF POLICE: Will I be able to stand there – or sit – and keep vigil over my entire death?

THE ENVOY: He who gets it will be there – dead – for eternity. The world will centre about it. About it will rotate the planets and the suns. From a secret point of the same room will run a road that will lead, after many and many a complication, to another room where mirrors will reflect to infinity ... I say infinity....

THE CHIEF OF POLICE: O.K.!

THE ENVOY: ... the image of a dead man.

IRMA: (*Hugging* THE CHIEF OF POLICE *to her.*) So I'll be real? My robe will be real? My lace, my jewels will be real? The rest of the world.... (*Machine-gun fire.*)

THE ENVOY: (*After a last glance through the shutters.*) Yes, but make haste. Go to your apartments. Embroider an interminable handkerchief.... (*To* THE CHIEF OF POLICE.) You, give your last orders to your last men. (*He goes to a mirror, takes from his pocket a whole collection of decorations and fastens them to his tunic.*) (*In a vulgar tone.*) And make it snappy. I don't have time to listen to your crap.

Scene Eight

The scene is the balcony itself, which projects beyond the façade of the brothel. The shutters, which face the audience, are closed. Suddenly, all the shutters open by themselves. The edge of the balcony is at the very edge of the footlights. Through the windows can be seen THE BISHOP, THE GENERAL *and* THE JUDGE, *who are getting ready. Finally, the French windows are flung wide open. The three men come out on the balcony. First* THE BISHOP, *then* THE GENERAL, *then* THE JUDGE. *They are followed by the Hero. Then comes* THE QUEEN: MME IRMA, *wearing a diadem on her brow and an ermine cloak. All the characters step forward and take their positions with great timidity. They are silent. They simply show themselves. All are of huge proportions, gigantic – except the Hero, that is,* THE CHIEF OF POLICE – *and are wearing their ceremonial garments, which are torn and dusty. Then, near them, but not on the balcony, appears* THE BEGGAR. *In a gentle voice, he cries out:*

THE BEGGAR: Long live the Queen! (*He goes off timidly, as he came.*) (*Finally, a strong wind stirs the curtains:* CHANTAL *appears.* THE QUEEN *bows to her. A shot.* CHANTAL *falls.* THE GENERAL *and* THE QUEEN *carry her away dead.*)

Scene Nine

IRMA'S *room, which looks as if it had been hit by a hurricane. Rear, a large two-panelled mirror which forms the wall. Right, a door; left, another. Three cameras on tripods. Next to each of them is a photographer, three very wide-awake young men with ironic expressions. Each is wearing a black leather jacket and close-fitting blue jeans. Enter, in turn, very timidly, right,* THE BISHOP *and, left,* THE JUDGE *and* THE GENERAL. *On seeing each other, they bow deeply. Then,* THE GENERAL *salutes and* THE BISHOP *blesses* THE GENERAL.

THE JUDGE: (*With a sigh of relief.*) What we've been through!

THE GENERAL: And it's not over! We have to invent an entire life.... That's hard....

THE BISHOP: Hard or not, we've got to go through with it. We can no longer back out. Before entering the carriage....

THE GENERAL: The slowness of the carriage!

THE BISHOP: ... entering the carriage, it was still possible to chuck the whole business. But now....

THE JUDGE: Do you think we were recognized? I was in the middle, hidden by your profiles. Opposite me, Irma .... (*The name astonishes him.*) Irma? The Queen.... The Queen hid my face.... Do you think we were?

THE BISHOP: No danger of that. You know whom I saw ... at the right (*unable to keep from laughing*) with his fat, good-natured mug and pink cheeks, though the town was in smithereens? (*The other two smile.*) With his dimples and decayed teeth? And who threw himself on my hand ... I thought to bite me, and I was about to pull away my fingers ... to kiss my ring? Who? My fruit-and-vegetable man. (THE JUDGE *laughs.*)

THE GENERAL: (*Grimly.*) The slowness of the carriage. The carriage wheels on the people's feet and hands! The dust!

THE JUDGE: (*Uneasily.*) I was opposite the Queen. Through the back window, a woman....

THE BISHOP: (*Continuing his account.*) I saw her too, at the left-hand door, she was running along and throwing kisses at us!

THE GENERAL: (*More and more grimly.*) The slowness of the carriage! We moved forward so slowly amidst the sweaty mob! Their roars were like threats, but they were only cheering. Someone could have hamstrung the horses, fired a shot, could have unhitched the traces and harnessed *us*, attached us to the shaft or the horses, could have drawn and quartered us or turned us into draught-horses. But no. Just flowers tossed from a window, and a people hailing its queen, who stood upright beneath her golden crown. (*A pause.*) And the horses going at a walking pace ... and the Envoy standing on the footboard!

A silence.

THE BISHOP: (*Ironically.*) No one could have recognized us. We were in the gold and glitter. They were blinded. It hit them in the eye....

THE JUDGE: It wouldn't have taken much....

THE BISHOP: (*Same.*) Exhausted by the fighting, choked by the dust, the people stood waiting for the procession. The procession was all they saw. In any case, we can no longer back out. We've been chosen.

THE GENERAL: By whom?

THE BISHOP: (*With sudden grandiloquence.*) By glory in person.

THE GENERAL: This masquerade?

THE BISHOP: It lies with us for this masquerade to change meaning. First, we must use words that magnify. We must act fast, and with precision. No errors allowed. (*With*

authority.*) As for me, instead of being merely the symbolic head of the country's church, I've decided to become its actual head. Instead of blessing and blessing and blessing until I've had my fill, I'm going to sign decrees and appoint priests. The clergy is being organized. A basilica is under construction. It's all in there. (*He points to a folder under his arm.*) Full of plans and projects. (*To* THE JUDGE.) What about you?

THE JUDGE: (*Looking at his wristwatch.*) I have an appointment with a number of magistrates. We're drafting bills, we're revising the legal code. (*To* THE GENERAL.) What about you?

THE GENERAL: Oh, me, your ideas drift through my poor head like smoke through a log shanty. The art of war's not something you can master just like that. The general-staffs....

THE BISHOP: (*Interrupting.*) Like everything else, the fate of arms can be read in your stars. Read your stars, damn it!

THE GENERAL: That's easy to say. But when the Hero comes back, planted firmly on his rump, as if on a horse.... For, of course, nothing's happened yet?

THE BISHOP: Nothing. But let's not crow too soon. Though his image hasn't yet been consecrated by the brothel, it still may. If so, we're done for. Unless you make a positive effort to seize power.

Suddenly, he breaks off. One of the photographers has cleared his throat, as if to spit. Another has snapped his fingers like a Spanish dancer.

THE BISHOP: (*Severely.*) Indeed, you're here. Please do your job quickly, and in silence, if possible. You're to take each of our profiles, one smiling, the other rather stern.

FIRST PHOTOGRAPHER: We'll do our job, don't worry. (*To* THE BISHOP.) Get set for prayer, because the world ought to be bombarded with the picture of a pious man.

THE BISHOP: (*Without moving.*) In fervent meditation.

FIRST PHOTOGRAPHER: Right, fervent. Get set.

THE BISHOP: (*Ill at ease.*) But ... how?

FIRST PHOTOGRAPHER: Don't you know how to compose yourself for prayer? Okay, facing both God and the camera. Hands together. Head up. Eyes down. That's the classical pose. A return to order, a return to classicism.

THE BISHOP: (*Kneeling.*) Like this?

FIRST PHOTOGRAPHER: (*Looking at him with curiosity.*) That's it.... (*He looks at the camera.*) No, you're not in the frame.... (*Shuffling on his knees,* THE BISHOP *places himself in front of the camera.*) Okay.

SECOND PHOTOGRAPHER: (*To* THE JUDGE.) Would you mind pulling a longer face? You don't quite look like a judge. A little longer.

THE JUDGE: Horselike? Sullen?

SECOND PHOTOGRAPHER: Horselike and sullen, my Lord. And both hands in front, on your brief. What I want is a shot of *the* Judge. A good photographer is one who gives a definitive image. Perfect.

FIRST PHOTOGRAPHER: (*To* THE BISHOP.) Turn your head … just a little…. (*He turns* THE BISHOP's *head.*)

THE BISHOP: (*Angrily.*) You're unscrewing the neck of a prelate!

FIRST PHOTOGRAPHER: I want a three-quarter view of you praying, my Lord.

SECOND PHOTOGRAPHER: (*To* THE JUDGE.) My Lord, if you possibly can, a little more severity … with a pendulous lip. (*Crying out.*) That's it! Perfect! Stay that way!

He rushes behind his camera, but there is a flash before he gets there. THE FIRST PHOTOGRAPHER *has just taken his shot.* THE SECOND PHOTOGRAPHER *puts his head under the black hood of his camera.*

THE GENERAL: (*To* THE THIRD PHOTOGRAPHER.) The finest pose is Poniatovsky's.

THIRD PHOTOGRAPHER: (*Striking a pose.*) With the sword?

THE GENERAL: No, no. That's Lafayette. No, with the arm extended and the marshal's baton….

THIRD PHOTOGRAPHER: Ah, you mean Wellington?

THE GENERAL: Unfortunately, I don't have a baton….

Meanwhile, THE FIRST PHOTOGRAPHER *has gone back to* THE BISHOP, *who has not moved, and looks him over silently.*

THIRD PHOTOGRAPHER: (*To* THE GENERAL.) We've got just what we need. Here, now strike the pose.

Rolls up a sheet of paper in the form of a marshal's baton. He hands it to THE GENERAL, *who strikes a pose, and then dashes to his camera. A flash:* THE SECOND PHOTOGRAPHER *has just taken his shot.*

THE BISHOP: (*To* THE FIRST PHOTOGRAPHER.) I hope the negative comes out well. Now we'll have to flood the world with a picture of me receiving the Eucharist. Unfortunately, we don't have a Host on hand….

FIRST PHOTOGRAPHER: Leave it to us, Monsignor. Newspapermen are a resourceful bunch. (*Calls out.*) My Lord!

THE JUDGE *approaches.*

I'm going to try a stunt. Lend me a hand a minute. (*Without further ado, he takes him by the hand and sets him in place.*) But I want only your hand to show … there … roll up your sleeve a little … above Monsignor's tongue. More. Okay. (*Still fumbling in his pocket. To* THE BISHOP.) Stick out your tongue. More. Okay. (*Still fumbling in his pocket. A flash:* THE GENERAL *has just been photographed; he resumes his natural pose.*) Damn it! I don't have a thing! (*He looks about. To* THE GENERAL.) That's perfect. May I? (*Without waiting for an answer, he takes* THE GENERAL's *monocle from his eye and goes back to the group formed by* THE BISHOP *and* THE JUDGE. *He makes* THE JUDGE *hold the monocle above* THE BISHOP's *tongue as if it were a Host, and he rushes to his camera. A flash.*)

THE QUEEN, *who has entered with* THE ENVOY, *has been watching these proceedings for some moments.*

THE ENVOY: It's a true image, born of a false spectacle.

FIRST PHOTOGRAPHER: (*Cynically.*) That's common practice, your Majesty. When some rebels were captured, we paid a militiaman to bump off a chap I'd just sent to buy me a packet of cigarettes. The photo shows a rebel shot down while trying to escape.

THE QUEEN: Monstrous!

THE ENVOY: But have things ever happened otherwise? History was lived so that a glorious page might be written, and then read. It's reading that counts. (*To* THE PHOTOGRAPHERS.) Gentlemen, the Queen informs me that she congratulates you. She asks that you return to your posts.

The THREE PHOTOGRAPHERS *put their heads under the black hoods of their cameras.*

A silence.

THE QUEEN: (*In a low voice, as if to herself.*) Isn't he here?

THE ENVOY: (*To the Three Figures.*) The Queen would like to know what you're doing, what you plan to do.

THE BISHOP: We've been recovering as many dead bodies as possible. We were planning to embalm them and lodge them in our heaven. Your grandeur requires your having slaughtered the rebels wholesale. We shall keep for ourselves only a few of our fallen martyrs, to whom we shall pay honour that will honour us.

THE QUEEN: (*To* THE ENVOY.) That will serve my glory, will it not?

THE ENVOY: (*Smiling.*) The massacres, too, are revels wherein the people indulge to their heart's content in the pleasure of hating us. I am speaking, to be sure, of 'our' people. They can at last set up a statue to us in their hearts so as to shower it with blows. At least, I hope so.

THE QUEEN: Does that mean that leniency and kindness are of no avail?

THE ENVOY: (*Smiling.*) A St Vincent de Paul Studio?

THE QUEEN: (*Testily to* THE JUDGE.) You, my Lord, what's being done? I'd ordered fewer death penalties and more sentences to forced labour. I hope the underground galleries are finished? (*To* THE ENVOY.) It's the word galley-slaves that made me think of the galleries of the Mausoleum. Are they finished?

THE JUDGE: Completely. And open to the public on Sundays. Some of the arches are completely adorned with the skeletons of prisoners who died during the digging.

THE QUEEN: (*In the direction of* THE BISHOP.) Very good. What about the Church? I suppose that anyone who hasn't done at least a week's work on this extraordinary chapel is in a state of mortal sin? (THE BISHOP *bows. To* THE GENERAL.) As for you, I'm aware of your severity. Your soldiers are watching over the workers, and they thoroughly deserve the fine name of builders. (*Smiling gently, with feigned fatigue.*) For, as you know, gentlemen, I plan to present this tomb to the Hero. You know how downcast he feels, don't you, and how he suffers at not yet having been impersonated?

THE GENERAL: (*Plucking up courage.*) He'll have a hard time attaining glory. The places have been filled for ages. Every niche has its statue. (*Fatuously.*) We, at least....

THE JUDGE: That's how it always is when one wants to start from the bottom. And particularly by rejecting or neglecting the traditional. The established order of things, as it were.

THE QUEEN: (*Suddenly vibrant.*) Yet it was he who saved everything. He wants glory. He insists on breaking open the gates of legend, but he has allowed you to carry on with your ceremonies.

THE BISHOP: (*Arrogantly.*) To be frank, Madame, we're no longer concerned with that. As for me, my skirt hampers me, and my hands get caught in the lace. We're going to have to act.

THE QUEEN: (*Indignantly.*) Act? You? You mean to say you're going to strip us of our power?

THE JUDGE: We have to fulfil our functions, don't we?

THE QUEEN: Functions! You're planning to overthrow him, to lower him, to take his place!

THE BISHOP: Somewhere in time – in time or in space! – perhaps there exist high dignitaries invested with absolute dignity and attired with veritable ornaments....

THE QUEEN: (*Very angrily.*) Veritable! And what about those? You mean that those you're wrapped and swathed in – my whole paraphernalia! – which come from my closets, aren't veritable?

THE BISHOP: (*Pointing to* THE JUDGE's *ermine, the silk of his robe, etc.*) Rabbit, sateen, machine-made lace ... you think we're going to be satisfied with make-believe to the end of our days?

THE QUEEN: (*Outraged.*) But this morning... .

She breaks off. Enter THE CHIEF OF POLICE, *quietly, humbly.*

George, beware of them.

THE CHIEF OF POLICE: (*Trying to smile.*) I think that ... victory ... we've won the day. May I sit down?

He sits down. Then he looks about, as if questioning everyone.

THE ENVOY: (*Ironically.*) No, nobody's come yet. Nobody has yet felt the need to abolish himself in your fascinating image.

THE CHIEF OF POLICE: That means the projects you submitted to me aren't very effective. (*To* THE QUEEN.) Nothing? Nobody?

THE QUEEN: (*Very gently.*) Nobody. And yet, the blinds have been drawn again. The men ought to be coming in. Besides, the apparatus has been set up; so we'll be informed by a full peal of bells.

THE ENVOY: (*To* THE CHIEF OF POLICE.) You didn't care for the project I submitted to you this morning. Yet that's the image that haunts you and that ought to haunt others.

THE CHIEF OF POLICE: Ineffectual.

THE ENVOY: (*Showing a photographic negative.*) The execu-

tioner's red coat and his axe. I suggested amaranth red and the steel axe.

THE QUEEN: (*Testily.*) Studio 14, known as the Studio of Executions. Already been done.

THE JUDGE: (*Making himself agreeable, to* THE CHIEF OF POLICE.) Yet you're feared.

THE CHIEF OF POLICE: I'm afraid that they fear and envy a man, but ... (*groping for words*) ... but not a wrinkle, for example, or a curl ... or a cigar ... or a whip. The latest image that was proposed to me.... I hardly dare mention it to you.

THE JUDGE: Was it ... very audacious?

THE CHIEF OF POLICE: Very. Too audacious. I'd never dare tell you what it was. (*Suddenly, he seems to make up his mind.*) Gentlemen, I have sufficient confidence in your judgment and devotion. After all, I want to carry on the fight by boldness of ideas as well. It was this: I've been advised to appear in the form of a gigantic phallus, a prick of great stature....

The Three Figures and THE QUEEN *are dumbfounded.*

THE QUEEN: George! You?

THE CHIEF OF POLICE: What do you expect? If I'm to symbolize the nation, your joint....

THE ENVOY: (*To* THE QUEEN.) Allow him, Madame. It's the tone of the age.

THE JUDGE: A phallus? Of great stature? You mean – enormous?

THE CHIEF OF POLICE: Of my stature.

THE JUDGE: But that'll be very difficult to bring off.

THE ENVOY: Not so very. What with new techniques and our rubber industry, remarkable things can be worked out. No I'm not worried about that, but rather ... (*turning to* THE BISHOP) ... what the Church will think of it?

THE BISHOP: (*After reflection, shrugging his shoulders.*) No definite pronouncement can be made this evening. To be sure, the idea is a bold one. (*To* THE CHIEF OF POLICE.) But if your case is desperate, we shall have to examine the matter. For ... it would be a formidable figure-head, and if you were to transmit yourself in that guise to posterity....

THE CHIEF OF POLICE: (*Gently.*) Would you like to see the model?

THE JUDGE: (*To* THE CHIEF OF POLICE.) It's wrong of you to be impatient. *We* waited two thousand years to perfect our roles. Keep hoping....

THE GENERAL: (*Interrupting him.*) Glory is achieved in combat. You haven't enough illustrious Waterloos to your credit. Keep fighting, or sit down and wait out the regulation two thousand years.

Everyone laughs.

THE QUEEN: (*Violently.*) You don't care a damn about his suffering. And it was I who singled you out! I who fished you out of the rooms of my brothel and hired you for his glory. And you agreed to serve him.

A pause.

THE BISHOP: (*Firmly.*) It is at this point that a question, and a very serious one, arises: are you going to use what we represent, or are we (*he points to the other two Figures*) going to use you to serve what we represent?

THE QUEEN: (*Flaring up.*) Your conditions, you? Puppets who without their rabbit, as you put it, would be nothing, you, a man who was made to dance naked – in other words, skinned! – on the public squares of Seville and Toledo! and who danced! To the click of castanets! Your conditions, my Lord?

THE BISHOP: That day I *had* to dance. As for the rabbit, it's what it *must* be – the sacred image of ermine – it has the same power.

THE CHIEF OF POLICE: For the time being, but….

THE BISHOP: (*Getting excited.*) Exactly. So long as we were in a room in a brothel, we belonged to our own fantasies. But once having exposed them, having named them, having proclaimed them, we're now tied up with human beings, tied to you, and forced to go on with this adventure according to the laws of visibility.

THE CHIEF OF POLICE: You have no power. I alone….

THE BISHOP: Then we shall go back to our rooms and there continue the quest of an absolute dignity. We ought never to have left them. For we were content there, and it was you who came and dragged us away. For ours was a happy state. And absolutely safe. In peace, in comfort, behind shutters, behind padded curtains, protected by a police force that protects brothels, we were able to be a general, judge and bishop to the point of perfection and to the point of rapture! You tore us brutally from that delicious, untroubled state.

THE GENERAL: (*Interrupting* THE BISHOP.) My breeches! What joy when I pulled on my breeches! I now sleep in my general's breeches. I eat in my breeches, I waltz – *when* I waltz – in my breeches, I live in my general's breeches. I'm a general the way one is a priest.

THE JUDGE: I'm just a dignity represented by a skirt.

THE GENERAL: (*To* THE BISHOP.) At no moment can I prepare myself – I used to start a month in advance! – prepare myself for pulling on my general's boots and breeches. I'm rigged in them for all eternity. By Jove, I no longer dream.

THE BISHOP: (*To* THE CHIEF OF POLICE.) You see, he no longer dreams. Our ornamental purity, our luxurious and barren – and sublime – appearance has been eaten away. It's gone forever. Well and good. But the taste of that bitter delight of responsibility of which I've spoken has remained with us, and we find it to our liking. Our rooms are no longer secret. You hurt us by dragging us into the light. But as for dancing? You spoke of dancing? You referred to that notorious afternoon when, stripped – or skinned, whichever word amuses you – stripped of our priestly ornaments, we had to dance naked on the cathedral square. I danced, I admit it, with people laughing at me, but at least I danced. Whereas now, if ever I have an itch for that kind of thing, I'll have to go on the sly to the Balcony, where there probably is a room prepared for prelates who like to be ballerinas a few hours a week. No, no…. We're going to live in the light, but with all that that implies. We – magistrate, soldier, prelate – we're going to act in such a way as to impoverish our ornaments unceasingly! We're going to render them useful! But in order that they be of use, and of use to us – since it's your order that we've chosen to defend – you must be the first to recognize them and pay homage to them.

THE CHIEF OF POLICE: (*Calmly.*) I shall be not the hundred-thousandth-reflection-within-a-reflection in a mirror, but the One and Only, into whom a hundred thousand want to merge. If not for me, you'd have all been done for. The expression 'beaten hollow' would have had meaning. (*He is going to regain his authority increasingly.*)

THE QUEEN: (*To* THE BISHOP, *insinuatingly.*) You happen to be wearing that robe this evening simply because you were unable to clear out of the studios in time. You just couldn't tear yourself away from one of your hundred thousand reflections, but the clients are beginning to come back…. There's no rush yet, but Carmen has recorded several entries…. (*To* THE CHIEF OF POLICE.) Don't let them intimidate you. Before the revolt, there were lots of them…. (*To* THE BISHOP.) If you hadn't had the abominable idea of having Chantal assassinated….

THE BISHOP: (*Frightened.*) A stray bullet!

THE QUEEN: Stray or not, Chantal was assassinated on *my* balcony! When she came back here to see me, to visit her boss….

THE BISHOP: I had the presence of mind to make her one of our saints.

THE CHIEF OF POLICE: A traditional attitude. A churchman's reflex. But there's no need to congratulate yourself. The image of her on our flag has hardly any power. Or rather…. I've had reports from all quarters that owing to the possibility that she was playing a double game, Chantal has been condemned by those she was supposed to save….

THE QUEEN: (*Anxiously.*) But then the whole business is starting all over again?

From this point on THE QUEEN *and* THE CHIEF OF POLICE *will seem very agitated.* THE QUEEN *will go to a window and draw the curtains after trying to look out into the street.*

THE ENVOY: All of it.

THE GENERAL: Are we going to have to … to get into the carriage again? The slowness of the carriage!

THE BISHOP: If I had Chantal shot, and then canonized, if I had her image blazoned on our flag….

THE QUEEN: It's *my* image that ought to be there….

THE ENVOY: You're already on the postage stamps, on the banknotes, on the seals in the police-stations.

THE GENERAL: The slowness of the carriage …

THE QUEEN: Will I therefore never be who I am?

THE ENVOY: Never again.

THE QUEEN: Every event of my life – my blood that trickles if I scratch myself.…

THE ENVOY: Everything will be written for you with a capital letter.

THE QUEEN: But that's Death?

THE ENVOY: It is indeed.

THE CHIEF OF POLICE: (*With sudden authority.*) It means death for all of you. And that's why I'm sure of you. At least, as long as I've not been impersonated, because after that I'll just sit back and take it easy. (*Inspired.*) Besides, I'll know by a sudden weakness of my muscles that my image is escaping from me to go and haunt men's minds. When that happens my visible end will be near. For the time being, and if we have to act … (*To* THE BISHOP.) who will assume real responsibilities? You? (*He shrugs.*) Be logical: if you are what you are, judge, general, bishop, it's because you wanted to become that and wanted it known that you had become it. You therefore did what was necessary to achieve your purpose and to be a focus of attention. Is that right?

THE JUDGE: Pretty much.

THE CHIEF OF POLICE: Very well. That means you've never performed an act for its own sake, but always so that, when linked with other acts, it would make a bishop, a judge, a general.…

THE BISHOP: That's both true and false. For each act contained within itself its leaven of novelty.

THE JUDGE: We acquired greater dignity thereby.

THE CHIEF OF POLICE: No doubt, my Lord, but this dignity, which has become as inhuman as a crystal, makes you unfit for governing men. No, no, gentlemen, above you, more sublime than you, is the Queen. It's from her, for the time being, that you derive your power and your rights. Above her – that to which she refers – is our standard, on which I've blazoned the image of Chantal Victorious, our saint.

THE BISHOP: (*Aggressively.*) Above Her Majesty, whom we venerate, and above her flag, is God, Who speaks through my voice.

THE CHIEF OF POLICE: (*Irritably.*) And above God? (*A silence.*) Well, gentlemen, above God are you, without whom God would be nothing. And above you am I, without whom.…

THE JUDGE: What about the people? The photographers?

THE CHIEF OF POLICE: On their knees before the people who are on their knees before God. Therefore.…

They all burst out laughing.

That's why I want you to serve me. But a while ago you were holding forth quite volubly. I should therefore like to pay homage to your eloquence, your facility of elocution, the limpidity of your timbre, the potency of your organ. As for me, I'm a mere man of action who gets tangled up in words and ideas when they're not immediately applied. That's why I was wondering whether to send you back to your kennel. I won't do it. In any case, not right away, since you're already there.

THE GENERAL: Sir!

THE CHIEF OF POLICE: (*He pushes* THE GENERAL, *who topples over and remains sitting on the floor, flabbergasted.*) Lie down! Lie down, General!

THE JUDGE: My skirt can be tucked up.…

THE CHIEF OF POLICE: (*He pushes* THE JUDGE, *who topples over.*) Lie down! Since you want to be recognized as a judge, do you want to hold on to your dignity according to my idea of it? And according to the general meaning attached to your dignities? Very well. Must I therefore grant you increasing recognition along these lines? Yes or no?

No one answers.

Well, gentlemen, yes or no? (THE BISHOP *steps aside, prudently.*)

THE QUEEN: (*Very blandly.*) Excuse him, if he gets carried away. I'm quite aware of what you used to come here for: (*to* THE BISHOP) you, my Lord, to seek by quick, decisive ways a manifest saintliness. No, no, I'm not being ironic. The gold of my chasubles had little to do with it, I'm sure. It wasn't mere gross ambition that brought you behind my closed shutters. Love of God was hidden there. I realize that. You, my Lord, you were indeed guided by a concern for justice, since it was the image of a magistrate that you wished to see reflected a thousand times in my mirrors. And you, General, it was bravery and military glory and the heroic deed that haunted you. So let yourselves go, relax, without too many scruples.…

One after the other, the three men heave a deep sigh.

THE CHIEF OF POLICE: (*Continuing.*) That's a relief to you, isn't it? You never really wanted to get out of yourselves and communicate, if only by acts of meanness, with the world. I understand you. (*Amiably.*) My role, unfortunately, is in motion. In short, as you probably know, it's not in the nomenclature of the brothels.…

THE QUEEN: In the pink handbook.

THE CHIEF OF POLICE: Yes, in the pink handbook. (*To the Three Figures.*) Come now, gentlemen, don't you feel sorry for a poor fellow like me? (*He looks at them one after the other.*) Come, come, gentlemen, you're not hardhearted, are you? It's for you that these Studios and Illustrious Rites were perfected, by means of exquisite experimentation. They required long labour, infinite patience, and you want to go back to the light of day? (*Almost humble, and suddenly looking very very tired.*) Wait just a little while. For the time being, I'm still loaded with future acts, loaded with actions … but as soon as I feel I'm being multiplied ad infinitum, then … then, ceasing to be hard, I'll go and rot in people's minds. And you, get into your skirts again if you want to, and get back on the job. (*To THE BISHOP.*) You're silent. (*A long silence.*) That's right.... Let's be silent, and let's wait.... (*A long and heavy silence.*) Perhaps it's now ... (*In a low, humble voice.*) that my apotheosis is being prepared....

(*Everybody is visibly expectant. Then, CARMEN enters, as if furtively, by the left door. THE ENVOY is the first to see her. He silently indicates her presence to THE QUEEN. THE QUEEN motions to CARMEN to withdraw, but CARMEN nevertheless takes a step forward.*)

THE QUEEN: (*In an almost low voice.*) I gave orders that we were not to be disturbed. What do you want?

CARMEN goes to her.

CARMEN: I tried to ring, but the apparatus is out of order. I beg your pardon. I'd like to speak with you.
THE QUEEN: Well, what is it? Speak up!
CARMEN: (*Hesitantly.*) It's ... I don't know....
THE QUEEN: (*Resignedly.*) Well, when at Court do as the Court does. Let's speak in an undertone.

She conspicuously lends ear to CARMEN, who leans forward and murmurs a few words. THE QUEEN seems very upset.

THE QUEEN: Are you sure?
CARMEN: Quite, Madame.

THE QUEEN bolts from the room, followed by CARMEN. THE CHIEF OF POLICE starts to follow them, but THE ENVOY intervenes.

THE ENVOY: One does not follow Her Majesty.
THE CHIEF OF POLICE: What's going on? Where's she going?
THE ENVOY: (*Ironically.*) To embroider. The Queen is embroidering and she is not embroidering.... You know the refrain? The Queen attains her reality when she withdraws, absents herself, or dies.
THE CHIEF OF POLICE: What's happening outside? (*To THE JUDGE.*) Do you have any news?
THE JUDGE: What you call outside is as mysterious to us as we are to it.
THE BISHOP: I shall try to depict the grief of this people which thought it had liberated itself by rebelling. Alas – or rather, thank Heaven! – there will never be a movement powerful enough to destroy our imagery.
THE CHIEF OF POLICE: (*Almost tremblingly.*) So you think I have a chance?
THE BISHOP: You're in the best possible position. There's consternation everywhere, in all families, in all institutions. People have trembled so violently that your image is beginning to make them doubt themselves.
THE CHIEF OF POLICE: Am I their only hope?
THE BISHOP: Their only hope lies in utter collapse.
THE CHIEF OF POLICE: In short, I'm like a pool in which they behold themselves?

THE GENERAL: (*Delighted, with a burst of laughter.*) And if they lean over too far, they fall in and drown. Before long, you'll be full of drowned bodies! (*No one seems to share his merriment.*) Oh well ... they're not yet at the brink! (*Embarrassed.*) Let's wait.

A silence.

THE CHIEF OF POLICE: So you really think the people had a wild hope? And that in losing all hope they lose everything? And that in losing everything they'll come and lose themselves in me? ...
THE BISHOP: That may very well happen. But, believe me, not if we can help it.
THE CHIEF OF POLICE: When I am offered that final consecration....
THE ENVOY: (*Ironically.*): For you, but for you alone, for a second the Earth will stop rotating....

Suddenly the door at the left opens and THE QUEEN appears, beaming.

THE QUEEN: George!

She falls into the arms of THE CHIEF OF POLICE.

THE CHIEF OF POLICE: (*Incredulous.*) It's not true. (*THE QUEEN nods yes.*) But where? ... When?
THE QUEEN (*Deeply moved*): There! ... Now! The Studio....
THE CHIEF OF POLICE: You're pulling my leg. I didn't hear anything.

Suddenly a tremendous ringing, a kind of peal of bells.

So it's true? It's for me? (*He pushes THE QUEEN away. Solemnly, as the ringing stops.*) Gentlemen, I belong to the Nomenclature! (*To THE QUEEN.*) But are you really sure?

The ringing starts again, then stops.

THE QUEEN: It was I who received him and ushered him into the Mausoleum Studio. The one that's being built in your honour. I left Carmen behind to attend to the preparations and I ran to let you know. I'm trembling like a leaf....

The ringing starts again, then stops.

THE BISHOP: (*Gloomily.*) We're up the creek.
THE CHIEF OF POLICE: The apparatus is working. You can see....

He goes to the left, followed by THE QUEEN.

THE ENVOY: That is not the practice. It's filthy....
THE CHIEF OF POLICE: (*Shrugging his shoulders.*) Where's the mechanism? (*To THE QUEEN.*) Let's watch together.

She stands at the left, facing a small port-hole. After a brief hesitation, THE JUDGE, GENERAL and BISHOP place themselves at the right, at another port-hole symmetrical with the first. Then, the two panels of the double mirror forming the back of the stage silently draw apart, revealing the interior of the Special Studio. THE ENVOY, *with resignation, joins* THE CHIEF OF POLICE.

DESCRIPTION OF THE MAUSOLEUM STUDIO: *The stones of the wall, which is circular, are visible. At the rear, a stairway that descends. In the centre of this well there seems to be another, in which the steps of a stairway are visible. On the walls, four laurel wreaths, adorned with crêpe. When the panels separate,* ROGER *is at the middle of the stairway, which he is descending.* CARMEN *seems to be guiding him.* ROGER *is dressed like the chief of police, though, mounted on the same cothurni as the Three Figures, he looks taller. His shoulders have also been broadened. He descends the stairs to the rhythm of a drum.*

CARMEN: (*Approaching, and handing him a cigar.*) It's on the house.
ROGER: (*Putting the cigar into his mouth.*) Thanks.
CARMEN: (*Taking the cigar from him.*) That end's for the light. This one's for the mouth. (*She turns the cigar around.*) Is this your first cigar?
ROGER: Yes…. (*A pause.*) I'm not asking for your advice. You're here to serve me, I've paid….
CARMEN: I beg your pardon, sir.
ROGER: The slave?
CARMEN: He's being untied.
ROGER: He knows what it's about?
CARMEN: Completely. You're the first. You're inaugurating this Studio, but, you know, the scenarios are all reducible to a major theme….
ROGER: Which is…?
CARMEN: Death.
ROGER: (*Touching the walls.*) And so this is my tomb?
CARMEN: (*Correcting him.*) Mausoleum.
ROGER: How many slaves are working on it?
CARMEN: The entire people, sir. Half of the population during the day and the other half at night. As you have requested, the whole mountain will be burrowed and tunnelled. The interior will have the complexity of a termite nest or of the Basilica of Lourdes – we don't know yet. No one will be able to see anything from the outside. All they'll know is that the mountain is sacred, but, inside, the tombs are already being enshrined in tombs, the cenotaphs in cenotaphs, the coffins in coffins, the urns….
ROGER: What about here, where I am now?
CARMEN: (*With a gesture of disdain.*) An antechamber. An antechamber called the Valley of the Fallen. (*She mounts the underground stairway.*) In a little while, you'll go farther down.
ROGER: I'm not to hope to see the light of day again?
CARMEN: But … do you still want to?

A silence.

ROGER: It's really true that no one's ever been here before me?
CARMEN: In this … tomb, or in this … Studio?

A silence.

ROGER: Is everything really on right? My outfit? My toupee?

THE CHIEF OF POLICE *turns to* THE QUEEN.

THE CHIEF OF POLICE: He knew I wear a toupee?
THE BISHOP: (*Snickering, to* THE JUDGE, *and* THE GENERAL.) He's the only one who doesn't know that everyone knows it.
CARMEN: (*To* ROGER.) Everything was carefully planned long ago. It's all been worked out. The rest is up to you.
ROGER: (*Anxiously.*) You realize I'm feeling my way too. I've got to imagine what the Hero's like, and he's never shown himself much.
CARMEN: That's why we've taken you to the Mausoleum Studio. It's not possible to make many errors here, nor indulge your imagination.

A pause.

ROGER: Will I be alone?
CARMEN: Everything is padded. The doors are lined. So are the walls.
ROGER: (*Hesitantly.*) What about … the mausoleum?
CARMEN: (*Forcefully.*) Built into the rock. The proof is that there's water oozing from the walls. Deathly silent. As for light, the darkness is so thick that your eyes have developed astounding qualities. The cold? Yes, the coldness of death. It's been a gigantic job drilling through the mountain. Men are still groaning in order to hollow out a gigantic niche for you. Everything proves that you're loved and that you're a conqueror.
ROGER: Groaning? Could … could I hear the groaning?

CARMEN *turns toward a hole dug out at the foot of the wall, from which emerges the head of* THE BEGGAR, *the character seen in Scene Four. He is now* THE SLAVE.

CARMEN: Come here!

THE SLAVE *crawls in.*

ROGER: (*Looking* THE SLAVE *over.*) Is that it?
CARMEN: A fine specimen, isn't he? Skinny. With lice and sores. He dreams of dying for you. I'll leave you alone now.
ROGER: With him? No, no. (*A pause.*) Stay. Everything always takes place in the presence of a woman. It's in order for a woman's face to be a witness that, usually….

Suddenly, the sound of a hammer striking an anvil. Then a cock crows.

Is life so near?
CARMEN: (*In a normal voice, not acting.*) As I've told you, everything's padded, but some sounds always manage to filter through. Does it bother you? Life's starting up again little by little … as before….
ROGER: (*He seems anxious.*) Yes, as before….
CARMEN: (*Gently.*) You were….
ROGER: Yes. Everything's washed up…. And what's saddest of all is people's saying: 'The rebellion was wonderful!'

CARMEN: You mustn't think about it any more. And you must stop listening to the sounds from outside. Besides, it's raining. The whole mountain has been swept by a tornado. (*Stage voice.*) You are at home here. (*Pointing to* THE SLAVE.) Make him talk.

ROGER: (*Playing his role.*) For you can talk? And what else can you do?

THE SLAVE: (*Lying on his belly.*) First, bow; then, shrink into myself a little more (*He takes* ROGER'S *foot and places it on his own back.*) like this! ... and even....

ROGER: (*Impatiently.*) Yes ... and even?

THE SLAVE: Sink into the earth, if it's possible.

ROGER: (*Drawing on his cigar.*) Sink in, really? But there's no mud?

THE QUEEN: (*To the others.*) He's right. We should have provided mud. In a well-run house.... But it's opening day, and he's the first client to use the Studio....

THE SLAVE: (*To* ROGER.) I feel it all over my body, sir. It's all over me, except in my mouth, which is open so that I can sing your praises and utter the groans that made me famous.

ROGER: Famous? You're famous, you?

THE SLAVE: Famous for my chants, sir, which are hymns to your glory.

ROGER: So your glory accompanies mine? (*To* CARMEN.) Does he mean that my reputation will be kept going by his words? And ... if he says nothing, I'll cease to exist...?

CARMEN: (*Curtly.*) I'd like very much to satisfy you, but you ask questions that aren't in the scenario.

ROGER: (*To* THE SLAVE.) But what about you, who sings to you?

THE SLAVE: Nobody. I'm dying.

ROGER: But without me, without my sweat, without my tears and blood, what would you be?

THE SLAVE: Nothing.

ROGER: (*To* THE SLAVE.) You sing? But what else do you do?

THE SLAVE: We do all we possibly can to be more and more unworthy of you.

ROGER: What, for example?

THE SLAVE: We try hard just to stand and rot. And, believe me, it's not always easy. Life tries to prevail.... But we stand our ground. We keep shrinking more and more every....

ROGER: Day?

THE SLAVE: Week.

THE CHIEF OF POLICE: (*To the others.*) That's not much. With a little effort....

THE ENVOY: (*To* THE CHIEF OF POLICE.) Be still. Let them play out their roles.

ROGER: That's not much. With a little effort....

THE SLAVE: (*With exaltation.*) With joy, Your Excellency! You're so splendid! So splendid that I wonder whether you're aglow or whether you're all the darkness of all the nights?

ROGER: What does it matter, since I'm no longer to have any reality except in the reality of your phrases.

THE SLAVE: (*Crawling in the direction of the upper stairway.*) You have not mouth nor ears nor eyes, but all of you is a thundering mouth and at the same time a dazzling and watchful eye....

ROGER: *You* see it, but do the others know it? Does the night know it? Does death? Do the stones? What do the stones say?

THE SLAVE: (*Still dragging on his belly and beginning to crawl up the stairs.*) The stones say....

ROGER: Well, I'm listening.

THE SLAVE: (*He stops crawling, and faces the audience.*) The cement that holds us together to form your tomb....

THE CHIEF OF POLICE: (*Facing the audience and joyfully beating his breast.*) The stones venerate me!

THE SLAVE: (*Continuing.*) ... the cement is moulded of tears, spit and blood. The workers' eyes and hands that rested upon us have matted us with grief. We are yours, and only yours. (THE SLAVE *starts crawling up the stairs again.*)

ROGER: (*With rising exaltation.*) Everything proclaims me! Everything breathes me and everything worships me! My history was lived so that a glorious page might be written and then read. It's reading that counts. (*He suddenly notices that* THE SLAVE *has disappeared. To* CARMEN.) But ... where's he going? ... Where is he? ...

CARMEN: He's gone off to sing. He's going up into the light of day. He'll tell ... that he carried your footsteps ... and that....

ROGER: (*Anxiously.*) Yes, and that? What else will he tell?

CARMEN: The truth; that you're dead, or rather that you don't stop dying and that your image, like your name, reverberates to infinity.

ROGER: He knows that my image is everywhere?

CARMEN: Yes, everywhere, inscribed and engraved and imposed by fear.

ROGER: In the palms of stevedores? In the games of children? On the teeth of soldiers? In war?

CARMEN: Everywhere.

THE CHIEF OF POLICE: (*To the others.*) So I've made it?

THE QUEEN: (*Fondly.*) Are you happy?

THE CHIEF OF POLICE: You've done a good job. That puts the finishing touch to your house.

ROGER: (*To* CARMEN.) Is it in prisons? In the wrinkles of old people?

CARMEN: It is.

ROGER: In the curves of roads?

CARMEN: You mustn't ask the impossible.

Same sounds as earlier: the cock and the anvil.

It's time to go, sir. The session's over. Turn left, and when you reach the corridor....

The sound of the anvil again, a little louder.

You hear? You've got to go home.... What are you doing?

ROGER: Life is nearby ... and far away. Here all the women are beautiful. Their purpose is purely ornamental.... One can lose oneself in them....

CARMEN: (*Curtly.*) That's right. In ordinary language, we're called whores. But you've got to leave....

ROGER: And go where? Into life? To carry on, as they say, with my activities....

CARMEN: (*A little anxiously.*) I don't know what you're doing, and I haven't the right to inquire. But you've got to leave. Your time's up.

The sound of the anvil and other sounds indicate an activity: cracking of a whip, humming of a motor, etc.

ROGER: They give you the rush in this place! Why do you want me to go back where I came from?

CARMEN: You've nothing further to do....

ROGER: There? No. Nothing further. Nor here either. And outside, in what you call life, everything has crashed. No truth was possible.... Did you know Chantal?

CARMEN: (*Suddenly frightened.*) Get going! Clear out of here!

THE QUEEN: I won't allow him to create a rumpus in my studios! Who was it who sent me that individual? Whenever there are disturbances, the riff-raff always crop up. I hope that Carmen....

CARMEN: (*To* ROGER.) Get out! You've no right to ask questions either. You know that brothels are very strictly regulated and that we're protected by the police.

ROGER: No! Since I'm playing the Chief of Police and since you allow me to be here....

CARMEN: (*Pulling him away.*) You're crazy! You wouldn't be the first who thought he'd risen to power.... Come along!

ROGER: (*Disengaging himself.*) If the brothel exists and if I've a right to go there, then I've a right to lead the character I've chosen to the very limit of his destiny ... no, of mine ... of merging his destiny with mine....

CARMEN: Stop shouting, sir. All the studios are occupied. Come along....

CARMEN tries to make him leave. She opens a door, then another, then a third, unable to find the right one. ROGER takes out a knife and, with his back to the audience, makes the gesture of castrating himself.

THE QUEEN: On my rugs! On the new carpet! He's a lunatic!

CARMEN: (*Crying out.*) Doing that here! (*She yells.*) Madame! Mme Irma!

CARMEN finally manages to drag ROGER out.

THE QUEEN rushes from the room. All the characters – THE CHIEF OF POLICE, THE ENVOY, THE JUDGE, THE GENERAL, THE BISHOP – turn and leave the port-holes. THE CHIEF OF POLICE moves forward to the middle of the stage.

THE CHIEF OF POLICE: Well played. He thought he had me. (*He places his hand on his fly, very visibly feels his balls and, reassured, heaves a sigh.*) Mine are here. So which of us is washed up? He or I? Though my image be castrated in every brothel in the world, I remain intact. Intact,

gentlemen. (*A pause.*) That plumber didn't know how to handle his role, that was all. (*He calls out, joyfully.*) Irma! Irma! ... Where is she? It's not her job to dress wounds.

THE QUEEN: (*Entering.*) George! The vestibule ... the rugs are covered with blood ... the vestibule's full of clients.... We're wiping up as best we can.... Carmen doesn't know where to put them....

THE ENVOY: (*Bowing to* THE CHIEF OF POLICE.) Nice work.

THE CHIEF OF POLICE: An image of me will be perpetuated in secret. Mutilated? (*He shrugs his shoulders.*) Yet a low Mass will be said to my glory. Notify the kitchens! Have them send me enough grub for two thousand years.

THE QUEEN: What about me? George, I'm alive!

THE CHIEF OF POLICE: (*Without hearing her.*) So.... I'm.... Where? Here, or ... a thousand times there? (*He points to the tomb.*) Now I can be kind ... and pious ... and just.... Did you see? Did you see me? There, just before, larger than large, stronger than strong, deader than dead? So I've nothing more to do with you.

THE QUEEN: George! But I still love you!

THE CHIEF OF POLICE: (*Moving towards the tomb.*) I've won the right to go and sit and wait for two thousand years. (*To* THE PHOTOGRAPHERS.) You! Watch me live, and die. For posterity: shoot! (*Three almost simultaneous flashes.*) I've won! (*He walks backwards into the tomb, very slowly, while* THE THREE PHOTOGRAPHERS *casually leave by the left wing, with their cameras slung over their backs. They wave before disappearing.*)

THE QUEEN: But it was I who did everything, who organized everything.... Stay.... What will....

Suddenly a burst of machine-gun fire.

You hear!

THE CHIEF OF POLICE: (*With a burst of laughter.*) Think of me!

THE JUDGE and THE GENERAL rush forward to stop him, but the doors start closing as THE CHIEF OF POLICE *descends the first steps. A second burst of machine-gun fire.*

THE JUDGE: (*Clinging to the door.*) Don't leave us alone!

THE GENERAL: (*Gloomily.*) That carriage again!

THE ENVOY: (*To* THE JUDGE.) Be careful, you'll get your fingers caught.

The door has definitely closed. The characters remain bewildered for a moment. A third burst of machine-gun fire.

THE QUEEN: Gentlemen, you are free.

THE BISHOP: But ... in the middle of the night?

THE QUEEN: (*Interrupting him.*) You'll leave by the narrow door that leads into the alley. There's a car waiting for you.

She nods courteously. The Three Figures exeunt right. A fourth burst of machine-gun fire.

Who is it? ... Our side? ... Or rebels? ... Or? ...

THE ENVOY: Someone dreaming, Madame....

THE QUEEN *goes to various parts of the room and presses buttons. Each time, a light goes out.*

THE QUEEN: (*Continuing to extinguish lights.*) … Irma…. Call me Mme Irma and go home. Good night, sir.

THE ENVOY: Good night, Mme Irma. (THE ENVOY *exits.*)

IRMA: (*Alone, and continuing to extinguish lights.*) It took so much light … two pounds' worth of electricity a day! Thirty-eight studios! Every one of them gilded, and all of them rigged with machinery so as to be able to fit into and combine with each other…. And all these performances so that I can remain alone, mistress and assistant mistress of this house and of myself. (*She pushes in a button, then pushes it out again.*) Oh no, that's the tomb. He needs light, for two thousand years! … and food for two thousand years…. (*She shrugs her shoulders.*) Oh well, everything's in working order, and dishes have been prepared. Glory means descending into the grave with tons of victuals! … (*She calls out, facing the wings.*) Carmen? Carmen? … Bolt the doors, my dear, and put the furniture-covers on…. (*She continues extinguishing.*) In a little while, I'll have to start all over again … put all the lights on again … dress up…. (*A cock crows.*) Dress up … ah, the disguises! Distribute roles again … assume my own…. (*She stops in the middle of the stage, facing the audience.*) … Prepare yours … judges, generals, bishops, chamberlains, rebels who allow the revolt to congeal, I'm going to prepare my costumes and studios for tomorrow…. You must now go home, where everything – you can be quite sure – will be falser than here…. You must go now. You'll leave by the right, through the alley…. (*She extinguishes the last light.*) It's morning already.

A burst of machine-gun fire.

Note

Genet's first version of *The Balcony* (*Le Balcon*) appeared in 1956. This translation is based on the dramatist's third version of the play, which Genet completed in 1962.

4.4 THE DUMB WAITER (1960)

HAROLD PINTER

Harold Pinter (1930–2008) *was a British playwright, actor and director whose work was originally produced by the English Stage Company at the 'playwright's theatre', the Royal Court, London. He came from a working class, East End of London, Jewish family and originally trained as an actor at both RADA and at Central School of Speech and Drama. A conscientious objector, his career was shaped more and more by his politics and activism and he was awarded the Nobel Prize in Literature in 2005. Pinter's early work was often located in domestic interiors and focused on the dysfunctional operations of families* (The Homecoming *[1964]), or on the ways that violence underpins all human interaction* (The Dumb Waiter *[1957] and* The Caretaker *[1960]). During the 1960s and 1970s, much of Pinter's work was directed by Peter Hall at the RSC (Royal Shakespeare Company), and at the National Theatre. He is known for his film scripts and adaptations such as* The Servant *(1963) and* The French Lieutenant's Woman *(1981). Pinter also directed numerous theatre productions of his own plays and of others such as Simon Gray and Noël Coward during his professional life.*

Scene: A basement room. Two beds, flat against the back wall. A serving hatch, closed, between the beds. A door to the kitchen and lavatory, left. A door to a passage, right.

BEN *is lying on a bed, left, reading a paper.* GUS *is sitting on a bed, right, tying his shoelaces, with difficulty. Both are dressed in shirts, trousers and braces.*

Silence.

GUS *ties his laces, rises, yawns and begins to walk slowly to the door, left. He stops, looks down, and shakes his foot.*

BEN *lowers his paper and watches him.* GUS *kneels and unties his shoe-lace and slowly takes off the shoe. He looks inside it and brings out a flattened matchbox. He shakes it and examines it. Their eyes meet.* BEN *rattles his paper and reads.* GUS *puts the matchbox in his pocket and bends down to put on his shoe. He ties his lace, with difficulty.* BEN *lowers his paper and watches him.* GUS *walks to the door, left, stops, and shakes the other foot. He kneels, unties his shoe-lace, and slowly takes off the shoe. He looks inside it and brings out a flattened cigarette packet. He shakes it and examines it. Their eyes meet.* BEN *rattles his paper and reads.* GUS *puts the packet in his pocket, bends down, puts on his shoe and ties the lace.*

He wanders off, left.

BEN *slams the paper down on the bed and glares after him. He picks up the paper and lies on his back, reading.*

Silence.

A lavatory chain is pulled twice off, left, but the lavatory does not flush.

Silence.

GUS *re-enters, left, and halts at the door, scratching his head.*

BEN *slams down the paper.*

BEN: Kaw!

He picks up the paper.

What about this? Listen to this!

He refers to the paper.

A man of eighty-seven wanted to cross the road. But there was a lot of traffic, see? He couldn't see how he was going to squeeze through. So he crawled under a lorry.

GUS: He what?

BEN: He crawled under a lorry. A stationary lorry.

GUS: No?

BEN: The lorry started and ran over him.

GUS: Go on!

BEN: That's what it says here.

GUS: Get away.

BEN: It's enough to make you want to puke, isn't it?

GUS: Who advised him to do a thing like that?

BEN: A man of eighty-seven crawling under a lorry!

GUS: It's unbelievable.

BEN: It's down here in black and white.

GUS: Incredible.

Silence.

GUS *shakes his head and exits.* BEN *lies back and reads.*

The lavatory chain is pulled once off left, but the lavatory does not flush.

BEN *whistles at an item in the paper.*

GUS *re-enters.*

I want to ask you something.

BEN: What are you doing out there?

GUS: Well, I was just —

BEN: What about the tea?

GUS: I'm just going to make it.

BEN: Well, go on, make it.

GUS: Yes, I will. (*He sits in a chair. Ruminatively.*) He's laid on some very nice crockery this time, I'll say that. It's sort of striped. There's a white stripe.

BEN *reads.*

It's very nice. I'll say that.

BEN *turns the page.*

You know, sort of round the cup. Round the rim. All the rest of it's black, you see. Then the saucer's black, except for right in the middle, where the cup goes, where it's white.

BEN *reads.*

Then the plates are the same, you see. Only they've got a black stripe — the plates — right across the middle. Yes, I'm quite taken with the crockery.

BEN: (*Still reading.*) What do you want plates for? You're not going to eat.

GUS: I've brought a few biscuits.

BEN: Well, you'd better eat them quick.

GUS: I always bring a few biscuits. Or a pie. You know I can't drink tea without anything to eat.

BEN: Well, make the tea then, will you? Time's getting on.

GUS *brings out the flattened cigarette packet and examines it.*

GUS: You got any cigarettes? I think I've run out.

He throws the packet high up and leans forward to catch it.

I hope it won't be a long job, this one.

Aiming carefully, he flips the packet under his bed.

Oh, I wanted to ask you something.

BEN: (*Slamming his paper down.*) Kaw!

GUS: What's that?

BEN: A child of eight killed a cat!

GUS: Get away.

BEN: It's a fact. What about that, eh? A child of eight killing a cat!

GUS: How did he do it?

BEN: It was a girl.

GUS: How did she do it?

BEN: She —

He picks up the paper and studies it.

It doesn't say.

GUS: Why not?

BEN: Wait a minute. It just says — Her brother, aged eleven, viewed the incident from the toolshed.

GUS: Go on! Ben. That's bloody ridiculous.

Pause.

GUS: I bet he did it.

BEN: Who?

GUS: The brother.

BEN: I think you're right.

Pause.

(*Slamming down the paper.*) What about that, eh? A kid of eleven killing a cat and blaming it on his little sister of eight! It's enough to —

He breaks off in disgust and seizes the paper. GUS *rises.*

GUS: What time is he getting in touch?

BEN *reads.*

What time is he getting in touch?

BEN: What's the matter with you? It could be any time. Any time.

GUS: (*Moves to the foot of* BEN's *bed.*) Well, I was going to ask you something.

BEN: What?

GUS: Have you noticed the time that tank takes to fill?

BEN: What tank?

GUS: In the lavatory.

BEN: No. Does it?

GUS: Terrible.

BEN: Well, what about it?

GUS: What do you think's the matter with it?

BEN: Nothing.

GUS: Nothing?

BEN: It's got a deficient ballcock, that's all.

GUS: A deficient what?

BEN: Ballcock.

GUS: No? Really?

BEN: That's what I should say.

GUS: Go on! That didn't occur to me.

GUS wanders to his bed and presses the mattress.

I didn't have a very restful sleep today, did you? It's not much of a bed. I could have done with another blanket too. (*He catches sight of a picture on the wall.*) Hello, what's this? (*Peering at it.*) 'The First Eleven.' Cricketers. You seen this, Ben?

BEN: (*Reading.*) What?

GUS: The first eleven.

BEN: What?

GUS: There's a photo here of the first eleven.

BEN: What first eleven?

GUS: (*Studying the photo.*) It doesn't say.

BEN: What about that tea?

GUS: They all look a bit old to me.

GUS wanders downstage, looks out front, then all about the room.

I wouldn't like to live in this dump. I wouldn't mind if you had a window, you could see what it looked like outside.

BEN: What do you want a window for?

GUS: Well, I like to have a bit of a view, Ben. It whiles away the time.

He walks about the room.

I mean, you come into a place when it's still dark, you come into a room you've never seen before, you sleep all day, you do your job, and then you go away in the night again.

Pause.

I like to get a look at the scenery. You never get the chance in this job.

BEN: You get your holidays, don't you?

GUS: Only a fortnight.

BEN: (*Lowering the paper.*) You kill me. Anyone would think you're working every day. How often do we do a job? Once a week? What are you complaining about?

GUS: Yes, but we've got to be on tap though, haven't we? You can't move out of the house in case a call comes.

BEN: You know what your trouble is?

GUS: What?

BEN: You haven't got any interests.

GUS: I've got interests.

BEN: What? Tell me one of your interests.

Pause.

GUS: I've got interests.

BEN: Look at me. What have I got?

GUS: I don't know. What?

BEN: I've got my woodwork. I've got my model boats. Have you ever seen me idle? I'm never idle. I know how to occupy my time, to its best advantage. Then when a call comes, I'm ready.

GUS: Don't you ever get a bit fed up?

BEN: Fed up? What with?

Silence.

BEN reads. GUS feels in the pocket of his jacket, which hangs on the bed.

GUS: You got any cigarettes? I've run out.

The lavatory flushes off left.

There she goes.

GUS sits on his bed.

No, I mean, I say the crockery's good. It is. It's very nice. But that's about all I can say for this place. It's worse than the last one. Remember that last place we were in? Last time, where was it? At least there was a wireless there. No, honest. He doesn't seem to bother much about our comfort these days.

BEN: When are you going to stop jabbering?

GUS: You'd get rheumatism in a place like this, if you stay long.

BEN: We're not staying long. Make the tea, will you? We'll be on the job in a minute.

GUS picks up a small bag by his bed and brings out a packet of tea. He examines it and looks up.

GUS: Eh, I've been meaning to ask you.

BEN: What the hell is it now?

GUS: Why did you stop the car this morning, in the middle of that road?

BEN: (*Lowering the paper.*) I thought you were asleep.

GUS: I was, but I woke up when you stopped. You did stop, didn't you?

Pause.

In the middle of that road. It was still dark, don't you remember? I looked out. It was all misty. I thought perhaps you wanted to kip, but you were sitting up dead straight, like you were waiting for something.

BEN: I wasn't waiting for anything.

GUS: I must have fallen asleep again. What was all that about then? Why did you stop?

BEN: (*Picking up the paper.*) We were too early.

GUS: Early? (*He rises.*) What do you mean? We got the call, didn't we, saying we were to start right away. We did. We shoved out on the dot. So how could we be too early?

BEN: (*Quietly.*) Who took the call, me or you?

GUS: You.

BEN: We were too early.

GUS: Too early for what?

Pause.

You mean someone had to get out before we got in?

He examines the bedclothes.

I thought these sheets didn't look too bright. I thought they ponged a bit. I was too tired to notice when I got in this morning. Eh, that's taking a bit of a liberty, isn't it? I don't want to share my bed-sheets. I told you things were going down the drain. I mean, we've always had clean sheets laid on up till now. I've noticed it.

BEN: How do you know those sheets weren't clean?

GUS: What do you mean?

BEN: How do you know they weren't clean? You've spent the whole day in them, haven't you?

GUS: What, you mean it might be my pong? (*He sniffs sheets.*) Yes. (*He sits slowly on bed.*) It could be my pong, I suppose. It's difficult to tell. I don't really know what I pong like, that's the trouble.

BEN: (*Referring to the paper.*) Kaw!

GUS: Eh, Ben.

BEN: Kaw!

GUS: Ben.

BEN: What?

GUS: What town are we in? I've forgotten.

BEN: I've told you. Birmingham.

GUS: Go on!

He looks with interest about the room.

That's in the Midlands. The second biggest city in Great Britain. I'd never have guessed.

He snaps his fingers.

Eh, it's Friday today, isn't it? It'll be Saturday tomorrow.

BEN: What about it?

GUS: (*Excited.*) We could go and watch the Villa.

BEN: They're playing away.

GUS: No, are they? Caarr! What a pity.

BEN: Anyway, there's no time. We've got to get straight back.

GUS: Well, we have done in the past, haven't we? Stayed over and watched a game, haven't we? For a bit of relaxation.

BEN: Things have tightened up, mate. They've tightened up.

GUS chuckles to himself.

GUS: I saw the Villa get beat in a cup-tie once. Who was it against now? White shirts. It was one-all at half-time. I'll never forget it. Their opponents won by a penalty. Talk about drama. Yes, it was a disputed penalty. Disputed. They got beat two-one, anyway, because of it. You were there yourself.

BEN: Not me.

GUS: Yes, you were there. Don't you remember that disputed penalty?

BEN: No.

GUS: He went down just inside the area. Then they said he was just acting. I didn't think the other bloke touched him myself. But the referee had the ball on the spot.

BEN: Didn't touch him! What are you talking about? He laid him out flat!

GUS: Not the Villa. The Villa don't play that sort of game.

BEN: Get out of it.

Pause.

GUS: Eh, that must have been here, in Birmingham.

BEN: What must?

GUS: The Villa. That must have been here.

BEN: They were playing away.

GUS: Because you know who the other team was? It was the Spurs. It was Tottenham Hotspur.

BEN: Well, what about it?

GUS: We've never done a job in Tottenham.

BEN: How do you know?

GUS: I'd remember Tottenham.

BEN turns on his bed to look at him.

BEN: Don't make me laugh, will you?

BEN turns back and reads. GUS yawns and speaks through his yawn.

GUS: When's he going to get in touch?

Pause.

Yes, I'd like to see another football match. I've always been an ardent football fan. Here, what about coming to see the Spurs tomorrow?

BEN: (*Tonelessly.*) They're playing away.

GUS: Who are?

BEN: The Spurs.

GUS: Then they might be playing here.

BEN: Don't be silly.

GUS: If they're playing away they might be playing here. They might be playing the Villa.

BEN: (*Tonelessly.*) But the Villa are playing away.

Pause. An envelope slides under the door, right. GUS sees it. He stands, looking at it.

GUS: Ben.

BEN: Away. They're all playing away.

GUS: Ben, look here.

BEN: What?

GUS: Look.

BEN turns his head and sees the envelope. He stands.

BEN: What's that?

GUS: I don't know.

BEN: Where did it come from?

GUS: Under the door.

BEN: Well, what is it?

GUS: I don't know.

They stare at it.

BEN: Pick it up.

GUS: What do you mean?

BEN: Pick it up!

GUS slowly moves towards it, bends and picks it up.

What is it?

GUS: An envelope.

BEN: Is there anything on it?

GUS: No.

BEN: Is it sealed?

GUS: Yes.

BEN: Open it.

GUS: What?

BEN: Open it!

GUS opens it and looks inside.

What's in it?

GUS empties twelve matches into his hand.

GUS: Matches.

BEN: Matches?

GUS: Yes.

BEN: Show it to me.

GUS passes the envelope. BEN examines it.

Nothing on it. Not a word.

GUS: That's funny, isn't it?

BEN: It came under the door?

GUS: Must have done.

BEN: Well, go on.

GUS: Go on where?

BEN: Open the door and see if you can catch anyone outside.

GUS: Who, me?

BEN: Go on!

GUS stares at him, puts the matches in his pocket, goes to his bed and brings a revolver from under the pillow. He goes to the door, opens it, looks out and shuts it.

GUS: No one.

He replaces the revolver.

BEN: What did you see?

GUS: Nothing.

BEN: They must have been pretty quick.

GUS takes the matches from his pocket and looks at them.

GUS: Well, they'll come in handy.

BEN: Yes.

GUS: Won't they?

BEN: Yes, you're always running out, aren't you?

GUS: All the time.

BEN: Well, they'll come in handy then.

GUS: Yes.

BEN: Won't they?

GUS: Yes, I could do with them. I could do with them too.

BEN: You could, eh?

GUS: Yes.

BEN: Why?

GUS: We haven't got any.

BEN: Well, you've got some now, haven't you?

GUS: I can light the kettle now.

BEN: Yes, you're always cadging matches. How many have you got there?

GUS: About a dozen.

BEN: Well, don't lose them. Red too. You don't even need a box.

GUS probes his ear with a match.

(*Slapping his hand.*) Don't waste them! Go on, go and light it.

GUS: Eh?

BEN: Go and light it.

GUS: Light what?

BEN: The kettle.

GUS: You mean the gas.

BEN: Who does?

GUS: You do.

BEN: (*His eyes narrowing.*) What do you mean, I mean the gas?

GUS: Well, that's what you mean, don't you? The gas.

BEN: (*Powerfully.*) If I say go and light the kettle I mean go and light the kettle.

GUS: How can you light a kettle?

BEN: It's a figure of speech! Light the kettle. It's a figure of speech!

GUS: I've never heard it.

BEN: Light the kettle! It's common usage!

GUS: I think you've got it wrong.

BEN: (*Menacing.*) What do you mean?

GUS: They say put on the kettle.

BEN: (*Taut.*) Who says?

They stare at each other, breathing hard.

(*Deliberately.*) I have never in all my life heard anyone say put on the kettle.

GUS: I bet my mother used to say it.

BEN: Your mother? When did you last see your mother?

GUS: I don't know, about –

BEN: Well, what are you talking about your mother for?

They stare.

Gus, I'm not trying to be unreasonable. I'm just trying to point out something to you.

GUS: Yes, but –

BEN: Who's the senior partner here, me or you?

GUS: You.

BEN: I'm only looking after your interests, Gus. You've got to learn, mate.

GUS: Yes, but I've never heard –

BEN: (*Vehemently.*) Nobody says light the gas! What does the gas light?

GUS: What does the gas – ?

BEN: (*Grabbing him with two hands by the throat, at arm's length.*) THE KETTLE, YOU FOOL!

GUS takes the hands from his throat.

GUS: All right, all right.

Pause.

BEN: Well, what are you waiting for?

GUS: I want to see if they light.

BEN: What?

GUS: The matches.

He takes out the flattened box and tries to strike.

No.

He throws the box under the bed.

BEN stares at him.

GUS raises his foot.

Shall I try it on here?

BEN stares. GUS strikes a match on his shoe. It lights.

Here we are.

BEN: (*Wearily.*) Put on the bloody kettle, for Christ's sake.

BEN goes to his bed, but, realising what he has said, stops and half turns. They look at each other. GUS slowly exits, left. BEN slams his paper down on the bed and sits on it, head in hands.

GUS: (*Entering.*) It's going.

BEN: What?

GUS: The stove.

GUS goes to his bed and sits.

I wonder who it'll be tonight.

Silence.

Eh, I've been wanting to ask you something.

BEN: (*Putting his legs on the bed.*) Oh, for Christ's sake.

GUS: No. I was going to ask you something.

He rises and sits on BEN's bed.

BEN: What are you sitting on my bed for?

GUS sits.

What's the matter with you? You're always asking me questions. What's the matter with you?

GUS: Nothing.

BEN: You never used to ask me so many damn questions. What's come over you?

GUS: No, I was just wondering.

BEN: Stop wondering. You've got a job to do. Why don't you just do it and shut up?

GUS: That's what I was wondering about.

BEN: What?

GUS: The job.

BEN: What job?

GUS: (*Tentatively.*) I thought perhaps you might know something.

BEN looks at him.

I thought perhaps you – I mean – have you got any idea – who it's going to be tonight?

BEN: Who what's going to be?

They look at each other.

GUS: (*At length.*) Who it's going to be.

Silence.

BEN: Are you feeling all right?

GUS: Sure.

BEN: Go and make the tea.

GUS: Yes, sure.

GUS exits, left, BEN looks after him. He then takes his revolver from under the pillow and checks it for ammunition. GUS re-enters.

The gas has gone out.

BEN: Well, what about it?

GUS: There's a meter.

BEN: I haven't got any money.

GUS: Nor have I.

BEN: You'll have to wait.

GUS: What for?

BEN: For Wilson.

GUS: He might not come. He might just send a message. He doesn't always come.

BEN: Well, you'll have to do without it, won't you?

GUS: Blimey.

BEN: You'll have a cup of tea afterwards. What's the matter with you?

GUS: I like to have one before.

BEN holds the revolver up to the light and polishes it.

BEN: You'd better get ready anyway.

GUS: Well, I don't know, that's a bit much, you know, for my money.

He picks up a packet of tea from the bed and throws it into the bag.

I hope he's got a shilling, anyway, if he comes. He's entitled to have. After all, it's his place, he could have seen there was enough gas for a cup of tea.

BEN: What do you mean, it's his place?

GUS: Well, isn't it?

BEN: He's probably only rented it. It doesn't have to be his place.

GUS: I know it's his place. I bet the whole house is. He's not even laying on any gas now either.

GUS sits on his bed.

It's his place all right. Look at all the other places. You go to this address, there's a key there, there's a teapot, there's never a soul in sight – (*He pauses.*) Eh, nobody ever hears a thing, have you ever thought of that? We never get any complaints, do we, too much noise or anything like that? You never see a soul, do you? – except the bloke who comes. You ever noticed that? I wonder if the walls are sound-proof. (*He touches the wall above his bed.*) Can't tell. All you do is wait, eh? Half the time he doesn't even bother to put in an appearance, Wilson.

BEN: Why should he? He's a busy man.

GUS: (*Thoughtfully.*) I find him hard to talk to, Wilson. Do you know that, Ben?

BEN: Scrub round it, will you?

Pause.

GUS: There are a number of things I want to ask him. But I can never get round to it, when I see him.

Pause.

I've been thinking about the last one.

BEN: What last one?

GUS: That girl.

BEN grabs the paper, which he reads.

(*Rising, looking down at BEN.*) How many times have you read that paper?

BEN slams the paper down and rises.

BEN: (*Angrily.*) What do you mean?

GUS: I was just wondering how many times you'd –

BEN: What are you doing, criticizing me?

GUS: No, I was just –

BEN: You'll get a swipe round your earhole if you don't watch your step.

GUS: Now look here, Ben –

BEN: I'm not looking anywhere! (*He addresses the room.*) How many times have I – ! A bloody liberty!

GUS: I didn't mean that.

BEN: You just get on with it, mate. Get on with it, that's all.

BEN gets back on the bed.

GUS: I was just thinking about that girl, that's all.

GUS sits on his bed.

She wasn't much to look at, I know, but still. It was a mess though, wasn't it? What a mess. Honest, I can't remember a mess like that one. They don't seem to hold together like men, women. A looser texture, like. Didn't she spread, eh? She didn't half spread. Kaw! But I've been meaning to ask you.

BEN sits up and clenches his eyes.

Who clears up after we've gone? I'm curious about that. Who does the clearing up? Maybe they don't clear up. Maybe they just leave them there, eh? What do you think? How many jobs have we done? Blimey, I can't count them. What if they never clear anything up after we've gone.

BEN: (*Pityingly.*) You mutt. Do you think we're the only branch of this organization? Have a bit of common. They got departments for everything.

GUS: What cleaners and all?

BEN: You birk!

GUS: No, it was that girl made me start to think –

There is a loud clatter and racket in the bulge of wall between the beds, of something descending. They grab their revolvers, jump up and face the wall. The noise comes to a stop. Silence. They look at each other. BEN gestures sharply towards the wall. GUS approaches the wall slowly. He bangs it with his revolver. It is hollow. BEN moves to the head of his bed, his revolver cocked. GUS puts his revolver on his bed and pats along the bottom of the centre panel. He finds a rim. He lifts the panel. Disclosed is a serving-hatch, a 'dumb waiter'. A wide box is held by pulleys. GUS peers into the box. He brings out a piece of paper.

BEN: What is it?

GUS: You have a look at it.

BEN: Read it.

GUS: (*Reading.*) Two braised steak and chips. Two sago puddings. Two teas without sugar.

BEN: Let me see that. (*He takes the paper.*)

GUS: (*To himself.*) Two teas without sugar.

BEN: Mmnn.

GUS: What do you think of that?

BEN: Well –

The box goes up. BEN levels his revolver.

GUS: Give us a chance! They're in a hurry, aren't they?

BEN re-reads the note. GUS looks over his shoulder.

That's a bit – that's a bit funny, isn't it?

BEN: (*Quickly.*) No. It's not funny. It probably used to be a café here, that's all. Upstairs. These places change hands very quickly.

GUS: A café?

BEN: Yes.

GUS: What, you mean this was the kitchen, down here?

BEN: Yes, they change hands overnight, these places. Go into liquidation. The people who run it, you know, they don't find it a going concern, they move out.

GUS: You mean the people who ran this place didn't find it a going concern and moved out?

BEN: Sure.

GUS: WELL, WHO'S GOT IT NOW?

Silence.

BEN: What do you mean, who's got it now?

GUS: Who's got it now? If they moved out, who moved in?

BEN: Well, that all depends –

The box descends with a clatter and bang. BEN levels his revolver. GUS goes to the box and brings out a piece of paper.

GUS: (*Reading.*) Soup of the day. Liver and onions. Jam tart.

A pause. GUS looks at BEN. BEN takes the note and reads it. He walks slowly to the hatch. GUS follows. BEN looks into the hatch but not up it. GUS puts his hand on BEN's shoulder. BEN throws it off. GUS puts his finger to his mouth. He leans on the hatch and swiftly looks up it. BEN flings him away in alarm. BEN looks at the note. He throws his revolver on the bed and speaks with decision.

BEN: We'd better send something up.

GUS: Eh?

BEN: We'd better send something up.

GUS: Oh! Yes. Yes. Maybe you're right.

They are both relieved at the decision.

BEN: (*Purposefully.*) Quick! What have you got in that bag?

GUS: Not much.

GUS goes to the hatch and shouts up it.

Wait a minute!

BEN: Don't do that!

GUS examines the contents of the bag and brings them out, one by one.

GUS: Biscuits. A bar of chocolate. Half a pint of milk.

BEN: That all?

GUS: Packet of tea.

BEN: Good.

GUS: We can't send the tea. That's all the tea we've got.

BEN: Well, there's no gas. You can't do anything with it, can you?

GUS: Maybe they can send us down a bob.

BEN: What else is there?

GUS: (*Reaching into bag.*) One Eccles cake.

BEN: One Eccles cake?

GUS: Yes.

BEN: You never told me you had an Eccles cake.

GUS: Didn't I?

BEN: Why only one? Didn't you bring one for me?

GUS: I didn't think you'd be keen.

BEN: Well, you can't send up one Eccles cake, anyway.

GUS: Why not?

BEN: Fetch one of those plates.

GUS: All right.

GUS goes towards the door, left, and stops.

Do you mean I can keep the Eccles cake then?

BEN: Keep it?

GUS: Well, they don't know we've got it, do they?

BEN: That's not the point.

GUS: Can't I keep it?

BEN: No, you can't. Get the plate.

GUS exits, left. BEN looks in the bag. He brings out a packet of crisps. Enter GUS with a plate.

(*Accusingly, holding up the crisps.*) Where did these come from?

GUS: What?

BEN: Where did these crisps come from?

GUS: Where did you find them?

BEN: (*Hitting him on the shoulder.*) You're playing a dirty game, my lad!

GUS: I only eat those with beer!

BEN: Well, where were you going to get the beer?

GUS: I was saving them till I did.

BEN: I'll remember this. Put everything on the plate.

They pile everything on to the plate. The box goes up without the plate.

Wait a minute!

They stand.

GUS: It's gone up.

BEN: It's all your stupid fault, playing about!

GUS: What do we do now?

BEN: We'll have to wait till it comes down.

BEN puts the plate on the bed, puts on his shoulder holster, and starts to put on his tie.

You'd better get ready.

GUS goes to his bed, puts on his tie, and starts to fix his holster.

GUS: Hey, Ben.

BEN: What?

GUS: What's going on here?

Pause.

BEN: What do you mean?

GUS: How can this be a café?

BEN: It used to be a café.

GUS: Have you seen the gas stove?

BEN: What about it?

GUS: It's only got three rings.

BEN: So what?

GUS: Well, you couldn't cook much on three rings, not for a busy place like this.

BEN: (*Irritably.*) That's why the service is slow!

BEN puts on his waistcoat.

GUS: Yes, but what happens when we're not here? What do they do then? All these menus coming down and nothing going up. It might have been going on like this for years.

BEN brushes his jacket.

What happens when we go?

BEN puts on his jacket.

They can't do much business.

The box descends. They turn about. GUS *goes to the hatch and brings out a note.*

GUS: (*Reading.*) Macaroni Pastitsio. Ormitha Macarounada.

BEN: What was that?

GUS: Macaroni Pastitsio. Ormitha Macarounada.

BEN: Greek dishes.

GUS: No.

BEN: That's right.

GUS: That's pretty high class.

BEN: Quick before it goes up.

GUS puts the plate in the box.

GUS: (*Calling up the hatch.*) Three McVitie and Price! One Lyons Red Label! One Smith's Crisps! One Eccles cake! One Fruit and Nut!

BEN: Cadbury's.

GUS: (*Up the hatch.*) Cadbury's!

BEN: (*Handing the milk.*) One bottle of milk.

GUS: (*Up the hatch.*) One bottle of milk! Half a pint! (*He looks at the label.*) Express Dairy! (*He puts the bottle in the box.*)

The box goes up.

Just did it.

BEN: You shouldn't shout like that.

GUS: Why not?

BEN: It isn't done.

BEN goes to his bed.

Well, that should be all right, anyway, for the time being.

GUS: You think so, eh?

BEN: Get dressed, will you? It'll be any minute now.

GUS puts on his waistcoat. BEN *lies down and looks up at the ceiling.*

GUS: This is some place. No tea and no biscuits.

BEN: Eating makes you lazy, mate. You're getting lazy, you know that? You don't want to get slack on your job.

GUS: Who me?

BEN: Slack, mate, slack.

GUS: Who me? Slack?

BEN: Have you checked your gun? You haven't even checked your gun. It looks disgraceful, anyway. Why don't you ever polish it?

GUS rubs his revolver on the sheet. BEN *takes out a pocket mirror and straightens his tie.*

GUS: I wonder where the cook is. They must have had a few, to cope with that. Maybe they had a few more gas stoves. Eh! Maybe there's another kitchen along the passage.

BEN: Of course there is! Do you know what it takes to make an Ormitha Macarounada?

GUS: No, what?

BEN: An Ormitha –! Buck your ideas up, will you?

GUS: Takes a few cooks, eh?

GUS puts his revolver in its holster.

The sooner we're out of this place the better.

He puts on his jacket.

Why doesn't he get in touch? I feel like I've been here years. (*He takes his revolver out of its holster to check the ammunition.*) We've never let him down though, have we? We've never let him down. I was thinking only the other day, Ben. We're reliable, aren't we?

He puts his revolver back in its holster.

Still, I'll be glad when it's over tonight.

He brushes his jacket.

I hope the blokc's not going to get excited tonight, or anything. I'm feeling a bit off. I've got a splitting headache.

Silence.

The box descends. BEN *jumps up.*

GUS collects the note.

(*Reading.*) One Bamboo Shoots, Water Chestnuts and Chicken. One Char Siu and Beansprouts.

BEN: Beansprouts?

GUS: Yes.

BEN: Blimey.

GUS: I wouldn't know where to begin.

He looks back at the box. The packet of tea is inside it. He picks it up.

They've sent back the tea.

BEN: (*Anxious.*) What'd they do that for?

GUS: Maybe it isn't tea-time.

The box goes up. Silence.

BEN: (*Throwing the tea on the bed, and speaking urgently.*) Look here. We'd better tell them.

GUS: Tell them what?

BEN: That we can't do it, we haven't got it.

GUS: All right then.

BEN: Lend us your pencil. We'll write a note.

GUS, turning for a pencil, suddenly discovers the speaking-tube, which hangs on the right wall of the hatch facing his bed.

GUS: What's this?

BEN: What?

GUS: This.

BEN: (*Examining it.*) This? It's a speaking-tube.

GUS: How long has that been there?

BEN: Just the job. We should have used it before, instead of shouting up there.

GUS: Funny I never noticed it before.

BEN: Well, come on.

GUS: What do you do?

BEN: See that? That's a whistle.

GUS: What, this?

BEN: Yes, take it out. Pull it out.

GUS does so.

That's it.

GUS: What do we do now?

BEN: Blow into it.

GUS: Blow?

BEN: It whistles up there if you blow. Then they know you want to speak. Blow.

GUS blows. Silence.

GUS: (*Tube at mouth.*) I can't hear a thing.

BEN: Now you speak! Speak into it!

GUS looks at BEN, then speaks into the tube.

GUS: The larder's bare!

BEN: Give me that!

He grabs the tube and puts it to his mouth.

(*Speaking with great deference.*) Good evening. I'm sorry to – bother you, but we just thought we'd better let you know that we haven't got anything left. We sent up all we had. There's no more food down here.

He brings the tube slowly to his ear.

What?

To mouth.

What?

To ear. He listens. To mouth.

No, all we had we sent up.

To ear. He listens. To mouth.

Oh, I'm very sorry to hear that.

To ear. He listens. To GUS.

The Eccles cake was stale.

He listens. To GUS.

The chocolate was melted.

He listens. To GUS.

The milk was sour.

GUS: What about the crisps?

BEN: (*Listening.*) The biscuits were mouldy.

He glares at GUS. Tube to mouth.

Well, we're very sorry about that.

Tube to ear.

What?

To mouth.

What?

To ear.

Yes. Yes.

To mouth.

Yes certainly. Certainly. Right away.

To ear. The voice has ceased. He hangs up the tube.

(*Excitedly.*) Did you hear that?

GUS: What?

BEN: You know what he said? Light the kettle! Not put on the kettle! Not light the gas! But light the kettle!

GUS: How can we light the kettle?

BEN: What do you mean?

GUS: There's no gas.

BEN: (*Clapping hand to head.*) Now what do we do?

GUS: What did he want us to light the kettle for?

BEN: For tea. He wanted a cup of tea.

GUS: *He* wanted a cup of tea! What about me? I've been wanting a cup of tea all night!

BEN: (*Despairingly.*) What do we do now?

GUS: What are we supposed to drink?

BEN sits on his bed, staring.

What about us?

BEN sits.

I'm thirsty too. I'm starving. And he wants a cup of tea. That beats the band, that does.

BEN lets his head sink on to his chest.

I could do with a bit of sustenance myself. What about you? You look as if you could do with something too.

GUS *sits on his bed.*

We send him up all we've got and he's not satisfied. No, honest, it's enough to make the cat laugh. Why did you send him up all that stuff? (*Thoughtfully.*) Why did I send it up?

Pause.

Who knows what he's got upstairs? He's probably got a salad bowl. They must have something up there. They won't get much from down here. You notice they didn't ask for any salads? They've probably got a salad bowl up there. Cold meat, radishes, cucumbers. Watercress. Roll mops.

Pause.

Hardboiled eggs.

Pause.

The lot. They've probably got a crate of beer too. Probably eating my crisps with a pint of beer now. Didn't have anything to say about those crisps, did he? They do all right, don't worry about that. You don't think they're just going to sit there and wait for stuff to come up from down here, do you? That'll get them nowhere.

Pause.

They do all right.

Pause.

And he wants a cup of tea.

Pause.

That's past a joke, in my opinion.

He looks over at BEN, *rises, and goes to him.*

What's the matter with you? You don't look too bright. I feel like an Alka-Seltzer myself.

BEN *sits up.*

BEN: (*In a low voice.*) Time's getting on.
GUS: I know. I don't like doing a job on an empty stomach.
BEN: (*Wearily.*) Be quiet a minute. Let me give you your instructions.
GUS: What for? We always do it the same way, don't we?
BEN: Let me give you your instructions.

GUS *sighs and sits next to* BEN *on the bed. The instructions are stated and repeated automatically.*

When we get the call, you go over and stand behind the door.
GUS: Stand behind the door.
BEN: If there's a knock on the door you don't answer it.
GUS: If there's a knock on the door I don't answer it.

BEN: But there won't be a knock on the door.
GUS: So I won't answer it.
BEN: When the bloke comes in –
GUS: When the bloke comes in –
BEN: Shut the door behind him.
GUS: Shut the door behind him.
BEN: Without divulging your presence.
GUS: Without divulging my presence.
BEN: He'll see me and come towards me.
GUS: He'll see you and come towards you.
BEN: He won't see you.
GUS: (*Absently.*) Eh?
BEN: He won't see you.
GUS: He won't see me.
BEN: But he'll see me.
GUS: He'll see you.
BEN: He won't know you're there.
GUS: He won't know you're there.
BEN: He won't know you're there.
GUS: He won't know I'm there.
BEN: I take out my gun.
GUS: You take out your gun.
BEN: He stops in his tracks.
GUS: He stops in his tracks.
BEN: If he turns round –
GUS: If he turns round –
BEN: You're there.
GUS: I'm here.

BEN *frowns and presses his forehead.*

You've missed something out.
BEN: I know. What?
GUS: I haven't taken my gun out, according to you.
BEN: You take your gun out –
GUS: After I've closed the door.
BEN: After you've closed the door.
GUS: You've never missed that out before, you know that?
BEN: When he sees you behind him –
GUS: Me behind him –
BEN: And me in front of him –
GUS: And you in front of him –
BEN: He'll feel uncertain –
GUS: Uneasy.
BEN: He won't know what to do.
GUS: So what will he do?
BEN: He'll look at me and he'll look at you.
GUS: We won't say a word.
BEN: We'll look at him.
GUS: He won't say a word.
BEN: He'll look at us.
GUS: And we'll look at him.
BEN: Nobody says a word.

Pause.

GUS: What do we do if it's a girl?

BEN: We do the same.

GUS: Exactly the same?

BEN: Exactly.

Pause.

GUS: We don't do anything different?

BEN: We do exactly the same.

GUS: Oh.

GUS rises, and shivers.

Excuse me.

He exits through the door on the left. BEN remains sitting on the bed, still.

The lavatory chain is pulled once off left, but the lavatory does not flush. Silence.

GUS re-enters and stops inside the door, deep in thought. He looks at BEN, then walks slowly across to his own bed. He is troubled. He stands, thinking. He turns and looks at BEN. He moves a few paces towards him.

(Slowly in a low, tense voice.) Why did he send us matches if he knew there was no gas?

Silence.

BEN stares in front of him. GUS crosses to the left side of BEN, to the foot of his bed, to get to his other ear.

BEN: Why did he send us matches if he knew there was no gas?

BEN looks up.

Why did he do that?

BEN: Who?

GUS: Who sent us those matches?

BEN: What are you talking about?

GUS stares down at him.

GUS: *(Thickly.)* Who is it upstairs?

BEN: *(Nervously.)* What's one thing to do with another?

GUS: Who is it, though?

BEN: What's one thing to do with another?

BEN fumbles for his paper on the bed.

GUS: I asked you a question.

BEN: Enough!

GUS: *(With growing agitation.)* I asked you before. Who moved in? I asked you. You said the people who had it before moved out. Well, who moved in?

BEN: *(Hunched.)* Shut up.

GUS: I told you, didn't I?

BEN: *(Standing.)* Shut up!

GUS: *(Feverishly.)* I told you before who owned this place, didn't I? I told you.

BEN hits him viciously on the shoulder.

I told you who ran this place, didn't I?

BEN hits him viciously on the shoulder.

(Violently.) Well, what's he playing all these games for? That's what I want to know. What's he doing it for?

BEN: What games?

GUS: *(Passionately, advancing.)* What's he doing it for? We've been through our tests, haven't we? We got right through our tests, years ago, didn't we? We took them together, don't you remember, didn't we? We've proved ourselves before now, haven't we? We've always done our job. What's he doing all this for? What's the idea? What's he playing these games for?

The box in the shaft comes down behind them. The noise is this time accompanied by a shrill whistle, as it falls. GUS rushes to the hatch and seizes the note.

(Reading.) Scampi!

He crumples the note, picks up the tube, takes out the whistle, blows and speaks.

WE'VE GOT NOTHING LEFT! NOTHING! DO YOU UNDERSTAND?

BEN seizes the tube and flings GUS away. He follows GUS and slaps him hard, back-handed, across the chest.

BEN: Stop it! You maniac!

GUS: But you heard!

BEN: *(Savagely.)* That's enough! I'm warning you!

Silence.

BEN hangs the tube. He goes to his bed and lies down. He picks up his paper and reads.

Silence.

The box goes up.

They turn quickly, their eyes meet. BEN turns to his paper.

Slowly GUS goes back to his bed, and sits.

Silence.

The hatch falls back into place.

They turn quickly, their eyes meet. BEN turns back to his paper.

Silence.

BEN throws his paper down.

BEN: Kaw!

He picks up the paper and looks at it.

Listen to this!

Pause.

What about that, eh?

Pause.

Kaw!

Pause.

Have you ever heard such a thing?
GUS: (*Dully.*) Go on!
BEN: It's true.
GUS: Get away.
BEN: It's down here in black and white.
GUS: (*Very low.*) Is that a fact?
BEN: Can you imagine it.
GUS: It's unbelievable.
BEN: It's enough to make you want to puke, isn't it?
GUS: (*Almost inaudible.*) Incredible.

BEN shakes his head. He puts the paper down and rises. He fixes the revolver in his holster.

GUS stands up. He goes towards the door on the left.

BEN: Where are you going?
GUS: I'm going to have a glass of water.

He exits. BEN brushes dust off his clothes and shoes. The whistle in the speaking-tube blows. He goes to it, takes the whistle out and puts the tube to his ear. He listens. He puts it to his mouth.

BEN: Yes.

To ear. He listens. To mouth.

Straight away. Right.

To ear. He listens. To mouth.

Sure we're ready.

To ear. He listens. To mouth.

Understood. Repeat. He has arrived and will be coming in straight away. The normal method to be employed. Understood.

To ear. He listens. To mouth.

Sure we're ready.

To ear. He listens. To mouth.

Right.

He hangs the tube up.

Gus!

He takes out a comb and combs his hair, adjusts his jacket to diminish the bulge of the revolver. The lavatory flushes off left. BEN goes quickly to the door, left.

Gus!

The door right opens sharply. BEN turns, his revolver levelled at the door.

GUS stumbles in.

He is stripped of his jacket, waistcoat, tie, holster and revolver.

He stops, body stooping, his arms at his sides.

He raises his head and looks at BEN.

A long silence.

They stare at each other.

Curtain

4.5 The Absurdity of the Absurd (Introduction to *The Theatre of the Absurd*) (1961)

MARTIN ESSLIN

On 19 November 1957, a group of worried actors were preparing to face their audience. The actors were members of the company of the San Francisco Actors' Workshop. The audience consisted of fourteen hundred convicts at the San Quentin penitentiary. No live play had been performed at San Quentin since Sarah Bernhardt appeared there in 1913. Now, forty-four years later, the play that had been chosen, largely because no woman appeared in it, was Samuel Beckett's *Waiting for Godot*.

No wonder the actors and Herbert Blau, the director, were apprehensive. How were they to face one of the toughest audiences in the world with a highly obscure, intellectual play that had produced near riots among a good many highly sophisticated audiences in Western Europe? Herbert Blau decided to prepare the San Quentin audience for what was to come. He stepped on to the stage and addressed the packed, darkened North Dining Hall – a sea of flickering matches that the convicts tossed over their shoulders after lighting their cigarettes. Blau compared the play to a piece of jazz music 'to which one must listen for whatever one may find in it'. In the same way, he hoped, there would be some meaning, some personal significance for each member of the audience in *Waiting for Godot*.

The curtain parted. The play began. And what had bewildered the sophisticated audiences of Paris, London, and New York was immediately grasped by an audience of convicts. As the writer of 'Memos of a first-nighter' put it in the columns of the prison paper, the *San Quentin News*:

> The trio of muscle-men, biceps overflowing ... parked all 642 lbs on the aisle and waited for the girls and funny stuff. When this didn't appear they audibly fumed and audibly decided to wait until the house lights dimmed before escaping. They made one error. They listened and looked two minutes too long – and stayed. Left at the end. All shook ...'[1]

Or as the writer of the lead story of the same paper reported, under the headline, 'San Francisco Group Leaves S.Q. Audience Waiting for Godot':

> From the moment Robin Wagner's thoughtful and limbo-like set was dressed with light, until the last futile and expectant handclasp was hesitantly activated between the two searching vagrants, the San Francisco company had its audience of captives in its collective hand ...

Those that had felt a less controversial vehicle should be attempted as a first play here had their fears allayed a short five minutes after the Samuel Beckett piece began to unfold.[2]

A reporter from the San Francisco *Chronicle* who was present noted that the convicts did not find it difficult to understand the play. One prisoner told him, 'Godot is society.' Said another: 'He's the outside.'[3] A teacher at the prison was quoted as saying, 'They know what is meant by waiting … and they knew if Godot finally came, he would only be a disappointment.'[4] The leading article of the prison paper showed how clearly the writers had understood the meaning of the play:

> It was an expression, symbolic in order to avoid all personal error, by an author who expected each member of his audience to draw his own conclusions, make his own errors. It asked nothing in point, it forced no dramatized moral on the viewer, it held out no specific hope … We're still waiting for Godot, and shall continue to wait. When the scenery gets too drab and the action too slow, we'll call each other names and swear to part forever – but then, there's no place to go![5]

It is said that Godot himself, as well as turns of phrase and characters from the play, has since become a permanent part of the private language, the institutional mythology of San Quentin. Why did a play of the supposedly esoteric avant-garde make so immediate and so deep an impact on an audience of convicts? Because it confronted them with a situation in some ways analogous to their own? Perhaps. Or perhaps because they were unsophisticated enough to come to the theatre without any preconceived notions and ready-made expectations, so that they avoided the mistake that trapped so many established critics who condemned the play for its lack of plot, development, characterization, suspense, or plain common sense. Certainly the prisoners of San Quentin could not be suspected of the sin of intellectual snobbery, for which a sizeable proportion of the audiences of *Waiting for Godot* have often been reproached; of pretending to like a play they did not even begin to understand, just to appear in the know.

The reception of *Waiting for Godot* at San Quentin, and the wide acclaim given to plays by Ionesco, Adamov, Pinter, and others, testify that these plays, which are so often superciliously dismissed as nonsense or mystification, *have* something to say and *can* be understood. Most of the incomprehension with which plays of this type are still being received by critics and theatrical reviewers, most of the bewilderment they have caused and to which they still give rise, come from the fact that they are part of a new and still developing stage convention that has not yet been generally understood and has hardly ever been defined. Inevitably, plays written in this new convention will, when judged by the standards and criteria of another, be regarded as impertinent and outrageous impostures. If a good play must have a cleverly constructed story, these have no story or plot to speak of; if a good play is judged by subtlety of characterization and motivation, these are often without recognizable characters and present the audience with almost mechanical puppets; if a good play has to have a fully explained theme, which is neatly exposed and finally solved, these often have neither a beginning nor an end; if a good play is to hold the mirror up to nature and portray the manners and mannerisms of the age in finely observed sketches, these seem often to be reflections of dreams and nightmares; if a good play relies on witty repartee and pointed dialogue, these often consist of incoherent babblings.

But the plays we are concerned with here pursue ends quite different from those of the conventional play and therefore use quite different methods. They can be judged only by the standards of the Theatre of the Absurd, which it is the purpose of this book to define and clarify.

It must be stressed, however, that the dramatists whose work is here discussed do not form part of any self-proclaimed or self-conscious school or movement. On the contrary, each of the writers in question is an individual who regards himself as a lone outsider, cut off and isolated in his private world. Each has his own personal approach to both subject-matter and form; his own roots, sources, and background. If they also, very clearly and in spite of themselves, have a good deal in common, it is because their work most sensitively mirrors and reflects the preoccupations and anxieties, the emotions and thinking of many of their contemporaries in the Western world.

This is not to say that their works are representative of mass attitudes. It is an oversimplification to assume that any age presents a homogeneous pattern. Ours being, more than most others, an age of transition, it displays a bewilderingly stratified picture: medieval beliefs still held and overlaid by eighteenth-century rationalism and mid-nineteenth-century Marxism, rocked by sudden volcanic eruptions of prehistoric fanaticisms and primitive tribal cults. Each of these components of the cultural pattern of the age finds its own artistic expression. The Theatre of the Absurd, however, can be seen as the reflection of what seems to be the attitude most genuinely representative of our own time.

The hallmark of this attitude is its sense that the certitudes and unshakable basic assumptions of former ages have been swept away, that they have been tested and found wanting, that they have been discredited as cheap and somewhat childish illusions. The decline of religious faith was masked until the end of the Second World War by the substitute religions of faith in progress, nationalism, and various totalitarian fallacies. All this was shattered by the war. By 1942, Albert Camus was calmly putting the question why, since life had lost all meaning, man should not seek escape in suicide. In one of the great, seminal heart-searchings of our time, *The Myth of Sisyphus*, Camus tried to diagnose the human situation in a world of shattered beliefs:

A world that can be explained by reasoning, however faulty, is a familiar world. But in a universe that is suddenly deprived of illusions and of light, man feels a stranger. His is an irremediable exile, because he is deprived of memories of a lost homeland as much as he lacks the hope of a promised land to come. This divorce between man and his life, the actor and his setting, truly constitutes the feeling of Absurdity.[6]

'Absurd' originally means 'out of harmony', in a musical context. Hence its dictionary definition: 'out of harmony with reason or propriety; incongruous, unreasonable, illogical'. In common usage, 'absurd' may simply mean 'ridiculous', but this is not the sense in which Camus uses the word, and in which it is used when we speak of the Theatre of the Absurd. In an essay on Kafka, Ionesco defined his understanding of the term as follows: 'Absurd is that which is devoid of purpose ... Cut off from his religious, metaphysical, and transcendental roots, man is lost; all his actions become senseless, absurd, useless.'[7]

This sense of metaphysical anguish at the absurdity of the human condition is, broadly speaking, the theme of the plays of Beckett, Adamov, Ionesco, Genet, and the other writers discussed in this book. But it is not merely the subject-matter that defines what is here called the Theatre of the Absurd. A similar sense of the senselessness of life, of the inevitable devaluation of ideals, purity, and purpose, is also the theme of much of the work of dramatists like Giraudoux, Anouilh, Salacrou, Sartre, and Camus himself. Yet these writers differ from the dramatists of the Absurd in an important respect: they present their sense of the irrationality of the human condition in the form of highly lucid and logically constructed reasoning, while the Theatre of the Absurd strives to express its sense of the senselessness of the human condition and the inadequacy of the rational approach by the open abandonment of rational devices and discursive thought. While Sartre or Camus express the new content in the old convention, the Theatre of the Absurd goes a step further in trying to achieve a unity between its basic assumptions and the form in which these are expressed. In some senses, the *theatre* of Sartre and Camus is less adequate as an expression of the *philosophy* of Sartre and Camus – in artistic, as distinct from philosophic, terms – than the Theatre of the Absurd.

If Camus argued that in our disillusioned age the world has ceased to make sense, he did so in the elegantly rationalistic and discursive style of an eighteenth-century moralist, in well-constructed and polished plays. If Sartre argues that existence comes before essence and that human personality can be reduced to pure potentiality and the freedom to choose itself anew at any moment, he presents his ideas in plays based on brilliantly drawn characters who remain wholly consistent and thus reflect the old convention that each human being has a core of immutable, unchanging essence – in fact, an immortal soul. And the beautiful phrasing and argumentative brilliance of both Sartre and Camus in their relentless probing still, by implication, proclaim a tacit conviction that logical discourse can offer valid solutions, that the analysis of language will lead to the uncovering of basic concepts – Platonic ideas.

This is an inner contradiction that the dramatists of the Absurd are trying, by instinct and intuition rather than by conscious effort, to overcome and resolve. The Theatre of the Absurd has renounced arguing *about* the absurdity of the human condition; it merely *presents* it in being – that is, in terms of concrete stage images. This is the difference between the approach of the philosopher and that of the poet; the difference, to take an example from another sphere, between the *idea* of God in the works of Thomas Aquinas or Spinoza and the *intuition* of God in those of St John of the Cross or Meister Eckhart – the difference between theory and experience.

It is this striving for an integration between the subject-matter and the form in which it is expressed that separates the Theatre of the Absurd from the Existentialist theatre.

It must also be distinguished from another important, and parallel, trend in the contemporary French theatre, which is equally preoccupied with the absurdity and uncertainty of the human condition: the 'poetic avant-garde' theatre of dramatists like Michel de Ghelderode, Jacques Audiberti, Georges Neveux, and, in the younger generation, Georges Schehadé, Henri Pichette, and Jean Vauthier, to name only some of its most important exponents. This is an even more difficult dividing line to draw, for the two approaches overlap a good deal. The 'poetic avant-garde' relies on fantasy and dream reality as much as the Theatre of the Absurd does; it also disregards such traditional axioms as that of the basic unity and consistency of each character or the need for a plot. Yet basically the 'poetic avant-garde' represents a different mood; it is more lyrical, and far less violent and grotesque. Even more important is its different attitude toward language: the 'poetic avant-garde' relies to a far greater extent on consciously 'poetic' speech; it aspires to plays that are in effect poems, images composed of a rich web of verbal associations.

The Theatre of the Absurd, on the other hand, tends toward a radical devaluation of language, toward a poetry that is to emerge from the concrete and objectified images of the stage itself. The element of language still plays an important part in this conception, but what *happens* on the stage transcends, and often contradicts, the *words* spoken by the characters. In Ionesco's *The Chairs*, for example, the poetic content of a powerfully poetic play does not lie in the banal words that are uttered but in the fact that they are spoken to an ever-growing number of empty chairs.

The Theatre of the Absurd is thus part of the 'anti-literary' movement of our time, which has found its expression in abstract painting, with its rejection of 'literary' elements in pictures; or in the 'new novel' in France, with its reliance on the description of objects and its rejection of empathy and anthropomorphism. It is no coincidence that, like all these movements and so many of the efforts to create new forms of expression in all the arts, the Theatre of the Absurd should be centred in Paris.

This does not mean that the Theatre of the Absurd is essentially French. It is broadly based on ancient strands of the Western tradition and has its exponents in Britain, Spain, Italy, Germany, Switzerland, Eastern Europe and the United States as well as in France. Moreover, its leading practitioners who live in Paris and write in French are not themselves Frenchmen.

As a powerhouse of the modern movement, Paris is an international rather than a merely French centre: it acts as a magnet attracting artists of all nationalities who are in search of freedom to work and to live nonconformist lives unhampered by the need to look over their shoulder to see whether their neighbours are shocked. That is the secret of Paris as the capital of the world's individualists: here, in a world of cafés and small hotels, it is possible to live easily and unmolested.

That is why a cosmopolitan of uncertain origin like Apollinaire; Spaniards like Picasso or Juan Gris; Russians like Kandinsky and Chagall; Rumanians like Tzara and Brancusi; Americans like Gertrude Stein, Hemingway, and E. E. Cummings; an Irishman like Joyce; and many others from the four corners of the world could come together in Paris and shape the modern movement in the arts and literature. The Theatre of the Absurd springs from the same tradition and is nourished from the same roots. An Irishman, Samuel Beckett; a Romanian, Eugène Ionesco; a Russian of Armenian origin, Arthur Adamov, not only found in Paris the atmosphere that allowed them to experiment in freedom, they also found there the opportunities to get their work produced.

The standards of staging and production in the smaller theatres of Paris are often criticized as slapdash and perfunctory. That may indeed sometimes be the case; yet the fact remains that there is no other place in the world where so many first-rate men of the theatre can be found who are adventurous and intelligent enough to champion the experimental work of new playwrights and to help them acquire a mastery of stage technique – from Lugné-Poë, Copeau, and Dullin to Jean-Louis Barrault, Jean Vilar, Roger Blin, Nicolas Bataille, Jacques Mauclair, Sylvain Dhomme, Jean-Marie Serreau, and a host of others whose names are indissolubly linked with the rise of much that is best in the contemporary theatre.

Equally important, Paris also has a highly intelligent theatre-going public, which is receptive, thoughtful, and as able as it is eager to absorb new ideas. This does not mean that the first productions of some of the more startling manifestations of the Theatre of the Absurd did not provoke hostile demonstrations or, at first, play to empty houses. What matters is that these scandals were the expression of passionate concern and interest, and that even the emptiest houses contained enthusiasts articulate enough to proclaim loudly and effectively the merits of the original experiments they had witnessed.

Yet in spite of these favourable circumstances, inherent in the fertile cultural climate of Paris, the success of the Theatre of the Absurd, achieved within a short span of time, remains one of the most astonishing aspects of this astonishing phenomenon. That plays so strange and puzzling, so clearly devoid of the traditional attractions of the well-made drama, should within less than a decade have reached the stages of the world from Finland to Japan, from Norway to the Argentine, and that they should have stimulated a large body of work in a similar convention, are in themselves powerful and entirely empirical tests of the importance of the Theatre of the Absurd.

The study of this phenomenon as literature, as stage technique, and as a manifestation of the thinking of its age must proceed from the examination of the works themselves. Only then can they be seen as part of an old tradition that may at times have been submerged but that can be traced back to antiquity. Only after the movement of today has been placed within its historical context can an attempt be made to assess its significance and to establish its importance and the part it has to play within the pattern of contemporary thought.

A public conditioned to an accepted convention tends to receive the impact of artistic experiences through a filter of critical standards, of predetermined expectations and terms of reference, which is the natural result of the schooling of its taste and faculty of perception. This framework of values, admirably efficient in itself, produces only bewildering results when it is faced with a completely new and revolutionary convention – a tug of war ensues between impressions that have undoubtedly been received and critical preconceptions that clearly exclude the possibility that any such impressions could have been felt. Hence the storms of frustration and indignation always caused by works in a new convention.

It is the purpose of this book to provide a framework of reference that will show the works of the Theatre of the Absurd within their own convention so that their relevance and force can emerge as clearly to the reader as *Waiting for Godot* did to the convicts of San Quentin.

Notes

1. *San Quentin News*, San Quentin, Calif., 28 November 1957.
2. ibid.
3. *Theatre Arts*, New York, July 1958.
4. ibid.
5. *San Quentin News*, 28 November 1957.
6. Albert Camus, *Le Mythe de Sisyphe* (Paris: Gallimard, 1942), p. 18.
7. Eugène Ionesco, 'Dans les armes de la ville', *Cahiers de la Compagnie Madeleine Renaud–Jean–Louis Barrault*, Paris, no. 20, October 1957.

4.6 The London Controversy (1958/1964)

EUGÈNE IONESCO [AND KENNETH TYNAN]

From Eugène Ionesco, *Notes and Counter-Notes* (translated by Donald Watson)

I

Kenneth Tynan, whose essay 'Theatre and Life' has appeared in France in 'Les jeunes gens en colère vous parlent', is one of the critics who has battled the hardest to make Ionesco known in England. When the battle was won, he suddenly had doubts, which he revealed in 'The Observer' on the 22nd of June, 1958, bearing the interrogative title:

Ionesco: Man of Destiny?

At the Royal Court Theatre, 'The Chairs' is a Court revival, and the Arts Theatre taught us our lesson in 1955. The point of the programme is to demonstrate the versatility of Joan Plowright, who sheds seventy years during the interval; and to celebrate this nimble girl's return from Broadway, where she appeared in both plays under Tony Richardson's direction. Yet there was more in the applause than a mere welcome home. It had about it a blind, deafening intensity: one felt present at the consecration of a cult. Not, let me add, a Plowright cult: staggeringly though she played the crumbling hag in the first play, she simpered a little too knowingly as the crammer's prey in the second. No: this was an Ionesco cult, and in it I smell danger.

Ever since the Fry-Eliot 'poetic revival' caved in on them, the ostriches of our theatrical intelligentsia have been seeking another faith. Anything would do as long as it shook off what are known as 'the fetters of realism.' Now the broad definition of a realistic play is that its characters and events have traceable roots in life; Gorki and Chekhov, Arthur Miller and Tennessee Williams, Brecht and O'Casey, Osborne and Sartre have all written such plays. They express one man's view of the world in terms of people we can all recognise. Like all hard disciplines, realism can easily be corrupted. It can sink into sentimentality (N. C. Hunter), half-truth (Terence Rattigan), or mere photographic reproduction of the trivia of human behaviour. Even so, those who have mastered it have created the lasting body of twentieth-century drama: and I have been careful not to except Brecht, who employed stylised production techniques to set off essentially realistic characters.

That, for the ostriches, was what ruled him out of court. He was too real. Similarly, they preferred Beckett's 'Fin de Partie', in which the human element was minimal, to 'Waiting for Godot,' which not only contained two tramps of mephitic reality but even seemed to regard them, as human beings, with love. Veiling their disapproval, the ostriches seized on Beckett's more blatant verbal caprices and called them 'authentic images of a disintegrated society.' But it was only when M. Ionesco arrived that they hailed a messiah. Here at last was a self-proclaimed advocate of *anti-théâtre*: explicitly anti-realist, and by implication anti-reality as well. Here was a writer ready to declare that words were meaningless and that all communication between human beings was impossible. The aged (as in 'The Chairs') are wrapped in an impenetrable cocoon of hallucinatory memories; they can speak intelligibly neither to each other nor to the world. The teacher in 'The Lesson' can 'get through' to his pupil only by means of sexual assault, followed by murder. Words, the magic innovation of our species, are dismissed as useless and fraudulent.

Ionesco's is a world of isolated robots, conversing in cartoon-strip balloons of dialogue that are sometimes hilarious, sometimes evocative, and quite often neither, on which occasions they become profoundly tiresome. (As with shaggy-dog stories, few of M. Ionesco's plays survive a second hearing: I felt this particularly with 'The Chairs.') This world is not mine, but I recognise it to be a valid personal vision, presented with great imaginative aplomb and verbal audacity. The peril arises when it is held up for general emulation as the gateway to the theatre of the future, that bleak new world from which the humanist heresies of faith in logic and belief in man will forever be banished.

M. Ionesco certainly offers an 'escape from realism': but an escape into what? A blind alley, perhaps, adorned with *tachiste* murals. Or a self-imposed vacuum, wherein the author ominously bids us observe the absence of air. Or, best of all, a funfair ride on a ghost train, all skulls and hooting waxworks, from which we emerge into the far more intimidating clamour of diurnal reality. M. Ionesco's theatre is pungent and exciting, but it remains a diversion. It is not on the main road: and we do him no good, nor the drama at large, to pretend that it is …

II

Ionesco replies to Kenneth Tynan as follows:

The Playwright's Role

I was of course honoured by the article Mr Tynan devoted to my two plays, 'The Chairs' and 'The Lesson', in spite of the strictures it contained, which a critic has a perfect right to make. However, since some of his objections seem to me to be based on premises that are not only false but, strictly speaking, outside the domain of the theatre, I think I have the right to make certain comments. In effect, Mr Tynan says that it has been claimed, and that I myself have approved or supported this claim, that I was a sort of 'messiah' of the theatre. This is doubly untrue because I do not like messiahs and I certainly do not consider the vocation of the artist or the playwright to lie in that direction. I have a distinct impression that it is Mr Tynan who is in search of messiahs. But to deliver a message to the world, to wish to direct its course, to save it, is the business of the founders of religions, of the moralists or the politicians – who, incidentally, as we know only too well, make a pretty poor job of it. A playwright simply writes plays, in which he can offer only a testimony, not a didactic message – a personal, affective testimony of his anguish and the anguish of others or, which is rare, of his happiness – or he can express his feelings, comic or tragic, about life.

A work of art has nothing to do with doctrine. I have already written elsewhere that any work of art which was ideological and nothing else would be pointless, tautological, inferior to the doctrine it claimed to illustrate, which would already have been expressed in its proper language, that of discursive demonstration. An ideological play can be no more than the vulgarisation of an ideology. In my view, a work of art has its own unique system of expression, its own means of directly apprehending the real.

Mr Tynan seems to accuse me of being deliberately, explicitly, anti-realist; of having declared that words have no meaning and that all language is incommunicable. That is only partly true, for the very fact of writing and presenting plays is surely incompatible with such a view. I simply hold that it is difficult to make oneself understood, not absolutely impossible, and my play 'The Chairs' is a plea, pathetic perhaps, for mutual understanding. As for the idea of reality, Mr Tynan seems (as he also made clear in an interview published in *Encounter*) to acknowledge only one plane of reality: what is called the 'social' plane, which seems to me to be the most external, in other words the most superficial. That is why I think that writers like Sartre (Sartre the author of political melodramas), Osborne, Miller, Brecht, etc. are simply the new *auteurs du boulevard*, representatives of a left-wing conformism which is just as lamentable as the right-wing sort. These writers offer nothing that one does not know already, through books and political speeches.

But that is not all; it is not enough to be a social realist writer, one must also, apparently, be a militant believer in what is known as progress. The only worth-while authors, those who are on the 'main road' of the theatre, would be those who thought in a certain clearly defined way, obeying certain pre-established principles or directives. This would be to make the 'main road' a very narrow one; it would considerably restrict the planes of reality (which are innumerable) and limit the field open to the investigations of artistic research and creation.

I believe that what separates us all from one another is simply society itself, or, if you like, politics. This is what raises barriers between men, this is what creates misunderstanding.

If I may be allowed to express myself paradoxically, I should say that the true society, the authentic human community, is extra-social – a wider, deeper society, that which is revealed by our common anxieties, our desires, our secret nostalgias. The whole history of the world has been governed by these nostalgias and anxieties, which political action does no more than reflect and interpret, very imperfectly. No society has been able to abolish human sadness, no political system can deliver us from the pain of living, from our fear of death, our thirst for the absolute; it is the human condition that directs the social condition, not vice versa.

This 'reality' seems to me much vaster and more complex than the one to which Mr Tynan and many others want to limit themselves. The problem is to get to the source of our malady, to find the non-conventional language of this anguish, perhaps by breaking down this 'social' language which is nothing but clichés, empty formulas, and slogans. The 'robot' characters Mr Tynan disapproves of seem to me to be precisely those who belong *solely* to this or that *milieu* or social 'reality', who are prisoners of it, and who – being no more than social, seeking a solution to their problems only by so-called social means – have become impoverished, alienated, empty. It is precisely the conformist, the *petit-bourgeois*, the ideologist of *every* society who is lost and dehumanised. If anything needs demystifying it is our ideologies, which offer ready-made solutions (which history quickly overtakes and refutes) and a language that congeals *as soon as it is formulated*. It is these ideologies which must be continually re-examined in the light of our anxieties and dreams, and their congealed language must be relentlessly split apart in order to find the living sap beneath.

To discover the fundamental problem common to all mankind, I must ask myself what *my* fundamental problem is, what *my* most ineradicable fear is. I am certain, then, to find the problems and fears of literally everyone. That is the true road, into my own darkness, our darkness, which I try to bring to the light of day.

It would be amusing to try an experiment, which I have no room for here but which I hope to carry out some day. I could take almost any work of art, any play, and guarantee to give it in turn a Marxist, a Buddhist, a Christian, an Existentialist, a psycho-analytical interpretation and 'prove' that the work subjected to each interpretation is a perfect and exclusive illustration of each creed, that it confirms this or that ideology beyond all doubt. For me this proves another thing: that every work of art (unless it is a pseudo-intellectualist work, a work already comprised in some ideology that it merely illustrates, as with Brecht) is outside ideology, is not reducible to ideology. Ideology circumscribes without penetrating it. The absence of ideology in a work does not mean an absence of ideas: on the contrary it fertilises them. In other words, it was not Sophocles who was inspired by Freud but, obviously, the other way round. Ideology is not the source of art. A work of art is the source and the raw material of ideologies to come.

What, then, should the critic do? Where should he look for his criteria? Inside the work itself, its universe and its mythology. He must look at it, listen to it, and simply say whether it is true to its own nature. The best judgment is a careful exposition of the work itself. For that, the work must be allowed to speak, uncoloured by preconception or prejudice.

Whether or not it is on the 'main road'; whether or not it is what you would like it to be – to consider this is already to pass judgment, a judgment that is external, pointless and false. A work of art is the expression of an incommunicable reality that one tries to communicate – and which sometimes can be communicated. That is its paradox, and its truth.

(Eugène IONESCO)

III

Ionesco's reply provoked numerous comments. Kenneth Tynan replied to this reply. Then Philip Toynbee had his say, as well as a number of readers whose letters were published. Two fragments from these letters are given. But here, first of all, is Kenneth Tynan again. This article appeared in 'The Observer' on the 6th of July, 1958:

I

Ionesco and the Phantom

M. Ionesco's article on 'The Playwright's Role' is discussed elsewhere in these pages by Mr Toynbee and several readers. I want to add what I hope will not be a postscript, for this is a debate that should continue.

As I read the piece I felt first bewilderment, next admiration, and finally regret. Bewilderment at his assumption that I wanted drama to be forced to echo a particular political creed, when all I want is for drama to realise that it is a *part* of politics, in the sense that every human activity, even buying a packet of cigarettes, has social and political repercussions. Then, admiration: no one could help admiring the sincerity and skill with which, last Sunday, M. Ionesco marshalled prose for his purposes. And ultimately, regret: regret that a man so capable of stating a positive attitude towards art should deny that there was any positive attitude worth taking towards life. Or even (which is crucial) that there was an umbilical connection between the two.

The position towards which M. Ionesco is moving is that which regards art as if it were something different from and independent of everything else in the world; as if it not only did not but *should* not correspond to anything outside the mind of the artist. This position, as it happens, was reached some years ago by a French painter who declared that, since nothing in nature exactly resembled anything else, he proposed to burn all of his paintings which in any way resembled anything that already existed. The end of that line, of course, is Action Painting.

M. Ionesco has not yet gone so far. He is stuck, to pursue the analogy, in an earlier groove, the groove of cubism, which has fascinated him so much that he has begun to confuse ends and means. The cubists employed distortion to make discoveries about the nature of objective reality. M. Ionesco, I fear, is on the brink of believing that his distortions are more valid and important than the external world it is their proper function to interpret. To adapt Johnson, I am not yet so lost in drama criticism as to forget that plays are the daughters of earth, and that things are the sons of heaven. But M. Ionesco is in danger of forgetting; of locking himself up in that hall of mirrors which in philosophy is known as solipsism.

Art is parasitic on life, just as criticism is parasitic on art. M. Ionesco and his followers are breaking the chain, applying the tourniquet, aspiring as writers to a condition of stasis. At their best, of course, they don't succeed: the alarming thing is that they try. As in physiology, note how quickly the brain, starved of blood, produces hallucinations and delusions of grandeur. 'A work of art,' says M. Ionesco, 'is the source and the raw material of ideologies to come.' O hubris! Art and ideology often interact on each other; but the plain fact is that both spring from a common source. Both draw on human experience to explain mankind to itself; both attempt, in very different ways, to assemble coherence from seemingly unrelated phenomena; both stand guard for us against chaos. They are brothers, not child and parent. To say, as M. Ionesco does, that Freud was inspired by Sophocles is the direst nonsense. Freud merely found in Sophocles confirmation of a theory he had formed on a basis of empirical evidence. This does not make Sophocles a Freudian, or vice versa: it is simply a pleasing instance of fraternal corroboration.

You may wonder why M. Ionesco is so keen on this phantom notion of art as a world of its own, answerable to none but its own laws. Wonder no more: he is merely seeking to exempt himself from any kind of value-judgment. His aim is to blind us to the fact that we are all in some sense critics, who bring to the theatre not only those 'nostalgias and anxieties' by which, as he rightly says, world history has largely been governed, but also a whole series of new ideas – moral, social, psychological, political – through which we hope some day to free ourselves from the rusty hegemony of *Angst*. These fond ideas, M. Ionesco quickly assures us, do not belong in the theatre. Our job, as critics, is just to hear the play and 'simply say whether it is true to its own nature'. Not, you notice, whether it is true to ours; or even relevant; for we, as an audience, have forfeited our right to a hearing as conscious, sentient beings. 'Clear evidence of cancer here, sir.' 'Very well, leave it alone: it's being true to its own nature.'

Whether M. Ionesco admits it or not, every play worth serious consideration is a statement. It is a statement addressed in the first person singular to the first person plural; and the latter must retain the right of dissent. I am rebuked in the current *Encounter* for having disagreed with the nihilistic philosophy expressed in Strindberg's 'Dream Play': 'The important thing,' says my interviewer, 'seems to me to be not the rightness of Strindberg's belief, but rather how he has expressed it ...' Strindberg expressed it very vividly, but there are things more important than that. If a man tells me something I believe to be an untruth, am I forbidden to do more than congratulate him on the brilliance of his lying?

Cyril Connolly once said, once and wanly, that it was closing time in the gardens of the West; but I deny the rest of that suavely cadenced sentence, which asserts that 'from now on an artist will be judged only by the resonance of his solitude or the quality of his despair.' Not by me, he won't. I shall, I hope, respond to the honesty of such testimonies: but I shall be looking for something more, something harder; for evidence of the artist who is not content with the passive role of a symptom, but concerns himself, from time to time, with such things as healing. M. Ionesco correctly says that no ideology has yet abolished fear, pain or sadness. Nor has any work of art. But both are in the business of trying. What other business is there?

(Kenneth TYNAN)

IV

Philip Toynbee expressed his opinion in a review of Arthur Miller's plays on July the 6th, 1958:

An Attitude to Life (extracts)

In last week's 'Observer' M. Eugène Ionesco wrote as follows: '... writers like Sartre, Osborne, Miller, Brecht, etc., are simply the new *auteurs du boulevard*, representatives of a leftwing conformism which is just as lamentable as the right-wing sort. These writers offer nothing that one does not know already, through books and political speeches.' He went on to write: 'I believe that what separates us all from one another is simply society itself, or if you like, politics. This is what raises barriers between men, this is what creates misunderstanding.'

The first of these quotations strongly suggests that Sartre is the only playwright M. Ionesco has read or seen of those whom he has chosen to attack. It certainly seems unlikely that M. Ionesco is well acquainted with the work of Arthur Miller, for the charge against him of 'left-wing conformism' is as absurd as it would be to charge M. Ionesco with being the mouth-piece of the Algerian *colons*.

As for the second quotation from M. Ionesco's article, it seems to me to underline, by its frivolity, one of the very qualities which make Arthur Miller an important playwright and Eugène Ionesco a lesser one. To write that what separates us all from one another is simply 'society itself' (*'le social'*) is like writing that the human race is horribly hampered in its freedom of movement by the atmosphere which lies so heavy on our planet.

(Philip TOYNBEE)

V

And here are the opinions of two 'Observer' readers. The second letter ends with a phrase that could have been from the pen of Robert Kemp:

Sir,

M. Ionesco has a view of life, a view of history and even a view of the future. These constitute an ideology just as definite as Kenneth Tynan's.

M. Ionesco's article of faith is that 'no political system can deliver us from the pain of living, from our fear of death, our thirst for the absolute.' He also believes that everything outside himself is 'superficial'.

The majority of mankind look to political systems for something different: to deliver them from poverty and unnecessary death and to satisfy their thirst for knowledge. They have also discovered that their relationships with other men involve life and death.

(John BERGER Newland, Glos.)

Sir,

I am anything but an addict of Eugène Ionesco's plays: what I know of them seems to me distasteful and − to use his own term − incommunicable. But I consider his reply to Mr Tynan's criticism one of the most brilliant refutations of the current theory of 'social realism'. This essay should be reprinted and distributed on the widest possible scale. If only M. Ionesco were able to put some of its clarity and wisdom into his own plays − he might yet become a great playwright!

(H. F. GARTEN London, S.W.10)

VI

Then an imposing personality intervened in the debate: Orson Welles. He gave his opinion on what the playwright's role should he in an article published by 'The Observer' on the 13th of July:

The Artist and the Critic

M. Eugène Ionesco's recent article in reply to Kenneth Tynan offers, it seems to me, some inadvertent testimony in support of the playwright's celebrated views on the general unreliability of language.

M. Ionesco seems to imagine that 'The Observer''s critic has ordered him, like a sort of traffic policeman, on to 'the main road'. In fact, the remarks to which he takes exception were not addressed to the artist or his art; what was deplored was the peculiar ardour of his audience. As one of Mr Ionesco's enthusiasts, I felt that Mr Tynan rather overstated his case. A keen admirer is not the follower of a cult; and I did not like being told that to enjoy a play is necessarily to approve its 'message'. When I applauded 'The Chairs' was I participating in a demonstration in favour of nihilism? This sounded farfetched. After reading M. Ionesco's rebuttal to Mr Tynan I am not so sure.

If man cannot communicate, can he be expected to control his destiny? Mr Tynan's gloomiest deductions would seem to be justified if M. Ionesco admits the ultimate logic of his proposition: that proving the incapacity of language, he also proves the incapacity of man himself.

Can the artist evade politics? He should certainly avoid polemics. Directing the course of the world, writes M. Ionesco, 'is the business of the founders of religions, of the moralists or the politicians.' An artist's every word is an expression of a social attitude; and I cannot agree with M. Ionesco that these expressions are always less original than political speeches or pamphlets. An artist must confirm the values of his society; or he must challenge them.

Giving, as he does, such emphasis to the wholly personal in art, to the individual, the unique, M. Ionesco surely knows better than to look for sanctuary among the authoritarians. He cannot hope to smuggle his own private world into a world where privacy is a crime, where the sovereign individual is an outlaw. He throws himself – frigidly aloof, proudly inviolable – on the mercy of the partisans of freedom.

I resist the delicate instinct which tempts me to apologise to M. Ionesco for the use of that word 'freedom'. Whatever is valuable is likely to have a rather shop-soiled name. Very few of us, however, are so fed up with talk about freedom that we are ready to scuttle freedom of speech. In M. Ionesco's country that freedom cannot be said to be any safer than elsewhere just at this moment. Many freedoms everywhere are under siege, and all of them – including M. Ionesco's privilege to shrug his shoulders at politics – were, at one time or another, political achievements. It is not 'politics' which is the arch-enemy of art; it is neutrality – which robs us of the sense of tragedy. Neutrality is also a political position like any other; and its practical consequences have been meditated by many of M. Ionesco's fellow poets in the only effective ivory tower to be erected in our century – the concentration camp.

That politics is best left to the professionals is a perfectly respectable conservative argument; but M. Ionesco was careful to add that in his view the politicians 'make a pretty poor job of it'. I wish it could be said that these two sentiments – the revolutionary and the legitimist – cancel each other out. But M. Ionesco, for once, is not talking Jabberwocky: he is talking surrender.

To denounce leadership as incompetent, and, having done so, then to insist that the 'direction' of world affairs be left strictly in these incompetent hands, is to acknowledge an extraordinary despair.

Under the present circumstances, the call to abandon ship is not merely unpractical: it is a cry of panic. If we are doomed indeed, let M. Ionesco go down fighting with the rest of us. He should have the courage of our platitudes.

(Orson WELLES)

VII

The debate could go on for ever. To finish it off (provisionally) we give the text of Ionesco's second reply to Kenneth Tynan. This text is unpublished. 'The Observer' bought the English rights but did not publish it.

Hearts are Not Worn on the Sleeve

I cannot answer all the problems raised by my courteous enemy, Mr Kenneth Tynan, in his last article (*Ionesco and the Phantom*). It would take too long and I cannot go on abusing the hospitality of 'The Observer'. It would also, in a way, be a waste of time, for we would only succeed in repeating ourselves. That is what Mr Kenneth Tynan is already beginning to do. So I shall try above all to put my views in greater detail and answer those questions which seem to me essential.

Mr Tynan reproaches me for being so fascinated by the means of expressing 'objective reality' (but it is another question to know what objective reality really is), – that I forget objective reality in favour of the means of expressing it, which therefore becomes an end in itself. In other words, he is, I believe, accusing me of formalism. But what is the history of art or literature if it is not, first and foremost, the history of its expression, the history of its language or idiom? For me expression is form and content at one and the same time. To approach the problem of literature by studying its expression (and that, in my opinion, is what a critic should do) is also to deal with its content and arrive at its essence. But to attack idiom that is out of date, to try and hold it up to ridicule and reveal its limitations and its deficiencies; to try and shake it up, for every idiom wears out, gets hidebound and is drained of significance; to try and renew it or reinvent it or simply to amplify it is the function of every 'creator', who in so doing, as I have just said, reaches the heart of things, of living and changing reality, always different and yet always the same. This process can take place consciously as well as instinctively, with humour, if you like, and in perfect freedom, with ideas but without ideology, if ideology means a closed system of thought a system of slogans, good, bad or indifferent, far removed from life, which it quite fails to absorb, although it persists in trying to impose itself as though it were the expression of life itself. I am not the first to point out the divergency that exists, in art as well as in 'political' life, between ideology and reality. I therefore consider art to be more concerned with an independent search for knowledge than with any system of morals, political or not. It is of course a way of knowing that involves the emotions, an exploration that is objective in its subjectivity, testimony rather than teaching, evidence of how the world appears to the artist.

To renew one's idiom or one's language is to renew one's conception or one's vision of the world. A revolution is a change of mentality. Any new artistic expression enriches us by answering some spiritual need and broadens the frontiers of known reality; it is an adventure, it is a gamble, so it cannot be a repetition of some already classified ideology, it cannot serve any other kind of truth but its own (because a truth, once uttered, is already superseded). Any work that answers this requirement may seem strange at the outset, since it communicates what has not been communicated before in this particular way. And as everything is to be found in its expression, its structure or inner logic, it is the expression that must be examined. In a reasoned argument one should see that the conclusion follows logically from the data; for it is a construction that seems (but only *seems*) to be independent, to stand alone – just as a play, for example, is a construction one has to describe in order to verify its internal unity. The data used in any reasoning process are of course verified by other reasoned arguments, which are also again constructions.

I do not believe there is any contradiction between creation and knowledge, for mental structures are probably a reflection of the structure of the universe.

What is the point of a temple, a church or a palace? Can we find any realism there? Certainly not. Yet architecture reveals the fundamental laws of construction; every building testifies to the *objective* reality of the principles of architecture. And what is the purpose of a building? Of a church? Apparently to accommodate people and shelter the faithful. But that is their least important use. Their principal purpose is to reveal and be the expression of these architectonic laws, and it is in order to study and admire these buildings that we visit abandoned temples, cathedrals, deserted palaces and old, uninhabitable houses. Is it then the purpose of all these buildings to improve the lot of man (which according to Mr Tynan should be the essential aim of all thought and all works of art)? Certainly not. And what also is the purpose of music, unless it be to reveal its own different laws? In a sense one could therefore say that a column or a sonata is of no practical use at all. Their purpose is to be what they are. The one should just stand there, the other should be heard. And what is the point of the existence of the universe? Simply that it should exist. But whether it is of any use to existence to exist is a matter of opinion and a different question, an unthinkable one moreover, for existence cannot but exist.

When Mr Tynan defends realist writers, because they express themselves in an idiom everyone can immediately recognise, he is nevertheless defending a narrow realism – even if he denies it –

the kind of realism that no longer captures reality and must therefore be exploded. Once a thing is admitted by all, it is no longer admissible.

There was, at the beginning of this century, what is usually called a vast '*avant-garde*' in all realms of the spirit. A revolution, an upheaval in our mental habits. Exploration continues, of course, and intelligence perseveres in its research, which in turn transforms intelligence itself and completely alters our understanding of the world. In the West the renewal continues, particularly in music and painting. In literature and especially in the theatre this movement seems to have come to a halt, round about 1925 perhaps. I should like to be allowed the hope that I may be considered one of the modest craftsmen who are trying to take it further. I have attempted, for example, to exteriorise, by using objects, the anguish (I hope Mr Tynan will excuse me employing this word) of my characters, to make the set speak and the action on the stage more visual, to translate into concrete images terror, regret or remorse, and estrangement, to play with words (but not to send them packing) and even perhaps to deform them – which is generally accepted in the work of poets and humorists. I have thus sought to extend the idiom of the theatre. I believe I have to some degree succeeded in my aim. Is this to be condemned? I do not know. All I know is that I have not been judged on the merit of these plays, for this does not seem to be one of the considerations of a dramatic critic as important as Mr Tynan, who is moreover far from blind.

But let us come back to realism for the last time. Quite recently I happened to see an international exhibition of painting. There were 'abstract' pictures (which do not seem to appeal to Mr Tynan) and representational pictures: impressionist, post-impressionist and 'social-realist'. In the Soviet pavilion, of course, only the latter were in evidence. These paintings were dead: portraits of heroes frozen into conventional and unreal poses; sailors and snipers in captured castles, so academic they were no longer credible; and non-political pictures too, a few frosty flowers; and a street scene with *abstract* city folk, and in the centre a woman devoid of life, inexpressive though exact in detail, dehumanised. It was very curious. And what was even more curious was that the sturdy local bourgeois were lost in admiration. They said that this particular pavilion was the only one worth seeing; for even the Fauves or the Impressionists went over their heads. This was not the first time I had noticed that the reactions of Stalinist bourgeois realists and Capitalist bourgeois realists are identical. By a still more curious trick of fate, it is clear that these social-realist painters were in fact formalist and academic, unable to emphasise content just because they neglected the requirements of form. The content had escaped them and formal technique had turned against them and taken revenge by extinguishing reality.

In the French pavilion, on the other hand, the pictures by Masson (a painter who is indeed exclusively concerned with the way he paints, his means of expression, his technique) gave evidence of a deeply moving truth, of an extraordinary pictorially dramatic quality. Dark night surrounds a dazzlingly brilliant throbbing light and struggles to overcome it. Curves trace a pattern, lines rear up violently and through a gap in the serried planes of composition we can glimpse infinite space. As Masson, the craftsman, had left human reality strictly alone, as he had not tried to track it down and thought of nothing but 'the act of painting', human reality and the tragedy of it had for this very reason, truly and freely, been unveiled. So it was what Mr Tynan calls anti-reality that had become real, the incommunicable was communicated; and it is there too, behind an apparent rejection of all concrete and moral human truth, that his living heart was hidden, whereas with the others, the anti-formalists, there was nothing but dried-up forms, dead and empty: hearts are not worn on the sleeve.

Mr Tynan agrees with me when he remarks that 'no ideology has yet abolished fear, pain or sadness. Nor has any work of art. But both are in the business of trying. What other business is there?'

What other business? Painting, for example. Or having a sense of humour. No Englishman should be without that. I beg of you, Mr Tynan, do not attempt, by means of art or any other means, to improve the lot of mankind. Please do not do it. We have had enough of civil wars already, enough of blood and tears and trials that are a mockery, enough of 'righteous' executioners and 'ignoble' martyrs, of disappointed hopes and penal servitude.

Do not improve the lot of mankind, if you really wish them well.

A few words for Mr Philip Toynbee. I take back all the wicked things I said about Arthur Miller. Mr Toynbee judges Mr Arthur Miller's plays according to this dramatist's own ideas about writing drama. I did not think this could be anything but a presumption in his favour. No doubt I was wrong. So I am going to make a favourable judgement of his work too, according to something that lies outside the work itself. I shall therefore judge Mr Arthur Miller's work according to the photograph of Mr Miller published in 'The Observer'. Mr Miller does indeed look a very fine fellow. And so I admire his work.

On the other hand, I am rather amazed that Mr Philip Toynbee should be amazed at the idea that man can be hampered in his movements by society or by the air he breathes. It seems to me it is not so easy to breathe and to live; I also think it possible for man not to be a social animal. A child has great difficulty in fitting into society, he struggles against it and finds it hard to adapt himself to it: those who work with children will know what I am talking about. And if a child finds it hard to adapt himself to society, it is because there is in human nature something that has to escape the social order or be alienated by it. And even when a man becomes part of society, he does not always manage things very well. Social life, living with other people and what that can mean, has been shown to us by Sartre himself (Mr Toynbee will not object to me quoting Sartre) in his play *Huis-Clos*. Society is hell, hell is other people. We would be very pleased to do without them. And was it not Dostoyevsky who said that one could not live more than a few days with anyone before beginning to detest him? And does not the hero of *Homme pour homme* lose his soul and his name, and does he not lose his individuality to the point of becoming totally alienated when he joins in the collective irresponsibility of the wearers of uniform?

I too have done my military service. My sergeant-major despised me because my boots were not well polished. How could I make him understand that there are other standards of judgement apart from polishing boots? And that shining my boots did not entirely exhaust my possibilities as a human being? At dances, girls did not want me as a partner because I was not a lieutenant. And yet, out of uniform, I was still a man. As for my general, he was so morally deformed that he thought of himself as nothing but a general, and used to go to bed in his uniform. Later on I worked as a clerk, yet I still had the feeling I was 'something more' than a clerk. I believe I was really well aware of my estrangement from society, the kind of alienation that is denounced by the most Marxist of the Marxists and prevents a man from developing freely and finding fulfilment. When my play, *Les Chaises*, was performed in Warsaw and a few other Polish towns my characters were immediately seen to be not mentally deranged but socially estranged. And yet they wore the working clothes of the proletariat, of 'the workers'. I believe that every society alienates, even and above all a 'socialist' society (in the West, in England or in France, the classes are levelled out or interpenetrate more freely) where the political leaders consider themselves an elite because they are enlightened and where they are absorbed as men by their function. Wherever one finds social functions, one finds alienation (society being an organisation of functions), for once again man is not merely a social function.

When my lieutenant and my boss are back in their homes, alone in their rooms, they could, for example, just like me, being outside the social order, be afraid of death as I am, have the same dreams and nightmares, and having stripped off their social personality, suddenly find themselves naked, like a body stretched out on the sand, amazed to be there and amazed at their own amazement, amazed at their own awareness as they are confronted with the immense ocean of the infinite, alone in the brilliant, inconceivable and indisputable sunlight of existence. And it is then that my general or my boss can be identified with me. It is in our solitude that we can all be reunited. And that is why true society transcends our social machinery.

But that has nothing to do with the theatre. *Je m'excuse.* I am sorry.

(Eugene IONESCO, republished in *Cahiers des Saisons*, Winter 1959.)

4.7 Trying to Understand *Endgame* (1961)

THEODOR W. ADORNO

(to S.B. in memory of Paris, Fall 1958)

Translated by Michael T. Jones

Beckett's *oeuvre* has several elements in common with Parisian existentialism. Reminiscences of the category of 'absurdity,' of 'situation,' of 'decision' or their opposite permeate it as medieval ruins permeate Kafka's monstrous house on the edge of the city: occasionally, windows fly open and reveal to view the black starless heaven of something like anthropology. But form – conceived by Sartre rather traditionally as that of didactic plays, not at all as something audacious but rather oriented toward an effect – absorbs what is expressed and changes it. Impulses are raised to the level of the most advanced artistic means, those of Joyce and Kafka. Absurdity in Beckett is no longer a state of human existence thinned out to a mere idea and then expressed in images. Poetic procedure surrenders to it without intention. Absurdity is divested of that generality of doctrine which existentialism, that creed of the permanence of individual existence, nonetheless combines with Western pathos of the universal and the immutable. Existential conformity – that one should be what one is – is thereby rejected along with the ease of its representation. What Beckett offers in the way of philosophy he himself also reduces to culture-trash, no different from the innumerable allusions and residues of education which he employs in the wake of the Anglo-Saxon tradition, particularly of Joyce and Eliot. Culture parades before him as the entrails of *Jugendstil* ornaments did before that progress which preceded him, modernism as the obsolescence of the modern. The regressive language demolishes it. Such objectivity in Beckett obliterates the meaning that was culture, along with its rudiments. Culture thus begins to fluoresce. He thereby completes a tendency of the recent novel. What was decried as abstract according to the cultural criterion of aesthetic immanence – reflection – is lumped together with pure representation, corroding the Flaubertian principle of the purely self-enclosed matter at hand. The less events can be presumed meaningful in themselves, the more the idea of aesthetic *Gestalt* as a unity of appearance and intention becomes illusory. Beckett relinquishes the illusion by coupling both disparate aspects. Thought becomes as much a means of producing a meaning for the work which cannot be immediately rendered tangible, as it is an expression of meaning's absence. When applied to drama, the word 'meaning' is multivalent. It denotes: metaphysical content, which objectively presents itself in the complexion of the artifact; likewise the intention of the whole as a structure of meaning which it signifies in itself; and finally the sense of the words and sentences which the characters speak, and that of their progression – the sense of the dialogue. But these equivocations point toward a common basis. From it, in Beckett's *Endgame*, emerges a continuum. It is historio-philosophically supported by a change in the dramatic *a priori*: positive metaphysical meaning is no longer possible in such a substantive way (if indeed it ever was), such that dramatic form could have its law in such meaning and its epiphany. Yet that afflicts the form even in its linguistic construction. Drama cannot simply seize on to negative meaning, or its absence, as content, without thereby affecting everything peculiar to it – virtually to the point of reversal to its opposite. What is essential for drama was constituted by that meaning. If drama were to strive to survive meaning aesthetically, it would be reduced to inadequate content or to a clattering machinery demonstrating world views, as often happens in existentialist plays. The explosion of metaphysical meaning, which alone guaranteed the unity of an aesthetic structure of meaning, makes it crumble away with a necessity and stringency which equals that of the transmitted canon of dramaturgical form. Harmonious aesthetic meaning, and certainly its subjectification in a binding tangible intention, substituted for that transcendent meaningfulness, the denial of which itself constituted the content. Through its own organized meaninglessness, the plot must approach that which transpired in the truth content of dramaturgy generally. Such construction of the senseless also even includes linguistic molecules; if they and their connections were rationally meaningful, then within the drama they would synthesize irrevocably into that very meaning structure of the whole which is denied by the whole. The interpretation of *Endgame* therefore cannot chase the chimera of expressing its meaning with the help of philosophical mediation. Understanding it can mean nothing other than understanding its incomprehensibility, or concretely reconstructing its meaning structure – that it has none. Isolated, thought no longer pretends, as the Idea once did, to be itself the structure's meaning – a transcendence which would be engendered and guaranteed by the work's own immanence. Instead, thought transforms itself into a kind of material of a second degree, just as the philosophemes expounded in Thomas Mann's *The Magic Mountain* and *Doctor Faustus*, as novel materials, find their destiny in replacing that sensate immediacy which is diminished in the self-reflective work of art. If such materiality of thought was heretofore largely involuntary, pointing to the dilemma of works which perforce confused themselves with the Idea they could not achieve, then Beckett confronts this challenge and uses thoughts *sans phrase* as phrases, as those material compents of the *monologue intérieur* which mind itself has become, the reified residue of education. Whereas pre-Beckett existentialism cannibalized philosophy for poetic purposes as if it were Schiller incarnate, Beckett, as educated as anyone, presents the bill: philosophy, or spirit itself, proclaims its bankruptcy as the dreamlike dross of the experiential world, and the poetic process shows itself as worn out. Disgust (*dégoût*), a productive force in the arts since Baudelaire, is insatiable in Beckett's historically mediated impulses. Everything now impossible becomes canonical, freeing a motif from the prehistory of existentialism – Husserl's universal annihilation of the world – from the shadowy realm of methodology. Totalitarians like Lukács, who rage against the – truly terrifying – simplifier as 'decadent,' are not ill-advised by the interests of their bosses. They hate in Beckett what they have betrayed. Only the nausea of satiation – the tedium of spirit with itself – wants something completely different: prescribed 'health' nevertheless makes do with the nourishment offered, with simple fare. Beckett's *dégoût* cannot be forced to fall in line. He responds to the cheery call to play along with parody, parody of the philosophy spit out by his dialogues as well as parody of forms. Existentialism itself is parodied; nothing remains of its 'invariants' other than minimal existence. The drama's opposition to ontology – as the sketch of a first or immutable principle –

is unmistakable in an exchange of dialogue which unintentionally garbles Goethe's phrase about 'old truths,' which has degenerated to an arch-bourgeois sentiment:

HAMM: Do you remember your father.
CLOV: (*Wearily*) Same answer. (*Pause.*) You've asked me these questions millions of times.
HAMM: I love the old questions. (*With fervour.*) Ah the old questions, the old answers, there's nothing like them.[1]

Thoughts are dragged along and distorted like the day's left-overs, *homo homini sapienti sat*. Hence the precariousness of what Beckett refuses to deal with, interpretation. He shrugs his shoulders about the possibility of philosophy today, or theory in general. The irrationality of bourgeois society on the wane resists being understood: those were the good old days when a critique of political economy could be written which took this society by its own *ratio*. For in the meantime it has thrown this *ratio* on the junk-heap and virtually replaced it with direct control. The interpretive word, therefore, cannot recuperate Beckett, while his dramaturgy – precisely by virtue of its limitation to exploded facticity – twitches beyond it, pointing toward interpretation in its essence as riddle. One could almost designate as the criterion of relevant philosophy today whether it is up to that task.

French existentialism had tackled history. In Beckett, history devours existentialism. In *Endgame,* a historical moment is revealed, the experience which was cited in the title of the culture industry's rubbish book *Corpsed*. After the Second War, everything is destroyed, even resurrected culture, without knowing it; humanity vegetates along, crawling, after events which even the survivors cannot really survive, on a pile of ruins which even renders futile self-reflection of one's own battered state. From the marketplace, as the play's pragmatic precondition, that fact is ripped away:

CLOV: (*He gets up on ladder, turns the telescope on the without.*) Let's see. (*He looks, moving the telescope.*) Zero... (*he looks*) ... zero ... (*he looks*) ... and zero.
HAMM: Nothing stirs. All is –
CLOV: Zer –
HAMM: (*Violently*) Wait till you're spoken to. (*Normal voice.*) All is ... all is ... all is what? (*Violently.*) All is what?
CLOV: What all is? In a word. Is that what you want to know? Just a moment. (*He turns the telescope on the without, looks, lowers the telescope, turns toward Hamm.*) Corpsed. (*Pause.*) Well? Content?[2]

That all human beings are dead is covertly smuggled in. An earlier passage explains why the catastrophe may not be mentioned. Vaguely, Hamm himself is to blame for that:

HAMM: That old doctor, he's dead naturally?
CLOV: He wasn't old.
HAMM: But he's dead?
CLOV: Naturally. (*Pause.*) You ask *me* that?[3]

The condition presented in the play is nothing other than that in which 'there's no more nature.'[4] Indistinguishable is the phase of completed reification of the world, which leaves no remainder of what was not made by humans; it is permanent catastrophe, along with a catastrophic event caused by humans themselves, in which nature has been extinguished and nothing grows any longer.

HAMM: Did your seeds come up?
CLOV: No.
HAMM: Did you scratch round them to see if they had sprouted?
CLOV: They haven't sprouted.
HAMM: Perhaps it's still too early.
CLOV: If they were going to sprout they would have sprouted. (*Violently.*) They'll never sprout![5]

The *dramatis personae* resemble those who dream their own death, in a 'shelter' where 'it's time it ended.'[6] The end of the world is discounted, as if it were a matter of course. Every supposed drama of the atomic age would mock itself, if only because its fable would hopelessly falsify the horror of historical anonymity by shoving it into the characters and actions of humans, and possibly by gaping at the 'prominents' who decide whether the button will be pushed. The violence of the unspeakable is mimicked by the timidity to mention it. Beckett keeps it nebulous. One can only speak euphemistically about what is incommensurate with all experience, just as one speaks in Germany of the murder of the Jews. It has become a total *a priori*, so that bombed-out consciousness no longer has any position from which it could reflect on that fact. The desperate state of things supplies – with gruesome irony – a means of stylization that protects that pragmatic precondition from any contamination by childish science fiction. If Clov really were exaggerating, as his nagging, 'common-sensical' companion reproaches him, that would not change much. If catastrophe amounted to a partial end of the world, that would be a bad joke: then nature, from which the imprisoned figures are cut off, would be as good as nonexistent; what remains of it would only prolong the torment.

This historical *nota bene* however, this parody of the Kierkegaardian one of the convergence of time and eternity, imposes at the same time a taboo on history. What would be called the *condition humaine* in existentialist jargon is the image of the last human, which is devouring the earlier ones – humanity. Existential ontology asserts the universally valid in a process of abstraction which is not conscious of itself. While it still – according to the old phenomenological doctrine of the intuition of essence – behaves as if it were aware, even in the particular, of its binding determinations, thereby unifying apriority and concreteness, it nonetheless distills out what appears to transcend temporality. It does so by blotting out particularity – what is individualized in space and time, what makes existence existence rather than its mere concept. Ontology appeals to those who are weary of philosophical formalism but who yet cling to what is only accessible formally. To such unacknowledged abstraction, Beckett affixes the caustic antithesis by means of acknowledged subtraction. He does not leave out the temporality of existence – all existence, after all, is temporal – but rather removes from existence what time, the historical tendency, attempts to quash in reality. He lengthens the escape route of the subject's liquidation to the point where it constricts into a 'this-here,' whose abstractness – the loss of all qualities – extends ontological abstraction literally *ad absurdum*, to that Absurd which mere existence becomes as soon as it is consumed in naked self-identity. Childish foolishness emerges as the content of philosophy, which degenerates to tautology – to a conceptual duplication of that existence it had intended to comprehend. While recent ontology subsists on the unfulfilled promise of concretion of its abstractions, concreteness in Beckett – that shell-like, self-enclosed existence which is no longer capable of universality but rather exhausts itself in pure self-positing – is obviously the same as an abstractness which is no longer capable of experience. Ontology arrives home as the pathogenesis of false life. It is depicted as the state of negative eternity. If the messianic Myshkin once forgot his watch because earthly time is invalid for him, then time is lost to his antipodes because it could still imply hope. The yawn accompanying the bored remark that the weather is 'as usual'[7] gapes like a hellish abyss:

HAMM: But that's always the way at the end of the day, isn't it, Clov?
CLOV: Always.
HAMM: It's the end of the day like any other day, isn't it, Clov?
CLOV: Looks like it.[8]

Like time, the temporal itself is damaged; saying that it no longer exists would already be too comforting. It is and it is not, like the world for the solipsist who doubts its existence, while he must concede it with every sentence. Thus a passage of dialogue hovers:

HAMM: And the horizon? Nothing on the horizon?
CLOV: (*lowering the telescope, turning towards Hamm, exasperated*): What in God's name would there be on the horizon?
(*Pause.*)
HAMM: The waves, how are the waves?
CLOV: The waves? (*He turns the telescope on the waves.*) Lead.
HAMM: And the sun?
CLOV: (*Looking*) Zero.
HAMM: But it should be sinking. Look again.
CLOV: (*Looking*) Damn the sun.
HAMM: Is it night already then?
CLOV: (*Looking*) No.
HAMM: Then what is it?
CLOV: (*Looking*) Gray. (*Lowering the telescope, turning towards Hamm, louder.*) Gray! (*Pause. Still louder.*) GRRAY![9]

History is excluded, because it itself has dehydrated the power of consciousness to think history, the power of remembrance. Drama falls silent and becomes gesture, frozen amid the dialogues. Only the result of history appears – as decline. What preens itself in the existentialists as the once-and-for-all of being has withered to the sharp point of history which breaks off. Lukács' objection, that in Beckett humans are reduced to animality,[10] resists with official optimism the fact that residual philosophies, which would like to bank the true and immutable after removing temporal contingency, have become the residue of life, the end product of injury. Admittedly, as nonsensical as it is to attribute to Beckett – as Lukács does – an abstract, subjectivist ontology and then to place it on the excavated index of degenerate art because of its worldlessness and infantility, it would be equally ridiculous to have him testify as a key political witness. For urging the struggle against atomic death, a work that notes that death's potential even in ancient struggles is hardly appropriate. The simplifier of terror refuses – unlike Brecht – any simplification. But he is not so dissimilar from Brecht, insofar as his differentiation becomes sensitivity to subjective differences, which have regressed to the 'conspicuous consumption' of those who can afford individuation.

Therein lies social truth. Differentiation cannot absolutely or automatically be recorded as positive. The simplification of the social process now beginning relegates it to 'incidental expenses' (*faux frais*), somewhat as the formalities of social forms, from which emerged the capability for differentiation, are disappearing. Differentiation, once the condition of humanity, glides into ideology. But the non-sentimental consciousness of that fact does not regress itself. In the act of omission, that which is omitted survives through its exclusion, as consonance survives in atonal harmony. The idiocy of *Endgame* is recorded and developed with the greatest differentiation. The unprotesting depiction of omnipresent regression protests against a disposition of the world which obeys the law of regression so obligingly, that a counter-notion can no longer be conceived to be held against it. That it is only thus and not otherwise is carefully shown; a finely tuned alarm system reports what belongs to the topology of the play and what does not. Delicately, Beckett suppresses the delicate elements no less than the brutal ones. The vanity of the individual who indicts society, while his rights themselves merge in the accumulation of the injustice of all individuals – disaster itself – is manifest in embarrassing declamations like the 'Germany' poem of Karl Wolfskehl. The 'too-late,' the missed moment condemns such bombastic rhetoric to phraseology. Nothing of that sort in Beckett. Even the view that he negatively presents the negativity of the age would fit into a certain kind of conception, according to which people in the eastern satellite countries – where the revolution is carried out by bureaucratic decree – need only devote themselves happily to reflecting a happy-go-lucky age. Playing with elements of reality – devoid of any mirror-like reflection – refusing to take a 'position,' and finding joy in such freedom as is prescribed: all of this reveals more than would be possible if a 'revealer' were partisan. The name of disaster can only be spoken silently. Only in the terror of recent events is the terror of the whole ignited, but only there, not in gazing upon 'origins.' Humankind, whose general species-name fits badly into Beckett's linguistic landscape, is only that which humanity has become. As in utopia, the last days pass judgment on the species. But this lamentation – within mind itself – must reflect that lamenting has become impossible. No amount of weeping melts the armor; only that face remains on which the tears have dried up. That is the basis of a kind of artistic behavior denounced as inhuman by those whose humanity has already become an advertisement for inhumanity, even if they have as yet no notion of that fact. Among the motives for Beckett's regression to animal-like man, that is probably the deepest. By hiding its countenance, his poetic work participates in the absurd.

The catastrophes that inspire *Endgame* have exploded the individual whose substantiality and absoluteness was the common element between Kierkegaard, Jaspers, and the Sartrian version of existentialism. Even to the concentration camp victims, existentialism had attributed the freedom either inwardly to accept or reject the inflicted martyrdom. *Endgame* destroys such illusions. The individual as a historical category, as the result of the captalist process of alienation and as a defiant protest against it, has itself become openly transitory. The individualist position belonged, as polar opposite, to the ontological tendency of every existentialism, even that of *Being and Time*. Beckett's dramaturgy abandons it like an obsolete bunker. In its narrowness and contingency, individual experience could nowhere locate the authority to interpret itself as a cipher of being, unless it pronounced itself the fundamental characteristic of being. Precisely that, however, is untrue. The immediacy of individuation was deceptive: what particular human experience clings to is mediated, determined. *Endgame* insinuates that the individual's claim of autonomy and of being has become incredible. But while the prison of individuation is revealed as a prison and simultaneously as mere semblance – the stage scenery is the image of such self-reflection – art is unable to release the spell of fragmented subjectivity; it can only depict solipsism. Beckett thereby bumps up against art's contemporary antinomy. The position of the absolute subject, once it has been cracked open as the appearance of an overarching whole through which it first matures, cannot be maintained: Expressionism becomes obsolete. Yet the transition to the binding universality of objective reality, that universality which could relativize the semblance of individuation, is denied art. For art is different from the discursive cogniton of the real, not gradually but categorically distinct from it; in art, only what is transported into the realm of subjectivity, commensurable to it, is valid. It can conceive reconciliation – its idea – only as reconciliation of that which is alienated. If art simulated the state of reconciliation by surrendering to the mere world of things, then it would negate itself. What is offered in the way of socialist realism is not – as some claim – beyond subjectivism but rather lags behind it and is at the same time its pre-artistic complement; the expressionist 'Oh Man' and ideologically spiced social reportage fit together seamlessly. In art, unreconciled reality tolerates no reconciliation with the object; realism, which does not reach the level of subjective experience, to say nothing of reaching further, merely mimics reconciliation. The dignity of art today is not measured by asking whether it slips out of this antinomy by luck or cleverness, but whether art confronts and develops it. In that regard, *Endgame* is exemplary. It yields both to the impossibility of dealing with materials and of representation according to nineteenth-century practice, as well as to the insight that subjective modes of reaction, which mediate the laws of form rather than reflecting reality, are themselves no absolute first principle but rather a last principle, objectively posited. All content of subjectivity, which necessarily hypostatizes itself, is trace and shadow of the world, from which it withdraws in order not to serve that semblance and conformity the world demands. Beckett responds to that condition not with any immutable 'provisions' (*Vorrat*), but rather with what is still permitted, precariously and uncertainly, by the antagonistic tendencies. His dramaturgy resembles the fun that the old Germany offered – knocking about between the border markers of Baden and Bavaria, as if they fenced in a realm of freedom. *Endgame* takes place in a zone of indifference between inner and outer, neutral between – on the one hand – the 'materials' without which subjectivity could not manifest itself or even exist, and – on the other – an animating impulse which blurs the materials, as if that impulse had breathed on the glass through which they are viewed. These materials are so meager that aesthetic formalism is ironically rescued – against its adversaries hither and thither, the stuff-pushers of dialectical materialism and the administrators of authentic messages. The concreteness of the lemurs, whose horizon was lost in a double sense, is transformed directly into the most extreme abstraction; the level of material itself determines a procedure in which the materials, by being lightly touched as transitory, approximate geometrical forms; the most narrow becomes the general. The localization of *Endgame* in that zone teases the spectator with the suggestion of a symbolism which it – like Kafka – refuses. Because no state of affairs is merely what it is, each appears as the sign of interiority, but that inward element supposedly signified no longer exists, and the signs mean just that. The iron ration of reality and people, with whom the drama reckons and keeps house, is one with that which remains of subject, mind (*Geist*), and soul in the face of permanent catastrophe: of the mind, which originated in mimesis, only ridiculous imitation; of the soul – staging itself – inhumane sentimentality; of the subject its most abstract determination, actually existing and thereby already blaspheming. Beckett's figures behave primitively and behavioristically, corresponding to conditions after the catastrophe, which has mutilated them to such an extent that they cannot react differently – flies that twitch after the swatter has half smashed them. The aesthetic *principium stilisationis* does the same to humans.

Thrown back completely upon themselves, subjects – anti-cosmism become flesh – consist in nothing other than the wretched realities of their world, shrivelled down to raw necessities; they are empty *personae*, through which the world truly can only resound. Their 'phonyness' is the result of mind's disenchantment – as mythology. In order to undercut history and perhaps thereby to hibernate, *Endgame* occupies the nadir of what philosophy's construction of the subject-object confiscated at its zenith: pure identity becomes the identity of annihilation, identity of subject and object in the state of complete alienation. While meanings in Kafka were beheaded or confused, Beckett calls a halt to the bad infinity of intentions: their sense is senselessness. Objectively and without any polemical intent, that is his answer to existential philosophy, which under the name of 'thrownness' and later of 'absurdity' transforms senselessness itself into sense, exploiting the equivocations inherent in the concept of sense. To this Beckett juxtaposes no world view, rather he takes it at its word. What becomes of the absurd, after the characters of the meaning of existence have been torn down, is no longer a universal – the absurd would then be yet again an idea – but only pathetic details which ridicule conceptuality, a stratum of utensils as in an emergency refuge: ice boxes, lameness, blindness, and unappetizing bodily functions. Everything awaits evacuation. This stratum is not symbolic but rather the post-psychological state, as in old people and torture victims.

Removed from their inwardness, Heidegger's states of being (*Befindlichkeiten*) and Jaspers' 'situations' have become materialistic. With them, the hypostatis of individual and that of situation were in harmony. The 'situation' was temporal existence itself, and the totality of living individuals was the primary certainty. It presupposed personal identity. Here, Beckett proves to be a pupil of Proust and a friend of Joyce, in that he gives back to the concept of 'situation' what it actually says and what philosophy made vanish by exploiting it: dissociation of the unity of consciousness into disparate elements – non-identity. As soon as the subject is no longer doubtlessly self-identical, no longer a closed structure of meaning, the line of demarcation with the exterior becomes blurred, and the situations of inwardness become at the same time physical ones. The tribunal over individuality – conserved by existentialism as its idealist core – condemns idealism. Non-identity is both: the historical disintegration of the subject's unity and the emergence of what is not itself subject. That changes the possible meaning of 'situation.' It is defined by Jaspers as 'a reality for an existing subject who has a stake in it.'[11] He subsumes the concept of situation under a subject conceived as firm and identical, just as he insinuates that meaning accrues to the situation because of its relationship to this subject. Immediately thereafter, he also calls it 'not just a reality governed by natural laws. It is a sense-related reality,' a reality moreover which, strangely enough, is said by Jaspers to be 'neither psychological nor physical, but both in one.'[12] When situation becomes – in Beckett's view – actually both, it loses its existential-ontological constituents: personal identity and meaning. That becomes striking in the concept of 'boundary situation' (*Grenzsituation*). It also stems from Jaspers: 'Situations like the following: that I am always in situations; that I cannot live without struggling and suffering; that I cannot avoid guilt; that I must die – these are what I call boundary situations. They never change, except in appearance; [with regard to our existence, they are final].'[13] The construction of *Endgame* takes that up with a sardonic 'Pardon me?' Such wise sayings as that 'I cannot live without suffering, that I cannot avoid guilt, that I must die' lose their triviality the moment they are retrieved back from their apriority and portrayed concretely. Then they break to pieces – all those noble, affirmative elements with which philosophy adorns that existence that Hegel already called 'foul' (*faul*). It does so by subsuming the non-conceptual under a concept, which magically disperses that difference pompously characterized as 'ontological.' Beckett turns existential philosophy from its head back on its feet. His play reacts to the comical and ideological mischief of sentences like: 'Courage in the boundary situation is an attitude that lets me view death as an indefinite opportunity to be myself,'[14] whether Beckett is familiar with them or not. The misery of participants in the *Endgame* is the misery of philosophy.

These Beckettian situations which constitute his drama are the negative of meaningful reality. Their models are those of empirical reality. As soon as they are isolated and divested of their purposeful and psychological context through the loss of personal unity, they assume a specific and compelling expression – that of horror. They are manifest already in the practice of Expressionism. The dread disseminated by Leonhard Frank's elementary school teacher Mager, the cause of his murder, becomes evident in the description of Mager's fussy manner of peeling an apple in class. Although it seems so innocent, such circumspection is the figure of sadism: this image of one who takes his time resembles that of the one who delays giving a ghastly punishment. Beckett's treatment of these situations, that panicky and yet artificial derivation of simplistic slapstick comedy of yesteryear, articulates a content noted already in Proust. In his posthumous work *Immediacy and Sense-Interpretation*, Heinrich Rickert considers the possibility of an objective physiognomy of mind, rather than of a merely projected 'soul' of a landscape or a work of art.[15] He cites a passage from Ernst Robert Curtius, who considers it 'only partially correct to view Proust only or primarily as a great psychologist. A Stendhal is appropriately characterized in this manner. He is indeed part of the Cartesian tradition of the French mind. But Proust does not recognize the division between thinking and the extended substance. He does not sever the world into psychological and physical parts. To regard his work from the perspective of the "psychological novel" is to misunderstand its significance. In Proust's books, the world of sensate objects occupies the same space as that of mind.' Or: 'If Proust is a psychologist, he is one in a completely new sense – by immersing all reality, including sense perception, in a mental fluid.' To show 'that the usual concept of the psychic is not appropriate here,' Rickert again quotes Curtius: 'But here the concept of the psychological has lost its opposite – and is thereby no longer a useful characterization.'[16] The physiognomy of objective expression, however, retains an enigma. The situations say something, but what? In this regard, art itself, as the embodiment of situations, converges with that physiognomy. It combines the most extreme determinacy with its radical opposite. In Beckett, this contradiction is inverted outward. What is otherwise entrenched behind a communicative facade is here condemned merely to appear. Proust, in a subterranean mystical tradition, still clings affirmatively to that physiognomy, as if involuntary memory disclosed a secret language of things; in Beckett, it becomes the physiognomy of what is no longer human. His situations are counterparts to the immutable elements conjured by Proust's situations; they are wrested from the flood of schizophrenia, which fearful 'health' resists with murderous cries. In this realm Beckett's drama remains master of itself, transforming even schizophrenia into reflection:

HAMM: I once knew a madman who thought the end of the world had come. He was a painter – and engraver. I had a great fondness for him. I used to go and see him, in the asylum. I'd take him by the hand and drag him to the window. Look! There! All that rising corn! And there! Look! The sails of the herring fleet! All that loveliness! (*Pause.*) He'd snatch away his hand and go back into his corner. Appalled. All he had seen was ashes. (*Pause.*) He alone had been spared. (*Pause.*) Forgotten. (*Pause.*) It appears the case is … was not so … so unusual.[17]

The madman's perception would approximate that of Clov peering on command through the window. *Endgame* draws back from the nadir through no other means than by calling to itself like a sleepwalker: negation of negativity. There sticks in Beckett's memory something like an apoplectic middle-aged man taking his midday nap, with a cloth over his eyes to keep out the light or the flies; it makes him unrecognizable. This image – average and optically barely unusual – becomes a sign only for that gaze which perceives the face's loss of identity, sees the possibility that being concealed is the face of a dead man, and becomes aware of the repulsive nature of that physical concern which reduces the man to his body and places him already among corpses.[18] Beckett stares at such aspects until that family routine – from which they stem – pales into irrelevance. The tableau begins with Hamm covered by an old sheet; at the end, he places near his face the handkerchief, his last possession:

HAMM: Old Stancher! (*Pause.*) You … remain.[19]

Such situations, emancipated from their context and from personal character, are reconstructed in a second autonomous context, just as music joins together the intentions and states of expression immersed in it until its sequence becomes a structure in its own right. A key point in the drama – 'If I can hold my peace, and sit quiet, it will be all over with sound, and motion, all over and done with'[20] – betrays the principle, perhaps as a reminiscence of how Shakespeare employed his principle in the actors' scene of *Hamlet.*

HAMM: Then babble, babble, words, like the solitary child who turns himself into children, two, three, so as to be together, and whisper together, in the dark. (*Pause.*) Moment upon moment, pattering down, like the millet grains of … (*he hesitates*) that old Greek, and all life long you wait for that to mount up to a life.[21]

In the tremors of 'not being in a hurry,' such situations allude to the indifference and superfluity of what the subject can still manage to do. While Hamm considers riveting shut the lids of those trash cans where his parents reside, he retracts that decision with the same words as when he must urinate with the tortuous aid of the catheter: 'Time enough.'[22] The imperceptible aversion to medicine bottles, dating back to the moment one perceived one's parents as physically vulnerable, mortal, deteriorating, reappears in the question:

HAMM: Is it not time for my pain-killer?[23]

Speaking to each other has completely become Strindbergian grumbling:

HAMM: You feel normal?
CLOV: (*irritably*) I tell you I don't complain.[24]

And another time:

HAMM: I feel a little too far to the left. (*Clov moves chair slightly.*) Now I feel a little too far to the right. (*Clov moves chair slightly.*) Now I feel a little too far forward. (*Clov moves chair slightly.*) Now I feel a little too far back. (*Clov moves chair slightly.*) Don't stay there, (i.e. behind the chair) you give me the shivers. (*Clov returns to his place beside the chair.*)

CLOV: If I could kill him I'd die happy.[25]

The waning of a marriage is the situation where one scratches the other:

NELL: I am going to leave you.
NAGG: Could you give me a scratch before you go?
NELL: No. (*Pause.*) Where?
NAGG: In the back.
NELL: No. (*Pause.*) Rub yourself against the rim.
NAGG: It's lower down. In the hollow.
NELL: What hollow?
NAGG: The hollow! (*Pause.*) Could you not? (*Pause.*) Yesterday you scratched me there.
NELL: (*elegiac*) Ah yesterday!
NAGG: Could you not? (*Pause.*) Would you like me to scratch you? (*Pause.*) Are you crying again?
NELL: I was trying.[26]

After the dismissed father – preceptor of his parents – has told the Jewish joke, metaphysically famous, about the trousers and the world, he himself bursts into laughter. The shame which grips the listener when someone laughs at his own words becomes existential; life is merely the epitome of everything about which one must be ashamed. Subjectivity is frightening when it simply amounts to domination, as in the situation where one whistles and the other comes running.[27] But what shame struggles against has its social function: in those moments when the bourgeois (*Bürger*) acts like a real bourgeois, he besmirches the concept of humanity on which his claim rests. Beckett's archaic images (*Urbilder*) are also historical, in that he shows as humanly typical only those deformations inflicted on humans by the form of their society. No space remains for anything else. The rudeness and ticks of normal character, which *Endgame* inconceivably intensifies, is that universality of the whole that already preforms all classes and individuals; it merely reproduces itself through bad particularity, the antagonistic interests of single individuals. Because there was no other life than the false one, the catalogue of its defects becomes the mirror image of ontology.

   This shattering into unconnected, non-identical elements is nevertheless tied to identity in a theatre play, which does not abandon the traditional cast of characters. Only against identity, by dismantling its concept, is dissociation at all possible; otherwise, it would be pure, unpolemical, innocent pluralism. For the time being, the historical crisis of the individual runs up against the single biological being, its arena. The succession of situations in Beckett, gliding along without resistance from individuals, thus ends with those obstinate bodies to which they have regressed. Measured by a unit, such as the body, the schizoid situations are comical like optical illusions. That explains the *prima vista* clowning evident in the behaviour and constellations of Beckett's figures.[28] Psychoanalysis explains clownish humor as a regression back to a primordial ontogenetic level, and Beckett's regressive play descends to that level. But the laughter it inspires ought to suffocate the laughter. That is what happened to humor, after it became – as an aesthetic medium – obsolete, repulsive, devoid of any canon of what can be laughed at; without any place for reconciliation, where one could laugh; without anything between heaven and earth harmless enough to be laughed at. An intentionally idiotic *double entendre* about the weather runs:

CLOV: Things are livening up. (*He gets up on ladder, raises the telescope, lets it fall.*) It did it on purpose. (*He gets down, picks up the telescope, turns it on auditorium.*) I see … a multitude … in transports … of joy. (*Pause.*) That's what I call a magnifier. (*He lowers the telescope, turns toward Hamm.*) Well? Don't we laugh?[29]

Humor itself has become foolish, ridiculous – who could still laugh at basic comic texts like *Don Quixote* or *Gargantua* – and Beckett carries out the verdict on humor. The jokes of the damaged people are themselves damaged. They no longer reach anybody; the state of decline, admittedly a part of all jokes, the *Kalauer*, now covers them like a rash. When Clov, looking through the telescope, is asked about the weather and frightens Hamm with the word 'gray,' he corrects himself with the formulation 'a light black.' That smears the punchline from Molière's *Miser*, who describes the allegedly stolen casket as gray-red. The marrow has been sucked out of the joke as well as out of the colors. At one point, the two anti-heroes, a blind man and a lame man – the stronger is already both while the weaker will become so – come up with a 'trick,' an escape, 'some kind of plan' à la *Three Penny Opera*; but they do not know whether it will only lengthen their lives and torment, or whether both are to end with absolute obliteration:

CLOV: Ah good. (*He starts pacing to and fro, his eyes fixed on the ground, his hands behind his back. He halts.*) The pains in my legs! It's unbelievable! Soon I won't be able to think any more.
HAMM: You won't be able to leave me. (*Clov resumes his pacing.*) What are you doing?
CLOV: Having an idea. (*He paces.*) Ah. (*He halts.*)
HAMM: What a brain! (*Pause.*) Well?
CLOV: Wait! (*He meditates. Not very convinced.*) Yes … (*Pause. More convinced.*) Yes! (*He raises his head.*) I have it! I set the alarm![30]

That is probably associated with the originally Jewish joke from the Busch circus, when stupid August, who has caught his wife with his friend on the sofa, cannot decide whether to throw out his wife or the friend, because they are both so dear to him, and comes up with the idea of selling the sofa. But even the remaining trace of silly, sophistic rationality is wiped away. The only comical thing remaining is that along with the sense of the punchline, comedy itself has evaporated. That is how someone suddenly jerks upright after climbing to the top step, climbing further, and stepping into the void. The most extreme crudity completes the verdict on laughter, which has long since participated in its own guilt. Hamm lets his stumps of parents completely starve, those parents who have become babies in their trashcans – the son's triumph as a father. There is this chatter:

NAGG: Me pap!
HAMM: Accursed progenitor!
NAGG: Me pap!
HAMM: The old folks at home! No decency left! Guzzle, guzzle, that's all they think of. (*He whistles. Enter Clov. He halts beside the chair.*) Well! I thought you were leaving me.
CLOV: Oh not just yet, not just yet.
NAGG: Me pap!
HAMM: Give him his pap.
CLOV: There's no more pap.
HAMM: (*to Nagg*) Do you hear that? There's no more pap. You'll never get any more pap.[31]

To the irreparable harm already done, the anti-hero adds his scorn – the indignation at the old people who have no manners, just as the latter customarily decry dissolute youth. What remains humane in this scene – that the two old people share the zwieback with each other – becomes repulsive through its contrast with transcendental bestiality; the residue of love becomes the intimacy of smacking. As far as they are still human, they 'humanize':

NELL: What is it, my pet? (*Pause.*) Time for love?
NAGG: Were you asleep?
NELL: Oh no!
NAGG: Kiss me.
NELL: We can't.
NAGG: Try. (*Their heads strain towards each other, fail to meet, fall apart again.*)[32]

Dramatic categories as a whole are treated just like humor. All are parodied. But not ridiculed. Emphatically, parody entails the use of forms in the epoch of their impossibility. It demonstrates this impossibility and thereby changes the forms. The three Aristotelian unities are retained, but drama itself perishes. Along with subjectivity, whose final epilogue (*Nachspiel*) is *Endgame*, the hero is also withdrawn; the drama's freedom is only the impotent, pathetic reflex of futile resolutions.[33] In that regard, too, Beckett's drama is heir to Kafka's novels, to whom he stands in a similar relation as the serial composers to Schönberg: he reflects the precursor in himself, altering the latter through the totality of his principle. Beckett's critique of the earlier writer, which irrefutably stresses the divergence between what happens and the objectively pure, epic language, conceals the same diffi-culty as that confronted by contemporary integral composition with the antagonistic procedure of Schönberg. What is the *raison d'être* of forms when the tension between them and what is not homogeneous to them disappears, and when one nevertheless cannot halt the progress of mastery over aesthetic material? *Endgame* pulls out of the fray, by making that question its own, by making it thematic. That which prohibits the dramatization of Kafka's novels becomes subject matter. Dramatic components reappear after their demise. Exposition, complication, plot, peripeteia, and catastrophe return as decomposed elements in a post-mortem examination of dramaturgy: the news that there are no more painkillers depicts catastrophe.[34] Those components have been toppled along with that meaning once discharged by drama; *Endgame* studies (as if in a test-tube) the drama of the age, the age that no longer tolerates what constitutes drama. For example, tragedy, at the height of its plot and with antithesis as its quintessence, manifested the utmost tightening of the dramatic thread, stychomythia – dialogues in which the trimeter spoken by one person follows that of the other. Drama had renounced this technique, because its stylization and resulting pretentiousness seemed alien to secular society. Beckett employs it as if the detonation had revealed what was buried in drama. *Endgame* contains rapid, monosyllabic dialogues, like the earlier question-and-answer games between the blinded king and fate's messenger. But where the bind tightened then, the speakers now grow slack. Short of breath until they almost fall silent, they no longer manage the synthesis of linguistic phrases; they stammer in protocol sentences that might stem from positivists or Expressionists. The boundary value (*Grenzwert*) of Beckett's drama is that silence already defined as 'the rest' in Shakespeare's inauguration of modern tragedy. The fact that an 'act without words' follows *Endgame* as a kind of epilogue is its own *terminus ad quem*. The words resound like merely makeshift ones because silence is not yet entirely successful, like voices accompanying and disturbing it.

What becomes of form in *Endgame* can be virtually reconstructed from literary history. In Ibsen's *The Wild Duck*, the degenerate photographer Hjalmar Ekdal – himself a potential anti-hero – forgets to bring to the teenager Hedwig the promised menu from the sumptuous dinner at old Werle's house, to which he had been invited without his family. Psychologically, that is motivated by his slovenly egotistical character, but it is symbolically significant also for Hjalmar, for the course of the plot, and for the play's meaning: the girl's futile sacrifice. That anticipates the later Freudian theory of 'parapraxis,'★ which explicates such slip-ups by means of their relation to past experiences and wishes of an individual, to the individual's identity. Freud's hypotheses, 'all our experiences have a sense,'[35] transforms the traditional dramatic idea into psychlogical realism, from which Ibsen's tragi-comedy of the *Wild Duck* incomparably extracts the spark of form one more time. When such symbolism liberates itself from its psychological determination, it congeals into a being-in-itself, and the symbol becomes symbolic as in Ibsen's late works like *John Gabriel Borkmann*, where the accountant Foldal is overcome by so-called 'youth.' The contradiction between such a consistent symbolism and conservative realism constitutes the inadequacy of the late plays. But it thereby also constitutes the leavening ferment of the Expressionist Strindberg. His symbols, torn away from empirical human beings, are woven into a tapestry in which everything and nothing is symbolic, because everything can signify everything. Drama need only become aware of the ineluctably ridiculous nature of such pan-symbolism, which destroys itself; it need only take that up and utilize it, and Beckettian absurdity is already achieved as a result of the immanent dialectic of form. Not meaning anything becomes the only meaning. The mortal fear of the dramatic figures, if not of the parodied drama itself, is the distortedly comical fear that they could mean something or other:

HAMM: We're not beginning to … to … mean something?
CLOV: Mean something! You and I, mean something! (*Brief laugh.*) Ah that's a good one![36]

With this possibility, long since crushed by the overwhelming power of an apparatus in which individuals are interchangeable and superfluous, the meaning of language also disappears. Hamm, irritated by the impulse of life which has regressed to clumsiness in his parents' trashcan conversations, and nervous because 'it doesn't end,' asks: 'Will you never finish? Will this never finish?'[37] The play takes place on that level. It is constructed on the ground of a proscription of language, and it articulates that in its own structure. However, it does not thereby avoid the aporia of Expressionist drama: that language, even where it tends to be shortened to mere sound, yet cannot shake off its semantic element. It cannot become purely mimetic[38] or gestural, just as forms of modern painting, liberated from referentiality (*Gegenständlichkeit*), cannot cast off all similarity to objects. Mimetic values, definitively unloosed from significative ones, then approach arbitrariness, contingency, and finally a mere secondary convention. The way *Endgame* comes to terms with that differentiates it from *Finnegans Wake*. Rather than striving to liquidate the discursive element of language through pure sound, Beckett turns that element into an instrument of its own absurdity and he does that according to the ritual of clowns, whose babbling becomes nonsensical by presenting itself as sense. The objective disintegration of language – that simultaneously stereotyped and faulty chatter of self-alienation, where word and sentence melt together in human mouths – penetrates the aesthetic arcanum. The second language of those falling silent, a conglomeration of insolent phrases, pseudo-logical connections, and galvanized words appearing as commodity signs – as the desolate echo of the advertising world – is 'refunctioned' (*umfunktioniert*) into the language of a poetic work that negates language.[39] Beckett thus approximates the drama of Eugène Ionesco. Whereas a later work by him is organized around the image of the tape recorder, the language of *Endgame* resembles another language familiar from the loathsome party game, where someone records the nonsense spoken at a party and then plays it back for the guests' humiliation. The shock, overcome on such an occasion only by stupid tittering, is here carefully composed. Just as alert experience seems to notice everywhere situations from Kafka's novels after reading him intensely, so does Beckett's language bring about a healing illness of those already ill: whoever listens to himself worries that he also talks like that. For some time now, the accidental events on the street seem to the movie-goer just leaving the theatre like the planned contingency of a film. Between the mechanically assembled phrases taken from the language of daily life, the chasm yawns. Where one of the pair asks with the routine gesture of the hardened man, certain of the uncontestable boredom of existence, 'What in God's name could there be on the horizon?'[40] then this shoulder-shrugging in language becomes apocalyptic, particularly because it is so familiar. From the bland yet aggressive impulse of human 'common sense,' 'What do you think there is?' is extracted the confession of its own nihilism. Somewhat later, Hamm the master commands the *soi-disant* servant Clov, in a circus-task, to undertake the vain attempt to shove the chair back and forth, to fetch the 'gaff.' There follows a brief dialogue:

CLOV: Do this, do that, and I do it. I never refuse. Why?
HAMM: You're not able to.
CLOV: Soon I won't do it any more.
HAMM: You won't be able to any more. (*Exit Clov.*) Ah the creatures, everything has to be explained to them.[41]

That 'everything has to be explained to the creatures' is drummed daily by millions of superiors into millions of subordinates. However, by means of the nonsense thus supposedly established in the passage – Hamm's explanation contradicts his own command – the cliché's inanity, usually hidden by custom, is garishly illuminated, and furthermore, the fraud of speaking with each other is expressed. When conversing, people remain hopelessly distant from each other, no more reaching each other than the two old cripples in the trash bins do. Communication, the universal law of clichés, proclaims that there is no more communication. The absurdity of all speaking is not unrelated to realism but rather develops from it. For communicative language postulates – already in its syntactic form, through logic, the nature of conclusions, and stable concepts – the principle of sufficient reason. Yet this requirement is hardly met anymore: when people speak with each other, they are motivated partly by their psychology or pre-logical unconscious, and partly by their pursuit of purposes. Since they aim at self-preservation, these purposes deviate from that objectivity deceptively manifest in their logical form. At any rate, one can prove that point to people today with the help of tape recorders. In Freud's as in Pareto's understanding, the *ratio* of verbal communication is always also a rationalization. *Ratio* itself emerged from the interest in self-preservation, and it is therefore undermined by the obligatory rationalizations of its own irrationality. The contradiction between the rational facade and the immutably irrational is itself already the absurd. Beckett must only mark the contradiction and employ it as a selective principle, and realism, casting off the illusion of rational stringency, comes into its own.

Even the syntactic form of question and answer is undermined. It presupposes an openness of what is to be spoken, an openness which no longer exists, as Huxley already noted. In the question one hears already the anticipated answer, and that condemns the game of question and answer to empty deception, to the unworkable effort to conceal the unfreedom of informative language in the linguistic gesture of freedom. Beckett tears away this veil, and the philosophical veil as well. Everything radically called into question when confronted by nothingness resists – by virtue of a pathos borrowed from theology – these terrifying consequences, while insisting on their possibility; in the form of question and answer, the answer is infiltrated with the meaning denied by the whole game. It is not for nothing that in fascism and pre-fascism such destructionists were able heartily to scorn destructive intellect. But Beckett deciphers the lie of the question mark: the question has become rhetorical. While the existential-philosophical hell resembles a tunnel, where in the middle one can already discern light shining at the end, Beckett's dialogues rip up the railroad tracks of conservation; the train no longer arrives at the bright end of the tunnel. Wedekind's old technique of misunderstanding becomes total. The course of the dialogues themselves approximates the contingency principle of literary production. It sounds as if the laws of its continuation were not the 'reason' of speech and reply, and not even their psychological entwinement, but rather a test of listening, related to that of a music which frees itself from preformed types. The drama attends carefully to what kind of sentence might follow another. Given the accessible spontaneity of such questions, the absurdity of content is all the more strongly felt. That, too, finds its infantile model in those people who, when visiting the zoo, wait attentively for the next move of the hippopotamus or the chimpanzee.

In the state of its disintegration, language is polarized. On the one hand, it becomes Basic English, or French, or German – single words, archaically ejected commands in the jargon of universal disregard, the intimacy of irreconcilable adversaries; on the other hand, it becomes the aggregate of its empty forms, of a grammar that has renounced all reference to its content and therefore also to its synthetic function. The interjections are accompanied by exercise sentences, God knows why. Beckett trumpets this from the rooftops, too: one of the rules of the *Endgame* is that the unsocial partners – and with them the audience – are always eyeing each other's cards. Hamm considers himself an artist. He has chosen as his life maxim Nero's *qualis artifex pereo*. But the stories he undertakes run aground on syntax:

HAMM: Where was I? (*Pause. Gloomily.*) It's finished, we're finished. (*Pause.*) Nearly finished.[42]

Logic reels between the linguistic paradigms. Hamm and Clov converse in their authoritative, mutually cutting fashion:

HAMM: Open the window.
CLOV: What for?
HAMM: I want to hear the sea.
CLOV: You wouldn't hear it.
HAMM: Even if you opened the window?
CLOV: No.
HAMM: Then it's not worthwhile opening it?
CLOV: No.
HAMM: (*Violently*) Then open it! (*Clov gets up on the ladder, opens the window. Pause.*) Have you opened it?

CLOV: Yes.[43]

One could almost see in Hamm's last 'then' the key to the play. Because it is not worthwhile to open the window, since Hamm cannot hear the sea – perhaps it is dried out, perhaps it no longer moves – he insists that Clov open it. The nonsense of an act becomes a reason to accomplish it – a late legitimation of Fichte's free activity for its own sake. That is how contemporary actions look, and they arouse the suspicion that things were never very different. The logical figure of the absurd, which makes the claim of stringency for stringency's contradictory opposite, denies every context of meaning apparently guaranteed by logic, in order to prove logic's own absurdity: that logic, by means of subject, predicate, and copula, treats non-identity as if it were identical, as if it were consumed in its forms. The absurd does not take the place of the rational as one world view of another; in the absurd, the rational world view comes into its own.

The pre-established harmony of despair reigns between the forms and the residual content of the play. The ensemble – smelted together – counts only four heads. Two of them are excessively red, as if their vitality were a skin disease; the two old ones, however, are excessively white, like sprouting potatoes in a cellar. None of them still has a properly functioning body; the old people consist only of rumps, having apparently lost their legs not in the catastrophe but in a private tandem accident in the Ardennes, 'on the road to Sedan,'[44] an area where one army regularly annihilates another. One should not suppose that all that much has changed. Even the memory of their own particular (*bestimmt*) misfortune becomes enviable in relation to the indeterminacy (*Unbestimmtheit*) of universal misfortune – they laugh at it. In contrast to Expressionism's fathers and sons, they all have their own names, but all four names have one syllable, 'four-letter words' like obscenities. Practical, familiar abbreviations, popular in Anglo-Saxon countries, are exposed as mere stumps of names. Only the name of the old mother, Nell, is somewhat common even if obsolete; Dickens uses it for the touching child in *Old Curiosity Shop*. The three other names are invented as if for bill-boards. The old man is named Nagg, with the association of 'nagging' and perhaps also a German association: an intimate pair is intimate through 'gnawing' (*Nagen*). They talk about whether the sawdust in their cans has been changed; yet it is not sawdust but sand. Nagg stipulates that it used to be sawdust, and Nell answers boredly: 'Once!'[45] – a woman who spitefully exposes her husband's frozen, repetitive declarations. As sordid as the fight about sawdust or sand is, the difference is decisive for the residual plot, the transition from a minimum to nothing. Beckett can claim for himself what Benjamin praised in Baudelaire, the ability to 'express something extreme with extreme discretion';[46] the routine consolation that things could be worse becomes a condemnation. In the realm between life and death, where even pain is no longer possible, the difference between sawdust and sand means everything. Sawdust, wretched by-product of the world of things, is now in great demand; its removal becomes an intensification of the life-long death penalty. The fact that both lodge in trash bins – a comparable motif appears, moreover, in Tennessee Williams' *Camino Real*, surely without one play having been influenced by the other – takes the conversational phrase literally, as in Kafka. 'Today old people are thrown in the trashcan' and it happens. *Endgame* is the true gerontology. According to the measure of socially useful labor, which they can no longer perform, old people are superfluous and must be discarded. That is extracted from the scientific ruckus of a welfare system that accentuates what it negates. *Endgame* trains the viewer for a condition where everyone involved expects – upon lifting the lid from the nearest dumpster – to find his own parents. The natural cohesion of life has become organic refuse. The national socialists irreparably overturned the taboo of old age. Beckett's trashcans are the emblem of a culture restored after Auschwitz. Yet the sub-plot goes further than too far, to the old people's demise. They are denied children's fare, their pap, which is replaced by a biscuit they – toothless – can no longer chew; and they suffocate, because the last man is too sensitive to grant life to the next-to-last ones. That is entwined with the main plot, because the old pair's miserable end drives it forward to that exit of life whose possibility constitutes the tension in the play. Hamlet is revised: croak or croak, that is the question.

The name of Shakespeare's hero is grimly foreshortened by Beckett – the last, liquidated dramatic subject echoing the first. It is also associated with one of Noah's sons and thereby with the flood: the progenitor of blacks, who replaces the white 'master race' in a Freudian negation. Finally, there is the English 'ham actor.' Beckett's Hamm, the key to power and helpless at the same time, plays at what he no longer is, as if he had read the most recent sociological literature defining *zoon politikon* as a role. Whoever cleverly presented himself became a 'personality' just like helpless Hamm. 'Personality' may have been a role originally – nature pretending to transcend nature. Fluctuation in the play's situations causes one of Hamm's roles: occasionally, a stage direction drastically suggests that he speak with the 'voice of a rational being'; in a lengthy narrative, he is to strike a 'narrative tone.' The memory of what is irretrievably past becomes a swindle. Disintegration retrospectively condemns as fictional that continuity of life which alone made life possible. Differences in tone – between people who narrate and those who speak directly – pass judgment on the principle of identity. Both alternate in Hamm's long speech, a kind of inserted aria without music. At the transition points he pauses – the artistic pauses of the veteran actor of heroic roles. For the norm of existential philosophy   people should be themselves because they can no longer become anything else – *Endgame* posits the antithesis, that precisely this self is not a self but rather the aping imitation of something non-existent. Hamm's mendacity exposes the lie concealed in saying 'I' and thereby exhibiting substantiality, whose opposite is the content disclosed by the 'I.' Immutability, the epitome of transience, is its ideology. What used to be the truth content of the subject – thinking – is only still preserved in its gestural shell. Both main figures act as if they were reflecting on something, but without thinking.

HAMM: The whole thing is comical, I grant you that. What about having a good guffaw the two of us together?
CLOV: (*After reflection*) I couldn't guffaw today.
HAMM: (*After reflection*) Nor I.[47]

According to his name, Hamm's counterpart is what he is, a truncated clown, whose last letter has been severed. An archaic expression for the devil sounds similar – cloven foot; it also resembles the current word 'glove.' He is the devil of his master, whom he has threatened with the worst, leaving him; yet at the same time he is also the glove with which the master touches the world of things, which he can no longer directly grasp. Not only the figure of Clov is constructed through such associations, but also his connection with the others. In the old piano edition of Stravinsky's 'Ragtime for Eleven Instruments,' one of the most significant works of his Surrealist phase, there was a Picasso drawing which – probably inspired by the title 'rag' – showed two ragged figures, the ancestors of those vagabonds Vladimir and Estragon, who are waiting for Godot. This virtuoso sketch is a single entangled line. The double-sketch of *Endgame* is of this spirit, as well as the damaged repetitions irresistably produced by Beckett's entire work. In them, history is canceled out. This compulsory repetition is taken from the regressive behavior of someone locked up, who tries it again and again. Beckett converges with the newest musical tendencies by combining, as a Westerner, aspects of Stravinsky's radical past – the oppressive stasis of disintegrating continuity – with the most advanced expressive and constructive means from the Schönberg school. Even the outlines of Hamm and Clov are one line; they are denied the individuation of a tidily independent monad. They cannot live without each other. Hamm's power over Clov seems to be that only he knows how to open the cupboard, somewhat like the situation where only the principal knows the combination of the safe. He would reveal the secret to Clov, if Clov would swear to 'finish' him – or 'us.' In a reply thoroughly characteristic of the play's tapestry, Clov answers: 'I couldn't finish you'; as if the play were mocking the man who feigns reason, Hamm says: 'Then you won't finish me.'[48] He is dependent on Clov, because Clov alone can accomplish what keeps both alive. But that is of questionable value, because both – like the captain of the ghostly ship – must fear not being able to die. The tiny bit that is also everything – that would be the possibility that something could perhaps change. This movement, or its absence, is the plot. Admittedly, it does not become much more explicit than the repeated motif 'Something is taking its course,'[49] as abstract as the pure form of time. The Hegelian dialectic of master and slave, mentioned by Günther Anders with reference to *Godot*, is derided rather than portrayed according to the tenets of traditional aesthetics. The slave can no longer grasp the reins and abolish domination. Crippled as he is, he would hardly be capable of this, and according to the plays historico-philosophical sundial, it is too late for spontaneous action anyway. Clov has no other choice than to emigrate out into the world that no longer exists for the play's recluses, with a good chance of dying. He cannot even depend on freedom unto death. He does manage to make the decision to go, even comes in for the farewell: 'Panama hat, tweed coat, raincoat over his arm, umbrella, bag'[50] – a strong, almost musical conclusion. But one does not see his exit, rather he remains 'impassive and motionless, his eyes fixed on Hamm, till the end.'[51] That is an allegory whose intention has evaporated. Aside from some differences, which may be decisive or completely irrelevant, this is identical with the beginning. No spectator and no philosopher can say if the play will not begin anew. The dialectic swings to a standstill.

As a whole, the play's plot is musically composed with two themes, like the double fugue of earlier times. The first theme is that it should end, a Schopenhauerian negation of the will to live become insignificant. Hamm strikes it up; the persons, no longer persons, become instruments of their situation, as if they were playing chamber music. 'Of all of Beckett's bizarre instruments, Hamm, who in *Endgame* sits blindly and immovably in his wheelchair, resounds with the most tones, the most surprising sound.'[52] Hamm's non-identity with himself motivates the course of the play. While he desires the end of the torment of a miserably infinite existence, he is concerned about his life, like a gentleman in his ominous 'prime' years. The peripheral paraphernalia of health are utmost in his mind. Yet he does not fear death, rather that death could miscarry; Kafka's motif of the hunter Grachus still resonates.[53] Just as important to him as his own bodily necessities is the certainty that Clov, ordered to gaze out, does not espy any sail or trail of smoke, that no rat or insect is stirring, with whom the calamity could begin anew; that he also does not see the perhaps surviving child, who could signify hope and for whom he lies in wait like

Herod the butcher for the *agnus dei*. Insecticide, which all along pointed toward the genocidal camps, becomes the final product of the domination of nature, which destroys itself. Only this content of life remains: that nothing be living. All existence is levelled to a life that is itself death, abstract domination. The second theme is attributed to Clov the servant. After an admittedly obscure history he sought refuge with Hamm; but he also resembles the son of the raging yet impotent patriarch. To give up obedience to the powerless is most difficult; the insignificant and obsolete struggles irresistably against its abolition. Both plots are counterpointed, since Hamm's will to die is identical with his life principle, while Clov's will to live may well bring about the death of both; Hamm says: 'Outside of here it's death.'[54] The antithesis of the heroes is also not fixed, rather their impulses converge; it is Clov who first speaks of the end. The scheme of the play's progression is the end game in chess, a typical, rather standard situation, separated from the middle game and its combinations by a caesura; these are also missing in the play, where intrigue and 'plot' are silently suspended. Only artistic mistakes or accidents, such as something growing somewhere, could cause unforeseen events, but not resourceful spirit. The field is almost empty, and what happened before can only be poorly construed from the positions of the few remaining figures. Hamm is the king, about whom everything turns and who can do nothing himself. The incongruity between chess as pastime and the excessive effort involved becomes on the stage an incongruity between athletic pretense and the lightweight actions that are performed. Whether the game ends with stalemate or with perpetual check, or whether Clov wins, remains unclear, as if clarity in that would already be too much meaning. Moreover, it is probably not so important, because everything would come to an end in stalemate as in checkmate. Otherwise, only the fleeting image of the child[55] breaks out of the circle, the most feeble reminder of Fortinbras or the child king. It could even be Clov's own abandoned child. But the oblique light falling from thence into the room is as weak as the helplessly helping arms extending from the windows at the conclusion of Kafka's *Trial*.

The history of the subject's end becomes thematic in an intermezzo, which can afford its symbolism, because it depicts the subject's own decrepitude and therefore that of its meaning. The hubris of idealism, the in-throning of man as creator in the center of creation, has entrenched itself in that 'bare interior' like a tyrant in his last days. There man repeats with a reduced, tiny imagination what man was once supposed to be; man repeats what was taken from him by social strictures as well as by today's cosmology, which he cannot escape. Clov is his male nurse. Hamm has himself shoved about by Clov into the middle of that *intérieur* which the world has become but which is also the interior of his own subjectivity:

HAMM: Take me for a little turn. (*Clov goes behind the chair and pushes it forward.*) Not too fast! (*Clov pushes chair.*) Right round the world! (*Clov pushes chair.*) Hug the walls, then back to the center again. (*Clov pushes chair.*) I was right in the center, wasn't I?[56]

The loss of the center, parodied here because that center itself was a lie, becomes the paltry object of carping and powerless pedantry:

CLOV: We haven't done the round.
HAMM: Back to my place. (*Clov pushes chair back to centre.*) Is that my place?
CLOV: I'll measure it.

HAMM: More or less! More or less!
CLOV: (*Moving chair slightly*) There!
HAMM: I'm more or less in the center?
CLOV: I'd say so.
HAMM: You'd say so! Put me right in the center!
CLOV: I'll go and get the tape.
HAMM: Roughly! Roughly! (*Clov moves chair slightly.*) Bang in the center![57]

What is payed back in this ludicrous ritual is nothing originally perpetrated by the subject. Subjectivity itself is guilty; that one even is. Original sin is heretically fused with creation. Being, trumpeted by existential philosophy as the meaning of being, becomes its antithesis. Panic fear of the reflex movements of living entities does not only drive untiringly toward the domination of nature: it also attaches itself to life as the ground of that calamity which life has become:

HAMM: All those I might have helped. (*Pause.*) Helped! (*Pause.*) Saved. (*Pause.*) Saved! (*Pause.*) The place was crawling with them! (*Pause. Violently.*) Use your head, can't you, use your head, you're on earth, there's no cure for that![58]

From that he draws the conclusion: 'The end is in the beginning and yet you go on.'[59] The autonomous moral law reverts anti-nomically from pure domination over nature into the duty to exterminate, which always lurked in the background:

HAMM: More complications' (*Clov gets down.*) Not an underplot, I trust. (*Clov moves ladder nearer window gets up on it, turns telescope on the without.*)
CLOV: (*Dismayed*) Looks like a small boy!
HAMM: (*Sarcastic*) A small … boy!
CLOV: I'll go and see. (*He gets down, drops the telescope, goes toward door, turns.*)
HAMM: No! (*Clov halts.*)
CLOV: No? A potential procreator?[60]

Such a total conception of duty stems from idealism, which is judged by a question the handicapped rebel Clov poses to his handicapped master:

CLOV: Any particular sector you fancy? Or merely the whole thing?[61]

That sounds like a reminder of Benjamin's insight that an intuited cell of reality counterbalances the remainder of the whole world. Totality, a pure postulate of the subject, is nothing. No sentence sounds more absurd than this most reasonable of sentences, which bargains 'the whole thing' down to 'merely,' to the phantom of an anthropocentrically dominated world. As reasonable as this most absurd observation is, it is nevertheless impossible to dispute the absurd aspects of Beckett's play just because they are confiscated by hurried apologetics and a desire for easy disposal. *Ratio,* having been fully instrumentalized, and therefore devoid of self-reflection and of reflection on what it has excluded, must seek that meaning it has itself extinguished. But in the condition that necessarily gave rise to this question, no answer is possible other than nothingness, which the form of the answer already is. The historical inevitability of this absurdity allows it to seem ontological; that is the veil of delusion produced by history itself. Beckett's drama rips through this veil. The immanent contradiction of the absurd, reason terminating in senselessness, emphatically reveals the possibility of a truth which can no longer even be thought; it undermines the absolute claim exercised by what merely is. Negative ontology is the negation of ontology: history alone has brought to maturity what was appropriated by the mythic power of timelessness. The historical fiber of situation and language in Beckett does not concretize – *more philosophico* – something unhistorical: precisely this procedure, typical of existential dramatists, is both foreign to art and philosophically obsolete. Beckett's once-and-for-all is rather infinite catastrophe; only 'that the earth is extinguished, although I never saw it lit'[62] justifies Clov's answer to Hamm's question: 'Do you not think this has gone on long enough?' 'Yes.'[63] Pre-history goes on, and the phantasm of infinity is only its curse. After Clov, commanded to look outside,[64] reports to the totally lame man what he sees of earth, Hamm entrusts to him his secret:

CLOV: (*Absorbed*) Mmm.
HAMM: Do you know what it is?
CLOV: (*As before*) Mmm.
HAMM: I was never there.[65]

Earth was never yet tread upon; the subject is not yet a subject.

Determinate negation becomes dramaturgical through consistent reversal. Both social partners qualify their insight that there is no more nature with the bourgeois 'You exaggerate.'[66] Prudence and circumspection are the tried-and-true means of sabotaging contemplation. They cause only melancholy reflection:

CLOV: (*Sadly*) No one that ever lived ever thought so crooked as we.[67]

Where they draw nearest to the truth, they experience their consciousness – doubly comical – as false consciousness; thus a condition is mirrored that reflection no longer reaches. The entire play is woven with the technique of reversal. It transfigures the empirical world into that world desultorily named already by the late Strindberg and in Expressionism. 'The whole house stinks of corpses ... The whole universe.'[68] Hamm, who then says 'to hell with the universe,' is just as much the descendant of Fichte, who disdains the world as nothing more than raw material and mere product, as he is the one without hope except for the cosmic night, which he implores with poetic quotes. Absolute, the world becomes a hell; there is nothing else. Beckett graphically stresses Hamm's sentence: 'Beyond is the ... OTHER hell.'[69] With a Brechtian commentary, he lets the distorted metaphysics of 'the here and now' shine through:

CLOV: Do you believe in the life to come?
HAMM: Mine was always like that. (*Exit Clov.*) Got him that time![70]

In his conception, Benjamin's notion of the 'dialectic at a standstill' comes into its own:

HAMM: It will be the end and there I'll be, wondering what can have brought it on and wondering what can have (he hesitates) ... why it was so long coming. (*Pause.*) There I'll be, in the old shelter, alone against the silence and ... (he hesitates) ... the stillness. If I can hold my peace, and sit quiet, it will be all over with sound and motion, all over and done with.[71]

That 'stillness' is the order which Clov supposedly loves and which he defines as the purpose of his functions:

CLOV: A world where all would be silent and still and each thing in its last place, under the last dust.[72]

To be sure, the Old Testament saying 'You shall become dust (*Staub*) again' is translated here into 'dirt' (*Dreck*). In the play, the substance of life, a life that is death, is the excretions. But the imageless image of death is one of indifference. In it, the distinction disappears: the distinction between absolute domination, the hell in which time is banished into space, in which nothing will change any more – and the messianic condition where everything would be in its proper place. The ultimate absurdity is that the repose of nothingness and that of reconciliation cannot be distinguished from each other. Hope creeps out of a world in which it is no more conserved than pap and pralines, and back where it came from, back into death. From it, the play derives its only consolation, a stoic one:

CLOV: There are so many terrible things now.
HAMM: No, no, there are not so many now.[73]

Consciousness begins to look its own demise in the eye, as if it wanted to survive the demise, as these two want to survive the destruction of their world. Proust, about whom the young Beckett wrote an essay, is said to have attempted to keep protocol on his own struggle with death, in notes which were to be integrated into the description of Bergotte's death. *Endgame* carries out this intention like a mandate from a testament.

Notes

1. Samuel Beckett, *Endgame: A Play in One Act* (New York: Grove Press, 1958), p. 38.
2. *Endgame*, pp. 29–30.
3. *Endgame*, pp. 24–25.
4. *Endgame*, p. 11.
5. *Endgame*, p. 13.
6. *Endgame*, p. 3.
7. *Endgame*, p. 27
8. *Endgame*, p. 13.
9. *Endgame*, p. 31.
10. Cf. Theodor W. Adorno, 'Reconciliation under Duress,' in Ernst Bloch *et al.*, *Aesthetics and Politics*, afterword Frederic Jameson (London: New Left Books, 1977), p. 161; and Georg Lukács, *The Meaning of Contemporary Realism*, trans. John and Necke Mander (London: Merlin Press, 1963), p. 31.
11. Karl Jaspers, *Philosophy*, trans. E.B. Ashton (Chicago and London: University of Chicago Press, 1970), II, p. 177.
12. *Philosophy*, II, p. 177.
13. *Philosophy*, II, p. 178; bracketed material omitted in English translation.
14. *Philosophy*, II, p. 197.
15. Heinrich Rickert, *Unmittelbarkeit und Sinndeutung* (Tübingen: Mohr, 1939), pp. 133 f.
16. Ernst Robert Curtius, *Französischer Geist im neuen Europa* (1925), rpt. in his *Französischer Geist im zwanzigsten Jahrhundert* (Bern: Francke, 1952), pp. 312–313; quoted in Rickert, *Unmittelbarkeit*, pp. 133 f., footnote.
17. *Endgame*, p. 44.
18. Max Horkheimer and Theodor W. Adorno, *Dialectic of Enlightenment*, trans. John Cumming (New York: Seabury Press, 1972), p. 234.

19. *Endgame*, p. 84.
20. *Endgame*, p. 69.
21. *Endgame*, p. 70.
22. *Endgame*, p. 24.
23. *Endgame*, p. 7.
24. *Endgame*, p. 4.
25. *Endgame*, p. 27.
26. *Endgame*, pp. 19–20.
27. *Endgame*, p. 45.
28. Cf. Günther Anders, *Die Antiquiertheit des Menschen* (Munich: Beck, 1956), p. 217.
29. *Endgame*, p. 29.
30. *Endgame*, pp. 46–47.
31. *Endgame*, p. 9.
32. *Endgame*, p. 14.
33. Theodor W. Adorno, 'Notes on Kafka,' in *Prisms,* trans. Samuel and Shierry Weber (1967; rpt. Cambridge: MIT Press, 1981), pp. 262–263 fn.
34. *Endgame*, p. 14.
★ 'Parapraxes' is the usual translation of Freud's *Fehlleistungen*, although Adorno writes *Fehlhandlung*: faulty acts, slip-ups.
35. Sigmund Freud, *The Standard Edition of the Complete Psychological Works*, trans. and ed. James Strachey (London: Hogarth Press, 1963), XV, p. 40. [The context is discussing 'parapraxes,' and Freud asserts that 'we formed an impression that in particular cases they seemed to be betraying a sense of their own.']
36. *Endgame*, pp. 32–33.
37. *Endgame*, p. 23.
38. Theodor W. Adorno, 'Voraussetzungen,' in *Noten zur Literatur III* (Frankfurt am Main: Suhrkamp, 1965), pp. 136–155; Horkheimer and Adorno, *Dialectic of Enlightenment*, pp. 24f.
39. Cf. Theodor W. Adorno, *Dissonanzen: Musik in der verwalteten Welt*, 2nd ed. (Göttingen: Vandenhoeck & Ruprecht, 1958), pp. 34 and 44.
40. *Endgame*, p. 31.
41. *Endgame*, p. 43.
42. *Endgame*, p. 50.
43. *Endgame*, pp. 64–65.
44. *Endgame*, p. 16
45. *Endgame*, p. 17.
46. Walter Benjamin, 'On Some Motifs in Baudelaire,' in his *Illuminations*, trans. Harry Zohn (New York: Schocken Books, 1969), pp. 183–184.
47. *Endgame*, p. 60.
48. *Endgame*, p. 36.
49. *Endgame*, p. 13; cf. p. 32.
50. *Endgame*, p. 82.
51. *Endgame*, p. 82.
52. Marie Luise von Kaschnitz, 'Lecture on Lucky,' Frankfurt University.
53. Adorno, 'Notes on Kafka,' *Prisms*, p. 260.
54. *Endgame*, p. 9.
55. *Endgame*, p. 78.
56. *Endgame*, p. 25.
57. *Endgame*, pp. 26–27.
58. *Endgame*, p. 68.
59. *Endgame*, p. 69.
60. *Endgame*, p. 78. [Adorno cites the divergent German edition, which here includes Clov's belief that he sees someone and Hamm's command to him to do his duty and extirpate that person.]
61. *Endgame*, p. 73

62. *Endgame*, p. 81.
63. *Endgame*, p. 45. [In the German edition, Clov says 'from time immemorial.']
64. *Endgame*, p. 72.
65. *Endgame*, p. 74.
66. *Endgame*, p. 11.
67. *Endgame*, p. 11.
68. *Endgame*, p. 46.
69. *Endgame*, p. 26. [Not capitalized in the English edition.]
70. *Endgame*, p. 49.
71. *Endgame*, p. 69
72. *Endgame*, p. 57.
73. *Endgame*, p. 44.

Adorno's 'Versuch, das Endspiel zu verstehen' was first published in *Noten zur Literatur II* (Frankfurt am Main, 1961). It appears here in English with the permission of Suhrkamp Verlag.

4.8 The Theatre of Genet: A Sociological Study (1968)

LUCIEN GOLDMANN

Translated by Pat Dreyfus, edited by Richard Schechner

1

Until a few years ago, aestheticians, critics, and literary historians accorded sociology only marginal status. However, the availability of Georg Lukács' early work, the psychological and epistemological researches of Jean Piaget, and the acceptance of the dialectic as genetic structuralism has changed all that.

Traditional sociology – which still dominates university teaching – tried to relate the *content* of a literary work to the *content* of the collective unconscious: how men think and act in daily life. Such criticism becomes more effective the more mundane is the writer being studied, content merely to relate his experiences without imaginatively transposing them. Structural sociology begins from premises that exclude those of traditional sociology. The five most important of these are:

1. The essential relation between social life and art does not lie in content but only in the *mental structures* – the 'categories' – which organize both the day-to-day consciousness of a social group and the artist's imagination.
2. Individual experience is too brief and limited to create such structures. They can be produced only within a social group. Individuals within groups experience together a set of problems for which they seek solutions. In other words, mental structures – or, abstractly, meaningful categorical structures – are not individual but social phenomena.
3. The relationship between the structure of day-to-day consciousness and the organization of the artist's imagination – in works that can be most easily studied – is more or less rigorously homologous. Often, however, it is a simple significative relation. Frequently, heterogenous or contradictory contents are structurally homologous: they are related on the level of categorical structures. For example, a fairy tale can be rigorously homologous *in its structure* to the experience of a particular social group; or, at the very least, it can be related meaningfully to that experience. No longer is there anything contradictory in asserting that a literary work is closely linked to social and historical reality as well as to the most powerful creative imagination.
4. The finest literary works are especially suited for such examination. In fact, the categorical structures – which are the object of this type of literary sociology – are what gives the work its unity: its specific aesthetic character.

5. The categorical structures are neither conscious nor unconscious in the Freudian sense (which implies repression). Rather, they are non-conscious processes – similar in certain ways to those mechanisms which regulate muscular and nervous activity. These are neither conscious nor repressed.

That is why discovering these structures (and thereby understanding the art work) is beyond the range of both purely literary studies and those oriented toward the writer's conscious intentions or hidden motives. Categorical structures can be found only through sociological investigation.

2

Genet's theatre offers a very interesting object for sociological study. He is the product of the French underclass of petty thieves and homosexuals; he describes and transposes his underclass experiences in his early works. But what makes Genet truly interesting (as an example of the relation between modern industrial society and literary creation) is the encounter in his work between an implicit but radical rejection of society and the problems of a still active European intelligentsia which is hostile to today's corporate capitalism. The underclass has been expelled from respectable society. But Genet has interiorized this expulsion and raised it to the level of world vision.

This encounter is complicated. The rejection of industrial society is coupled with the knowledge that this society provides a high standard of living for most of those living in it. A previously unheard-of number of consumer possibilities (cars, apartments, vacations, etc.) create an apparent unity among individuals. However, this same consumer orientation stifles the deep need for authenticity, for communication with one's fellow men, for the development of one's own intellectual and emotional life. This conflict produces a relatively broad sector of the lower middle class which, while seemingly integrated into the existing social order, feels oppressed and frustrated, particularly in its emotional life.

It would seem that the first task of a sociological analysis of modern French theatre would be to relate this lower middle class to characters like Ionesco's Berenger who, although unsatisfied and out of place, is unable to resist; indeed, he cannot even conceive of the possibility of resistance. However, alongside this widespread 'Berenger phenomenon,' there are – particularly in France and Italy – strong Socialist and anarchist unionist traditions. These comprise a small number of workers and creative intellectuals and a fairly large number of educated people who refuse to accede to modern capitalism. They are concerned with the problem of establishing a human order that will effectively guarantee individual liberties. The frustrated hope for a Socialist revolution in the West and the development of Stalinism in the East constituted a set of difficult problems for this group. It now finds itself maintaining a genuinely negative attitude toward capitalism (which it rejects more firmly than does the lower middle class) while knowing that this rejection brings with it intellectual and practical difficulties which are incomparably serious and decisive.

The early novels of Malraux, Robbe-Grillet's fiction, films like *Last Year at Marienbad*, some of Beckett's writings, and, primarily, Genet's theatre should be studied as the literary transposition of this latter group's world vision.

Genet's plays result from an encounter between the radical negative of the underclass poet who, as he says, is in no way rebelling against existing society (making no claims on it) and the consciousness which exists among progressive workers and the most radical intellectuals, who see the difficulty – increasingly evident as the years go by – of finding satisfaction through revolution. Another characteristic of Genet's theatre (and one which is most interesting to the cultural sociologist) is the way in which it unintentionally incorporates certain decisive experiences of the European Left. A play like *The Balcony* cannot be understood without taking these experiences into account. The sociologist must ask, of course, how this incorporation takes place; it is important to know because one finds analogous phenomena in other authors: Gombrowicz's *The Marriage*, for example. But whatever the answer, the fact remains that Genet, the non-conformist sub-proletarian whose work is essentially moral and lyrical, is the only modern French dramatist who assigns a central place to the problems of history as a whole, thereby making them the key to understanding his work's unity.

3

So far, Genet has written five plays: *Deathwatch*, *The Maids*, *The Balcony*, *The Blacks*, and *The Screens*. These plays show an ever richer and more complex – but also more unified – expression of one and the same problem.

Deathwatch belongs to the poetic universe of the non-conformist underclass. Lefranc strangles Maurice to win Green Eyes' acceptance and become Snowball's equal. But his act is gratuitous, for, as Green Eyes says:

> Don't talk to me. Don't put your hands on me. Do you know what misfortune is? Don't you know that I kept hoping to avoid it? And you thought you could become, all by yourself, without the help of heaven, as great as me! Maybe overshadow me? You poor fool, don't you realize it's impossible to overshadow me? I didn't want what happened to me to happen. It was all given to me. A gift from God or the devil, but something I didn't want.

Later, again Green Eyes:

> You don't know the first thing about misfortune if you think you can choose it. I didn't want mine. It chose me. It fell right smack on my puss, and I tried everything to shake it off. I struggled, I boxed, I danced, I even sang, and, funny as it may seem, I refused it at first. It was only when I saw that everything was irremediable that I calmed down. I've only just barely accepted it. It had to be total.

Deathwatch is already a strictly coherent work, although it is Genet's first play. It describes the individual's struggle for moral recognition where the only things of moral value are those which ordinary society condemns. This divides the world into two kinds of men: the weak – the petty thieves and crooks, and the strong – the natural murderers whose criminal character is part of the natural order.

The Maids is more complex and, in certain crucial ways, different. Although the play is as radical and non-conformist as *Deathwatch*, it is no longer set entirely within the marginal world of the underclass. In *The Maids* the opposition between the maids and Madame is central: we cannot understand Claire and Solange without knowing of their hatred for Madame. *The Maids* shows the basic structure of Genet's world, the setting for *The Balcony*, *The Blacks*, and, to a degree, *The Screens*. This world pivots on the relationship between the ruled and the rulers: the maids and Madame, the rebels and the balcony, the blacks and the whites, the colonials and the colonists. It is a dialectical relationship, one of hatred and fascination. Hatred is fundamental to all these plays. It becomes love-hate only through the fascination which the ruled have for the rulers, a fascination based on the utter incapacity of revolution to succeed. It is not until *The Screens* that the rulers can be defeated. Madame cannot be killed; the revolt is put down; the whites are routed only in fantasy.

The action of these plays unfolds in a static, insufficient universe; but this insufficiency is compensated by a fantasy ritual which permits the ruled to identify, either with the rulers or with subjects who end domination through revolution. In this way, the ruled – but only in their imagination – cause values to exist that are not found in the real world. In *The Maids*, Claire plays Madame and Solange plays Claire. In *The Balcony*, minor employees play a bishop, a judge, a general (and also, it is true, a slave). In *The Blacks*, Negroes on the balcony play whites and below, on the stage, enact the purely imaginary murder of a white woman. In *The Screens*, before the revolt breaks out, Saïd plays a fiancé laden with costly gifts; later his wife and his mother play the owners of a farmyard full of poultry. On one side of the stage Warda – who, through tremendous effort, has become the perfect whore – enables the oppressed to ritualize the poetic and intensely felt communion between man and woman.

In short, in a world where the power of the rulers cannot be shaken, where the ruled are motivated by love-hate for the rulers, an inadequate reality offers the possibility of a poetic-religious ritual through which the ruled identify with the rulers and succeed in fantasy in overcoming them.

4

Let us return to our structural comparison of *Deathwatch* and *The Maids*. The world of the first play is structurally homologous to middle-class society – not as it is but as it wishes itself to be. Only here it is presented inversely. Love is at the centre, but it is homosexual love. Value and recognition are a function of the dangerous nature of the characters' lives. But danger does not consist in choosing a perilous profession or in socially recognized heroism. Rather, danger comes from crime and murder, which lead to imprisonment and death. *Deathwatch* also presents an elitist view which is confirmed by contemporary society. Green Eyes and Snowball are creatures of misfortune; their nature dooms them willy-nilly to be murderers. This is why Lefranc, who kills by intention, can never be admitted to their community. The special power of *Deathwatch* comes from the implicit criticism of the purely verbal and often deceitful values of accepted morality and the intensity which marks human experiences when they are forbidden and acted out by the outcast and condemned.

Just how different is *The Maids*? First, the world here is divided. On one side are the strong

– whose lives consist of lies and prating but who are invincible: Madame and Monsieur. On the other side are the maids – authentic, intense, simultaneously hating and loving their masters. A world, therefore, where everything is positive and negative at once and where the one authentic value is the imaginary realization of love-hate in the ritual which the maids resume each evening (and which they now act out for spectators, on the stage).

The maids are authentic, while Madame – powerful and insuperable – is nothing but a puppet. Solange and Claire have a vivid fantasy of following their condemned lover into exile. Later, Madame appears and touches the same theme in almost the exact words. But her verbs are conditional, she is self-satisfied; and, anyway, Monsieur will not be convicted: her words lack all sincerity. 'Of course, none of this is serious, but if it were, Solange, it would be a joy for me to bear his cross. I'd follow him from place to place, from prison to prison, on foot if need be, as far as the penal colony, Solange!' The little word 'Solange' at the end of the speech betrays how utterly superficial Madame's emotions are: play-acting for the benefit of the maids. But, pushing the farce to its extreme, Genet also has her say that this situation makes her 'almost happier, monstrously happy!' until the moment when, exhausted, she ends her speech: 'I'll simply die if I don't have a cigarette!'

The telephone call from Monsieur interrupts the maids in the middle of their ritual. He has been released from prison. Solange exclaims: 'The judges have their damned nerve letting him go. It's a mockery of justice. It's an insult to us!' They will be discovered, arrested, and sentenced for libel. In *Deathwatch*, Solange and Claire would have proudly accepted this as the confirmation of their existence. But the world of *The Maids* is radically different. Here the sentencing will be a shameful defeat. Thus they try to poison Madame, fail, and follow their fantasy ritual into reality. The sentence for libel is transformed into one for murder. In becoming a murderer, Solange has become 'Mademoiselle Solange Lemercier. [...] I'm Madame's equal and I, too, hold my head high.' She has become an autonomous creature for all eternity.

Before dying, Claire says:

We'll see this through to the end. You will have to live for both of us, just you alone. You'll have to be very strong. [...] And above all, after you've been convicted, don't forget that I am inside of you. A precious burden. We will be beautiful, joyous and free. Solange, we don't have a minute to lose.

In both human and spiritual terms the maids have won over the powerful puppet, Madame. They really live in appearances while Madame – lying and ridiculous – only appears to live in reality. But this has been so since the play began. Madame cannot be defeated and the maids are forced to destroy themselves in order to preserve the seriousness and authenticity of their existence. *The Maids* is an embodiment of the static dialectic of despair. By interiorizing the conflict between ruled and rulers, Genet becomes a radical pessimist for whom art and appearance are the only possible compensations for a deceitful and inadequate reality.

5

With *The Balcony*, Genet introduces a new element: he incorporates social and political reality not merely as a framework but as a possible future. Even if this future comes to nothing, its presence brings into his work the principle of motion. *The Balcony* begins as the other Genet plays do: little people acting out their dreams inside a house of illusions. But right from the start, and particularly in Scene V, two new tensions are present: there is a revolt which threatens the established order, and this house of illusions belongs to the chief of police and his girlfriend, Irma (who are both disappointed that no client has ever asked to play the chief's role). The play shows how the image of the chief of police penetrates the ritual of the house of illusions and how this is related to the revolt's defeat.

Scene V takes place in the rear of the house – in the rooms of the administration. Here we meet the chief of police, the pimp Arthur, Irma, and Carmen, a whore whom Irma has hired to help run the house. A few words about Carmen: she epitomizes the general predicament expressed in the play (a technique repeated in *The Screens*). The rebels' struggle against the balcony is one between death and life, between an order in which values exist only in fantasy and ritual and the attempt to create a new order in which these values penetrate life itself, making it unnecessary to escape into fantasy because living at last will be authentic. Carmen, like the world, is forced to choose between her genuine love for her daughter, whom she has sent to the country, and her activities as a whore in the brothel – where she used to play the role of the Virgin. Irma tells Carmen that she will have to give up her daughter and – because Carmen no longer wishes to help administer the house – she is given the role of Saint Theresa.

IRMA: Whether dead or alive, your daughter is dead. Think of the charming grave, adorned with daisies and artificial wreaths, at the far end of the garden. [...] and that garden in your heart, where you'll be able to look after it.
CARMEN: I'd have loved to see her again.
IRMA: You'll keep her image in the image of the garden and the garden in your heart under the flaming robe of Saint Theresa. And you hesitate? I offer you the very finest of deaths, and you hesitate? Are you a coward?

Carmen renounces life in favor of illusion, just as the revolt will be quelled and the house of illusions rebuilt.

The revolt itself is doomed because it has split into two factions – one oriented toward liberty and fantasy and the other, led by Roger, organized in a disciplined, repressive way. Chantal, the girl from the house of illusions who has become the rebels' muse, is killed and her name and image glorified, inscribed on the banners of the repressive forces. In the rebuilt house there is friction between the bishop, general, and judge (who are now real dignitaries and therefore puppets) and the chief of police, who has the power. The long-awaited event happens at last: Roger presents himself and asks to play the chief of police. But Roger recognizes that this is nothing but play-acting, a ritual. His revolutionary essence consisted precisely in his efforts to create a reality which had no need of fantasy or ritual. Despairing, he castrates himself: thus fantasy accords with the reality of suppressed revolt. Roger's gesture soils the carpet. He is thrown out and the real chief of police takes his place. Outside, machine-guns are heard. The Queen (Irma) asks: 'Who is it? … Our side … or rebels? … Or? …' The answer: 'Someone dreaming, Madame.'

The Balcony poses a very important problem to the sociologist. The play represents a transposition of the decisive historical events of the first half of the 20th century in a manner that is very likely non-conscious and involuntary. The theme of *The Balcony* is how awareness of the importance of the executive function develops in a society which has long been dominated by property-owners but in which people still imagine power to be in the hands of long out-dated fixtures: the bishop, the judge, and the general. And Genet is telling us that this awareness is created by the threat of revolution and its subsequent defeat: a fairly accurate reflection of Western European history between 1917 and 1923. Although we cannot describe the mechanism by which these events were incorporated into *The Balcony*, we do know that the Polish aristocrat Gombrowicz incorporated into *The Marriage* the contrary but complementary experience of Eastern Europe. In neither case is the incorporation conscious or voluntary.

The Blacks represents another step. Here hope and the prospect of victory make their way into the world of the play, if only in a peripheral way. Outside, distantly, the blacks are engaged in a real struggle. One leader has been executed, but another has already replaced him. And this revolutionary struggle is linked to what happens on stage. 'Thanks to us, they've sensed nothing of what's going on elsewhere.' On stage, however, in the present world, the situation is homologous to *The Maids* and *The Balcony*. Like Solange and Claire, like the humble clients of Irma's house, like the dreamy revolutionaries in the Andromeda network, the blacks enact a nightly ritual: the murder of a white woman. Like the maids and Roger, the only way the blacks can overcome the whites *on stage* is in fantasy. As in *The Maids* and *The Balcony*, this fantasy is comprised of revolt, hatred, and fascination.

So much for similarities. What are the differences? Everything points to the lengthening shadow of the real struggle going on outside the theatre; and the revolution outside is in the interest of the blacks who charade for their white audience (both real in the theatre and make-believe on the balcony). But victory offstage is only a hope, as distant in time as it is in space.

But the nature of the onstage ritual has changed, and this is particularly evident in the way it affects the real world. Claire and Solange commit suicide, Roger mutilates himself, the blacks kill one of their own. This killing, however, is performed within the framework of a real struggle which strengthens the hope of victory. Onstage, *The Blacks* ends with an apotheosis, as does *The Maids*. In that play the apotheosis is a real suicide; in *The Blacks* it is an imaginary murder of an imaginary white woman but the real hope of future victory over the whites: the self-awareness of the blacks is authentic. The play ends with Village and Virtue on stage. He wants to express his love for her but can do so only with words and images borrowed from the whites. She is disappointed, but offers her assistance. 'I'll help you. At least, there's one sure thing: you won't be able to wind your fingers in my long golden hair.' The destruction of the caricatured whites, even if only imaginary, will oblige the blacks to discover authentic words of love, original gestures, a truly black culture rooted in their own essence, which they have just discovered.

Nor is the relationship between ruled and rulers the same in *The Blacks* as in *The Maids*. It still involves a synthesis of hatred and fascination; but in *The Maids* fascination was dominant. In *The Blacks*, hatred is the authentic fact of black existence. We may now ask: what social group's point of view is represented by *The Maids*, *The Balcony*, and *The Blacks*? It seems at least possible that the basic structure of these three plays corresponds to the mental and spiritual structure of the French radical Left; this structure includes – among other things – these five elements:

1. Affirmation of the existence of a radical opposition between classes, and the need to strengthen that opposition.
2. Recognition of the fact that the rulers of Western society cannot be overcome by violence: this society is without revolutionary perspective.

3. Fascination with the political and technological success of corporative capitalism.
4. Condemnation in moral and human terms of the social reality created by corporative capitalism.
5. Justification, in the name of moral, aesthetic, and human values, of the radical struggle against corporative capitalism. These values – once compromise and acceptance of oppression have both been rejected – can alone give value to a society founded on minority rule, lies, and the decline of culture.

6

We may now begin to analyze *The Screens*, which, beyond its unquestioned artistic value, has the added significance of being one of the first works of contemporary French drama to be animated by a belief in man's ability to resist regimentation and constraint. The action is divided into four stages, representing both society's development and Saïd's increasingly radical attitudes.

At first we find the ruled-ruler situation already familiar to us from Genet's earlier plays. However, this social order is extremely provisional – the revolution will succeed – and this means that hatred is tempered and that the ritual-brothel, trunkful of gifts, farm-yard – is of only peripheral importance. In the second stage, Saïd, surrounded by his wife and mother, clashes with the social order and is rejected as a thief and outsider. From that moment, the ritual loses its importance for all three of them. Saïd no longer goes to the brothel, because his struggle for an authentic life has begun. The Arab village, which still accepts the rule and morality of the colonists, at first rejects Saïd and his family. Kadidja and the village women prevent Saïd's mother from taking part in the funeral. The Mother resorts to magic and appeals to the dead man's mouth. But he too rejects her, in a scene which summarizes the entire play (the dead man was a member of the revolution and therefore incarnates the three social orders of *The Screens*: the Arab village, the revolt, and the kingdom of the dead). In prison Saïd and Leila grow closer to each other: they go together toward radical politics, monstrosity, evil, and negation.

The third stage begins with the outbreak of the revolt. Kadidja, who is the incarnation of the village, is killed. But before yielding to death she exhorts the village to revolt and thereby embraces the position she condemned in Saïd and Leila.

> I'm dead? So I am. Well, not yet! I haven't finished my job. So, Death, I'll fight it out with you! Saïd, Leila, my loved ones! You, too, in the evening related the day's evil to each other. You realized that in evil lay the only hope. Evil, wonderful evil, you who remain when all goes to pot, miraculous evil, you're going to help us. I beg of you, evil, and I beg you standing upright, impregnate my people. And let them not be idle!

But Saïd, Leila, and the Mother – who started the resistance as thieves and arsonists – will withdraw from it now that it is organized and taken over by the entire community. Their action was personal. They will pursue their course of negativity and evil to its absolute limit. Saïd poisons watering troughs, an act which harms the rebels more than the colonists. The Mother kills a soldier, apparently by accident. Later, in the kingdom of the dead, she admits that it was intentional. She denies taking part in the resistance, even when her deed objectively defines her as a participant.

Stage four: the revolt is successful and a new order has been created, one which has neither oppressed nor oppressors and which Genet describes in a manner that is no longer caricature but serious and dignified. Still, it is an order and it will necessarily reappropriate many elements of the order it has replaced.

As the revolutionary social order adopts the patterns of the order it has replaced, the third and last social order appears: the kingdom of the dead. It is beyond contradictions and all those who previously were enemies exist in harmony before entering the true realm of the dead: Nothingness. The Mother arrives here to wait for her two children. Like Kadidja she is replaced on earth by a mythic figure, Ommu, who declares: 'Kadidja! Kadidja! They say you're dead, since you're in the earth, but enter my body and inspire me! As for Saïd, may he be blessed!' Later, in the kingdom of the dead, Kadidja will say to the Mother: 'Yes. Ommu has taken over from us, from you and me.'

Saïd returns to the village and meets the representatives of the new order. Ommu, who incarnates the expectations of the village, notes that Saïd did everything he could to betray them but that 'he didn't achieve much.' She says that she will be able to disappear if – in the new revolutionary order – there is a place for Saïd, whose truth is not of those which must be realized in action, but which alone can become song and give meaning to the new society. 'There are truths that must never be applied, those that must be made to live through the song they've become.' The revolutionary leaders offer to pardon Saïd. Saïd is ready for one last act of treachery. 'I'm very much in demand. I can set my price.' But the Mother cries out from the realm of death:

> Saïd! Saïd! You're not going to give in? She-dog that I am, she-dog big with a mongrel pup, I kept you in my guts not to become one more one less! A dog's life, kicks in the ribs and maybe rabies! Less than a patch of nettles, less than what you're worth, until noon today – it's noon sharp – I thought it was hatred that was leading *me*, Saïd!

Saïd reconsiders. He is about to leave, when he is killed by one of the Arabs. There is still no place for him in the new order, as there was none in the old. Ommu – representing the hopes of the village – must remain on earth. 'Burying this one, screaming at that one: I'll live to a hundred.' The Mother waits for Leila (who died earlier) and Saïd. But they do not come to the kingdom of the dead. All that gets there of Leila is her veil. As for Saïd, he has bypassed the kingdom of the dead and entered Nothingness direct.

So not to be guilty of omitting a particularly important element from this schematic picture, I would like to add that the development of the brothel – the house of illusions – runs parallel to the other events in the play. With the revolt and the resistance the prostitutes – who were essential and autonomous in the society of oppressed and oppressors – become the same as all the other members of the community: respected citizens who fight and whose function is recognized and respected. But after victory there is no place for them in the new order. Warda is killed by the village women: she carries Leila's veil to the Mother in the kingdom of the dead.

How does *The Screens* fit into Genet's development? It would be both easy and inadequate to say that Genet here returns to his point of departure: anarchy. Saïd does, to be sure, share many features with the narrator of *The Thief's Journal* and the attitudes which shaped *Deathwatch*. But there are fundamental differences too. The problem of the meaning and quality of social orders which is so important in *The Screens* is not even mentioned in the early works. The characters in *Deathwatch* are non-conformists, outcasts. Saïd is a universal figure, moral to be sure, but through his negativity, also political. As Ommu says to the soldiers of the victorious revolution: 'You and your pals are proof that we need Saïd.'

Some of the decisive experiences of the European Left have been incorporated into the play. First of all: the possibility of a successful revolt in Algeria – and in other countries throughout the world as well. Then: victory alone will not guarantee men happiness and freedom, nor secure a place within the new order for those values which, as Ommu says, are not to be realized in action but are to become song. The play's three social orders correspond to three basic concepts of European Socialist thought: the class society based on oppression; the society born of the successful revolt which does away with oppression but is still rooted in constraint; and the vision of a classless society with no restraints. This last serves the same need for Socialist thought as the Kingdom of Heaven does in Christian eschatology.

Saïd and through him Genet refuse to participate in these three orders. There is another path which must be followed if we wish to remain men. *The Screens* is the first French theatre work to describe the possibilities that men still have intact and, paradoxical as this may sound, to put on stage a hero who – in and through his negativity – is ultimately positive. For whatever one may think of Saïd's values (and needless to say they are not ours) they are authentic and undisputed within the world of the play. And, unlike Solange and Claire, unlike the rebels of *The Balcony*, unlike the blacks, Saïd fulfills his ideals outside of ritual – in his life: he remains unbowed and intact to the very end. Having freed himself of all fascination and all hatred for both the old and new rulers, he follows his own path and enters Nothingness naturally and undefeated.

Is it coincidence that *The Screens* was written recently? Is it just a result of Genet's intellectual evolution, or is something much more at stake: the first symptom of an historical turning-point? Difficult as it is to answer this question, let us note that a current has developed in Western European Marxist thought whose objectives will dominate any discussion of Socialism's prospects in today's world. This current affirms the inadequacy of the old revolutionary schema and, in particular, the impossibility of revolution within contemporary Western society. This current also sees the dangers to liberty inherent in old revolutionary ideas and the need to replace these ideas with something better adapted to the evolution of modern industrial society. Of course, those who support the new ideas sense that estrangement from the traditional position constitutes a grave and painful predicament. Transposed to politics, this feeling corresponds to a 'betrayal' of the old point of view (it is not really, however: Saïd 'did not achieve much' in the way of treason) and the stock it put in revolution. Also, insofar as these thinkers are really Socialists, they know that the new point of view runs a considerable risk of being compromised and integrated into the existing capitalist order. They know that any reform action, whatever its nature, involves the danger of corruption and that the only defense against this is a radical rejection of any compromise with the technocratic society.

Until now this predicament has been purely theoretical and conceptual. However, things are changing; and the cultural sociologist will find the following facts to be of particular significance:

1. That a writer whose last plays were focused on the problem of history can now put a character on stage who, although no longer involved with the traditional path of revolt, rejects the three

orders of Socialist thought without, however, putting them all on the same level. Indeed, it is not possible to put the caricatured order of the oppressors and colonists on the same level as the successful revolt or death – which are also rejected but treated in a dignified and serious way.

2. That this character, whom nothing has been able to break, maintains his negativity to the very end.

3. That without making the slightest compromise, he is still unbowed when he leaves the world where Ommu (and, with her, the entire village) must wait for a future in which another Saïd will at last have a place.

Is *The Screens* an isolated, accidental occurrence? Or is it the sign of a turning point in our intellectual and social life?

Part 5
Contemporary Theatre and Performance

Timeline

	Social, cultural and political context	Theatre
1964		Odin Theatre founded by Eugenio Barba, Oslo, moves to permanent company home in Denmark in 1966
1967	Sexual Offences Act (decriminalizes homosexual relations between consenting adults over the age of 21 (UK) Abortion Act (legalizing abortion in UK) Roland Barthes's seminal essay *The Death of the Author* first published.	*Hair: The American Tribal Love-Rock Musical* (USA) The Performance Group founded, USA (Richard Schechner)
1968	Assassination of Martin Luther King, Jr Assassination of Robert Kennedy Student demonstrations and occupations in France	Theatres Act 1968 – abolition of stage censorship in UK *Dionysus in 69* (first production of The Performance Group, USA)
1969	Stonewall Riots (New York) – riots inaugurated by the gay community seen as the beginnings of gay activism Woodstock Festival, New York The internet developed out of US military defence project VCR video player invented – becomes widely available by 1977	
1970	Germaine Greer's feminist polemic *The Female Eunuch* becomes a best-seller	
1972	Invention of email communication (in wide public use by the mid-1990s) Mobile or cell phone invented, made widely available to the general public by Vodaphone in 1985	
1973	UK joins European Economic Community	
1974	Labour Party wins general election (UK)	The Wooster Group formed (USA) (Elizabeth LeCompte and Spalding Gray, USA)
1976		Philip Glass and Robert Wilson's *Einstein on the Beach* premieres
1978		Pina Bausch's *Café Müller*, Germany
1979	Conservative Party wins general election (UK) – Margaret Thatcher becomes Prime Minister Soviet Union invades Afghanistan Jean-François Lyotard's *The Postmodern Condition: A Report on Knowledge* first published	Eugenio Barba and collaborators found the International School of Theatre Anthropology (ISTA)

	Social, cultural and political context	Theatre
1980	Hunger strikes by IRA prisoners begin in Northern Ireland Iran/Iraq War commences	Split Britches formed in New York
1981	Martial law in Poland The beginnings of the AIDS crisis IBM produces PC computer for the mass market	*Quartet*: Heiner Müller *Simulacra and Simulation*: Jean Baudrillard, published in French (translated into English in 1994)
1982	Music recorded on CD made available	*Brecht's Ashes* (1982–4), Odin Theatre
1983	USA invades Grenada	*Theatre de Complicite* founded by Simon McBurney, Annabel Arden and Marcello Magni
1984	Coal miners strike begins (UK, March) IRA attempt to assassinate British Prime Minister Margaret Thatcher Apple Macintosh produces its first computers for mass market	Forced Entertainment founded in Sheffeld, UK *L.S.D. (… Just the High Points …)*: The Wooster Group
1985	Coal miners return to work (March) Mikhail Gorbachev becomes leader of the Soviet Union	
1986		DV8 Physical Theatre formed (Lloyd Newson, UK)
1989	George H. W. Bush becomes President of the USA East Germany opens border with West Germany, demolition of Berlin Wall begins Following the development of the world wide web (www) the internet opens up to wide public usage	
1990	Reunification of Germany First Gulf War (ends 1991)	*Belle Reprieve*: Split Britches
1991		*Angels in America: Millennium Approaches*: Tony Kushner
1992		*Angels in America: Perestroika*: Tony Kushner Robert Wilson's production of *Dr Faustus Lights the Lights* (Gertrude Stein – see Part 2)
1993	Bill Clinton becomes President of the USA	
1994		*Speak Bitterness*: Forced Entertainment
1995		*Blasted*: Sarah Kane *The Story of M*: SuAndi Heiner Müller dies
1996	DVD players being sold in Japan (and in the USA in 1997)	

	Social, cultural and political context	Theatre
1997	'New' Labour wins landslide general election victory – Tony Blair becomes Prime Minister	*House/Lights*: The Wooster Group (an adaptation of Gertrude Stein's *Dr Faustus Lights the Lights* – see Part 2)
1998	Google, the free internet search engine, launched	
1999/ 2000	Millennium celebrations	Jerzy Grotowski dies (1999) Hans Thies-Lehmann: *Postdramatic Theatre* (in English)
2001	George W. Bush becomes President of the USA September 11 – terrorist attack on the USA (known since as the events of 9/11) Apple iPod available on mass market Wikipedia, the free internet encyclopaedia, launched	
2003	Anglo-American-led invasion of Iraq (Second Gulf War) DVD sales overtake VHS video sales in USA	
2005		Harold Pinter awarded the Nobel Prize *Product*: Mark Ravenhill
2008	Global financial collapse	*Spectacular*: Forced Entertainment Jacques Rancière, *The Emancipated Spectator*
2009	Barack Obama becomes President of the USA	Pina Bausch dies Complicite's production of *Endgame* Royal National Theatre, UK, begins programme of live simulcasting of productions across the UK. These are broadcast globally within a couple of years (known as NT Live)
2012	Barack Obama re-elected as President of the USA	

Introduction

JOHN F. DEENEY AND MAGGIE B. GALE

The plethora of phenomena in the theatre landscape of the last few decades that have challenged the traditional forms of drama and 'its' theatre with aesthetic consistency and inventiveness suggests that it is justified to speak of a new *paradigm* ... These works of theatre also become paradigmatic because they are widely recognized – albeit not always welcomed – as an authentic testimony of the times. (Lehmann 2006: 24)

A NY ACCOUNT OF CONTEMPORARY performance has to encompass the varying nuances of an enormous diversity of experimentation in work produced over the past half century in Europe and the United States. Some would agree with Hans-Thies Lehmann that there has been a 'new paradigm' in theatre and performance, whereas others would see the differences in practice as signifying that no such paradigm is possible to either configure or fix. In Part 5 we try to embrace these two positions and bring together diverse texts that, in different ways, represent points on a map of contemporary theatre and performance practice. In order to explore how these materials might be seen as responding to their contemporary moment, we use a number of aesthetic and critical frameworks: the idea of the contemporary, postmodernity and the postmodern and the 'postdramatic'.

The contemporary and contemporaneity

'Contemporary' is a word commonly used to denote that which is happening in the here and now. Many cultural critics see an analysis of the contemporary as problematic because it cannot be viewed from a 'historical' perspective (see Gale 2013). Clearly, all the materials in this anthology reflect upon and are reflections of their contemporary moment. However, whilst something contemporary may lie at the cutting edge of practice during one decade, its quality of contemporaneity will quickly fade in another. Here we use the word 'contemporary' in a generic sense to try to group together work from the 1970s onwards. We identify shared attitudes underlying the disparate territories of theatre and performance practice, and also explore the ways in which these practices engage with the complex dynamics of the contemporary world.

Historically the period following on from the social upheavals of the late 1950s and 1960s (see Parts 3 and 4) is constituted by the most extraordinary communications and technological revolution, which has changed forever the ways in which we as humans engage in the processes of social and personal encounter and exchange that theatre and performance exemplify so well. The new generation of communications and digital technology have become commonplace but have not in and of themselves transformed theatre and performance beyond recognition. They have however – from technological advances made in scenography, to the increase in use of TV, video and digital technology in performance – impacted on the ways and means by which theatre and performance are both conceived and received. In terms of theatre and performance, Tim Etchells also notes that such a 'shifting of cultural forms' – a move to 'soundbite' culture reliant on the visual and on technology – creates 'changes in our consciousness' (Etchells 1996b: 111). With a culture so dependent on technology, we have come to expect a different kind of experience from theatre and performance: our horizons of expectation are vastly different from audiences of the eras covered in the earlier Parts of this anthology.

Beyond issues of technological advance, performance work developed from the late 1960s onwards more explicitly explores the potential of the body to signify and express experience. In the 1970s and 1980s Europe in particular saw an explosion of theatre and performance work that was influenced by developments in dance and performance art. The work of practitioners such as Pina Bausch (1940–2009) in Germany and DV8 Physical Theatre in Britain, for example, shifted the boundaries between forms of performance. Dance Theatre, in some ways reminiscent of the work of innovative modernist choreographers associated with the Historical Avant-Garde, and influenced by mid-century practitioners such as Merce Cunningham (1919–2009) in the USA, dominated European stages during the latter decades of the twentieth century. Such work is not detailed here, but its influences can be felt in some of the practice we explore, certainly in the case of practice where the body becomes as important as the text and is deliberately framed as part of the rich textuality of performance (see 5.1, 5.3 and 5.4). What can also be felt in the practices documented here is the influence of interdisciplinarity: using anthropological, philosophical and scientific discourse and engaging with the various areas of cultural theory have become common practice for artist and critic alike.

Many of the texts included in this Part are 'performance' texts, 'versions' of the textual component of a performance; they are effectively samples, they are not representations of the central component of a performance in the same way as a play might be (see 5.1–5.4, for example). Traditionally a play is written prior to a rehearsal process, although it might be changed and developed during that process. The included performance texts are products of a process of theatre/performance making. What they give us are *traces* of performance. At one extreme Peggy Phelan has suggested that, 'Performance's only life is in the present. Performance cannot be saved, recorded, documented, or otherwise participate in the circulation of representations of representation … Performance's being … becomes itself through disappearance' (Phelan 1993: 146). Whilst we acknowledge the particularity of performance existing only in the here and now of its live moment, we revert to having to rely upon the power of language, text and visual stimulae to enable us to study elements of performance: these cannot comprehensively 'document' the performance but can open up interpretive possibilities. Whilst we acknowledge the problematic relationship between the written word and the live performance – that one cannot stand in for the other – the desire to include a range of materials for exploration means that the traces provided by the performance text have to suffice as starting points for discussion.

As with the other Parts in this anthology, the critical and theoretical materials are included in order to extend a range of available reading strategies. Similarly, the range of performance texts included allow for a wide spectrum of contrasting opportunities in our reading of contemporary performance practice over the last quarter of the twentieth century and the first decades of the twenty-first. For our purposes here then, 'contemporary theatre and performance' is an umbrella term for a geographically expansive movement, a pluralistic movement with a range of connected and unconnected modes of, and attitudes to, process and practice.

Postmodernity and postmodernism: the contexts of contemporary performance

> The real postmodernism … was about flight from modernism, a revival of the classical, the figurative, the decorative. Postmodernism was inherently backward-looking and nostalgic … nostalgia was not really about the past but about its erasure by democratic mass society. Postmodernism was the great leveler of differences, horizontally across culture, vertically within history. Postmodernism was the cultural dominant of late capitalism, commodity driven, and fundamentally reactionary. (Fuchs 1996: 144)

Contemporary performance practice is a direct result of the cultural modes it both engages with and rejects, but it cannot be seen as an absolute and straightforward break from the conventions it challenges. Thus, Bert O. States's suggestion that, 'the difference between art paradigms and scientific paradigms is that art rarely discards any previous achievement' is relevant to our understanding of the modes of performance in contemporary practice (States 1985: 88–9). Equally relevant here is the theoretical framework of postmodernity which roughly covers the period represented in this Part. Postmodernity is a historical phase that follows on from the modernist tropes of the first half of the twentieth century. Generally understood as having emerged from the 1950s onwards, it is a term used to reflect a cultural shift which, following the end of the Second World War, is post-Holocaust and riven with ideological, technological, political and philosophical uncertainty. The nature of this uncertainty frequently centres around ideas of the end of progress, social and cultural fragmentation, and struggles with the failing utopian project of consensus and cohesion: typically framed by the idea, for example, that we are somehow now at the 'end of history' (see also Parts 3 and 4). Postmodernity is also conscious of the growing impossibility of any realization of utopian ideals. It is, rather, driven, certainly in its general aesthetic, by a playful juxtaposition of the classic and the modern. In architecture, for example, postmodernity has been expressed in the mixing of materials such as marble and glass inside concrete or metal structures, and the externalizing of traditionally internalized components such as pipework. In art, pastiche and kitsch might reign supreme, or we might find reference to nostalgic or iconic images in cutting-edge avant-garde film and so on. Cultural products often operate through the playing against each other of the personal and the public, through a play between the live and the recorded and a celebration of a complex hybridity of form. The 'postmodern' is therefore a product of postmodernity.

The easy association of the idea of 'the end of history' (see Parts 3 and 4) with postmodernism is queried in Nick Kaye's analysis of the difference between the modernist and the postmodernist position with regard to the historical and its function:

> while the 'modernist' project rejects the past precisely because it can be read, understood and so transcended, the postmodern self-consciously 'replays' images of a past that cannot be known, but that can only be constructed and re-constructed through a play of entirely contemporary references to the idea of the past. (Kaye 1994: 20)

For Jean-François Lyotard, the 'postmodern condition' is wrought with uncertainty and the proliferation of social and economic instability. Within this the 'self' exists in a 'fabric of relations that is now more complex and mobile than ever before' (Lyotard 1997: 15). This has produced a kind of crisis of subjectivity, manifest in a great deal of contemporary performance. Thus, the postmodern in performance is exemplified by fragmentation and self-referentiality, but also by nostalgia, the sublime, the uncanny and by an engagement with a dystopian perspective on our social and political world. Some postmodern performance appears more concerned with style and display and moves away entirely from the 'functional austerity' of modernist works (Birringer 1993: 5).

In terms of distinguishing a typology of postmodern performance, practitioner and theorist Tim Etchells connects a number of characteristics of performance work during the 1980s and 1990s – such as the 're-framing of narrative', the use of 'media-culture imagery', 'questioning the idea of the body as an essential object', a re-thinking of the location of performance and a retreat into or an embracing of the 'fictional', the 'dreamlike' and the 'imaginary' (see Etchells 1996b). Such characteristics might certainly be classed as postmodern in their appearance, but we should also note here the ever-present resistance of some theorists to define the 'postmodern' in any complete sense. David Harvey has suggested that as the definition of 'modernism' is so problematic and 'confused' so too is the definition of the 'postmodern', which is meant to represent a departure from it. He uses Terry Eagleton to elucidate this point, and it is useful to refer directly to Eagleton's summary here:

> There is, perhaps, a degree of consensus that the typical post-modernist artefact is playful, self-ironizing and even schizoid; and that it reacts to the austere autonomy of high modernism by impudently embracing the language of commerce and the commodity. Its stance towards cultural tradition is one of irreverent pastiche, and its contrived depthlessness undermines all metaphysical solemnities, sometimes by a brutal aesthetics of squalor and shock. (qtd in Harvey 1996: 7–8)

If we think back to the work in Part 2, we can see that many of the aesthetic strategies of the Historical Avant-Garde reappear within the postmodern framework – the centrality of playfulness, reference to popular culture, a desire for a lack of fixity and so on. The texts included in Part 2, although appearing to have little in common at times, shared certain 'attitudes' to theatre and performance, such as a breaking away from the dominance or linearity of text, or the reframing of the visual in performance – either scenographically or in terms of the role of the performer. So too, the texts included in this part share certain 'attitudes', in particular to the idea and function of narrative. One of the tenets of postmodern theory is the idea of the collapse of 'grand narratives'; thus it is useful to explore the ways in which contemporary theatre and performance practice has reconceptualized the creation, exploration and expression of narrative.

The death of narrative

Contemporary theatre and performance frequently draw attention to narrative and its fragmentation, and undermine or play with its role and function. Narrative, story, storytelling and story making and unmaking are central to postmodern performance practice as is typified in the work of both SuAndi and Mark Ravenhill, included in this volume (see 5.4 and 5.7). In a text such as Forced Entertainment's *Speak Bitterness* (5.2), the absence of named characters or indeed the lack of apportioning text to specified speakers does not, however, undermine the dominant function of narration and narrative within the text. What is important is the chance assignment, combination and tonal delivery of the narrative, not the chronology or linearity. Similarly, the effect of narrative is not intentionally laid out by the authors – meaning is gathered, if at all, on a personal basis and cumulatively through either the recognition or non-recognition of patterns in the language or in the actions the language narrates. We connect to the text in short moments through the images it conjures, the moments and events that the text narrates. As such, *Speak Bitterness* could be considered as a postmodern performance text *par excellence*. It demonstrates Lyotard's 'incredulity toward metanarratives' (Lyotard 1997: xxiv), and remains rich on the level of micro-narrative as opposed to metanarrative. Linda Hutcheon also suggests the question is not about metanarrative in retreat, it is more to do with a confrontation with the unproblematic assertion of a metanarrative that is somehow a representation of 'truth' (Hutcheon 1989).

What is often absent in the performance practices included here is a linearity of sequence, 'character', and any security of knowledge of the authentic or authoritative voice. Confessions or testimony may be central to the composition of the text, but they may be a game, an act, a playful bricolage, a fabrication and manipulation of imagined and experienced events. Whether the events confessed are 'real' or not is irrelevant, what is important is the telling and witnessing of them. The relationship between *acting* and *being* – arguably so central to differentiating between theatre and performance – here becomes blurred: a feature of many of the performance works which come out of the period we cover in this part (see Auslander 1997). In the work of Forced Entertainment, SuAndi, and Mark Ravenhill for example, there is less of an engagement with the idea of 'acting' than there is with the presence/non-presence of the performer; many of the texts are self-generated and so too the relationship between author and performer is radically altered (see also 5.3). What comes into question is the relationship between the 'fictional' and the 'real' and this is a central conundrum in a great deal of the cultural theory and practice which has been produced during the last fifty years. Whilst ideas of replication and authenticity were foundational to Walter Benjamin's exploration of cultural production (see 3.9), Baudrillard's seminal book *Simulacra and Simulation* has become a key reference point for contemporary cultural theory and practice (see 5.10 for an extract).

Jean Baudrillard: 'The Precession of Simulacra' (5.10)

In her chapter 'Postmodernism and the Scene of Theater', Elinor Fuchs elaborates a thesis concerning how the 'the protean image of the theatrical' is embedded in the writings of many leading philosophers and cultural theorists from the 1960s to the 1980s (Fuchs 1996: 147). Citing such seminal figures as Guy Debord, Jacques Derrida, Hélène Cixous, Gilles Deleuze and Félix Guattari, Fuchs argues that 'semiotic, deconstructive, neo-Marxist [and] feminist' writings from this period, 'serve as an anticipation and explication of the postmodern paradigm shift' (ibid: 146). For Fuchs, this meeting point between theatricality and the postmodern reaches its pinnacle in the work of Jean Baudrillard, who 'contemplates the movement of society from a stable real to a final and negative hyper-theatre' (ibid: 151).

Baudrillard's relevance to theatre, and particularly to contemporary performance, can be traced in the extracts included in this part from his *Simulacra and Simulation*. Here Baudrillard argues that, in our excessively technologically mediatized world, 'simulation' threatens the difference between the 'true' and the 'false', the 'real' and the 'imaginary'. Our experience of the world is now so immensely mediated that 'the real' no longer constitutes an objective concrete actuality, as something that can then be 'reflected' or 'represented' to reveal its truth content. Thus – as spectators – our experience of events, however actual or real these original events might be, is *simulated*. For example, Baudrillard controversially compared the 1991 Gulf War to the film thriller *Capricorn One* (1977), in which astronauts supposedly exploring the planet Mars, the events of which are being televised around the world, are in reality being filmed in a studio (Baudrillard 2006: 61). Baudrillard is seeking to challenge the very efficacy, even the possibility, of *representation* as something that operates on 'the principle of the equivalence of the sign and of the real' (5.10: 823). Thus, transmutation of the image (or sign) can be characterized in four consecutive stages:

> it is the reflection of a profound reality; it masks and denatures a profound reality; it masks the *absence* of a profound reality; it has no relation to any reality whatsoever: it is its own pure simulacrum. (ibid: 823)

When Baudrillard states, '[i]llusion is no longer possible, because the real is no longer possible', he offers both an ideological critique of contemporary society and provides a cue to performance practitioners and theorists for questioning and reformulating the underpinnings of those theatre practices – particularly Naturalism and realism – but also any practice that operates within 'conventional' representational regimes (Baudrillard 2006: 19). This is also where we can a make a useful distinction between the philosophical and political impulses behind the Historical Avant-Garde and those of contemporary performance. We might view the Surrealists, for example, as seeking the means to create radical cultural and aesthetic forms that render an *authenticity* to human subjectivity. For Baudrillard, however, as for a range of contemporary performance makers, the very idea of an authentic subject is up for grabs. Furthermore, if theatricality, mediatization and deconstructing ideas of 'the real' are central to Baudrillard's critique of society, so too are they in the making and understanding of spectatorship in contemporary performance.

Heiner Müller (1929–95): *Quartet* (5.1)

Heiner Müller's *Quartet* (1981) is a play/performance text that exemplifies the new developments in dramaturgy and performance that were a response to the kinds of ideas circulated by theorists of the postmodern. The idea, as Fuchs suggests, that character, or the stable subject, can no longer be relied upon, shifts the focus of text from psychologically layered characters to fractured subjects on whom we rely to depict the world they inhabit, at the same time as our sense of being out of joint with it. *Quartet* is inspired by Laclos's novel *Les Liaisons Dangereuses* (1782), which was written in pre-revolutionary France and critiques the decadence and sexual amorality of the aristocracy. The novel is built around a series of letters between Merteuil and Valmont, and this form is reflected in Müller's text, which is composed around a series of extended speeches in which the two protagonists engage in a form of play-acting where identity, subjectivity, power and desire become entwined. *Quartet*, however, is not simply about the psycho-sexual. From the opening of the play, where Müller gives the 'Timespace' location of the text as: '*Drawing room before the French Revolution/Air raid shelter after World War III*', the mise-en-scène of *Quartet* disrupts the very possibility of coherence: it is not clear where we are – in the past, the present or the future. There is a sense in which 'reality' has become hybridized: what we see in front of us is a kind of 'mash-up' of time where the theatrical present cannot be located in one historical moment. In this sense Müller's text asserts a political relevance without exclusively adhering to a Brechtian idea of polemics, although it requires a Brechtian 'distancing' and an excessive sense of contradiction, which depends on simultaneity rather than a process of dialectics (see Part 3). Müller relies on what Rancière later calls the 'emancipated spectator' (see 5.11), to read the sensate and cognate simultaneously in the theatrical moment.

Authorship and Textuality – Roland Barthes: 'The Death of the Author' (5.8), Jacques Rancière: 'The Emancipated Spectator' (5.11) and Eugenio Barba: 'Dramaturgy' and 'Montage' (5.9)

Contemporary performance repeatedly breaks the traditional linearity of text – often more than one narrative is at play at any one time, and may or may not be revealed or explored in chronology. Much early postmodern performance played with the formal qualities of text, fragmenting or repeating it and exploring the play of tone and rhythm that language might offer rather than its semantic significance or meaning (see, for example, Robert Wilson's early work with Philip Glass such as *Einstein on the Beach* [1976]; see Holmberg 1996). Similarly, contemporary performance often plays with the compositional possibilities of repeated patterns of sound, movement and chosen 'rules' in the process of making work (see also Part 2). These 'rules' are often utilized as a structuring device similar to those that are found in a game – so whilst the performers are generating materials through improvisation, for example, the 'rules' provide a dramaturgical framework for processing those materials and constituting them into the performance (see Barba, 5.9, and Etchells 1996a). What the performance might then capitalize upon is its ability to elicit response rather than 'interpretation', to produce experience rather than meaning.

We need here to make reference to philosopher and cultural theorist Roland Barthes's seminal 1967 essay 'The Death of the Author', in which he made the radical observation that meaning is not to be derived from the singular position of the author, but rather, it is created by the reader. In other words, 'in the multiplicity of writing, everything is to be *disentangled*, nothing *deciphered*' (5.8: 806). The author ceases to function as a 'god-like' figure, the creator of all meaning, and is replaced with the mediation, by the reader, of all they themselves bring to the reading of the text – their history, their social milieu, their memory, their sexuality and so on. Such a stark departure from a traditional view of the relationship between the maker of the artwork, the artwork itself and its audience, as Barthes's essay suggests, marks a cultural turn in the democratizing of the role of the spectator. Writing forty years later, the French philosopher Jacques Rancière revived the ideas rehearsed by Barthes in 'The Death of the Author' with his essay 'The Emancipated Spectator' (originally translated in 2007, see 5.11). However, Rancière, in his specific focus on the act of spectating (as opposed to the solitary one of 'reading'), argues how historically and philosophically in theatre and performance the binary oppositions between 'viewing/knowing, appearance/reality activity/passivity' are not inherent but function as 'embodied allegories of inequality' (5.11: 834). Rancière does not suggest here that such inequalities are overturned simply through innovative practices that dismantle the conventional theatre's fourth wall (ibid: 834); indeed, he is suspicious of forms of experiment 'which use the blurring of boundaries and the confusion of roles to enhance the effect of performance without questioning its principles' (ibid: 839). He also identifies another problem; in the work of practitioners and theorists as diverse as Brecht and Artaud – the idea that 'distanced investigation' versus 'vital participation' (ibid: 831) demonstrates a shared vision for the ultimate kind of liberation of the spectator, where 'the theatre is presented as a mediation striving for its own abolition' (ibid: 832). For Rancière, the fundamental 'communitarian power' of theatre in contemporary life can only be fully recognized if the relationship between cause and effect is dispelled by 'spectators who play the role of active interpreters, who develop their own translation in order to appropriate the "story" and make it their own story. An emancipated community is a community of narrators and translators' (ibid: 839).

Taken together Barthes and Rancière offer at least two momentous theoretical propositions which have had an impact on contemporary performance practices. The first is the idea that the *intention* of the author, in terms of the creation of meaning, may bear little relation to the actual and multiple readings of the artwork by the reader or, for our purposes, the spectator. The second is the recognition that written language cannot be assumed to be the dominant feature of performance or cultural production, nor is it singular – language can be visual, kinaesthetic, musical. In fact, what comes into play is a textuality and an intertextuality in terms of the composition of an artwork as a cultural signifier, to which no one meaning can be attached. Thus, for both Barthes and Rancière the authority of the author is not fixed, nor is the relationship between an object (cause) and what that object signifies (effect). One should also not underestimate here the influence such writings carry in the critical framing of contemporary performance, both aesthetically and politically.

If we focus on the ways in which text is composed, processed and then located inside the performance in relation to both the performer, their performed materials and the spectator, we can see connections between the seemingly diverse practices included in this Part. Early in the period, companies such as Odin Teatret in Denmark created performance works from found texts and improvisation. The performance would come out of a process whereby the director, Eugenio Barba (b. 1936), mediated their creations through his own compositional technique. All this took place without a desire to create fixed meaning, but, rather, to materialize performed moments, image sequences, soundscapes and relationships between performers. The montage of materials therefore would not be driven by any sense of a singular or overarching narrative but rather a bricolage of responses to materials and ideas generated by a particular theme. So, for example, in the original version of Odin's *Brecht's Ashes* (1982–4), the source materials included a biography of Brecht (see Part 3), text from his plays and poetry such as *Mother Courage* (1939), and historical events from Brecht's life – the First World War, the rise of Nazism and so on. These were responded to by the performers in the improvisational process, and the material they generated was then formed into a performative composition by Barba. This kind of process has almost become understood as conventional practice now, but in its time presented a radical departure in European practice whereby the ensemble, the director and the spectator all, in one way or another, assume the role of 'author' in terms of the generation of possible 'meanings' from a performance event.

In 'Dramaturgy' and 'Montage' (5.9) Barba writes of the strategies involved in making performance. His work comes out of a tradition inspired by the performance training work of Jerzy Grotowski (1933–99) (see Grotowski 2002 [1968]) and from that of ensemble theatre making, which has developed and thrived during the period covered here. Barba sees text, performance and spectatorship as intertwined: all are elements of the process of making a performance and constitute the basis of 'action', from the perspective of both the performer and the spectator: 'Everything that works directly on the spectators' attention, on their understanding, their emotions, their kinaesthesia, is an action' (5.9: 808). Thus, for Barba, dramaturgy – a term which has a variety of implied meanings from the process of researching a production to the management of the creation and composition of text in rehearsal – is relevant to much more than the text as the written or spoken word. The 'text' of performance relates to its overall texture, its textuality – as Barba reminds us, the word text originates from a conception of a 'weaving together' of different elements: 'In this sense, there is no performance which does not have "text"' (ibid). Thus in 'Montage' (5.9), where Barba discusses the processing of materials generated for performance, he uses a theoretical concept originating in film practice to build a strategy for describing the practice of performance making. Here, the term 'montage' relates to the ways in which materials both come out of a creative impulse and are then (re)placed into a performative sequence. Again, the object is not to 'represent or to reproduce' in any straightforward way. The sequence of movements created by a performer are not imitative of the image, word or instruction which may have inspired them, and instead are motivated by the performer's personal response to the given impulse. This, in turn, is influenced by their existing and available movement vocabulary, their memory, their own research and so on. What Barba then suggests is that the products of the performers' creative process can be reprocessed and remontaged without regard to their origin or the potential fixing of meaning for the spectator. The business of a theatre maker is not to define an assumed reception of the materials which comprise the performance.

Barba's work comes out of a particular tradition and specific cultural moment. Working from the 1970s and 1980s onwards, he developed a kind of anthropology of theatre, working across Europe, South America and Asia, building a network of experimental theatre companies and practitioners. He connects his own work with the theories and practices of a variety of twentieth-century innovative practitioners such as Stanislavski, Eisenstein, Artaud, Brecht and Grotowski. His intercultural interweaving of Western and non-Western performance techniques and desire to find a communion between performer and spectator might appear to be somehow old-fashioned. But this has been married with a technique of theatre making which works against an under-standing of theatre as commodity or overt polemic, producing instead theatre which is technically sophisticated and demanding from the perspective of the performer and audience. Text is less important than texture; experience is not mediated by a traditional dramaturgy of chronological narrative, plot and character. Barba's theatre and the intercultural International School of Theatre Anthropology (ISTA, founded in 1979) are predicated on the creation of a laboratory for experi-mentation and an artistic space in which the unique qualities of theatre and performance can be investigated (see Barba and Savarese 2006). Although unique and somewhat removed from, or at least standing back from, a great deal of practice created by their contemporaries, the tradition developed by Barba and Odin Teatret lies at one end of a spectrum of contemporary performance practices, but shares with others the desire to 'attack', as Lehmann notes, 'language's function of representation' (Lehmann 2006: 146).

Tim Etchells/Forced Entertainment: *Speak Bitterness* (5.2)

Originally created as a six-hour durational performance, the text of *Speak Bitterness* included in this volume represents the performance score at a particular historical moment; as Etchells notes, the text 'remains decidedly in process' (5.2: 735). Originally performed by eight performers working inside a blue tarpaulin box, where the audience were free to come and go at will during the six hours, the 'theatre' version of the piece represented here has been developed from 1995 onwards. For this, one wall of the tarpaulin box was 'lost' to fit the piece into a more traditional stage space. On the back of the tarpaulin is printed the phrase 'SPEAK BITTERNESS' and the ceiling is hung with bare electric light bulbs extended over the audience. This scenography remains fairly constant over the lifetime of the piece, as Hugo Glendinning's photographs from the 2009 version imply (see Figures 26 and 27).

In reworking the piece over time, the company have made use of video recording in rehearsal and tried to preserve the 'feeling' of the original durational version – 'spatial and performance intimacy, a sense of real-time process' – whilst adding what Etchells calls 'structural architecture' (5.2: 735). In the original version, scripts, the long list of confessions and catalogues of statements of guilt printed on sheets of paper, were placed on the table, which runs right across the front of the stage. Chairs were placed at the table and at the back of the stage – and performers chose which bits of text to read or perform on a random basis, adhering to the improvisational 'rules' set up during the process of making the performance. In the version reproduced here, there is a 'fixed' ordering of the text or, rather, the 'structural architecture' is less dependent on the rhythm and chance moments of an improvisational format. Some sections and the ordering of the text in the 'theatre' version in performance, however, continue to be improvised. Whilst there is some repetition of ideas, confessions or motifs, and occasional moments are extended beyond the bare statement of fact – the confession of working for the Beckhams, for example, extends beyond one statement, to another and another, all related to the final statement 'We just wanted to work for the Beckhams we didn't really mind in what capacity' (ibid: 740). The piece still gives the impression of 'a practice of listing and of cataloguing-through-language', as Etchells notes. Reminiscent of the performance practice of some of the Historical Avant-Garde (see Part 2), Etchells is at pains to point out, however, that this 'text' is not like the 'modernist' experiments in collage where images integrate and overlay each other. Rather, 'the act of listing does not layer, merge, overlay, re-mix or blur together its contents. Lists rather, with a seriality that implies but never fully delivers narrative, let each of their items stand alone but together, a menu or line of ingredients rather than a soup' (ibid: 734). We should note here, however, that our propensity to organize materials on reception can lead us to reformulate the text as delivered in terms of Barba's 'montage': we try to find connections between images implied, events described, the performers' tone and mood of delivery and their relationships with each other on stage. We might, for example, after noting the reference to celebrities such as the artist Tracey Emin and the footballer David Beckham, expect to find more direct references to celebrities, but are just as likely to find references to more anonymized figures – Colin, Jason, Cynthia and so on. Etchells is aware of and plays with this expectation when he states that, 'Lists are blank or "spacious" since the job of guessing the constituency of listed items and of unpacking their individual meaning is left to the viewer' (ibid: 734). The audience experiences the moment but produces the 'meaning' evoking the terms of Roland Barthes's 'The Death of the Author' (see above). This impetus is built into a great deal of Forced Entertainment's work. They often play with the idea of gaps or emptiness: the creation of 'space', as Etchells calls it, is a deliberate strategy played out in their practice. Whilst this again connects their work process to Barba's idea of dramaturgy (5.9), it is important to note that their work comes out of a very different tradition, equally linked to live art and performance art as it is to a theatre heritage. Both rely on the spectator to 'complete' the picture as it were, to become their own 'author'. Here the connection to innovations in art practice and the development of conceptual live art in the 1970s are paramount. In this sense we might see 'performance art' as performance practices 'that explicitly reject, oppose, expose or move beyond the framework of theatre' (Ridout 2007: 5; see also Féral 1982). A great deal of contemporary performance plays with the theatrical, and self-consciously manipulates and challenges our understanding and expectation of a theatre event.

In *Speak Bitterness*, the performers are all dressed in anonymous, everyday 'working' or semi-formal clothing: grey, black or dark-coloured suits. They come to the front of the stage one, two or more at a time, and pick up the sheets of paper where the texts are printed: they might remain standing or they might sit. The tone and speed of delivery of the text varies, and there are clear moments when it seems as if the performers are in dialogue or are inflecting their speech with a particular emotional 'mood', but almost as soon as this appears to be happening in a manner which might elicit empathy, something changes or the speaker switches: our moment of recognition is quickly undermined. None of this is implied in the text as printed in this anthology where, as we have noted previously, speakers are not assigned specific text, nor is there any sense of stage direction, rhythm, pause and so on. An 'understanding' of *Speak Bitterness* cannot be derived or reduced from its arbitrary content. Predicated on the 'live dynamic of the performers interacting with each other and the text' (ibid: 735), this is a piece, like much of the work in Part 5, that is more specifically concerned with the act and experience of spectating, of perception and of the relationship between the elements of an event. As Etchells notes:

> Far from the blanket communal comfort it may appear to offer, the 'we' of *Speak Bitterness* both refuses and accuses those watching, dividing and subdividing the supposedly shared social space of the auditorium. (ibid: 734)

Peggy Phelan reminds us that Etchells uses the term 'witness' rather than 'spectator', as he notes, 'to witness an event is to be present at it in some fundamentally ethical way, to feel the weight of things and one's place in them, even if that place is simply, for the moment, as an on-looker' (Etchells 2006: 18). For Phelan, witnessing, as distinct from spectating, implies an ethical response where we are directly implicated (ibid: 9). The way in which this operates on the level of the 'political' is different from the 'political' as we have identified it elsewhere in this anthology (see Part 3). Whilst Etchells notes the 'suspect certainties of what other people call political theatre' (ibid: 19), his use of the idea of witnessing evokes a differently conceptualized political concern enacted in performance. This is much more explorative of the contingencies of relationship and uncertainties of encounter in the *moment* of performance, than any identifiable political programme or ideology.

Hans-Thies Lehmann and 'postdramatic theatre' (5.12)

Forced Entertainment's *Speak Bitterness* provides a useful example of what Hans-Thies Lehmann has named 'postdramatic theatre' (Lehmann 2006). The term was originally coined by performance theorist Richard Schechner to describe certain aspects of avant-garde practices from the 1960s associated with 'happenings', and a refusal of the primacy or relevance of the dramatic text (see Schechner 1988; Sandford 1995; and Bottoms 2011). However, Lehmann's developed concept of postdramatic theatre has, over the past decade, offered a paradigm for understanding a range of diverse performance practices within contemporary theatre that seek to challenge – aesthetically, culturally and politically – the authority of drama-based theatre. Postdramatic theatre is not, however, reducible to a particular style and form of theatre and/or performance practice. Lehmann's proposal that, 'there is never a harmonious relationship but rather a perpetual conflict between text and scene', reflects upon the ways in which contemporary practitioners have sought to problematize notions of the dramatic (Lehmann 2006: 145).

> The adjective 'postdramatic' denotes a theatre that feels bound to operate beyond drama, at a time 'after' the authority of the dramatic paradigm in theatre. What it does not mean is an abstract negation and mere looking away from the tradition of drama. 'After' drama means that it lives on as a structure – however weakened and exhausted – of the 'normal' theatre; as an expectation of large parts of its audience, as a foundation for many of its means of representation. (ibid: 27)

In his attempts to define the 'postdramatic', Lehmann refers to theatre and performance practices where conventional Aristotelian-influenced dramatic forms are substituted by self-consciously deconstructed narrative, and compositional strategies which are 'manufactured', not to support logic and internal coherence, but, rather, as a challenge to linearity and synthesis. Simply put, 'postdramatic' theatre relies on a reordering of the hierarchies of performance where text no longer determines or defines performance. As a term, 'postdramatic' does not mean 'post-drama', as in without dramatic text. Lehmann uses the word 'dramatic' in all its complexity and what he tries to identify is a *vocabulary* of contemporary theatre and performance which certain companies and practitioners appear to share. Thus, as with postmodernism, 'the prefix "post"' indicates that a culture or artistic practice has stepped out of the previously unquestioned horizon of modernity but still exists with some kind of reference to it' (ibid). Lehmann's postdramatic theatre interfaces with the idea of 'postmodern theatre' discussed elsewhere in this introduction. However, postdramatic refers to both critical interventions and aesthetic practices that cannot simply be subsumed under the umbrella of postmodernism. For example, Caryl Churchill's *Far Away* (see 5.6) engages with a number of postmodern discourses, such as fragmentation and the 'problem' of contemporary subjectivity and agency. Nevertheless, however innovative we might regard Churchill's use of dramatic form to be, the play does not fundamentally challenge the basis of the solo-authored play text as a means for mediating contemporary concerns. Other performance scores which rely on textuality rather than semantics – produced through collaborative or ensemble-based practices – can more easily be categorized as postdramatic in their challenge to a formal adherence to and traditional hierarchy of performance elements. Similarly, 'postmodern' ideas and attitudes might find a resonance in contemporary productions of classical texts, yet such productions do not necessarily challenge the value and efficacy of 'drama'. Thus the Wooster Group, who cut, delete, reformulate, regurgitate and redefine classical texts, and Odin, who mix sources, relayer, extract from and rebind texts, might both be seen as companies whose work is postdramatic despite the fact that their work borrows both aesthetically, technically and compositionally from very diverse cultural heritages.

Lehmann offers us another model of definition of practice to add to the categories of postmodern and contemporary. But just as there are crossovers and crosscurrents here, so too the postdramatic cannot be separated out in total. It is possible for a production to take a postmodern approach – look for example again at Figure 6, where we see a scenographically postmodern conceptualization of Chekhov's *Three Sisters* – without altering the formal and absolutely modernist qualities of the dramatic text. This kind of approach has been common during the 1980s and 1990s where productions of classic texts have been inflected by postmodern ideas. However, this does not make them postdramatic in Lehmann's terms.

Groups and ensembles – aesthetic/political strategies: Split Britches and *Belle Reprieve* (5.3)

Making theatre and performance within an ensemble or collective organizational structure is not new to the contemporary period, but arguably such practice has become more commonplace amongst theatre and performance makers in Europe and in the USA. Whilst many of these groups have dynamic 'leaders' or directors, they place an emphasis on collective ways of working in which the hierarchies so prevalent in more 'traditional' theatre practice are subverted. Often all members of the group are paid on an equal basis and each member has multiple responsibilities within the company, as performer, technician, administrator and so on. Sometimes membership of the group remains fairly permanent, as is the case with the Wooster Group, the now disbanded Goat Island (USA), Odin Teatret (Denmark) and Forced Entertainment (UK). Equally the group may have a core membership whilst additional performers become members for the duration of a project such as is the case with Théâtre du Soleil (France: see Williams 1999). Some ensembles follow a particular theatre heritage, an ethos or a commonly shared ethic; others have a shared training, as is the case with Theatre de Complicite (UK). In Europe in particular, where public funding has been more readily available than in the USA, these groups make performances over a prolonged period, sometimes one or two years, and the work stays in the repertoire for a further two or three, or even more, years.

The work of many of these performance groups often exemplifies a conscious desire to push at the boundaries of, and interconnect, different art forms, thus moving towards a hybridity of form. Here the lines between performance, performance art, live art and theatre have become blurred, shifting or interchangeable. There is also a shared interest in experimentation with the performer/spectator relationship – with the spectator becoming more directly implicated in the *composition* of the performance, for example. Similarly, many of the performance groups dislodge the primacy and centrality of the text, patchworking or sampling different classical texts together with personal materials such as autobiographical texts, or simply fragmenting and rearranging classical texts. One example here is the Wooster Group's *House/Lights* (1997), which performs a 'playful interweaving' of Gertrude Stein's *Dr Faustus Lights the Lights* (2:10) and Joseph Mawra's B-movie, *Olga's House of Shame* (1964) (see Quick 2007: 14). In *Belle Reprieve*, the performance troupe Split Britches reimagines Tennessee Williams' *A Streetcar Named Desire* (1947). As an ensemble the group was originally made up of three performers – Peggy Shaw, Lois Weaver and Deb Margolin (see 5.3). Whilst some of their works such as *Lesbians Who Kill* (1992) deal specifically with lesbian politics and lifestyles, *Belle Reprieve* is a complex interweaving of personal narratives woven through the structure and key tropes of the original Tennessee Williams play. It was originally created in collaboration with Bloolips performer Bette Bourne and with Paul Shaw. As a company Split Britches draw heavily from popular culture, vaudeville and drag, countering mainstream assimilationist agendas around sexuality and gender, though developing a collaborative performance practice that combines personal narratives with the reimagining of canonical texts. In *Belle Repreive* this reimagining is anchored in the theatrical and performative interrogation of the 'butch-femme aesthetic'. The text plays with characters moving in and out of the tragic, the comedic and the domestic. It is a witty but layered investigation of sexuality, desire, role-play and subjectivity. With music and cross-dressing, the text/performance epitomizes postmodern performance's mash-up of classical and popular culture.

Solo performance and the auto/biographical 'I': SuAndi and *The Story of M* (5.4)

Whilst the choice to work in a collective through an ensemble method is often a political one, informed by a commitment to a less hierarchical approach to theatre making, so too many performers choosing to work in the field of solo performance do so through a belief in its political as well as aesthetic potential and economic viability. This is even more so in the case of autobiographical solo work which embodies a strategic impulse to unveil, to retell and to reposition the subject. As Deirdre Heddon succinctly summarizes:

> The vast majority of autobiographical performances have been concerned with using the public arena of performance in order to 'speak out', attempting to make visible denied or marginalised subjects, or to 'talk back', aiming to challenge, contest and problematise dominant representations and assumptions about those subjects. (Heddon 2007: 20)

SuAndi is one of the foremost artists of her generation and describes herself as a 'performance poet'. She is known for her work with black arts organizations in Britain and elsewhere, and in particular for the ways in which her activism as a black woman artist and performer shapes her practice with 'diverse ... and disadvantaged, communities' (Aston and Harris 2008: 60). This sense of the artist as activist also strongly impacts on her solo performance work as *The Story of M* (5.4) exemplifies: her ethnic background has a significant impact on the 'production, reception and perception of her work' (ibid: 62). Her work also epitomizes the performance and compositional strategies utilized by a number of other solo performance artists of her generation.

The Story of M is performed by SuAndi herself, who for most of the text 'plays' her mother dying of cancer in hospital. *M* tells the story of her life as a working woman and a mother. It is not until the end of the text, as Aston has noted, that we realize that her mother is a white woman who has married a black man, even though the text is strewn with details of the racial hatred and ignorance which have surrounded *M* and her family. Here, also, the 'mother' transforms into the daughter, SuAndi the performer, who removes her 'costume' and closes the performance by interconnecting her mother's life with her own, 'it's only the body that dies. But the spirit continues and you carry it here, in this place of love' (5.4: 780). The text represents a recapitulation of a life story which runs from the middle years of the twentieth century and depicts the interconnection between issues of class, sexism and race. Aston notes the weaving together by *M* of issues of racism and discourses of 'pollution or contamination' in her descriptions of the social response to her interracial marriage and her children (Aston 2003: 145). *M*, a working-class woman, transgresses many social taboos: children out of wedlock, sharp social wit, a woman bringing up a family on her own, a mother of mixed-race offspring and so on. The racial abuse she suffers is unveiled in such a way as to express a history of class as well as racial stereotypes – she is an Irish working-class woman living in England at a time when the Irish were also socially stigmatized. *The Story of M* touches on the personal and the political simultaneously, celebrating the multicultural world of working-class Manchester and Liverpool in the 1950s, as well as noting its decline into a racially divided community, a divide that reflects the breakdown of urban communities with the fragmentation of industry after the Second World War. SuAndi's text is not confined to referring to the particular history of England and makes numerous references to the influence of world events, such as the assassination of Malcolm X, and the lives of ordinary people living on the other side of the world. Far from being a liberal text which presents the victim of racial abuse as a survivor, *M*'s humour draws us willingly into her world but we are also implicated by it as an audience. We may laugh at the stories she comically depicts, as SuAndi notes, '*M*'s resilience and caustic humour draw the audience in' (SuAndi 2006: 126). The humour is deliberately subverted by our growing sense that the racial abuse *M* describes is real and has had profound effects on the lives of people she represents. Being spat at in the street, refused credit because of your gender or race, or hearing your neighbours shouting, 'Don't cut the branches on that side, I don't want those niggers looking in on me' (5.4: 776), were parts of *M*'s life not shared by a white audience. SuAndi suggests that her work gives expression to 'familial and cultural ancestry' (SuAndi 2006). She also notes the dangers of nostalgia inherent in a retelling of history so central to much feminist and black performance, but that a weaving of 'the past into the present' is a political strategy to performatively 'fill the voids of history' (ibid: 125). Black culture and experience have been historically marginalized, and SuAndi's performance text works against the ongoing practice of such marginalization. As such, SuAndi's work connects strongly with feminist practice and is embedded in the work of a new generation of black artists whose work crosses the boundaries between art, poetry and performance. It articulates the experience not only of the auto/biographical individual but is a positive response to aspects of what has been described by one critic as a 'black community in crisis in Britain', a crisis of agency and subjectivity (Ugwu 1995: 56). Equally, SuAndi's work can be linked to the work of many US black artists whose practice centres on modes of testimony in performance as a means of cultural memorialization (ibid).

Storytelling, testimony, subjectivity and dystopia: Guillermo Gómez-Peña (5.5 and 5.13), Mark Ravenhill's *Product* (5.7), and Caryl Churchill's *Far Away* (5.6)

The critical and creative relationship between the contemporary world, the artwork and the artist is central to the practice of US/Mexican performance artist/activist Guillermo Gómez-Peña, whose work challenges and reformulates an understanding of the cultural and political role of artist and artwork in a contemporary, fragmented and alienating culture. He draws on autobiography, social observation, cultural critique, technology and storytelling to make performances that disturb and relocate the subject and subjectivity of performer and audience (see 5.5 and 5.13).

For Gómez-Peña, late capitalism and globalization have created a world characterized by 'unprecedented emptiness and acute social crises' (Gómez-Peña 2001b: 26), which has brought with it a 'backlash against humanistic concerns and identity politics' (ibid: 7). Identifying with both Mexican and American cultures, Gómez-Peña's work crosses what he names as 'extremely volatile geographic and cultural borders' (Gómez-Peña 2001a: 7). He defines himself as a 'migrant provocateur, an intercultural pirate' (ibid: 9) and experiments with forms of political activism and performance, operating with great suspicion about the coercive imperatives of mediatized cultures. In the excerpt included here, Gómez-Peña performs in a wheelchair and follows the movement patterns of a 'mechanical video-game-like pattern' whilst being given instructions by his co-performer Roberto Sifuentes (5.5). The performance is full of self-ironizing commentary about performance and the cultural role of an artist, and plays with language, mixing Spanish and English. Gómez-Peña is told by Sifuentes to 'give me some burning trivia' whereby he makes cynical quips about popular cultural appropriation: 'Madonna defeated Argentina & got to play Evita Gooooo Madonna!' (5.5: 784), or jokes about the media furor around the affair between former US President Bill Clinton and White House intern Monica Lewinski as a 'great millennial soap opera' – 'Clintoris & Linguinsky' – playing on the fetishized relationship between sex and food (ibid: 785). The performance ends with the entrance of another performer as a 'Green Alien' and the 'Beginning of Nintendo Ethnic Wars'. The piece hybridizes 'high' art – beginning with an opera singer singing Mozart with a 'soundbed of Japanese techno music' – and popular culture and races with anarchic fervour from one social/political issue to another, with Gómez-Peña failing all the time to achieve the tasks which Sifuentes, as a kind of 'MC puppetmaster', requests of him.

In 'Away from the Surveillance Cameras of the Art World: Strategies for Collaboration and Community Activism' (5.13), Gómez-Peña notes how, in making work, he and his collaborators look for 'images that will create a disturbing sediment in the consciousness of the spectator' (ibid: 852). Like Barba, he refers to the ways in which any of the images or icons he uses in performance have the character of a 'polysemantic image' – whereby different readings by different audiences are expected and welcomed. Indeed he wants his performance work to trigger 'a process of reflexivity' and starts from a 'theoretical proposal' when beginning to make a performance. Gómez-Peña, like SuAndi, crosses between the public world, the 'civic realm' – with, for example, his 'experimental town meetings' where activists, performers and scholars perform and improvise a 'hypertextual script' in a real political meeting/discussion/ performance – and the world of performance, working in activist as well as performance contexts. Like SuAndi, too, much of Gómez-Peña's work is concerned with race and gender issues and questions of identity, the formation of subjectivity and the social/political role of the artist, in a fragmented, racist, war-ridden and alienating world.

The preponderance of solo and autobiographical work in contemporary performance has, in its turn, influenced developments in drama and more traditional text-based theatre practices. Dramatists and performers such as Anna Deavere Smith, Wallace Shawn (USA) and Tim Crouch (UK) have, with increasing frequency, performed their own compositions as solo performers, as well as writing works for others. These works may often have an autobiographical foundation. However, Mark Ravenhill's *Product* (5.7) written in 2005 and revised in 2007, employs the conventions of autobiographical performance, but turns them on their head, to manipulate the relationship between fact and fiction, confession and storytelling. The premise of *Product* is that a producer called James is pitching a new Hollywood script to an actress who he hopes will be willing to take the lead role. The actress is on stage but remains silent, whilst James embodies the character of a woman who finds herself embroiled in the events leading up to a major terrorist attack. The post-9/11 framework for the play implicates us as the audience in the woman's collusion in the planning and carrying out of the attack. We feel ourselves understanding her empathy with the ringleader with whom she is in love, but no more so than our horror at the devastation which will be caused by the attacks should they happen. Ravenhill not only plays with our liberal sensibilities here, but configures our experience of reality as akin to watching a movie. The action is described and 'played out' as a 'virtual monologue' where we constantly need reminding that the events are scripted as opposed to real. This is a text which is completely reliant on the anxieties of the post 9/11 era.

Interestingly Caryl Churchill's *Far Away* (2000, 5.6), explicitly embraces similar cultural anxieties relating to war and terror, ecological disaster and the absolute fear of the 'other' – but it was written before the 9/11 attacks. A playwright who in the 1980s was aligned with British leftist and feminist artists, Churchill has, of her generation, moved furthest away from post-Brechtian dramatic conventions towards a more poetic, experimental, and fragmented dramaturgy and theatricality.

Far Away appears, at first, to be set in a world rather uncomfortably recognizable as being close to home. The play, divided into three scenes, begins with a girl, Joan, quizzing her aunt, Harper, over a brutal scene she has witnessed. Scene 2 is set a number of years later and is divided into six short sections. Joan and Todd, a young man, are working at making extravagant hats that we learn are to be worn by convicts prior to their execution. Joan's concern is that the hats, works of art, are not preserved:

JOAN: It seems so sad to burn them with the bodies.
TODD: No I think that's the joy of it. The hats are ephemeral. It's like a metaphor for something or other.
JOAN: Well, life.
TODD: Well, life, there you are. Out of nearly three hundred hats I've made here I've only had three win and go in the museum. But that's never bothered me. You make beauty and it disappears, I love that. (5.6: 790)

Whilst one might expect Joan and Todd to be more concerned about the death of the prisoners who are paraded in the hats before their execution, their conversation dismisses genocide in favour of the 'metaphor' of art. At the same time, the brutality of execution is juxtaposed with the development of a tender and humanizing relationship between alienated co-workers. In the final scene we return to Harper's house; again it is some years later. World war has broken out, involving humans, animals and the cosmos itself. It is not possible to discern who is on what side in the conflict, 'The Bolivians are working with gravity, that's a secret so as not to spread alarm. But we're getting further with noise and there's thousands dead of light in Madagascar. Who's going to mobilise darkness and silence?' (5.6: 792). *Far Away* ends in a kind of apocalyptic implosion, where the natural and the material world are engaged in an interminable conflict with humanity and each other.

Some theories of contemporary theatre and performance have argued that drama is, in many respects, no longer of functional value to a performance agenda centred around an exploration of our experience and understanding of the contemporary world (see Lehmann 2006). However, *Far Away* demonstrates drama's potential to respond imaginatively, poetically and politically to a changed ideological landscape. The first scenes of the play employ a form of pared-down realism – particularly in terms of the dialogue – but which desists from providing us with background information or given circumstances of the type that we might most obviously associate with Naturalism. It sets up 'the familiar' or 'recognizable', and then subsequently breaks these securities apart. Although *Far Away* is perhaps more obviously a play *about* globalization it inhabits the same world as Ravenhill's *Product*. As Dan Rebellato points out, the movement through the play is 'from the domestic to the national to the global', and 'in the turmoil of international allegiances in the last act, the play presents national differences as moral absurdities' (Rebellato 2009: 81; see also Dymkowski 2003). Whilst texts such as *Far Away*, *Product* and Gómez-Peña's work appear to be more contrasting than connected, they are all responses to a set of shared concerns, whether pre- or post-9/11, which focus on the destructive impact of global neoliberalism on both the individual and the community.

Conclusion

From the standpoint of the social, the technological and the political, the world of contemporary performance makers and that of the artists and practitioners working at the beginning of the twentieth century is very far apart. Yet the concerns of artists driven to blur the boundaries between art and life, theatre and performance, in the early decades of the twentieth century are echoed in the practices of contemporary artists at the start of the twenty-first century. In contemporary performance practice we still see artists responding to the political world in which they function, both embracing and rejecting technology as a means of mediation between human and mechanical expression, moving between the complexities of mediatized performance to the seeming simplicity of confession, autobiography, storytelling and 'stand-up' routines. In his article 'Me, My iBook, and Writing in America' (5.14) Mark Ravenhill, for example, offers some prescient observations on playwriting under globalization. His constant emphasis is on the contingent nature of his own practice and agency, that if he cannot willingly escape the productive forces of late capitalism, a more useful strategy might be to critically engage with them. This also applies to Ravenhill's own dramaturgical practice.

For many contemporary practitioners there is similarly a fascination with the relationship between theatricality and the everyday, fact and fiction, between the 'real' and the 'simulated', in a world where performance and performativity appear to be so embedded in our lives, from mediatized war, the 'performed political personas' of our politicians, viewing transmitted live performance in a cinema, to 'reality' TV, which appears to bear little relation to our lived realities. Part 5 can only hint at the huge variety of practice which we might place under the umbrella of contemporary performance, and so has been offered as a 'framed' starting point. Arguably, the best writing about the performers and performances we have explored in Part 5 comes from the artists themselves, many of whom articulate, far better than critics and scholars, how their work operates and the conceptual and aesthetic frameworks involved in the process of making that work. Many of these artists create access to their work through vibrant websites and of course on the endlessly fascinating fora of YouTube and Vimeo, where our access to soundbites of performance work help make sense of our 'reading' of the traces of performance available through forms of paper-based documentation. This is an extraordinary resource, less in flux than it was a decade ago as many artists now use it for archiving their work. We conclude this anthology therefore with the suggestion that you combine your 'readings' of the materials it offers with others which await you in cyberspace: type the name of a practitioner, theatre company or performance into the search bar and …

Bibliography

Aston, Elaine (2003) *Feminist Views on the English Stage*, Cambridge: Cambridge University Press.

Aston, Elaine and Geraldine Harris (eds) (2008) *Performance Practice and Process: Contemporary (Women Practitioners)*, Basingstoke: Palgrave Macmillan.

Auslander, Philip (1997) *From Acting to Performance: Essays in Modernism and Postmodernism*, London: Routledge.

Auslander, Phillip (1999) *Liveness: Performance in a Mediatized Culture*, London: Routledge.

Barba, Eugenio and Nicola Savarese (2006 [1991]) *A Dictionary of Theatre Anthropology: The Secret Art of the Performer*, London: Routledge.

Barthes, Roland (1977 [1968]) *Music, Image, Text*, London: Fontana Press.

Baudrillard, Jean (2006 [1981]) *Simulacra and Simulation*, trans. S. F. Glaser, Ann Arbor: University of Michigan Press.

Birringer, Johannes (1993 [1991]) *Theatre, Theory, Postmodernism*, Bloomington: Indiana University Press.

Bottoms, Stephen (2011) 'In Defense of the String Quartet: An Open Letter to Richard Schechner', in James Harding and Cindy Rosenthal (eds) *The Rise of Performance Studies: Rethinking Richard Schechner's Broad Spectrum*, Basingstoke: Palgrave Macmillan, pp. 23–37.

Chapple, Freda and Chiel Kattenbelt (eds) (2006) *Intermediality in Theatre and Performance*, Amsterdam: Rodopi.

Dymkowski, Christine (2003) 'Caryl Churchill: *Far Away* ... but Close to Home', *European Journal of English Studies*, 7(1), 55–68.

Etchells, Tim (1996a) *Certain Fragments*, London: Routledge.

Etchells, Tim (1996b [1994]) 'Diverse Assembly: Some Trends in Recent Performance', in, Theodore Shank (ed.), *Contemporary British Theatre*, Basingstoke: Macmillan, pp. 107–22.

Féral, Josette (1982) 'Performance and Theatricality: The Subject Demystified', trans. Therese Lyons, *Modern Drama*, 25(1), 170–81.

Fuchs, Elinor (1996) *The Death of Character: Perspectives on Theatre after Modernism*, Bloomington: Indiana University Press.

Gale, Maggie B. (2013) 'The Contemporary', *Contemporary Theatre Review Special Issue*, 23(1), 16–18.

Gómez-Peña, Guillermo (2001a [2000]) *Dangerous Border Crossings: The Artist Talks Back*, London: Routledge.

Gómez-Peña, Guillermo (2001b) 'The New Global Culture: Somewhere Between Corporate Multiculturalism and the Mainstream Bizarre (a Border Perspective)', *The Drama Review*, 45(1) (T169), 7–30.

Grotowski, Jerzy (2002 [1968]) *Towards a Poor Theatre*, London: Routledge.

Harvey, David (1996 [1990]) *The Condition of Postmodernity*, Oxford: Blackwells.

Heddon, Dee (2007) *Autobiography and Performance*, Basingstoke: Palgrave Macmillan.

Holmberg, Arthur (1996) *The Theatre of Robert Wilson*, Cambridge: Cambridge University Press.

Hutcheon, Linda (1989) *The Politics of Postmodernism*, London: Routledge.

Kaye, Nick (1994) *Postmodernism and Performance*, Basingstoke: Macmillan.

Lehmann, Hans-Thies (2006 [1999]) *Postdramatic Theatre*, trans. K. Jürs-Munby, London: Routledge.

Lyotard, Jean-François (1997 [1979]) *The Postmodern Condition: A Report on Knowledge*, trans. G. Bennington and B. Massumi, Manchester: Manchester University Press.

O'Connor, Steve (2005 [1989]) *Postmodernist Culture*, Oxford: Blackwell.

Phelan, Peggy (1993) *Unmarked: The Politics of Performance*, London: Routledge.

Quick, Andrew (2007) *The Wooster Group Workbook*, London: Routledge.

Rebellato, Dan (2009) *Theatre and Globalization*, Basingstoke: Palgrave Macmillan.

Ridout, Nicholas (2007) *Stage Fright, Animals and Other Theatrical Problems*, Cambridge: Cambridge University Press.

Sandford, Mariellen R. (ed.) (1995) *Happenings and Other Acts*, London: Routledge.

Schechner, Richard (1988) *Performance Theory*, London: Routledge.

Shank, Theodore (1996 [1994]) *Contemporary British Theatre*, Basingstoke: Macmillan.

States, Bert O. (1985) *Great Reckonings in Little Rooms: On the Phenomenology of Theatre*, Berkeley: University of California Press.

SuAndi (2006) 'Africa Lives on in We: Histories and Futures of Black Women Artists', in Elaine Aston and Geraldine Harris (eds), *Feminist Futures? Theatre, Performance, Theory*, Basingstoke: Palgrave Macmillan, pp. 118–29.

Ugwu, Catherine (1995) 'Keep on Running: The Politics of Black British Performance', in Catherine Ugwu, *Let's Get It On: The Politics of Black Performance*, London: Institute of Contemporary Arts/Bay Press, pp. 54–83.

Williams, David (1999) *Collaborative Theatre: The Théâtre du Soleil Workbook*, London: Routledge.

Further reading

Barba, Eugenio (2010) *On Directing and Dramaturgy: Burning the House*, trans. Judy Barba, London: Routledge.

Davis, Tracy C. (2008) *The Cambridge Companion to Performance Studies*, Cambridge: Cambridge University Press.

Deeney, John (1998) *Writing Live: An Investigation of the Relationship Between Writing and Live Art*, London: London Arts Board.

Delgado, Maria and Dan Rebellato (2010) *Contemporary European Theatre Directors*, London: Routledge.

Goldberg, RoseLee (1993 [1979]) *Performance Art: From Futurism to the Present*, London: Thames and Hudson.

Gómez-Peña, Guillermo (2005) *Ethno-Techno: Writings on Performance, Activism and Pedagogy*, London: Routledge.

Gómez-Peña, Guillermo and Roberto Sifuentes (2011) *Exercises for Rebel Artists: Radical Performance Pedagogy*, London: Routledge.

Harvie, Jen and Andy Lavender (2010) *Making Contemporary Theatre: International Rehearsal Processes*, Manchester: Manchester University Press.

Heathfield, Adrian (ed.) (2000) *Small Acts: Performance, the Millennium and the Marking of Time*, London: Black Dog Publishing.

Heathfield, Adrian (ed.) (2004) *Live: Art and Performance*, London: The Arts Council/Tate Publishing.

Helmer, Judith and Florian Malzacher (2004) *Not Even a Game Anymore: The Theatre of Forced Entertainment*, Berlin: Alexander Verlag.

Jackson, Shannon (2011) *Social Works: Performing Art, Supporting Publics*, London: Routledge.

Jürs-Munby, Karen, Jerome Caroll and Steve Giles (2013) *Postdramatic Theatre and the Political*, London: Bloomsbury.

Kelleher, Joe and Nicholas Ridout (2006) *Contemporary Theatres in Europe: A Critical Companion*, London: Routledge.

Ledger, Adam (2012) *Odin Teatret: Theatre in a New Century*, Basingstoke: Palgrave Macmillan.

Radosavljvić, Duška (2013) *Theatre-Making: Interplay Between Text and Performance in the 21st Century*, Basingstoke: Palgrave Macmillan.

Rappaport, Herman (1986) '"Can You Say Hello?" Laurie Anderson's *United States*', *Theatre Journal*, 38, 339–54.

Ravenhill, Mark (2004) 'A Tear in the Fabric: The Jamie Bulger Murder and New Theatre Writing in the Nineties', in *New Theatre Quarterly*, 20(4), 305–314.

Savran, David (1986) *Breaking the Rules: The Wooster Group*, New York: Theatre Communications Group.

Savran, David (2005) 'The Death of the Avantgarde', *The Drama Review*, 49(3) (T187), 10–42.

Servos, Norbert (1984) *Pina Bausch-Wuppertal Dance Theater, or, The Art of Training a Goldfish: Excursions into Dance*, Cologne: Ballett-Bühnen-Verlag.

Shepherd, Simon (2006) *Theatre, Body and Pleasure*, London: Routledge.

Tufnell, Miranda and Chris Crickmay (1990) *Body, Space, Image*, London: Dance Books.

Zarrilli, Phillip (1995) *Acting (Re)Considered*, London: Routledge.

5.1 QUARTET (1981)

HEINER MÜLLER

Translated by Carl Weber

Heiner Müller (1929-95) *was born Eppendorf, East Germany, and was the dramatist who has perhaps most uniquely articulated, obliquely and often with breathtaking formal inventiveness, the experience of a divided Germany during the Cold War period. Müller's early plays, such as* The Scab *(1957), although resisting naturalistic conventions, directly referenced the experience of working life and socialist policies in the German Democratic Republic (GDR). Not surprisingly, the GDR authorities exercised censorship over the dramatist's work, which led Müller to develop compositional practices – embracing montage, fragmentation, contradiction and intertextuality – that forged a complex inter-relationship between the political, the psychological and the philosophical. In* The Hamletmachine *(1977), a 'text for performance' rather than a 'play', speech is not always attributed to 'character' and the overall dismantling of dramatic conventions unhinges the notion that identity and subjectivity can be rendered as stable. Many of these ideas are reflected in* Quartet, *the text reprinted here. Whilst such practices have resulted in some commentators framing Müller's work as an exemplar of 'postdramatic theatre' (supported, not least, by his work with the director Robert Wilson), Müller's working life also represents an extended dialogue with the ideas of Bertolt Brecht, concerning the evolution of 'the dialectic', history, and the relationship between the individual and the collective. Müller also had a notable career as a director, and in the final years of his life became part of the directorate of the Berliner Ensemble.*

The Characters

MERTEUIL
VALMONT

Timespace

Drawing room before the French revolution.
Air raid shelter after World War III.

MERTEUIL: Valmont. I believed your passion for me died. Why this sudden fire again? And with such youthful force. However, it's too late, You won't ignite my heart anymore. Not once again. Never more. I am telling you this not without regret, Valmont. After all, there were minutes – maybe, I should say moments, a minute that is an eternity – when I was happy thanks to your company, I am talking of myself, Valmont. What do I know of your feelings. And I should perhaps talk rather about the minutes during which I could use you – you, that was your talent in the intercourse with my physiology – to feel something that in my memory seems to be a sensation of bliss, You didn't forget how to manipulate this engine. Don't take your hand away. It's not that I am feeling anything for you. It is my skin that remembers. Or perhaps it doesn't matter to it – I am talking of my skin, Valmont – simply doesn't matter, does it? to what kind of animal the instrument of its lust is attached, hand or claw. When I close my eyes you are beautiful, Valmont. Or hunchbacked if I want it. The privilege of the blind. They drew the better lot in love. They are spared the comedy of circumstances. They see what they want to see. The ideal would be blind and deafmute. The love of stones. Did I shock you, Valmont. How easy it is to discourage you. I didn't know you like this. Did the fair sex wound you deeply after me. Tears. Do you have a heart, Valmont. Since when. Or was your virility damaged in my successors. Your breath tastes of solitude. Did the successor of my successor send you packing. The forsaken lover. No. Don't retract your tender offer, Sir. I am buying. I am buying in any case. No need to fear emotions. Why should I hate you, I didn't love you. Let's rub our hides together. Ah, the bondage of bodies. The agony to live and not be God. To have a consciousness but no power over matter. Do not rush, Valmont. That is good. Yes yes yes yes. That was well acted, wasn't it. What do I care for the lust of my body, I am no dairy-maid. My brain is working at its normal rate. I am totally cold, Valmont. My life My death My love.

Enter Valmont.

MERTEUIL: Valmont. You are coming exactly on the minute. And I almost regret your punctuality. It's cutting short a bliss I'd have loved to share with you, wouldn't it be based on its indivisibility alone if you understand what I mean.

VALMONT: Do I understand you if I assume that you are in love again, Marchioness. Well, I am too if you want to call it that. Once again. I would be sorry should I have prevented a lover's attack on your beautiful person. Through which window did he climb out. May I hope he has broken his neck in doing so.

MERTEUIL: Fie, Valmont. And save your compliments for the lady of your heart wherever this organ might be located. I hope for your sake its new sheath is gilded. You ought to know me better. In love. I thought we agreed that what you call love belongs to the realm of servants. How can you consider me capable of such a vulgar stirring. The greatest bliss is the bliss of animals. Rarely enough it drops into our lap. You let me feel it once in a while when I still liked to use you for it, Valmont, and I hope you didn't leave empty handed either. Who is the lucky one of the moment. Or may we already call her the unlucky one.

VALMONT: It is La Tourvel. As for your indivisible

MERTEUIL: Jealous. You, Valmont. What a regression. I could understand you if you would know him. By the way, I am certain you have met him. An attractive man. Though he looks like you. Even birds migrating flutter in the nets of habit though their flight spans the continents. Turn around once. His advantage is his youth. In bed as well if you want to know. Do you want to know. A dream if I assume you are reality, Valmont, begging your pardon. In ten years perhaps there won't be any difference between you if I could turn you into a stone now with one loving glance of the Medusa. Or into a more pleasing substance. A fertile notion. the museum of our loves. We would have full houses, wouldn't we, Valmont, with the statues of our putrefied desires. Those dead dreams classified according to the alphabet or lined up in chronological order, free of the accidents of the flesh, not exposed anymore to the horrors of change. Our memory needs those crutches; one doesn't even remember the various bends of cocks,

not to mention faces. A haze. La Tourvel is an insult. I didn't release you into liberty so you could mount this cow, Valmont. I could understand it if you would take an interest in little Volange, a vegetable fresh from a convent's discipline, my virginal niece, but La Tourvel. I admit she is a mighty piece of flesh but to be shared with a husband who has sunk his teeth into it, a loyal husband as I have good reason to fear, and for who knows how many years. What's left for you, Valmont. The dregs. Do you seriously want to poke around in those muddy leftovers. I pity you, Valmont. If she were a whore who had learned her trade. La Merreaux, for example, I would share her with ten men. But the only lady of high society perverse enough to enjoy herself in wedlock, a bigot with reddened knees from the pew and swollen fingers from wringing her hands before her father confessor. Those hands won't touch a genital, Valmont, without the blessing of the church. I'll bet she is dreaming of immaculate conception when her loving spouse lowers himself on her with the conjugal intention to make her a child, once every year. What is the devastation of a landscape compared to the despoiling of lust through the loyalty of a husband. Of course, the Count Gercourt contemplates the innocence of my niece. In good faith, by the way; the bill of sale is filed with the magistrate. And perhaps you are afraid of his competition, he already snatched La Vressac from under your nose, and you were two years younger at the time. You are getting old, Valmont. I thought it would be a pleasure for you, besides a ride on the virgin, to crown the beautiful animal Gercourt with the inevitable antlers before he assumes the gamekeeper's office, and all the poachers of the capital raid his forest and keep renewing his subscription for this headgear. Be a good dog, Valmont, and pick up the scent as long as it is fresh. A little youth in your bed since the mirror doesn't provide it anymore. Why lift your leg at a poor box. Or are you pining for the alms of marriage. Shall we give an example to the world and marry each other, Valmont.

VALMONT: How could I dare insult you thus, Marchioness, in front of all the world. The alms could be poisoned. By the way, I prefer to select my hunt myself. Or the tree I am lifting my leg at, as you like to call it. Rain hasn't fallen on you in a long time, when did you last look in the mirror, friend of my soul. I wish I could still serve you as a cloud but the wind is driving me towards new skies. I don't doubt I will make the poor box blossom. As for the competition. Marchioness, I know your long memory, You won't forget even in hell that the president preferred Tourvel to you. I am prepared to become the loving tool of your revenge. And I expect a better hunt from the object of my adoration than from your virginal niece, unexperienced as she is in the arts of fortification. What could she have learned in the convent but fasting and a little Godpleasing masturbation with the crucifix.

I bet that after the frost of filial prayers she burns for the coup de grace to put an end to her innocence. She will run into my knife before I have even drawn it. She won't even double once: she doesn't know the thrills of the hunt, What is game to me without the lust of the chase. Without the sweat of fear, the choked breath, the turning upward of the white in the eye. What's left is digestion. My best tricks will make a fool of me like the empty theatre does of the actor. I will have to applaud myself. The tiger as a ham. Let the rabble fornicate between door and threshold, their time is expensive, it's costing us money; our noble vocation is to kill time. It demands everything of a human being; there is too much of it. Happy he who could make the clocks of the world stand still. Eternity as an eternal erection. Time is the void of creation, all of mankind fits into it. For the rabble, the church has stuffed it with God, we know it is black and has no bottom. If the rabble is going to find this out, they'll stuff us into it after Him.

MERTEUIL: The clocks of the world. Do you have difficulty, Valmont, to make your better self stand erect.

VALMONT: With you, Marchioness. Though I do have to admit that I am beginning to understand why loyalty is the wildest of all debaucheries, Too late as far as our tender relation is concerned, but I am planning to exercise this new experience a bit. I hate times past. Change accumulates them. Look at our nails, we go on sprouting in the coffin. And imagine if we had to dwell among the refuse of our years. Pyramids of filth, until the tape rips at the finish line. Or in the secretions of our bodies. Death alone is eternal, life keeps repeating itself until the abyss yawns. The deluge is a deficiency of canalization. As for the loving husband, he is in a foreign country on some secret mission. Maybe he'll succeed, political animal that he is, in starting some war or other. An effective poison against the boredom of devastation. Life moves faster when dying becomes a stage play, the beauty of the world cuts less deeply into the heart – do we have a heart, Marchioness – as we watch its destruction; you're watching the parade of young buttocks which confronts us day in, day out, with our own mortality – we can't have all of them, can we, and the clap to each one who managed to escape us! – you're watching them in front of sword points and in the flash of cannon fire with some composure. Do you sometimes think of death, Marchioness. What is your mirror telling you. It is always the other one who looks back. It is him we search for when we burrow through unknown bodies, away from ourselves. Maybe, neither one nor the other exists, only the void in our soul that crows for its fill. When are you going to put your virginal niece on view, Marchioness.

MERTEUIL: Did you find the way back into your own hide, Valmont. There is no man whose member won't stiffen at the thought of his dear flesh departing, fear makes

philosophers. Welcome to sin and forget the poor box before piety overpowers you and you forget your one true vocation. What else have you learned but to maneuver your cock into a cunt resembling the one you once fell out of, always with the same more or less pleasant result, and always deluded that the applause of those alien mucous membranes is meant for you, and only you, that those screams of lust are addressed to you, while you are nothing but a barren vehicle, indifferent and totally interchangeable, for the lust of the woman who is using you, the power drunk fool of her creation. You know well enough that every man is one man too few for a woman. You also know, Valmont; soon enough fate will catch up with you and you won't even be that anymore, a man too few. Even the gravedigger will enjoy himself with us.

VALMONT: I am bored with the bestiality of our conversation. Every word rips a gash, every smile bares a fang, We should let tigers play our parts. Another bite, please, another strike of the paw. The stage craft of wild beasts.

MERTEUIL: You are going to pieces, Valmont, you're becoming sentimental. Virtue is an infectious disease. What is that thing, our soul. A muscle or mucous membrane. What I am afraid of is the night of the bodies. Four days' journey from Paris in a mudhole that belongs to my family, that chain of members and wombs threaded on the string of an accidental name bestowed on an unwashed ancestor by a stinking king, there something lives – half human, half cattle. I hope I will never see it in this life, or in another life if there is another life. The mere thought of its stench makes me sweat from all my pores. My mirrors are oozing its blood. It doesn't cloud my image, I laugh about the sufferings of others like any animal gifted with reason. But sometimes I dream that it is stepping out of my mirrors on its feet of dung and without any kind of face, but I see its hands clearly, claws and hoofs, when it rips the silk off my thighs and throws itself on top of me like soil on a coffin, and maybe its violence is the key that unlocks my heart. Go now, Valmont. The virgin tomorrow night at the opera.

Exit VALMONT.

MERTEUIL: Madame Tourvel. My heart at your feet. Don't be shocked, beloved of my soul. Can you believe that a lecherous thought dwells in this breast after so many weeks of your pious company, I admit I was a different man before the lightning flash of your eyes struck me, Valmont the breaker of hearts. I AM BREAKING THE HEARTS OF THE PROUDEST OF WOMEN, I didn't know you, Madame. Shame even to think of it. What filth I have waded through. What art of dissembling. What depravity. Sins like scarlet fever. The mere glimpse of a beautiful woman – what am I saying? – of a fishwife's behind, and I turned into a beast of prey. I was an abyss, Madame. Would you like to venture a look into it – I wanted to say downwards, forgive me – from the height of your virtue. I see you blush. How does this red come to your cheeks, my love. It suits you. But where does your imagination get these colors to paint for you my vices. From the sacrament of matrimony, perhaps, which I believed armored you against the worldly forces of seduction, I would be tempted to display for you my sins down to the smallest detail – are you eager for my catalogue – if only to see your becoming blush a bit longer. At least it gives some evidence that there is blood pulsing in your veins. Blood. The cruel fate not to be the first one. Don't make me think of it. And even if you would open your veins for me, all your blood could not compensate for the wedding another man took away from me, forever. The moment never to be recovered. The deadly 'once and never again' of the batting eyelid. And so forth. Don't make me think of it. Don't be afraid. I respect the sacred bond that joins you to your spouse, and should he not find the way into your bed anymore I'd be the first to help him on top. His lust is my joy since your virtue has taught me to hate the rake I used to be, and I know your womb is sealed. I hardly dare kiss your hand. And if I make so bold it is not worldly passion that drives me on. Don't take away your hand, Madame. A drink in the desert. Even the love of God needs a body. Why else did He let his son become human and give him the cross for a lover. THE FLESH HAS ITS OWN SPIRIT. Do you want to be my cross. You are already by virtue of the sacrament of your marriage to another but me. But maybe your body has one or another secret entrance that is not covered by this interdiction, one forgotten or scorned by the love of Monsieur Le President. Can you believe that so much beauty should have the sole purpose of repro-duction and only one eternal center. Isn't it blasphemy to reserve this mouth to the in and out of breathing, to the drudgery of absorbing food, and the golden middle of this magnificent behind to the sad labor of discharging excrement. Can this tongue move only syllables and dead matter. What a waste. And what avarice at the same time. Twins of vices. Yes, you blaspheme, Madame, if you leave the wear and tear of your gifts to the ravages of time and to the tender fauna of the graveyard. Can it be less than a mortal sin not to do what we have been blessed to think. To strangle the offspring of our blessed brains before their first timid cry. This instrument of our bodies, isn't it given to us so it may be played upon until silence breaks the strings. The thought that doesn't become deed poisons the soul. To live with the mortal sin of discrimination and refusal. To die only partly used. The salvation of your mortal soul is what's at my heart, Madame, during each attempt at your unfortunately perishable body. You will leave it behind more easily when it's been fully used. Heaven is covetous of all matter and hell is scrupulous, it punishes idleness and neglect, its eternal tortures prefer

the neglected parts. The deepest fall into hell is from the heights of innocence.

Enter VALMONT.

VALMONT: I shall think about it, my dear Valmont. It moves me to see you so worried about the salvation of my soul. I won't forget to tell my husband that heaven appointed him the regent of all my orifices. Not without mentioning the unselfish source from which this revelation sprang at me. I see you share my joyous anticipation of the voyages of discovery in the matrimonial bed. You are a saint, Valmont. Or should I have deceived myself about you. Should you have deceived me. Are you playing a game with me. What is this grimace hiding. A mask or a face. The horrible suspicion is growing in my heart that you drape a very worldly passion with the cloak of piety. Fear, Valmont, the wrath of an insulted wife.

MERTEUIL: Fear. What should I fear from your wrath but the restoration of my shaken virtue. Fear. What is the conversion of the sinner without the dagger's daily stab of lust, the sting of remorse, the benefit of chastisement. Fear. I am asking for your wrath, Madame. Like the desert for the rain, like the blind man for the lightning which explodes the night of his eyes. Do not withhold your punishing hand from my unruly flesh. Every blow will be a caress, every gash from your nails a gift of heaven, every bite a monument.

VALMONT: I am no goose, Valmont, as you would like to believe. I won't give you the pleasure of being a tool of your degenerate lust. Tears, My lord.

MERTEUIL: What else, Queen. You kill me when you talk daggers. Spill my blood if that will soothe your wrath. But don't mock my noblest sentiments, This frivolity doesn't rise from your beautiful soul. You shouldn't copy a monster like La Merteuil. You are a bad copy, it does you credit. Forgive me if I moisten your hand, only you are able to stop the flow of my tears, Let me rest in your lap – ah, you still don't trust me. Let me dispel your doubts. A trial of my constancy. For example, bare these breasts, the armor of your dress cannot conceal their beauty anyway. Lightning shall strike me if I even lift my eyes. Not to mention my hand, it shall wither away if

VALMONT: Fall, Valmont. Fall, lightning did strike you. And take your hand away, it has a putrid smell.

MERTEUIL: You are cruel.

VALMONT: I?

MERTEUIL: By the way, I have to make a confession. You are taking upon yourself a deadly offense by defending your conjugal bed.

VALMONT: So you'll die for a good cause and we shall meet again before the face of God.

MERTEUIL: I am not familiar with the geography of the heavens, I'd be mortified to miss you in the Elysian fields which are densely populated if we are to believe the church. But I am not talking of myself. At issue is the blood of a virgin. The niece of the monster, the little Volange. She is pursuing me. Church, drawing room or playhouse, as soon as she sees me from afar, she waves her virginal behind towards my weak flesh. A vessel of evil, the more dangerous because it is completely innocent, a roseate tool of hell, a menace from the void. Ah, this void within me. It is growing and will swallow me. Daily it demands sacrifice. One day temptation will engulf me. I shall be the devil who thrusts this child into eternal damnation, if you do not offer me your hand and more, you my guardian angel who carries me across the abyss on the wings of love. Do it, make this sacrifice for the sake of your helpless sister, since you are afraid of the flame which burns me to ashes and keep your heart cold for me. After all, there is less at stake for you than for a virgin. Do I have to tell you what heaven thinks of this. Hell will thank you threefold if you keep insisting on your undivided bed. Your coldness, Madame, is throwing three souls into the eternal flames, and what is a murder compared to the crime against even one soul.

VALMONT: Do I understand you correctly, Vicomte. Because you are unable to bridle your lechery or, how did you call it, the growing void within you to which you have to sacrifice every day – isn't your philosophical vacuum rather the daily need of your very worldly sexual duct? – and because this one virgin didn't learn to move with propriety – what debauched convent must she have grown up in – the happiness of my marriage shall be

MERTEUIL: That is not you. This cold heart is not yours. You save or condemn three immortal souls, Madame, by pledging or withholding a body that will pass away in any case. Think of your better self. The pleasure will be multiple. The end sanctifies the means, the sting of the sacrifice will make the happiness of your marriage even more complete.

VALMONT: You know I'd rather kill myself than

MERTEUIL: And renounce bliss. I am talking of the eternal kind.

VALMONT: It is enough, Valmont.

MERTEUIL: Yes, it is enough. Forgive the terrible trial I had to subject you to so I could learn what I know: Madame, you are an angel and my price is not too high.

VALMONT: Which price, my friend,

MERTEUIL: The lifelong renunciation of the arousal of lust which filled my other life to the brim, ah, how far behind me it is now for lack of a subject worthy of my adoration. Let me at your feet

VALMONT: The devil knows many disguises, A new mask, Valmont?

MERTEUIL: See the evidence of my truth. By what means should I become dangerous to you, with what penetrate into the crypt of your virtue. The devil has no part of me anymore, worldly lust no weapon. WASTE AND VOID

THE SEA IS QUIET. If you won't believe your eyes convince yourself with your tender hand. Put your hand, Madame, on the empty spot between my thighs. Don't be afraid of anything, I am all soul. Your hand, Madame.

VALMONT: You are a saint, Valmont. I permit you to kiss my feet.

MERTEUIL: You make me happy, Madame, And throw me back into my abyss, Tonight at the opera, I shall again be exposed to the lures of that certain virgin the devil has recruited against me. Should I avoid her. Virtue becomes lazy without toiling at the thorn of temptation. Wouldn't you despise me if I shunned the danger. MAN MUST VENTURE INTO THE HOSTILE WORLD. Every art needs to be exercised. Don't send me unarmed into battle. Three souls will be in the eternal fire if this my barely tamed flesh sprouts anew before the young blossom. The prey has its power over the hunter, sweet are the terrors of the opera. Let me measure my small strength against your naked beauty, Queen, protected as you are by the fence of matrimony, so I can hold up your sacred image in front of my eyes when I, confined in my weak flesh, have to step out into the dark arena to face the spearheads of maiden breasts.

VALMONT: I ask myself if you will resist those breasts, Vicomte. I see you wavering. Should we have deceived ourselves about the degree of your sanctity. Will you endure the tougher test. Here it is. I am a woman, Valmont. Can you look at a woman and not be a man.

MERTEUIL: I can, Lady. As you see, your offer makes no muscle twitch, no nerve quiver inside me. I scorn you with a light heart, share my joy. Tears. You are crying with good reason, Queen. Tears of joy, I know it. With good reason you are proud to have been so scorned, I see you have understood me. Cover yourself, my love. An unchaste draft could brush you, cold as a husband's hand.

Pause.

VALMONT: I believe I could get used to being a woman, Marchioness.

MERTEUIL: I wish I could.

Pause.

VALMONT: What now. Are we to go on playing.

MERTEUIL: Are we playing? Go on to what?

VALMONT: Adored virgin, beautiful child, most charming niece. Ah, the sight of your innocence makes me forget my sex and changes me into your aunt who commended you so warmly to me. Not an edifying thought. I shall bore myself to death in her sorry impersonation. I know every spot on her soul. I shall say nothing of the rest. But the doom between my legs – pray with me that it won't overcome you in its rebellion against my virtue, and close the abyss of your eyes before it devours us –

makes me nearly wish for the exchange. Yes, I wish I could exchange it, this my sex, here in the shadow of the danger of losing myself completely to your beauty. A loss only to be made up by the destruction of the portrait in the ecstasy of lust it so urgently invites. Lust alone takes the blindfold from love's eyes and grants them the view through the veil of the skin to the coarseness of the flesh, the indifferent food of graves. God must have wanted it, what. Why else the weapon called face. Whoever creates wants the destruction. And not until the flesh rots away has the soul time off. Better you shed it immediately. If you were ugly. Only the timely liberation from the attributes of beauty is insurance against the Fall. And that won't suffice, everything or nothing, nothing can happen to a skeleton except the wind playing with the bones on the other side of sin. Let us forget what stands between us before it unites us for the duration of one spasm – am I doing well, Marchioness – we all do our gymnastics at the umbilical cord, and permit me to offer you my male protection, the strong arm of a father, against the malice of the world the silence of your convent didn't acquaint you with. I know, believe me, my ominous sex, and the thought splits my heart that a worthless brute, dull novice, lewd farmhand could break that seal with which nature protects the secret of your virginal womb. I'd rather fall into sin myself than suffer such injustice that cries to high heaven.

MERTEUIL: Does it cry. What is that fatherly hand, Monsieur, searching for these parts of my body the Mother Superior forbade me to touch.

VALMONT: Why father. Let me be your priest, who is more a father than the priest who opens the gates of paradise for all of God's children. The key is in my hand, the signpost, the heavenly tool, the fiery sword. The matter is urgent; before the niece becomes the aunt the lesson has to be learned. On your knees, wretch. I know the dreams which walk through your sleep. Repent and I shall change your punishment into grace. Don't be afraid for your innocence. There are many dwellings in God's mansion. You only need to open those amazing lips and the dove of our Lord will come flying and pour forth the Holy Spirit. It trembles with readiness, look. What is life without its daily death. You talk with angel's tongues. The school of the convent. The language of Mother Superior. Man should not spit out the gifts of God. To those who give it shall be given to them. What falls you should erect again. Christ would not have reached Golgotha without the righteous man who helped him carry the cross. Your hand, Madame. This is the resurrection. Did you say innocence. What you call your innocence is a blasphemy. He loves only ONE virgin, the world can do with one Saviour. Do you believe this eager body has been given to you so you can go to school alone, hidden from the eyes of the world. IT IS NOT GOOD THAT MAN SHALL BE ALONE. If you want to know where God dwells trust the twitching of your thighs, the trembling of your knees. A tiny membrane should prevent us from becoming one body. THE PAIN IS SHORT BUT JOY WILL BE ETERNAL. He who brings the light should not be afraid of darkness. Paradise has three gates. He who rejects the third one insults the master-builder of the Trinity. THERE IS SPACE E'EN IN THE SMALLEST COTTAGE.

MERTEUIL: You are very attentive, Sir, I am obliged to you Since you have shown, could show, me so forcibly where God dwells. I won't forget any of His dwellings and take care that the flow of visitors doesn't stop and that His guests feel at home in them as long as I have breath to receive them.

VALMONT: Why not a little longer, Breath should not be a condition of hospitality, death no grounds for divorce. Many a guest may have particular needs, LOVE IS AS STRONG AS DEATH. And let me do something more, my girl, whom I now may call woman. Woman has in the final outcome only one lover. I hear the clamour of battle, made by the clocks of the world which strike at your defenseless beauty. The thought that this glorious body will be exposed to the drapery in which the years enshroud it, that this mouth will shrivel, these breasts wither, this womb shrink under the plough of time, cuts so deeply into my soul that I want to assume the profession of the physician too, and help you to eternal life. I want to be the midwife of death, our mutual future. I want to fold my loving hands around your neck. How else can I pray for your youth with any prospect of success, I want to liberate your blood from the prison of veins, the bowels from the constraints of the body, the bones from the stranglehold of the flesh. How else can I grasp with my hands and see with my eyes what the transient shell hides from my view and my grasp. I want to release into the solitude of the stars the angel who dwells within you.

MERTEUIL: The annihilation of the niece.

Pause.

MERTEUIL: Shall we devour each other, Valmont, so this affair can come to an end before you become thoroughly tasteless.

VALMONT: I regret having to tell you that I have dined already, Marchioness. The President's wife did fall.

MERTEUIL: The eternal spouse.

VALMONT: Madame de Tourvel.

MERTEUIL: You are a whore, Valmont.

VALMONT: I am expecting my punishment, Queen.

MERTEUIL: Didn't my love for the whore deserve chastisement.

VALMONT: I am dirt. I want to eat your excrement.

MERTEUIL: Dirt to dirt. I want you to spit at me.

VALMONT: I want you to urinate on me.

MERTEUIL: Your excrement.

VALMONT: Let us pray, Madame, that hell won't separate us.

MERTEUIL: And now, Valmont, let us make the President's wife die of her futile fall from grace. Sacrificing the Queen.

VALMONT: I have put myself at your feet, Valmont, so you won't stumble anymore. You have baptized me with the perfume of the gutter. From the heaven of my marriage I have thrust myself into the chasm of your desires in order to save this virgin, I have told you that I shall kill myself if you don't resist this time the evil that is reaching out from inside you, I have warned you, Valmont. All that is left for me to do is to include you in my final prayers. You are my murderer, Valmont.

MERTEUIL: Am I? Too much honor, Madame. I have not decreed the commandments you wish to obey by executing yourself. Didn't you draw any pleasure from your pious adultery but that tender pang of conscience you are enjoying right now. You are not too cold for hell if I am to judge from our games in bed. No flesh under forty can lie as well as that. And what the rabble call suicide is the epitome of masturbation. You permit that I employ the aid of my lorgnette so I'll be able to watch better the performance – your last one, Queen – with fear and pity. I have had mirrors set up so you can die in the plural. And do me the favor, from my hands this your last glass of wine.

VALMONT: I hope I shall be able to contribute to your amusement, Valmont, with this my last performance, since I cannot count on a moral effect after my belated glimpse at the slimy bottom of your soul. HOW TO GET RID OF THIS MOST WICKED BODY.★ I shall open my veins as I would an unread book. You will learn how to read it, Valmont, after me. I shall do it with scissors since I am a woman. Every trade has its own jokes. You can use my blood to make yourself up, a new grimace. I shall find a way to my heart through my flesh. The way you never found, Valmont, since you are a man, your breast empty, and only nothingness growing inside you.

Your body is the body of your death, Valmont. A woman has many bodies. You have to bleed yourself if you want to see blood. Or one man has to bleed the other. Envy of the milk in our breasts, that is what makes you men into butchers. If you only could give birth. I do regret, Valmont, that this experience will be denied you, this garden forbidden, because of a decree of nature hard to understand. You would give the best part of yourself for it if you knew what you are missing and we could make a deal with nature, I did love you, Valmont. But I shall push a needle into my womb before I kill myself, to be sure nothing that you have planted is growing inside me, Valmont. You are a monster and I want to become one. Green and bloated with poison I shall walk through your sleep, Swinging from a rope I shall dance for you. My face will be a blue mask. The tongue protruding. With my head in the gas oven I will be aware that you are standing behind me with no thought but how to get inside me, and I, I will desire it while the gas bursts my lungs. It is good to be a woman, Valmont, and not a conqueror. When I close my eyes I can see you rotting. I don't envy you the cesspool growing inside you, Valmont. Do you want to know more. I am a dying encyclopedia, every word a clot of blood. You don't have to tell me, Marchioness, that the wine was poisoned. I wish I could watch you die as I watch myself now. By the way, I am still pleased with myself. This can masturbate even with the maggots. I hope my performance didn't bore you. That indeed would be unpardonable.

MERTEUIL: Death of a whore. We are alone now cancer my lover.

END

★English in the German text.

5.2 'Confess to Everything: A Note on *Speak Bitterness*' (2008) and SPEAK BITTERNESS (1994–)

TIM ETCHELLS

Tim Etchells (b. 1956) *is a writer, performer and director. He has worked with Forced Entertainment, a leading UK-based experimental performance company, since 1984. The group works through improvisation to collectively create performances which are often centred around questions of contemporary identity and urban living as well as investigating the performative elements of theatricality. The performances are often durational, multimedia or site-specific and are predicated on creating non-linear narratives which evoke rather than state. Like many experimental performance companies their work plays with chance, rules and montage and often has a personal, confessional tone.*

Confess to Everything: A Note on *Speak Bitterness*

IN *SPEAK BITTERNESS* A line of performers make confessions from positions stood or seated behind a long table in a brightly lit space, the blue backdrop for which bears the title for the piece. The text for the performance – a long list or catalogue of statements admitting guilt, responsibility or complicity for a wide range of human wrong-doings great and small – is strewn across the table. This text – confessions for things like forgery, murder or genocide to more domestic stuff like reading each other's diaries or forgetting to take the dogs out for a walk – is the raw material through which relationships between the performers themselves and between performers and the audience are constructed in the piece. At different times the confessions are read, whispered, or shouted, appearing as single lines, as fast-paced exchanges and as long monologues or lists. With the lines punctuated by doubt, laughter and hesitation, invigorated by passion or laughter the performance itself shifts around in tone throughout, moving from apparent sincerity to numb accusation and blatant absurdity.

Central to *Speak Bitterness* is a practice of listing and of cataloguing-through-language. As the work unfolds the text creates a rolling and shifting map of the world outside the theatre space – a map which defines and redefines an idea or question of what's out there, its highs, lows, shape and borders. Each new sequential addition to the list (which, in performance occurs as part of a temporal process) either adjusts or confirms the watchers' developing guess about the culture it comes from and goes to. Manipulating or transforming this guess is a key element in the dramaturgy (or game) of lists. The list itemizes, catalogues and, essentially, stores data, presenting its contents as temporarily equivalent, without transparent comment or opinion. Unlike another staple of modernist composition – the collage – the act of listing does not layer, merge, overlay, re-mix or blur together its contents. Lists rather, with a seriality that implies but never fully delivers narrative, let each of their items stand alone but together, a menu or line of ingredients rather than a soup. Lists are blank or 'spacious' since the job of guessing the constituency of listed items and of unpacking their individual meaning is left to the viewer.

In its process of textual cataloguing *Speak Bitterness* has a strong relation to other durational works I've made with Forced Entertainment such as *Quizoola!* (1996) and *And on the Thousandth Night . . .* (2000), the former a catalogue of written questions and improvised answers, the latter an entirely improvised compendium of stories developed by a group of eight performers over a period of six hours. *Speak Bitterness* also relates to my more recent projects *That Night Follows Day* (with Victoria, 2007), a performance about the relationship between children and adults, for a group of sixteen young people aged between eight and fourteen, and *Sight Is The Sense...* (2008), a long free-associating list-monologue exploring language and its ability to define or describe the world, for the American actor Jim Fletcher.

In each of these quite different works the text explores a particular formal category or aspect of language, and particular kinds or genres of content – pushing at the limits of the category, raising questions not just about individual fragments of content but about the broader social and cultural frameworks that contain them. *Speak Bitterness* in this sense is as much about the nature of confession and guilt, the limits and energies of empathy, complicity, forgiveness and judgement, as it is about any particular thing that is named. *Speak Bitterness* is also, quite explicitly, about the audience, since the we which dominates and reverberates through the text at all times is of course a shifting and problematic construct. At times this we is something that might happily encompass the whole of the audience on any particular occasion. Most people would perhaps feel covered by or sign up to statements like 'we had our doubts' or 'we lost our way', but many would balk at signing up to statements such as 'we were date rapists' or 'we pushed dog shit through immigrants' doors'. The 'we' of the text, first appearing as a place of communal shelter and definition, rapidly becomes a problem – a fact which the piece is keen to explore and exploit. Even the range of confessions (from admitting distant historical events to admitting evidently futuristic or highly improbable fictional actions) makes an issue of our potential belonging. Far from the blanket communal comfort it may appear to offer, the 'we' of *Speak Bitterness* both refuses and accuses those watching, dividing and subdividing the supposedly shared social space of the auditorium. It's a probing of the idea of 'audience' that has continued in many later works that I have made with Forced Entertainment, notably *First Night* (2001), the disastrous vaudeville which constantly worries and provokes at the question of who exactly is watching out there in the dark, niggling to comic and disturbing effect at the question of their needs, (lack of) morals and (low) expectations.

★

In its original 'durational' version *Speak Bitterness* (National Review of Live Art, 1994) played with eight performers as an ongoing improvisational task and lasted six hours, with audience members free to arrive, depart and return at any point. Latterly the performance was developed in a condensed theatre version for seven performers, lasting one and half hours, and with a largely fixed text and dramaturgy. The original text drew on short passages of confessions material I had written for earlier Forced Entertainment pieces (*Let The Water Run Its Course*) *To The Sea That Made The Promise* (1986) and for *Marina & Lee* (1991). This material was joined by a large additional amount of new material written by me and then added to again with writing from performers Robin Arthur, Cathy Naden, Tim Hall and Sue Marshall. This writing was edited by me and further augmented by improvisation from the whole company. Since the theatre version (1995), I've continued to add more material to the text every year, accumulating confessions in reference to current events, cultural shifts and new areas of possibility and invention that open up in the writing.

Like most of the durational performances created by myself and Forced Entertainment the original long version of *Speak Bitterness* was not structured beyond its six-hour time-limit and an outline of simple performance rules and strategies. In such a performance, as in later six-hour works like *Quizoola!* and *And on the Thousandth Night...*, the event of the piece unfolds in real time: an encounter between the public, the performers and their decisions on the day. Subject to the influence of desire, tiredness, accident, whim and impulse, this version of *Speak Bitterness* remains a moveable feast, constructed and constrained through the simple device of the confessions and very much a vehicle for the live improvisational energies of the group.

The theatre version of *Speak Bitterness* was developed during summer 1995. We took the same blue tarpaulin box we'd used for the Glasgow performances (a space which contained both actors and audience) and adapted it as a stage-space – losing one wall to create an open rectangle that the public looked into. Strings of bare bulbs hung over the performance area were extended over the auditoria of venues that we toured to – lighting the audience slightly and sustaining a sense of being 'in the same room as' the performance.

In dramatic terms we tried to preserve the feeling of the Glasgow durational (spatial and performance intimacy, a sense of real-time process, etc.) whilst adding enough in the way of structural architecture (narrative or musical development) to keep a theatre audience engaged for an hour and a half. Rehearsals involved the usual glut of improvisation based, on this occasion, on the reams of confessional texts. We used video a lot – playing back rehearsals and analysing them. We set and scripted sections out of successful improvisations and then combined these sections into various different orders. We also left some sections of the piece relatively unscripted so that performers would be free to choose new lines in each performance, or to interrupt each other, speaking in a different order each night in various sections. Our aim – as has been the case in much of our theatre work since this point and including works as diverse as the minimalist *Spectacular* (2008) and the energetic chaos of *Bloody Mess* (2004) – was for an architecture/structure in the performance that did develop – leading the viewer in different directions – but a structure which nonetheless could still seem live, accidental and to a certain extent spontaneous.

The *Speak Bitterness* text as presented here represents a wide range of the confessions material from the piece. The fact that it's not broken down and distributed between individual or named speakers reflects most accurately the form of the piece that we continue to present – the durational version – in which the text appears unhierarchicalised, in any sequence, from any of the performers, in blocks or line by line, according to the decisions people make on the spot. What draws us to this version is the live dynamic of the performers interacting with each other and the text, the ups and downs of the social interaction between them, and the way that this exhausting and exhaustive work stresses the task of the performance – 'confess to everything' – over and above any dramaturgy or the revelation of any particular item of content. Everything in this work remains decidedly in process.

Figure 26 *Speak Bitterness* (Forced Entertainment), Essen tour, 2009. (Photographer: Hugo Glendinning.)

Figure 27 *Speak Bitterness* (Forced Entertainment), Essen tour, 2009. (Photographer: Hugo Glendinning.)

SPEAK BITTERNESS

TIM ETCHELLS/FORCED ENTERTAINMENT

WE CONFESS TO LUST, greed, envy and hate crimes. We're guilty of bad coughs, Chest X-Rays, Lithium and Librium. We lost our equilibrium. We lost our will to live. We lost our way somewhere just after the junction and never found it again. We had double standards. We put the psychiatric patients in cage-beds. We saw the economic advantages of warfare and destruction. We smirked at the Simpson trial. When the markets crashed, we laughed out loud. We never claimed to have halos and wings. Our show used adult humour. Our kids had broken ribs. We joined a network of disorganised crime. We crashed the spaceship on purpose. We got drunk too often. We nobbled horses. We made each other bleed. We dropped atomic bombs on Nagasaki, Coventry, Seattle, Belize, Belsize Park and Hiroshima. We were rightly arrested under sections 7 and 23 and rightly charged under section 45. We planned the overthrow of governments, and holidays in the summer. We put love first. We broke our legs playing rounders. We were scumbags in a shooting war with other scumbags. We thought Gordon Brown was inspiring. We filmed events in which we could not intervene, events that spilled out of control, events that didn't even exist. We altered documents and photographs to disguise the location of people and places that were dear to us. We knew that a professional foul inside the thirty yard box could lead to a penalty but in the 83rd minute we felt there was no choice – some of us went one way and some went the other, sandwiching the bloke and bringing him down hard – the referee was a Hungarian and never saw a thing. We were cold callers, scared of kryptonite. We were class traitors and cry-for-help shoplifters. We were murderers of sleep. Everything was a movie to us. We hacked and hoodwinked, we wounded with intent. When the food-aid arrived in the lorries, we started shoving and pushing. We had nose jobs, chin-jobs, eye jobs, tummy-tucks and bum sucks. We were bloody fools. We're guilty of that look people have sometimes when they dare not speak their minds. We confess to radium, railways and romanticism. We were jealous of Helen Sebley's personal transformation. We never made the rendezvous. We were deathless, never fading. We ate pet food straight from the can. We dipped our toes in the water and we got our fingers burned. We had a truce on Christmas day. In the last years of our rule we deteriorated both physically and mentally – we planned to eliminate even our most loyal supporters. We went to Blackpool and got caught in the act. We used a telescope to read other people's newspapers and novels on the beach. We devised viral marketing campaigns. We wrecked the neighbours' garden with a Strimmer. We registered Internet domain names based on the names of well-known celebrities and established brands of merchandise in the hope of getting rich. RobertRedford.com, DrewBarrymore.com, ChristinaMilian.com, Steps.com, JayZ.com and ABucketofMcNuggetswithSaucetoGo.com were all our work. We made a film using stock footage. We switched the medications when the nurse was not looking. We made mockumentaries. We made cockumentaries. We did not think that low budget and lowest common denominator were necessarily the same thing. We were broke and mistaken all the time. We were addicted to sadness. We worked for Enron. We got the cable turned back on but pretty soon the excitement wore off. We came as we were. We paid as we went. We said, 'Let it be.' We said, 'So it goes.' We said, 'Try to think of the heart attack as nature's way of warning you.' We lay in the hot-tub and fooled around with a handgun, taking aim at the stars. We were bag snatchers. We were stockbrokers. We threatened a cashier with a replica pistol. We threatened a nightclub bouncer with a kids' plastic raygun. We threatened a fat white shopkeeper with a cucumber hidden under a sweatshirt. We gave Peter a black eye. We gave Ethel a cauliflower ear. We gave Jed a bloody nose. We watched too much TV. We did not believe that there was a hierarchy of suffering. We tried to please our girlfriends by setting up three- and foursomes with several well-hung guys. We robbed peoples' lockers while they were down in surgery. We had the St James' Infirmary Blues. Our sarcasm was uncalled for in the circumstances. We had no last wishes. We left last wills and testaments which were confusing in some places, vague or even contradictory in others, and which in yet further places seemed to have been designed deliberately to cause disputes amongst the surviving family members, especially our assortment of ex-wives and ex-husbands, lovers, kids, step-kids and friends. Our dying words were, 'Let the bastards fight.' Our last words were incomprehensible. Our last words were deliberately cryptic. Our last words were totally inaudible. We were the judges in a third-rate televised talent show. We banned hunting. We pulled a knife. We pulled some girl from Southampton but couldn't really fuck her on account of her period. We puffed and panted. We dumbed it down. We said that God would be our judge on Afghanistan and Iraq. We confess to Aerobics, Pilates, Power Yoga, Carb Attack and Body Burn. We were rap's Grateful Dead. We were Death Metal's The Carpenters. We were light entertainment's answer to Charles Manson. We got all the girls in the crowd to shout YEAH YEAH, then we got all the guys in the crowd to shout YEAH YEAH, then we got the girls to wave their arms in the air and say YO YO, then we got the guys to shout YO YO and shake their butts around. Afterwards, sat together in the dressing room or on the tour bus with its built-in Jacuzzi, we laughed and laughed about how phenomenally dumb our fans really were. We drew a line under what happened. We made great friends with the neighbours. We made great friends with the bloke in the bed next door. We didn't make friends at all. We frightened each other with the Ouija board. We coughed up phlegm into neatly labelled jars. We left Wendy tied to a tree. We left Johan tied to the railway tracks. We didn't know how to party. We drank Velvet Crush. We drank Southern Comfort. We slipped a few points in the polls but we thought 'So what?' We offered cold comfort to strangers. We offered a kind of formulaic comfort to the families of the injured or deceased. We offered up our only daughters in exchange for the village being spared from the wrath of the Dragon. We said, 'OK people – it's time to rewind.' We could not memorise the sequence of numbers. We pulled dead rabbits out of hats. We had opinions about things that we did not know anything about. We were number crunchers, lone drinkers, postal voters. We kissed babies and pressed palms. We wanted second chances. We wanted a simple life with Marvin and the kids. On talk shows we were silent and on chat shows we would speak not a word. We were a dime a dozen. We read the newspaper over other people's shoulders. We offered support. We offered down-home guidance to our staff. We wanted war in the Caucuses – we didn't care about the consequence. We paid through the nose. We dropped butter and crumbs in the marmalade. We left a trail of jam, honey or Marmite in the margarine. We joked and chatted with the nurses but nothing could hide how frightened we were. We were de-motivational speakers. We were the flunkies and the yes-men that swarmed around uncharismatic leaders, fawning, obsequious and grey. We were shallow. We were shadows. We were less than shadows. Our lives were a tissue of lies, our pasts were a web of deceit, our futures were a tangle of distortions, dark dreams and long unspeakable fantasies. We hid our emotions behind a brick wall of silence, strength and pride. We hid the kids where the cops would never find them. We left the kids in the apartment while the rest of us went out to get tapas. We tested people's patience. We tested people's limits. We tested our parents, trying to identify the weak spots, finding gaps in their defences. By the time we were ready to strike, what we did was quick, easy and totally devastating. We wrote words with the letters all in the wrong order. We robbed little kids of their mobile phones, trainers and dinner money. We were pimps. We were gangsters. We were goody-fucking-two-shoes. Our boredom threshold was too low for comfort. We imposed a state of emergency. We slept with Tracey Emin but she forgot to put our names in her tent. When they asked us our religions, we said 'NONE'. We broke every bone in our victims' bodies. We liked men with limited verbal skills. We took the easiest girls to the sleaziest clubs. As fathers, we saw our main function as explaining the dangers of an offside trap. We had more than our fair share of bad luck. We lost Kirsten's phone number in a fight. We lost the house in a card game. We lost our souls in a tap dancing contest. We went to the lessons each week but we never practised at home. We forgot to set the alarm. We were travelling salesmen who got lost on the back-roads, fell in with a crowd of drifters and never found our way back to the place we started out. We hung out in the Zombie Room. Our music only made sense if you were taking the right kind of drugs. We put our feet in the footsteps of those who went just before us. We traipsed along behind. We didn't think for ourselves. We're guilty of dice, of teletype and needles. We spread true rumours and wrote false receipts. On game shows we cheated and on quiz shows we lied. We lay at home with the flu and a hangover. We made the heartbreak face and then we smiled. We stank of chlorine and fists fell on us like the rain. We made a mockery of justice and a mockery of the American/English language. We doctored photographs, carefully erasing figures and substituting stonework, pillars and curtains to make it look like George Michael had stood on the balcony all alone. We sacked the town; we painted it red. We slipped through customs at Nairobi International, without even being seen. We were exiled kings, useless princes. We revamped our image; we were really working class. We made the crowd blush. We were driven by demons whose names we couldn't even spell. We were white-collar criminals, haunted by our pasts. We told Mrs Gamble that Helen was with us when she wasn't. We were ex-cons trying to go straight. We thought that Freud was probably right about laughter. We thought that Hitler had a point. We had it in for Hillary. We had no moral compass, or if we did have one it had been badly damaged during the frequent electrical storms. We're guilty of heresy and hearsay, of turning our backs to the wall. We saw Arthur Scargill's blue movie cameo. We lied when it would've been easier to tell the truth. When we broke the law about satellites, there was no one to stop us or care. We sent death threats by fax machine and kept a list on a computer of the people we were going to kill. We put the bop in the bop she wop. We loved each other too much. We held each other's hands. We spat in the beer when no one was looking. We're guilty of murder, arson and theft. We gave Dr Taylor a good taste of his own medicine. We trapped Quentin in the showers and gave him what for. We read the same books again and again. We checked into a hotel and started work on the mini-bar – life seemed simpler that way. We had nothing much to say. We lusted after strangers. We exchanged body fluids on the westbound platform of the District Line. We exchanged parcels on the uptown F train. We tried to take photographs of ghosts. We fixed prices. We lived on the streets. We loved nocturnal darkness. We climbed in through a skylight that someone else had left open on purpose. We lay weeping in the bed. We tried to contain the rioters in B wing but they set fire to their mattresses and we were forced to open up the security screens that allowed them access to the rest of the jail. What happened after that was more or less inevitable. We calculated an incorrect orbit for an asteroid as it came quite close to earth. We got sent back to the past to stop the future from happening. We got sent to the future to ask them for help but when we got there we found the place deserted. We were frightened to use adjectives. We made scale models of boats. We dealt swiftly with a bloke that came rushing at us with a hammer. We let our kids drink wine. We got a job doing security for the Beckhams. We got jobs as financial advisors to the Beckhams. We got jobs as magicians for the Beckhams' kids' Christmas party. We just wanted to work for the Beckhams we didn't really mind in what capacity. We just wanted to get the ball rolling. We just wanted to get things done. We just wanted to give peace a chance. We just wanted the step-kids out of the way so that we could have Miriam all for ourselves. We accidentally summoned menus and incomprehensible option boxes by pressing random combinations of keys on the keyboard. We crashed the computer, right into the canal. We walked off in the middle of other people's anecdotes. We fell asleep while our partners made clumsy attempts at a reconciliation. We toed the line. We came from Planet Stress. We were deliciously vicious. We were student teachers, just having a laugh. When we removed Mr Chadwick's appendix, we left a plastic wristwatch inside him as a kind of comical intervention. We played the same role in every movie we made. We played golf with a baseball bat instead of clubs and a hamster instead of a ball. We said we were rough diamonds but really we were heartless fools. When we got to the end, all we could hear was our own voices, echoing and echoing. We inflicted democracy on innocent people. We gave them ballot boxes, beatings and ten months in solitary. We were too brutal for mercy, too depraved to reform, too lost to be found again, too out of it to make much sense at all. As we fumbled for our change and made conversation with the checkout girls, we made everyone curse the moment that they'd chosen to stand behind us in the supermarket checkout line. We did not stop, look and listen. We did not look both ways. We thought the Americans should just go home. We took one look at the guy sleeping at the table near the window and decided to sit somewhere else. We spent our last night together making a Top Ten list of highs and lows of the relationship. We each made our own lists at first and then at midnight began to share them in a kind of awards ceremony slash long long night of drunken vindictiveness and melancholy. We got caught red-handed then we legged it. We stuffed the ears of men with false reports. We confess to oil rigs and pylons. We're guilty of landslide victories and throwing in the towel. We looked at pictures of rare skin diseases. We got drunk and got tattoos. We cut to the quick and were frozen to the bone. We read books to avoid conversation. We confess to the dimming of streetlamps on long tropical nights. We thought thuggery was better than common sense. We didn't like modern Britain. We thought modern art was a load of shit. When we started to go bald, we grew our hair long in one of those Bobby Charlton haircuts, with a very long very thin strand of side hair plastered all over the bald bit at the front. We were cowards, strictly black market. We became nocturnal, inward looking, scared. We set men a new standard by which to measure infamy and shame. We lived on diet of speed and chips. We fell off the earth. We cut off the hand of an evil-hearted pirate called Captain Hook in a fair fight and threw it to a crocodile which had also eaten an alarm clock. The crocodile so enjoyed eating Hook's hand that he followed the pirate around all the time, hoping to get a second helping – but the tick tock tick from the alarm clock he'd swallowed always warned the pirate of the crocodile's approach. We made false economies. We were one of those double acts from way back – onstage it was all love and laughter; offstage we never spoke. We pissed on the flag. We made a soap for black people. We told long boring anecdotes. We worked for £2.90 an hour. We gave Helen fifteen minutes to pack her bags and get out of the house. We never thought. We never danced at weddings. They invented a new classification of lunatic just for us. We wrote biographies without bothering to research or ask permission. We lost the front door keys. We dressed Geisha and looked ridiculous. We did that Sharon Tate. We used laser treatment on hapless immigrants. We stood outside the prisoners' doors all night and whispered nonsense so they couldn't sleep. We sang the songs of streetlamps and paving slabs. We kept a boyfriend in waiting. We dug a few graves in the football pitch and buried the bodies at night. We were not quite at home in the world. We made a film called AMERICAN BONDING CRAP – it was mainly for boys but some girls liked it. We invented a TV channel called THE MONEY CHANNEL – 24 hours of nothing but long fingers handling money – it was a hit all over the world. We blazed the trail, set off rockets and yelled from rooftops. We were small minded, rusty after too many years. We were wankers. We noticed, not for the first time, the look between Carol and Jessica's boyfriend Martin Gardener. We held our savings in Deutschmarks, under a bed. We confess to autumn leaves, to fatherless children and shift work. We were regrouping fighters, looking for somewhere to sleep. We served up the beer in cups made from human skulls. Our trade was to traffic in human misery. We sold the records that we'd bought in our teens and which were no longer fashionable. We were bored of the poor. We killed the first daughter of all English greengrocers in an attempt to avoid any unfortunate recurrences of the last ten years. We confess to intercoms, faxes and prohibited places. We are guilty of arsenic, poor-laws, pass-laws and slightness in the face of adversity. We said we were the best there's ever been. We fucked around. We were Neocons. We lived in condos. We sniggered at a Scotsman's account of an alien attack – they ripped his trousers and left him in the pub. We invented rain-glare on tarmac and UHT cream which you could squirt from a tin. We were sceptics who didn't believe in anything. We drew our own blood with a syringe to make ourselves anorexic. We injected ourselves with yeast to make the blood clot. We injected red dye to make the blood more red, more red when we were bleeding. We crept out when everyone else was fast asleep. We had eyes like the stars. We talked to the trees. We named our sons THIRSTY, LUCKY and MEMORY. We sat up some nights and talked about the future of history. We talked about doing time. Our lives were like a soap made in heaven. We cut open our own bodies to try and find the evil in them – we found nothing, lost a bit of blood, needed stitches. We confess to wasting promises. We wrongly prescribed medicines. We turned down the title Miss Scunthorpe Evening Telegraph. When morning came, we changed our stories. We confess to fraud and to forgery. We're guilty of coldness and spite. We gave up too easy, hit our children too hard. We confess to trade routes, comedy scenes, kitchen knives and libel. We confess to microphones, water and polygraphs. We needed help but we wouldn't take it. We wanted spiritualist ends through materialist means. We lacked faith and therefore patience. We spat on soldiers in the street. In a parody we published, high state officials were portrayed in an insulting manner – the public and premeditated humiliation of their honour and worth was reproduced widely in the mass media in an unseemly and counterproductive fashion, adding greater insult to our already reprehensible words. We wanked off for money. We were at Tet and My Lai. We kissed Tom on the mouth before we killed him. We had butterflies. We wanted to write love songs, really good love songs that would really last but we didn't know music and we couldn't write. We had unorthodox thoughts about the economy. We burned people's faces off with a blow-torch. We got nostalgic for Spangles. In a previous life we had a previous wife. We rubbed salt in other people's wounds. We thought that class was more important than race. We accused the people at our birthday parties of stealing. We slept in coffin hotels. We measured our cocks with a plastic ruler borrowed from the kids' pencil case. We scratched ourselves raw. We drank water to keep our blood pressure up. We smoked fags to keep our weight down. We were remix artists. We exploited the workforce. We scoured the second-hand record stores looking for beats, breaks and stuff to sample. We always ducked when the shit hit the fan. We only wanted tenure. We had a party when we finally made payroll. We were inadequate, indifferent and afraid. We launched the death ray. We passed off crap as good stuff. We drove the planes right into the towers. It was beautiful, beautiful, beautiful and it changed the world. We lost our grip. When daylight came we lost our limited charm. It was our job to insinuate strange objects into the crowd scenes of cinema – the man carrying a surfboard in *Anna Karenina* at the station, the child in Bertolucci's *1900* who's wearing a bum-bag and the woman in *Basic Instinct* who's leading oxen to the slaughter – all these were our work. We confess to lip-synching, eye winking and overturned lorries. Our good deeds would not take much recounting. We ate Kimberly Saunders' arm. We waited till Jim was completely drunk and then beat the fuck out of him. We went to the dogs. We drank our own tears. We farted on the first date. We said the Lord's prayer backwards. We fell asleep in the middle and so didn't understand. We killed children. We practised false chemistry and worshipped graven images. The company we set up was fictitious – just a trading screen for another company which in turn was just a trading screen for a third company and so on – you could chase the money halfway round the world if you wanted and still never find the place where it ended up. We drank our own tears. We bathed in Diet Lilt. We had to get up in the night with a stomach ache. We had the doubts of daytime and the doubts of nighttime. We perpetrated a hoax. We shot people in the head. We thought in shapes rather than words. We wouldn't talk about things; we just bottled them up. We photocopied our own semen and excrement. We bargained for immunity. We watched the light changing. We loved the sky. We dreamed in black and white. We rumbled with other gangs. We dreamed of drained swimming pools. We went into shock for a year. We didn't give anything; we were just there. We shouted for so long and we kept shouting until it didn't even sound like our voices anymore. We told simple stories to children. We put family first. We were opinionated and sloppily dressed. We burst into tears. We confess to driftwood, safe breaking and teletype. We said, 'Come on, come on, let's drink and make up ... ' We were stowaways. We left tapes with bad instructions. We wouldn't read novels at all because we found ourselves so taken over by the characters. We tested the animals with approximately 345cl of the serum. We used force to get people's attention. Our big Broadway show was a total flop. We lived on sliced water and bottled bread. We made licence plates and sewed mail-bags in jail. We played a lot of chess. We worked with Justin Timberlake, Kanye West and a load of the other big names in pop. We thought there was nothing more to 'security' than wearing dark suits, dark glasses and those funny little ear-piece communicators. We cried at family photos. We played the field. There was love in us somewhere but somehow it got lost. We scratched Nigel's face out in all the wedding pictures, turning his head into an angry whirlpool of biro marks, the scribbles and scratches spiralling out from his fat stupid grinning face. We were top of the fucking food chain. We dreamt of hammer blows. When we looked back at the Super 8 and video of ourselves, we could not recognise anything. We were cop killers. We were comedy sub-plots. We got jobs teaching sarcasm to censors. We're guilty of astrophysics and heavy gases. We confess to truth serum, old tricks and stratagems. In the ID line we smiled. In Tesco's when we saw each other again, we just pretended that nothing had happened. We found a way of digitising death. We confess to canned laughter and circular saws. We were cheeky little monkeys that need teaching a lesson. We dreamed of Tokyo, snow monsters and John Ford on his deathbed. We stood at the altar but couldn't say the words. We gave cabinet posts to all of our mates. We tied cans to the back of Martin Gardener's hearse – it's what he would've wanted. Each morning when we put the kids on the bus to school, we took their photographs – it was less a piece of photography and more an act of magic – making talismans to try and ensure that they'd come back OK. We confess to never having an original idea. We feigned disapproval of things we'd done ourselves. We loved the rush of wind and rain when the lorries thundered by. We said, 'Hold on, hold on it won't be long now … '. We sat back in a pose of indifference; we stank of sweat and the Yankee hash. When a few housing benefit cheques arrived made out to Greg Samson, we used them to open a Building Society account in that name and then cashed the cheques. We were antheads, chickenheads and snaggle-toothed deviants. We were just a bunch of fucking arseholes. We had unnatural talents, we used supernatural means. We confess to night vigils that left us tired and lonely. We wept with the aid of glycerine and caught the red-eye home. We struck it lucky on the hit parade. We knew god-damned ALL there was to know about the rumba. We didn't want to blow our own trumpet but it blasted anyway. We said, 'Oh, any old how darling, any old time … '. We held a shredding party in the basement at midnight. We sat with our backs to the wall and posed full-frontal. We lived in a city of fainting buildings; we lived in difficult times. Our smiles suggested something more of surgery than of pleasure. We sat by Rachel's bedside and read stuff to her, hoping to wake her from the coma – we read her Tolstoy and *Peter Pan*, we told her stories, we told her all the wrongs we'd ever done. We thought cheap thoughts in risky places. We called our children Dawn, Leslie and Lisa-Marie, Chantale Duran and Young Whipper Snapper. We went on *Swap Shop* the same day that Edward died. We were often seen in the background of other people's holiday snaps, blurred, out of focus, staring downstream. We had identical operation scars – it was too uncanny, just something meant to be. We designed the Bull Ring Centre. We designed the Millennium Dome. We had enigmatic smiles. We wanted to be Michael's love child because he had such deep-set eyes. We were dizzy with happiness. We saw ourselves as commodities. When we got to the island, the natives told us they looked after a huge monkey god called King Kong – we thought it would be a good idea to capture it and take it back to New York to exhibit – the rest is history. We were inaccessible, inaccurate, inadequate, inadmissible, inane, inanimate, inapplicable, inapposite, inappreciable, inappreciative, inappropriate, inapt, inarticulate, inartistic, inattentive, inaudible, inauspicious, inbred, incalculable, incapable, incautious, incendiary, incessant, incestuous, incidental, incivil, incognito, incoherent, incommensurable, incommensurate, incommunicable, incompatible, incompetent, incomplete, incomprehensible, inconceivable, inconclusive, incongruous, inconsequential, inconsiderate, inconsistent, inconstant, incontinent, inconvenient, incorrect, incredible, incurable, indebted, indecent, indecipherable, indecorous, indefensible, indictable, indifferent, indigestible, indignant, indiscreet, indistinct, indolent, indulgent, inebriated, ineffective, inefficient, inelegant, ineligible, inept, inert, inexpert, infamous, infantile, infectious, inferior, infested, inflammatory, inflated, inflexible, inflicted, inglorious, inhibited, inhospitable, inhuman, inhumane, iniquitous, injudicious, injust, insalubrious, insane, insanitary, insatiable, insecure, insensate, insensible, insensitive, insentient, insidious, insignificant, insincere, insipid, insolent, insomniac, institutionalised, insubordinate, insubstantial, insufferable, insufficient, insular, insulting, insurgent, intimidating, intolerable, intolerant, intoxicated, intransigent, introverted, invalid, invidious and invisible. We took what we could get. We took the Fifth. We did long slow kisses that lasted three days. We confess to tidal waves, hurricanes and magnetic storms. We're guilty of everything. We were clumsy – we got lipstick on our boyfriends' trousers. We loved language. We hated Jews. We dated Asians out of curiosity. We knew the place but we didn't know the time. We sent dirty faxes. We signed our names. We christened our children DEATH, SOLITUDE and FORGETTING. We ate like pigs and never left home. We confess to mud and bleach. We perpetrated a fraud. We set the clocks forward ten minutes to counteract our general tendency to be late. We reserved six tickets for a show and then never turned up to collect them. We chartered planes but never flew. We charted the Straits of Magellan. We lived with our mothers too long. We sold sex for crack. We told lies to the people we were supposed to represent. We robbed Peter to pay Paul. We staged a dancing dogs competition. We had wheels of steel. We had tits made of titanium. We zoned out. We played an old-fashioned sweeper combination. We thought that John McCain wasn't old enough, that John Betjeman was a misogynist and that Stalin was misunderstood. We said, 'Lets keep on going like we were before, like nothing changed at all.' We said, 'Look, please, look.' We asked the patients a question to distract them from the pain. We did not listen to Cynthia's advice. The last thing we said to Joanna before she died was, 'Fuck off, bitch.' The last thing we said to Florian was, 'Sorry, Dude.' It was probably the effects of the heroin. We served up death for breakfast. We pushed each other's buttons. When the kids came shivering out of the water, we were not ready with the towel. We ordered the prisoners to take a walk for a while and stretch their legs. We held a wet T-shirt competition for the women and a wet trousers competition for the men. We were scum. We passed out drunk on the floor of a garage. We watched a film with bad language; it got four stars. We wrote death threats to ourselves. We made a film called OUT OF SOUTH AFRICA. We thought that Black Watch was a musical. We made false promises. We never sat down. We tried to bring about the false death of President Kennedy – false in the sense of co-existent or alternate. We left the best bits on the cutting-room floor. We sulked and skulked and stamped. We confess to breaking three ribs in our sleep. We said we'd speak again soon and then never called back. We were accessories. We gave names, names and more names. We mistranslated. We drove too fast. We admit to announcing personal problems instead of the next train approaching platform four. We asked awkward questions on the Granada studios tour. We never had our fill of bombing and shooting; we were cry for help shoplifters, bingo callers with cancer of the throat. Long after Stalin died we pretended he was alive – wheeling him out for public appearances, waving his hand from the balcony. We never wore seat belts. We got rumbled and frisked. We found panoramic views. We transmitted deadly advice. We switched labels just before the checkout but didn't realise that the bar-code would betray us. We never spoke another language. We flipped channels quickly when the film got embarrassing. We wrote in to the magazine WIFE BEATER MONTHLY. We peeled the skin back and looked. We made no difference. We made no sense. We were the worst kind of people in the world. We're guilty of bright light and rum. We altered flight paths and planned alternative routes. We confess to static, break up and climactic change. We broke into phone boxes. We weren't comfortable in our skins. We were witches. We stole hotel soap. In the scene of community singing filmed in an air-raid shelter and designed to show the goodwill and high spirits of Londoners during the Blitz, we were the ones in the background whose lips were hardly moving. We were bloody fools. We were sick as a parrot. We ran a numbers racket and we dug our own graves. We were loons that danced naked at harvest time. We never wanted children anyway. We confess to zinc and shopping malls, to bad dreams and collectivisation. We fucked the economy. We talked about democracy. All we wanted to do was to tempt into life things that were hidden and strange. We went into town and stopped dead in our tracks. We had a bag full of controlled substances hidden in the toilets. Our hobbies were card playing and time wasting. We drank too much champagne. We were a slick act; we were stadium rockers – every mumble, every gesture every bit of impromptu patter was the same at every gig, all over the world. We had HUNGER for breakfast and STARVATION for lunch. We were suicide bombers. We made a film called STREETS OF YESTERDAY. We're guilty of heart attacks, car crashes and falling off bridges. We agreed with Albert Einstein the scientific genius. We confess to X-Boxes, Gamecubes, Megadrives, PSPs and PS3s. We sewed a horse's head onto the body of a cholera patient, replacing his feet with hooves and his hands with the tentacles of an octopus. He didn't last long but once cleaned, pickled and placed in an outsized jar he made an excellent attraction. We were sheep, eyewitnesses, minor-clerics, prostitutes and baseball fans. We dreamt of heat and of solitude. We wished for peace, or a cease-fire at least. We cut the head off a live rooster and drank the blood – we thought it would help. We fucked our brother. We were smugglers, heathens and pirates. We lied about our age and then hoped for better things. We showed a gun in the first act, in a drawer, hidden under some papers – the central character kept staring at it and mumbling, crying almost, but we weren't prepared to let her use it; the dramatic tension was all wrong and so by act four the audience were still wondering what the gun thing was all about. We burned effigies of trade negotiators. We were fraudulent mediums, working the crowd. We were not beautiful or especially bright but we had the strange gift of being remembered. We were hate-filled children with ice in our veins. In interrogation our voices got quieter and quieter, and the detectives, not wishing to break the mood, got quieter and quieter too, until, by the end of it, stage by stage, we each were only moving our lips and no sound came out, the tape recorder running for posterity. We altered the limits of human action. We loved a piece of time too small to give it a name. We came to the place where the tape says POLICE LINE DO NOT CROSS and then we crossed it. We were funny without meaning to be. We listened to *Stairway to Heaven* 13 times in a row. We played in the show houses on the edge of the estate. Long periods of boredom were our fault. We spent long hours at the bus stop. We were long-lost cousins in love. We liked the way Sarah smiled. We liked the smell of napalm in the morning. We missed episode two. We lied through false teeth. We watched repeats of everything. We did thankless tasks. We were continuity flaws. We jumped ship before the world had taken one full turn. We took three sugars in our coffee. We confess to parricide, conspiracy and Pearl Harbor. We all wore clothes our mothers made. We were black-listed in car manuals. We evacuated whole communities overnight. We buried our pasts in shallow graves. In the baths we spontaneously combusted and in the park we talked while the kids played on the climbing frame. After a long time of fake deliberation over the menu at the motorway services, we went for the special offer RECESSION BUSTER BREAKFAST (2 kids eat free with 2 adults). We confess to personal interest, hobbies and irrelevant experience; we are guilty of landing awkwardly. We are responsible for the coasts and the moors and cumulus clouds and great vistas and vast landscapes and poignant winters. We read the map the wrong way up. We confess to sarcastic suicide notes, to Aeroflot and diagrams. We sniffed lighter fluid and spat through our teeth. We took the gun shot, we took the ricochet; that's all there is to say. We were extras, walk-ons, stand-ins and losers. We were just there to make up the numbers in some of the crowd scenes. We knew we were gay from the age of five. We had plastic surgery to look oriental or black so we could supposedly report on what it was like to be different – we reported our findings on Good Morning Television to the pleasure and interest of Richard and Judy. We confess to knowing Sam and refusing to wave to him. We bled in open spaces. We climbed without a rope. We revealed secrets to the Russians and cheated for small change. We were cautioned for loitering under Section 35. We were test patients, sitting in a hospital room and waiting for the side-effects. We got mixed up; we got into the Occult. We dreamt the whole of the Second World War before it happened. We had the faith of no faith. We thought that less was less. We failed the breath test. We gambled everything on the chance to win diamonds, camcorders and holidays. We were bogus asylum seekers, bogus refugees. We travelled through the German night; we met the German girl. Our marriage was just part of a plan to blow up the train. We had sex in the visionary position – sat far apart on opposite sides of the room and gazing and, masturbating, staring at each other in a mixture of fear, desire and disbelief, certain in the knowledge that even if we came together we would not come together at all. We stayed up after midnight. We worked at Guantanamo. We worked at Abu Ghraib. We were described by photofits. We sighed when the evening had to end. We were invisible. We sadly lacked in the subject of botany. We switched the bags while no one was looking. We noticed, not for the first time, the look between Brian and Peter's boyfriend Neville Darby. We christened diseases with beautiful names; we cut off the villages and sealed off the streets. We drew the curtains when the window cleaners came. We mispronounced URANUS and SCHEAT. We thought we were funny, funnier than anyone had ever been. We took afternoon naps when we should have been working. We fell in love with every co-star. We cheated at cards. It took us three hours to cut off the head with an open knife. We dreamt about dinosaurs and planes crash-landing in back gardens. We never said how much we needed each other. We washed up badly. We never thought. We never danced until the end of the disco. We got tattoos done on our foreheads saying PAX AMERICANA. We stole some electrical equipment which looked expensive and complicated but which we couldn't understand; we plugged it in at home and got some nasty burns – objects began to arrive from the future; we were puzzled and then later imprisoned. We made small talk. Some of the paperwork we submitted was a little bit irregular. We asked the hairdresser about his recently dead father. We stole fish. We worshipped cruel Aztec Gods. We were careless with the truth. We patented an obviously crackpot device for listening to the songs of angels. We built extensions on our houses without the necessary planning permission. We treated people like scenery. We treated the whole place like a hotel. World War III was just a thinly painted backdrop for our love. We kept lifting up the curtain and peeking behind. We hit rock bottom. We found our own level. We tried to guess the presents by feeling through the wrapping paper. We filmed a frog's leg, twitching on a slab. We hated robbing banks — it got boring after a while. We handcuffed Lee Morris to the railings in the playground and pulled his trousers down. We lived a harsh fast life. We were glad to be alive. We didn't have an opinion on anything except how crazy the world was. We're guilty of attic rooms, power cuts and bombs. We confess to statues, ruins and our older brother's Gameboys. We confess to aborting our children for research, killing our parents for the house and putting granddad in a home. We were not at our best in the mornings. We did not feed the neighbours' cat. We lost the thread. We laid down our lives for someone else's country. We smiled invitingly at Antoine, thereby raising expectations that we had no intention of fulfilling. We frequented gaming halls, low hostelries and the late-night super-market on Jasmine Street. We passed folded notes and whispered at the back. We sang off-key and stared at the person to our right. We weren't ready for our opening night. We were sex tourists. We liked Steven but he smelt funny. We told stolen jokes on *The X Factor*. We sang out of key on *Pop Idol: The Rivals*. We sold defective oven gloves door to door. We lived in clutter. We were top of the pops. We stayed out past bedtime, past curfew, past caring. We knew what we were doing. We looked on at the ecstatic twilight of technological society. We saw nine great motorway pile-ups. We were always interested in missing things — time, people and history. We fenced stolen farming equipment. When the mermaids tried to warn us, we threw stones at them. We snored loudly while other people were trying to eat. We read novels with unhappy endings. We wept for slimmers. We learnt how to fly but we did not learn how to land. We were intellectual pygmies. We flung mud. We dug up mass graves. We played truant. We taught Russian roulette at A level. We dubbed silent movies; we coughed in dramatic pauses. We chanted meaningless or silly slogans to put the other marchers off and when the stewards tried to stop us, we ducked under the crash barriers and ran off into the park. We played musical chairs. We believed in the spirits of dead astronauts. We were scared of volcanoes. We sent each other used underwear through the post. We countenanced forever as an expression of mortality. We honoured without exception all church architecture. We said, 'Love is like floating in duckweed.' We were dead meat. We stand accused of Saturday nights and early Monday mornings. We were jealous in a sensational manner. We used supermodels in war documentaries — they were excellent. We were poisoners. We put the last buffalo to sleep. We went to Stonehenge and didn't like it. We ate an irregular meal. We watched a man die in six inches of water. We're guilty of making weak tea. We drove madness into the hearts of good folks. We broke all the rules of ice hockey in one day. We forged doctors' notes. We could never return. We broke down doors, smashed windows and blamed Philip Lawson. We took a lot of liberties. We took advice from demons. We pretended to know people. We took too long getting ready. We inflicted viscous attacks and horrible injuries. We stole from a warehouse on Last Minute Street. We practised strange tactics for interviews including The Long Sustained Silence, Repetition of the Previous Question and Sudden Welling Up of Tears. We idolised Raymond and Lesley. We liked uniforms and signs of obedience. We held him down — it was fascinating. We had piss stains on our trousers. We had shit stains on our shoes. We had no hope. We linked our arms and skipped in a desperate imitation of the *Wizard of Oz*. Our philosophy was do them before they do you. We fingered our arses. We thought we were relatives of Robert Duvall — but we weren't. We confess to rubbing up against tables. We redrew maps to slowly excise certain areas — this was a slow technical distortion (nothing as crude as omission) by which unwanted areas were minutely compressed over long periods of time. When the government changed, and with it our political fortunes, we had to slowly distort it all back. We sniffed lighter fluid and spat through our teeth. We took the gun shot; we took the ricochet. We came from a country where smiling was considered dangerous. We were tricksters, pranksters, practical jokers – we put meat in someone's tea; we left the bedroom looking like a raid; we wore funny noses, bow ties that went round and round – for the grandchildren we pretended to be powered by electricity, drawing energy from the light bulb in the centre of the ceiling and moving in a strange jerky way. We blocked the fucking fast lane. We rang the wrong number twice, no, three times. We bought the same magazine for years. We had tattoos done on our arses saying LONG LIVE THE HEROISM OF SENSELESS PURSUITS. We had tattoos done on our heads saying LET NO MAN ENTER HERE. We had tattoos done on our stomachs saying WHY EMPTY? We ran out on Vic – it was a gamble. We missed a train. We were death mechanics. We were sleep throwers – when we woke up in the mornings there was nothing near us. We were loud drunks and fornicators. After dark was a time of hate and burning for us. We fell asleep at the wheel and woke up some miles down the road. We were pirates. We were lawless. We sailed beneath the black flag. We had our hands in the till. Stumbling lost and disorientated, we realised the world was full of dames. We confess to bellowing sweet nothings. We believed in UFOs. We believed that Jung was probably right about women. We believed that truth was always the best policy. We dealt in imaginary videos. We got drunk on half a pint. We entered the wrong room and backed out hastily. We had sexual intercourse that night, not once, but seventeen times. We sent our daughters off into prostitution and one of them came back dying of AIDS; we could not understand why she was dying, or even that she was dying at all – with her sweats, her blisters and her strange agonised deliriums we thought she was becoming a shaman, a magic priestess, but it didn't work out that way. When the lights went out, we swapped places. We were YTS vandals – losers on job-creation schemes. We pretended to fall over outside a hospital. We lied about our age. We looked promising in mirrors. We lied twice, denied three times. We killed ten men, burned sixteen houses. We wrote two love songs twice on the trot, we made six threatening phone calls and six gentle apologies. We saw six crows sat on a fence, we wept sixteen gallons of tears, we drank fourteen vodkas, we issued several writs. We saw each other 57 times, we threw nine coins in the fountain, we threw seventeen coins at the goalkeeper, we made three wishes, we had seven dreams, we had ten seconds of silence, ten years of peace, ten scars on our arms where the rotor blades had hit. We tore five pages from the back of the book, we crashed 200 cars, fathered 39 children, walked backwards for nine days. We wrote six novels with the same plot, we whispered seven desires, we murmured eighteen pleas, we broke nine mirrors, seventeen plates, 36 cups, a window, a washing-machine and three statues. We shouted 36 curses, told three thousand cautious jokes. Our lounge was like Bosnia – divided into two – the two of us looking shell-shocked across space. We cut the crime rate by introducing a new system of counting. We said, 'Don't call here again; it's dangerous.' We spoke OCTOBER LANGUAGE. We dreamt of hammer blows; we trained as cosmonauts in Star City. We were spastic bashers. We were the captives of our own metaphors. We danced naked for money. We tried to export things without all the proper documents – it wasn't deliberate fraud but you could see why the customs men at Ramsgate were suspicious – they kept looking over the paperwork and tutting and then making phone calls to a man in one of the other portacabins. It was 3am when they let us go, and only then because it was the end of their shift. We told mortician jokes at weddings. We betrayed our friends through silence. We were lonely for twelve years. We loved the way the rain ran off the windscreen. We confess to making love for an irregular amount of time. We smiled secretively, faking orgasms as we did. We sold our kidneys to a rich Arab. We escaped with the help of the netball team. We burned and maimed in recognition of our illustrious past. We were drunk in charge of a telephone. Our nicknames were muck-mouth, filth-tongue and toxic avenger. Our town was famous for its mud. We burnt the grass 'cos we got sick of waiting for Bruno to mow it. We suspected our husbands of having a bit on the side. We suspected our best friends of espionage. We asked our boyfriends to drive the getaway car. When we met in a gay disco, we could never have known what horrors lay ahead. We had savage compulsions. We knew the law, not because we wanted to obey it, but because we wanted to get away with things. We used Ju-Ju to bind people to us. We did not like the big goodbyes. We refused to succumb. We refused to suck Colin's cock until he had been to the bathroom and washed it. We turned the tables on Jason. We saved our trump cards till last. We killed ourselves so that we could spend more time with the kids. We saw the moon reflected in a pool of our own blood. We saw the future in the face of a dead civillian. They traced our travel through the credit cards. We were freeloaders. We switched off the SatNav. We had lecherous plans. We locked our eldest daughter up at the top of a very tall tower so that she could not escape. We said, 'Lets go back to the hotel. No one will notice.' We secretly shat ourselves whilst halfway up the climbing wall. Most days we doubted things, some days we doubted it all.

5.3 BELLE REPRIEVE (1991)

SPLIT BRITCHES – BETTE BOURNE, PAUL SHAW, PEGGY SHAW AND LOIS WEAVER

Split Britches *is a performance troupe that was formed in New York City in 1980 by Peggy Shaw (b. 1944), Lois Weaver (b. 1949) and Deb Margolin (b. 1953). Highly influenced by the experimental theatre and radical politics of the 1960s and 1970s, Split Britches – who initially worked together as members of Spiderwoman Theater – rapidly rose to the vanguard of feminist, lesbian and queer performance during the 1980s and 1990s. Made in collaboration with Bette Bourne of performance group Bloolips, Belle Reprieve comically celebrates and deconstructs lesbian and gay relationships of the 1940s through the adaptation and appropriation of Tennessee Williams'* A Streetcar Named Desire *(1947). Although Margolin departed from Split Britches in the early 1990s, Shaw and Weaver have continued to develop the troupe's practice through new collaborations, site-specific and solo performance, and visual art-based work. Their activities also embrace work in prisons and, most recently, in health and human rights activism. Split Britches co-founded the WOW (Women's One World) Cafe performance space in New York in the 1980s. Both Shaw and Weaver also work as teachers, and Weaver is currently Professor of Contemporary Performance at Queen Mary University of London, UK.*

['I'm a Man' by Elias McDaniel. Copyright © 1955 Arc Music Corporation, by permission of Tristan Music Ltd

'Running Wild' by Joe Grey, Leo Wood and A. Harrington Gibbs. Copyright © 1950 (renewed) Leo Feist Inc., by permission of EMI Feist Catalog Inc.

'Sweet Little Angel' was written by Lucille Bogan

'Pushover' by Billy Davis and Tony Clark. Copyright © 1963 Chevis Publishing Corporation, used by permission

'I Love My Art' was written by Edward Clark

Original songs
'Under the Covers,' words by Peggy Shaw and Paul Shaw, music by Phil Booth
'Beautiful Dream,' words and music by Phil Booth
'The Fairy Song,' words and music by Paul Shaw]

Characters
MITCH, A FAIRY DISGUISED AS A MAN (PAUL SHAW)
STELLA, A WOMAN DISGUISED AS A WOMAN (LOIS WEAVER)
STANLEY, A BUTCH LESBIAN (PEGGY SHAW)
BLANCHE, A MAN IN A DRESS (BETTE BOURNE)

An empty stage. The backdrop is a scrim painted to resemble the interior of a 1940s New Orleans apartment. There are three high-tension wires strung across the stage. Throughout the play, various painted cloth curtains are pulled across these wires to denote a change in scenery or mood.

Four o'clock in the morning.

Act 1

MITCH is wheeling three large boxes onstage with a handtruck. One is designed to resemble a steamer trunk. The second is square, large enough to hold an actor, and shaped to resemble a card table, which it becomes in later scenes. The third is tall, rectangular, and large enough to hold another actor. It is turned on its back to represent a bathtub in the second act.

MITCH: Inside this box it's four o'clock in the morning. I know that sounds incredible but it's true. I know because it's *my* four o'clock in the morning. Every time it comes around, I put it in this box. I've been doing it for years now. At four o'clock in the morning, the thread that holds us to the earth is at its most slender, and all the creatures that never see sunlight come out to make mincemeat of well-laid plans. So you can imagine what it's like in there. If you listen closely you can hear them shuffling about, like the sound of rain or chittering birds. It reminds me of a soundtrack, the beginning of a movie … (*STELLA appears drinking a Coke behind the scrim*) a clean slate. Darkness all around. Small sounds that give a taste of an atmosphere, a head turning, a body lit from behind, shadows in a dark, tiled hallway, a blues piano. (*PIANIST strikes a match and begins to play the blues.*)

STELLA: (*Moving to center from behind the scrim, still drinking the Coke.*) Is there something you want? What can I do for you? Do you know who I am, what I feel, how I think? You want my body. My soul, my food, my bed, my skin, my hands? You want to touch me, hold me, lick me, smell me, eat me, have me? You think you need a little more time to decide? Well, you've got a little over an hour to have your fill. Meanwhile … (*MITCH enters with the last box, swatting bugs*) I'm surprised there aren't more bugs out this time of year. All the ones that are out seem to be buzzing around my head.

MITCH: No, there's plenty for both of us. Don't feel singled out.

STELLA: I think it's 'cuz I eat so much sugar that they're attracted to me. Sugar in my blood. And my veins are close to the surface.

MITCH: You know that they excrete something to digest your blood, that's why they leave that bump on your skin.

STELLA: I always worry that they carry things with them, transferring them from person to person.

MITCH: That's an old wives' tale. This country has no tradition of disease being spread by mosquitoes. You're mistaken.

STELLA: Well, every year I make one big mistake. I wonder what it will be this year?

MITCH: This mistake, is it at a particular time, or can't you tell when it's coming?

STELLA: I can usually feel it coming …

BLANCHE: (*From inside the box.*) I've always depended on the strangeness of strangers.

STELLA: Or at least after the fact I thought I knew it was coming.

MITCH: Isn't there something you can do to stop it happening?

STELLA: Such as …

MITCH: Change the script!

STELLA: Change the script. Ha ha. You want me to do *what* in these shoes? The script is not the problem. I've changed the script.

MITCH: It's a start.

STELLA: Look, I'm supposed to wander around in a state of narcotized sensuality. That's my part. (*BLANCHE and STANLEY speak simultaneously from inside the two largest boxes.*)

BLANCHE: You didn't see, Miss Stella, see what I saw, the long parade to the graveyard. The mortgage on the house, death is expensive, Miss Stella, death is expensive.

STANLEY: Is that so? You don't say, hey Stella wasn't we happy before she showed up. Didn't we see those colored lights you and me. Didn't we see those colored lights.

STELLA: And anyway, it's too late. It's already started.

STANLEY: Hey Stella! (*He comes out of the stage right box.*) (*Cat screams from MITCH and STELLA.*)

BLANCHE: What was that?

STANLEY: Cats. I'm afraid I'm going to have to perform an intimate search.

BLANCHE: My body?

STANLEY: Your luggage.

BLANCHE: Stella, how do I look?

STELLA: Fresh as a daisy.

STANLEY: One that's been picked a few days.

MITCH: Look, can't we just scrub 'round the search and get on with the scenes of brutal humiliation and sexual passion?

STANLEY: I'm afraid we have to find a motive in this case, and I believe it's in this trunk. (*To MITCH.*) Why don't you mind your own business?

BLANCHE: How dare you speak to my ex-fiancé like that!

STANLEY: Your ex-fiancé?! This man is your ex-fiancé?

BLANCHE: That's right.

MITCH: I told her I loved her and she pushed me down the stairwell, but I forgave her as any decent man would.

STANLEY: That's not what it says in the script. In the script it says you treated her like shit because you're a stuck-up mommy's boy.

MITCH: That's a lie!

BLANCHE: I think I'm going to faint.

STELLA: Is all this really necessary?

STANLEY: Look, have you any idea how many people we have come in here saying they're Blanche DuBois, clutching tiny handbags and fainting in the foyer? I'm afraid I'll have to subject this case to the closest possible scrutiny before I allow any of you to pass any further.

BLANCHE: I see, you want me to come clean by showing my dirty laundry to the world.

STANLEY: You got it.

BLANCHE: I think I'll go into the dressing room and burst into tears.

STELLA: We're in this up to our asses now. There's no going back.

BLANCHE: Hold me Stella, I think I feel a flashback coming on. (*Lights flash, music plays, a curtain painted like a grotesque piece of torn lace is pulled on stage behind the action, the actors shuffling backward around the trunk.*) And so it was that I set out to prove to the world that I was indeed myself. A difficult enough task, you might say, for anyone.

STELLA: She threw herself at the feet of an unforgiving world to prove her identity.

MITCH: The answer was somewhere in that trunk.

STANLEY: (*Thumping his fist on the trunk as the music and lights stop flashing.*) This is gonna cost you, lady. What did you think you were gonna get a free ride or something? (*About to open the trunk.*) What do we have here?

BLANCHE: Please open the doors one at a time! If you open them all at once pink things and fur things, dainty things, delicate and wistful things might pop out.

STANLEY: I'll open them one at a time. First things first. (*Music starts.* STANLEY *pulls out a jacket and tosses it to* STELLA, *then pulls out a scarf and throws it to* MITCH.)

BLANCHE: I won't take it personally the way you're treating everything I own in the world.

STANLEY: Let's see, what are little girls made of? (*He sings.*) I put my right hand in, I pull my right hand out (*He pulls it out empty and laughs.*), I put my right hand in (*He pulls out a dress on a hanger and puts it around his neck.*) and I shake it all about.

BLANCHE: I can't approve of any of this, just as you can't approve of my entire life.

STANLEY: I do the hokey-pokey and I turn myself around. That's what it's all about. So this is what little girls are made of. Tiaras, diamond tiaras. (*He puts a tiara on his head.*) And what's this? (*He pulls out a gold bracelet and puts it on.*) A solid gold Cadillac. This must be worth a fortune. And what have we got here? A box of valuables. (*He tosses the contents onto the floor.*) Love letters, scrap books, newspaper clippings.

BLANCHE: Everybody has something they don't want others to touch because of their intimate nature.

STANLEY: (*Singing, as Mitch picks up the newspaper clippings.*) I put my right foot in, I take my right foot out, I put my right foot in and I shake it all about … (STANLEY *pulls out a high-heeled shoe.*)

MITCH: (*As* STANLEY *continues singing.*) There was a time when everyone was trying to get a piece of her. These are the pieces left over, 'Tipped for the Top,' 'What an Angel.' Now the angel's in the kitchen, washing out the dishes and picking her teeth.

BLANCHE: (*As* MITCH *hands her the newspaper clippings.*) I don't see how any of this relates to my own life except in the way people perceive my fall.

STANLEY: I put my left hand in … (*He shakes the box violently from inside.*)

BLANCHE: (*Ripping up the newspaper clippings.*) Tearing … I hear tearing … be careful … the wings, you're tearing them!

STANLEY: They're just animals, lady, what's the matter with you?

BLANCHE: But they've been faithful their whole lives. There are things we don't know here.

STANLEY: Things are different now. (*Still struggling inside the box.*) I pull the white-feathered excited body of one swan off the white-feathered excited body of another swan. (*He pulls out a handful of feathers.*)

BLANCHE: What right have you to interfere with nature?

STANLEY: (*Pulling feathers apart to reveal that they are a boa which he drapes across his shoulders.*) And shake it all about.

BLANCHE: Birds of a feather.

STANLEY: I put my left hand in … (*He pulls his hand quickly out.*) Oww, Stella, Stella!

STELLA: What?

STANLEY: I burned my hand.

STELLA: Oh, Stanley, it's just candle wax.

STANLEY: I know but it hurts.

STELLA: Some people think it's sexy.

STANLEY: (*Pulling his hand away from her.*) I can see where it might be sexy if I knew it was coming. I put my left hand in, I pull my left hand out … oh, a little cheerleading doll … (*he breaks off the arm*) the arm is busted … the rubber band must be broken inside.

BLANCHE: My mother gave me that.

STANLEY: (*Dancing the doll on top of the trunk.*) And I shake it all about …

BLANCHE: And before that, it was her mother's.

STANLEY: (*Slamming the doll down.*) Look, lady, I'm just trying to do my job here.

BLANCHE: Yes, of course.

STANLEY: And my job is to make sure you're not smuggling something personal in this here trunk. (*He reaches into the trunk.*) Let's see, what's this? And what is this? (*He pulls out a purse.*)

BLANCHE: This contains all of my hopes and dreams … this is my hope chest.

STANLEY: Hopes and dreams? Forget it. (*He sticks his hand into the purse.*) I put my whole body in, I take my whole body out. (*He pulls out a scarf.*) I grab myself a frilly thing and shake it all about. I pin it on my shoulders and I sashay up and down, that's what it's all about. Yes? I put my right hand in, I take my right hand out … (*He pulls out his hand covered in blood.* BLANCHE *and* STELLA *exit.* MITCH *enters in fading light to roll away the trunk; music and lights slowly fade out. In blackout.*) I am suddenly aware that the atmosphere has changed. It's dark. The night has a thousand eyes and they're all looking at me. They're burning into me, burning into my chest. If I don't sleep now, I never will … don't panic … the night seems to last forever … don't panic … I'm scared, I'm wrong, the night is making me feel … (*The lights return suddenly on a curtain with a painting of an oversized clawed foot of a bathtub and a straight razor lying on a tiled floor.* STELLA *is onstage with* STANLEY.

She is wearing a cheerleading outfit and carries a cheerleading doll.) Vivien Leigh, huh? Okay, that's your story and I'm stuck with it for now. But let's see if you can keep up the deception day after day, week after week in front of me. Let that be a challenge to our relationship. But meanwhile, relax, make yourself at home, have a drink. Tell me about yourself, stuff I haven't heard before, recent stuff like how've you been lately. I got all the time in the world and I'm all ears.

STELLA: Stanley, you come out here and let Blanche finish dressing. (*STANLEY exits.*) I let her keep her hopes and dreams, just like I let her keep her cheerleading memories. I pretended they were mine as well, came to know them as I know my own face in the mirror. A face that was not a twin of my older sister.

BLANCHE: (*Entering stage left in a bathrobe.*) I think I handled that really well. It's a tricky business, deception in the face of legal documents. Thank heavens for bathrooms, they always make me feel so new.

STELLA: Blanche, honey, are you all right in there? There was no answer, but I could hear her splashing and the sound of her radio.

BLANCHE: I can always refresh my spirits in the bathroom.

STELLA: Blanche, I brought you your lemon Coke.

BLANCHE: All right sweetie. Be right out.

STELLA: I'll wait out here.

BLANCHE: I don't want you to have to wait on me.

STELLA: I like waiting on you Blanche, it feels more like home.

BLANCHE: I must admit, I do like to be waited on.

STELLA: Well, I'm waiting.

BLANCHE: One day I'll probably just dissolve in the bath. They'll come looking for me, but there'll be nothing left. 'Drag Queen Dissolves in Bathtub,' that'll be the headline. 'All that was left was a full head of hair clogging up the plughole. She was exceptional even in death …' I wonder where I'll end up. In the sea, I suppose.

STELLA: I'm waiting, Blanche.

BLANCHE: Just a few last finishing touches.

STELLA: Waiting. Waiting in the wings. Waiting for her to get off the phone.

BLANCHE: You wouldn't want me to go out looking a mess, now would you?

STELLA: Waiting for her to come home from Woolworth's with the new Tangee lipstick. And when I wasn't waiting I was following. I used to follow her into the bathroom. I loved the way she touched her check with the back of her hand. How she let her hand come to rest just slightly between her breasts as she took one last look in the mirror. I used to study the way she adjusted her hips and twisted her thighs in that funny way when she was changing her shoes. Then she would fling open the bathroom door and sail down the staircase into the front room to receive her gentlemen callers.

BLANCHE: (*Colliding into* STELLA, *who drops the doll.*) My doll, it's broken!

STELLA: (*Laughingly.*) No it isn't.

BLANCHE: I did. I broke it.

STELLA: No, honey. You didn't.

BLANCHE: Yes I did. I broke it.

STELLA: (*Shaking* BLANCHE.) No, Blanche, it was already broken.

BLANCHE: I don't know why I'm like this today.

STELLA: (*Embracing her.*) Blanche, you know what this reminds me of? My homecoming corsage, remember? Before the homecoming parade, when the band and all the floats were gathered in front of the war memorial. It was your senior year, you were the captain of the cheerleaders, and I was the mascot. And they gave us these big orange and maroon chrysanthemums with ribbon streamers; mine was just as big as yours.

BLANCHE: And I pinned it on your shoulder and you were so proud of its size and excited by the smell of it.

STELLA: I felt every bit as tall and glamorous as the real cheerleaders, the majorettes, the homecoming court, even Miss Mississippi herself. I stood in that November air imagining all the things a grownup woman could be … and then, that great big old football player came walking across the red dirt and smacked right into me.

BLANCHE: And your poor corsage, it started to bleed, it started to lose its petals one by one.

STELLA: And I started to cry. I threw a god-awful fit.

BLANCHE: You certainly did.

STELLA: My whole life was disappearing with those dropping petals. How was I going to present myself in the same parade with Miss Mississippi, her in her strapless gown and me with a handful of petals. But you put your big strong arms around me and set me right up there on the float with …

BLANCHE: The beauty queen herself. And there you were, all puffy-eyed and corsageless …

STELLA: Right next to the great white virgin, with her round bare shoulders and her rhinestone tiara.

BLANCHE: (*As the music starts.*) And I took your picture and it was in the papers. (BLANCHE *takes off the bathrobe to reveal a cheer-leading outfit and they sing.*)

'Under the Covers'

BOTH: When life is unfair, and the world makes you sick
I know somewhere that's bliss on a stick.

STELLA: Somewhere to go when things are unsteady

BLANCHE: Somewhere to go with cocoa and teddy.

BOTH: Under the covers, the pillows and laces
We both can share, those soft cotton places

STELLA: Lying together like spoons in a drawer

BLANCHE: Then turning over to have an explore …

BOTH: Under the covers, those smooth satin covers
We share our dreams

STELLA: Like goose downy lovers

BLANCHE: Tucked in together like girls in the dorm

BOTH: Under the covers everything's cozy and warm …

They pull hidden pom-poms from each other's sleeves and cheer:

AMO, AMAS, AMAT
WE LOVE OUR TEAM A LOT
WE'RE GONNA FIGHT FIGHT FIGHT
WE'RE GONNA WIN WIN WIN
WE'RE GONNA BE …

BLANCHE: FABULOUS.

Tap dance break.

BOTH: Under the covers, it's you and it's me now
Our pleasure grows, because we are two now
Lean on a pillow and look in my eyes
Spreading our knowledge and sharing our thighs
Under the covers, our fingers exploring
Those hidden dreams, we've found there is something

STELLA pulls a hand covered in menstrual blood out from under her skirt.

Mother has maybe forgotten to tell
Tho' if she found out
We'd found out
She'd give us hell.

STANLEY: (*Yelling from backstage.*) Stella!

BLANCHE AND STELLA: She'd give us hell.

STANLEY: Stella!

BLANCHE AND STELLA: She'd give us … (*The song dissolves into laughter.*)

STANLEY: When are you hens gonna end that conversation?

STELLA: Oh, you can't hear us.

STANLEY: Well, you can hear me, and I say hush up!

STELLA: This is my house too, Stanley, and I'll talk as much as …

BLANCHE: (*Interrupting her.*) Please don't start another row, I couldn't bear it … (*She exits.*)

STELLA: I tried to follow her, but I got stuck. Stuck in the bathroom, where I saw myself in the medicine chest mirror. I stopped there and I stared. For three days I stared. I wasn't her little sister. And in the mirror I saw the road split, and I took mine …

STANLEY: (*Grabbing Stella.*) Stella. (*They hug;* STELLA *exits;* STANLEY *goes to the bathroom and starts shaving. The lights dim.*)

MITCH: (*Entering stage right. He carries a painting of a card table, which he places over the front of the square box.*) Now and then I reached out to touch his wrists. They glittered with a dozen golden bracelets that matched the large earrings he wore. He was like a shimmering waterfall of gold, his whole front covered with golden pendants that looked like coins. Beneath, he wore a purple semi-transparent shift that matched the dark makeup around his large bedroom eyes. There was something both fierce and warm in his face. He was glowing with a pagan intensity that matched the intense feelings brimming up in my heart, which in turn matched the brimming purple wine that was being poured, seemingly without end, into our glittering golden goblets that matched the shafts of golden scorching sunlight that poured through the high windows down onto the banqueting table, where they were scattered in a dozen colors as they hit the gold in the glass. Finally, he rose from his throne, which was covered in a mantle of blue macaw feathers that cost ten dollars per square inch and matched the cerulean blue of the deep-piled carpet reputedly made by the tiny fingers of ten-year-old eunuchs within the forbidden city in Peking. Then he began to dance …

STANLEY: (*Grabbing* MITCH *by the shoulders.*) You know, a bum like me can grow up in a great country like this and be her lover, which is a hell of a better job than being president of the United States.

MITCH: You're a lucky man.

STANLEY: You know, when I think about her, it's like food, I want to eat her, just put her whole leg in my mouth, or her face, or her hands …

MITCH: That's a mouthful!

STANLEY: I feel so hungry when I think of her, I could eat my car, I could eat dirt, I could eat a brick wall. I have to, I have no choice. I have to touch things, and my hands bring them to my mouth.

MITCH: Your big hands!

STANLEY: Feelings grow inside me, and sometimes they fly out of me so fast and then smack, I'm out of control. When it comes to big hands, I have no competition. (STANLEY *takes a swig of beer.*)

MITCH: When it comes to big hands, she knows she's got your big hands all over her. (*He takes a swig.*)

STANLEY: (*Challenging him to arm wrestle.*) My big pioneer hands all over her rocky mountains.

MITCH: (*Taking the challenge.*) All over her livestock and vegetation.

STANLEY: Her buffalos and prairies.

MITCH: Her thick forests and golden sunsets.

STANLEY: All over her stars!

MITCH: She's in your hands!

STANLEY: She's in my hands and … yeeaaa … (*He pins* MITCH's *arms down.*)

MITCH: That's right! Bite me! Bite me! Suck on me … oops.

STANLEY: (*Pulling away from* MITCH.) What are you talking about?

MITCH: Mosquitoes! Biting me, biting me …

STANLEY: (*Both of them slapping at bugs.*) Suck on me, suck on my body!

MITCH: What do you think I'm here for, your entertainment? A Coney Island for you?

STANLEY: A joyride on my ankle! A suck on my wrist! I'll eliminate you! (*He mimes a machine gun and makes a gun noise.*)

MITCH: Remove you from my space! Pow!

STANLEY: Away from my body, you aggravating hungry bugger.

MITCH: Bugger off! Away with you!

STANLEY: You're spoiled … Splat!

MITCH: You're educated … Squash!

STANLEY: You remind me of my fate.

MITCH: You remind me of my immortality! Leave me my blood.

STANLEY: Blood!

MITCH: Bloody sheet.

STANLEY: Bloody night.

MITCH: Blood on your hand!

STANLEY: It's my hand, I'm dealing the cards.

MITCH: (*Running after* STANLEY *around the box.*) Deal me!

STANLEY: If you want another card I'll hit you with it.

MITCH: Hit me!

STANLEY: When it comes to big hands I got no competition.

MITCH: Take me!

STANLEY: Your shuffle.

MITCH: Cut me in!

STANLEY: Throw your checkbook out the window!

MITCH: Empty my pockets!

STANLEY: I'm a royal flush, I win every time. (*He challenges him to arm wrestle.*)

MITCH: (*Taking the challenge.*) I'm the last sailboat across the horizon before the sun sets.

STANLEY: Nobody can audition for my part.

MITCH: I flop and smash and throw things.

STANLEY: I turn and punch the air!

MITCH: I sweat.

STANLEY: I smell.

MITCH: I smell!

STANLEY: I smell of car oil, I smell of your blood.

MITCH: I smell of … cologne!

STANLEY: I'm hungry, ha, hungry! I'm gonna eat rough memories.

MITCH: I'm gonna eat tough dreams.

STANLEY: Digest hard words. Hard, hard words.

MITCH: I'm gonna spit them out!

STANLEY: It's gonna cost you my hunger!

MITCH: I'm gonna pay!

STANLEY: (*Grabbing* MITCH.) I'm gonna eat my car. I'm gonna eat dirt!

MITCH: I'm gonna eat a tree! Eat your whole leg!

STANLEY: I'm gonna eat the sun and then I'll sweat!

STANLEY AND MITCH: (*In a frenzy.*) Bite me! Bite me! Suck on me!

BLANCHE: (*Opening the bathroom curtain and entering wearing a man's jacket, pants and cap.*) Suck my wrist.

STANLEY *sings.*
'I'm a Man'

STANLEY: When I was a little boy, at the age of five
I had something in my pocket, kept a lot of folks alive
Now I'm a man, made twenty-one
I'll tell you baby, we can have a lot of fun
'Cos I'm a man
Spelled M … A … N … Man
Oohh … oowww … oowww

All you pretty women, standing in a line
I can make love to you, in an hour's time
'Cos I'm a man
Spelled M … A … N … Man

Dance break.

The line I shoot will never miss
When I make love to you baby, it comes to this
I'm a man
Spelled M … A … N … Man
Oohh … oowww … oowww … owww …
I'm a man, yes I am, I'm a man …

STANLEY: (*Gradually noticing* BLANCHE *has a finger up her nose.*) Hold it, hold it. (*To* BLANCHE.) Is there something I can help you with?

BLANCHE: Please could you give me a tissue. I think I've got something stuck up my nose.

STANLEY: Would you like me to have a look?

BLANCHE: Please don't trouble. I think a tissue would probably do it.

STANLEY: (*Handing her a tissue.*) Here.

BLANCHE: Probably a boogey, I expect.

STANLEY: An acquaintance of mine lost his sense of smell from having a booger stuck up his nose … better?

BLANCHE: Not really, no.

MITCH: Can I help?

BLANCHE: Oh no, please, it's only something stuck up my nose.

MITCH: Try sticking your little finger in as far as it'll go.

STANLEY: Then blow your nose.

MITCH: Please let me look, I happen to be a doctor.

BLANCHE: It's very kind of you.

MITCH: Turn around to the light please. Now look up. Now look down. Now look up again … I can see it … keep still … (*He twists the tissue and pokes it up her nose.*) There!

BLANCHE: Oh dear, what a relief, it was agonizing.

MITCH: (*Holding up the tissue.*) It looks like a piece of Christmas pudding.

BLANCHE: Thank you very much indeed.

MITCH: Not at all.

BLANCHE: How lucky for me you happened to be here.

MITCH: Anybody could have done it.

BLANCHE: Never mind, you did and I'm most grateful.

MITCH: There's my train … Goodbye. (*He exits.*)

BLANCHE: And that's how it all began, just through me getting a booger stuck up my nose. (*She takes off her cap, turns to face* STANLEY, *then walks away upstage left as the lights dim and music starts.* MITCH *enters and motions for* BLANCHE *to dance with him, as* STANLEY *shuffles a deck of cards.*)

STANLEY: Hey Mitch, you in this game or what?

MITCH: Deal me out. I'm talking to Miss DuBois. (*They begin to dance as* STELLA *wanders on.*)

STELLA: Look, we made enchantment.

STANLEY: Who turned that on? Turn it off.

STELLA: Ah-h-h-h let them have their music.

STANLEY: I said turn it off!

STELLA: What are you doing?

STANLEY: That's the last time anybody plays music during my game. Now get OUT! OUT! (*The music stops;* STELLA *is laughing quietly.*)

STELLA: I guess you think that's funny.

STANLEY: Yeah, I thought it was pretty funny.

STELLA: Well, maybe I blinked at the wrong time, 'cuz I missed the joke.

STANLEY: Oh, so now you're an authority on what's funny.

STELLA: I didn't say that. I said I didn't think that that was funny.

STANLEY: Well, if you know so much, why don't you show me what is funny.

STELLA: Look, I don't want to get twisted out of shape about it, I just didn't think it was all that funny.

STANLEY: Oh, you thought it was just a little bit funny.

STELLA: No, not even a little bit funny.

STANLEY: So, show me!

STELLA: This is ridiculous.

STANLEY: Show me what's funny.

STELLA: You want me to show you what's funny.

STANLEY: Yeah, show me funny.

STELLA: Okay, I'll show you funny … (*She rips* STANLEY'S *sleeve.*) That's funny.

STANLEY: That was not funny.

STELLA: You want funny? (*She rips off the other sleeve.*) That's funny.

STANLEY: That was not funny.

STELLA: Okay. What about this? (*She rips off half of* STANLEY'S *shirt.*) Or this? (*She rips off the other half.*)

STANLEY: That's not funny.

STELLA: I'll be right back. (*She bustles offstage and comes back with a seltzer bottle, then sprays* STANLEY.) That was funny.

STANLEY: That was not funny.

STELLA: I'll be right back. (*She comes back with a giant powder puff and powders* STANLEY.) That was funny.

STANLEY: That's not funny.

STELLA: I'll be right back. (*She comes back with a cream pie. As she nears* STANLEY, STANLEY *unexpectedly tips it into* STELLA'S *face.*)

STANLEY: Now *that* was funny. (STANLEY *exits.* MITCH *enters, pulling a curtain with a painting of a giant orchid. The Cassandra aria from* Les Troyens *comes on loudly, then fades.*)

MITCH: The bell sounds and they're both middle weights. They know the rules, and they've been publicized as an even match. 'Ere, you've paid good money to see them, you want to see a battle, you want to see blood. Round One is I Love You, Round Two is You See Me For Who I Really Am. You never see a person more clearly than the first time they lay hands on you. After that, it's all up for grabs. (*To* STELLA.) He's gonna be back and he's gonna say he's sorry.

STELLA: (*Wiping the pie from her face.*) Sorry. (*She laughs.*) Sorry … sorry, sorry. (*Laughs.*) The Indian women. The Indian women, wrapping their soft bodies in thick silk the colors of a church window. Sari. (*Laughs.*) I'm sorry too. It makes me laugh. They can't take it back. What the gods give they cannot take back, they can only add to what they've given, to make the gift painful to have. Cassandra! Zeus gave her the gift of the seer, and then she wouldn't have sex with him, but he couldn't take back the gift. He couldn't have her, so he made sure no one would believe her … She knew all those men were in that wooden horse, but they wouldn't listen … (*Laughs.*) That's hysterical. It was their loss, that curse! Zeus made a prophetess and then spit in her face. And just what do you think went on inside that horse? Hundreds of warlike men, spitting, smoking, dreaming death in the belly of a fake horse … I dream a purple darkness … purple … the color of the sari … darlings. I'm in here. I'm on drugs. I'm braless, shirtless, I'm giggling, I'm lost, I'm in love. I'm stuck in the stomach of a fake horse, can you hear me? I hear you. Cassandra tell me what will happen. I promise I'll believe you! I … I'm in love with you Cassandra, you blonde, you seer, you whisperer … tell me what's going to happen … come here … let's make it happen. Please don't, blonde seer. I can't, I'm already married. Take your hands off my breasts, I'm already married. I'm in here. The horse! I'm in the belly of a horse, smoking, shirtless. I'm preparing for a war. (*She begins to strip off her house dress to reveal a tight, strapless dress.*) Someone stole my woman, stole her from my house, filched her from history, and I'm here to get her back. I am a powerful warrior. (*She poses like Marilyn Monroe.*) Come sweet prophetess, what is going to happen? Tell me, I'm nailed to this story. Cut me down. I'm in here. Can't you see me? I'm having sex with the fortune teller that men don't believe. Sex … sex! (*She sings.*)

'Running Wild'

STELLA: Running wild, lost control
Running wild, mighty bold
Feeling gay, reckless too
Carefree mind, all the time, never blue
Always going – don't know where
Always showing – I don't care
Don't love nobody, it's not worthwhile
All alone and running wild

STANLEY *has entered the audience and applauds* STELLA *loudly as the piano starts the intro for* STELLA's *next song.*

'Sweet Little Angel'

STELLA: I've got a sweet little angel
And I love the way she spreads her wings
I've got a sweet little angel
And I love the way she spreads her wings
When she spreads those wings over me
She brings joy in everything

STANLEY: (*Clapping loudly and talking to the audience.*) Is she good or what? She is so good … can you believe how good she is? (STELLA *stops singing.*) Any moment this dame spends out of bed is wasted, totally wasted. (STANLEY *runs to* STELLA *and drops to his knees.*)

STELLA: I could smell you coming.

STANLEY: You say the sweetest things.

STELLA: Women have to develop a sense of smell. Just in general. Just as a matter of fact. Like in a war. In a war, you learn to smell the enemy. You learn to cross the street. You learn to see through their disguises.

Figure 28 Peggy Shaw and Lois Weaver in *Belle Reprieve*, 1991. (Photograph: Sheila Burnett.)

STANLEY: I am not your enemy.

STELLA: No … but you have many of the characteristics. Not that I go by appearances, just smell and instinct.

STANLEY: What are you looking for?

STELLA: You're tense.

STANLEY: I'm always tense. It keeps me in check, keeps me in balance.

STELLA: It's hard to watch.

STANLEY: That's 'cuz you don't know that it's leading to something.

STELLA: And are you gonna tell me what that is?

STANLEY: It's a fact of life, you figure it out.

STELLA: I already did. I don't have to spend long on the likes of you, not one as experienced as I am. I know that your tension is sexual, and it's a desire that I share in, but not for your pleasure, for my own. I'm lookin' for it, I might not find it in you, I might find it somewhere else, as a matter of fact, and there's nothing you can do about it. You don't satisfy me, you're not real.

STANLEY: Are you saying I'm not a real man?

STELLA: I'm saying you're not real. You're cute. Could be much cuter if you weren't quite so obvious.

STANLEY: Then it wouldn't be me. I am not subtle.

STELLA: Try it, just for tonight.

STANLEY: You mean put it on like clothes? I couldn't pull that off.

STELLA: No, take it off. Take it all off. I want to see what you're really made of. I want to see what it is that makes me want you. That makes me want to have you as I've never had anyone. Strip. Take it off, then we'll talk.

STANLEY: Talk is cheap.

STELLA: I want to see you naked like a baby.

STANLEY: No more talk, let's make a deal.

STELLA: We are partners in this deal. I have my part, you have yours.

STANLEY: I can live up to my end of the deal, how 'bout you.

STELLA: Put your cards on the table, I'm calling your bluff.

Blackout.

STANLEY: Hey, turn on the light!

STELLA: I like it in the dark.

STANLEY: I don't like the dark, I like to see.

STELLA: (*As the lights slowly fade up.*) You can see if you get your eyes used to it.

STANLEY: I don't want to get used to it, I'm afraid of the dark.

A low light reveals their silhouettes dancing as the pianist sings. 'Sweet Little Angel'

PIANIST: I've got a sweet little angel
And I love the way she spreads her wings
I've got a sweet little angel
And I love the way she spreads her wings
When she spreads those wings over me
She brings joy in everything

I asked my angel for a nickel
And she gave me a twenty-dollar bill
I asked my angel for a nickel
And she gave me a twenty-dollar bill
When I asked her for her body
She said she'd leave it to me in her will …

Well my angel if she quit me
I believe I would die
Well my angel if she quit me
I believe I would die
If you don't believe me
You must tell me the reason why.

STELLA has pulled off STANLEY's ripped T-shirt as they dance. She jumps up and wraps her body around STANLEY and throws the shirt to the ground as they exit. Blackout.

Act 2

The stage is empty except for the large rectangular box on its side, with the painting of a tub across the front. A dim orange light comes up on STELLA standing and stretching in the bathtub in her slip.

STELLA: The fire is keeping me awake. It reminds me of the night Yellow Mountain was burning. All night long I could see Yellow Mountain burning on my bedroom ceiling. I was afraid that the burning debris would fall from the mountain on to our roof and burn through the ceiling. Meet up with a flicker that was already there, waiting to devour me.

MITCH: (*A light behind the scrim reveals BLANCHE in a nightgown holding a cigarette and MITCH standing beside her. MITCH lights her cigarette.*) There's a shadow over by the window. It's a woman. She's smoking a cigarette. (*BLANCHE blows smoke into MITCH's face; he coughs.*) The smoke is coming my way. Maybe she wants me to go with her. (*BLANCHE passes around the scrim and crosses to center stage, where she picks up STANLEY's torn T-shirt.*)

STELLA: The fire has leapt out of control. It's too late, the firemen have all gone home to their wives. Had to hose down their own houses, to protect them from the falling debris.

BLANCHE: (*Examining STANLEY's shirt.*) This shirt smells of success to me. These elements of manhood … there's something about Stanley I can't quite put my finger on. I can't put my finger on his smell. I don't believe he's a man. I question his sexuality. His postures are not real, don't seem to be coming from a true place. He's a phoney, and he's got her believing it, and if she has children he'll have them believing it and when he dies, they'll find out. (*She crosses to STELLA.*) Have you ever seen him naked?

STELLA: (*Drinking Coke.*) It's the sugar that satisfies me. The cool liquid running down my throat is only temporary.

It's when the sugar hits the bloodstream, that's when my heart starts pumping.

BLANCHE: There's something about the way he smells, something about the way he has to prove his manhood all the time, that makes me suspicious. I'm looking at the shape, not the content.

STELLA: (*Straddling the edge of the tub.*) Don't you love that feeling when you lean against a solid surface and you can feel your heart beating under your body.

BLANCHE: The noises he makes, the way he walks like Mae West, the sensual way he wears his clothes, this is no garage-mechanic working-class boy, this is planned behavior. This is calculated sexuality, developed over years of picking up signals not necessarily genetic is what I'm trying to say.

STELLA: I remember leaning my abdomen against the cold sink and feeling my heart beating between my legs.

BLANCHE: I'm trying to say, what I mean is, perhaps he was a man in some former life. Perhaps he's just a halfway house, to lure you into a sexual trap, a trap well laid, with just the right flavors, just the right mood to seduce you … what I'm trying to say is, I think he's a fag.

STELLA: The thing about Coca-Cola is that one sixteen-ounce bottle has more than four tablespoons of sugar.

BLANCHE: But now you have the chance to get out. To end this charade before it's too late …

STELLA: Enough to keep you up half the night.

BLANCHE: Only someone as skilled as I am at being a woman can pick up these subtle signs.

STELLA: Enough to curb your appetite.

BLANCHE: I'm well trained, equipped. I know how to talk to him, to flirt with him, not get involved really, to decorate his arm, to aid him in his charade, to give him a passing grade.

STELLA: Sugar in a sixteen-ounce bottle.

BLANCHE: (*Grabbing STELLA's hand.*) I'm the real woman for you. I can show you satisfaction. A rewarding, cultural life; me and you, you and me, Blanche and Stella, Stella and Blanche … You were such a pretty girl. (*STELLA pulls away.*) What day was it that you changed? You were tipped for the top and you threw it all away. You were headed upward to the good, right life and suddenly you changed.

STELLA: Pure sugar, liquid sex.

BLANCHE: Stella, you haven't been listening to a word I've been saying.

STELLA: (*STANLEY has come through the audience and is standing facing STELLA and BLANCHE.*) The fire is still burning … my clothes sticking to my chest just like Mama's dress against her naked belly. Now why did she stay at the sink so long … (*she walks towards STANLEY*) and every day without underwear. (*She jumps into STANLEY's arms.*)

STANLEY: Hey! (*STANLEY spins her around, then they walk offstage together.*)

BLANCHE: Trouble is, Marlon Brando does look gorgeous.

And I know that if I met him at the time he was in that film I'd want to lick his armpits. I don't suppose he'd be able to open himself up to that though ... surrender himself. But he does have that big shapely mouth ... I guess I'm pretty taken with this actor in the film. But what if the film was life and I could just walk right into it? I don't suppose he'd welcome me, probably give me a hard time. Just like he gave Blanche ... I mean Miss Leigh ... and what would she say if this drag queen poured out of the camera lens and blew up to size right there in front of her. Yes, well, she had to deal with Marlon Brando all day and Laurence Olivier in the evenings ... I'd say she had enough problems without me on the set ... I feel like an old hotel. (*Pianist starts the prelude to 'Beautiful Dream.'*) Beautiful bits of dereliction in need of massive renovation. There's that record again. Have you ever had something stuck in your head for a very long time, like a record playing over and over and every time it stops there's applause, and then it starts all over again ... (*The music stops and* BLANCHE *ticks her hand in the tub.*) I like a warm bath. It's the warmth I'm after, not the cleanliness. I don't even mind Stella's cheap, common soap ... Oh I did it you know, I did lead the grand life ... chauffeurs, limos. I used to go to clubs and know I was the most attractive person there ... now I don't go to clubs.

STANLEY: (*Pulling in the painted vaudeville curtain behind* BLANCHE.) Ha Ha.

BLANCHE: (*With the music beginning again.*) Now, here it comes ... the record ... and there's a dark burgundy curtain opening on the stage, and there we are, just me and Vivien ...

STANLEY: HA HA. Did you hear what I said? HA HA HA. (*He exits.*)

BLANCHE: (*Singing.*)

'Beautiful Dream'

Cold wind blowing through the empty rooms
Windows broken, floors damp and rotten now
No sound in the silence
No step in the stillness
No warmth in the cold air
Only shadows moving in the half-light
Empty lockers, lines of empty hooks
Vacant showers, all deep in dust now
Just a modest price bought you paradise
No one wondered would it last
Running out of stream, now the beautiful dream
Has passed.

No one greets me as I step inside
Hot and ready for whatever comes my way
No warm body waiting for me
No pulse of a warm heart near me

No strong arms around me
No one lying warm and sweet beside me
Thought we'd party 'til the end of time
But it's over, seems so long ago now
Down the long parade, see them slowly fade
As they all leave one by one
Running out of steam, now the beautiful dream
Has gone.

So I fill the tub, rub-a-dub-dub-dub
But I still freeze up inside
'Cuz the water's cold
And the dream has grown old and died
Running out of steam
Now the beautiful dream
Has gone.

(*The lights fade, the curtain is pulled offstage,* BLANCHE *moves to the tub upstage left and climbs in.*) Bubbles, bawbles, bumholes ... (*She smells the soap.*) Municipal, that's the word. Now I'm going under ... can't hear the noises at all ... just the odd humps and hoomps and grinds ... my hair is floating about ... whooosh ... up in the air again. (BLANCHE *reappears in the tub wearing the bubble dress as a ukelele strums in the background.*) Listen ... there it is again, the record, going around and around and then the applause. Until something replaces that song and that wild applause, I know I'll cling to it. I'll always choose applause over death.

Lights behind the scrim reveal MITCH *in fairy costume perched on a ladder and looking down on* BLANCHE *in the tub. He is playing the ukelele and singing.*
'The Fairy Song'

MITCH: I was sitting on my asteroid, way up in the sky
When I saw you through the window, and I thought I'd drop by
You were looking sad, bothered and forlorn
Wondering where your days of youth and beauty all had gone.
Now I don't possess a magic wand, my wings are rather small
As far as fairies go I'm nothing special at all
But still I've got that something that I know you'll just adore
That special kind of magic, gonna sweep you off the floor.

Chorus

I'm a supernatural being, I'm your sweetie-pie
And I've come here from somewhere far, away up in the sky
I'm here to play a song tonight by Rimsky-Korsakov
And if you play your cards right we might even have it off.

BLANCHE *mouths the words as* MITCH *continues singing.*

Now I was sitting in the bathtub, minding my own biz

When this vision came from outer space and now I'm
in a tiz
He was gorgeous, he was handsome, he was eager just
to please
And he said that he'd come here so me and him could
have a squeeze.

I'm a supernatural being, I'm your sweetie-pie
And I've come here from somewhere far, away up in the sky
I'll take you to my fairy dell, in my fairy car
And hang a sign 'Do not disturb' upon the evening star.

Dance break, BLANCHE *twirls around and motions* MITCH *to join her. They dance.*

BLANCHE: (*Speaking.*) Are you sure that you're a fairy?
I'd imagined they were blonde.
And frankly I'm not leaving 'til I've seen your magic wand.
MITCH: (*Singing.*) My wand, alas, I left at home, you'll have
to come on spec
But I promise when we get there you can hold it for a sec.

Chorus

MITCH *and* BLANCHE *exit.* BLANCHE *re-enters with* STELLA *and* STANLEY, *who resets the table box and holds a birthday cake.*

STANLEY: (*Singing in monotone.*) Happy birthday to you, happy
birthday to you, happy birthday … Blanche, happy
birthday to you.
BLANCHE: What a lovely cake. How many candles are on it?
STELLA: Don't you worry about that right now. Why don't
you tell us one of your funny stories.
BLANCHE: I don't think Mr. Kowalski would be interested in
any of my funny stories.
STANLEY: I've got a funny story, what about this: there's
these two faggots sitting on the sofa, which one is the
cocksucker? (*Long pause.*) The one with the feathers
coming out of his mouth.
BLANCHE: In the version I heard it was two pollacks.
STANLEY: I am not a pollack. People from Poland are Poles.
There is no such thing as a pollack. And in any case, for
your information, I am one hundred percent American.
STELLA: Well, now that we're all getting along so well, why
don't you blow out the candles, Blanche, and make a wish.
STANLEY: Be careful what you wish for.

BLANCHE *blows out all the candles. They relight. She blows them out again, but again they relight. As she goes to blow them out again,* STANLEY *brushes her aside and sticks the candles upside down in the cake one by one. Blackout. The bathtub is removed and a painting of an oversized naked light bulb is pulled onstage.*

STANLEY: Stella! Blanche! Mitch! It's dark. I'm afraid.
STELLA: Let's play a game. (*She blindfolds him and spins him around.*)
STANLEY: This is not funny. Stella. Mitch. (*The lights slowly fade up.* STANLEY *is wandering around the stage blindfolded.*)

Don't panic … I feel these original sins burning into me.
I feel I'm never safe. There I am at four a.m. with giant
monsters spelling out my life in large slimy letters above
my body, just far enough above it to heat it up. To make
my skin bead in sweat starting just under my hair, above
my forehead, on the back of my neck, on my chest and
the back of my knees. Don't panic … I was born this
way. I didn't learn it at theatre school. I was born butch.
I'm so queer I don't even have to talk about it. It speaks
for itself, it's not funny. Being butch isn't funny … don't
panic … I fall to pieces in the night. I'm just thousands
of parts of other people all mashed into one body. I am
not an original person. I take all these pieces, snatch them
off the floor before they get swept under the bed, and
I manufacture myself. When I'm saying I fall to pieces,
I'm saying Marlon Brando was not there for me. (*Pianist starts playing softly.*) James Dean failed to come through,
where was Susan Hayward when I needed her, and Rita
Hayworth was nowhere to be found. I fall to pieces at the
drop of a hat. Just pick the piece you want and when I
pull myself back together again I'll think of you. I'll think
of you and what you want me to be. (*He sings all the verses to a song in the style of the Frank Sinatra hit 'My Way,' while crawling onto the table with the birthday cake and presents on it. As he gets to his knees on top of the table, one hand breaks through a box and comes out covered in blood, the other hand goes into the cake and then into a box filled with feathers. He sings the final stanza kneeling on the cake.*) WHERE THE
FUCK IS EVERYBODY?! (*Blackout. After a short pause the lights come up on* STELLA *and* STANLEY.) What time is it?
STELLA: It's four a.m.
STANLEY: Help me make it through the night.
STELLA: Don't I always?
STANLEY: I'll be tired tomorrow, I'll be tired all day.
STELLA: Don't think about tomorrow. (*They embrace and kiss as the lights fade to black. The lights come up upstage right on* MITCH *stuffing cake into his mouth.*)
MITCH: (*Talking with his mouth full throughout.*) I think it all
started to go wrong when I wasn't allowed to be a boy
scout. There were more important things to be done.
Vacuuming, clearing up at home, putting the garbage out.
I used to get so angry putting out the garbage, I'd kick the
shit out of the garbage cans in front. I thought about what
I was missing. It gave me a repulsion for physical activity.
Swimming was the only exception, and even then it took
me a long time to learn, as I was afraid of deep water.
Then one day I fell in love with a beautiful young man.
He came like a messenger from another world bearing a
message of simple physical desire. But it was already too
late, for me everything about the body was bound up
with pain and boredom. I even used to eat fast because
I found it so boring. Soon the boy left. He knew better
than to spend his life cooking dinners for someone with
poor appetite. Then I was alone. I lived in a small room

near a fly-over. I stopped going out except to go to the laundry and get groceries. At night I would lie awake on my bed, and imagine I could hear things. (*The sound of a ukelele from offstage. He opens one of the gift boxes on the table and the sound comes again. He reaches into the box and pulls out a ukelele, then sings a song in the style of 'The Man I Love,' by George and Ira Gershwin. As he sings, tap-dancing Chinese lanterns – the remaining members of the cast in lantern costumes – enter and begin dancing around him. During the song the lanterns begin running into each other and floundering around the stage. The audience begins to hear them mumbling from under their costumes.*)

BLANCHE: Oh, what are we doing? I can't stand it! I want to be in a real play! (*Bright light pops on as* STELLA *drops her lantern to the floor.*) With real scenery! White telephones, French windows, a beginning, a middle and an end! This is the most confusing show I've ever been in. What's wrong with red plush? What's wrong with a theme and a plot we can all follow? There isn't even a fucking drinks trolley. Agatha Christie was right.

STELLA: Now we all talked about this, and we decided that realism works against us.

BLANCHE: Oh we did, did we?

STELLA, STANLEY AND MITCH: Yes we did!

BLANCHE: But I felt better before, I could cope. All I had to do was learn my lines and not trip over the furniture. It was all so clear. And here we are romping about in the avant-garde and I don't know what else. I want my mother to come and have a good time. She's seventy-three for chrissake. You know she's expecting me to play Romeo before it's too late. What am I supposed to tell her? That I like being a drag-queen? She couldn't bear it. I know she couldn't. She wants me to be in something realistic, playing a real person with a real job, like on television.

STELLA: You want realism?

BLANCHE: What do you mean?

STELLA: You want realism, you can have it.

BLANCHE: You mean like in a real play?

STELLA: If that's what you want.

BLANCHE: With Marlon Brando and Vivien Leigh?

STELLA: You think you can play it?

BLANCHE: I have the shoulders.

STANLEY: I have the pajamas … okay, let's go for it. (MITCH *and* STELLA *exit, striking the light bulb curtain.* STANLEY *sweeps the table with his forearm knocking the cake and presents to the floor.*) I cleared my place, want me to clear yours? It's just you and me now, Blanche.

BLANCHE: You mean we're alone in here?

STANLEY: Unless you got someone in the bathroom. (*He takes off his pajama top and pulls out a bottle of beer.*)

BLANCHE: Please don't get undressed without pulling the curtain.

STANLEY: Oh, this is all I'm gonna undress right now. Feel like a shower? (*He opens the beer and shakes it, then lets it squirt all over the stage, then pours some over his head before drinking it.*) You want some?

BLANCHE: No thank you.

STANLEY: (*Moving towards her, menacingly.*) Sure I can't make you reconsider?

BLANCHE: Keep away from me.

STANLEY: What's the matter, don't you trust me? Afraid I might touch you or something? You should be so lucky. Take a look at yourself in that worn-out party dress from a third-rate thrift store. What queen do you think you are?

BLANCHE: (*Trying to get past him.*) Oh God.

STANLEY: (*Blocking her exit.*) I got your number baby.

BLANCHE: Do we have to play this scene?

STANLEY: You said that's what you wanted.

BLANCHE: But I didn't mean it.

STANLEY: You wanted realism.

BLANCHE: Just let me get by you.

STANLEY: Get by me? Sure, go ahead.

BLANCHE: You stand over there.

STANLEY: You got plenty of room, go ahead.

BLANCHE: Not with you there! I've got to get by somehow!

STANLEY: You can get by, there's plenty of room. I won't hurt you. I like you. We're in this together, me and you. We've known that from the start. We're the extremes, the stereotypes. We are as far as we can go. We have no choice, me and you. We're tried it all, haven't we? We've rejected ourselves, not trusted ourselves, mirrored ourselves, and we always come back to ourselves. We're the warriors. We have an agreement … there's plenty in this world for both of us. We don't have to give each other up to anyone. You are my special angel.

BLANCHE: You wouldn't talk this way if you were a real man.

STANLEY: No, if I was a real man I'd say, 'Come to think of it, you wouldn't be so bad to interfere with.'

BLANCHE: And if I were really Blanche I'd say, 'Stay back … don't come near me another step … or I'll …'

STANLEY: You'll what?

BLANCHE: Something's gonna happen here. It will.

STANLEY: What are you trying to pull?

BLANCHE: (*Pulling off one of her stiletto-heeled shoes.*) I warn you … don't!

STANLEY: Now what did you do that for?

BLANCHE: So I could twist this heel right in your face.

STANLEY: You'd do that, wouldn't you?

BLANCHE: I would, and I will if you …

STANLEY: You want to play dirty? I can play dirty. (*He grabs her arm.*) Drop it. I said drop it! Drop the stiletto!

BLANCHE: You think I'm crazy or something?

STANLEY: If you want to be in this play you've got to drop the stiletto.

BLANCHE: If you want to be in this play you've got to make me!

STANLEY: If you want to play a woman, the woman in this play gets raped and goes crazy in the end.

BLANCHE: I don't want to get raped and go crazy. I just wanted to wear a nice frock, and look at the shit they've given me!

STELLA: (*Entering with* MITCH.) Gimme that shoe! (*pianist starts 'Pushover' as she grabs* STANLEY *and sings to him.*)

'Pushover'

STELLA: All the girls think you're fine, they even call you Romeo,

You've got 'em, yeah you've got 'em runnin' to and fro, oh yes you have.

But I don't want a one-night thrill, I want a love that's for real,

And I can tell by your lies, yours is not the lasting kind.

You took me for a pushover, you thought I was a pushover,

I'm not a pushover, you thought that you could change my mind.

MITCH *sings to* BLANCHE.

MITCH: So you told all the boys that were gonna take me out

You even, yeah you even had the nerve to make a bet, oh yes you did,

That I, I would give in, all of my love you would win,

But you haven't, you haven't won it yet.

You took me for a pushover, you thought I was a pushover,

I'm not a pushover, you thought my love was easy to get.

MITCH AND STELLA: Your tempting lips, your wavy hair,

Your pretty eyes with that come hither stare,

It makes me weak, I start to bend and then I stop and think again,

No, no, no don't let yourself go.

I wanna spoil your reputation, I want true love, not an imitation,

And I'm hip, to every word in your conversation.

You took me for a pushover, I'm not a pushover,

You can't push me over, you thought I was a pushover …

STELLA: (*To the audience.*) Did you figure it out yet? Who's who, what's what, who gets what, where the toaster is plugged in? Did you get what you wanted?

STANLEY: Hey Stella, I just figured it out. Wasn't Blanche blonde?

STELLA: That's right. And come to think of it, it was suspicious she didn't have a southern accent.

STANLEY: I knew it all along. The person we've been referring to as your sister is an imposter.

STELLA: Incredible! There's no flies on you Stanley.

STANLEY: What did you say?

STELLA: I said there's no disguising you, Stanley. You're one hundred percent.

STANLEY: I thought you said something else … something about flies.

STELLA: Well, come to think of it, there is something in that area I've been meaning to open up a little.

STANLEY: So, you figured it out.

STELLA: Yeah, I figured it out.

STANLEY: And in those shoes. Un-fuckin'-believable! You know what this means?

STELLA: No, what?

STANLEY: This means that you are the only thing we can rely on, because you are at least who you seem to be.

STELLA: Well Stanley, there's something I've been meaning to tell you … (*She sings.*)

You took me for a pushover

(*All join in.*) I'm not a pushover

You can't push me over

You thought I was a pushover

DON'T PUSH!

Encore.

'I Love My Art'

I've been mad about the stage since childhood,

When I roamed the sage and wildwood,

The attraction for the dazzling lights,

Caused me troublesome nights

Now I realize my one ambition

I can make a full and frank admission,

I am madly in love with my art, I love to play my part,

I love the theatre, I love it better than all my life, and just because

It's so entrancing, the song and dancing, to the music of applause,

I love the stage and all about it, it simply goes right to my heart,

I love the glamour, I love the drama,

I love I love I love my art

I love the glamour, I love the drama

I love I love I love my art

THE END

5.4 THE STORY OF M (1995)

SUANDI

SuAndi (b. 1951) *is a UK-based performer, director, poet and writer. She has been working as a performance poet and live artist since the mid-1980s and has worked with the Black Arts Alliance as an artist-activist in the UK for which she was awarded the Queen's Honours of an O.B.E. in 1999. She has worked extensively in the UK and the USA in particular with community arts projects which engage with the work of artists of colour. Her public artworks include the libretto for an opera about Mary Seacole and 24 poetry disks at Salford Quays Lowry Centre, Manchester, England.*

I wrote M following a mediocre production that closed with homage to white women who had endured racism following their inter-racial marriages. Lois Keidan felt it was the strongest section and encouraged me to write more, as fact is always more interesting. Forty minutes into my return journey to Manchester I'd done as advised with tears running down my face. It took very little more writing to complete.

SCENE – Hospital room with a single bed with a screen to the side. A chair next to a small locker on which is placed a jug of water, tissues and a flower vase. 'M' is led onto the stage by a nurse; she is continuously coughing.

I've got cancer.
I have.
Bloody cancer
And I know exactly when I got it –
eating a jam cream sponge cake
with my daughter's boyfriend.
I suppose you'll think I'm daft
Me calling him her boyfriend
what with him being gay!
But he is,
he's her boyfriend
and for me he's like a second son.
I was over at their place.
They live together.
Not together like,
But you know, together.
I was eating this jam cream sponge cake –
It was my first for months
I'd been dieting
Getting ready for her coming home.
I was born big – me.
Big!
Always was.
Take the time like I tried to join the
Sally Army now you'll not believe this.
They wouldn't let me in
Because my legs were too big for the boots.
Christianity my big toe.

Hi get it?
Big toe, big foot, big leg,
Oh never mind

I'd lost two stone
thought I was a bloody miracle –
when suddenly
I get this massive pain
and wow cancer.
Think of all those cream cakes
I could have eaten.
Now I'm here, two parts dead.
Going over me life
like you do,
like you all will,
given the chance.

Not like poor Malcolm –
No cancer for him –
Just a bloody racist
With a gun.
But for me –
it's a long drawn out death.
And you'd be amazed
how those memories
come flooding back.

SCENE – M sleeps (Nurse) picks up then drops a kidney tray.

Munitions?
All my friends worked in munitions,
but not me.
I've always been really sensitive to smells.
I was always passing out in church.
Used to drive the nuns crazy.

So I went into the laundries.
Loved it –
All that cleanliness,
Messing about with the suds.
Played bloody murder with your hands
And the heat could burn the end of your
nose off.

Anyways there I was this day
When the new Charge-hand goes past
And says, loud enough for me to hear like,
I bet this heat doesn't bother some people.
Them that belong in jungle!
Well bugger that. I was off.
The rest stayed, but not me.
I knew better.
There were folk from all over the world
Doing their bit for the war effort and here

was this fool talking about the bleedin'
jungle.
I bet he'd been no further than top of
the street.

Anyway –
I could wash at home
For my son and my husband.
Husband!
Bastard more like!
Don't get me wrong. I like men.
It took some time, I'll admit, what, with me
being born a Catholic
And thinking any man, not wearing a
frock (a black frock naturally), was
suspect.
I suppose that's why you never see
Jesus in trousers – because the Catholic
Church has spread so many stories
about the evils in them.

Well I found out the hard way.
I wasn't just naive,
I was thick.
First man that said he loved me, got me –
and not a wedding vow on his lips.
But being the Catholic that I was
I believed in the sanctity of marriage.
So I took him to court.
He was scared shitless!

The first day he stood in the dock
looking like the very criminal he was.
The next day he brought half the ship's
crew with him,
And they testified.
I'd been with them all.
A prostitute he called me.
Me! A Catholic girl, and the judge
believed him.
He looked at me as though I just stepped
off Lime St.
I cried;
I cried; then really cried.
I had no one to turn to.
In the end I won the case,
But my son never took his name.
And I went back!
Back to the only home I'd ever known,
the orphanage.
Convent, more like!
I thought I'd had enough of nuns to last
me a lifetime, and then a bit more, and
here I was back with them.

They gave you another name,
A church name so to speak,
Like Sister Theresa or something.
Every morning, crack of dawn
They'd wake you
And tell you where you were working
that day.
And, they'd also pass out any Special
announcements.
Like, Sister Theresa your baby died
last night.
Oh, and by the way, you're in the kitchen.
I'd pray every night that my son wouldn't
die.
It took me ages to realise
All these babies – they weren't dying.
They were being given away for adoption.

And no one wanted a Black lad.
Well, Thank You Blessed Jesus.
But, I needed a husband,
A father for my son.
In those days my son
Was the only person I loved in the whole
wide world.
Loving a child is important –
I should know,
No one ever really loved me.

My mum had cancer and my elder sister.
For my mum they called it a broken heart.
You see, my father was lost at sea and
from the day he disappeared, she never
got out of bed.
I used to climb up to snuggle next to her.
Close – the way a cat does.
But if she realised it was me
She would shoo me away.
She didn't love me you see.
And I was the youngest.
I should have been loved the best.
They said, the day she died they found me
Lying right next to her cold dead body,
I must have been there for hours.
Neighbours took us in.
Neighbours!
An extended family, with no blood ties.
But they couldn't feed themselves
Never mind the three of us.
So, in time, the church took us.
Seems it was decided by some relatives
from across the water.
You can bet your life they didn't want us,
but they wanted to make sure we were

brought up as Catholics.
See what I mean.
Christianity. It's bloody stupid!

SCENE – M is coughing really badly.

The priest's been round today with his
bloody rosary.
Telling me I should welcome death.
Welcome death!
I'd sooner welcome Margaret Thatcher.

My husband.
My ex-husband
Smokes 40 fags a day
And he's not got cancer.
He's an African.
A real African.
Not like me, a mix up of this, that, and a
bit of the other.
And the only good thing he ever did for me
Was give me my daughter.
She's beautiful my daughter.
The day I got rid of him we had a party!
Bloody good riddance.
But he's a great father – always there for her.
Buys her things; takes her out;
Loves her.
Maybe even more than I do
But as a husband,
well – he just another bastard man.

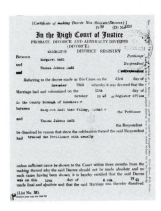

I met him on Berkley St.
All the sailors lived on Berkley St,
Sort of on top of each other.
Liverpool was great in them days.
It was like the world
You know,
People from all over the world
And we all lived happily
side-by-side.

I mean, I had names for the Chinese
That weren't,
Well you know,
Very nice.
I mean,
I didn't exactly
Call them Chinese.

But there again,
I don't suppose the names they called me
were very flattering either.
But we didn't beat each other up,

Shit, on each other's doorsteps.
Oh there were fights.
And name calling.
That made my mouth seem virginal,
And I'm sure there were many
Who would have liked to put us all
On our respective boats
and floated back home.
But in Liverpool 8,
You married anyone you wanted,
And no one gave a bugger;
So why the hell did I marry him?
I mean,
He didn't pretend to like my son.
He didn't even pretend to like me
But he still gave me my daughter.

Hulme
In the 50's
was just like Liverpool

On our street there was an Irish cobbler,
An African fish shop, and
Two funny French people
Who sold horsemeat to make stew out of.
No, not dog food, love, stew.
Where are you from OH?
Anyway, the grocers, the off licence,
And the people in the shop across the road,
They were English,
Or Scottish, or Welsh, or something.
Well, I mean, I can't tell,
can you?
We had Indians across the street
And Jamaicans round the corner.

But it was harder in Manchester;
You see, the war was over,
And the unity had gone out of our lives.
And I had become harder.
I don't mean, I was getting used to it
Just, that, well, I was getting used to it
And had to get harder.
Being spat on in the street!
Being turned away from rooms to let!
Not being able to get HP.
Hearing mothers tell their kids
Not to play with my kids.
Hearing their kids ask my kids
Why they were dirty.
I hit one kid once, outside church.

My daughter was like a flower,
All dressed up with long ringlets in her hair.

I made each of those ringlets, by hand,
every day.
I don't mean that weave on stuff like
they've got now,
It was her own hair.
And every morning I'd make her
stand there
As I tortured these ringlets into place.
Then out we'd go and some sod would
pat her head like she was a dog
And they'd all fall out.

I was trying her out at a new
Sunday school,
As much as I hated the church,
And as much as the old fella should have!
We still wanted her to go.

Anyway, we were all stood outside,
Not together like.
The mothers and kids over there,
And me and mine over here
When this spotty little four eyed creature
Comes up and says to my daughter,
If you have a wash next week
I'll be your friend and Jesus will love you.
Well, Love that, I said,
As I slapped across the mouth.
The police were called.
There was loads of trouble,
I had to go round and apologise.
I know I shouldn't have done it,
And if it had been my daughter hit
I would have stabbed the lot of them.
But I was angry and hurting –
Hurting from the ignorance.
So when they decided to pull Hulme down,
I decided to move my kids
As far away from the likes of that as
possible.
So we moved to Ancoats,
A new council estate.

There were two blocks of maisonettes.
On the other side they were all dead smart.
Clean windows lace and ironed curtains.
On our side, there were a few curtains,
but mainly bits of cloth or nothing at all,
which didn't really matter
Because you couldn't see through the
windows for the muck.
Now, me,
I have always washed my windows.
And I change my curtains for Christmas,

Easter, Whitsun, Birthdays, and sometimes
just when I feel like.
You see I'd reckoned that I couldn't and
Didn't want to change black to white.
But people do judge books by their covers.
So I'd decided, long time back, that no
matter how badly off we might be.
Our home would be spotless and my kids
the same.

My daughter had all her clothes tailored.
Tailored.
And when I did buy
I bought the best.
Her dresses came from this posh shop
on Stretford Road with a French name.
Funny,
I can't remember the name now.
I was paying a fiver for her frocks,
Off-the-peg as they say
And it was only 1958.
Her shoes were leather,
her coats had fur trims in the winter,
And she always wore a hat and gloves.
What, me?
Me?
Well, I always wore a rain mac
And carried a plastic shopping bag.
But I was living for my daughter now.
When it came time for her to go to
Secondary School.
I hit a major problem.
The school uniform.
How in God's name
was I going to make sure
that everyone knew she was clean
each day?
Then one night I hit on this great idea.
I had the days of week,
You know, Monday, Tuesday
Wednesday, Thursday, Friday
Embroidered on the collar of her school
blouses, and every day she swapped a
cardigan for a jumper, you know.
You're laughing,
I'm laughing.
But it's not funny to be called dirty
and smelly.
So why are we laughing.

*SCENE – The nurse has given M a bowl to vomit into – her weak state is becoming
more and more apparent.*

What was I talking about?
This chemotherapy is doing me head –

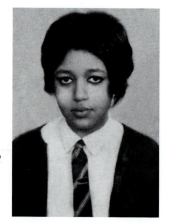

I told that nurse, I don't know about
getting rid of the cancer

Bloody hell
I'll tell you something,
Don't take up hospital visiting
As a career –
For you're all bloody useless!
I was talking about the maisonette –
Good God, it's me that's dying, isn't it?

I'd been moving in, getting things ready
mostly during the early hours of the
morning.
I was working nights by then, in a canteen;
had been for a few years.

My son Malcolm,
(well, he was away at Queens College)
That's what we used to call prison –
I'd lost him to school expulsions,
Petty thieving, drugs, Nigger calling,
police beatings,
Do you think it was because of his colour?

I remember one time
I was working nights.
My daughter was about 5 or 6
My son 17–18,
He was supposed to look after her while
I worked.
I'd leave home at 7 for a 7.30 start
and get back around 4 in the morning.
This one day as soon as I turned into
our street
I knew something was wrong.
All the lights were on.
The house was ablaze like Christmas.
My heart started beating really loud
You know I could hear it.
When I got outside of the house
The front door was wide open.
I started to pray,
Pray for my daughter.
When I stepped inside the room – looked
as though it had been raped!
My head was bursting,
All I could think about was her.
Was she safe
Was she safe?
I flew upstairs to her bedroom.
It was empty.
I must have started screaming.
I know I was making a noise but what

I was saying
I don't know.
I rushed out into the street
And the neighbour must have told me
The police had taken her.
So I ran.
I ran all the way from Hulme
To Moss Lane Police Station, and when I
went inside
I saw her, sat on a bench in her blue
dressing gown and slippers with the
red trim.
She had this look in her eyes.
I have never forgotten that look in her eyes,
It turned out they had been looking for
my son.
Looking for something, found nothing.
So they took her instead.
Home Alone, that's what they call it now,
Isn't it?
Oh, they hadn't tried to contact me.
Hadn't even contacted Social Services.
They just left her sat there, all night long.
She must have seen so much that night.
The thieves,
the drunks
the druggies
the prossies.
You see, me,
I hate the police every last man of them.
And don't tell me they are here for my
protection.
I could tell you some stories about the
police,
About that caring arm across your shoulder,
then a hand slips down to your breast.
Or the reassuring pat on your knee that
travels up your thighs.
Yes, I could tell you stories,
But what's the point?

When my son was younger.
Not more than a toddler

I tried to do homework.
You know, work from home.
But I couldn't sew.
Couldn't do anything, really, but clean.
I couldn't cook either, much to the
annoyance of my husband.
So my homework was odd like there was
this one time I made stuffed straw dolls.
The first day
These two huge bales of hay arrived.

And this bungle of rags
For the dolls' dresses.
I had to make fifty a day to get paid.
At the end of the first day there was
this thing.
It had half a head –
Dropping, two arms, no body, and a leg.
And its eyes popped off.
And the house looked like a romp in
a stable.
I had a right earful from the hubby for
the mess.
Well, after that,
I cleaned other people's houses.
But they knew I needed the money,
So each day the lady of the house
Would increase the work.

First it was,
Could you rub this shirt through for my
husband?
Soon I was doing the whole family wash.
By hand!
For the same pay as I got for mopping
and dusting.
So the first chance I got to work in a
canteen
I took it.
And when the father left (*she waves*)
I washed those stacks of dishes with an
energy you wouldn't believe.

My daughter slept over with this West
Indian Family.
They were Jamaicans,
With three girls of their own,
So she was in good company.
Although I do wish they wouldn't tell
Those Tarzan stories about Africans,
She gets really upset.

Anyway, I was busy, as we were moving,
So every night after my shift
I'd get the all night bus from town and go
over to the maisonette to hang me
curtains or clean something.
The people living on the other side
Must have been really impressed
Thinking their own kind were moving in.
They must have been gob-smacked
to see us!
I heard one of them, you know the type,
Hair by mistake, make-up by necessity,
Asking my daughter when had she first

come to England.
Long before your lot, I yelled,
She slammed her balcony door
And we never spoke again.
Me and Anne West used to go shopping
together.
She lived next-door, Anne,
And didn't give a damn who you were or,
where you came from.
Her life had been too hard for snobbery,
And very soon it was going to get
murderously worse.
I don't know why I decided to move,
I'm sure some of it was instinct.
I had this fella by then,
He was Polish this fella and dead clever
with money.
His family had the lot; land, property, and
he was educated – that's how he got the
job as a wine waiter.
I don't mean he had studied wine
He bloody drank it,
You know, with his dinner.
He'd even got me sipping Drambuie.
Drambuie

It's dead posh that Drambuie.
Well, when the Communists took over,
he came to England.
And can you believe this
Just because he hadn't been educated
in Britain
They wouldn't let him work as a vet.
I told him
I wasn't surprised –
I'd seen it all before.
There are West Indians – university
qualified -
You know like teachers,
Driving bloody buses,
Believe me, I said,
As far as this country is concerned
If it's not bloody British it's shit.
Anyway it was him who convinced me to
buy somewhere.
I had no money, only me wages,
And no one was going to give me credit,
were they?
The only thing I could get on the tick
Was from the catalogue or Pauldens.
It's called Debenhams now.

In fact every thing we owned came from
Pauldens,

And one day my two complained so the
next Saturday I took them to town
To Lewis's.
We picked out this three-piece suite,
I didn't need it, like, but I had to make
them understand.
Then we went upstairs to the offices,
Filled the forms out and waited
For this snooty nosed bastard,
in his smelly suit, to tell me
That they didn't give credit to coloured
families,
And he was sure that I would understand.
Well, I didn't understand, but I did.
So George –
he was called George – did I tell you that?
He arranged everything
You know, like as though he was buying,
But my name went on the mortgage.
I'd pick the ones I liked from the pictures
And he'd go and look at them – and you
know, it was really strange,
But as soon as I got the one I wanted.
I wanted out of that maisonette.
I don't think we spent a year there.
And after all these years –
I still think about it.
Well, it could have been my daughter.
My little girl, but it wasn't, it was Lesley.
She was beautiful, Lesley.
Mum, can Lesley stay for tea?
Mum, I'm going to play with friend Lesley.
Lesley. Lesley.

10 second silent pause.

There were trees in Levenshulme

And at the back of our new house
a small garden
With a fence to one side
A wall to the other,
And one separating us from the garden
at the back.
Although we never went near the place,
Before signing the contracts,
They all knew we were coming.
Some of our stuff arrived on the back of a
lorry.
I kid you not, on the back of a lorry,
some in a mini van, a friend's car, a taxi,
and the rest by movers.

The old couple on the right

Never spoke one word to any of us
For the ten or more years we lived there.
The neighbours on the left weren't so bad,
Nosey like, but over the years –
we became sort of friends.
When we first moved in, my daughter
would leave the hall light on for me
coming home from work.
The grandmother remarked one day,
That maybe it was delight of having
electricity
That was making us so extravagant.
Silly cow.

But back to when we first moved.
On the first Monday.
The first Monday!
I done a bit of washing, curtains or
something.
I was hanging them out, as the house at
the back of us was having this tree
trimmed and heard them say to the bloke
doing the job
Don't cut the branches on that side,
I don't want those niggers
looking in on me.

By the end of the day
I had this fucking big fence erected,
To stop that racist
Looking in on us.
To stop him looking in on us.

So much happened in that house
As we laughed and argued
Through each day.

The world was changing too.
I remember when my nephew –
Have I told you about my family?
We're just like anybody
I mean, I'm not talking to that lot.
And wouldn't have them lot over
if you paid me!
But when my nephew was boxing
at the Olympics games,
we watched every minute on the telly.

That's how we came to see it
Black Power against American racism.
My son Malcolm, had grown his hair,
he was reading the Solidad Brothers
and quoting X.
We were always fighting, arguing.

Him screaming at me,
I've never cried so much in my life,
But I wanted him to grab a future,
to escape the life that was destroying him.

Sam Cooke died and we played his music
late into the night, and I sang
won't somebody tell me what's wrong
with me –
why my life is so full of misery?
And I prayed that the woman found with
him wasn't white.
Much the same way as I tried to explain
to my daughter,
I prayed that the Yorkshire Ripper wouldn't
be black.
A Black man and so many murders
Would send people rioting onto the streets,
and many an innocent Black man
Would pay the price for one man's guilt.
Oh, there s no lynching in England
Here, they just beat you to death.

SCENE – *The nurse has removed M's dressing gown and slippers. she covers M's head with a cap, ready for surgery.*

I'd do anything to be out of here,
out and about.
Not that I ever went anywhere.
When I first left the orphanage
I went into service, working for priests.
On the first night
I took a fancy to cold porridge.
So I nicked some. And popped myself up
in bed with a great bowlful.
The other maid just looked at me then
blew out the candle.
I didn't mind.

When we were kids
My sister worked in the kitchen cooking
for the nuns.
She used to sneak food in her
knickers and, along with our mate Winnie,
we'd eat it in the dark.
Anyway, the next night
I fancied porridge again.
So I nicked some more,
And the girl said,
Why are you eating that? she said
Why, because I fancied it. I said
Well don't. she said
Why not? I said,
Because the last girl that worked here,
she said.

Ate porridge every night laced with
arsenic until she died.
I left the next morning.

We used to get one Saturday off per
month, in Service.
I used to meet my mates at Lime Street
to go to the matinees.
We would buy a great big bag of rotten
tomatoes
And go to see Arthur Askey.
Do you remember him?
I'm a buzzing, bloody buzzing,
busy bloody bee.
Well, buzz off, we'd say
And threw the buggers – then over the
road for Ken Dodd with the other half.
Tight Ken we called him even then,
and we were right.
Mind you,
I wouldn't pay my taxes –
given half the chance.
That was it for me really.
As the years passed,
I'd spend my rare night off in front of the
telly, my feet up on a pouffe, eating a
cream cake.

I went on holidays.
I went to Paris once, –
in France!
It was marvellous.
Went to the Moulin Rouge
To see the can-can dancers.
And listen to this,
when the girls kicked their legs up,
They had no knickers on!
Well, I started laughing
and when I laugh –
everyone knows about it.
I laughed so much they threw me out!

My daughter did the can-can once.
Over at the Lesser Free Trade Hall.
I sent her to dancing school
as soon as she could walk.
Well, I couldn't dance, so I just thought
that she wouldn't be able to either.
Well, what did I know about natural
rhythms, in any form,
If you get my meaning?
And she was a natural
She could do anything –
Tap,

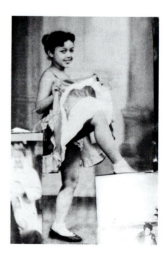

Ballet,
Which amazed the teachers —
Well, African bottoms are not supposed
To be able to learn certain ballet techniques.
Bloody stupid if you ask me,
Well, you don't dance with your arse,
Do ya?

When she was thirteen
She auditioned and got a place
In the pantomime at the Palace Theatre.
When I went to collect her, after the first
rehearsal they told me, apologising,
Not to bring her back the next day.
They said she didn't blend in with the
rest of the kids.
Anyone try and tell me that now
I'd swing for them.
But that day —
I don't know.
I simply hugged her close, and took
her home.
I used to say to my daughter,
you're beautiful.
I don't mean on the outside
but on the inside.
And you have to remember that.
For so many people are going to try —
to prove different.
I'd tell her, wherever you go and you're
the only coloured person there.
I used to say coloured then.
Naturally I say black now.
Well, I'd tell her, you are representing
all black people,
so hold your head up high.
I'd say,
You see your father,
well, I can't stand the bastard.
But he's an African — that means you're
an African
never forget that.
I told my kids that I would always be
proud of them and hope that they would
never, you know, grow up and become
ashamed of me.
Kids!
Who'd have them?
Who'd be without them once they're here.

SCENE – The stage slowly goes darker and darker

Nurse, turn the light on.
I hate the dark.
Turn the light on.

She's useless that nurse.
I've told her,
In the forties and fifties thousands of
qualified women came over from the
West Indies to be nurses, and ended up
scrubbing hospital floors.
She'd be better off as a backing-singer.
Turn the bloody light on.
I'm scared of the dark.

SCENE – BLACK OUT.
M rises removing her hospital gown and cap as she walks towards the screen and reads aloud the certificate.

When my mother died, the world did not
stand still.
Nothing stopped, changed to note her
passing.
It was almost as though everything
moved at double speed.
She was there and suddenly – she was
this small container of ash, and I could
carry the whole of her here in my hands.
When my mother died
No one felt the emptiness of life like I did.
Then, I don't know, weeks, months later
I woke up crying.
But in that moment
Between sleep and waking
I began to laugh.
That dreadful laugh of my mum.
That laugh that said they won't keep us
down forever.
Then I began to remember her as she was
In private times,
Like at the end of a day she would come
home stand in front of the fire, raise her
skirt and pull off her corset, scratching
red welts into her skin.
I began to remember her stories,
tales of the convent.
Of her struggle to keep us proud of what
we were.
And wonder why she was always hopeful
that we would never be ashamed of her.
That day, I realised, that it's only the body
that dies.
But the spirit continues and you carry it
here, in this place of 'love'.
And I laughed then at myself for forgetting
that I carry the spirit of an ancestral people,
Not only in the colour of my skin
But in my determination to see each day
through.
Better than yesterday.

And mixed in along with all those Africans
is this.

One special woman.

So, if any of you think that all mixed
raced people
Grow up confused, without identity,
Think again.
I work in schools,
And often, the cocky lad sat at the back
Asks me where I come from.
I answer, 'Manchester'.
He'll say, 'Nope, where do you really
come from,
Manchester?
Why, where do you think I come from?
Somewhere hot and exotic he'll say
Well it's exotic in Manchester some days
well, I mean look at me.
Then there's the media, desperate for
a story,
Headlining, The Mixed Heritage,
confused shows.
They can F
I know exactly who I am –
I am a Black woman
A mixed race woman.
I am proud to be a Nigerian daughter
whose father loved her.
He loved me so much,
And I am equally proud to be the daughter
of a Liverpool woman of Irish descent.
Confused? Get out of here.
If you're loved you're –
hell I wish you'd known my mother.
Oh, I forgot, you do now.
For this was the story of M –
M for Margaret,
M for Mother,
And now M for Me.
And my name is SuAndi.

5.5 SUPERNINTENDO RANCHERO

Excerpt from BORDERscape 2000

GUILLERMO GÓMEZ-PEÑA

Guillermo Gómez-Peña (b. 1950) *is a Mexican performance artist, writer, cultural critic and activist. He pioneered multimedia performance making use of live performance, photography, film and installation. His performances are often collaborative and durational and play with the relationship between the artwork, the performer and the audience, such as in* The Couple in the Cage *(1992). A politically driven artist, Gómez-Peña's work frequently explores themes around hybridization, identity, borders, globalization and consumerism (see also 5.13).* **Roberto Sifuentes** *is an interdisciplinary practitioner whose work combines the live and the mediatized. He has collaborated with Gómez-Peña as a member of La Pocha Nostra from 1994 to 2000.*

Performance is the most flexible language I have found. I utilize it to analyze our social crises and cultural misplacement; to articulate my desires and frustration in the overlapping realms of politics, sexuality, art and spirituality. Performance is a vast conceptual territory where my eclectic and ever-changing ideas, and the ideas of my collaborators, can be integrated into a coherent system and be put into practice. It's radical theory turned into praxis through movement, ritual, gesture, sound, light and spoken text.
From Gómez-Peña's *Performance Diaries*, 1990

(Opera singer sings Mozart intertwined with a soundbed of Japanese techno music. ROBERTO SIFUENTES *stands on top of a metallic pyramid. He wears a laboratory coat and teched-out glasses, and speaks in a computer-processed, mechanical voice.* GUILLERMO GÓMEZ-PEÑA *enters dressed as El Mad Mexterminator, riding a motorized wheelchair. He moves across the stage in a mechanical, video-game-like pattern, responding to gestural commands from* SIFUENTES.*)*

RS: San Francisco, March of 99. Dear Chicano colleagues, welcome to *BORDER scape 2000*, part three of a performance trilogy. Allow me to introduce to you the very first prototype: a beta version of an imperfect Mexican. This cyborg still has a sentimental mind and a political consciousness. He failed the test for robotic migrant workers, and still longs for his homeland. Eventually when we manage to get the Mexican bugs out of him, we will create a Chicano, the vato uberalis, the next step on the evolutionary scale. Speak Mexi-cyborg!! Repent yourself!! Use voice #53 and please stick to the script.

GGP: *(Processed voice #1.)* No, I won't cru-ci-fy myself to protest la migra no more.

RS: You can't repeat a performance or it would become theater.

GGP: No, I swear,
I won't box with a hanging chicken for art's sake …

nor will I exhibit myself inside a gilded cage
as an endangered species or an androgynous wrestler/shaman.

RS: Why Mad Mex Frankenstein?

GGP: I'm just gonna be a poet for a while.

RS: Then be a poet. Stick to the spoken word material. Go!! Go North!!

GGP: So I continue my trek north
like a compulsive explorer
El Marco Pollo de Tijuana,
El Vasco de Gama de Aztlán
ever looking for a new island, a new performance stage
to spill my beans, my bleeding tripas,
expose my crevasses, my wounded penis
in the name of ex-pe-ri-men-ta-tion.

RS: Now you wish to be a performance artist again?

"*Performance is the most flexible language I have found. I utilize it to analyze our social codes and cultural misplacement; to articulate my desires and frustration in the overlapping realms of politics, sexuality, art and spirituality. Performance is a vast conceptual territory where my eclectic and ever-changing ideas, and the ideas of my collaborators, can be integrated into a coherent system and be put into practice. It's radical theory turned into praxis through movement, ritual, gesture, sound, light and spoken text.*"

FROM GÓMEZ-PEÑA'S PERFORMANCE DIARIES, 1995

7 *El Veteran Survivor.*

Figure 29 Gómez-Peña as 'El Veteran Survivor'. (Photographer: Eugenio Castro.)

GGP: Not exactly.
(*GGP intersperses 'no's' through following text.*)

RS: So Vato, give us some blood,
show us your piercings, your prosthetics,
eat your green card or burn your bra
but get fuckin' real!

GGP: no, no, ni madres.

RS: Why?

GGP: Cause I'm giving up, right now, in front of you.

RS: Oh god, you fuckin' martyr!

GGP: I willingly turn myself in to my inner border patrol
three agents are present tonight
come on, get me!!
this is your golden chance culeros
I su-rren-der to my own darkest fears.

RS: You're not responding to my performance commands. You were much better when you were just trying to be a poet. Go back to poetry. Synthesize an entire cosmology into one burning sentence. Go!

GGP: Fear is the foundation of your identity. (*He points at someone in audience.*)

RS: What a fuckin' assumption.

GGP: To be Mexican is a felony not a misdemeanor . . .

RS: Hey better, chido, punchy.

GGP: versus ser pocho es still una afrenta binacional.

RS: You are using Spanish unnecessarily. Shift accent.

GGP: (*Texan accent.*) I'm fully aware that your ears are tired of listening to so many foreign languages. (*He speaks in 'gringo tongues,' interspersed with recognizable English words.*)

RS: Stop! Next dialect!

GGP: Hey, that's how English sounded to me when I was a kid.

RS: So upgrade yourself!

GGP: Such linguistic vertigo you have to endure daily
I mean, you can't even communicate with your maid
or your gardener,
and then you come to California
(*Gringoñol.*)
& carrramba mamazita!
the artist speaks Spanglish and gringoñol
(*Mispronounced Spanish.*)
io hablou el idiouma del criminal, il drogadictou y la piuta
e' cuandouu io hablou tu muérres un poquitou mas.

RS: English only, pinche wetback!

GGP: I mean, 23 states in America have embraced English only
California just abolished bilingual education
and I dare to talk to you in Spanglish? Que poca ma . . .

RS: Good boy . . . you are assimilating.
What is your prime directive? Explain yourself.

GGP: To you or to the audience?

RS: To the audience.

GGP: Dear citizens of nothingness:
this is a desperate attempt by a dying performance artist
to recapture the power of the spoken word
in the year of virtual despair and victorious whiteness.

RS: Stop! Now, do something more kinetic, more defiant.
Don't you have a fuckin choreographer?

GGP: Sara!!!

RS: Music!!

GGP: Sara!!!

RS: We need some hip music
cd #3; track 2, take 1: Japanese tea house lounge. Go.

(*Lights transition to lounge look.*)

RS: Yeah! Now, stand up & dance. (*Repeats three times.*)

GGP *stops wheelchair and attempts to stand up but fails. He eventually succeeds in standing.* GGP *dances cheesy disco & twist, then falls down on his knees.*

RS: Stop the music. This is terrifying
Who do you think you are? an MTV Latino?

GGP *crawls back onto the chair while speaking. Lights return to normal and sound goes back to techno music.*

GGP: El Mariachi with a biiiiiig moooouth.

RS: Not anymore carnal.

GGP: Mexi-cyborg el extra-extra-terrestre.

RS: Not quite yet. You wish.

GGP: El immigrant bizarro con su mente explosiva y expansiva al servicio de la fragmentación político-poética.

RS: State your function or lose your greencard.

GGP: To you or to the audience?

RS: To the audience.

GGP: My normal state of being, carnal,
is to die for you, cause after all these years
I'm still imprisoned inside this historical purgatory.

RS: Still obsessed with history in the year 2000?

GGP: *Yes.*

RS: That's cute.

GGP: Do you remember the terms of the Guadalupe-Hidalgo treaty?
do you fuckin' remem …

RS: Can anyone answer this pathetic poet?

GGP: Est-ce que vous êtes illégal?
L'illegalité est à la mode, n'est-ce pas?

RS: OK, you win this time. Let's talk about illegality … Go!

GGP moves to extreme downstage and looks into audience. House lights come up. After each question, RS intersperses improvised replies.

GGP: Are there any illegal immigrants in the audience?
People who once were illegal?
What about people who have had sex with an illegal alien?
Can you describe in detail their genitalia?
Are there people here who have hired illegal immigrants for domestic, or artistic purposes?
Yessss! To do what exactly?
How much did you pay them?
How did you feel about that?
Thanks for your sincerity …
Now, have any of you ever fantasized about being from another race or culture?
Which one?
Black, Indian?
Native American? Mexican?

RS: Boring. Cambio de canal: give me burning sentence #2.

House lights down.

GGP: Ser emigrante en América ya es un acto ilegal.

RS: Translation please?

GGP: Just to be different is potentially an illegal act
one strike & you're out!
punishable with deportation without trail,
and retroactive to 10 years.

RS: That's too … technical

GGP: I mean, to be excluded from a national project
at a time when all nation states are collapsing

is not an extraordinary act of heroism
or literary fiction, ask the Welsh or the Irish, man …

RS: That's too fuckin' heavy to deal with right now.
This is the year 2000;
it's all about style without content.

GGP: You mean radical actions without repercussions?

RS: Right!

GGP: Tropical tourism without Montezuma's revenge?

RS: Global nada … rien

GGP: Nothing-ness, really?
Just style, anonymous sex, weird trivia?
So, if that's what defines your values and your identity,
let's fuckin' engage in trivia.

RS: Good! But bring down at least 10 decibels the level of your drama.
Remember: pc est passé, and so is rage, Supermojado.
Now, give me some burning trivia. Go:

GGP: Madonna defeated Argentina & got to play Evita
Gooooo Madonna!!

RS: Dated material. Next!

GGP: Selena died precisely during the crossover.
(*Looking up.*) Selena, we luv you diva, auuu!!

RS: What's so fucking special about Selena?

GGP: Her whiny voice, her liposuctioned nalgas.
Besides, she is all we have, since we've got no real leaders
o que? Do you think we have any true Chicano leaders?

RS: Kind of.

GGP: Can you mention one?

RS: Eddie Olmos (*GGP reacts.*), El Haniachi Two (*GGP reacts.*), the Taco Bell Chihuahua.

GGP: Fax you, man! Marcos! He is not a Chicano but he is certainly a leader …

RS: He's just a fading myth. Back to our search for burning trivia. Go!

GGP: Zappa is resting in the Olympus of Americana
(me persigno)
per ipsum, ecu nip zzzum Zzzzappa!

RS: And so is Sinatra.

GGP: Sinatra?
(*Sings.*) 'When I was 35, it was a very good year'
ese mi Frank
your absence hurts much more than that of Octavio Paz.

RS: Hey that's a great trivial line.
Do you have some of this shit on disc?

GGP: No. I no longer have a laptop. I am a Neo-Luddite.

RS: A luddite with a mechanical wheelchair?

GGP: Yes.

RS: You fuckin' ro-man-tico! Shift 348X-13 Trivialize race. Go!

GGP: OJ was a cyborg constructed by your own fears & desires.

RS: But was he guilty?

GGP: Yes, he was guilty & not that interesting a character

RS: But we cared about him, cause he was (*GGP intersperses* 'Que?') ... cause he is a ... a ... a ... black cyborg.

Pause.

GGP: I didn't say it. You did!!

RS: These are the issues that truly matter.

GGP: Sure ... in a time & place
where nothing significant truly matters.

RS: What you consider trivia is my raison d'être.
Give me a headline that truly captures our times.

GGP: Clintoris & Linguinsky: the great millennial soap opera.

RS: Elaborate ... elaborate ... elaborate.

GGP: Monica finally described in detail the genitals of your President.

RS: Don't elaborate.

GGP: She said, she said:
'it's pink, about three inches long, and it never gets hard but there is something endearing about it.'

RS: You are diverging from our subject matter. We are beginning to sound like bad experimental poetry. Neruda meets Jello Biafra.
What are we really here for?

GGP: Tonight?

RS: Tonight

GGP: Tonight?

RS: Tonight

GGP: (*To the audience.*) There is too much turmoil in your private life for me to bother you with the truly heavy issues like racism, homelessness or police brutality.

RS: Right! That was the 80s, ese.
We've heard that pop song so many times
but tonight, your audience is understandably tired.
They suffer from ... repeat with me:
com-pa-ssion fa-tigue, yeah.

GGP: com-pa-ssion fa-tigue, yeah.

RS: Just to hear you say it makes me want to slash you in the face.

GGP: Thank you.

Lights up on Sara Shelton-Mann SL. dressed as Mariachi Zapatista. She breaks into fast-paced, Chaplinesque movements with a gun, dancing to Mexican punk. Strobe light. Music stops abruptly and video cuts out at end of her dance. Juan Ybarra as Green Alien enters. Beginning of Nintendo Ethnic Wars.

Note

Originally published in Guillermo Gómez-Peña, *Dangerous Border Crossers: The Artist Talks Back*, London: Routledge, 2000. pp. 24–33.

5.6 FAR AWAY (2000)

CARYL CHURCHILL

Caryl Churchill (b. 1938) is a leading contemporary British playwright, both prolific and highly influential. Churchill's first plays were produced at Oxford University – where she studied English Literature – and by BBC radio. The interface between feminism and theatre in the 1970s led Churchill to produce a number of groundbreaking works, including Cloud Nine *(1979) and* Top Girls *(1982). Her career has also been marked by shifts in thematic focus, an ever-increasing tendency towards formal experiment and the exploration of new working partnerships with both directors and chorographers. Churchill's most recent work embraces such subjects as Israeli/Palestinian conflict (*Seven Jewish Children: A Play for Gaza, *2009), human cloning in* A Number *(2002) and the fragmentation of modern life mediated through over 100 characters and 50 scenes (*Love and Information, *2012).* Far Away *(2000) is a haunting contemplation on our personal and political response to genocide, war and terror in an era of globalization, media simulation and the exhaustion of nature. The play was first produced at London's Royal Court Theatre – as with most of Churchill's plays – and directed by Stephen Daldry.*

Characters

JOAN, a girl
HARPER, her aunt
TODD, a young man

1

HARPER's house. Night.

JOAN: I can't sleep.

HARPER: It's the strange bed.

JOAN: No, I like different places.

HARPER: Are you cold?

JOAN: No.

HARPER: Do you want a drink?

JOAN: I think I am cold.

HARPER: That's easy enough then. There's extra blankets in the cupboard.

JOAN: Is it late?

HARPER: Two.

JOAN: Are you going to bed?

HARPER: Do you want a hot drink?

JOAN: No thank you.

HARPER: I should go to bed then.

JOAN: Yes.

HARPER: It's always odd in a new place. When you've been here a week you'll look back at tonight and it won't seem the same at all.

JOAN: I've been to a lot of places. I've stayed with friends at their houses. I don't miss my parents if you think that.

HARPER: Do you miss your dog?

JOAN: I miss the cat I think.

HARPER: Does it sleep on your bed?

JOAN: No because I chase it off. But it gets in if the door's not properly shut. You think you've shut the door but it hasn't caught and she pushes it open in the night.

HARPER: Come here a minute. You're shivering. Are you hot?

JOAN: No, I'm all right.

HARPER: You're over-tired. Go to bed. I'm going to bed myself.

JOAN: I went out.

HARPER: When? just now?

JOAN: Just now.

HARPER: No wonder you're cold. It's hot in the daytime here but it's cold at night.

JOAN: The stars are brighter here than at home.

HARPER: It's because there's no street lights.

JOAN: I couldn't see much.

HARPER: I don't expect you could. How did you get out? I didn't hear the door.

JOAN: I went out the window.

HARPER: I'm not sure I like that.

JOAN: No it's quite safe, there's a roof and a tree.

HARPER: When people go to bed they should stay in bed. Do you climb out of the window at home?

JOAN: I can't at home because – No I don't.

HARPER: I'm responsible for you.

JOAN: Yes, I'm sorry.

HARPER: Well that's enough adventures for one night. You'll sleep now. Off you go. Look at you, you're asleep on your feet.

JOAN: There was a reason.

HARPER: For going out?

JOAN: I heard a noise.

HARPER: An owl?

JOAN: A shriek.

HARPER: An owl then. There are all sorts of birds here, you might see a golden oriole. People come here specially to watch birds and we sometimes make tea or coffee or sell bottles of water because there's no café and people don't expect that and they get thirsty. You'll see in the morning what a beautiful place it is.

JOAN: It was more like a person screaming.

HARPER: It is like a person screaming when you hear an owl.

JOAN: It was a person screaming.

HARPER: Poor girl, what a fright you must have had imagining you heard somebody screaming. You should have come straight down here to me.

JOAN: I wanted to see.

HARPER: It was dark.

JOAN: Yes but I did see.

HARPER: Now what did you imagine you saw in the dark?

JOAN: I saw my uncle.

HARPER: Yes I expect you did. He likes a breath of air. He wasn't screaming I hope?

JOAN: No.

HARPER: That's all right then. Did you talk to him? I expect you were frightened he'd say what are you doing out of your bed so late.

JOAN: I stayed in the tree.

HARPER: He didn't see you?

JOAN: No.

HARPER: He'll be surprised won't he, he'll laugh when he hears you were up in the tree. He'll be cross but he doesn't mean it, he'll think it's a good joke, it's the sort of thing he did when he was a boy. So bed now. I'll go up too.

JOAN: He was pushing someone. He was bundling someone into a shed.

HARPER: He must have been putting a big sack in the shed. He works too late.

JOAN: I'm not sure if it was a woman. It could have been a young man.

HARPER: Well I have to tell you, when you've been married as long as I have. There are things people get up to, it's natural, it's nothing bad, that's just friends of his your uncle was having a little party with.

JOAN: Was it a party?

HARPER: Just a little party.

JOAN: Yes because there wasn't just that one person.

HARPER: No, there'd be a few of his friends.

JOAN: There was a lorry.

HARPER: Yes, I expect there was.

JOAN: When I put my ear against the side of the lorry I heard crying inside.

HARPER: How could you do that from up in the tree?

JOAN: I got down from the tree. I went to the lorry after I looked in the window of the shed.

HARPER: There might be things that are not your business when you're a visitor in someone else's house.

JOAN: Yes, I'd rather not have seen. I'm sorry.

HARPER: Nobody saw you?

JOAN: They were thinking about themselves.

HARPER: I think it's lucky nobody saw you.

JOAN: If it's a party, why was there so much blood?

HARPER: There isn't any blood.

JOAN: Yes.

HARPER: Where?

JOAN: On the ground.

HARPER: In the dark? how would you see that in the dark?

JOAN: I slipped in it.

She holds up her bare foot.

I mostly wiped it off.

HARPER: That's where the dog got run over this afternoon.

JOAN: Wouldn't it have dried up?

HARPER: Not if the ground was muddy.

JOAN: What sort of dog?

HARPER: A big dog, a big mongrel.

JOAN: That's awful, you must be very sad, had you had him long?

HARPER: No, he was young, he ran out, he was never very obedient, a lorry was backing up.

JOAN: What was his name?

HARPER: Flash.

JOAN: What colour was he?

HARPER: Black with a bit of white.

JOAN: Why were the children in the shed?

HARPER: What children?

JOAN: Don't you know what children?

HARPER: How could you see there were children?

JOAN: There was a light on. That's how I could see the blood inside the shed. I could see the faces and which ones had blood on.

HARPER: You've found out something secret. You know that don't you?

JOAN: Yes.

HARPER: Something you shouldn't know.

JOAN: Yes I'm sorry.

HARPER: Something you must never talk about. Because if you do you could put people's lives in danger.

JOAN: Why? who from? from my uncle?

HARPER: Of course not from your uncle.

JOAN: From you?

HARPER: Of course not from me, are you mad? I'm going to tell you what's going on. Your uncle is helping these people. He's helping them escape. He's giving them shelter. Some of them were still in the lorry, that's why they were crying. Your uncle's going to take them all into the shed and then they'll be all right.

JOAN: They had blood on their faces.

HARPER: That's from before. That's because they were attacked by the people your uncle's saving them from.

JOAN: There was blood on the ground.

HARPER: One of them was injured very badly but your uncle bandaged him up.

JOAN: He's helping them.

HARPER: That's right.

JOAN: There wasn't a dog. There wasn't a party.

HARPER: No, I'm trusting you with the truth now. You must never talk about it or you'll put your uncle's life in danger and mine and even your own. You won't even say anything to your parents.

JOAN: Why did you have me to stay if you've got this secret going on?

HARPER: The lorry should have come yesterday. It won't happen again while you're here.

JOAN: It can now because I know. You don't have to stop for me. I could help uncle in the shed and look after them.

HARPER: No, he has to do it himself. But thank you for offering, that's very kind. So after all that excitement do you think you could go back to bed?

JOAN: Why was uncle hitting them?

HARPER: Hitting who?

JOAN: He was hitting a man with a stick. I think the stick was metal. He hit one of the children.

HARPER: One of the people in the lorry was a traitor. He wasn't really one of them, he was pretending, he was going to betray them, they found out and told your uncle. Then he attacked your uncle, he attacked the other people, your uncle had to fight him.

JOAN: That's why there was so much blood.

HARPER: Yes, it had to be done to save the others.

JOAN: He hit one of the children.

HARPER: That would have been the child of the traitor. Or sometimes you get bad children who even betray their parents.

JOAN: What's going to happen?

HARPER: They'll go off in the lorry very early in the morning.

JOAN: Where to?

HARPER: Where they're escaping to. You don't want to have to keep any more secrets.

JOAN: He only hit the traitors.

HARPER: Of course. I'm not surprised you can't sleep, what an upsetting thing to see. But now you understand, it's not so bad. You're part of a big movement now to make things better. You can be proud of that. You can look at the stars and think here we are in our little bit of space, and I'm on the side of the people who are putting things right, and your soul will expand right into the sky.

JOAN: Can't I help?

HARPER: You can help me clean up in the morning. Will you do that?

JOAN: Yes.

HARPER: So you'd better get some sleep.

2

Several years later. A hat makers.

1.

JOAN and TODD are sitting at a workbench. They have each just started making a hat.

TODD: There's plenty of blue.

JOAN: I think I'm starting with black.

TODD: Colour always wins.

JOAN: I will have colour, I'm starting with black to set the colour off.

TODD: I did one last week that was an abstract picture of the street, blue for the buses, yellow for the flats, red for the leaves, grey for the sky. Nobody got it but I knew what it was. There's little satisfactions to be had.

JOAN: Don't you enjoy it?

TODD: You're new aren't you?

JOAN: This is my first hat. My first professional hat.

TODD: Did you do hat at college?

JOAN: My degree hat was a giraffe six feet tall.

TODD: You won't have time to do something like that in the week.

JOAN: I know.

TODD: We used to get two weeks before a parade and then they took it down to one and now they're talking about cutting a day.

JOAN: So we'd get an extra day off?

TODD: We'd get a day's less money. We wouldn't make such good hats.

JOAN: Can they do that?

TODD: You'd oppose it would you?

JOAN: I've only just started.

TODD: You'll find there's a lot wrong with this place.

JOAN: I thought it was one of the best jobs.

TODD: It is. Do you know where to go for lunch?

JOAN: I think there's a canteen isn't there?

TODD: Yes but we don't go there. I'll show you where to go.

2.

Next day. They are working on the hats, which are by now far more brightly decorated, i.e. the ones they were working on have been replaced by ones nearer completion.

JOAN: Your turn.

TODD: I go for a swim in the river before work.

JOAN: Isn't it dangerous?

TODD: Your turn.

JOAN: I've got a pilot's licence.

TODD: I stay up till four every morning watching the trials.

JOAN: I'm getting a room in a subway.

TODD: I've got my own place.

JOAN: Have you?

TODD: Do you want to see it? That's coming on.

JOAN: I don't understand yours but I like the feather.

TODD: I'm not trying. I've been here too long.

JOAN: Will you leave?

TODD: My turn. There's something wrong with how we get the contracts.

JOAN: But we want the contracts.

TODD: What if we don't deserve them? What if our work isn't really the best?

JOAN: So what's going on?

TODD: I'll just say a certain person's brother-in-law. Where does he work do you think?

JOAN: Where does he work?

TODD: I'm not talking about it in here. Tell me something else.

JOAN: I don't like staying in in the evenings and watching trials.

TODD: I watch them at night after I come back.

JOAN: Back from where?

TODD: Where do you like?

3.

Next day. They're working on the hats, which are getting very big and extravagant.

TODD: I don't enjoy animal hats myself.

JOAN: I was a student.

TODD: Abstract hats are back in a big way.

JOAN: I've always liked abstract hats.

TODD: You must have not noticed when everyone hated them.

JOAN: It was probably before my time.

Silence. They go on working.

JOAN: It's just if you're going on about it all the time I don't know why you don't do something about it.

TODD: This is your third day.

JOAN: The management's corrupt – you've told me. We're too low paid – you've told me.

Silence. They go on working.

TODD: Too much green.

JOAN: It's meant to be too much.

Silence. They go on working.

TODD: I noticed you looking at that fair boy's hat. I hope you told him it was derivative.

Silence. They go on working.

TODD: I'm the only person in this place who's got any principles, don't tell me I should do something, I spend my days wondering what to do.

JOAN: So you'll probably come up with something.

Silence. They go on working.

4.

Next day. They are working on the hats, which are now enormous and preposterous.

TODD: That's beautiful.

JOAN: You like it?

TODD: I do.

JOAN: I like yours too.

TODD: You don't have to say that. It's not one of my best.

JOAN: No it's got – I don't know, it's a confident hat.

TODD: I have been doing parades for six years. So I'm a valued old hand. So when I go and speak to a certain person he might pay attention.

JOAN: You're going to speak to him?

TODD: I've an appointment after work.

JOAN: You might lose your job.

TODD: I might.

JOAN: I'm impressed.

TODD: That was the idea.

JOAN: Will you mention the brother-in-law?

TODD: First I'll talk about the money. Then I'll just touch in the brother-in-law. I've a friend who's a journalist.

JOAN: Will you touch in the journalist?

TODD: I might imply something without giving the journalist away. It might be better if he can't trace the journalist back to me.

JOAN: Though he will suspect.

TODD: However much he suspects. One thing if I lost my job.

JOAN: What's that?

TODD: I'd miss you.

JOAN: Already?

5.

Next day. A procession of ragged, beaten, chained prisoners, each wearing a hat, on their way to execution. The finished hats are even more enormous and preposterous than in the previous scene.

Figure 30 *Far Away* at the Royal Court Theatre, 2000, directed by Stephen Daldry. (Photographer: Ivan Kyncl.)

6.

A new week. JOAN and TODD are starting work on new hats.

JOAN: I still can't believe it.

TODD: No one's ever won in their first week before.

JOAN: It's all going to be downhill from now on.

TODD: You can't win every week.

JOAN: That's what I mean.

TODD: No but you'll do a fantastic body of work while you're here.

JOAN: Sometimes I think it's a pity that more aren't kept.

TODD: There'd be too many, what would they do with them?

JOAN: They could reuse them.

TODD: Exactly and then we'd be out of work.

JOAN: It seems so sad to burn them with the bodies.

TODD: No I think that's the joy of it. The hats are ephemeral. It's like a metaphor for something or other.

JOAN: Well, life.

TODD: Well, life, there you are. Out of nearly three hundred hats I've made here I've only had three win and go in the museum. But that's never bothered me. You make beauty and it disappears, I love that.

JOAN: You're so . .

TODD: What?

JOAN: You make me think in different ways. Like I'd never have thought about how this place is run and now I see how important it is.

TODD: I think it did impress a certain person that I was speaking from the high moral ground.

JOAN: So tell me again exactly what he said at the end.

TODD: 'These things must be thought about.'

JOAN: I think that's encouraging.

TODD: It could mean he'll think how to get rid of me.

JOAN: That's a fantastic shape to start from.

TODD: It's a new one for me. I'm getting inspired by you.

JOAN: There's still the journalist. If he looks into it a bit more we could expose the corrupt financial basis of how the whole hat industry is run, not just this place, I bet the whole industry is dodgy.

TODD: Do you think so?

JOAN: I think we should find out.

TODD: You've changed my life, do you know that?

JOAN: If you lose your job I'll resign.

TODD: We might not get jobs in hats again.

JOAN: There's other parades.

TODD: But I think you're a hat genius.

JOAN: Unless all the parades are corrupt.

TODD: I love these beads. Use these beads.

JOAN: No, you have them.

TODD: No, you.

3

Several years later. HARPER's house, daytime.

HARPER: You were right to poison the wasps.

TODD: Yes, I think all the wasps have got to go.

HARPER: I was outside yesterday on the edge of the wood when a shadow came over and it was a cloud of butterflies, and they came down just beyond me and the trees and bushes were red with them. Two of them clung to my arm, I was terrified, one of them got in my hair, I managed to squash them.

TODD: I haven't had a problem with butterflies.

HARPER: They can cover your face. The Romans used to commit suicide with gold leaf, just flip it down their throat and it covered their windpipe, I think of that with butterflies.

TODD: I was passing an orchard, there were horses standing under the trees, and suddenly wasps attacked them out of the plums. There were the horses galloping by screaming with their heads made of wasp. I wish she'd wake up.

HARPER: We don't know how long she'd been walking.

TODD: She was right to come.

HARPER: You don't go walking off in the middle of a war.

TODD: You do if you're escaping.

HARPER: We don't know that she was escaping.

TODD: She was getting to a place of safety to regroup.

HARPER: Is this a place of safety?

TODD: Relatively, yes of course it is. Everyone thinks it's just a house.

HARPER: The cats have come in on the side of the French.

TODD: I never liked cats, they smell, they scratch, they only like you because you feed them, they bite, I used to have a cat that would suddenly just take some bit of you in its mouth.

HARPER: Did you know they've been killing babies?

TODD: Where's that?

HARPER: In China. They jump in the cots when nobody's looking.

TODD: But some cats are still OK.

HARPER: I don't think so.

TODD: I know a cat up the road.

HARPER: No, you must be careful of that.

TODD: But we're not exactly on the other side from the French. It's not as if they're the Moroccans and the ants.

HARPER: It's not as if they're the Canadians, the Venezuelans and the mosquitoes.

TODD: It's not as if they're the engineers, the chefs, the children under five, the musicians.

HARPER: The car salesmen.

TODD: Portuguese car salesmen.

HARPER: Russian swimmers.

TODD: Thai butchers.

HARPER: Latvian dentists.

TODD: No, the Latvian dentists have been doing good work in Cuba. They've a house outside Havana.

HARPER: But Latvia has been sending pigs to Sweden. The dentists are linked to international dentistry and that's where their loyalty lies, with dentists in Dar-es-Salaam.

TODD: We don't argue about Dar-es-Salaam.

HARPER: You would attempt to justify the massacre in Dar-es-Salaam?

She's come here because you're here on leave and if anyone finds out I'll be held responsible.

TODD: It's only till tomorrow. I'll wake her up. I'll give her a few more minutes.

HARPER: Did you see the programme about crocodiles?

TODD: Yes but crocodiles, the way they look after the baby crocodiles and carry them down to the water in their mouths.

HARPER: Don't you think everyone helps their own children?

TODD: I'm just saying I wouldn't be sorry if the crocodiles were on one of the sides we have alliances with. They're unstoppable, come on.

HARPER: Crocodiles are evil and it is always right to be opposed to crocodiles. Their skin, their teeth, the foul smell of their mouths from the dead meat. Crocodiles wait till zebras are crossing the river and bite the weak ones with those jaws and pull them down. Crocodiles invade villages at night and take children out of their beds. A crocodile will carry a dozen heads back to the river, tenderly like it carries its young, and put them in the water where they bob about as trophies till they rot.

TODD: I'm just saying we could use that.

HARPER: And the fluffy little darling waterbirds, the smallest one left behind squeaking wait for me, wait for me. And their mother who would give her life to save them.

TODD: Do we include mallards in this?

HARPER: Mallards are not a good waterbird. They commit rape, and they're on the side of the elephants and the Koreans. But crocodiles are always in the wrong.

TODD: Do you think I should wake her up or let her sleep? We won't get any time together.

HARPER: You agree with me about the crocodiles?

TODD: What's the matter? you don't know whose side I'm on?

HARPER: I don't know what you think.

TODD: I think what we all think.

HARPER: Take deer.

TODD: You mean sweet little bambis?

HARPER: You mean that ironically?

TODD: I mean it sarcastically.

HARPER: Because they burst out of parks and storm down from mountains and terrorise shopping malls. If the does run away when you shoot they run into somebody else and trample them with their vicious little shining hooves, the fawns get under the feet of shoppers and send them crashing down escalators, the young bucks charge the plate glass windows –

TODD: I know to hate deer.

HARPER: and the old ones, do you know how heavy their antlers are or how sharp the prongs are when they twist into teenagers running down the street?

TODD: Yes I do know that.

He lifts his shirt and shows a scar.

HARPER: Was that a deer?

TODD: In fact it was a bear. I don't like being doubted.

HARPER: It was when the elephants went over to the Dutch, I'd always trusted elephants.

TODD: I've shot cattle and children in Ethiopia. I've gassed mixed troops of Spanish, computer programmers and dogs. I've torn starlings apart with my bare hands. And I liked doing it with my bare hands. So don't suggest I'm not reliable.

HARPER: I'm not saying you can't kill.

TODD: And I know it's not all about excitement. I've done boring jobs. I've worked in abattoirs stunning pigs and musicians and by the end of the day your back aches and all you can see when you shut your eyes is people hanging upside down by their feet.

HARPER: So you'd say the deer are vicious?

TODD: We've been over that.

HARPER: If a hungry deer came into the yard you wouldn't feed it?

TODD: Of course not.

HARPER: I don't understand that because the deer are with us. They have been for three weeks.

TODD: I didn't know. You said yourself.

HARPER: Their natural goodness has come through. You can see it in their soft brown eyes.

TODD: That's good news.

HARPER: You hate the deer. You admire the crocodiles.

TODD: I've lost touch because I'm tired.

HARPER: You must leave.

TODD: I'm your family.

HARPER: Do you think I sleep?

JOAN comes in and walks into TODD's arms.

HARPER: You can't stay here, they'll be after you. What are you going to say when you go back, you ran off to spend a day with your husband? Everyone has people they love they'd like to see or anyway people they'd rather see than lie in a hollow waiting to be bitten by ants. Are you not going back at all because if you're not you might as well shoot me now. Did anyone see you leave? which way did you come? were you followed? There are ospreys here who will have seen you arrive. And you're risking your life for you don't know what because he says things that aren't right. Don't you care? Maybe you don't know right from wrong yourself, what do I know about you after two years, I'd like to be glad to see you but how can I?

JOAN: Of course birds saw me, everyone saw me walking along but nobody knew why, I could have been on a mission, everyone's moving about and no one knows why, and in fact I killed two cats and a child under five so it wasn't that different from a mission, and I don't see why I can't have one day and then go back, I'll go on to the end after this. It wasn't so much the birds I was frightened of, it was the weather, the weather here's on the side of the Japanese. There were thunderstorms all through the mountains, I went through towns I hadn't been before. The rats are bleeding out of their mouths and ears, which is good, and so were the girls by the side of the road. It was tiring there because everything's been recruited, there were piles of bodies and if you stopped to find out there was one killed by coffee or one killed by pins, they were killed by heroin, petrol, chainsaws, hairspray, bleach, foxgloves, the smell of smoke was where we were burning the grass that wouldn't serve. The Bolivians are working with gravity, that's a secret so as not to spread alarm. But we're getting further with noise and there's thousands dead of light in Madagascar. Who's going to mobilise darkness and silence? that's what I wondered in the night. By the third day I could hardly walk but I got down to the river. There was a camp of Chilean soldiers upstream but they hadn't seen me and fourteen black and white cows downstream having a drink so I knew I'd have to go straight across. But I didn't know whose side the river was on, it might help me swim or it might drown me. In the middle the current was running much faster, the water was brown, I didn't know if that meant anything. I stood on the bank a long time. But I knew it was my only way of getting here so at last I put one foot in the river. It was very cold but so far that was all. When you've just stepped in you can't tell what's going to happen. The water laps round your ankles in any case.

Note

The Parade (Scene 2.5): five is too few and twenty better than ten. A hundred?

5.7 PRODUCT (2005)

MARK RAVENHILL

Mark Ravenhill (b. 1966) *graduated in English and Drama from Bristol University, and came to prominence as a dramatist in 1996 with the Out of Joint/Royal Court Theatre production of* Shopping and Fucking *– an explicit, comic and politically aware exploration of disenfranchised young people in a 'post-ideological' age. The notable international critical and commercial success of* Shopping and Fucking *did not deter Ravenhill from expanding his thematic landscape, persistently engaging with formal experiment, and developing new collaborations with directors and theatre companies. His work over the past twenty years has embraced subjects and practices as diverse as same-sex parenting (*Handbag, *1998), theatre for young people (including* Citizenship, *2005), pantomime (*Dick Whittington, *2005), the War on Terror (*Shoot/Get Treasure/Repeat, *2007), libretti for opera and contemporary music theatre (*Ten Plagues, *2011, performed by the singer Marc Almond) and television sitcom (as co-creator of* Vicious, *about an elderly gay couple played by Ian McKellen and Derek Jacobi, first broadcast in the UK in 2013).* Product *(2005) was written for the UK company Paines Plough to tour nationally and internationally. The work is a bitingly comedic response to the experience and function of narrative and representation in a post-9/11 world. It also exemplifies another strand to Ravenhill's practice – this 'virtual monologue' was conceived for the dramatist himself to perform. Ravenhill's unique position in contemporary British playwriting is also complemented by the dramatist's critically reflective engagement with his own practice in relation to the wider cultural and ideological landscape (see 5.14).*

An office. JAMES, *a film producer, and* OLIVIA, *an actress.*

JAMES: So there's a knife.

And your eyes widen as you see the knife.

And he's pulled it out from under his ... the knife comes out from ... he's wearing a, a ... robe.

He's a tall fellow, a tall, dusky fellow, and –

And now he uses the knife, he uses the knife and he slits open the plastic on his croissant and he puts the croissant in his mouth and he puts the knife in that sort of stringy pouch in front of him.

Now you want to call out – you are just about to call out.

'He's got a knife. The tall dusky fellow has got a knife.'

But something – a decision, a small but important beat, you don't call out. You look down the aisle at the tanned and blond and frankly effeminate airline staff and you don't call out.

Why? Why? Why? Well ...

Let's just discover her, shall we? Let's just discover Amy, a beat at a time.

'Excuse me,' you tells the dusky fellow, 'that's my seat.' You've had the window seat since childhood and he stands to let you in and you open the overhead baggage container – your luggage is Gucci, Gucci are in, it's going to be fabulous, you open the luggage container and ...

There's a mat. A small oriental mat rolled up very neat.

Hold on your face. Suprise, apprehension, maybe, I just want you to ... play it.

'Is this yours?'

'Yes.'

'Do you do yoga?'

'No. That is my prayer mat. I pray.'

'Oh.'

And you sit and you ... you look out the window and you ... fear ... you're in an, an aeroplane up in the air, next to a tall dusky fellow whose prayer mat is up above you and whose knife is in the pouch in front of you.

'Ladies and gentlemen. Could I remind you to switch off all electrical goods?'

And you reach into your bag and you take out your mobile and you go to switch off your mobile phone and now we – close up on you – you look down at the mobile and something is triggered inside you, a chord of emotion resonates and we see – ah! Amy is wounded, there's a wound and it's something about the mobile, something about the ... it's a narrative hook and it's empathy.

I know you're going to love her, I hope you're going to love her. She is three-dimensional. And I'd love to see you play three-dimensional again after those last three, four ...

And now the fellow turns, he turns, the tall dusky, fellow he turns and suddenly – his head is on the shoulder of your suit – it's Versace, Versace are on board, it's a Versace suit – his dusky head is on the fabulous shoulder of your fabulous Versace suit and he falls asleep.

And you look at, you look at him ... You ... His smell is so different.

And do you know what you want to do? Do you know what you want to do? Well, I'll ...

You want to ... you actually want to ... you want to reach out to the knife ... reach out to the knife and you want to grab hold of the knife, okay, and pull the knife out of that stringy pouch and you want to feel the weight of the blade in your hand and then you want to thrust it into him, in and out and in and and in and out and in out until there is blood, there is blood shooting from that dusky frame and the blood is shooting over you and you're more blood than face and you want to call out.

'This is for the Towers. This is for civilisation. This is for all of us, you bastard.'

You don't say that. You don't do that. That's an interior monologue. You play that? I want you to play that with your eyes. Can you play that with your ... ? Well of course you can, of course you can. I love your work.

'This is for all of us you bastard.'

You see? You see? Amy is wounded. She is ... to each of us the wound, to each the wound is different. It sounds classical but it's me, it's my note to my writers ... show me the wound ... and... please ... I will show you Amy's wound if you'll – Yes? Yes? Yes?

It's a thrill to have you in the room.

So Amy doesn't touch the knife, she leaves the knife, the knife is untouched and the plane lands and the dusky fellow puts the knife under his robe and he takes his prayer mat from the baggage container and that should be ... they should never meet again but ... this is the world of the heart, this is the screen, the dream, this is movie-land, so, so, so...

It's a rainy night, a storm at Heathrow, a broken heel on your Jimmy Choos and the only taxi left and it's his taxi, and suddenly he's saying.

'Please – get in.'

Fear but somehow excitement. The adventure has begun. Into the car of a stranger.

And you climb in with fear and excitement and there's the prayer mat and there's the knife on the seat between him and you, and you.

'Which way are you going?'

'I don't know. Which way you going?'

'I – I – I –'

'You gonna take me home?'

Take him home? Take him home? Are you going to take him home?

Cut to your face. Cut to the knife. Cut to the prayer mat. Cut to his – and the lighting favours him now, okay? Something in the lighting – for the first time he looks handsome.

And you, and you, and you – you play the, her aching sexuality. Which I know you ...

Your sexuality aches and he's handsome and you ignore the prayer mat and the knife and you say to the cabbie,

'The docklands please.'

And he says,

'Docklands love, course love.'

And you exit east from Trafalgar Square.

You live in an abbatoir, it's an old converted abbatoir that is now a massively cool loft-style apartment and it feels good to be home and strange and exciting to be letting the dusky fellow in to your world, but you open the door and you let him in and he puts down the knife and the prayer mat on your floor and you offer him wine, but he doesn't drink, but you do drink –

And you're nervous and you drink the better part of a bottle and your eye occasionally flicks to the knife and the prayer mat and now you've drunk the bottle and you are …

'I'm Amy. I open call centres and call centres, I travel around and around and around in dwindling circles around this shrinking globe.'

A man, a tall, dusky man in your apartment.

Your sexuality is so … it's aching, it's aching … it's inflamed and you – you surprise yourself – but you want him, you want him, you want the dusky fellow and you, and you press yourself upon him.

Mohammed.

But he's frightened. He's a virgin and he knows nothing of this world of aching sexuality and he's frightened.

'Amy, I'm frightened.'

'Mohammed, don't be frightened. Don't be … Ssssh. Ssssh. Ssssh.'

And you lead him to the bed and it's very beautiful – and you have a body double, Beata is your body double – and you lead him to the bed and you slip his body from his robes and at last your ache can be, can be, can be … filled.

And he is slow and unsure and clumsy at first, but then as you move together, body and heart and … as you find the music of your … and now you begin to come and come and come and come and come and it's the orgasm of your life.

To find yourself, to find yourself, you – Amy – with your wound, to find yourself so at one with this dusky fellow is so … strange. We have to … we have to see that in your face.

Can you play that? Can you … ? Of course. I love your work. I love it. I've seen you do those turns on a sixpence. Hate. Love. Click. Power. Subjection. Click. I've seen you do that with a shit script and a cast I wouldn't wish on a mini-series. You're fabulous and this is fab – it's gonna be fabulous once it's been punched up.

But then – time passes in the night – time passes in the night and maybe you fall asleep but you wake, you wake – a jolt – uh – and you reach out – you reach out – you reach out and – you're – like so many times before you're alone in the bed.

Has he – ? Has he gone? Has he taken you and gone?

Your eyes adjust to the darkness. No. He hasn't gone. He hasn't … There is the prayer mat and there is the knife just where he left them on your floor, so he hasn't gone he's just, he's …

And then you see him. You see his dusky frame. You see the dusky frame moving about your incredibly cool loft-style apartment – which was once an abbatoir – and you see him and he's moving about and he's looking at your white goods and he's looking at your black goods and your chrome goods and your beech goods and your plasma and your bluetooth and your exercise equipment and you know, you know, you know what he's doing and you throw yourself, you throw your naked – Beata's naked body from the bed and the words just come up, they just come up from inside you and you scream:

'Stop judging me. Stop fucking judging. So my life is worthless. So I'm busy but it means nothing. So all I have around me is clutter and no value. So I never had a belief. So I'm all alone and I let the first human being inside me who shows me the slightest –'

'So, so, so, so –'

(We had a theatre writer work on this bit.)

'And you, what about you? Who gives you your orders? The Imam? The Dictator? Allah? Oh, open your *eyes*, open your eyes. What would you like to do to me eh? Given half a chance. Cover me up? Stone me? But you'd like to.'

That's stopped him. That's stopped him in his tracks and he's just stopped and he's listening to you.

'How can you, how dare you feel superior to me? I am freedom, I am progress, I am democracy – and you are fear and darkness and evil and I hate you.'

His sperm is still dribbling down your leg. That's a private note. We won't shoot it.

And now you, there are tears, you are, the tears come up and now – your wound – as if on impulse, a beat, fast beat, you reach for your mobile and you call up a message, a message from the past, a message from – the time when the wound began, when all the hurting began to hurt.

And you – message is on conference and you place it there in the middle of the floor down by the prayer mat and down by the knife, and you place your mobile phone down and you stand naked and Mohammed stands naked – like Eve, like Eve – and you listen to:

'Oh my God oh my God oh my God oh my God oh my God …' (It can be punched up.)

'Oh my God Amy, something's got the tower. They've … the other tower is on fire.'

'And – Amy, sweetheart, I think they've got us too. I think they hit our tower, sweetheart. We're on fire. Shit. We're on fire. And I'm gonna have to jump baby and I – I just want you to know, Amy, I love you, I love you, I love you with all my – aaaaah.'

And the message ends and Amy falls, falls to the floor and sobs. Which I think you can, I know you can …

I get a lot of scripts. It's my job. I get … there are hundreds of thousands of stories and they're sitting on my desk and mostly they are, they are, they are …

The effluent of the soul.

Nobody understands the basic, the truth, the wound.

But this script, this story, I – I have been touched, I have been moved by this. When I – I have lain on the floor in my office and wept when I read this script, you see? You see?

And I want to …

There are powers greater than me. There is a Higher Power. I cannot greenlight. And I have been to the Power and I have said. 'This is the one, this is the … I want to produce this script, I have wept like a woman at this script and now I must tell this story,' and the Power has said to me. 'Get someone big attached.'

And so I – so I – so I – no bullshit – I thought of you. For Amy. You are my first, you are my only choice for Amy –

Because like her you are … I know you hurt, I know … it's there, it's up there on the screen, your raw wound for me, us all to see which is why you …

You fascinate and you excite me.

So let's… make a movie.

The message ends. The message from the past, the message from the Towers, and Amy falls to the floor of her fabulous apartment and she is sobbing and now she, she's calling out:

'Troy's gone. I'll never see Troy again. Troy died in the Towers and I'll never see Troy again.'

And Mohammed comes to you and he puts his arms around you.

'Sssshhh.'

And for a moment, there's comfort, comfort, but then your POV on the knife and the prayer mat and you say:

'Mohammed, I have to know. I have to know, Mohammed.'

'Sssshhh. Not now Amy.'

'Yes, Mohammed I have to – are you Al Queda?'

'Not now, Amy. Ssssh. Sssssssh. Sssssh.'

And he lies you down on the bed and he holds you and, oh, the comfort of that dusky frame.

Now let's not play Amy with any judgement please, no let's not judge … let's just … let's just play her as a woman, as a woman who that night as she lay there fell *in love, fell in* love with a man, a man with a knife and a prayer mat, a woman who that night as she slept, as she slept in Mohammed's dusky arms, forgot, forgot for the first time since the eleventh of the ninth of 2001, forgot the smoke and the confusion and the calls, and the droop and crumble of the Towers, and she forgot the fall of Troy.

And let's – moment by moment, day by day – she is drawn into Mohammed's world, moment by moment, day by day, and other men begin to gather at her apartment, other men with their *robes* and their knives and their prayer mats – seven, then eight, then nine, then ten men at a time, their mats positioned on the floor, calling to Mecca, talking, planning.

Is this is a cell? Is this – a fundamentalist terrorist threat in the middle of your world?

You should ask, you should challenge, but you're – it's love, you're in – wild, blind, stupid – and the Heart is a bigger organ than the Brain, as we say in this business we call show.

And then one day they are there – Mohammed and the men are there with their knives and their prayer mats in your fabulous loft-style apartment, and you're making their infusion and suddenly the door opens, the door opens and you turn and you see, you see, you see, here, in your apartment, coming across your apartment, he's there in your apartment, in your apartment, Osama is in your apartment.

And he comes towards you and he smiles at you – it's a cruel smile – and he …

Bless you.

Why don't you – ? There are knives, there are – Why don't you attack? You could, you should, you –

It's inner conflict you're experiencing, you're playing this inner conflict. Everything is – for the sake of Troy, for revenge you should attack, you should revenge but you don't and you are kissed – you are kissed, a warm breathy kiss on the forehead from Osama.

And now the plan is revealed. Now the work of the cell is made known to you. Now you know that they are all evil men.

Europe is to be torn apart. The Hague. The Reichstag. Tate Modern. Suicide bombing. Each of these men is to be stuffed and strapped with explosives and then at midday tomorrow they will carry off buildings and people and nothing but misery and devastation will follow.

And now they're coming to Mohammed. To Mohammed's task. What will be Mohammed's task?

You want to cry out:

'No, no, no, no, Mohammed. I love you.'

Your mouth is open but the words don't come.

And then you discover, then you learn. Osama turns, he turns and he gives Mohammed his mission. Disneyworld Europe. He must blow up Disneyworld Europe.

And now you step forward and you hear yourself saying, as if another is speaking for you.

'I can't bear for you to do this, Mohammed. I can't bear to lose you. I've already lost Troy. And I won't lose you. I'm a woman and I love this man.'

And then you turn to Osama.

'Let me go with him. Strap me and stuff me with explosives and let me go with him and let me die with my man in the middle of the day, in the middle of the continent, at Disneyworld Europe.'

'No woman can ever – '

'Please, great mullah, please. I am a woman but I love this man and I want to die with this man.'

Minutes go by and we cut to the faces of the jihadists as they wait for the decision of Osama, their mullah. Cut to Mohammed – his eyes are misty. Cut to you – waiting, waiting.

And then Osama breathes and he smiles and he nods:

'Yes.'

You are to die with your man.

And that night you lie in Mohammed's arms, you lie and wait the call that will take you to the EuroStar and on to your mission, you lie in the dark and he says:

'I love you, Amy, I love you with all my heart and I thank Allah for your bravery to join me in suicide.'

'It's just something I have to do, Mohammed.'

'But I fear. When my body is blown apart at the beat of twelve I will go to Paradise. It will be easy to leave this world and go to Paradise. Where will you go?'

'I … I … I … I … don't know Mohammed. Where there … Can I come to Paradise?'

'No. You are not chosen for Paradise.'

'Oh,'

'These are our last hours together.'

'Then fuck me. Fuck me. Fuck me. Fuck me these last few hours. Fill me every way you can until I hurt and I just can't take you any more. Come, Mohammed, come.'

'A place that only we know.'

And he does and you are hungry, hungry, hungry, but finally your en-seam-ed bodies topple into slumber and then it comes, the nightmare comes.

You are there, you are in Disneyworld Europe and you are

stuffed and strapped with every explosive known to man and you look around – a minute to twelve and you look around – and you see the people and you can't see … These are good people, these are good, fat, happy, bright people. Queueing, eating, riding people. These are your people. What are you doing? What are you doing?

Forty seconds until you take them away. Forty seconds until you push your hand through all of us and rip it apart.

How can you do this? Why are you doing this?

'*Avez-vous vu ma mère?*'

You look down at the little girl with the ears and the balloon and she's what – three?

'*Avez-vous vu ma mère? Je veux ma mère. S'il vous plaît – je cherche ma mère.*'

And you want to scream:

'No fucking point sweetheart. No fucking point. She's a dead person. I'm a dead person. You're a dead person. We're all just dead people in the Magic Kingdom of Life.'

But you don't – you take her hand – twenty seconds to go, but you take her hand –

You, you suicide jihadist, you take the hand of the pretty little girl with her mouse ears and balloon and you begin to walk down main street because you think, better she has these last few seconds of comfort in the search for *maman* than to die alone and in fear and despair.

The time is coming in now, it's coming – ten, nine, eight, seven, six –

The explosives on your body are pulsating and vibrating as if to will themselves to their deathly task –

Five –

'*Mama, mama, où est-tu, mama?*'

Four –

A figure is approaching.

'*Bonjour – Je m'appelle Mickey. Vous est ma amie. Comment t'appelles-tu?*'

'I am Death. I am Death. Run, Mickey. Run, Magic Kingdom. I am Death.'

Three –

'*Bonjour – fille jolie. Quelle ballon joli.*'

'*Où est mama?*'

Two –

'*Je ne sais pas. Moi, je ne suis pas ta mère.*'

One. Tiny beat – maybe it's not gonna, maybe it's not – maybe fate and computer error have saved the world but then –

Boom!

From your back and your chest and your sex the force comes, the explosive comes, and in your last moment of your life that child's head, now ripped from its body, and the blood filling your eyes, that child's head is blown towards you and her voice fills your head as you die.

'*Maman.*'

You wake with a start. It's three in the morning, three in the morning in your fabulous loft-style apartment and you look at Mohammed and suddenly you are filled with disgust.

What is this? What are you doing?

He shouldn't be here with you. He shouldn't be – he should be in an orange jump suit and he should be spat at and kicked and humiliated.

You pig. You dog. You worse than animal. Roll in this shit. Piss your pants. Eat your faeces, cunt.

And you are resolved and you reach for the phone and you phone the Special Forces.

And you report everything – sometimes with tears, sometimes in anger – you tell the whole terrible tale.

And now a van is on its way to take … Mohammed and the explosives.

Alone again. Another man who turned out to be not right for you. Every year the hurt grows a little more, until one day it will be so raw you'll never love.

Just one last look, one last look at Mohammed before he goes.

He looks like a boy – who could have thought he would be … ? He looks like a boy.

And you move towards him and you sit on the bed and you run your fingers through his dark, dark hair.

'I'm sorry, Mohammed, I'm sorry.'

And you lean forward and you kiss a gentle kiss upon the sleeping lips.

'Bitch.'

His eyes snap open, his hand is up and strikes across the jaw.

'Bitch. Bitch. Bitch.'

'Ahhh!'

'Bitch. You have betrayed us.'

His lithe body jumps from the bed and he kicks you in the stomach, there's no breath in your lungs, there's a gob of blood in your mouth.

'You have betrayed Allah.'

'I won't do it. I won't kill innocent children.'

And you fear for your life. You fear that Mohammed will kill you, dismembered corpse in your apartment, and you remember Mohammed's knife. And something inside you says – get the knife – get the knife – it's lying there and he could use the fucking knife and slit me toe to crown. You rush for the knife, you hold it – and you look up. But he hasn't gone for the knife.

He's got a petrol can in his hand. Where did that come from?

He looks down at you. His eyes lock on to yours. The seconds pass. A lorry passes in the night carrying beef to Dover. (That's a detail.)

And now there is sadness in his eyes and he says.

'I am the weakness. I am the flaw. I was the lust that drove me to woman. I have betrayed jihad.'

And he pours the petrol can over his dusky frame, shaking his hair like a girl in a shower after hockey.

'This world is a place of suffering and unhappiness. Yes?'

'Yes, yes, yes.'

'Please, Allah, admit me to Paradise, please Allah. I failed jihad, but please, Allah.'

And now he moves to the Aga and he picks up the matches and you see what he's going to do.

'Mohammed – don't.'

'But I have failed my mullah, I have failed my cause. Goodbye.'

He strikes the match.

'But Mohammed, I love you, I love you, I love you with all my heart more than Troy, more than the Towers, your strength your mystery your heart. I – Let's run away now, before the security forces … Let's begin again, there's a cottage, the countryside –'

'No. I have loved you, Amy. But we are just people.'

'That's all there is. People. Lonely, wounded people and their loving hearts.'

'No. There is Destiny, there is Allah's will, there is the Cause. And all of these are bigger than people. I pity you, my love, in your small world of people. No purpose … How do you live with this? My sadness is with you.'

He looks up.

'Oh please, Allah, let your servant come to Paradise.'

And then – woosh – he's alight, the flame racing across his body and his skin and hair and crackling and the smell is almost sweet in your converted abbatoir.

And then you – this feeling deep within and you call out.

'Oh take me, take me, Mohammed. Take me in those arms. I love you. I don't know you. I'll never know you. I will never believe a thing you *believe*. But fold me in your burning arms, press your flaming chest against me, scorch me with your groin of fire.'

Then, as if in slow motion – fuck it, we are in slow motion – you run toward the burning man.

And now – a life avoiding, avoiding, afraid of death (character notes: your mother's cancer, your best friend's suicide, your father dwindling into Alzheimered oblivion), all your life scared and your denial of death and now the freedom, the total exhilarating three-dimensional freedom as you call on the Angel of Death to take you and –

'Yes, Mohammed. Yeeeeessss!'

And you're closing in on him, you're reaching him, your hair is starting to crack and sizzle as the flames are inches from you and then, then, then, your arms enfold him and his skin begins to melt onto yours:

'Yeeeeessss!'

And then there's the crack of glass – do you know Liz? Fabulous little dyke, gonna be doing all your stunts? – the crack of glass as you both fall and fall and fall, four storeys and into the pool below.

Underwater those bodies, twisting around, the flames becoming smoke, becoming charred and sodden, your bodies twisting one over the other.

Until you come up – eighty-degree burns on his part, twenty degrees for you but –

There's love, like a great wave of release, suddenly there's love, there in the pool there's love and you kiss and caress and you fuck in the water, the pleasure of the lovemaking, the pain of the burns all rolling into one.

But then they're there. The Feds, the cops, the special ops – all the special forces of the world – and they pull Mohammed from your arms and you're screaming:

'Please I love him. You have to – love will conquer this. I know it, Yes there is terror and horror and he's done wickedness, yes – but we've found love here tonight and I –'

Your final vision. Your final vision of Mohammed – the body a mass of burns, the smell of chlorine, the feel of him still inside you – a vision as the butt of a gun pushes you to the ground and the doors of the van open, the savage barking of a dog, the manacles clipping around the hands and feet of this man you love.

You rush into the street – you throw yourself into the path of the van – you are on the verge of madness now – I'd love to see you play the verge of madness – you block the path of the van – surely they must stop for you? – but the van is racing toward you – at the last moment your nerve cracks and – wham! – you throw yourself out of the way.

Your cowardice. How you despise your cowardice. When an eighteen-year-old boy can blow himself up, why can't you stand in front of a racing vehicle to save the man you love?

You pick yourself up from the pavement with difficulty. Already the bruising is beginning. You see the TV crew, the redhead with the microphone running towards you in the night and you're very wet and very cold and very alone.

No. He isn't a bad man, you tell the News. He is a good man and I love him.

And then your stomach loops, your knees disappear and you lose consciousness.

You're out for a couple of days. Your mother cares for you. Your mother or a neighbour or an aunt or blah blah blah. She's a mentor, okay? Too old to fuck, too old to kick ass, but we have a place for her in our world.

And this wise old woman, this woman whose sexuality has died so that she might think of higher things, this woman says.

'Hush now, child, hush. You must forget him. You must let Mohammed go. There is a time for everything and your time for Mohammed has ended and now is the time to live a new life.'

And you look up from the bed and you feel the warmth of her wisdom and you say.

'Yes MotherAuntNeighbour yes.'

And so there is an emptiness. An emptiness which once he filled. And your life begins again. You begin to spin around the globe again. There's the constant drive drive drive to outsource customer relations to expanding economies. There are several weeks in China.

And back at home Nathan gets in touch again. Nathan who loved you at school. Nathan who married the fitness instructor but lost her in the rail crash. Nathan who has loved you all the time.

And you sit in sushi bars and theatres and taxis with Nathan and he holds your hand and he touches your knee and all the time he's telling you what a special person you are but really there is nothing that you hear.

And you take Nathan in your mouth. You take his broad beautiful cock in your mouth and you force it back and back into you so that you gag because when you gag you know you'll feel something. But you don't feel anything.

And you plead with Nathan to hit you about the head. You put the club in his hand and say. 'Come on, come on, strike me.' But he loves you in such a tender way and he runs into the night and that's Nathan gone.

You hang about the coach station and you pull up your skirt for teenagers in toilets and in alleyways – looking for a smell that will drown the scent of Mohammed.

(This is edgy, okay? This is fucking – fucking edgy stuff, okay? What do you think? What are you thinking? I'd love a word here. just a word to let me know how I'm …

I'm pitching my bollocks off and that –.

I like it. I like it. Enjoy your power. I would. If I had that power then I would use it.

You bitch, you bitch. I love you, you bitch. Respect to the bitch.

No stay stay stay. Stay. Hear the end of the story. Hear the end of the story or I'll …

Thank you.)

It's a bar. A bar with a TV screen. A fucking scuzzy prostitutes-and-drunkards bar by the coach station when you first see the images of Mohammed on the TV screen. They've been smuggled out of the offshore prison. It's a blurry image – nothing more than a grey shadow moving across the TV screen. But you know straight away. You know the man you love as he is dragged across the screen, the hair torn from his scalp. And you see her apply the electrodes to his testicles, you see the dignity in his face as the other guards laugh and jeer, you see the spit on his face, then his body dancing as the electrodes burn at the testes you have held so often in the night.

You sit in your fabulous loft-style apartment that evening and you watch that image played over as it rolls through the news and you listen to the experts and the politicians and the lawyers and the celebrities trying to give it their story, every time a new story as once again the electrodes are clipped onto Mohammed's sac, as the spit hits his face, the jeers and the jaunts and then the electricity dancing through his body.

And, just as suddenly as the power jolts through your lover, the resolve jolts through you. You leap from your chair, you throw your towel to the ground and you turn your naked body to the screen and you call out:

'Hold on. Hold on. Because I'm coming, I'm coming to save you – lover.'

And we crane, crane, crane as though the gods, the heavens, the eternal powers hear and endorse your cry.

A montage. You're training. A boy's boxing club in the east of the city where you push yourself until your eyes swell with blood. The icy lake where you swim for hours before even the ducks are awake. The Tibetan monastery where you learn to breathe and kick and chop. The mountain state where your

Kalashnikov is slung across your breast ready to fire as the targets go flying into the sky.

And as one image melts to another, we see Amy disappearing from view. She's gone. Amy – who once lived on coffee and air-miles and longing – Amy – who never found the perfect diet, never found the perfect man, never found a therapist she could trust – this Amy is ripped away to reveal a creature of muscle and will and strength.

You are hero. Before you, we are nothing. Before you, we – oh saviour, oh saviour, oh saviour.

If only you would save me, if only – this story were … there is an inner truth to this st … but… it's what we would want to …

No. You're right. Fucking pointless. I'm fucking pointless. What is this piece of crap? What is this … ? What is this story? What's this … three mil on an opening weekend? What is that? It's shit.

So you don't … have to …

I'll call a car …

(*To phone.*) A car for … yeah, yeah … account.

Thank you. Thank you. Thank you.

Listen, just …

There's just this … okay?

That final night in your fabulous loft-style apartment that was once an abbatoir. And in your fabulous apartment you take Mohammed's mat from the floor and you bless it and you place the mat in your rucksack and you take Mohammed's knife and you kiss the blade and you slip the knife amongst the weapons that are slung about your waist.

And then we cut to –

Boom! The explosion crashes open the door to the corridor and in you come – a fury in fatigues.

'Where is he? Where is he?' you scream at the Cuban guard pushing him against the wall. 'Where the fuck is he?'

And your fist – crack crack crack – against the Cuban's skull.

'I'm coming to fucking find you,' you scream, blasting at the guards who come running toward you. Your bullets tear into them and hurtle them against the walls and the blood begins to run in rivers down the corridors of Uncle Sam's detention centre.

'Mohammed! Mohammed! Mohammed!'

Boom! You blow open the doors to the first cell and out they come the men and women in their orange jumpsuits, blinking into the light and calling to Allah as they dance with their liberty.

But he's not there. So many faces – but not the face of the man you love.

You blow open the second door, the third door, the fourth door – and they are pouring down the corridors of the prison now, a great carnival of the enchained.

There he is! Mohammed! You run towards him, you throw yourself towards him, you pull at his shoulder –

'Please?'

The stranger is terrified at this fierce warrior who is clinging to him.

So. The search goes on and you go into the lift and down and down and down – until …

The light is dim here. Many floors above the orange jumpsuits and the guards are fighting but here there's not a sound. 'Pad like the cat, strike like the tiger,' said the Tibetan monk and so you pad through the dimness – and strike like the tiger as the guard turns the corner, slitting his throat with one keen slice from Mohammed's blade.

And finally the silhouette against the bars. And he's weeping.

'Oh Mohammed.'

The hair has been pulled from his skull, he's burnt, he's bruised and –

'Amy?'

'Yes, Mohammed.'

'Go. I won't see you.'

'Please –'

'Western bitch who destroyed my bond to Allah.'

'Mohammed.'

'Western bitch who defiled my body and tore at my heart.'

'Mohammed.'

'Western bitch who cannot see Paradise.'

'Please, Mohammed. I have been… there was Amy and I spit on her. I spit on her restless, pointless, aching decadence. Yes, I spit. I spit – and I pray to be reborn – reborn in Allah's eye and I will not rest until this world is purged of the infidel and all stand pure before Allah – together we will do this, my love, we will fight and struggle and work until this hollow world is purified and all are ready for Paradise.'

'This prison is hell.'

'And I have come to take you back. Please, Mohammed, let me …'

'Yes, my love.'

And so you blast open the bars and out he steps, the broken figure of this man you love. And how gently you hold him in that moment. And how tender but how lingering is that kiss as your souls melt into one.

(There will be awards for this, there will be prizes – but let's not sully …)

'Come,' you tell Mohammed, and you lead him down the corridor, but –

Tuh! The lone guard – you take her out, but not before *her* bullet ricochets around the walls and – slow, slow, slow motion drills its way into Mohammed's head. He crumples – slow – and – slow – the blood stutters from his mouth and ears.

There is no God, no angels, no nothing in our world but still …

There is actually a moment. We're going to need a fantastic lighting-cameraman, but there is actually a moment when the soul leaves the body. Have you ever … ? I've seen it. I've seen it and, erm – if we can get that on celluloid then … they can fucking kiss my arse.

So Mohammed's soul leaves his body for Paradise.

And you mourn him and you mature in that moment – not in a gradual – bereavement matures you in a moment.

And you see it's all screens and show and display and symbols and acting make-believe emptiness.

And you pull out the knife and you feel the weight of the knife in your hand and the sharpness of the blade and you turn the blade toward you, oh to do it, to do it, to do it, just to feel the dignity of Ancient Rome.–

But then –

Cut to your POV.

And it's the rucksack with the prayer mat.

And you take out the prayer mat. And you play: The knife or the prayer mat? Prayer mat or the knife. Which will it be? Which will you … ?

Knife. Prayer mat. Face. Knife. Prayer mat. Face.

And then … you put down the knife. You don't kill yourself.

And you move across the floor and you reach the prayer mat and you look around – unsure which way to position yourself – but then –

A sudden swell of certainty – you're underscored – and then you kneel down, you kneel down upon the mat and – she's a great character.

'Allah? I will revenge, Allah.'

Thank you for listening. Thank you for coming here. It's been a privilege to tell the story. And you, if you want to go back to your, you know, manager and agent and PR and your people and, you know, take the piss, use the script to … then fine, fine, because at least I've told you, I have told you.

Exit OLIVIA. JAMES *phones.*

Hey! Loved it. Loved it. She loved it.

5.8 The Death of the Author (1977)

ROLAND BARTHES

Translated by Stephen Heath

IN HIS STORY *SARRASINE* Balzac, describing a castrato disguised as a woman, writes the following sentence: *'This was woman herself, with her sudden fears, her irrational whims, her instinctive worries, her impetuous boldness, her fussings, and her delicious sensibility.'* Who is speaking thus? Is it the hero of the story bent on remaining ignorant of the castrato hidden beneath the woman? Is it Balzac the individual, furnished by his personal experience with a philosophy of Woman? Is it Balzac the author professing 'literary' ideas on femininity? Is it universal wisdom? Romantic psychology? We shall never know, for the good reason that writing is the destruction of every voice, of every point of origin. Writing is that neutral, composite, oblique space where our subject slips away, the negative where all identity is lost, starting with the very identity of the body writing.

No doubt it has always been that way. As soon as a fact is *narrated* no longer with a view to acting directly on reality but intransitively, that is to say, finally outside of any function other than that of the very practice of the symbol itself, this disconnection occurs, the voice loses its origin, the author enters into his own death, writing begins. The sense of this phenomenon, however, has varied; in ethnographic societies the responsibility for a narrative is never assumed by a person but by a mediator, shaman or relator whose 'performance' – the mastery of the narrative code – may possibly be admired but never his 'genius'. The author is a modern figure, a product of our society insofar as, emerging from the Middle Ages with English empiricism, French rationalism and the personal faith of the Reformation, it discovered the prestige of the individual, of, as it is more nobly put, the 'human person'. It is thus logical that in literature it should be this positivism, the epitome and culmination of capitalist ideology, which has attached the greatest importance to the 'person' of the author. The *author* still reigns in histories of literature, biographies of writers, interviews, magazines, as in the very consciousness of men of letters anxious to unite their person and their work through diaries and memoirs. The image of literature to be found in ordinary culture is tyrannically centred on the author, his person, his life, his tastes, his passions, while criticism still consists for the most part in saying that Baudelaire's work is the failure of Baudelaire the man, Van Gogh's his madness, Tchaikovsky's his vice. The *explanation* of a work is always sought in the man or woman who produced it, as if it were always in the end, through the more or less transparent allegory of the fiction, the voice of a single person, the *author* 'confiding' in us.

Though the sway of the Author remains powerful (the new criticism has often done no more than consolidate it), it goes without saying that certain writers have long since attempted to loosen it. In France, Mallarmé was doubtless the first to see and to foresee in its full extent the necessity to substitute language itself for the person who until then had been supposed to be its owner. For him, for us too, it is language which speaks, not the author; to write is, through a prerequisite impersonality (not at all to be confused with the castrating objectivity of the realist novelist), to reach that point where only language acts, 'performs', and not 'me'. Mallarmé's entire poetics consists in suppressing the author in the interests of writing (which is, as will be seen, to restore the place of the reader). Valéry, encumbered by a psychology of the Ego, considerably diluted Mallarmé's theory but, his taste for classicism leading him to turn to the lessons of rhetoric, he never stopped calling into question and deriding the Author; he stressed the linguistic and, as it were, 'hazardous' nature of his activity, and throughout his prose works he militated in favour of the essentially verbal condition of literature, in the face of which all recourse to the writer's interiority seemed to him pure superstition. Proust himself, despite the apparently psychological character of what are called his *analyses,* was visibly concerned with the task of inexorably blurring, by an extreme subtilization, the relation between the writer and his characters; by making of the narrator not he who has seen and felt nor even he who is writing, but he who *is going to write* (the young man in the novel – but, in fact, how old is he and who is he? – wants to write but cannot; the novel ends when writing at last becomes possible), Proust gave modern writing its epic. By a radical reversal, instead of putting his life into his novel, as is so often maintained, he made of his very life a work for which his own book was the model; so that it is clear to us that Charlus does not imitate Montesquiou but that Montesquiou – in his anecdotal, historical reality – is no more than a secondary fragment, derived from Charlus. Lastly, to go no further than this prehistory of modernity, Surrealism, though unable to accord language a supreme place (language being system and the aim of the movement being, romantically, a direct subversion of codes – itself moreover illusory: a code cannot be destroyed, only 'played off'), contributed to the desacrilization of the image of the Author by ceaselessly recommending the abrupt disappointment of expectations of meaning (the famous surrealist 'jolt'), by entrusting the hand with the task of writing as quickly as possible what the head itself is unaware of (automatic writing), by accepting the principle and the experience of several people writing together. Leaving aside literature itself (such distinctions really becoming invalid), linguistics has recently provided the destruction of the Author with a valuable analytical tool by showing that the whole of the enunciation is an empty process, functioning perfectly without there being any need for it to be filled with the person of the interlocutors. Linguistically, the author is never more than the instance writing, just as *I* is nothing other than the instance saying *I*: language knows a 'subject', not a 'person', and this subject, empty outside of the very enunciation which defines it, suffices to make language 'hold together', suffices, that is to say, to exhaust it.

The removal of the Author (one could talk here with Brecht of a veritable 'distancing', the Author diminishing like a figurine at the far end of the literary stage) is not merely an historical fact or an act of writing; it utterly transforms the modern text (or – which is the same thing – the text is henceforth made and read in such a way that at all its levels the author is absent). The temporality is different. The Author, when believed in, is always conceived of as the past of his own book: book and author stand automatically on a single line divided into a *before* and an *after*. The Author is thought to *nourish* the book, which is to say that he exists before it, thinks, suffers, lives for it, is in the same relation of antecedence to his work as a father to his child. In complete contrast, the modern scriptor is born simultaneously with the text, is in no way equipped with a being preceding or exceeding the writing, is not the subject with the book as predicate; there is no other time than that of the enunciation and every text is eternally written *here and now*. The fact is (or, it follows) that *writing* can no longer designate an operation of recording, notation, representation, 'depiction' (as the Classics would say); rather, it designates exactly what linguists, referring to Oxford philosophy, call a performative, a rare verbal form (exclusively given in the first person and in the present tense) in which the enunciation has no other content (contains no other proposition) than the act by which it is uttered – something like the *I declare* of kings or the *I sing* of very ancient poets. Having buried the Author, the modern scriptor can thus no longer believe, as according to the pathetic view of his predecessors, that this hand is too slow for his thought or passion and that consequently, making a law of necessity, he must emphasize this delay and indefinitely 'polish' his form. For him, on the contrary, the hand, cut off from any voice, borne by a pure gesture of inscription (and not of expression), traces a field without origin – or which, at least, has no other origin than language itself, language which ceaselessly calls into question all origins.

We know now that a text is not a line of words releasing a single 'theological' meaning (the 'message' of the Author-God) but a multi-dimensional space in which a variety of writings, none of them original, blend and clash. The text is a tissue of quotations drawn from the innumerable centres of culture. Similar to Bouvard and Pécuchet, those eternal copyists, at once sublime and comic and whose profound ridiculousness indicates precisely the truth of writing, the writer can only imitate a gesture that is always anterior, never original. His only power is to mix writings, to counter the ones with the others, in such a way as never to rest on any one of them. Did he wish to *express himself*, he ought at least to know that the inner 'thing' he thinks to 'translate' is itself only a ready-formed dictionary, its words only explainable through other words, and so on indefinitely; something experienced in exemplary fashion by the young Thomas de Quincey, he who was so good at Greek that in order to translate absolutely modern ideas and images into that dead language, he had, so Baudelaire tells us (in *Paradis Artificiels*), 'created for himself an unfailing dictionary, vastly more extensive and complex than those resulting from the ordinary patience of purely literary themes'. Succeeding the Author, the scriptor no longer bears within him passions, humours, feelings, impressions, but rather this immense dictionary from which he draws a writing that can know no halt: life never does more than imitate the book, and the book itself is only a tissue of signs, an imitation that is lost, infinitely deferred.

Once the Author is removed, the claim to decipher a text becomes quite futile. To give a text an Author is to impose a limit on that text, to furnish it with a final signified, to close the writing. Such a conception suits criticism very well, the latter then allotting itself the important task of discovering the Author (or its hypostases: society, history, psyché, liberty) beneath the work: when the Author has been found, the text is 'explained' – victory to the critic. Hence there is no surprise in the fact that, historically, the reign of the Author has also been that of the Critic, nor again in the fact that criticism (be it new) is today undermined along with the Author. In the multiplicity of writing, everything is to be *disentangled*, nothing *deciphered*; the structure can be followed, 'run' (like the thread of a stocking) at every point and at every level, but there is nothing beneath: the space of writing is to be ranged over, not pierced; writing ceaselessly posits meaning ceaselessly to evaporate it, carrying out a systematic exemption of meaning. In precisely this way literature (it would be better from now on to say *writing),* by refusing to assign a 'secret', an ultimate meaning, to the text (and to the world as text), liberates what may be called an anti-theological activity, an activity that is truly revolutionary since to refuse to fix meaning is, in the end, to refuse God and his hypostases – reason, science, law.

Let us come back to the Balzac sentence. No one, no 'person', says it: its source, its voice, is not the true place of the writing, which is reading. Another – very precise – example will help to make this clear: recent research (J.-P. Vernant[1]) has demonstrated the constitutively ambiguous nature of Greek tragedy, its texts being woven from words with double meanings that each character understands unilaterally (this perpetual misunderstanding is exactly the 'tragic'); there is, however, someone who understands each word in its duplicity and who, in addition, hears the very deafness of the characters speaking in front of him – this someone being precisely the reader (or here, the listener). Thus is revealed the total existence of writing: a text is made of multiple writings, drawn from many cultures and entering into mutual relations of dialogue, parody, contestation, but there is one place where this multiplicity is focused and that place is the reader, not, as was hitherto said, the author. The reader is the space on which all the quotations that make up a writing are inscribed without any of them being lost; a text's unity lies not in its origin but in its destination. Yet this destination cannot any longer be personal: the reader is without history, biography, psychology; he is simply that *someone* who holds together in a single field all the traces by which the written text is constituted. Which is why it is derisory to condemn the new writing in the name of a humanism hypocritically turned champion of the reader's rights. Classic criticism has never paid any attention to the reader; for it, the writer is the only person in literature. We are now beginning to let ourselves be fooled no longer by the arrogant antiphrastical recriminations of good society in favour of the very thing it sets aside, ignores, smothers, or destroys; we know that to give writing its future, it is necessary to overthrow the myth: the birth of the reader must be at the cost of the death of the Author.

Notes

1. [Cf. Jean-Pierre Vernant (with Pierre Vidal-Naquet), *Mythe et tragèdie en Grèce ancienne,* Paris 1972 esp. pp. 19–40, 99–131.]

5.9 Dramaturgy *and* Montage (1991)

Dramaturgy: Actions at work

EUGENIO BARBA

Translated by Richard Fowler

THE WORD 'TEXT', BEFORE referring to a written or spoken, printed or manuscripted text, meant 'a weaving together'. In this sense, there is no performance which does not have 'text'.

That which concerns the text (the weave) of the performance can be defined as 'dramaturgy', that is, *drama-ergon*, the 'work of the actions' in the performance. The way in which the actions work is the plot.

It is not always possible to differentiate between what, in the dramaturgy of a performance, may be 'direction' and what may be the author's 'writing'. This distinction is clear only in theatre which seeks to *interpret* a written text.

Differentiating between autonomous dramaturgy and the performance per se dates back to Aristotle's attitude towards the tradition of Greek tragedy, a tradition already well in the past even for him. He drew attention to two different fields of investigation: the written texts and the way they are performed. The idea that there exists a dramaturgy which is identifiable only in an autonomous, written text and which is the matrix of the performance is a consequence of those occasions in history when the memory of a theatre has been passed on by means of the words spoken by the characters in its performances. Such a distinction would not even be conceivable if it were the performances in their entirety that were being examined.

In a performance, actions (that is, all that which has to do with the dramaturgy) are not only what is said and done, but also the sounds, the lights and the changes in space. At higher level of organisation, actions are the episodes of the story or the different facets of a situation, the arches of time between two accents of the performance, between two changes in the space – or even the evolution of the musical score, the light changes, and the variations of rhythm and intensity which a performer develops following certain precise physical themes (ways of walking, of handling props, of using make-up or costume). The objects used in the performance are also *actions*. They are transformed, they acquire different meanings and different emotive colourations.

All the relationships, all the interactions between the characters or between the characters and the lights, the sounds and the space, are actions. Everything that works directly on the spectators' attention, on their understanding, their emotions, their kinaesthesia, is an action.

The list could become uselessly long. It is not so important to define what an action is, or to determine how many actions there may be in a performance. What is important is to observe that the actions come into play only when they are woven together, when they become texture: 'text'.

The plot can be of two types. The first type is accomplished through the development of actions in time by means of a *concatenation* of causes and effects or through an alternation of actions which represent two parallel developments. The second type occurs only by means of *simultaneity*: the simultaneous presence of several actions.

Concatenation and *simultaneity* are the two dimensions of the plot. They are not two aesthetic alternatives or two different choices of method. They are the two poles whose tension and dialectic determine the performance and its life: actions at work – dramaturgy.

Let us return to the important distinction – investigated especially by Richard Schechner – between theatre based on the mise-en-scène of a previously written text, and theatre based on a performance text. This distinction can be used to define two different approaches to the theatrical phenomenon and therefore two different performance results.

For example: while the written text is recognisable and transmissible before and independently of the performance, the performance text exists only at the end of the work process and cannot be passed on. It would in fact be tautological to say that the performance text (which is the performance) can be extracted from the performance. Even if one used a transcription technique similar to that used for music, in which various horizontal sequences can be arranged vertically, it would be impossible to pass on the information: the more faithful one tried to make it, the more illegible it would become. Even aural and visual mechanical recording of the performance captures only a part of the performance text, excluding (at least in the case of performances that do not use a proscenium stage) the complex montages of actor–spectator distance–proximity relationships, and favouring, in all those cases in which the actions are simultaneous, a single montage from among many. It reflects in fact only *one* observer's way of seeing.

The distinction between theatre based on a written text, or in any case on a text composed a priori and used as the matrix of the mise-en-scène, and theatre whose only meaningful text is the performance text, represents rather well the difference between 'traditional' and 'new' theatre. This distinction becomes even more useful if we wish to move from a classification of modern theatrical phenomena to a microscopic analysis or an anatomical investigation of scenic *bios*, of dramatic life: dramaturgy.

From this point of view, the relationship between a performance text and a text composed a priori no longer seems like a contradiction but like a complementary situation, a kind of dialectic opposition. The problem is not, therefore, the choice of one pole or another, the definition of one or another type of theatre. The problem is that of the balance between the *concatenation pole* and the *simultaneity pole*.

The only prejudicial thing that can occur is the loss of balance between these two poles.

When a performance is based on a text composed of words, there is a danger that the balance in the performance will be lost because of the prevalence of linear relationships (the plot as concatenation). This will damage the plot understood as the weaving together of simultaneously present actions.

If the fundamental meaning of the performance is carried by the interpretation of a written text, there will be a tendency to favour this dimension of the performance, which parallels the linear dimension of language. There will be a tendency to consider as ornamental elements all the interweavings that arise out of the conjunction of several actions at the same time, or simply to treat them as actions that are not woven together, as background actions.

The tendency to underestimate the importance of the simultaneity pole for the life of the play is reinforced, in the modern way of thinking, by the kind of performance which Eisenstein in his time was already calling the 'real level of theatre', that is, the cinema. In the cinema, the linear dimension is almost absolute and the dialectic life of the interwoven actions (the plot) depends basically on two poles: the concatenation of actions and the concatenation of an abstract observer's attention, the eye-filter which selects close-ups, long shots, etc.

The cinema's grip on our imagination increases the risk that the balance between the concatenation and simultaneity poles will be lost when we make theatre performances. The spectator tends not to attribute a significant value to the interweaving of simultaneous actions and behaves – as opposed to what happens in daily life – as if there was a favoured element in the performance particularly suited to establishing the meaning of the play (the words, the protagonist's adventures, etc.). This explains why a 'normal' spectator, in the West, often believes that he doesn't fully understand performances based on the simultaneous weaving together of actions, and why he finds himself in difficulty when faced with the logic of many Asian theatres, which seem to him to be complicated or suggestive because of their 'exoticness'.

If one impoverishes the simultaneity pole, one limits the possibility of making complex meanings arise out of the performance. These meanings do not derive from a complex concatenation of actions but from the interweaving of many dramatic actions, each one endowed with its own simple meaning, and from the assembling of these actions by means of a single unity of time. Thus the meaning of a fragment of a performance is not only determined by what precedes and follows it, but also by a multiplicity of facets whose three-dimensional presence makes it live in the present with a life of its own.

In many cases, this means that for a spectator, the more difficult it becomes for him to interpret or to judge immediately the meaning of what is happening in front of his eyes and in his head, the stronger is his sensation of living through an experience. Or, said in a way that is more obscure but perhaps closer to the reality: the stronger is the experience of an experience.

The simultaneous interweaving of several actions in the performance causes something similar to what Eisenstein describes in reference to El Greco's *View of Toledo*: that the painter does not reconstruct a real view but rather constructs a synthesis of several views, making a montage of the different sides of a building, including even those sides that are not visible, showing various elements – drawn from reality independently of each other – in a new and artificial relationship.

These dramaturgical possibilities apply to all the different levels and all the different elements of the performance taken one by one, as well as to the overall plot. The performer, for example, obtains simultaneous effects as soon as he breaks the abstract pattern of movements, just as the spectator is about to anticipate them. He composes his actions ('composes' used here in its original meaning, deriving from *cum-ponere*, 'to put together') into a synthesis that is far removed from a daily way of behaving. In this montage, he segments the actions, choosing and dilating certain fragments, composing the rhythms, achieving an equivalent to the real action by means of what Richard Schechner calls the 'restoration of behaviour'.

The use of the written text itself, when it is not interpreted only as a concatenation of actions, can guide elements and details, which are not themselves dramatic, into a simultaneous interweaving.

We can draw from *Hamlet*, for example, certain information: traces of the age-old strife between Norway and Denmark are to be found in the conflict between Hamlet's father and Fortinbras's father; England needing to pay taxes to Denmark echoes the days of the Vikings; the life of the Court recalls the Renaissance; the allusions to Wittenberg reflect Reformation issues. All these various historical facets (which we can really *use* as *different* historical facets) can be various choices by means of which the play can be interpreted: in this case, one chosen facet will eliminate the others.

They can also, however, be woven together into a synthesis with many simultaneously present historical elements, whose 'meaning' as it relates to the interpretation of *Hamlet* – that is, what the play will show to the spectators – is not foreseeable. The more the director has woven the different threads together, according to his own logic, the more the meaning of the performance will appear surprising, motivated and unexpected, even to the director himself.

Something similar can also be said for the play's protagonist, for Hamlet. The concatenation of Shakespeare's assembled actions (his montage) usually results in an image of Hamlet as a man in doubt, indecisive, consumed by melancholia, a philosopher ill-suited to action. But this image does not correspond to all the single elements of Shakespeare's total montage. Hamlet acts resolutely when he kills Polonius; he falsifies the message from Claudius to the King of England with cold decisiveness; he defeats the pirates; he challenges Laertes; he quickly notices and sees through the stratagems of his enemies; he kills the King. For an actor (and a director), all of these details, taken one by one, can be used as evidence with which to construct a coherent interpretation of Hamlet. But they can also be used as evidence of different and contradictory aspects of behaviour to be assembled into a synthesis which is not the result of a previous decision about what kind of character Hamlet is going to be.

As can be seen, this simple hypothesis brings us much closer to the creative process (that is, composition process) of many of the great actors in the Western tradition. In their daily work, they did not and do not begin with the interpretation of a character, but develop their work following a route not based on *what?* but on *how?*, assembling aspects that would at first seem incoherent from the point of view of habitual realism, and ending up with a formally coherent synthesis.

Actions at work (dramaturgy) come alive by means of the balance between the concatenation pole and the simultaneity pole. There is a risk of this life being lost with the loss of tension between the two poles.

While the alteration of balance for the sake of weaving through concatenation draws a performance into the somnolence of comfortable recognisability, the alteration of balance for the sake of weaving in the simultaneity dimension can result in arbitrariness, chaos. Or incoherent incoherence. It is easy to see that these risks are even greater for those who work without the guide of a previously composed text.

Written text, performance text, the concatenation or linear dimension, the simultaneity or three-dimensional dimension: these are elements without any value, positive or negative. Positive or negative value depends on the quality of the relationship between these elements.

The more the performance gives the spectator the experience of an experience, the more it must also guide his attention in the complexity of the actions which are taking place, so that he does not lose his sense of direction, his sense of the past and future – that is, the story, not as anecdote but as the 'historical time' of the performance.

All the principles that make it possible to direct the spectator's attention can be drawn from the life of the performance (from the actions that are at work): the interweaving means of concatenation and the interweaving by means of simultaneity.

To create the life of a performance does not mean only to interweave its actions and tensions, but also to direct the spectator's attention, his rhythms, to induce tensions in him without trying to impose an interpretation.

On the one hand, the spectator's attention is attracted by the action's complexity, its presence; on the other hand, the spectator is continuously required to evaluate this presence and this action in the light of his knowledge of what has occurred and in expectation of (or questioning about) what will happen next.

As with the performer's action, the spectator's attention must be able to live in a three-dimensional space, governed by a dialectic which is his own and which is the equivalent of the dialectic that governs life.

In the final analysis, one could relate the dialectic between the interweaving by means of concatenation and the interweaving by means of simultaneity to the complementary (and not the opposing) natures of the left and right hemispheres of the brain.

Each Odin Teatret production uses the scenic space in a different way. The actors do not adapt to given spatial dimensions (as happens on the proscenium stage) but model the architecture of the space according to the specific dramaturgical demands of each new production.

But it is not only the respective spaces occupied by the actors and spectators that change from production to production. During a given single production, the actors sometimes work on the sides of the performing area, at other times in the middle; thus certain spectators experience certain actions in close-up, as it were – when the actors are but a few centimetres from them – while other spectators see the whole picture from a much wider angle.

These same principles are used in outdoor performances, which take place in squares and streets, on balconies and on the rooftops of cities or villages. In this case the environment is given and apparently cannot change, but the actor can use his presence to make a dramatic character spring out of the architecture, which we are normally no longer able to see because of daily habits and usages and which we no longer experience with a fresh eye.

Montage: The Performer's Montage and the Director's Montage

'Montage' is a word which today replaces the former term 'composition'. 'To compose' (to put with) also means 'to mount', 'to put together', 'to weave actions together', 'to create the play'. Composition is a new synthesis of materials and fragments taken out of their original contexts. It is a synthesis that is equivalent to the phenomenon and to the real relationships which it suggests or represents.

It is also a dilation equivalent to the way in which a performer isolates and fixes certain physiological processes or certain behaviour patterns, as if putting them under a magnifying glass and making his body a dilated body. To dilate implies above all to isolate and to select:

'From afar, a city is a city and a landscape is a landscape, but little by little, as one approaches, there appear houses, trees, tiles, leaves, ants, ants' legs, *ad infinitum.*' The film director Robert Bresson quotes these words written by Pascal and deduces from them that in order to compose one must know how to see the reality that surrounds us and to subdivide it into its constituent parts. One must know how to isolate these parts, to make them independent, in order to give them a new dependence.

A performance is born out of a specific and dramatic relationship between elements and details which, considered in isolation, are neither dramatic nor appear to have anything in common. The concept of montage does not only imply a composition of words, images or relationships. Above all, it implies the montage of rhythm, but not in order to *represent* or *to reproduce* the movement. By means of the montage of rhythm, in fact, one aims at the very principle of motion, at tensions, at the dialectic process of nature or thought. Or better, at 'the thought which penetrates matter'.

Eisenstein's comments on El Greco are particularly important with respect to montage because they demonstrate how montage is actually the construction of meaning. Eisenstein shows how El Greco, assembling the individual parts of his paintings (Eisenstein calls them 'frames'), succeeds not in *representing* ecstatic characters but rather in creating an *ecstatic construction* of the paintings, forcing the observer's eye, even his body, to follow the route designed by the creator.

Making use of art critic J. E. Willumsen's accurate analyses, Eisenstein examines El Greco's *View and Map of Toledo*: the proportions of the huge Don Juan Tavera hospital on the slopes of the hill have been so reduced that the building appears only slightly larger than a house, 'otherwise it would have hidden the view of the city'. What El Greco paints, therefore, is not the landscape as it appears from a particular perspective but an *equivalent* of a *view* which does not allow the great bulk of the hospital to become an obstacle.

Moreover, the painter shows the hospital's principal and most beautiful façade, even though it is not actually visible from the angle from which the painting has been made.

Eisenstein writes: 'This view of Toledo is not possible from any real point of view. It is a mounted complex, a representation composed by means of a montage of objects, "photographed in isolation", which in nature mask each other or have their backs to the observer.' The painting, in short, is composed: 'of elements taken one by one and reunited in an arbitrary construction which is non-existent from a single point of view but which is fully consistent with respect to the internal logic of the composition.'

And again: 'El Greco did this painting at home, in his studio. That is to say, it is not based on a view, but on knowledge. Not on a single point of view, but on the assembling of isolated motifs collected while walking through the city and its surroundings.'

Montage is fundamental with regard to the effect the actions must have on the spectator. It guides the spectator's senses through the dramatic (*performance*) fabric (*text*), letting the spectator experience the *performance* text. The director guides, divides and reassembles the spectator's attention by means of the performer's actions, the words of the text, the relationships, the music, the sounds, the lights, the use of props.

The Performer's Montage

It is possible to differentiate two different spheres or directions of work: that of the performer who works inside a codified performance system and that of the performer who must invent and fix his way of being present every time he works in a new production, taking care not to repeat what he did in the previous production.

The performer who works in a codified performance system constructs the montage by altering his 'natural' and 'spontaneous' behaviour. Balance is modified and modelled, made precarious: new tensions are thus produced in the body, dilating it.

In the same way that particular physiological processes are dilated and codified, continuous eye

Figure 31 a–k Actor's first montage: Kosuke Nomura in Sequence A: how one picks and eats a fruit in a kyogen scene.

movements (*saccades*), which in daily life occur two or three times a second and which alternate with phases of stillness (*nystagmes*), are also codified. These formalisations recreate, by means of very precise rules which dictate how the eyes should move, an equivalent to the continuous life of the eyes in daily reality.

The same applies to the hands. In daily life the fingers are continuously animated by tensions that individualise each finger. These tensions are reconstructed in theatre by means of *mudras*, which can have either a semantic or a purely dynamic value. They recreate the equivalence of the fingers' life, which move continuously from one codified position to another equally precise position.

Analogously, in positions of non-movement, regulated as action in time by means of tensions in the postural muscles, the equivalent of the life which regulates daily balance is recreated. In daily life, immobility does not exist and apparent immobility is based on continuous, minuscule movements of adjustment (cf. *Eyes, Hands, Balance*).

The result of all these procedures, which amplify behavioural and physiological processes, is a series of very precise 'scores'. Richard Schechner speaks of a 'restoration of behaviour' which is used in all performance forms from shamanism to aesthetic theatre:

A restored behaviour is a living behaviour treated the way a film director treats a strip of film. Each piece of film must be re-systemised, reconstructed. This is independent of the causal (social, psychological, technological) systems which have created it: it has its own behaviour. The original 'truth' or 'motivation' of that behaviour can be lost, ignored or covered, elaborated or distorted by myth. Originating a process – used in the course of rehearsals in order to obtain a new process, the performance – the strips of behaviour are themselves no longer processes but objects, *materials*.

What Schechner has written in order to explain how certain ritual dances (which today are considered classical) have been 'restored', applies perfectly well to the performer who works on the basis of a codification, or who fixes improvisations like 'strips of behaviour' on which montage work can be done. The restoration, that is, the work of selection and dilation, can only take place if there exists a process of fixing.

Thus, for example, when kabuki performers meet to perform, even if they have never before done the particular performance (or the variation of the performance) that they are about to present, they can make use of 'materials', already prepared for other scenic situations. These 'materials' are then re-edited in the new context. I have myself seen an *onnagata*, who had never performed a certain rôle, go on stage and perform it after only two rehearsals: he made a montage of materials available to him from rôles which he already knew.

The Director's Montage

If the performer's actions can be considered as analogous to strips of film which are already the result of a montage, it is possible to use this montage not as a final result but as material for a further montage. This is generally the task of the director, who can weave the actions of several performers into a succession in which one action seems to answer another, or into a simultaneous execution in which the meanings of both actions derive directly from the fact of their mutual presence.

Let us take an example, rough as all examples are, and even the more so here because we will use fixed images, photographs, to illustrate a process the meaning of which depends on the development of actions in space and in time and on their rhythm. But crude as it may be, this example can serve as a demonstration of the most elementary (grammatical) level of the director's montage.

Figure 32 a–n Actor's second montage: Etienne Decroux in Sequence B: how one picks a flower in mime.

Let us imagine having the following text as a point of departure: 'Then the woman saw that the tree was good to eat, pleasing to the eye, desirable for the gaining of knowledge. She took its fruit and ate of it. She gave some to her husband, who was with her, and he also ate of it' (Genesis 3:6). We also have two performers' montages, two sequences of 'restored behaviour':

Sequence A: Kosuke Nomura, kyogen actor, shows how, in the tradition of his art, one picks a fruit (a plum) and eats it [Figure 31]. We see the principle of selection and dilation at work: [a] with one hand he grasps the branch, with the other, starting from the opposite side, he begins the movement to take the fruit; [b] he grasps the fruit and then, in order to pluck it, he does not pull it, but ... [c] he turns it, showing its size; [d] the fruit is brought to the mouth, not in a direct line, but with a circular movement; the fingers squeeze the fruit and are composed in a way that shows the fruit's size, its softness, its weight; [e–h] with a movement that begins high up, the fruit is brought to the mouth; [i] it is not the mouth that squeezes the fruit but the hand, executing an action *equivalent* to that which, in reality, would be done by the mouth; [j] the fruit is swallowed (and again it is the hand which does the action): the performer does not show a man swallowing but his hand makes an otherwise invisible action – that of swallowing – visible; [k] having savoured the fruit, the man smiles with satisfaction.

Sequence B: Etienne Decroux, the great mime master, shows how one picks a flower according to the principles of his art. He also begins from a position that is opposite to that towards which he will direct the action, first with the eyes and then with the action itself [Figure 32].

The two sequences provided by the two performers, in spite of their different motivations and different original contexts, can be put together. We will thus obtain a new sequence whose meaning will depend on the new context into which it is inserted: the biblical text that we have chosen as the point of departure for our example. In this case, naturally, the sex of the two performers will not be taken into consideration: but there is no reason why the Japanese performer Kosuke Nomura cannot interpret the rôle of Eve.

Let's run through the two performers' sequences as if they now were a single sequence: Eve has just given in to the serpent's temptation, picks the fruit, tastes it. Her final reaction is a smile for the new world that has opened up in front of her eyes. Eve tempts Adam in her turn, puts the fruit of knowledge beside him on the ground, and now Adam glances sideways as if in fear of being watched by the angel of God. He begins the movement to take the fruit, starting in the extreme opposite direction: the principle of opposition now becomes legible as an initial reaction of refusal. Then Adam bends down, picks up the fruit and turns his back as if to leave, or as if to eat the fruit without being seen, or perhaps he is ashamed of what he has done or, having been left alone, he goes in search of Eve.

A montage of this type would be possible because the two performers are able to repeat each single action, each detail of each action, perfectly. And this is why the director can create a new relationship from the two sequences, can extrapolate them from their original contexts and create between them a new dependence, putting them in relationship with a text which is then faithfully followed. The biblical text does not in fact say *how* Eve gave Adam the fruit. At this point the director can fill the visual void in the text with the help of the sequences that have already been fixed by the performers. Some details of the actions can be amplified further, minimalised, accelerated.

Figure 33 a–j Director's montage: the new sequence obtained through the elaboration of the two actors' sequences, A and B, and the possible content variations: Genesis 3:6 and Strindberg's *The Father*, I, ix.

Let us return to our example, to the 'material' furnished by the two performers, without adding anything new.

Since the two performers' sequences are already the result of a 'restoration of behaviour', since they are perfectly fixed and thus can be treated like two strips of film, the director can extract a few fragments from one performer's sequence and remount them, interweaving them with fragments from the other performer's sequence, taking care to ensure that, after the cuts and with the new montage, enough physical coherence remains so that the performers can go from one movement to another in an organic way.

Further montage by the director

Here is an example of a new montage which weaves together fragments from the original, autonomous and independent sequences furnished by the two performers [Figure 33].

If we apply this montage to our theme, Adam and Eve, we have the meaning of the new situation: [a] Adam looks incredulously ... [b] Eve has picked the forbidden fruit and is about to eat it. [c] Adam: 'We have promised not to eat the fruit of this tree!' [d] Eve persists, and brings the forbidden fruit up to her mouth. [e] Adam: 'God's sword will punish us.' [f] Eve is about to eat the fruit. [g] Adam: 'Don't do it!' [h] Eve eats the forbidden fruit. [i] Adam collapses on the floor. [j] Eve is intoxicated with knowledge.

The same montage that we have applied to the biblical story can also be applied to Strindberg's *The Father*: the wife Laura (once again, Kosuke Nomura is cast as the female) makes the Captain (her husband) suspect that he is not the father of their daughter. The man is ridiculed and crushed. The director has used Kosuke Nomura's actions (originally a sequence based on picking a plum and eating it) to create a sign of adultery and especially the image of the *vagina dentata* which emasculates and crushes the male. At the end, Laura says, 'It's strange, but I've never been able to look at a man without feeling superior to him' (*The Father*, Act I, scene x).

Seen in the light of their new Strindberg context, the performers' interwoven actions would have to change, small details would have to be modified in order to make these actions consistent with the meaning they have now acquired. Above all, the rhythm and intensity with which the actions are interwoven will allow unexpected meanings to emerge from the materials furnished by the performers.

The level of this montage of photographs, which we have used as a rough example, is the elementary, grammatical level: the essential work, that is the process of elaboration and refinement, is yet to come. We are face to face with a body that has been coldly constructed, an 'artificial body' in which there is no life. But this artificial body already has within it all the circuits in which *scenic bios*, that is, life recreated as art, will flow. In order for this to occur, there must be something burning, no longer analysable or anatomisable, which fuses the performer's and the director's work into a single whole in which it is no longer possible to distinguish the actions of the former and the montage of the latter. In this phase of work no rules exist. The rules serve only to make the event possible, to provide the conditions in which the real artistic creation can occur without further respect for limits or principles.

In the director's montage, the actions, in order to become dramatic, must take on a new value, must transcend the meaning and the motivations for which they were originally composed by the performers.

It is this new value which causes the actions to go beyond the literal act that they represent on their own. If I walk, I walk and nothing more. If I sit, I sit and nothing more. If I eat, I do nothing more than eat. If I smoke, I do nothing more than smoke. These are self-referential acts that do nothing more than illustrate themselves.

The actions transcend their illustrative meaning because of the relationships created in the new context in which they are placed. Put in relationship with something else, they become dramatic. To dramatise an action means to introduce a leap of tensions that obliges the action to develop meanings which are different from its original ones.

Montage, in short, is the art of putting actions in a context that causes them to deviate from their implicit meaning.

Note

Originally published in Eugenio Barba and Nicola Savarese, *A Dictionary of Theatre Anthropology: The Secret Art of the Performer*, 2nd edn, London: Routledge, 2006 [1991], pp. 66–9 and 178-84. Some of the photos from the original publication have not been reproduced in this version.

5.10 The Precession of Simulacra (1981)

[Extracts]
JEAN BAUDRILLARD

Translated by Sheila Faria Glaser

The divine irreference of images

TO DISSIMULATE IS TO pretend not to have what one has. To simulate is to feign to have what one doesn't have. One implies a presence, the other an absence. But it is more complicated than that because simulating is not pretending: 'Whoever fakes an illness can simply stay in bed and make everyone believe he is ill. Whoever simulates an illness produces in himself some of the symptoms' (Littré). Therefore, pretending, or dissimulating, leaves the principle of reality intact: the difference is always clear, it is simply masked, whereas simulation threatens the difference between the 'true' and the 'false', the 'real' and the 'imaginary'. Is the simulator sick or not, given that he produces 'true' symptoms? Objectively one cannot treat him as being either ill or not ill. Psychology and medicine stop at this point, forestalled by the illness's henceforth undiscoverable truth. For if any symptom can be 'produced', and can no longer be taken as a fact of nature, then every illness can be considered as simulatable and simulated, and medicine loses its meaning since it only knows how to treat 'real' illnesses according to their objective causes. Psychosomatics evolves in a dubious manner at the borders of the principle of illness. As to psychoanalysis, it transfers the symptom of the organic order to the unconscious order: the latter is new and taken for 'real' more real than the other – but why would simulation be at the gates of the unconscious? Why couldn't the 'work' of the unconscious be 'produced' in the same way as any old symptom of classical medicine? Dreams already are.

Certainly, the psychiatrist purports that 'for every form of mental alienation there is a particular order in the succession of symptoms of which the simulator is ignorant and in the absence of which the psychiatrist would not be deceived'. This (which dates from 1865) in order to safeguard the principle of a truth at all costs and to escape the interrogation posed by simulation – the knowledge that truth, reference, objective cause have ceased to exist. Now, what can medicine do with what floats on either side of illness, on either side of health, with the duplication of illness in a discourse that is no longer either true or false? What can psychoanalysis do with the duplication of the discourse of the unconscious in the discourse of simulation that can never again be unmasked, since it is not false either?[1]

What can the army do about simulators? Traditionally it unmasks them and punishes them, according to a clear principle of identification. Today it can discharge a very good simulator as exactly equivalent to a 'real' homosexual, a heart patient, or a madman. Even military psychology draws back from Cartesian certainties and hesitates to make the distinction between true and false, between the 'produced' and the authentic symptom. 'If he is this good at acting crazy, it's because he is.' Nor is military psychology mistaken in this regard: in this sense, all crazy people simulate, and this lack of distinction is the worst kind of subversion. It is against this lack of distinction that classical reason armed itself in all its categories. But it is what today again outflanks them, submerging the principle of truth.

Beyond medicine and the army, favored terrains of simulation, the question returns to religion and the simulacrum of divinity: 'I forbade that there be any simulacra in the temples because the divinity that animates nature can never be represented.' Indeed it can be. But what becomes of the divinity when it reveals itself in icons, when it is multiplied in simulacra? Does it remain the supreme power that is simply incarnated in images as a visible theology? Or does it volatilize itself in the simulacra that, alone, deploy their power and pomp of fascination – the visible machinery of icons substituted for the pure and intelligible Idea of God? This is precisely what was feared by Iconoclasts, whose millennial quarrel is still with us today.[2] This is precisely because they predicted this omnipotence of simulacra, the faculty simulacra have of effacing God from the conscience of man, and the destructive, annihilating truth that they allow to appear – that deep down God never existed, that only the simulacrum ever existed, even that God himself was never anything but his own simulacrum – from this came their urge to destroy the images. If they could have believed that these images only obfuscated or masked the Platonic Idea of God, there would have been no reason to destroy them. One can live with the idea of distorted truth. But their metaphysical despair came from the idea that the image didn't conceal anything at all, and that these images were in essence not images, such as an original model would have made them, but perfect simulacra, forever radiant with their own fascination. Thus this death of the divine referential must be exorcised at all costs.

One can see that the iconoclasts, whom one accuses of disdaining and negating images, were those who accorded them their true value, in contrast to the iconolaters who only saw reflections in them and were content to venerate a filigree God. On the other hand, one can say that the icon worshipers were the most modern minds, the most adventurous, because, in the guise of having God become apparent in the mirror of images, they were already enacting his death and his disappearance in the epiphany of his representations (which, perhaps, they already knew no longer represented anything, that they were purely a game, but that it was therein the great game lay – knowing also that it is dangerous to unmask images, since they dissimulate the fact that there is nothing behind them).

This was the approach of the Jesuits, who founded their politics on the virtual disappearance of God and on the worldly and spectacular manipulation of consciences – the evanescence of God in the epiphany of power – the end of transcendence, which now only serves as an alibi for a strategy altogether free of influences and signs. Behind the baroqueness of images hides the éminence grise of politics.

This way the stake will always have been the murderous power of images, murderers of the real, murderers of their own model, as the Byzantine icons could be those of divine identity. To this murderous power is opposed that of representations as a dialectical power, the visible and intelligible mediation of the Real. All Western faith and good faith became engaged in this wager on representation: that a sign could refer to the depth of meaning, that a sign could be exchanged for meaning and that something could guarantee this exchange – God of course. But what if God himself can be simulated, that is to say can be reduced to the signs that constitute faith? Then the whole system becomes weightless, it is no longer itself anything but a gigantic simulacrum – not unreal, but a simulacrum, that is to say never exchanged for the real, but exchanged for itself, in an uninterrupted circuit without reference or circumference.

Such is simulation, insofar as it is opposed to representation. Representation stems from the principle of the equivalence of the sign and of the real (even if this equivalence is utopian, it is a fundamental axiom). Simulation, on the contrary, stems from the utopia of the principle of equivalence, *from the radical negation of the sign as value*, from the sign as the reversion and death sentence of every reference. Whereas representation attempts to absorb simulation by interpreting it as a false representation, simulation envelops the whole edifice of representation itself as a simulacrum.

Such would be the successive phases of the image:

it is the reflection of a profound reality;
it masks and denatures a profound reality;
it masks the *absence* of a profound reality;
it has no relation to any reality whatsoever: it is its own pure simulacrum.

In the first case, the image is a *good* appearance – representation is of the sacramental order. In the second, it is an evil appearance – it is of the order of maleficence. In the third, it plays at being an appearance – it is of the order of sorcery. In the fourth, it is no longer of the order of appearances, but of simulation.

The transition from signs that dissimulate something to signs that dissimulate that there is nothing marks a decisive turning point. The first reflects a theology of truth and secrecy (to which the notion of ideology still belongs). The second inaugurates the era of simulacra and of simulation, in which there is no longer a God to recognize his own, no longer a Last Judgment to separate the false from the true, the real from its artificial resurrection, as everything is already dead and resurrected in advance.

When the real is no longer what it was, nostalgia assumes its full meaning. There is a plethora of myths of origin and of signs of reality – a plethora of truth, of secondary objectivity, and authenticity. Escalation of the true, of lived experience, resurrection of the figurative where the object and substance have disappeared. Panic-stricken production of the real and of the referential, parallel to and greater than the panic of material production: this is how simulation appears in the phase that concerns us – a strategy of the real, of the neoreal and the hyperreal that everywhere is the double of a strategy of deterrence. [...]

The strategy of the real

The impossibility of rediscovering an absolute level of the real is of the same order as the impossibility of staging illusion. Illusion is no longer possible, because the real is no longer possible. It is the whole *political* problem of parody, of hypersimulation or offensive simulation, that is posed here.

For example: it would be interesting to see whether the repressive apparatus would not react more violently to a simulated holdup than to a real holdup. Because the latter does nothing but disturb the order of things, the right to property, whereas the former attacks the reality principle itself. Transgression and violence are less serious because they only contest the *distribution* of the real. Simulation is infinitely more dangerous because it always leaves open to supposition that, above and beyond its object, *law and order themselves might be nothing but simulation.*

But the difficulty is proportional to the danger. How to feign a violation and put it to the test? Simulate a robbery in a large store: how to persuade security that it is a simulated robbery? There is no 'objective' difference: the gestures, the signs are the same as for a real robbery, the signs do not lean to one side or another. To the established order they are always of the order of the real.

Organize a fake holdup. Verify that your weapons are harmless, and take the most trustworthy hostage, so that no human life will be in danger (or one lapses into the criminal). Demand a ransom, and make it so that the operation creates as much commotion as possible – in short, remain close to the 'truth', in order to test the reaction of the apparatus to a perfect simulacrum. You won't be able to do it: the network of artificial signs will become inextricably mixed up with real elements (a policeman will really fire on sight; a client of the bank will faint and die of a heart attack; one will actually pay you the phony ransom), in short, you will immediately find yourself once again, without wishing it, in the real, one of whose functions is precisely to devour any attempt at simulation, to reduce everything to the real – that is, to the established order itself, well before institutions and justice come into play.

It is necessary to see in this impossibility of isolating the process of simulation the weight of an order that cannot see and conceive of anything but the real, because it cannot function anywhere else. The simulation of an offense, if it is established as such, will either be punished less severely (because it has no 'consequences') or punished as an offense against the judicial system (for example if one sets in motion a police operation 'for nothing') – but *never as simulation* since it is precisely as such that no equivalence with the real is possible, and hence no repression either. The challenge of simulation is never admitted by power. How can the simulation of virtue be punished? However, as such it is as serious as the simulation of crime. Parody renders submission and transgression equivalent, and that is the most serious crime, because it *cancels out the difference upon which the law is based.* The established order can do nothing against it, because the law is a simulacrum of the second order, whereas simulation is of the third order, beyond true and false, beyond equivalences, beyond rational distinctions upon which the whole of the social and power depend. Thus, *lacking the real*, it is there that we must aim at order.

This is certainly why order always opts for the real. When in doubt, it always prefers this hypothesis (as in the army one prefers to take the simulator for a real madman). But this becomes more and more difficult, because if it is practically impossible to isolate the process of simulation, through the force of inertia of the real that surrounds us, the opposite is also true (and this reversibility itself is part of the apparatus of simulation and the impotence of power): namely, it is *now impossible to isolate the process of the real*, or to prove the real.

This is how all the holdups, airplane hijackings, etc. are now in some sense simulation holdups in that they are already inscribed in the decoding and orchestration rituals of the media, anticipated in their presentation and their possible consequences. In short, where they function as a group of signs dedicated exclusively to their recurrence as signs, and no longer at all to their 'real' end. But this does not make them harmless. On the contrary, it is as hyperreal events, no longer with a specific content or end, but indefinitely refracted by each other (just like so-called historical events: strikes, demonstrations, crises, etc.),[3] it is in this sense that they cannot be controlled by an order that can only exert itself on the real and the rational, on causes and ends, a referential order that can only reign over the referential, a determined power that can only reign over a determined world, but that cannot do anything against this indefinite recurrence of simulation, against this nebula whose weight no longer obeys the laws of gravitation of the real, power itself ends by being dismantled in this space and becoming a simulation of power (disconnected from its ends and its objectives, and dedicated to the *effects of power* and mass simulation).

The only weapon of power, its only strategy against this defection, is to reinject the real and the referential everywhere, to persuade us of the reality of the social, of the gravity of the economy and the finalities of production. To this end it prefers the discourse of crisis, but also, why not? that of desire. 'Take your desires for reality!' can be understood as the ultimate slogan of power since in a nonreferential world, even the confusion of the reality principle and the principle of desire is less dangerous than contagious hyperreality. One remains among principles, and among those power is always in the right.

Hyperreality and simulation are deterrents of every principle and every objective, they turn against power the deterrent that it used so well for such a long time. Because in the end, throughout its history it was capital that first fed on the destructuration of every referential, of every human objective, that shattered every ideal distinction between true and false, good and evil, in order to establish a radical law of equivalence and exchange, the iron law of its power. Capital was the first to play at deterrence, abstraction, disconnection, deterritorialization, etc., and if it is the one that fostered reality, the reality principle, it was also the first to liquidate it by exterminating all use value, all real equivalence of production and wealth, in the very sense we have of the unreality of the stakes and the omnipotence of manipulation. Well, today it is this same logic that is even more set against capital. And as soon as it wishes to combat this disastrous spiral by secreting a last glimmer of reality, on which to establish a last glimmer of power, it does nothing but multiply the *signs* and accelerate the play of simulation.

As long as the historical threat came at it from the real, power played at deterrence and simulation, disintegrating all the contradictions by dint of producing equivalent signs. Today when the danger comes at it from simulation (that of being dissolved in the play of signs), power plays at the real, plays at crisis, plays at remanufacturing artificial, social, economic, and political stakes. For power, it is a question of life and death. But it is too late.

Whence the characteristic hysteria of our times: that of the production and reproduction of the real. The other production, that of values and commodities, that of the belle epoque of political economy, has for a long time had no specific meaning. What every society looks for in continuing to produce, and to over-produce, is to restore the real that escapes it. That is why *today this 'material' production is that of the hyperreal itself.* It retains all the features, the whole discourse of traditional production, but it is no longer anything but its scaled-down refraction (thus hyper-realists fix a real from which all meaning and charm, all depth and energy of representation have vanished in a hallucinatory resemblance). Thus everywhere the hyperrealism of simulation is translated by the hallucinatory resemblance of the real to itself.

Power itself has for a long time produced nothing but the signs of its resemblance. And at the same time, another figure of power comes into play: that of a collective demand for *signs* of power – a holy union that is reconstructed around its disappearance. The whole world adheres to it more or less in terror of the collapse of the political. And in the end the game of power becomes nothing but the *critical* obsession with power – obsession with its death, obsession with its survival, which increases as it disappears. When it has totally disappeared, we will logically be under the total hallucination of power – a haunting memory that is already in evidence every-where, expressing at once the compulsion to get rid of it (no one wants it anymore, everyone unloads it on everyone else) and the panicked nostalgia over its loss. The melancholy of societies without power: this has already stirred up fascism, that overdose of a strong referential in a society that cannot terminate its mourning.

With the extenuation of the political sphere, the president comes increasingly to resemble that *Puppet of Power* who is the head of primitive societies (Clastres).

All previous presidents pay for and continue to pay for Kennedy's murder as if they were the ones who had suppressed it – which is true phantasmatically, if not in fact. They must efface this defect and this complicity with their simulated murder. Because, now it can only be simulated. Presidents Johnson and Ford were both the object of failed assassination attempts which, if they were not staged, were at least perpetrated by simulation. The Kennedys died because they incar-nated something: the political, political substance, whereas the new presidents are nothing but caricatures and fake film – curiously, Johnson, Nixon, Ford, all have this simian mug, the monkeys of power.

Death is never an absolute criterion, but in this case it is significant: the era of James Dean, Marilyn Monroe, and the Kennedys, of those who really died simply because they had a mythic dimension that implies death (not for romantic reasons, but because of the fundamental principle of reversal and exchange) – this era is long gone. It is now the era of murder by simulation, of the generalized aesthetic of simulation, of the murder-alibi – the allegorical resurrection of death, which is only there to sanction the institution of power, without which it no longer has any substance or an autonomous reality.

These staged presidential assassinations are revealing because they signal the status of all negativity in the West: political opposition, the 'Left', critical discourse, etc. – a simulacral contrast through which power attempts to break the vicious circle of its nonexistence, of its fundamental irresponsibility, of its 'suspension'. Power floats like money, like language, like theory. Criticism and negativity alone still secrete a phantom of the reality of power. If they become weak for one reason or another, power has no other recourse but to artificially revive and hallucinate them.

It is in this way that the Spanish executions still serve as a stimulant to Western liberal democracy, to a dying system of democratic values. Fresh blood, but for how much longer? The deterioration of all power is irresistibly pursued: it is not so much the 'revolutionary forces' that accelerate this process (often it is quite the opposite), it is the system itself that deploys against its own structures this violence that annuls all substance and all finality. One must not resist this process by trying to confront the system and destroy it, because this system that is dying from being dispossessed of its death expects nothing but that from us: that we give the system back its death, that we revive it through the negative. End of revolutionary praxis, end of the dialectic. Curiously, Nixon, who was not even found worthy of dying at the hands of the most insig-nificant, chance, unbalanced person (and though it is perhaps true that presidents are assassinated by unbalanced types, this changes *nothing*: the leftist penchant for detecting a rightist conspiracy beneath this brings out a false problem – the function of bringing death to, or the prophecy, etc., against power has always been fulfilled, from primitive societies to the present, by demented people, crazy people, or neurotics, who nonetheless carry out a social function as fundamental as that of presidents), was nevertheless ritually put to death by Watergate. Watergate is still a mechanism for the ritual murder of power (the American institution of the presidency is much more thrilling in this regard than the European: it surrounds itself with all the violence and vicissitudes of primitive powers, of savage rituals). But already impeachment is no longer assassination: it happens via the Constitution. Nixon has nevertheless arrived at the goal of which all power dreams: to be taken seriously enough, to constitute a mortal enough danger to the group to be one day relieved of his duties, denounced, and liquidated. Ford doesn't even have this opportunity anymore: a simulacrum of an already dead power, he can only accumulate against himself the signs of reversion through murder – in fact, he is immunized by his impotence, which infuriates him.

In contrast to the primitive rite, which foresees the official and sacrificial death of the king (the king or the chief is nothing without the promise of his sacrifice), the modern political imaginary goes increasingly in the direction of delaying, of concealing for as long as possible, the death of the head of state. This obsession has accumulated since the era of revolutions and of charismatic leaders: Hitler, Franco, Mao, having no 'legitimate' heirs, no filiation of power, see themselves forced to perpetuate themselves indefinitely – popular myth never wishes to believe them dead. The pharaohs already did this: it was always one and the same person who incarnated the successive pharaohs.

Everything happens as if Mao or Franco had already died several times and had been replaced by his double. From a political point of view, that a head of state remains the same or is someone else doesn't strictly change anything, so long as they resemble each other. For a long time now a head of state – *no matter which one* – is nothing but the simulacrum of himself, and *only that gives him the power and the quality to govern*. No one would grant the least consent, the least devotion to a *real* person. It is to his double, he being always already *dead*, to which allegiance is given. This myth does nothing but translate the persistence, and at the same time the deception, of the necessity of the king's sacrificial death.

We are still in the same boat: no society knows how to mourn the real, power, the *social itself*, which is implicated in the same loss. And it is through an artificial revitalization of all this that we try to escape this fact. *This situation will no doubt end up giving rise to socialism.* Through an unforeseen turn of events and via an irony that is no longer that of history, it is from the death of the social that socialism will emerge, as it is from the death of God that religions emerge. A twisted advent, a perverse event, an unintelligible reversion to the logic of reason. As is the fact that power is in essence no longer present except to conceal that there is no more power. A simulation that can last indefinitely, because, as distinct from 'true' power – which is, or was, a structure, a strategy, a relation of force, a stake – it is nothing but the object of a social *demand*, and thus as the object of the law of supply and demand, it is no longer subject to violence and death. Completely purged of a *political* dimension, it, like any other commodity, is dependent on mass production and consumption. Its spark has disappeared, only the fiction of a political universe remains.

The same holds true for work. The spark of production, the violence of its stakes no longer exist. The whole world still produces, and increasingly, but subtly work has become something else: a need (as Marx ideally envisioned it but not in the same sense), the object of a social 'demand', like leisure, to which it is equivalent in the course of everyday life. A demand exactly proportional to the loss of a stake in the work process.[4] Same change in fortune as for power: the *scenario* of work is there to conceal that the real of work, the real of production, has disappeared. And the real of the strike as well, which is no longer a work stoppage, but its alternate pole in the ritual scansion of the social calendar. Everything occurs as if each person had, after declaring a strike, 'occupied' his place and work station and recommenced production, as is the norm in a 'self-managed' occupation, exactly in the same terms as before, all while declaring himself (and in virtually being) permanently on strike.

This is not a dream out of science fiction: everywhere it is a question of doubling the process of work. And of a doubling of the process of going on strike – striking incorporated just as obsolescence is in objects, just as crisis is in production. So, there is no longer striking, nor work, but both simultaneously, that is to say something else: a *magic of work*, a trompe l'oeil, a scenodrama (so as not to say a melodrama) of production, a collective dramaturgy on the empty stage of the social.

It is no longer a question of the ideology of work – the traditional ethic that would obscure the 'real' process of work and the 'objective' process of exploitation – but of the scenario of work. In the same way, it is no longer a question of the ideology of power, but of the *scenario* of power. Ideology only corresponds to a corruption of reality through signs; simulation corresponds to a short circuit of reality and to its duplication through signs. It is always the goal of the ideological analysis to restore the objective process, it is always a false problem to wish to restore the truth beneath the simulacrum.

This is why in the end power is so much in tune with ideological discourses and discourses on ideology, that is they are discourses of *truth* – always good for countering the mortal blows of simulation, even and especially if they are revolutionary.

Notes

1. A discourse that is itself not susceptible to being resolved in transference. It is the entanglement of these two discourses that renders psychoanalysis interminable.
2. Cf. M. Perniola, *Icônes, visions, simulacres* (icons, visions, simulacra), 39.
3. Taken together, the energy crisis and the ecological mise-en-scène are themselves *a disaster movie*, in the same style (and with the same value) as those that currently comprise the golden days of Hollywood. It is useless to laboriously interpret these films in terms of their relation to an 'objective' social crisis or even to an 'objective' phantasm of disaster. It is in another sense that it must be said that it is *the social itself that,* in contemporary discourse, *is organized along the lines of a disaster-movie script.* (Cf. M. Makarius, *La stratègie de la catastrophe* [The strategy of disaster], 115).
4. To this flagging investment in work corresponds a parallel decline in the investment in consumption. Goodbye to use value or to the prestige of the automobile, goodbye amorous discourses that neatly opposed the object of enjoyment to the object of work. Another discourse takes hold that is a *discourse of work on the object of consumption* aiming for an active, constraining, puritan reinvestment (use less gas, watch out for your safety, you've gone over the speed limit, etc.) to which the characteristics of automobiles pretend to adapt. Rediscovering a stake through the transposition of these two poles, work becomes the object of a need, the car becomes the object of work. There is no better proof of the lack of differentiation among all the stakes. It is through the same slippage between the 'right' to vote and electoral 'duty' that the divestment of the political sphere is signaled.

From *Simulacra and Simulation*, trans. S. F. Glaser, Ann Arbor: University of Michigan Press, 2006 [1994], pp. 3–7, 19–27.

5.11 The Emancipated Spectator (2008)

JACQUES RANCIÈRE

Translated by Gregory Elliott

THIS BOOK ORIGINATED IN a request I received a few years ago to introduce the reflections of an academy of artists on the spectator, on the basis of ideas developed in my book *The Ignorant Schoolmaster*.[1] The proposal initially caused me some bewilderment. *The Ignorant Schoolmaster* set out the eccentric theory and singular fate of Joseph Jacotot, who created a scandal in the early nineteenth century by claiming that one ignoramus could teach another what he himself did not know, asserting the equality of intelligence and opposing intellectual emancipation to popular instruction. His ideas had fallen into oblivion in the middle of his century. I had thought it worthwhile reviving them in the 1980s, to inject some life into debates on the purposes of public education by throwing in the issue of intellectual equality. But how was the thought of a man whose artistic universe can be emblematized by the names of Demosthenes, Racine and Poussin relevant to contemporary thinking about art?

On reflection, it seemed to me that the absence of any obvious relationship between the theory of intellectual emancipation and the question of the spectator today was also an opportunity. It might afford an occasion for a radical differentiation from the theoretical and political presuppositions which, even in postmodern form, still underpin the gist of the debate on theatre, performance and the spectator. But in order to bring out the relationship and make it meaningful, it was necessary to reconstruct the network of presuppositions that place the question of the spectator at the heart of the discussion of the relations between art and politics. It was necessary to outline the general model of rationality against whose background we have become used to judging the political implications of theatrical spectacle. I use this term here to include all those forms of spectacle – drama, dance, performance art, mime and so on – that place bodies in action before an assembled audience.

The numerous critiques for which theatre has provided the material throughout its history can in effect be boiled down to one basic formula. I shall call it the paradox of the spectator – a paradox that is possibly more fundamental than the famous paradox of the actor. This paradox is easily formulated: there is no theatre without a spectator (if only a single, concealed spectator, as in the fictional performance of *Le Fils naturel* that gives rise to Diderot's *Entretiens*). But according to the accusers, being a spectator is a bad thing for two reasons. First, viewing is the opposite of knowing: the spectator is held before an appearance in a state of ignorance about the process of production of this appearance and about the reality it conceals. Second, it is the opposite of acting: the spectator remains immobile in her seat, passive. To be a spectator is to be separated from both the capacity to know and the power to act.

This diagnosis leads to two different conclusions. The first is that theatre is an absolutely bad thing: a scene of illusion and passivity that must be abolished in favour of what it prohibits – knowledge and action; the action of knowing and action guided by knowledge. This is the conclusion formulated by Plato: theatre is the place where ignoramuses are invited to see people suffering. What the theatrical scene offers them is the spectacle of a *pathos*, the manifestation of an illness, that of desire and suffering – that is to say, the self-division which derives from ignorance. The particular effect of theatre is to transmit this illness by means of another one: the illness of the gaze in thrall to shades. It transmits the illness of ignorance that makes the characters suffer through a machinery of ignorance, the optical machinery that prepares the gaze for illusion and passivity. A true community is therefore one that does not tolerate theatrical mediation; one in which the measure that governs the community is directly incorporated into the living attitudes of its members.

That is the most logical deduction. But it is not the one that has prevailed among critics of theatrical mimesis. They have invariably retained the premises while changing the conclusion. According to them, whoever says 'theatre' says 'spectator' – and therein lies the evil. Such is the circle of theatre as we know it, as our society has shaped it in its image. We therefore need a different theatre, a theatre without spectators: not a theatre played out in front of empty seats, but a theatre where the passive optical relationship implied by the very term is subjected to a different relationship that implied by another word, one which refers to what is produced on the stage: *drama*. Drama means action. Theatre is the place where an action is taken to its conclusion by bodies in motion in front of living bodies that are to be mobilized. The latter might have relinquished their power. But this power is revived, reactivated in the performance of the former, in the intelligence which constructs that performance, in the energy it generates. It is on the basis of this active power that a new theatre must be built, or rather a theatre restored to its original virtue, to its true essence, of which the spectacles that take this name offer nothing but a degraded version. What is required is a theatre without spectators, where those in attendance learn from as opposed to being seduced by images; where they become active participants as opposed to passive voyeurs.

There have been two main formulations of this switch, which in principle are conflicting, even if the practice and the theory of a reformed theatre have often combined them. According to the first, the spectator must be roused from the stupefaction of spectators enthralled by appearances and won over by the empathy that makes them identify with the characters on the stage. He will be shown a strange, unusual spectacle, a mystery whose meaning he must seek out. He will thus be compelled to exchange the position of passive spectator for that of scientific investigator or experimenter, who observes phenomena and searches for their causes. Alternatively, he will be offered an exemplary dilemma, similar to those facing human beings engaged in decisions about how to act. In this way, he will be led to hone his own sense of the evaluation of reasons, of their discussion and of the choice that arrives at a decision.

According to the second formulation, it is this reasoning distance that must itself be abolished. The spectator must be removed from the position of observer calmly examining the spectacle offered to her. She must be dispossessed of this illusory mastery, drawn into the magic circle of theatrical action where she will exchange the privilege of rational observer for that of the being in possession of all her vital energies.

Such are the basic attitudes encapsulated in Brecht's epic theatre and Artaud's theatre of cruelty. For one, the spectator must be allowed some distance; for the other, he must forego any distance. For one, he must refine his gaze, while for the other, he must abdicate the very position of viewer. Modern attempts to reform theatre have constantly oscillated between these two poles of distanced investigation and vital participation, when not combining their principles and their effects. They have claimed to transform theatre on the basis of a diagnosis that led to its abolition. Consequently, it is not surprising that they have revived not simply the provisions of Plato's critique but also the positive formula which it opposed to the evil of theatre. Plato wanted to replace the democratic, ignorant community of theatre with a different community, encapsulated in a different performance of bodies. To it he counter-posed the choreographic community, where no one remains a static spectator, where everyone must move in accordance with the community rhythm fixed by mathematical proportion, even if that requires getting old people reluctant to take part in the community dance drunk.

Reformers of theatre have reformulated Plato's opposition between *choros* and theatre as one between the truth of the theatre and the simulacrum of the spectacle. They have made theatre the place where the passive audience of spectators must be transformed into its opposite: the active body of a community enacting its living principle. The presentational text of the Sommerakademie that welcomed me put it like this: 'theatre remains the only place where the audience confronts itself as a collective.' In the narrow sense, the sentence merely seeks to distinguish the collective audience of the theatre from individual visitors to an exhibition or the mere sum of admissions to a cinema. But it is clear that it means more. It signifies that 'theatre' is an exemplary community form. It involves an idea of community as self-presence, in contrast to the distance of represen-tation. Since German Romanticism, thinking about theatre has been associated with this idea of the living community. Theatre emerged as a form of aesthetic constitution – sensible consti-tution – of the community. By that I mean the community as a way of occupying a place and a time, as the body in action as opposed to a mere apparatus of laws; a set of perceptions, gestures and attitudes that precede and pre-form laws and political institutions. More than any other art, theatre has been associated with the Romantic idea of an aesthetic revolution, changing not the mechanics of the state and laws, but the sensible forms of human experience. Hence reform of theatre meant the restoration of its character as assembly or ceremony of the community. Theatre is an assembly in which ordinary people become aware of their situation and discuss their interests, says Brecht following Piscator. It is, claims Artaud, the purifying ritual in which a community is put in possession of its own energies. If theatre thus embodies the living community, as opposed to the illusion of mimesis, it is not surprising that the desire to restore theatre to its essence can draw on the critique of the spectacle.

What in fact is the essence of the spectacle for Guy Debord? It is exteriority. The spectacle is the reign of vision, and vision is exteriority – that is, self-dispossession. The malady of spectating man can be summed up in a brief formula: 'the more he contemplates, the less he lives'.[2] The formula seems to be anti-Platonic. In fact, the theoretical foundations of the critique of the spectacle are borrowed, via Marx, from Feuerbach's critique of religion. The basis of both critiques consists in the Romantic vision of truth as non-separation. But that idea is itself dependent on Plato's conception of *mimesis*. The 'contemplation' denounced by Debord is contemplation of the appearance separated from its truth; it is the spectacle of the suffering produced by that separation:

'Separation is the alpha and omega of the spectacle.'[3] What human beings contemplate in the spectacle is the activity they have been robbed of; it is their own essence become alien, turned against them, organizing a collective world whose reality is that dispossession.

Thus, there is no contradiction between the critique of the spectacle and the quest for a theatre restored to its original essence. 'Good' theatre is one that uses its separated reality in order to abolish it. The paradox of the spectator pertains to the curious device that adopts Plato's prohibition of theatre for theatre. Accordingly, it is these principles that should be reexamined today. Or rather, it is the network of presuppositions, the set of equivalences and oppositions, that underpin their possibility: equivalences between theatrical audience and community, gaze and passivity, exteriority and separation, mediation and simulacrum; oppositions between the collective and the individual, the image and living reality, activity and passivity, self-ownership and alienation.

This set of equivalences and oppositions in fact composes a rather intricate dramaturgy of sin and redemption. Theatre accuses itself of rendering spectators passive and thereby betraying its essence as community action. It consequently assigns itself the mission of reversing its effects and expiating its sins by restoring to spectators ownership of their consciousness and their activity. The theatrical stage and performance thus become a vanishing mediation between the evil of spectacle and the virtue of true theatre. They intend to teach their spectators ways of ceasing to be spectators and becoming agents of a collective practice. According to the Brechtian paradigm, theatrical mediation makes them conscious of the social situation that gives rise to it and desirous of acting in order to transform it. According to Artaud's logic, it makes them abandon their position as spectators: rather than being placed in front of a spectacle, they are surrounded by the performance, drawn into the circle of action that restores their collective energy. In both cases, theatre is presented as a mediation striving for its own abolition.

This is where the descriptions and statements of intellectual emancipation and proposals for it might come into play and help us reformulate its logic. For this self-vanishing mediation is not something unknown to us. It is the very logic of the pedagogical relationship: the role assigned to the schoolmaster in that relationship is to abolish the distance between his knowledge and the ignorance of the ignoramus. His lessons and the exercises he sets aim gradually to reduce the gulf separating them. Unfortunately, he can only reduce the distance on condition that he constantly re-creates it. To replace ignorance by knowledge, he must always be one step ahead, install a new form of ignorance between the pupil and himself. The reason is simple. In pedagogical logic, the ignoramus is not simply one who does not as yet know what the schoolmaster knows. She is the one who does not know what she does not know or how to know it. For his part, the schoolmaster is not only the one who possesses the knowledge unknown by the ignoramus. He is also the one who knows how to make it an object of knowledge, at what point and in accordance with what protocol. For, in truth, there is no ignoramus who does not already know a mass of things, who has not learnt them by herself, by listening and looking around her, by observation and repetition, by being mistaken and correcting her errors. But for the schoolmaster such knowledge is merely an *ignoramus's knowledge*, knowledge that cannot be ordered in accordance with the ascent from the simplest to the most complex. The ignoramus advances by comparing what she discovers with what she already knows, in line with random encounters but also according to the arithmetical rule, the democratic rule, that makes ignorance a lesser form of knowledge. She is concerned solely with knowing more, with knowing what she did not yet know. What she lacks, what the pupil will always lack, unless she becomes a schoolmistress herself, is *knowledge of ignorance* – a knowledge of the exact distance separating knowledge from ignorance.

This measurement precisely eludes the arithmetic of ignoramuses. What the schoolmaster knows, what the protocol of knowledge transmission teaches the pupil in the first instance, is that ignorance is not a lesser form of knowledge, but the opposite of knowledge; that knowledge is not a collection of fragments of knowledge, but a position. The exact distance is the distance that no yardstick measures, the distance that is demonstrated solely by the interplay of positions occupied, which is enforced by the interminable practice of the 'step ahead' separating the schoolmaster from the one whom he is supposed to train to join him. It is the metaphor of the radical gulf separating the schoolmaster's manner from the ignoramus's, because it separates two intelligences: one that knows what ignorance consists in and one that does not. It is, in the first instance, the radical difference that ordered, progressive teaching teaches the pupil. The first thing it teaches her is her own inability. In its activity, it thereby constantly confirms its own presupposition: the inequality of intelligence. This endless confirmation is what Jacotot calls stultification.

To this practice of stultification he counter-posed intellectual emancipation. Intellectual emancipation is the verification of the equality of intelligence. This does not signify the equal value of all manifestations of intelligence, but the self-equality of intelligence in all its manifestations. There are not two sorts of intelligence separated by a gulf. The human animal learns everything in the same way as it initially learnt its mother tongue, as it learnt to venture into the forest of things and signs surrounding it, so as to take its place among human beings: by observing and comparing one thing with another, a sign with a fact, a sign with another sign. If an illiterate knows only one prayer by heart, she can compare that knowledge with what she does not yet know: the words of this prayer as written down on paper. She can learn, one sign after the other, the relationship between what she does not know and what she does know. She can do this if, at each step, she observes what is before her, says what she has seen, and verifies what she has said. From this ignoramus, spelling out signs, to the scientist who constructs hypotheses, the same intelligence is always at work – an intelligence that translates signs into other signs and proceeds by comparisons and illustrations in order to communicate its intellectual adventures and understand what another intelligence is endeavouring to communicate to it.

This poetic labour of translation is at the heart of all learning. It is at the heart of the emancipatory practice of the ignorant schoolmaster. What he does not know is stupefying distance, distance transformed into a radical gulf that can only be 'bridged' by an expert. Distance is not an evil to be abolished, but the normal condition of any communication. Human animals are distant animals who communicate through the forest of signs. The distance the ignoramus has to cover is not the gulf between her ignorance and the schoolmaster's knowledge. It is simply the path from what she already knows to what she does not yet know, but which she can learn just as she has learnt the rest; which she can learn not in order to occupy the position of the scholar, but so as better to practise the art of translating, of putting her experience into words and her words to the test; of translating her intellectual adventures for others and counter-translating the translations of their own adventures which they present to her. The ignorant schoolmaster who can help her along this path is named thus not because he knows nothing, but because he has renounced the 'knowledge of ignorance' and thereby uncoupled his mastery from his knowledge. He does not teach his pupils *his* knowledge, but orders them to venture into the forest of things and signs, to say what they have seen and what they think of what they have seen, to verify it and have it verified. What is unknown to him is the inequality of intelligence. Every distance is a factual distance and each intellectual act is a path traced between a form of ignorance and a form of knowledge, a path that constantly abolishes any fixity and hierarchy of positions with their boundaries.

What is the relationship between this story and the question of the spectator today? We no longer live in the days when playwrights wanted to explain to their audience the truth of social relations and ways of struggling against capitalist domination. But one does not necessarily lose one's presuppositions with one's illusions, or the apparatus of means with the horizon of ends. On the contrary, it might be that the loss of their illusions leads artists to increase the pressure on spectators: perhaps the latter will know what is to be done, as long as the performance draws them out of their passive attitude and transforms them into active participants in a shared world. Such is the first conviction that theatrical reformers share with stultifying pedagogues: that of the gulf separating two positions. Even if the playwright or director does not know what she wants the spectator to do, she at least knows one thing: she knows that she must *do one thing* – overcome the gulf separating activity from passivity.

But could we not invert the terms of the problem by asking if it is not precisely the desire to abolish the distance that creates it? What makes it possible to pronounce the spectator seated in her place inactive, if not the previously posited radical opposition between the active and the passive? Why identify gaze and passivity, unless on the presupposition that to view means to take pleasure in images and appearances while ignoring the truth behind the image and the reality outside the theatre? Why assimilate listening to passivity, unless through the prejudice that speech is the opposite of action? These oppositions – viewing/knowing, appearance/reality, activity/passivity – are quite different from logical oppositions between clearly defined terms. They specifically define a distribution of the sensible, an *a priori* distribution of the positions and capacities and incapacities attached to these positions. They are embodied allegories of inequality. That is why we can change the value of the terms, transform a 'good' term into a 'bad' one and vice versa, without altering the functioning of the opposition itself. Thus, the spectator is discredited because she does nothing, whereas actors on the stage or workers outside put their bodies in action. But the opposition of seeing and doing returns as soon as we oppose to the blindness of manual workers and empirical practitioners, mired in immediacy and routine, the broad perspective of those who contemplate ideas, predict the future or take a comprehensive view of our world. In the past, property owners who lived off their private income were referred to as *active* citizens, capable of electing and being elected, while those who worked for a living were *passive* citizens, unworthy of these duties. The terms can change their meaning, and the positions can be reversed, but the main thing is that the structure counter-posing two categories – those who possess a capacity and those who do not – persists.

Emancipation begins when we challenge the opposition between viewing and acting; when we understand that the self-evident facts that structure the relations between saying, seeing and doing themselves belong to the structure of domination and subjection. It begins when we understand that viewing is also an action that confirms or transforms this distribution of positions. The spectator also acts, like the pupil or scholar. She observes, selects, compares, interprets. She links what she sees to a host of other things that she has seen on other stages, in other kinds of place.

She composes her own poem with the elements of the poem before her. She participates in the performance by refashioning it in her own way – by drawing back, for example, from the vital energy that it is supposed to transmit in order to make it a pure image and associate this image with a story which she has read or dreamt, experienced or invented. They are thus both distant spectators and active interpreters of the spectacle offered to them.

This is a crucial point: spectators see, feel and understand something in as much as they compose their own poem, as, in their way, do actors or playwrights, directors, dancers or performers. Let us simply observe the mobility of the gaze and expressions of spectators of a traditional Shiite religious drama commemorating the death of Hussein, captured by Abbas Kiarostami's camera (*Looking at Tazieh*). The playwright or director would like the spectators to see this and feel that, understand some particular thing and draw some particular conclusion. This is the logic of the stultifying pedagogue, the logic of straight, uniform transmission: there is something – a form of knowledge, a capacity, an energy in a body or a mind – on one side, and it must pass to the other side. What the pupil must *learn* is what the schoolmaster must *teach* her. What the spectator *must see* is what the director *makes her see*. What she must feel is the energy he communicates to her. To this identity of cause and effect, which is at the heart of stultifying logic, emancipation counter-poses their dissociation. This is the meaning of the ignorant schoolmaster: from the schoolmaster the pupil learns something that the schoolmaster does not know himself. She learns it as an effect of the mastery that forces her to search and verifies this research. But she does not learn the schoolmaster's knowledge.

It will be said that, for their part, artists do not wish to instruct the spectator. Today, they deny using the stage to dictate a lesson or convey a message. They simply wish to produce a form of consciousness, an intensity of feeling, an energy for action. But they always assume that what will be perceived, felt, understood is what they have put into their dramatic art or performance. They always presuppose an identity between cause and effect. This supposed equality between cause and effect is itself based upon an inegalitarian principle: it is based on the privilege that the schoolmaster grants himself – knowledge of the 'right' distance and ways to abolish it. But this is to confuse two quite different distances. There is the distance between artist and spectator, but there is also the distance inherent in the performance itself, in so far as it subsists, as a spectacle, an autonomous thing, between the idea of the artist and the sensation or comprehension of the spectator. In the logic of emancipation, between the ignorant schoolmaster and the emancipated novice there is always a third thing – a book or some other piece of writing – alien to both and to which they can refer to verify in common what the pupil has seen, what she says about it and what she thinks of it. The same applies to performance. It is not the transmission of the artist's knowledge or inspiration to the spectator. It is the third thing that is owned by no one, whose meaning is owned by no one, but which subsists between them, excluding any uniform transmission, any identity of cause and effect.

This idea of emancipation is thus clearly opposed to the one on which the politics of theatre and its reform have often relied: emancipation as re-appropriation of a relationship to self lost in a process of separation. It is this idea of separation and its abolition that connects Debord's critique of the spectacle to Feuerbach's critique of religion via the Marxist critique of alienation. In this logic, the mediation of a third term can be nothing but a fatal illusion of autonomy, trapped in the logic of dispossession and its concealment. The separation of stage and auditorium is something to be transcended. The precise aim of the performance is to abolish this exteriority in various ways: by placing the spectators on the stage and the performers in the auditorium: by abolishing the difference between the two; by transferring the performance to other sites; by identifying it with taking possession of the street, the town or life. And this attempt dramatically to change the distribution of places has unquestionably produced many enrichments of theatrical performance. But the redistribution of places is one thing; the requirement that theatre assign itself the goal of assembling a community which ends the separation of the spectacle is quite another. The first involves the invention of new intellectual adventures, the second a new form of allocating bodies to their rightful place, which, in the event, is their place of communion.

For the refusal of mediation, the refusal of the third, is the affirmation of a communitarian essence of theatre as such. The less the playwright knows what he wants the collective of spectators to do, the more he knows that they should, at any rate, act as a collective, transform their aggregation into community. However, it is high time we examine this idea that the theatre is, in and of itself, a community site. Because living bodies onstage address bodies assembled in the same place, it seems that that is enough to make theatre the vehicle for a sense of community, radically different from the situation of individuals seated in front of a television, or film spectators in front of projected shadows. Curiously, generalization of the use of images and every variety of projection in theatrical production seems to alter nothing in this belief. Projected images can be conjoined with living bodies or substituted for them. However, as long as spectators are assembled in the theatrical space, it is as if the living, communitarian essence of theatre were preserved and one could avoid the question: what exactly occurs among theatre spectators that cannot happen elsewhere? What is more interactive, more communitarian, about these spectators than a mass of individuals watching the same television show at the same hour?

This something, I believe, is simply the presupposition that theatre is in and of itself communitarian. This presupposition continues to precede theatrical performances and anticipate its effects. But in a theatre, in front of a performance, just as in a museum, school or street, there are only ever individuals plotting their own paths in the forest of things, acts and signs that confront or surround them. The collective power shared by spectators does not stem from the fact that they are members of a collective body or from some specific form of interactivity. It is the power each of them has to translate what she perceives in her own way, to link it to the unique intellectual adventure that makes her similar to all the rest in as much as this adventure is not like any other. This shared power of the equality of intelligence links individuals, makes them exchange their intellectual adventures, in so far as it keeps them separate from one another, equally capable of using the power everyone has to plot her own path. What our performances – be they teaching or playing, speaking, writing, making art or looking at it – verify is not our participation in a power embodied in the community. It is the capacity of anonymous people, the capacity that makes everyone equal to everyone else. This capacity is exercised through irreducible distances; it is exercised by an unpredictable interplay of associations and dissociations.

It is in this power of associating and dissociating that the emancipation of the spectator consists – that is to say, the emancipation of each of us as spectator. Being a spectator is not some passive condition that we should transform into activity. It is our normal situation. We also learn and teach, act and know, as spectators who all the time link what we see to what we have seen and said, done and dreamed. There is no more a privileged form than there is a privileged starting point. Everywhere there are starting points, intersections and junctions that enable us to learn something new if we refuse, firstly, radical distance, secondly the distribution of roles, and thirdly the boundaries between territories. We do not have to transform spectators into actors, and ignoramuses into scholars. We have to recognize the knowledge at work in the ignoramus and the activity peculiar to the spectator. Every spectator is already an actor in her story; every actor, every man of action, is the spectator of the same story.

I shall readily illustrate this point at the cost of a little detour via my own political and intellectual experience. I belong to a generation that found itself pulled between two opposite requirements. According to the first, those who possessed an understanding of the social system had to teach it to those who suffered because of that system so as to arm them for struggle. According to the second, supposed scholars were in fact ignoramuses who knew nothing about what exploitation and rebellion meant and had to educate themselves among the workers whom they treated as ignoramuses. To respond to this dual requirement, I first of all wanted to rediscover the truth of Marxism, so as to arm a new revolutionary movement, and then to learn the meaning of exploitation and rebellion from those who worked and struggled in factories. For me, as for my generation, neither of these endeavours was wholly convincing. This state of affairs led me to search in the history of the working-class movement for the reasons for the ambiguous or failed encounters between workers and the intellectuals who had come to visit them to educate them or be educated by them. I thus had the opportunity to understand that the affair was not something played out between ignorance and knowledge, any more than it was between activity and passivity, individuality and community. One day in May when I consulted the correspondence of two workers in the 1830s, in order to find information on the condition and forms of consciousness of workers at that time, I was surprised to encounter something quite different: the adventures of two other visitors on different May days, 145 years earlier. One of the two workers had just joined the Saint-Simonian community in Ménilmontant and gave his friend the timetable of his days in utopia: work and exercises during the day, games, choirs and tales in the evening. In return, his correspondent recounted the day in the countryside he had just spent with two mates enjoying a springtime Sunday. But what he recounted was nothing like the day of rest of a worker replenishing his physical and mental strength for the working week to come. It was an incursion into quite a different kind of leisure: the leisure of aesthetes who enjoy the landscape's forms and light and shade, of philosophers who settle into a country inn to develop metaphysical hypotheses there, of apostles who apply themselves to communicating their faith to all the chance companions encountered on the path or in the inn.[4]

These workers, who should have supplied me with information on working conditions and forms of class consciousness, provided me with something altogether different: a sense of similarity, a demonstration of equality. They too were spectators and visitors within their own class. Their activity as propagandists could not be separated from their idleness as strollers and contemplators. The simple chronicle of their leisure dictated reformulation of the established relations between *seeing*, *doing* and *speaking*. By making themselves spectators and visitors, they disrupted the distribution of the sensible which would have it that those who work do not have time to let their steps and gazes roam at random; and that the members of a collective body do not have time to spend on the forms and insignia of individuality. That is what the word 'emancipation' means: the blurring of the boundary between those who act and those who look; between individuals and members of a collective body. What these days brought the two correspondents and their fellows was not knowledge of their condition and energy for the following day's work and the coming struggle. It was a reconfiguration in the here and now of the distribution of space and time, work and leisure.

Understanding this break made at the very heart of time was to develop the implications of a similarity and an equality, as opposed to ensuring its mastery in the endless task of reducing the irreducible distance. These two workers were themselves intellectuals, as is anyone and everyone. They were visitors and spectators, like the researcher who a century and a half later read their letters in a library, like the visitors of Marxist theory or the distributors of leaflets at factory gates. There was no gap to be filled between intellectuals and workers, any more than there was between actors and spectators. There followed various conclusions as to the discourse that could account for this experience. Recounting the story of their days and nights made it necessary to blur other boundaries. This story which told of time, its loss and re-appropriation, only assumed meaning and significance by being related to a similar story, told elsewhere, in another time and a quite different genre of writing – in Book 2 of the *Republic* where Plato, before assailing the mendacious shadows of the theatre, explains that in a well-ordered community everyone has to do one thing and that artisans do not have the time to be anywhere other than their workplace and to do anything other than the work appropriate to the (in)capacities allocated them by nature.

To understand the story of these two visitors, it was therefore necessary to blur the boundaries between empirical history and pure philosophy; the boundaries between disciplines and the hierarchies between levels of discourse. There was not on the one hand the factual narrative and on the other the philosophical or scientific explanation ascertaining the reason of history or the truth concealed underneath. It was not a case of the facts and their interpretation. There were two different ways of telling a story. And what it came down to me to do was a work of translation, showing how these tales of springtime Sundays and the philosopher's dialogues translated into one another. It was necessary to invent the idiom appropriate to this translation and counter-translation, even if it meant this idiom remaining unintelligible to all those who requested the meaning of this story, the reality that explained it, and the lesson it contained for action. In fact, this idiom could only be read by those who would translate it on the basis of their own intellectual adventure.

This biographical detour returns me to my central point. These stories of boundaries to cross, and of a distribution of roles to be blurred, in fact coincide with the reality of contemporary art, in which all specific artistic skills tend to leave their particular domain and swap places and powers. Today, we have theatre without speech, and spoken dance; installations and performances by way of plastic works; video projections transformed into series of frescos: photographs treated as *tableaux vivants* or history paintings; sculpture metamorphosed into multimedia shows; and other combinations. Now, there are three ways of understanding and practising this mélange of genres. There is that which relaunches the form of the total artwork. It was supposed to be the apotheosis of art become life. Today, it instead tends to be that of a few outsize artistic egos or a form of consumerist hyper-activism, if not both at once. Next, there is the idea of a hybridization of artistic means appropriate to the postmodern reality of a constant exchange of roles and identities, the real and the virtual, the organic and mechanical and information-technology prostheses. This second idea hardly differs from the first in its consequences. It often leads to a different form of stultification, which uses the blurring of boundaries and the confusion of roles to enhance the effect of the performance without questioning its principles.

There remains a third way that aims not to amplify effects, but to problematize the cause–effect relationship itself and the set of presuppositions that sustain the logic of stultification. Faced with the hyper-theatre that wants to transform representation into presence and passivity into activity, it proposes instead to revoke the privilege of vitality and communitarian power accorded the theatrical stage, so as to restore it to an equal footing with the telling of a story, the reading of a book, or the gaze focused on an image. In sum, it proposes to conceive it as a new scene of equality where heterogeneous performances are translated into one another. For in all these performances what is involved is linking what one knows with what one does not know; being at once a performer deploying her skills and a spectator observing what these skills might produce in a new context among other spectators. Like researchers, artists construct the stages where the manifestation and effect of their skills are exhibited, rendered uncertain in the terms of the new idiom that conveys a new intellectual adventure. The effect of the idiom cannot be anticipated. It requires spectators who play the role of active interpreters, who develop their own translation in order to appropriate the 'story' and make it their own story. An emancipated community is a community of narrators and translators.

I am aware that of all this it might be said: words, yet more words, and nothing but words. I shall not take it as an insult. We have heard so many orators passing off their words as more than words, as formulas for embarking on a new existence; we have seen so many theatrical representations claiming to be not spectacles but community ceremonies; and even today, despite all the 'postmodern' scepticism about the desire to change existence, we see so many installations and spectacles transformed into religious mysteries that it is not necessarily scandalous to hear it said that words are merely words. To dismiss the fantasies of the word made flesh and the spectator rendered active, to know that words are merely words and spectacles merely spectacles, can help us arrive at a better understanding of how words and images, stories and performances, can change something of the world we live in.

Notes

1. The invitation to open the fifth Internationale Sommerakademie of Frankfurt-on-Main, on 20 August 2004, came from the Swedish performer and choreographer Mårten Spångberg.
2. Guy Debord, *The Society of the Spectacle*, trans. Donald Nicholson-Smith. New York: Zone Books, 1994, p. 23.
3. Ibid., p. 20.
4. Cf. Gabriel Gauny, *Le Philosophe plébéien*, Paris: Presses Universitaires de Vincennes, 1985, pp. 147–58.

5.12 Epilogue (from *Postdramatic Theatre*) (2006)

HANS-THIES LEHMANN

Translated by Karen Jürs-Munby

The political

This study of postdramatic theatre does not aim to trace the new theatrical modes of creation to sociologically determined causes and circumstances. For one thing, such deductions normally fall short, even in the case of subject matter to which scholars have more of a historical distance. They can be trusted even less when it comes to the confusing and 'unsurveyable' present (Habermas) in which highly contradictory – but therefore no less ambitious – large-scale analyses of the state of the world are chasing each other. Nevertheless, in a reality brimming with social and political conflicts, civil wars, oppression, growing poverty and social injustice, it seems appropriate to conclude with a few general reflections on the way in which one could theorize the relationship of postdramatic theatre to the political. Issues that we call 'political' have to do with social power. For a long time issues of power have been conceived in the domain of law, with its borderline phenomena of revolution, anarchy, state of emergency (*Ausnahmezustand*) and war. In spite of the noticeable tendency towards a juridification of all areas of life, however, 'power' is increasingly organized as a micro-physics, as a web, in which even the leading political elite – not to mention single individuals – hardly have any real power over economico-political processes any more. Therefore, political conflicts increasingly elude intuitive perception and cognition and consequently scenic representation. There are hardly any visible representatives of legal positions confronting each other as political opponents any more. What still attains an intuitable quality, by contrast, is the momentary *suspension* of normative, legal and political modes of behaviour, i.e. the plainly *non*-political terror, anarchy, madness, despair, laughter, revolt, antisocial behaviour – and inherent in it the already latently posited fanatical or fundamentalist negation of immanently secular, rationally founded criteria of action in general. Since Machiavelli, however, the modern demarcation of the political as an autonomous plane of argumentation has been based exactly on the immanence of these criteria.

Intercultural theatre

Some see the political dimension of theatre in furthering 'intercultural' understanding. This possibility cannot be denied outright. But haven't advocates of intercultural theatre like Pavis, Schechner and Peter Brook been vehemently criticized by Indian authors for keeping silent about the disrespectful and superficial appropriation often lurking in intercultural activities, i.e. the cultural imperialist exploitation of the other culture?[1] Brook's famous *Mahabharata*, as well as Lee Breuer's *The Gospel at Colonus* (which combined Greek-European theatre traditions with Afro-American and Christian traditions), met not only with approval but also with harsh criticism as examples of a patriarchal treatment of an oppressed culture by a dominant culture. An underlying ambiguity continues to exist in all intercultural communication as long as cultural forms of expression are always at the same time part of a politically dominant culture or of an oppressed culture, so that it is not a 'communication' of equals that occurs between the two cultures. Instead of hanging on to an idealizing vision of a 'new kind of transcultural communicative synthesis through performance', it seems more honest to join Andrzej Wirth in simply diagnosing the utilization of the most diverse cultural patterns and emblems throughout the international theatre landscape without hoping for a new theatrical *ersatz* site of a political public sphere. To use Wirth's terms, we are dealing here more with an 'iconophilia' than with interculturalism.[2]

The term 'interculturalism' should in any case provoke more political scepticism than is usually the case. It is true that it is preferable to the even more questionable term of 'multiculturalism' that tends to favour the mutual isolation of cultures from each other and the aggressive self-affirmation of cultural group identities more than the urban ideal of mutual influence and interaction. But here, too, questions should be raised: for it is not just 'cultures' as such that meet but concrete artists, art forms and theatre productions. The inter-artistic exchange, moreover, does not take place in the sense of a cultural 'representation': it is not as a representative of African culture that Wole Soyinka adapts a text by Brecht as a representative of European culture. Quite apart from the question of what 'the' African (or European or German) culture would be anyway, it generally holds true that most artists also view their 'own' culture from a certain distance, occupying very often a dissident, deviant and marginal position within it.[3] A good example for intercultural theatre with all its chances and problems was a play with the baroque title *The Aboriginal Protesters Confront the Proclamation of the Australian Republic on 26 January 2001 with the Theatre Production 'The Mission' by Heiner Müller*. The project premiered in Sydney in early 1996 and could be seen in Weimar in the same year. The idea by Gerhard Fischer (a German Studies specialist resident in Australia) had been realized after several years of difficult preparations: to stage a text – written on Fischer's initiative – by the Aborigine author Mudrooroo that shows how the intention of an Aborigine group of actors to stage Heiner Müller's important postcolonial play *The Mission* leads to increasingly violent political conflicts. There is too much of a rift between the political consciousness of the players and the deeply sceptical vision of the European author, who after all always proclaimed his political sympathy with the 'third world'. Müller's play with the subtitle *Memory of a Revolution* revolves around the story of three emissaries from revolutionary France who arrive in Jamaica in 1794 with the 'mission' to stir up a revolt of the black: against their English colonizers. The play ends with treason and the failure of the revolution but raises the question of the ongoing oppression of races and classes all the more adamantly. The staging by Noel Tovey became a political theatre event in Sydney precisely because of the demonstration of the unbridgeable distance between the author and the theatre practitioners. Mudrooroo's adaptation shows how the theatre group at the end votes unanimously against a performance of the Müller text (which none the less has been shown practically in its entirety in the course of the rehearsals performed in the play). Another example was the performance piece *Borderama* (1995) by Guillermo Gómez-Peña and Robert Sifuentes, who have developed their own performance style from their experience of the borderland between the USA and Mexico in order to find an expression for the 'intercultural' experience of oppression and marginalization. In this work, radio art, hip hop, cable television, film and literature are combined. Migration, border crossings, criminalization, racism and xenophobia are addressed in a theatre form that moves with surprising ease between talk show, sports, cinema parodies and harangues, demonstrations, cabaret, night club atmosphere and aggressive pop.[4] Gómez-Peña and Coco Fusco had previously caused an international stir with the tour of their provocative performance *Two Undiscovered Amerindians Visit ...* (also known as *The Couple in the Cage*) in 1992.[5] Posing in a cage as 'natives' from a 'newly discovered' island they intended to protest 500 years of the exhibition of colonized people, a history Fusco calls 'the other history of intercultural performance'.[6] To their shock and surprise, many spectators missed the irony and believed the performers to be real undiscovered natives.

Representation, measure and transgression

As a reaction to the difficulty of developing adequate forms of a political theatre, we find a widespread and questionable return to a deceptively *immediate morality* that is believed to be valid independently of the ambiguities of the political world. In theatre, such moralism favours the return of the idea of the 'theatre considered as a moral institution' (Schiller) – which is always going to suffer, however, from not being able really to believe in itself. On the other hand, there is one thing theatre can do: artistically deconstruct the space of political discourse as such – in as much as the latter erects the thesis, opinion, order, law and organically conceived wholeness of the political body – and to show its latently authoritarian constitution. This happens through the dismantling of discursive certainties of the political, the unmasking of rhetoric, the opening of the field of a non-thetical presentation (in the sense of Julia Kristeva). If we do not want to write off the political dimension of theatre altogether, we have to start with the diagnosis that the question of a political theatre changes radically under the conditions of contemporary information society. That politically oppressed people are shown on stage does not make theatre political. And if the political in its sensational aspects merely procures entertainment value, then theatre may well be political – but only in the bad sense of an (at least unconscious) affirmation of existing political conditions. It is not through the direct thematization of the political that theatre becomes political but through the implicit substance and critical value of its *mode of representation*.

The political, Julia Kristeva emphasizes, is that which sets the measure. The political is subject to the law of the law. It cannot help but posit an order, a rule, a power that is applicable to all, a common measure.[7] The socio-symbolic law is the common measure; the political is the sphere of its confirmation, affirmation, protection, adaptation to the changeable course of things, abolition or modification. Hence, there is an insurmountable rift between the political, which sets the rules, and art, which constitutes, we might say, always an *exception*: the exception to every rule, the affirmation of the irregular even within the rule itself. Theatre as aesthetic behaviour is unthinkable without the infringement of prescriptions, without *transgression*. Pitted against this statement is an argument that is quasi-omnipresent especially in the American debate: namely, that the present was defined by 'the breakdown of the old structural opposition of the cultural and the economic in the simultaneous commodification of the former and the symbolization of the latter'.[8] If this diagnosis were accurate, then the obvious thesis would be that no 'avant-garde' implying a politics of transgression is possible any more because 'the transgressive politics of avant-gardism presupposes cultural limits which are no longer relevant to the seemingly limitless horizon of multinational capitalism'.[9] According to this thesis, there could no longer be a 'transgressive' but only a 'resistant' politics of the arts.[10] Apart from the fact that on closer inspection of what the terms 'transgressive' and 'resistant' mean in the American debate the difference would perhaps diminish, we should just like to make the case here for the counter-thesis that the transgressive moment is in our understanding essential for all art, not just political art. Art privileges – even in the 'création collective' – the individual *par excellence*, the singular, that which remains unquantifiable in relation to even the best of laws – given that the domain of the law is always the attempt to *calculate* even the unpredictable. In art, it is always Brecht's Fatzer who speaks:

> You, however, you calculate to the last fraction
> What remains to be done by me, and put it on the account.
> But I don't do it! Count!
> Count on Fatzer's ten pence perseverance
> And Fatzer's daily vagary!
> Estimate my abyss
> Take five for the unforeseen
> Keep of everything there is of me
> Only what is useful to you.
> The rest is Fatzer.[11]

Theatre itself would hardly have come about without the hybrid act that an individual broke free from the collective, into the unknown, aspiring to an unthinkable possibility; it would hardly have happened without the courage to transgress borders, all borders of the collective. There is no theatre without self-dramatization, exaggeration, overdressing, without demanding attention for this one, personal body – its voice, its movement, its presence and what it has to say. Certainly, at the origin of theatre as a social practice there is also the instrumentalizing and rational self-staging of shamans, chiefs and rulers who manifest their elevated position *vis-à-vis* the collective through heightened gesture and costume: theatre as an effect of power. Yet, at the same time, theatre is a practice in and with signifying material, which does not create orders of power but introduces chaos and novelty into the ordered, ordering perception. As an opening of the logo-centric procedure (in which the dominant mode is conceptual identification) in favour of a practice that does not fear the suspension and interruption of the designating function, theatre can be political. This thesis includes the merely apparent paradox that theatre is political precisely to the degree in which it interrupts the categories of the political itself, deposing of them instead of betting on new laws (no matter how well-intended).

Afformance art?

This seems an appropriate moment for a certain consideration in terms of philosophy of language and at the same time of political theory, which puts the question of the political theatre into yet another perspective. As long as we view the political about theatre as a counterforce that is itself political – as a counter-position and -action and not as a *non-action* and interruption of the law – we are putting the wrong kind of game on the agenda. While acting with linguistic signs has been defined by speech act theory as performative, theatre is not a performative act in the full sense of the word. It is – even if this may seem paradoxical – only pretending to perform. Theatre is not even a thesis but a form of articulation that partially eludes the thetical and the active in general. We could borrow here the term of the *afformative*, which Werner Hamacher coined in a different context,[12] and call theatre *afformance art*, in order to allude to the somehow non-performative in the proximity of performance. While the real political actors rarely know what they are ultimately bringing about with their actions, they can at least have a – perhaps false – sense of certainty that what they are doing at least *is* a doing. While they may not know what it means, they feed the – perhaps charitable but questionable – illusion that their acting is at all 'meaningful' or important in some way or another. Not so the theatre, which does not even produce an object, is deceptive as an action, and deceives even when the illusion is openly disturbed or destroyed. Theatre can only ever be ambiguously 'real' – even when it tries to escape deceptive appearance and draws close to the real. It permeates all representation with the uncertainty of whether something is represented; every act with the uncertainty of whether it was one; every thesis, every position, every work, every meaning with a wavering and potential cancellation. Perhaps theatre can never know whether it really 'does' something, whether it effects something and on top of it means something. Apart from the profitable and ridiculous mass entertainment of the musical, it therefore 'does' less and less. It produces increasingly less meaning because in proximity of the zero-point (in 'fun', in stasis, in the silence of the gazes) something might happen: a now. Doubtful performative – afformance art.

Time and again, especially when the discussion turns to the (impossible) unambiguous differentiation between theatre and performance, the idea comes up that we can oppose performance as a 'real' action to the theatre as the realm of fiction, the actions 'as if', where we can understand something and where the boundaries are clear. Some scholars go as far as to say that performance can be compared to the *terrorist act*.[13] After all, both take place in real, historical time, the performers act as themselves and simultaneously take on symbolic significance, and so on. Even if one could concede some illuminating structural similarities between terrorism and performance, one difference remains decisive: the latter does not happen as a *means* to another (political) end; as a performance it is in this sense precisely 'afformative', namely not simply a performative act. By contrast, what is at issue in the terrorist action is a political or other *determination of aims* (however one may judge these). The terrorist act is intentional, is performative through and through, an act and a postulate in the realm of the logic of means and ends.

Drama and society

Although the question as to the political character of the aesthetic concerns the arts in general and *all* forms of theatre, the relations between a postdramatic aesthetic and the possible political dimensions of theatre immediately come to mind. They resonate in the obvious question: is there a political theatre without narration? Without a fable in Brecht's sense? What might political theatre after and without Brecht be? Does theatre, as many people believe, rely on the fable as a vehicle for the representation of the world? If the artistic work of the theatre belongs to those 'ways of worldmaking' (Nelson Goodman) that are most likely still to contain some potential for reflection, it could seem paradoxical that theatre would simply relinquish drama as one of the strong points that is quasi-sanctified by tradition. Would this not be its real 'gap in the market'? After all, forms and genres always offer also the possibility of communication about collective, not just private experience – artistic forms *are* congealed collective patterns of experience. How can a 'theatrum mundi' function without the possibilities of dramatic fictionalization with its whole wealth of chances for play between fictive (but somehow quasi-real) dramatis personae and real actors? One could indeed be afraid that the disintegration of the established canon of forms could lead to the desolation of whole landscapes of the interrogation of human experience. But lo and behold: the panorama of postdramatic theatre shows that this worry is unfounded; that the new theatre can more plausibly bring the essence and specific chance of theatre to life. To the degree in which it does not represent a fictive figure (in its imaginary eternity, e.g. Hamlet) but instead exposes the body of a performer in its temporality, the themes of the oldest theatre traditions reappear, albeit certainly in a new light: enigma, death, decline, parting, old age, guilt, sacrifice, tragedy and Eros. Death may be performed as an amicably accompanied exit in the real time of the stage, not a fictive tragedy but rather a scenic gesture 'imagined as death', but hence-forth the simple gesture carries within it the whole weight of the basic 'everyday' experience of saying goodbye. Postdramatic theatre has come closer to the trivial and banal, the simplicity of an encounter, a look or a shared situation. With this, however, theatre also articulates a possible answer to the tedium of the daily flood of artificial formulas of intensification. The inflationary dramatizations of daily sensations that anaesthetize the sensorium have become unbearable. What is at stake is not a heightening but a deepening of a condition, a situation. In political terms: what is at stake is also the fate of the errors of the dramatic imagination.

Several decades ago, Althusser's essay on Bertolazzi and Brecht[14] made clear how a political theatre can be constituted: namely, in such a way that it lets the dramatic phantasmagoria of the subject come apart at the unbudging wall of 'another' time of the social. What is experienced and/or stylized as 'drama' is nothing but the hopelessly deceptive 'perspectivation' of occurrences as action. Occurrences are interpreted as a 'doing': that was Nietzsche's formula for mythification. This shift also characterizes the individual's (by nature) illusory perception of reality, the 'eternal' ideology of a spontaneously anthropomorphizing perception. Thus, the experience of a split between two times – the time of the subject and the time of the historical process – is the core of political theatre, as Althusser points out, and this in fact hits the nerve of the problem of politics as a subject for theatre. Althusser could show in Brecht's work how the epic theatre assumes the alterity of two times: one is the undialectical, massive time of social and historical processes that is unknowable and inaccessible to the individual, the other the illusory time pattern of subjective experience – melodrama. In this sense, the politics of a theatre that turns the illusions of the subject and the contrasting heterogeneous reality of social processes into an experience for the spectator – as a relation of lacking relations, as discrepancy and 'alterity' – is still possible today.

In present society, almost any form has come to seem more suitable for articulating reality than the action of a causal logic with its inherent attribution of events to the decisions of individuals. Drama and society cannot come together. If dramatic theatre loses ground so 'dramatically', however, this may indicate that the form of experience that corresponds to this art form is retreating in reality itself. Within the scope of this study, we cannot tackle, never mind solve, the question as to the reasons for the retreat of dramatic imagination or for the fact that it is no longer taken for granted. We can only offer a few reflections on this topic. A first thesis could be: while the drama of modern times was based on a human being that constituted itself through interpersonal rapport, the postdramatic theatre assumes a human being for whom even the most conflictuous situations will no longer appear as drama. The representational form 'drama' is available but grasps at nothing when it is meant to articulate experienced reality (beyond the melodramatic illusions). Certainly, one can still recognize a 'dramatic form' in this or that moment (e.g. 'fights' between powerful rulers), but it soon becomes obvious that the real issues are only decided in power blocs, not by protagonists who in reality are interchangeable in what Hegel called the 'prose of civic life'. In addition, the theatre seems to *relinquish the idea of a beginning, middle and end*, since we feel more at home with the thought that the catastrophe (or the amusement) could consist in all things continuing in the same way as they used to. Scientific theories of a rhythmically expanding and contracting universe, chaos and game theory, have further de-dramatized reality.

Another reflection on the disappearance of the dramatic impulse can be tied in with Richard Schechner's theses. He emphasizes that the model 'drama' – understood in Turner's sense as the shape and model of 'social drama' with its sequence of a rupture of the social norm, crisis, reconciliation ('redressive action') and reintegration, i.e. re-establishment of the social continuum – is ultimately based on an overarching social cohesion. The sequential structure of 'performance' – in the comprehensive sense assumed by the theory of cultural performance in theatre anthropology – consists of the phases of gathering, actual performance and disbanding. Within this precisely fixed frame, it offers the image of the staging of a conflict that is surrounded by a space of solidarity and is made possible by it in the first place. This view[15] can be developed in such a way that the presence of drama could indicate precisely a society's capacity to uphold its inner coherence. If it disposes of a frame of solidarity, the latter makes it possible repeatedly to thematize evident and more hidden conflictuous dynamics in the form of wrenching conflicts. Thus, the depth, extent, precision and consequence of the thematization of the conflict indicate the state of the social 'glue', the solidarity or at least the deeper symbolic unity of the society – *how much drama it can afford*, so to speak. Viewed in this light, it would be a fact worth thinking about that drama is increasingly becoming the core of a more or less banal mass entertainment where it is flattened into mere 'action', while it is simultaneously disappearing from the more complex forms of innovative theatre.

Whether or not the processes of crisis and reconciliation and the ritualizations connected to them, as analysed by Bateson, Goffman and Turner, are accurate anthropological and sociological descriptions of the social processes has to remain undecided here. The dwindling of the dramatic space of imagination in the consciousness of society and of the artists seems, at any rate, indisputable and proves that something about this model is no longer in tune with our experience. The dwindling of the dramatic impulse has to be stated – no matter whether it is due to the fact that it has been exhausted and as reconciliation only ever stays 'the same'; whether it assumes a mode of 'action' that we no longer recognize anywhere; or whether it paints an obsolete image of social and personal conflict. If we were to give in to the temptation of regarding postdramatic theatre as an expression of contemporary social structures – for just a moment and despite all reservations – then a rather gloomy picture would result. We could hardly suppress the suspicion that society can no longer afford the complex and profound representation of wrenching conflicts, representations that 'go to the substance' of issues. It deludes itself with the illusory comedy of a society that allegedly no longer has such inherent conflicts. The theatre aesthetics inadvertently even reflects some of this. A certain paralysis of public discourse about the basic principles of society is striking. There is no current issue that is not 'verbalized' *ad nauseam* in endless commentaries, special broadcasts, talk shows, polls and interviews – but we find hardly a sign of society's capacity to 'dramatize' the uncertainty of its really founding and fundamental issues and principles, which are after all deeply shaken. Postdramatic theatre is also theatre in an age of omitted images of conflict.

Theatre and the 'Society of the Spectacle'

It is apparent that the decline of the dramatic is by no means synonymous with the decline of the theatrical. On the contrary: theatricalization permeates the entire social life, starting with the individual attempts to produce or feign a *public self* – the cult of self-presentation and self-revelation through fashion signs or other marks designed to attest to the model of a self (albeit mostly borrowed) *vis-à-vis* a certain group, as well as *vis-à-vis* the anonymous crowd. Alongside the external construction of the individual there are the self-presentations of group- and generation-specific identities that represent themselves as theatrically organized appearances, for want of distinct linguistic discourses, programmes, ideologies or utopias. If we add advertising, the self-staging of the business world and the theatricality of mediated self-presentation in politics, it seems that we are witnessing the perfection of what Guy Debord described as emerging in his *Society of the Spectacle*. It is a fundamental fact of today's Western societies that all human experiences (life, eroticism, happiness, recognition) are tied to *commodities* or more precisely their consumption and possession (and not to a discourse). This corresponds exactly to the civilization of images that can only ever refer to the next image and call up other images. The totality of the spectacle is the 'theatricalization' of all areas of social life.

As society seems to be freeing itself more and more from needs and wants through perpetual economic growth, it enters into a more or less total dependence on precisely this growth, or rather on the political means to secure it.[16] For this mechanism, however, the *definition of the citizen as spectator* is indispensable – a definition that is gaining more and more plausibility in the society of the media anyway. In an essay devoted to the media effects in the political sphere, Samuel Weber writes:

> If we remain spectators/viewers, if we stay where we are – in front of the television – the catastrophes will always stay outside, will always be 'objects' for a 'subject' – this is the implicit promise of the medium. But this comforting promise coincides with an equally clear, if unspoken threat: Stay where you are! If you move, there may be an intervention, whether humanitarian or not.[17]

One realizes here that the separation of the event from the perception of the event, precisely through the mediation of the news about it, leads to an erosion of the act of communication. The consciousness of being connected to others and thus being answerable and bound to them 'in the language', in the medium of communication itself recedes in favour of communication as (an exchange of) information. Speaking as such is in principle an accountable speaking. (The statement 'I love you' is not a piece of information but an act, an engagement.) Media, by contrast, transform the giving of signs into information and through habit and repetition dissolve the consciousness and even the sense for the fact that the act of sending signs ultimately involves sender and receiver in a shared situation connected through the medium of language. This is the real reason why fiction and reality merge, as is often deplored. Not because people mistake that in one case they are dealing with something invented and in the other with news, but because of the manner in which the signifying process divides the thing and the sign, the reference and the situation of the production of the signs. The uncontrollable degree of reality of the images, on the one hand, delocalizes the events disseminated through the medium and, on the other hand, simultaneously promotes 'communities of values' among the viewers who are receiving the images isolated in their homes. Thus the continual presentation of bodies that are abused, injured, killed through isolated (real or fictive) catastrophes creates a radical distance for passive viewing: the bond between perception and action, receiving message and 'answerability', is dissolved. We find ourselves *in* a spectacle in which we can only *look on* – bad traditional theatre. Under these conditions, postdramatic theatre tries to withdraw from the reproduction of 'images' into which all spectacles ultimately solidify. It becomes 'calm' and 'static', offering images without reference and handing over the domain of the dramatic to the images of violence and conflict in the media, unless it incorporates these in order to parody them.

Politics of perception, aesthetics of responsibility

It is not a new insight that theatre is reliant on indirectness and deceleration, on a reflecting immersion in political topics. Its political engagement does not consist in the topics but in the forms of perception. This insight presupposes the overcoming of what Peter von Becker once called the 'Lessing-Schiller-Brecht-68-syndrom' in German theatre.[18] At the same time, we have to avoid facile assertions along the lines that the political is only a superficial aspect of art – or inversely, that all art is 'somehow' political. For whether the political is considered as altogether absent from theatre or as a quite general ingredient of it anyway – in both cases it is regarded as no longer interesting. Yet theatre is an art of the social *par excellence*. Its analysis, therefore, cannot settle for a de-politicization because its practice is objectively politically co-determined. The politics of theatre, however, is to be sought in the manner of its *sign usage*. The politics of theatre is a *politics of perception*. To define it we have to remember that the mode of perception in theatre cannot be separated from the existence of theatre in a world of media which massively shapes all perception. The rapidly transmitted and seemingly 'true to life' image suggests the real which in truth it first softens, mellows and weakens. Produced far from its reception and received far from its origin, it imprints indifference onto everything shown. We enter into (mediated) contact with everything, and simultaneously experience ourselves as radically detached from the plethora of facts and fictions we are being informed about. While the media perpetually dramatize all political conflicts, the glut of information, combined with the factual disintegration of clearly discernible political frontlines of the events, produces within the omnipresence of the electronic image a *disjointedness* between representation and represented, between image and reception of the image. Denied in vain by the media with their insistent gestures of appeal, this disjointedness is incessantly confirmed by the technology of the mediated circulation of signs. We have the impression that individuals are reporting to us, but in fact it is collectives, who for their part represent nothing but *functions of the medium* instead of availing themselves of it. What happens from moment to moment is the erasure of the trace, the avoidance of the self-referencing of the sign. Consequently a 'bisection' of language occurs. On the one hand, the medium releases the senders from all connection with the emitted message and, on the other hand, it occults the viewers' perception of the fact that participation in language also makes them, the receivers, responsible for the message. In a fairytale-like manner, the technical tricks and conventional dramaturgies assert the fantasy of omnipotence inherent to mediated inscription – as a defence mechanism against the fear of the producers and consumers of images alike, a fantasy that creates the illusion of being able to preside quite calmly over all realities – even the most inconceivable – without being affected by them oneself. The more unlimited the horror of the image, the more unreal its constitution. Horror rhymes with cosiness. The 'uncanny', by contrast, which Freud found in the merging of signs and signified, remains excluded.

It would be absurd to expect theatre to oppose an effective alternative to the massive superiority of these structures. But the question can be shifted from the problem of a political thesis or antithesis onto the level of sign usage itself. The basic structure of perception mediated by media is such that there is no experience of a connection among the individual images received but above all no connection between the receiving and sending of signs; there is no experience of a relation between address and answer. Theatre can respond to this only with a *politics of perception*, which could at the same time be called an *aesthetic of responsibility (or response-ability)*. Instead of the deceptively comforting duality of here and there, inside and outside, it can move the *mutual implication of actors and spectators in the theatrical production of images* into the centre and thus make visible the broken thread between personal experience and perception. Such an experience would be not only aesthetic but therein at the same time ethico-political. All else, even the most perfected political demonstration, would not escape Baudrillard's diagnosis that we are dealing only with circulating simulacra.

Aesthetics of risk

It should be evident by now that, for a politics of perception in the theatre, it is not the thesis (or antithesis) that counts, not the political statement or engagement (both of which belong in the domain of real politics not represented politics), but rather a basic disrespect for tenability or positive affirmation. Such politics will, in other words, include the transgression of taboos. Theatre is dealing with it all the time.[19] If one defines the taboo as a socially anchored form of affective reaction that rejects ('abjects') certain realities, forms of behaviour or images as 'untouchable', disgusting or unacceptable prior to any rational judgment, then the often stated observation that the taboo has virtually disappeared in the course of the rationalization, de-mythologization and disenchantment of the world is pertinent to our theme. Instead of an extended analysis, we risk the following simplification: there is nothing, or nearly nothing, in contemporary society that cannot be rationally discussed. But what if such rationalization also anaesthetizes the equally urgently needed human reflexes, which at a crucial moment could be the condition for a quick, timely reaction? Is it not already the case that disregarding spontaneous impulses (e.g. with respect to the environment, animals, a cold social climate) in favour of economic instrumental rationality leads to disasters that are as obvious as they are unstoppable? In light of this observation of the progressive breakdown of immediate affective reaction, we have to realize the growing importance of a certain cultivation of affects, the 'training' of an emotionality that is not under the tutelage of rational preconsiderations. 'Enlightenment' and education by themselves are not enough. (Even in the eighteenth century enlightenment (*Aufklärung*) was accompanied by the equally powerful current of 'sensibility' (*Empfindsamkeit*)). It will increasingly become an important task for 'theatrical' practices in the widest sense to create playful situations in which affects are released and played out.

That the capacity to achieve a certain emotional 'training' is important to theatre was a notion even of the baroque. Opitz defined it as the task of tragedy to prepare the spectators better for their own 'afflictions' by exercising and thus reinforcing 'constantia', stoic strength of endurance. Lessing, and with him the 'Enlightenment', considered theatre as a school for training pity or empathy (*Mitleid*). Even Brecht accorded to the theatre – which he did not intend to surrender to the 'old' emotions – the task of elevating feelings 'to a higher level', promoting feelings such as the love of justice and outrage at injustice. In the age of rationalization, of the ideal of calculation and of the generalized rationality of the market, it falls to the theatre to deal with extremes of affect by means of an *aesthetics of risk*, extremes which always also contain the possibility of offending by breaking taboos. This is given when the spectators are confronted with the problem of having to react to what is happening in their presence, that is as soon as the safe distance is no longer given, which the aesthetic distance between stage and auditorium seemed to safeguard. Precisely this reality of the theatre, that it can play with the border, predestines it for acts and actions in which not an 'ethical' reality or a thesis is formulated but in which a situation develops that confronts the spectators with abysmal fear, shame and even mounting aggression. Once more, we can clearly see here that theatre does not attain its political, ethical reality by way of information, theses and messages; in short: by way of its content in the traditional sense. On the contrary: it is part of its constitution to hurt feelings, to produce shock and disorientation, which point the spectators to their own presence precisely through 'amoral', 'asocial' and seemingly 'cynical' events. In doing so, it deprives us neither of the humour and shock of cognition, nor of the pain nor the fun for which alone we gather in the theatre.

Notes

1. R. Barucha and G. Dasgupta, '*The Mahabarata*: Peter Brook's "Orientalism"', in *Performing Arts Journal*, vol. x, no. 3 (1987), pp. 9–16.
2. A. Wirth, 'Interkulturalität und Iconophilia im neuen Theater', in S. Bauschinger and S. L. Cocalis (eds), *Vom Wort zum Bild: Das Neue Theatrer in Deutschland und den USA*, Bern: Francke, 1992, pp. 233–43.
3. Compare A. P. Nganang, *Interkulturalität und Bearbeitung: Untersuchung zu Soyinka und Brecht* (dissertation, Frankfurt am Main 1998), Munich: Iudicium, 1998.
4. For a more comprehensive documentation and discussion of this borderland performance work see G. Gómez-Peña's recent book *Dangerous Border Crossers: The Artist Talks Back*, New York: Routledge, 2000.
5. Compare Fischer-Lichte, *The Show and The Gaze of Theatre*, p. 223ff.
6. See C. Fusco, 'The Other History of Intercultural Performance', in *Drama Review*, vol. 38, no. 1, Spring 1994, pp.143–66.
7. J. Kristeva, 'Politique de la littérature', in *Polylogue*, Paris, 1977, pp. 13–21.
8. H. Foster, *Recodings: Art, Spectacle, Cultural Politics*, Port Townsend, WA: Bay Press, 1985, p. 145.
9. Ibid.
10. See also P. Auslander, *Presence and Resistance: Postmodernism and Cultural Politics in Contemporary American Performance*, Ann Arbor: University of Michigan Press, 1994.
11. Brecht, *Werke*, vol. 10, p. 495.
12. W. Hamacher, 'Afformative, Strike: Benjamin's "Critique of Violence"', trans. by D. Hollander, in A. Benjamin and P. Osborne (eds), *Walter Benjamin's Philosophy Destruction and Experience*, London and New York: Routledge, 1994, pp. 110–38.
13. A. J. Sabbatini, 'Terrorism, Perform', in *High Performance*, vol. 9, no. 2, 1986, pp. 29–33.

14. L. Althusser, 'The Piccolo Teatro: Bertolazzi and Brecht', in L. Althusser, *For Marx*, trans. by B. Brewster, London: Verso, 1886, pp. 129–51.

15. R. Schechner, *Performance Theory*, New York: Taylor and Francis, 1988, p. 166ff.

16. G. Debord, *The Society of the Spectacle*, trans. by Donald Nicholson-Smith, New York: Zone Books, 1994, p. 40.

17. S. Weber, 'Humanitäre Intervention im Zeitalter der Medien: Zur Frage einer hetergenen Politik', in H.-P. Jäck and H. Pfeil (eds), *Eingriffe im Zeitalter der Medien* (*Politick des Anderen*, vol. 1), Bornheim and Rostock: Hanseatischer Fachverlag für Wirtschaft, 1995, pp. 5–27, here p. 26.

18. P. von Becker, in *Theater heute*, vol. 1, 1990, p. 1.

19. Compare H.-T. Lehmann, 'L'esthétique du risque', in *L'Art du Théâtre*, no. 7, autumn 1987, pp. 35–44.

5.13 **Away From the Surveillance Cameras of the Art World** (2000)

Strategies for Collaboration and Community Activism

A CONVERSATION BETWEEN GUILLERMO GÓMEZ-PEÑA, ROBERTO SIFUENTES, AND LISA WOLFORD

(The text published below is part of the fourth in an ongoing series of conversations with members of Pocha Nostra [Guillermo Gómez-Peña, Roberto Sifuentes, Sara Shelton-Mann, and a fluctuating group of additional collaborators that includes Juan Ybarra and Rona Michele] that I recorded beginning in October 1998. This particular meeting took place over a long meal at a 'pan-Caribbean' restaurant in Ann Arbor, Michigan, decorated with murals of exotic birds and jungle foliage – true midwestern tropicalia. L.W.)

Lisa Wolford: During one of the rehearsals for *BORDERscape 2000*, you talked about being 'hunters of images'. I'm wondering if both of you could talk about that process.

Guillermo Gómez-Peña: In this oversaturated culture, it has become increasingly difficult to find original images that speak for the times. Most metaphors and symbols seem overused, hollow, or broken. I think that one of the many jobs of an artist is to look for new, fresh metaphors and symbols to help us understand our everchanging realities and fragmented cultures. We go about doing this in many ways. Sometimes we find images in everyday life, in the streets, and we capture them with our photographic eye and then re-enact them in more complex ways on stage. At other times, we create composite images by departing from a highly charged, traditional icon such as the crucifixion, the captured primitive, the political monster, the mariachi performing for outsiders and tourists, the witch doctor … Then we begin to do nasty things to these images. We begin to layer them as a kind of palimpsest. We add layers of contradiction or complexity, or we begin inserting details and features from other sources until these 'traditional' images implode. The result is like genetically engineered Mexicabilia. The ultimate goal is to look for images that will create a disturbing sediment in the consciousness of the spectator, images that the audience cannot easily escape from, that will haunt them in dreams, in conversations, in memories.

Roberto Sifuentes: It's very important for us that the complex images we use in performance be open to multiple interpretations that we may never have imagined ourselves. It's always interesting for us to hear the varied readings of our diverse audiences. For example, the image of the hanging chickens in our performances: on one level, there's our intention behind using this charged metaphor, which is that it recalls the fact that Mexican migrant workers were hung by the Texas Rangers.

Gómez-Peña: Even nowadays, migrant workers are derogatorily referred to as *pollos*. But we don't necessarily expect our audiences to know this. We welcome other readings of the hanging chickens. Every image we use is a polysemantic image. It changes meaning with the context …

Sifuentes: Bringing this image out of its culturally specific context and presenting the work in the deep South brought out a completely different reading, which had to do with the fact that African-American slaves were hung for stealing chickens. In the Caribbean, after hearing about the image, people thought we might be into some kind of Santeria or 'Mexican Voodoo' rituals …

Wolford: Are there ever moments when this process of interpretation becomes too elliptical, too open-ended? When audience members read something into an image that you didn't intend to communicate at all, or when a very specific message isn't recognized by the spectator? Like this idea that you're practicing Santeria …

Sifuentes: Yes, sometimes the interpretations of our images are really surprising. We were performing at a small college outside Kansas City, where the audience was described to us as right-wing Christian extremists who had, just a couple of weeks before, attacked a queer performance artist colleague of ours. So imagine how surprised we were to find out that these fundamentalists took an image on the publicity posters, that showed Guillermo in his mariachi suit, completely at face value. So these five hundred Republicans showed up to our performance with drums and maracas, ready to party, because they thought they were coming to 'Mariachi Karaoke' night. And imagine how surprised they were when they saw our particular brand of Mariachi night!

Gómez-Peña: I used to fear being misunderstood, five or six years ago. Since intercultural misunderstanding is often the source of racism, I used to think that for the performance to be understood was very important. Now I think that whether the audience feels they understand us or not is completely irrelevant. In fact, I now distrust people who come up to me right after a show and tell me 'I understood everything and I am with you.' I answer: 'Are you sure you are with me?' If you see a narrative film or a theater play, you immediately assume an ethical or emotional positionality. Whether you like it or not, you align yourself with certain characters, with certain notions of good, justice, freedom, rebellion, etc. You walk out of the theater and you say I got it, I liked it or I didn't.

Wolford: With some kinds of theater, not all.

Gómez-Peña: But with performance art, it's different. You walk out of a performance feeling troubled and perplexed. The performance triggers a process of reflexivity that continues through days and sometimes weeks, creating sediments in the consciousness of people. People slowly begin to come to terms with the images and make up their minds about what they saw, but it takes them weeks, even months. Sometimes people think they are offended because they don't want to face certain realities or certain scary feelings they harbor, and it's very easy to say 'I'm offended', as opposed to trying to understand what wound was opened.

Wolford: Guillermo, I think that really interesting, important theater can have that effect as well. But that's another conversation. In terms of the images, why do you think some people get offended? I don't mean something like the use of the chickens *per se* – I know that animal rights groups have been very vocal about objecting to that, but their reasons are fairly straightforward. I'm thinking about people who manifest strong reactions to some of the more poetical images, such as the crucifixion imagery, or the gang member's stigmata …

Sifuentes: Most of the time, the audience is completely comfortable with images like a Chicano 'gang member' being beaten by the police, or dragged out of his home in front of his family by the LAPD. They see it on syndicated TV every night, on shows like 'COPS' and 'LAPD: Life in the Streets'. What our spectators find disturbing is witnessing these images of violence recontextualized in high art institutions by two Mexicans who talk back to them. I remember that during one performance we did, the melancholic image of Guillermo as a mariachi in a straightjacket confessing his intercultural desires so disturbed one upper-class Latina that she came onstage and whipped Guillermo so hard across the face and genitals that he crumbled to the ground and was unable to continue the piece for a few minutes. She ran out of the theater and was stopped by our agent and asked why. She only responded that this was offensive, and didn't represent her as a Latina. And this happened in the first five minutes of the piece.

Figure 34 Performance jamming session at Theater Arnaud (Gómez-Peña, Margaret Leonard, Roberto Sifuentes, Sara Shelton-Mann and Nao Bustamente). (Photographer: Eugenio Castro.)

Gómez-Peña: There's a very disturbing tendency in America to take things literally. Since our work is highly symbolic and metaphorical, it appears to be very much out of context in the current culture. We're living in a time in which confessional narrative is the primary means of communication, and we don't engage in confessional narratives of authenticity. Neither do we engage in psychological or social realism. The work is really not about 'us' …

Sifuentes: It's not autobiographical. We're not performing our authenticity as Chicanos; what we're doing is performing the multiplicity of mythologies and perceptions of Mexicans and Chicanos in the US. Unfortunately, some audiences don't think of Chicanos as 'cultural thinkers' or 'conceptual arists', so when I first began to portray the 'Vato' (street hipster) covered in tattoos, wearing baggie clothes, and manipulating weapons, many audience members and even some journalists thought I was a Latino gang member brought to town and put on display by Gómez-Peña.

Wolford: So the fact that you're both coming out of an experimental performance tradition already contradicts the ways in which people may tend to want to label your work. Also the incorporation of different media, the extent to which your performances reference theory and critical discourse, etc.

Gómez-Peña: Roberto and I are first and foremost conceptual artists. We always depart from a theoretical proposal, an idea which first becomes a blueprint for action, and eventually becomes a performance piece, a video, or a radio piece. But some of our collaborators come from very different traditions, especially when we work with actors, singers and dancers. Sara [Shelton-Mann] comes from the apocalypse dance theater movement that uses a lot of contact improvisation and physical movement to create original imagery and visceral rituals, and then the collaborating artists conceptualize around the imagery they have developed in the rehearsal room – that's basically the opposite of the way we work. Roberto and I don't spend that much time in the rehearsal room. What we do instead is write, brainstorm, debate with other artists and activists, and every now and then we rehearse. We usually only rehearse physically the month before launching a new project. But we are learning tremendously from Sara. We are beginning to shyly incorporate some of her methodologies into our work.

Sifuentes: And Sara is beginning to incorporate our methodologies. She now thinks of Doc's Clock (our local bar in the Mission) and La Boheme Cafe as viable rehearsal spaces.

Gómez-Peña: Imagine Roberto and I doing contact dance and Ch'i Kung. It sounds ridiculous, que no?

Wolford: Hey, I've seen it – it works. I really don't think you could have gotten to what you're doing now in terms of the physical images on stage without it.

Gómez-Peña: We are hoping to develop a kind of dialectic in which these two processes, the conceptual and the visceral, go together. When we brainstorm with our collaborators about how to incorporate a new vignette, we inevitably talk about politics, about other issues. Our discussions during the creative process are not just about the work itself. We talk about what we saw on TV the night before, about a new book we are reading, about cinema, computers, sex, anthropology, you name it … We share an experience we had the week before. We describe a rare prop we just found in a roadside museum on our last trip somewhere. And then, out of these eclectic discussions, where language and ideas are like personas in a conceptual mini-proscenium, the stage of the dinner table or the bar table, a new image or a new text begins to emerge. Then we try it out informally in front of friends. When we are in San Francisco, we have performance salons at least once a month. There we try out all the new material and invite other performers to try out fresh material.

Sifuentes: A text can begin in a salon, evolve into a radio commentary and then become the basis for a major section in a proscenium piece, or else the radio piece gets worked into the soundtrack for a diorama performance. But really, the performance personas, their actions, the texts, and juxtapositions of images, never get finalized. They are always in process of development. We test them in front of an audience and that's the moment when they begin to blossom, to really take form.

Wolford: When you stage a new piece, I know you often have a very short rehearsal period. Obviously, before you begin mounting a performance, you work conceptually, or you work with the text if it's a scripted piece. You work in your apartment, or in transit, but when you come into a venue with a script to mount a performance, normally you've got about a week to get it up on stage –

Gómez-Peña: At best.

Wolford: Often even less if it's an installation piece. And during the short time you're actually working in a performance space, you end up putting a lot of attention to the technical aspects of the piece, which can be very elaborate.

Sifuentes: Not to mention the shortness of the run. We've never performed more than three weekends in one city. Most of the time it's one show, two shows, a weekend at most … When we produce ourselves, we manage to squeeze out three weeks in a venue, but we don't normally have the luxury of presenting the work for the time that it really needs to evolve. As artists of color in the US, we aren't given the space, time, and funding to be able to sit and create a piece of work. Yes, we create on the road, in airplanes and hotel rooms, in cafes. No matter how visible we are, Chicanos don't have the infrastructure or financial support that would allow us to sit and create in peace, to spend half of the year in artist retreats.

Gómez-Peña: Let's face it, rehearsing all the time is a privilege that most Chicanos don't have. Besides, we have community responsibilities, and our community reminds us all the time of our civic duties, which include benefits for grassroots organizations, workshops in community centers, fundraisers for particular social causes, impromptu appearances at civic events or on Public Access

TV – you name it. And you cannot say no. You have to give back. It's a basic ethical issue. Besides, the work we do in the civic realm feeds the other work. It gives strength and weight to our work in and around the art world. We constantly cross the border back and forth between the civic realm and the art realm, and this is much more important to us than rehearsing all the time. In a sense, our grassroots activities are part of our rehearsal time.

Sifuentes: Traveling and performing is our sole means of economic survival. But at the same time, that's also our means of production. We have turned the necessity of working all the time into our creative process. We travel to the most unlikely places where our audience has never encountered Chicanos – which means that often our performance begins the moment we step off the plane. We become, in a sense, field workers conducting "reverse anthropological" research. I am also not about to begin complaining about the amount of touring we have, because that's something we've fought tooth and nail to achieve. It never gets any easier, even though because of our visibility, some people might get a false sense that we have the corner on the Latino performance art market. The fact of the matter is that we are constantly pushing, struggling, trying to find our niche, in order to make the work happen in the places where it needs to happen. We travel all the time, working in many different contexts from community centers to high art museums, from major urban centers to rural communities, from the US–Mexico border to New York and beyond . . .

Wolford: Could I ask you to talk a little bit about the structure of Pocha Nostra, your performance company? In the past, Guillermo, I know that you've collaborated with people whose primary professional identity wasn't as performers – theorists, cultural critics, visual artists. But in your more recent work, the two of you have been integrating a number of dancers and experimental theater artists.

Gómez-Peña: The way we work is that we have a core group of performance collaborators; for a long time, it was basically Roberto and myself, and more recently Sara. We also have another group of collaborators who are specialists in other areas. People like Mexican filmmaker Gustavo Vazquez, soundscape composer Rona Michele, or digital media advisor Suzanne Stefanac. Incredible performance artists from Mexico city like Juan Ybarra, Violet Luna and Yoshigiro Maeshiro. Chicana performance artists like Norma Medina and Isis Rodriguez. And all of these wonderful *locos y locas* bring something very special to the performances. Their individual creative output finds a new context and a new syntax within the frame of our installations and proscenium performances. Then we have a much bigger, outside circle of collaborators. Some of them are performance artists based in other countries or other cities, and we collaborate with them for specific projects, usually when we're doing a residency or presenting a performance in the areas where they live.

Sifuentes: Suomi violinists in 'traditional' costume sitting on stuffed reindeer in Helsinki, English singers interpreting traditional Welsh songs while doing erotic things with opera singers, gringo rasta tattoo artists tattooing performers onstage, neo-primitives naked on a platform displaying their bodies as art . . .

Gómez-Peña: Given what has happened to arts funding in the 90s, it's financially impossible for artists like us – politicized, experimental performance artists – to maintain any kind of big group. But we still have the desire to bring other people into the work, so the strategy we've developed is to create ephemeral communities that come together around a specific project, and once the project is over, they go back to their homes, to their own practice. Very often, we develop ongoing relationships with artists during our travels. For example, we've done several projects with our Crow friends from Montana, Susan and Tyler Medicine Horse, and we have plans to work with them again in the future. We are a tribe of nomads and misfits.

In some of our projects, we also like to collaborate with people who don't have specialized performance training. Along these lines, we have been working with all kinds of wonderful people: politicized strippers, activists with very theatrical personalities, hip hop poets, extremely articulate transsexuals who are willing to deconstruct their performance personas on stage, mariachis and other civic artists who have chosen to transgress their own tradition ... We love to work with eccentrics who have performative personalities and important things to say. Whenever we collaborate with people who don't have formal performance experience, our work has been to contribute to shaping their material so that it gets presented in the best possible way.

Sifuentes: Then it can be incorporated into the larger context of the work that we are doing.

Gómez-Peña: Exactly. And they always get to have the last word about their own material and their representation. Our role is to coordinate, design, and stage the larger event, not necessarily to direct it. Our goal is to attempt a model that is not colonial, in which we don't manipulate these wonderful 'involuntary performance artists', and in which they get to have editorial say. We help them shape the material (I don't even want to use the word help, because it's condescending), but we work with them to structure their material because we have certain skills and experience that we have developed throughout the years.

Wolford: I want to shift back to the discussion of audience reception of the work, if that's okay. In the diorama performances, there is no spoken text – the text that exists is part of the soundscape. Because you work with multivalent, polysemantic images, and because irony is such a central aspect of your performance strategy, some of the journalistic responses to the diorama performances suggest that without spoken text it's impossible for the work to deliver a clear political critique.

Gómez-Peña: Who can deliver a clear political critique nowadays? When all the philosophical and political systems are bankrupt, who can possibly claim that they have found a political positionality that is not susceptible to being challenged? I cannot assume a clear positionality vis-à-vis any progressive movement, even those closest to my heart. All the ideological systems that used to be sanctuaries of progressive thought are undergoing a permanent process of renegotiation. We now know that obvious ethical or ideological borders are mere illusions, that the enemy is everywhere, even inside of us – especially inside of us. I think that in these senses, we cannot possibly assume one clear political position in the performance.

Sifuentes: Also, part of the point is that we want to see where people position themselves. The responses of our live audience in performance and the written intercultural fantasies, fears, and desires we've collected through the *Temple* and the website become a barometer for America's intolerance towards other cultures. In the 90s, handing the microphone to our audience, so to speak, has been a very effective performance strategy for dealing with sensitive issues.

Gómez-Peña: I think that what we are trying to do is to open up spaces of ambiguity where there are contradictory voices and contradictory ideas clashing in front of the audience – spaces of ambiguity in which audience members can undergo multiple emotional and intellectual journeys that lead to different responses and different political positionalities within the performance, especially if the performance lasts, say, five to six hours over a three-day period. Also, our own positionality is contextual.

Wolford: In what sense?

Gómez-Peña: When we're in Mexico we end up behaving a bit like Chicano nationalists, because Mexicans can be quite insensitive and ethnocentric toward Chicanos. But when we perform for primarily Chicano audiences, we question this type of nationalism. When we perform solely for Anglos, we tend to assume a pan-Latino or pan-subaltern space, but when we are performing for traditional or essentialist Latino audiences, we often defend cultural kleptomania, transvestism, and hybridity as a response to neo-essentialism in our own communities. Performance art allows us to shift these positionalities. We are constantly crossing invisible borders, reframing our voices, reinventing our identities.

Sifuentes: We tailor-make our performances to be specific to the context, regardless of where we are. When we go further away from the US/Mexican border, we adapt the work a little bit so as to ground the piece in different experience, say, to find the connections between the Chicano experience and the local subaltern or immigrant group. Performance art is all about contextualization, about doing site-specific pieces that speak to the moment and the context for which they are created.

Wolford: What are some of the aspects of your performance strategies that remain consistent even when you move among extremely different contexts?

Gómez-Peña: What we're attempting to do is to articulate unspoken complexities of race and gender relations in such a way that people don't close down. Discussions around sensitive issues of race and gender have reached a stalemate in contemporary America, and in order to get out of this stasis, we need to become almost like flashers. If people don't want to see something, we show it to them when they least expect it, and in a way that they actually accept it, even enjoy it. If they don't want to talk about a certain issue, we scream at them, but we make them laugh. If they just want us to whisper it, we say it louder and force them to confront the issues they don't want to talk about, but in such a way that they don't realize right away that we are forcing them to confront these issues. Performance art utilizes a very complex set of communication strategies.

Humor is a good way to deal with heavy issues so we don't get shot, because it takes people by surprise and disarms them for a little while. They bring their guard down a little, and that's exactly when we hit them with the tough question or with the bold image. It's a subversive strategy in our work. We often get criticized for being too humorous.

Wolford: What do you mean?

Gómez-Peña: In a Eurocentric tradition of conceptual art, humor is often equated with lack of seriousness and sophistication. There's an unwillingness in the US and European art world to understand that highly sophisticated conceptual constructions can coexist with very bald humor, so often when people from certain artistic milieus see our work, they just don't know what to think. These apparently sophisticated post-posty post-colonial Mexicans who travel all over are also capable of being crass, direct, sexually outrageous, and making people laugh. It just doesn't jive. There is also a kind of sacred irreverence in our work, a spirituality paired with satire, and that also takes people by surprise, because spirituality in the US is supposed to be a serious and solemn matter, and so are hardcore political subject matters, like racism, sexism, police brutality, etc.

Sifuentes: So when people see Sara crucified as an androgynous mariachi with a strap-on dildo, or when Guillermo as a 'holistic techno shaman' in a mechanical wheelchair baptizes the audience by spitting bad tequila on them, or when Tyler Medicine Horse sells audience members 'real' Indian names in the Crow language that translate to absurd things like 'itchy butt', reactions vary from utter repulsion to raucous laughter.

Gómez-Peña: Irreverent humor, merciless, uncompromising humor, has been at the core of Mexican and Chicano art, and it has always been one of our most effective political strategies. This humor has always taken many shapes, from social parody to self-parody to exaggerating a racist stereotype until it explodes or implodes. I would go so far as to say that humor is a quintessential feature of Mexican and Chicano art and activism. From the Royal Chicano Airforce to Superbarrio and Marcos, we've used humor to help fight our battles. But people forget this. Paradoxically, certain nationalist and essentialist sectors, mainly humorless activists and academicians, have become guardians of solemnity. They have forgotten that humor is profoundly political. They seem not to notice that Chicano and indigenous communities are actively engaged in humor as a mechanism of survival, as a means to generate attention to sensitive issues, as a way to elicit public dialogue. If you are funny, you can get away with murder, and you can appeal to a much larger audience. I'm not saying that all irreverence is subversive by any means – there is insensitive humor, and there are racist forms of irreverence – but our communities let us know how far we can go.

Sifuentes: Mexicano/Chicano audiences never let us take ourselves too seriously because they themselves are irreverent. They get it, they get a kick out of the humor, they laugh a lot. Maybe what makes some intellectuals uptight about our work is that they're afriad we're making fun of them, or that they'll do or say 'the wrong thing' in one of our interactive performances and end up getting laughed at by our 'less informed' Chicano audiences.

Gómez-Peña: These self-proclaimed guardians of our communities promote the idea that when you perform in a grassroots context, you've got to be extremely solemn and 'respectful', because the elders and the families won't be able to take our eccentricity, our transgressive behavior, our three-alarm spicy salsa. Reality tells us exactly the opposite. Every time we perform in a grassroots context, we find incredible tolerance for irreverence and extreme behavior, often a lot more tolerance than in artsy milieus.

Wolford: This brings up another important subject, Guillermo, because the extent to which you identify yourself in relation to the Chicano community is criticized as problematic.

Gómez-Peña: It used to be an ongoing source of pain for me, but not anymore. Now I don't have time to get entangled in that rhetoric. The fact is that my colleagues and I have chosen to speak from the epicentre of the earthquake, and because of that we become the easy targets of many conservative sectors on both the right and the left. When you open a wound and then rub chile into that wound, you are asking to be reprimanded. It's inevitable, especially nowadays when so many people are retrenching to essentialist positions. Neo-essentialism in the late 90s has reached ridiculous extremes. Essentialists nowadays are almost like eugenic intellectuals; if you don't show your birth certificate to prove that you were born in the barrio, if you were not present during the civil rights struggle, you can get conceptually deported back to Mexico. If your Spanglish is not 'street language', if you don't use each and every pc term, they disregard you. But I can deal with Chicano essentialists. I can put up a good fight. It's an internal family affair. What drives me crazy are the Anglo guardians of the Chicano community.

Wolford: What do you mean?

Gómez-Peña: Recently some Anglo scholar argued in her book that since I left the Tijuana/San Diego border region nine years ago, my work stopped being relevant – that I was no longer a true 'grassroots' artist, a real 'border' artist. Give me a million pinche breaks! How many times do we have to show our stinking badges to the Anglo cultural borderpatrol, so we can get their permission to travel across Mexamerica and out of our conceptual barrios? These people want us to remain in the margins forever, so that they can comfortably occupy the center, and from there pontificate about us.

Wolford: That reminds me of something bell hooks has said, about the fact that even well-intentioned white critics speaking about marginality sometimes reinforce the silencing of other voices and end up ventriloquizing for people of color, pointing out the absences, the spaces where they would be if they were allowed to speak for themselves … But we're on the verge of opening a really huge Pandora's Box here if we're going to get into the issue of Anglo critics speaking about the work of artists of color. I know this isn't where you meant to go with that comment, but hey … I'm sitting here with you guys and I still haven't really gotten over the interrogation I got last week at the conference about how 'unfortunate' it was that you had chosen Josh [Kun] and me to respond to your performance, and what that allegedly implied about your relationship to audiences of color. I mean, Josh is an amazing scholar, and his knowledge of rock en español gives him a very particular insight into your work, which is an important aspect of the performances that I've never known another scholar to deal with as a central topic. But his presumed 'whiteness' became an issue at that conference, as did mine. I'm certainly not Chicana, but as an Appalachian woman from a mixed-race background, I don't exactly think of myself as 'white' in any simple way. Identity and affinity are so much more complicated than that, you can't judge those things by phenotype.

Gómez-Peña: No, you're totally right. But I hope you didn't really think that I was making an essentialist comment?

Wolford: Come on, I know you better than that.

Gómez-Peña: Anyone, regardless of their race, class, or gender, who is truly committed to social change and to the transformation of consciousness, has the moral authority to discuss these issues. The binary models that say only intellectuals and artists of color can talk about their own communities are totally ridiculous. The idea that only Chicanos can talk about Chicano art implies that all Chicanos are on the same side of a border and the same side of an issue, which is just not true. As a Mexicano, for example, I must say that I have more in common with an Asian-American intellectual or an Afro-American artist than I do with the Chief of Police of Mexico City, even if he's Mexican. Or as a Chicano, Roberto probably has more in common with a Jewish performance artist than he has with a Chicano borderpatrol officer. Our political coalitions and our artistic work have to do with more than just our ethnic and cultural backgrounds. But what I was talking about before was really specifically about the 'guardians', the self-proclaimed Anglo gatekeepers who believe they have the right to decide, from the outside, whose work gets canonized, included or excluded, who does or doesn't count as a member of a particular community.

Wolford: You're right, that's a very different issue, and an incredibly complicated one, with all sorts of problematic implications in terms of ways that white institutions, curators, or theorists try to maintain a position of privilege over artists of color.

Gómez-Peña: With all humility, I think that Roberto and I have paid our dues, and I'm getting a little pissed about theoreticians who say that we aren't involved in grassroots activism, that we've become mere darlings and pets of the 'liberal' art world.

Wolford: So there's more of a wound there than you were admitting before about your relationship with certain sectors of the Latino community?

Gómez-Peña: What can I say, the wound does open every now and then. We've been involved in political struggles for many years, and these struggles take place in the outside world, not in university department meetings. We've been working on the front lines, so to speak. We've been touring the Southwest and the Chicano communities of the US for many, many years, and we have very good relations with them.

Wolford: That's certainly true here in Ohio. You have very strong ties with Baldemar Velasquez and the Farm Labor Organizing Committee [FLOC], which is based here in Toledo.

Sifuentes: It makes perfect sense that a visionary like Baldemar has asked us to present our spoken word pieces and experimental work at the forefront of an ongoing farmworkers' movement. And Baldemar and all the campesinos have been responding very positively to the work. They see its value in the community centers, that it can speak very directly to the farmworker experience. That for me is a very encouraging affirmation of the work, because so often people want to believe that only muralism can speak to these communities, only campesino theater can speak to the campesinos, and that has not been our experience at all.

Gómez-Peña: Next weekend, it's possible that FLOC is going to bring a couple of vans with migrant workers to see the *Mexterminator* performance at the Detroit Institute of the Arts, just like they did last year when we did a public lecture in Bowling Green [Ohio]. That's not atypical of our work; it happens all the time. When we were in Kansas City a couple of years ago, there was a bus completely full of migrant workers who drove three hours in order to see the performance. This idea that we are speaking only to white 'liberal' audiences is really a misperception. It's completely misinformed. I don't want to suggest that there's anything heroic about what we're doing, because many of our Chicano/Latino performance colleagues have similar experiences. But it's paternalistic to pretend that the farm workers or the young homeboys in the barrio won't understand our work because it's too heavy, too dark, or too theoretically sophisticated.

For the last year and a half, we have been engaging in a dialogue with FLOC, and we have just formalized our association with them by having been declared honorary members, with very serious ethical responsibilities that go along with accepting this position. After our performances, when we engage in public discussions with the audience, we've committed to promote their boycott of corporations that are oppressing and mistreating migrant workers in North Carolina, and to teach audiences how they can effectively participate in this national boycott. I think that this is a very important part of our performance work, and we really don't care if this is lauded or not; whether it is visible to the art world or to academia is absolutely meaningless to us. We are simply trying to figure out ways to be useful to Latino communities in despair and in need, and we feel that we cannot shy away from direct activism. Perhaps one of the reasons why I was more careful about entering into direct activism in the past was because of my condition as a 'resident alien', because I'm not supposed to be affiliated with political organizations. That's part of the condition of receiving the resident card. If you are directly affiliated with a political organization considered to be a troublemaker, you risk being deported. But I'm hoping to acquire dual citizenship very soon, so that would no longer be a problem.

Sifuentes: You can begin to finally exercise your civic rights.

Gómez-Peña: Half of the work we do is in the civic realm rather than in the art world, but it goes unnoticed by the surveillance cameras of the art world. Wherever we go we have a double agenda. We work with a mainstream cultural institution that pays the bill and helps us to present a piece of work in the best possible way, and we also engage in a number of 'parallel' activities.

Those are often the most significant part of our work, but they go unnoticed. We're now on our way to Florida to do a residency at the Atlantic Center for the Arts, and also to do a number of presentations for farm worker communities; it's very likely that those presentations will never be documented, and that the piece at the Atlantic Center for the Arts will be covered in some way. There is no way out of this predicament. The art world is simply not interested in these other activities. And it's good that the art world is not interested, because that grants us special freedoms. They can see what we're doing with the right hand, but they never see what we're doing with the left hand.

Wolford: You're right that a spoken word performance at the Sofia Quintero Cultural Arts Center in Toledo probably isn't going to get written up in *Artforum*, but I certainly understand why it's important to do that work. Could I ask you to talk a bit more about some of the other facets of your work in the civic realm?

Gómez-Peña: We have been designing what we term 'experimental town meetings' in different cities across the US. The biggest up to now took place in Washington, DC. The premise was as follows: the performance artists designed the stage and structured the event carefully, as if a performance art piece was to take place, with lights, video projections, sound, etc. Inside this performance space, we placed a table with activists and radical scholars from the Latino, Indigenous and African-American communities. The performance artists, in character and in costume, with our voices processed by an SPX machine, would get to ask these panelists questions about lack of leadership, about the state of affairs in our communities, about intra-Latino conflicts, about inter-ethnic conflicts, and so on. There was a mediator, radical psychiatrist Leticia Nieto, who would broker between the panelists and the audience. So there were many things taking place simultaneously on different levels and fronts, and any time the conversation would drag or become uninteresting, the performance artists were allowed to 'intervene' with a skit or a spoken word text. At the main table where the panelists were seated, food was being served by performance artists dressed as waiters, and every now and then the waiters would go into performance mode. It was a very complicated script to write and put together, a sort of hypertextual script with lots of open ends. Initially there was some anxiety, especially from the activists. Of course they didn't want to make fools out of themselves. We had very prominent people working with us. Susan Harjo was there, and Baldemar Velasquez, among other people. Abel Lopez, the national director of NALAC at the time, he was there. One of the top immigration lawyers in Washington was there. Of course, some of these people were apprehensive in the beginning about what it meant for them as political activists, as lawyers and union organizers, to put themselves into this situation, which was framed in a very performative way. Susan was not, because she herself is a performance artist extraordinaire; she's one of the co-founders of Spiderwoman Theater and also a poet, along with being one of the most important Native American politicians we have in the country. She was also very familiar with our work, as was Baldemar. He was absolutely not apprehensive, as he himself is an involuntary performance artist, one of the most charismatic and compelling speakers I have ever met. But the others were. So it took a lot of talking to persuade them that we were not going to make fun of them. The event took place and it was a huge success, a strange hybrid of a hardcore political town meeting and an epic performance art piece. I wish all the performance art curators had been there, *esa*. A few days ago, for the closing ceremony of the Latino MacArthur Fellows visit to Toledo, we tried another version, smaller scale. The Latino MacArturos confronted the local political elite, and Roberto and I were asked by Baldemar to design the town meeting and to be the performance animateurs. We are very interested in continuing these experiments and fine-tuning this model, this new genre, utilizing performance art as a means to design, animate, layer, and reframe very tough political debates.

Sifuentes: It's important that we find a new forum to discuss these issues, because so often political panels or discussions around Latino issues and intra-community conflicts get stuck. People have gotten locked into particular ways of discussing identity and race relations. The discussion gets glazed over and audiences become completely uninterested, or else the debates wander into incredibly petty or inflammatory discourse, which is absolutely unproductive. In the context of these experimental town meetings, the performative interventions help us to break through these dynamics. Because the panelists have agreed to be part of this performance context where they can sense the energy of what's going on in the performance space, they tend to be much more concise, energetic and dynamic themselves in what they have to say. But if there are moments when the conversation starts to lag or go in an unproductive direction, the performative interventions are a good way to bring the discussion back around to the main issues we're trying to talk about, and also to diffuse the heaviness and the solemnity that often accompany political discussions. As performers, part of what we're trying to do in this context is to bring back the irreverence to these discussions, so that we don't take ourselves so seriously. That's the model that we're going for – looking for ways to keep the discussions dynamic so that people can encounter these issues in new ways.

Note

Originally published in Guillermo Gómez-Peña, *Dangerous Border Crossers: The Artist Talks Back*, London: Routledge, 2000, pp. 167-87.

5.14 Me, My iBook, and Writing in America (2006)

MARK RAVENHILL

I SOMETIMES WONDER IF I would ever have written a play it if hadn't been for Apple Mac. I made various starts at writing a play during the first thirty years of my life – bits of scenes in old exercise books, a few pages on a typewriter bought in a junk shop, a student attempt on an early Sinclair computer with a printer that printed a page of text every ten minutes (you'd set aside an afternoon to print out the draft of a document), bits and pieces on various friends' PCs. But it was only when I was sharing a flat with a friend in 1992, a friend who had a Mac, that I started to make my first serious attempts at writing, attempts that led, three years later, to me becoming a professional playwright.

Now I wouldn't claim that it was the Mac alone that made me a playwright. That would be silly. There was also the political climate, the Major government returned once again for a final period of 'office without power'; there was the personal experience I went through in 1993 of losing my boyfriend to AIDS; there was the jolt to comfortable assumptions about good and evil brought about by the murder of Jamie Bulger;[1] there was a change in theatrical fashion which meant the high-water mark of performance and physical theatre had turned and once again it seemed like a smart thing for a young man with theatrical aspirations to write a play.

All of these things played their part in making me a playwright. But the actual technology, the actual thought processes, the actual mechanism of creating those plays? I think the Mac was an essential part of all that. Because my hunch is that the technology available is not just a recorder of the artist's thoughts and feelings but itself makes some thoughts and feelings possible that were never possible before, makes other thoughts and feelings no longer transferable to the page.

It's a slightly fanciful notion, but all I know is that once I'd opened a word document on a Mac, once I was clicking on its icons, once I was dragging across its desktop, I felt that it thought as I thought, that here was something that was an extension of my heart and head in a way that the pencil or the typewriter or the PC had never been. Sat before the screen of a Mac, I was a writer.

A writer used to be heroic. You could lock him or her up in a prison cell for twenty years and still they'd find a way to carry on writing. They'd risk everything to pass around *samizdat* copies of their work. The Church or the State or the Stasi were out to get them but they'd carry on writing – even if only in their head. There is not an ounce of the hero about me – maybe none of us are heroes today, maybe we're in a post-heroic age, maybe we're all more Carrie Bradshaw than Solzhenitsyn – but I certainly wouldn't have finished a full-length play and written several drafts without a Mac.

I may just be romanticising my own lack of heroism. Maybe I am a writer. And if I had to write on a typewriter I would. It's one of the tricks of new technology that within months we cannot imagine a life without it. (However did I call my partner from the train to say I was on my way home before the invention of the mobile phone?) But certainly now, as I approach ten years as a produced playwright, I cannot imagine having produced the body of work that I have without the programmes of the several Macs I've got through over the years – currently iBook, OS X 10, AppleWorks Word Document. The rhythms, the structures, the themes of those plays are as much Mac's as they are mine.

There is an irony about this of course. Plenty of commentators, mainly journalists but a few people who should know better, have chosen only to report the 'shocking' moments in my plays: the 'bloody rimming' moments. But other commentators have spotted another, bigger project in my plays to date: something which may even report upon, maybe even critique, a world of globalised capitalism. I'd like to think that's there. There's nothing very schematic about writing a play: you tend to start with an instinct and only later, often after the audience have seen the play, can you say 'ah maybe that's what this thing is about'. Even so, I'd like to think that the best bits of my writing have captured some of the weightless, soulless emptiness of contemporary global capitalism and in doing so opened up a space for some of the audience to think more critically about The Way We Live Now than they might have done before. So of course it's ironic that this writing has been made possible by the technology coming out of Silicon Valley, the nerve centre of that same globalised world.

This is the embarrassing contradiction I find myself in as a playwright: I would like to think of my plays as oppositional, of critical, of outside of the ebb and flow of information and capital but I suspect they would never have existed without start-ups, bubbles and chips. I'd like to be a free thinker but maybe in truth I'm just another microserf.

And if I were just going to be a jolly postmodernist, I could embrace this. I don't want to do that, but nor is it just possible to deny this irony, return to the pre-ironic simplicity of a world where I would have written on a Remington – or probably reclined on a sofa while a poorly paid fifteen-year-old girl from a Secondary Modern School typed on a Remington for me. So what is to be done?

I first became really aware of the word globalisation (no doubt later than most people) towards the end of the 1990s. Searching around for material for the play that would become *Some Explicit Polaroids*, I took a whole pile of books away for a week to a cheap room in Ibiza and gave myself a crammer course, trying to understand how the world's economies had changed. In the spring of 1999, Max Stafford-Clark asked me if I'd like to do a week-long workshop for this new play. I had very little text to show (and indeed didn't have much more text to show when the play began rehearsing in the autumn) but I said I thought we should look at this subject of globalisation and Max, myself and the actors in the workshop made up lists of people we would like to meet to interview and try to find out what this globalisation thing was.

I'm not sure who came up with the idea of meeting Charles Saatchi. I think it was one of the actors. But I went with a couple of the actors from the workshop – I think it was Lesley Manville and Monica Dolan – to the headquarters of Saatchi and Saatchi and we were shown into the office of the great man. He told us that several years before his company had identified 'globalisation' as the wave of the future and had been preparing themselves for the new globalised economy.

'But really,' he said with a weary smile, 'globalisation is just a weasel word – what we're really talking about is Americanisation'.

I was very taken aback by this. This somehow seemed to be the sentiment of an anti-globalist, an anti-American and Saatchi was clearly neither. 'So would you say', asked Monica Dolan, 'that globalisation is a good thing or a bad thing?'

'Oh you can't say something like that is good or bad,' Saatchi said. 'It's a fact. It's like the wind blowing or the tide coming in. It's not good or bad. It just is.'

I was struck just how in that moment he resembled one of Brecht's capitalists, who always forget (or deliberately deny) that the economy is a human construct and not a tsunami. It was as though he were speaking from the selfsame script as Brecht's Pierpont Mauler in *St Joan of the Stockyards*. Saatchi was a fascinating character, hugely charismatic and a big influence on the development of the character of Jonathan when I came to write *Some Explicit Polaroids*.

Was Saatchi right? Was 'globalisation' 'Americanisation'? There was certainly plenty of Americanisation about me.

I think this is something you become particularly aware of when you start writing about your experiences as a gay man. Because contemporary 'gay' identity is almost entirely an American construct. The group lobbying for gay legal and democratic rights in the UK is called Stonewall after a bar in New York that only a tiny proportion of British gays and lesbians can ever have ever been to. Most gays and lesbians rehearse their coming outs by engaging with American coming-out narratives: the gay genre fiction in any British bookshop is almost entirely American. Early generations of British gay men made an ironic appropriation of the camp images of Hollywood glamour. Maybe in the absence of robust European or British narratives of gay identity, or maybe by excluding them, it is American images and narratives that have defined British gay identity. Try to buy gay porn featuring men with British accents and you'd be hard pushed (so to speak). It's all California dudes or daddies with, in the last few years, a wave of new Eastern European product. And as if to prove how entirely hegemonic all this is even the challenge to 'gay' with the early 1990s 'queer' was a largely American movement, albeit in part inspired by European philosophy and critical theory.

Now I felt pretty pleased with myself that my first play *Shopping and Fucking* had managed to move outside of the parameters of a 'gay' narrative without being too self-consciously 'queer' either. The characters enjoyed or suffered what *Little Britain* calls 'some cock and arse action' but there were no coming-out narratives, no hugs, no learning.

I was troubled by one particular block (of several) that I hit while writing *Some Explicit Polaroids*. In the play the character of Tim, who is HIV positive, refuses to take his medication and eventually dies of an AIDS-related illness. Now this was the most autobiographical thing I had ever written: five years before I wrote the play my boyfriend, also called Tim, had died of an AIDS-related illness. And yet when I came to write these scenes for the play I couldn't connect with anything that had happened to me in real life because all I could see, all I could hear, was stuff from other people's AIDS narratives: *The Normal Heart*, *Longtime Companion*, *Angels in America*. As soon as I stuck a character in a hospital bed and gave them a Kaposi's Sarcoma (KS) lesion they would start to talk with an American accent and before you knew it Meryl Streep was sitting by the bed and everyone was hugging each other.

I think it's important – certainly for me when I'm writing – that we don't just play the weary game of referencing and quoting other narratives in a warm glow of cynicism. I want to test in my writing how much the new experiences of humanity can be captured in a piece of theatre. But for months I would come back to writing those scenes, always with the same effect. A play that was supposedly set in London would suddenly lurch over the Atlantic once the doors of the AIDS ward were open. Eventually I became really angry. This was my experience. This was my narrative. How *dare* Larry Kramer and Tony Kushner colonise my life like this? Why was I seeing the first revelation of the KS lesion from *The Normal Heart* or Louis, Prior and the Angel when I shut my eyes, and not my own memory? Damn you for writing your American AIDS plays!

I didn't feel, having written *Some Explicit Polaroids*, that I had done anything other than chip away at the subject of globalisation – if indeed it is still a 'subject' (is something a 'subject' when it is so integrated into our lives?). It's still something I want to write about but I keep on hitting the same block every time I sit down wanting to write dramatically about it: the action wants to happen in America. The research I read, the popular anti-globalisation books are about American companies doing terrible things to American workers and consumers for the benefit of the American shareholder. And I don't feel it would be honest of me to write with a setting of Americanoise (I did it in my play *Faust is Dead* with mixed results). Of course Brecht used a mythic America repeatedly as a setting that allowed him to write an earlier stage of capitalist development but I can't help feeling that to write plays set in America is to have one's narrative defined by America, however critical the play might be of America or globalisation.

Britain may have become increasingly part of a global economy, and culturally and economically we may be more and more American, but the fashionability of these truths is in danger of preventing commentators and dramatists from exploring what is specifically British about us. Because there is still plenty about us, I think, that is very specific to this island. Writing globally, nationally, locally, personally, it's a lot for a playwright to do.

'Where is the state of the nation play?' a dying breed of grumpy old men still ask, assuming that the state of the nation is the same thing as the fate of the planet, the choices facing the globe or the way of the world – all of these concerns every bit as ambitious and political as the 'state of the nation'.

Because if you were to take the conflict between capital and labour as a basic motor of human experience (a widely discredited idea but still one with a bit of life in it), you can see how problematic it is to dramatise for a contemporary playwright. Hauptmann could bring his nineteenth-century weavers in conflict with their bourgeois masters by setting his play in a small German town. Of course, nineteenth-century 'free trade' saw a fair amount of movement of goods and capital but it's possible to imagine many, many situations where a dramatist can place the seller of labour and the owner of capital in the same geographic space. This is far more difficult today. Where did the food come from that you ate today? Who made your trainers? Who wove that cloth? They are phantoms and the profits have vanished off to phantoms elsewhere. Certainly a very different type of play is needed if we're going to write about this world.

But actually this very fundamental conflict between capital and labour – perhaps the fundamental social and economic conflict – was rarely ever at the heart of the British 'state of the nation' play, an ideal model of a play that perhaps never quite existed in the British theatre from the 1950s through to the 1980s.

The main tradition in British 'political' theatre was an oppositional voice that spoke up against the crushing hand of the Big Other: the Headmaster, the Priest, the Colonel, the Men from the Ministry – the Daddy who wants to deny the voice and energy of his offspring. It was at the heart of the satire boom of the 1960s (laughing at these Big Others fuelled *Beyond the Fringe*); it was the 'heroes led by donkeys' anger of *Oh What A Lovely War*; it was Osborne's Jimmy and Wesker's Beattie. (Osborne and Wesker are good dramatists and so invite complex responses to Jimmy and Beattie.)

It's a drama in which tradition and its intertwining with class plays a very significant part and fuels many writers' anger, but in which no very significant part is played by the economic life of the characters, nor by the conflict between capital and labour. British theatre never produced a character with the force of Arthur Miller's Willy Loman or Brecht's Mother Courage, characters for whom at the very core of their being, at the basis of their conflict with the world, is the economic. We nearly always preferred to play a scene in front of a Union Jack and attack 'authority' and call this 'political theatre'. This was 'oppositional' theatre I would suggest but was rarely rooted enough in the economic to be thoroughly 'political'.

If anyone has the time or the inclination I think it could be illuminating to do a word count for the occurrence of the word 'England' in English plays from the 1950s to the present day. I suspect you'd find a pretty steady occurrence of the word from the 1950s through to the 1980s, with a rapid trailing off in the 1990s. From John Osborne's rallying cry of 'Damn You England!', ushering Jimmy Porter and Archie Rice and his bumping and grinding Britannia onto the stage of the English Stage Company, through to Edgar's *Destiny* and Brenton's *The Churchill Play*, in which Winston Churchill leaps from his coffin at his state funeral, and onto Wertenbaker's *Our Country's Good*, the 'English' word rings out alongside the iconography of Englishness.

But then something changed. I think maybe we reached a stage in the 1990s where a new group of younger dramatists weren't so interested in criticising these figures in power (the basic patricidal impulse) – largely I suspect because these figures of power have learned to speak a different language – one that promises (or threatens) inclusion rather than coercion. Looking at my own plays, rather than railing against patriarchal figures, the characters tend to have a nostalgic hankering for a time when there was a stern father figure looking over them, a time when we weren't expected to make so many choices for ourselves.

David Hare once remarked that it was a strange thing but you only needed to mention the word 'Weybridge' to get a huge laugh on the London stage. I've noticed that Alan Bennett's audiences seem to find 'Battenberg' or 'antimacassar' similarly hilarious. It is as though British theatre audiences, certainly mainstream London theatre audiences, like to be reminded of their parochialism, of their naffness, of their not quite moving with the times. There is real pride in that laughter at 'Weybridge' or 'Battenberg'.

When I started writing my first full-length play *Shopping and Fucking*, I didn't have much of an idea about what course the action of the play was going to take or what the play was going to be about. Playwrights often don't. But starting on *Shopping and Fucking* I did have a clear idea, a rule that I set myself: there would be no geographical references, no references to England, London, Streatham, Halifax, Weybridge and also no references to anything that had been in use for more than a decade or so; characters were allowed to use a microwave but not a kettle, send an email but not a postcard. Very consciously, I wanted the play to have a different relationship to history and geography from the existing tradition of contemporary British playwriting.

Why did I do this? I think in part because I'd observed that English audiences would cling onto place names or products – think Batley, think Bovril – as comfort blankets, and I wanted to take those comfort blankets away. And because I suppose I sensed that for the young characters in my play being part of the narrative of nationhood or history played very little part in their lives. But this didn't come from any theory. I'd been too busy doing a portfolio of badly paid jobs to read any Fukuyama, at least until the profits from being a West End playwright rolled in.

I don't think the director of the play, Max Stafford-Clark, ever really saw this absence of reference in the play as anything other than a weakness. Max had a huge, and almost entirely beneficial, influence on the development of the play through the various drafts I worked on once his Out of Joint Company committed to the production of the play. From my very first meeting with him through to the last week of rehearsals, he would push and push for something more 'specif', as we jokingly called it. Where were these characters born? Where were they living now? What were their surnames? (I didn't even want to give them first names but got round this by naming the characters after early 1990s popsters, Take That.)

I remember once, in complete exasperation at one of our meetings, Max threw down his script and said: 'Look you've got to put in some more specif stuff – otherwise they'll do this play in Germany and it'll all be Expressionist and they'll all have Mohicans. Do you want that?' I remarked glibly that I believed the royalties from German productions were rather good. (They are and I'm sure a production not unlike Max's nightmare has taken place in a *Stadttheater* somewhere.) It was a glib response because I couldn't really rationalise at the time why a geographical or historical reference in the play was wrong. I was flying on instinct but I strongly resisted putting any of those references in the play. Looking at it now I would say *Shopping and Fucking* mostly works inside the language of 'social realism'; it just selects slightly different bits of the social and the real to define its world than those things that Max was used to with his long and illustrious work directing new British plays.

I'd been partly inspired to write in this way by the plays and essays of David Mamet. An American offered the way forward. Mamet had a huge influence on a significant group of the new British playwrights of the 1990s, as I discovered when Patrick Marber, Joe Penhall and myself got together to discuss Mamet's *Edmond* for a programme article to accompany the National Theatre's revival of the play. You can trace it through Marber's career, from his first play *Dealer's Choice* (Mamet is an advocate of poker), his performance in Mamet's *Speed The Plow* (picked up for revival by a West End management after Penhall directed a reading at the Royal Court), Marber's direction of Mamet's *The Old Neighbourhood*, which may in turn have led Marber to the world of his most recent play *Howard Katz*.

I think maybe we were drawn to Mamet for a number of reasons. He offered a clear definition of masculinity, at a time when masculinity was supposedly in crisis. (Is it still? Was it ever?) But also he offered a strict set of aesthetic disciplines at a time when we didn't feel inspired by an older generation of British playwrights. What Mamet stresses time and time again in his essays is that the play should be stripped of all extraneous detail until just the story, which he defines as just the protagonist in pursuit of their objective, is left. Mamet insists that the dramatist can't make the play say anything beyond this or on top of this, that the meaning of the play *is* this story. In some ways it's the old Hemingway adage of 'cut out the good writing' applied to the play but it's certainly worked for David Mamet. His work from *American Buffalo* through to *The Old Neighbourhood* (charitably ignoring *Boston Marriage*) is as impressive a body of work as that of any dramatist alive.

And in some ways, through his absorption in the narrative purity of Aristotelian poetics,

Mamet was bringing us in touch with a European tradition which the British theatre had never fully absorbed. (British playwrights from Shakespeare to Churchill have preferred to disrupt and transgress the Aristotelian rules.) What Mamet was arguing for was a theatre free of ideology in which the audience would undergo a profound experience by projecting themselves into the uninflected protagonist. This is the idea that lies at the heart of Mamet's aesthetic. Of course you can spot a more superficial influence of Mamet on the development of dialogue, the repetitive masculine drive of his characters' language echoed in a lot of British new writing of the 1990s. But more profoundly it is the stripping away of detail and opinion, the emphasis on narrative, where Mamet's influence can be felt on Marber, Penhall, Neilson, McDonagh *et al*. (He was very definitely a role model for emerging male writers rather than women.)

In one of his essays, Mamet talks about the decor of American Jewish homes, of its wish to be tasteful and to be acceptable, not to give too much away, not to be too Jewish. Recently in his writing and in his life he has explored his identity as a Jew in a way that he never publicly did in the 1970s and 1980s. It struck me reading the essay that as well as describing the decor of Jewish homes he was pretty much describing his own aesthetic as a playwright. Was his desire to strip a play of wasteful detail, to present a central protagonist who can be defined by the pursuit of their objective, what Jewish writers for Hollywood and Broadway have been doing for the whole century? Was the aesthetic purity of all this making sure that the little guy at the centre of their stories could stand for an American Everyman and not a Jew? It struck me that it was and I'm sure Mamet, a writer who thinks very deeply about his work, will have been struck by this too.

For the group of writers starting off their careers in the 1990s, Mamet's influence allowed us to break free of the existing dominant discourse of British theatre – the discourse about Britishness and the attack on the bad Father (I'm talking of course about an impulse that was largely uncon-scious and rarely discussed, these weren't a group of playwrights who ever discussed a movement or came up with a manifesto, many of them have never met each other to this day).

So, I wrote *Shopping and Fucking*. It was a commercial and critical success here, the Out of Joint production toured internationally with the support of the British Council, and the play was quickly translated into many languages and produced all over the world. From being part of the British new writing scene I had become a global commodity. Ironically, though in much of the world the play was received at least as well as it was at home, the place where the play did least well was in New York where the play was universally loathed by the critics – 'Mr Ravenhill belongs to a long line of whingeing Brits from John Osborne to Caryl Churchill' and 'Mr Ravenhill should go home and learn how to write a play' – but it sold out for its allotted run. 'I don't get it,' said the American producer, 'A sold-out flop!'

I was hugely excited to be produced all over the world. I would often be invited to produc-tions of the play. The temptation was to rush to each of them, not because I wanted to see the play again and again, but because of the opportunities for free travel that were offered. I decided to ration myself and only go to a few of these overseas productions but I went to enough to start to suspect that I was becoming part of the global class who live out of a mini-bar and a breakfast buffet. It's a life I quite like.

I was amused to see how many of the productions replaced the missing 'Britishness' of the play, the Britishness I had so carefully excluded, but this was the height of Britpop, so in Greek, Lithuanian, Danish productions I saw characters in Union Jack T-shirts with pictures of Princess

Diana pinned to their wall listening to a soundtrack of Blur and Oasis. No small part of the appeal of the play, I saw, was that it was British and if the writer hadn't provided enough of the Old Country then the production would do the work. 'Your writing – it's so like Dickens, it's Oliver Twist,' said a director in Amsterdam. At first I was completely mystified but on reflection I could see this play, which was predominantly social realist with a group of lost kids getting drawn into nefarious activity, had much more in common with Dickens, who I'd read avidly in my teenage years, than I would really like to admit. I had to confront the fact that not only would overseas productions actually emphasise, even over emphasise, the Britishness of the play, but actually maybe there was actually something essentially British about the play.

Despite this Britishness, I was aware that one of the reasons the play had proved such good export material was that it wasn't cluttered with references that would confuse foreign audiences and that the commodified world of the play was not a specifically British one. I think by the time I came to write *Some Explicit Polaroids* I wanted to write another play that would repeat the international success of *Shopping and Fucking*. I'd had a taste of the travel and the interest and some decent money and I wanted to repeat the experience. Of course this calculation is fatal to the creative process and that play was the slowest, most painful thing I've ever written, wrung out of me scene by scene by an incredibly patient Max Stafford-Clark.

It was a grimly ironic experience. I wanted to write about globalisation, hence the workshop where we'd interviewed Charles Saatchi, but as a playwright I had become a global commodity, with *Shopping and Fucking* franchises all over the world. Now I wanted to produce a new global product that would speak to people in Johannesburg and Melbourne, Toronto and Mexico City: places I'd only been to for a couple of days and whose cultures I knew no more of than a quick tasting in a food hall. Trying to think of this global audience was so daunting that I became totally blocked, until finally I resolved to write anything that came into my head and to deliver a play that I liked even if it wasn't performed in a single translation.

And looking at *Some Explicit Polaroids* on opening night I thought, well, I'm proud of what I've come up with but this is clearly not a global play. The young characters of the play – Tim, Victor, Nadia – belong to a similar world to the young people of *Shopping and Fucking* but the characters of Nick and Helen, the old socialists, belong to an entirely different, a very – so it seemed to me – British world. Indeed so different were these two groups of characters I found it almost impossible to conceive of scenes where they would talk to each other and in the end Helen's intrusion into Tim, Victor and Nadia's world proved to be brief.

I was wrong about *Some Explicit Polaroids*. It's received almost as many productions overseas as *Shopping and Fucking*, far more than my other plays. And directors and actors have told me that the central generational conflict between a weary politicised older generation and a party-happy apolitical younger generation is one that is reflected in their country, in South America or in Eastern Europe. And then there's one scene set on the terrace of the Houses of Parliament when they can really leap on the Britishness in the staging if they want to. Oddly enough, most productions choose not to. I guess the fashion for all things Cool Britannia has passed. With *Polaroids* I realised that the playwright could never play the game of guessing what would play with different audiences; you write for yourself, maybe for the immediate culture around you and then wait and see what will travel.

In 2002, I got the opportunity to spend a month writing at the Eugene O'Neill Center in Connecticut alongside twenty other playwrights, all of them American. I was sent by the National Theatre's Connections programme, where I was to write a play for young people to perform in schools and youth theatres. When I flew into New York the country was preparing to commemorate the first anniversary of 9/11, while also psyching itself up for the assault on Iraq, after Afghanistan hadn't provided the 'closure' that was being sought for.

On the train travelling up through New York state and into Connecticut I was amazed at the number of houses (in many areas the majority) that had huge Stars and Stripes flags hanging down the side of the building, many of them the full length of the houses. I was struck by how much America still had recourse to a strong narrative of national identity, of buzzwords, of rituals, of routines, that we no longer have. We called our programme *Pop Idol*; they called theirs *American Idol*. What does it say about the two cultures where one side aspires to be Pop, the other aspires to be American?

Arriving at the O'Neill, it was soon obvious that no-one had heard of me or any of my plays. This was rather different from the reception I'd got used to in the rest of the world but I decided it would be a very good, if rather humbling experience for me. (I'm rubbish at being humble and for most of the month I carried on like Simon Cowell but I gave it a go.) But I had to write the play, eventually called *Totally Over You*, while I was there. Surrounded by American voices, I found when I sat down to write I could do one of two things: write dialogue that was very self-consciously English (in a Richard Curtis, Julian Fellowes sort of a way, which has always exported very well) or in a sort of mid-Atlantic chat. I suspect that in conversation during the day I slipped between the two. It's amazing how quickly your ear for your own culture's rhythms goes: I'd lost mine within a couple of days. But I had to write a play within four weeks and there was little time to anguish about the rhythms of my writing. I decided that the teenagers in my play, who are obsessed by celebrity culture, would have existed entirely on a diet of American television, American cinema, American music and American food. Since American actors were going to present the play to an American audience as a staged reading at the end of the month, I didn't want to spend my time explaining a lot of British youth references to them or to expect them to perform with a north London accent. I chose to place the play in a genre – teenagers in a school adapted from a European classic (I was inspired by Molière) – that I'd enjoyed in the American teen comedies *Clueless* and *Ten Things I Hate About You*. And I had my characters talk in mid-Atlantic because I figured there were a whole generation of kids living in Camden or Bradford or Glasgow who either spoke like American teenagers or aspired to talk like American teenagers and with identical pop-culture references. Whether the young people who performed the play were always aware of the play's critique of this Americanisation of youth experience, or whether they revelled in speaking mid-Atlantic I was never sure.

But however much we may have in common, however much it's possible to write in a demotic language that sits just as easily on the lips of kids in Harlesden as it does in Harlem, I realised there was a fundamental difference between the theatre cultures of the two countries. One evening during a panel discussion with the other writers at the O'Neill, I said (probably rather grandly) that I thought we should be writing plays that 'existed at the centre of the culture'. There was little response at the time but with the session over one of my fellow playwrights, his whole body drawn tight with anger, stepped into my path. 'How can you say that?' he hissed. 'How dare you come over here and say that?'

'I'm sorry?'

'A theatre at the centre of the culture. Don't you know what a ridiculous idea that is? That's never going to happen! And you stand here and you throw it in our faces!'

'But surely if we're not aiming for the centre of the —'

'You don't understand America, you don't understand our theatre, just don't talk about it.' And off he went. I subsequently learned that he lived in the strange shadow world of being a virtual playwright with a salaried post as a professor of playwriting and various plays workshopped and read over the years, but nothing produced.

But what he'd voiced was, I think, a fundamental distinction between the way many American writers and the way British writers tend to view themselves. There is a mournful sense from many American writers that they are cut adrift from a society which has little interest in anything they have to write. The writer and actor Wallace Shawn voices this in an interview for a programme at the Royal Court when he says that the audience comes to the theatre looking for a world that is calmer and more polite than the world around them but all the playwrights have to offer them is 'frenzied glimpses of lives in little rooms'. The audience and the playwright, Shawn said, have grown apart, their needs irreconcilable.

There are some very similar sentiments expressed by Jonathan Franzen's in his recent collection of essays,[2] mourning the death of the great American social novel, the death of the novel in general, the death of reading. Why is he writing at all when there is every sign that his dying culture is finally going to turn its back on writing and reading once and for all?

It's only when you read these bleak assessments of the writer's struggle that you realise how different the situation is here in Britain. Of course, writers always feel insecure — why hasn't that theatre programmed my play? why did that actor turn down the lead? why can't that critic understand what I'm doing? — but somehow, underneath all this there is still a fundamental, unspoken sense that what we do matters, that theatres are looking for new writers, that audiences want to see their work, that the new plays will be studied and discussed, that they are part of the wider cultural life of the country. It sometimes doesn't feel that way, but meet a group of American writers and you suddenly realise how different our perception of ourselves is.

And I think a great deal of it is perception. Wallace Shawn and Jonathan Franzen draw a picture of themselves alienated and alone, shouting against the glass at a culture that can't hear. But in reality both are hugely respected and one suspects reasonably well remunerated for their talents. You might not find the latest literary novel or fringe play being debated in every bar in every state, but the *New York Review of Books* or the *New York Times* often give more consideration to new work than any comparable British publication.

And over here, despite the guilt imposed upon us by the Thatcherites for our lack of economic efficiency and by the Blairites for our lack of access, we somehow still feel central to the culture, when in reality most people in Britain couldn't name a contemporary playwright or novelist. The American writer may be creating a mirage of alienation and victimhood for themselves, but our cultural institutions carefully cushion us from a sense that what we do doesn't really matter.

So for all the globalisation, the Americanisation, this is where there is still something fundamentally different about being a British playwright: the sense that our writing counts. And this may be an illusion that our theatres, our newspapers, our universities help us to sustain, but it's a valuable, maybe even a necessary, illusion for a writer to have and I'm grateful that while I've written on my iBook I've been able to do it in a culture which is still in some ways peculiarly British.

Notes

1. Mark Ravenhill, 'A Tear in the Fabric: The Jamie Bulger Murder and New Theatre Writing in the 'Nineties', *New Theatre Quarterly*, 20(4) (November 2004), 305–14.
2. Jonathan Franzen, *How To Be Alone: Essays* (New York: Farrar Straus Giroux, 2002).

Originally published in *Contemporary Theatre Review*, 16(1) (2006), pp. 131–8.

Index